Lecture Notes in Computer Science 2870

Edited by G. Goos, J. Hartmanis, and J. van Leeuwen

Springer
Berlin
Heidelberg
New York
Hong Kong
London
Milan
Paris
Tokyo

Dieter Fensel Katia Sycara
John Mylopoulos (Eds.)

The Semantic Web - ISWC 2003

Second International Semantic Web Conference
Sanibel Island, FL, USA, October 20-23, 2003
Proceedings

Springer

Volume Editors

Dieter Fensel
DERI, located at the Universities of Galway and Innsbruck
E-mail: dieter.fensel@uibk.ac.at

Katia Sycara
Carnegie Mellon University, School of Computer Science
Pittsburgh, PA 15213, USA
E-mail: katia@cs.cmu.edu

John Mylopoulos
University of Toronto, Department of Computer Science
40 St. George Street, rm 7266
Toronto, Canada M5S 2E4
E-mail: jm@cs.toronto.edu

Cataloging-in-Publication Data applied for

A catalog record for this book is available from the Library of Congress.

Bibliographic information published by Die Deutsche Bibliothek
Die Deutsche Bibliothek lists this publication in the Deutsche Nationalbibliografie; detailed bibliographic data is available in the Internet at <http://dnb.ddb.de>.

CR Subject Classification (1998): C.2, H.3, H.4, H.5, F.3, I.2, K.4

ISSN 0302-9743
ISBN 3-540-20362-1 Springer-Verlag Berlin Heidelberg New York

Springer-Verlag Berlin Heidelberg New York
a member of BertelsmannSpringer Science+Business Media GmbH

http://www.springeronline.com

Printed in Germany

Typesetting: Camera-ready by author, data conversion by PTP Berlin GmbH
Printed on acid-free paper SPIN: 10964071 06/3142 5 4 3 2 1 0

Preface

These proceedings contain the papers accepted for presentation at the Second International Semantic Web Conference (ISWC 2003) held on Sanibel Island, Florida, U.S.A., October 20–23, 2003. Following the success of ISWC 2002 that was held in Sardinia in June 2002, ISWC 2003 enjoyed a greatly increased interest in the conference themes.

The number of submitted papers more than doubled compared with ISWC 2002 to 283. Of those, 262 were submitted to the research track and 21 to the industrial track. With rare exceptions, each submission was evaluated by three program committee members whose reviews were coordinated by members of the senior program committee. This year 49 papers in the research track and 9 papers in the industrial track were accepted.

The high quality of ISWC 2003 was the result of the joint effort of many people. First of all we would like to thank the authors for their high-quality submissions and the members of the program committee for their reviewing and review coordination efforts. We would like to extend special thanks to Christoph Bussler for chairing the industrial track, to Mike Dean for his help with the conference management software, the web site, and conference publicity, and to Massimo Paolucci for helping with the organization of the proceedings and arranging sponsorships. We would also like to thank Jeff Bradshaw for local organization; Jerome Euzenat for financial organization; Asun Gomez-Perez for organizing the tutorials; Sheila McIlraith and Dimitris Plexousakis for organizing the workshops; Raphael Malyankar for organizing the poster sessions; Jeff Heflin for organizing the software demonstrations; Steffen Staab for coordinating the semantic markup; Atanas Kiryakov for handling registrations; Ying Ding for organizing sponsorships; and the sponsors for their financial support.

October 2003 Katia Sycara, John Mylopulos, Dieter Fensel

Organizing Committee

General Chair	Dieter Fensel (University of Innsbruck, Austria)
Program Chair	Katia Sycara (Carnegie Mellon University, USA)
Program Co-chair	John Mylopoulos (University of Toronto, Canada)
Tutorial Chair	Asun Gomez-Perez (Polytechnic University of Madrid, Spain)
Workshops Chairs	Sheila McIlraith (Stanford University, USA) Dimitris Plexousakis (University of Crete, Greece)
Industrial Track Chair	Christoph Bussler (Oracle, USA)
Poster Chair	Raphael Malyankar (Arizona State University, USA)
Finance Chair	Jerome Euzenat (INRIA, Rhone-Alpes, France)
Publicity Chair	Mike Dean (BBN, USA)
Local Arrangements Chair	Jeff Bradshaw (University of West Florida, USA)
Sponsor Chairs	Ying Ding (University of Innsbruck, Austria) Massimo Paolucci (Carnegie Mellon University, USA)
Demonstration Chair	Jeff Heflin (Lehigh University, USA)
Registration Chair	Atanas Kiryakov (Sirma AI, Ltd., Bulgaria)

Senior Program Committee

Paolo Atzeni (Università di Roma, Tre, Italy)
Sonia Bergamaschi (University of Modena, Italy)
Stefano Ceri (Politecnico di Milano, Italy)
Umesh Dayal (Hewlett-Packard, USA)
Stefan Decker (USC ISI, USA)
Oren Etzioni (University of Washington, USA)
Alon Halevy (University of Washington, USA)
Frank van Harmelen (Vrije Universiteit, Amsterdam, The Netherlands)
Masahiro Hori (Kansai University, Japan)
Ian Horrocks (University of Manchester, UK)
Vipul Kashyap (National Library of Medicine, USA)
Roger King (University of Colorado, USA)
Ora Lassila (Nokia, USA)
David Martin (SRI, USA)
Brian McBride (Hewlett-Packard, UK)
Robert Meersman (Vrije Universiteit, Brussels, Belgium)
Riichiro Mizoguchi (Osaka University, Japan)
Peter Patel-Schneider (Lucent, USA)
Guus Schreiber (University of Amsterdam, The Netherlands)

Zbigniew Ras (University of North Carolina, USA)
Amit Sheth (University of Georgia, USA)
Rudi Studer (University of Karlsruhe, Germany)
Gerhard Weikum (University of Saarland, Germany)

Program Committee

Karl Aberer (École Polytechnique Federale de Lausanne, Switzerland)
Sudhir Agarwal (University of Karlsruhe, Germany)
Giuseppe Amato (ISTI-CNR, Italy)
Yuan An (University of Toronto, Canada)
Anjo Anjewierden (University of Amsterdam, The Netherlands)
Anupriya Ankolekar (Carnegie Mellon University, USA)
Budak Arpinar (University of Georgia, USA)
Andreas Becks (Fraunhofer Institute, Germany)
Domenico Beneventano (University of Modena, Italy)
Bettina Berendt (Humboldt University, Berlin, Germany)
Abraham Bernstein (University of Zurich, Switzerland)
Keith Bessette (University of Connecticut, USA)
Harold Boley (National Research Council, Canada)
Alex Borgida (Rutgers University, USA)
Omar Boucelma (LSIS-CNRS, France)
Paolo Bouquet (University of Trento, Italy)
Paolo Bresciani (ITC-IRST, Italy)
Jeen Broekstra (Aidministrator, The Netherlands)
Mark Burstein (BBN, USA)
Jorge Cardoso (University of Madeira, Portugal)
Jeremy Carroll (Hewlett-Packard, UK)
Vassilis Christophides (ICS-FORTH, Greece)
Nigel Collier (National Institute of Informatics, Japan)
Isabel Cruz (University of Illinois at Chicago, USA)
Susan Davidson (University of Pennsylvania, USA)
Maarten de Rijke (University of Amsterdam, The Netherlands)
Jos De Roo (Agfa-Gevaert, The Netherlands)
Mike Dean (BBN, USA)
Steven Demurjian (University of Connecticut, USA)
Thuong Doan (University of Connecticut, USA)
Chris Dollin (Hewlett-Packard, UK)
Martin Dzbor (Open University, UK)
David Embley (Brigham Young University, USA)
Skevos Evripidou (University of Cyprus, Cyprus)
Wenfei Fan (Bell Laboratories and Temple University, USA)
Richard Fikes (Stanford University, USA)
Tim Finin (University of Maryland, Baltimore County, USA)

Martin Frank (USC ISI, USA)
Jeremy Frumkin (University of Arizona, USA)
Norbert Fuchs (University of Zurich, Switzerland)
Avigdor Gal (Technion, Israel)
Jonathan Gelati (University of Modena, Italy)
Yolanda Gil (USC ISI, USA)
Paolo Giorgini (University of Trento, Italy)
Carole Goble (University of Manchester, UK)
Benjamin Grosof (MIT, USA)
William Grosso (SDForum, USA)
Francesco Guerra (University of Modena, Italy)
Nicola Guarino (CNR, Italy)
Siegfried Handschuh (University of Karlsruhe, Germany)
Andreas Hotho (University of Karlsruhe, Germany)
Zachary Ives (University of Pennsylvania, USA)
Anupam Joshi (University of Maryland, Baltimore County, USA)
Gerti Kappel (Vienna University of Technology, Austria)
Alfons Kemper (University of Passau, Germany)
Matthias Klusch (DFKI, Germany)
Manuel Kolp (University of Louvain, Belgium)
Donald Kossmann (Technical University of Munich, Germany)
Yannis Labrou (Fujitsu, USA)
Georg Lausen (University of Freiburg, Germany)
Alain Leger (France Telecom, France)
Chen Li (University of California, Irvine, USA)
Ling Liu (Georgia Tech, USA)
Bertram Ludaescher (University of California, San Diego, USA)
Robert MacGregor Manolescu (USC ISI, USA)
Ioana Manolescu (INRIA, France)
Ryusuke Masuoka (Fujitsu, USA)
Massimo Marchiori (W3C and University of Venice, Italy)
Frank McCabe (Fujitsu, USA)
Luke McDowell (University of Washington, USA)
Sergey Melnik (University of Leipzig, Germany)
Daniele Montanari (Enidata SpA, Italy)
Pavlos Moraitis (University of Cyprus, Cyprus)
Boris Motik (FZI, Germany)
Enrico Motta (Open University, UK)
Haralambos Mouratidis (University of Sheffield, UK)
Claire Nedellec (MIG-INRA, France)
Natasha F. Noy (Stanford University, USA)
Borys Omelayenko (Vrije Universiteit, Amsterdam, The Netherlands)
Massimo Paoluccci (Carnegie Mellon University, USA)
Terry Payne (University of Southampton, UK)
Adam Pease (Teknowledge, USA)

Loris Penserini (Università Politecnica delle Marche, Italy)
Charles Phillips (University of Connecticut, USA)
Christoph Quix (RWTH Aachen, Germany)
Erhard Rahm (University of Leipzig, Germany)
Matt Richardson (University of Washington, USA)
Thomas Russ (USC ISI, USA)
Mareike Schoop (RWTH Aachen, Germany)
Ronny Siebes (Vrije Universiteit, Amsterdam, The Netherlands)
Munindar Singh (North Carolina State University, USA)
Michael Sintek (DFKI, Germany)
Divesh Srivastava (Bell Laboratories, USA)
Steffen Staab (University of Karlsruhe, Germany)
Heiner Stuckenschmidt (Vrije Universiteit, Amsterdam, The Netherlands)
Gerd Stumme (University of Karlsruhe, Germany)
Valentina Tamma (University of Liverpool, UK)
Herman ter Horst (Philips, The Netherlands)
Walt Truszkowski (NASA, USA)
Maria Vargas-Vera (Open University, UK)
Panos Vassiliadis (University of Ioannina, Greece)
Daniel Veit (University of Karlsruhe, Germany)
Guido Vetere (IBM, Italy)
Maurizio Vincini (University of Modena, Italy)
Claude Vogel (CONVERA, USA)
Raphael Volz (University of Karlsruhe, Germany)
Gottfried Vossen (University of Muenster, Germany)
Jan Wielemaker (University of Amsterdam, The Netherlands)
Stuart Williams (Hewlett-Packard, UK)
Carlo Zaniolo (University of California, Los Angeles, USA)

Patrons and Sponsors

Patrons

Platinum

Gold

Silver

Table of Contents

Foundations

Ontological Reasoning

Semantic Web Services

Security, Trust, and Privacy

Agents and the Semantic Web

Information Retrieval

Multi-media

Tools and Metodologies

Applications

Industrial Track

Representing the UMLS® Semantic Network Using OWL
(Or "What's in a Semantic Web Link?")

Vipul Kashyap[1] and Alex Borgida[2]

[1] LHCNBC, National Library of Medicine,
8600 Rockville Pike, Bethesda, MD 20894
[2] Department of Computer Science, Rutgers University,
New Brunswick, NJ 08903

Abstract. The Semantic Network, a component of the Unified Medical Language System® (UMLS), describes core biomedical knowledge consisting of semantic types and relationships. It is a well established, semi-formal ontology in widespread use for over a decade. We expected to "publish" this ontology on the Semantic Web, using OWL, with relatively little effort. However, we ran into a number of problems concerning alternative interpretations of the SN notation and the inability to express some of the interpretations in OWL. We detail these problems, as a cautionary tale to others planning to publish pre-existing ontologies on the Semantic Web, as a list of issues to consider when describing formally concepts in any ontology, and as a collection of criteria for evaluating alternative representations, which could form part of a methodology of ontology development.

1 Introduction

The Unified Medical Language System® (UMLS®) project was initiated in 1986 by the U.S. National Library of Medicine (NLM). Its goal is to help health professionals and researchers use biomedical information from *a variety of different sources* [1]. The UMLS consists of (i) biomedical concepts and associated strings, comprising the Metathesaurus (*MT*), (ii) a Semantic Network (*SN*) [2], and (iii) a collection of lexical tools (including SPECIALIST lexicon). Both data and tools are integrated in the UMLS Knowledge Source Server[1] and used in a large variety of applications (e.g. PubMed[2], ClinicalTrials.gov[3]). The *MT* provides a common structure for integrating more than 95 source biomedical vocabularies, organized by "concept" (cluster of terms representing the same meaning). The *SN* is a structured description of core biomedical knowledge consisting of semantic types and relationships, used to categorize *MT* concepts, with the *SN* being viewed by some as a semi-formal ontology. It (along with the *MT*) has been in use for more than a decade in the context of information retrieval applications. We expected to "publish" the *SN* on the Semantic Web by expressing it in OWL with relative ease, since there have been lots

[1] http://umlsks.nlm.nih.gov
[2] http://www.ncbi.nlm.nih.gov/entrez/query.fcgi
[3] http://www.clinicaltrials.gov

D. Fensel et al. (Eds.): ISWC 2003, LNCS 2870, pp. 1–16, 2003.

of papers that discuss the representation of medical terminologies using OWL style notations, called description logics (*DLs*) (e.g., [11][17][26][27]). Besides, there are numerous papers on the UMLS, including ones specifically about the semantics of the *SN* [2].

We ran into a number of difficulties in this undertaking. Some obstacles were due to ambiguities in the semantics of the *SN* notation or the under-specification of the notation (e.g., what can be inferred from the absence of edges?). Other problems were due to the inability to express the *SN* as OWL axioms which would provide the desired inferences, and the difficulty of making choices between multiple possible representations. We detail these problems: (i) as a cautionary tale to others wanting to publish ontologies on the semantic web, (ii) as a list of issues/alternatives to be considered in the process, and (iii) explore criteria for choosing among the above alternatives. We discuss next the motivation for expressing the *SN* and *MT* using OWL.

Motivation: Formal Representations of Biomedical Knowledge

Biomedical vocabularies and ontologies have always played a critical role in the context of healthcare information. For example, clinical and hospital information systems have used terms from a variety of biomedical vocabularies to specify codes for healthcare transactions and other pieces of information. eGov initiatives such as consolidated health informatics[4] (CHI) and government regulations such as HIPAA[5] have standardized on biomedical vocabularies included in the UMLS, for example, SNOMED, ICD-9-CM. Vocabularies such as the Medical Subject heading (MeSH), a component of the UMLS, have also been developed to help better specify queries for full text retrieval and for annotation of research articles in PubMed. Therefore the main motivations for a *formal* representation of biomedical knowledge are: (a) creation and maintenance of *consistent* biomedical terminology; (b) enabling translations of concepts across multiple autonomous vocabularies; and (c) improved specification of queries for information retrieval. An instance of the latter is the annotation of MEDLINE documents using descriptors built with concepts from the MeSH vocabulary [20]. For example, the semantics of the keyword "mumps" can be qualified by the subheading "complication", which can be conjoined with the main heading "pancreatitis" qualified by "etiology", to produce the MeSH descriptor `(Mumps/CO AND Pancreatitis/ET)`. This semi-formal descriptor can be used to improve text retrieval by use as a label or as part of a query. It can also be expressed more precisely using a Description Logic concept like $\exists$`complication.Mumps` $\sqcap$ $\exists$`etiology.Pancreatitis`, thus allowing for inferences during query answering. The above applications require functionality enabled by the use of OWL and its associated DL reasoner:

- Recognizing inconsistent (empty) concepts/relationships, and faulty subclass/ sub-property relationships (for creation and consistency maintenance).
- Recognizing concept equivalence (for creation/merging of terminologies, and matching of search queries and document annotations).
- Determining the position of a concept expression in a given hierarchy (to enable vocabulary merging into a directed acyclic graph (DAG) structure).

---

[4] http://www.jrfii.com/chi/

[5] http://www.cms.hhs.gov/hipaa/

- Determining the closest parents and children of a concept in the DAG (for concept translations e.g., [6]).
- Subsumption checking to tighten estimates of semantic distance between concepts, and to limit navigation of the DAG (for concept translations [6], and determination of relevant articles and result ranking for IR.)

We discuss next the "Vanilla" *SN* and its naïve OWL representation. Section 3 then presents various possible interpretations of "links" in the *SN* (prompting the sub-title of the paper as a twist on the famous paper by W. Woods [12]), and the resulting multiple representations. Section 4 discusses possible criteria that might be used to choose between these multiple representations. Conclusions and ongoing/future work are presented in Section 5.

2 The ("Vanilla") Semantic Network and OWL

We start by relating the simple, uncontroversial aspects of the *SN* to the OWL ontology language. The *SN* is a typical semantic network (see Figure 1) with nodes (called "semantic types") and links ("semantic relationships"). The types are organized into two high level hyponym/is-a hierarchies rooted at **`Entity`** and **`Event`**. Intuitively, but not formally, types are organized either by their inherent properties (e.g., a `Mammal` is a `Vertebrate` with constant body temperature) or by certain attributed characteristics (e.g., `ProfessionalGroup` is a set of individuals classified by their vocation). As illustrated in Figure 1, a `MentalBehavioralDysfunction` is a `DiseaseOrSyndrome`, which in turn is a `PathologicFunction`. The relationships used in the SN are also organized in a (shallow) is-a hierarchy, with 5 roots: (a) **`physically_related_to:`** e.g., `part_of`; (b) **`spatially_related_to:`** e.g., `surrounds`, (c) **`temporally_related_to:`** e.g., `precedes`, (d) **`functionally_related_to:`** e.g., `performs`, (e) **`conceptually_related_to:`** e.g., `measures`, `property_of`. For example, the relationship root **`functionally_related_to`** has several is-a children, including `affects` which in turn has many children, including `manages` and `treats`. As is, the relationships in the semantic network are binary.

In order to represent the above on the Semantic Web, RDF Schema (RDFS) would seem to be sufficient. However, RDFS cannot deal with some more advanced aspects of the *SN* to be presented below, and is not equipped to provide the kinds of inferences we had asked for earlier, thus leading us to consider OWL [22]. OWL, based on DAML+OIL [4], is intended to describe the terminology of a domain in terms of *classes/concepts* describing sets of individuals, and *properties/roles* relating these. An ontology consists of a set of *axioms* that assert characteristics of these classes and properties. OWL DL is a kind of *DL* – a logic with clear, formal semantics, (usually corresponding to a subset of First Order Predicate Calculus,) with desirable computational properties (e.g. decidable decision procedures). As in all *DL*, classes can be names (URIs) or *composite expressions*, and a variety of *constructors* are provided for building class expressions. The expressive power of the language is determined by the class (and property) constructors provided, and by the kinds of axioms allowed. Table 1 summarizes these for the underlying OWL. The connection between the *DL* notation and OWL's RDF syntax is shown by the translation of the disjunctive *DL* concept `Bacterium` $\cup$ `Virus`:

```
<owl:Class>
     <owl:unionOf rdf:parseType="Collection">
          <owl:Class rdf:about="#Bacterium"/>
          <owl:Class rdf:about="#Virus"/>
     </owl:unionOf>
</owl:Class>
```

In a *DL* representation of the UMLS Semantic Network, it is natural to associate *SN* semantic types with *DL* primitive concepts. So, the node `Organism` corresponds to *DL* concept `Organism`, which would be represented in OWL as the class `<owl:Class rdf:ID="Organism"/>`.

An *SN* relationship, such as `process_of`, corresponds to a *DL* primitive role, `process_of`, which would be translated to OWL object properties. In the simplest case, one could associate with a relationship the source and destination of the edge as the "domain" and "range" specification:

```
<owl:ObjectProperty rdf:ID="process_of">
               <rdfs:domain rdf:resource="#BiologicFunction">
               <rdfs:range rdf:resource="#Organism">
</owl:ObjectProperty>
```

However, as we shall see in the next section, this translation could be controversial.

Axioms originate from inheritance hierarchies of the various types and relationships. Thus the type/relationship hierarchy in the *SN* can be represented as a collection of subclass/subproperty axioms such as:

`Fungus` ⊆ `Organism` *(sub-types using <owl:subClassOf>)*
`Virus` ⊆ `Organism`
`part_of` ⊆ `physically_related_to` *(sub-relationships using <owl:subPropertyOf>)*
`contains` ⊆ `physically_related_to`

Some relationships in the *SN* have inverses, which is specified through axioms involving the inverseOf role constructor

`part_of` ≡ `has_part`$^{-}$ *(asymmetric property)*
`adjacent_to` ≡ `adjacent_to`$^{-}$ *(symmetric property)*

3 Semantics of a "Link" in the UMLS Semantic Network

SN types, relationships and their hierarchies, as well as inverses have clear corresponding OWL/DL constructs. However, there are serious difficulties in accurately capturing the semantics of the *SN*, due both to the under-specified meaning of the notion of "link" between two semantic types, and the somewhat unusual inferences/constraints that are associated with them in *SN*. We explore next various possible interpretations of "link", proposing OWL axioms for each, identifying when necessary new *DL* constructs needed. We then evaluate each in light of additional special "inferences" required in the *SN*, such as the notions "domain and range inheritance", "inheritance blocking" and "polymorphic relationships".

3.1 Multiple Interpretations of a "Link"

Consider the following simple diagram, with link labeled "causes" connecting two nodes, Bacteria and Infection:

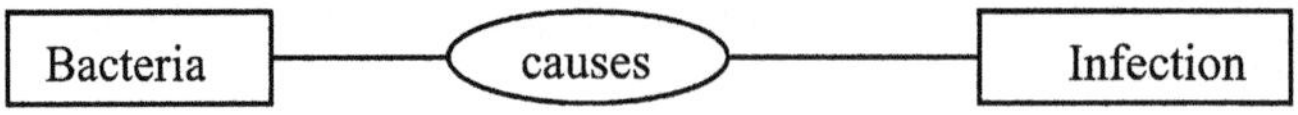

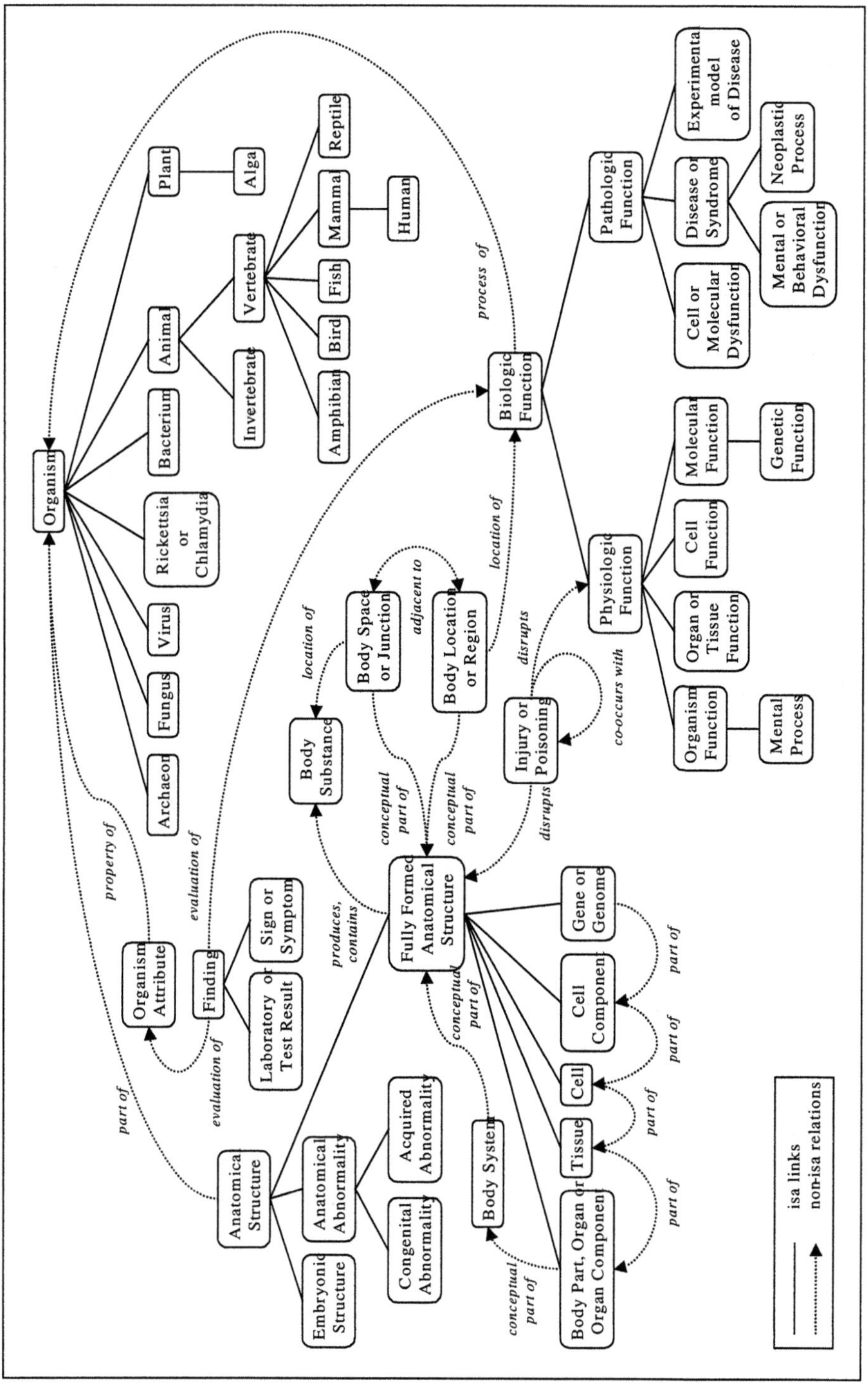

Fig. 1. A portion of the UMLS Semantic Network [23]

Table 1. OWL/RDF constructors and axioms

Constructor/Axiom	DL Syntax	Example
intersectionOf	$C_1 \cap \ldots \cap C_n$	Bacterium ∩ Animal
unionOf	$C_1 \cup \ldots \cup C_n$	Bacterium ∪ Virus
complementOf	$\neg C$	¬Plant
oneOf	$\{ x_1, \ldots, x_n \}$	{aspirin, tylenol}
allValuesFrom	$\forall P.C$	∀partOf.Cell
someValuesFrom	$\exists P.C$	∃processOf.Organism
hasValue	$\exists P.\{x\}$	∃treatedBy{aspirin}
top concept	$\top$	ENTITY
bottom concept	$\bot$	NOTHING
subClassOf	$C_1 \subseteq C_2$	Human ⊆ Animal ∩ Biped
sameClassAs	$C_1 \equiv C_2$	Man ≡ Human ∩ Male
subPropertyOf	$P_1 \subseteq P_2$	part_of ⊆ physically_related_to
samePropertyAs	$P_1 \equiv P_2$	has_temperature ≡ has_fever
disjointWith	$C_1 \subseteq \neg C_2$	Vertebrate ⊆ ¬Invertebrate
sameIndividualAs	$\{x_1\} \equiv \{x_2\}$	{aspirin}≡{acetyl_salicylic_acid}
differentIndFrom	$\{x_1\} \subseteq \neg\{x_2\}$	{aspirin} ⊆ ¬{tylenol}
inverseOf	$P_1 \equiv P_2^{-}$	has_evaluation ≡ evaluation_of⁻
transitiveProperty	$P^+ \subseteq P$	part_of⁺ ⊆ part_of
functionalProperty	$\top \subseteq \leq 1\, P$	T ⊆ ≤ 1 has_genetic_profile
inverseFunctionalPropty	$\top \subseteq \leq 1\, P^{-}$	T ⊆ ≤ 1 is_genetic_profile_of⁻
domain	$\exists P.\top \subseteq C$	∃evaluation_of.T ⊆ Finding
range	$\top \subseteq \forall P.C$	T ⊆ ∀evaluation_of.DiagnosticTest

Rector [9] identifies 5 possible interpretations of the above, corresponding to the English statements:

"**All** bacteria cause {**each/only/some**} infection(s)"

"**Some** bacteria cause {**all/some**} infections".

Since semantic web ontology languages emphasize describing relationships in terms of domains and ranges, let us also consider some statements using these notions. We start with defining two operators δ and ρ as follows:

$$\delta(\mathbf{P}) = \{x \mid (\exists y)P(x, y)\} \text{ and } \rho(\mathbf{P}) = \{y \mid (\exists x)P(x, y)\}$$

These operators define two sets for presentation purposes and under some interpretations they might correspond to the domain/range interpretations associated with RDFS, and DAML+OIL/OWL. These operators suggest three more interpretations.

"The set of Bacteria {**equals / is contained in/contains**} δ(causes)."

"The set of Infections {**equals/ is contained in /contains**} ρ(causes)."

Consider now representing each of the above 8 cases using *DLs*. *DL* descriptions can be used to represent δ(**P**) and ρ(**P**) as follows:

$$\delta(\mathbf{P}) \equiv \exists \texttt{causes}.\top, \quad \rho(\mathbf{P}) \equiv \exists \texttt{causes}^{-}.\top$$

we have the following axioms for the last three cases above:

- **"δ/ρ equals":**

  axioms: ∃causes.T ≡ Bacteria, ∃causes⁻.T ≡ Infection

- **"δ/ρ subsumed":**
  axioms: $\exists$causes.T $\subseteq$ Bacteria, $\exists$causes^{-}.T $\subseteq$ Infection
  It may be noted that this corresponds to the domain/range interpretations specified in the RDFS, DAML+OIL/OWL context [24] [25].
- **"δ/ρ subsumes":**
  axioms: Bacteria $\subseteq$ $\exists$causes.T, Infection $\subseteq$ $\exists$causes^{-}.T

For the 5 possible statements discussed earlier, we have:

- **"All/some"** (*"All bacteria cause some infection"*) :
  axiom: Bacteria $\subseteq$ $\exists$causes.Infection
- **"All/only"** (*"All bacteria cause only infections."*):
  axiom: Bacteria $\subseteq$ $\forall$causes.Infection
- **"All/each"** (*"All bacteria cause each infection."*) This interpretation corresponds to the FOL formula:
  ($\forall$x)(Bacteria(x) $\wedge$ ($\forall$y)(Infection(y) $\rightarrow$ causes(x,y)))
  $\equiv$ ($\forall$x)(Bacteria(x) $\wedge$ ($\forall$y)($\neg$causes(x,y) $\rightarrow$ $\neg$Infection(y)))
  This can be represented as a subsumption axiom using the role complement operator in *DLs*:
  axiom: Bacteria $\subseteq$ $\forall\neg$causes.$\neg$Infection
  or using the special concept constructor $\forall$**C.r** (*"objects related by r to all objects in C"*), which has been investigated by Lutz and Sattler [13]:
  Bacteria $\subseteq$ $\forall$Infection.causes
  In either case, we go beyond the limits of OWL.
- **"Some/some"** (*"Some bacteria cause some infections."*) This interpretation can be represented in a number of different ways, though none using axioms of the kinds described in **Table 1**. The alternatives include:
  (i) "There is *some* state of the world where a bacterium causes an infection"
  axiom: Bacteria $\not\subseteq$ ($\leq$ 0 causes Infection) or
  axiom: "Bacteria $\cap$ $\exists$causes.Infection **is consistent**"
  (ii) "A bacterium causes an infection in every possible state of the world"
  axiom: "**the concept** (Bacteria $\cap$ $\exists$causes.Infection) **is never empty**"
  It is the latter which corresponds to the desired logical formula ($\exists$x)($\exists$y)(Bacteria(x) $\wedge$ Infection(y) $\wedge$ causes(x,y)); it can be expressed using a new kind of axiom, concerning the cardinality of *concepts*[6], which was introduced by Baader et al [8]:
  axiom: $\geq$ 1 (Bacteria $\cap$ $\exists$causes.Infection)
- **"Some/any"** (*"Some bacteria cause all infections."*) This requires a combination of the two previous techniques
  axiom: $\geq$ 1 (Bacteria $\cap$ $\forall\neg$causes.$\neg$Infection)

A summary of the above interpretations and corresponding encodings may be viewed in Table 2, at the end of this section. We consider next three aspects of the *SN*, some corresponding to inferences and some to constraints, and evaluate the above listed encodings with them in mind.

---

[6] $\geq$ 1 C) is encoded in OWL by asserting the following axioms: T $\subseteq$ $\exists$P.{b} and {b} $\subseteq$ $\exists$P^{-}.C, where b is a new atomic individual and P is a new role.

3.2 δ and ρ Inheritance

The "is-a" link gives rise to "inheritance" relationships, a hallmark of semantic networks. For example, the type `BiologicFunction` has a relationship `process_of` to the type `Organism` in the semantic network (Figure 1) – to be written henceforth as `process_of(BiologicFunction,Organism)`. By inheritance, the descendants of `BiologicFunction` such as `PhysiologicFunction`, `MentalProcess`, etc. are all understood to have the `process_of` relationship to `Organism`. Surprisingly, *SN* also assumes inheritance on the "range" of the relationship, i.e., `process_of(BiologicFunction,Animal)`, `process_of(PhysiologicFunction, Animal)` also hold. An encoding of *SN* will be said to support δ-inheritance if, given (an encoding of) P(A,B), and a concept C such that $C \subseteq A$, (the encoding of) P(C,B) is entailed; and ρ-inheritance is supported if for a D such that $D \subseteq B$, P(A,D) is entailed. Consider now whether/how the encodings discussed in Section 3.1 support δ-inheritance and ρ-inheritance.

- **"δ/ρ equals":** This encoding doesn't support δ-inheritance or ρ-inheritance: from P(A,B) we have $\delta(P) \equiv A$, and if P(C,B) were to be true, then $\delta(P) \equiv C$, which means that A must have been equal C.
- **"δ/ρ subsumed":** This encoding also doesn't support δ-inheritance or ρ-inheritance, since $\{C \subseteq A,\ \delta(P) \subseteq A\}$ doesn't entail $\delta(P) \subseteq C$.
- **"δ/ρ subsumes":** Interestingly , this encoding supports both δ-inheritance and ρ-inheritance, because $C \subseteq A \subseteq \delta(P)$ entails $C \subseteq \delta(P)$, and $D \subseteq B \subseteq \rho(P)$ entails $D \subseteq \rho(P)$, so that the representation of P(C,D) holds.
- **"All/some":** The encoding of P(A,B) as $A \subseteq \exists P.B$ supports δ-inheritance, but not ρ-inheritance since from $C \subseteq A$ and $D \subseteq B$ we get $C \subseteq \exists P.B$ but not $C \subseteq \exists P.D$
- **"All/only":** The encoding $A \subseteq \forall P.B$ behaves like the previous one, supporting δ-inheritance, but not ρ-inheritance.
- **"All/each":** The encoding $A \subseteq \forall\neg P.\neg B$ supports δ-inheritance as in the previous cases. It also supports ρ-inheritance since $D \subseteq B$ entails $\forall\neg P.\neg B \subseteq \forall\neg P.\neg D$, so that $A \subseteq \forall\neg P.\neg D$ holds.
- **"Some/some":** The encoding $(\geq 1\ (A \sqcap \exists P.B))$ doesn't support δ-inheritance or ρ-inheritance because the addition of $C \subseteq A$ and $D \subseteq B$ doesn't entail either $(\geq 1\ (C \sqcap \exists P.B))$ or $(\geq 1\ (A \sqcap \exists P.D))$.
- **"Some/all":** The encoding $(\geq 1\ (A \sqcap \forall\neg P.\neg B))$ doesn't support δ-inheritance, but supports ρ-inheritance: Since $D \subseteq B$ entails $\forall\neg P.\neg B \subseteq \forall\neg P.\neg D$, we can infer $(A \sqcap \forall\neg P.\neg B) \subseteq (A \sqcap \forall\neg P.\neg D)$, and hence $(\geq 1\ (A \sqcap \forall\neg P.\neg D))$ holds if $(\geq 1\ (A \sqcap \forall\neg P.\neg B))$ holds.

In general, if an encoding does not support some form of inheritance, we will need to explicitly assert axioms corresponding to the missed inheritance inferences.

3.3 Inheritance Blocking

In some cases there will be a conflict between the placement of types in the *SN* and the links to be inherited. For example, `process_of(MentalProcess,Plant)` is inherited from `process_of(BiologicFunction,Organism)` though this is an undesirable inference, since plants are not sentient beings. For this purpose, the *SN* provides a mechanism to explicitly "block" inheritance.[7] In general, whenever a mechanism does *not* support a form of inheritance, it can deal with blocking by simply not adding explicitly the axioms. However, when inheritance is a logical consequence of the axioms, preventing the relationship from holding would normally lead to logical inconsistency. Rather than rely on "default/non-monotonic reasoning", which however is quite complex, we will instead adopt the approach of *modifying* axioms whenever exceptions are encountered. This approach will be made easier in our case by the fact that the *SN* does not support multiple inheritance. Let us look then at ways to block inheritance in those cases where it does occur:

- **"δ/ρ subsumes":** Let $C_1 \subseteq A$ and $D_1 \subseteq B$, and suppose that although $P(A,B)$ holds, we don't want the property P to be inherited to C_1 and D_1. We could specify: $A \cap \neg C_1 \subseteq \delta(P)$ and $B \cap \neg D_1 \subseteq \rho(P)$. However, suppose $C_2 \subseteq A$ and $D_2 \subseteq B$, and we also want to block $P(C_2,D_2)$; then asserting $A \cap \neg(C_1 \cup C_2) \subseteq \delta(P)$ and $B \cap \neg(D_1 \cup D_2) \subseteq \rho(P)$ has the unintended effect of blocking the links $P(C_1,D_2)$ and $P(C_2,D_1)$. To **compensate** for this, one could explicitly add axioms specifying $P(C_1,D_2)$ and $P(C_2,D_1)$.
- **"All/each":** Recall that the encoding $A \subseteq \forall\neg P.\neg B$ supports both δ-inheritance and ρ-inheritance. Suppose we are given $C_1, C_2 \subseteq A$ and $D_1, D_2 \subseteq B$, and we want to block $P(C_1,D_1)$ and $P(C_2,D_2)$. We can start by asserting $A \cap \neg(C_1 \cup C_2) \subseteq \forall\neg P.(\neg(B \cap \neg(D_1 \cup D_2)))$. But once again we need to add ***compensating axioms*** $C_2 \subseteq \forall P.\ D_1$ and $C_1 \subseteq \forall P.\ D_2$ to represent the links $P(C_1,D_2)$ and $P(C_2,D_1)$, which could no longer be deduced.
- **"All/only":** To block the δ-inheritance of $P(C_1,B)$ when $P(A,B)$ and $C_1 \subseteq A$, replace the axiom $A \subseteq \forall P.B$ by $A \cap \neg(C_1 \cup \ldots) \subseteq \forall P.B$, so that exceptions are explicitly noted.
- **"All/some"** is similar to **"all/only"**.
- **"Some/all":** To block ρ-inheritance of $P(A,D)$ when $P(A,B)$ and $D_1 \subseteq B$, use the axiom $\geq 1\ (A \cap \forall\neg P.(\neg B \cup D_1))$ instead of $\geq 1\ (A \cap \forall\neg P.\neg B)$.
- **"Some/some":** Although this representation does not support either δ-inheritance and ρ-inheritance, and hence has no problem with blocking, it does have an interesting property: $\{(\geq 1\ (A \cap \exists P.B)),\ A' \supseteq A\ ,\ B' \supseteq B\}$ entails $(\geq 1\ (A' \cap \exists P.B))$ and $(\geq 1\ (A \cap \exists P.B'))$, which suggests that if $P(A,B)$ is asserted then $P(A',B')$ can be deduced for all *super-classes* A' of A and B' of B. This undesirable "upwards inheritance" can be blocked by specifying axioms such as $(\leq 0\ (A' \cap \exists P.B))$ and $(\leq 0\ (A \cap \exists P.B'))$.

3.4 Polymorphic Relationships

Polymorphic relationships are ones whose arguments, i.e., domain and range values can be instances of multiple classes. One (benign) source of such polymorphism is

---

[7] The *SN* also allows blocking to be applied to ***all*** children, without explicitly having to list all possible pairs. So from P(A, B), P(C, D) is blocked for *any* descendants C of A and D of B. We do not examine this feature here for lack of space.

inheritance – it is called "subtype polymorphism" in Programming Languages. However, in UMLS SN, the same relationship can be stated to connect pairs of types that are not is-a related. For example, in Figure 1, we have, among others

```
location_of(BodySpaceorJunction,BodySubstance)
location_of(BodyLocationOrRegion,BiologicFunction)
contained_in(BodySubstance,EmbryonicStructure)
contained_in(BodySubstance,FullyFormedAnatomicalStructure)
```

Such examples, with edges $P(A_1, B_1)$ and $P(A_2, B_2)$, exhibit what might be called "ad-hoc polymorphism/overloading" in Object Oriented languages. One could interpret this to be equivalent to the introduction of two new relationships, P_1 and P_2, adding the axiom $P \equiv P_1 \cup P_2$, and modeling $P(A_1, B_1)$ and $P(A_2, B_2)$ with $P_1(A_1, B_1)$ and $P_2(A_2, B_2)$. Unfortunately, OWL does not support property union; and even if it did, the above encoding is ***non-incremental*** in the sense that we must detect cases of overloading, and *remove* earlier axioms, replacing them with new ones. Such non-locality seems unavoidable for blocking, which is inherently non-monotonic, but is otherwise undesirable since it makes it difficult to maintain sets of axioms.

Some intuitions related to polymorphism which may be useful to evaluate alternatives are: (i) When $A_1 \cap A_2$ and $B_1 \cap B_2$ are empty, as in the first pair above, the constraints should not affect each other. (ii) When $A_1 \equiv A_2 \equiv A$, as in the second example pair above, the encoding should not require R to be the empty relation if $B1 \cap B2 \equiv \emptyset$. Consider again the encodings from Section 3.1.

- **"δ/ρ subsumed":** From $\{\delta(P) \subseteq A_1, \delta(P) \subseteq A_2, \rho(P) \subseteq B_1, \rho(P) \subseteq B_2\}$ we get $\{\delta(P) \subseteq A_1 \cap A_2, \rho(P) \subseteq B_1 \cap B_2\}$, which means that case (i) above is miss-handled. It may be noted that this case corresponds to the RDFS, DAML+OIL/OWL interpretation of multiple ranges and domains [24][25].
- **"δ/ρ subsumes":** While the above intuitions are satisfied, $\{A_1 \subseteq \delta(P), A_2 \subseteq \delta(P), B_1 \subseteq \rho(P), B_2 \subseteq \rho(P)\}$ entails $\{A_1 \cup A_2 \subseteq \delta(P), B_1 \cup B_2 \subseteq \rho(P)\}$, so it seems we get $P(A_1 \cup A_2, B_1 \cup B_2)$ from $P(A_1,B_1)$ and $P(A_2,B_2)$. This is overly permissive, since it gives rise to *unintended* models, when $(x,y) \in P$, $x \in A_1$, $y \in B_2$ or $x \in A_2$, $y \in B_1$.

The previous two cases are ones where using sub-properties is appropriate.

- **"All/only":** The encoding $\{A_1 \subseteq \forall P.B_1, A_2 \subseteq \forall P.B_2\}$ supports polymorphism properly in the case when the A's are disjoint, but in case (ii) above we get $A \subseteq \forall P.(B_1 \cap B_2) \equiv \forall P.\bot \equiv (\leq 0\ P)$, which does not allow A to be related to anything via P, thus contradicting our intuitions for (ii). Therefore, we must replace the original axioms $\{A_1 \subseteq \forall P.B_1, A_2 \subseteq \forall P.B_2\}$ by a new set $\{(A_1 \cap \neg A_2) \subseteq \forall P.B_1, (\neg A_1 \cap A_2) \subseteq \forall P.B_2, (A_1 \cap A_2) \subseteq \forall P.(B_1 \cup B_2)\}$, another case of non-incrementality.
- **All/each, all/some, some/each, some/some**: All these encodings support polymorphism following an analysis similar to the previous case.

3.5 Summary

The various encoding schemes and their suitability for the three special aspects of *SN*, viz. domain and range inheritance, inheritance blocking and polymorphic relationships are summarized in Table 2.

Table 2. Interpretation, axioms and support for *SN* requirements

Interpretation	Encoding	δ/ρ Inheritance	Inheritance Blocking	Polymorphic Relations
δ/ρ equals	$\delta(P) \equiv A$ $\rho(P) \equiv B$	No/No	N/A	No
δ/ρ subsumed	$\delta(P) \subseteq A$ $\rho(P) \subseteq B$	No/No	N/A	Missed model
δ/ρ subsumes	$A \subseteq \delta(P)$ $B \subseteq \rho(P)$	Yes/Yes	Exceptions + compensation	Unintended model
all / some	$A \subseteq \exists P.B$	Yes/No	Exception in axiom	ok
all / only	$A \subseteq \forall P.B$	Yes/No	Exception in axiom	Modification
some / some	$\geq 1(A \cap \exists P.B)$	No/No	N/A	ok
some / all	$\geq 1(A \cap \forall\neg P.\neg B)$	No/Yes	Exception in axiom	ok
all / each	$A \subseteq \forall\neg P.\neg B$	Yes/Yes	Exceptions + compensation	ok

4 First Steps towards a Representation Choice Methodology

In the previous section we considered a list of alternative encodings of the *SN* into *DL*. We now propose an (incomplete) set of questions that could guide ontology developers in making choices among alternative representations in a formal ontology language such as OWL; these might form the basis of a methodological framework. The questions fall into several categories:

(a) Does the encoding support the "inferences" of the original notation?
(b) Does the encoding support inferences needed by expected applications?
(c) Does the encoding provide a reasonable intuitive model of the domain?
(d) Is the encoding supported by the formal ontology language and its reasoner?

Let us examine the alternatives from Section 3 in this regard as a way of illustrating and adding details to the list given below.

(a) Support for Inferences of the Notation

After identifying a number of possible representations for the node+link notation of *SN*, in Section 3, we looked to see which provided a logically consistent mechanism for performing inferences *explicitly, though informally, sanctioned by the notation.* Surprisingly, it appears that for *SN* the **"all/each"** encoding most closely captures these intuitions, with "**δ/ρ subsumes**" as the next best encoding. Several other aspects need to be considered, when dealing with graphical notations:

Does an encoding entail unintended inferences?

The "some/some" statement has the effect of "upwardly" inheriting a link to all the superclasses of the nodes associated with the link. This requires the ontology developer to identify such situations and assert axioms to prevent them.

Can/should something be inferred from the absence of a link?

It is not clear in *SN* whether links should be read as type constraints in programming languages: what is not explicitly permitted is forbidden. If so, the encoding $A \subseteq \forall P.B$

doesn't prohibit instances of ¬A being related to B. To prevent this, we would have to add the axiom (¬A ⊆ ≤ 0 P).

Should relationships be inferred to be asymmetric by default?
This is a special case of the previous general "default negation". According to [2], in the *SN*, links are "*usually asymmetric – MedicalDevice prevents Pathologic Function but not vice versa*"; moreover one can specify it: adjacent_to ≡ adjacent_to⁻. Axioms to this effect can be added automatically during translation, although asymmetricity again requires non-standard axioms: ¬(P ≡ P-).

Are the is-a children of nodes disjoint?
In the *SN*, there are some examples where this is not the case. Horrocks and Rector [17] give good arguments that the proper way to model ontologies is to start with trees of disjoint primitive concepts, and *define* everything else in terms of them.

(b) Support for Intended Application
If it is important to detect inconsistency in an ontology without overloading [11] e.g., {hasGender(FATHER,{male}), hasGender(FATHER,{female})}, where the relationship hasGender relates a concept FATHER to concepts represented as enumerations, e.g. {male}, {female}. An encoding of the form A ⊆ ∀P.B will not infer inconsistency, unless one also adds A ⊆ ∃P.T. Alternately, if the application uses only a limited set of inferences (e.g., because the form of the questions asked is limited), then one may not need to represent difficult kinds of axioms (e.g., properties being asymmetric). Such criteria can be criticized on the grounds that an ontology is supposed to be "application neutral", although there is always some arbitrary decision to be made about what is included and what is not.

(c) Reasonableness of the domain model
A strong case can be made that one should start first with an idea of how the world should be *modeled* – what are individuals, properties, etc, in the domain of discourse, and how concepts related to them, tied to the denotational semantics of the formal notation. The standard interpretation of a concept is a set of individual objects in the world, connected by properties (DL denotational semantics). Thus, causes (Bacteria, Infection) constrains the way in which any particular individual bacterium can be related by "causes" to a case of infection. So the questions are:

What are the intuitive encodings?
The "**all/some**" encoding Bacteria ⊆ ∃cause.Infection seems to be the representation of choice in several sophisticated medical ontologies developed with DL-knowledgeable collaborators [10][11], although in any state of the world some bacteria may not cause any infection. On the other hand, the "**all/only**" encoding Bacteria ⊆ ∀cause.Infection, is most frequently used in object-centered representations (e.g., [16]), though it runs into problems with polymorphism, since some bacteria might cause rashes and infections. Either way, interpretations such as "*all bacteria cause all infections*", or "*there is a bacterium that causes some infection*" seem quite odd, and were in fact rejected out of hand in [9].

Is an alternative interpretation possible?
The above seems rather discouraging for the **"all/each"** encoding, even though it satisfies all the *SN* requirements. However, suppose we prefix the relationship names by *"can/could_have/could_be"*: *"a bacterium could be the cause of any case of infection"*. The resulting reading is much more reasonable, and may explain the inheritance and polymorphism properties of the *SN*, especially when noting that most relationships in the *SN* (unlike `fatherOf,` say) can be read this way.

The **"some/some"** reading – "some bacterium causes some infection", also seems to be unnatural, but interestingly McCray and Nelson explicitly endorse it: "**a relation is only established if at least some members of a set map onto at least one member of another set linked by the relationship**"[2]. The explanation for this may be that in the medical informatics community, concepts such as INFECTION are viewed by many as having kinds of infections, rather than specific cases of those infections, as instances. This is hinted at by the UMLS terminology of "labeling" concepts in the MT by the semantic types in the SN, rather than saying that the MT concepts are subclasses of semantic types, which form a high-level ontology. We note that this approach has been successful in the context of medical research literature search/retrieval, and propose this as an interesting topic of future research in the OWL/RDF context.

(d) Representation and inference in ontology language
Can the desired encoding be expressed in the ontology language of choice?
Given that the Semantic Web appears to be settling on a common ontology language (OWL) it is clearly important to encode the axioms in the constructs of this language. In this respect the representations based on role operators (negation, disjunction) and concept cardinality appear to be unsatisfactory. (But see below.)

Can the interpretation be represented using less "expensive" terms?
In addition to addressing the previous issue, reformulating an encoding using different constructors/axioms could provide significant computational benefits in view of the wealth of information about the computational complexity of various collections of DL concept and role constructors (e.g., see [7]) .

Is there some (better) way to capture the desired encoding knowing the technology used to implement the reasoner for the ontology language?
We have seen that one encoding of the some/some interpretation uses a language extension proposed by Baader et al. [8], who used esoteric techniques (based on "Hintikka trees" and automata), to reason about theses. There is an alternate encoding using nominals (individuals), and we saw that for the case of $(\geq 1\ C)$, there is even a solution in the basic ALC DL. Similarly, the axiom $\top \sqsubseteq \forall P.C$ can be reasoned withmuch more efficiently by some tableaux reasoners than the logically equivalent $\exists P^{-}.\top \sqsubseteq C$

Are there acceptable approximations to concepts/axioms?
Another approach to deal with the limited expressiveness of the ontology language, or the complexity of reasoning, is by representing concepts and/or axioms in an *approximate* way; this requires understanding what kinds of questions applications

need to have answered, in order to evaluate the price of information loss. Consider the axiom $P \equiv P_1 \cup P_2$, used in property polymorphisms. To avoid property union, not available in OWL, we can assert $P_1 \subseteq P$ and $P_2 \subseteq P$. Approximation of disjunction using hierarchies has been considered in [18], and there has been considerable research on approximation in *DLs* [19].

5 Conclusions and Future Work

We have reviewed in this paper some of our experiences with representing in OWL, a well established semi-formal ontology, the UMLS Semantic Network, which has been in use for over a decade in the context of medical informatics. Whereas the representation of the "vanilla" *SN* was straightforward, we encountered obstacles representing the semantics of "links" in the *SN*, especially in the context of requirements such as δ/ρ inheritance, inheritance blocking and polymorphism. This led us to investigate the possible interpretations and encodings of a "link" in the *SN*. We did not use role transitivity and number restrictions, but did use class disjunctions, role hierarchies, axioms, inverses, all and some property restrictions. The encodings were evaluated based on their support to *SN* requirements above. The various issues enumerated in this context should be considered by ontology and content developers while formally describing concepts in an ontology. Among the criteria we have identified are (i) support for inferences desired, (ii) intuitiveness of the resulting denotational semantic model, (iii) representation and effective reasoning in the ontology language. The latter involves formal worst case complexity results about the cost of reasoning, direct exploitation of the reasoner technology underlying the ontology language, and the possibility of approximate representation. We hope that the parts of a methodology provided above will be helpful to ontology developers that have embarked on the task of expressing their ontologies using OWL. We observe that although some of our problems could have been avoided if *SN* would have had a formal semantics. However, even starting with a language with equivalent translations to OWL, is not enough, since questions related to expressibility and intended modeling semantics, among others, still remain.

At the NLM, we are exploring various research issues related to the Semantic Web [3], both in the context of enhancing existing biomedical applications and for enabling new applications. Some ongoing investigations are: (a) The Semantic Vocabulary Interoperation project [21], which aims to provide tools and techniques to translate a term in a source biomedical vocabulary (e.g., ICD-9-CM) to a target biomedical vocabulary (e.g., SNOMED) by using the knowledge present in the *SN* and *MT*; (b) Potential improvement for searching and retrieving text and citation information by annotation of biomedical content using semantic web markup languages such as RDF and OWL; and (c) Enhancement and consistency maintenance of biomedical vocabularies based on reasoning with OWL descriptions as proposed in [5].

Acknowledgements. We would like to acknowledge helpful discussions with Alexa McCray, Olivier Bodenreider and Sergio Tessari. Support for this work was provided by the Oak Ridge Institute for Science and Education (ORISE).

References

[1] Lindberg D, Humphreys B, McCray A. "The Unified Medical Language System." Methods Inf Med 1993:32(4):281–91.

[2] McCray A, Nelson S. "The representation of meaning in the UMLS." Methods Inf Med 1995:34(1–2):193–201

[3] Berners-Lee T, Hendler J, Lassila O. "The Semantic Web." Scientific American, May 2001. http://www.sciam.com/2001/0501issue/0501berners-lee.html

[4] Horrocks I. "DAML+OIL: A Description Logic for the Semantic Web." IEEE Bulletin for the Technical Committee on Data Engineering, 2002.

[5] Stevens R., Goble R., Horrocks I. and Bechhofer S. "Building a Bioinformatics Ontology using OIL." IEEE Information Technology in Biomedicine, special issue on Bioinformatics, Vol 6(2):135–141, June 2002.

[6] Mena E, Kashyap V, Illarramendi A and Sheth A. "Imprecise answers in a Distributed Environment: Estimation of Information Loss for Multiple Ontology-based Query Processing." Int. J. of Cooperative Information Systems (IJCIS), 9(4), December 2000.

[7] "The Description Logic Handbook: Theory, Implementation and Applications." F. Baader, D. Calvanese, D. McGuiness , D. Nardi and P F Patel-Schneider (editors), Cambridge University Press, 2003.

[8] Baader F, Buchheit F, and Hollunder B. "Cardinality Restrictions on Concepts." Artificial Intelligence, 88(1–2):195–213, 1996.

[9] Rector A L, Rogers J and colleagues. "Introduction to Ontologies." Tutorial presented at the AMIA Annual Symposium 2002.

[10] Rector A L, Bechhofer S K, Goble C A, Horrocks I, Nowlan W A, Solomon W D. "The GRAIL Concept Modelling Language for Medical Terminology." Artificial Intelligence in Medicine, Volume 9, 1997

[11] Gangemi A, Pisanelli D M and Steve G. "An overview of the ONIONS project: Applying ontologies to the integration of medical terminologies." Data and Knowledge Engineering, 31(2):183–220, 1999.

[12] Woods W A. "What's in a link: Foundations for Semantic Networks." In R. J. Brachman and H J Levesque (editors), Readings in Knowledge Representation, 218–241. Morgan Kaufman Publishers, 1985

[13] Lutz C and Sattler U. "Mary likes all Cats." Proc. 2000 Int. Workshop on Description Logics (DL 2000).

[14] http://phd1.cs.yale.edu:8080/umls/UMLSinDAML/NET/SRSTR.daml

[15] Horrocks, I. "The FaCT system." In Proc. Int. Conf. Tableaux '98, Springer-Verlag LNCS 1397, pp. 307–312, May 1998.

[16] Calvanese D, Lenzerini M and Nardi D. "Unifying Class-Based Representation Formalisms." Journal of Artificial Intelligence Research (JAIR) 11: 199–240 (1999)

[17] Horrocks I., and Rector A. "Experience building a large, re-usable medical ontology using a description logic with transitivity and concept inclusions." Proc. Workshop on Ontological Engineering, AAAI Spring Symposium (AAAI'97).

[18] Borgida, A., and Etherington, D.W. "Hierarchical Knowledge Bases and Efficient Disjunctive Reasoning." Proc. KR'89, pp. 33–43

[19] Brandt S., Küsters R., and Turhan A.-Y. "Approximating ALCN-Concept Descriptions." In Proc. of the 2002 Int. Workshop on Description Logics (DL 2002).

[20] Medical Subject Headings – Home Page, http://www.nlm.nih.gov/mesh/meshhome.html

[21] The Semantic Vocabulary Interoperation Project, http://cgsb2.nlm.nih.gov/~kashyap/projects/SVIP.html

[22] OWL Web Ontology Language Guide, http://www.w3.org/TR/2003/WD-owl-guide-20030331/

[23] McCray, A. T. and Bodenreider O. "A Conceptual Framework for the Biomedical Domain." In R. Green, C. A. Bean and S. H. Myaeng, (editors), The Semantics of Relationships: An Interdisciplinary Perspective, Kluwer Academic Publishers, 2002
[24] http://www.w3.org/TR/rdf-mt/#rdfs_interp
[25] http://www.daml.org/2001/03/model-theoretic-semantics
[26] Schulz, S. and Hahn, U. "Medical Knowledge Re-engineering – converting major portions of the UMLS into a terminological knowledge base". International Journal of Medical Informatics 64(2–3):207–221 (2001).
[27] Cornet, R. and Abu-Henna, A. "Evaluation of a frame-based Ontology. A formalization-oriented Approach". In Proceedings of MIE 2002.

Reducing OWL Entailment to Description Logic Satisfiability

Ian Horrocks[1] and Peter F. Patel-Schneider[2]

[1] Department of Computer Science
University of Manchester
horrocks@cs.man.ac.uk
[2] Bell Labs Research
Lucent Technologies
pfps@research.bell-labs.com

Abstract. We show how to reduce ontology entailment for the OWL DL and OWL Lite ontology languages to knowledge base satisfiability in (respectively) the $\mathcal{SHOIN}(\mathbf{D})$ and $\mathcal{SHIF}(\mathbf{D})$ description logics. This is done by first establishing a correspondence between OWL ontologies and description logic knowledge bases and then by showing how knowledge base entailment can be reduced to knowledge base satisfiability.

1 Introduction

The aim of the Semantic Web is to make web resources (not just HTML pages, but a wide range of web accessible data and services) more readily accessible to automated processes. This is to be done by augmenting existing *presentation* markup with *semantic* markup, i.e., meta-data annotations that describe their content [2]. According to widely known proposals for a Semantic Web architecture, ontologies will play a key role as they will be used as a source of shared and precisely defined terms that can be used in such metadata [15].

The importance of ontologies in semantic markup has prompted the development of several ontology languages specifically designed for this purpose. These include OIL [7], DAML+OIL [10] and OWL [4]. OWL is of particular significance as it has been developed by the W3C Web Ontology working group, and is set to become a W3C recommendation.

The proposed OWL recommendation actually consists of three languages of increasing expressive power: OWL Lite, OWL DL and OWL Full. Like OWL's predecessor DAML+OIL, OWL Lite and OWL DL are basically very expressive description logics with an RDF syntax. They can therefore exploit the considerable existing body of description logic research, e.g., to define the semantics of the language and to understand its formal properties, in particular the decidability and complexity of key inference problems [6]. OWL Full provides a more complete integration with RDF, but its formal properties are less well understood, and key inference problems would certainly be

D. Fensel et al. (Eds.): ISWC 2003, LNCS 2870, pp. 17–29, 2003.

much harder to compute.[1] In this paper we will, therefore, concentrate on the provision of reasoning services for OWL Lite and OWL DL.

1.1 OWL Reasoning

Reasoning with ontology languages will be important in the Semantic Web if applications are to exploit the semantics of ontology based metadata annotations, e.g., if semantic search engines are to find pages based on the semantics of their annotations rather than their syntax. As well as providing insights into OWL's formal properties, OWL's relationship to expressive description logics provides a source of algorithms for solving key inference problems, in particular satisfiability. Moreover, in spite of the high worst case complexity of reasoning in such description logics, highly optimised implementations of these algorithms are available and have been shown to work well with realistic problems. Two difficulties arise, however, when attempting to use such implementations to provide reasoning services for OWL:

1. OWL's RDF syntax uses frame-like constructs that do not correspond directly to description logic axioms; and
2. as in RDF, OWL inference is defined in terms of ontology entailment rather than ontology satisfiability.

The obvious solution to the first problem is to define a mapping that decomposes OWL frames into one or more description logic axioms. It turns out, however, that the RDF syntax used in OWL cannot be directly translated into any "standard" description logic because it allows the use of anonymous individuals in axioms asserting the types of and relationships between individuals. The obvious solution to the second problem is to reduce entailment to satisfiability. Doing this naively would, however, require role negation, and this is not supported in any implemented description logic reasoner.

In this paper we will show that, in spite of these difficulties, ontology entailment in OWL DL and OWL Lite can be reduced to knowledge base satisfiability in the $\mathcal{SHOIN}(\mathbf{D})$ and $\mathcal{SHIF}(\mathbf{D})$ description logics respectively. This is achieved by mapping OWL to an intermediate description logic that includes a novel axiom asserting the non-emptiness of a class, and by using a more sophisticated reduction to satisfiability that both eliminates this constructor and avoids the use of role negation.

This is a significant result from both a theoretical and a practical perspective: it demonstrates that computing ontology entailment in OWL DL (resp. OWL Lite) has the same complexity as computing knowledge base satisfiability in $\mathcal{SHOIN}(\mathbf{D})$ ($\mathcal{SHIF}(\mathbf{D})$), and that description logic algorithms and implementations (such as RACER [8]) can be used to provide reasoning services for OWL Lite. Unfortunately, the design of "practical" algorithms for $\mathcal{SHOIN}(\mathbf{D})$ is still an open problem – the search for such algorithms must obviously be a high priority within the Semantic Web research community.

[1] Inference in OWL Full is clearly undecidable as OWL Full does not include restrictions on the use of transitive properties which are required in order to maintain decidability [13].

2 The OWL Web Ontology Language

As mentioned in Section 1, OWL [4] is an ontology language that has recently been developed by the W3C Web Ontology Working Group. OWL is defined as an extension to RDF in the form of a vocabulary entailment [9], i.e., the syntax of OWL is the syntax of RDF and the semantics of OWL are an extension of the semantics of RDF.

OWL has many features in common with description logics, but also has some significant differences. The first difference between OWL and description logics is that the syntax of OWL is the syntax of RDF. OWL information is thus encoded in RDF/XML documents [1] and parsed into RDF Graphs [14] composed of triples. Because RDF Graphs are such an impoverished syntax, many description logic constructs in OWL are encoded into several triples. Because RDF Graphs are graphs, however, it is possible to create circular syntactic structures in OWL, which are not possible in description logics. Subtle interactions between OWL and RDF cause problems with some of these circular syntactic structures.

The second difference between OWL and description logics is that OWL contains features that do not fit within the description logic framework. For example, OWL classes are objects in the domain of discourse and can be made instances of other concepts, including themselves. These two features, also present in RDF, make a semantic treatment of OWL quite different from the semantic treatment of description logics.

2.1 OWL DL and OWL Lite

Fortunately for our purpose, there are officially-defined subsets of OWL that are much closer to description logics. The larger of these subsets, called OWL DL, restricts OWL in two ways. First, unusual syntactic constructs, such as descriptions with syntactic cycles in them, are not allowed in OWL DL. Second, classes, properties, and individuals (usually called concepts, roles and individuals in description logics) must be disjoint in the semantics for OWL DL.

Because of the syntactic restrictions in OWL DL, it is possible to develop an abstract syntax for OWL DL [16] that looks much like an abstract syntax for a powerful frame language, and is not very different from description logic syntaxes. This is very similar to the approach taken in the OIL language [7]. The abstract syntax for OWL DL has classes and data ranges, which are analogues of concepts and concrete datatypes in description logics, and axioms and facts, which are analogues of axioms in description logics. Axioms and facts are grouped into ontologies, the analogue of description logic knowledge bases, which are the highest level of OWL DL syntax.

The constructors used to form OWL DL descriptions and data ranges are summarised in Figure 1, where A is a class name, C (possibly subscripted) is a description, o (possibly subscripted) is an individual name, R is an object (or abstract) property, T is a datatype property,[2] B is a datatype, D is a data range, v (possibly subscripted) is a data value and ℓ, m, n are non-negative integers; elements {enclosed in braces} can be repeated zero or more times and elements [enclosed in square brackets] are optional. The details of these constructors can be found in the OWL documentation [4].

[2] An object property is one that associates pairs of individuals; a datatype property associates an individual with a data value.

Classes
A
intersectionOf($C_1 \ldots C_n$)
unionOf($C_1 \ldots C_n$)
complementOf(C)
oneOf($o_1 \ldots o_n$)
restriction(R $\{$allValuesFrom(C)$\}$ $\{$someValuesFrom(C)$\}$ $\{$value(o)$\}$ [minCardinality(n)] [maxCardinality(m)] [cardinality(ℓ)])
restriction(T $\{$allValuesFrom(D)$\}$ $\{$someValuesFrom(D)$\}$ $\{$value(v)$\}$ [minCardinality(n)] [maxCardinality(m)] [cardinality(ℓ)])
Data Ranges
B
oneOf($v_1 \ldots v_n$)

Fig. 1. OWL DL Constructors

Descriptions and data ranges can be used in OWL DL axioms and facts to provide information about classes, properties, and individuals. Figure 2 provides a summary of these axioms and facts. The details of these constructors can also be found in the OWL documentation [4]. In particular, Figure 2 ignores annotations and deprecation, which allow uninterpreted information to be associated with classes and properties, but which are not interesting from a logical point of view.

Because of the semantic restrictions in OWL DL, metaclasses and other notions that do not fit into the description logic semantic framework can be ignored. In fact, OWL DL has a semantics that is very much in the description logic style, and that has been shown to be equivalent to the RDF-style semantics for all of OWL [16]. Again, we will not present all of this semantics, instead concentrating on its differences from the usual description logics semantics.

There is a subset of OWL DL, called OWL Lite, the motivation for which is increased ease of implementation. This is achieved by supporting fewer constructors than OWL DL, and by limiting the use of some of these constructors. In particular, OWL Lite does not support the `oneOf` constuctor (equivalent to description logic *nominals*), as this constructor is known to increase theoretical complexity and to lead to difficulties in the design of practical algorithms [11]. In Section 5 we will examine these differences in more detail, and explore their impact on the reduction from OWL entailment to description logic satisfiability.

2.2 Semantics for OWL DL

The semantics for OWL DL is fairly standard by description logic standards. The OWL semantic domain is a set whose elements can be divided into abstract objects (the abstract domain), and datatype values (the datatype or concrete domain, written $\Delta_{\mathrm{D}}^{\mathcal{I}}$). Datatypes

Class Axioms
Class(A partial $d_1 \ldots d_n$)
Class(A complete $d_1 \ldots d_n$)
EnumeratedClass(A $o_1 \ldots o_n$)
DisjointClasses($d_1 \ldots d_n$)
EquivalentClasses($d_1 \ldots d_n$)
SubClassOf(d_1 d_2)
Property Axioms
DatatypeProperty(U super(U_1) ... super(U_n) [Functional] domain(d_1) ... domain(d_m) range(r_1) ... domain(r_l))
ObjectProperty(P super(P_1) ... super(P_n) [inverseOf(P_0)] [Functional] [InverseFunctional] [Symmetric] [Transitive] domain(d_1) ... domain(d_m) range(e_1) ... domain(e_l))
EquivalentProperties($U_1 \ldots U_n$)
SubPropertyOf(U_1 U_2)
EquivalentProperties($P_1 \ldots P_n$)
SubPropertyOf(P_1 P_2)
Facts
Individual([o] type(d_1) ... type(d_1) value(p_1 v_1) ... value(p_1 v_1))
SameIndividual($o_1 \ldots o_n$)
DifferentIndividuals($o_1 \ldots o_n$)

Fig. 2. OWL DL Axioms and Facts (simplified)

in OWL are derived from the built-in XML Schema datatypes [3]. Datatype values are denoted by special literal constructs in the syntax, the details of which need not concern us here.

An interpretation in this semantics is officially a four-tuple consisting of the abstract domain and separate mappings for concept names, property names, and individual names (in description logics, the mappings are usually combined to give a two-tuple, but the two forms are obviously equivalent). OWL DL classes are interpreted as subsets of the abstract domain, and for each constructor the semantics of the resulting class is defined in terms of its components. For example, given two classes C and D, the interpretation of the intersection of C and D is defined to be the intersection of the interpretations of C and D. Datatypes are handled by means of a mapping $\cdot^{\mathbf{D}}$ that interprets datatype names as subsets of the concrete domain and data names (i.e., lexical representations of data values) as elements of the concrete domain.

OWL DL axioms and facts result in semantic conditions on interpretations. For example, an axiom asserting that C is a subclass of D results in the semantic condition that the interpretation of C must be a subset of the interpretation of D, while a fact asserting that a has type C results in the semantic condition that the interpretation of a must be an element of the set that is the interpretation of C. An OWL DL ontology O is satisfied by an interpretation $\mathcal{I}$ just when all of the semantic conditions resulting from the axioms and facts in $\mathcal{O}$ are satisfied by $\mathcal{I}$.

The main semantic relationship in OWL DL is entailment – a relationship between pairs of OWL ontologies. An ontology O_1 entails an ontology O_2, written $O_1 \models O_2$,

Constructor Name	Syntax	Semantics
atomic concept **A**	A	$A^{\mathcal{I}} \subseteq \Delta^{\mathcal{I}}$
datatypes **D**	D	$D^{\mathbf{D}} \subseteq \Delta^{\mathcal{I}}_{\mathbf{D}}$
abstract role $\mathbf{R}_A$	R	$R^{\mathcal{I}} \subseteq \Delta^{\mathcal{I}} \times \Delta^{\mathcal{I}}$
datatype role $\mathbf{R}_{\mathbf{D}}$	U	$U^{\mathcal{I}} \subseteq \Delta^{\mathcal{I}} \times \Delta^{\mathcal{I}}_{\mathbf{D}}$
individuals **I**	o	$o^{\mathcal{I}} \in \Delta^{\mathcal{I}}$
data values	v	$v^{\mathcal{I}} = v^{\mathbf{D}}$
inverse role	R^{-}	$(R^{-})^{\mathcal{I}} = (R^{\mathcal{I}})^{-}$
conjunction	$C_1 \sqcap C_2$	$(C_1 \sqcap C_2)^{\mathcal{I}} = C_1^{\mathcal{I}} \cap C_2^{\mathcal{I}}$
disjunction	$C_1 \sqcup C_2$	$(C_1 \sqcup C_2)^{\mathcal{I}} = C_1^{\mathcal{I}} \cup C_2^{\mathcal{I}}$
negation	$\neg C_1$	$(\neg C_1)^{\mathcal{I}} = \Delta^{\mathcal{I}} \setminus C_1^{\mathcal{I}}$
oneOf	$\{o_1, \ldots\}$	$\{o_1, \ldots\}^{\mathcal{I}} = \{o_1^{\mathcal{I}}, \ldots\}$
exists restriction	$\exists R.C$	$(\exists R.C)^{\mathcal{I}} = \{x \mid \exists y. \langle x\rangle y \in R^{\mathcal{I}} \text{ and } y \in C^{\mathcal{I}}\}$
value restriction	$\forall R.C$	$(\forall R.C)^{\mathcal{I}} = \{x \mid \forall y. \langle x, y\rangle \in R^{\mathcal{I}} \rightarrow y \in C^{\mathcal{I}}\}$
atleast restriction	$\geqslant n\, R$	$(\geqslant n\, R)^{\mathcal{I}} = \{x \mid \sharp(\{y. \langle x, y\rangle \in R^{\mathcal{I}}\}) \geqslant n\}$
atmost restriction	$\leqslant n\, R$	$(\leqslant n\, R)^{\mathcal{I}} = \{x \mid \sharp(\{y. \langle x, y\rangle \in R^{\mathcal{I}}\}) \leqslant n\}$
datatype exists	$\exists U.D$	$(\exists U.D)^{\mathcal{I}} = \{x \mid \exists y. \langle x, y\rangle \in U^{\mathcal{I}} \text{ and } y \in D^{\mathbf{D}}\}$
datatype value	$\forall U.D$	$(\forall U.D)^{\mathcal{I}} = \{x \mid \forall y. \langle x, y\rangle \in U^{\mathcal{I}} \rightarrow y \in D^{\mathbf{D}}\}$
datatype atleast	$\geqslant n\, U$	$(\geqslant n\, U)^{\mathcal{I}} = \{x \mid \sharp(\{y. \langle x, y\rangle \in U^{\mathcal{I}}\}) \geqslant n\}$
datatype atmost	$\leqslant n\, U$	$(\leqslant n\, U)^{\mathcal{I}} = \{x \mid \sharp(\{y. \langle x, y\rangle \in U^{\mathcal{I}}\}) \leqslant n\}$
datatype oneOf	$\{v_1, \ldots\}$	$\{v_1, \ldots\}^{\mathcal{I}} = \{v_1^{\mathcal{I}}, \ldots\}$
Axiom Name	**Syntax**	**Semantics**
concept inclusion	$C_1 \sqsubseteq C_2$	$C_1^{\mathcal{I}} \subseteq C_2^{\mathcal{I}}$
object role inclusion	$R_1 \sqsubseteq R_2$	$R_1^{\mathcal{I}} \subseteq R_2^{\mathcal{I}}$
object role transitivity	$\mathsf{Trans}(R)$	$R^{\mathcal{I}} = (R^{\mathcal{I}})^{+}$
datatype role inclusion	$U_1 \sqsubseteq U_2$	$U_1^{\mathcal{I}} \subseteq U_2^{\mathcal{I}}$
individual inclusion	$a : C$	$a^{\mathcal{I}} \in C^{\mathcal{I}}$
individual equality	$a = b$	$a^{\mathcal{I}} = b^{\mathcal{I}}$
individual inequality	$a \neq b$	$a^{\mathcal{I}} \neq b^{\mathcal{I}}$
concept existence	$\exists C$	$\sharp(C^{\mathcal{I}}) \geqslant 1$

Fig. 3. Syntax and semantics of $\mathcal{SHOIN}^{+}(\mathbf{D})$

exactly when all interpretations that satisfy O_1 also satisfy O_2. This semantic relationship is different from the standard description logic relationships, such as knowledge base and concept satisfiability. The main goal of this paper is to show how OWL DL entailment can be transformed into DL knowledge base (un)satisfiability.

3 $\mathcal{SHOIN}(\mathbf{D})$ and $\mathcal{SHIF}(\mathbf{D})$

The main description logic that we will be using in this paper is $\mathcal{SHOIN}(\mathbf{D})$, which is similar to the well known $\mathcal{SHOQ}(\mathbf{D})$ description logic [11], but is extended with inverse roles ($\mathcal{I}$) and restricted to unqualified number restrictions ($\mathcal{N}$). We will assume throughout the paper that datatypes and data values are as in OWL.

Let $\mathbf{A}, \mathbf{R}_A, \mathbf{R}_\mathbf{D}$, and $\mathbf{I}$ be pairwise disjoint sets of *concept names*, *abstract role names*, *datatype (or concrete) role names*, and *individual names*. The set of $\mathcal{SHOIN}(\mathbf{D})$-roles is $\mathbf{R}_A \cup \{R^- \mid R \in \mathbf{R}_A\} \cup \mathbf{R}_\mathbf{D}$. In order to avoid considering roles such as R^{--} we will define $\mathsf{Inv}(R)$ s.t. $\mathsf{Inv}(R) = R^-$ and $\mathsf{Inv}(R^-) = R$. The set of $\mathcal{SHOIN}(\mathbf{D})$-concepts is the smallest set that can be built using the constructors in Figure 3.

The $\mathcal{SHOIN}(\mathbf{D})$ axiom syntax is also given in Figure 3. (The last axiom in Figure 3 forms an extension of $\mathcal{SHOIN}(\mathbf{D})$, which we call $\mathcal{SHOIN}^+(\mathbf{D})$, which is used internally in our translation.) A *knowledge base* $\mathcal{K}$ is a finite set of axioms. We will use $\sqsubseteq\!\!\!*$ to denote the transitive reflexive closure of $\sqsubseteq$ on roles, i.e., for two roles S, R in $\mathcal{K}$, $S \sqsubseteq\!\!\!* R$ in $\mathcal{K}$ if $S = R$, $S \sqsubseteq R \in \mathcal{K}$, $\mathsf{Inv}(S) \sqsubseteq \mathsf{Inv}(R) \in \mathcal{K}$, or there exists some role Q such that $S \sqsubseteq\!\!\!* Q$ in $\mathcal{K}$ and $Q \sqsubseteq\!\!\!* R$ in $\mathcal{K}$. A role R is called *simple* in $\mathcal{K}$ if for each role S s.t. $S \sqsubseteq\!\!\!* R$ in $\mathcal{K}$, $\mathsf{Trans}(S) \notin \mathcal{K}$ and $\mathsf{Trans}(\mathsf{Inv}(S)) \notin \mathcal{K}$. To maintain decidability, a knowledge base must have no number restrictions on non-simple roles [13].

The semantics of $\mathcal{SHOIN}^+(\mathbf{D})$ is given by means of an interpretation $\mathcal{I} = (\Delta^\mathcal{I}, \cdot^\mathcal{I})$ consisting of a non-empty domain $\Delta^\mathcal{I}$, disjoint from the datatype (or concrete) domain $\Delta^\mathcal{I}_\mathbf{D}$, and a mapping $\cdot^\mathcal{I}$, which interprets atomic and complex concepts, roles, and nominals according to Figure 3. (In Figure 3, $\sharp$ is set cardinality.)

An interpretation $\mathcal{I} = (\Delta^\mathcal{I}, \cdot^\mathcal{I})$ *satisfies* a $\mathcal{SHOIN}^+(\mathbf{D})$-axiom under the conditions given in Figure 3. An interpretation satisfies a knowledge base $\mathcal{K}$ iff it satisfies each axiom in $\mathcal{K}$; $\mathcal{K}$ is *satisfiable* (*unsatisfiable*) iff there exists (does not exist) such an interpretation. A $\mathcal{SHOIN}(\mathbf{D})$-concept C is satisfiable w.r.t. a knowledge base $\mathcal{K}$ iff there is an interpretation $\mathcal{I}$ with $C^\mathcal{I} \neq \emptyset$ that satisfies $\mathcal{K}$. A concept C is *subsumed* by a concept D w.r.t. $\mathcal{K}$ iff $C^\mathcal{I} \sqsubseteq D^\mathcal{I}$ for each interpretation $\mathcal{I}$ satisfying $\mathcal{K}$. Two concepts are said to be equivalent w.r.t. $\mathcal{K}$ iff they subsume each other w.r.t. $\mathcal{K}$. A knowledge base $\mathcal{K}_1$ entails a knowledge base $\mathcal{K}_2$ iff every interpretation of $\mathcal{K}_1$ is also an interpretation of $\mathcal{K}_2$.

We define a notion of entailment in $\mathcal{SHOIN}^+(\mathbf{D})$ in the same way as it was defined for OWL DL. It is easy to show that $\mathcal{K} \models \mathcal{K}'$ iff $\mathcal{K} \models A$ for every axiom A in $\mathcal{K}'$.

The description logic $\mathcal{SHIF}(\mathbf{D})$ is just $\mathcal{SHOIN}(\mathbf{D})$ without the oneOf constructor and with the atleast and atmost constructors limited to 0 and 1. $\mathcal{SHIF}^+(\mathbf{D})$ is related to $\mathcal{SHOIN}^+(\mathbf{D})$ in the same way.

4 From OWL DL Entailment to $\mathcal{SHOIN}(\mathbf{D})$ Unsatisfiability

We will now show how to translate OWL DL entailment into $\mathcal{SHOIN}(\mathbf{D})$ unsatisfiability. The first step of our process is to translate an entailment between OWL DL ontologies into an entailment between knowledge bases in $\mathcal{SHOIN}^+(\mathbf{D})$. Then $\mathcal{SHOIN}^+(\mathbf{D})$ entailment is transformed into unsatisfiability of $\mathcal{SHOIN}(\mathbf{D})$ knowledge bases. (Note that concept existence axioms are eliminated in this last step, leaving a $\mathcal{SHOIN}(\mathbf{D})$ knowledge base.)

OWL fragment F	Translation $\mathcal{F}(F)$
Individual($x_1 \ldots x_n$)	$\exists(\mathcal{F}(x_1) \sqcap \ldots \sqcap \mathcal{F}(x_n))$
type(C)	$\mathcal{V}(C)$
value($R\ x$)	$\exists R.\mathcal{F}(x)$
value($U\ v$)	$\exists U.\{v\}$
o	$\{o\}$

Fig. 4. Translation from OWL facts to $\mathcal{SHOIN}^+(\mathbf{D})$

4.1 From OWL DL to $\mathcal{SHOIN}(\mathbf{D})$

An OWL DL ontology is translated into a $\mathcal{SHOIN}^+(\mathbf{D})$ knowledge base by taking each axiom and fact in the ontology and translating it into one or more axioms in the knowledge base. For OWL DL axioms, this translation is very natural, and is almost identical to the translation of OIL described by Decker et al. [5]. For example, the OWL DL axiom Class(A complete $C_1 \ldots C_n$) is translated into the pair of $\mathcal{SHOIN}^+(\mathbf{D})$ axioms $A \sqsubseteq \mathcal{V}(C_1) \sqcap \ldots \sqcap \mathcal{V}(C_n)$ and $\mathcal{V}(C_1) \sqcap \ldots \sqcap \mathcal{V}(C_n) \sqsubseteq A$, where $\mathcal{V}$ is the obvious translation from OWL classes to description logic concepts, again very similar to the transformation described by Decker et al. [5]. Similarly, an OWL DL axiom `DisjointClasses(`$C_1 \ldots C_n$`)` is translated into the $\mathcal{SHOIN}^+(\mathbf{D})$ axioms $\mathcal{V}(C_i) \sqsubseteq \neg\mathcal{V}(C_j)$ for $1 \leq i < j \leq n$.

The translation of OWL DL facts to $\mathcal{SHOIN}^+(\mathbf{D})$ axioms is more complex. This is because facts can be stated with respect to anonymous individuals, and can include relationships to other (possibly anonymous) individuals. For example, the fact Individual(type(C) value(R Individual(type(D)))) states that there exists an individual that is an instance of class C and is related via the property R to an individual that is an instance of the class D, without naming either of the individuals.

The need to translate this kind of fact is the reason for introducing the $\mathcal{SHOIN}^+(\mathbf{D})$ existence axiom. For example, the above fact can be translated into the axiom $\exists(C \sqcap \exists R.D)$, which states that there exists some instance of the concept $C \sqcap \exists R.D$, i.e., an individual that is an instance of C and is related via the role R to an instance of the concept D. Figure 4 describes a translation $\mathcal{F}$ that transforms OWL facts into a $\mathcal{SHOIN}^+(\mathbf{D})$ existence axioms, where C is an OWL class, R is an OWL abstract property or $\mathcal{SHOIN}^+(\mathbf{D})$ abstract role, U is an OWL datatype property or $\mathcal{SHOIN}^+(\mathbf{D})$ datatype role, o is an individual name, v is a data value, and $\mathcal{V}$ is the above mentioned translation from OWL classes to $\mathcal{SHOIN}^+(\mathbf{D})$ concepts.

Theorem 1. *The translation from OWL DL to $\mathcal{SHOIN}^+(\mathbf{D})$ preserves equivalence. That is, an OWL DL axiom or fact is satisfied by an interpretation $\mathcal{I}$ if and only if the translation is satisfied by $\mathcal{I}$.*[3]

The above translation increases the size of an ontology to at most the square of its size. It can easily be performed in time linear in the size of the resultant knowledge base.

[3] The statement of the theorem here ignores the minor differences between OWL DL interpretations and $\mathcal{SHOIN}^+(\mathbf{D})$ interpretations. A stricter account would have to worry about these stylistic differences.

Axiom A	Transformation $\mathcal{G}(A)$
$c \sqsubseteq d$	$x : c \sqcap \neg d$
$\exists c$	$\top \sqsubseteq \neg c$
$\mathsf{Trans}(r)$	$x : \exists r.\exists r.\{y\} \sqcap \neg\exists r.\{y\}$
$r \sqsubseteq s$	$x : \exists r.\{y\} \sqcap \neg\exists s.\{y\}$
$f \sqsubseteq g$	$x : \bigsqcup_{z \in \mathbf{V}} \exists f.\{z\} \sqcap \neg\exists g.\{z\}$ for $\mathbf{V}$ = the set of data values in $\mathcal{K}$, plus one fresh data value for each datatype in $\mathcal{K}$
$a = b$	$a \neq b$
$a \neq b$	$a = b$

Fig. 5. Translation from Entailment to Unsatisfiability

4.2 From Entailment to Unsatisfiability

The next step of our process is to transform $\mathcal{SHOIN}^+(\mathbf{D})$ knowledge base entailment to $\mathcal{SHOIN}(\mathbf{D})$ knowledge base unsatisfiability. We do this to relate our new notion of description logic entailment to the well-known operation of description logic knowledge base unsatisfiability.

We recall from Section 3 that $\mathcal{K} \models \mathcal{K}'$ iff $\mathcal{K} \models A$ for every axiom A in $\mathcal{K}'$. We therefore define (in Figure 5) a translation, $\mathcal{G}$, such that $\mathcal{K} \models A$ iff $\mathcal{K} \cup \{\mathcal{G}(A)\}$ is unsatisfiable, for $\mathcal{K}$ a $\mathcal{SHOIN}(\mathbf{D})$ knowledge base and A a $\mathcal{SHOIN}(\mathbf{D})$ axiom. In this transformation we have need of names of various sorts that do not occur in the knowledge base or axiom; following standard practice we will call these fresh names. Throughout the translation, x and y are fresh individual names.

Most of the translations in $\mathcal{G}$ are quite standard and simple. For example, an object role inclusion axiom $r \sqsubseteq s$ is translated into an axiom that requires the existence of an individual that is related to some other individual by r but not by s, thus violating the axiom. The only unusual translation is for datatype role inclusions $f \sqsubseteq g$. Because data values have a known "identity" (rather like individuals under the unique name assumption), a fresh value cannot be used to simulate an existentially quantified variable that could be interpreted as any element in the datatype domain (in the way the fresh nominal is used in the case of an object role inclusion axiom). Instead, it is necessary to show that the relevant inclusion holds for every data value that occurs in the knowledge base, plus one fresh data value (i.e., one that does not occur in the knowledge base) for each datatype in $\mathcal{K}$. Because there are no operations on data values, it suffices to consider only these fresh data values in addition to those that occur in the knowledge base.

The translation $\mathcal{G}$ increases the size of an axiom to at most the larger of its size and the size of the knowledge base. It can easily be performed in time linear in the larger of the size of the axiom and the size of the knowledge base. (If datatype role inclusions are not used, then $\mathcal{G}$ increases the size of an axiom by atmost a constant amount.)

The translation $\mathcal{G}$ eliminates concept existence axioms from the knowledge base $\mathcal{K}'$ on the right-hand side of the entailment. Our last step is to eliminate concept existance axioms from the knowledge base $\mathcal{K}$ on the left-hand side of the entailment. We do this by applying a translation $\mathcal{E}(\mathcal{K})$ that replaces each axiom of the form $\exists C \in \mathcal{K}$ with an axiom $a : C$, for a a fresh individual name. It is obvious that this translation preserves

OWL fragment F	Translation $\mathcal{F}'(F)$
Individual($x_1 \ldots x_n$)	$\mathcal{F}'(a : x_1), \ldots, \mathcal{F}'(a : x_n)$ for a a fresh individual name
a : type(C)	$a : \mathcal{V}(C)$
a : value(R x)	$\langle a, b \rangle : R, \mathcal{F}'(b : x)$ for b a fresh individual name
a : value(U v)	$\langle a, v \rangle : U$
$a : o$	$a = o$

Fig. 6. Translation from OWL Lite facts to $\mathcal{SHIF}^+(\mathbf{D})$

satisfiability, can be easily performed, and only increases the size of a knowledge base by a linear amount.

Theorem 2. *Let $\mathcal{K}$ and $\mathcal{K}'$ be $\mathcal{SHOIN}^+(\mathbf{D})$ knowledge bases. Then $\mathcal{K} \models \mathcal{K}'$ iff the $\mathcal{SHOIN}(\mathbf{D})$ knowledge base $\mathcal{E}(\mathcal{K}) \cup \{\mathcal{G}(\mathcal{A})\}$ is unsatisfiable for every axiom A in $\mathcal{K}'$.*

4.3 Consequences

The overall translation from OWL DL entailment to $\mathcal{SHOIN}(\mathbf{D})$ can be performed in polynomial time and results in a polynomial number of knowledge base satisfiability problems each of which is polynomial in the size of the initial OWL DL entailment. Therefore we have shown that OWL DL entailment is in the same complexity class as knowledge base satisfiability in $\mathcal{SHOIN}(\mathbf{D})$.

Unfortunately, $\mathcal{SHOIN}(\mathbf{D})$ is a difficult description logic. Most problems in $\mathcal{SHOIN}(\mathbf{D})$, including knowledge base satisfiability, are in NExpTime [17]. Further, there are as yet no known optimized inference algorithms or implemented systems for $\mathcal{SHOIN}(\mathbf{D})$. The situation is not, however, completely bleak. There is an inexact translation from $\mathcal{SHOIN}(\mathbf{D})$ to $\mathcal{SHIN}(\mathbf{D})$ that turns nominals into atomic concept names. This translation could be used to produce a partial, but still very capable, reasoner for OWL DL. Moreover, as is shown in the next section, the situation for OWL Lite is significantly different.

5 Transforming OWL Lite

OWL Lite is the subset of OWL DL that

1. eliminates the `intersectionOf`, `unionOf`, `complementOf`, and `oneOf` constructors;
2. removes the `value` construct from the `restriction` constructors;
3. limits cardinalities to 0 and 1;
4. eliminates the `enumeratedClass` axiom; and
5. requires that description-forming constructors not occur in other description-forming constructors.

Axiom A	Transformation $\mathcal{G}(A)$
$a : C$	$a : \neg C$
$\langle a, b\rangle : R$	$b : B, a : \forall R.\neg B$ for B a fresh concept name
$\langle a, v\rangle : U$	$a : \forall U.\overline{v}$

Fig. 7. Extended Transformation from Entailment to Unsatisfiability

The reason for defining the OWL Lite subset of OWL DL was to have an easier target for implementation. This was thought to be mostly easier parsing and other syntactic manipulations.

As OWL Lite does not have the analogue of nominals it is possible that inference is easier in OWL Lite than in OWL DL. However, the transformation above from OWL DL entailment into $\mathcal{SHOIN}(\mathbf{D})$ unsatisfiability uses nominals even for OWL Lite constructs. It is thus worthwhile to devise an alternative translation that avoids nominals.

There are three places that nominals show up in our transformation:

1. translations into $\mathcal{SHOIN}^+(\mathbf{D})$ of OWL DL constructs that are not in OWL Lite, in particular the `oneOf` constructor;
2. translations into $\mathcal{SHOIN}^+(\mathbf{D})$ axioms of OWL DL `Individual` facts; and
3. the transformation to $\mathcal{SHOIN}(\mathbf{D})$ unsatisfiability of $\mathcal{SHOIN}^+(\mathbf{D})$ entailments whose consequents are role inclusion axioms or role transitivity axioms.

The first of these, of course, is not a concern when considering OWL Lite.

The second place where nominals show up is in the translation of OWL `Individual` facts into $\mathcal{SHOIN}(\mathbf{D})$ axioms (Figure 4). In order to avoid introducing nominals, we can use the alternative transformation $\mathcal{F}'$ given in Figure 6. Note that, in this case, the translation $\mathcal{V}(C)$ does not introduce any nominals as we are translating OWL Lite classes.

The new transformation does, however, introduce axioms of the form $a : C$, $\langle a, b\rangle : R$ and $\langle a, v\rangle : U$ that we will need to deal with when transforming from entailment to satisfiability. We can do this by extending the transformation $\mathcal{G}$ given in Figure 5 as shown in Figure 7. The extension deals with axioms of the form $\langle a, b\rangle : R$ using a simple transformation, described in more detail by [12], and with axioms of the form $\langle a, v\rangle : U$ using a datatype derived from the negation of a data value (written $\overline{v}$).

The third and final place where nominals show up is in the transformation of entailments whose consequents are object role inclusion axioms or role transitivity axioms.

Object role inclusion axioms can be dealt with using a transformation similar to those given in Figure 7 (and described in more detail in [12]), which does not introduce any nominals. This is shown in the following lemma:

Lemma 1. *Let K be an OWL Lite ontology and let A be an OWL Lite role inclusion axiom stating that r is a subrole of s. Then $K \models A$ iff $\mathcal{E}(K) \cup \{x : B \sqcap \exists r(\forall s^-.\neg B)\}$ is unsatisfiable for x a fresh individual name, and B a fresh concept name.*

Transitivity axioms can be dealt with by exploiting the more limited expressive power of OWL Lite, in particular its inability to describe classes, datatypes or properties whose interpretations must be non-empty but finite (e.g., classes described using the `oneOf` constructor). As a result of this more limited expressive power, the only way to deduce the transitivity of a property r is to show that the interpretation of r cannot form any chains (i.e., consists only of isolated tuples, or is empty). This observation leads to the following lemma:

Lemma 2. *Let K be an OWL Lite ontology and let A be an OWL Lite role transitivity axiom stating that r is transitive. Then* $K \models A$ *iff* $\mathcal{E}(K) \cup \{x : \exists r(\exists r \top)\}$ *is unsatisfiable for* x *a fresh individual name (i.e., r forms no chains).*

The above lemmas, taken together, show that OWL Lite entailment can be transformed into knowledge base unsatisfiability in $\mathcal{SHIF}(\mathbf{D})$, plus some simple (and easy) tests on the syntactic form of a knowledge base. A simple examination shows that the transformations can be computed in polynomial time and result in only a linear increase in size.

As knowledge base satisfiability in $\mathcal{SHIF}(\mathbf{D})$ is in ExpTime [17] this means that entailment in OWL Lite can be computed in exponential time. Further, OWL Lite entailment can be computed by the RACER description logic system [8], a heavily-optimised description logic reasoner, resulting in an effective reasoner for OWL Lite entailment.

6 Conclusion

Reasoning with ontology languages will be important in the Semantic Web if applications are to exploit the semantics of ontology based metadata annotations. We have shown that ontology entailment in the OWL DL and OWL Lite ontology languages can be reduced to knowledge base satisfiability in, respectively, the $\mathcal{SHOIN}(\mathbf{D})$ and $\mathcal{SHIF}(\mathbf{D})$ description logics. This is so even though some constructs in these languages go beyond the standard description logic constructs.

From these mappings, we have determined that the complexity of ontology entailment in OWL DL and OWL Lite is in NExpTime and ExpTime respectively (the same as for knowledge base satisfiability in $\mathcal{SHOIN}(\mathbf{D})$ and $\mathcal{SHIF}(\mathbf{D})$ respectively). The mapping of OWL Lite to $\mathcal{SHIF}(\mathbf{D})$ also means that already-known practical reasoning algorithms for $\mathcal{SHIF}(\mathbf{D})$ can be used to determine ontology entailment in OWL Lite; in particular, the highly optimised RACER system [8], which can determine knowledge base satisfaction in $\mathcal{SHIF}(\mathbf{D})$, can be used to provide efficient reasoning services for OWL Lite.

The mapping from OWL DL to $\mathcal{SHOIN}(\mathbf{D})$ can also be used to provide complete reasoning services for a large part of OWL DL, or partial reasoning services for all of OWL DL. In spite of its known decidability, however, the design of "practical" decision procedures for $\mathcal{SHOIN}(\mathbf{D})$ is still an open problem. The search for such algorithms must obviously be a high priority within the Semantic Web research community.

References

[1] D. Beckett. RDF/XML syntax specification (revised). W3C Working Draft, 2003. Available at `http://www.w3.org/TR/2003/WD-rdf-syntax-grammar-20030123`.

[2] T. Berners-Lee. *Weaving the Web*. Harpur, San Francisco, 1999.

[3] P. V. Biron and A. Malhotra. XML schema part 2: Datatypes. W3C Recommendation, 2001. Available at `http://www.w3.org/TR/2003/WD-xmlschema-2-20010502/`.

[4] M. Dean, D. Connolly, F. van Harmelen, J. Hendler, I. Horrocks, Deborah L. McGuinness, Peter F. Patel-Schneider, and Lynn Andrea Stein. Web ontology language (OWL) reference version 1.0. W3C Working Draft, 2003. Available at `http://www.w3.org/TR/2003/WD-owl-ref-20030331`.

[5] S. Decker, D. Fensel, F. van Harmelen, I. Horrocks, S. Melnik, M. Klein, and J. Broekstra. Knowledge representation on the web. In *Proc. of the 2000 Description Logic Workshop (DL 2000)*, pages 89–98, 2000.

[6] F. M. Donini, M. Lenzerini, D. Nardi, and W. Nutt. The complexity of concept languages. *Information and Computation*, 134:1–58, 1997.

[7] D. Fensel, F. van Harmelen, I. Horrocks, D. McGuinness, and P. F. Patel-Schneider. OIL: An ontology infrastructure for the semantic web. *IEEE Intelligent Systems*, 16(2):38–45, 2001.

[8] V. Haarslev and R. Möller. RACER system description. In *Proc. of the Int. Joint Conf. on Automated Reasoning (IJCAR 2001)*, volume 2083 of *Lecture Notes in Artificial Intelligence*, pages 701–705. Springer, 2001.

[9] P. Hayes. RDF semantics. W3C Working Draft, 2003. Available at `http://www.w3.org/TR/2003/WD-rdf-mt-20030123`.

[10] I. Horrocks, P. F. Patel-Schneider, and F. van Harmelen. Reviewing the design of DAML+OIL: An ontology language for the semantic web. In *Proc. of the 18th Nat. Conf. on Artificial Intelligence (AAAI 2002)*, 2002.

[11] I. Horrocks and U. Sattler. Ontology reasoning in the $\mathcal{SHOQ}$ description logic. In B. Nebel, editor, *Proc. of the 17th Int. Joint Conf. on Artificial Intelligence (IJCAI 2001)*, pages 199–204. Morgan Kaufmann, 2001.

[12] I. Horrocks, U. Sattler, S. Tessaris, and S. Tobies. How to decide query containment under constraints using a description logic. In *Proceedings of the 7th International Conference on Logic for Programming and Automated Reasoning (LPAR'2000)*, Lecture Notes in Artificial Intelligence. Springer-Verlag, 2000.

[13] I. Horrocks, U. Sattler, and S. Tobies. Practical reasoning for expressive description logics. In Harald Ganzinger, David McAllester, and Andrei Voronkov, editors, *Proc. of the 6th Int. Conf. on Logic for Programming and Automated Reasoning (LPAR'99)*, number 1705 in Lecture Notes in Artificial Intelligence, pages 161–180. Springer, 1999.

[14] G. Klyne and J. J. Carroll. Resource description framework (RDF): Concepts and abstract syntax. W3C Working Draft, 2003. Available at `http://www.w3.org/TR/2003/WD-rdf-concepts-20030123`.

[15] O. Lassila and R. R. Swick. Resource description framework (RDF) model and syntax specification. W3C Recommendation, 1999. Available at `http://www.w3.org/TR/1999/REC-rdf-syntax-19990222`.

[16] P. F. Patel-Schneider, P. Hayes, I. Horrocks, and F. van Harmelen. Web ontology language (OWL) abstract syntax and semantics. W3C Working Draft, 2003. Available at `http://www.w3.org/TR/2003/WD-owl-ref-20030331`.

[17] S. Tobies. *Complexity Results and Practical Algorithms for Logics in Knowledge Representation*. PhD thesis, LuFG Theoretical Computer Science, RWTH-Aachen, Germany, 2001.

RDFS(FA) and RDF MT: Two Semantics for RDFS

Jeff Z. Pan and Ian Horrocks

Department of Computer Science,
University of Manchester, UK M13 9PL
{pan,horrocks}@cs.man.ac.uk

Abstract. RDF Schema (RDFS) has a non-standard metamodeling architecture, which makes some elements in the model have dual roles in the RDFS specification. As a result, this can be confusing and difficult to understand and, more importantly, the specification of its semantics requires a non-standard model theory. This leads to semantic problems when trying to layer conventional first order languages, like DAML+OIL, on top of RDFS. In this paper we will first demonstrate how this problem with RDFS can be solved in a sub-language of RDFS – RDFS(FA), which introduces a Fixed layer metamodeling Architecture to RDFS, based on a (relatively) standard model-theoretic semantics. Logical layer Semantic Web languages such as DAML+OIL and OWL can, therefore, be built on top of both the syntax and semantics of RDFS(FA). We will also compare this approach with the existing RDF Model Theory and discuss the advantages and disadvantages of the two approaches.

1 Introduction

The Semantic Web [1] is a vision of the next generation Web, in which the current rendering markup, which specifies how to display Web resources for human consumption, will be enhanced with semantic markups (often called annotations), which will specify the meaning of Web resources so as to make them more accessible to automatic processes. Ontologies [16] will play an important role in the Semantic Web as a source of precisely defined important terms and properties in the domain, which can then be used in annotations, for communication.

There is a functional architecture [1,12] of semantic Web languages. On the bottom, XML (eXtensible Markup Language) [2] is used as syntax. On top of XML, RDF (Resource Description Framework) [10] is a simple metadata language, which provides a simple and general model of semantic assertions of the Web. E.g., RDF can be used to add annotations to Web resources. On top of RDF, RDF Schema (RDFS) [3] is a schema language (as well as a very simple Web ontology language), which provides facilities to define terms used in annotations. More powerful (logical layer) ontology languages, e.g. OIL [6,7], DAML-ONT [9], DAML+OIL [17] and OWL [5], are expected to stand on top of RDFS and supply a richer set of modelling primitives. Unfortunately, the relationships between adjacent layers aren't clearly specified, especially that between RDFS and more powerful ontology languages, e.g. DAML+OIL and OWL.

D. Fensel et al. (Eds.): ISWC 2003, LNCS 2870, pp. 30–46, 2003.

Initially RDF and RDFS had no formal model theory, nor any formal meaning at all. This made them unlikely foundations for the Semantic Web. As earlier works [11,4] pointed out, RDFS has a non-standard and non-fixed layer metamodeling architecture, which makes some elements in the model have dual roles in the RDFS specification. In other words, multiple modelling primitives seems to be implicitly represented by a single RDFS primitive (see Section 2 for more details). Therefore, it makes the RDFS specification itself rather confusing and difficult to understand for the modelers. One of the consequences is that when DAML+OIL is layering on top of RDFS, it uses the syntax of RDFS only, but defines its own semantics [18] for the ontological primitives of RDFS.

To clear up any confusion, [12] proposed RDFS(FA)[1], a sub-language of RDFS, which provides a Fixed layer metamodeling Architecture for RDFS. The implicitly represented modelling primitives in RDFS are explicitly stratified into different strata (layers) of RDFS(FA). Thus RDFS(FA) has clear semantics and there are no dual roles in RDFS(FA). Subsequently RDF Model Theory (RDF MT) [8] gave an official semantics for RDF and RDFS, justifying the dual roles by treating both classes and properties as objects in the universe. So RDF MT is another approach to clear up the kinds of confusion that can arise in RDFS.

In the remainder of this paper, we will first illustrate the kinds of confusion that can arise in RDFS (Section 2). We will then present the design philosophy and stratification of RDFS(FA), which were not covered by [12], and describe how RDFS(FA) clears up any possible confusion of RDFS (Section 3). For the purpose of comparison, we will also explain how RDF MT formalises RDFS (Section 4) and then compare the advantages and disadvantages of these two approaches (Section 5). Finally we will discuss what conclusions we can draw from the above comparison in Section 6.

2 RDFS Architecture

The Resource Description Framework (RDF) [10] and its schema extension, RDF Schema Specification (RDFS) [3] form the lowest two layers of the Semantic Web. RDF is a foundation for processing metadata, which provides interoperability between applications that exchange machine-readable information on the Semantic Web. RDFS provides a standard mechanism for declaring classes and (global) properties as well as defining relationships between classes and properties, using RDF syntax. As a schema layer language, RDFS is responsible to define a basic metamodeling architecture for Web ontology languages. RDFS, however, has a non-standard and non-fixed layer metamodeling architecture, which makes some elements in the model appear to have multiple roles - multiple modelling primitives seem to be implicitly represented by a single RDFS primitive.

Figure 1 shows an example of dual roles of some RDFS elements in a directed labelled graph. The top three ellipses represent three RDFS built-in modelling primitives rdfs:Class, rdfs:Resource and rdfs:Property. The rest is a very simple ontology. There are two classes in this ontology, where eg:Researcher is an

[1] `http://DL-Web.man.ac.uk/rdfsfa/`

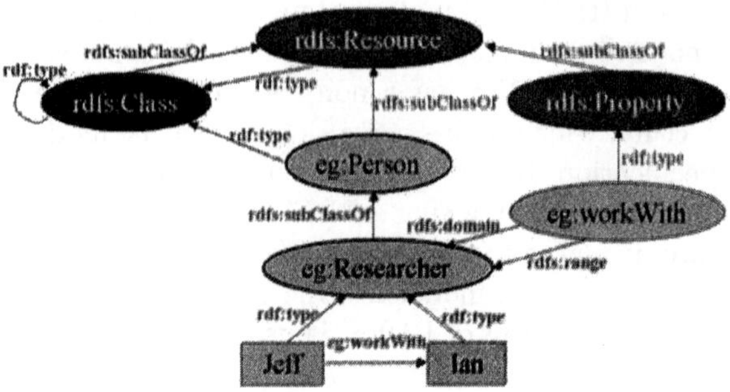

Fig. 1. An Example of Dual Roles in RDFS

rdfs:subClassOf eg:Person. eg:workWith is a property, whose rdfs:domain and rdfs:range are both eg:researcher. There are two instances of eg:Researcher, they are objects Ian and Jeff.

In this example, there seem to be more than one role for rdf:type and rdfs:subClassOf. For instance, rdf:type is used between objects and ontology classes (i.e. Jeff and eg:Researcher) and between ontology classes and built-in classes (i.e. eg:Person and rdfs: Class) etc. Similarly, rdfs:subClassOf is used between two ontology classes (i.e. eg:Researcher and eg:Person) and between two built-in classes (i.e. rdfs:Class and rdfs:Resource) etc.

Furthermore, there is a strange situation for rdfs:Class and rdfs:Resource as discussed in [12]. On the one hand, rdfs:Resource is an instance of rdfs:Class. On the other hand, rdfs:Class is a sub-class of rdfs:Resource. Thus rdfs:Resource is an instance of its sub-class?!

While RDF is mainly used as standard *syntax*, RDFS is expected to be the lowest layer to provide *semantics* for the Semantic Web. However, the existence of dual roles in RDFS makes it difficult to give clear semantics to RDFS. E.g. it is unclear whether rdfs:Resource should be interpreted as an instance or a super-class of rdfs:Class. This might partially explain why Brickley and Guha [3] didn't define the semantics for RDFS. Up to now, there are at least two ways to clear up any confusion and give a clear semantics to the schema language: RDFS(FA) and RDF MT. We will present them individually in the following two sections.

3 RDFS(FA)

In [12] we proposed a sub-language of RDFS - RDFS(FA), which provides a Fixed layer metamodeling Architecture for RDFS. RDFS(FA) eliminates dual roles by defining the modelling primitives *explicitly*, instead of implicitly.

We call the solution *stratification*. The universe of discourse is divided up into different strata (layers). Built-in modelling primitives of RDFS are stratified into different strata of RDFS(FA), so that certain modelling primitives belong to a certain stratum (layer). Different prefixes, e.g. o-, l- or m-, are used to label which stratum modelling primitives belong to. The semantics of modelling primitives

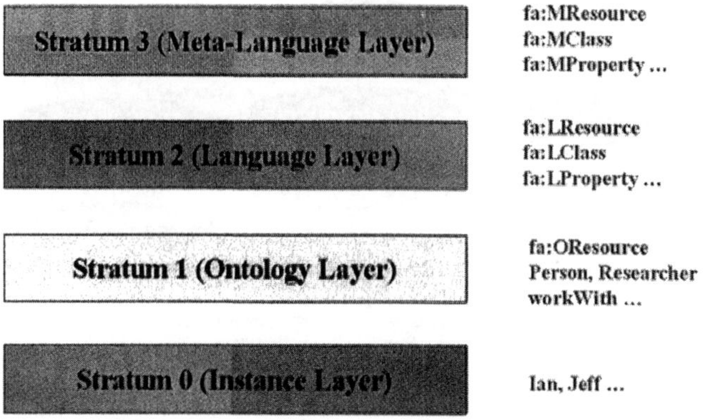

Fig. 2. Metamodeling Architecture (Four Strata) of RDFS(FA)

depend on the stratum they belong to. All these strata form the metamodeling architecture of RDFS(FA). Theoretically there can be infinite number of strata, while in practice, four strata are usually enough [12].

Figure 2 shows the metamodeling architecture (four strata) of RDFS(FA). Here are stratum 0,1,2 and 3. Some people like to call them layers, then they are called the Instance Layer, the Ontology Layer, the Language Layer and the Meta-Language Layer respectively.

Resources in the Instance Layer are objects, e.g. Ian and Jeff. Resources in the Ontology Layer are ontology classes, e.g. Person and Researcher, and ontology properties, e.g. workWith. Resources in the Language Layer are used to define and describe resources in the Ontology Layer, e.g. fa:LClass and fa:LProperty, and resources in the Meta-Language Layer are used to define and describe resources in the Language Layer.

As seen in Figure 2, rdfs:Resource is stratified into three layers, i.e. fa:OResource in the Ontology Layer, fa:LResource in the Language Layer and fa:MResource in the Meta-Language Layer. The same thing happens to rdfs:Class and rdfs:Property. They are stratified into the Language Layer and the Meta-Language Layer.

3.1 No Dual Roles in RDFS(FA)

There are no dual roles in RDFS(FA). Let's visit the same example again, but this time in RDFS(FA) (see Figure 3). As we mentioned earlier, rdfs:Resource and rdfs:Class are stratified into different layers in RDFS(FA), such that fa:OResource is an instance of fa:LClass, and fa:LClass is a sub-class of fa:LResource, while fa:LResource is an instance of fa:MClass.

As far as rdf:type and rdfs:subClassOf in RDFS(FA), rdf:type is stratified into fa:o-type, fa:l-type and fa:m-type[2] where

[2] In order to make it more readable, we change the syntax a bit and use fa:o-type, fa:l-type and fa:m-type, instead of fa:otype, fa:ltype and fa:mtype in [12].

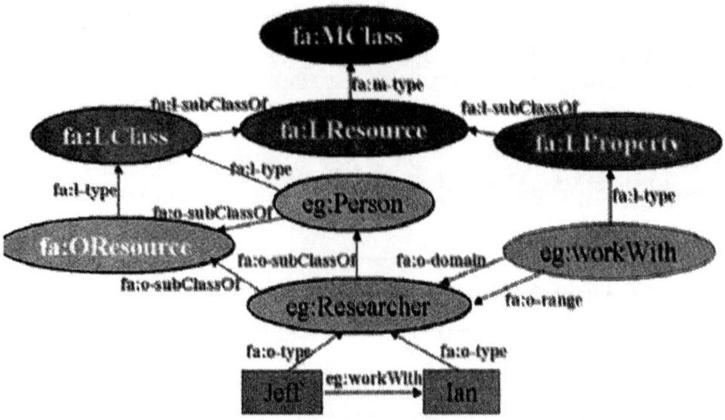

Fig. 3. No Dual Roles in RDFS(FA)

- fa:o-type is used between objects and ontology classes, e.g. Jeff and eg:Researcher;
- fa:l-type is used between resources in the Ontology Layer and resources in the Language Layer, such as eg:Person and fa:LClass, as well as eg:workWith and fa:LProperty;
- fa:m-type is used between resources in the Language Layer and resources in the Meta-Language Layer, e.g. fa:LResource and fa:MClass.

Similarly, rdfs:subClassOf is stratified into fa:o-subClassOf, fa:l-subClassOf and fa:m-subClassOf:

- fa:o-subClassOf is used between two ontology classes, such as eg:Researcher and eg:Person;
- fa:l-subClassOf is used between two classes in the Language Layer, e.g. fa:LClass and fa:LResource;
- fa:m-subClassOf is used between two classes in the Meta-Language Layer.

3.2 Design Philosophy

We discuss the design philosophy of RDFS(FA) in this section. The principle is to build the fixed layer metamodeling architecture on the basis of semantics. There are two groups of fundamental modelling primitives in RDFS(FA), which are classes primitives and property primitives.

What is the semantics of a class primitive in RDFS(FA)? A Class primitive is interpreted as a set of objects or a set of sets. E.g. in Figure 3, eg:Researcher is a class in the Ontology Layer, since it is mapped to a set of objects (e.g. Ian and Jeff). For the same reason, eg:person is also a class. In the Language Layer, fa:LClass is a class since it is mapped to a set of sets (such as eg:Person and eg:Research). fa:Property is also class primitive, since it is mapped to a set of sets (such as eg:workWith).

What is the semantics of a property primitive in RDFS(FA)? A property primitive is interpreted as a set of binary relationships (or pairs) between two instance of class primitive(s) in the same stratum. E.g. in Figure 3, eg:workWith is a property primitive, since it is mapped to a set of binary relationships between two instances of eg:Researcher in the same stratum (the Ontology Layer). fa:o-subClassOf is also a property primitive, since it is mapped to a set of binary relationships between two instances of fa:LClass in the same stratum (the Language Layer).

Once a property primitive is defined in a certain stratum, it can be used in the adjacent lower stratum. E.g. in Figure 3, once eg:workWith is defined in stratum 1 (the Ontology Layer), it can be used in stratum 0 (the Instance Layer), e.g. Jeff eg:workWith Ian. Once fa:o-subClassOf is defined in stratum 2 (the Language Layer), it can be used in stratum 1 (the Ontology Layer), such as eg:Researcher fa:o-subClassOf eg:Person.

The only exceptions are the type properties, because they are just the instance-of relationships, and always cross adjacent strata (layers). Please note that the type properties are very special, because they are just the *connections* between the two groups of fundamental primitives.[3]

3.3 Formal Description

Based on the design philosophy, we will give a formal description of the stratification of RDFS(FA) in this section. To clarify the presentation, we will not consider datatypes and values in this section; they will be discussed in Section 3.4.

Let V be a vocabulary, which is a set of urirefs. V is divided into disjoint sets $V_0, V_1, V_2, \ldots$, the vocabularies used in strata 0,1,2 ... respectively, where all the individual names are in V_0, and the names of class/property primitives are in $V_{i+1} (i \geq 0)$.

Let $\mathbf{R}_i$, $\mathbf{C}_i$, $\mathbf{P}_i$ be the modelling primitives which are interpreted as the sets of all resources, all classes and all properties respectively in stratum i. According to the design philosophy, since their *instances* are in stratum i, $\mathbf{R}_i$, $\mathbf{C}_i$, $\mathbf{P}_i$ are classes in stratum $i+1$. For example, $\mathbf{R}_1$, $\mathbf{C}_1$ and $\mathbf{P}_1$ are fa:LResource, fa:LClass and fa:LProperty respectively; fa:LResource is mapped to the *set* of all resources in stratum 1 (the Ontology Layer), fa:LClass is mapped to the *set* of all ontology classes (such as eg:Person) in stratum 1, and fa:LProperty is mapped to the *set* of all ontology properties (such as eg:workWith) in stratum 1; since their instances are in stratum 1, fa:LResource, fa:LClass and fa:LProperty exist in stratum 2.

Let $\mathbf{D}_i$ be the domain in stratum i and IE be an interpretation function.

We start from stratum 0. Every individual name $x \in V_0$ is mapped to an object in the domain $\mathbf{D}_0$:

$$IE(x) \in \mathbf{D}_0,$$

the set of all the resources in stratum 0 (the interpretation of $\mathbf{R}_0$) is $\mathbf{D}_0$:

$$IE(\mathbf{R}_0) = \mathbf{D}_0.$$

[3] They are properties *and* are used to join classes and their instances.

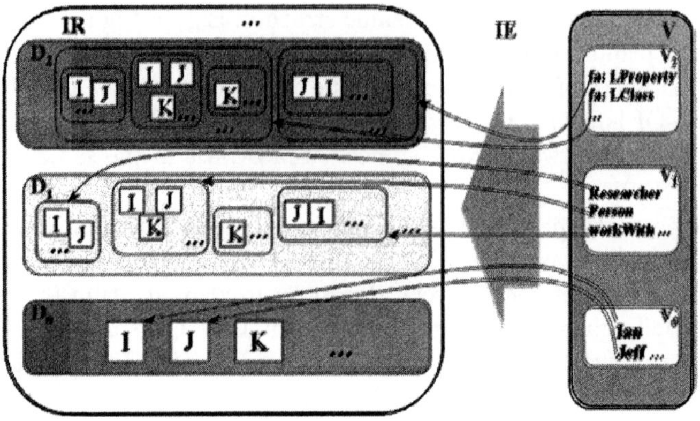

Fig. 4. Interpretation of RDFS(FA)

In stratum $i+1$ (where $i = 0, 1, 2, \ldots$), the set of all resources is equal to the domain of stratum i+1:

$$IE(\mathbf{R}_{i+1}) = \mathbf{D}_{i+1},$$

the domain $\mathbf{D}_{i+1}$ is equal to the union of the set of all classes and the set of all properties in stratum $i+1$:

$$IE(\mathbf{R}_{i+1}) = IE(\mathbf{C}_{i+1}) \cup IE(\mathbf{P}_{i+1})$$

Each class primitive $c_{i+1} \in V_{i+1}$ is interpreted as a set of resources in stratum i:

$$IE(c_{i+1}) \subseteq IE(\mathbf{R}_i),$$

and each property primitive $p_{i+1} \in V_{i+1}$ is interpreted as a set of pairs of resources in stratum i:

$$IE(p_{i+1}) \subseteq IE(\mathbf{R}_i) \times IE(\mathbf{R}_i).$$

The $type_{i+1}$ property is interpreted as a set of pairs, where the first resource is in stratum i, and the second resource is a class in stratum $i+1$:

$$IE(type_{i+1}) \subseteq IE(\mathbf{R}_i) \times IE(\mathbf{C}_{i+1}).$$

Since $IE(c_{i+1}) \subseteq IE(\mathbf{R}_i)$, we have $IE(c_{i+1}) \in 2^{IE(\mathbf{R}_i)}$, i.e. $IE(c_{i+1}) \in 2^{\mathbf{D}_i}$. According to the intended interpretation of $\mathbf{C}_{i+1}$, we have

$$IE(\mathbf{C}_{i+1}) = 2^{\mathbf{D}_i}.$$

Similarly, since $IE(p_{i+1}) \subseteq IE(\mathbf{R}_i) \times IE(\mathbf{R}_i)$, we have $IE(p_{i+1}) \in 2^{IE(\mathbf{R}_i) \times IE(\mathbf{R}_i)}$, i.e. $IE(p_{i+1}) \in 2^{\mathbf{D}_i \times \mathbf{D}_i}$. According to the intended interpretation of $\mathbf{P}_{i+1}$, we have

$$IE(\mathbf{P}_{i+1}) = 2^{\mathbf{D}_i \times \mathbf{D}_i}.$$

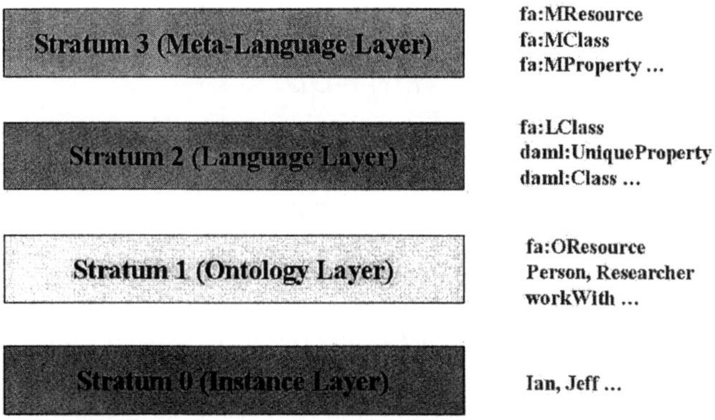

Fig. 5. DAML+OIL and the Stratification of RDFS(FA)

Since $IE(\mathbf{R}_{i+1}) = \mathbf{D}_{i+1} = IE(\mathbf{C}_{i+1}) \cup IE(\mathbf{P}_{i+1})$,we have

$$\mathbf{D}_{i+1} = 2^{\mathbf{D}_i} \cup 2^{\mathbf{D}_i \times \mathbf{D}_i}.$$

The pair $\langle IR, IE \rangle$ is an interpretation for RDFS(FA), where

$$IR = \mathbf{D}_0 \cup \mathbf{D}_1 \cup \mathbf{D}_2 \cup \cdots.$$

Figure 4 illustrates the interpretation of RDFS(FA). Vocabularies in stratum 0 (the Instance Layer), e.g. Ian and Jeff, are interpreted as objects (i.e., resources of D_0). Vocabularies for ontology classes (in V_1), such as eg:Researcher and eg:Person, are interpreted as sets of objects. Vocabularies for ontology properties (in V_1), such as eg:workWith, are interpreted as sets of pairs of objects. In stratum 2 (the Language Layer), fa:LClass is interpreted as a set of sets of objects (a set of ontology classes), and fa:LProperty is interpreted as a set of sets of pairs of objects (a set of ontology properties).

3.4 RDFS(FA) and DAML+OIL

The semantics of DAML+OIL is consistent with the stratification of RDFS(FA). Its constructs are defined in stratum 1 and 2. As shown in Figure 5, daml:Thing is in stratum 1 (the Ontology Layer) and daml:Class, daml:UniqueProperty and daml:Datatype are in stratum 2 (the Language Layer). The semantics of DAML+OIL covers stratum 0 and 1 (see below).

Since DAML+OIL supports datatypes, the domain in stratum 0 is divided into two disjoint sets, the "object domain" **OD** and "datatype domain" **DD**[4] such that $\mathbf{D}_0 = \mathbf{OD} \cup \mathbf{DD}$.

In stratum 0, every individual name $x \in V_0$ is interpreted as an object in the domain **OD**:

$$IE(x) \in \mathbf{OD},$$

[4] Note that datatype domain (a set) is in stratum 1, since it is a set of data values that are in stratum o.

every literal $t \in V_0$ is interpreted as a data value in the domain **DD**

$$IE(t) \in \mathbf{DD},$$

and the set of all the resources in stratum 0 (the interpretation of $\mathbf{R}_0$) is $\mathbf{D}_0$

$$IE(\mathbf{R}_0) = \mathbf{D}_0 = \mathbf{OD} \cup \mathbf{DD}.$$

In stratum 1, each class primitive $c_1 \in V_1$ is interpreted as a set of objects:

$$IE(c_1) \subseteq \mathbf{OD},$$

each datatype name $d_1 \in V_1$ is interpreted as a set of data values:

$$IE(d_1) \subseteq \mathbf{DD},$$

each object property $p_1^o \in V_1$ is interpreted as a set of pairs of objects:

$$IE(p_1^o) \subseteq \mathbf{OD} \times \mathbf{OD},$$

each datatype property $p_1^d \in V_1$ is interpreted as a set of pairs, where the first resource is an object and the second resource is a data value:

$$IE(p_1^d) \subseteq \mathbf{OD} \times \mathbf{DD}.$$

In general, DAML+OIL, and other logical layer Semantic Web languages, can be built on top of both the syntax and semantics of RDFS(FA). Furthermore, the stratification of RDFS(FA) can benefit such logical layer Semantic Web languages by offering possibilities of extending them in stratum 3 (the Meta-Language Layer). It can also help avoiding "layer mistakes" [12] in DAML+OIL.

4 RDF Model Theory

Another way to clear up the kinds of confusion of RDFS is RDF Model Theory (RDF MT) [12], which gives a precise semantic theory for RDF and RDFS. It is a W3C working draft when this paper is being written.

An interpretation in the RDF model theory is a triple $\langle \mathbf{IR}, IEXT, IS \rangle$, where **IR** is the domain (of resources); IS is a function that maps URI references to elements of **IR**; and $IEXT$ is a partial function (called extension function) from **IR** to the powerset of $\mathbf{IR} \times \mathbf{IR}$. In RDF MT, meaning is given to properties by first mapping the property URI references to an object of the domain of discourse via IS. The domain object is then mapped into a set of pairs via $IEXT$.

In RDF MT, all resources (including all classes and properties) are objects (see Figure 6). IS maps the URI references of resources to objects in the domain **IR**, e.g. IS maps rdfs:subClassOf to object S, or IS(rdfs:subClassOf) , rdf:type to object T, or IS(rdf:type), rdfs:Class to object C, or IS(rdfs:Class) etc. **IP**, which is a set of all property objects, is a special sub-set of **IR**.

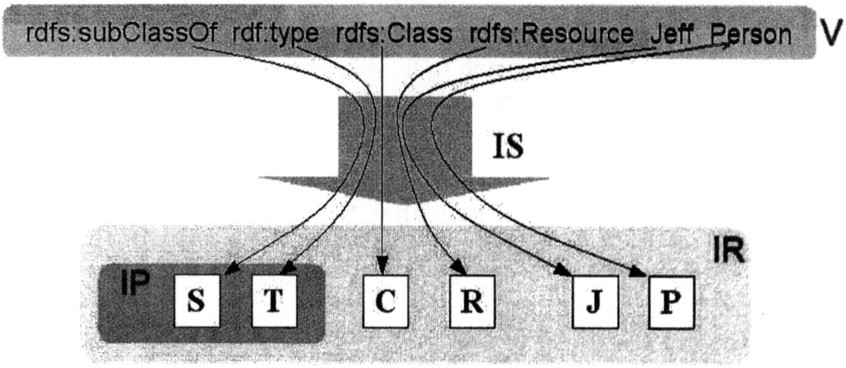

Fig. 6. Resources in RDF MT

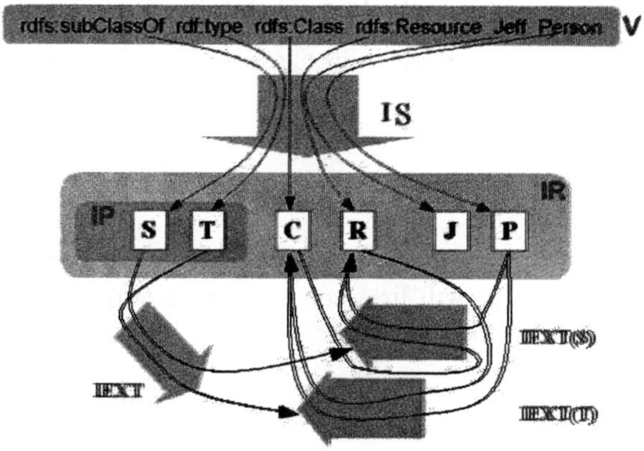

Fig. 7. Interpretation of RDF MT

Extension function $IEXT$ maps property objects to their extensions. E.g. in Figure 7, $IEXT$ maps S to $IEXT$(S), which is a set of pairs {⟨P,R⟩, ⟨C,R⟩}. $IEXT$ maps T to $IEXT$(T), which is a set of pairs {⟨P,C⟩, ⟨R,C⟩}. Class primitives are not fundamental primitives in RDF MT. Class extension $ICEXT$ is defined through the extension of IS(rdf:type):

$$ICEXT(x) = \{y \mid \langle y, x\rangle \text{ is in } IEXT(IS(\text{rdf:type}))\}$$

In Figure 7, $IEXT$(T)={⟨P,C⟩, ⟨R,C⟩}, so P and R are in ICEXT(C).

4.1 No Confusion in RDF MT

RDF MT justifies dual roles in RDFS by treating classes and properties as objects. In other words, class primitives in RDF MT are interpreted as objects that can have non-empty class extensions; property primitives in RDF MT are interpreted as objects that can have non-empty extensions. Even though it is a bit strange to some people, there is no confusion in RDF MT.

Let's revisit the same example in RDF MT. rdfs:Class and rdfs:Resource are mapped to objects C and R in the domain of resource by IS, therefore rdfs:Class is rdfs:subClassOf rdfs:Resource means the pair of R and C is in the extension of the rdfs:subClassOf object S

$$\langle \mathrm{C,R} \rangle \in IEXT(\mathrm{S})$$

while rdfs:Resource is instance of rdfs:Class means the pair of R and C is in the extension of the rdf:type object T

$$\langle \mathrm{R,C} \rangle \in IEXT(\mathrm{T}).$$

According to the definition of $ICEXT$, we have

$$\mathrm{R} \in ICEXT(\mathrm{C}).$$

In this way, the situation between rdfs:Class and rdfs:Resource is given a well defined meaning.

5 Comparing the Two Approaches

In Section 3 and 4, we described two approaches to clear up any confusion of RDFS. In this section, we will first compare these two approaches, and then discuss their advantages and disadvantages.

5.1 Main Differences

On how to clear up the confusion of RDFS, RDFS(FA) stratifies dual roles into different strata and defines modelling primitives explicitly; while RDF MT justifies dual roles by treating classes and properties as objects, making dual roles a feature, instead of a problem, of the language.

Differences in Syntax. RDFS(FA) provides extra syntax to add restriction of stratification, so as to enable the layering style of RDFS, and to avoid dual roles. Since elements of RDFS(FA) exist in different strata of the domain of discourse, (prefixes of) symbols of elements should indicate this fact. E.g. fa:OResource is in stratum 1 (the Ontology Layer), fa:LProperty is in stratum 2 (the Language Layer), and fa:MClass is in stratum 3 (the Meta-Language Layer). [5]

Secondly, valid RDFS(FA) statements should be consistent with the design philosophy (see Section 3.2) of RDFS(FA). If one defines a class in stratum $i+1$, then the instances of that class should be in stratum i, e.g.

[5] Note that properties, except the type properties, are always used one stratum lower than the one where they are defined, e.g. fa:o-subClassOf is defined in stratum 2 (the Language Layer) and used in stratum 1 (the Ontology Layer).

```
<fa:LClass rdf:about=‘‘\#Person’’>
</fa:LClass>
```

Since fa:LClass is in stratum 2 (the Language Layer), the Class "Person" should be in stratum 1 (the Ontology Layer).

Similarly, if one defines a property in stratum $i+1$, then the classes as the domain and range of the property should be in stratum $i+1$ as well.

```
<fa:LProperty rdf:about=‘‘\#hasFriend’’>
  <fa:o-domain rdf:resource=‘‘\#Person’’/>
  <fa:o-range rdf:resource=‘‘\#Person’’/>
</fa:LProperty>
```

Furthermore, RDFS(FA) distinguishes its predefined property primitives (such as fa:o-type and fa:o-domain etc) from user-defined properties (such as eg:hasFriend). For instance, users are not allowed to define sub-properties of fa:o-type. In RDFS, however, there is no such restriction.

Differences in Semantics. Besides differences in syntax, there are also differences in semantics between RDFS(FA) and RDF MT.[6]

First of all, RDFS is more expressive than RDFS(FA). The reason for being less expressive is that the stratification of RDFS(FA) disallows most cross-stratum binary relationships (except the type properties). However, it could be argued that these kinds of relationship are too confusing for most users.

Secondly, there are different *fundamental* primitives in RDFS(FA) and RDF MT. In RDFS(FA), both class and property primitives are fundamental primitives, i.e., both are directly interpreted by the interpretation function IE. As seen in Section 3.3, RDFS(FA) class primitives in stratum $i+1$ are interpreted as sets of elements in stratum i, while property primitives in stratum $i+1$ are interpreted as sets of pairs of elements in stratum i. The type properties are *special* properties: their interpretations are just the *instance-of* relationships.

In RDF MT, although both class and property primitives are objects, *only* property primitives are fundamental primitives, i.e., only property primitives can be given non empty extensions by $IEXT$. The class extension $ICEXT$ is simply derived from the $IEXT$ extension of the rdf:type object. Note, however that although the rdf:type property is used to define membership of classes, in all other respects it is treated in the same way as any other property.

Thirdly, RDFS(FA) and RDF MT interpret property (and class) primitives in different ways. In RDFS(FA) (and conventional FOL), property (class) symbols are directly mapped to a set of pairs of elements (elements) in the domain. While in RDF MT, on the other hand, meaning is given to property and class symbols by first mapping them (via IS) to objects in the domain. A property object is then mapped (via $IEXT$) to a set of pairs of objects in the domain.

Based on the differences between RDFS(FA) and RDF MT, we will discuss their advantages and disadvantages in next section.

[6] Readers are advised to refer to Figure 4 and 7 for better understanding of these differences.

5.2 Advantages of RDF MT (Disadvantages of RDFS(FA))

Since there is no restriction of stratification, RDF MT (RDFS) is more expressive than RDFS(FA). This advantage of RDF MT is believed to be consistent with the following philosophy: anyone can say anything about anything. In RDF MT, this means

- properties can be defined between any two resources;
- any resource can be an instance of any resource (including itself).

However, this *"unlimited"* expressive power can lead to problems, as we will see in the following section.

5.3 Disadvantages of RDF MT (Advantages of RDFS(FA))

The syntax rules in RDFS are very weak, and there are not many restrictions on writing RDFS triples. As a result, this can be confusing and difficult to understand and, more importantly, the specification of its semantics requires a non-standard model theory, i.e. RDF MT.

This leads to semantic problems when trying to layer[7] conventional FOL, like DAML+OIL and OWL. E.g., as DAML+OIL is more expressive than RDFS, a large and more complex set of semantic conditions[8] is required to capture the meaning and characteristic of its additional constructs. It is very difficult to get such semantic conditions correct, not to mention that one should also prove that they are right.

There are at least three known problems if we extend RDFS with more expressive FOL constructs, e.g. conjunctions and qualified number restrictions, and extend RDF MT to so called "RDF+ MT" to give meaning to this extended language. These known problems are: (i) too few entailments; (ii) contradiction classes; (iii) size of the universe.

Too Few Entailments. Entailment is the key idea which connects model-theoretic semantics to real-world applications. What is entailment? In RDF MT, entailment means "If A entails B, then any interpretation that makes A true also makes B true," so that an assertion of A already contains the same "meaning" as an assertion of B [12].

[13] first addressed the problem of too few entailments and gave the following example: if John is an instance of the class Student ⊓Employee⊓European, is John an instance of the class Employee ⊓Student?

In RDFS(FA) and FOL, the answer is simply "yes", since Student⊓Employee⊓ European is a sub-class of Employee ⊓Student, so every instance of the former class is also an instance of the later one.

[7] RDFS, in some sense, is a very limited language, and serves as the bottom semantic layer of Semantic Web languages. So it is both necessary and desirable to layer more expressive ontology languages on top of it.

[8] Since the constructs of RDFS are simple, the set of semantic conditions for RDFS is relatively small.

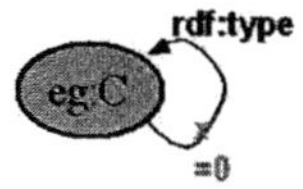

Fig. 8. Contradiction Classes

However, in "RDF+ MT", since every concept is also an object, "John is an instance of the concept Student⊓Employee ⊓European" can't guarantee there exists an object for Employee ⊓Student in all the interpretations that make "John is an instance of the concept Student⊓ Employee⊓European" true. So the answer in RDF+ MT is "no".

In this case, the "RDF+ MT" semantics seems to be broken, because the semantics of an ontology language should give meaning to any possible class expressions. In order to fix the problem, one can/should introduce comprehension axioms to add all possible missing objects into the domain, e.g. the Employee ⊓Student in this example. But that is surely a very difficult task. Theoretically, it is yet to be proved that proper objects are all added into the universe, no more and no less. Practically, there will be infinite numbers of possible class expressions.[9] It is still unknown whether there exists a practical approach to solve the problem.

Contradiction Classes. [13,14] also addressed the problem of contradiction classes. In RDFS, resources can be defined as instances of themselves, and rdf:type is treated as any other property. So, if the extended language supports qualified number restrictions, one can define a class eg:C as an instance of itself, and add a cardinality constraint "=0" on the rdf:type property (see Figure 8). It is impossible for one to determine the membership of this class. If an object is an instance of this class, then it isn't, because instances should have no rdf:type property pointing to itself. But if it isn't then it is. This is a contradiction class.

One might argue that we can simply avoid defining such classes. However, with the comprehension axioms (see Section 5.3.1), we must add all possible class objects into the domain, and the above contradiction class is one of them. In this way, all the interpretations will have such contradiction classes, and thus have ill-defined class memberships. Again, the "RDF+ MT" semantics seems to be broken[10]. RDFS(FA) does't have this problem, because the type properties are not treated as ordinary properties.

Size of the Universe. Like RDF MT, in "RDF+ MT" there is a pre-defined vocabulary (e.g. rdf:type, rdfs:Property etc), terms from which are mapped to

[9] Think about all the possible conjunctions, disjunctions, exist restrictions, value restrictions and qualified number restrictions ...

[10] One might solve the problem by making the comprehension axioms more complex. It is yet to be proved that we keep the objects of all possible contradiction classes outside the universe.

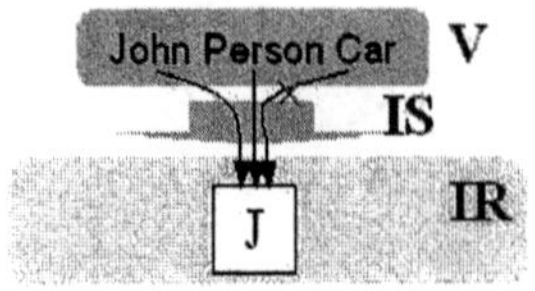

Fig. 9. Size of the Universe

elements of the universe. Thus these elements *must* exist in all the possible interpretations. A problem arises if we set constraints on the size of the universe. Even if we don't consider such pre-defined vocabulary, this problem still exists. Here is an example.

Let us consider the following question: is it possible to have an interpretation such that John is a member of Person, but not a member of Car, and there is only one object in the universe?

In RDFS(FA) and FOL, the answer is simply "yes". There is only one object in the universe, and John is interpreted as that object. The Person class thus has one instance, i.e. the interpretation of John. The Car class has no instances. So it is possible to have such an interpretation.

But it is impossible to have only one object in the "RDF+ MT" universe in this example. Since classes are also objects, John, Person and Car should all be mapped to the only one object in the universe (see Figure 9). However, since the interpretation of John is a member of Person, but not a member of Car, Person and Car should be different. Thus there should be at least two objects in the universe. In other words, the required interpretation is impossible in "RDF+ MT", and the answer to our question is "no".

This example shows that the interpretation of RDF MT has different features than the interpretation of standard FOL model theoretic semantics. This raises the question as to whether it is possible to layer FOL languages on top of both the syntax and semantics of RDFS.

6 Discussion

As we have seen, RDFS has a non-standard and non-fixed layer metamodeling architecture, which makes some elements in the model have dual roles in the RDFS specification. This can be confusing and difficult to understand for modelers. One of the consequences is that when DAML+OIL is layering on top of RDFS, it uses the syntax of RDFS only, and defines its own semantics for the ontological primitives of RDFS.

Up to now, there are at least two approaches to clear up the kinds of confusion that can arise w.r.t. RDFS: RDFS(FA) and RDF MT. RDFS(FA), as a sub-language of RDFS, clears up any confusions via stratification, while RDF MT justifies dual roles by treating classes and properties as objects.

The advantage of RDF MT is that it is more expressive than RDFS(FA), because it doesn't have the restriction of stratification. The philosophy is that anyone can say anything about anything. Properties can be defined between any two resources, and a resource can be an instance of any resource (including itself). Some people, however, worry about this "unlimited" expressive power, in particular when layering more expressive languages on top of RDFS.

The advantage of RDFS(FA) is that FOLs, e.g. DAML+OIL, can be built on top of both the syntax and semantics of RDFS(FA). Furthermore, the stratification of RDFS(FA) can benefit such logical layer Semantic Web languages by offering possibilities of extending them in stratum 3 (the Meta-Language Layer).

The disadvantage of RDF MT is that there are at least three known problems if we extend RDFS with more expressive FOL constructs, and extend RDF MT to the so called "RDF+ MT" to give meaning to this extended language (see Section 5.3). Moreover, layering FOL on top of RDFS doesn't lead directly to any "computational pathway", i.e. it is not clear whether/how applications would be able to reason with languages layered on top of RDFS.

Generally speaking, on the one hand, RDF MT allows for a larger number of models of the universe, and can represent more heterogeneous states of affairs. On the other hand, RDFS(FA) allows more expressive ontology languages, e.g. DAML+OIL, to be layered on top of it, so that people can say more things about a smaller number of (more homogeneous) models of the universe.

It has yet to be proved that RDF MT can be extended to give a coherent meaning to more expressive ontology languages[11]. Moreover, it is not clear if the more heterogeneous models supported by RDF MT would be needed in many realistic applications. Given that the set of RDFS(FA) statements is a subset of the set of RDFS statements, one possible solution would be to support both semantics, with users able to choose if they are willing to use the layering style of RDFS to facilitate the extension of the language with more expressive modelling primitives. This solution could provide a good guideline for more expressive logical ontology languages designed on top of RDFS, and for users to be aware of the above problems when they choose to use the non-layering style of RDFS.

Acknowledgments. We would like to thank Peter Patel-Schneider for discussion on the stratification of RDFS(FA), and Peter Aczel for discussion on non-well founded sets.

References

1. T. Berners-lee. Semantic Web Road Map. W3C Design Issues. URL `http://www.w3.org/DesignIssues/Semantic.html`, Oct. 1998.
2. T. Bray, J. Paoli, C. M. Sperberg-McQueen, and E. Maler. Extensible Markup Language (XML) 1.0 (Second Edition) – W3C Recommendation 6 October 2000. Technical report, World Wide Web Consortium, 2000. Available at `http://www.w3.org/TR/REC-xml`.

[11] Note that in OWL the RDFS-compatible model-theoretic semantics has the same consequence as the direct semantics on OWL ontologies, *only* when the separate vocabulary restriction is satisfied [15].

3. D. Brickley and R. Guha. Resource Description Framework (RDF) Schema Specification 1.0. W3C Recommentdation, Mar. 2000.
4. J. Broekstra, M. Klein, S. Decker, D. Fensel, F. van Harmelen, and I. Horrocks. Enabling Knowledge Representation on the Web by Extending RDF Schema. In *Proc. of the 10th WWW conf. (WWW10)*, Hong Kong, May 2001.
5. M. Dean, D. Connolly, F. van Harmelen, J. Hendler, I. Horrocks, D. L. McGuinness, P. F. Patel-Schneider, and L. A. S. eds. OWL Web Ontology Language 1.0 Reference. URL `http://www.w3.org/TR/owl-ref/`, Nov 2002.
6. D. Fensel, I. Horrocks, F. van Harmelen, S. Decker, M. Erdmann, and M. Klein. OIL in a nutshell. In *Proc. of the 12th Eur. Workshop on Knowledge Acquisition, Modeling, and Management (EKAW'00)*, pages 1–16, 2000.
7. D. Fensel, F. van Harmelen, I. Horrocks, D. L. McGuinness, and P. F. Patel-Schneider. OIL: An ontology infrastructure for the semantic web. *IEEE Intelligent Systems*, 16(2):38–45, 2001.
8. P. Hayes. RDF Model Theory. Apr 2002. W3C Working Draft, URL `http://www.w3.org/TR/rdf-mt/`.
9. J. Hendler and D. L. McGuinness. The DARPA Agent Markup Language. *IEEE Intelligent Systems*, 15(6):67–73, 2000.
10. O. Lassila and R. R.Swick. Resource Description Framework (RDF) Model and Syntax Specification – W3C Recommendation 22 February 1999. Technical report, World Wide Web Consortium, 1999.
11. W. Nejdl, M. Wolpers, and C. Capella. The RDF Schema Specification Revisited. In *Modelle und Modellierungssprachen in Informatik und Wirtschaftsinformatik, Modellierung 2000*, Apr. 2000.
12. J. Z. Pan and I. Horrocks. Metamodeling Architecture of Web Ontology Languages. In *Proc. of the 2001 Int. Semantic Web Working Symposium (SWWS 2001)*, July 2001. URL `http://www.cs.man.ac.uk/ panz/Zhilin/download/Paper/Pan-Horrocks-rdfsfa-2001.pdf`.
13. P. F. Patel-Schneider. Layering the Semantic Web: Problems and Directions. In *Proc. of the 2002 Int. Semantic Web Conf. (ISWC 2002)*, Jun 2002.
14. P. F. Patel-Schneider. Two Proposals for a Semantic Web Ontology Language. In *2002 International Description Logic Workshop*, Apr 2002.
15. P. F. Patel-Schneider, P. Hayes, and I. Horrocks. OWL Web Ontology Language Semantics and Abstract Syntax. Technical report, Mar. 2003. W3C Working Draft, URL `http://www.w3.org/TR/2003/WD-owl-semantics-20030331/`.
16. M. Uschold and M. Gruninger. Ontologies: Principles, Methods and Applications. *The Knowledge Engineering Review*, 1996.
17. F. van Harmelen, P. F. Patel-Schneider, and I. Horrocks. Reference Description of the DAML+OIL(March 2001) Ontology Markuk Language. DAML+OIL Document. Available at `http://www.daml.org/2000/12/reference.html`, Mar. 2001.
18. F. van Harmelen, P. F. Patel-Schneider, and I. Horrocks. A Model-Theoretis Semantics of DAML+OIL(March 2001). DAML+OIL Document, URL `http://www.daml.org/2001/03/model-theoretic-semantics.html`, Mar. 2001.

Web Ontology Reasoning with Datatype Groups

Jeff Z. Pan and Ian Horrocks

Department of Computer Science,
University of Manchester, UK M13 9PL
{pan,horrocks}@cs.man.ac.uk

Abstract. When providing reasoning services for ontology languages such as DAML+OIL and OWL, it is necessary for description logics to deal with "concrete" datatypes (strings, integers, etc.) as well as "abstract" concepts and relationships. In this paper, we present a new approach, the datatype group approach, to integrating DLs with multiple datatypes. We discuss the advantages of such approach over the existing ones and show how a tableaux algorithm for the description logic $\mathcal{SHOQ}(\mathbf{D_n})$ can be modified in order to reason with datatype groups.

1 Introduction

Datatypes are important in the Semantic Web ontologies and applications, because most of which need to represent, in some way, various "real world" properties such as size, weight and duration, and some other complex user defined datatypes. Reasoning and querying over datatype properties are important and necessary if these properties are to be understood by machines.

For instance, e-shops may need to classify items according to their sizes, and to reason that an item which has height less than 5cm and the sum of length and width less than 10cm belongs to a class, called "small-items", for which no shipping costs are charged. Accordingly the billing system will charge no shipping fees for all the instances of the "small-items" class.

Various Web ontology languages, such as RDF(S) [4], OIL [5], DAML+OIL[1] [7] and OWL[2], have witnessed the importance of datatypes in the Semantic Web. All of them support datatypes. For instance, the DAML+OIL language supports unary datatype predicates and qualified number restrictions on unary datatype predicates, e.g. a "less than 21" predicate could be used with the datatype property *age* to describe objects having age less than 21.[3]

Description Logics (DLs)[1], a family of logical formalisms for the representation of and reasoning about conceptual knowledge, are of crucial importance to

1 http://www.daml.org/
2 http://www.w3.org/2001/sw/WebOnt/
3 It is important to distinguish between a unary predicate such as "less than 21", which is true of any number x that is less than 21, and a binary predicate such as "less than", which is true of any pair of numbers x, y where x is less than y.

D. Fensel et al. (Eds.): ISWC 2003, LNCS 2870, pp. 47–63, 2003.

the development of the Semantic Web. Their role is to provide formal underpinnings and automated reasoning services for Semantic Web ontology languages such as OIL, DAML+OIL and OWL.

Using datatypes within Semantic Web ontology languages presents new requirements for DL reasoning services. Firstly, such reasoning services should be compatible with the XML Schema type system[3], and may need to support many different datatypes. Furthermore, they should be easy to extend when new datatypes are required.

DL researchers have been working on combining DLs and datatypes for quite a long time. Bader and Hanschke [2] first presented the concrete domain approach, Lutz [10] studied the effect on complexity of adding concrete domains to a range of DLs, Horrocks and Sattler [8] proposed the $\mathcal{SHOQ}(\mathbf{D})$ DL which combines DLs and type systems (e.g. the XML Schema type system), and more recently Pan and Horrocks [12] presented the $\mathcal{SHOQ}(\mathbf{D_n})$ DL, which extends $\mathcal{SHOQ}(\mathbf{D})$ with n-ary datatype predicates and qualified number restrictions.

To reason with $\mathcal{SHOQ}(\mathbf{D})$ and $\mathcal{SHOQ}(\mathbf{D_n})$, type checkers are introduced to work with DL "concept reasoners". By using a separate type checker, we can deal with an arbitrary conforming set of datatypes and predicates without compromising the compactness of the concept language or the soundness and completeness of the decision procedure [8]. Whenever new datatypes are required, only the type checkers need to be updated and the DL concept reasoner can be reused. The result is a framework that is both robust and flexible.

To support type systems and type checkers, in this paper, we present the datatype group approach, which extends existing approaches in order to overcome problems and limitations such as counter-intuitive negation, disjointness of different datatypes and mixed datatype predicates. We then describe an algorithm for reasoning with $\mathcal{SHOQ}(\mathbf{D_n})$, which improves on the one presented in [12] by allowing simpler "deterministic" type checkers to be used.

Next section, we will show the expressive power of the $\mathcal{SHOQ}(\mathbf{D_n})$ DL by an example of using n-ary datatype predicates.

2 An Example: Using Datatypes

Maybe you still remember the "small-items" example presented in last section, in which `the sum of ... less than 10cm` is an n-ary datatype predicate. In this section, we give another example of using n-ary (this time n=2) datatype predicates to support unit mapping.

Example 1 Miles and Kilometers.[4] Unit mapping is important because of the variety of units. For instance, you can find more than one hundred and sixty

[4] This example is inspired by a discussion about datatypes in the www-rdf-logic mailing list:
`http://lists.w3.org/Archives/Public/www-rdf-logic/2003Mar/0048.html`.

length units in `http://www.chemie.de/`[5]. This example concerns the mapping between the units of mile and kilometer.

Firstly, we define two datatypes to represent the units of mile and kilometer. Since the positive float is not a built-in XML Schema datatype, we define two derived XML Schema datatypes[6] lengthInMile and lengthInKMtr, as follows:

```
<xsd:schema xmlns:xsd="http://www.w3.org/2001/XMLSchema}"
                xmlns="http://www.example.org/length-units.xsd}">
  <xsd:simpleType name="lengthInMile">
    <xsd:restriction base="xsd:float">
      <xsd:minInclusive value="0/>
    </xsd:restriction base="xsd:float">
  </xsd:simpleType>
  <xsd:simpleType name="lengthInKMtr">
    <xsd:restriction base="xsd:float">
      <xsd:minInclusive value="0/>
    </xsd:restriction base="xsd:float">
  </xsd:simpleType>
</xsd:schema>
```

We can then make use of these datatypes in DAML+OIL ontologies.[7] E.g., if we have datatype properties "length-mile" and "length-kmtr" defined in a river ontology:

```
<rdf:RDF
        xmlns="http://www.example.org/river#"
          ...
   xmlns:unit="http://www.example.org/length-units.xsd">
   <owl:DataTypeProperty rdf:ID="length">
     <rdfs:range rdf:resource="xsd:float"/>
   </owl:DataTypeProperty>
   <owl:Class rdf:ID="River"/>
   <owl:DataTypeProperty rdf:ID="length-mile">
     <rdfs:subPropertyOf rdf:resource="\#length"/>
     <rdfs:domain rdf:resource="\#River"/>
     <rdfs:range rdf:resource="unit:lengthInMile"/>
   </owl:DataTypeProperty>
   <owl:DataTypeProperty rdf:ID="length-kmtr">
     <rdfs:subPropertyOf rdf:resource="\#length"/>
     <rdfs:domain rdf:resource="\#River"/>
     <rdfs:range rdf:resource="unit:lengthInKMtr"/>
   </owl:DataTypeProperty>
```

[5] `http://www.chemie.de/tools/units.php3?language=e\&property=m`

[6] When we talk about XML Schema datatype in this paper, we mean XML Schema simple types.

[7] OWL currently does not support the use of derived datatypes.

we can describe the length of the Yangtze river as 3937.5 miles *and* 6300 kilometers:

```
<River rdf:ID="Yangtze">
  <length-mile rdf:datatype="unit:lengthInMile">3937.5</length>
</River>
<River rdf:ID="Yangtze">
  <length-kmtr rdf:datatype="unit:lengthInKMtr">6300</length>
</River>
```

We can specify the mapping between miles and kilometers using a binary datatype predicate. Sadly, XML Schema does not support n-ary datatype predicates. We have used an XML style syntax to present this predicate in `http://www.example.org/length-units.xsd` as follows:[8]

```
<predicate name="kmtrsPerMile" arity="2">
  <par var="i" base="lengthInKMtr">
  <par var="j" base="lengthInMile">
  <constraint val="i=1.6*j">
</predicate>
```

The binary (with $arity = 2$) datatype predicate "kmtrsPerMile" is defined over the datatypes "lengthInKMtr" and "lengthInMile".

Now we can add a restriction to the "River" class and require that the value of the "length-kmtr" property be 1.6 times that of the "length-mile" property. Again, we could imagine an extension of a language such as OWL to support the use of n-ary datatype predicates:

```
<owl:Class rdf:about="River">
  <rdfs:subClassOf>
    <owl:NaryRestriction>
      <owl:onProperties rdf:parseType="Collection">
        <owl:DatatypeProperty rdf:ID="length-kmtr">
        <owl:DatatypeProperty rdf:ID="length-mile">
      </owl:onProperties>
      <owl:allTuplesSatisfy rdf:resource="unit:kmtrsPerMile"/>
    </owl:NaryRestriction>
  <rdfs:subClassOf>
</owl:Class>
```

Note that, in the above restriction, the order of the properties in the `onProperties` list is significant, and "kmtrsPerMile" is a datatype predicate whose arity must match the number of properties in the `onProperties` list. Such restriction is expressible in the $\mathcal{SHOQ}(\mathbf{D_n})$ DL (see section 4).

[8] Currently we are also working on extending the common DL Interface DIG/1.1 to support n-ary datatype predicates in a similar manner.

One example of reasoning with the above ontology and datatypes is to check whether a large set of instances of the ontology class River are consistent with the above restriction of the River class. ◇

As we hope the above example shows, n-ary datatype predicates would be very useful in Semantic Web ontologies and applications. In next section, we will start to investigate how to provide DL reasoning services for ontologies and datatypes.

3 Concrete Domains and Datatype Groups

As mentioned in Section 1, Description Logic researchers have been working on combining DLs and datatypes for quite a long time, although they might not always have used the term "datatype". It was Baader and Hanschke [2] who first presented a rigorous treatment of datatypes, which they called "concrete domains". Lutz [9] presents a survey of DLs with concrete domains, concentrating on the effect on complexity and decidability of adding concrete domains to various DLs. More recently, Horrocks and Sattler [8] proposed a new approach to cope with datatypes structured by a type system. In the rest of this section, we will briefly describe the above two approaches, explaining their advantages and disadvantages in coping with multiple datatypes, then extend these approaches and present the datatype group approach.

3.1 The Concrete Domain Approach

A "concrete domain" is formally defined as followed:

Definition 1 *(***Concrete Domain.***)* A concrete domain $\mathcal{D}$ consists of a pair $(\Delta_\mathcal{D},\Phi_\mathcal{D})$, where $\Delta_\mathcal{D}$ is the domain of $\mathcal{D}$ and $\Phi_\mathcal{D}$ is a set of predicate names. Each predicate name P is associated with an arity n, and an n-ary predicate $P^\mathcal{D} \subseteq \Delta_\mathcal{D}^n$. Let $\mathbf{V}$ be a set of variables. A predicate conjunction of the form

$$c = \bigwedge_{j=1}^{k} P_j(v_1^{(j)}, \dots, v_{n_j}^{(j)}), \tag{1}$$

where P_j is an n_j-ary predicate and the $v_i^{(j)}$ are variables from $\mathbf{V}$, is called *satisfiable* iff there exists a function δ mapping the variables in c to data values in $\Delta_\mathcal{D}$ s.t. $(\delta(v_1^{(j)}), \dots, \delta(v_{n_j}^{(j)})) \in P_j^\mathcal{D}$ for $1 \leq j \leq k$. Such a function δ is called a *solution* for c. A concrete domain $\mathcal{D}$ is called *admissible* iff

1. $\Phi_\mathcal{D}$ is closed under negation[9] and contains a name $\top_\mathcal{D}$ for $\Delta_\mathcal{D}$ and
2. the satisfiability problem for finite conjunctions of predicates is decidable.

[9] Closed under negation requires that if $P \in \Phi_\mathcal{D}$, then $\overline{P} \in \Phi_\mathcal{D}$.

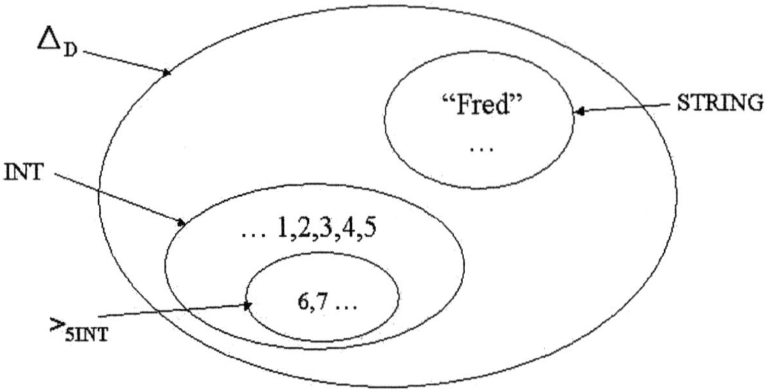

Fig. 1. The $>_5$ and $\leq_5$ Datatype Predicates

By $\overline{P}$, we denote the name for the negation of the predicate P, i.e., if the arity of P is n, then $\overline{P}^{\mathcal{D}} = \Delta_{\mathcal{D}}^n \setminus P^{\mathcal{D}}$. ◇

Here is an example of a concrete domain.

Example 2 The Concrete Domain. $\mathcal{N} = (\Delta_{\mathcal{N}}, \Phi_{\mathcal{N}})$, where $\Delta_{\mathcal{N}}$ is the set of nonnegative integers and $\Phi_{\mathcal{N}} = \{\geq, \geq_n\}$.[10] $\mathcal{N}$ is not admissible since $\Phi_{\mathcal{N}}$ doesn't satisfy condition 1 of admissible in Definition 1; in order to make it admissible we would have to extend $\Phi_{\mathcal{N}}$ to $\{\top_{\mathcal{N}}, \bot_{\mathcal{N}}\} \cup \{<, \geq, <_n, \geq_n\}$. ◇

The introduction of concrete domains in Baader and Hanschke [2] gives a firm basis for integrating DLs with datatypes. More examples of admissible concrete domains can be found in Section 2.4 of [10]. We can integrate an arbitrary concrete domain $\mathcal{D}$ into the $\mathcal{ALC}$ DL and give the $\mathcal{ALC}(\mathcal{D})$ DL. The syntax and semantics of this DL are described in [2,10]. The new concept expression (about datatypes) of $\mathcal{ALC}(\mathcal{D})$ is the predicate restriction $P(u_1, \ldots, u_n)$, where P is a predicate name in $\Phi_{\mathcal{D}}$ and $u_1, \ldots, u_n$ are feature chains.[11]

Although the concrete domain approach does a very good job in combining DLs with *one* concrete domain, there are some problems when combining DLs with more than one concrete domain, especially in the context of Web ontology reasoning.

Negated Datatypes. In the concrete domain approach, when two admissible concrete domains $\mathcal{D}_1$ and $\mathcal{D}_2$ are combined to form a new concrete domain $\mathcal{D}_1 \oplus \mathcal{D}_2$, the interpretation of the negation of each predicate name $P_j \in \Phi_{\mathcal{D}_1}$

[10] Note that $\geq$ is a binary predicate and $\geq_n$ is a unary predicate.
[11] See [2,10] for more about feature chains.

will be modified from $\overline{P_j}^{\mathcal{D}_1} = \Delta_{\mathcal{D}_1}^{n_j} \setminus P_j^{\mathcal{D}_1}$ to $\overline{P_j}^{\mathcal{D}_1 \oplus \mathcal{D}_2} = (\Delta_{\mathcal{D}_1} \cup \Delta_{\mathcal{D}_2})^{n_j} \setminus P_j^{\mathcal{D}_1}$. We can see that $\overline{P_j}^{\mathcal{D}_1 \oplus \mathcal{D}_2}$ equals to $\overline{P_j}^{\mathcal{D}_1}$ union a set of n_j-ary tuples involving type errors, where at least one of the variables of P_j is mapped to a data value in $\mathcal{D}_2$ instead of $\mathcal{D}_1$. Counting type errors in the negations of datatype predicates may be counter-intuition. Let's see an example.

Example 3 The $>_5$ and $\leq_5$ Datatype Predicates. We first only consider the concrete domains *INT*, where datatype predicates $>_5, \leq_5 \in \Phi_{INT}$. We have $\overline{>_5}^{INT} = \leq_5^{INT}$ (see figure 1). When we consider two concrete domain *INT* and *STRING*, we might still expect that $\overline{>_5}^{INT \oplus STRING}$ only include the *integers* that are not in $>_5^{INT}$, e.g., the integer 3. However, since $\overline{>_5}^{INT \oplus STRING} = (\Delta_{INT} \cup \Delta_{STRING}) \setminus >_5^{INT}$, the string "Fred" is also in $\overline{>_5}^{INT \oplus STRING}$. ◇

As well as being counter-intuitive, the change in the interpretation of $\overline{P_j}$ does not fit well with the idea of using type checkers to work with DL reasoner. We will come back to this in Section 3.3.

Disjoint Domains. The concrete domain approach requires that two concrete domains be disjoint with each other if they are to be combined to form a new concrete domain. This does not accord with XML Schema datatypes, where some datatypes can be sub-types of other datatypes.

Mixed Datatype Predicates. The "kmtrsPerMile" example illustrates another limitation of the concrete domain approach: all of the arguments to a predicate must be from the same concrete domain. The example shows that in some cases it may be useful to have predicates taking arguments of different datatypes.

3.2 The Type System Approach

To solve the "disjoint domains" problem mentioned in the previous section, Horrocks and Sattler [8] proposed a new approach to combine DLs and *type systems* (e.g. XML Schema type system). A type system typically defines a set of "base datatypes", such as *integer* or *string*, and provides a mechanism for deriving new datatypes from existing ones. In this approach, multiple datatypes may be defined over a *universal concrete domain.*

Definition 2 *(***Universal Concrete Domain.***)* The universal concrete domain $\mathbf{D}$ consists of a pair ($\Delta_{\mathbf{D}}$,Φ^1), where $\Delta_{\mathbf{D}}$ is the domain of all datatypes and Φ^1 is a set of datatype (unary datatype predicate) names. Each datatype name d is associated with a unary datatype predicate $d^{\mathbf{D}} \subseteq \Delta_{\mathbf{D}}$. Let $\mathbf{V}$ be a set of variables, a datatype conjunction of the form

$$c_1 = \bigwedge_{j=1}^{k} d_j(v^{(j)}), \tag{2}$$

where d_j is a (possibly negated) datatype from Φ^1 and the $v^{(j)}$ are variables from $\mathbf{V}$, is called *satisfiable* iff there exists a function δ mapping the variables in c_1 to data values in $\Delta_{\mathbf{D}}$ s.t. $\delta(v^{(j)}) \in d^{\mathbf{D}}$ for $1 \leq j \leq k$. Such a function δ is called a *solution* for c_1. By $\overline{d}$, we denote the name for the negation of the datatype d, and $\overline{d}^{\mathbf{D}} = \Delta_{\mathbf{D}} \setminus d^{\mathbf{D}}$.

A set of datatypes Φ^1 is called *conforming* iff $\Delta_{\mathbf{D}}$ is disjoint with the abstract domain $\Delta^{\mathcal{I}}$ and the satisfiability problem for finite conjunctions of datatypes over Φ^1 is decidable. ◇

In this approach, the universal concrete domain $\mathbf{D}$ is treated as the only concrete domain,[12] with datatypes being unary predicates over $\mathbf{D}$. Datatypes are considered to be sufficiently structured by type systems, which may include a derivation mechanism and built-in ordering relation. The satisfiability problem (2) is, therefore, much easier than that of the concrete domain approach (1).

Example 4 Miles and Kilometers. *(cont.)* As shown in Example 1, lengthInMile and lengthInKMtr can be defined as derived XML Schema datatypes of FLOAT. In $\mathbf{D}$, lengthInMile, lengthInKMtr and FLOAT are datatype names of Φ^1. Since there are no n-ary datatype predicate names in Φ^1, it is not possible to represent the binary datatype predicate kilosPerMile using this approach. ◇

The type system approach provides an easy way to combine DLs with XML Schema datatypes. Horrocks and Sattler [8] integrated the universal concrete domain ($\mathbf{D}$) as well as nominals ($\mathcal{O}$) into the $\mathcal{SHQ}$ DL to give the $\mathcal{SHOQ}(\mathbf{D})$ DL. In order to make $\mathcal{SHOQ}(\mathbf{D})$ decidable, feature chains are not allowed. In addition, roles are divided into disjoint sets of abstract roles and concrete roles. The datatype constructs included in $\mathcal{SHOQ}(\mathbf{D})$ are datatype exists $\exists T.d$ and datatype value $\forall T.d$, where T is a concrete role and d is a datatype name in Φ^1. Detailed discussions on the differences in datatype handling between $\mathcal{SHOQ}(\mathbf{D})$ and $\mathcal{ALC}(\mathcal{D})$ can be found in [11].

The main disadvantage of the type system approach is that it doesn't support n-ary datatype predicates. Furthermore, since the interpretation of $\overline{d}$ is defined as $\Delta_{\mathbf{D}} \setminus d^{\mathbf{D}}$, the negated datatypes problem mentioned in Section 3.1 still exists.

Example 5 The $>_5$ and $\leq_5$ Datatype Predicates. *(cont.)* Let us revisit Figure 1 in the type system approach. Now $INT, >_5, \leq_5, STRING$ are datatype names in Φ^1. Although the interpretation of $\overline{INT}$ is fine (the integer 3 is not in $\overline{INT}^{\mathbf{D}}$ and the string "Fred" is), the interpretation of $\overline{>_5}$ is still quite "strange": both the integer 3 and the string "Fred" are in $\overline{>_5}^{\mathbf{D}}$. ◇

This example suggests that we might want to deal with base datatypes and derived datatypes in different manners.

[12] In [8]'s notation, $\mathbf{D}$ refers to Φ^1 the set of datatypes. We call it Φ^1 in order to make it more consistent with $\Phi_{\mathcal{D}}$ in Definition 1.

3.3 The Datatype Group Approach

In this section we describe an extension of the type system approach which we call the datatype group approach. Our motivation is to provide an easy and intuitive way to cope with datatypes structured by type systems, and to support n-ary datatype predicates such that (i) the interpretations of negations of datatype predicates does not change when new datatypes are introduced into a datatype group, and (ii) it is possible to reuse existing concrete domain algorithms for the satisfiability problem of predicate conjunctions (1). A "datatype group" is formally defined as follows.

Definition 3 (Datatype Group.) *A datatype group* $\mathcal{G}$ is a tuple $(\Delta_{\mathbf{D}},\mathbf{D}_{\mathcal{G}},\Phi^1_{\mathcal{G}},\Phi_{\mathcal{G}})$, where $\Delta_{\mathbf{D}}$, which is disjoint with the abstract domain $\Delta^{\mathcal{I}}$, is the datatype domain covering all datatypes, $\mathbf{D}_{\mathcal{G}}$ is a set of base datatype names, $\Phi^1_{\mathcal{G}}$ is a set of derived datatype names and $\Phi_{\mathcal{G}}$ is a set of predicate names. Each base datatype name $d \in \mathbf{D}_{\mathcal{G}}$ is associated with a base datatype $d^{\mathbf{D}} \subseteq \Delta_{\mathbf{D}}$, each derived datatype name $d' \in \Phi^1_{\mathcal{G}}$ is associated with a derived datatype $d'^{\mathbf{D}} \subseteq d^{\mathbf{D}}$, where $d \in \mathbf{D}_{\mathcal{G}}$, and each predicate name $P \in \Phi_{\mathcal{G}}$ is associated with an arity n ($n > 1$) and a n-ary predicate $P^{\mathbf{D}} \subseteq d_1^{\mathbf{D}} \times \ldots \times d_n^{\mathbf{D}} \subseteq \Delta^n_{\mathbf{D}}$, where $d_1 \ldots d_n \in \mathbf{D}_{\mathcal{G}} \cup \Phi^1_{\mathcal{G}}$.

The domain function $\mathsf{dom}(p, i)$ returns the domain of the i-th argument of the (possibly unary) predicate p, where datatypes can be regarded as unary predicates. According to the above definition, $\mathsf{dom}(p, i)$ is defined as

1. for each $d \in \mathbf{D}_{\mathcal{G}}$, $\mathsf{dom}(d, 1) = \Delta_{\mathbf{D}}$;
2. for each $d' \in \Phi^1_{\mathcal{G}}$, $\mathsf{dom}(d', 1) = d^{\mathbf{D}}$;
3. for each $P \in \Phi_{\mathcal{G}}$, $\mathsf{dom}(P, i) = d_i^{\mathbf{D}}$ $(1 < i \leq n)$ if the arity of P is n.

Let $\mathbf{V}$ be a set of variables. We will consider predicate conjunctions over $\mathcal{G}$ of the form

$$\mathrm{C} = \bigwedge_{j=1}^{k} p_j(v_1^{(j)}, \ldots, v_{n_j}^{(j)}), \tag{3}$$

where p_j is an n_j-ary predicate in $\mathbf{D}_{\mathcal{G}} \cup \Phi^1_{\mathcal{G}} \cup \Phi_{\mathcal{G}}$, and the $v_i^{(j)}$ are variables from $\mathbf{V}$. A predicate conjunction C is called *satisfiable* iff there exists a function δ mapping the variables in C to data values in $\Delta_{\mathbf{D}}$ s.t. $\langle \delta(v_1^{(j)}), \ldots, \delta(v_{n_j}^{(j)}) \rangle \in p_j^{\mathbf{D}}$ for $1 \leq j \leq k$. Such a function δ is called a *solution* for C. A datatype group $\mathcal{G}$ is *conforming* iff

1. $\mathbf{D}_{\mathcal{G}}$, $\Phi^1_{\mathcal{G}}$ and $\Phi_{\mathcal{G}}$ are closed under negation,
2. a binary inequality predicate $\neq_i \in \Phi_{\mathcal{G}}$ is defined for each datatype $d_i \in \mathbf{D}_{\mathcal{G}}$, and
3. the satisfiability problem for finite predicate conjunctions over $\mathcal{G}$ is decidable.

By $\overline{p}$, we denote the negation of the (possibly unary) predicate p, if the arity of p is n ($n \geq 1$), then $\mathsf{dom}(\overline{p}, 1) = \mathsf{dom}(p, 1), \ldots, \mathsf{dom}(\overline{p}, n) = \mathsf{dom}(p, n)$ and $\overline{p}^{\mathbf{D}} = \mathsf{dom}(p, 1) \times \ldots \times \mathsf{dom}(p, n) \setminus p^{\mathbf{D}}$.

For convenience, we use $\top_{\mathbf{D}}$ as the name of $\Delta_{\mathbf{D}}$ and $\bot_{\mathbf{D}}$ as the name of the negation of $\top_{\mathbf{D}}$. ◇

A datatype group $\mathcal{G}$ is a natural n-ary predicate extension (introducing $\Phi_{\mathcal{G}}$) of the universal concrete domain $\mathbf{D}$, where the set Φ^1 of datatype names is divided into the set $\mathbf{D}_{\mathcal{G}}$ of base datatype names and the set $\Phi^1_{\mathcal{G}}$ of derived datatype names. The division is motivated by having different interpretation settings for their negations. The domain function $\mathsf{dom}(p,i)$ is defined for this purpose, so that the interpretation of the negation of datatypes and datatype predicates can be more intuitive, and do not change when new datatypes are introduced. Here is an example.

Example 6 The $>_5$ and $\leq_5$ Datatype Predicates. *(cont.)* A datatype group $\mathcal{G}$ can be defined as

$$\begin{aligned}(&\Delta_{\mathbf{D}},\\ &\mathbf{D}_{\mathcal{G}} := \{INT, \overline{INT}, STRING, \overline{STRING}\},\\ &\Phi^1_{\mathcal{G}} := \{>_5, \leq_5\},\\ &\Phi_{\mathcal{G}} := \{\neq_{INT}, =_{INT}, \neq_{STRING}, =_{STRING}\}),\end{aligned}$$

where $\overline{INT}^{\mathbf{D}} = \mathsf{dom}(INT,1) \setminus INT^{\mathbf{D}} = \Delta_{\mathbf{D}} \setminus INT^{\mathbf{D}}$, and $\overline{>_5}^{\mathbf{D}} = \mathsf{dom}(>_5,1) \setminus >_5^{\mathbf{D}} = INT^{\mathbf{D}} \setminus >_5^{\mathbf{D}} = \leq_5^{\mathbf{D}}$. Therefore the integer 3 is in $\overline{>_5}^{\mathbf{D}}$ but not in $\overline{INT}^{\mathbf{D}}$, while the string "Fred" is in $\overline{INT}^{\mathbf{D}}$ but not in $\overline{>_5}^{\mathbf{D}}$. ◇

Since the datatype group approach supports n-ary datatype predicates, we can now present the binary predicate kilosPerMile in the miles and kilometers example.

Example 7 Miles and Kilometers. *(cont.)* A datatype group $\mathcal{G}_2$ can be defined as

$$\begin{aligned}(&\Delta_{\mathbf{D}},\\ &\mathbf{D}_{\mathcal{G}_2} := \{FLOAT, \overline{FLOAT}\},\\ &\Phi^1_{\mathcal{G}_2} := \{lengthInMile, \overline{lengthInMile}, lengthInKMtr, \overline{lengthInKMtr}\},\\ &\Phi_{\mathcal{G}_2} := \{kmtrsPerMile, \overline{kmtrsPerMile}, \neq_{FLOAT}, =_{FLOAT}\}),\end{aligned}$$

where $\overline{kmtrsPerMile}^{\mathbf{D}} = \mathsf{dom}(kmtrsPerMile,1) \times \mathsf{dom}(kmtrsPerMile,2) \setminus kmtrsPerMile^{\mathbf{D}} = lengthInKmtr^{\mathbf{D}} \times lengthInMile^{\mathbf{D}} \setminus kmtrsPerMile^{\mathbf{D}}$. ◇

There is a close relationship between a conforming datatype group with only one base datatype and an admissible concrete domain.

Lemma 4 An admissible concrete domain $(\Delta_{\mathcal{D}}, \Phi_{\mathcal{D}})$ is a conforming datatype group $\mathcal{G} = (\Delta_{\mathbf{D}},\ \mathbf{D}_{\mathcal{G}} := \{\mathcal{D}\},\ \Phi^1_{\mathcal{G}}, \Phi_{\mathcal{G}})$, where $\Phi^1_{\mathcal{G}}$ is the set of unary predicate names in $\Phi_{\mathcal{D}}$ and $\Phi_{\mathcal{G}}$ is set of n-ary ($n > 1$) predicate names in $\Phi_{\mathcal{D}}$, if there exists a binary inequality predicate $\neq_{\mathcal{D}} \in \Phi_{\mathcal{D}}$.

Proof. Immediate consequence of Definition 1 and 3. □

Now we show how two conforming datatype groups $\mathcal{G}_1$ and $\mathcal{G}_2$ can be combined to form a new datatype groups $\mathcal{G}_1 \oplus \mathcal{G}_2$. It turns out (Lemma 6 and 7) that the combination is also conforming in many cases.

Definition 5 Assume that $\mathcal{G}_1$ and $\mathcal{G}_2$ are conforming datatype groups. Then $\mathcal{G}_1 \oplus \mathcal{G}_2$ can be constructed as $(\Delta_{\mathbf{D}}, \mathbf{D}_{\mathcal{G}_1 \oplus \mathcal{G}_2} := \mathbf{D}_{\mathcal{G}_1} \cup \mathbf{D}_{\mathcal{G}_2}, \Phi^1_{\mathcal{G}_1 \oplus \mathcal{G}_2} := \Phi^1_{\mathcal{G}_1} \cup \Phi^1_{\mathcal{G}_2}, \Phi_{\mathcal{G}_1 \oplus \mathcal{G}_2} := \Phi_{\mathcal{G}_1} \cup \Phi_{\mathcal{G}_2})$. ◇

Note that for a predicate p in either $\mathcal{G}_1$ or $\mathcal{G}_2$ $\overline{p}^{\mathbf{D}}$ doesn't changed after the combination.

Lemma 6 If $\mathcal{G}_1$ and $\mathcal{G}_2$ are conforming datatype groups where $\mathbf{D}_{\mathcal{G}_1} \cap \mathbf{D}_{\mathcal{G}_2} = \emptyset$, then $\mathcal{G}_1 \oplus \mathcal{G}_2$ is also a conforming datatype group.

Proof. Obviously $\mathcal{G}_1 \oplus \mathcal{G}_2$ satisfies the first two conditions of a conforming datatype group. Now we only focus on the third condition. Assume that a predicate conjunction

$$\mathrm{C} = \bigwedge_{j=1}^{k} P_j(v_1^{(j)}, \ldots, v_{n_j}^{(j)})$$

is given, where P_j are predicates of $\mathcal{G}_1 \oplus \mathcal{G}_2$.

1. If a variable v occurs as an argument of (possibly unary) predicates from both datatype groups, then C is not satisfiable, because $\mathbf{D}_{\mathcal{G}_1}$ and $\mathbf{D}_{\mathcal{G}_2}$ are disjoint.
2. Otherwise, C can be split into two predicate conjunctions C_1 and C_2 such that they are predicate conjunctions in $\mathcal{G}_1$ and $\mathcal{G}_2$ respectively and no variable occurs in both conjunctions. Therefore, we observe that C is satisfiable iff the satisfiability tests of the respective datatype groups succeed for C_1 and C_2. □

Note that we don't need to cope with disjunctions in the combination, while in the corresponding Lemma for $\mathcal{D}_1 \oplus \mathcal{D}_2$ (Lemma 2.4 in [2]) in the concrete domain approach, disjunctions must be handled because of type errors.

If the set of datatypes and predicates in a conforming datatype group $\mathcal{G}_1$ is a sub-set of the set of datatypes and predicates in another conforming datatype group $\mathcal{G}_2$, then trivially $\mathcal{G}_1 \oplus \mathcal{G}_2$ is also conforming.

Lemma 7 If $\mathcal{G}_1$ and $\mathcal{G}_2$ are conforming datatype group where $\mathbf{D}_{\mathcal{G}_1} \cup \Phi^1_{\mathcal{G}_1} \cup \Phi_{\mathcal{G}_1} \subseteq \mathbf{D}_{\mathcal{G}_2} \cup \Phi^1_{\mathcal{G}_2} \cup \Phi_{\mathcal{G}_2}$, then $\mathcal{G}_1 \oplus \mathcal{G}_2$ is also a conforming datatype group.

Proof. Immediate consequence of Definition 5, obviously $\mathcal{G}_1 \oplus \mathcal{G}_2$ is equivalent to $\mathcal{G}_2$. □

Lemma 6 and 7 give guidelines on how to build complex conforming datatype groups from simple ones. Based on the definition of a datatype group, we can define a type checker which works with a DL reasoner to answer datatype queries.

Definition 8 A *type checker* is a program that takes as input a finite predicate conjunction C over (one of) the conforming datatype group(s) it supports, and answers *satisfiable* if C is satisfiable and *unsatisfiable* otherwise. ◇

It is possible for a DL reasoner to work with many type checkers. Firstly, in the datatype group approach, the interpretation of $\overline{p}$ ($p \in \mathbf{D}_{\mathcal{G}} \cup \Phi^1_{\mathcal{G}} \cup \Phi_{\mathcal{G}}$) doesn't change when new datatypes are introduced, so the interpretation of each $\overline{p}$ supported by a type checker won't be affected by the existence of other type checkers. Secondly, assuming that the set of base datatypes of the conforming datatype group supported by each type checker is disjoint from each other, Lemma 6 shows that the combined datatype group of all these datatype groups supported by the type checkers is also conforming.

4 $\mathcal{SHOQ}(\mathbf{D_n})$

In this section, we give the definition of the $\mathcal{SHOQ}(\mathbf{D_n})$ DL that supports reasoning with datatype groups. Note that in DLs we talk about *concepts* and *roles* where in Web ontology languages we usually talk about *classes* and *properties.*

Definition 9 *($\mathcal{SHOQ}(\mathbf{D_n})$* **Syntax and Semantics.***)* Let $\mathbf{C}$, $\mathbf{R} = \mathbf{R}_A \uplus \mathbf{R}_\mathbf{D}$, $\mathbf{I}$ be disjoint sets of concept, abstract and concrete role and individual names. For R and S roles, a *role axiom* is either a role inclusion, which is of the form $R \sqsubseteq S$ for $R, S \in \mathbf{R}_A$ or $R, S \in \mathbf{R}_\mathbf{D}$, or a transitivity axiom, which is of the form $\mathsf{Trans}(R)$ for $R \in \mathbf{R}_A$. A *role box* $\mathcal{R}$ is a finite set of role axioms. A role R is called *simple* if, for $\underline{\sqsubseteq}^*$ the transitive reflexive closure of $\sqsubseteq$ on $\mathcal{R}$ and for each role S, $S \,\underline{\sqsubseteq}^*\, R$ implies $\mathsf{Trans}(S) \notin \mathcal{R}$.

The set of concept terms of $\mathcal{SHOQ}(\mathbf{D_n})$ is inductively defined. As a starting point of the induction, any element A of $\mathbf{C}$ is a concept term (atomic terms). Now let C and D be concept terms, o be an individual, R be a abstract role name, $T_1, \ldots, T_n$ be concrete role names, S be a simple role name, P be an n-ary datatype predicate name. Then complex concepts can be built using the operators shown in Figure 2.

The semantics is defined in terms of an interpretation $\mathcal{I} = (\Delta^\mathcal{I}, \cdot^\mathcal{I})$, where $\Delta^\mathcal{I}$ (the abstract domain) is a nonempty set and and $\cdot^\mathcal{I}$ (the interpretation function) maps atomic and complex concepts, roles and nominals according to Figure 2. Note that $\sharp$ denotes set cardinality, $\Delta_\mathbf{D}$ is the datatype domain and $\mathsf{dom}(P, i)$ is the domain function in a datatype group.

An interpretation $\mathcal{I} = (\Delta^\mathcal{I}, \cdot^\mathcal{I})$ satisfies a role inclusion axiom $R_1 \sqsubseteq R_2$ iff $R_1^\mathcal{I} \subseteq R_2^\mathcal{I}$, and it satisfies a transitivity axiom $\mathsf{Trans}(R)$ iff $R^\mathcal{I} = (R^\mathcal{I})^+$. An interpretation satisfies a role box $\mathcal{R}$ iff it satisfies each axiom in $\mathcal{R}$. A $\mathcal{SHOQ}(\mathbf{D_n})$-concept C is satisfiable w.r.t. a role box $\mathcal{R}$ iff there is an interpretation $\mathcal{I}$ with $C^\mathcal{I} \neq \emptyset$ that satisfies $\mathcal{R}$. Such an interpretation is called a *model* of C w.r.t. $\mathcal{R}$. A concept C is *subsumed* by a concept D w.r.t. $\mathcal{R}$ iff $C^\mathcal{I} \sqsubseteq D^\mathcal{I}$ for each interpretation $\mathcal{I}$ satisfying $\mathcal{R}$. Two concepts are said to be equivalent (w.r.t. $\mathcal{R}$) iff they mutually subsume each other (w.r.t. $\mathcal{R}$). ◇

Construct Name	Syntax	Semantics
atomic concept	A	$A^{\mathcal{I}} \subseteq \Delta^{\mathcal{I}}$
abstract role	R	$R^{\mathcal{I}} \subseteq \Delta^{\mathcal{I}} \times \Delta^{\mathcal{I}}$
concrete role	T	$T^{\mathcal{I}} \subseteq \Delta^{\mathcal{I}} \times \Delta_{\mathbf{D}}$
nominals	$\{o\}$	$\{o\}^{\mathcal{I}} \subseteq \Delta^{\mathcal{I}}, \sharp\{o\}^{\mathcal{I}} = 1$
conjunction	$C \sqcap D$	$(C \sqcap D)^{\mathcal{I}} = C^{\mathcal{I}} \cap D^{\mathcal{I}}$
disjunction	$C \sqcup D$	$(C \sqcup D)^{\mathcal{I}} = C^{\mathcal{I}} \cup D^{\mathcal{I}}$
negation	$\neg C$	$(\neg C)^{\mathcal{I}} = \Delta^{\mathcal{I}} \setminus C^{\mathcal{I}}$
exists restriction	$\exists R.C$	$(\exists R.C)^{\mathcal{I}} = \{x \in \Delta^{\mathcal{I}} \mid \exists y.\langle x, y\rangle \in R^{\mathcal{I}} \wedge y \in C^{\mathcal{I}}\}$
value restriction	$\forall R.C$	$(\forall R.C)^{\mathcal{I}} = \{x \in \Delta^{\mathcal{I}} \mid \forall y.\langle x, y\rangle \in R^{\mathcal{I}} \rightarrow y \in C^{\mathcal{I}}\}$
atleast restriction	$\geqslant nS.C$	$(\geqslant nS.C)^{\mathcal{I}} = \{x \in \Delta^{\mathcal{I}} \mid \sharp\{y.\langle x, y\rangle \in S^{\mathcal{I}} \wedge y \in C^{\mathcal{I}}\} \geq n\}$
atmost restriction	$\leqslant nS.C$	$(\leqslant nS.C)^{\mathcal{I}} = \{x \in \Delta^{\mathcal{I}} \mid \sharp\{y.\langle x, y\rangle \in S^{\mathcal{I}} \wedge y \in C^{\mathcal{I}}\} \leq n\}$
datatype exists	$\exists T_1, \cdots, T_n.P_n$	$(\exists T_1, \cdots, T_n.P_n)^{\mathcal{I}} = \{x \in \Delta^{\mathcal{I}} \mid \exists y_1 \cdots y_n.y_i \in \mathsf{dom}(P_n, i)$ $\wedge \langle x, y_i\rangle \in T_i^{\mathcal{I}}$ (for $1 \leq i \leq n$) $\wedge \langle y_1, \cdots y_n\rangle \in P_n^{\mathbf{D}}\}$
datatype value	$\forall T_1, \cdots, T_n.P_n$	$(\forall T_1, \cdots, T_n.P_n)^{\mathcal{I}} = \{x \in \Delta^{\mathcal{I}} \mid \forall y_1 \cdots y_n.y_i \in \mathsf{dom}(P_n, i)$ $\wedge \langle x, y_i\rangle \in T_i^{\mathcal{I}}$ (for $1 \leq i \leq n$) $\rightarrow \langle y_1, \cdots y_n\rangle \in P_n^{\mathbf{D}}\}$
datatype atleast	$\geqslant mT_1, \ldots, T_n.P_n$	$(\geqslant mT_1, \ldots, T_n.P_n)^{\mathcal{I}} = \{x \in \Delta^{\mathcal{I}} \mid \sharp\{\langle y_1 \cdots y_n\rangle \mid y_i \in \mathsf{dom}(P_n, i)$ $\wedge \langle x, y_i\rangle \in T_i^{\mathcal{I}}$ (for $1 \leq i \leq n$) $\wedge \langle y_1, \cdots y_n\rangle \in P_n^{\mathbf{D}}\} \geq m\}$
datatype atmost	$\leqslant mT_1, \ldots, T_n.P_n$	$(\leqslant mT_1, \ldots, T_n.P_n)^{\mathcal{I}} = \{x \in \Delta^{\mathcal{I}} \mid \sharp\{\langle y_1 \cdots y_n\rangle \mid y_i \in \mathsf{dom}(P_n, i)$ $\wedge \langle x, y_i\rangle \in T_i^{\mathcal{I}}$ (for $1 \leq i \leq n$) $\wedge \langle y_1, \cdots y_n\rangle \in P_n^{\mathbf{D}}\} \leq m\}$

Fig. 2. Syntax and Semantics of $\mathcal{SHOQ}(\mathbf{D_n})$

Note that the use of domain function $\mathsf{dom}(P, i)$ in the semantics of datatype constructs in $\mathcal{SHOQ}(\mathbf{D_n})$ is to ensure that every $\mathcal{SHOQ}(\mathbf{D_n})$-concept can be converted into an equivalent one in negation normal form (NNF), i.e., with negations only applying to concept names. This is important for tableau algorithms, which typically operate only on concepts in NNF.

Example 8 Miles and Kilometers. *(cont.)* The *River* concept can be defined as a sub-concept of the $\mathcal{SHOQ}(\mathbf{D_n})$-concept $\forall$ *length-kmtr,length-mile*.`kmtrsPerMile`, that is, *River* $\sqsubseteq$ $\forall$*length-kmtr,length-mile*.`kmtrsPerMile`. ◇

5 A Tableaux Algorithm for $\mathcal{SHOQ}(\mathrm{D_n})$

A key feature of DLs is the provision of reasoning services. These services can be used to support the design and deployment of ontologies using DL based ontology languages such as DAML+OIL and OWL. In common with other expressive DLs, we can use a tableau algorithm that checks concept satisfiability w.r.t. a role box in order to provide reasoning services for $\mathcal{SHOQ}(\mathbf{D_n})$: a range of reasoning problems, including subsumption and satisfiability w.r.t. a terminology (ontology) can be reduced to concept satisfiability [8]. As space is limited, and as the algorithm is similar to those presented in [8,12], we will not describe it in detail here. Instead, we will sketch some of its more interesting features, and in particular those related to reasoning with datatype groups. The interested reader is referred to the online technical report[13] [13] for full details and proofs of the algorithm's soundness and completeness.

As with any tableau algorithm, the basic idea is to try to prove the satisfiability of a concept C (w.r.t. a role box $\mathcal{R}$) by building a model of C, i.e., (a structure that closely corresponds to) an interpretation $\mathcal{I}$ that satisfies $\mathcal{R}$ and in which $C^{\mathcal{I}}$ is not empty. The algorithm works on a (set of) tree(s), where nodes are labeled with sets of sub-concepts of C, and edges are labeled with sets of roles occurring in C. Nodes (edges) in the tree correspond to elements (tuples) in the interpretation of the concepts (roles) with which they are labeled. Normally, a single tree is initialised with a root node labeled $\{C\}$.

The algorithm exhaustively applies tableau rules that decompose the syntactic structure of the concepts in node labels, either expanding node labels, adding new edges and nodes to the tree(s), or merging edges and nodes. The application of a rule effectively explicates constraints on the interpretation implied by the concepts to which the rule was applied. E.g., if $A \sqcap B$ is in the label of a node x then the $\sqcap$-*rule* adds both A and B to the label, explicating the fact that if $x \in (A \sqcap B)^{\mathcal{I}}$, then both $x \in A^{\mathcal{I}}$ and $x \in B^{\mathcal{I}}$. Similarly, if $\exists R.A$ is in the label of a node x, then the $\exists$-*rule* adds a new node y labelled $\{A\}$ with an edge between x and y labeled $\{R\}$, explicating the fact that if $x \in (\exists R.A)^{\mathcal{I}}$, then there must exist a node y such that $\langle x, y\rangle \in R^{\mathcal{I}}$ and $y \in A^{\mathcal{I}}$.

An attempt to build a model fails if an obvious contradiction, often called a *clash*, is generated, e.g., if the label of some node contains both D and $\neg D$ for some concept D; it is successful if no more rules can be applied, and there are no clashes. It is relatively straightforward to prove that a concept is satisfiable if and only if the rules can be applied in such a way that a model is successfully constructed. The computational complexity of the algorithm stems from the fact that some rules are non-deterministic (e.g., the rule dealing with disjunctions); in practice this is dealt with by backtracking when a clash is detected, and trying a different non-deterministic rule application.

Various refinements of this basic technique are required in order to deal with a logic as expressive as $\mathcal{SHOQ}(\mathbf{D_n})$. In the first place, the algorithm operates on a forest of trees, as an additional tree must be constructed for each nominal in C (see Figure 2); a form of cycle check called *blocking* must also be used in order to guarantee termination [6]. In the second place, the algorithm needs to use a type checker to check constraints on the interpretation derived from datatype exists, value, atleast and atmost concepts.

5.1 Datatype Reasoning

Logics like $\mathcal{SHOQ}(\mathbf{D})$ and $\mathcal{SHOQ}(\mathbf{D_n})$ are designed so that reasoning about datatypes and values can be separated from reasoning about concepts and roles – this is the reason for the strict separation of the domains and of abstract and concrete roles. The result of the separation is that node labels can contain either concepts or datatypes and values, but never a mixture. This allows node labels

[13] `http://DL-Web.man.ac.uk/Doc/shoqdn-proofs.pdf`

containing datatypes and values to be checked using a separate type checker, with inconsistencies in such labels being treated as an additional clash condition. E.g., if a node label includes the concepts $\exists T.\texttt{string}$ and $\forall T.\texttt{real}$, then a new concrete node will be generated labeled string, real, and when checked with the type checker this would (presumably) return a clash on the grounds that there is no element that is in the interpretation of both `string` and `real`.

With $\mathcal{SHOQ}(\mathbf{D_n})$ the situation is more complex because it is necessary to deal with both n-ary predicates and datatype cardinality constraints that may be qualified with n-ary predicates. The algorithm deals with n-ary predicates by keeping track of tuples of concrete nodes that must satisfy datatype predicates, and it deals with datatype cardinality constraints by keeping track of inequalities between tuples of concrete nodes that were generated by the datatype $\geqslant_P -rule$ in order to explicate datatype atleast concepts (merging such tuples could lead to non-termination as the $\geqslant_P -rule$ might be applied again and cause new tuples to be generated).

The predicate relationships between (the values represented by) concrete nodes are taken into consideration by the type checker, which can check predicate conjunctions (see Definition 8). In the algorithm described in [12], the type checker must also ensure that the solution is consistent with inequalities between tuples of concrete nodes. This means that it must be extended to deal with non-deterministic reasoning, because $\langle t_{j1}, \ldots, t_{jn} \rangle \dot{\neq} \langle t_{k1}, \ldots, t_{kn} \rangle$ is equivalent to

$$(t_{j1} \dot{\neq} t_{k1}) \cup \ldots \cup (t_{jn} \dot{\neq} t_{kn}) \tag{4}$$

In the new algorithm, this non-deterministic reasoning is pushed back into the tableau reasoner, which is already able to cope with non-determinism arising, e.g., from disjunction concepts. This is done by adding concepts "equivalent" to (4) to the node labels containing the relevant datatype atleast concept. For this purpose, we use concepts of the form

$$(\forall T_1^{C_{j1}}, T_1^{C_{k1}}. \neq_{d_{P_n,i}}) \sqcup \ldots \sqcup (\forall T_n^{C_{jn}}, T_n^{C_{kn}}. \neq_{d_{P_n,i}}), \tag{5}$$

where $C = \; \geqslant mT_1, \ldots, T_n.P_n$, is the datatype atleast concept in question, $T_1^{C_{j1}}, T_1^{C_{k1}}, \ldots, T_n^{C_{jn}}, T_n^{C_{kn}}$ are *superscripted concrete roles* and $\neq_{d_{P_n,i}}$ is the inequality predicate for the datatype $\mathsf{dom}(P_n, i)$ (recall that each datatype in a datatype group must be equipped with an inequality predicate). The superscripted concrete roles are generated by the $\geqslant_P -rule$ and used to link the node x containing C to the new concrete nodes that the rule generates. The form of the superscript means that a superscripted role acts as a unique (w.r.t. the node x) name for a given concrete node. The result is that if ever two tuples created by applying the $\geqslant_P -rule$ to C are merged, then the type checker will return a clash. This is because, whichever way the $\sqcup - rule$ is applied to the disjunction (5), the predicate relationships will include $x \neq x$ for some concrete node x.

6 Discussion

As we have seen, using datatypes within Semantic Web ontology languages (such as DAML+OIL and OWL) presents new requirements for DL reasoning services. We have presented the datatype group approach, which extends the type system approach with n-ary predicates and a new treatment of predicate negation, so as to make it possible to use type checkers with DL reasoners. We have also sketched an improved algorithm for reasoning with $\mathcal{SHOQ}(\mathbf{D_n})$ using datatype groups. Type checkers for datatype groups should be easy to implement as we do not have to deal with disjunctions of predicate terms. Moreover, the similarity of conforming datatype groups and admissible concrete domains can be exploited in order to identify suitable datatype groups.

The resulting framework is both robust and extensible. On the one hand, most complex reasoning tasks take place within the well understood and provably correct tableau algorithm. On the other hand, it is relatively easy to add support for new datatypes and predicates, and this does not require any changes to the tableaux algorithm itself. An implementation of the algorithm along with a simple type checker (supporting integers and strings) is currently underway (based on the FaCT system), and will be used to evaluate empirical performance.

Although existing Web ontology languages such as DAML+OIL and OWL do not support n-ary predicates, we believe that they are useful/essential in many realistic applications, and will be a prime candidate for inclusion in future extensions of these languages. The algorithm we have presented could be used to provide reasoning support for such extended Web ontology languages.

Acknowledgements. We would like to thank Ulrike Sattler, since the work presented here extends the original work on $\mathcal{SHOQ}(\mathbf{D})$. Thanks are also due to Carsten Lutz for his helpful discussion on inequality predicates.

References

[1] F. Baader, D. L. McGuiness, D. Nardi, and P. Patel-Schneider, editors. *Description Logic Handbook: Theory, implementation and applications.* Cambridge University Press, 2002.

[2] Franz Baader and Philipp Hanschke. A Schema for Integrating Concrete Domains into Concept Languages. In *Proc. of the 12th Int. Joint Conf. on Artificial Intelligence (IJCAI'91)*, pages 452–457, 1991.

[3] Paul V. Biron and Ashok Malhotra. Extensible Markup Language (XML) Schema Part 2: Datatypes – W3C Recommendation 02 May 2001. Technical report, World Wide Web Consortium, 2001. Available at `http://www.w3.org/TR/xmlschema-2/`.

[4] Dan Brickley and R.V. Guha. Resource Description Framework (RDF) Schema Specification 1.0. W3C Recommentdation, URL `http://www.w3.org/TR/rdf-schema`, Mar. 2000.

[5] Dieter Fensel, Frank van Harmelen, Ian Horrocks, Deborah L. McGuinness, and Peter F. Patel-Schneider. OIL: An ontology infrastructure for the semantic web. *IEEE Intelligent Systems*, 16(2):38–45, 2001.

[6] I. Horrocks, U. Sattler, and S. Tobies. Practical Reasoning for Expressive Description Logics. In H. Ganzinger, D. McAllester, and A. Voronkov, editors, *Proc. of the 6th Int. Conf. on Logic for Programming and Automated Reasoning (LPAR'99)*, pages 161–180, 1999.
[7] Ian Horrocks and Peter F. Patel-Schneider. The generation of DAML+OIL. In *Proc. of the 2001 Description Logic Workshop (DL 2001)*, pages 30–35. CEUR Electronic Workshop Proceedings, `http://ceur-ws.org/Vol-49/`, 2001.
[8] Ian Horrocks and Ulrike Sattler. Ontology reasoning in the $\mathcal{SHOQ}$(D) description logic. In *Proc. of the 17th Int. Joint Conf. on Artificial Intelligence (IJCAI 2001)*, pages 199–204, 2001.
[9] C. Lutz. Description logics with concrete domains – a survey. In *Advances in Modal Logics Volume 4*. World Scientific Publishing Co. Pte. Ltd., 2002.
[10] Carsten Lutz. *The Complexity of Reasoning with Concrete Domains*. PhD thesis, Teaching and Research Area for Theoretical Computer Science, RWTH Aachen, 2001.
[11] Jeff Z. Pan. Web Ontology Reasoning in the $\mathcal{SHOQ}(\mathbf{D_n})$ Description Logic. In *Carlos Areces and Maartin de Rijke, editors,Proceedings of the Methods for Modalities 2 (M4M-2)*, Nov 2001. ILLC, University of Amsterdam.
[12] Jeff Z. Pan and Ian Horrocks. Reasoning in the SHOQ(Dn) Description Logic. In Ian Horrocks and Sergio Tessaris, editors, *Proc. of the 2002 Int. Workshop on Description Logics (DL-2002)*, Apr. 2002.
[13] Jeff Z. Pan and Ian Horrocks. Reasoning in the $\mathcal{SHOQ}(\mathbf{D_n})$ Description Logic (Online Proofs), 2003.

Merging Topics in Well-Formed XML Topic Maps

Richard Widhalm and Thomas A. Mueck

University Of Vienna
Institute for Computer Science and Business Informatics
Rathausstr. 19
1010 Vienna, Austria
rwidhalm@gmx.at
mueck@ifs.univie.ac.at

Abstract. Topic Maps are a standardized modelling approach for the semantic annotation and description of WWW resources. They enable an improved search and navigational access on information objects stored in semi-structured information spaces like the WWW. However, the according standards ISO 13250 and XTM (XML Topic Maps) lack formal semantics, several questions concerning e.g. subclassing, inheritance or merging of topics are left open. The proposed TMUML meta model, directly derived from the well known UML meta model, is a meta model for Topic Maps which enables semantic constraints to be formulated in OCL (object constraint language) in order to answer such open questions and overcome possible inconsistencies in Topic Map repositories. We will examine the XTM merging conditions and show, in several examples, how the TMUML meta model enables semantic constraints for Topic Map merging to be formulated in OCL. Finally, we will show how the TM validation process, i.e., checking if a Topic Map is well formed, includes our merging conditions.

1 Introduction

The Topic Maps standard ISO 13250 [7] as well as XTM (XML Topic Maps) [12] provide for the semantic characterization of information objects across the WWW or company-controlled intranet or extranet platforms. They externally describe the underlying information objects (documents, web pages, etc.) without changing them. With Topic Maps, which are syntactically based on XML (or SGML for ISO13250), semantic networks consisting of topics and their relationships can be built, thus enhancing the flexibility of search queries and navigational access on the underlying information objects. They can be used as a flexible, generic index for knowledge bases. In a topic map, every real world subject (equal if a WWW resource or an abstract thing) is represented by a *topic*. Each topic may be an instance of several *topic types* (which are also topics), may have several lexical *names* in different *scopes* (where a scope is the area where the according name for the topic is said to be valid and each scope

D. Fensel et al. (Eds.): ISWC 2003, LNCS 2870, pp. 64–79, 2003.

is described by a set of topics) and may show several *occurrences* in different WWW resources. An occurrence is a link, typed by a topic, to an information object. Topics can be interrelated via n-ary *associations*, where each topic plays a certain *role* which is again expressed by another topic. Associations can be typed via a topic. Further, it is possible to create generalization hierarchies for topic types, association types and occurrence types. Occurrences, names and associations can be placed within a scope. Each topic T has an *identificator*, which can be a WWW resource or another topic, indicating or itself being the subject for which T stands. Furthermore, Topic Maps define two topics T_1 and T_2 as identical, if they are identified by the same resource or if they both exhibit the same name N in the same scope S. In that case, they shall be merged to a single topic bearing all the characteristics of the original topics. In this paper, we will focus on the issue of merging topics. We will show how the TMUML meta model lets one formulate the actual XTM merging conditions with the OCL (*object constraint language*), defined within the UML specification [9]. We will also show specific circumstances under which merging would not be desirable, although the XTM criteria would be met. Therefore, we will inspect the consequences of the merging of two topics of a different kind (like an association type merged with an occurrence type). Consequently, we present suggestions for additional OCL constraints showing how the TMUML meta model can help to overcome such issues. Of course, the presented constraints are only considered as suggestions that may further be extended or only partially applied according to specific needs. The following section briefly introduces the TMUML meta model, succeeded by an overview about related work. Afterwards, we will describe the synonymy relation used for merging in the TMUML meta model. Chapter 5 expresses the XTM merging rules in OCL and adds a further, implicated merging rule. Afterwards, we will inspect situations of merging different kinds of topics (like association types, occurrence types, topic types or topic instances) and show the processing steps within our XTM validation and the functionality of the OCL checker. The conclusion will point out the meaningfulness of merging in largely designed Topic Maps systems and give a prospect on our further work.

2 Topic Maps and the TMUML Meta Model

In [19] and [20], the TMUML meta model has been presented, including a detailed description as well as the according class diagrams. It is a meta model for Topic Maps, directly derived from the UML meta model. It does not make use of all of the UML meta model components, only those which are also relevant for Topic Maps (like `Association` or `GeneralizableElement`). Note that topics are divided into the meta classes `TopicType` (for topics used as types for other topics), `TopicObject` (topics not functioning as types but as instances of types), `AssociationTopicType` (similar to the UML `AssociationClass`, representing types for association instances) and `OccurrenceType` (types for occurrences). The `TopicAssociationEnd` defines, like the `AssociationEnd` in UML, the allowed `TopicType` for a role within the according `TopicAssociation`, and also

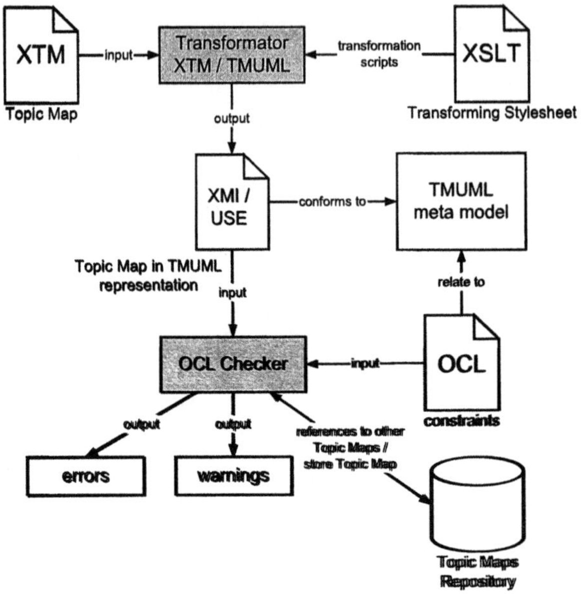

Fig. 1. Topic Maps validation process

its multiplicity. Base names and its subvariants are all represented by `TopicName` (which may be part of a name hierarchy). See [19] and [20] for a detailed description of the TMUML meta model. The TMUML meta model enables our process for validating the well-formedness of a topic map. Fig. 1 schematically shows our approach in the context of validating an XTM topic map before storing it within a repository.

First, the XTM topic map is transformed into an UML representation. For the transformation, XSLT would be an appropriate method, while for the representation, the XMI metadata interchange format [10] or the USE syntax (see [5]) could be used. While the first alternative provides more openness, the second will fit perfectly if using the USE tool for validating OCL constraints. The OCL checker is the component which is responsible for validating the UML representation of the topic map against the OCL constraints that make up well-formedness. For our testing purposes, we used the USE tool, but any other tool capable of OCL validation may be used instead. The OCL checker is then responsible for generating appropriate error and warning messages. After proving a topic map to be valid, it can be inserted into a repository. Also, reading repository data may be important for the OCL checker, in case topics could be merged according to the name based merging principle (see section 5).

The following example shows the definition of a simple OCL constraint, stating that no `Topic` shall be identified by itself.

```
context Topic
 inv C_Topic_identifiedByItself:
  not self.identificator()->exists(e | e = self)
```

It makes use of the operation `identificator()`, which is defined in the context of `Topic` and retrieves all `Identificators` that are related to the context `Topic` via an `Identification` relationship in the TMUML meta model. An `Identificator` may be a subject constituting resource, a subject indicating resource or another topic (see [12]).

```
identificator() : Set(Identificator) =
 self.identifiedBy->collect(i : Identification | i.identificator)->asSet
```

3 Related Work

An early work on constraining Topic Maps is [14], where several suggestions for constraints at the instance layer of a topic map are given (without a formal method). An overview about the idea behind constraints for Topic Maps in general can be found in [6]. In [11], Ontopia describes their own solution for a Topic Maps constraint language, called OSL (*Ontopia Schema Language*). It allows for a more constrained and precisely defined Topic Maps schema definition, but again is not usable for constraining the Topic Maps meta model. With OSL, the types and roles allowed within certain association types may be specified, but, for example, the effects of subclassing association types in general are not treated (the semantics of inheritance). Our method is best suitable for solving the second kind of problem, while it may also be used for the first kind. A similar approach is sketched by the TMCL [13], the *Topic Maps Constraint Language*, although it has not yet surpassed the level of a requirements suggestion. [2] presents a formal model for Topic Maps, consisting only of topics and associations, which are contained in a *homogenous* hypergraph. Meta associations like instancing, subclassing or scoping are contained in a *shift* hypergraph, that compounds components of the homogenous hypergraph and thus establishes semantic layers (e.g. separating role types, topic types or association types). Although this approach applies formal semantics to Topic Maps using hypergraphs, it does not mention additional constraints on the Topic Maps meta model or how they can be applied. Our approach goes beyond that and provides means for the automation of semantic constraints using OCL and USE (or comparable OCL tools). Moreover, the hypergraph model does only distinguish between topics and associations, while names, occurrences or resources have to be modelled by topics. Actually, names have different properties compared to topics in the Topic Maps meta model. Names can not be merged or have occurrences or have names etc. Further, there may be difficulties due to the fact that the semantics of the associations in the shift hypergraph (denoted as θ) is only determined by the semantic layers of the connected topics. For example, there may be different meanings of connections from a role type to a topic type, one may mean a "subclass" relation, the other may mean a type constraint for the topic members playing the role type in the according association type.

Additional information on Topic Maps can be found in [8], [18], [1] and [3]. The first gives an introduction to the fundamental concepts of Topic Maps and introduces a system architecture for applications based on a distributed

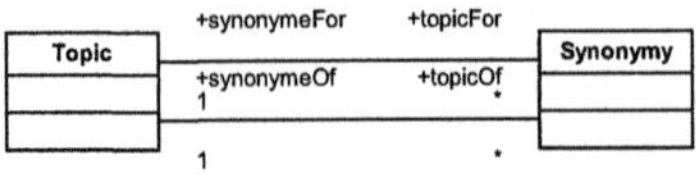

Fig. 2. The Synonymy relation

Topic Maps repository. The second describes a webbased search engine based on a Topic Maps repository, from the conceptual approaches up to a pseudocode, including a prototypic query language. The third publication discusses a range of possible application areas for Topic Maps, while the fourth presents preliminary guidelines to the design of certain topic maps. Detailed information on OCL can be found in the according specification [9] and in [17]. In [4], uncertainties in the semi-formal OCL specification are discussed. In [16], a formal semantics for the OCL is introduced.

4 The Synonymy Relation

XTM defines that two topics T_1 and T_2 shall be merged to one single topic T_3, that inherits all characteristics of T_1 and T_2 (names, occurrences, association memberships, types), if T_1 and T_2 meet some merging criteria and can therefore be deemed to reify (stand for) the same subject. Unfortunately, this would mean that they could not be separated from each other. This should be possible in the context of a Topic Maps repository: in the case one wants to remove the topic map TM_1, which contains T_1, T_2 which belongs to the topic map TM_2 should remain in the repository, in the state it was before the merging with T_1. For this reason, we will keep topics which shall be merged separated in the TMUML meta model, but interrelate them via a `Synonymy` relationship, an equivalence relationship which we have to introduce in our TMUML meta model. Fig. 2 shows the additional class `Synonymy` and its associations.

When removing a previously merged `Topic` T, the topics which have been merged with T can still remain in the repository, only their `Synonymy` link to T will be removed.

In our set of constraints, every time we refer to a Topic T or its characteristics, we also have to refer to the characteristics of all the `Topics` $TSYN_i, i = 1, .., n$, which are directly or transitively connected to T via a `Synonymy` relation. We do this by providing an OCL operation called `closure()` yielding the transitive closure of a `Topic` T, formally
$\{T \cup \{TSYN_i | TSYN_i \text{ is (transitively) synonymous to } T; i = 1, .., n\}\}$.

```
Topic::closure() : Set (Topic) =
 let strt : Set(Topic) = oclEmpty(Set(Topic)) in
  self.synonymesRec (strt)
```

`strt` denotes a local variable of the type `Set(Topic)`, initialized with an empty set of `Topics`. `synonymesRec` is an operation in the context of `Topic` that takes a set S of `Topics` as argument and returns for a `Topic` T a set of `Topics` containing T and the Topics returned by recursively calling synonymesRec (which takes S extended by T) for all Topics directly connected to T via the Synonymy relation.

```
Topic::synonymesRec(s : Set(Topic)) : Set(Topic) =
 Set{self}->union (
  self.topicOf.synonymeFor->select (f |
   s->excludes(f)).synonymesRec (s->including(self))
  )->union (
  self.topicFor.synonymeOf->select (f |
   s->excludes(f)).synonymesRec (s->including(self))
  )->asSet
```

Thus, by calling T.closure(), we receive T and all other Topics that are synonymous to T. Further, to determine whether two Topics are equal, we can not simply compare the two Topics, we have to find out if one is contained within the closure of the other. We therefore provide the operation Topic::equals(), which is defined as follows.

```
Topic::equals(t : Topic) : Boolean =
 self.closure()->exists (c_t | c_t = t)
```

5 Merging Conditions

XTM defines two merging conditions. The *naming constraint-based merge* [12] says that two Topics T_1 and T_2 have to be merged if T_1 has a base name N_1 in the scope S_1, and T_2 has a base name N_2 in scope S_2, and N_1 and N_2 are equal strings and S_1 and S_2 are equal sets of Topics. We define this condition as an OCL operation called Topic::nameBasedMerge(b: Topic), which checks whether the context Topic may be merged with b due to the naming constraint-based merge.

```
Topic::nameBasedMerge(b : Topic) : Boolean =
 (self.closure().nameForTopic->exists (s_n |
  b.closure().nameForTopic->exists (b_n |
   s_n.value = b_n.value and s_n.equalScope (b_n))))
```

Here, ScopableElement::equalScope (s: ScopableElement) is used to compare the scopes of two ScopableElements, which are names in our case (Occurrences and Associations are also ScopableElements. It uses two other operations, which are also defined within the context of ScopableElement.

```
ScopableElement::scope() : Set(ScopingElement) =
 self.scopedBy.scope->asSet
ScopableElement::compareScope (other: ScopableElement) : Boolean =
 self.scope()->forAll (
  self_t | other.scope()->select(
   other_t | other_t.oclAsType(Topic).equals(self_t.oclAsType(Topic))
  )->size = 1)
ScopableElement::equalScope (s : ScopableElement) : Boolean =
 self.compareScope (s) and s.compareScope (self)
```

Note that `Topic.nameForTopic` yields all `TopicNames` for a `Topic`, `Topic-Name.value` is the lexical represenation of a name, and `ScopableElement.scope()` yields the set of `Topics` (which are `ScopingElements`) making up the scope of a `ScopableElement`.

The other XTM merging condition is called *subject-based merge* [12] and says that two `Topics` T_1 and T_2 have to be merged if T_1 has an `Identificator` I_1, and T_2 an `Identificator` I_2, where the URIs of I_1 and I_2 are equal or $T_1 = I_2$ or $T_2 = I_1$. Note that also in this operation we have to excessively use `Topic::closure()`.

```
Topic::subjectBasedMerge(b : Topic) : Boolean =
 (self.closure().identificator()->select (i |
  i.oclIsTypeOf (Topic)).oclAsType(Topic).closure()->includes (b))
 or (self.closure().identificator()->exists (
   s_i | b.closure().identificator()->exists (
    b_i | b_i.URI = s_i.URI ))
  )
 or (self.closure().identificator()->select (i |
   i.oclIsTypeOf (Topic)).oclAsType(Topic).closure()->exists (
    s_i | b.closure().identificator()->select (i |
     i.oclIsTypeOf (Topic)).oclAsType(Topic).closure()->exists (
      b_i | b_i.URI = s_i.URI ))
  )
```

Further, note that the determination of URI equality is not discussed in this paper and therefore, for the time being, simplified by comparing the URI strings. Instead, the information objects that can be reached by the specific URIs should be compared, and also time (timestamps) may play an important role. See also [15] for more details on URIs.

We will call two `Topics` T_1 and T_2, which meet one of the two XTM merging conditions, *candidates for merging*, as they should be merged according to XTM, but this merging and its consequences has to be examined and possibly prohibited due to some resulting complications.

A situation where merging is still not possible, even if one of the aforementioned conditions would be met, is, when the two candidate `Topics` T_1 and T_2 both have a `SubjectConstitutingResource` (which means, the resource is the subject itself) as `Identificator` - call them SCR_1 and SCR_2 - and SCR_1 is different from SCR_2 (they have different URIs). In XTM, only one `SubjectConstitutingResource` is possible for a `Topic`, which is quite intuitive. Fig. 3 shows this issue schematically. There, T_1 is synonymous to T_2 due to having an equal base name in the same scope $\{T_s\}$. Because they both exhibit a `SubjectConstitutingResource` as `Identificator`, differing from each other, the OCL checker has to raise an error.

We have to check this situation in our validation process and therefore suggest an appropriate operation called `Topic::noDifferentSCR (b:Topic)`. It uses an operation called `Topic::ownSCRIdentificators()`, which is defined in the following.

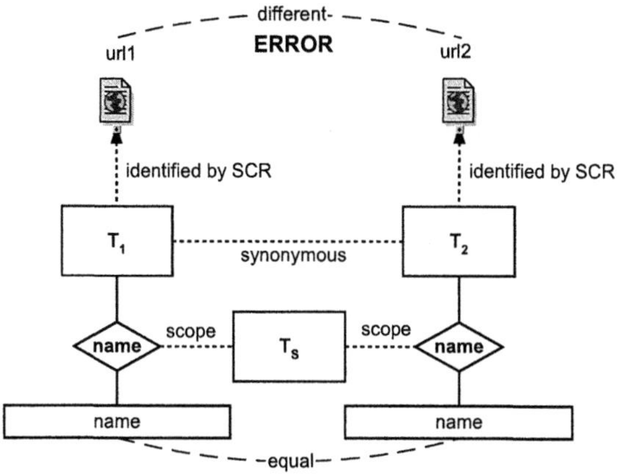

Fig. 3. Different SubjectConstitutingResources as Identificator

```
Topic::noDifferentSCR(b : Topic) : Boolean =
 not self.ownSCRIdentificators()->exists (i_self |
  b.ownSCRIdentificators()->excluding(i_self)->exists (i_b |
   i_self.URI != i_b.URI ))

Topic::ownSCRIdentificators () : Set (SubjectConstitutingResource) =
 self.closure().identificator()->select (i |
  i.oclIsTypeOf(SubjectConstitutingResource)).
   oclAsType(SubjectConstitutingResource)->asSet
```

6 Merging Different Kinds of Topics

What is yet unconsidered in the merging criteria is the fact that the two `Topics` T_1 and T_2, which are candidates for merging due to one of the merging conditions, can be of a different kind. The possible kinds are: `TopicType (TT)`, `TopicObject (TO)`, `AssociationTopicType (AT)` and `OccurrenceType (OT)`. We will use the abbreviations (in brackets) for the four kinds of `Topics`.

In the following, we will examine many of the possible combinations (refer to our further work for a full description of all combinations, including an extensive description of the combination AT - AT) and find out for any combination, if merging shall be prohibited due to the possibility of a semantic inconsistence or not.

6.1 TT - TT, TO - TO, OT - OT

First, we will examine the merging of two `TopicTypes` TT_1 and TT_2. A `TopicType` TT_1 may define a `TopicAssociationEnd` of an AT, where the `multiplicity_min` (the lower bound of the multiplicity) is greater than 0. Look at the example in fig. 4. Some constraint, which will not be shown in this work

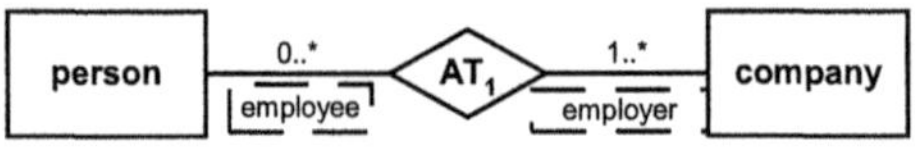

Fig. 4. Example for a Multiplicity Constraint on an AT

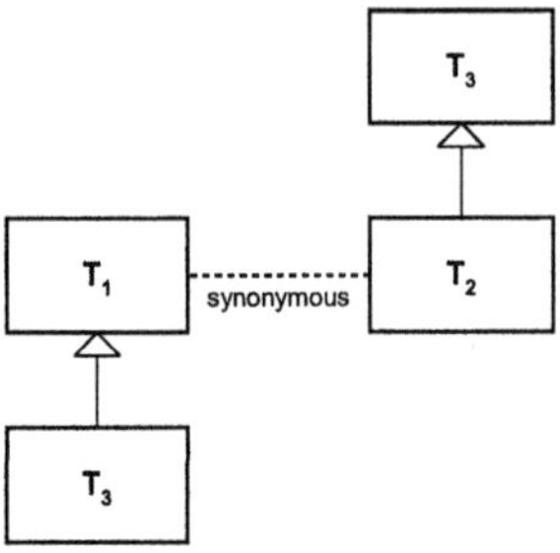

Fig. 5. Circular Inheritance After Merging

due to space reasons, will have to guarantee that every instance of "person" is connected to at least one company via a `TopicAssociation` of type AT_1. Thus, when merging the `TopicType` "person" with some other `TopicType` T_2, all instances of T_2 will also have to have at least one `TopicAssociation` of type AT_1. We will call this the *MultiplicityMinProblem*. This can be realized either by formulating an operation that does this check before merging (called from inside the preconditions of the merge operation), or by an invariant that has to hold any time and yields false after merging.

A further problem may arise when TT_1 and TT_2, which are candidates for merging, define the roles of the two `TopicAssociationEnds` TAE_1 and TAE_2 of the same AT. When desiring unique roles within the same AT, the appropriate OCL invariant will yield false after merging TT_1 and TT_2. We will call this the *UniqueRolesProblem*. Finally, the *CircularInheritanceProblem* may arise after merging, so that TT_1 and TT_2 are then in a circular generalization relationship chain. Fig. 5 shows this schematically.

A circular inheritance prohibiting constraint, like the one adopted by the TMUML meta model from the UML `GeneralizableElement` (constraint 3 for `GeneralizableElement` in [9]), would yield false after merging. Again, these problems can also be checked by OCL operations before performing the merge operation.

By merging two `TopicObjects` TO_1 and TO_2, TO_1 is afterwards instance of its own TTs and the TTs of TO_2. The *MultiplicityMinProblem*, as described in the previous section, may also arise here. `TopicObjects` may also define the role of some property of an AT, so in this case, the *UniqueRolesProblem* also may arise.

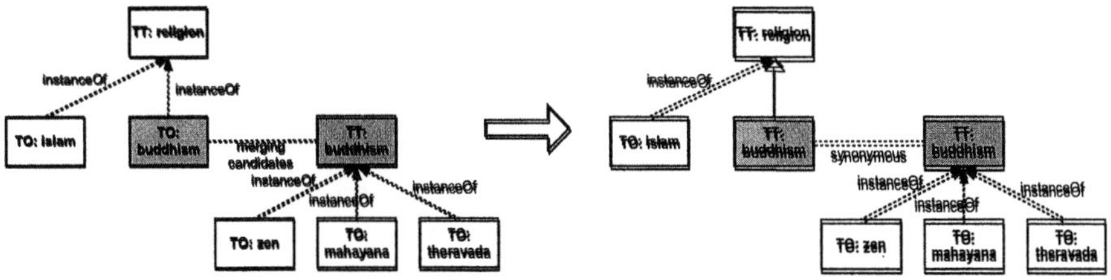

Fig. 6. Merging TT - TO

At the moment, there is no mechanism to constrain an OT to be only applicable to several TTs (like the TopicAssociationEnds do for ATs). Therefore, the merging of two OccurrenceTypes OT_1 and OT_2 should be no problem.

6.2 TT - TO, AT - TO, OT - TO

When merging two Topics of a different kind, the question arises whether the resulting Topics should be of the one kind or of the other. Similarly, when establishing a Synonymy relation in our TMUML meta model for two different kinds of Topics, we have to agree upon one kind for both Topics. In the case of merging TT_1 with TO_2, it is not possible to change TT_1 to TO_1, because TT_1 could have subtypes and may be used in TopicAssociationEnds as type constraints. But changing TO_2 to TT_2 would be an appropriate measurement, requiring every class-instance relation from TO_2 to some TT_{2super} to be transformed by the merging operation to a subtype relation from the resulting TT_2 to the original TT_{2super}. This works, because a TO does not have any further capabilities in the TMUML meta model than a TT has, and a TT may also play a role within an association instance (see also [19]). Fig. 6 shows an example. There, the Topics "TT:buddhism" and "TO:buddhism" are candidates for merging. "TO:buddhism" has to be converted to "TT:buddhism", and the class-instance relation between "TO:buddhism" and "TT:religion" is converted to a subtype relation.

Note that also in the TT-TO case, a *UniqueRolesProblem* may occur after merging. The following OCL operation is called `Topic::changeToTT (t: TopicType)`, where the context Topic is the TO, t is the TT and `TopicObject._class` is a TMUML relation to the TTs of the context TO.

```
Topic::changeToTT(t : TopicType)
 pre changeToTT_pre:
  self.oclIsTypeOf (TopicObject)
  and self.closure()->includes(t)
 post changeToTT_post:
  self.oclIsTypeOf (TopicType) and
  self.oclAsType(TopicType).parent().oclAsType(TopicType)->
asSet->includesAll(
    self@pre.closure()->excluding(t).oclAsType(TopicObject)._class)
```

After calling this operation after the merge operation, which already set the `Synonymy` relation between the TO and TT, no `Topic::closure()` contains both a TT and a TO. Note that this strategy is a suggestion - of course, other strategies can be realized with OCL constraints. The merging of a TT and TO could in general be prohibited, which would be a more performant, but also a more restrictive solution. The two cases of merging an AT with a TO or an OT with a TO can be treated similar to the TT - TO case. As a TO has no instances and no more capabilities in the TMUML meta model than an AT, the TO can be converted to and AT after merging the TO and the AT. Note that an AT can also be a member of a `TopicAssociationEndInstance` (see [19]). The same is true for an OT and a TO. For space reasons, the operations `Topic::changeToAT(t : AssociationTopicType)` and `Topic::changeToOT(t : OccurrenceType)` are not shown here.

6.3 TT - AT, TT - OT

Converting an AT_2 to a TT_2, when merging TT_1 and AT_2, will often be impossible, as AT_2 may have a supertype AT_{2super}, and TT_1 cannot be subtype of an AT (a TT has no `TopicAssociationEnds`). Intuitively, in this situation we will try to specialize TT_1 and convert it to AT_1. As AT_1`.properties()` will (after the conversion from a TT to an AT) obviously be empty, AT_1 simply will have the same properties as AT_2 after the merge (for the definition of `AT.properties`, which yields the `TopicAssociationEnds` of an AT, taking inheritance into account, see [19] or [20]). On the other hand, TT_1 and all its subtypes must not have any instances (TOs), because this would mean these TOs should actually be `TopicAssociations` after the merge, which is not possible. Moreover, all supertypes of TT_1 are neither allowed to have any instances, because after converting TT_1 to AT_1, each direct or transitive supertype TT_x of AT_1 has to be abstract (if not so, TT_x would be a class containing both `TopicObjects` and `TopicAssociations`, which are fundamentally different constructs in Topic Maps). Thus, this kind of merging will rarely be possible, which seems intuitive, as it would mean a mixing of topics and associations, which are fundamentally different meta constructs within Topic Maps. Nevertheless, the following shows the formal representation of our suggested strategy, represented by the OCL operation `Topic::checkATTT(b : Topic)`, which yields true if the context `Topic` is a `TopicType` and all its supertypes and subtypes, which are also `TopicTypes`, have no instances. This operation is used inside the merge operation to determine the possibility of the merging of two candidate `Topics`. Note that `allParents()` recursively yields all supertypes of a `TopicType`, with respect to its closure, and `allChildren()` does so for its subtypes.

```
Topic::checkATTT(b : Topic) : Boolean =
 self.oclIsTypeOf(AssociationTopicType)
 and b.oclIsTypeOf(TopicType)
 and b.oclAsType(TopicType).allTTInstancesSuperAndSub()->isEmpty

TopicType::allTTInstancesSuperAndSub() : Set (TopicObject) =
 self.allTTInstances()->union (self.allTTparentInstances())
```

```
TopicType::allTTInstances() : Set (TopicObject) =
 self.typeClosure()._instance->union(self.allChildren()->select (c |
 c.oclIsTypeOf(TopicType)).oclAsType(TopicType)._instance)->asSet

TopicType::allTTparentInstances() : Set (TopicObject) =
 self.typeClosure()._instance->union(self.allParents()->select (p |
 p.oclIsTypeOf(TopicType)).oclAsType(TopicType)._instance)->asSet

TopicType::typeClosure() : Set (TopicType) =
 self.closure()->select (c |
  c.oclIsTypeOf(TopicType)).oclAsType(TopicType)->asSet
```

Note that `TopicType._instance` yields the set of direct instances (TOs) of the context TT.

6.4 AT - OT

Converting AT_1 to an OT_1 may only work in the case all supertypes and subtypes of AT_1, which are also ATs, have no `TopicAssociationEnds`, which would be a rather theoretical situation. Converting OT_2 to an AT_2 would only work, if OT_2 had neither instances (Occurrences) nor subtypes. Thus, we will simply prohibit merging of AT_1 and OT_2. At last, the OCL checker should report a warning that the merging of two candidate `Topics` was avoided.

7 Merging Inside the OCL Checker

In the previous sections, we have discussed the merging of different kinds of `Topics` and its effects on the consistency and well-formedness of a topic map and presented several additional constraints to avoid merging in certain situations. Finally, we will take a short look at the processing steps inside the OCL checker, which is not only responsible for checking all OCL invariants, it also has to perform merging by establishing the according `Synonymy` relations. Merging inside the OCL checker can be divided into the following three steps, where the set of processed topic maps may be, for example, all the topic maps within a repository and a new topic map to be stored into the repository:
For all Topics T_1, T_2 in the set of processed topic maps

1. check, if T_1 and T_2 are candidates for merging and - if they are of a different kind - if they can be merged
2. if T_1 and T_2 should be merged, establish a `Synonymy` relation between T_1 and T_2
3. if T_1 and T_2 should be merged, and T_1 is of a different kind than T_2, change the kind of T_1 or T_2 so that T_1 and T_2 are of the same kind

The core of the first step is the following operation `Topic::canMerge (b : Topics)`, which simply calls the already presented check operations.

```
Topic::canMerge(b : Topic) : Boolean =
 (subjectBasedMerge(b) or nameBasedMerge(b))
 and typeOfMergePossible(b) and noDifferentSCR(b)
```

While the first two operation calls are for checking the XTM merging conditions, and the last one checks an additional condition implied by the XTM merging conditions, `Topic::typeOfMergePossible(b : Topics)` encapsulates our suggested strategies for merging different kinds of `Topics`. It contains calls to `Topic::tOMP (b: Topic)` in both directions, which is the actual application of our suggestions. There, operations like `checkATTT()` are called. Note that in this version, issues like the *UniqueRolesProblem* (section 6.1) are not checked in advance, merging is optimistically performed and may lead to an according constraint violation afterwards, which is reported by the OCL checker. Performing all checks before establishing the `Synonymy` relation, would call for additional OCL operations to be called from within `tOMP()`.

```
Topic::typeOfMergePossible(b : Topic) : Boolean =
 self.tOMP (b) or b.tOMP (self)

Topic::tOMP(b : Topic) : Boolean =
 b.oclIsTypeOf(TopicObject)
 or (self.oclIsTypeOf(TopicType) and b.oclIsTypeOf(TopicType))
 or (self.oclIsTypeOf(OccurrenceType) and b.oclIsTypeOf(OccurrenceType))
 or (self.checkATTT (b))
```

If T_1`.canMerge(`T_2`)` yields true, the `Synonymy` relation can be established by T_1`.merge(`T_2`)`. This operation has to be implemented by an according method, in OCL we can only formulate its pre- and post-conditions.

```
Topic::merge(b : Topic)
 pre merge_pre:
  self.canMerge(b) and not self.closure()->excluding(self)->includes(b)
 post merge_post_Synonymy:
  self.closure()->excluding(self)->includes(b)
```

For the third step, a method `Topic::change (b : Topic)` has to be implemented, which checks the kinds of T_1 and T_2 and subsequently calls the appropriate `changeToXX()` operation, if the kind of T_1 or T_2 has to be changed. One example for this would be the `changeToTT(b: TopicType)` operation presented in section 6.2. The postcondition of `change()` has to state that all `Topics` in the closure of the context `Topic` have to be of the same kind. We omit this for space reasons.

Fig. 7 schematically shows the processing steps of the OCL checker. At first, the previously introduced three merging steps are performed. Afterwards, all other constraints (OCL invariants for inheritance, instancing, etc.) are checked. If errors are to be reported, the OCL checker does so and stops further work, the topic map is considered not well-formed (and therefore can not be stored into a repository). Otherwise, if some merging has happened, the whole processing has to be repeated, as one merging may cause a further merging to happen. This situation is shown in fig. 8.

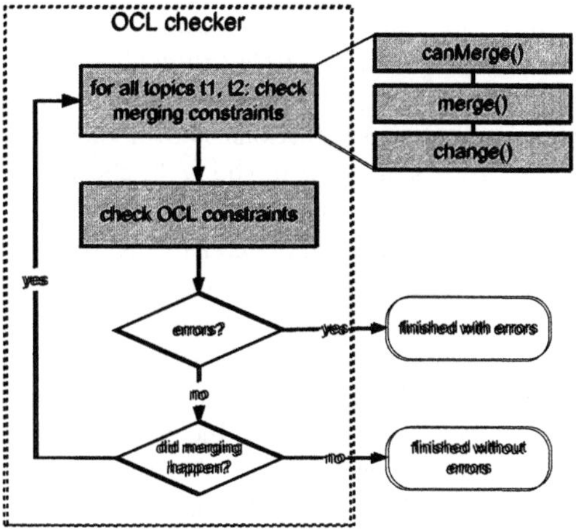

Fig. 7. Process Steps of the OCL Checker

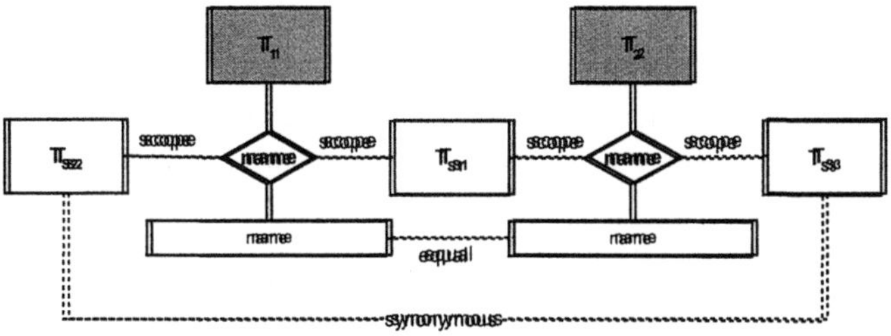

Fig. 8. One Merge Causing a Further Merge

There, T_1 has a name in the scope $\{TS_1, TS_2\}$, and T_2 has the same name in the scope $\{TS_1, TS_3\}$. In a first processing cycle of the OCL checker, T_1 and T_2 are considered to stand for different subjects and are therefore not merged. Suppose that TS_2 and TS_3 are merged (due to identifying the same subject). Then, T_1 and T_2 had the name in the same scope and could also be merged, but only in the second processing cycle of the OCL checker. These processing cycles have to be implemented by a fix-point algorithm, stopping if either an error occurred (a constraint was violated) or a complete cycle has run without performing a single merge. This is shown in fig. 7.

8 Conclusion

In this paper, we have treated the merging of topics in XTM in detail. We have shown how the XTM merging conditions can be realized with the TMUML meta model and presented the according OCL constraints and operations. These operations and constraints can be tested straightforwardly with the USE tool

[5], which helps creators of Topic Maps systems trying out different strategies and their implications. We identified further difficulties when merging different kinds of topics, including association types, occurrence types, topic types and topic instances. After presenting suggestions to overcome these difficulties using OCL, we sketched the processing steps of the OCL checker, which is the central component for validating the well-formedness of topic maps.

All in all, the more voluminous and extensive a Topic Maps system is designed to be, the more important is the issue of merging. At this point, we want to emphasize the duality of merging. On one hand, it provides a great gain in extending existent knowledge by additional facts and information. Two topics may be part of topic maps of different authors. When their associations, occurrences, names and types are combined due to merging, the resulting topic holds the knowledge about a subject of both of the authors. One may learn from the other, and the quality of search queries against topic maps as well as the navigational access on topic maps may enormously benefit from the combined information about a subject.

On the other hand, merging that is applied "silently", simply checking the existing conditions, may always cause subjectively undesired effects. Consider the case two authors both created a topic with the same name, but the second author added another name that the first author would not recognize as a valid name for the topic. No merging process could automatically detect and avoid such situations. Therefore, a notification system seems very important to be integrated with a Topic Maps repository. Every merging should be reported (e.g. by e-Mail, a newsletter system or at least a common logging file or database) to the originators of the merged topics, so that they can verify the semantic impacts of the merge and possibly correct undesired effects (or even manually take back the merge). Another strategy can be adding a special attribute, let us call it "mergeable", to each topic, providing a flag that may avoid merging the topic in any case, even if it would have to be merged according to XTM. The drawback would be that possibly merging would happen quite rarely, and it would be a proprietary extension to XTM.

Our further work will contain an explicit description of the transformation of XTM to a UML compliant, intermediate format like XMI [9] or the USE syntax. The implementation of this transformation together with the implementation of the OCL checker will make up a validator for well-formed XTM Topic Maps, where OCL constraints can dynamically be added or modified in the according USE file and need not be hard-coded into the OCL checker.

References

1. Ahmed, K.: Topic Maps for repositories. Proceedings XML Europe 2000. GCA, Paris (2000).
2. Auillans, P., de Mendez, P.O., Rosenstiehl, P., Vatant, B.: A formal model for Topic Maps. International Semantic Web Conference (ISWC) 2002. http://www.mondeca.com/english/publications_-_doc.htm, last visited 23.2.2003

3. Baird, C.: Topic Map Cartography - a discussion of Topic Map authoring. Proceedings XML Europe 2000. GCA, Paris (2000)
4. Gogolla, M., Richters, M.: On constraints and queries in UML. In: Schader, M., Korthaus, A. (eds.): The Unified Modeling Language - Technical Aspects and Applications, p. 109-121. Physica, Heidelberg (1998)
5. Gogolla, M., Richters, M.: Development of UML Descriptions with USE. In: Tjoa A.M., Shafazand, H., Badie K. (eds.): Proc. 1st Eurasian Conf. Information and Communication Technology (EURASIA'2002). LNCS, Springer Verlag, Berlin Heidelberg New York (2002)
6. Gronmo, G.O.: Creating semantically valid topic maps. Proceedings XML Europe 2000. GCA, Paris (2000)
7. ISO/IEC 13250: Information technology - SGML Applications - Topic Maps. International Organization for Standardization, Geneve, Switzerland (1999)
8. Mueck, T.A., Widhalm, R.: Schlagwort - Topic Maps. Wirtschaftsinformatik, 3:297-300. Verlag Vieweg, Wiesbaden (2001)
9. Object Management Group: OMG UML Specification Version 1.3. http://www.omg.org./uml/, last visited 1. 8. 2002
10. Object Management Group: XMI XML Metadata Interchange, Version 1.1. http://cgi.omg.org/docs/ad/99-10-02.pdf, last visited 2. 8. 02
11. Ontopia: The Ontopia Schema Language Reference Specification, Version 1.3. http://www.ontopia.net/omnigator/docs/schema/spec.html, last visited 23. 10. 2002
12. Pepper, S., Moore, G. et al: XML Topic Maps (XTM) 1.0. Topic Maps Authoring Group (2001). http://www.topicmaps.org/xtm/1.0/, last visited 19. 6. 2001
13. Pepper, S.: Draft requirements, examples and a "low bar" proposal for Topic Map Constraint Language. ISO/IEC JTC 1/SC34/WG3 (2001). http://www.y12.doe.gov/sgml/sc34/document/0226.htm, last visited 1. 8. 2002
14. Rath, H.H.: Technical Issues on Topic Maps. Proceedings MetaStructures 99. GCA, Alexandria, VA (1999)
15. IETF (Internet Engineering Task Force) RFC 2396: Uniform Resource Identifiers (URI): Generic Syntax. IETF (1998). http://www.ietf.org/rfc/rfc2396.txt, last visited 17. 1. 2003
16. Richters, M., Gogolla, M.: On formalizing the UML object constraint language OCL. In: Tok-Wand, L. (ed.): Proc. 17th Int. Conf. Conceptual Modeling (ER'98), p. 449-464. LNCS Vol. 1507, Springer Verlag, Berlin Heidelberg New York (1998)
17. Warmer, J., Kleppe, A.: The object constraint language - precise modeling with UML. Addison-Wesley (1999).
18. Widhalm, R., Mueck, T.A.: Topic Maps - Semantische Suche im Internet. Springer Verlag, Heidelberg (2002).
19. Widhalm, R., Mueck, T.A.: Web metadata semantics - on the road to well-formed topic maps. In: Ozsu T. et al. (eds.): Proc. 2nd Int. Conf. On Web Information Systems Engineering (WISE), vol. 2, p. 141-150. IEEE Computer Society, Los Alamitos, CA (2002).
20. Widhalm, R., Mueck, T.A.: Well-formed Topic Maps. Submitted to SoSyM, Journal on Software & System Modeling. Springer Verlag, Berlin Heidelberg New York (2003)

Semantic Processing of the Semantic Web*

Kunal Patel and Gopal Gupta

Applied Logic, Programming-Languages and Systems (ALPS) Laboratory
Department of Computer Science
University of Texas at Dallas
{kkp025000,gupta}@utdallas.edu

Abstract. We develop a semantics based approach to process information on the semantic web. We show how Horn logic can be used to denotationally capture the semantics of mark-up languages designed for describing resources on the semantic web (such as RDF). The same approach can also be used to specify the semantics of query languages for the semantic web. The semantics of both the resource description languages and the query languages are executable and when put together can be used to compute answers to semantic web queries. The main advantage of this semantic-based approach to processing the semantic web is that these executable semantics can be developed extremely quickly. Thus, as the semantic web mark-up languages evolve rapidly, their implementations can be developed at the same pace. In this paper, we present our approach based on denotational semantics and Horn logic. Our approach is quite general, and applicable to any description format (XML, RDF, DAML, etc.), though in this paper we illustrate it via RDF (Resource Description Framework).

1 Introduction

With increased importance of the Web in our daily lives and national economy, researchers have been looking for ways to make the WEB documents more expressive. That is, designing ways to mark-up WEB documents so that more information can be automatically inferred from them compared to what is possible with HTML. These efforts have resulted in XML (the eXtensible Mark Language) family of notation. While XML allows one to go beyond HTML, it does not take one quite far enough, since the meaning of various tags in a particular XML have to still be agreed upon. The Semantic Web [2] effort goes beyond XML by including metadata information in the document itself.

A problem with any interchange format for the semantic web is that it has to be turned into an "executable" notation, so that new information that is logically implied by the information given in the document can be automatically inferred (computed). Turning a mark-up language into an "executable" entity usually requires writing a compiler like program that maps the language to a

* Authors are partially supported by US NSF grants CCR 99-00320, CCR 98-20852, EIA 01-09347, INT 99-04063, and the US Environmental Protection Agency.

D. Fensel et al. (Eds.): ISWC 2003, LNCS 2870, pp. 80–95, 2003.

notation whose semantics is mathematical; information that is implied can then be inferred automatically from this mathematical semantics.

In this paper, we develop a systematic framework for rapidly translating semantic web formats to notations that are executable. Our framework relies on Horn logic and denotational semantics. Essentially, the denotational semantics of the mark up notation is written in Horn logic. If the semantics is executable, the *denotation* of a document (i.e., the meaning assigned to the document by the semantics) written in that notation is also executable and can be used to infer information implied in that document. Denotational semantics of a language consists of three components: syntax, semantic algebras, and valuation functions. All three components can be specified in Horn logic. The interesting aspect about using Horn logic for specifying denotational semantics is that both the syntax as well as the semantic specification is executable. The syntax specification validates a document, while the semantic specification maps it to its executable mathematical semantics (called its denotation). The denotation of the document can then be employed for inferring implied information (i.e., querying the document). Since both the syntax and semantics are denotationally specified in Horn logic, they are declarative, and thus can be developed very rapidly.

As a result, as the mark-up language or a resource description notation rapidly evolves, its executable semantics can be developed with the same rapid pace. Thus, our framework can be used for computing the executable semantics of XML [19], RDF [25], as well as DAML [1] and OWL [15]. Providing automatic means of translating RDF descriptions into notations that are executable, not only specifies the meaning of the descriptions, but also produces a representation of the descriptions from which inferences can automatically be made using traditional automatic theorem provers, problem solvers, and other inference engines.

In the rest of this paper, we expound on our approach to semantic processing of the semantic web. For illustration purposes we use RDF and show how RDF documents can be rapidly translated into Horn logic (pure Prolog) using the Horn logical denotational method. This Prolog code can be queried to infer (or compute) information that is implied by the document. In a similar vain we show that query languages designed for resource description formats (e.g., RDQL for RDF) can be translated into Horn logic using a Horn logical denotational approach. A RDQL query is thus translated into a Prolog query, and if the semantics of RDF and RDQL are developed in a consistent manner, than the Prolog query obtained from RDQL can be executed on Prolog data obtained from the RDF document.

Horn logic has played an important role in the Semantic Web enterprise and has been used in the past to develop systems for querying RDF documents [34, 16]. The novel contribution of this paper is to show that a semantics based approach that relies on Horn Logic is sufficient to automatically (and rapidly) obtain such systems.

2 A Semantics Based Approach to Translation

If more information is to be inferred from a document written using a mark-up language, then it has to be semantically mapped into an (executable) notation which is amenable to drawing inferences, e.g., via querying. That is, the document has to be syntactically transformed into an executable notation in a manner that preserves its semantics. A relatively easy approach to accomplish this is to express the formal semantics of the mark-up language in terms of this executable notation. Such an approach has been developed in [23] using Horn Logic and denotational semantics. In this approach, to translate one notation, say $\mathcal{L}_s$ to $\mathcal{L}_t$, the denotational semantics of $\mathcal{L}_s$ is given in terms of the language constructs of $\mathcal{L}_t$. All components of this semantics are coded in Horn logic rendering it executable. Given a program/document coded in $\mathcal{L}_s$, its denotation under this semantics is the program/document coded in $\mathcal{L}_t$. The executable semantics thus acts as a translator. Because this semantics is denotational (declarative), it can be specified quickly. Additionally, since the translator is obtained automatically from semantics, it is provably correct w.r.t. the specification.

Thus, assuming that we have RDF as the mark-up language, the semantics of RDF can be given denotationally in terms of an executable notation such as Horn Logic (pure Prolog). Likewise, given a query language such as RDQL, its semantics can also be given denotationally in terms of Horn Logic. This Prolog translated query can be executed w.r.t. the Prolog translated RDF document to compute the query results.

2.1 Denotational Semantics

Denotational Semantics [32] is a well-established methodology for the design, description, and analysis of programming languages. In the denotational semantics approach, the semantics of a programming language/notation is specified in terms of mathematical entities, such as sets and functions. The denotational semantics of a language $\mathcal{L}$ has three components: (i) *syntax specification:* maps sentences of $\mathcal{L}$ to parse trees; it is commonly specified as a grammar in the BNF format; (ii) *semantic algebra:* represents the mathematical objects used for expressing the meaning of a program written in the language $\mathcal{L}$; these mathematical objects typically are sets or domains (partially ordered sets, lattices, etc.) along with associated operations to manipulate the elements of the sets; (iii) *valuation functions:* these are functions mapping parse trees to elements of the semantic algebras.

Given the denotational semantics of a language $\mathcal{L}$, and a program $\mathcal{P}_\mathcal{L}$ written in $\mathcal{L}$, the denotation of $\mathcal{P}_\mathcal{L}$ w.r.t. the denotational semantics can be obtained by applying the top-level valuation function to the parse tree of $\mathcal{P}_\mathcal{L}$. The denotation of $\mathcal{P}_\mathcal{L}$ is an entity that is amenable to formal mathematical processing, and thus has a number of applications. For example, it can be used to prove properties of $\mathcal{P}_\mathcal{L}$, or it can be transformed to obtain other representations of $\mathcal{P}_\mathcal{L}$ (e.g., a compiled representation that can be executed more efficiently [20]). In this paper we assume that the reader is familiar with formal semantics. A detailed exposition can be found in [32].

2.2 Horn Logical Semantics

Traditional denotational definitions express syntax as BNF grammars, and the semantic algebras and valuation functions using λ-calculus. The Horn Logical Semantics of a language uses Horn-clause logic (or pure Prolog) to code all three components of the denotational semantics of a language [20]. This simple change in the notation for expressing denotational semantics, while resulting in loss of some declarative purity, leads to a number of applications [20]. There are two major advantages [20]. First, a parser can be obtained from the syntax specification with negligible effort: the BNF specification of a language $\mathcal{L}$ can be trivially translated to a *Definite Clause Grammar* (DCG) [35,31]. This syntax specification, coded as a DCG, can be loaded in a Prolog system, and a parser automatically obtained. This parser can be used to parse programs written in $\mathcal{L}$ and obtain their parse trees. The semantic algebra and valuation functions can also be coded in Horn clause logic. Second, Horn logical semantics can be used for automatic verification [20].

Since both the syntax and semantics of the specification are expressed as logic programs, they are both executable. These syntax and semantic specifications can be loaded in a logic programming system and "executed," given a program written in $\mathcal{L}$. This provides us with an interpreter that computes the semantics of programs written in the language $\mathcal{L}$.

2.3 Semantics-Based Language Translation

Horn logical semantics also provides a formal basis for *language translation.* Specification of a translator can be seen as an exercise in semantics. Essentially, the meaning or semantics of the language $\mathcal{L}_s$ can be given in terms of the constructs of the language $\mathcal{L}_t$. This meaning consists of both syntax and semantic specifications. If these syntax and semantic specifications are executable, then the specification itself acts as a translation system, providing a provably correct translator. The task of specifying the filter from $\mathcal{L}_s$ to $\mathcal{L}_t$ consists of specifying the definite clause grammar (DCG) for $\mathcal{L}_s$ and $\mathcal{L}_t$ and the appropriate valuation predicates which essentially relate (map) parse tree patterns of $\mathcal{L}_s$ to parse tree patterns of $\mathcal{L}_t$. Let $\mathcal{P}_s(S_s, T_s)$ be the top level predicate for the DCG of $\mathcal{L}_s$ that takes a sentence S_s of $\mathcal{L}_s$, parses it and produces the parse tree T_s for it. Let $\mathcal{P}_t(S_t, T_t)$ be the top level predicate for the DCG of $\mathcal{L}_t$ that takes a sentence S_t of $\mathcal{L}_t$, parses it and produces the parse tree T_t for it. Let $\mathcal{M}_{st}(T_s, T_t)$ be the top level valuation predicate that relates parse trees of $\mathcal{L}_s$ and $\mathcal{L}_t$. Then the relation

$$\texttt{translate}(S_s, S_t) \texttt{ :- } \mathcal{P}_s(S_s, T_s),\ \mathcal{M}_{st}(T_s, T_t),\ \mathcal{P}_t(S_t, T_t).$$

declaratively specifies the equivalence of the source and target sentence under the semantic mapping given. The `translate` predicate can be used for obtaining S_t given S_s (and *vice versa*).

Note that because the semantics is specified denotationally, the syntax and semantics specification of a language are guided by its BNF grammar: there is one syntax rule in the syntax specification per BNF production and one semantics rule in the semantics specification per BNF production. Occasionally, however, some auxiliary predicates may be needed while defining valuation predicates for semantics. Also, if a Prolog interpreter is to be used, extra syntax rules may be introduced if the BNF grammar has left recursive rules which need to be eliminated in the DCG (by converting to right-recursive rules).

3 Semantic Processing of the Semantic Web

In the context of the web, our semantics based approach to translation has a number of applications. First, to provide interoperability on the web, translators can be built that translate one format into another. Indeed this approach has been applied to translate one XML to another [23,21], as well as to convert HTML to VoiceXML in an attempt to make the web accessible via audio [11]. This helps in increasing the usability of the regular (i.e., non-semantic) web. Second, syntactic mark-up can be translated into an executable notation which can be queried to infer more knowledge from documents. This permits sophisticated applications to be deployed on the semantic web.

In this paper we explore the applications of our technique to the semantic web enterprise. We considered two languages: (i) RDF, that has been used for marking up semantic content on the web, and (ii) RDQL, that has been used for querying the semantic web. Both are denotationally translated into Horn logic using the approach outlined, to aid in processing queries to the semantic web.

Let's first consider specifying the semantics of RDF. The ("triples") statements of the RDF data model can be thought of as the equivalent of ground facts in a logic based language. Consequently, logic based approaches to information management and querying map very simply onto the RDF model. We have developed a complete denotational semantics of RDF, which consists of syntax specification and semantic specification.

3.1 Syntax Specification

We specify the syntax of RDF as a definite clause grammar. As stated earlier, DCG rules for RDF can be easily obtained from its BNF specification. The syntax specification in the DCG format automatically yields a parser. The formal grammar for RDF described in [25] was used to obtain the DCG. The following examples illustrate some rules from the formal grammar of RDF and their corresponding DCG rules. Note that the formal grammar in [25] is given in the Extended BNF form, while the DCG corresponds to a BNF.

```
EBNF Grammar rule:
 description ::= '<rdf:Description' idAboutAttr? bagIdAttr? propAttr* '/>'
                 | typedNode
```

```
DCG rules:
 description(descr(IAA,BIA,PA)) --> ['<rdf:Description'], idaboutattr(IAA),
                                     bagidattr(BIA), propattrs(PA), ['/>'].
 description(descr(IAA,BIA)) -->
          ['<rdf:Description'], idaboutattr(IAA), bagidattr(BIA), ['/>'].
 description(descr(IAA,PA)) -->
          ['<rdf:Description'], idaboutattr(IAA), propattrs(PA), ['/>'].
 description(descr(IAA)) --> ['<rdf:Description'], idaboutattr(IAA),['/>'].
 description(descr(BIA,PA)) -->
          ['<rdf:Description'], bagidattr(BIA), propattrs(PA), ['/>'].
 description(descr(BIA)) --> ['<rdf:Description'], bagidattr(BIA), ['/>'].
 description(descr(PA)) --> ['<rdf:Description'], propattrs(PA), ['/>'].
 description(descr([])) --> ['<rdf:Description'], ['/>'].
 description(descr(TN)) --> typenode(TN).
 propattrs(PA)-->propattr(PA).
 propattrs((PA,PAs))-->propattr(PA), propattrs(PAs).
```

The above EBNF grammar rule states that a description consists of the '`rdf:Description`' tag followed by an optional id describing what the document is about, followed by an optional id for the associated bag, followed by zero or more property attributes, and terminating with the symbol '`/>`'. The DCG rules corresponding to this EBNF rule is also shown above. This DCG is slightly extended, so that the parse tree of the document is recursively synthesized during the parsing process. The parse tree of the document generated is passed to the semantic valuation predicates, for mapping to its denotation.

Another example EBNF rule and its correspond DCG rules are shown below.

```
EBNF Grammar rule:
    propAttr ::= typeAttr | propName '="' string '"'

DCG rules:
    propattr(propattr(TA))-->typeattr(TA).
    propattr(propattr(PN,S))-->propname(PN),['="'],string(S),['"'].
```

The following example shows an input RDF statement and the corresponding output that is obtained from the DCG,

```
RDF statement:
   <rdf:RDF>
        <rdf:Description about="http://www.w3.org">
            <s:Publisher>World Wide Web Consortium</s:Publisher>
            <s:Title>W3C Home Page</s:Title>
            <s:Date>1998-10-03T02:27</s:Date>
        </rdf:Description>
   </rdf:RDF>

Output from DCG (after parsing):
  R = r(o(descr(idaboutattr(aboutattr(
              uriref(string("http://www.w3.org")))),
```

```
    (propertyelt(propname(qname(nsprefix(s), name(publisher))),
          value(string("World Wide Web Consortium)),
          propname(qname(nsprefix(s), name(publisher)))),
     propertyelt(propname(qname(nsprefix(s), name(title))),
          value(string(W3C Home Page)),
          propname(qname(nsprefix(s), name(publisher)))),
     propertyelt(propname(qname(nsprefix(s), name(date))),
          value(string(1998-10-03T02:27)),
          propname(qname(nsprefix(s), name(date)))
  ))) ) )
```

3.2 Semantic Specification

RDF statements can be represented as logical expressions. However, instead of defining a triple (P, S, O) directly we adopt the approach of [26] and define it as a ternary relation "property": property(S, P, O).
which means resource S has property P with value O. The reason is that developing statements about properties would lead to unwanted higher order statements. Our goal is to keep the semantics first order, not simply because we are interested in using a logic programming based framework, but also because higher order logics quickly become intractable and inefficient. Therefore, we represent RDF document as a set of assertions having three arguments. These assertions are generated during semantic processing, which uses the parse tree produced from the syntax specification as input. The output parse tree obtained is semantically processed to identify the subject, predicate and object, which in turn, are used to generate the ground facts. The semantic function is specified denotationally in Horn Logic. The semantic function (actually, a predicate) maps the parse tree to a database of ground facts.

The following example illustrate fragments of rules used to map property elements to a list of ground facts. The rules essentially map the corresponding parse tree obtained in the semantic phase to the subject, predicate and object values in order to generate the Prolog fact database. The property elements are processed recursively to obtain the list of facts.

```
description(descr(IAA,PE),IAASTR,PROSTR,VALSTR) :-
          idaboutattr(IAA,IAASTR), propertyelts(PE,PROSTR,VALSTR,IAASTR).

propertyelts((PE,PEs),PROSTR,VALSTR,IAASTR) :-
         propertyelt(PE,IAASTR,PROSTR,VALSTR),
         assemble(IAASTR,PROSTR,VALSTR)
         propertyelts(PEs,PROSTR1,VALSTR1,IAASTR).
```

In the first rule, the value of IAASTR, which corresponds to the "subject" argument of the property predicate, is obtained from the parse tree. The value of IAASTR is then used to retrieve the values of the "predicate" argument and the "object" argument of the property predicate to assemble the related facts. We can regard the predicate property as an operation in the semantic algebra.

The following examples illustrate some RDF statements and their corresponding denotation generated as ground facts by our semantic specification.

```
RDF statement 1:
   <rdf:RDF>
       <rdf:Description about="http://www.w3.org/Home/Lassila">
           <s:Creator>
                <rdf:Description about="http://www/w3.org/staffID/85740">
                   <v:Name>Ora Lassila</v:Name>
                   <v:Email>lassila@w3.org</v:Email>
                 </rdf:Description>
            </s:Creator>
       </rdf:Description>
   </rdf:RDF>
```

```
DENOTATION of statement 1:
   property("http://www.w3.org/Home/Lassila", creator,
                              "http://www.w3.org/staffID/85740").
   property("http://www.w3.org/staffID/85740", name, ora lassila).
   property("http://www.w3.org/staffID/85740", email, lassila@w3.org).
```

The RDF model also defines the concept of containers. Frequently, it is necessary to refer to a collection of resources; for example, to say that a work was created by more than one person, or to list the students in a course. RDF containers are used to hold such lists of resources or literals. A container object can be a *bag*, a *sequence* or an *alternative*. To semantically map the container tag, we make use of structures which holds such list of resources or literals. The name of the structure identifies the type of the container (a bag, a sequence or an alternative). The first argument of the structure is reserved for the ID of the container. If there is no ID for the container then this argument takes the default value of `noid`. The second argument of the structure is a list of resources or literals contained within the container. The following example illustrates the bag container.

Consider an RDF rendition of the information contained in the following sentence: “The students in course 6.001 are Amy, Tim, John and Mary.” The corresponding RDF document and its denotation generated by our semantics is shown below.

```
RDF statement 2:
    <rdf:RDF>
       <rdf:Description about="http://mycollege.edu/courses/6.001">
          <s:students>
             <rdf:Bag>
                <rdf:li resource="http://mycollege.edu/students/Amy"/>
                <rdf:li resource="http://mycollege.edu/students/Tim"/>
                <rdf:li resource="http://mycollege.edu/students/Mary"/>
             </rdf:Bag>
          </s:students>
       </rdf:Description>
    </rdf:RDF>
```

```
DENOTATION of statement 2:
   property("http://mycollege.edu.courses/6.001", students,
            bag("StudentsOf6.001", ["http://mycollege.edu/students/Amy",
                                "http://mycollege.edu/students/Tim",
                                "http://mycollege.edu/students/Mary"]))
```

In the above example the ID of the Bag container is "StudentsOf6.001" and the Bag contains three resources.

In addition to making statement about web resources, RDF can also be used for making statements about other RDF statements. These are referred to as *higher order statements.* In order to express higher order statements RDF defines a model of a statement. This model of a statement has four properties, namely, subject, predicate, object and type, and is also known as a reified statement. The semantics of reified statements is defined with the help of a a new predicate called `statement`. By assigning internal ids, higher order statements can be represented in Horn logic. To achieve this, the first argument of the "statement" is bound to a unique id which links this reified statement to its other properties. The second argument of "statement" is the subject of the reified statement, the third argument is the predicate of the reified statement and the fourth argument is the object of the reified statement. Other additional statements made about this reified statement use the unique id to refer to the reified statement. The following example shows the semantic mapping of a higher order statement.

Consider the statement: "Ralph Swick says that Ora Lassila is the creator of the resource http://www.w3.org/Home/Lassila." The RDF document generated for this statement and the corresponding denotation generated by our semantics is shown below. Note that the two predicates in the denotation are joined via the unique id `id007`.

```
RDF statement 3:
 <rdf:RDF>
   <rdf:Description>
     <rdf:subject resource="http://www.w3.org/Home/Lassila"/>
     <rdf:predicate resource="http://description.org/schema/Creator"/>
     <rdf:object>Ora Lassila</rdf:object>
     <rdf:type resource="www.w3.org/1999/02/22-rdf-syntax-ns#Statement"/>
     <a:attributedTo>Ralph Swick</a:attributedTo>
   </rdf:Description>
 </rdf:RDF>
```

```
DENOTATION of statement 3:
   statement(id007, "http://www.w3.org/Home/Lassila",
                "http://description.org/schema/Creator", Ora Lassila)
   property(id007, attributedTo, Ralph Swick)
```

The semantics of other RDF constructs are similarly defined. Name-spaces are also easily handled by associating name-space identifiers with their corresponding URI via a predicate. Details are omitted due to lack of space. The whole semantic specification for RDF has indeed been developed. The semantic specification coupled with syntax specification can produce the denotation of any arbitrary RDF document as a set of logic programming ground facts.

3.3 Syntax and Semantics of RDQL

Several RDF Query languages and systems have been recently proposed. These proposals either take the "database approach" or the "knowledge base approach" to query language design (see [9]). The database approach interprets an RDF document primarily as an XML document, which leads to several drawbacks described in [9]. For this reason, all of the recently presented RDF Query languages and systems adhere to the knowledge base approach, explicitly dealing with RDF triples instead of document trees. It is easy to see that the knowledge base approach of RDF querying fits our approach quite well: queries can be expressed as (Horn logic) rules, which can be processed with respect to the denotation of the RDF document using a Logic Programming engine.

The semantics of RDF Query languages like RDQL [9], RQL [3], RDFDBQL [30] or SQUISH [12] can be expressed in Horn logic, using the approach described above. We choose RDQL as an example RDF Query language. RDQL(RDF Data Query Language) is an implementation of SQL-like query language for RDF. It treats RDF as data and provides query with triple patterns and constraints over a single RDF model. An RDQL query is of the form:

```
SELECT vars
FROM documents
WHERE expressions
AND filters
USING Namespace declarations
```

where `SELECT` clause indicates which RDQL variables should be returned by the query; the `FROM` clause of the query indicates the RDF sources to be queried (each source is enclosed by angle brackets(<&>)); while the `WHERE` clause indicates the constraints that RDF triples (subject, predicate, object) that constitute the solution must satisfy. The `WHERE` part is expressed by a list of restrictions separated by commas, each restriction takes the form (subject, predicate, object) where the subject, predicate and object can be a literal value or a RDQL variable. Finally, the `USING` clause declares all the name spaces that will be used for RDF properties.

RDQL queries are also converted to Horn Logic queries, using the same method as described for RDF statements. A syntax specification for RDQL as a DCG is developed based on the RDQL formal grammar described in [9]. The denotational semantics of RDQL as a mapping from parse trees to logic programming facts and queries is also specified. Given a RDQL query, its denotation can be viewed as a query coded in logic programming. The logic programming coded query can be executed on top of the logic programming coded database obtained denotationally from the RDF document. The following example shows a sample RDQL query and its corresponding denotation that is generated:

```
RDQL Query:                        DENOTATION:
   SELECT ?a ?b                       :- property(X, pred, Y), Y > 250.
   WHERE (?a, pred, ?b)
   AND    ?b > 250
```

3.4 An Example

The following example shows some RDF statements and RDQL queries. The Prolog denotation corresponding to these statements and queries is also shown.

```
RDF statement:
  <rdf:RDF>
       <rdf:Description about="http://www.abc.org">
            <s:Author>John</s:Author>
            <s:Title>ABC Home Page</s:Title>
            <s:Hits>200</s:Hits>
       </rdf:Description>
       <rdf:Description about="http://www.pqr.org">
            <s:Author>Tom</s:Author>
            <s:Title>PQR Home Page</s:Title>
            <s:Hits>350</s:Hits>
       </rdf:Description>
  </rdf:RDF>

RDF DENOTATION:
    property("http://www.abc.org", author, john).
    property("http://www.abc.org", title, abc home page).
    property("http://www.abc.org", hits, 200).
    property("http://www.pqr.org", author, Tom).
    property("http://www.pqr.org", title, pqr home page).
    property("http://www.pqr.org", hits, 350).

Query in RDQL (constraints):
    SELECT ?a ?b
    WHERE (?a, hits, ?b)
    AND    ?b > 250

RDQL DENOTATION:
    :- property(X, hits, Y), Y > 250.
```

Once the denotation of RDF and RDQL is obtained in terms of logic programming, the RDQL query can be executed on top of the data provided by RDF using a logic programming engine. For example, execution of the query

```
:- property(X, hits, Y), Y > 250.
```

will yield the answer

```
X = "http://www.pqr.org", Y = 350.
```

4 An Extended Example

In this section we give a slightly extended example that illustrates how the techniques discussed in this paper can be applied to build an on-line application that integrates, combines and deduces information that is on the semantic web to assist users in performing tasks. These examples are motivated from the *semantic web challenge* [6]. While a true semantic web is still far, our research efforts reported here, we believe, will bring us one step closer.

Consider the case of disaster management. Given the Semantic Web, we should be able to use and integrate data from various sources to provide actual and accurate support in a disaster situation (e.g., the flood in Germany in August 2002 or the forest fires in the USA). Possible information sources in this case are (i) weather information, (ii) maps from geographical information systems (iii) News sites and (iv) satellite images. We assume that this information is available as RDF documents, which are denotationally mapped to a logic program using our technique. Thus, from the weather information sites we can obtain information as shown below (instead of showing the RDF, we give an English description). We kept the level of treatment very simple, in reality, the RDF document and the information generated may be more complex.

Today it is rainy in plano:
`property(plano, weathertoday, rainy).`
The weather in plano will be cold tomorrow:
`property(plano, weathertomorrow, cold).`
Plano will have sunny weather next week:
`property(plano, weathernextweek, sunny).`

Similarly, from the transport information RDF we can obtain the following data:

Frisco can be reached by bus#1: `property(frisco, access, bus#1).`
Plano can be reached by bus#2; `property(plano, access, bus#2).`
Plano can be reached by bus#3; `property(plano, access, bus#3).`

Information regarding routes can be obtained from the map sites. The following predicates are generated from the RDF documents of the Map sites:

Bus#1 runs on route 75N: `property(bus#1, route, 75N).`
Bus#2 runs on route 635-North: `property(bus#2, route, 635-North).`
Bus#3 runs on plano road: `property(bus#3, route, plano-road).`

Similarly from the news sites we can obtain the following information:

Route 635-North is closed for construction:
`property(635-North, status, nonoperational).`
Bus #3 is not operational today:
`property(bus#3, status, nonoperational).`

From the Medical information sites we can obtain the following data:

Hospital#1 is located in plano.	`property(hospital#1, location, plano).`
Hospital#2 is located in frisco.	`property(hospital#2, location, frisco).`
`20 beds are free in Hospital#1.`	`property(hospital#1, freebeds, 20).`
`30 beds are free in Hospital#2.`	`property(hospital#2, freebeds, 30).`

With the above data we can provide answers to various different queries. These queries, posed in RDQL, are denotationally translated into Horn logic. The English equivalent of the RDQL queries, and their corresponding denotations are given below.

What weather is predicted in plano tomorrow?:

```
:- property(plano, weathertomorrow, X).
```

By which bus can one reach frisco today?:

```
:- property(frisco, access, X),
   property(X, route, Y),
   property(Y, status, Z), Z ≠ nonoperational.
```

Which hospitals in plano have free beds?:

```
:- property(X, location, plano),
   property(X, freebeds, Y), Y > 0.
```

Are bus services to Plano operational today?:

```
:- property(plano, access, B), property(B, route, T),
   property(T, status, X), X ≠ nonoperational.
```

While these queries are relatively simple, more complex queries can be asked, and as long as they are expressible in RDQL, they can be processed using our approach.

5 Discussion

The approach outlined in this paper for turning a syntactically marked-up document into a semantically understandable, executable form is quite universal. In fact, it has been applied to quite diverse scenarios [23]. For example, it has been used to map complex, multiple notations used by bioinformatics systems to each other [23] so that they are inter-operable; it has been used to systematically translate relational databases (data as well as queries) to object-oriented databases [14], as well as to translate Braille based mark-up notation (called Nemeth Math notation [10]) for mathematics to LaTeX. In the context of the Web, this approach has been used to automatically generate validating parsers from XML DTDs (the semantics of the language used to describe DTDs is expressed in terms of a DCG [22]; the generated DCG acts as a validating parser for the input XML DTD) and for translating HTML documents to VoiceXML in order to make the Web accessible via audio [11]. Currently, work is in progress to use our semantics based methodology for interfacing intelligent multi-agent systems with other agents through DAML [1].

In the context of querying, this approach has been applied to reason about properties of real-time systems [24] where a real-time system specified as a timed-automata is denotationally mapped to a constraint logic program over reals [27]. The generated CLP(R) program is queried to reason about timing properties. A similar approach has been used to verify properties of the Bay Area Rapid Transit system specification; in this case, the design of the BART system specified in Ada is semantically mapped to a logic program, which is then queried to prove *safety* and *liveness* properties [28].

Our approach to querying RDF documents illustrates the power of logic, since not only the target executable notation is based on logic, the means of semantically translating RDF into logic also relies on logic. The importance of logic in realizing the semantic web is well-realized by the community, our paper provides yet another venue where logic can help in piecing together a true semantic-web. The main advantage of our approach is that the semantic translators can be rapidly developed. In fact, it took us only a few weeks of work to specify the syntax and semantics of both RDF and RDQL. As a result, as mark-up languages for the web rapidly evolve, as they have from HTML to XML to DAML to RDF, they can be processed and queried with the same rapidity.

6 Related Work

RDF provides a good framework for effectively storing and retrieving data, especially if multiple heterogeneous vocabularies are involved. Several concepts have been proposed so far concentrating on different goals (e.g. expressiveness, performance). Our concept follows the approach of applying Logic Programming as it provides the expressivity that we need to build generic transformation services.

A number of tool already exist that exploit the relationship between the W3C's RDF and Logic Programming (see [17]). Such efforts include TRIPLE [34], a layered rule language that aims to support applications in need of RDF reasoning and transformation. The core language is based on Horn logic which is syntactically extended to support RDF primitives like name-spaces, resources and statements. Metalog [29] is another query/logical-reasoning system for the semantic web. Metalog views an RDF statement in the logical setting as just a binary predicate involving the subject and the literal. The Metalog schema extends plain RDF with a "logical layer," enabling expression of arbitrary logical relationships within RDF. SiLRI (Simple Logic Based RDF Interpreter) [16] is a main-memory logic-based inference engine implemented in JAVA. It implements a major part of Frame Logic and has support for RDF. The implemented semantics include well-founded semantics and the rule language allows general logic programs. Various other RDF Query languages like RQL [3], R-DEVICE [4], RDFQL [5], Versa [7], N3 [8], RDQL [9], have also been developed and used.

All these approaches require considerable implementation effort, making it hard for them to keep up with the pace of evolution of the semantic web. In contrast, our approach has firm semantic foundations and allows for rapid mapping to executable denotations that can be used for inferring information implicit in Semantic Web documents.

7 Conclusions

In this paper we presented a semantics-based approach to mapping mark-up languages to executable notations so that documents coded in these mark-up languages can be queried further. Our approach is based on denotational semantics and Horn logic. In the denotational approach, the semantics of a language is expressed in the mathematical formalism of the λ-calculus. We adopted an approach in which Horn logic instead of the λ-calculus is the formalism used to express the semantics. We demonstrated our approach by developing the Horn logical denotational semantics for RDF and RDQL, and showing how it leads to their becoming executable. The main advantage of our approach is that documents can be rapidly mapped to their executable semantics, which can be used for querying them. Using this approach we were able to develop a complete semantics of RDF in a few of weeks of work. A complete Horn logical executable semantics of RDF and RDQL indeed will be publicly available shortly.

References

1. DARPA Agent Mark-up Language. `http://www.daml.org`.
2. The Semantic Web. `http://www.semanticweb.org`.
3. RQL: The RDF Query Language. `http://139.91.183.30:9090/RDF/RQL/`
4. R-DEVICE. `http://lpis.csd.auth.gr/systems/r-device.html`
5. Intellidimension. Intellidimension's RDF Gateway. See `http://www.intellidimension.com/RDFGateway`
6. The Semantic Web Challenge. `http://challenge.semanticweb.org/`.
7. Versa: An RDF Query Language. `http://rdfinference.org/versa-about.xml?xslt=index.xslt`
8. RDF:Notation3. `http://www.gingerall.com/charlie/ga/html/rdf-notation3.html`
9. RDQL: Jena toolkit – RDQL Query Language. `http://www.hpl.hp.com/semweb/rdql.html`
10. N. Annamalai, G. Gupta, et al. INSIGHT: A System for Translating Braille based Mathematical Documents to LaTeX. In *Proc. HCI 2003*. pp 1245–1249.
11. N. Annamalai. An Extensible Translator from HTML to VoiceXML. MS Thesis. May 2002. University of Texas at Dallas.
12. J. Broekstra, A. Kampman, and F. van Harmelen. Sesame:A Generic Architecture for Storing and Querying RDF and RDF Schema. In *Proc. International Semantic Web Conference*. Springer LNCS 2342, 2002.
13. A. S. Christophides, V. Plexousakis, D. Karvounarakis, and M. Scholl. RQL: A declarative query language for RDF. In *11th Int'l World Wide Web Conference (WWW'02)*, 2002.

14. N. Datta. A Semantic based approach to Interoperation between Object Querly Language and ODBC. MS thesis. New Mexico State University. Aug. 2000.
15. M. Dean, D. Connolly, et al. OWL Web Ontology Language 1.0 Reference. W3C Working Draft, Mar 2003. `http://www.w3.org/TR/owl-ref/`.
16. S. Decker, D. Brickley, J. Sarrela, J. Angele. SiLRI (Simple Logic Based RDF Interpreter). `http://www.aifb.uni-karlsruhe.de/~sde/rdf/`.
17. S. Decker. Logic Databases on the Semantic Web: Challenges and Opportunities. In *Proc. Int'l Conf. on Logic Programming*. Springer LNCS. 2002. pp. 20–21
18. R. V. Guha Rdfdb : An RDF database. `http://rdfdb.sourceforge.net`. 2000.
19. C. Goldfarb, P. Prescod. The XML Handbook. Prentice Hall. 1998.
20. G. Gupta "Horn Logic Denotations and Their Applications," *The Logic Programming Paradigm: A 25 year perspective* Springer Verlag. pp. 127–160.
21. G. Gupta, Building the Tower of Babel: Interconverting XMLs for Interoperability. Proc. In *7th Int'l Conf. on Computers Helping People with Special Needs (ICCHP00)*. pp. 267–272.
22. G. Gupta, X. Zhou. Automatic Generation of Validating Parsers for XML. Internal Report. U.T. Dallas. 2001.
23. G. Gupta, H-F. Guo, A. Karshmer, E. Pontelli, et al. Semantic-Based Filtering: Logic Programming's Killer App? In *4th Int'l Symp. on Practical Aspects of Declarative Languages*, Springer LNCS 2257, pp. 82–100, 2002.
24. G. Gupta, E. Pontelli. "A Constraint-based Approach to Specification and Verification of Real-time Systems," In *Proc. Real-time Symposium*, IEEE Press. pp. 230–239. 1997.
25. P. Hayes (editor). RDF Model Theory. W3C Working Draft `http://www.w3.org/TR/rdf-mt/`
26. G. Karvounarakis RDF Query languages: A state-of-the-art, 1998. `http://139.91.183.30:9090/RDF/publications/state.html`.
27. J. L. Lassez and J. Jaffar. Constraint logic programming. In *Proc. 14th ACM POPL*, 1987.
28. L. King, G. Gupta, E. Pontelli. Verification of a Controller for BART: An Approach based on Horn Logic and Denotational Semantics. In *High Integrity Software Systems*. Kluwer Academic Publishers.
29. Massimo Marchiori, Janne Saarela. Query + Metadata + Logic = Metalog, `http://www.w3.org/TandS/QL/QL98/pp/metalog.html`
30. L. Miller RDF Query : Squish QL, 2001. `http://swordfish.rdfweb.org/rdfquery/`
31. R. A. O'Keefe. The Craft of Prolog. MIT Press. 1990.
32. D. Schmidt. *Denotational Semantics: a Methodology for Language Development.* W.C. Brown Publishers, 1986.
33. D. Schmidt. Programming language semantics. In CRC Handbook of Computer Science, Allen Tucker, ed., CRC Press, Boca Raton, FL, 1996. Summary version, ACM Computing Surveys 28–1 (1996) 265–267.
34. M. Sintek, S. Decker. TRIPLE: An RDF Query, Inference and Transformation Language. `http://triple.semanticweb.org`.
35. L. Sterling & S. Shapiro. The Art of Prolog. MIT Press, '94.

Viewing the Semantic Web through RVL Lenses*

Aimilia Magkanaraki[1], Val Tannen[2**], Vassilis Christophides[1], and Dimitris Plexousakis[1]

[1] Institute of Computer Science, FORTH, Vassilika Vouton,
P.O.Box 1385, GR 71110, Heraklion, Greece and
Department of Computer Science, University of Crete,
P.O.Box 2208, GR 71409, Heraklion, Greece
{aimilia,christop,dp}@ics.forth.gr

[2] Department of Computer and Information Science, University of Pennsylvania,
200 South 33rd Street Philadelphia, Pennsylvania 19104-6389
val@cis.upenn.edu

Abstract. Personalized access and content syndication involving diverse conceptual representations of information resources are two of the key challenges of real-scale Semantic Web (SW) applications, such as e-Commerce, e-Learning or e-Science portals. RDF/S represents nowadays the core SW language for creating and exchanging resource descriptions worldwide. Unfortunately, full-fledged view definition languages for the RDF/S data model are still missing. We propose *RVL*, a view definition language capable of creating not only virtual resource descriptions, but also virtual RDF/S schemas from (meta)classes, properties, as well as, resource descriptions available on the Semantic Web. *RVL* exploits the functional nature and type system of the RQL query language in order to navigate, filter and restructure complex RDF/S schema and resource description graphs.

1 Introduction

The syndication and personalization of web resources, including semantic reconciliation and integration of heterogeneous metadata, are nowadays emerging as key challenges for Semantic Web [5] applications, such as e-Learning, e-Commerce or e-Science portals. Metadata provide the means to describe resources, thereby facilitating their manipulation both by applications and humans. The core Semantic Web (SW) language for creating and exchanging resource descriptions worldwide is the **Resource Description Framework/Schema Language** (RDF/S) [16,9], which provides i) a *Standard Representation Language* [16] for metadata based on *directed labelled graphs* in which nodes are called *resources* (or *literals*) and edges are called *properties*; ii) a *Schema Definition Language* (RDFS) [9] for creating vocabularies of labels for these graph nodes (called *classes*) and edges (called *property types*); and iii) an *XML* [8] *syntax* for expressing metadata and schemas.

* This work was partially supported by the EU project SeLeNe (IST-2001-39045).

** Work performed during the visit of the author at ICS-FORTH.

D. Fensel et al. (Eds.): ISWC 2003, LNCS 2870, pp. 96–112, 2003.

The declarative access to the metadata repository of a SW application is facilitated by RDF/S query languages, such as *RQL* [14], a typed, functional query language for uniformly navigating/filtering on RDF/S graphs at all abstraction levels (metaschema, schema and data). However, a query language is not enough. As with any query language, formulating queries on data with complex organizations may require schema knowledge beyond the needs of a given application. This difficulty can be alleviated by the use of *views*, which create *virtual* schemas and resource descriptions reflecting only the users' conception of a specific application domain. In relational databases, the standard query language, SQL, serves also as a view definition language. However, for Semantic Webs represented as RDF/S graphs, a view should not be restricted to a query returning part of the SW, as *RQL* queries do. Instead, it should extend to the restructuring of class and property hierarchies, allowing the creation of new resources and property values, and even new classes and property types. To the best of our knowledge, no language for defining such views has been proposed before. In this paper we introduce RVL (RDF View Language), an expressive view definition language designed to play this role. *RVL* provides users with the ability to define a view in the same way in which they write normal RDF/S schemas and resource descriptions, defining classes and "populating" them with resources. By exploiting the *RQL* type system and the distinction of abstraction layers in an RDF/S application, *RVL* captures the desired functionality through the use of just two operators. In essence, schema creation is treated as the instantiation of appropriate metaclasses.

The organization of the paper is as follows: Section 2 motivates the use of the *RVL* view definition language by means of an e-Learning portal example and exhibits a first sample of the functionality it supports. Section 3 unfolds the expressiveness of *RVL* by presenting the operators it specifies and their respective functionality, while Section 4 complements the presentation of *RVL* by presenting existing related approaches. Lastly, Section 5 concludes this paper by presenting directions for future work.

2 A Motivating Example

Educational portals aggregate and classify in a semantically meaningful way various online resources for different educational audiences (e.g., instructors, learners, etc.). The main resources of information in such Portals are called *learning objects* (LO) containing any kind of material (e.g., a web page, a ppt presentation, a book, a Java applet, etc.) which can be used or referenced (using, for instance, URIs [4]) during technology supported learning. To enable effective search in educational portals, LOs are described according to e-Learning metadata standards, such as IEEE/LOM, ARIADNE or IMS[1] [19]. E-Learning schemas and LO descriptions can be easily represented in RDF/S.

In Figure 1 we present the RDF/S description schema and base of such a portal. The upper part of the figure presents a simplified RDF/S schema for descri-

[1] http://ltsc.ieee.org/wg12/, http://ariadne.unil.ch/Metadata/, www.imsglobal.org/

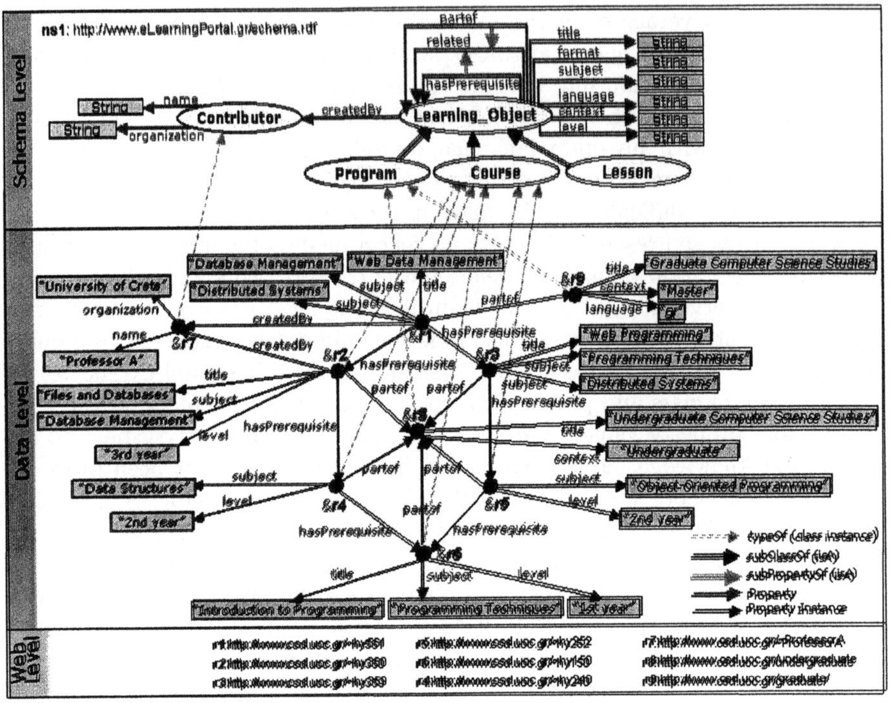

Fig. 1. An example e-Learning Portal application

bing *LOs* using attributes with information about their content (*title*, *subject*, *language*, *format* etc.), as well as their pedagogical value (educational *context* and *level*, learning objectives and time, etc.). Specialization of learning material at different granularity levels is represented by the *rdfs:subClass*-es (class subsumption) *Program*, *Course*, *Lesson* or more specific components, such as notes, assignments, exams, figures or simulation programs. Relationships between LOs like *hasPrerequisite* capturing learning dependency graphs or *partof* capturing learning material composition trees, are defined as *rdfs:subProperty*-'s (property subsumption) of the abstract relationship *related*[2]. Finally, LOs may be also related to other classes of resources through relationships like *createdBy* ranging over instances of the class *Contributor*, which are described in turn by attributes like *name* and *organization*.

The lower part of Figure 1 illustrates the descriptions of some LOs provided by the web site of the Computer Science Department of the University of Crete (CSD UoC). For instance, the LO *&r1* is of *rdf:type Course* and has a *title* attribute with value "Web Data Management" and two *subject* attributes with values "Database Management" and "Distributed Systems". In addition, *&r1* is *part of* *&r9* (i.e., the graduate studies *Program* of the CSD UoC), has two *prerequisite* courses *&r2* (with *title* "Files and Database") and *&r3* (with *title*

[2] According to e-Learning standards other specializations are also possible [19].

"Web Programming") and it has been *createdBy* the *Contributor &r7* with *name* "Professor A" and *organization* "University of Crete". The other LOs illustrated in Figure 1 are described in a similar way.

Searching LOs in such Semantic Web portals relies on declarative query languages for RDF/S descriptions, such as *RQL* [14]. Although portals usually provide appropriate GUIs for assisting users during searching, the formulation of effective queries depends heavily on the understanding of the portal's description "schema". Such RDF/S schema graphs can be quite complex, especially when multiple schemas are employed to describe LOs available on the Web. Therefore, having a central access point to the wealth of LOs is a mixed blessing, if the user must be aware of too much detail in order to search the portal. To enhance the user's experience, we need the ability to personalize the way the portal can be viewed, by providing simpler virtual schemas that reflect a user's perception (e.g., for instructors or learners) of the application domain. *RVL*, the view definition language we describe in this paper, provides this ability. For instance, consider a simple virtual schema (view) for instructors, which shows only database course material and its authors. This schema can be specified with the *RVL* statements presented in the bottom-right part of Figure 2 taking as input the RDF/S description base of Figure 1. The output of these view statements is the RDF/S virtual schema and resource descriptions presented at the top-right part of Figure 2 in an XML serialization.

In RDF/S the uniqueness of (meta)schema labels and the ability to describe resources using labels from several schemas is ensured by the XML namespace facility [7]. Thus, in our example we use the *RVL* statement:

```
CREATE NAMESPACE myview=&http://www.ics.forth.gr/LO.rdf#
```

Descriptive labels are prefixed by the namespace of the schema to which they belong (e.g., *ns1#Learning_Object*), forming in this way unique URIs. This is particularly important in the open and diverse Web world and even more so when defining views, where virtual, but different, copies of old schema labels, such as class and property names, are considered.

The second *RVL* statement in our example "creates" the virtual classes `Author` and `DBCourse` and the virtual properties `creates` and `name`:

```
VIEW rdfs:Class("DBCourse"),rdfs:Class("Author"),
     rdf:Property("creates", Author, DBCourse),
     rdf:Property("name", Author, xsd:string);
```

where *rdfs:Class* and *rdf:Property* are two core metaclasses provided in the default RDF/S namespaces. The semantics of these namespaces along with the XML Schema datatypes is built-in in *RVL*/*RQL* and the corresponding namespace prefixes (e.g., *rdf*, *rdfs*,*xsd*) can thus be omitted, while we can use the `USING NAMESPACE` clause to declare the namespaces used in view statements. As we will see in the next section, *RVL* also provides the ability to create virtual subsumption hierarchies or even to filter/restructure existing ones.

The third *RVL* statement "populates" the virtual classes and properties defined in the view with appropriate instances copied from the source schema illustrated in Figure 1:

RQL:

```
<?xml version="1.0" encoding="UTF-8" ?>
<rdf:RDF xmlns:rdf="http://www.w3.org/1999/02/22-rdf-
  syntax-ns#">
<rdf:Bag>
   <rdf:li>
      <rdf:Seq>
         <rdf:li rdf:type="resource" rdf:resource="&r1"/>
         <rdf:li rdf:type="resource" rdf:resource="&r7"/>
         <rdf:li rdf:type="string">Professor A</rdf:li>
      </rdf:Seq>
   </rdf:li>
   <rdf:li>
      <rdf:Seq>
         <rdf:li rdf:type="resource" rdf:resource="&r2"/>
         <rdf:li rdf:type="resource" rdf:resource="&r7"/>
         <rdf:li rdf:type="string">Professor A</rdf:li>
      </rdf:Seq>
   </rdf:li>
</rdf:Bag>
</rdf:RDF>
```

```
SELECT Y, X, W
FROM {Y;ns1:Course}ns1:createdBy{X}.
     ns1:name{W}, {Y}ns1:subject{Z}
WHERE Z like "Database Management"
USING NAMESPACE
ns1=&www.eLearningPortal.gr/schema.rdf#
```

RVL:

```
<?xml version="1.0" ?>
<rdf:RDF xml:lang="en"
    xmlns:rdf="http://www.w3.org/1999/02/22-rdf-syntax-ns#"
    xmlns:rdfs="http://www.w3.org/2000/01/rdf-schema#"
    xmlns:xsd="http://www.w3.org/2001/XMLSchema#">
<rdfs:Class rdf:ID="Author"/>
<rdfs:Class rdf:ID="DBCourse"/>
<rdf:Property rdf:ID="creates">
   <rdfs:domain rdf:resource="#Author"/>
   <rdfs:range rdf:resource="#DBCourse"/>
</rdf:Property>
<rdf:Property rdf:ID="name">
   <rdfs:domain rdf:resource="#Author"/>
   <rdfs:range rdf:resource="http://www.w3.org/2001/XMLSchema#string"/>
</rdf:Property>
<DBCourse rdf:about="&r1"/>
<DBCourse rdf:about="&r2"/>
<Author rdf:about="&r7">
    <creates rdf:resource="&r1"/>
    <creates rdf:resource="&r2"/>
    <name>Professor A</name>
</Author>
</rdf:RDF>
```

```
CREATE NAMESPACE
          myview=&http://www.ics.forth.gr/LO.rdf#
VIEW rdfs:Class("DBCourse"),
     rdfs:Class("Author"),
     rdf:Property("creates", Author, DBCourse),
     rdf:Property("name", Author, xsd:string) ;
VIEW DBCourse(Y),Author(X),creates(X, Y),name(X, W)
FROM {Y;ns1:Course}ns1:createdBy{X}.ns1:name{W},
     {Y}ns1:subject{Z}
WHERE Z like "Database Management";
USING NAMESPACE
 ns1=&www.eLearningPortal.gr/schema.rdf#,
 xsd=&http://www.w3.org/2001/XMLSchema#,
 rdf=&http://www.w3.org/1999/02/22-rdf-syntax-ns#,
 rdfs=&http://www.w3.org/2000/01/rdf-schema#
```

Fig. 2. Comparing *RQL* to *RVL*

```
VIEW DBCourse(Y),Author(X),creates(X,Y),name(X,W)
FROM {Y;ns1:Course}ns1:createdBy{X}.ns1:name{W},
     {Y}ns1:subject{Z}
WHERE Z like "Database Management";
```

This statement works much like a query on the portal description base. In fact, to emphasize the connection, we present on the left side of Figure 2 an *RQL* query that has the same `FROM` and `WHERE` clauses as the *RVL* statement. In the top-left of the figure we give the XML serialization of the result of this query.

As we see, an *RVL* `FROM` clause consists of *RQL* [14] path expressions facilitating navigation through complex schemas and description bases and binding of introduced variables. Filtering conditions on these variable bindings are stated in the `WHERE` clause. For instance, the *RQL* path expression `{Y;ns1:Course}-ns1:createdBy{X}.ns1:name{W}` will match all instances of class *Course* and their associated *createdBy* properties, which link them to some instance of *Contributor* and its *name* value. For each such match, we get a binding that maps Y to the *Course* resource, X to the *Contributor* and W to the *name* value. In a similar way, the path expression `{Y}ns1:subject{Z}` is evaluated and the involved variable bindings are filtered according to the `WHERE` clause, as well as, to the implicit join condition imposed by the presence of the same variable, Y, in both path expressions. Notice however the difference between the result of the *RQL* query and the output of the *RVL* view definition in Figure 2. Although their input is the same RDF/S graph, *RVL* is capable of producing virtual schemas and resource descriptions instead of simple variable bindings represented in some (nested) tabular form.

This functionality is ensured by the `VIEW` clause, where appropriate population functions are used taking as parameters the variable bindings produced by the `FROM-WHERE` filter. For instance, the virtual class `DBCourse` is populated with instances (bound to variable Y) of the original class *Course* having a property *subject* valued "Database Management". The virtual class `Author` is populated with instances (bound to variable X) of the base class *Contributor*, which are the range values of the property *createdBy* applied to *Course* resources. In other words, `Author` is populated with all the contributors who have created a database course. Virtual properties are populated with pairs of resources (e.g., `creates` is populated with authors having created database courses) or pairs of resources-values (e.g., `name` is populated with the names of database course authors). One of the most salient *RVL* features is its ability to create virtual schemas by simply populating the two core RDF/S metaclasses *Class* (e.g., with schema classes `Author` and `DBCourse`) and *Property* (e.g., with schema properties `creates` and `name`). For someone interested only in database learning material, this view is much easier to understand. One can then easily formulate queries *on the view*, such as the following one in *RQL*:

```
SELECT Y
FROM {X}myview:creates{Y}, {X}myview:name{Z}
WHERE Z = "Professor A"
USING NAMESPACE myview=&http://www.ics.forth.gr/LO.rdf#
```

This query should retrieve the database courses created by the author named "Professor A".

3 RVL: A View Definition Language for RDF/S

Motivated by the previous example, a fundamental question one can naturally pose, is *"what is a good specification of views for the RDF/S data model?"*. We have designed *RVL* as a conceptually simple language enabling both humans and applications to understand view specifications as normal RDF/S schemas and resource descriptions. More precisely, an *RVL* view specifies a **virtual description schema** graph (or **virtual schema** for brevity). Its extension corresponds to a **virtual description base** graph (or **virtual base** for brevity), which is a valid instance of the virtual view schema. Thus, *RVL* views produce new RDF/S (meta)classes and properties which are **virtual** and their instances are computed from the **source** base(s) or schema(s) using the *RVL* program specifying the view. This program defines essentially the *mapping* (i.e., transformation) of the input (i.e., source) to the output (i.e., virtual) RDF/S graph(s).

3.1 RVL Design Choices

In order to design an effective RDF/S view specification language, we have addressed the following issues:

1. How are the virtual schema (meta)classes and properties of a view related to the source description schema(s)?
2. How are the virtual base resources and property values of a view related to source description base(s)?
3. What is the expressiveness of the input/output transformations supported by the view specification language?
4. How can the output of view specifications be used in queries and other views?

In the sequel, we will present the main design choices for *RVL* in response to the above fundamental issues.

Logical Data Independence is one of the most important properties that a view definition language should respect (recall the ANSI-SPARC three-level architecture [3]). It essentially requires that view specifications should be independent of those of the source schemas and bases, while the semantics of existing virtual schemas should not be altered by the definition of new ones. For this reason, the scope of virtual (meta)class and property definitions is determined in *RVL* by the namespace of the view. This is particularly useful since *RVL* allows us to not only create *new* (meta)classes and properties (as in Figure 2), but to also *import* in a view existing ones from the source schemas given as input. Imported (meta)classes and properties are simply replicated in the virtual schema and do not interfere with those at the source. Moreover, as we will see in Section 3.2, virtual subsumption hierarchies (for both classes and properties) could also be defined in a view, which are not necessarily present in the source schemas. Instead of creating a global subsumption hierarchy mixing both virtual and source (meta)classes and properties, an *RVL* virtual schema refers only to the subsumption relationships explicitly established between the virtual (meta)classes and properties. The separation of virtual from source (meta)classes and properties in *RVL* leads to smaller virtual schemas easier to understand and manage.

View Instantiation Capabilities. Besides the population of virtual (meta)classes and properties using, for instance, *RQL* queries (see Figure 2) over the original description base (i.e., **object-preserving views**), an *RVL* virtual schema can also be instantiated in the view (i.e., **object-generating views**) specification. These instances exist only during the activation of the view and their identifiers are generated by appropriate Skolem functions. As a matter of fact, the entire virtual schema specified in a view is essentially a new instance of the default RDF/S meta-schema (class and property names are used as unique identifiers)! As we will see in Section 3.2, this functionality is also useful in cases where virtual resource descriptions may have both a dynamic part populated with resources from the original base and a static one populated exclusively at the view level. *RVL* is powerful enough to support both kinds of view instantiation, while instances of the source schemas are simply copied into the view extension, thereby acquiring a virtual hypostasis.

Transformation Expressiveness is the cornerstone of the *RVL* design in order to cope with a wide range of heterogeneities found in real-scale Semantic Web applications [15,6]. Therefore, a view specification language should provide the ability to both create (for personalization purposes) and reconciliate (for mediation purposes) quite different conceptual representations of the same application domain. For this reason, *RVL* is equipped with *expressive restructuring* capabilities enabling users to change the abstraction level (i.e., metaschema, schema, data) in which a particular view construct is defined. As we will detail in Section 3.2, *RVL* is capable of "promoting" literals or resources of the original description base to virtual classes, as well as of "demoting" metaclasses of the original description schema to virtual classes of the view. This ability is ensured by the expressiveness of the *RQL* query language to query RDF/S information at all abstraction levels and the polymorphic type system of the *RVL* population functions (i.e., the `VIEW` clause) (see Table 1 in Appendix).

Closure of View Language. On the one hand, one should be able to query *RVL* views, as in the case of source schemas and description bases. Since *RVL* views introduce virtual schemas, one can use their namespace to formulate *RQL* queries (see previous section) retrieving (part of) the RDF/S graph specified by the view program. On the other hand, one should be able to create views using both source and virtual schemas. We can distinguish between two levels of view specification reuse: inside a virtual schema (intra-) and across (inter-) virtual schemas. Intra-view reuse is not supported by *RVL*, since it gives the possibility to define the extension of a virtual (meta)class based on the extension of another virtual construct of the same view. To ensure data independence and avoid cyclic declarations of virtual classes which are hard to grasp, we impose the following restriction: the `FROM` clause of *RQL* queries defining the population of the view constructs cannot refer to information (schema and data) of the view being defined. Only inter-view reuse is supported by *RVL* for creating virtual (meta)classes and properties by employing other virtual schemas. This process results in a cascade of virtual schema specifications, which ensures that the constructs of a virtual schema used in the definition of another virtual schema have already been defined.

The above design decisions were taken with the objective of devising a clear and expressive RDF/S view specification language required by a large spectrum of Semantic Web applications. In the sequel, we will detail how *RVL* implements this functionality.

3.2 RVL Operators

RVL reduces the creation of virtual schemas and description bases down to the use of two operators, namely the **instantiation** and the **subsumption** operators. In order to ensure the validity of their application and infer the type of virtual constructs, the operands of the *RVL* operators must be of a specific type, which is checked during compilation w.r.t the *RQL*/*RVL* type system using

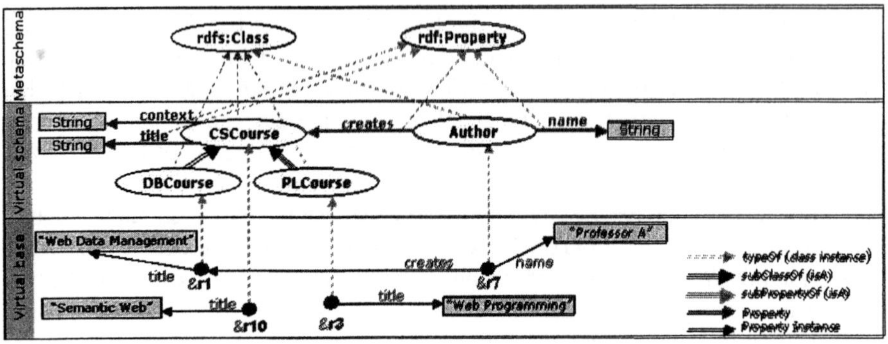

Fig. 3. A more complex *RVL* view

the typing rules presented in Table 1 in Appendix. In addition, the presence of this type system, facilitates a more compact declaration of view statements in the sense that the type of one entity in the source schema or base can be reused as such in the view. This ability does not prohibit users to alter the type of one element using the instantiation operator, as we will subsequently see in this section.

In the following, we will sketch the functionality supported by each operator by using the more complex view illustrated in Figure 3. This virtual schema is defined as a view on the schema of the motivating example in Figure 1 and refers to computer science courses —especially database and programming languages courses— and their authors. In each case, we cite the typing rule of Table 1 applicable for the specific operator.

The Instantiation Operator, denoted "`()`", exploits the existence of abstraction layers in an RDF/S graph to support: (a) the creation/import of virtual (meta)classes and properties and (b) the population of virtual (meta)classes and properties. The instantiation of a virtual construct should be performed only with resources at the immediate lower abstraction level (see rules `9-12` in Table 1). Changing the type of an RDF/S entity in an *RVL* view compared to a source schema or base (e.g., a literal to a class, or a metaclass to a class) is also supported using more complex *RVL* expressions.

Let us examine the functionality of the instantiation operator by means of the example view illustrated in Figure 3. In the simplest case, we are interested in creating new virtual classes as follows (see rule `3`):

```
VIEW Class("Author"),Class("CSCourse"),Class("DBCourse"),Class("PLCourse");
```

The first operand of "`()`" is the (meta)class (e.g., *Class*) one wants to populate with a new instance identified by the string value of the second operand (e.g., `Author`). Virtual metaclasses of classes and properties can be also created by instantiating the *RVL* built-in (meta)metaclasses *rvl:MetaClass* and *rvl:MetaProperty* (see rules `1` and `2` respectively). In order to import a part (i.e., a *set*) of the classes defined in a source schema, we need first to use an *RQL* filter in order to identify which classes (or properties) are going to be imported into the virtual schema and then, use the instantiation operator in the VIEW clause, as depicted by the following example (see rule 3):

```
VIEW Class(X)
FROM Class{X}
WHERE namespace(X) = ns1 and X < ns1:Learning_Object;
```

The *RQL* path expression *Class*{*X*} in the FROM clause introduces a variable X ranging over all classes, while the WHERE clause filters X bindings only to the subclasses (direct or transitive) of *Learning_Object* defined in the schema namespace *ns*1. The instantiation operator "()" in the VIEW clause simply creates new instances of *Class* for each successful binding of class variable X. Since in this case we are importing in the virtual schema classes as provided by the source schema, we can omit the explicit call to the instantiation operator by just writing VIEW X.

This abbreviation cannot be used when we transform ("promote" or "demote") the abstraction level (i.e., metaschema, schema, data) of constructs specified in the view w.r.t. their level in the source schema and base. Assuming, for instance, that the values of the property *subject* are not simple strings but terms from a structured vocabulary (e.g., ACM Computing Classification System[3]), one can easily create virtual classes from these values using the following *RVL* statement (see rule 3):

```
VIEW Class(X)
FROM ns1:subject{X};
```

In this example, string values will be used as unique names of the so created virtual classes. For this purpose, the instantiation operator uses appropriate Skolem functions: for two equal *subject* values, only one virtual class is created. This ability offers a great flexibility in view specification, especially in environments with highly diverse modelling of resource descriptions.

As far as **properties** are concerned, *RVL* follows the RDF/S approach to consider properties as first-class citizens. Thereby, their definition is independent of the definition of the class they are attributed to, while they can be specialized forming subsumption hierarchies. The restriction posed by the *RQL*/*RVL* data model is that the domain and range of a property must always be defined and be unique, thus the creation of a (virtual) property is accompanied with the definition of its domain and range classes (or metaclasses or literal types). To accommodate this peculiarity, the instantiation operator has a slightly different syntax. The first operand of the instantiation operator corresponds to the name of the core metaclass of properties (*Property*), the second to the name of the virtual property, the third to its domain and the fourth to its range. In the simplest case, we are interested in creating new virtual properties as follows (see rule 4):

```
VIEW Property("creates", Author, CSCourse),
     Property("name", Author, xsd:string),
     Property("context", CSCourse, xsd:string),
     Property("title", CSCourse, xsd:string);
```

[3] http://www.acm.org/class/1998/

This view statement creates four new instances of the metaclass *Property* uniquely identified by their names: the virtual property `creates` emanating from the virtual class `Author` and ranging over the virtual class `CSCourse`, as well as the virtual attributes `name`, `context` and `title` of type `string` having as domain respectively the virtual classes `Author` and `CSCourse`.

Due to the functional nature of *RVL*, the operands of the instantiation operator are not restricted to atoms (constants or variables), but can also be other *RVL*/*RQL* expressions of an appropriate type. For instance, we could define *inverse* properties using the following *RVL* statement (see rule 4):

```
VIEW Property("creator",range(ns1:createdBy),domain(ns1:createdBy));
```

In this example, the virtual property `creator` is created with domain and range the virtual classes `Contributor` and `Learning_Object` respectively returned by the employed *RQL* functions. This is an example of another possible *RVL* abbreviated expression: the domain and range virtual classes `Contributor` and `Learning_Object` are defined in the view at the same time as the property `creator`. The complete syntax of the `VIEW` clause comprises the expressions: `Class(domain(ns1:createdBy))` and `Class(range(ns1:createdBy))`.

As in the case of classes, we can import in the view a part (i.e., a *set*) of the properties defined in a source schema as follows (rule 4):

```
VIEW Property(P, CSCourse, range(P))
FROM Property{P}
WHERE domain(P)=ns1:Learning_Object and P < ns1:related;
```

According to our example of Figure 1, this *RVL* statement creates two instances of the metaclass *Property* with names `partof` and `hasPrerequisite` with domain the already defined virtual class `CSCourse` and with the same ranges as in the source schema identified by the namespace `ns1`.

Besides creating virtual schemas we also need to populate the virtual classes and properties specified in the view. The same instantiation operator is used for this purpose taking this time operands of different types. The additional restriction imposed in the case of properties is that the resources at the data level to which a property is attributed are instances of the domain and range classes of the property at schema level. The following two *RVL* statements populate the virtual classes and properties we defined above for the example of Figure 3 (see rules `11` and `12` respectively):

```
VIEW DBCourse(Y),creates(X,Y),Author(X),name(X,W),context(Y,Z),title(Y,K)
FROM {Y;ns1:Course}ns1:createdBy{X}.ns1:name{W}, {Y}ns1:context{Z},
     {Y}ns1:title{K}, {Y}ns1:subject{L}
WHERE L like "Database Management";
VIEW PLCourse(Y),creates(X,Y),Author(X),name(X,W),context(Y,Z),title(Y,K)
FROM {Y;ns1:Course}ns1:createdBy{X}.ns1:name{W}, {Y}ns1:context{Z},
     {Y}ns1:title{K}, {Y}ns1:subject{L}
WHERE L like "*Programming*";
```

The virtual class `DBCourse` (`PLCourse`) is populated with instances of the source class *Course* having a property *subject* valued "Database Management" ("Programming Techniques" or "Object-Oriented Programming"). The virtual class `Author` is populated in both cases by *Contributor* instances having created (property *createdBy*) *Course* instances on the desired *subject*. Virtual properties are populated in a similar way (`DBCourse` and `PLCourse` are defined as subclasses of `CSCourse` in the next section).

As a last example we illustrate how virtual classes (or properties) can be populated with virtual resources residing exclusively at the view. Assuming that an instructor wants also to include within the virtual base `CSCourses` published by himself, he/she can issue the following *RVL* statement (rules `11` and `12`):

```
VIEW CSCourse(&http://www.mycourses.net/~SemWeb),
     title(&http://www.mycourses.net/~SemWeb, "Semantic Web");
```

As we will see in the next subsection, by defining `DBCourse` and `PLCourse` as subclasses of `CSCourse`, the final population of `CSCourse` will contain its proper instances, as well as, those of its subclasses.

In more complex situations, an instructor may want to populate the `DBCourse` virtual class with resources from a source base, while complete their description manually, by adding, for instance, a learning `objective` property:

```
VIEW DBCourse(X),objective(X,"research tutorial")
FROM {X;ns1:Course}ns1:subject{Y},
WHERE Y like "Database Management";
```

The above *RVL* statement will create for each LO instance of `DBCourse` an `objective` property with value "research tutorial" (the property is assumed to be already defined in the view).

The Subsumption Operator, denoted "`< >`", is mainly used for defining virtual sub-(meta)classes or subproperties. Some restrictions are imposed on the use of this operator by the *RQL*/*RVL* data model. First, cycles in virtual class (or property) subsumption hierarchies are not allowed. Second, the domain and range of a property must be subsumed by the domain and range of its super properties. In addition, the subsumption operator is applicable on operands of the same type ((meta)/class and property types), since the formulation of hierarchies between entities of different type is meaningless (see rules `5-8` in Table 1).

In the simplest case one wants to explicitly define the subsumption relationship between two virtual (meta)classes or properties, as for instance in the following *RVL* statements:

```
VIEW CSCourse<DBCourse>;
VIEW CSCourse<PLCourse>;
```

The second operand (e.g., `DBCourse`) of "`< >`" is declared to be a subclass (or a subproperty) of the first one (e.g., `CSCourse`). Both operands in this example are of type class (see rule `7`).

As we have seen in the previous subsection, *RVL* gives us the ability to import a part of the source schema into the view. Using the subsumption operator in conjunction with *RQL* filters, we are able to import not only the source classes (or property) names but entire subsumption hierarchies from a source schema, as depicted in the following example:

```
VIEW $X<$Y>
FROM $X{;$Y}
WHERE namespace($X)=&www.eLearningPortal.gr/schema.rdf# and
      namespace($Y)=&www.eLearningPortal.gr/schema.rdf#;
```

The *RQL* path expression in the FROM clause essentially traverses the class subsumption hierarchy of the source schema identified by the namespace www.eLearningPortal.gr/schema.rdf. Then, for each binding of the class variable $\$X$ (e.g., to *Learning_Object*), the variable $\$Y$ is bind to the corresponding (direct of transitive) subclasses (e.g., to *Course*). The result of the original *RQL* query produces essentially a Cartesian product of each class with its subclasses. The use of the subsumption operator in the VIEW clause with operands the variables $\$X$ and $\$Y$ results in the reconstruction in the view of the original subsumption hierarchy of the source schema. It should be stressed that the above *RQL* path expression considers a complete transitive closure of the subsumption hierarchy (i.e., there are all the paths from a node to its ancestors up to the root). This is extremely useful when filtering conditions on class (or property) names are also used in the WHERE clause. For instance, the exclusion from the view of some source classes (e.g., *Program*) results into a "connected" hierarchy relating through subsumption subclasses (e.g., figures, exams, etc) to their ancestors(s) (e.g., *Learning_Object*). Since the use of appropriate labelling schemes for class (or property) DAGS [10] alleviates the need for actually computing the transitive closure, the subsumption operator can easily produce a *minimal* form in which redundant relationships are removed.

The *RVL* examples presented in this section were just indicative of *RVL*'s expressiveness. Consider the spectrum of possible views which can be defined by changing the operands of the subsumption and instantiation operators and by exploiting the querying capabilities of *RQL*. This expressiveness allows us to think of *RVL* as a powerful transformation mechanism for RDF/S schema and resource description graphs. In addition, *RVL* allows to capture in a view several modelling constructs recently proposed in OWL [11], such as inverse properties, synonyms of classes and properties or complex class definitions using boolean expressions and existential/universal quantifiers (supported by *RQL* filters).

4 Related Work

Several view specification languages have been proposed in the database literature. The most relevant to *RVL* is work conducted in the context of ODMG-compliant object-oriented DBMS, such as O_2 [1,18], MultiView [17], Chimera [13] and K2 [21]. These view specification languages extend the relational approach for defining views as "named queries" with features for creating virtual object schemas. Apart from the differences between the ODMG and RDF/S data models (e.g., sub-properties, multiple classification of objects, etc.) or between the underlying design choices (e.g., in transformation expressiveness), the main novelty of *RVL* compared to these languages lies in its flexibility to create virtual classes (or properties) using *RQL* queries. This functionality is particularly useful for Semantic Web applications managing large schemas in a peer-to-peer way.

Some view specification languages have also been proposed for the RDF/S data model. In [22], set-based operations have been introduced in order to define object-preserving views using an untyped version of *RQL*. Opposite to *RVL*, the logical data independence of views is violated by this language, since virtual and source classes are merged into one global schema, while restructuring constructs for subsumption hierarchies are not supported. An alternative approach has been proposed in [12], which relies on F-logic rules to define only virtual description bases. Unlike *RVL*, this language does not provide the means to define virtual RDF/S schema graphs using, for instance, meta-schema instantiation capabilities. In the same spirit, [2] proposes a variation of *RQL* in order to produce as a query result an output RDF resource description graph instead of variable bindings in some tabular form. To the best of our knowledge, *RVL* is the first language offering a full-fledged view specification for the RDF/S model.

5 Summary and Future Work

We have presented *RVL*, a language that brings a new kind of capability to the management of RDF/S metadata: users can create virtual schemas and resource descriptions customized to the needs of specific applications. By distinguishing the abstraction layers in an RDF/S application and by exploiting the *RQL* type system, *RVL* realizes the virtual schema creation as the instantiation of appropriate metaclasses and achieves its target functionality through the use of only two operators: the *instantiation* and the *subsumption* operators.

Several issues need to be dealt with in order to fully support a view definition mechanism for RDF/S. One of them is the *composition* of queries formulated against a view with the definition of the view in order to produce queries against the original RDF/S data that can be actually evaluated (thus avoiding the computation of the view data in its entirety). In relational databases composing SQL queries with SQL view definitions is fairly straightforward. Composing *RQL* queries with *RVL* views is more challenging and is a research target for us [20]. Another important issue is checking the *consistency* of view definitions, i.e., checking whether the graph they produce satisfies the constraints of our model. Again, we wish to develop methods for consistency checking that avoid the naive approach in which the entire view data is constructed and then validated. Lastly, although we have argued for the benefits of defining virtual views, it is possible to implement an *RVL* engine that would actually compute and *materialize* the views. Such a capability would be of interest in metadata transformation applications where, for example, subsidiary but independently functioning portals are created from a given central one. This raises the classical problem of maintenance/update of materialized views, a complex problem long pondered upon by the database community. In the context of RDF/S, this problem is even more interesting, due to the peculiarities of the data model.

References

1. Abiteboul, S., Bonner, A.: Objects and Views. In: Proceedings of the ACM SIGMOD International Conference on Management of Data, Denver, Colorado (1991) 238–247
2. Aidministrator Nederland bv: SeRQL user manual, Version:0.4 (2003), http://sesame.aidministrator.nl/publications/SeRQL
3. ANSI/X3/SPARC Study Group on Database Management Systems. Interim Report. ACM SIGMOD Bulletin 7, N2 (1975)
4. Berners-Lee, T., Fielding, R., Masinter, L.: Uniform Resource Identifiers (URI): Generic Syntax. RFC 2396, http://www.ietf.org/rfc/rfc2396.txt
5. Berners-Lee, T., Hendler, J., Lassila, O.: The Semantic Web. In: Scientific American (May, 2001), http://www.sciam.com/2001/0501issue/0501berners-lee.html
6. Bernstein, P., Levy, A., Pottinger, R.: A Vision for Management of Complex Models. Microsoft Research Technical Report MSR-TR-2000-53 (2000), http://research.microsoft.com/scripts/pubs/view.asp?TR_ID=MSR-TR-2000-53
7. Bray, T., Hollander, D., Layman, A.: Namespaces in XML. W3C Recommendation (1999)
8. Bray, T., Paoli, J., Sperberg-McQueen, C.M., Maler, E.: Extensible Markup Language (XML) 1.0 (Second Edition). W3C Recommendation (2000)
9. Brickley, D., Guha, R.V.: Resource Description Framework Schema (RDF/S) Specification 1.0. W3C Candidate Recommendation (2000)
10. Christophides, V., Plexousakis, D., Scholl, M., Tourtounis, S.: On Labeling Schemes for the Semantic Web. In: Proceedings of the 12th International World Wide Web Conference (WWW'03), Budapest, Hungary (2003)
11. Dean, M., Connolly, D., Van Harmelen, F., Hendler, J., Horrocks, I., McGuinness, D., Patel-Schneider, P., Stein, L.A.: OWL Web Ontology Language 1.0 Reference. W3C Working Draft (2002)
12. Decker, S., Sintek, M., Nejdl, W.: TRIPLE: A Logic for Reasoning with Parameterized Views over Semi-Structured Data. Technical Report (2002), http://www.kbs.uni-hannover.de/Arbeiten/Publikationen/2002/triple_views.pdf
13. Guerrini, G., Bertino, E., Catania, B., Garcia-Molina, J.: A Formal Model of Views for Object-Oriented Database Systems. Theory and Practice of Object Systems, 3(**3**) (1997) 157–183
14. Karvounarakis, G., Alexaki, S., Christophides, V., Plexousakis, D., Scholl, M.: RQL: A Declarative Query Language for RDF. In: Proceedings of the Eleventh International World Wide Web Conference 2002, Honolulu, Hawaii, USA (2002) 592–603
15. Klein, M.: Combining and Relating Ontologies: An Analysis of Problems and Solutions. In: Proceedings of the IJCAI'01 Workshop on Ontologies and Information Sharing, Seattle, USA (2001)
16. Lassila, O., Swick, R.: Resource Description Framework (RDF) Model and Syntax Specification. W3C Recommendation (1999)
17. Rundensteiner, E.: MultiView: A Methodology for Supporting Multiple View Schemata in Object-Oriented Databases. In: Proceedings of the 18th International Conference on Very Large Data Bases, Vancouver, Canada (1992) 187–198
18. Souza dos Santos, C., Abiteboul, S., Delobel, C.: Virtual Schemas and Bases. In: M. Jarke, J. Bubenko and K. Jeffery (editors): Proceedings of the Fourth International Conference on Extending Database Technology, St John's College, Cambridge, UK. Lecture Notes in Computer Science No. 779 (1994) 81–94

19. Stratakis, M., Christophides, V., Keenoy, K., Magkanaraki, A.: E-Learning Standards. SeLeNe Project Deliverable 2.1 (2003), http://www.dcs.bbk.ac.uk/ãp/projects/selene/
20. Tannen, V., Christophides, V., Karvounarakis, G., Koffina, I., Kokkinidis, G., Magkanaraki, A., Plexousakis, D., Serfiotis, G.: The ICS-FORTH SWIM: A Powerful Semantic Web Integration Middleware. Submitted for publication (2003)
21. Tannen, V., Davidson, S.B, Harker, S.: The Information Integration System K2. In: Bioinformatics: Managing Scientific Data, T. Critchlow and Z. Lacroix eds., Elsevier (2003)
22. Volz, R., Oberle, D., Studer, R.: Views for light-weight web ontologies. In: Proceedings of the ACM Symposium on Applied Computing SAC 2003, Melbourne, Florida, USA (2003)

Appendix: *RVL* Typing Rules

The type system foreseen by *RQL* [14] specifies a set of types, namely the `metaclass of classes` (MC) (τ_{M_c}), `metaclass of properties` (MP) (τ_{M_p}),

Table 1. *RVL* Typing rules

Operation	Typing Rule	
`MC creation`	$\dfrac{e_1:\omega_C, e_2:\tau, \tau \in \{string, \tau_{M_c}, \tau_{M_p}, \tau_C, \tau_P, \tau_U\}}{e_1(e_2) : \tau_{M_c}}$	(1)
`MP creation`	$\dfrac{e_1:\omega_P, e_2:\tau, \tau \in \{string, \tau_{M_c}, \tau_{M_p}, \tau_C, \tau_P, \tau_U\}}{e_1(e_2) : \tau_{M_p}}$	(2)
`Class creation`	$\dfrac{e_1:\tau_{M_c}, e_2:\tau, \tau \in \{string, \tau_{M_c}, \tau_{M_p}, \tau_C, \tau_P, \tau_U\}}{e_1(e_2) : \tau_C}$	(3)
`Property Creation`	$\dfrac{e:\tau_{M_p}, e_1:\tau_1, \tau_1 \in \{string, \tau_{M_c}, \tau_{M_p}, \tau_C, \tau_P\} \quad e_2:\tau_2, \tau_2 \in \{\tau_{M_c}, \tau_{M_p}, \tau_C\}, e_3:\tau_3, \tau_3 \in \{\tau_{M_c}, \tau_{M_p}, \tau_C, \tau_L\}}{e(e_1, e_2, e_3) : \tau_P[\tau_2, \tau_3]}$	(4)
`MC subsumption`	$\dfrac{e_1:\tau_{M_c}, e_2:\tau_{M_c}}{e_1 < e_2 >: [\tau_{M_c}, \tau_{M_c}]}$	(5)
`MP subsumption`	$\dfrac{e_1:\tau_{M_p}, e_2:\tau_{M_p}}{e_1 < e_2 >: [\tau_{M_p}, \tau_{M_p}]}$	(6)
`Class subsumption`	$\dfrac{e_1:\tau_C, e_2:\tau_C}{e_1 < e_2 >: [\tau_C, \tau_C]}$	(7)
`Property Subsumption`	$\dfrac{e_1:\tau_P, e_2:\tau_P}{e_1 < e_2 >: [\tau_P, \tau_P]}$	(8)
`MC population`	$\dfrac{e_1:\tau_{M_c}, e_2:\tau_C}{e_1(e_2) : \tau_C}$	(9)
`MP population`	$\dfrac{e_1:\tau_{M_p}, e_2:\tau_P}{e_1(e_2) : \tau_P}$	(10)
`Class population`	$\dfrac{e_1:\tau_C, e_2:\tau_U}{e_1(e_2) : \tau_U}$	(11)
`Property population`	$\dfrac{e:\tau_P, e_1:\tau_1, \tau_1 \in \{\tau_U, \tau_C, \tau_P\}, e_2:\tau_2, \tau_2 \in \{\tau_U, \tau_C, \tau_P, \tau_L\}}{e(e_1, e_2) : [\tau_1, \tau_2]}$	(12)

`class` (τ_C), `property` ($\tau_P[\tau,\tau]$), `resource URIs` (τ_U), `literal` (τ_L) (XML Schema data types), `bag` ($\{.\}$), `sequence` ($[.]$) and `alternative` ($(.)$) types. The notation $\tau_P[\tau,\tau]$ for property types indicates the exact type of its domain (metaclass and class types) and range (metaclass, class and literal types) (first and second position in the sequence). For brevity, we use the notation τ_P for property types. *RVL* extends this type system by specifying two more metaschema types, ω_C and ω_P, used by the instantiation operator to created user-defined metaclasses of classes and properties respectively. The restrictions and inferences specified by *RVL* are captured by the typing rules presented in Table 1. Each rule represents the drawing of a conclusion (the part below the horizontal line) on the basis of a premise (the part above the horizontal line). For instance, rule 12 states that: "*If e is an expression of property type and* e_1 *and* e_2 *are expressions of types* τ_1 *(resource, class or property) and* τ_2 *(resource, class, property or literal) respectively, then* $e(e_1, e_2)$ *is a valid expression of type sequence of types* τ_1 *and* τ_2*. Otherwise, a type error is returned*".

Infrastructure for Web Explanations

Deborah L. McGuinness and Paulo Pinheiro da Silva

Knowledge Systems Laboratory,
Stanford University, Stanford CA 94305
{dlm,pp}@ksl.stanford.edu

Abstract. The Semantic Web lacks support for explaining knowledge provenance. When web applications return answers, many users do not know what information sources were used, when they were updated, how reliable the source was, or what information was looked up versus derived. The Semantic Web also lacks support for explaining reasoning paths used to derive answers. The Inference Web (IW) aims to take opaque query answers and make the answers more transparent by providing explanations. The explanations include information concerning where answers came from and how they were derived (or retrieved). In this paper we describe an infrastructure for IW explanations. The infrastructure includes: an extensible web-based registry containing details on information sources, reasoners, languages, and rewrite rules; a portable proof specification; and a proof and explanation browser. Source information in the IW registry is used to convey knowledge provenance. Representation and reasoning language axioms and rewrite rules in the IW registry are used to support proofs, proof combination, and semantic web agent interoperability. The IW browser is used to support navigation and presentations of proofs and their explanations. The Inference Web is in use by two Semantic Web agents using an embedded reasoning engine fully registered in the IW. Additional reasoning engine registration is underway in order to help provide input for evaluation of the adequacy, breadth, and scalability of our approach.

1 Introduction

Inference Web (IW) aims to enable applications to generate portable and distributed explanations for any of their answers. IW addresses needs that arise with systems performing reasoning and retrieval tasks in heterogeneous environments such as the web. Users (humans and computer agents) need to decide when to trust answers from varied sources. We believe that the key to trust is understanding. Explanations of knowledge provenance and derivation history can be used to provide that understanding [16]. In the simplest case, users would retrieve information from individual or multiple sources and they may need knowledge provenance (e.g., source identification, source recency, authoritativeness, etc.) before they decide to trust an answer. Users may also obtain information from systems that manipulate data and derive information that was implicit rather than explicit. Users may need to inspect the deductive proof trace that was used

D. Fensel et al. (Eds.): ISWC 2003, LNCS 2870, pp. 113–129, 2003.

to derive implicit information before they trust the system answer. Many times proof traces are long and complex so users may need the proof transformed (or abstracted) into something more understandable that we call an explanation. Some users may agree to trust the deductions if they know what reasoner was used to deduce answers and what data sources were used in the proof. Users may also obtain information from hybrid and distributed systems and they may need help integrating answers and solutions. As web usage grows, a broader and more distributed array of information services becomes available for use and the needs for explanations that are portable, sharable, and reusable grows. Inference web addresses the issues of knowledge provenance with its registry infrastructure. It also addresses the issues of proof tracing with its browser. It addresses the issues of explanations (proofs transformed by rewrite rules for understandability) with its language axioms and rewrite rules. IW addresses the needs for combination and sharing with its portable proof specification.

In this paper, we include a list of explanation requirements gathered from past work, literature searches, and from surveying users. We present the Inference Web architecture and provide a description of the major IW components including the portable proof specification, the registry [17] (containing information about inference engines, proof methods, ontologies, and languages and their axioms), the explanation mechanism, and the justification browser. We also provide some simple usage examples. We conclude with a discussion of our work in the context of explanation work and state our contributions with respect to trust and reuse.

2 Background and Related Work

Recognition of the importance of explanation components for reasoning systems has existed in a number of fields for many years. For example, from the early days in expert systems (e.g., MYCIN [18]), expert systems researchers identified the need for systems that understood their reasoning processes and could generate explanations in a language understandable to its users. Inference Web attempts to stand on the shoulders of past work in expert systems, such as MYCIN and the Explainable Expert System [20] on generating explanations.

IW also builds on the learnings of explanation in description logics (e.g., [1,2, 13,14]) which attempt to provide a logical infrastructure for separating pieces of logical proofs and automatically generating follow-questions based on the logical format. IW goes beyond this work in providing an infrastructure for explaining answers in a distributed, web-based environment possibly integrating many question answering agents using multiple reasoners. IW also attempts to integrate learnings from the theorem proving community on proof presentation(e.g., [4,9]) and explanation (e.g., [12]), moving from proof tracing presentation to abstractions and understandable explanations. IW attempts to learn from this and push the explanation component started in Huang's work and also add the emphasis on provenance and distributed environments.

The work in this paper also builds on experience designing query components for frame-like systems [3,10,13] to generate requirements. The foundational work in those areas typically focus on answers and only secondarily on information supporting the understanding of the answers. In our requirements gathering effort, we obtained requirements input from contractors in DARPA-sponsored programs concerning knowledge-based applications (the High Performance Knowledge Base program[1], Rapid Knowledge Formation Program[2], and the DARPA Agent Markup Language Program[3]) and more recently, the ARDA AQUAINT[4] and NIMD[5] programs and DARPA's IPTO Office programs. We also gathered requirements from work on the usability of knowledge representation systems (e.g., [15]) and ontology environments (e.g., [8]). We have also gathered needs from the World Wide Web Consortium efforts on CWM[6] and the related reasoner effort on Euler[7]. Finally, we gathered knowledge provenance requirements from the programs above and from previous work on data provenance from the database community(e.g., [5]).

3 Requirements

If humans and agents need to make informed decisions about when and how to use answers from applications, there are many things to consider. Decisions will be based on the quality of the source information, the suitability and quality of the reasoning/retrieval engine, and the context of the situation. Particularly for use on the web, information needs to be available in a distributed environment and be interoperable across applications.

3.1 Support for Knowledge Provenance

Even when search engines or databases simply retrieve asserted or "told" information, users (and agents) may need to understand where the source information came from with varying degrees of detail. Similarly, even if users are willing to trust the background reasoner in a question answering environment, they may need to understand where the background reasoner obtained its ground facts. Information about the origins of asserted facts, sometimes called provenance, may be viewed as meta information about told information. Knowledge provenance requirements may include:

- Source name (e.g., CIA World Fact Book). If facts are encountered in multiple sources, any integrated solution needs to have a way of identifying from which source information was taken.

[1] http://reliant.teknowledge.com/HPKB/
[2] http://reliant.teknowledge.com/RKF/
[3] http://www.daml.org
[4] http://www.ic-arda.org/InfoExploit/aquaint/
[5] http://www.ic-arda.org/Novel_Intelligence/
[6] http://www.w3.org/2000/10/swap/doc/cwm.html
[7] http://www.agfa.com/w3c/euler/

- Date and author(s) of original information and any updates
- Authoritativeness of the source (is this knowledge store considered or certified as reliable by a third party?)
- Degree of belief (is the author certain about the information?)
- Degree of completeness (Within a particular scope, is the source considered complete. For example, does this source have information about all of the employees of a particular organization up until a some date? If so, not finding information about a particular employee would mean that this person is not employed, counting employees would be an accurate response to number of employees, etc.)

The information above could be handled with meta information about content sources and about individual assertions. Additional types of information may be required if users need to understand the meaning of terms or implications of query answers.

- Term or phrase meaning (in natural language or a formal language)
- Term inter-relationships (ontological relations including subclass, superclass, part-of, etc.)

3.2 Support for Reasoning Information

Once systems do more than simple retrieval, additional requirements result. If information is manipulated as a result of integration, synthesis, abstraction, deduction, etc., then users may need access to a trace of the manipulations performed along with information about the manipulations as well as information about the provenance. We refer to this as reasoning traces or proof traces. Requirements as a result of reasoning may include the following:

- The reasoner used
- Reasoning method (e.g., tableaux, model elimination, etc.)
- Inference rules supported by the reasoner
- Reasoner soundness and completeness properties
- Reasoner assumptions (e.g., closed world vs. open world, unique names assumption, etc.)
- Reasoner authors, version, etc.
- Detailed trace of inference rules applied (with appropriate variable bindings) to provide conclusion
- Term coherence (is a particular definition incoherent?)
- Were assumptions used in a derivation? If so, have the assumptions changed?
- Source consistency (is there support in a system for both A and $\neg$A)
- Support for alternative reasoning paths to a single conclusion

3.3 Support for Explanation Generation

While knowledge provenance and proof traces may be enough for expert logicians when they attempt to understand why an answer was returned, usually they are inadequate for a typical user. For our purposes, we view an explanation as a transformation of a proof trace into an understandable justification for an answer. With this view in mind, we consider techniques for taking proofs and proof fragments and rewriting them into abstractions that produce the foundation for what is presented to users. In order to handle rewriting, details of the representation and reasoning language must be captured along with their intended semantics. Requirements for explanations may include:

- Representation language descriptions (e.g., DAML+OIL, OWL, RDF, ...)
- Axioms capturing the semantics of the representation languages
- Description of rewriting rules based on language axioms

3.4 Support for Distributed Proofs

Much of the past work on explanation, whether from expert systems, theorem proving, or description logics, has focused on single systems or integrated systems that either use a single reasoner or use one integrated reasoning system. Systems being deployed on the web are moving to distributed environments where source information is quite varied and sometimes question answering systems include hybrid reasoning techniques. Additionally multi-agent systems may provide inference by many applications. Thus many additional requirements for proofs and their explanations may arise from a distributed architecture. Some requirements we are addressing are listed below:

- Reasoner result combinations (if a statement is proved by one system and another system uses that statement as a part of another proof, then the second system needs to have access to the proof trace from the first system).
- Portable proof interlingua (if two or more systems need to share proof fragments, they need an language for sharing proofs).

3.5 Support for Proof Presentation

If humans are expected to view proofs and their explanations, presentation support needs to be provided. Human users will need some help in asking questions, obtaining manageable size answers, asking followup question, etc. Additionally, even agents need some control over proof requests. If agents request very large proofs, they may need assistance in breaking them into appropriate size portions and also in asking appropriate follow-up questions. Requirements for proof presentation may include:

- A method for asking for explanations (or proofs)
- A way of breaking up proofs into manageable pieces
- A method for pruning proofs and explanations to help the user find relevant information
- A method for allowing proof and explanation navigation (including the ability to ask followup questions)
- A presentation solution compatible with web browsers
- A way of seeing alternative justifications for answers

4 Use Cases

Every combination of a query language with a query-answering environment is a potential new context for the Inference Web. We provide two motivating scenarios. Consider the situation where someone has analyzed a situation previously and wants to retrieve this analysis. In order to present the findings, the analyst may need to defend the conclusions by exposing the reasoning path used along with the source of the information. In order for the analyst to reuse the previous work, s/he will also need to decide if the source information used previously is still valid (and possibly if the reasoning path is still valid).

Another simple motivating example arises when a user asks for information from a web application and then needs to decide whether to act on the information. For example, a user might use a search engine interface or a query language such as DQL[8] for retrieving information such as "zinfandels from Napa Valley" or "wine recommended for serving with a spicy red meat meal" (as exemplified in the wine agent example in the OWL guide document [19]). A user might ask for an explanation of why the particular wines were recommended as well as why any particular property of the wine was recommended (like flavor, body, color, etc.). The user may also want information concerning whose recommendations these were (a wine store trying to move its inventory, a wine writer, etc.). In order for this scenario to be operationalized, we need to have the following:

- A way for applications (reasoners, retrieval engines, etc.) to dump justifications for their answers in a format that others can understand. This supports the distributed proofs requirements above. To solve this problem we introduce a portable and sharable proof specification.
- A place for receiving, storing, manipulating, annotating, comparing, and returning meta information used to enrich proofs and proof fragments. To address this requirement, we introduce the Inference Web registry for storing the meta information and the Inference Web registrar web application for handling the registry. This addresses the issues related to knowledge provenance.
- A way to present justifications to the user. Our solution to this has multiple components. First the IW browser is capable of navigating through proof dumps provided in the portable proof format. It can display multiple formats including KIF[9] and English. Additionally, it is capable of using rewrite rules (or tactics) to abstract proofs in order to provide more understandable explanations. This addresses the issues related to reasoning, explanations, and presentation.

5 Inference Web

Inference Web contains both data used for proof manipulation and tools for building, maintaining, presenting, and manipulating proofs. Figure 1 presents an

[8] http://www.daml.org/2002/08/dql/

[9] http://logic.stanford.edu/kif/kif.html

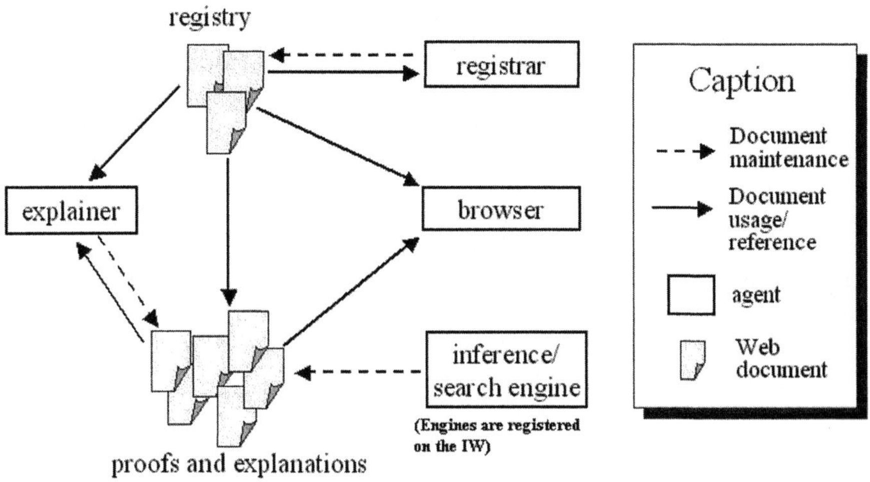

Fig. 1. Inference Web framework overview.

abstract and partial view of the Inference Web framework[10]. There, Inference Web data includes proofs and explanations published anywhere on the web. Inference and search engines can generate proofs using the IW format. The explainer, an IW tool, can abstract proofs into explanations. Inference Web data also has a distributed repository of meta-data including sources, inference engines, inference rules and ontologies. In addition to the explainer, Inference Web tools include a registrar for interacting with the registry, a browser for displaying proofs, and planned future tools such as proof web-search engines, proof verifiers, proof combinators, and truth maintenance systems. In this paper, we limit our discussion to the portable proofs (and an associated parser), registry (and the associated registrar tools), explanations, and the browser.

5.1 Portable Proof

The Inference Web provides a proof specification written in the web markup language DAML+OIL[11] [7]. Proofs dumped in the portable proof format become a portion of the Inference Web data used for combining and presenting proofs and for generating explanations. Our portable proof specification includes two major components of IW proof trees: inference steps and node sets. Proof metadata as described in Section 5.2 are the other components of our proof specification.

Figure 2 presents a typical dump of an IW node set. Each node set is labeled by a well formed formula (WFF) written in KIF. (In this example, the node set is labeled with a WFF stating that the color of `W1` is `?x` or the value of the color property of `Wine1` is the item of interest.) The node set represents a

[10] A more detailed view is available at http://ksl.stanford.edu/software/IW/details.shtml

[11] An OWL version is coming soon.

statement and the last step in a deductive path that led a system to derive the statement. It is a set because there could be multiple deductive paths leading to the statement.

Figure 2 shows an instance of a node set, an inference step, and a reference to an inference rule. There is no source associated with this node set since it is derived (although it could be derived and associated with a source). If it had been asserted, it would require an association to a source, which is typically an ontology that contains it. In general, each node set can be associated with multiple, one, or no inference steps as described by the `iw:isConsequentOf` property of the node set in Figure 2. A proof can then be defined as a tree of inference steps explaining the process of deducing the consequent sentence. Thus, a proof can physically vary from a single file containing all its node sets to many files, each one containing a single node set. Also, files containing node sets can be distributed in the web. Considering the IW requirement that proofs need to be combinable, it is important to emphasize that an IW proof is a forest of trees since the nodes of a proof tree are sets of inference steps. In contrast with typical proof trees that are composed of nodes rather than node sets, every theorem in an IW proof can have multiple justifications.

An inference step is a single application of an inference rule, whether the rule is atomic or derived as discussed in Section 5.2. Inference rules (such as modus ponens) can be used to deduce a consequent (a well formed formula) from any number of antecedents (also well formed formulae). Inference steps contain pointers to proof nodes of its antecedents, the inference rule used, and any variable bindings used in the step. The antecedent sentence in an inference step may come from inference steps in other node sets, existing ontologies, extraction from documents, or they may be assumptions.

With respect to a query, a logical starting point for a proof in Inference Web is a proof fragment containing the last inference step used to derive a node set that contains the answer sentence for the query. Any inference step can be presented as a stand alone, meaningful proof fragment as it contains the inference rule used with links to its antecedents and variable bindings. The generation of proof fragments is a straightforward task once inference engine data structures storing proof elements are identified as IW components. To facilitate the generation of proofs, the Inference Web provides a web service that dumps proofs from IW components and uploads IW components from proofs. This service is a language-independent facility used to dump proofs. Also, it is a valuable mechanism for recording the usage of registry entries.

The IW infrastructure can automatically generate follow-up questions for any proof fragment by asking how each antecedent sentence was derived. The individual proof fragments may be combined together to generate a complete proof, i.e., a set of inference steps culminating in inference steps containing only asserted (rather than derived) antecedents. When an antecedent sentence is asserted, there are no additional follow-up questions required and that ends the complete proof generation. The specification of IW concepts used in Figure 2 is available at http://www.ksl.stanford.edu/software/IW/spec/iw.daml.

```
<?xml version='1.0'?> <rdf:RDF (...)>
<iw:NodeSet rdf:about='../sample/IW1.daml#IW1'>
    <iw:NodeSetContent>
      <iw:KIF>
         <iw:Statement>(wines:COLOR W1 ?x)</iw:Statement>
      </iw:KIF>
    </iw:NodeSetContent>
    <iw:isConsequentOf rdf:parseType='daml:collection'>
         (a NodeSet can be associated to a set of Inference steps)
     <iw:InferenceStep>
        <iw:hasInferenceRule rdf:parseType='daml:collection'>
          <iw:InferenceRule rdf:about='../registry/IR/GMP.daml'/>
        </iw:hasInferenceRule>
        <iw:hasInferenceEngine rdf:parseType='daml:collection'>
           <iw:InferenceEngine rdf:about='../registry/IE/JTP.daml'/>
         </iw:hasInferenceEngine>
         (...)
        <iw:has Antecedent rdf:parseType='daml:collection'>
            (inference step antecedents are IW files with their own URIs)
          <iw:NodeSet rdf:about='../sample/IW3.daml#IW3'/>
          <iw:NodeSet rdf:about='../sample/IW4.daml#IW3'/>
        </iw:hasAntecedent>
        <iw:hasVariableMapping
               rdf:type='http://www.daml.org/2001/03/daml+oil#List'/>
        (...)
      </iw:InferenceStep>
    </iw:isConsequentOf>
  </iw:NodeSet>
</rdf:RDF>
```

Fig. 2. An Inference Web Proof.

5.2 Registry

The IW registry is a hierarchical interconnection of distributed repositories of information relevant to proofs and explanations. Entries in the registry contain the information linked to in the proofs. Every entry in the registry is a file written in DAML+OIL. Also, every entry is an instance of a registry concept. *InferenceEngine*, *Language* and *Source* are the core concepts in the registry. Other concepts in the registry are related to one of these core concepts.

In order to interact with the IW registry, the IW provides a web agent registrar that supports users in updating or browsing the registry. The registrar may grant update or access privileges on a concept basis and it may define and implement policies for accessing the registry. The current demonstration registrar is available at: http://onto.stanford.edu:8080/iwregistrar/.

The *InferenceEngine* is a core concept since every inference step should have a link to at least one entry of *InferenceEngine* that was responsible for instantiating the inference step itself. For instance, Figure 2 shows that the `iw:hasInferenceEngine` property of `iw:InferenceStep` has a pointer to `JTP.-`

`daml`, which is the registry meta information about Stanford's JTP[12] model-elimination theorem prover. Inference engines may have the following properties associated with them: name, URL, author(s), date, version number, organization, etc. *InferenceRule* is one of the most important concepts associated with *InferenceEngine*. With respect to an inference engine, registered rules can be either atomic or derived from other registered rules.

A screen shot from an IW registrar interface browsing the entry for the generalized modus ponens (GMP) rule is presented in Figure 3. GMP is an atomic inference rule for JTP[13]. Each of the inference rules includes a name, description, optional example, and optional formal specification. An inference rule is formally specified by a set of sentences patterns for its premises, a sentence pattern for its conclusion, and optional side conditions. Patterns and conditions are specified using KIF and a set of name conventions for KIF arguments. For example, an argument `@Si` such as the `@S1` and `@S2` in Figure 3 says that it can be bound to a sentence while `@SSi` says that it can be bound to a set of sentences. Many reasoners also use a set of derived rules that may be useful for optimization or other efficiency concerns. One individual reasoner may not be able to provide a proof of any particular derived rule but it may point to another reasoner's proof of a rule. Thus, reasoner-specific rules can be explained in the registry before the reasoner is actually used to generate IW proofs. Inference Web thus provides a way to use one reasoner to explain another reasoner's inference rules. (This was the strategy used in [2] for example where the performance tableaux reasoner was explained by a set of natural-deduction style inference rules in the explanation system.) This strategy may be useful for explaining heavily optimized inference engines. Inference Web's registry, when fully populated, will contain inference rule sets for many common reasoning systems. In this case, users may view inference rule sets to help them decide whether to use a particular inference engine.

Inference engines may use specialized language axioms to support a language such as DAML or RDF. *Language* is a core IW concept. Axiom sets such as the one specified in [11] may be associated with a *Language*. The axiom set may be used as a source and specialized rewrites of those axioms may be used by a particular theorem prover to reason efficiently. Thus proofs may depend upon these language-specific axioms sets called *LanguageAxiomSet* in the IW. It is worth noting that an entry of *Language* may be associated with a number of entries of *LanguageAxiomSet* as different reasoners may find different sets of axioms to be more useful. For example, JTP uses a horn-style set of DAML axioms while another reasoner may use a slightly different set. Also, an entry of an *Axiom* can be included in multiple entries of *LanguageAxiomSet*. The content attribute of *Axiom* entries contains the axiom stated in KIF.

Source is the other core concept of the registry. *Source* is specialized into five basic classes: *Person*, *Team*, *Publication*, *Ontology*, and *Organization*. At

[12] http://www.ksl.stanford.edu/software/jtp/

[13] GMP or any rule may be atomic for one reasoner while it may be derived for another reasoner.

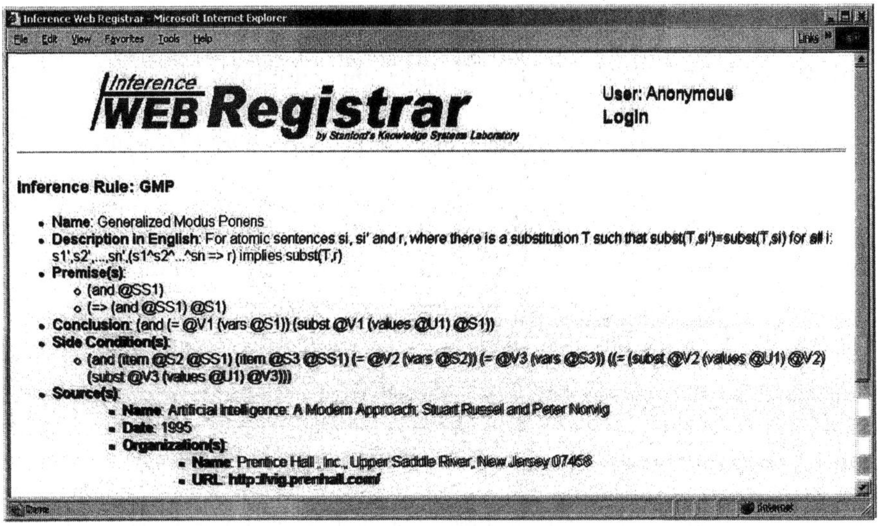

Fig. 3. Sample registry entry for an inference rule.

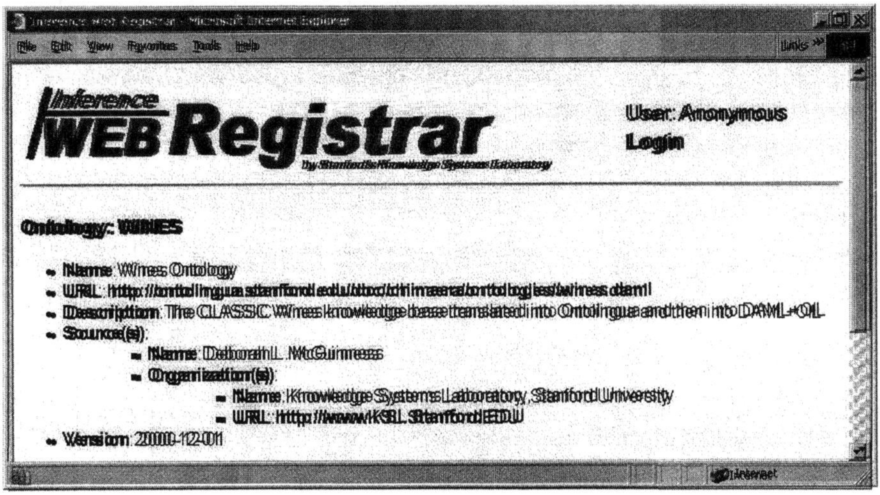

Fig. 4. Sample registry entry for an ontology.

the moment, we are expanding the specification of (authoritative) sources as required. Thus, we are keeping a minimal description of these sources in the initial specification used in the IW. Entries of *Ontology*, for example, describe stores of assertions that may be used in proofs. It can be important to be able to present information such as ontology source, date, version, URL (for browsing), etc. Figure 4 contains a sample ontology registry entry for the ontology used in our wine examples.

5.3 Explanations

Although essential for automated reasoning, inference rules such as those used by theorem provers and registered in the registry as *InferenceRule* entries are often inappropriate for "explaining" reasoning tasks. Moreover, syntactic manipulations of proofs based on atomic inference rules may also be insufficient for abstracting machine-generated proofs into some more understandable proofs [12]. Proofs, however, can be abstracted when they are rewritten using rules derived from axioms and other rules. Axioms in rewriting rules are the elements responsible for aggregating some semantics in order to make the rules more understandable. Entries of *DerivedRule* are the natural candidates for storing specialized sets of rewriting rules. In the IW, tactics are rules associated with axioms, and are used independent of whether a rule is atomic or derived.

Many intermediate results are "dropped" along with their supporting axioms, thereby abstracting the structure of proofs. The user may always ask follow-up questions and still obtain the detail, however the default explanation provides abstracted explanations. The general result is to hide the core reasoner rules and expose abstractions of the higher-level derived rules. An example of an IW explanation is described in the Inference Web web page at: http://www.ksl.stanford.edu/software/iw/Ex1/. The implementation of the IW explainer is work in progress. The explainer algorithm generate explanations in a systematic way using the derived rules related to a selected language axiom set.

5.4 Browser

Inference Web includes a browser that can display both proofs and their explanations in a number of proof styles and sentence formats. Initially, we include the "English", "Proof" and "Dag" styles and the restricted "English" and "KIF" formats[14]. We also expect that some applications may implement their own displays using the IW API. The browser implements a lens metaphor responsible for rendering a fixed number of levels of inference steps depending on the lens magnitude setting. The prototype browser allows a user to see up to five levels of inference steps simultaneously along with their derived sentences and antecedent sentences.

Figure 5 presents two levels of inference step for one wine use case in Section 4. Prior to this view, the program has asked what wine to serve with a seafood course. In Figure 5, one can see that `New-course`, which is the selected meal course, requires a drink that has a white color since it is a seafood course. The sentences are formatted in English and the lens magnitude is two, thus the browser displays the inference steps used to derive it including its antecedents and the antecedent's derivations.

We believe that one of the keys to presentation of justifications is breaking proofs into separable pieces. Since we present fragments, automatic follow-up

[14] Current investigations are underway for an N3 format as well.

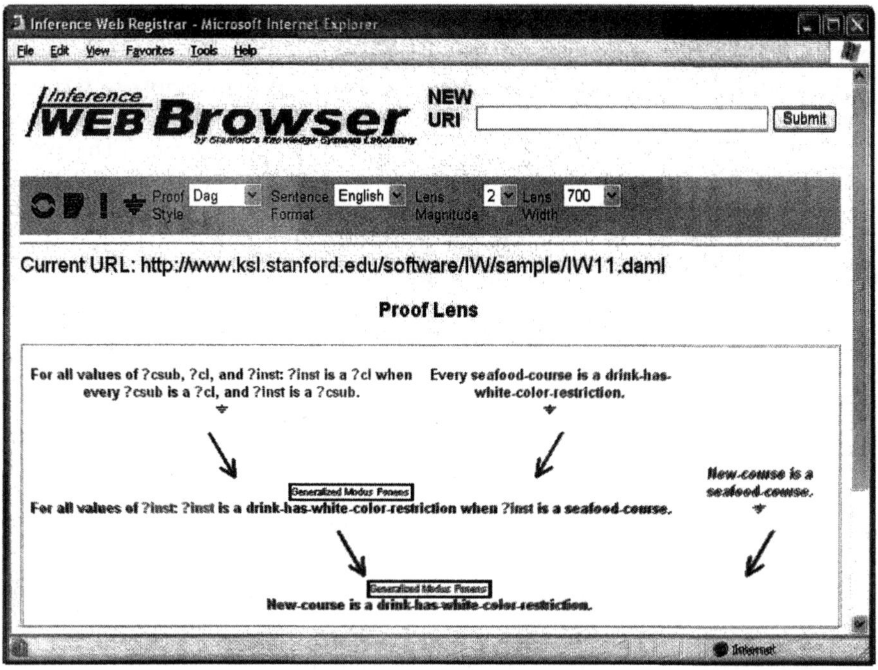

Fig. 5. An Inference Web Browser screen.

question support is a critical function of the IW browser. Every element in the viewing lens can trigger a browser action. The selection of an antecedent refocuses the lens on an antecedent's inference step. For other lens elements, associated actions present registry meta-information. The selection of the consequent presents details about the inference engine used to derive the actual theorem. The selection of an inference rule presents a description of the rule. The selection of the source icon beside sentences associated with source documents presents details about sources where the axiom is defined. In Figure 5, selecting the consequent would present information about JTP - the inference engine used to derive it. Selecting GMP - the inference rule, would present information about JTP's Generalized Modus Ponens rule as presented in Figure 3.

6 Contributions and Future Work

The Wine Agent[15] and the DAML Query Language Front-End[16] are Semantic Web agents supported by the Inference Web. These agents are based on the Stanford's JTP theorem prover that produces portable proofs. The IW registry is populated with JTP information: one *InferenceEngine* entry for the reasoner

[15] http://onto.stanford.edu:8080/wino/

[16] http://onto.stanford.edu:8080/dql/servlet/DQLFrontEnd

itself, nine entries for its primitive inference rules, one entry for its set of DAML axioms, and 56 entries for the axioms.

Beyond just explaining a single system, Inference Web attempts to incorporate best in class explanations and provide a way of combining and presenting proofs that are available. It does not take one stance on the form of the explanation since it allows deductive engines to dump single or multiple explanations of any deduction in the deductive language of their choice. It provides the user with flexibility in viewing fragments of single or multiple explanations in multiple formats. IW simply requires inference rule registration and portable proof format.

Revisiting the Inference Web requirements in Section 3, we can identify the following contributions:

- *Support for knowledge provenance* is provided by: the portable proof specification that allows node sets to be associated with sources; and the registry that supports meta information for annotating sources.
- *Support for reasoning information* is provided by: the proof specification that supports a comprehensive representation of proof trees; and the registry that supports meta information for annotating inference engines along with their primitive inference rules. Also, the proof specification provides support for alternative justifications by allowing multiple inference steps per node set and the proof browser supports navigation of the information.
- *Support for explanation generation* is provided by the registry that supports both formal and informal information about languages, axioms, axiom sets, derived and rewrite rules. Rewrite rules provide the key to abstracting complicated proofs into more understandable explanations. The proof support for alternative justifications allows derivations to be performed by performance reasoners with explanations being generated by alternative reasoners aimed at human consumption.
- *Support for distributed proofs* are provided by the IW architecture. Portable proofs are specified in the emerging web standard DAML+OIL so as to leverage XML-, RDF-, and DAML-based information services. Proof fragments as well as entire proofs may be combined and interchanged.
- *Support for proof presentation* is provided by a lightweight proof browsing using the lens-based IW browser. The browser can present either pruned justifications or guided viewing of a complete reasoning path.

We are currently extending SRI's SNARK[17] theorem prover to produce portable proofs and simultaneously populating the IW registry with SNARK information. Also, we are in the process of discussing the registration of the W3C's CWM[18] theorem prover in the Inference Web.

Future work includes the registration of more inference engines. Explanations for some proofs can be automatically created as presented in http://www.

[17] http://www.ai.sri.com/~stickel/snark.html
[18] http://www.w3.org/2000/10/swap/doc/cwm.html

ksl.stanford.edu/software/IW/Ex1. Currently, we are developing tools for generating tactics that are required for explaining other proofs. We also intend to provide specialized support for why-not questions expanding upon [6] and [13]. We are also looking at additional support for proof browsing and pruning. We have also initiated conversations with the verification community in order to provide a portable proof and registry format that meets their needs as well as meeting the needs of the applications that require explanation. Initial discussions at least for utilizing registry inference rule information with "correct-by-construction" software environments such as Specware[19] appear promising.

7 Conclusion

Inference Web enables applications to generate portable explanations of their conclusions. We identified the support for knowledge provenance, reasoning information, explanation generation, distributed proofs, and proof presentation as requirements for explanations in the web. We described the major components of IW - the portable proof specification based on the emerging web language-DAML (soon to be updated to OWL) supporting proofs and their explanations, the registry, and the IW proof browser. We described how Inference Web features provide infrastructure for the identified requirements for web explanations. We facilitated use in a distributed environment by providing IW tools for registering and manipulating proofs, proof fragments, inference engines, ontologies, and source information. We also facilitated interoperability by specifying the portable proof format and providing tools for manipulating proofs and fragments. We have implemented the IW approach for two Semantic Web agents based on JTP and are in discussions with additional reasoner authors to include more reasoning engines. We have presented the work at government sponsored program meetings(RKF, DAML, AQUAINT, and NIMD) to gather input from other reasoner authors/users and have obtained feedback and interest. Current registration work includes SRI's SNARK and W3C's CWM.

Acknowledgments. Many people have provided valuable input to our work. Thanks in particular go to colleagues at KSL including Richard Fikes, Jessica Jenkins, Gleb Frank, Eric Hsu, Bill MacCartney, Rob McCool, Sheila McIlraith, and Yulin Li for input on JTP, our specification or applications. Also thanks go to a number of colleagues in some government programs who provided input including Hans Chalupsky, Peter Clark, Ken Forbus, Ken Murray, and Steve Reed. All errors, of course are our responsibility.

This work is supported by the following grants DARPA F30602-00-2-0579, N66001-00-C-8027, NBCHD030010, and ARDA H278000*000 and H768000*000/4400049114.

[19] http://www.kestrel.edu/HTML/prototypes/specware.html

References

[1] Alex Borgida, Enrico Franconi, and Ian Horrocks. Explaining *ACL* Subsumption. In *Proc. of the 14th European Conf. on Artificial Intelligence (ECAI2000)*, pages 209–213. IOS Press, 2000.

[2] Alex Borgida, Enrico Franconi, Ian Horrocks, Deborah L. McGuinness, and Peter F. Patel-Schneider. Explaining *ALC* Subsumption. In *Proc. of the International Workshop on Description Logics (DL'99)*, pages 33–36, Linköping, Sweden, July 1999.

[3] Alex Borgida and Deborah L. McGuinness. Asking Queries about Frames. In *Proceedings of Fifth International Conference on the Principles of Knowledge Representation and Reasoning*, Cambridge, Massachusetts, November 1996. Morgan Kaufmann.

[4] Robert Boyer, Matt Kaufmann, and J. Moore. The Boyer-Moore Theorem Prover and Its Interactive Enhancements. *Computers and Mathematics with Applications*, 29(2):27–62, 1995.

[5] Peter Buneman, Sanjeev Khanna, and Wang-Chiew Tan. Why and Where: A Characterization of Data Provenance. In *Proceedings of 8th International Conference on Database Theory*, pages 316–330, January 2001.

[6] Hans Chalupsky and Tom Russ. WhyNot: Debugging Failed Queries in Large Knowledge Bases. In *Proc. of the 14th Innovative Applications of Artificial Intelligence Conference (IAAI-02)*, pages 870–877, 2002.

[7] Dan Connolly, Frank van Harmelen, Ian Horrocks, Deborah L. McGuinness, Peter F. Patel-Schneider, and Lynn Andrea Stein. DAML+OIL (March 2001) Reference Description. Technical Report Note 18, World Wide Web Committee (W3C), December 2001.

[8] Aseem Das, Wei Wu, and Deborah L. McGuinness. Industrial Strength Ontology Management. In Isabel Cruz, Stefan Decker, Jerome Euzenat, and Deborah L. McGuinness, editors, *The Emerging Semantic Web*. IOS Press, 2002.

[9] Amy Felty and Dale Miller. Proof Explanation and Revision. Technical Report MSCIS8817, University of Pennsylvania, 1987.

[10] Richard Fikes, Pat Hayes, and Ian Horrocks. DAML Query Language (DQL) Abstract Specification. Technical report, W3C, 2002.

[11] Richard Fikes and Deborah L. McGuinness. An Axiomatic Semantics for RDF, RDF-S, and DAML+OIL (March 2001). Technical Report Note 18, W3C, December 2001.

[12] Xiaorong Huang. Reconstructing Proofs at the Assertion Level. In *Proceedings of CADE-94*, LNAI-814, pages 738–752. Springer, 1994.

[13] Deborah L. McGuinness. *Explaining Reasoning in Description Logics.* PhD thesis, Rutgers University, 1996.

[14] Deborah L. McGuinness and Alex Borgida. Explaining Subsumption in Description Logics. In *Proc. of the 14th International Joint Conference on Artificial Intelligence*, pages 816–821, Montreal, Canada, August 1995. Morgan Kaufmann.

[15] Deborah L. McGuinness and Peter Patel-Schneider. From Description Logic Provers to Knowledge Representation Systems. In Franz Baader, Diego Calvanese, Deborah McGuinness, Daniele Nardi, and Peter Patel-Schneider, editors, *The Description Logic Handbook: Theory, Implementation, and Applications*, pages 265–281. Cambridge University Press, 2003.

[16] Deborah L. McGuinness and Paulo Pinheiro da Silva. Trusting Answers on the Web. In Mark T. Maybury, editor, *New Directions in Question Answering.* AAAI/MIT Press. To appear.

[17] Deborah L. McGuinness and Paulo Pinheiro da Silva. Registry-Based Support for Information Integration. In *Proceedings of IJCAI-2003 Workshop on Information Integration on the Web (IIWeb-03)*, pages 117–122, Acapulco, Mexico, August 2003.

[18] Edward Hance Shortliffe. *Computer-Based Medical Consultations: MYCIN*. Elsevier/North Holland, New York, NY, USA, 1976.

[19] Michael Smith, Deborah L. McGuinness, Raphael Volz, and Chris Welty. Web Ontology Language (OWL) Guide Version 1.0. Technical Report Working Draft, World Wide Web Committee (W3C), 2003.

[20] W. Swartout, C. Paris, and J. Moore. Explanations in Knowledge Systems: Design for Explainable Expert Systems. *IEEE Intelligent Systems*, June 1991.

Semantic Coordination: A New Approach and an Application

Paolo Bouquet[1,2], Luciano Serafini[2], and Stefano Zanobini[1]

[1] Department of Information and Communication Technology – University of Trento
Via Sommarive, 10 – 38050 Trento (Italy)
{bouquet,zanobini}@dit.unitn.it
[2] ITC-IRST – Istituto per la Ricerca Scientifica e Tecnologica
Via Sommarive, 14 – 38050 Trento (Italy)
serafini@itc.it

Abstract. Semantic coordination, namely the problem of finding an agreement on the meaning of heterogeneous semantic models, is one of the key issues in the development of the Semantic Web. In this paper, we propose a new algorithm for discovering semantic mappings across hierarchical classifications based on a new approach to semantic coordination. This approach shifts the problem of semantic coordination from the problem of computing linguistic or structural similarities (what most other proposed approaches do) to the problem of deducing relations between sets of logical formulae that represent the meaning of concepts belonging to different models. We show how to apply the approach and the algorithm to an interesting family of semantic models, namely hierarchical classifications, and present the results of preliminary tests on two types of hierarchical classifications, web directories and catalogs. Finally, we argue why this is a significant improvement on previous approaches.

1 Introduction

One of the key issues in the development of the Semantic Web is the problem of enabling machines to exchange meaningful information/knowledge across applications which (i) may use autonomously developed models of locally available data (local models), and (ii) need to find a sort of agreement on what local models are about to achieve their users' goals. This problem can be viewed as a problem of *semantic coordination*[1], defined as follows: (i) all parties have an interest in finding an agreement on how to map their models onto each others, but (ii) there are many possible/plausible solutions (many alternative mappings across local models) among which they need to select the right, or at least a sufficiently good, one.

In environments with more or less well-defined boundaries, like a corporate Intranet, the semantic coordination problem can be addressed by defining and using shared models (e.g., ontologies) throughout the entire organization[2]. However, in open environments,

[1] See the introduction of [6] for this notion, and its relation with the notion of *meaning negotiation*.
[2] But see [4] for a discussion of the drawbacks of this approach from the standpoint of Knowledge Management applications.

D. Fensel et al. (Eds.): ISWC 2003, LNCS 2870, pp. 130–145, 2003.

like the Semantic Web, this "centralized" approach to semantic coordination is not viable for several reasons, such as the difficulty of "negotiating" a shared model of data that suits the needs of all parties involved, the practical impossibility of maintaining such a model in a highly dynamic environment, the problem of finding a satisfactory mapping of pre-existing local models onto such a global model. In such a scenario, the problem of exchanging meaningful information across locally defined models seems particularly tough, as we cannot presuppose an *a priori* agreement, and therefore its solution requires a more dynamic and flexible form of "peer-to-peer" semantic coordination.

In this paper, we address an important instance of the problem of semantic coordination, namely the problem of coordinating hierarchical classifications (HCs). HCs are structures having the *explicit* purpose of organizing/classifying some kind of data (such as documents, records in a database, goods, activities, services). The problem of coordinating HCs is significant for at least two main reasons:

- first, HCs are widely used in many applications[3]. Examples are: web directories (see e.g. the Google^{TM} Directory or the Yahoo!^{TM}Directory), content management tools and portals (which often use hierarchical classifications to organize documents and web pages), service registry (web services are typically classified in a hierarchical form, e.g. in UDDI), marketplaces (goods are classified in hierarchical catalogs), PC's file systems (where files are typically classified in hierarchical folder structures);
- second, it is an empirical fact that most actual HCs (as most concrete instances of models available on the Semantic Web) are built using structures whose labels are expressions from the language spoken by the community of their users (including technical words, neologisms, proper names, abbreviations, acronyms, whose meaning is shared in that community). In our opinion, recognizing this fact is crucial to go beyond the use of syntactic (or weakly semantic) techniques, as it gives us the chance of exploiting the complex degree of semantic coordination implicit in the way a community uses the language from which the labels of a HC are taken.

The main technical contribution of the paper is a logic–based algorithm, called CTXMATCH, for coordinating HCs. It takes in input two HCs H and H' and, for each pair of concepts $k \in H$ and $k' \in H'$, returns their semantic relation. The relations we consider in this version of CTXMATCH are: k is less general than k', k is more general than k', k is equivalent to k', k is compatible with k', and k is incompatible with (i.e., disjoint from) k'. The formal semantics of these relations will be made precise in the paper.

With respect to other approaches to semantic coordination proposed in the literature (often under different "headings", such as schema matching, ontology mapping, semantic integration; see Section 6 for references and a detailed discussion of some of them), our approach is innovative in three main aspects: (1) we introduce a new method for making explicit the meaning of nodes in a HC (and in general, in structured semantic models) by combining three different types of knowledge, each of which has a specific role; (2) the result of applying this method is that we are able to produce a new representation

[3] For an interesting discussion of the central role of classification in human cognition see, e.g., [15,7].

of a HC, in which all relevant knowledge about the nodes (including their meaning in that specific HC) is encoded as a set of logical formulae; (3) mappings across nodes of two HCs are then deduced via logical reasoning, rather then derived through some more or less complex heuristic procedure, and thus can be assigned a clearly defined model-theoretic semantics. As we will show, this leads to a major conceptual shift, as the problem of semantic coordination between HCs is no longer tackled as a problem of computing linguistic or structural similarities (possibly with the help of a thesaurus and of other information about the type of arcs between nodes), but rather as a problem of deducing relations between formulae that represent the meaning of each concept in a given HC. This explains, for example, why our approach performs much better than other ones when two concepts are intuitively equivalent, but occur in structurally very different HCs.

The paper goes as follows. In Section 2 we introduce the main conceptual assumptions of the new approach we propose to semantic coordination. In Section 3 we show how this approach is instantiated to the problem of coordinating HCs. Then we present the main features of CtxMatch the proposed algorithm for coordinating HCs (Section 4). In the final part of the paper, we sum-up the results of testing the algorithm on web directories and catalogs (Section 5) and compare our approach with other proposed approaches for matching schemas (Section 6).

2 Our Approach

The approach to semantic coordination we propose in this paper is based on the intuition that there is an essential conceptual difference between coordinating generic abstract structures (e.g., arbitrary labelled graphs) and coordinating structures whose labels are taken from the language spoken by the community of their users. Indeed, the second type of structures give us the chance of exploiting the complex degree of semantic coordination implicit in the way a community uses the language from which the labels are taken. Most importantly, the status of this linguistic coordination at a given time is already "codified" in artifacts (e.g., dictionaries, but today also ontologies and other formalized models), which provide senses for words and more complex expressions, relations between senses, and other important knowledge about them. Our aim is to exploit these artifacts as an essential source of constraints on possible/acceptable mappings across HCs.

To clarify this intuition, let us consider the HCs in Figure 1, and suppose they are used to classify images in two multi-media repositories. Imagine we want to discover the semantic relation between the nodes labelled `MOUNTAIN` in the two HCs on the left hand side, and between the two nodes `FLORENCE` on the right hand side. Using knowledge about the meaning of labels and about the world, we understand almost immediately that the relation between the first pair of nodes is "less general than" (intuitively, the images that one would classify as images of mountains in Tuscany is a subset of images that one would classify under images of mountains in Italy), and that the relation between the second pair of nodes is "equivalent to" (the images that one would classify as images of Florence in Tuscany are the same as the images that one would classify under images of Florence in Italy). Notice that the relation is different, even though the two pairs of HCs

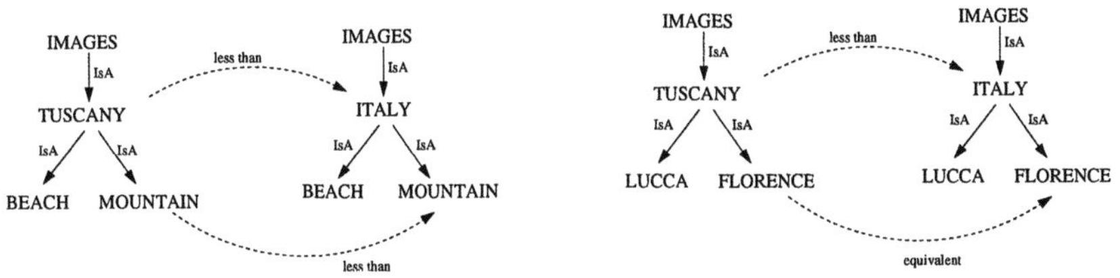

Fig. 1. Coordinating HCs

are structurally very similar. How do we design a technique of semantic coordination which exploits the same kind of facts to achieve the same results?

The approach we propose is based on three basic ideas. First of all, exploiting the degree of coordination implicit in the fact that labels are taken from language requires to make explicit the meaning of labels associated to each node in a HC. We claim that this can be done only of we properly take into account three distinct levels of semantic knowledge:

Lexical knowledge: knowledge about the words used in the labels. For example, the fact that the word 'image' can be used in the sense of a picture or in the sense of personal facade, and the fact that different words may have the same sense (e.g., 'picture' and 'image');

Domain knowledge: knowledge about the relation between the senses of labels in the real world or in a specific domain. For example, the fact that Tuscany is part of Italy, or that Florence is in Italy;

Structural knowledge: knowledge deriving from how labels are arranged in a given HC. For example, the fact that the concept labelled `MOUNTAIN` classifies images, and not books.

Let us see how these three levels can be used to explain the intuitive reasoning described above. Consider the mapping between the two nodes `MOUNTAIN`. Linguistic meaning can be used to assume that the sense of the two labels is the same. Domain knowledge tells us, among other things, that Tuscany is part of Italy. Finally, structural knowledge tells us that the intended meaning of the two nodes `MOUNTAIN` is images of Tuscan mountains (left HC) and images of Italian mountains (right HC). All these facts together allow us to conclude that one node is less general than the other one. We can use similar reasoning for the two nodes `FLORENCE`, which are structurally equivalent. But exploiting domain knowledge, we can add the fact that Florence is in Tuscany (such a relation doesn't hold between mountains and Italy in the first example). This further piece of domain knowledge allows us to conclude that, beyond structural similarity, the relation is different.

Second, this analysis of meaning has an important consequence on our approach to semantic coordination. Indeed, unlike all other approaches we know of, we do not use lexical knowledge (and, in our case, domain knowledge) to improve the results of structural matching (e.g., by adding synonyms for labels, or expanding acronyms). Instead, we combine knowledge from all three levels to build a new representation of the problem, where the meaning of each node is encoded as a logical formula, and relevant domain knowledge and structural relations between nodes are added to nodes as sets of axioms that capture background knowledge about them.

This, in turn, introduces the third innovative idea of our approach. Indeed, once the meaning of each node, together with all relevant domain and structural knowledge, is encoded as a set of logical formulae, the problem of discovering the semantic relation between two nodes can be stated not as a matching problem, but as a relatively simple problem of logical deduction. Intuitively, as we will say in a more technical form in Section 4, determining whether there is an equivalence relation between the meaning of two nodes becomes a problem of testing whether the first implies the second and vice versa (given a suitable collection of axioms, which acts as a sort of background theory); and determining whether one is less general than the other one amounts to testing if the first implies the second. As we will say, in the current version of the algorithm we encode this reasoning problem as a problem of logical satisfiability, and then compute mappings by feeding the problem to a standard SAT solver.

3 Semantic Coordination of Hierarchical Classification

In this section we show how to apply the general approach described in the previous section to the problem of coordinating HCs. Intuitively, a classification is a grouping of things into classes or categories. When categories are arranged into a hierarchical structure, we have a hierarchical classification. Formally, the hierarchical structures we use to build HCs are *concept hierarchies*, defined as follows in [8]:

Definition 1 (Concept hierarchy). A concept hierarchy *is a triple* $H = \langle K, E, l \rangle$ *where* K *is a finite set of nodes,* E *is a set of arcs on* K*, such that* $\langle K, E \rangle$ *is a rooted tree, and* l *is a function from* $K \cup E$ *to a set* L *of labels.*

Given a concept hierarchy H, a classification can be defined as follows:

Definition 2 (Classification). A classification *of a set of objects* D *in a concept hierarchy* $H = \langle K, E, l \rangle$ *is a function* $\mu : K \to 2^D$.

We assume that the classification function μ in Definition 2 satisfies the following *specificity principle*: an object $d \in D$ is classified under a category k, if d is about k (according to the some criteria, e.g., the semantic intuition of the creator of the classification!) and there isn't a more specific concept k' under which d could be classified[4].

Prototypical examples of HCs are the web directories of many search engines, for example the Google^{TM} Directory, the Yahoo!^{TM} Directory, or the Looksmart^{TM} web directory. A tiny fraction of the HCs corresponding to the Google^{TM} Directory^{TM} and to the Yahoo!^{TM}Directory is depicted in Figure 2.

Intuitively, the problem of semantic coordination arises when one needs to find relations between categories belonging to distinct (and thus typically heterogeneous) HCs. Imagine the following scenario. You are browsing the Google^{TM} Directory on the left hand side of Figure 2, and find out that the documents classified under the category

[4] See for example Yahoo!^{TM} instruction for "Finding an appropriate Category" at http://docs.yahoo.com/info/suggest/appropriate.html.

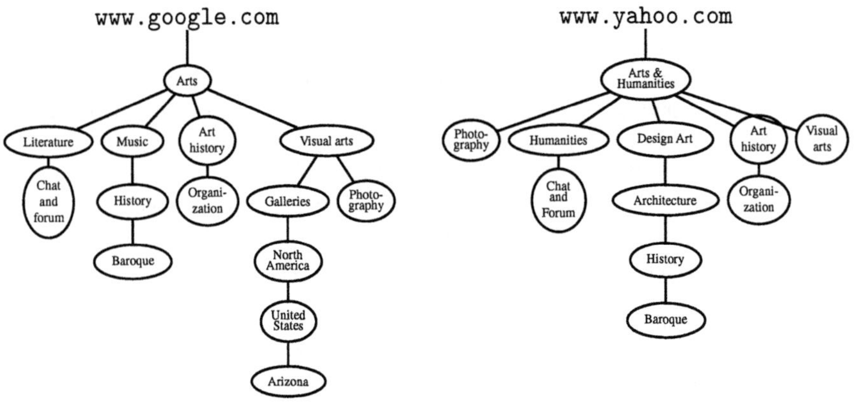

Fig. 2. Examples of concept hierarchies (source: Open Directory and Yahoo!Directory)

labelled `Baroque` are very relevant for your work on Baroque music. So you would like to ask the system to find out for you whether there are categories in different hierarchical classifications (e.g., the Yahoo!^{TM}Directory) which have the same meaning as, or a meaning related to, the category `Baroque` in the directory you are currently browsing[5]. Formally, we define the problem of semantic coordination as the problem of discovering mappings between categories in two distinct concept hierarchies H and H':

Definition 3 (Mapping). *A mapping M from $H = \langle K, E, l\rangle$ to $H' = \langle K', E', l'\rangle$ is a function $M : K \times K' \to rel$, where rel is a set of symbols, called the* possible relations.

The set rel of possible relations depends on the intended use of the structures we want to map. Indeed, in our experience, the intended use of a structure (e.g., classifying objects) is semantically much more relevant than the type of abstract structures involved to determine how a structure should be interpreted. As the purpose of mapping HCs is to discover relations between nodes (concepts) that are used to classify objects, five possible relations can hold between two nodes k_s and k_t belonging to different HCs: $k_s \xrightarrow{\supseteq} k_t$ (k_s is more general than k_t); $k_s \xrightarrow{\subseteq} k_t$ (k_s is less general than k_t); $k_s \xrightarrow{\equiv} k_t$ (k_s is equivalent to k_t); $k_s \xrightarrow{*} k_t$ (k_s is compatible with k_t); $k_s \xrightarrow{\perp} k_t$ (k_s is disjoint from k_t). Later in the paper we'll provide a formal definition of these five relations.

4 The Algorithm: CtxMatch

CtxMatch takes the concept hierarchies of two HCs as input and returns a mapping between their nodes. The algorithm has the following two main steps:

Semantic explicitation: The meaning of each node k in a concept hierarchy H is made explicit in a logical formula $w(k)$. This formula approximates the intended meaning of the node k in H. For instance the formulae associated with the two nodes labeled

[5] Similar examples apply to catalogs. Here we use web directories, as they are well-known to most readers and easy to understand.

FLORENCE on the right hand side of Figure 1 will approximate the meanings "images of Florence, a city in Tuscany" and "images of Florence, a city in Italy", respectively.

Semantic comparison: The problem of finding the semantic relation between two nodes $k \in H$ and $k' \in H'$ is encoded in a satisfiability problem, involving the formulae $w(k)$ and $w(k')$, and a background theory T containing properties (axioms) relevant for the relation between $w(k)$ and $w(k')$. So, to prove that the two nodes FLORENCE in Figure 1 are equivalent, we deduce the logical equivalence between the formulas associated to the nodes by using the domain axioms "Florence is a city of Tuscany" and "Tuscany is a region of Italy".

In the version of the algorithm presented here, we use WORDNET [12] as a source of both lexical and domain knowledge. However, WORDNET could be replaced by another combination of a linguistic resource and a domain knowledge resource.

4.1 Semantic Explicitation

In this phase we make explicit the meaning of each node into a logical formula. Let us see how lexical, domain, and structural knowledge is exploited in this phase. Consider Figure 2. Using lexical knowledge, we associate linguistic senses to labels. For example, the label "Arizona" is associated with two senses corresponding to "a state in southwestern United States" or a "glossy snake". Domain knowledge and structural knowledge are used to filter out some of the possible senses.

Semantic explicitation is performed in two phases: *linguistic interpretation* and *contextualization.*

Linguistic Interpretation. In this first phase we provide an interpretation of the labels independently from the structure in which they occur. Let $H = \langle K, E, l \rangle$ be a concept hierarchy and L_H the set of labels associated to the nodes and edges of a hierarchy H by the function l. In this phase we associate to each label $s \in L_H$ a logical formula representing all possible linguistic interpretations of that label allowed by the lexical knowledge available.

Definition 4 (Label interpretation). *Given a logic W, a* label interpretation *in W is a function $li : L_H \to wff(W)$, where $wff(W)$ is a set of well formed formulas of W.*

The choice of W depends on how expressive one wants to be in the approximation of the meaning of nodes, and on the complexity of the NLP techniques used to process labels. In our first implementation we have adopted the propositional fragment of description logic with $\sqcup$, $\sqcap$ and $\neg$, whose primitive concepts are the synsets of WORDNET that we associate to each label. Labels are processed by text chunking (via Alembic chunker [10]), and translation of the connectives into a logical form according to the following rules:

- coordinating conjunctions and commas are interpreted as a disjunction;
- prepositions, like 'in' or 'of', are interpreted as a conjunction;
- expressions denoting exclusion, like 'except' or 'but not', are interpreted as negations.

We access WORDNET to attach to each word in each label its set of senses. When two or more words in a label are contained in WORDNET as a single expression (a so-called multiword), the corresponding senses are selected and, in the basic logical form, the intersection between the two words is substituted by the multiword.

Example 1.

- $li(\texttt{Baroque}) = \texttt{baroque\#1}$, the unique sense of 'Baroque' presents in WORDNET;
- $li(\texttt{Arizona}) = \texttt{arizona\#1} \sqcup \texttt{arizona\#2}$, i.e., the disjunction of the two possible senses of 'Arizona';
- $li(\texttt{Chat and Forum}) = \texttt{chat\#1} \sqcup \texttt{chat\#2} \sqcup \texttt{chat\#3} \sqcup \texttt{forum\#1} \sqcup \texttt{forum\#2} \sqcup \texttt{forum\#3}$ i.e. the disjunction of the meaning of 'chat' and 'forum' taken separately (both 'chat' and 'forum' have tree senses in WORDNET);
- $li(\texttt{Classic Music}) = ((\texttt{classic\#1} \sqcup \ldots) \sqcap (\texttt{music\#1} \sqcup \ldots)) \sqcup \texttt{classic\_music\#1}$ either the conjunction of the meaning of 'classic' (with n senses) and the meaning of 'music' (with m sense) taken separately, or the multiword 'classic music' considered as a whole concept, ('classic music' is a multiword in WORDNET).

Contextualization. The aim of this phase is to determine the component of the meaning of a node's label that depends on its position in the concept hierarchy associated to a HC. To this end, we introduce the notion of *focus* of a concept k in a hierarchy H, denoted by $f(k, H)$. Intuitively, the focus is the smallest sub-tree of H that one should take into account to determine the meaning of k in H. In CTXMATCH, the focus is defined as follows:

Definition 5 (Focus). *The* focus *of a node $k \in K$ in a concept hierarchy $H = \langle K, E, l \rangle$, is a finite concept hierarchy $f(k, H) = \langle K', E', l' \rangle$ such that: $K' \subseteq K$, and K' contains exactly k, its ancestors, and their children; $E' \subseteq E$ is the set of edges between the concepts of K'; l' is the restriction of l on K'.*

This definition of focus is motivated by observations on how we humans use HCs. When searching for documents in a HC, we incrementally construct the meaning of a node k by navigating the classification from the root to k. During this navigation, we have access to the labels of the ancestors of k, and also to the labels of their siblings. This information is used at each stage to select the node we want to access[6].

Given a focus $f(k, H)$ and the linguistic interpretation $li(.)$ of the labels of all its nodes, the phase called *contextualization* defines a formula $w(k)$ which is called the *structural interpretation* of the node k. We first set $w(k) := li(l(k))$ (i.e., $w(k)$ is the linguistic interpretation of the label associated to k), then we refine this definition via *sense filtering* and *sense composition*.

[6] This definition of focus is appropriate for HCs. With structures used for different purposes, different definitions of focus should be used. For example, if a concept hierarchy is used to represents an XML-schema, the meaning of a node is determined also by the meaning of its sub-nodes, so a more suitable definition of focus $f(k, H)$ would include for example the sub-tree rooted at k.

Sense Filtering is a heuristic method by which we keep only the senses of a linguistic interpretation that a node k is more likely to have, and discharge the other ones. To this end, we analyze the relations between the senses of k and the senses of the other nodes in the focus. For example, if $w(k) = \texttt{arizona\#1} \sqcup \texttt{arizona\#2}$, the sense `arizona#2` (i.e., the snake) can be discharged if $f(k, H)$ contains the sense `United States#1` (the United States of America), and the focus does not contain any sense that is somehow related with snakes.

Sense Composition enriches the meaning of a node's label by combining its linguistic interpretation with structural information and domain theory. For HCs, the rule is that the structural meaning of a concept k is formalized as the conjunction of the senses associated to all its ancestors; this makes sense, if we consider how we interpret the relation between a node and its ancestors in a classification. In CTXMATCH, some interesting exceptions are handled. For example, in the Yahoo!™Directory, `Visual arts` and `Photography` are sibling nodes under `Arts & Humanities`; since in WORDNET photography is in a is–a relationship with visual art, the node `Visual arts` is re-interpreted as visual arts with the exception of photography, and is then formalized in description logic as: $\texttt{visual art\#1} \sqcap \neg\, \texttt{photography\#1}$.

4.2 Computing Semantic Relations via SAT

After semantic explicitation is over, the problem of discovering semantic relations between two nodes k and k' in two HCs can be reduced to the problem of checking if a logical relation holds between the formulas $w(k)$ and $w(k')$; this is done again on the basis of domain knowledge. In CTXMATCH, the existence of a logical relation is checked as a problem of propositional satisfiability (SAT), and then computed via a standard SAT solver. The SAT problem is built in two steps. First, we select the portion B of the available domain knowledge which is relevant to the structural interpretation $w(k)$ and $w(k')$ of the two nodes k and k'; then we compute the logical relation between $w(k)$ and $w(k')$ which are implied by B.

Definition 6 (Background theory). *Let $\phi = w(k)$ and $\psi = w(k')$ be the structural interpretations of two nodes k and k' of two hierarchical classifications H_1 and H_2 respectively. Let T be a theory (a set of axioms) in the logic where ϕ and ψ are expressed. The* portion of T relevant to the semantic relation of ϕ and ψ, *denoted by $B(\phi, \psi)$ is a subset of T, such that for any subset B' of T, with $B(\phi, \psi) \subseteq B'$, we have that*

$$B' \models \alpha_{\phi,\psi} \text{ iff } B(\phi, \psi) \models \alpha_{\phi,\psi}$$

where $\alpha_{\phi,\psi}$ is a formula obtained by combining ϕ and ψ by replacing all the atomic proposition of α either with ϕ or with ψ.

In the first version of CTXMATCH, the background theory B is built by transforming WORDNET relations between senses in a set of subsumption axioms as follows:

1. $\texttt{s\#k} \equiv \texttt{t\#h}$: `s#k` and `t#h` are synonyms (i.e., they are in the same synset);
2. $\texttt{s\#k} \sqsubseteq \texttt{t\#h}$: `s#k` is either a hyponym or a meronym of `t#h`;

3. $\texttt{t\#h} \sqsubseteq \texttt{s\#k}$: $\texttt{s\#k}$ is either a hypernym or a holonym of $\texttt{t\#h}$;
4. $\neg\texttt{t\#k} \sqsubseteq \texttt{s\#h}$: $\texttt{s\#k}$ belongs to the set of opposite meanings of $\texttt{t\#h}$ (if $\texttt{s\#k}$ and $\texttt{t\#h}$ are adjectives) or, in case of nouns, that $\texttt{s\#k}$ and $\texttt{t\#h}$ are different hyponyms of the same synset.

To build $B(\phi, \psi)$ from WordNet, we adopt heuristic rules that turned out to produce satisfactory results. The idea is to extract the smallest set of axioms which provide semantic relations between senses that occur in ϕ and ψ. However, different sources (e.g., domain specific ontologies) and different heuristic rules may be used to build the background theory for ϕ and ψ.

Example 2. Suppose that we want to discover the relation between `Chat and Forum` in the Google^{TM} Directory and `Chat and Forum` in the Yahoo!^{TM}Directory in Figure 2. From WordNet we can extract the following relevant axioms: $\texttt{art\#1} \sqsubseteq \texttt{humanities\#1}$ (the sense 1 of 'art' is an hyponym of the sense 1 of 'humanities'), and $\texttt{humanities\#1} \sqsupseteq \texttt{literature\#2}$ (the sense 1 of 'humanities' is an hyperonym of the sense 2 of 'literature').

Once we have extracted a suitable background theory, we are ready to state a SAT problem for each possible relation in rel between any two nodes k and k' belonging to different HCs. In CtxMatch, we use the following encoding:

relation	SAT Problem
$k_s \xrightarrow{\supseteq} k'_t$	$B \models w(k_t) \sqsubseteq w(k_s)$
$k_s \xrightarrow{\subseteq} k_t$	$B \models w(k_s) \sqsubseteq w(k_t)$
$k_s \xrightarrow{\perp} k_t$	$B \models w(k_s) \sqcap w(k_t) \sqsubseteq \perp$
$k_s \xrightarrow{\equiv} k_t$	$B \models w(k_t) \sqsubseteq w(k_s)$ and $B \models w(k_s) \sqsubseteq w(k_t)$
$k_s \xrightarrow{*} k_t$	$w(k_s) \sqcap w(k_t)$ is consistent in B

B is the portion of the background theory relevant to k_s and k_t. The idea under this translation is to see WordNet senses (contained in $w(k)$ and $w(k')$) as sets of documents. For instance the concept `art#i`, corresponding to the first WordNet sense of art, is though as the set of documents speaking about art in the first sense. Using the set theoretic interpretation of mapping given in definition 7, we have that mapping can be translated in terms of subsumption of $w(k)$ and $w(k')$. Indeed subsumption relation semantically corresponds to the subset relation.

Example 3. The problem of checking whether `Chat and Forum` in Google^{TM} is, say, less general than `Chat and Forum` in Yahoo!^{TM} amounts to a problem of satisfiability on the following formulas:

$$\phi = (\texttt{art\#1} \sqcap \texttt{literature\#2} \sqcap (\texttt{chat\#1} \sqcup \texttt{forum\#1}))$$
$$\psi = (\texttt{art\#1} \sqcup \texttt{humanities\#1}) \sqcap \texttt{humanities\#1} \sqcap (\texttt{chat\#1} \sqcup \texttt{forum\#1})$$
$$B(\phi, \psi) = (\texttt{art\#1} \sqsubseteq \texttt{humanities\#1}), (\texttt{humanities\#1} \sqsupseteq \texttt{literature\#2})$$

It is easy to see that from the above axioms we can infer $B(\phi, \psi) \models \phi \sqsubseteq \psi$.

5 Testing the Algorithm

In this section, we report from [17] some results of the first tests on CTXMATCH. The tests were performed on real HCs (i.e., pre-existing classifications used in real applications), and not on *ad hoc* HCs.

In [1], a testing methodology is defined which is based on an ideal situation where two agents have the same set of documents and proceed to classify them into two different HCs following the *specificity principle* (see Section 3). Then, we can define the following criterion of correctness for mapping elements:

Definition 7 (Correctness of a mapping element[7]). *Let H_s to H_t be the concept hierarchies of two HCs. Let k_s and k_t denote any pair of nodes of H_s and H_t respectively. Let μ_s and μ_t denote two classifications of a set of documents D in H_s and H_t respectively. Then:*

1. $k_s \xrightarrow{\supseteq} k_t$ *is correct if for all* μ_s *and* μ_t, $\mu_s(k_s{\downarrow}) \supseteq \mu_t(k_t{\downarrow})$;
2. $k_s \xrightarrow{\subseteq} k_t$ *is correct if for all* μ_s *and* μ_t, $\mu_s(k_s{\downarrow}) \subseteq \mu_t(k_t{\downarrow})$;
3. $k_s \xrightarrow{\equiv} k_t$ *is correct if* $k_s \xrightarrow{\subseteq} k_t$ *is correct and* $k_s \xrightarrow{\supseteq} k_t$ *is correct;*
4. $k_s \xrightarrow{\perp} k_t$ *is correct if for all* μ_s *and* μ_t, $\mu_s(k_s{\downarrow}) \cap \mu_t(k_t{\downarrow}) = \emptyset$;
5. $k_s \xrightarrow{*} k_t$ *is correct if there is pair* μ_s *and* μ_t *such that* $\mu_s(k_s{\downarrow}) \cap \mu_t(k_t{\downarrow}) \neq \emptyset$.

where $\mu(c{\downarrow})$ is the union of $\mu(d)$ for any d in the subtree rooted at c. A mapping is correct if all its elements are correct.

5.1 Experiment 1: Matching Google with Yahoo!

The aim of this experiment was to evaluate the CTXMATCH algorithm over portions of the Google™ Directory and the Yahoo!™ Directory about overlapping domains. The test was performed on the two sub-hierarchies 'Architecture' and 'Medicine' available in Google™ and Yahoo!™. The results, expressed in terms of precision and recall, are reported in the following table:

	Architecture		Medicine	
Relations	Pre.	Rec.	Pre.	Rec.
equivalence $\xrightarrow{\equiv}$	.75	.08	.88	.09
less general than $\xrightarrow{\subseteq}$	.84	.79	.86	.61
more general than $\xrightarrow{\supseteq}$	.94	.38	.97	.35

[7] The semantics introduced in Definition 7 can be viewed as an instance of the compatibility relation between contexts as defined in Local Models Semantics [13,5]. Indeed, suppose we take a set of documents D as the domain of interpretation of the local models of two contexts c_1 and c_2, and each concept as a unary predicate. If we see the documents associated to a concept as the interpretation of a predicate in a local model, then the relation we discover between concepts of different contexts can be viewed as a compatibility constraint between the local models of the two concepts. For example, if the algorithm returns an equivalence between the concepts k_1 and k_2 in the contexts c_1 and c_2, then it can be interpreted as the following constraint: if a local model of c_1 associates a document d to k_1, then any compatible model of c_2 must associate d to k_2 (and vice versa); analogously for the other relations.

We observe that the use of domain knowledge allowed us to discover non trivial mappings. For example, an inclusion mapping was computed between `Architecture /History/Periods_and_Styles/Gothic/Gargoyles` and `Architecture/History/ Medieval` as a consequence of the relation between `Medieval` and `Gothic` that can be found in WordNet. This kind of semantic mappings are very difficult to find using a keyword–based approach.

5.2 Experiment 2: Product Re-classification

The second test was in the domain of e–commerce. In the framework of a collaboration with a worldwide telecommunication company, the matching algorithm was applied to re-classify the HC of the 'equipment and accessories' office (used to classify company suppliers) into UNSPSC[8] (version 5.0.2).

To evaluate the results of the re-classification, consider the different results between CtxMatch and the baseline matching process[9]:

	Baseline classification		**Matching classification**	
Total items	194	100%	194	100%
Rightly classified	75	39%	134	70%
Wrongly classified	91	50%	16	8%
Non classified	27	14%	42	22%

Given the 194 items to be re-classified, the baseline process found 1945 possible nodes, but only 75 out of the 1945 proposed nodes are correct. The baseline, a simple string-based matching method, is able to capture a certain number of re-classifications, but the percentage of error is quite high (50%), with respect to the one of correctness (39%). Concerning the results of CtxMatch, the percentage of success is significantly higher (70%) and, even more relevant, the percentage of error is minimal (8%).

6 Related Work

CtxMatch shifts the problem of semantic coordination from the problem of matching (in a more or less sophisticated way) semantic structures (e.g., schemas) to the problem of deducing semantic relations between sets of logical formulae. Under this respect, to the best of our knowledge, there are no other works to which we can compare ours.

However, it is important to see how CtxMatch compares with the performance of techniques based on different approaches to semantic coordination. There are four other

[8] UNSPSC (Universal Standard Products and Services Classification) is an open global coding system that classifies products and services. UNSPSC is extensively used around the world for electronic catalogs, search engines, e–procurement applications and accounting systems.

[9] The baseline has been performed by a simple keyword based matching which worked according to the following rule: for each item description (made up of one or more words) gives back the set of nodes, and their paths, which maximize the occurrences of the item words.

Table 1. Comparing CtxMatch with other methods

	graph matching	CUPID	MOMIS	GLUE	CtxMatch
Structural knowledge	•	•	•		•
Lexical knowledge		•	•	•	•
Domain knowledge				•	•
Instance-based knowledge				•	
Type of result	Pairs of nodes	Similarity measure ∈ [0..1] between pairs of nodes	Similarity measure ∈ [0..1] between pairs of nodes	Similarity measure ∈ [0..1] between pairs of nodes	Semantic relations between pairs of nodes

families of approaches that we will consider: graph matching, automatic schema matching, semi-automatic schema matching, and instance based matching. For each of them, we will discuss the proposal that, in our opinion, is more significant. The comparison is based on the following five dimensions: (1) if and how structural knowledge is used; (2) if and how lexical knowledge is used; (3) if and how domain knowledge is used; (4) if instances are considered; (5) the type of result returned. The general results of our comparison are reported in Table 1.

In graph matching techniques, a concept hierarchy is viewed as a tree of labelled nodes, but the semantic information associated to labels is substantially ignored. In this approach, matching two graphs G_1 and G_2 means finding a sub-graph of G_2 which is isomorphic to G_2 and report as a result the mapping of nodes of G_1 into the nodes of G_2. These approaches consider only structural knowledge and completely ignore lexical and domain knowledge. Some examples of this approach are described in [21,20,19,18, 14].

CUPID [16] is a completely automatic algorithm for schema matching. Lexical knowledge is exploited for discovering linguistic similarity between labels (e.g., using synonyms), while the schema structure is used as a matching constraint. That is, the more the structure of the subtree of a node s is similar to the structure of a subtree of a node t, the more s is similar to t. For this reason CUPID is more effective in matching concept hierarchies that represent data types rather than hierarchical classifications. With hierarchical classifications, there are cases of equivalent concepts occurring in completely different structures, and completely independent concepts that belong to isomorphic structures. Two simple examples are depicted in Figure 3. In case (a), CUPID does not match the two nodes labelled with `ITALY`; in case (b) CUPID finds a match between the node labelled with `FRANCE` and `ENGLAND`. The reason is that CUPID combines in an additive way lexical and structural information, so when structural similarity is very strong (for example, all neighbor nodes do match), then a relation between nodes is inferred without considering labels. So, for example, `FRANCE` and `ENGLAND` match because the structural similarity of the neighbor nodes is so strong that labels are ignored.

MOMIS (Mediator envirOnment for Multiple Information Sources) [2] is a set of tools for information integration of (semi-)structured data sources, whose main objective is to define a global schema that allow an uniform and transparent access to the data stored in a set of semantically heterogeneous sources. One of the key steps of MOMIS

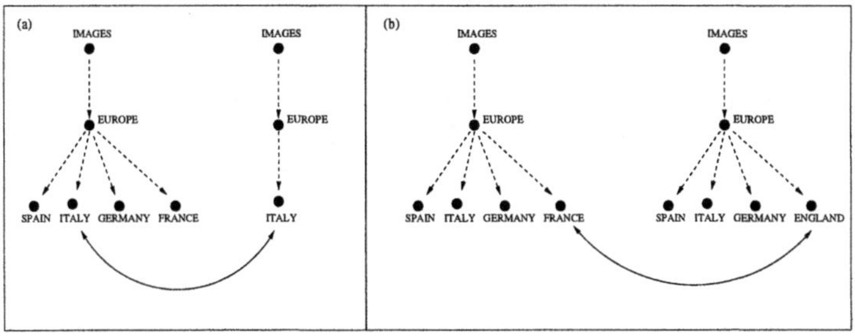

Fig. 3. Two example of mappings from CTXMATCH

is the discovery of overlappings (relations) between the different source schemas. This is done by exploiting knowledge in a Common Thesaurus together with a combination of clustering techniques and Description Logics. The approach is very similar to CUPID and presents the same drawbacks in matching hierarchical classifications. Furthermore, MOMIS includes an interactive process as a step of the integration procedure, and thus, unlike CTXMATCH, it does not support a fully automatic and run-time generation of mappings.

GLUE [11] is a taxonomy matcher that builds mappings taking advantage of information contained in instances, using machine learning techniques and domain-dependent constraints, manually provided by domain experts. GLUE represents an approach complementary to CTXMATCH. GLUE is more effective when a large amount of data is available, while CTXMATCH is more performant when less data are available, or the application requires a quick, on-the-fly mapping between structures. So, for instance, in case of product classification such as UNSPSC or Eclss (which are pure hierarchies of concepts with no data attached), GLUE cannot be applied. Combining the two approaches is a challenging research topic, which can probably lead to a more precise and effective methodology for semantic coordination.

7 Conclusions

In this paper we presented a new approach to semantic coordination in open and distributed environments, and an algorithm (called CTXMATCH) that implements this method for hierarchical classifications. The algorithm has already been used in a peer-to-peer application for distributed knowledge management (the application is described in [3]), and is going to be applied in a peer-to-peer wireless system for ambient intelligence [9].

An important lesson we learned from this work is that methods for semantic coordinations should not be grouped together on the basis of the type of abstract structure they aim at coordinating (e.g., graphs, concept hierarchies), but on the basis of the intended use of the structures under consideration. In this paper, we addressed the problem of coordinating concept hierarchies when used to build hierarchical classifications. Other possible uses of structures are: conceptualizing some domain (ontologies), describing services (automata), describing data types (schemas). This "pragmatic" level (i.e., the use) is essential to provide the correct interpretation of a structure, and thus to discover the correct mappings with other structures.

The importance we assign to the fact that HCs are labelled with meaningful expressions does not mean that we see the problem of semantic coordination as a problem of natural language processing (NLP). On the contrary, the solution we provided is mostly based on knowledge representation and automated reasoning techniques. However, the problem of semantic coordination is a fertile field for collaboration between researchers in knowledge representation and in NLP. Indeed, if in describing the general approach one can assume that some linguistic meaning analysis for labels is available and ready to use, we must be very clear about the fact that real applications (like the one we described in Section 4) require a massive use of techniques and tools from NLP, as a good automatic analysis of labels from a linguistic point of view is a necessary precondition for applying the algorithm to HC in local applications, and for the quality of mappings resulting from the application of the algorithm.

The work we presented in this paper is only the first step of a very ambitious scientific challenge, namely to investigate what is the minimal common ground needed to enable communication between autonomous entities (e.g., agents) that cannot look into each others head, and thus can achieve some degree of semantic coordination only through other means, like exchanging examples, pointing to things, remembering past interactions, generalizing from past communications, and so on. To this end, a lot of work remains to be done. On our side, the next steps will be: extending the algorithm beyond classifications (namely to structures with purposes other than classifying things); generalizing the types of structures we can match (for example, structures with non hierarchical relations, e.g. roles); going beyond WordNet as a source of lexical and domain knowledge; allowing different lexical and/or domain knowledge sources for each of the local structures to be coordinated. The last problem is perhaps the most challenging one, as it introduces a situation is which the space of "senses" is not necessarily shared, and thus we cannot rely on that information for inferring a semantic relation between labels of distinct structures.

References

1. P. Avesani. Evaluation framework for local ontologies interoperability. In *MeaN-02 – AAAI workshop on Meaning Negotiation*, Edmonton, Alberta, Canada, 2002.
2. Sonia Bergamaschi, Silvana Castano, and Maurizio Vincini. Semantic integration of semistructured and structured data sources. *SIGMOD Record*, 28(1):54–59, 1999.
3. M. Bonifacio, P. Bouquet, G. Mameli, and M. Nori. Kex: a peer-to-peer solution for distributed knowledge management. In D. Karagiannis and U. Reimer, editors, *Fourth International Conference on Practical Aspects of Knowledge Management (PAKM-2002)*, Vienna (Austria), 2002.
4. M. Bonifacio, P. Bouquet, and P. Traverso. Enabling distributed knowledge management. managerial and technological implications. *Novatica and Informatik/Informatique*, III(1), 2002.
5. A. Borgida and L. Serafini. Distributed description logics: Directed domain correspondences in federated information sources. In R. Meersman and Z. Tari, editors, *On The Move to Meaningful Internet Systems 2002: CoopIS, Doa, and ODBase*, volume 2519 of *LNCS*, pages 36–53. Springer Verlag, 2002.

6. P. Bouquet, editor. *AAAI-02 Workshop on Meaning Negotiation*, Edmonton, Canada, July 2002. American Association for Artificial Intelligence (AAAI), AAAI Press.
7. G. C. Bowker and S. L. Star. *Sorting things out: classification and its consequences*. MIT Press., 1999.
8. A. Büchner, M. Ranta, J. Hughes, and M. Mäntylä. Semantic information mediation among multiple product ontologies. In *Proc. 4th World Conference on Integrated Design & Process Technology*, 1999.
9. P. Busetta, P. Bouquet, G. Adami, M. Bonifacio, and F. Palmieri. K-Trek: An approach to context awareness in large environments. Technical report, Istituto per la Ricerca Scientifica e Tecnologica (ITC-IRST), Trento (Italy), April 2003. Submitted to UbiComp'2003.
10. D. S. Day and M. B. Vilain. Phrase parsing with rule sequence processors: an application to the shared CoNLL task. In *Proc. of CoNLL-2000 and LLL-2000*, Lisbon, Portugal, September 2000.
11. A. Doan, J. Madhavan, P. Domingos, and A. Halevy. Learning to map between ontologies on the semantic web. In *Proceedings of WWW-2002, 11th International WWW Conference, Hawaii*, 2002.
12. Christiane Fellbaum, editor. *WordNet: An Electronic Lexical Database*. The MIT Press, Cambridge, US, 1998.
13. C. Ghidini and F. Giunchiglia. Local Models Semantics, or Contextual Reasoning = Locality + Compatibility. *Artificial Intelligence*, 127(2):221–259, April 2001.
14. Jeremy Carroll Hewlett-Packard. Matching rdf graphs. In *Proc. in the first International Semantic Web Conference - ISWC 2002*, pages 5–15, 2002.
15. G. Lakoff. *Women, Fire, and Dangerous Things*. Chicago Unversity Press, 1987.
16. Jayant Madhavan, Philip A. Bernstein, and Erhard Rahm. Generic schema matching with cupid. In *The VLDB Journal*, pages 49–58, 2001.
17. B.M. Magnini, L. Serafini, A. Doná, L. Gatti, C. Girardi, and M. Speranza. Large–scale evaluation of context matching. Technical Report 0301–07, ITC–IRST, Trento, Italy, 2003.
18. Tova Milo and Sagit Zohar. Using schema matching to simplify heterogeneous data translation. In *Proc. 24th Int. Conf. Very Large Data Bases, VLDB*, pages 122–133, 24–27 1998.
19. Marcello Pelillo, Kaleem Siddiqi, and Steven W. Zucker. Matching hierarchical structures using association graphs. *Lecture Notes in Computer Science*, 1407:3–??, 1998.
20. Jason Tsong-Li Wang, Kaizhong Zhang, Karpjoo Jeong, and Dennis Shasha. A system for approximate tree matching. *Knowledge and Data Engineering*, 6(4):559–571, 1994.
21. K. Zhang, J. T. L. Wang, and D. Shasha. On the editing distance between undirected acyclic graphs and related problems. In Z. Galil and E. Ukkonen, editors, *Proceedings of the 6th Annual Symposium on Combinatorial Pattern Matching*, volume 937, pages 395–407, Espoo, Finland, 1995. Springer-Verlag, Berlin.

Interoperability on XML Data

Laks V.S. Lakshmanan[1*] and Fereidoon Sadri[2**]

[1] UBC, Vancouver, BC, Canada,
laks@cs.ubc.edu
[2] UNCG, Greensboro, NC, USA,
sadri@uncg.edu

Abstract. We study the problem of interoperability among XML data sources. We propose a lightweight infrastructure for this purpose that derives its inspiration from the recent semantic web initiative. Our approach is based on enriching local sources with semantic declarations so as to enable interoperability. These declarations expose the semantics of the information content of sources by mapping the concepts present therein to a common (application specific) vocabulary, in the spirit of RDF. In addition to this infrastructure, we discuss tools that may assist in generating semantic declarations, and formulation of global queries and address some interesting issues in query processing and optimization.

1 Introduction

Interoperability and data integration are long standing open problems with extensive research literature. Much of the work in the context of federated databases focused on integrating schemas by defining a global schema in an expressive data model and defining mappings from local schemas to the global one. More recently, in the context of integration of data sources on the internet, the so-called global-as-view and local-as-view paradigms have emerged out of projects such as TSIMMIS [22] and Information Manifold (IM) [14]. All of these have primarily concerned themselves with relational abstractions of data sources. Recently, the advent of XML as a standard for online data interchange holds much promise toward promoting interoperability and data integration. But XML, being a syntactic model, in itself cannot make interoperability happen automatically. Two main challenges to overcome are: (i) data sources may model XML data in heterogeneous ways, e.g., using different nestings or groupings or interchanging elements and attributes, and (ii) sources may employ different terminology, a classic problem even in multi-database interoperability. While earlier approaches to integration can be extended to handle XML, they suffer from significant overhead of designing a commonly agreed upon global schema. Can we interoperate without this overhead?

* Supported by NSERC.
** Supported by NSF grant IIS-0083312.

D. Fensel et al. (Eds.): ISWC 2003, LNCS 2870, pp. 146–163, 2003.

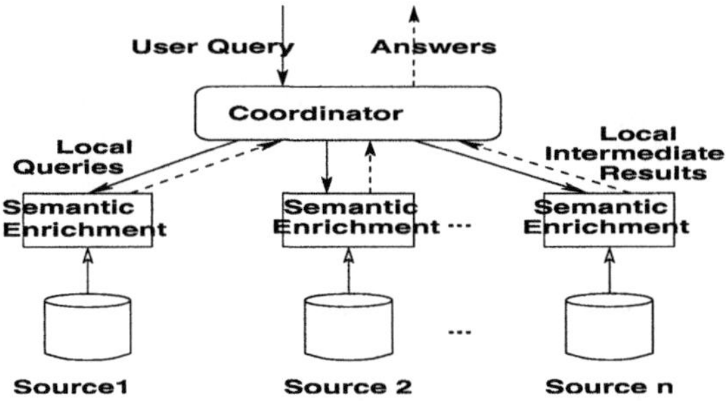

Fig. 1. An architecture for semantic markup and query processing.

Indeed, there are a few recent proposals that do overcome the need for a global schema – Halevy et al. [10] and Miller et al. [18]. We will discuss them in detail in Section 5. In a nutshell, both of these approaches rely on source to source mappings. One problem here is that requiring such mappings for all pairs is too tedious and cumbersome. In order to mitigate this, one can merely insist, as [10] does, that the graph of pairs with available mappings be connected. A second problem is that when a source s_i is mapped to source s_j, if s_j does not have some of the concepts present in s_i, then they will be lost. E.g., s_i may include the `ISBN` for all its books while s_j may not.

Independently of all this, there has been a lot of recent excitement around the *semantic web* [21] initiative, coming with its own host of technologies such as resource description framework (RDF) [20] and ontology description languages such as DAML+OIL, OWL, and XTM [8,17,23]. The promise of the semantic web is to expose the semantics of the information content of web resources (including text, audio, video, etc.) using common transparent vocabulary thus taking the web to a higher semantic level, enabling easy exchange of data and applications. Can we leverage these developments and create a lightweight scalable infrastructure for interoperability? We believe the answer is yes and take the first steps toward this creation here.

Our thesis is that each source('s administrator) interested in participating in data and application sharing should "enrich" itself with adequate semantic declarations. These declarations would essentially expose the semantic concepts present in the source using common, but possibly application specific, terminology, in the spirit of the semantic web initiative and frameworks such as RDF. Queries across data sources so enriched can be composed over this common vocabulary, being agnostic to the specific modeling constructs or terminologies employed in the local sources. A detailed example motivating these issues appears in Section 2. A suggested architecture for semantic enrichment and query processing is depicted in Figure 1. Other architectures such as peer to peer are also possible.

We make the following contributions in this paper.

- We describe a lightweight infrastructure based on local semantic declarations for enabling interoperability across data sources (Section 3).

```
<!ELEMENT store (warehouse*)>
<!ELEMENT warehouse (city, state, item*)>
<!ELEMENT item (id, name, description)>
<!ATTLIST warehouse id ID #REQUIRED>
```

DTD: Source1

```
<!ELEMENT store (items, warehouses)>
<!ELEMENT items (item*)>
<!ELEMENT item (id, name, description)>
<!ELEMENT warehouses (warehouse*)>
<!ELEMENT warehouse (city, state)>
<!ATTLIST item warehouse-id IDREFS #REQUIRED>
<!ATTLIST warehouse id ID #REQUIRED>
```

DTD: Source2

```
<!ELEMENT store (items,warehouses,inventory)>
<!ELEMENT items (i-tuple*)>
<!ELEMENT i-tuple (id,name,description)>
<!ELEMENT warehouses (w-tuple*)>
<!ELEMENT w-tuple (id,city,state)>
<!ELEMENT inventory (inv-tuple*)>
<!ELEMENT inv-tuple (item-id,warehouse-id)>
```

(Relational) **DTD: Source3**

Fig. 2. Schema of three sources.

- These declarations are mapping rules that map data items in a source to a common vocabulary, inspired by RDF. Checking the validity of these mappings involves checking certain key constraints. We illustrate this issue and show how this checking can be done in general (Section 3).
- A user query, when translated against the data sources will in general lead to exponentially many inter-source queries and a linear number of intra-source queries. The former are more expensive and their elimination/optimization is an important problem. We show under what conditions inter-source queries can be eliminated altogether. We also develop a generic technique for optimizing inter-source queries (Section 4).
- Optimizing inter-source queries requires us to infer key and foreign key constraints that hold for the predicates defining the vocabulary, given the source schema (e.g., XML schema or DTD) and the mappings. While previous work has addressed the derivation of key constraints, we develop an algorithm for inferring foreign key constraints (Section 4.3).

2 A Motivating Example

Consider a federation of catalog sales stores maintaining their merchandise information as shown in Figure 2.

Consider the query "For each state, list the state information and all (distinct) items available in warehouses in that state." How can we express this query? There are two sources of complexity in writing this query (say in XQuery):

- For each source, the user has to write source specific "access code" involving XPath expression specific to it.
- The query, in general, is *not* the union of three intra-source queries, as we must consider combinations of state/warehouse pairs in one source with warehouse/item pairs in others. As a result, the resulting query is a complex union of a large number of "joins" across sources in addition to the three intra-source queries.

In addition to the obvious burden on the user for composing such queries, without further knowledge, they are hard to optimize. *Note that even if we were to employ source-source mapping techniques of [10] or [18], the second of these difficulties does not go away.* The reason is that not every concept present in a source may have a counterpart in the source it is mapped to.

What we would ideally like is for the user to be able to write such queries easily, preferably by referring to some common vocabulary infrastructure created for the application on hand. The infrastructure should alleviate the burden on the user of source specific access code writing. Besides, we want the query expression to be simple to compose and to comprehend. Finally, we would like query optimization to be handled by the system.

The main idea behind our approach is based on the observation that ontology specification frameworks such as RDF [20] and OWL [17] provide mechanisms for specifying metadata about a source that includes, not only metadata such as the author and creation date, but also the semantic concepts present therein. This is normally done by specifying concepts (*i.e.* classes or types of objects) and their properties (*i.e.* predicates describing relationships among objects). We will use the terms *property* and *predicate* interchangeably in this paper. E.g., suppose we have the following common vocabulary (properties) defined for describing catalog sales applications: [1]

`item-itemId`, `item-name`, `item-description`, `item-warehouse`, `warehouse-warehouseId`, `warehouse-city`, `warehouse-state`

Each property takes two arguments where the arguments are required to play specific roles. In the spirit of RDF, the first argument is always a URI, which is interpreted as an identifier. The second argument can be a URI or a basic type. E.g., `item-name` takes two arguments where the first argument is the URI of an item whereas the second is a literal name string. The properties `item-itemId` and `warehouse-warehouseId` provide the mappings between the URIs and database-style identifiers of these objects. The roles of the (two) arguments of the other predicates is often self-evident from the predicate names. This is in line with RDF convention where a URI is associated with each subject, property (predicate), and value (or object). For lack of space, we do not show the RDF specs. In fact, in the spirit of semantic web, we may expect that in addition to the semantic marking up of each source, there may be additional ontological mappings (expressed in languages such as OWL [17]) that relate concepts in a class hierarchy as well as specify additional constraints on them. A final point is that an RDF-based semantic marking up for a large source can be tedious. Furthermore, storing the RDF marking up explicitly is redundant and wastes considerable space. To address these concerns, we can: (i) write a transformation program in, say XSLT that transforms an XML document into the required RDF markup specs, and (ii) make use of tools that assist in the writing of the XSLT program.

[1] In addition to the classes `item, warehouse, state`.

```
item-itemId((f_I($I),$I)       <- source1/store/warehouse/item/id $I.
item-name(f_I($I),$N)          <- source1/store/warehouse/item $X, $X/id $I, $X/name $N.
item-warehouse(f_I($I),f_W($W)) <- source1/store/warehouse $X, $X/item/id $I, $X/@id $W.
warehouse-state(f_W($W),$S)    <- source1/store/warehouse $X, $X/@id $W, $X/state $S.

item-itemId(f_I($I),$I)        <- source2/store/items/item/id $I.
item-name(f_I($I),$N)          <- source2/store/items/item $X, $X/id $I, $X/name $N.
item-warehouse(f_I($I),f_W($W)) <- source2/store/items/item $X, $X/id $I, $X/@warehouse-id $W.
warehouse-state(f_W($W),$S)    <- source2/store/warehouses/warehouse $X, $X/@id $W, $X/state $S.

item-itemId(f_I($I),$I)        <- source3/store/items/i-tuple/id $I.
item-name(f_I($I),$N)          <- source3/store/items/i-tuple $X, $X/id $I, $X/name $N.
item-warehouse(f_I($I),f_W($W)) <- source3/store/inventory/inv-tuple $X, $X/item-id $I, $X/warehouse-id $W.
warehouse-state(f_W($W),$S)    <- source3/store/warehouses/w-tuple $X, $X/id $W, $X/state $S.
```

Fig. 3. Mappings.

We expect users (local source administrators) will create such transformations or mappings with the aid of tools. In the paper, for simplicity, in place of the complex syntax of XSLT, we use a fragment of XPath together with predicates to express the mappings. An example mapping program for some of the properties of data sources of Figure 2 appears in Figure 3. We have used URI-generating functions f_I and f_W in the following mappings. A *URI-generating* function is a one-to-one function that takes an identifier of an object and generates a unique URI for that object. A simple scheme can be employed for URI generation. For example, for an item id `$I`, f_I(`$I`) = `baseURI/item#$I`. This simplifies the task of determining whether two URIs correspond to the same object. This can be accomplished by stripping away the `baseURI` components, and comparing the extension for equal (or equivalent) object ids.

Global queries can now be formulated using these vocabulary predicates. No knowledge of local sources is needed for this task.

Example 1 (A global query). Revisit the query "For each state, list the state information and all (distinct) items available in warehouses in that state." For simplicity, we have assumed different sources are using the same domain for item ids (such as the manufacturer's item id), and the same URI-generating functions for each domain[2]. We can formulate this query as follows:

```
for $S in distinct-values(warehouse-state/tuple/state)
return <state> {$S}
  for $X in warehouse-state/tuple[state=$S]
      $Y in item-warehouse/tuple[warehouse=$X/warehouse]
      $Z in item-itemId/tuple[item=$Y/item]
  return
   <item> <id> {distinct($Z/itemId)} </id> <item>
  </state>
```

Note that the only information needed to formulate this query is the knowledge that the federation contains the vocabulary predicates – `item-warehouse`

[2] In general, local sources may use their own id domains and URI-generating functions. In such cases, mappings (for example between local item ids and manufacturer's item ids) should be available to relate different id domains and URIs in order to make interoperability possible.

listing items and the warehouses for each item, `warehouse-state` listing warehouses and their respective states, and `item-itemId` relating URIs to database-style identifiers. Also note that, in general, each source in the federation may have none, some, or all of the predicates specified in the global query.

The rest, optimization and execution of query, is the responsibility of the system. We will discuss query optimization and processing in Section 4. ■

3 Local Source Declarations

The main idea behind our approach is to provide a simple yet powerful model for semantic markups for local information sources that makes interoperability possible. Any approach to interoperability and integration is ultimately dependent on standards, common vocabularies, and higher level declarations that relate vocabularies to each other. Our approach is based on *ontologies.* An application specific ontology specifies the classes (concepts) and predicates (properties) that are needed for the modeling of the application. For example, in our catalog stores application, the classes are `items`, `warehouses`, `cities`, `states`, etc., and properties are `item-itemId`, `item-name`, `item-description`, `item-warehouse`, `warehouse-warehouseId`, `warehouse-city`, and `warehouse-state`.

Where do ontologies come from? And aren't they a little like a global schema which we wanted not to have to assume? Firstly, currently there are several efforts underway toward developing just such ontologies [4] (also see the bibliography ontology in [16]). We envisage that groups of parties engaged in specific applications will converge to standard ontologies. Secondly, unlike the problem with global schema, we are *not* attempting to determine a commonly agreed upon global schema into which local source schemas can be mapped. Rather, the idea is that whenever a source/site wants to join an interoperability effort, it must map its data to the standard ontology that already exists. In other words, we get the global schema for free, as long as an application specific standard ontology exists.

In general, we expect ontologies containing the following information to be useful for interoperability:

- Property names and usages.
- Domain and range of each property. We will treat this as the two arguments of the corresponding predicate. For example, the property `item-warehouse` takes two arguments, which are URIs for item (domain) and warehouse (range), respectively.
- Key and cardinality information for predicates. For example, `person` is the key in `person-salary`, and `person-child` is [1-2]-to-n.
- Additional type information for arguments. For example, in the predicate `person-salary`, the type information for salary may specify additional information such as currency, and period (*e.g.* annual, monthly, bi-weekly).

If different terminologies are used in the declaration of the semantic contents of different sources, then higher-level declarations (typically domain level ontologies) relating the concepts and properties of different applications in the domain (which are used by different sources) are needed to make interoperability possible.

A local source exists in its native model (XML data, relational, spreadsheet, etc.). To make interoperability possible, the user (or local database administrator) should (1) choose the set of properties from a relevant ontology to model the source contents, and (2) provide *mappings* (or transformation rules) that map source data to the properties.

3.1 Mappings

Once the set of properties to model the contents of a source has been determined, mappings from XML data (or other source types) to properties should be established. The language we use to specify XML-to-property mappings is based on a (subset of) XPath and is similar to mapping languages (also called *transformation rules*) in the literature (For example, [9]). The mapping for a binary property p has the following form

```
p(f($X), g($Y)) <- path1 $G, $G/path2 $X, $G/path3 $Y.
```

where `$X` and `$Y` correspond to the arguments of p, `f($X)` is either $X itself, or f_X`($X)`, where f_X is the URI-generating function for objects `$X` of type X, and similarly for `g($Y)`. The variable `$G` is called the *glue* variable, and is used to restrict the (`$X`,`$Y`) pairs to have the same `$G` ancestor element in the document.

We envision tools to assist users (or database administrators of local sources) in defining the mappings. The graphical interface displays the structure of the XML document as a graph. To specify the mapping for a property `p`, three nodes in the XML schema graph should be selected by the user to determine (1) and (2): Variables associated with each of the arguments, respectively, and (3): The glue variable. Normally, the node specifying the glue variable is the least common ancestor of the first two nodes that specify the arguments. Sometimes, gluing may be accomplished by equating values of elements related to the first two argument elements. The user should also specify whether URI-generating functions are applied to the first and/or second argument. To be consistent with RDF, we require the first argument to be a URI. Hence, if `$X` is not a URI, then a URI-generating function must be applied to it.

Example 2 (Mapping Tool). In the schema graph of source 1 (below) user selects a property **item-warehouse** from an appropriate ontology, and specifies the three nodes **id**, **@id**, and **warehouse** for argument1, argument2, and glue, respectively. He also specifies that URI-generating functions should be applied to the arguments. The following mapping is then generated by the tool.

```
item-warehouse(f_I($I),f_W($W)) <- source1/store/warehouse $X,
                                   $X/item/id $I, $X/@id $W
```

```
            store
              |*
          warehouse
       /  |     \   \*
   @id city state item
                  / | \
              id name description
```

Note that the type of the URI-generating functions is determined by type information contained in the ontology. For example, since the domain of `item-warehouse` (*i.e.*, its first argument) is of type `item`, then the URI-generating function for items, f_I, is applied to the first argument. Similarly, f_W, the URI-generating function for warehouses, is applied to the second argument. ■

The mapping tool can also assist the user by performing certain *type* and *role* checking on the arguments of the predicate, and verifying or deriving integrity constraints for the predicates. The extent to which the tool can succeed in these tasks depends on the richness of local source (native) declarations of types and constraints. For example, a rich declaration for XML data would use a powerful schema declaration language (such as XML Schema) and contain elaborate integrity constraints satisfied by source data.

Example 3. For the property `warehouse-state`, the ontology may specify that the first argument should be an identifier for warehouses, and should be the key for the property. These requirements can be verified by the tool if adequate declarations exist for the sources. For example, in the DTD of source 1, the `@id` attribute of `warehouse` is of type `ID`, hence it is an identifier for `warehouse`. As a result, f_W`($id)` is also an identifier for warehouse (recall that URI-generating functions are one-to-one). Alternatively, if XML Schema was used, the requirements could be derived from the following constraint[3] $(\epsilon, (source1/store/warehouse, (\{@id\})))$ using techniques of [9]. ■

We will study the problem of deriving foreign key constraints (or referential integrity constraints) for the properties from XML source schema specifications and mapping rules (Section 4.3). These constraints play a very important role in query optimization in this approach. Davidson et al. [9] have studied the problem of deriving or verifying functional dependencies from XML key constraints. Their algorithms can be used by the mapping tool for the verification of mapping correctness by checking argument roles and constraints that should be satisfied by the properties.

4 Query Translation, Processing, and Optimization

In this section, we discuss query specification and translation, and present algorithms for the optimization and efficient processing of queries. Recall that we

[3] Which says in the context of the whole document, attribute `@id` uniquely identifies a warehouse.

use the terms *property* and *predicate* interchangeably. The latter is used predominantly in this section to emphasize the relational view of properties (in the database sense). Our simple model of binary predicates significantly simplifies the task of query formulation. The federation consists of local sources, where the content of each source has been declared by a set of predicates, together with data mappings to these predicates. Let's assume, for the time being, that all local declarations use the same ontology. We will relax this assumption later in Section 4.4. In this case, the "global schema" is simply the collection of all local predicates.

Given a predicate p, a source i may contain a fragment of p, which we denote by p_i. In general, fragments of the same predicate at different sources may contain overlapping data. We refer to the (conceptual) union of all fragments p_i of a predicate p as the *global* predicate p.

A query is formulated in terms of global predicates and predicate fragments. The query processor architecture is shown in Figure 1. A naive implementation approach is to materialize these predicates at the coordinator using the local mapping specifications, and then execute the query using materialized predicates. This approach will be very inefficient in general.

A better approach involves expanding the query by replacing each global predicate by the union of its fragments. The outcome, in general, consists of a collection of *local* (*i.e.*, intra-source) and *inter-source* sub-queries, the results of which should be combined to obtain the answer to the query. The coordinator is in charge of query expansion, query preparation and transformation (to local native schemas), and coordination of sub-query execution at different sources. It then collects results of the sub-queries and combines them to form the final answer.

A local sub-query is one where all the predicate fragments specified in the sub-query belong to the same source. A local sub-query can be rewritten in the native model of the source, and executed locally at that source. We will demonstrate this with an example below.

In an inter-source query, fragments from different sources are specified. We present various techniques for the translation, optimization, and processing of inter-source queries (Section 4.2). Processing these queries normally involves data transmission between sources so optimizing inter-source queries is important.

Example 4 (A local query). Let's consider the global query Q of Example 1. The local sub-query obtained from Q for source 1 is obtained by substituting predicate fragments `warehouse-state-1`, `item-warehouse-1`, and `item-itemId-1` for the corresponding predicates in Q.

The local query is then transformed by substituting its variable declarations by variable declarations obtained from mappings for source 1 (see Figure 3). We also make the observation that URIs were generated for the predicates (properties) to be consistent with RDF. When translating back to the native source data, we can use the object identifier instead of its corresponding URI. This follows from the fact that URI-generating functions are one-to-one. For example, `@id` is used instead of f_W (`@id`) in the transformation of our query. The resulting sub-query for source 1 is shown below.

```
for $S in distinct-values(source1/store/warehouse/state)
return <state> {$S}
  for $XG in source1/store/warehouse[state=$S],
      $YG in source1/store/warehouse[@id=$XG/@id]
  return <item> <id> {distinct($YG/item/id)} </id> <item>
  </state>
```

The last step for local queries is native query optimization, which may be carried out by the coordinator, the source, or both. In this example, the optimizer realizes **$XG** and **$YG** are the same, and eliminates one to get the following local query to be executed by the local source. Physical query optimization by a source follows this logical optimization.

```
for $S in distinct-values(source1/store/warehouse/state)
return <state> {$S}
  for $XG in source1/store/warehouse[state=$S]
  return
   <item> <id> {distinct($XG/item/id)} </id> <item>
  </state>
```

Algorithm 1 (Local Sub-query Generation for an XML Source)

Input: Global query Q, source mappings m_i for source i

Output: Local sub-query Q_i at source i resulting from Q.

Method: The idea is to replace variable declarations of Q with variable declarations of source i using the mapping rules m_i. Certain details should be observed in this translation as follows:

(1) If a variable declaration **$X** in Q corresponds to a *tuple* of a predicate p, then replace it by the declaration for the *glue* variable in the mapping rule for p in m_i.

(2) If a variable declaration **$X** in Q corresponds to an *argument* of a predicate p, and the declaration also has a selection condition on the other argument, then replace it by the declaration for the *glue* variable in the mapping rule for p in m_i, and include the selection condition as well.

(3) If a variable declaration **$X** in Q corresponds to an *argument* of a predicate p, and rule (2) above does not apply, then replace it by the declaration for the argument obtained from the mapping rule for p in m_i.

(4) If a URI is used in Q, then Q_i will use its corresponding object id. (Note: we are assuming global queries do not ask for URIs. Otherwise, only for the output, Q_i applies the URI-generating function to the corresponding object id.)

(5) Variables declared in Q with respect to an `object-objectId` predicate do not need a counterpart declaration in Q_i if the `object-objectId` predicate is joined with another predicate p having the same `object` as one of its arguments. In such cases the declaration in Q_i corresponding to p can supply the required variable.

Example 5. Consider our running query Q of Example 1, and its local sub-query Q_1 of Example 4 (before the final local optimization step). Variables \$X and \$Y in Q correspond to step (1) of the algorithm. In Q_1 they are replaced by \$XG and \$YG (their corresponding glue variables). Query Q does not contain any variables corresponding to step (2). An example would be the following declaration: `for $X in warehouse-state/tuple[state=$S]/warehouse`. Variable \$S in Q corresponds to step (3). The condition ... `[@id=$XG/@id]` in $Q1$ is an example of step (4). It resulted from ... `[warehouse=$X/warehouse]` in Q. Finally, as an example of step (5) of the algorithm, Q_1 does not have a variable that corresponds to `$Z` is Q. The output `$Z/itemID` has been replaced by `$YG/item/id` in Q_1. ∎

4.1 When Can Inter-source Processing Be Eliminated?

A global query often involves more than one predicate. If there are n sources and the query involves m predicates, then the expansion of the query results in $O(n^m)$ queries. Only $O(n)$ of these queries are local queries. The rest are expensive inter-source queries.

We are interested in characterizing cases where inter-source queries can be eliminated. If we can eliminate all inter-source queries, then we have reduced the number of queries to $O(n)$, instead of $O(n^m)$. In the remainder of this section we will study a simple case where the global query involves the joining of two binary predicates. Results of this section can be extended to more general cases.

Let the global query involve the join of predicates $p(A, B)$ and $q(B, C)$ on argument B. Our Example 1 was of this type, joining `item-warehouse` and `warehouse-state` on the `warehouse` argument. In general, predicate fragments from different sources contain overlapping data. Often a `distinct` clause must be used in the query to deal with multiplicities that result from this data duplication.

Consistency Condition: We say a predicate p satisfies the *consistency condition*, provided: (i) whenever the constraint $p(\alpha) \rightarrow p(\beta)$ holds in p, then it holds for every fragment p_i; (ii) if for fragments p_i and p_j we have $t_i \in p_i$, $t_j \in p_j$, such that $t_i(\alpha) = t_j(\alpha)$, then $t_i(\beta) = t_j(\beta)$.

The following theorem characterizes the cases where inter-source joins are not needed. Let Q be a query involving the join of $p(A, B)$ and $q(B, C)$, and suppose Q has the `distinct` clause to eliminate duplicates. Let k be a source.

Theorem 1. Suppose the key constraint $B \rightarrow C$ holds in q. No inter-source processing involving p_k is needed if and only if the following conditions hold: (1) The consistency condition holds for q, and (2) There is a foreign key constraint from p_k to q_k on the attribute B.

Proof. (*if*) We should show that any tuple in the join of p_k with q_i, $i \neq k$, is also in the join of p_k with q_k. Let $(a, b, c) \in p_k \bowtie q_i$. Then $(a, b) \in p_k$ and $(b, c) \in q_i$. By the foreign key constraint, there exists a tuple $(b, c') \in q_k$, for some c'. By the consistency requirement, and since q satisfies $B \rightarrow C$, we have $c' = c$, hence $(b, c) \in q_k$. It follows that $(a, b, c) \in p_k \bowtie q_k$.

(*only if*) We should show that if any of the conditions does not hold, then $p_k \bowtie q_i$, $i \neq k$, can contain a tuple that is not in $p_k \bowtie q_k$ (nor in any other $p_k \bowtie q_j$, $j \neq k$ and $j \neq i$). First, assume the consistency condition does not hold. Then, p_k and q_i can contain tuples (a, b) and (b, c), respectively. But q_k can have a tuple (b, c'), $c \neq c'$. Similarly, other q_j's may contain $(b, c")$, $c \neq c"$, or contain no tuple t_j where $t_j(A) = a$. Hence, the tuple (a, b, c) is only in $p_k \bowtie q_i$. The case when q_k does not satisfy $B \rightarrow C$ is similar. Finally, if the foreign key constraint from p_k to q_k does not hold, then p_k and q_i can contain tuples (a, b) and (b, c), respectively. But other q_j's, $j \neq i$ (including q_k) may contain no tuple t_j where $t_j(A) = a$. Again, the tuple (a, b, c) is only in $p_k \bowtie q_i$. ∎

We should emphasize that in this theorem we are assuming *only local information in the form of key and foreign key constraints, plus a consistency condition which is basically a statement of correctness of data across sources.* If other forms of constraints are permitted, the theorem can be extended by relaxing the conditions. An extension of the theorem is given below.

In Section 4.3 we discuss how referential integrities for predicates (properties) can be derived from local source native XML specifications and the predicate mappings. We also present an example (Example 6) in that section demonstrating that conditions of Theorem 1 are satisfied by source 1 for our running query example.

Relaxing the Conditions of Theorem 1

The first condition of Theorem 1 states that the argument B of $q(B, C)$ is the key for q. There are cases where the argument is not a key, but, semantically, a functional relationship exists. Consider, for example, the predicate `person-child`. It has two arguments. The first argument is a URI for person. The second argument is also a person URI (for a child of the first argument). The constraint that should hold is: Each person (URI) determines the *set* of his/her children (URIs). A relaxed consistency condition states the equality of the *sets* of associated objects:

Relaxed Consistency Assumption: We say a predicate p satisfies the (relaxed) consistency condition $p(\alpha) \rightarrow [p(\beta)]$ if for every pair of fragments p_i and p_j of p and $a \in p_i(\alpha) \cap p_j(\alpha)$ we have $\{t_i(\beta) \mid t_i \in p_i \text{ and } t_i(\alpha) = a\} = \{t_j(\beta) \mid t_j \in p_j \text{ and } t_j(\alpha) = a\}$.

The relaxed version of Theorem 1 is as follows.

Theorem 2. Let $p(A, B)$ and $q(B, C)$ be the predicates, and k be a source. If the following conditions hold: (1) The relaxed consistency condition $B \rightarrow [C]$ holds for q, and and (2) There is a referential integrity constraint from p_k to q_k on the attribute B.

Then no inter-source joins involving p_k is needed.

Proof. Proof is similar to the proof of Theorem 1 and is omitted. ∎

4.2 Efficient Inter-source Processing (When Needed)

Let's consider a query involving the join of predicates p and q, and concentrate on the inter-source processing of $p_i \bowtie q_j$, $i \neq j$. We will discuss several approaches. The optimization process, in general, will need a *cost-based* approach which estimates the cost of different approaches and selects the best.

A Naive Algorithm. A naive approach for calculating $p_i \bowtie q_j$ is to ship one complete document to the other site, and then proceed as before by transforming variable declarations of the query to variable declarations on the documents (that are now locally available) and executing the query locally.

Algorithm 2. A more promising approach for calculating $p_i \bowtie q_j$, $i \neq j$ is to first materialize one of the predicates locally and send it to the other site. Then only transform query variable declarations on the second predicate to its corresponding document, and execute the query (using the first predicate and the second document). For example, p_i can be materialized at site i and shipped to site j. Then query is transformed to one that uses predicate p_i and the document at site j. This approach may be more efficient than the first approach since the volume of data transferred may be significantly lower (predicate p_i versus the whole document at site i.) ■

If certain conditions hold, we can use the *semi anti-join* approach discussed below in the calculation of inter-source joins. The idea is to *avoid* generation of duplicate answers, thereby further optimizing query processing.

Assume the global query involves join of predicates $p(A, B)$ and $q(B, C)$. Conditions under which semi anti-join approach can be used in the calculation of inter-source joins are: (1) The global query has a `distinct` qualifier, and (2) The key constraints $A \rightarrow B$ and $B \rightarrow C$ and the consistency condition hold for p and q. (This condition can be reduced to relaxed consistency conditions $A \rightarrow [B]$ and $B \rightarrow [C]$ for p and q.)

The semi anti-join technique: When calculating inter-source join $p_i \bowtie q_j$ as a step towards calculating $p \bowtie q$, proceed as follows:

(1) Let the partial result of $p \bowtie q$ calculated so far be r. Ship $r[A]$ to site i.
(2) At site i, generate $p'_i = \{t \mid t \in p_i, t(A) \notin r[A]\}$.
(3) Ship p'_i to site j.
(4) Calculate $p'_i \bowtie q_j$.
(5) Combine the result with r to obtain the updated partial result.

We also present a variation on the semi anti-join algorithm that may be more efficient in some cases.

The maintenance of the partial result in the above algorithm may be expensive to the extent of making the overall join calculation sub-optimal. In the following version of the algorithm each source maintains its own partial result. The initial partial result at site i is $p_i \bowtie q_i$ which is calculated locally.

The modified semi anti-join technique: Let r_i be the (local) partial result at site i. To calculate $p_i \bowtie q_j$:

(1) At site i, generate $p'_i = \{t \mid t \in p_i, t(A) \notin r_i[A]\}$.
(2) Ship p'_i to site j.
(3) Calculate $p'_i \bowtie q_j$.
(4) Combine the result with r_j to obtain the updated partial result at site j.

4.3 Deriving Referential Integrities from XML Schema and Constraints

Theorem 1 can be used for query optimization to determine inter-source joins that can be avoided. To apply this theorem we need to know key and foreign key constraints on the predicates of each source. Results of [9] can be used to derive key constraints for predicates from schema specification and key constraints of the underlying XML data. In this section we study the problem of deriving referential integrity and foreign key constraints for the predicates.

Consider two binary predicates, p and q, with the following mappings. `$G` and `$H` are the glue variables of each rule, respectively.

```
p($X, $Y) <- path1 $G, $G/path2 $X, $G/path3 $Y.
q($Z, $W) <- path4 $H, $H/path5 $Z, $H/path6 $W.
```

Theorem 3 (referential integrities). If the following conditions hold for $p(A, B)$ and $q(B, C)$, then there is a referential integrity from p to q on B.

1. `path1/path3 = path4/path5`. Further, the element associated with `path1/path3` (or `path4/path5`) is declared by the source schema declaration to have non-null values.
2. The element associated with `path4/path6` is declared by the source schema declaration (i) to be required and (ii) to have non-null values. ■

Example 6. Let's revisit Example 1. This query involves the join of predicates `item-warehouse` and `warehouse-state`. Let's consider source 1. If we can verify the conditions of Theorem 1 for the fragments of these predicates at source 1, we can eliminate all inter-source joins involving `item-warehouse-1`. The first condition, namely $B \rightarrow C$ in `warehouse-state-1`(B, C), was verified in Example 3. The second condition, namely foreign key constraint from `item-warehouse-1` to `warehouse-state-1`, can be verified using Theorem 3. The mappings for these predicates were given in Section 2. From the DTDs in Figure 2, it is easy to verify that `path1/path3` = `source1/store/warehouse/@id` = `path4/path5`, and `@id` is a required attribute. For Condition 2, we notice `path4/path6` = `source1/store/warehouse/state`, and `state` element is also required.

If the conditions of Theorem 1 can also be verified for sources 2 and 3, then no inter-source processing at all is needed and query can the whole query can be processed by computing local queries and then combining the results. ■

4.4 Case of Multiple Ontologies

Up to this point, we had assumed local declarations used the same ontology for all sources. In this section, we relax this assumption and investigate the case where multiple ontologies are used in local declarations. We show how this affects query specification and translation, and argue that our query optimization techniques remain largely unchanged under the new model.

It has been argued that Description Logics (DL) provide the mathematical basis for ontology languages. In fact, OWL itself has been inspired and influenced by DL [3,7]. We will use DL in our discussions rather than the more verbose RDF or OWL specifications. An ontology specification, modeled as a DL theory, contains a set of base concepts and properties. New concepts and properties can be declared using base or already declared concepts and properties using operators of the DL. A concept is interpreted as a set of objects (belonging to, or having the type of, that concept), and a property is interpreted as a relationship among its underlying concepts. Several DLs have been proposed for ontology specifications, such as $\mathcal{DLR}$ and $\mathcal{SHIQ}$ [3,7], which differ in their set of operators and declaration power. The main goal has been to identify the language that provides the desired functionality, without becoming computationally undecidable or infeasible. DLs also provide mechanisms to declare concept hierarchies (taxonomies) and constraints.

When multiple ontologies are used in local declarations, providing interoperability is only possible if we are able to relate concepts and properties of different ontologies. This can be achieved if higher-level declarations relating ontologies are available, or through the use of tools that discover relationships among ontologies and produce the higher-level declarations.

There are recent investigations into the problem of *integration of ontologies.* It has been argued that a mechanism similar to the view mechanism in database systems is required for ontology integration in the general case [7]. In this section, we will concentrate on simple cases of ontology relationships that occur frequently in practice. More complicated cases need further investigation.

Given two ontologies O_1 and O_2, we study the case where concepts and properties of the two ontologies are related by *equivalence* and *sub-concept/sub-property* relationships, denoted by the symbols $\doteq$ and $\dot{\sqsubseteq}$. We say concepts (or properties) C_1 and C_2 in O_1 and O_2 are equivalent, $C_1 \doteq C_2$, if they are semantically the same concept (property). Similarly, $C_1 \dot{\sqsubseteq} C_2$ if C_1 is semantically a subconcept (subproperty) of C_2. The usual axioms apply to $\doteq$ and $\dot{\sqsubseteq}$, namely, (1) $\dot{\sqsubseteq}$ is reflexive, transitive, and antisymmetric, and (2) $C_1 \doteq C_2$ *iff* $C_1 \dot{\sqsubseteq} C_2$ and $C_2 \dot{\sqsubseteq} C_1$. It is important to note that $C_1 \dot{\sqsubseteq} C_2$ does *not* mean the extension of C_1 in a specific source is a subset of the extension of C_2 in another source. It merely states a semantic relationship between concepts across ontologies.

Recall that when a single ontology was used for all local declarations, we interpreted a global property p as the union of its fragments p_i for each source i. We extend this view to the case of multiple ontologies related by $\doteq$ and $\dot{\sqsubseteq}$ relationships as follows. Let p_i be a property at source i. Concept/property p_i is from ontology O_i. We interpret the *global* property p as the union of all properties that are equivalent to or subproperty of p_i, namely, $p = \bigcup\{q_j \mid q_j \dot{\equiv} p_i \text{ or } q_j \dot{\sqsubseteq} p_i\}$.

In this way, global queries can use a language that is the combination of the ontologies in the federation. Any symbol from any ontology can be used in the formulation of the query, and it is interpreted according to the semantics discussed above. Translation of queries to local and inter-source sub-queries is also a simple extension of the case for single ontology: The source-j fragments of a predicate p in the query are q_j's where $q_j \dot{\equiv} p$ or $q_j \dot{\sqsubseteq} p$. Note that, *unlike the case for single ontology, here a source may have more than one fragment corresponding to a concept or property.* For example, a source may have properties `student-salary` and `staff-salary` which are sub-properties (and, hence, fragments) of `person-salary`. The first step of the translation algorithm replaces each property in the query with the union of its fragments, and generates a set of local and inter-source queries. Once this is done, the translation of sub-queries to local (native) models and their optimization can proceed as discussed in previous sections for the single ontology case.

5 Related Work

Data integration has received significant attention since the early days of databases. Most approaches to data integration involve *deriving* a global schema, which integrates local schemas. Then mappings are provided between the global schema and local schemas. There are two general approaches: *local as view* where local sources are considered as views of the global; and *global as view* where rules are provided to derive global data from local sources. There are a number of excellent surveys and discussions on data integration and related topics [5,11,12, 13,19].

A more recent approach attempts at providing data sharing by mapping sources to each other. These approaches eliminate the need for deriving the global schema, and hence eliminate a substantial overhead in system design and creation. The approach of [10] is particularly attractive as it does not require schema mappings between every pair of sources. Rather, schema mappings can be *composed* to derive new mappings. Hence, it suffices for a source to provide a mapping to one other source, preferably the one closest to its structure. Every source-pair needs to be connected by a sequence of these peer-to-peer mappings. This approach works well when sources have more or less the same information content. Otherwise some concepts in a source may not have counterparts in another source, and the mapping will lose these concepts. The loss will be further propagated by mapping compositions. The Clio project has made significant contributions to the problems of data and schema integration from various source types (legacy, relational, object-oriented, semistructured) [2,15,18]. Their approach is based on providing tools to map any two schemas to each other, and hence it can be used for source-source as well as source-global approaches. Amann et al. [1] propose mappings of XML sources into a global schema using the local as view approach and propose algorithms for query rewriting and optimization.

Our approach differs from most of the previous approaches in that we provide simple but powerful declarations that are local to each source. Global interoperability is then obtained by using the predicates (properties) declared for each source.

Effective query optimization in our approach depends on rich schema specification and consistency rules declaration for local sources, and the ability to derive key and foreign key (or referential integrity) constraints for the predicates. There has been a lot of recent interest in the declaration of constraints for XML data, and derivation of constraints when XML data is stored as relational. Buneman et al. study the question of constraints declaration for XML [6]. The problem of propagating XML key constraints to relational is studied in [9]. They provide algorithms to determine, given XML key constraints and XML to relational transformation rules, whether a given FD is implied by the XML key constraints. We can utilize these results, as well as our results in Section 4.3, to derive key and foreign key constraints that are used in query optimization.

6 Conclusion

The vision behind our project is to create a lightweight scalable infrastructure for interoperating over XML data sources. Thereto, we presented an approach that derives its inspiration from the semantic web initiative, specifically RDF and OWL, to semantically mark up the information contents of data sources using application specific common vocabulary, by means of mappings, specified in a language like XSLT. User queries are expressed over this vocabulary and are translated into source specific access code and optimized. We addressed issues of eliminating or optimizing the costly inter-source queries as well as inference of integrity constraints over the vocabulary predicates, across the mapping rules. We are currently implementing a prototype system incorporating these ideas. Our ongoing work addresses various exciting technical challenges arising from this investigation.

References

1. B. Amann, C. Beeri, I. Fundulaki, and M. Scholl. Querying XML sources using an ontology-based mediator. In *Proceedings of International Conference on Cooperative Information Systems*, pages 429–448, 2002.
2. P. Andritsos, R. Fagin, A. Fuxman, L. M. Haas, M. A. Hernández, C.-T. Ho, A. Kementsietsidis, R. J. Miller, F. Naumann, L. Popa, Y. Velegrakis, C. Vilarem, and L.-L. Yan. Schema management. *IEEE Data Engineering Bulletin*, 25(3), 2002.
3. F. Baader, I. Horrocks, and U. Sattler. Description logics as ontology languages for the semantic web. In D. Hutter and W. Stephan, editors, *Festschrift in honor of Jörg Siekmann*, Lecture Notes in Artificial Intelligence. Springer, 2003. To appear.

4. T. Berners-Lee and E. Miller. The semantic web lifts off. *ERCIM News*, 51, pp. 9–11, 2002.
5. P. A. Bernstein. Applying model management to classical meta data problems. In *Proceedings of Conference on Innovative Data Systems Research*, 2003.
6. P. Buneman, S. B. Davidson, W. Fan, C. S. Hara, and W.-C. Tan. Keys for XML. *Computer Networks*, 39(5):473–487, 2002.
7. D. Calvanese, G. D. Giacomo, and M. Lenzerini. A framework for ontology integration. In *Proceedings of Semantic Web Working Symposium*, 2001.
8. The DARPA agent markup language (DAML). `http://www.daml.org/`.
9. S. Davidson, W. Fan, C. Hara, and J. Qin. Propagating XML constraints to relations. In *Proceedings of IEEE International Conference on Data Engineering*, 2003.
10. A. Halevy, O. Etzioni, A. Doan, Z. Ives, J. Madhaven, L. McDowell, and I. Tatarinov. Crossing the structure chasm. In *Proceedings of Conference on Innovative Data Systems Research*, 2003.
11. A. Y. Halevy. Answering queries using views. *The VLDB Journal*, 10(4):270–294, 2001.
12. *IEEE Data Engineering Bulletin*, 25(3), 2002. Special issue on Integration Management.
13. M. Lenzerini. Data integration: A theoretical perspective. In *Proceedings of ACM Symposium on Principles of Database Systems*, pages 233–246, 2002.
14. A. Y. Levy, A. Rajaraman, and J. J. Ordille. Querying heterogeneous information sources using source descriptions. In *Proceedings of International Conference on Very Large Databases*, pages 251–262, 1996.
15. R. J. Miller, M. A. Hernández, L. M. Haas, L.-L. Yan, C. T. H. Ho, R. Fagin, and L. Popa. The Clio project: Managing heterogeneity. *SIGMOD Record*, 30(1), 2001.
16. E. Mena. `http://sol1.cps.unizar.es:5080/OBSERVER/ontologies.html`.
17. OWL web ontology language. `http://www.w3c.org/TR/owl-features`.
18. L. Popa, Y. Velegrakis, R. J. Miller, M. A. Hernández, and R. Fagin. Translating web data. In *Proceedings of International Conference on Very Large Databases*, 2002.
19. E. Rahm and P. A. Bernstein. A survey of approaches to automatic schema matching. *The VLDB Journal*, 10(4):334–350, 2001.
20. Resource description framework (RDF). `http://www.w3c.org/RDF/`.
21. Semantic web. `http://www.w3c.org/2001/sw/`.
22. The TSIMMIS project home page.
`http://www-db.stanford.edu/tsimmis/tsimmis.html`.
23. XML topic maps (XTM). `http://www.topicmaps.org/xtm/`.

C-OWL: Contextualizing Ontologies

Paolo Bouquet[1,2], Fausto Giunchiglia[1,2], Frank van Harmelen[3], Luciano Serafini[1], and Heiner Stuckenschmidt[3]

[1] ITC-IRST, Trento, Italy
[2] DIT - University of Trento, Trento, Italy
[3] AI Department, Vrije Universiteit Amsterdam, The Netherlands

Abstract. Ontologies are *shared* models of a domain that encode a view which is common to a set of different parties. Contexts are *local* models that encode a party's subjective view of a domain. In this paper we show how ontologies can be contextualized, thus acquiring certain useful properties that a pure shared approach cannot provide. We say that an ontology is contextualized or, also, that it is a *contextual ontology*, when its contents are kept local, and therefore not shared with other ontologies, and mapped with the contents of other ontologies via explicit (context) mappings. The result is *Context OWL (C-OWL)*, a language whose syntax and semantics have been obtained by extending the OWL syntax and semantics to allow for the representation of contextual ontologies.

1 Introduction

The aim of the Semantic Web is to make information on the World Wide Web more accessible using machine-readable meta-data. In this context, the need for explicit models of semantic information (terminologies and background knowledge) in order to support information exchange has been widely acknowledged by the research community. Several different ways of describing information semantics have been proposed and used in applications. However we can distinguish two broad approaches which follow somehow opposite directions:

Ontologies are *shared* models of some domain that encode a view which is common to a set of different parties [15];
Contexts are *local* (where *local* is intended here to imply *not shared*) models that encode a party's view of a domain [11,12,9].

Thus, ontologies are best used in applications where the core problem is the use and management of common representations. Many applications have been developed, for instance in bio-informatics [7], or for knowledge management purposes inside organizations [6]. Contexts, instead, are best used in those applications where the core problem is the use and management of local and autonomous representations with a need for a limited and controlled form of globalization (or, using the terminology used in the context literature, maintaining *locality* still guaranteeing semantic *compatibility* among representations [9]). Examples of uses of contexts are the classifications of documents [4], distributed knowledge

D. Fensel et al. (Eds.): ISWC 2003, LNCS 2870, pp. 164–179, 2003.

management [1], the development and integration of catalogs [8,2], peer-to-peer applications with a large degree of *autonomy* of the peer nodes but still with a strong need of *coordination* [13,16] (with autonomy and coordination being the behavioral counterpart of the semantic need of locality and compatibility).

Contexts and ontologies have both strengths and weaknesses. It can be argued that the strengths of ontologies are the weaknesses of contexts and vice versa. On the one hand, the use of ontologies enables the parties to communicate and exchange information. Shared ontologies define a common understanding of specific terms, and thus make it possible to communicate between systems on a semantic level. On the weak side, ontologies can be used only as long as consensus about their contents is reached. Furthermore, building and maintaining (!) them may become arbitrarily hard, in particular in a very dynamic, open and distributed domain like the Web. On the other hand, contexts encode not shared interpretation schemas of individuals or groups of individuals. Contexts are easier to define and to maintain. They can be constructed with no consensus with the other parties, or only with the limited consensus which makes it possible to achieve the desired level of communication and only with the "relevant" parties. On the weak side, since contexts are local to parties, communication can be achieved only by constructing explicit mappings among the elements of the contexts of the involved parties; and extending the communication to new topics and/or new parties requires the explicit definition of new mappings.

Depending on their attitude, from an epistemological point of view, some people would argue that ontologies are all we need, while others would argue the exact contrary, namely that contexts are all we need. Our attitude in this paper is quite pragmatical. We believe that ontologies and contexts have both some advantages and that, therefore, they should be integrated in the representational infrastructure of the Semantic Web. Thus, on the one hand, the intended meaning of terms provided by parties which are willing to share information can be more easily captured with an ontology (or a set of shared ontologies). On the other hand, multiple ontologies (or sets or shared ontologies) which contain information which *should not* be integrated (an obvious example being information which is mutually inconsistent) should be contextualized. We say that an ontology is contextualized, or that it is a *contextual ontology*, when its contents are kept local (and therefore not shared with other ontologies) and are put in relation with the contents of other ontologies via explicit mappings.

Our approach in this paper is as follows. We take the notion of ontology as the core representation mechanism for representing information semantics. To this end, we start from the standard Web ontology language OWL [14]. Notice that from OWL we inherit the possibility to have shared ontologies. We show, providing some motivating examples, that OWL cannot model certain situations (Section 4). Finally, we provide an extension of OWL, that we call *Context OWL* (*C-OWL*), which allows us to deal with all the examples of Section 4. C-OWL integrates in a uniform way the, somehow orthogonal, key architectural features of contexts and ontologies and the consequent semantic level differences.

The main technical contributions of this paper are the following:

1. We provide a (somewhat synthetic) description of OWL and its semantics, restating Patel-Schneider and Hayes' semantics [15], in a formal framework more adequate to be extended (adapted) with a contextualized interpretation. These are the contents of Section 3.
2. We modify the OWL semantics to make it able to deal with the motivating examples reported in Section 4. These are the contents of Section 5.
3. We define the C-OWL syntax by taking the OWL syntax and by adding *bridge rules*, which allow to relate, at the syntactic and at the semantic level, concepts, roles and individuals in different ontologies. We call a set of bridge rules between two ontologies a *context mapping*. Thus a *contextual ontology* is an OWL ontology embedded in a space of other OWL ontologies and related to them via context mappings. We define the C-OWL semantics by taking the modified OWL semantics, as defined in Section 5. These are the contents of Section 6.

The semantics of C-OWL is obtained by modifying the OWL semantics [15] using the ideas and notions originally developed in the semantics of context (the, so called, Local Models Semantics [9,10]). Bridge rules were originally defined in [11] and further studied in [9,10,4,3]. The bridge rules proposed in this paper were first defined in [5]. Finally the constructs for representing bridge rules have been taken from the context markup language CTXML [4].

2 Ontologies vs. Contexts, or Globalize vs. Localize

At the architectural level, the crucial difference between the notions of context and ontology is in how mappings among multiple models are constructed:

- in OWL, mappings are not part of the language. The ability of combining models is restricted to the import of complete models and to the use of the imported elements by direct reference. Via the import mechanism, a set of local models is *globalized* in a unique shared model (which, however, keeps track of the original distinctions). It is assumed that references to external statements are only made for statements from imported models, however, this is strictly speaking not required. As a consequence, mappings rather implicitly exist in terms of mutual use of statements across models. Further, there are two ways of treating external statements: we can either treat the referred statement as a single fact with no further implications that the one it directly encodes, or we can use the complete model containing the fact as additional knowledge. This latter view is the one adopted in OWL, and it is the one we will consider in the following.
- in context-based approaches, local models are kept *localized*. A limited and completely controlled form of globalization is obtained by using explicit mappings. In this approach, mappings are regarded as projections of a local representation onto another, and are first class modelling elements with a

unique identity. In other words, also mappings are viewed as part of a local representation. This view makes it possible to have multiple alternative mappings between the same pair of contexts, and to define mappings in one direction that differ from the mappings in the opposite direction.

This different bias towards localization/globalization, and the consequent very different treatment of mappings lead to important semantic differences. OWL is mainly inspired by the Tarskian style semantics of propositional description logics. A model theoretic semantics is provided by mapping the elements of existing models into an abstract domain, where concepts are represented by sets, relation by sets of tuples and instances by elements of that domain. When reasoning is performed across different models, then these models are assumed to share the interpretation domain. Thus, as a consequence, the mappings between two models become part of the overall model and define constraints on the elements of the original two models.

The situation is quite different when we move to contexts. In the Local Models Semantics, each context uses a local set of models and a local domain of interpretation. Relations between these local interpretation domains are established by *domain relations* which explicitly codify how elements in one domain map into elements of the other domain. Domain relations are indexed by source and target domain, making them irreversible and non-transitive; and bridge rules modify only the target context, leaving the source unaffected.

3 A Global Semantics for OWL

According to [15], an OWL ontology is a set of annotated *axioms* and *facts*, plus import references to other ontologies. OWL ontologies can be referenced by means of a URI. Ontologies can also have annotations that can be used to record authorship and other information associated with an ontology. Since annotation directives have no effect on the semantics of OWL ontologies in the abstract syntax, we ignore them. We concentrate on the OWL-DL fragment of OWL. This language is equivalent to the SHOIQ(D+) DL, i.e., SHIQ(D+) extended with an equivalent of the oneOf constructor. The proposed framework can be restricted or generalized to OWL-lite and OWL-full, respectively.

Let I be a set of indexes, standing for a set of URI's of onotlogies. For instance I contains `http://www.w3.org/2002/07/owl`. Let also $\mathbb{C}$, $\mathbb{R}$ and $\mathbb{O}$ be the sets of strings that can used to denote concepts, roles and individuals respectively. The disjoint union of $\mathbb{C}$, $\mathbb{R}$ and $\mathbb{O}$ is denoted with $\mathbb{L}$.

Definition 1 (OWL Ontology). *An* OWL Ontology *(or simply an* ontology*) is a pair $\langle i, O_i\rangle$, where $i \in I$ and $O_i = \langle T_i, A_i\rangle$ where T and A are a T-box and an A-box respectively in the SHOIQ(D+) description logic on $\mathbb{L} \cup (I \times \mathbb{L})$. $\langle i, O_i\rangle$ is an ontology with index i.*

Suppose that $C, D, E, F \in \mathbb{C}$ and $r, s \in \mathbb{R}$. The following are examples of concepts that can appear in O_i.

$$C, \quad i{:}C, \quad C \sqcap D, \quad j{:}E, \quad C \sqcap (j{:}E), \quad \exists r.C \sqcup D, \quad \exists(j{:}s).C \sqcup (j{:}F) \qquad (1)$$

Every expression occurring in O_i without an index is intended to be in the language defined by O_i, L_i. The expressions appearing in O_i with indexes j are supposed to be defined in O_j; therefore they appear in O_j without index. We introduce the notions of *local language* and *foreign language.*

Definition 2 (Local language). *A* local concept, *w.r.t. i, is an element of* $\mathbb{C}$ *that appears in* O_i *either without indexes or with index equal to i.* Local roles *and* local individuals *are defined analogously. The set of local concepts, local roles, and local individuals w.r.t. i are denoted by* $\mathbb{C}_i$, $\mathbb{R}_i$, *and* $\mathbb{O}_i$. *The* local language *to i,* $\mathbb{L}_i$, *is the disjoint union of them.*

Local objects of a language L_i are also called *i-objects.* For notational convenience, in the following we always use the colon notation. Thus, for instance, that local concepts $C \in \mathbb{C}_i$ of an ontology O_i are written as $i : C$. A *foreign concept,* or equivalently a *non local concept,* w.r.t. $i \in I$, is a concept that appears in O_i but is defined in some ontology O_j. Foreign concepts are referred with the notation $j{:}c$. An analogous definition can be given for roles and individuals.

Definition 3 (Foreign language). *For any* $j \neq i$, *a* j-foreign concept *w.r.t.* i *is an element of* $\mathbb{C}$ *that appears in* O_i *with index* j. j-foreign roles *and* j-foreign individuals *are defined analogously. The j-foreign language w.r.t. i is the disjoint union of them.*

Among the concepts described in (1), C and D are local concepts w.r.t. i and r is a local role (w.r.t. i), while E and is a j-foreign concept and s is a j-foreign role. By means of foreign concepts, roles and individuals, two ontologies can refer to the *same* semantic object defined in a third ontology.

Definition 4 (OWL space). *An* OWL space *is a family of ontologies* $\{\langle i, O_i \rangle\}_{i \in I}$ *such that every* O_i *is an ontology, and for each* $i \neq j$, *the j-foreign language of* O_i *is contained in the local language of* O_j.

Moving to semantics, the idea is now to restate the semantics in [15] making explicit reference to the notions of local and foreign language. This distinction, crucial for the work developed in the next section, is not made in [15].

The semantics for OWL spaces defined in [15] is based on the intuition that, in OWL, as in RDF, a data type denotes the set of data values that is the value space for the data type. Concepts denote sets of individuals. Properties relate individuals to other information, and are divided into two disjoint groups, data-valued properties and individual-valued properties. Data-valued properties relate individuals to data values; individual-valued properties relate individuals to other individuals.

In the following we assume that any domain we introduce (denoted by Δ possibly with indexes) contains the union of the value spaces of the OWL data types and Unicode strings.

Definition 5 (OWL interpretation [15]). *An* OWL interpretation *for the OWL space* $\{\langle i, O_i \rangle\}_{i \in I}$, *is a pair* $\mathcal{I} = \langle \Delta^{\mathcal{I}}, (.)^{\mathcal{I}} \rangle$, *where* $\Delta^{\mathcal{I}}$, *contains a non-empty set of objects (the resources) and* $(.)^{\mathcal{I}}$ *is a function such that*

1. $\mathcal{I}(i, C) \subseteq \Delta^{\mathcal{I}}$ *for any* $i \in I$ *and* $C \in \mathbb{C}_i$;
2. $\mathcal{I}(i, r) \subseteq \Delta^{\mathcal{I}} \times \Delta^{\mathcal{I}}$ *for any* $i \in I$ *and* $r \in \mathbb{R}_i$;
3. $\mathcal{I}(i, o) \in D^{\mathcal{I}}$ *for any* $i \in I$ *and* $o \in \mathbb{O}_i$;

Notice that $(.)^{\mathcal{I}}$ can be extended to all the complex descriptions of SHIQ(D+) as usual. Statements contained in the A-box and the T-box (i.e., facts and axioms) of an ontology O of an OWL space $\{\langle i, O_i\rangle\}_{i\in I}$ can be verified/falsified by an interpretation according the axioms written in [15].

We call the above interpretation, a *global interpretation*, to emphasize the fact that language is interpreted against a global domain. We call the overall approach, the *global semantics* approach to OWL.

Definition 6 (OWL axiom and fact satisfiability [15]). *Given an* OWL interpretation $\mathcal{I}$ *for* $\{\langle i, O_i\rangle\}_{i\in I}$, $\mathcal{I}$ *satisfies a fact or an axiom* ϕ *of the* O_i *according to the rules defined in the table "Interpretation of Axioms and Facts" of [15]. An OWL interpretation* $\mathcal{I}$ *satisfies an OWL space* $\{\langle i, O_i\rangle\}_{i\in I}$, *if* $\mathcal{I}$ *satisfies each axiom and fact of* O_i, *for any* i.

Notice that we do not give any interpretation of the possibility for O_i to import another ontology O_j. However, from the logical point of view, importing O_j into O_i can be thought of as duplicating all the statements of O_j in O_i.

4 Motivating Examples

We provide some examples which cannot be represented with the current syntax and semantics of OWL. These examples show the need to enrich ontologies with the capability to cope with:

1. *the directionality of information flow*: we need to keep track of the source and the target ontology of a specific piece of information;
2. *Local domains*: we need to give up the hypothesis that all ontologies are interpreted in a single global domain;
3. *Context mappings*: we need to be able to state that two elements (concepts, roles, individuals) of two ontologies, though being (extensionally) different, are *contextually* related, for instance because they both refer to the same object in the world.

Example 1 (Directionality). Consider two ontologies O_1 and O_2 and suppose that O_2 is an extension of O_1, i.e., O_2 imports O_1 and adds it some new axiom. Directionality is fulfilled if the axioms added to O_2 should not affect what is stated in O_1. Consider the case where O_1 contains the axioms $A \sqsubseteq B$ and $C \sqsubseteq D$; furthermore, suppose that O_2 contains the axiom $B \sqsubseteq C$. We would like to derive $A \sqsubseteq D$ in O_2 but not in O_1.

Let us see how the global semantics behaves in this case. Let $\{\langle 1, O_1\rangle, \langle 2, O_2\rangle\}$ be the OWL space containing O_1 and O_2. Let A, B, C, and B be 1 local concepts. Suppose that O_1 contains the axioms $A \sqsubseteq B$ and $C \sqsubseteq D$. Suppose that O_2

imports O_1, this implies that O_2 contains $1{:}A \sqsubseteq 1{:}B$ and $1{:}C \sqsubseteq 1{:}D$. Finally suppose that O_2 contains the extra axiom $1 : B \sqsubseteq 1 : C$. We have that any interpretation of $\{\langle 1, O_1\rangle, \langle 2, O_2\rangle\}$, should be such that $(1{:}A)^{\mathcal{I}} \subseteq (1{:}B)^{\mathcal{I}} \subseteq (1{:}C)^{\mathcal{I}} \subseteq (1{:}D)^{\mathcal{I}}$; and therefore $(1{:}A)^{\mathcal{I}} \subseteq (1{:}D)^{\mathcal{I}}$. This means that $1{:}A \sqsubseteq 1{:}D$ is a logical consequence of the statements contained in the OWL space and, therefore, that directionality is not fulfilled.

Example 2 (A special form of directionality: the propagation of inconsistency). Consider the previous example and suppose that O_2 contains also the following two facts: $1{:}A(a)$ and $1{:}\neg D(a)$. O_2 is inconsistent, but we want to avoid the propagation of inconsistency to O_1. However, this is not possible as the fact that there is no interpretation that satisfies the axioms in O_2, automatically implies that there is no interpretation for the whole OWL space, either.

Example 3 (Local domains). Consider the ontology O_{WCM} of a worldwide organization on car manufacturing. Suppose that O_{WCM} contains the "standard" description of a car with its components. The domain of interpretation of this ontology is the totality of cars with their components. Clearly such a domain should be abstract enough so that it has not be changed whenever a new car appears on the earth. For instance, the extension of the concept car in this ontology will not be the set of actual physical cars in circulation, rather it will be some set of abstract objects for generic cars. Suppose also that this ontology contains two individual constants Diesel and Petrol for Diesel engine and petrol engine, and an axiom stating that a car has only one engine which is either Diesel or petrol, and that these two engines are different.

$$\mathsf{Car} \sqsubseteq (\exists 1)\mathsf{hasEngine}.\{\mathsf{Diesel}, \mathsf{Petrol}\} \tag{2}$$
$$\mathsf{Diesel} \neq \mathsf{Petrol} \tag{3}$$

A car manufacturing company, say Ferrari, decides to adopt the WCM standard and imports it in its ontology, O_{Ferrari}, used to describe Ferrari's production. Since Ferrari produces many petrol engines, a set of local constants for engines are added, eg. F23 and F34i, as well as the axiom, stating that the engine of a Ferrari is either an F23 or an F34i

$$\mathsf{Ferrari} \sqsubseteq (\mathsf{WCM{:}car} \sqcap (\exists 1)(\mathsf{WCM{:}hasEngine}).\{\mathsf{F23}, \mathsf{F23}\}) \tag{4}$$
$$\mathsf{F23} \neq \mathsf{F34i} \tag{5}$$

According to the global semantics we have that any interpretation of the OWL space containing O_{WCM} and O_{Ferrari} is such that, either $(\mathsf{F23})^{\mathcal{I}_{\mathsf{Ferrari}}} = (\mathsf{Diesel})^{\mathcal{I}_{\mathsf{WCM}}}$ or $(\mathsf{F34i})^{\mathcal{I}_{\mathsf{Ferrari}}} = (\mathsf{Diesel})^{\mathcal{I}_{\mathsf{WCM}}}$, which is not what we want as Ferrari produces only petrol engines. The main problem here is the diversity of the domains between O_{Ferrari} and O_{WCM}. Indeed since in O_{WCM} it is not possible to list all the existing engines, this domain is abstracted to two abstract objects called Petrol and Diesel. In O_{Ferrari}, instead, this enumeration is possible and, therefore, the domain is more specific. Ultimately, the two domains are at two different level of abstraction and cannot be merged in a single one.

Example 4 (Context mappings). Suppose we have an ontology O_{FIAT} describing cars from a manufacturing point of view, and a completely independent ontology O_{Sale} describing cars from a car vendor point of view. The two concepts of car defined in the two ontologies, (that can be referred by Sale: Car and FIAT : Car) are very different and it makes no sense for either ontology to import the concept of car from the other. The two concepts are not extensionally equivalent and the instances of FIAT:Car do not belong to Sale : Car and vice-versa. On the other hand the two concepts describe the same real-world class of objects from two different points of view, and there can be many reasons for wanting to integrate this information. For instance one might need to build a new concept which contains (some of) the information in Sale: Car and in FIAT: Car. This connection cannot be stated via OWL axioms, as, for instance

$$\mathsf{Sale{:}Car} \equiv \mathsf{FIAT{:}Car}$$

implies that

$$\mathsf{Car}^{\mathcal{I}_{\mathsf{Sale}}} = \mathsf{Car}^{\mathcal{I}_{\mathsf{FIAT}}}$$

i.e., that the two classes coincide at the instance level.

In this example, the problem is not only at the semantic level. As the following section will show, handling this example requires an extension of the OWL syntax.

5 A Semantics for Contextual Ontologies

In this section we incrementally extend/modify the OWL global semantics, and in the last subsection, also its syntax, in order to be able to model the above examples.

5.1 Directionality

We modify the definition of interpretation given above according to the intuition described in [3]. The main idea is that we split a global interpretation into a family of (local) interpretations, one for each ontology. Furthermore, we allow for an ontology to be locally inconsistent, i.e., not to have a local interpretation. In this case we associate to O_i a special "interpretation" $\mathcal{H}$, called a *hole*, that verifies any set of axioms, possibly contradictory.

Definition 7 (Hole). *A* Hole *is a pair* $\langle \Delta^{\mathcal{H}}, (.)^{\mathcal{H}} \rangle$, *such that* $\Delta^{\mathcal{H}}$ *is a nonempty set and* $(.)^{\mathcal{H}}$ *is a function that maps every constant of* $\mathbb{O}_i$ *into an element of* $\Delta^{\mathcal{H}}$, *every concept of* $\mathbb{C}_i$ *in the whole* $\Delta^{\mathcal{H}}$ *and every role of* $\mathbb{R}_i$ *into the set* $\Delta^{\mathcal{H}} \times \Delta^{\mathcal{H}}$. $\mathcal{H}$ *is called a hole on* Δ^{H}.

Analogously to what done in [3], the function $(.)^{\mathcal{H}}$ can be extended to complex descriptions and complex roles in the obvious way.

Definition 8 (Satisfiability in a hole). $\mathcal{H}$ *satisfies all the axioms and facts, i.e., if* ϕ *is an axiom or a fact,* $\mathcal{H} \models \phi$.

Definition 9 (OWL interpretation with holes). *An* OWL interpretation with holes *for the OWL space* $\{\langle i, O_i\rangle\}_{i\in I}$*, is a family* $\mathcal{I} = \{\mathcal{I}_i\}_{i\in I}$*, where each* $\mathcal{I}_i = \langle \Delta^{\mathcal{I}_i}, (.)^{\mathcal{I}_i}\rangle$*, called the* local interpretation *of* O_i*, is either an interpretation of* L_i *on* $\Delta^{\mathcal{I}_i}$*, or it is a hole for* L_i *on* $\Delta^{\mathcal{I}_i}$*, and for all* $i \in I$*, each* $\Delta^{\mathcal{I}_i}$ *coincides an are equal to a set denoted by* $\Delta^{\mathcal{I}}$.

Each $(.)^{\mathcal{I}_i}$ can be extended in the usual way to interpret local descriptions. Foreign descriptions are interpreted by the combination of the different $(.)^{\mathcal{I}_i}$ for each $i \in I$. In particular for any concept, role or individual of the alphabet L_j, $(.)^{\mathcal{I}_i}$ can be extended to be the same as $(.)^{\mathcal{I}_j}$. Namely:

$$(j\!:\!x)^{\mathcal{I}_i} = (x)^{\mathcal{I}_j} \tag{6}$$

which can intuitively be read as, "the meaning of the j-foreign concept $j : x$ occurring in O_i is the same as the meaning of x occurring in O_j". Since all interpretations share the same domain, this semantics is well founded. Namely, the interpretation of j-foreign concepts in i are contained in the domain of i, $\Delta^{\mathcal{I}_i}$. In the following we give some examples of $(.)^{\mathcal{I}_i}$, for which we suppose that $C, D \in \mathbb{C}_i$ and $r \in \mathbb{R}_i$ and $D, F \in \mathbb{C}_j$ and $s \in \mathbb{R}_j$.

$$C^{\mathcal{I}_i} = \begin{cases} \text{Any subset of } \Delta^{\mathcal{I}_i} \text{ if } \mathcal{I}_i \neq \mathcal{H}_i \\ \Delta^{\mathcal{I}} \text{ otherwise} \end{cases}$$

$$(C \sqcap D)^{\mathcal{I}_i} = \begin{cases} (C)^{\mathcal{I}_i} \cap (D)^{\mathcal{I}_i} \text{If } \mathcal{I}_i \neq \mathcal{H}_i \\ \Delta^{\mathcal{I}} \text{ otherwise} \end{cases}$$

$$(j : E)^{\mathcal{I}_i} = \begin{cases} (E)^{\mathcal{I}_j} \text{If } \mathcal{I}_i \neq \mathcal{H}_i \\ \Delta^{\mathcal{I}} \text{ otherwise} \end{cases}$$

$$(C \cap j : E)^{\mathcal{I}_i} = \begin{cases} (C)^{\mathcal{I}_i} \cap (E)^{\mathcal{I}_j} \text{If } \mathcal{I}_i \neq \mathcal{H}_i \\ \Delta^{\mathcal{I}} \text{ otherwise} \end{cases}$$

Definition 10 (Axiom satisfiability). *Given an* OWL interpretation with holes, $\mathcal{I}$ *for* $\{\langle i, O_i\rangle\}_{i\in I}$, $\mathcal{I}$ *satisfies a fact or an axiom* ϕ *of the* O_i*, in symbols* $\mathcal{I} \models i : \phi$ *if* $\mathcal{I}_i \models \phi$*. An OWL interpretation* $\mathcal{I}$ *satisfies an OWL space* $\{\langle i, O_i\rangle\}_{i\in I}$*, if* $\mathcal{I}$ *satisfies each axiom and fact of* O_i *for each* i.

Notice that interpretations with hole can behave differently in different ontologies. Thus, for instance, the same axiom can be satisfied in an ontology and not satisfied in another. Consider for instance the OWL interpretation with holes $\{\mathcal{I}_1, \mathcal{I}_2, \mathcal{H}_3\}$, where $\mathcal{I}_1$ and $\mathcal{I}_2$ are not holes. Suppose that $(A)^{\mathcal{I}_1} \not\subseteq (B)^{\mathcal{I}_2}$. Then we have that $1\!:\!A \sqsubseteq 1\!:\!B$ is not satisfied if it occurs in O_2, while it is satisfied if it occurs in O_3.

If every $\mathcal{I}_i$ is not a hole, the interpretation given of Definition 9 coincides with the global interpretation, as defined in Section 3. Let us analyze what happens when some $\mathcal{I}_i$ is a hole.

Example 5 (Examples 1 and 2 formalized). Consider the OWL interpretation with holes, $\mathcal{I} = \{\mathcal{I}_1, \mathcal{I}_2\}$ defined as follows

1. $\Delta^{\mathcal{I}_1} = \{a, b, c, d\}$, $A^{\mathcal{I}_1} = \{a\}$, $B^{\mathcal{I}_1} = \{a, b\}$, $C^{\mathcal{I}_1} = \{c\}$, $D^{\mathcal{I}_1} = \{c, d\}$,
2. $\Delta^{\mathcal{I}_2} = \{a, b, c, d\}$, and $\mathcal{I}_2 = \mathcal{H}_2$, i.e. $\mathcal{I}_2$ is a hole.

$\mathcal{I}$ is an interpretation for the OWL space containing O_1 and O_2, since

1. $\mathcal{I}_1 \models A \sqsubseteq B$, $\mathcal{I}_1 \models C \sqsubseteq D$, and $\mathcal{I}_1 \not\models A \sqsubseteq D$, by construction of $\mathcal{I}_1$,
2. $\mathcal{I}_2 \models 1{:}A \sqsubseteq 1{:}B$, $\mathcal{I}_2 \models 1{:}B \sqsubseteq 1{:}C$, and $\mathcal{I}_2 \models 1{:}C \sqsubseteq 1{:}D$, because $\mathcal{I}_2$ is a hole.

Notice that $\mathcal{I}$ is an interpretation that satisfies O_2 (i.e., $1{:}A \sqsubseteq 1{:}B$ $1{:}B \sqsubseteq 1{:}C$, and $1{:}C \sqsubseteq 1{:}D$)], without making $A \sqsubseteq D$ true in O_1.

To formalize Example 2, we consider the same interpretation as above. This interpretation satisfies any axiom in O_2 ($\mathcal{I}_2$ is a hole) still keeping O_1 consistent ($\mathcal{I}_1$ is an interpretation which is not a hole and which satisfies O_1).

5.2 Local Domains

The OWL semantics described in the previous section assumes the existence of a unique shared domain, namely, that each ontology describes the properties of the whole universe. In many cases this is not true as, for instance, an ontology on cars is not supposed to speak about medicines, or food. The idea here is to associate to each ontology a *local domain*. Local domains may overlap as we have to cope with the case where two ontologies refer to the same object.

Definition 11 (OWL interpretation with local domains). *An* OWL interpretation with local domains *for the OWL space* $\{\langle i, O_i\rangle\}_{i\in I}$, *is a family* $\mathcal{I} = \{\mathcal{I}_i\}_{i\in I}$, *where each* $\mathcal{I}_i = \langle \Delta^{\mathcal{I}_i}, (.)^{\mathcal{I}_i}\rangle$, *called the* local interpretation *of* O_i, *is either an interpretation of* L_i *on* $\Delta^{\mathcal{I}_i}$, *or a hole.*

Definition 11 is obtained from Definition 9 simply by dropping the restriction on domain equality. The interpretation $(.)^{\mathcal{I}_i}$ is extended to complex concepts, roles, and individuals, in the usual way. We have to take care, however, that j-foreign concepts, roles, and individuals used in O_i could be interpreted (by the local interpretation $\mathcal{I}_j$) in a (set of) object(s) which are not in the local domain $\Delta^{\mathcal{I}_i}$. Indeed, to deal with this problem, we have to impose that any expression occurring in O_i should be interpretable in the local domain $\Delta^{\mathcal{I}_i}$. As a consequence, we restrict the interpretation of any foreign concept $C \in \mathbb{C}_j$, any foreign role $r \in \mathbb{R}_j$ and any foreign individual $a \in \mathbb{O}_j$ as follows:

1. $(j{:}C)^{\mathcal{I}_i} = (C)^{\mathcal{I}_j} \cap \Delta^{\mathcal{I}_i}$
2. $(j{:}r)^{\mathcal{I}_i} = (r)^{\mathcal{I}_j} \cap (\Delta^{\mathcal{I}} \times \Delta^{\mathcal{I}})$
3. $(j{:}a)^{\mathcal{I}_i} = (a)^{\mathcal{I}_j}$

Notice that point 3 above implicitly imposes that if a j-foreign constant $j{:}a$ is used in the ontology O_i, then its interpretation in j, i.e., $a^{\mathcal{I}_j}$, must be contained in the domain $\Delta^{\mathcal{I}_i}$. Let us now see how we can deal with Example 3.

Example 6 (Example 3 formalized). Consider the OWL interpretation with local domains, $\mathcal{I} = \{\mathcal{I}_{\mathsf{WCM}}, \mathcal{I}_{\mathsf{Ferrari}}\}$ for the OWL space containing O_{WCM} and O_{Ferrari}. Suppose that Δ_{WCM} contains two constants d_1 and d_2, which are the interpretations of petrol and diesel, respectively. Suppose that $\Delta_{\mathsf{Ferrari}}$ contains two constants d_1 and d_3 which are the interpretations of F23 and F34i, respectively. Suppose also that $(\mathsf{hasAngine})^{\mathcal{I}_{\mathsf{WCM}}} = \{\langle c_1, d_1\rangle, \langle c_2, d_2\rangle\}$, where c_1 and c_2 are object for cars in both Δ_{WCM} and $\Delta_{\mathsf{Ferrari}}$. If can be verified that the axioms (2–5) are verified by the interpretation $\mathcal{I}$ and that it is the case that no Ferrari engine is a diesel.

5.3 Context Mappings

We have concepts, roles and individuals local to different ontologies and domains of interpretation. A context mapping allows us to state that a certain property holds between elements of two different ontologies. Thus, for instance, in Example 4, one possible mapping could allow us to say that the class Car in the ontology O_{FIAT} contains the same cars as (or, as we say, is contextually equivalent to) the class of Car defined in the ontology O_{Sale}. As from Example 4 this cannot be done via local axioms within an ontology.

The basic notion towards the definition of context mappings are *bridge rules.*

Definition 12 (Bridge rules). *A* bridge rule from i to j is a statement of one of the four following forms,

$$i:x \xrightarrow{\sqsubseteq} j:y, \quad i:x \xrightarrow{\sqsupseteq} j:y, \quad i:x \xrightarrow{\equiv} j:y, \quad i:x \xrightarrow{\perp} j:y, \quad i:x \xrightarrow{*} j:y,$$

where x and y are either concepts, or individuals, or roles of the languages L_i and L_j respectively.

A mapping between two ontologies is a set of bridge rules between them.

Definition 13 (Mapping). *Given a OWL space* $\{\langle i, O_i\rangle\}_{i\in I}$ *a* mapping M_{ij} *from* O_i *to* O_j *is a set of bridge rules from* O_i *to* O_j*, for some* $i, j \in I$.

Mappings are directional, i.e., M_{ij} is not the inverse of M_{ji}. A mapping M_{ij} might be empty. This represents the impossibility for O_j to interpret any i-foreign concept into some local concept. Dually M_{ij} might be a set of bridge rules of the form $i:x \xrightarrow{\equiv} j:y$ for any element x (concept, role, and individual) of O_i. This represents the operation of mapping all of O_i into an equivalent subset of O_j. If this subset is O_j itself then this becomes the contextual mapping version of the OWL import operation. However, notice that importing O_i into O_j is not the same as mapping O_i to O_j with M_{ij}. In both cases information goes from i to j. The difference is that, in the former case, O_j duplicates the information of i- foreign elements without any change, while, in the latter, O_j translates (via the mapping M_{ij}) the semantics of O_i into its internal (local) semantics.

Definition 14 (Context space). *A context space is a pair composed of an OWL space* $\{\langle i, O_i\rangle\}_{i\in I}$ *and a family* $\{M_{ij}\}_{i,j\in I}$ *of mappings from* i *to* j*, for each pair* $i, j \in I$.

To give the semantics of context mappings we extend the definition of OWL interpretation with local domains with the notion of *domain relation.* A domain relation $r_{ij} \subseteq \Delta^{\mathcal{I}_i} \times \Delta^{\mathcal{I}_j}$ states, for each element in $\Delta^{\mathcal{I}_i}$ to which element in $\Delta^{\mathcal{I}_j}$ it corresponds to. The semantics for bridge rules from i to j can then be given with respect to r_{ij}.

Definition 15 (Interpretation for context spaces). *An interpretation for a context space* $\langle\{\langle i, O_i\rangle\}_{i\in I}, \{M_{ij}\}_{ij\in I}\rangle$ *is composed of a pair* $\langle\mathcal{I}, \{r_{ij}\}_{i,j\in I}\rangle$. *where* $\mathcal{I}$ *is an OWL interpretation with holes and local domains of* $\{\langle i, O_i\rangle\}_{i\in I}$ *and* r_{ij}*, the domain relation from* i *to* j*, is a subset of* $\Delta^{\mathcal{I}_i} \times \Delta^{\mathcal{I}_j}$.

Definition 16 (Satisfiability of bridge rules[1]).

1. $\mathfrak{I} \models i{:}x \xrightarrow{\sqsubseteq} j{:}y$ *if* $r_{ij}(x^{\mathcal{I}_i}) \subseteq y^{\mathcal{I}_j}$;
2. $\mathfrak{I} \models i{:}x \xrightarrow{\sqsupseteq} j{:}y$ *if* $r_{ij}(x^{\mathcal{I}_i}) \supseteq y^{\mathcal{I}_j}$;
3. $\mathfrak{I} \models i{:}x \xrightarrow{\equiv} j{:}y$ *if* $r_{ij}(x^{\mathcal{I}_i}) = y^{\mathcal{I}_j}$;
4. $\mathfrak{I} \models i{:}x \xrightarrow{\bot} j{:}y$ *if* $r_{ij}(x^{\mathcal{I}_i}) \cap y^{\mathcal{I}_j} = \emptyset$;
5. $\mathfrak{I} \models i{:}x \xrightarrow{*} j{:}y$ $r_{ij}(x^{\mathcal{I}_i}) \cap y^{\mathcal{I}_j} \neq \emptyset$;

A interpretation for a context space is a model for it if all the bridge rules are satisfied.

When x and y are concepts, say C and D, the intuitive reading of $i{:}C \xrightarrow{\sqsubseteq} j : D$, is that the i-local concept C is more specific than the j-concept D. An analogous reading can be given to $i : C \xrightarrow{\sqsupseteq} j : D$. The intuitive reading of $i : C \xrightarrow{\bot} j : D$ is that C is disjoint from D. Finally, the intuitive reading of $i{:}C \xrightarrow{*} j{:}D$ is that C and D are two concepts which are compatible. When x and y are individuals, then $i : x \xrightarrow{\sqsubseteq} j : y$ states that y is a more abstract representation of the object represented by x in i (intuitively, there might be more than one x's corresponding to the same y) Vive-versa $i{:}x \xrightarrow{\sqsupseteq} j{:}y$ states that y is a less abstract (more concrete) representation of the object represented by x in i (intuitively there might be more than one y's corresponding to the same x). $i{:}x \xrightarrow{\equiv} j{:}y$ states that x and y are at the same level of abstraction. Notice that, we add $i{:}a \xrightarrow{\equiv} j{:}a$ for any individual a of Δ_i and Δ_j we reduce to the case of OWL interpretation with holes and local domains). $i{:}x \xrightarrow{\bot} j{:}y$ states that x and y denotes completely unrelated objects. While $i{:}x \xrightarrow{*} j{:}y$ states that x and y might be related.

[1] In this definition, to be more homogeneous, we consider the interpretations of individuals to be sets containing a single object rather than the object itself.

Example 7 (Example 4 and 3 formalized). The fact that SaleCar describes the *same* set of objects from two different points of view, can be captured by asserting the bridge rule:

$$\mathsf{Sale}:\mathsf{Car} \xrightarrow{\equiv} \mathsf{FIAT}:\mathsf{Car} \tag{7}$$

The domain relation from O_{Sale} to O_{FIAT} of any contextual interpretation satisfying (7) will be such that $r_{ij}(\mathsf{Car})^{\mathcal{I}_{\mathsf{Sale}}} = (\mathsf{Car})^{\mathcal{I}_{\mathsf{FIAT}}}$.

Contextual mappings can also be used to better formalize example 3. If, for instance, we want to state that F23 and F34i are two petrol engines, we can state the following bridge rules from O_{WCM} to O_{Ferrari}.

$$\mathsf{WCM}:\mathsf{Petrol} \xrightarrow{\sqsupseteq} \mathsf{Ferrari}:\mathsf{F23} \tag{8}$$

$$\mathsf{WCM}:\mathsf{Petrol} \xrightarrow{\sqsupseteq} \mathsf{Ferrari}:\mathsf{F34i} \tag{9}$$

The domain relation form O_{WCM} to O_{Ferrari} that satisfies the above axioms is such that $r_{\mathsf{WCM},\mathsf{Ferrari}}(\mathsf{Petrol}^{\mathcal{I}_{\mathsf{WCM}}}) \supseteq \{\mathsf{F23}^{\mathcal{I}_{\mathsf{Ferrari}}}, \mathsf{F34i}^{\mathcal{I}_{\mathsf{Ferrari}}}\}$.

6 Context OWL

As from Section 5, in C-OWL, directionality and local domains can be dealt with by maintaining the OWL syntax unchanged and by suitably modifying the OWL semantics. In practice this means that a C-OWL model will look exactly the same as a OWL model. However, from an operational point of view, certain operations that are allowed in OWL will no longer be allowed in C-OWL. In particular, for what concerns directionality, the facts of the source domain will not be accessible in the target domain while, for what concerns local domains, each ontology will be able to use only the individuals in its local domain.

As from Section 5.3, dealing with context mappings is more complex and requires also an extension of the OWL syntax (with the proper semantics, as provided in that section). In particular, we need to add constructs for representing bridge rules and, within them, domain relations. We propose below a syntax for C-OWL which basically replicates the constructs for bridge rules defined within CTXML. CTXML has two main components:

1. contexts, which in the first proposal, as described in [4], are very simple representational devices and allow only for hierarchical classifications; and
2. mappings between contexts, namely a set of bridge rules.

C-OWL can therefore be straightforwardly obtained from CTXML by substituting the language for representing contexts in item 1 with OWL, and by keeping item 2 unchanged. As a consequence, C-OWL has the full representational power of OWL when we boil down to using ontologies, and the full representational power of CTXML when we boil down to using contextual information. The further nice property of C-OWL is that the two components are

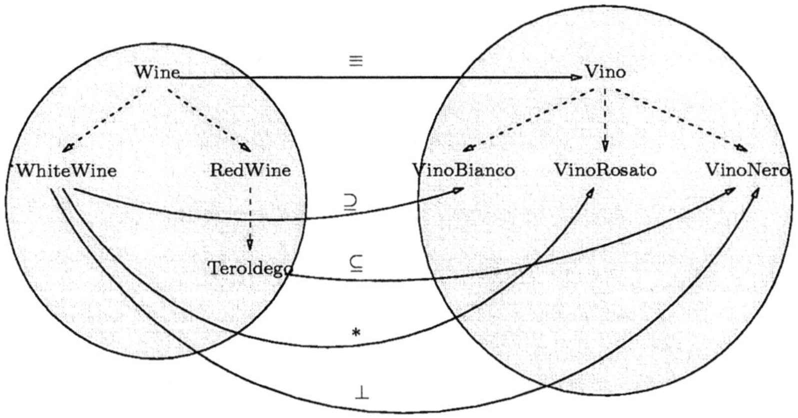

Fig. 1. A C-OWL mapping from the ontology "wine" to the ontology "vino".

```
;;;;; http://www.example.org/whine-to-vino.map;;;;;

<cowl:mapping>
  <rdfs:comment>Example of a mapping of wine into vino</rdfs:comment>
  <cowl:sourceOntology  rdf:resource="http://www.example.org/wine.owl"/>
  <cowl:targetOntology  rdf:resource="http://www.example.org/vino.owl"/>

  <cowl:bridgRule cowl:br-type="equiv">
     <cowl:sourceConcept rdf:resource="http://www.example.org/wine.owl#wine"/>
     <cowl:targedConcept rdf:resource="http://www.example.org/vino.owl#vino"/>
  </cowl:bridgRule>

  <cowl:bridgRule cowl:br-type="onto">
     <cowl:sourceConcept rdf:resource="http://www.example.org/wine.owl#RedWine"/>
     <cowl:targedConcept rdf:resource="http://www.example.org/vino.owl#VinoRosso"/>
  </cowl:bridgRule>

  <cowl:bridgRule cowl:br-type="into">
     <cowl:sourceConcept rdf:resource="http://www.example.org/wine.owl#Teroldego"/>
     <cowl:targedConcept rdf:resource="http://www.example.org/vino.owl#VinoRosso"/>
  </cowl:bridgRule>

  <cowl:bridgRule cowl:br-type="compat">
     <cowl:sourceConcept rdf:resource="http://www.example.org/wine.owl#WhiteWine"/>
     <cowl:targedConcept rdf:resource="http://www.example.org/vino.owl#Passito"/>
  </cowl:bridgRule>

  <cowl:bridgRule cowl:br-type="incompat">
     <cowl:sourceConcept rdf:resource="http://www.example.org/wine.owl#WhiteWine"/>
     <cowl:targedConcept rdf:resource="http://www.example.org/vino.owl#VinoNero"/>
  </cowl:bridgRule>
```

Fig. 2. A C-OWL mapping.

completely orthogonal and one can use the ontology or the contextual component in a totally independent manner.

A contextual ontology is therefore the pair: OWL ontology, set of C-OWL mappings, where each C-OWL mapping is a set of bridge rules with the same target ontology. A C-OWL mapping has therefore the following form:

1. A mapping identifier (URI)
2. A source context containing an OWL ontology (URI of an ontology)
3. A target context containing an OWL ontology (URI of an ontology)
4. A set of bridge rules from the local language of the source ontology to the local language of the target ontology. Each mapping is composed of three elements:
   a) a source element, which is either a concept, a role or an individual of the source ontology;
   b) a target element, which is either a concept, a role or an individual of the target ontology, with the restriction that this element must be of the same type as the source element.
   c) the type of mapping which is one of $\xrightarrow{\sqsubseteq}$, $\xrightarrow{\sqsupseteq}$, $\xrightarrow{\bot}$ and $\xrightarrow{*}$.

The proposal of a precise syntax for C-OWL is out of the scope of this paper. However the XML representation of the mapping between the two ontologies about wine given in Figure 1 will look something like Figure 2 (Teroldego is a very nice Trentino red wine).

7 Conclusion

In this paper we have shown how the syntax and the semantics of OWL can be extended to deal with some problems that couldn't otherwise be dealt with. The result is C-OWL (Context OWL), an extended language with an enriched semantics which allows us to contextualize ontologies, namely, to localize their contents (and, therefore, to make them not visible to the outside) and to allow for explicit mappings (bridge rules) which allow for limited and totally controlled forms of global visibility.

This is only the first step and a lot of research remains to be done. The core issue at stake here is the tension between how much we should share and globalize (via ontologies) and how much we should localize with limited and totally controlled forms of globalization (via contexts).

References

1. M. Bonifacio, P. Bouquet, G. Mameli, and M. Nori. Kex: a peer-to-peer solution for distributed knowledge management. In D. Karagiannis and U. Reimer, editors, *Fourth International Conference on Practical Aspects of Knowledge Management (PAKM-2002)*, Vienna (Austria), 2002.
2. M. Bonifacio, A. Doná, A. Molani, and L. Serafini. Context matching for electronic market places – a case study. Technical report, ITC IRST, March 2003. Available at `sra.itc.it/people/serafini/distribution/BDMS-mar-2002.pdf`.
3. A. Borgida and L. Serafini. Distributed description logics: Directed domain correspondences in federated information sources. In R. Meersman and Z. Tari, editors, *On The Move to Meaningful Internet Systems 2002: CoopIS, Doa, and ODBase*, volume 2519 of *LNCS*, pages 36–53. Springer Verlag, 2002.

4. P. Bouquet, A. Donà, L. Serafini, and S. Zanobini. ConTeXtualizedlocal ontology specification via ctxml. In P. Bouquet, editor, *Working Notes of the AAAI-02 workshop on Meaning Negotiation. Edmonton (Canada). July 28, 2002.* AAAI, AAAI Press, 2002.
5. P. Bouquet, B. Magnini, L. Serafini, and S. Zanobini. A sat-based algorithm for context matching. In P. Blackburn, C. Ghidini, and R. Turner, editors, *Proc. of Fourth International and Interdisciplinary Conference on Modeling and Using Context (Context'03)*, LNAI. Springer Verlag, 2003. To appear.
6. J. Davies, D. Fensel, and F. van Harmelen, editors. *Towards the Semantic Web: Ontology-Driven Knowledge Management.* John Wiley, 2002.
7. Gene ontologytm consortium. Web site. `http://www.geneontology.org/`.
8. M. R. Genesereth, A. M. Keller, and O. Duschka. Infomaster: An information integration system. In *Proceedings of 1997 ACM SIGMOD Conference*, 1997.
9. C. Ghidini and F. Giunchiglia. Local models semantics, or contextual reasoning = locality + compatibility. *Artificial Intelligence*, 127(2):221–259, April 2001.
10. C. Ghidini and L. Serafini. Distributed First Order Logics. In D. Gabbay and M. de Rijke, editors, *Frontiers Of Combining Systems 2*, Studies in Logic and Computation, pages 121–140. Research Studies Press, 1998.
11. F. Giunchiglia. Contextual reasoning. *Epistemologia, special issue on I Linguaggi e le Macchine*, XVI:345–364, 1993. Short version in Proceedings IJCAI'93 Workshop on Using Knowledge in its Context, Chambery, France, 1993, pp. 39–49. Also IRST-Technical Report 9211-20, IRST, Trento, Italy.
12. F. Giunchiglia and L. Serafini. Multilanguage hierarchical logics, or: how we can do without modal logics. *Artificial Intelligence*, 65(1):29–70, 1994. Also IRST-Technical Report 9110-07, IRST, Trento, Italy.
13. F. Giunchiglia and I. Zaihrayeu. Making peer databases interact – a vision for an architacture supprting data coordination. In *Proceedings of the Conference on Information Agents (CIA)*, Madrid (Spain), 2002. LNCS.
14. D.L. McGuinness and F. van Harmelen. Owl web ontology language overview. `http://www.w3.org/TR/2003/WD-owl-features-20030331/`, March 2003.
15. P.F. Patel-Schneider, P. Hayes, and I. Horrocks. Web Ontology Language (OWL) Abstract Syntax and Semantics. Technical report, W3C, `www.w3.org/TR/owl-semantics/`, February 2003.
16. L. Serafini, F. Giunchiglia, J. Mylopoulos, and P. Bernstein. Local relational model: a logical formalization of database coordination. In P. Blackburn, C. Ghidini, and R. Turner, editors, *Proc. of Fourth International and Interdisciplinary Conference on Modeling and Using Context (Context'03)*, LNAI. Springer Verlag, 2003. To appear.

Web Ontology Language Requirements w.r.t Expressiveness of Taxonomy and Axioms in Medicine

Christine Golbreich[1], Olivier Dameron[2], Bernard Gibaud[2], and Anita Burgun[1]

[1] Laboratoire d'Informatique Médicale,
Faculté de Médecine, Av du Pr. Léon Bernard, 35043 Rennes France
Christine.Golbreich@uhb.fr,
Anita.Burgun@univ-rennes1.fr
[2] Laboratoire IDM, UPRES-EA 3192
Faculté de Médecine, Av. du Pr. Léon Bernard, 35043 Rennes Cedex France,
{Olivier.Dameron,Bernard.Gibaud}@chu-rennes.fr

Abstract. An important issue is to know whether Web ontology languages, meet the expected requirements of expressiveness and reasoning. This paper aims at contributing to this question in evaluating and comparing several languages. After describing the needs of a Semantic Web in medicine, it analyses Protégé and DAML+OIL primitives on a concrete medical ontology, the brain cortex anatomy ontology. It draws conclusions about the requirements that a Web ontology language should meet for the representation of medical taxonomy and axioms. The expressiveness of DAML+OIL or OWL DL seems suited to describe the complex taxonomic knowledge. But rules are required for representing the deductive knowledge (dependencies between relations) and to support several tasks (ontology construction, maintenance, verification, query of heterogeneous distributed information sources). Finally, the paper evaluates the features of the next standard OWL and of an hybrid language CARIN-*ALN* with respect to these requirements.

1 Introduction

A major challenge for the Web is to evolve towards a « Semantic Web », in which information may have explicit semantics, enabling human and machines to make a better use of information, and better integrate available data. The semantic markup of data is a means to reach this goal. Ontologies play a central role in the Semantic Web, since they define the vocabulary for such semantic markup. Thus an important issue is to know whether Web Ontology Languages, meet the requirements of expressiveness and reasoning that may be expected from the Web communities. This paper aims at contributing to this question in evaluating two ontology languages, Protégé [15] and DAML+OIL[5] by using them to represent a concrete ontology in the medical domain, the brain cortex anatomy ontology. This experiment pointed out some lacking of expressiveness that a Web Ontology Language shall overcome and enabled to state important features to provide w.r.t expressiveness of the taxonomy and axioms, for meeting the biomedical community usual requirements.

D. Fensel et al. (Eds.): ISWC 2003, LNCS 2870, pp. 180–194, 2003.

Section 2 gives a brief overview of the major Web uses expected from the biomedical community. Section 3 presents motivation for a Web brain cortex ontology. Section 3 presents the main features of Protégé and DAML+OIL, the precursor of the future W3C standard OWL [18]. Section 5 analyses Protégé and DAML+OIL expressiveness on the brain cortex anatomy ontology and draws conclusions about the requirements that a Web ontology language should meet for the representation of medical taxonomy and axioms. Section 6 compares formal languages for representing medical ontologies and discusses requirements of the biomedical community for a Semantic Web Ontology language.

2 Biomedical Community Web Uses

Semantic Web shall improve existing Web-based applications and enable new uses of the Web for the biomedical community. Searching and getting easily information on the web, and using it for decision making are the major needs regarding the web in medicine.

Search on the web concerns all actors of the medical field: medical doctors, researchers, patients, as well as manufacturers e.g. from the pharmaceutical or medical device industry. Current search engines are mostly based on the use of keywords, and therefore may return non relevant information, due to homonymy, synonymy, hyponymy-hypernymy etc. The solution retained in documents repositories is to index and search documents using « descriptors » from a thesaurus, rather than keywords. This is the approach actually used with thesauri such as Digital Anatomist [22], or MEDLINE[1], based on the MeSH thesaurus. Existing thesauri and languages like the Unified Medical Language System UMLS™ [14] or the Medical Subject Headings, MeSH[2] provide a very significant basis that cannot be ignored. However, they have limitations. The lack of precision of the concepts definitions may lead to non-shared meanings, which may jeopardize reuse and interoperability. Some highly specific concepts may be absent (cf. § 3). The rapid evolution of medical knowledge and the very dynamic nature of web information require frequent updates, enforcing a strict version management, as well as detection of inconsistencies that might result of updates or modifications.

Medicine has now evolved to a more scientific discipline, highly specialized, and therefore exercised collectively. Thus, the sharing of medical data of increasing volume and complexity has become critical to guarantee seamless healthcare delivery. The setting up of medical data repositories, centralized or federated on the web, and articulated around common ontologies, is of critical importance for modern research. This is particularly crucial in multi-disciplinary domains of research – such as neurosciences [26], [3] – that require the sharing of both knowledge and data. The feasibility of this sharing assumes the proper alignment of several domain ontologies (e.g. clinical neurology, psychiatry, neuroimaging, anatomy, genomics, neural models, neurochemistry). The case of imaging is also important, since signals and images need to be described, in order to make their content and context e.g. their

---

1 http://www.ncbi.nlm.nih.gov/entrez/query.fcgi

2 http://www.nlm.nih.gov/mesh/

acquisition protocol explicit. Biological molecular and Genomics databanks are another obvious illustration.

Moreover, the problem is not limited to information sharing. What is at stake is also to be able to *use* this information for decision making. This also includes many aspects: for instance access to clinical guidelines and protocols (patient management, prescription) and reference to optimal clinical management (evidence-based medicine), which are fields where the Semantic Web should bring - at a reasonable price - meaningful contributions [23]. One should also mention decision support brought by knowledge-based systems, which is much harder to implement, because it requires medical data in machine-understandable form, as well as structured knowledge, in order to adequately interpret and process this data.

The Semantic Web languages should contribute to better address those needs. A formal language with a clear semantics for representing ontologies (§ 4.2), should allow a formal definition of concepts, facilitating precise and shared concepts meaning, automatic consistency checking, automatic concepts classification. Its extension by a rule formalism (§ 5.2), should allow the definition of inferences leading to a more powerful search, as well as the query of heterogeneous and distributed information sources.

3 Brain Cortex Anatomy Ontology

The use of anatomy as a ground to model many fields of medicine [22] is a first motivation for a Web ontology of anatomy, that could be shared as a common reference in these fields [3]. Modeling anatomy has been pursued in several works such as Galen [21] or Digital Anatomist [22]. However, they are much focused on the general level of organs and do not provide detailed descriptions of specific organ structures. They are missing a fine-grained description of the brain cortex. Moreover, a general ontology of brain cortex anatomy should be reusable in various applications: teaching, decision support for clinical practice, and neuroimaging data sharing among collaborating research centers, for instance in order to improve the statistical significance of research findings through the use of larger populations of subjects. Therefore, another reason to achieve a Web ontology of anatomy is to provide a model of anatomy independent from application, that could be usable by humans as well as for different software. For all these reasons, it is important to develop a Web ontology of brain cortex anatomy.

Modeling brain cortex anatomy requires to explicitly define the meaning and properties of the domain concepts and their relations. The definitions of the anatomical concepts in the following examples are based on anatomy atlases such as [17], and terminology sources such as NeuroNames [2]. For instance, a « brain hemisphere » is informally defined as an anatomical part of the cortex which is lateralized (i.e. located either on the right or on the left side), which includes five anatomical subdivisions called lobes (frontal, temporal, parietal, occipital and limbic lobes) and occupies a specific region of space. A medical ontology like the brain cortex ontology involves many different relations: specialization (e.g. frontal lobe is a lobe), part-of (e.g. opercular pars of inferior frontal gyrus is a part of inferior frontal gyrus), topological, causal relations etc. Representing the brain cortex relations arise some difficulty because they are not independent. For instance, dependencies between composition and topological relationships have been studied in [27], while propagation of relations along transitive role, for instance location of a disease is inherited across patrimony: "has-location propagates -via part-of" is analyzed in [20]. In order to insure consistency, a stratified representation of brain cortex anatomy with a spatial stratum representing space regions occupied by anatomical entities has been advocated in [4]. In that way, the relations between anatomical concepts can be defined from topological relationships associating the regions they take up. With these definitions, the symbolic model of anatomy can be related to anatomical imaging data, which in turn can be used as localization support for functional activities or pathological elements. Furthermore, dependencies between anatomical relations can be derived from properties of topological relations, and could be automatically inferred. But this requires a formalism that allows the explicit representation of terminological knowledge (concepts, relations, and taxonomical organization) with classification services and also of deductive knowledge (axioms) with capability of handling inferences.

4 Representation

Two representation languages have been used to represent the ontology, a frame-based language supported by the Protégé-2000 editor, and DAML+OIL based on the description logics *SHIQ* supported by the OILEd editor.

4.1 Ontology in Protégé

Knowledge representation in Protégé is based on frames. Protégé-2000 is a graphical and easy-to-use ontology-editing tool developed at Stanford University The class inheritance hierarchy is visualized as a tree (Fig.1) multiple inheritance is allowed. Users define and organize classes, subsumption relationships, properties and property values. Metaclasses and hierarchy of metaclasses can be defined. A UMLS™ widget has been developed [13]. It allows users who are developing and populating their

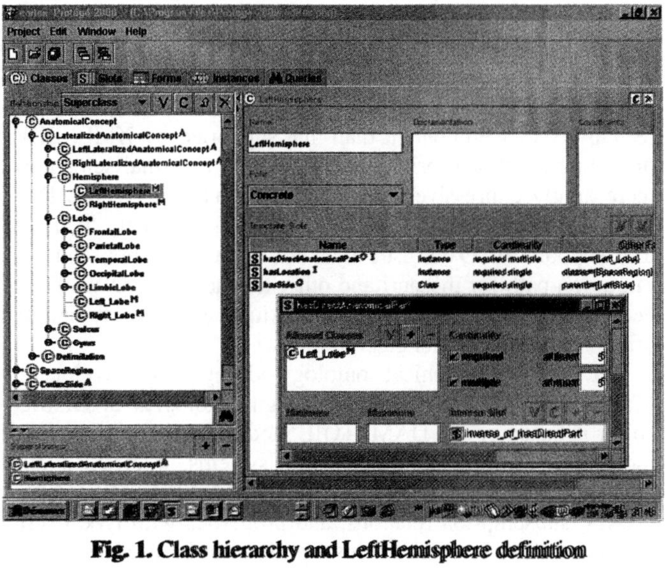

Fig. 1. Class hierarchy and LeftHemisphere definition

knowledge bases in Protégé to search and import UMLS™ elements directly into Protégé-2000. Other on-line resources can be used in a similar manner for knowledge acquisition in Protégé, e.g., WordNet [14].

For example, a « brain hemisphere » is defined as an anatomical part of the cortex which is lateralized (i.e. located either on the right or on the left side), includes five anatomical subdivisions called lobes (frontal, temporal, parietal, occipital and limbic lobes) and occupies a specific region of space. «Left hemispheres» are represented in Protégé by the class `LeftHemisphere`, subclass of `Hemisphere` and of `LeftLateralizedAnatomicConcept` whose slots are inherited but some of them overloaded: slots `hasSide restriction: LeftSide`, `hasDirectAnatomicalPart restriction: LeftLobe`, facets `at least`, `at most` with value 5 (Fig. 1), etc. This representation only expresses that a hemisphere has 5 lobes, each types confused. It would be difficult with frames (but possible) to represent that a hemisphere has exactly one lobe of each type, frontal, temporal, etc. (Ex14 gives the DAML+OIL representation).

4.2 Ontology in DAML+OIL

DAML+OIL [5] is a semantic markup language for Web resources designed by the W3C OntoGroup (Ontology Working Group) in order to go beyond the simple presentation of information on the Web, by offering a solution that supports interoperability, understanding and reasoning with these information. DAML+OIL, comes from DARPA results about DAML (American Agent Markup Language) [11] and from OIL [8]. DAML+OIL borrows its intuitive modeling primitives to frames, its syntax to the Web languages XML and RDF, its formal semantics and reasoning to description logics (DLs). From a formal point of view, DAML+OIL can be seen to be equivalent to the expressive description logic *SHIQ* with the addition of the oneOf constructor and datatypes (Table 1). It also supports the definition of a set of axioms (Table 2). DAML+OIL can make use of the Fast Classification of Terminology system FaCT (http://www.cs.man.ac.uk/~horrocks/FaCT/), which enables to reason on ontologies (consistency checking, classification). DAML+OIL, is the precursor of the future W3C Web Ontology Language OWL [18], intended "to facilitate machine readability of web content than that supported by XML, RDF, and RDF Schema, by providing additional primitives along with a formal semantics". OWL provides three increasingly expressive sublanguages: OWL Lite, OWL DL, and OWL Full. OWL Lite is less expressive, thus according to its designer, "it should be simpler to provide tool support for OWL Lite than for the two others, and easier to provide a quick migration path for thesauri and other taxonomies". OWL-DL offers completeness and decidability. OWL Full with its maximal expressivity and syntax freedom of RDF, offers no computational guarantees.

OILEd is a graphical ontology-editing tool developed by the University of Manchester. It allows users to design ontologies in DAML+OIL [5]. The OILEd editor is based on the DAML+OIL model. While OILEd uses graphical user-interface metaphors common to frame-based systems, it offers a more expressive ontology language based on Description Logics, including reasoning services. Users define classes, subsumption relations, and properties with type restriction (Fig. 2). Opposed to frames editors, complex descriptions can be used as slot value, without having to

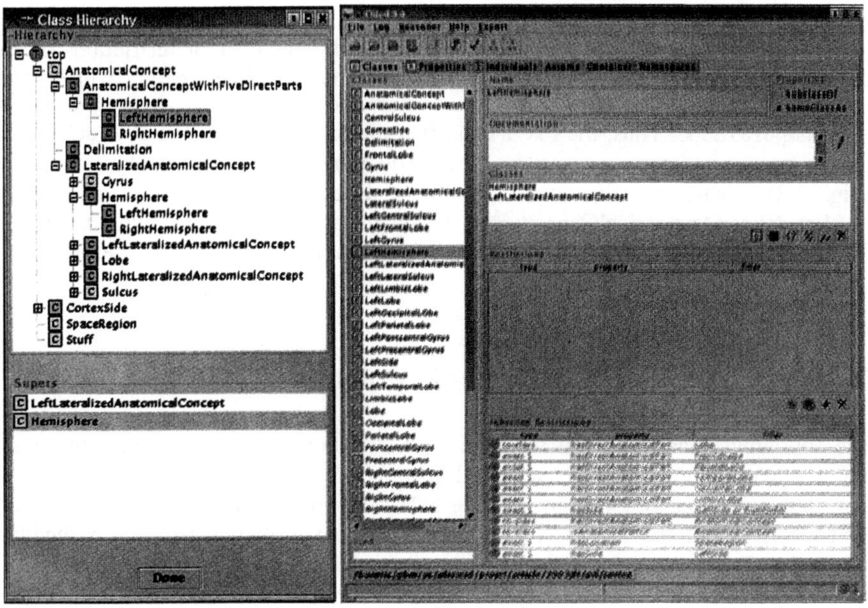

Fig. 2. Left: Post-classification hierarchy - Right : LeftHemisphere definition with OILEd

be named. Axioms allow for representing additional knowledge, e.g. the fact that two classes are disjoint.

The next examples illustrate the rigorous formalization of concepts and taxonomy in DAML+OIL, and their automatic classification supported by FaCT.

Ex1. */An anatomical concept is composed of direct parts, which are anatomical concepts, occupies exactly one region of space*

AnatomicalConcept:= (∀ hasDirectAnatomicalPart AnatomicalConcept)
∧(= 1 hasLocation SpaceRegion)

Ex2. */A lateralized concept is located either on the right side, or on the left side of the cortex, one can distinguish right-sided lateralized concepts and left-sided lateralized concepts/*

LateralizedAnatomicalConcept:= AnatomicalConcept
∧ (= 1 hasSide LeftSide ∨ RightSide)
LeftLateralizedAnatomicalConcept:= LateralizedAnatomicalConcept
∧ (∀ hasSide LeftSide) resp. RightLateralizedAnatomicalConcept

Ex3. */An hemisphere is a lateralized concept whose direct parts are lobes, each part being of a distinct type (i.e. frontal lobe, parietal lobe, occipital lobe, limbic lobe, temporal lobe/*

Hemisphere := LateralizedAnatomicalConcept
∧ (∀ hasDirectAnatomicalPart Lobe)
∧ (= 1 hasDirectAnatomicalPart FrontalLobe)
∧ (= 1 HasDirectAnatomicalPart ParietalLobe)
∧ (= 1 hasDirectAnatomicalPart OccipitalLobe)
∧ (= 1 hasDirectAnatomicalPart LimbicLobe)
∧ (= 1 hasDirectAnatomicalPart TemporalLobe)

Ex4. */A left (resp. right) hemisphere (resp. lobe etc.) is an hemisphere (resp. lobe etc.) located on the left (resp. right) side Fig.4 /*

*LeftHemisphere **:=** LeftLateralizedAnatomicalConcept ∧ Hemisphere*

The `LeftHemisphere` concept is defined as a Hemisphere as well as a `LeftLateralizedAnatomicalConcept`, together with a number of restrictions on its direct parts (Ex3). Consequently, it has exactly 5 direct parts, which are: `LeftFrontalLobe` `LeftParietalLobe` `LeftOccipitalLobe` `LeftLimbicLobe` `LeftTemporalLobe`. Thus, the FaCT classifier automatically classifies it as subsumed by `FiveDirectPartAnatomicalConcept` as shown on the Post-classification hierarchy (**Fig. 2**), whereas it was firstly defined as only subsumed by LeftLateralizedAnatomicalConcept and Hemisphere. This example exhibits how a formal language like DAML+OIL allows a finer-grained description than Protégé and the benefits of automatic classification.

5 Requirements and Lacking of Expressiveness

The following examples from the brain cortex anatomy ontology present the main features that are covered by Protégé or DAML+OIL (§ 5.1), and the requirements of expressiveness that they do not meet (§ 5.2). Thus this study enables to draw first conclusions about the expressiveness expected from a Web language for medical ontologies. For each example, the number refers to the Protégé-2000 and DAML+OIL constructor or axiom e.g. subsumption, equivalence that have been used, denoting a specific requirement of expressiveness (§ 6 column 2 – 3 Table 1 Table 2).

5.1 Maximum Expressiveness Required

The following examples 1 to 14 exhibit that OWL Lite is not sufficient, and that the enhanced expressiveness of OWL DL is at least required for representing the brain cortex ontology, since for instance disjunction, negation, disjoint union are needed

Ex5. ***disjointWith*** *is needed to represent disjunction (#9)*
/ Hemisphere, Lobe, Gyrus et Sulcus are disjoint classes /
`disjointWith (Hemisphere Lobe Gyrus Sulcus)`

Ex6. ***disjunction*** *is required (#2)*
/Lateralized anatomical concept are either right or left/
`LateralizedAnatomicalConcept := AnatomicalConcept`
`∧ (= 1 hasSide LeftSide ∨ RightSide)`

Ex7. ***negation*** *is needed (#5)*
/ Class of the anatomical concepts that are not lateralized /
`NonLateralizedAnatomicalConcept:= AnatomicalConcept`
`∧ ¬ LateralizedAnatomicalConcept`

Ex8. ***disjointUnionOf*** *is a primitive needed to represent a partition of A into a list of concepts (#10)*
/A side of the brain cortex is either right or left but not both/
`disjointUnionOf(CortexSide LeftSide RightSide)`
/A lobe is one of the following types : frontal, parietal, temporal, occipital, limbic lobe /
`disjointUnionOf(Lobe FrontalLobe ParietalLobe TemporalLobe OccipitalLobe LimbicLobe)`
/An hemisphere is either a right hemisphere or a left hemisphere /
`disjointUnionOf(Hemisphere LeftHemisphere RightHemisphere)`

Ex9. ***≡ (equivalent)*** *is needed to represent classes equivalence (#8)*
/The left lobe concept is equivalent to left lateralized anatomical concept and lobe/
`LeftLobe ≡ LeftLateralizedAnatomicalConcept ∧ Lobe`

Ex10. $\subseteq$ *subsumption is needed to represent class or relation specialization hierarchies (#11)*
/The relation hasAnatomicalPart is a specialization of hasDirectAnatomicalPart /
`hasDirectAnatomicalPart ⊆ hasAnatomicalPart`

Ex11. *transitive is needed for representing transitive relations (#14)*
/has-part is transitive (hasDirectPart no)/
`Slot-def has-part TransitiveProperty`

Representing such property features (reflexivity, symmetry, transitivity) is required. For example, transitivity enables to elicit the distinction between hasDirectAnatomicalPart and hasAnatomicalPart. The latter corresponds to the transitive closure of hasDirectAnatomicalPart, e.g. direct anatomical parts of hemispheres are lobes, thus anatomical parts of hemispheres are lobes and gyri. DAML+OIL provides such a possibility while Protégé does not.

Ex12. ***inverse relation*** *is needed (#13)*
/inverse of hasLocation/
`isLocatedIn inverseOf hasLocation`

Ex13. ***equivalence of relations*** *must be represented (#12)*
/concept A is anatomical part of a concept B if and only if the space occupied by A is a subspace of that occupied by B/
`isAnatomicalPartOf ≡ (isLocatedIn o isSubAreaOf o hasLocation)`

From this definition, constraints on body spaces can be inferred for two anatomical concepts A and B linked by isAnatomicalPartOf, and inversely A isAnatomicalPartOf B can be inferred from their respective regions. Moreover, equivalence between relations is crucial to merge several Web ontologies.

Ex14. ***cardinality*** *and non exclusive constraints on relations have to be represented (n°6)*
/An hemisphere is a lateralized concept whose direct parts are lobes and which has exactly one lobe of each type/

```
Hemisphere := LateralizedAnatomicalConcept
∧ (∀ hasDirectAnatomicalPart Lobe)
∧ (= 1 hasDirectAnatomicalPart FrontalLobe)
∧ (= 1 HasDirectAnatomicalPart ParietalLobe)
∧ (= 1 hasDirectAnatomicalPart OccipitalLobe)
∧ (= 1 hasDirectAnatomicalPart LimbicLobe)
∧ (= 1 hasDirectAnatomicalPart TemporalLobe)
```

DAML+OILs allow for representing such constraints whereas Protégé does not.

5.2 Needs of a Rule Layer

OWL DL is not yet sufficient. The next examples show needs that are not covered by Protégé and DAML+OIL, and exhibit that the expressiveness of rules is required. Indeed, the brain cortex ontology involves a lot of deductive knowledge, like dependencies between relationships (§ 3), that cannot be represented with DLs. Compositions of relation (Ex15) and relations whose arity is more than 2 are also needed (Ex16), but cannot be represented by these languages.

Ex15. ***composition*** *between relations is not provided but required*
/ a concept which has a location, which is included in a region, occupied by another concept C' /
`isLocatedIn ° isSubAreaOf ° hasLocation`

A possible solution for representing composition is using rules.

Ex16. ***n-ary relation*** *is not provided but required*

/ ternary relation: a sulcus is a separator for two lobes, or two gyri, or one gyrus one lobe/

```
Separation := AnatomicalConcept ∧ (= 1 separator Sulcus)      (1)
∧ (= 2 separate Lobe ∨ Gyrus)
parts(S, V) ∧ 1stPart(V, A) ∧ 2ndPart(V, B) → separation(S, A, B)
                                                              (2)
```

Frames and description logics allow only binary relations. Possible solutions for representing n-ary relations include relation reification, i.e. to represent it by a concept, e.g. Separation (1), and rules (2) like CARIN-*ALN* rules [9].

Ex17. *inference rule is not provided but required (#15)*

Rule # 1 : IF A is part of B THEN A has the same side as B

```
isAnatomicalPartOf (A,B) ∧ hasSide (B,C) → hasSide (A,C)
```

Rule#2 : IF a functional activity A is located in a part B of an anatomical structure C, THEN A is also located in the anatomical structure C.

```
isFunctionallyLocatedIn (A,B) ∧ isAnatomicalPartOf (B,C) →
isFunctionallyLocatedIn (A,C)
```

Rules are needed to support several tasks: (1) to generate the concepts and/or the relationships that associate them, for the ontology construction and its updates, (2) to check the ontology consistency for knowledge verification, (3) to combine or connect knowledge for managing multiple ontologies, (4) to process queries, or formulate conjunctive queries over multiple heterogeneous sources for an information integration system

Ontology construction. There are a lot of dependencies between the multiple concepts of the ontology and their relations. It is difficult, even quite impossible, to create all them or to maintain the ontology by hand. Adding a concept or a relationship may trigger the chaining creation of many other concepts or relationships. For instance, when stating that central sulcus separates the preCentral gyrus and the postCentral gyrus, additional separation relationships are derived, whose corresponding knowledge has to be added in the ontology, that is from the following facts F1, F2, F3, and Rule R1 the conclusion C is derived, and the corresponding knowledge should be added.

```
Rule R1: hasPart(A, B) ∧ ¬ hasPart(B, C) ∧ separates(S, A, C) →
separates(S, B, C)

PreCentralGyrus is an anatomical part of frontalLobe     (F1)
frontallobe and parietalLobe have no common part         (F2)
centralSulcus separates precentralGyrus and parietalLobe (F3)
centralSulcus separates frontalLobe and parietalLobe     (C)
```

For example, a single rule such as « if a sulcus S separates two gyri G1, G2 that belong to distinct lobes (G1 is part of L1, G2 is part of L2), then S separates G1 from L2, G2 from L1, and L1 from L2 » would generate 221 relations in the brain cortex ontology presented in [4].

Therefore, it is proposed to build by hand a minimal initial set of independent concepts and relationships, to represent all the dependencies by a rules base, then to automatically generate all the knowledge infered in applying the rule base.

A first experience has been done to test this approach, which needs further investigation. Rules are implemented in Prolog, the domain of variables is the set of AnatomicalConcepts. Each concept of the ontology is represented by a constant e.g. CentralSulcus is represented by the constant c-centralSulcus, relations between concepts are represented by facts e.g. separates (c-centralSulcus c-precentralGyrus c-parietalLobe (F3). Using this trick to represent the ontology concepts, roles, and rules in the same logical framework, it has been possible to generate new concepts of the ontology from a first set of « independant » concepts. But for that, it has been necessary to translate the knowledge of the ontology already represented in DAML+OIL into Prolog. A unified formalism integrating rules and DL would be more suited. It would prevent from duplicating the structural knowledge already described in the ontology, and from translation errors. The rules KB should represent only the deductive part of knowledge.

Consistency checking. When updating the ontology, it should be checked that added concepts and relationships do not conflict with previous ones e.g. a left-lateralized concept cannot be a part of a right-lateralized concept, and conversely. Constrainst like the Rule R2 together with the above *Rule # 1*,enable to check such inconsistencies. After saturation, all the inconsistent concepts are explicitely reported.

Rule R2 : `hasSide(X, leftSide) ∧ hasSide(X, rightSide) → ⊥`

Such a rule base serve as a conceptual model of consistency (similar to the usual approach for validation of knowledge bases), that can be used to check the ontology consistencty.

Managing multiple ontologies. Ontologies of related domains may have to be combined. For example, an ontology of brain anatomy may have to be merged with an ontology of the anatomy of the whole body. Both may be connected to an ontology of pathologies, in order to provide a disease localization support. Merging, or connecting ontologies requires to handle new dependencies. For instance, a tumor located in the part of an organ is also located in the organ. Such propagation of relations along transitive role as "part-of" are very frequent in medicine. However, all these dependencies cannot be statically and manually generated. Defining rules like R3 expressing the dependency of relations is a solution to manage them dynamically and automatically.

Rule R3: `tumor(T) ∧ anatomicalConcept(A) ∧ anatomicalConcept(B) ∧ hasAnatomicalPart(A, B) ∧ locatedIn(T, B) → locatedIn(T, A)`

Processing or representing queries. Rules like R3 are required for processing queries such as "retrieve all images showing a tumor in the frontal lobe". Indeed, it is wanted to obtain all the images showing either (1) any type of tumor in a frontal lobe, (2) tumors in any specialization of frontal lobe e.g. in the left frontal lobe, (3) but also tumors located in any part of a frontal lobe, or (4) any combination of the three previous cases, e.g. "a glioblastom in the left precentral gyrus", which is a specific tumor located in a specific part of a frontal lobe, has to be found.

These different use cases highlight both the benefits that can be expected from rules for building, managing and insuring ontologies consistency, and the necessity to rely on such explicit rules for managing multiple ontologies and representing or processing queries. Therefore, OWL DL is not sufficient, and a unified formalism integrating rules and description logics, would provide an elegant solution to construct, maintain, combine, and exploit ontologies.

5.3 Needs of Metaclass and of Modularity and Reuse Mechanisms

OWL DL might be not sufficient for some applications, and OWL Full required to represent metaclasses that may be needed and are not provided by OWL DL. For instance, metaclasses are a possible means for connecting an ontology like the cortex anatomy ontology with existing medical standards like UMLS™. Since Metaclass exist in Protégé, defining a metaclass with a slot 'UMLS-ID' connecting the ontology concepts to the UMLS™ concepts is possible in Protégé, but not in DAML+OIL. They may also become necessary for compatibility when merging several anatomical models, as advocated in [16]. Although it is not impossible, manipulating metaclasses in description logics is not straightforward. However metaclasses are legal in OWL-Full, but with no computational guarantees.

Ex18. ***metaclasses*** *are not provided in DAML+OIL (and OWL DL) but may be required (#16)*
/The class FrontalLobe, instance of the metaclass MetaAnatomicalConcept, is related by the property UMLS-ID to the UMLS Concept Unique Identifier C0016733/

```
<MetaAnatomicalConcept rdf:ID="FrontalLobe">
<UMLS-ID rdf:resource="&rdfs;Literal">C0016733</UMLS-ID>
```

Modularity and reuse mechanisms, similar to those proposed in software engineering, for modular specifications, are not provided but are also required to import ontologies or to reuse a general ontology, while respecting semantics constraints.

5.4 Results

Using PROTEGE 2000 and DAML+OIL for the brain cortex ontology pointed out a number of limitations of these languages and has led to the following conclusions about requirements of expressiveness that a Web ontology language should cover:

- First, representing the brain cortex anatomy ontology led to difficulties with both languages, but many limitations of Protégé are overcome by DAML+OIL, thanks to the enhanced expressiveness of *SHIQ* description logics versus frames.
- Next, it comes out that most DAML+OIL constructors (Table 1) and axioms (Table 2) in particular negation, disjunction, inverse, were needed for the ontology and would certainly be in a Web language for biomedical ontologies
- Equivalence of classes or relations, subclass and subproperty are key axioms to assert relationships between classes and relations of separately developed ontologies, thus are specially required for managing several Web ontologies.
- Finally, the main limitation encountered with DAML+OIL, and that the future Web Ontology Language shall overcome, is the lack of rules (§ 5.2)
- Metaclasses is a possible means for expressing compatibility of ontologies with the existing medical standard terminologies like UMLS™. Modularity and reuse mechanisms are required respectively for assembling elementary ontologies into more complex ones or for reusing more general ontologies

In conclusion, an expressive DL similar to DAML+OIL is suited to express the complex taxonomic knowledge, but rules are also required to enable representing the deductive knowledge necessary for supporting several tasks (ontology construction, maintenance, verification etc.). They might also be useful for representing predicates of arbitrary arity. Inferential services related to both formalisms are required. Finally, metaclasses might be used to take advantage of the existing medical standard terminologies. However to keep computational guarantees, other solutions shall be found.

6 Discussion

W3C standards but also other formal languages are available for Web ontologies. Table 1 and Table 2 compare the main class constructors and axioms supported by Protégé-2000 and DAML+OIL, which is quite similar to OWL-DL, to those of OWL Lite which is less expressive, and of CARIN-*ALN* [9], an hybrid language combining DL and rules.

From a formal point of view, DAML+OIL (and OWL DL) is quite equivalent to the description logics *SHIQ* extended by the oneOf constructor and datatypes together with a nice set of algebraic axioms. It can make use of the FaCT system which provides a reasoner with sound and complete tableaux algorithms to reason on ontologies, thus supports automatic tasks like ontology consistency checking, concepts classification, instantiation. CARIN-*ALN* is based on the less expressive *ALN* description logics, but combines it with a powerful rules language. OntoClass provides for CARIN-*ALN* the same services as FaCT, but subsumption and satisfiability are polynomial instead of exponential. Moreover, thanks to its rules, CARIN–*ALN* can serve as a query language to integrate heterogeneous sources via mediators built with PICSEL [9] (were queries reformulation is decidable).

The above study leads to conclude that ideally an hybrid language integrating an expressive DL with rules, similar to CARIN–*ALN* or TRIPLE [24] would benefit to medical ontologies. Besides, it might serve as a query language in order to search medical information on the Web and to query heterogeneous sources. But, combining description logics with rules implies to restrict, either the description logics part or/and the form of rules, to remain decidable and to have sound and complete algorithms [12]. An open question is to define a relevant subclass of DL and of rules to be integrated into a uniform language, suited to represent medical ontologies.

Table 1. Main class constructors (used in the brain cortex ontology)

Constructor	Protégé 2000	DAML-OIL (DL syntax)	Example	OWL Lite	CARIN-*ALN*
1. conjunction	multiple hierarchy	$C1 \wedge C2$	Ex4	$C1 \wedge C2$, for named C1, C2	$C1 \wedge C2$
2. disjunction	**No**	$C1 \vee C2$	Ex2	**No**	**No**
3. universal	Yes	$\forall$ r.C	Ex1	$\forall$ r.C	$\forall$ r C
4. existential	**No**	$\exists$ r.C	not used.	$\exists$ r.C	**No**
5. negation	**No**	$\neg$ C	Ex7	No	$\neg$C for C primitive
6. cardinality	single or multiple	$\leq$ n r C $\geq$ n r C = n r C	Ex14	$\leq$ n r C $\geq$ n r C = n r C for n = 0 or 1	$\leq$ n r $\geq$ n r

Table 2. Main axioms (used in the brain cortex ontology ontology)

Axiom	Protégé 2000	DAML-OIL (DL syntax)	Example	OWL Lite	CARIN-*ALN*
7.subsumption	Yes	subClassOf $C1 \subseteq C2$	Ex10	subClassOf $C1 \subseteq C2$	$C1 \subseteq C2$ C1primitive
8. class equivalence	**No**	sameClassAs $C1 \equiv C2$	Ex9	sameClassAs $C1 \equiv C2$	**No**
9. exclusion	**No**	disjointWith $C1 \subseteq \neg C2$	Ex5	**No**	$C1 \wedge C2 \subseteq \bot$ C1, C2 primitive
10. disjoint union	**No**	disjointUnionOf $C \equiv C1 \vee C2$ $C1 \wedge C2 \subseteq \bot$	Ex8	**No**	**No**
11. subproperty	Yes	subPropertyOf $r1 \subseteq r2$	Ex10	subPropertyOf $r1 \subseteq r2$	**No**
12. property equivalence	**No**	samePropertyAs $r1 \equiv r2$	Ex13	samePropertyAs	**No**
13. inverse	Yes	InverseOf $r1 \equiv r2^{-1}$	Ex12	inverseOf	**No**
14. transitivity	No	transitive	Ex11	transitiveProperty	**No**
15. Rule	No	**No**	Ex17	**No**	Carin-rule
16. Metaclass	Yes	**No**	Ex18	**No**	**No**

This study about expressiveness is a first step, to go further it should be useful that the main usage of a Semantic Web expected by the biomedical community are more precisely specified and its strong requirements stated: are decidability, sound and complete algorithms, efficient reasoning, essential or not?

7 Conclusion

Most people nowadays agree that a Web ontology language shall have formal semantics. We believe that it shall be enough expressive to allow a fine and precise representation of both terminological and deductive complex knowledge. But it has also to provide efficient means to reason with huge ontologies: (1) automatic ontology classification and consistency checking, and also (2) services for querying heterogeneous and distributed sources, (3) modularity and reuse mechanisms for assembling elementary ontologies into more complex ones or reusing more general ontologies. Thus, OWL is a good candidate for the taxonomic part, but it is not sufficient and should be extended by rules for representing the deductive component of knowledge. However, the combination of an expressive DL e.g. *ALNR* with rules as Datalog, enlarges the search space. The challenge is to identify an hybrid formalism combining a subclass of OWL with rules, that allows to remain decidable and to have sound and complete algorithms for subsumption and satisfiability, and also if possible good properties for the reformulation of queries upon heterogeneous information sources. A trade-off shall be found in restricting, either OWL to an appropriate sublanguage or/and the form of rules to appropriate versions of Datalog/RuleML. OWL Full with the syntactic freedom of RDF allows metaclasses, but offers no computational guarantees. Another important challenge, particular important for the biomedical domain, is to find suited solutions for relating formal ontologies to existing domain thesauri, that cannot be ignored, and for modular specification of Web ontologies.

References

1. Bechhofer S., Horrocks I., Goble C., Stevens R. OILEd: a Reason-able Ontology Editor for the Semantic Web. Proceedings of KI2001, Joint German/Austrian conference on Artificial Intelligence, Vienna. Springer LNAI Vol. 2174, (2001) 396–408
2. Bowden, DM and Martin, RF. NeuroNames Brain Hierarchy, Neuroimage,2 (1995) 63–83
3. Brinkley J.F. and Rosse C. Imaging informatics and the Human Brain Project : the role of structure, Yearbook of Medical Informatics (2002) 131–148
4. Dameron O., Burgun A., Morandi X., Gibaud B. Modelling dependencies between relations to insure consistency of a cerebral cortex anatomy knowledge base. Proceedings of Medical Informatics in Europe (2003)
5. DAML+OIL Reference Description. Dan Connolly, Frank van Harmelen, Ian Horrocks, Deborah L. McGuinness, Peter F. Patel-Schneider, and Lynn Andrea Stein. W3C Note 18 December 2001. http://www.w3.org/TR/daml+oil-reference.
6. Extensible Markup Language (XML) 1.0 (Second Edition). Tim Bray, Jean Paoli, C. M. Sperberg-McQueen, and Eve Maler, eds. (2000). http://www.w3.org/TR/REC-xml.
7. Fellbaum C, ed. WordNet: an electronic lexical database. Cambridge, MIT Press (1998)
8. Fensel D., van Harmelen F., Horrocks I., McGuinness D.L., and Patel-Schneider P. F. OIL An ontology infrastructure for the semantic web. IEEE Intel. Systems, 16(2) 38–45 (2001)
9. Goasdoue, F., Lattes, V., Rousset, M.C. The Use Of Carin Language and Algorithms for Information Integration: The PICSEL System International Journal of Cooperative Information Systems, 9(4): 383–401, 2000.
10. Gomez-Perez A., Corcho O., Ontology languages for the Semantic Web, IEEE Intelligent Systems 17, 4 54–60, 2002.
11. Hendler, J., McGuinness, D.L. The DARPA Agent Markup Language. IEEE Intelligent Systems 16(6) 67–73, 2000.
12. Levy A. Y, Rousset MC, The Limits on Combining Recursive Horn Rules with Description Logics, AAAI/IAAI, Vol. 1, 1996.
13. Li Q, Shilane P, Noy NF, Musen MA Ontology acquisition from on-line knowledge sources. Proc. AMIA Symp. 497–501, 2000.
14. Lindberg D.A, Humphreys, B.L. McCray AT. The Unified Medical Language System. Meth. Inf Med Aug; 32(4) (1993) 281–91
15. Noy N. F. Sintek M, Decker S.,. Crubezy M, Fergerson R. W., & Musen M. A.. Creating Semantic Web Contents with Protege-2000. IEEE Intelligent Systems 16(2): 60–71, 2001. http://protege.stanford.edu
16. Noy NF, Musen MA, Mejino JLV Jr., Rosse C. Pushing the Envelope: Challenges in a Frame-Based Representation of Human Anatomy. Technical Report, (2002). (http://smi-web.stanford. edu/pubs/SMI_Abstracts/SMI-2002-0925.html)
17. Ono M, Kubik, S and Abernathey, Geog Thieme Verlag, Atlas of the Cerebral Sulci, Thieme Medical Publishers Inc., (1990).
18. OWL Web Ontology Language 1.0 Reference. Mike Dean, Dan Connolly, Frank van Harmelen, James Hendler, Ian Horrocks, Deborah L. McGuinness, Peter F. Patel-Schneider, and Lynn Andrea Stein. W3C Working Draft 12 November 2002 http://www.w3.org/TR/owl-ref/. OWL Web Ontology Overview :W3C Working Draft 4 March 2003

19. RDF/XML Syntax Specification (Revised) Dave Beckett, ed. W3C Working Draft 23 January 2003. Latest version is available at http://www.w3.org/TR/rdf-syntax-grammar/.
20. Rector A. Analysis of propagation along transitive roles: Formalisation of the GALEN experience with Medical Ontologies, 2002 International Workshop on Description Logics DL2002, Toulouse, France, April 19–21, (2002) .
21. Rector. A., Nowlan W.A. and the GALEN Consortium, The GALEN Project Computer Methods and Programs in Biomedicine, 45, 75–78, 1993.
22. Rosse C, Mejino JL, Modayur BR, Jakobovits R, Hinshaw KP, Brinkley JF. Motivation and organizational principles for anatomical knowledge representation: the digital anatomist symbolic knowledge base. J Am Med Inform Assoc. 1998 Jan–Feb; 5(1):17–40.
23. Sakai Y. Metadata for evidence based medicine resources, Proc. Int'l Conf. On Dublin Core and Metadata Applications 2001, 81–85, 2001.
24. Sintek M., Decker S, TRIPLE An RDF Query, Inference, and Transformation Language. DDLP'2001, Japan, (2001).
25. Sure Y., Erdmann M., Angele J., Staab S., Studer R. and Wenke D. OntoEdit: Collaborative Ontology Engineering for the Semantic Web. In Proc. of the first Inter. Semantic Web Conference 2002, June 9–12 2002, Sardinia, Italy, (2002).
26. Toga A.W. Neuroimage databases : the good, the bad and the ugly, Nature reviews neuroscience vol. 3 302–309, 2002.
27. Varzi A. Parts, Wholes, and Part-Wholes Relations: the Prospects of Mereotopology. Data and Knowledge Engineering, 259–286, 1996.

Automating DAML-S Web Services Composition Using SHOP2

Dan Wu[1], Bijan Parsia[2], Evren Sirin[1], James Hendler[1], and Dana Nau[1]

[1] University of Maryland,
Computer Science Department,
College Park MD 20742, USA
{dandan,evren,hendler,nau}@cs.umd.edu
[2] University of Maryland, MIND Lab,
8400 Baltimore Ave, College Park MD 20742, USA
bparsia@isr.umd.edu

Abstract. The DAML-S Process Model is designed to support the application of AI planning techniques to the automated composition of Web services. SHOP2 is an Hierarchical Task Network (HTN) planner well-suited for working with the Process Model. We have proven the correspondence between the semantics of SHOP2 and the situation calculus semantics of the Process Model. We have also implemented a system which soundly and completely plans over sets of DAML-S descriptions using a SHOP2 planner, and then executes the resulting plans over the Web. We discuss the challenges and difficulties of using SHOP2 in the information-rich and human-oriented context of Web services.

1 Introduction

As Web services – that is, programs and devices accessible via standard Web protocols – proliferate, it becomes more difficult to find the specific service that can perform the task at hand. It becomes even more difficult when there is no single service capable of performing that task, but there are combinations of existing services that could. Sufficiently rich, machine-readable descriptions of Web services would allow the creation of novel, compound Web services with little or no direct human intervention. Semantic Web languages, such as the Web Ontology Language (OWL) [1] or DAML+OIL[2], provide the foundations for such sufficiently rich descriptions.

In May 2001, the DARPA Agent Markup Language (DAML) Program released the first version of DAML-S [4], a set of ontologies for describing the properties and capabilities of Web services. The purpose of DAML-S markup of Web services is to support effective automation of various Web services related activities including service discovery, composition, execution, and monitering.

For our work, we are motivated by issues related to automated Web services composition. One part of DAML-S, namely its process ontology, provides a standard language for describing the composition of Web services. Several metaphors have been used in developing this semantic markup of Web services including

D. Fensel et al. (Eds.): ISWC 2003, LNCS 2870, pp. 195–210, 2003.

viewing Web services as primitive and complex actions with preconditions and effects.

Given a representation of services as actions, we can exploit AI planning techniques for automatic service composition by treating service composition as a planning problem. Ideally, given a user's objective and a set of Web services, a planner would find a collection of Web services requests that achieves the objective. We believe that HTN planning is especially promising for this purpose, because the concept of task decomposition in HTN planning is very similar to the concept of composite process decomposition in DAML-S process ontology. In this paper, we explore how to use the SHOP2 HTN planning system[5,6] to do automatic composition of DAML-S Web services.

This paper is organized in the following manner. In Section 2, we describe a sample scenario for our research. In Section 3, we give the background knowledge about DAML-S process ontology and SHOP2. In Section 4, we present our approach for automatic Web services composition. In Section 5, we describe the implementation. In Section 6, we summarize some related work. And finally, in Section 7, we conclude our work and present some future research directions. Throughout this paper, we use the example we described in Section 2 to illustrate our approach. But our work is designed to be domain-independent and is not restricted to only this example.

2 Motivating Example

The example we describe here is based loosely on a scenario described in the Scientific American article about the Semantic Web [7]. Suppose Bill and Joan's mother goes to her physician complaining of pain and tingling in her legs and the physician proposes the following sequence of activities:

- A prescription for Relafen, an anti-inflammatory drug;
- An MRI scan and an electromyography, both of these are diagnostic tests to try to determine possible causes for the symptoms;
- A follow-up appointment with the physician to discuss the results of the diagnostic tests.

Bill and Joan need to do the following things for their mother:

- Fill the prescription at a pharmacy;
- Make appointments to take their mother to the two treatments;
- Make an appointment for the doctor's follow-up meeting.

For the three appointment times, there are the following preferences and constraints:

- For the two treatments:
  - Bill and Joan would prefer two appointment times that are close together scheduled at one or two nearby places, so that only one person needs to drive, and that person drives only once.

    - Otherwise, they would prefer two appointment times on different days, so that each person needs to drive once.
- The appointment time for doctor's follow up check must be later that the appointment times for the two treatments.
- An appointment time must fit the schedule of the person that will drive to the appointment.

Assume that there are the requisite Web services for finding appointment times and making appointments at the relevant clinics, Bill and Joan could use those services to schedule their mother's appointments. It would be difficult for Bill and Joan to finish their task with an optimal plan by consulting the Web services manually, because:

- They may have to try every available pair of close appointment times at any two nearby treatment centers in order to find one that fits their schedules.
- Furthermore, if they first choose an appointment time for one treatment and then find they have to use this same time for the other treatment, then they will have to reschedule the first appointment.

Instead, suppose we use the DAML-S process ontology to encode a description of how to compose Web services for tasks such as the one faced by Bill and Joan. If we have an agent technology which can find an execution path based on this predefined task decompositions, then we can perform Bill and Joan's Web services composition task automatically.

3 Background

3.1 DAML-S

In the DAML-S process ontology, services are modelled as processes. There are three kinds of processes: *atomic* processes, *composite* processes and *simple* processes. In DAML-S, an *atomic* process is a model of a "single step" (from the point of view of the client) Web service that is directly executed to accomplish some task. Executing an *atomic* process consists of calling the corresponding Web-accessible program with its input parameters bound to particular values. A *composite* process represents a compound Web service, i.e., it can be decomposed into other *atomic* or *composite* processes. The decomposition of a *composite* process is specified through its control constructs. The set of control constructs includes: **Sequence**, **Unordered**, **Choice**, **If-Then-Else**, **Iterate**, **Repeat-Until**, **Repeat-While**, **Split** and **Split+Join**. A simple process is an abstraction of an atomic or composite process (or of a possibly empty set of these). It is not considered to be directly executable, but provides an abstract view of an action. Like atomic processes, simple processes are, themselves, single-step, but unlike atomic processes, it's possible to peek at the internal structure of a simple process (if available) or to replace the simple process with an expansion of it.

In the process ontology, each process has several properties, including, *(optional) inputs*, *preconditions*, (conditional)*outputs* and (conditional) *effects*. *preconditions* specify things that must be true of the world in order for an agent to execute a service. *effects* characterize the physical side-effects that execution of a Web-service has on the world. *inputs* and *outputs* correspond to knowledge preconditions and effects. That is, necessary states of our knowledge base before execution and modifications to our knowledge base as a result of the execution. Note that not all services have physical side-effects, in particular, services that are strictly information-providing do not. Here is part of the DAML-S definition of an atomic process called PharmacyLocator used in our treatment scheduling example:

```
<daml:Class rdf:ID="PharmacyLocator">
  <rdfs:subClassOf rdf:resource=
    "http://www.daml.org/services/daml-s/0.7/Process.daml
    #AtomicProcess"/>
</daml:Class>

<rdf:Property rdf:ID="LocationPreference">
  <rdfs:subPropertyOf rdf:resource=
    "http://www.daml.org/services/daml-s/0.7/Process.daml
    #input"/>
  <rdfs:domain rdf:resource="#PharmacyLocator"/>
  <rdfs:range rdf:resource= "http://www.mindswap.org/services/
    shop2/concepts.daml#LocationPreference"/>
  </rdf:Property>
```

The process model of a compound Web service includes the designation of the top-level composite process corresponding to that service plus a decomposition of that composite process into a structured collection of (perhaps further decomposed) subprocesses.[1] Web services composition is sometimes thought of as the process of generating a (potentially) complexly structured composite process description which is subsequently executed. On this model, composite processes are the *output* of composition. In this paper, we take composite processes as *input* to a planner, that is, as descriptions of *how* to compose a sequence of single step actions. Thus, for us, the goal of automated Web services composition is find a collection of atomic processes instances which form an execution path for some top-level composite process.

3.2 SHOP2

SHOP2 is a domain-independent HTN planning system, which won one of the top four awards out of the 14 planners that competed in the 2002 International

[1] Here, we assume that a compound Web service always has a complete decomposition bottoming out in atomic processes. Such a composite process is *exectuable*.

Planning Competition. HTN planning is an AI planning methodology that creates plan by task decomposition. This is a process in which the planning system decomposes tasks into smaller and smaller subtasks, until primitive tasks are found that can be performed directly.

One difference between SHOP2 and most other HTN planning systems is that SHOP2 plans for tasks in the same order that they will later be executed. Planning for tasks in the order that those task will be performed makes it possible to know the current state of the world at each step in the planning process, which makes it possible for SHOP2's precondition-evaluation mechanism to incorporate significant inferencing and reasoning power, including the ability to call external programs. This makes SHOP2 ideal as a basis for integrating planning with external information sources, including Web based ones.

In order to do planning in a given planning domain, SHOP2 needs to be given the knowledge about that domain. A SHOP2 knowledge base consists of operators and methods (plus, various non-action related facts and axioms). Each operator is a description of what needs to be done to accomplish some primitive task, and each method tells how to decompose some compound task into partially ordered subtasks.

Definition 1 (Operator). A SHOP2 operator is an expression of the form $(h(\overrightarrow{v})$ *Pre Del Add*) where

- $h(\overrightarrow{v})$ represents a primitive task with a list of input parameters $\overrightarrow{v}$
- *Pre* represents the operator's preconditions
- *Del* represents the operator's delete list which includes the list of things that will become false after operator's execution.
- *Add* represents the operator's add list which includes the list of things that will become true after operator's execution.

Definition 2 (Method). A SHOP2 method is an expression of the form $(h(\overrightarrow{v})$ *Pre* $T)$ where

- $h(\overrightarrow{v})$ represents a compound task with a list of input parameters $\overrightarrow{v}$
- *Pre* represents the method's preconditions
- T represents a partially ordered list of subtasks which consist the decomposition of $h(\overrightarrow{v})$.

In addition to the usual logical atoms, preconditions of SHOP2 methods and operators may also contain calls to external programs and assignments to variables. These are useful for integrating planning with queries to information sources on the Web. For example, the following expression

$$(\text{assign } v \text{ (call } f \; t_1 \; t_2 \ldots t_n))$$

will bind the variable symbol v with the result of calling external procedure f with arguments $t_1 \; t_2 \ldots t_n$.

Definition 3 (Planning Problem). A planning problem for SHOP2 is a triple (S, T, D), where S is initial state, T is a task list, and D is a domain description. By taking (S, T, D) as input, SHOP2 will return a plan $P = (p_1 p_2 ... p_n)$, a sequence of instantiated operators that will achieve T from S in D.

4 From DAML-S to SHOP2

The execution of an atomic process is a call to the corresponding web accessible program with its input parameters instantiated.[2] The execution of a composite process ultimately consists in the execution of a collection of specific atomic processes. Instead of directly executing the composite process as a program on a DAML-S interpreter, we can treat the composite process as specification for how to compose a sequence of atomic process executions. In this section, we will show how to encode a composite process composition problem as a SHOP2 planning problem, so SHOP2 can be used with DAML-S Web services descriptions to automatically generate a composition of Web services calls.

4.1 Encoding DAML-S Process Models as SHOP2 Domains

In this section, we introduce an algorithm for translating a collection of DAML-S process models K into a SHOP2 domain D. In our translation, we make the following assumption:

Assumption 1. Given a collection of DAML-S process models $K = \{K_1, K_2, \ldots, K_n\}$, we assume:

- *All atomic processes defined in K can either have effects or outputs, but not both.* According to the situation calculus based semantics of DAML-S[8], *outputs* characterize knowledge effects of executing Web services and *effects* characterize physical effects for executing Web services. An atomic process with only outputs models an strictly information-providing Web service. And an atomic process with only effects models an world-altering Web service. In general, we don't want to actually affect the world during planning. However, we do want to gather certain information from information-providing Web services, which entails executing them at plan time. To enable information gathering from Web services at planning time, we require that the atomic processes to be either exclusively information-providing or exclusively world-altering.
- *There is no composite process in K with DAML-S's **Split** and **Split+Join** control constructs.* SHOP2 currently doesn't handle concurrency. Therefore in our translation, we only consider DAML-S process models that have no composite process using **Split** and **Split+Join** control construct. We also assume only a non-concurrent interpretation of **Unordered** (as permitted

[2] Here, we assume that before the execution of an atomic process the preconditions for executing the atomic process have been satisfied.

by DAML-S). We intend to address how to extend SHOP2 to handle concurrency in the future work.

We encode a collection of DAML-S process definitions K into a SHOP2 domain D as follows:

- For each atomic process with effects in K, we encode it as a SHOP2 operator that simulates the effects of the world-altering Web service.
- For each atomic process with output in K, we encode it as a SHOP2 operator whose precondition include a call to the information-providing Web service.
- For each simple or composite process in K, we encode it as one or more SHOP2 methods. These methods will tell how to decompose an HTN task that represents the simple or composite process.

The following algorithm shows how to translate a DAML-S definition of an atomic process with only effects into a SHOP2 operator.[3]

TRANSLATE-ATOMIC-PROCESS-EFFECT(Q)
Input: a DAML-S definition Q of an atomic process A with only effects.
Output: a SHOP2 operator O.
Procedure:

1. $\overrightarrow{v}$ = the list of input parameters defined for A in Q
2. *Pre* = conjunct of all preconditions of A, as defined in Q
3. *Add* = collection of all positive effects of A, as defined in Q
4. *Del* = collection of all negative effects of A, as defined in Q
5. Return $O = (A(\overrightarrow{v})\ \mathit{Pre}\ \mathit{Del}\ \mathit{Add})$

The above algorithm translates each atomic DAML-S definition into a SHOP2 operator that will simulate the effects of a world-altering Web service by changing its local state via an operator. Such Web services will never be executed at planning time, for obvious reasons.

The following algorithm shows how to translate a DAML-S definition of an atomic process with only outputs into a SHOP2 operator.

TRANSLATE-ATOMIC-PROCESS-OUTPUT(Q)
Input: a DAML-S definition Q of an atomic process A with only outputs.
Output: a SHOP2 operator O.
Procedure:

1. $\overrightarrow{v}$ = the list of input parameters defined for Aas in Q
2. *Pre* = a conjunct of all the preconditions of A, as defined in Q, plus one more precondition of the form (assign y (call Monitor A $\overrightarrow{v}$)), where Monitor is a procedure which will handle SHOP2's call to Web services
3. *Add* $= y$
4. *Del* $= \emptyset$
5. Return $O = (A(\overrightarrow{v})\ \mathit{Pre}\ \mathit{Del}\ \mathit{Add})$

[3] Conditional effects can be easily encoded into SHOP2 operators. Here, for simplicity, we assume that effects (and outputs) are not conditional.

The above algorithm translates each atomic DAML-S definition into a SHOP2 operator that will call the information-providing Web service in its precondition. In this way, the information-providing web service is executed during the planning process. The operator for these atomic processes are entirely "book-keeping", thus none of these operators will appear in the final plan.

The following algorithm shows how to translate a DAML-S definition of a simple process into SHOP2 method(s).

TRANSLATE-SIMPLE-PROCESS(Q)
Input: a DAML-S definition Q of a simple process S.
Output: a collection of SHOP2 methods M.
Procedure:

1. $\overrightarrow{v}$ = the list of input parameters defined for Sas in Q
2. *Pre* = conjunct of all preconditions of S as defined in Q
3. $(b_1, \ldots, b_m)$ = the list of atomic and composite processes that realizes or collapse into S as defined in Q.
4. for i = 1, ..., m
   - $M_i = (S(\overrightarrow{v})\ Pre\ b_i)$
5. return $M = \{M_1, \ldots, M_m\}$

The following algorithm shows how to translates a DAML-S definition of a composite process with **Sequence** control construct into a SHOP2 method.

TRANSLATE-Sequence-PROCESS(Q)
Input: a DAML-S definition Q of a composite process C with **Sequence** control construct.
Output: a SHOP2 method M.
Procedure:

1. $\overrightarrow{v}$ = the list of input parameters defined for Cas in Q
2. *Pre* = conjunct of all preconditions of C as defined in Q
3. B = **Sequence** control construct of C as defined in Q
4. $(b_1, \ldots, b_m)$ = the sequence of component processes of B as defined in Q
5. T = ordered task list of $(b_1, \ldots b_m)$
6. Return $M = (C(\overrightarrow{v})\ Pre\ T)$

The algorithms for translating composite processes with other control constructs such as **Unordered**, **Choice**, **If-Then-Else**, **Iterate**, **Repeat-Until** and **Repeat-While** control constructs are similar to the one for **Sequence**, and so we omit the details here.

To keep the above pseudocode simple, we did not specify the recursive translations within a composite process. E.g., What happens if we have a **Sequence** of **If-Then-Else** or further nestings? Our way for handling this problem is to treat each control construct within a composite process as a composite process. For above example, in our translation, we will have a SHOP2 method for the composite process with **Sequence** construct construct and a method for each nested **If-Then-Else** control construct.

Also we did not explicitly describe how our algorithm handles composite processes with outputs. In DAML-S, one can specify that an output of a composite process is equal to an output of one of its subprocesses whenever the composite process is instantiated. Also, for a composite process with a **Sequence** control construct, one can specify that the output of one subprocess is an input to another subprocesses. SHOP2 does not have the concept of an output, but we handle this problem by assigning a unique number to each instance of a SHOP2 domain's methods and operators. There is a, predicate $(O_{utput} I_{nstance} V_{alue})$, which indicates for each method or operator instance $I_{nstance}$ the value V_{alue} of the particular output O_{utput}.

4.2 Encoding DAML-S Web Services Composition Problem as SHOP2 Planning Problem

A formal semantics has been given for DAML-S service description in terms of an action theory based on the situation calculus [8] [9]. The following definition of a DAML-S service composition problem follows naturally from this semantics.

Definition 3 (DAML-S Service Composition). Let $K = \{K_1, K_2, \ldots, K_m\}$ be a collection of DAML-S process models satisfying Assumption 1 (from section 4.1), T be a top level composite process defined in K and $\vec{c}$ be a list of input parameters instance for T, S_0 be the initial state,and $P = (p_1, p_2, \ldots, p_n)$ be a sequence of atomic processes defined in K with input parameters instance $\vec{c_1}, \vec{c_2}, \ldots, \vec{c_n}$ respectively. Then P is a composition for $T(\vec{c})$ with respect to K in S_0 iff in action theory, we can prove:

$$\Sigma \vdash (\exists s)(Do(T(\vec{c}), S_0, s))$$

with $p_1(\vec{c_1}), p_2(\vec{c_2}), \ldots, p_n(\vec{c_n})$ as an instance of s. Here

- Σ is the axiomatization of K and S_0 as defined in action theory.
- $T(\vec{c})$ is the complex action defined for T as in action theory with input parameters instance $\vec{c}$
- $p_1(\vec{c_1}), p_2(\vec{c_2}), \ldots, p_n(\vec{c_n})$ are the primitive actions defined for atomic processes $p_1, p_2, \ldots, p_n$ as in action theory with input parameters instances $\vec{c_1}, \vec{c_2}, \ldots, \vec{c_n}$.
- *Do* is an additional extralogical symbol defined in situation calculus and action theory. Intuitively, $Do(\delta, s, s')$ will macro-expand into a situation calculus formula that says that it is possible to reach situation s' from situation s by executing a sequence of actions specified by δ.

We first state a theorem about a special case.

Theorem 1. Let $K = \{K_1, K_2, \ldots, K_n\}$ be a collection of DAML-S process models satisfying assumption 1 but also no atomic processes with outputs, T be a top level composite process defined in K, $\vec{c}$ be a list of input parameters instances for T, and S_0 be the initial state. Let $P = (p_1, p_2, \ldots, p_n)$ be a sequence of atomic processes defined in K with input parameters instance $\vec{c_1}, \vec{c_2}, \ldots, \vec{c_n}$ respectively. Let D = **TRANSLATE-PROCESS-MODEL**(K). Then P is a composition for $T(\vec{c})$ with respect to K in S_0 iff P is a plan for planning problem (S_0, T($\vec{c}$), D).

Outline of Proof. We have proven that a service composition problem and its corresponding SHOP2 planning problem map to the same theorem proving problem in action theory.

We now generalize the above theorem to remove the restriction of no atomic processes with the outputs.

As shown in the **TRANSLATE-ATOMIC-PROCESS-OUTPUT** procedure earlier, the precondition for the operator translated from an atomic process with output, SHOP2 will call a Monitor procedure to handle SHOP2's call to external information-providing Web services. This Monitor will monitor the current state of SHOP2, so that information can only be added into the current state if it has not been changed by the planner. We assume here that information will not be changed by other agents during SHOP2 planning time and we will address this problem in the future work.

Soundness and completeness proofs of classical planners assume that the preconditions can be evaluated relative to the current state. However, if a precondition involves call to the external program, this is no longer the case. We have to guarantee that all programs calls to be

- executable (with all parameters grounded)
- terminable (with finite computation)
- repeatable (with same result for the same call)

to ensure that the planner is sound and complete.

Given the dataflow model of DAML-S, no atomic process is, in fact, executed unless all its necessary inputs are bound, we know that when we call an information-providing service, all of its parameters must be grounded. If we can assume that information provided by all Web services will not change during SHOP2 planning time and all web services invocations are terminable, then we can establish the soundness and completeness proof of SHOP2.

Theorem 2. Let $K = \{K_1, K_2, \ldots, K_n\}$ be a collection of DAML-S process models satisfying assumption in Section 4.1, T be a top level composite process defined in K and $\vec{c}$ be a list of input parameters instance for T, S_0 be the initial state. $K_a = K$ - {atomic processes with outputs in K} and P be a sequence of atomic processes defined in K with input parameters instance $\vec{c_1}, \vec{c_2}, \ldots, \vec{c_n}$ respectively. Let D = **TRANSLATE-PROCESS-MODEL**(K). D_a = **TRANSLATE-PROCESS-MODEL**(K_a). If every execution of the information-providing Web services defined in K is guaranteed to terminate, then P is a plan for planning problem ($\emptyset$, $T(\vec{c})$, D) iff P is a plan for planning problem (S_0, $T(\vec{c})$, D_a).

Outline of Proof. Because calls to the information-providing services are always terminable, information is always available whenever needed. Therefore, SHOP2 will have the same planning process for two problems.

5 Implementation

To realize our agent technology, we started with an implementation of a DAML-S to SHOP2 translator. This translator is a Java program that reads in a collection of DAML-S process definitions files and outputs a SHOP2 domain file. As shown in the translation algorithm in section 4.1, when planning for any problem in this domain, SHOP2 will actually call the information-providing Web services to collect information while maintaining the ability of backtrack by merely simulating the effect of world-altering Web services. The output of SHOP2 is a sequence of world-altering Web services calls that can be subsequently executed.

We built a monitor which handles SHOP2's calls to external information-providing Web services during planning. We wrote a DAML-S Web services executor which communicates with SOAP based Web services described by DAML-S groundings to WSDL descriptions of those Web services. Upon SHOP2's request, the monitor will call this DAML-S Web services executor to execute the corresponding Web service. Since the information-providing services are always defined as atomic processes, the service is executed by invoking the WSDL service in the grounding. The monitor also caches the responses of the information-providing Web services to avoid invoking a Web service with same parameters more than once during planning. This will save the network communication times and improve planning efficiency, and establishes the repeatability condition required for proving SHOP2's soundness and completeness. Also information can only be added into the current state if it has not been changed by the planner. We assume that the cached information will not be changed by other agents during planning and we will generalize this in our future work.

We also built a SHOP2 to DAML-S plan converter, which will convert a the plan produced by SHOP2 to DAML-S format which can be directly executed by the DAML-S executor.

We ran our scenario from section 2 on this system. In doing so:

- Our system communicated with real Web services. Unfortunately, the current Web services available on the Web have only WSDL descriptions without any semantic markup. Therefore, we created DAML-S markup for the WSDL decriptions of these online services and for some services it was also necessary to create the WSDL descriptions since the service was only offered via filling a form on a web page such as CVS Online Pharmacy Store. It was not possible to use real services for some of the services either because none was available as Web services, e.g. a doctor's agent providing the patient's prescription, or it was infeasible to use a real Web service for the demo, e.g. making an appointment with a doctor each time the program is executed. For these services, we implemented Web services to simulate these functionalities.
- We built Web services that allow the access to user's personal information sources. For example, it is necessary to learn the user's schedule to be able to

generate a plan for the example task in our demo. It is possible to get this information from the sources available on the user's machine such as a Personal Information Manager like Microsoft's Outlook. We have implemented "local" SOAP based services that will retrieve this kind of information. WSDL and DAML-S descriptions are also generated for these local services so that they can be composed and executed in the same way as other remotely available services.
Finally, some information gathering services were implemented as direct Java calls from SHOP2 over a Java/SHOP2 bridge. For example, we have a service which asks the user for acceptable distances to the treatment center by popping up a window on the user's client to accept input. Changing the data entered at this point will possibly yield a different plan to be generated allowing the planner produce custom plans depending on personal preferences.
- We also encoded a description of how to compose Web services for tasks such as the one faced by Bill and Joan in section 2 in DAML-S. The description is given as a DAML-S composite process that is composed of several other composite processes that are defined as sequence, choice or unordered processes. This DAML-S description constitutes the top level composite process described in Section 4.2 and is translated into a SHOP2 domain for planning. We encode most of the constraints mentioned in section 2 as Web service preconditions. Right now, there is no standard process modelling language for specifying Web service preconditions. Therefore, we directly encode the Web services preconditions in SHOP2 format.

To test the effectiveness of our approach, we have run SHOP2 on several instances of the problem described in Section 2. These problem instances varied from cases where it was easy to schedule satisfactory appointments to a case in which no nearby treatment centers had treatment time slots that were close together, so that Bill and Joan would both have to drive Mom for treatments on separate days. In all of these cases, SHOP2 was easily able to find the best possible solution. Fig. 1 shows a snapshot of some information collected during SHOP2 planning process and a plan produced by SHOP2.

6 Related Work

McIlarith and Son [10] proposed an approach to building agent technology based on the notion of generic procedures and customizing user constraints. They argue that an augmented version of the logic programming language Golog provides a natural formalism for programming Web services. These contributions are realized in their development of the ConGolog interpreter which communicates with Web services via the Open Agent Architecture (OAA) but the service and procedure ontologies are written in first-order logic. Our system more directly supports the use of existing Web services by being able to ground directly in the existing WSDL services rather than creating a separate execution system for semantically described services. Also, we suspect that their approach will not be as efficient as an HTN planner.

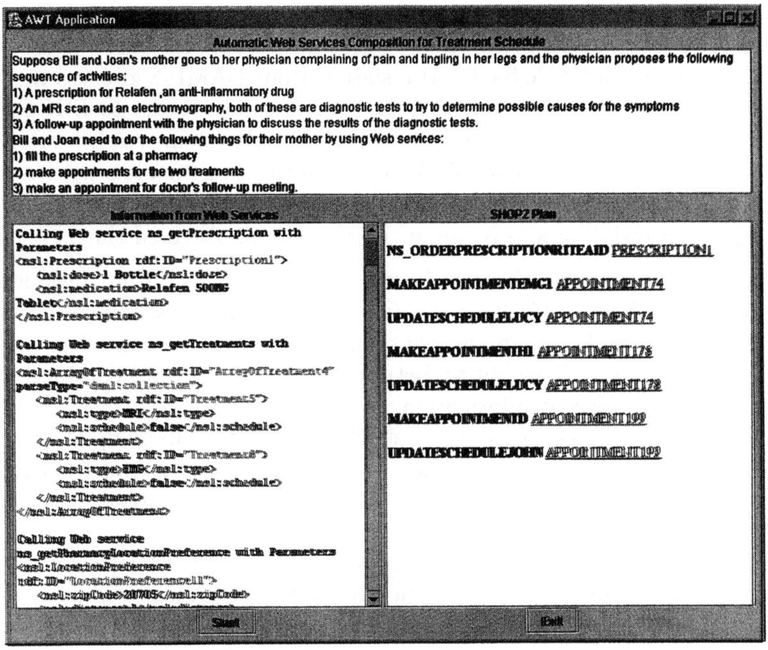

Fig. 1. Example Running Result

Matskin and Mao [11] applies software synthesis and composition methods to Web services composition. Their work is based on similarities between Web service composition and component-based system development in software engineering. They use DAML-S for service descriptions and adopt Structural Synthesis Program (SSP) method for automated service composition. Service composition is based on the input-output information of services components and requires little domain knowledge. This approach treats each service as an atomic entity without inspecting the internal process model and therefore lacks the ability to reason about different decompositions in a composite process.

RETSINA is an open multi-agent system that provides infrastructure for different types of deliberative, goal directed agents. RETSINA system includes a planner [13] based on the HTN planning paradigm. The RETSINA planner also extends HTN planning by adding interleaving of planning and execution which basically allows the acions execute before a plan is completely formed, similar to our approach. Paolucci et al. [13] also describes using RETSINA planner in the context of creating autonomous Web services that can automatically interact with each other. However, authors do not give details about how the HTN planning is employed in the system. It is not clear whether DAML-S Process Model was used or planning domain was given a priori to the planner agent. For this reason, we cannot make a comparison with our approach.

7 Conclusion

In this paper, we have defined a translation from DAML-S process models to the SHOP2 domains, and from DAML-S composition tasks to SHOP2 planning problems. We have described our implemented system which performs this translation, uses an extended SHOP2 implementation to plan with and over the translated domain, and then executes the resulting plans. In the process of defining the translation and building the system, we observed that:

- In our current approach, the planner always executes output producing actions as it plans. While this is fine for many situations, it may not always be appropriate. For example, the execution of some Web services may take a very long time. It would be better if the planner could continue to plan while waiting for this information.
- In our paper, we assume that all effects are physical. In complex situations, there may be other changes, such as in the mental states of the agents involved, that are not modelled. We will explore this problem in our future work.
- There is a fundamental difference between exclusively information providing and possibly world-altering atomic processes. We typically want to execute information providing atomic processes at various points in the planning process, while we never want to execute world-altering ones. Contrariwise, at composition execution time, the primary interest is in the execution of world-altering processes. Indeed, in our system we do not include any information providing processes in compositions. Furthermore, currently we do not permit world-altering processes to be information providing, at least in the sense that they must have no outputs. This simplification made the system fairly easy to implement without substantial modification of SHOP2. Mapping information-gathering processes to so-called "book-keeping" operators may be somewhat unaesthetic. It seems possible to encode them directly as external code calls in preconditions for the processes that receive the information as input, or more generally as part of the axiomatic inferential structure of the planner's state, though this would probably require some substantial dataflow analysis.

  Information providing (whether exclusively so, or not) is and is likely to be a significant fraction of the available and salient Web services. Many Web contexts seem to be *information rich* but *action poor*. In such environments, we'd want to reconsider the strict partition of services into exclusively information providing and output free. For example, world-altering services with outputs might supply information needed to decide subsequent courses of action. Clearly, such a service shouldn't be executed at planning time, which suggests that we will need to investigate generating conditional plans by SHOP2 style HTN planning.

  Conditional plans will also help eliminate the constraint on information change during planning. Currently, both for theoretical and practical reasons, we only execute an information providing process once during planning for any given input, and subsequently retrieve a cached result. Given

SHOPs speed, this is not that unreasonable a restriction for many cases, but conditional plans would permit planning for various contingencies.

These considerations raise a host of issues regarding plan time vs. composition execution time execution of information providing processes, including those of deciding which such processes to execute only during planning, only during plan execution, and during both. Furthermore, in complex, long running planning sessions, it might make sense to refresh the monitors cache for certain services at intervals. Presumably, DAML-S descriptions will be enriched to help support the requisite analysis. We intend to explore these issues in future work.

- Compared the complexities raised above, composite processes raise no additional or special problems — encoding them as SHOP2 methods seems correct and straightforward, modulo the need to extend SHOP2 to handle concurrency.
- Simple processes are the odd duck of the lot. Though various members of the DAML-S coalition have suggested, in conversation, that simple processes were intended to support HTN planning, we found them niether necessary, nor convenient, nor useful. In part, their lack of a clear semantics, particularly with regard to the relationship of their inputs, outpus, preconditions, and effects to those of their corresponding atomic or composite processes. Furthermore, while the language of the technical overview[3] suggests that a given simple process can be a view of one atomic process or one composite process, but not both, neither the langauge nor the ontology actually require this restriction. We speculated that this would make simple processes useful for specifying a range of alternative composition paths, but it wasn't clear that this was really more convenient (for our purposes) than using the **Choice** control construct.

Acknowledgments. This work was supported in part by Air Force Research Laboratory grant F30602-00-2-0505.

References

1. Dean, M., Connolly, D., van Harmelen, F., Hendler, J., Horrocks, I., McGuinness, D.L., Patel-Schneider, P. F. and Stein, L. A.: Web Ontology Language (OWL) Reference Version 1.0. Recent Trends and Developments. W3C Working Draft 12 November 2002, http://www.w3.org/TR/2002/WD-owl-ref-20021112/
2. Horrocks, I., van Harmelen, F., Patel-Schneider, P., Berners-Lee, T., Brickley, D., Connoly, D., Dean, M., Decker, S., Fensel, D., Hayes, P., Heflin,J., Hendler, J., Lassila, O., McGuinness, D., and Stein, L. A.: DAML+OIL. http://www.daml.org/2001/03/daml+oil-index.html (2001)
3. The DAML Services Coalition: DAML-S:Semantic Markup for Web Services. Technical Overview. http://www.daml.org/services/daml-s/0.7/daml-s.html (2002)
4. The DAML Services Coalition(Ankolekar, A., Burstein, M., Hobbs, J.R., Lassila, O., Martin, D. , McDermott, D., McIlraith, S.A., Narayanan, S., Paolucci, M., Payne, T., Sycara, K.):DAML-S: Web Service Description for the Semantic Web. Proceedings of the First International Semantic Web Conference (2002)

5. Nau, D., Munoz-Avila, H., Cao, Y., Lotem, A., Mitchell, S.:Total-Order Planning with Partially Ordered Subtasks. Proceedings of the Seventeenth International Joint Conference on Artificial Intelligence (2001)
6. Nau, D., Au, T., Ilghami,O., Kuter, U., Murdock, J. W., Wu, D., Yaman, F.: SHOP2: An HTN Planning Environment. To appear in Journal of Artificial Intelligence Research (2003)
7. Berners-Lee, T., Hendler, J., Lassila, O.:The Semantic Web. Scientific American (2001)
8. Narayanan, S., McIlraith, S.: Simulation, Verification and Automated Composition of Web Services. Proceedings of the Eleventh International World Wide Web Conference, Honolulu, Hawaii (2002)
9. Reiter, R.: Knowledge In Action: Logical Foundations for Specifying and Implementing Dynamical Systems, The MIT Press (2001)
10. McIlraith, S., Son, T.: Adapting Golog for Composition of Semantic Web Services. Proceedings of the Eighth International Conference on Knowledge Representation and Reasoning, Toulouse, France, (2002)
11. Matskin, M., Rao, J.: Value-Added Web Services Composition Using Automatic Program Synthesis. Web Services, E-Business, and the Semantic Web, CAiSE 2002 International Workshop, WES 2002, Toronto, Canada, (2002)
12. Paolucci, M., Shehory, O., Sycara,K.: Interleaving planning and execution in a multiagent team planning environment. Electronic Transactions of Artificial Intelligence, (2001)
13. Paolucci, M., Sycara,K., Kawamura, T.: Delivering semantic web services. Technical Report CMU-RI-TR-02-28, Robotics Institute, Carnegie Mellon University, Pittsburgh, PA, December 2002

Surfing the Service Web

Sudhir Agarwal[1], Siegfried Handschuh[1], and Steffen Staab[1,2]

[1] AIFB, University of Karlsruhe
{agarwal,sha,sst}@aifb.uni-karlsruhe.de,
http://www.aifb.uni-karlsruhe.de/WBS
[2] Ontoprise GmbH, 76131 Karlsruhe, Germany,
http://www.ontoprise.com/

Abstract. The way that web services are currently being developed places them beside rather than within the existing World Wide Web. In this paper we present an approach that combines the strength of the World Wide Web, viz. interlinked HTML pages for presentation and human consumption, with the strength of semantic web services, viz. support for semi-automatic composition and invocation of web services that have semantically heterogeneous descriptions. The objective we aim at eventually is that a human user can seamlessly surf the existing World Wide Web and the emerging web services and that he can easily compose and invoke Web services on the fly without being a software engineer. This paper presents our framework, OntoMat-Service, which trades off between having a reasonably easy to use interface for web services and the complexity of web service workflows. It is not our objective that everybody can produce arbitrarily complex workflows of web services with our tool, the OntoMat-Service-Surfer. However, OntoMat-Service aims at a service web, where simple service flows are easily possible — even for the persons with not much technical background, while still allowing for difficult flows for the expert engineer.

1 Introduction

The Stencil Group defines web services as: loosely coupled, reusable software components that semantically encapsulate discrete functionality and are distributed and programmatically accessible over standard internet protocols. Though this definition captures the broad understanding of what web services are, it raises the question, what web services have to do with the web. Even if HTTP is used as a communication protocol and XML/SOAP to carry some syntax this appears to be a rather random decision than a deeply meaningful design.

We believe that it makes sense to actually integrate the strengths of the conventional World Wide Web, viz. lightweight access to information in a highly-distributed setting, with the strengths of web wervices, viz. execution of functionality by lightweight protocols in a highly-distributed setting. To seamlessly integrate the two aspects we envision a *service web* that uses XHTML/XML/RDF to transport information and a web service framework to invoke operations and a

D. Fensel et al. (Eds.): ISWC 2003, LNCS 2870, pp. 211–226, 2003.

framework, OntoMat-Service, to bind the two aspects together. OntoMat-Service offers an infrastructure, OntoMat-Service-Surfer, that allows

- for seamlessly browsing conventional web pages, including XHTML advertisements for web services;
- for direct, manual invocation of an advertised web service as a one-off use of the service;
- for tying web service advertisements to each other when browsing them;
- for tying web service advertisements to one's own conceptualization of the web space when browsing them; and
- for invoking such aggregated web services.

For these objectives, we build on numerous existing technologies like RDF [9], ontologies [2] or WSDL [1]. To integrate the web and web services into the service web, we make specific use of a new type of *semantic annotation* [6], namely *deep annotation* [7].

The paper proceeds as follows. We first describe a simple use case for OntoMat-Service (cf. section 2), including a detailed WSDL description of a web service used for the running example. In section 3, we describe the process that allows to turn web services into a service web and that lets a user surfing the web with OntoMat-Service-Surfer exploit the very same tool to aggregate and invoke web services. The first step of this process, i.e. advertising web services in a form that combines presentation for human and machine agent consumption, is sketched in section 4. The second step of this process, i.e. using browsing and semantic deep annotation to tie together conceptual descriptions, is described in section 5. The third step comprises the generation of simple web service flows and is described in section 6. The fourth and final step described in section 7 deals with the invocation of web service flows. Before we conclude, we overview some related work.

2 Use Case

A typical use case supported by OntoMat-Service is the following (adapted from a larger scenario in [11]): An employee in a small enterprise needs a new laptop. In order to buy one he defines the characteristics of the laptop like processor speed, disk size, etc. Based on the configuration of the laptop he collects offers from laptop vendors. When he receives an offer he also solicits insurance terms from a third party. Once the most reasonable laptop and the best insurance contract terms are determined, the employee purchases the laptop and closes the service contract.

In our scenario, we assume a laptop vendor and an insurer offering web services with two operations each, i.e. `getLaptopOffer` / `buyLaptop` and `getInsuranceTerms` / `closeServiceContract`, respectively. The sequence of operations that must be executed by the customer is depicted in Figure 1.

The laptop vendor and the insurer being web service providers describe their web services with WSDL documents. In Figure 2, we show

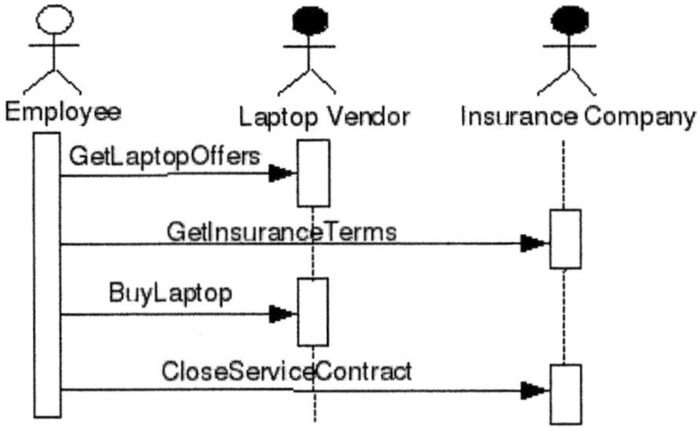

Fig. 1. Sequence Diagram for the Use Case

```
<?xml version="1.0" encoding="UTF-8"?> <definitions
name="LaptopService"
    targetNamespace="http://laptop.wsdl/laptop/"
    <types>
       <rdf:RDF>
          <rdfs:Class rdf:ID="Laptop">
             <rdfs:label>Laptop</rdfs:label>
          </rdfs:Class>
          <rdf:Property rdf:ID="diskSpace">
             <rdfs:label>diskSpace</rdfs:label>
             <rdfs:range rdf:resource="&rdfs;Literal"/>
             <rdfs:domain rdf:resource="#Laptop"/>
          </rdf:Property>
           ...
          <rdf:Property rdf:ID="price">
             <rdfs:label>price</rdfs:label>
             <rdfs:range rdf:resource="&rdfs;Literal"/>
             <rdfs:domain rdf:resource="#Laptop"/>
          </rdf:Property>
           ...
        </rdf:RDF>
    </types>
    <message name="getOffersRequest">
        <part name="processorSpeed" type="rdf:ID=processorSpeed"/>
        <part name="diskSpace" type="rdf:ID=diskSpace"/>
    </message>
    <message name="getOffersResponse">
        <part name="laptopOffers" type="rdf:ID=laptops"/>
    </message>
        ...
    <portType name="LaptopService">
        <operation name="getLaptopOffers" parameterOrder="processorSpeed diskSpace">
            <input message="tns:getOffersRequest" name="getOffersRequest"/>
            <output message="tns:getOffersResponse" name="getOffersResponse"/>
        </operation>
        ...
    </portType>
</definitions>
```

Fig. 2. Web Service Description of Laptop Vendor

```
@prefix rdfs: <http://www.w3.org/rdf-schema#>. @prefix : <#>.
@prefix a rdf:Type.
```

Fig. 3. N3 shortcuts

how a conventional WSDL document of the laptop vendor located at `http://laptop-vendor.de/lap top.wsdl` might look like.[1]

The WSDL document describes:

- *Data type definitions* in the XML element `types`. They are only sketched in figure 2 as they correspond to the laptop vendor's ontology depicted in N3[2] in figure 4. Thereby, we assume the definitions given in Figure 3. In our running example, the WSDL document of the laptop vendor, we describe the class Laptop.
- *Messages* that a service sends and/or receives and that constitute the web service operations in the XML element `portType`. For instance, our running example specifies '`getOffersRequest`' that a potential customer would send to the laptop vendor to solicit an offer. `getOffersRequest` must be provided with two arguments, namely processor speed and disk size. It returns a set of laptop offers with properties such as specified in the vendor ontology (cf. WSDL document in Figure 2 and vendor ontology in Figure 4).

WSDL provides a naming convention for URIs such that each conceptual element (e.g., `types`, `portType`, etc.) of a WSDL document can be uniquely referenced. Such a URI consists of a `targetNamespace` pointing to the location of the WSDL document and to element names of the WSDL document. For example, the URI `http://laptop.wsdl/laptop/#part(getOffersRequest/diskSpace)` refers to the second part (`diskSpace`) of the message `getOffersRequest` of the WSDL document in Figure 2 (cf. [1] for further specifications).

The web service description of the insurer looks similarly. We here only mention that the insurer provides the operations `getInsuranceTerms` and `closeServiceContract`. `getInsuranceTerms` requires a description of Laptop (according to the insurer's ontology in Figure 5) and a timePeriod, for which the contract is supposed to run. `getInsuranceTerms` returns a set of insurance terms available.

In the remainder of the paper, we assume that the customer has the plan depicted in Figure 1. However, in our running example, we will mostly focus on the first two steps to illustrate our framework.

[1] The single ideosyncrasy we have here is that the WSDL document employs RDFS in order to describe the data structures instead of the more common XML schema — though actually WSDL does not require XML Schema and it allows RDFS.

[2] Notation 3 or N3 is basically equivalent to RDF in its XML syntax, but more compact. Cf. http://www.w3.org/DesignIssues/Notation3

```
:Laptop a rdfs:Class.
:price rdfs:domain :Laptop;
       rdfs:range :rdfs:Literal.
:diskSpace rdfs:domain :Laptop;
           rdfs:range :rdfs:Literal.
:processorSpeed rdfs:domain :Laptop;
                rdfs:range :rdfs:Literal.
:laptopID rdfs:domain :Laptop;
          rdfs:range :rdfs:Literal.

:Offer a rdfs:Class.
:laptops rdfs:domain :Offer;
         rdfs:range :Laptop.

:Sale a rdfs:Class.
:laptop rdfs:domain :Sale;
        rdfs:range :Laptop.
:creditCardNumber rdfs:domain :Sale;
                  rdfs:range :Literal.
:customerReceipt rdfs:domain :Sale;
                 rdfs:range :Literal.
```

Fig. 4. Ontology of the laptop vendor

```
:Laptop a rdfs:Class.
:id rdfs:domain :Laptop;
    rdfs:range :Literal.

:ContractTerms a rdfs:Class.
:laptop rdfs:domain :ContractTerms;
        rdfs:range :Laptop.
:timePeriod rdfs:domain :ContractTerms;
            rdfs:range :Literal.
:price rdfs:domain :ContractTerms;
       rdfs:range :Literal.
```

Fig. 5. Ontology of the insurance company

```
:Product a rdfs:Class.
:id rdfs:domain :Product; rdfs:range :Literal.

:HardDisk a :Product.
:diskSize rdfs:domain :HardDisk; rdfs:range :Literal.
:Computer a :Product.
:hasHDD rdfs:domain :Computer; rdfs:range :HardDisk.
:price rdfs:domain :Computer; rdfs:range :Literal.
:cpuSpeed rdfs:domain :Computer; rdfs:range :Literal.

:Agent a :rdfs:Class.
:Company a :Agent.
:creditCardNumber rdfs:domain :Company; rdfs:range :Literal.

:Purchase a :rdfs:Class.
:hasBuyer rdfs:domain :Purchase; rdfs:range :Agent.
:hasObject rdfs:domain :Purchase; rdfs:range :Product.

:Insurance a :rdfs:Class.
:hasObject rdfs:domain :Insurance; rdfs:range :Product.
:price rdfs:domain :Insurance; rdfs:range :Literal.
:timePeriod rdfs:domain :Insurance; rdfs:range :Literal.
```

Fig. 6. Ontology of the customer

3 Overview of the Complete Process of OntoMat-Service

Figure 7 shows the complete process of our framework, OntoMat-Service. First, the figure consists of process steps, which are illustrated by a circle representing the step and a person icon representing the logical role of the person who executes the step, viz. service provider, annotating Service Web surfer and a user invoking a Web Service. The two latter roles typically coincide. Second, the figure comprises information that is used by a person or by OntoMat-Service-Surfer in a process step.

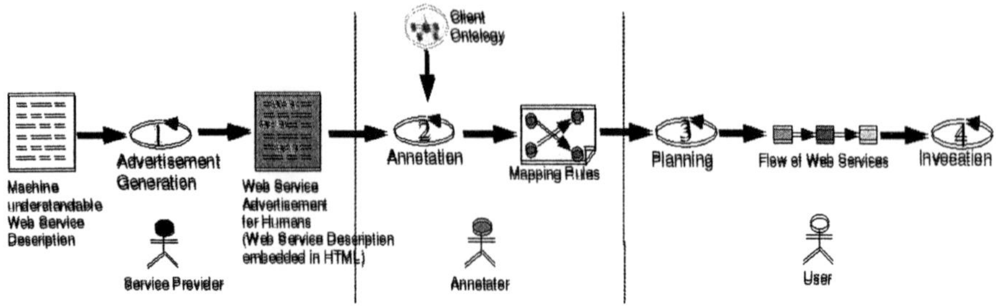

Fig. 7. The Complete Process of OntoMat-Service

The four main steps run as follows:

Init: OntoMat-Service starts with a common WSDL web service description by the service provider (e.g., Figure 2). Obviously, the WSDL document is primarily intended for use by a machine agent or a software engineer who has experience with web services. It is not adequate for presenting it to a user who is 'only' expert in a domain.

Web Service Presentation (Step 1): In the first step, the web service provider makes the web service presentation readable as a nicely formatted (X)HTML document — possibly including advertisements, cross-links to other HTML pages or services, or other items that make the web page attractive to the potential customer (cf. Section 4 for details).
Thereby, it is important that the understandable, but informal description of the web service is implicitly annotated to relate the textual descriptions to their corresponding semantic descriptions in their WSDL document.
Step 1 is a manual step that may be supported by tools such as *WSDL Documentation Generator* from *http://www.xmlspy.com*. However, we would not assume that tools like *WSDL Documentation Generator* would be sufficient to generate an amenable presentation, as they still produce rather rigid and technically oriented descriptions.

Result 1: Human understandable web page that advertises the web service and embeds/refers to machine understandable web service descriptions (WSDL + ontology).

Deep Annotation (Step 2): At a client side, a potential user of the web service browses the web page. OntoMat-Service-Surfer shows the web page like a conventional browser. In addition, OntoMat-Service-Surfer highlights human-understandable items (e.g. text phrases) that associate an underlying machine-understandable semantics.
The logical role of the user here is one of an annotator/surfer. He can decide to just view the page and proceed directly to step 4 (described below). Alternatively, he can decide to map some of the terminology used in the web page of the web service to his own terminology (or to the terminology of someone else).

For the latter purpose, he loads an ontology into OntoMat-Service-Surfer (if it is not already pre-loaded). Then he aligns terminology mentioned in the web page by drag'n'drop-ping it onto the ontology loaded into OntoMat-Service-Surfer. OntoMat-Service-Surfer generates mapping rules from these annotations that bridge between the ontology of the service provider and the ontology loaded into OntoMat-Service-Surfer (cf. Section 5 for details).
Typically, the user will map to more than one web service, i.e. often he will map to different ontologies.

Result 2: Sets of mapping rules between web service ontologies and pre-loaded ontology.

Web Service Planning (Step 3): At the client side, a user might view the web services as well as their annotations that yield mapping rules. The third logical role here is one of a service planner and invocator (this logical role is shared between the third and fourth step). For this purpose, the user decides to select

- a set of web service operations he wants to use and
- a set of mapping rules he wants to use.

The reader may note that very frequently the roles of an annotator/surfer and a service invocator will just coincide. Hence, the two selections just mention will take place implicitly — just by the web service pages he has browsed and the annotations that the service invocator has performed in step 2 of the OntoMat-Service process.

Once the two selections have been performed im- or explicitly, a module for web service planning will compute logically possible web service flows. For this objective, web service planning may employ a rich set of knowledge: goals, pre-conditions of web services, post-conditions of web services, previous similar cases, etc. In the current version of OntoMat-Service we just exploit the pre- and post-conditions derived from mapping one web service output to another web service input via the customer ontology. The web service description in the associated WSDL document describes what types are required for the input of a web service and what types appear in the output of a web service. Since data that wanders from one web service to the next can only proceed if types are compatible, OntoMat-Service-Surfer can compute a restricted set of possible web service flows (cf. Section 6).

Though in general this model may be too weak to compute complex flows it is quite sufficient and straightforward to use with a small number of selected and semantically aligned web services — such as an end user or prototype builder will use.

Result 3: Sets of possible web service flows.

Web Service Invocation (Step 4): The final user, i.e. the invocator, can select one such flow from the list or modify any, if none of them fits his needs. Obviously, he can always create a new flow on his own. Once the user has a flow, that fulfils his current needs, he invocates the flow (cf. Section 7). During the execution, the tranformation of the data of one ontology to another will happen automatically via the mapping rules. The user achieves his goal at the completion of the invocation of the web service flow.

```
<html><head><title>Laptop Vendor Service</title></head> <body><h1
align="center">Laptop Vendor Service</h1> <p><h2>getLaptopOffers</h2>
This service delivers the top offers of the laptops available in
the city. We have the largest archive of the laptop offers for the
city. So, the possibility that you find your desired laptop at a
reasonable price is very high. Just try it and get convinced from
our great offers. <ul><li> <span
wsdlLocation="http://laptop-vendor.de/laptop.wsdl"
elementURI="http://laptop.wsdl/laptop/#part(getOffersRequest/processorSpeed)">
<b>Processor speed</b> </span> Specifies the speed of the
processor. Please use only the units "MHz" and "GHz". For example,
"2GHz", "1.4GHz" and "1600MHz" are valid whereas "1800" or
"170000KHz" are invalid. </li><li> <span
wsdlLocation="http://laptop-vendor.de/laptop.wsdl"
elementURI="http://laptop.wsdl/laptop/#part(getOffersRequest/diskSpace)">
<b>Disk space</b> </span> Specifies the disk space. Please use
only the units "GB" and "MB". For example, "20GB", "30.5GB" are
valid whereas "40" or "25000KB" are invalid. </li><li> <span
wsdlLocation="http://laptop-vendor.de/laptop.wsdl"
elementURI="http://laptop-vendor.wsdl/laptop/#part(getOffersResponse/laptopOffers)">
<b>Top Offers</b> </span> This is the list of the most reasonable
offers available in the city that fulfill your requirements.
</li></ul></p>
                              ...
</body></html>
```

Fig. 8. Web Service Description as HTML Page

4 Semantic Web Page Markup for Web Services

In this section we show how a web service provider can semantically annotate the web pages describing his web services. Such a combined presentation allows for improved ways to find the web services (e.g., by a combined syntactic/semantic search engine) and it enables a user to define mapping rules between the ontology used in the web service description and the client's ontology.

The basic idea is that a conventional HTML page about the web service and web service parameters is extended by URIs referring to conceptual elements of the corresponding WSDL documents. To carry these two pieces of information, we use `wsdlLocation` and `elementURI` inside the `span` tags. In Figure 8, we show how such an web service advertisement(HTML page) for the laptop vendor service might look like.

When such an HTML page is opened in OntoMat-Service-Surfer, the `span` tags are interpreted and elements between `<span>` and `</span>` are highlighted to support the annotation step described in the next section.

5 Browsing and Deep Annotation

In this section, we describe the second main step of the OntoMat-Service process. This step consists of browsing web pages about web services with OntoMat-Service-Surfer. Thereby, the user may deep-annotate [7] these web pages generating mapping rules between a client ontology and the ontologies referred to in the WSDL documents as a 'side effect'. We call this action 'deep-annotation' as its purpose is not to provide semantic annotation about the surface of what is being annotated, this would be the web page, but about the semantic structures in the background, i.e. the WSDL elements.

Thus, this step is about web service discovery by browsing and using information retrieval engines like Google as well as about reconciling semantic heterogenity between different web services, such as described in the WSDL documents and the web service ontologies they embed or refer to.

5.1 User Interaction

Service Browsing. With OntoMat-Service-Surfer the user can surf the service web, i.e. he can browse the web pages of web service advertisements and OntoMat-Service-Surfer highlights semantic annotations added by the web service provider. OntoMat-Service-Surfer indicates semantically-annotated web service elements, e.g. input parameters, by graphical icons on the web page. Thus, the user may easily identify relevant terminology that needs to be aligned with his own ontology.

As an alternative to deep annotation, the ontology browser in OntoMat-Service-Surfer may also visualize the underlying service ontology. OntoMat-Service-Surfer is able to interpret the description of web service operations and provide a corresponding form interface. The user may then directly proceed to web service invocation (Section 7) and invoke a concrete web service operations with data he provides via this generic form interface.

Deep Annotation. The user selects an ontology to be used for annotation and loads it into OntoMat-Service-Surfer. The user annotates the web service by drag'n'dropping highlighted items from the web page into the ontology browser of OntoMat-Service-Surfer. Doing so, he does not only extend the web page with metadata (which is possible), but most important here he establishes mappings between concepts, relations and attributes from the ontology used by the web service provider to his client ontology.

In the following we describe the deep-annotation of the vendor web service shown in Figure 9. The web page advertising the web service describes the `getLaptopOffer` operation and constitutes the context for the usage of the vendor ontology. The aim of the annotator is to translate the terminology used in the description of `getLaptopOffer` (cf. the WSDL document in Figure 2 and the vendor ontology in Figure 4) into his client ontology (Figure 6).

By drag'n'drop, one generates a graph of instances, relations between instances and attribute values of instances in the browser that visualizes the client ontology (cf. the left pane depicted in Figure 9).

When performing a drag'n'drop one will create a literal instance, if one drop's an instance of the vendor ontology onto a concept in the client ontology, or a literal value, if one drop's an attribute value of an instance onto an attribute in the client ontology. For instance, dropping 'IBM' onto the concept company would create a corresponding literal instance in the client ontology, dropping '7MB' creates a corresponding attribute value to a selected instance in the client ontology.

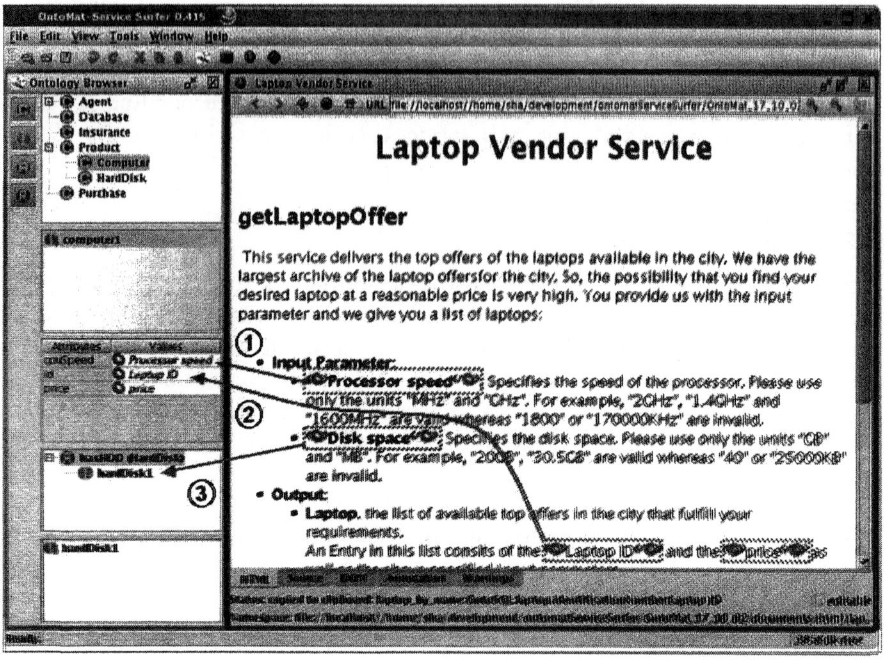

Fig. 9. Screenshot of OntoMat-Service-Surfer annotating vendor service

If one drop's a concept A from the vendor ontology onto a client ontology concept B, one will create a *generic instance*. A generic instance is just a variable that states that concept A in the vendor ontology corresponds to concept B in the client ontology.[3]

Thus, one may compile different types of instances in the client ontology. Each graph of non-separable, newly created instances and values in the client ontology corresponds to a mapping rule. For instance, one may *(i)*, drag'n'drop 'processorSpeed (from vendor ontology) onto cpuSpeed (from client ontology) that belongs to Computer (again in the client ontology). Thereby, *(ii)*, a generic instance is created for Computer with value Laptop (as cpuSpeed belongs to Computer and processorSpeed belongs to Laptop). The corresponding N3 notation reads as:

```
@prefix vendor: <http://laptop.wsdl/laptop/#>
@prefix client: <http://www.company.de/company.daml#>
vendor:Laptop a :GenericInstance; a client:Computer;
                                   client:cpuSpeed vendor:processorSpeed.
vendor:processorSpeed a :GenericInstance.
```

Its interpretation as a mapping is in first order logic:

```
FORALL X,Y (instanceOf(X,Computer) AND cpuSpeed(X,Y))
        <- (instanceOf(X,vendor:Laptop) AND vendor:processorSpeed(X,Y)).
```

[3] Corresponding generalizations exist for attributes and relationships.

One may trace the later drag'n'drop action in Figure 9, where action 1 picks up 'Processor Speed' with its underlying web service parameter processorSpeed (cf. the markup `elementURI="http://laptop.wsdl/laptop/#part(getLaptopOfferRequest/processorSpeed)"` in Figure 8). He drops onto the attribute that comes closest in his client ontology, viz. the aforementioned cpuSpeed, and generates the consequences just mentioned. Similarly, the second text item "Disk Space" being annotated with the input parameter `diskSpace` is handled in action 2. This time, however, the annotator must also create a hasHDD relationship between the generic instance hardisk1 and the generic instance of computer1 to build a larger graph representing a mapping rule with two generic attribute values (on cpuSpeed and diskSpace). Finally, the annotator maps the output parameters in action 3 (cf. Figure 9).

5.2 Mapping Rules Derived from Annotation

The results of deep annotation are mapping rules between the client ontology and each service ontology. The annotator may publish the client ontology and the mapping rules derived from annotations. This enables third parties (in particular logical roles that follow in the OntoMat-Service process) to execute the services on the basis of the semantics defined in the client ontology.

The mapping rules are defined in F-Logic. F-logic is a deductive, object-oriented database language that combines the declarative semantics and expressiveness of deductive database languages with the rich data modelling capabilities supported by object oriented model [8]. The annotator does not have to write F-logic rules. They are generated automatically by the OntoMat-Service-Surfer. Figure 10 and Figure 11 give the reader an intuition of how such automatically generated mapping rules look like when visualized with the OntoEdit plugins OntoMap (cf., [7]). Figure 10 shows the mapping from the company ontology to the vendor ontology which is a result from the annotation effort indicated in Figure 9. The result for the corresponding mapping of the insurer's ontology in depicted in Figure 11.

6 Web Services Planning

In this step, the web service end consumer selects the web service operations, he wants to use to accomplish certain tasks at hand. By making such a selection, he restricts the sets of relevant mapping rules. The inputs and outputs of web services are specified in the web service description documents of the web services. By considering the mapping rules and the information about the input and output types of web services, the planning component is able to infer valid web service flows.

If the output of a web service operation A is of type t and the input of another web service operation B is also of type t, then the service operations A and B can be plugged together (first A then B). Since, different web service providers will have different ontologies in general, this approach can only infer

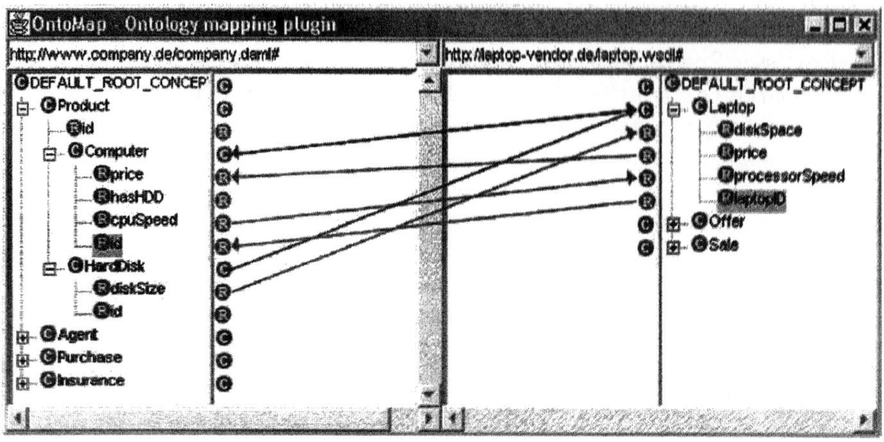

Fig. 10. Mapping between Client Ontology (left window) and Vendor Ontology (right window)

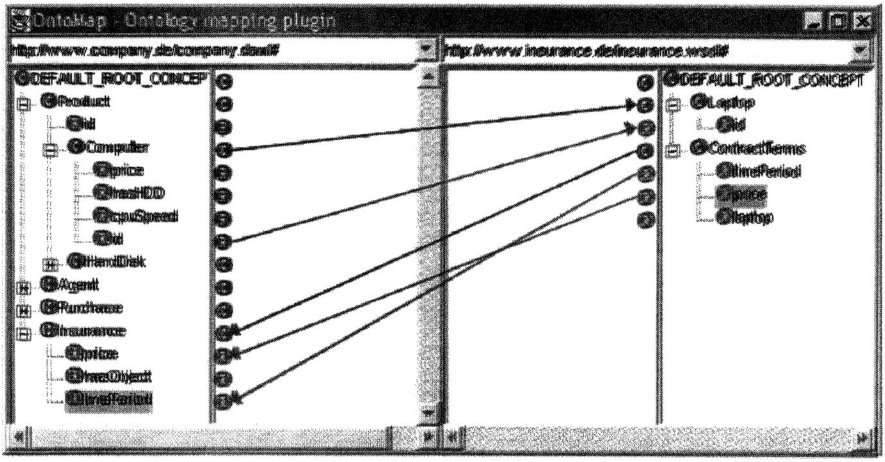

Fig. 11. Mapping between Client Ontology (left window) and Insurer's Ontology (right window)

web service flows in which all the web services are provided by one web service provider. However, web service flows consisting of web service operations from different providers can be inferred by using the restrictions contained in sets of mapping rules. For example, if the output of a service A is of type t_1 and the input of another web service B is of type t_2 and there is a mapping rule from t_1 to t_2, the services A and B can be plugged together (first A then B). In our running example, the service `getInsuranceTerms` can be called only after `getLaptopOffer`, since the former requires a `laptop`, which is the output of `getOffer`.

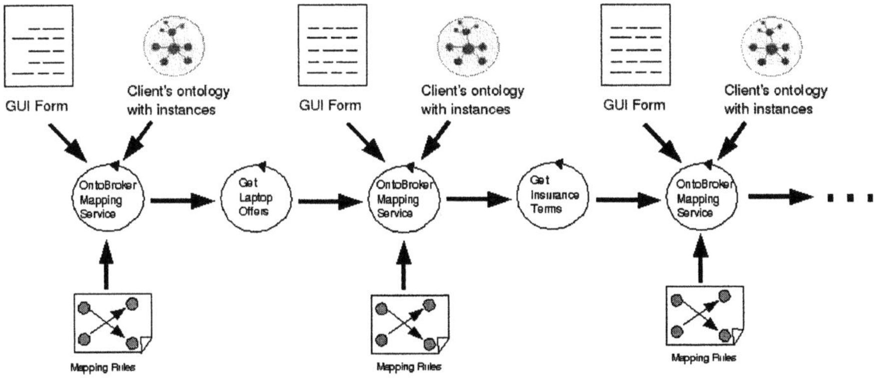

Fig. 12. Service Flow in our Running Example

7 Web Services Invocation

Finally, the user is presented with a list of feasible flows consisting only of web services selected by him in the previous step. The user chooses a flow from the list and invokes it.

The actual invocation is performed by a generic web services client engine. This engine takes a flow of web services as input. When the user requests the invocation of such a flow, the engine calls the web services in the order as specified in the flow. The invocation engine can be configured in a way such that data required from the client is retrieved automatically from client's ontology (with instances) during the invocation. The execution component communicates with OntoBroker [4], whenever mapping between concepts is required (cf. Figure 12).

The invocation component differentiates between the following cases (cf. Figure 12):

- **There are no mapping rules:** In this case, the user is provided with a form like interface, in which he has to enter required data according to the ontology of the respective web service provider to proceed the execution.
- **Automatic retrieval of data from client's ontology is not configured and mapping rules are defined:** In this case, the user is provided with a form like user interface, in which he has to enter required data according to his own (client's) ontology.
- **Automatic retrieval of data from client's ontology is configured and mapping rules are defined:** In this case, the invocation runs fully automatically.

This kind of approach is a generalization of common approaches to invocation of single web service operations. Let us consider this simple case in our framework: If a user wants to manually call only one web service operation, he will skip the definition of mapping rules. The flow will consist of only one web service operation. When executing the single web service operation, the invocation engine will request data from the user via a form interface that reflects the ontology of the service provider (because no mapping rule exists).

8 Related Work

In this paper we provide an original framework, OntoMat-Service, to embed the process of web service discovery (here: by browsing web pages and retrieving web pages from search engines like Google), composition (here: by deep annotation and reasoning over logically possible configurations), and invocation (here: by OntoMat-Service-Surfer, and the mapping to a client ontology). The consideration of semantic heterogenity is germane to OntoMat-Service. It offers semantic translations as one of its core modules.

OntoMat-Service does not aim at a web service discovery, composition and invocation that is intelligent in the sense that it completely automates the task that typically the user is supposed to do. Rather, it provides an interface, OntoMat-Service-Surfer, that supports the intelligence of the user and guides him to add semantic information such that only few logically valid paths remain to be chosen from by the user.

To fully pursue such an objective, one needs a large set of different modules. We have built on our existing experience and tool framework for semantic annotation (cf. [6,7]) and for logical reasoning [4]. We have not yet dealt with the issue of web service flow execution and monitoring that is certainly needed to complement our current version of OntoMat-Service.

Closest to our approach come frameworks that facilitate the building of web service flows. A number of software systems are available to facilitate manual composition of programs, and more recently web services. Such programs, which include a diversity of workflow tools [18,5], and more recently service composition aids such as BizTalk Orchestration [10] enable a software engineer to manually specify a composition of programs to perform some task — though they typically neglect the aspect of semantic heterogenity that is core to OntoMat-Service.[4]

Web Services Invocation Framework (WSIF) [16] is an open source framework to execute any web service, that can be described by a WSDL document. However, it does not support the execution of a flow of web services.

Some technologies have been proposed that use some form of semantic markup of web services in order to automatically compose web services to perform some desired task (e.g., [13,3,12]). In [13], the authors use situation calculus for representing web service description and petri nets for describing the execution behavious of web services. In [3], the authors present an architecture of intelligent brokers that offer problem solving methods that can be configured and used by the users according to their needs. In [12] the authors propose an extended version of Golog for formalizing the provision of high-level generic procedures and customization of constraints. In [15], the authors propose a rule

[4] BizTalk even allows for XML-based (non-semantic) translations of data.

based expert system to automatically compose web services from existing web services.

On the one hand most recent experiences from such advanced projects like IBrow, however, have shown that these automatic composition techniques cannot yet been carried over to an open world setting. There one needs to tightly integrate the user of a web service — such as we do in OntoMat-Service. On the other hand OntoMat-Service can obviously be extended in the future to consider more types of automatic semantic matchmaking, service discovery [14,17] and configuration of web services into the web planning phase.

9 Discussion

In this paper we have described OntoMat-Service, an original framework to tie together the World Wide Web and web services into a Service Web. Germane to OntoMat-Service is its blending of browsing the Web, aggregating conceptual descriptions and web services and then investigating and invoking them from one platform.

We have also presented OntoMat-Service-Surfer, a tool that constitutes a prototype implementation of OntoMat-Service. Currently, our prototype understands WSDL with RDF(S) for web service descriptions, but its flexible architecture allows easy integration of more powerful web service description languages like DAML-S [2].

Clearly, one must be aware of what OntoMat-Service and OntoMat-Service-Surfer can do and what they can't do. OntoMat-Service is not intended to cater to businesses that want to establish durable, complex and high-quality web service connections with intricate interactions. For this objective, the integration by semantic annotation may provide a quick, first prototype, but semantic annotation cannot provide arbitrary complex mapping rules or arbitrary complex workflows. On the other hand, OntoMat-Service allows exactly for easily building a prototype web service integration and it allows for users with domain knowledge to participate in the Service Web — without programming.

OntoMat-Service opens up many interesting questions that need to be solved in the future, such as

- how to automate the way that Web Services are presented to the World;
- how to make compiled flows understandable to their users; or
- how to characterize the boundaries of what functionality can be aggregated and executed.

Eventually, OntoMat-Service and OntoMat-Service-Surfer, in conjunction with their counterparts in semantic annotation [6] and deep annotation [6], open up the possibility to bring Web pages, databases and Web Services into one coherent framework and thus progress the Semantic Web to a large Web of data and services.

Acknowledgements. A part of this work was funded by the SemIPort project of the federal ministry of education and research (BMBF).

References

1. Web service description language (wsdl) version 1.2, March 2003.
2. Anupriya Ankolekar, Mark Burstein, Jerry R. Hobbs, Ora Lassila, Drew McDermott, David Martin, Sheila A. McIlraith, Srini Narayanan, Massimo Paolucci, and et al. Terry Payne. Daml-s: Web service description for the semantic web. In *1st Int'l Semantic Web Conf. (ISWC 02)*, 2002.
3. V. Richard Benjamins, Enric Plaza, Enrico Motta, Dieter Fensel, Rudi Studer, Bob Wielinga, Guus Schreiber, and Zdenek Zdrahal. Ibrow3 – an intelligent brokering service for knowledge-component reuse on the world wide web. In *Proc.11th Banff Knowledge Acquisition for Knowledge-Based System Workshop (KAW98)*, 1998.
4. S. Decker, M. Erdmann, D. Fensel, and R. Studer. Ontobroker: Ontology based access to distributed and semi-structured information. In *DS-8 – Proceedings of the Conference on Database Semantics*, pages 351–369, 1999.
5. C.A. Ellis and G.J. Nutt. Modelling and enactment of workflow systems. *Application and Theory of Petri Nets*, LNCS 691:Modelling and enactment of workflow systems, 1993.
6. S. Handschuh and S. Staab. Authoring and annotation of web pages in cream. In *Proceedings of the 11th International World Wide Web Conference, WWW 2002, Honolulu, Hawaii, May 7–11, 2002*, pages 462–473. ACM Press, 2002.
7. S. Handschuh, S. Staab, and R. Volz. On deep annotation. In *Proceedings of the 12th International World Wide Web Conference, WWW 2003, Budapest, Hungary, May 20–24, 2003 (to appear)*. ACM Press, 2003.
8. Michael Kiefer, Georg Lausen, and James wu. Logical foundations of object oriented and frame-based languages. *Journal of the ACM*, 1995.
9. O. Lassila and R. Swick. Resource description framework (RDF) model and syntax specification. Technical report, W3C, 1999. W3C Recommendation. http://www.w3.org/TR/REC-rdf-syntax.
10. D. et al. Lowe. *BizTalk(TM) Server: The Complete Reference.*, November 2001.
11. Alexander Maedche and Steffen Staab. Services on the move – Towards p2p-enabled semantic web services. In *Proceedings of the 10th International Conference on Information Technology and Travel & Tourism, ENTER 2003, Helsinki, Finland, 29th–31st January 2003*. Springer, 2003.
12. S. McIlraith and T. Son. Adapting golog for composition of semantic web services. In *Proc 8th International Conference on Principles of Knowledge Representation and Reasoning*, 2002.
13. Srini Narayanan and Sheila McIlraith. Simulation, verification and automated composition of web services. In *WWW2002*, May 2002.
14. M. Paolucci, T. Kawmura, T. Payne, and K. Sycara. Semantic matching of web services capabilities. In *First Int. Semantic Web Conf.*, 2002.
15. Shankar R. Ponnekanti and Armando Fox. Sword: A developer toolkit for building composite web services. In *Proceedings of the 11th International World Wide Web Conference, WWW 2002, Honolulu, Hawaii, May 7–11, 2002*. ACM Press, 2002.
16. Apache Web Services Project. Web services invocation framework.
17. Katia P. Sycara, Matthias Klusch, Seth Widoff, and Jianguo Lu. Dynamic service matchmaking among agents in open information environments. *SIGMOD Record*, 28(1):47–53, 1999.
18. van der Aalst and W..M..P. Woflan. A petri-net-based workflow analyzer, systems analysis – modelling – simulation. 35(3):345–357, 1999.

Adapting BPEL4WS for the Semantic Web: The Bottom-Up Approach to Web Service Interoperation

Daniel J. Mandell and Sheila A. McIlraith

Dept. Computer Science, Knowledge Systems Laboratory, Stanford University
Stanford, CA, 94305-9020, USA
{dmandell,sam}@ksl.stanford.edu

Abstract. Towards the ultimate goal of seamless interaction among networked programs and devices, industry has developed orchestration and process modeling languages such as XLANG, WSFL, and recently BPEL4WS. Unfortunately, these efforts leave us a long way from seamless interoperation. Researchers in the Semantic Web community have taken up this challenge proposing top-down approaches to achieve aspects of Web Service interoperation. Unfortunately, many of these efforts have been disconnected from emerging industry standards, particularly in process modeling. In this paper we take a bottom-up approach to integrating Semantic Web technology into Web services. Building on BPEL4WS, we present integrated Semantic Web technology for automating customized, dynamic binding of Web services together with interoperation through semantic translation. We discuss the value of semantically enriched service interoperation and demonstrate how our framework accounts for user-defined constraints while gaining potentially successful execution pathways in a practically motivated example. Finally, we provide an analysis of the forward-looking limitations of frameworks like BPEL4WS, and suggest how such specifications might embrace semantic technology at a fundamental level to work towards fully automated Web service interoperation.

1 Introduction

For many, the long-term goal of the Web services effort is seamless interoperation among networked programs and devices. Once achieved, many see Web services as providing the infrastructure for universal plug-and-play and ubiquitous computing [30]. To integrate complex, stateful interactions among services, most of the major industry players have proposed some form of business process integration, orchestration, or choreography model. These include WSCI, BPML, XLANG, WSFL, WSCL, BPSS, the Web Services Architecture, and most recently BPEL4WS from IBM, Microsoft, BEA, SAP, and Siebel [7]. Unfortunately, as we discuss in this paper, these standards and their associated computing machinery still place us a long way from seamless interoperability.

In parallel with these industry efforts, the Semantic Web [4] community has been developing languages and computing machinery for making Web content unambiguously interpretable by computer programs, with a view to automation of a diversity of Web tasks. Efforts include the development of expressive languages

D. Fensel et al. (Eds.): ISWC 2003, LNCS 2870, pp. 227–241, 2003.

based on artificial intelligence technology, including RDF [17], RDF(S), DAML+OIL [12,29], and most recently a proposal for the Ontology Web Language (OWL) [10,21,26]. In the area of Web Services, the Semantic Web community has argued that true interoperation requires description of Web Services in an expressive language with a well-defined semantics. To this end, they have developed OWL-S (previously DAML-S), an OWL (previously DAML+OIL) ontology for Web services [8]. Similarly, researchers have developed automated reasoning machinery to address some of the more difficult tasks necessary for seamless interoperation including a richer form of automated Web service discovery [25], semantic translation [20], and the ultimate challenge, automated Web Service composition [24,22,14]. Unfortunately, most of these efforts have been top-down approaches building on artificial intelligence and automated reasoning technology, sometimes grounding them in WSDL [6], but often times avoiding connection with evolving industry standards.

In this paper we take a bottom-up approach to incorporating Semantic Web technology into Web services. We argue that to achieve the long-term goal of seamless interoperability, Web services must embrace many of the representation and reasoning ideas proposed by the Semantic Web community and in particular by the Semantic Web services community. Nevertheless, we acknowledge that Web standards defined by industry efforts will shape the evolution of Semantic Web services. From this viewpoint we take the leading candidate for business process modeling on the Web, BPEL4WS, and its associated computational machinery, BPWS4J, and augment them with Semantic Web technology. In Section 2, we provide a reference example that we use to illustrate our contributions. In Section 3 we introduce BPEL4WS, demonstrate its use on the example, and characterize its level of automation. In Section 4, we extend BPEL4WS with a Semantic Discovery Service and introduce semantic translations to advance the level of interoperability provided by BPEL4WS. We discuss the architecture of our software, demonstrate it with respect to our reference example, and analyze its merits and shortcomings. In Section 5, we outline directions for Web service interoperation frameworks to achieve tighter integration between infrastructure and Semantic Web technologies. We conclude by highlighting the distinct features brought to Web service interoperation through richly expressive Semantic Web languages and well-defined semantics, and suggesting how interoperation frameworks might incorporate semantic markup and reasoning to achieve seamless automation of Web services.

2 A Motivating Example

To realize the value added by automated interoperation it is helpful to have a real-world example in mind. Consider the task of taking out a loan on the Web. In the absence of automation, the user invests considerable resources visiting numerous sites, determining appropriate service providers, entering personal information and preferences repeatedly, integrating information, and waiting for responses. We would prefer that the user enters information once and receives the expected results from the most appropriate services with minimal additional assistance. One possible interaction model follows:

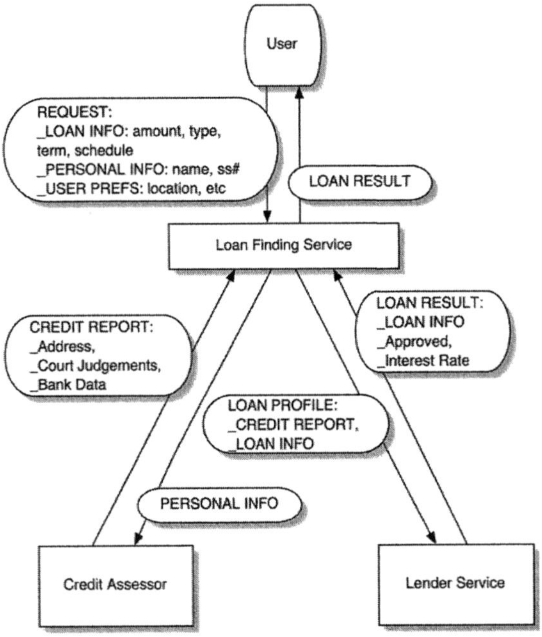

Fig. 1. An interaction model for the loan example domain.

In this scenario, the user sends a single request to a loan finding service containing personal information, the type of loan desired, and some provider preferences. The loan finder distributes its work among two partner services: a credit assessor, which consumes the user's personal information and provides a credit history report, and a lender service, which consumes a credit report and a loan request and returns a rejection or a loan offer and its terms. The loan finder first invokes a credit assessor to generate a credit report for the user, which it then passes to the lender service along with the user's personal information. The lender service generates a result, which the loan finder reports to the user. It is no longer required that the user enter information multiple times, determine which services are appropriate, or standby to bridge output from one service to another as input. These responsibilities have been offloaded to the loan finding service and its *service provider*—the party responsible for the form and function of the loan finding service.

This interaction model is appealing for the user, but switching perspectives to that of the service provider, it remains to show how service partners are selected, ordered, invoked, and integrated.

3 Automated Web Service Execution

A number of specifications and software packages are available to automate the execution of hand-written Web service compositions. Among them are BPEL4WS [7], WSCI [2], and BPML [1]. In this section we will focus on the most recently leading player, BPEL4WS (*Business Process Execution Language for Web Services*).

3.1 BPEL4WS and BPWS4J

The BPEL4WS specification co-authored by IBM, Microsoft, BEA, SAP, and Siebel Systems merges ideas from Microsoft's XLANG [28] and IBM's WSFL [18]. It provides a notation for describing interactions of Web services as *business processes*, following in the tradition of *workflow* modeling [31,13]. Workflow in BPEL4WS is directed by traditional control structures such as *if, then, else,* and *while-loop*. Services are integrated by treating them as *partners* that fill *roles* in a BPEL4WS *process model.* The communication-level parameters of the partner services are described in accompanying WSDL documents. The process model describes a program that orchestrates the interaction of the service partners. The key components of the process model are: *partners*, which associate a Web service defined in an accompanying WSDL document with a particular role; *variables*, which contain the messages passed between partners and correspond to messages in accompanying WSDL documents; *fault handlers*, which deal with known and unexpected exceptions in the spirit of the *try-catch* programming construct; and *flow*, which lists the *activities* defining the control flow of the process.

The BPWS4J engine [15], released by IBM alongside of BPEL4WS, implements a subset of the features defined in the BPEL4WS specification. The BPWS4J engine consumes a BPEL4WS document and WSDL documents defining the bindings for the BPEL4WS process and its partners. It then establishes a single endpoint for accessing the BPEL4WS process as a Web service.

3.2 BPEL4WS and the Loan Example

In order to model the workflow in Figure 1, a service provider writes each of the above elements into a BPEL4WS document. For our current purposes it is worth examining the `<partners>` element.

In a BPEL4WS document modeling the interaction in Figure 1, the loan finding service interacts with three `<partners>` corresponding to the user, the credit assessor service, and the lender service. Note that the loan finding service in Figure 1 is not a partner because it corresponds to the BPEL4WS process itself. The element might be written as follows:

```
<partners>
  <partner name="user"
     serviceLinkType="lns:loanCustomerLinkType"
                partnerRole="user"/>
  <partner name="assessor"
     serviceLinkType="lns:USCreditAssessorLinkType"
                partnerRole="assessor"/>
  <partner name="lender"
     serviceLinkType="lns:loanLenderLinkType"
                partnerRole="lender"/>
</partners>
```

The `serviceLinkType` attribute selects a communication-level agreement between partners. The `partnerRole` attribute identifies which role the partner plays and which the loan finding service plays. Each role is bound elsewhere in the BPEL4WS element space to a WSDL portType.

3.3 Critical Analysis of BPEL4WS Automation

BPWS4J enables automated Web service execution, and BPEL4WS opens the way for automated service discovery by leaving service partners unbound at design time. Both the engine and the specification, however, have shortcomings that limit their ability to provide a foundation for seamless interoperability.

3.3.1 Limitations in BPWS4J

Although a mechanism for dynamic partner assignment is outlined in the BPEL4WS specification, the version of BPWS4J available at the time of writing omits the service reference assignment feature, so a dynamically discovered service could not be bound to a partner role within BPWS4J. BPWS4J, then, enables automated Web service execution, but not automated Web service discovery.

Without automated discovery, the service provider is responsible for choosing service partners *a priori* and preconcerting them into an effective unit. Because partner services are chosen prior to receiving the user's request, the system cannot customize partner selection for the user's specific needs or preferences. It is possible that the service selects suboptimal service partners, either because the service provider lacks a comprehensive list of potential partners at design time, or because of the difficulty in finding partners whose solution generalizes for all users. In the case of the loan example, it is possible that the user prefers to use an in-state lender because in-state loans offer tax incentives from the user's state government. If the service provider defines the lending partner prior to the user's request, the user's preference is ignored. Additionally, discovering and integrating the service partners manually places greater responsibility and maintenance demands on the service provider than in the automated case.

3.3.2 Limitations of BPEL4WS

More interesting than engine-specific limitations are those inherent in the form and content of the BPEL4WS specification. Descriptions of executable and abstract processes in BPEL4WS are not declarative; they are not encoded in a manner that facilitates symbolic manipulation. As such, they are not well suited to many of the automated reasoning tasks envisioned by Semantic Web services [23].

For example, the task of binding service partners to physical ports can, theoretically, occur at runtime in BPEL4WS. Nevertheless, the description of those service partners is done via WSDL portType definitions. Effective dynamic service binding cannot be performed by solely matching WSDL messaging interfaces. Service partners should be selected based on functional, nonfunctional and behavioral descriptions of what a service does, and how it does it. Further, we argue that such descriptions must be encoded in an ontology language (e.g., [26]).

Restricting service descriptions to the expressivity of strictly syntactic WSDL interfaces limits the integration of service partners that operate on messages that have different syntax but are semantically compatible. For example, perhaps the only appropriate credit assessor for an ex-UK resident provides `UKCreditReports` while the lending service consumes `USCreditReports`. Even if these messages differed only in their representation of dates, an interoperation system that cannot recognize the semantic compatibility of the credit reports could fail to realize a potentially successful integration. Likewise, service partners that are syntactically identical, but semantically incompatible, because different messages are described using the same name, will cause binding of functionally incompatible services.

At the heart of the problem is BPEL4WS's reliance on describing services using XML and XMLSchema. XML provides a rudimentary content language, but lacks the constructs to describe complex relationships between Web resources. While XMLSchema augments XML with a data model and enables datatyping, the semantics of XML is underspecified. Further, XMLSchema is not sufficiently expressive to create and relate rich datatypes. In contrast, RDF and RDF(S) provide a rudimentary ontology language. Not only do they provide a data model for XML, but they also enable the representation of classes, properties, domain and range, and sub-class plus super-class hierarchies. Still further expressive is OWL, and its predecessor, DAML+OIL, which also include a well-defined semantics and the ability to define complex relationships between properties of objects in an ontology. By describing services in DAML+OIL or OWL, not only do we get a more expressive language for describing service partners, but also tools for automatically reasoning about those services [16]. With the absence of automated reasoning in BPEL4WS, it is the BPEL4WS author's responsibility to manually construct a process model that follows the operational semantics of its service partners.

4 Automated Service Discovery, Customization, and Semantic Translation

In this section we present work that extends BPWS4J with customized, dynamic binding of service partners and semantic translation to address shortcomings presented in Section 3. To enable these features, we need to consider three issues:

1. How to formally represent descriptions of potential service partners
2. How to store, query and reason about such descriptions to discover appropriate partners
3. How to integrate discovered partners into the BPWS4J engine

Our approach adopts Semantic Web technologies to address the first issue, and these are described in Section 4.1. In Section 4.2, we present novel work in the form of a *Semantic Discovery Service,* which addresses the last two issues.

4.1 Supporting Technologies

We adopt several key Semantic Web technologies to enable the description of services in a computer interpretable format and the discovery of services with desired properties.

4.1.1 DAML-S

DAML-S[1] is an ontology for describing Web services based on DAML+OIL. As a DAML+OIL ontology, DAML-S has a well-defined semantics, making it computer-interpretable and unambiguous. It also enables the definition of Web services content vocabulary in terms of objects and complex relationships between them, including class, subclass, and cardinality restrictions.

The DAML-S upper ontology comprises three components:

1. *ServiceProfile* - Relates and builds upon the type of content in UDDI, describing the properties of a service necessary for automatic discovery, such as what the services offers, its inputs and outputs, and its preconditions and effects.
2. *ServiceModel* - Describes a service's process model (the control flow and data-flow involved in using the service). It is designed to enable automated composition and execution of services.
3. *ServiceGrounding* - Connects the process model description to communication-level protocols and message descriptions in WSDL.

In this section, we focus on the ServiceProfile as a declarative descriptor of Web service properties enabling automated, customized service discovery and semantic translation. We collect DAML-S service profiles into a repository and exploit their semantics to query for partners based on descriptions of the partners' desired properties.

4.1.2 DAML Query Language

We adopt the *DAML Query Language* (DQL) [11] as our formal language and protocol for querying repositories of DAML-S service profiles. DQL defines the construction of queries over a repository comprised of DAML+OIL sentences. In our case, the repository is a *knowledge base* (KB) of DAML-S service profiles. DQL queries are handled by a DQL server, which interfaces with an *automated reasoner* operating over the KB. The reasoner determines which profiles satisfy the query restrictions. The DQL server answers the query by returning matching profiles in a series of *answer bundles*.

4.1.3 Java Theorem Prover

We use the *Java Theorem Prover* (JTP) [16] as the DQL server's automated reasoner. JTP is a hybrid reasoning system based on first-order logic model elimination. JTP is a particularly compelling candidate for our work because of its special purpose DAML+OIL reasoner. Since the reasoner is based on the axiomatic semantics of DAML+OIL, performance can be augmented by efficient storage of DAML+OIL sentences as triples and pre-computation of common queries.

4.2 The Semantic Discovery Service

DAML-S provides us with means to formally represent the form and function of Web services, and DQL/JTP provide us with sufficiently powerful machinery to query such descriptions. With these technologies in hand, it remains to integrate semantic service description querying into BPWS4J. Since the current release of BPWS4J is not

[1] The DAML-S ontology has recently been translated to OWL, and renamed OWL-S [8].

immediately extensible, we construct a *Semantic Discovery Service* (SDS) to work within BPWS4J's perspective as an aggregator of Web services.

The SDS sits between a BPWS4J process and its potential service partners. Instead of routing requests to previously selected partners, BPWS4J directs them to the SDS through a locally bound Web service interface. In order for the SDS to dynamically discover customized service partners, SDS messages contain (1) the parameters to be sent to a discovered service partner, and (2) the required service partner attributes, including functional and user constraints, expressed in DAML-S sentences. The SDS then locates appropriate service partners and serves as a dynamic proxy between the BPWS4J engine and the discovered partners. With this interface come two important properties of interactions with the SDS:

1. The SDS is agnostic as to the content of the service descriptions and invocation messages it receives.
2. The SDS is stateless, with no knowledge of prior interactions, and no service-specific properties.

These properties grant the SDS portability between any BPWS4J actions and processes.

Further information about the SDS and demonstration code is available online at (http://ksl.stanford.edu/sds).

4.3 Automated Service Customization

Automated service customization refers to the automatic selection of partners to meet preferences and constraints specific to each user. A user's request might contain preferences for a service's physical location, side effects, quality of service and security guarantees, and many other properties.

In our approach to automated service customization, user constraints are encoded as DAML-S sentences in requests to BPWS4J. Because the BPEL4WS author expects each service partner to exhibit particular functional behavior, the BPEL4WS process may also add constraints on the functional classes of service partners. These constraints are applied to the `functionalClass` property of service profiles in the KB. `functionalClass` properties, in turn, point to an ontology of service functions contained in the KB. In the absence of a computer interpretable operational semantics, referencing ontological representations of functional classes facilitates manual service composition by allowing the service partner and BPEL4WS to agree upon expected behavior.

Once the SDS receives a request for a partner service invocation, the SDS wraps the request's DAML-S restrictions inside a DQL query and sends them to the DQL server. The DQL server invokes the JTP DAML+OIL reasoner to compute the set of DAML-S service profiles meeting the query criteria. Matching DAML-S profiles are returned to the SDS as answer bundles. The SDS selects a partner from the answer bundles and invokes the partner's endpoint with the message parameters supplied by BPWS4J. The partner does its work and responds to the SDS, which in turn forwards the response to BPWS4J. BPWS4J recovers flow control, and continues executing the process model, invoking the SDS whenever a customized Web service invocation is needed (see Figure 2).

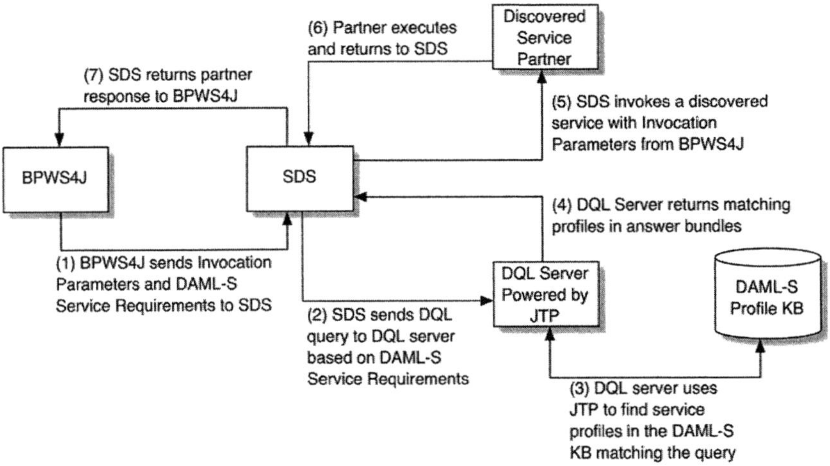

Fig. 2. Interaction flow between BPWS4J, SDS, DQL server, & discovered service partners.

4.4 Automated Semantic Translation

A key feature of semantically enriched data structures is their translatability within the context of automated reasoning. In goal-directed reasoning, an automated reasoner can exploit the semantic equality of syntactically distinct classes of objects to increasethe number of potentially successful execution pathways. Within the context of Web services, *semantic translation* refers to redefining well-defined data types in terms of their relationships to one another via implicit or explicit translational axioms. Semantic translation increases Web service interoperability by facilitating automatic translation of the inputs and outputs of service partners so they may interact seamlessly.

The SDS provides automated semantic translation for Web service discovery. Our approach uses a recursive *back-chaining* algorithm to determine a sequence of service invocations, or *service chain*, which takes the input supplied by BPWS4J and produces the output desired by BPWS4J. Our translational axioms are encoded as translation programs exposed as Web services. The algorithm invokes the DQL server to discover services that produce the desired outputs. If the SDS does not have a required input, the algorithm searches for a translator service that outputs the required input and adds it to the service chain. The process is recursive and terminates when it constructs a successful service chain, or the profiles in the KB (or some bounded subset) are exhausted.

The following pseudocode representation of the algorithm returns a service chain, if one exists in the KB, producing the desired output while consuming only the available inputs:

```
Initialization:
weHave = {inputs provided by BPWS4J process};
weWant = {output desired by BPWS4J process};
Step:
findServiceChain (weHave, weWant) {
```

```
  svcs = getServicesOutputtingWeWant(weWant);
  foreach service in svcs {
    chain = new chain;
    foreach input in service.inputs {
      if input not in weHave {
      newSvcs = findServiceChain(weHave, service.inputs);
      chain.add(newSvcs);
      }
    }
    if all service.inputs in weHave {
      chain.add(service);
      return chain;
    }
  }
  return null; // no chain found
}
```

Note that this algorithm fits our purposes for a small DAML-S KB, but the worst-case execution time grows exponentially in the number of inputs we allow. To improve performance we could utilize a heuristic that eliminates low scoring services from the `svcs` list based on a scoring function, e.g., the minimal distance between inputs we desire and the service's outputs in a taxonomy tree, as described in [25]. Additionally, we could favor service partners requiring fewer inputs.

Also note that we only account for inputs and outputs in translation because the translator services are of the same functional class. The translation services we describe are merely implementations of translational axioms and have no preconditions or side effects.

4.5 SDS and the Loan Example

We now consider the SDS in the context of the loan finding example from Sections 2 and 3. Assume that the user has recently moved to California, USA from the United Kingdom, so that the only potential credit-reporting agency is based in the UK. This credit assessor produces credit reports of class `UKCreditReport`. BPWS4J must then invoke a service that inputs a `UKCreditReport` and outputs a `LoanResult`. The behavior of the service is enforced by BPWS4J requiring that the partner be of functional class `creditAssesor`, which is defined in an ontology as described in Section 4.3. Assume further that the user must get a loan from a US lender and, moreover, wishes to borrow from a California-based lender (to take advantage of in-state tax incentives). The SDS may locate a CA-based lender of the required functional class using automated customization, but if the only such available lender requires a `USCreditReport` as an input the SDS would fail to discover an appropriate lender. The BPWS4J process would report that the request could not be completed.

With semantic translation, the user's request becomes satisfiable. We introduce into the DAML-S KB the profile for a `DateTranslator` service of functional class `semanticTranslator` that translates between `USCreditReport` and `UKCreditReport` classes. Assume that this service implements a semantic translation axiom that, for simplicity, properly declares that the credit reports are identical except that the US version represents dates as `MM/DD/YYYY`, while the UK version uses `DD/MM/YYYY`. Since the `DateTranslator` service requires a `UKCreditReport` as an input, and the SDS has one available, the algorithm adds the `DateTranslator` to the chain. The service chain (`assessor→DateTranslator→lender`) now consumes a `UKCreditReport` and produces a `LoanResult` as desired by the BPWS4J process. The SDS executes the service chain and returns the `LoanResult` to BPWS4J.

4.6 Characterization of SDS Automation

We now characterize the level of automation provided by BPWS4J extended with a Semantic Discovery Service within the broader context of Web service interoperation. As in Section 3, the BPWS4J engine provides automated Web service execution given a BPEL4WS process model. In this section, we introduce the Semantic Discovery Service, which extends BPWS4J with customized, dynamic service binding and semantic translation. These capabilities enlarge the space of potentially successful executions, and allow the framework to account for user-defined constraints in partner selection.

The SDS does not, however, enable *automated Web service composition*. This notion is regarded in the Semantic Web community as the determination of an execution plan to accomplish an objective given a current state, and adapting that plan as state changes without human intervention. Despite the fact that our implementation does discover and execute a sequence of services to produce a desired output from provided inputs, the fundamental workflow defined in the BPEL4WS document is intentionally unchanged, as we discuss below.

The reasoning performed by the SDS is purely communicative and ignores services' preconditions and effects, aside from those accounted for implicitly by their functional classes. To reason about preconditions and effects is to reason about what a service does. In the case of BPWS4J, the service provider performs this reasoning manually by defining a BPEL4WS process that utilizes a predefined number of service partners with expected operational semantics and an execution ordering. As such, the service provider imposes a particular decomposition of the process, making it inappropriate for the SDS to perform automated service composition for two reasons. First, recomposing a process without knowing the intended side effects of the original composition (i.e., those intended by the service provider) runs the risk of composing services with unintended side effects. Second, even if the SDS did have a formal description of the expected effects of the service partners – for example, an operational semantics defined by a DAML-S *ServiceModel* – recomposing the process into a new workflow reproduces the work of BPWS4J and the service provider, so the SDS would be replacing the very system it is supposed to complement. Enabling automated Web service composition within BPWS4J and similarly featured frameworks requires fundamentally redefining their roles and capabilities towards reasoning about abstract objectives and services described in languages with well-defined semantics. To so do, frameworks will need to shift from an *interface-oriented* perspective on Web services to one that is *functionally-oriented*.

5 Future Directions for Web Service Interoperation Systems

In this Section we briefly outline some directions for Web service interoperation frameworks to facilitate fuller integration between infrastructure and Semantic Web technologies. We consider automating service discovery and then service composition in turn, grounded in our critique and extension of BPEL4WS.

5.1 Adapting BPEL4WS for Automated Service Discovery, Customization, and Semantic Integration

As discussed in Section 3.3.2, the central shortcoming in BPEL4WS giving rise to the need for the Semantic Discovery Service is its reliance on XML and XMLSchema for describing Web service partners (for now we set aside shortcomings in the current implementation of the BPWS4J engine). BPEL4WS could subsume the capabilities provided by the SDS by relaxing its dependence on XML in favor of higher-level descriptions in a language like DAML-S. DAML-S service profiles can be used to query for service partners, as in the SDS, and the DAML-S service grounding can be used to connect the high-level description to communication level protocols like WSDL (see [8] for details), saving the final binding to portTypes until runtime. BPEL4WS engines could easily query repositories for services using their built-in communication-level functionality.

5.2 Adapting BPEL4WS for Automated Service Composition

Automating service composition with frameworks like BPEL4WS requires a more substantial evolution, shifting its perspective as an execution framework for predefined process models to that of an automated reasoner over abstract goals. Execution plans devised to attain such goals must be adjustable as execution state changes.

Several working systems developed by researchers in the Semantic Web community perform this function [22,24,20]. These frameworks share two key components necessary to automate Web service composition. The first is a declarative representation of the capabilities of each Web service in a semantically well-defined language that is computer interpretable, as employed by the SDS or the modified version of BPEL4WS suggested in Section 5.1. Further, this information must abstractly describe the service's function as well as its form. While BPEL4WS's predecessors, XLANG and WSFL, had a well-defined semantics for describing the execution of a workflow, to date BPEL4WS has not been shown to maintain this property. Adopting the DAML-S *ServiceModel* would shift the perspective of the interoperation framework towards being functionally-oriented on service partners. Partners could then be chosen based on functional and operational constraints in addition to their communication-level properties. In the case of the loan finding example, the *ServiceModel* would formally declare how the service functions, the potential side effects, and the necessary preconditions so that automated reasoning machinery could appropriately manipulate it to determine a composition. The runtime execution of the model would be determined by an automated reasoner within the

BPEL4WS engine, allowing far greater flexibility in successfully completing the user's request. In a loan finding scenario, for example, there are clearly many more ways to get a loan than the "assessor-lender" model. The composition system could propose, for example, an advance on the user's credit card, government subsidized assistance, or other solutions that meet the user's objective but may be more financially desirable or practical.

As implied above, the second necessary component to automated Web service composition is appropriate computational machinery to manipulate service descriptions to produce a composition. All of the composition work from the Semantic Web mentioned above employs such machinery operating on some model with a formal executional semantics. For example, Karmasim [24] uses reachability analysis over Petri nets. McIlraith and Son's work [22] uses Prolog and a subset of first-order logic. McDermott's work [20] likewise uses a logic-based automated reasoning system. All of these approaches, while powerful, reveal the need for further research, particularly in integration with industrial efforts. Importantly, however, this work highlights the spectrum of approaches interoperation frameworks could employ to increase their power and flexibility.

6 Conclusion

Seamless interoperability among networked programs and devices is critical for Web services to provide an infrastructure for the vision of ubiquitous computing. We argued here that industry has taken us a step in this direction with computing machinery for automated service execution, while the Semantic Web community has developed powerful representation and reasoning technology but has remained largely disconnected from the industrial effort. In acknowledgement of the fact that Web service technology will continue to evolve from emerging industry standards, we developed software from the bottom-up that extends industrial machinery with Semantic Web technology to enable automated service discovery, customization, and semantic translation. By integrating our technology, the industrial system gained the following capabilities:

1. Automatic, runtime binding of service partners
2. Selection between multiple service partners based on user-defined preferences and constraints
3. Integration of service partners with syntactically distinct but semantically translatable service descriptions

We further argued that these capabilities approach the limit of automated service interoperation with current industrial machinery. Extending manual composition frameworks with automated composition machinery supplants provider-defined workflows with potentially undesirable recompositions. Achieving automated Web service composition requires a fundamental shift in industrial frameworks from executing predefined process models to computing and adapting execution plans from abstract objectives. In particular, in order for industry to achieve this shift, it is critical that:

1. Web service providers publish unambiguous, computer-interpretable declarations of Web service form and function, at a level of detail commensurate with the task, and in a language with a well-defined semantics

2. Web service interoperation frameworks embed automated reasoning technology into their systems and specifications that is capable of reasoning about semantic descriptions of Web services.

With the Semantic Web grounded in firm industrial support, we can begin to attain the manifold benefits of fully integrated, Web-wide distributed computation.

Acknowledgements. We would like to acknowledge Jessica Jenkins for her help in writing DAML-S queries and profiles and Rob McCool for his help in integrating DQL with JTP. We also thank Francisco Curbera and Bill Nagy for helpful conversations about BPWS4J, and Srini Narayanan for his useful thoughts throughout this work. We gratefully acknowledge the financial support of the US Defense Advanced Research Projects Agency DARPA Agent Markup Language (DAML) research grant #F30602-00-2-0579-P00001 and CALO research grant #NBCHD030010. Finally, we also gratefully acknowledge financial support from the Stanford Networking Research Center.

References

1. Arkin, A. Business Process Modeling Language. http://www.bpmi.org/bpml.esp
2. Arkin, A., Askary, S., Fordin, S., Jekeli,, W., Kawaguchi, K., Orchard, D., Pogliani, S., Riemer, K., Struble, S., Takacsi-Nagy, P., Trickovic, I., Zimek, S. Web Service Choreography Interface. http://wwws.sun.com/software/xml/developers/wsci/
3. Bellwood, T., Clément, L., Ehnebuske, D., Hately, A., Hondo, M., Husband, Y., Januszewski, K., Lee, S., McKee, B., Munter, J., von Riegen, C. UDDI Version 3.0, 2002. http://www.uddi.org/pubs/uddi-v3.00-published-20020719.htm
4. Berners-Lee, T., Hendler, J., Lassila, O. The Semantic Web, Scientific American, May, 2001.
5. Box, D., Ehnebuske, D., Kakivaya, G., Layman, A., Mendelsohn, N., Nielsen, H., Thatte, S., Winer, D. Simple Object Assess Protocol (SOAP) 1.1. W3C Technical report, 2000. http://www.w3.org/TR/SOAP/
6. Christensen, E., Curbera, F., Meredith, G., and Weerawarana, S. Web Services Definition Language. Technical report, W3C, 2001. http://www.w3c.org/TR/wsdl
7. Curbera, F., Goland, Y., Klein, J., Leymann, F., Roller, D., Thatte, S., Weerawarana, S. Business Process Execution Language for Web Services. http://www.ibm.com/developerworks/library/ws-bpel/
8. DAML Services Coalition. DAML-S and OWL-S . http://www.daml.org/services/
9. DAML Services Coalition (alphabetically A. Ankolekar, M. Burstein, J. Hobbs, O. Lassila, D. Martin, D. McDermott, S. McIlraith, S. Narayanan, M. Paolucci, T. Payne, K. Sycara). DAML-S: Web Service Description for the Semantic Web. Proceedings of the International Semantic Web Conference (ISWC), pp. 348–363, July, 2002.
10. Dean, M., Connolly, D., van Harmelen, F., Hendler, J., Horrocks, I., McGuinness, D., Patel-Schneider, P., and Stein, L. OWL Web Ontology Language 1.0 Reference. http://www.w3.org/TR/2002/WD-owl-ref-20020729/
11. Fikes, R., Hayes, P., Horrocks, I. DAML Query Language, Abstract Specification, 2002. http://www.daml.org/2002/08/dql/dql
12. Fikes, R. and McGuinness, D. An Axiomatic Semantics for RDF, RDF-S, and DAML+OIL, Manuscript. March, 2001. http://www.daml.org/2001/03/axiomatic-semantics.html

13. Georgakopoulos, D., Hornick, M., Sheth, A. An Overview of Workflow Management: From Process Modeling to Workflow Automation Infrastructure. Distributed and Parallel Databases, 3(2):119–153, 1995.
14. Hendler, J. and McGuinness, D. The DARPA Agent Markup Language. IEEE Intelligent Systems, Tends and Controversies, pp. 6–7, November/December 2000.
15. IBM. BPWS4J. http://www.alphaWorks.ibm.com/tech/bpws4j
16. Frank, G. "A General Interface for Interaction of Special-Purpose Reasoners within a Modular Reasoning System", Proceedings of the 1999 AAAI Fall Symposium on Question Answering Systems, pp. 57–62, 1999.
17. Lassila, O., Swick, R. Resource Description Framework (RDF) Model and Syntax Specification.W3C Recommendation, 22 February, 1999. http://www.w3.org/TR/REC-rdf-syntax.
18. Leymann, F. Web Services Flow Language. http://www-3.ibm.com/software/solutions/webservices/pdf/WSFL.pdf
19. McDermott, Drew. "Estimated-Regression Planning for Interactions with Web Services", Proceedings of the AI Planning Systems Conference (AIPS'02), June, 2002.
20. McDermott, D., Burstein, M., and Smith, D. Overcoming ontology mismatches in transactions with self-describing agents. In Proc. Semantic Web Working Symposium, pp. 285–302, 2001.
21. McGuinness, D. and van Harmelen, F. Feature Synopsis for OWL Lite and OWL. http://www.w3.org/TR/2002/WD-owl-features-20020729/
22. McIlraith, S. and Son, T. Adapting Golog for Composition of Semantic Web Services. Proceedings of the Eighth International Conference on Knowledge Representation and Reasoning (KR2002), pp. 482–493, April, 2002.
23. McIlraith, S., Son, T.C. and Zeng, H. Semantic Web Services. IEEE Intelligent Systems. Special Issue on the Semantic Web. 16(2):46–53, March/April, 2001. Copyright IEEE, 2001.
24. 24. Narayanan, S. and McIlraith, S. Simulation, Verification and Automated Composition of Web Services. Proceedings of the Eleventh International World Wide Web Conference (WWW-11), May, 2002.
25. Paolucci, M., Kawamura, T., Payne, T., Sycara, K. Semantic Matching of Web Services Capabilities. Proceedings of the 1st International Semantic Web Conference (ISWC), pp. 333–347, 2002.
26. Patel-Schneider, P., Horrocks I., and van Harmelan, F. OWL Web Ontology Language 1.0 Abstract Syntax. http://www.w3.org/TR/2002/WD-owl-absyn-20020729/
27. Proposal for Web Services Choreography Working Group Charter. W3C Architecture Domain. http://www.w3.org/2002/ws/arch/2/09/chor-proposal.html
28. Thatte, S. XLANG: Web Services for Business Process Design. http://www.gotdotnet.com/team/xml_wsspecs/xlang-c/default.htm
29. van Harmelen, F. and Horrocks, I. FAQs on OIL: the Ontology Inference Layer. IEEE Intelligent Systems, Trends and Controversies, pp. 3–6, November/December, 2000.
30. Weiser, M. "Some Computer Science Problems in Ubiquitous Computing," Communications of the ACM, July, 1993.
31. Workflow Management Coalition. The Workflow Reference Model. Document Number TC00–1003, Workflow Management Coalition Office, Avenue Marcel Thirty 204, 1200 Brussels, Belgium, 1994.

Request Rewriting-Based Web Service Discovery

Boualem Benatallah[1], Mohand-Said Hacid[2], Christophe Rey[3], and Farouk Toumani[3]

[1] SCSE, UNSW, Sydney, Australia
boualem@cse.unsw.edu.au
[2] LIRIS, UCB Lyon I, France
mshacid@liris.univ-lyon1.fr
[3] LIMOS, UBP, France
{rey,ftoumani}@isima.fr

Abstract. One of the challenging problems that Web service technology faces is the ability to effectively discover services based on their capabilities. We present an approach to tackle this problem in the context of DAML-S ontologies of services. The proposed approach enables to select the combinations of Web services that *best match* a given request Q and effectively computes the extra information with respect to Q (e.g., the information required by a service request but not provided by any existing service). We study the reasoning problem associated with such a matching process and propose an algorithm derived from hypergraphs theory.

Keywords: Semantic Web Services, Web Services Discovery, Description Logics, Hypergraphs

1 Introduction

Semantic Web services are emerging as a promising technology for the effective automation of services discovery, combination, and management [1,2,3]. Semantic Web services aim at leveraging two major trends in Web technologies, namely *Web services* and *Semantic Web*:

- Web services build upon XML as vehicle for exchanging messages across applications. The basic technological infrastructure for Web services is structured around three major standards: SOAP, WSDL, and UDDI [4,5]. These standards provide the building blocks for service description, discovery, and communication. While Web services technologies have clearly influenced positively the potential of the Web infrastructure by providing programmatic access to information and services, they are hindered by lack of rich and machine-processable abstractions to describe service properties, capabilities, and behavior. As a result of these limitations, very little automation support can be provided to facilitate effective discovery, combination, and management of services. Automation support is considered as the cornerstone to provide effective and efficient access to services in large, heterogeneous, and dynamic environments [6,4,3].

D. Fensel et al. (Eds.): ISWC 2003, LNCS 2870, pp. 242–257, 2003.

- Semantic Web aims at improving the technology to organise, search, integrate, and evolve Web-accessible resources (e.g., Web documents, data) by using rich and machine-understandable abstractions for the representation of resources semantics. Efforts in this area include the development of ontology languages such as RDF, DAML, and DAML+OIL [7].

By leveraging efforts in both Web services and semantic Web, semantic Web services paradigm promises to take Web technologies a step further by providing foundations to enable automated discovery, access, combination, and management of Web services. Efforts in this area focus on providing rich and machine understandable representation of services properties, capabilities, and behavior as well as reasoning mechanisms to support automation activities [1,8,2,3,9,10]. Examples of such efforts include the DAML-S [9] initiative and the WSMF-Web Services Modeling Framework [2]. Work in this area is still in its infancy. Many of the objectives of the semantic Web services paradigm, such as dynamic discovery and composition remain largely to be reached. Our work focuses on the issue of dynamic discovery of Web services. The notion of *dynamic discovery* (or simply service discovery) refers to systems in which requesters search through registries to discover and then invoke services supporting the capabilities they require.

This paper focuses on the reasoning aspects to automate the discovery of Web services. Our aim is to ground the discovery of Web services on a semantic comparison between a requester query and available Web services. We tackle this problem in the context of DAML-S service ontologies. In DAML-S, service requests as well as service capabilities are characterized, among others, in terms of their inputs and outputs. We propose a novel matching algorithm for discovering services. The matching algorithm takes as input a service request (or query) Q and a DAML-S ontology $\mathcal{T}$, and computes the best combination of Web services that satisfies *as much as possible* the outputs of the query Q and that requires *as little as possible* of inputs that are not provided in Q.

The main contributions of our approach are:

- We propose to view service discovery as a rewriting process in which a requester query Q is rewritten into the closest description E expressed as a conjunction of (some) Web services of a given ontology $\mathcal{T}$. Our approach features a global reasoning mechanism that goes beyond a simple pair-wise comparison between a service request and service offers.
- We propose a matching process that goes beyond simple subsumption tests between a service request and service advertisements.
  As emphasized in [11], a Web service discovery algorithm should support flexible matching since it is unrealistic to expect service requests and service offers to be exactly equivalent. To cope with this requirement, we propose to use a *difference operation* on service descriptions. Such an operation enables to extract from a subset of Web service descriptions the part that is semantically common with a given service request and the part that is semantically different from the request. Knowing the former and the latter allows to select relevant Web services and then to choose the best ones.

We investigate the reasoning problem associated to such a discovery process and its relationship with the expressiveness of the service description language. Then we propose a service discovery algorithm derived from hypergraphs theory. We show that this problem is similar to the so-called *best covering problem* investigated in [12,13]. In this paper we extend our previous results to deal with DAML-S ontologies of services.

The remainder of this paper is organized as follows: Section 2 motivates the role of ontologies to associate formal semantics with service descriptions and outlines the overall structure of a DAML-S ontology. Section 3 formalizes the proposed service discovery approach in the context of DAML-S ontologies. An overview of a service discovery algorithm is given in Section 4 and together with some preliminary experimental results are presented in Section 5. We review related work and give concluding remarks in Section 6.

2 Describing Web Services with DAML-S

Ontologies *"are formal and consensual specifications of conceptualisations that provide a shared and common understanding of a domain, an understanding that can be communicated across people and application systems"* [3]. The semantic Web community propose ontologies as means to address semantic heterogeneity among Web-accessible information sources and services. Ontologies are used to provide meta-data for the effective manipulation of available information including discovering information sources and reasoning about their capabilities. RDF, DAML, and DAML+OIL are examples of ontology languages [7]. In the area of Web services, ontologies promise to take interoperability a step further by providing rich description and modeling of services properties, capabilities, and behavior. DAML-S[1] is a DAML-OIL ontology for describing Web services. In this section, we give a brief overview of DAML-S as our approach relies on DAML-S to describe service properties and capabilities.

2.1 DAML-S Ontologies: An Overview

DAML-S employs the ontology structuring mechanisms of DAML+OIL to describe the properties and capabilities of Web services in a computer-interpretable form, thereby facilitating the automation of Web service discovery, invocation, composition and execution. As a DAML+OIL ontology, DAML-S has a well-defined semantics. It supplies a core set of markup language constructs for describing Web services in terms of classes (concepts) and complex relationships between them.

A DAML-S ontology of services is structured in three main parts [9]:

- *ServiceProfile* describes the capabilities and parameters of the service. It is used for advertising and discovering services.

[1] http://www.daml.org/services/

- *ServiceModel* gives a detailed description of a service's operation. Service operation is described in terms of a process model, which details both the control structure and data flow structure of the service required to execute a service.
- *ServiceGrounding* specifies the details of how to access the service, via messages (e.g., communication protocol, message formats, addressing, etc).

The service profile provides information about a service that can be used by an agent to determine if the service meets its needs. It consists of three types of information: a (human readable) *description* of the service; the *functional behavior* of the service which is represented as a transformation from the inputs required by the service to the outputs produced; and several *functional attributes* which specify additional information about a service (e.g., the cost of the service).

In the DAML-S approach, a service profile is intended to be used by providers to advertise their services as well as by service requesters to specify their needs. An example[2] of a very simple *book selling* service is given below.

2.2 Example

BookSellingService is a simple service which given a book title returns the price of that book. The advertisement below shows that the service accepts as input a string and generates as output instances of the concept Price as defined in a given ontology dummyOnt.

```
<profile:Profile rdf:ID="BookSellingService">
 <profile:serviceName>BookSellingService</profile:serviceName>
 ...
 <input>
  <profile:ParameterDescription rdf:ID="BookTitle">
    <profile:parameterName>bookTitle</profile:parameterName>
    <profile:restrictedTo rdf:resource="http://../XMLSchema.xsd#string"/>
  </profile:ParameterDescription>
 </input>
 <output>
  <profile:ParameterDescription rdf:ID="Price_Output">
    <profile:parameterName>Price</profile:parameterName>
    <profile:restrictedTo rdf:resource="dummyOnt.daml#Price"/>
  </profile:ParameterDescription>
 </output>
</profile:Profile>
```

A request for a service is expressed in the same format. For example, the previous profile description can also be used to express a request that looks for a service that accepts as input a string and generates as outputs instances of Price.

[2] This example is inspired from [11].

3 Characterizing Services Discovery Automation

In this section, we describe an approach for matching a service request with service advertisements. Given a service request (or query) Q and a DAML-S ontology $\mathcal{T}$ of services, we want to compute the best combinations of Web services that satisfy *as much as possible* the outputs of the request Q and that require *as little as possible* of inputs that are not provided in the description of Q. We call such combinations of Web services *best profile covers* of Q using $\mathcal{T}$. This problem is similar to the *best covering problem* [12,13,14]. We describe hereafter how the best covering problem can be extended to DAML-S ontologies.

3.1 Best Covering Profile Descriptions

To formally define the notion of *best profile cover* it is necessary to be able to characterize the notion of *"extra information"*, i.e., the information contained in one service profile description and not contained in the request description. For that, a *difference or subtraction* operation on service descriptions is required. As explained below, this requirement has an impact on the expressiveness of the ontology description language.

Characterizing the Ontology Description Language. Our approach uses Description Logics (DLs) [15] as a formal framework. DLs are a family of logics that were developed to model complex hierarchical structures and to provide a specialized reasoning engine to do inferences on these structures. Recently, DLs have heavily influenced the development of the semantic Web languages. For example, DAML+OIL, the ontology language used by DAML-S, is in fact an alternative syntax for a very expressive Description Logic [16].

A DL allows to represent domain of interest in terms of *concepts or descriptions* (unary predicates) that characterize subsets of the objects (*individuals*) in the domain, and *roles* (binary predicates) over such domain. Concepts are denoted by expressions formed by means of special constructors. Examples of DL constructors are given below:

- the symbol $\top$ is a concept description which denotes the top concept while the symbol $\bot$ stands for the inconsistent (bottom) concept,
- concept conjunction ($\sqcap$), e.g., the concept description $parent \sqcap male$ denotes the class of fathers (i.e., male parents),
- the universal role quantification ($\forall R.C$), e.g., the description $\forall child.male$ denotes the set of individuals whose children are all male.
- the number restriction constructor ($\geq n\ R$) e.g., the description ($\geq 1\ child$) denotes the class of parents (i.e., individuals having at least one children).

Let C, D be two concept descriptions. In the sequel, we use the expression $C \equiv D$ to denote equivalence between concept descriptions and $|C|$ to denote the size[3] of a concept C (i.e., the number of occurrences of concept and role names in C).

[3] Usually, $|C|$ is computed using a given canonical form of C.

We consider description logics with a difference operator between concept descriptions. Roughly speaking, the difference of two descriptions C and D, expressed using $C-D$, is defined as being a description containing all information which is a part of the description C but not a part of the description D [17]. However, it is worth noting that, in some description logics, $C - D$ may be a set of descriptions which are not semantically equivalent. Teege [17] provides sufficient conditions to characterize the logics where the difference operation is always semantically unique and can be implemented in a simple syntactical way by computing the set difference of subterms in a conjunction. According to [17], *structural subsumption* is a sufficient condition that allows to identify such logics. However, it is worth noting that the definition of structural subsumption given in [17] is different from the one usually used in the literature (e.g., see [15] for the usual definition). Nevertheless, the result given in [17] is still interesting in practice since there exist many description logics with this property. Examples of such logics include the quite expressive language $\mathcal{L}_1$ [17] , which contains the following constructors:

- $\sqcap, \sqcup, \top, \bot, (\geq\ n\ R)$, existential role quantification ($\exists R.C$) and existential feature quantification ($\exists f.C$) for concepts, where C denotes a concept, R a role and f a feature (i.e., a functional role),
- bottom ($\bot$), composition ($\circ$), differentiation ($|$) for roles,
- bottom ($\bot$) and composition ($\circ$) for features.

Currently, our approach does not consider the full expression power of the DAML+OIL language. We consider a subset of DAML+OIL for which a structural subsumption[4] algorithm exists. In the sequel, we use the term *restricted DAML-S ontologies* to denote DAML-S ontologies which are defined using sublanguages of DAML+OIL with structural subsumption.

The extension of our approach to consider more expressive description logics is currently under investigation. Such an extension requires the definition of a restricted difference operator to deal with the cases where the difference operation is not semantically unique.

Statement of the Problem. Now let us introduce some basic definitions that allow to extend the best covering problem to DAML-S service profiles.

Let $\mathcal{T} = \{S_i, i \in [1,n]\}$ be a restricted DAML-S ontology and $E \equiv S_l \sqcap \ldots \sqcap S_p$, with $l, p \in [1,n]$ and $l \leq p$, be a conjunction of some services occurring in $\mathcal{T}$. We denote by $I(E)$ (respectively, $O(E)$) the concept obtained by the conjunction of all the inputs (respectively, the outputs) occurring in the profile section of all the services S_i, for all $i \in [l,p]$. In the same way, we write $I(Q)$ (respectively, $O(Q)$) to denote the concept obtained by the conjunction of all the inputs (respectively, the outputs) occurring in the profile section of a given query Q.

Definition 1. ***Profile cover (Pcover)***
A profile cover, called Pcover, of Q using $\mathcal{T}$ is a conjunction E of some services S_i from $\mathcal{T}$ such that: $O(Q) - O(E) \not\equiv O(Q)$.

[4] In this paper we use the term *structural subsumption* in the sense of [17].

Hence, a Pcover of a query Q using $\mathcal{T}$ is defined as being any conjunction of Web services occurring in $\mathcal{T}$ that share some outputs with Q.

The following two definitions allow to characterize more precisely the remaining descriptions both in the outputs of the query Q (hereafter called the *Prest*) and in the inputs of its cover E (hereafter called the *Pmiss*).

Definition 2. ***Profile rest (Prest) and Profile miss (Pmiss)***
Let Q be a service request and E be a Pcover of Q using $\mathcal{T}$.

- *The profile rest of Q with respect to E, written $Prest_E(Q)$, is defined as follows: $Prest_E(Q) \equiv O(Q) - O(E)$.*
- *The profile missing information of Q with respect to E, written $Pmiss_E(Q)$, is defined as follows: $Pmiss_E(Q) \equiv I(E) - I(Q)$.*

Now we can define the notion of best cover with respect to service profiles as follows.

Definition 3. ***best profile cover***
A conjunction E of some services of an ontology $\mathcal{T}$ is called a best profile cover of Q using $\mathcal{T}$ iff:

- *E is a Pcover of Q using $\mathcal{T}$, and*
- *there doesn't exist a Pcover E' of Q using $\mathcal{T}$ such that $(|Prest_{E'}(Q)|, |Pmiss_{E'}(Q)|) < (|Prest_E(Q)|, |Pmiss_E(Q)|)$, where $<$ stands for the lexicographic order.*

The *best profile covering problem* is then defined as the problem of computing all the best profile covers of Q using $\mathcal{T}$. From the results already shown for the best covering problem [13], it follows that the best profile covering problem is NP-Hard.

3.2 Illustrating Example

This example illustrates how the notion of best profile cover can be used to match a service request with service advertisements. Let us consider an ontology of Web services containing the following three services:

- *ToTravel* allowing to reserve a trip given an itinerary (i.e., the departure point and the arrival point) and the arrival time and date.
- *FromTravel* allowing to reserve a trip given an itinerary and the departure time and date.
- *Hotel* allowing to reserve a hotel given a destination place, a period of time expressed in terms of the check-in date and the check-out date.

Due to lack of space, we do not provide the complete profile descriptions of these services. Table 1 shows the inputs and the outputs concepts of the three Web services. We assume that, the service profiles refer to concepts that are defined in the restricted[5] DAML-OIL ontology of tourism given in Table 2. For

[5] In this example, we use a description language made of the following constructors: concept conjunction ($\sqcap$), universal role quantification ($\forall R.C$) and the at least number restriction constructor ($\geq nR$).

Table 1. Input and Output service parameters.

Service	Inputs	Outputs
ToTravel	Itinerary, Arrival	TripReservation
FromTravel	Itinerary, Departure	TripReservation
Hotel	Destination, StayDuration	HotelReservation

Table 2. Example of a tourism ontology.

Itinerary ≡	(≥ 1 departurePlace) ⊓ (∀ departurePlace.Location) ⊓ (≥ 1 arrivalPlace) ⊓ (∀ arrivalPlace.Location)
Arrival ≡	(≥ 1 arrivalDate) ⊓ (∀ arrivalDate.Date) ⊓ (≥ 1 arrivalTime) ⊓ (∀ arrivalTime.Time)
Departure ≡	(≥ 1 departureDate) ⊓ (∀ departureDate.Date) ⊓ (≥ 1 departureTime) ⊓ (∀ departureTime.Time)
Destination ≡	(≥ 1 destinationPlace) ⊓ (∀ destinationPlace.Location)
StayDuration ≡	(≥ 1 checkIn) ⊓ (∀ checkIn.Date) ⊓ (≥ 1 checkOut) ⊓ (∀ checkOut.Date)
TripReservation ≡	...
HotelReservation ≡	...
CarRental ≡	...

clarity reasons, we use the usual DL syntax instead of the DAML-OIL syntax to describe the ontology. In Table 2, the description of the concept Itinerary denotes the class of individuals whose departure places (respectively arrival places) are instances of the concept Location. Moreover, the individual belonging to this class must have at least one departure place (the constraint (≥ 1 departurePlace)) and at least one arrival place (the constraint (≥ 1 arrivalPlace)). The input of the service ToTravel is obtained by the conjunction of all its inputs as follows: `I(ToTravel)` ≡ `Itinerary` ⊓ `Arrival`. By replacing the concepts Itinerary and Arrival by their descriptions, we obtain the following equivalent description:

`I(ToTravel)` ≡ (≥ 1 departurePlace) ⊓ (∀ departurePlace.Location) ⊓ (≥ 1 arrivalPlace) ⊓ (∀ arrivalPlace.Location) ⊓ (≥ 1 arrivalDate) ⊓ (∀ arrivalDate.Date) ⊓ (≥ 1 arrivalTime) ⊓ (∀ arrivalTime.Time)

The inputs and the outputs of the other Web services can be computed in the same way.

Now, let us consider a service request Q that looks for a vacation package that combines a trip with a hotel and a car rental, given a departure place, an arrival place, a departure date, a (hotel) destination place and the check-in and check-out dates. The inputs and outputs of the query Q can be expressed by the following descriptions which, again, refer to some concepts of the tourism ontology given in Table 2:

$I(Q)$ ≡ (≥ 1 departurePlace) ⊓ (∀ departurePlace.Location) ⊓ (≥ 1 arrivalPlace) ⊓ (∀ arrivalPlace.Location) ⊓ (≥ 1 departureDate) ⊓ (∀ departureDate.Date) ⊓ (≥ 1 destinationPlace) ⊓ (∀ destinationPlace.Location) ⊓ (≥ 1 checkIn) ⊓ (∀ checkIn.Date) ⊓ (≥ 1 checkOut) ⊓ (∀ checkOut.Date)

$O(Q)$ ≡ TripReservation ⊓ HotelReservation ⊓ CarRental

The matching between the service request Q and the three advertised services given above can be achieved by computing the best profile covers of Q using these services. The result will be the following:

Best profile cover	Prest	Pmiss
FromTravel, Hotel	CarRental	departureTime

In this example, there is only one best profile cover of Q corresponding to the description $\texttt{E} \equiv \texttt{Hotel} \sqcap \texttt{FromTravel}$. The selected services generate the concepts `TripReservation` and `HotelReservation` which are part of the output required by the query Q. From the service descriptions we can see that no Web service supplies the concept CarRental. Hence, the best profile covers of Q will have exactly the following profile rest: $\texttt{Prest}_{\texttt{E}}(\texttt{Q}) \equiv \texttt{carRental}$. This rest corresponds to the output of the query that cannot be generated by any advertised service. Moreover, the **Pmiss** column shows the information (the role departureTime) required as input of the selected services but not provided in the query inputs. More precisely, the best profile covers of Q will have exactly the following profile missing information: $\texttt{Pmiss}_{\texttt{E}}(\texttt{Q}) \equiv (\geq 1\texttt{departureTime}) \sqcap (\forall \texttt{departureTime.Time})$. It is worth noting that, although the solution $\texttt{E}' \equiv \texttt{Hotel} \sqcap \texttt{ToTravel}$ generates the same outputs (i.e., the concepts `TripReservation` and `HotelReservation`), it will not be selected because its **Pmiss** is greater than the one of the first solution (it contains the roles arrivalTime and arrivalDate).

4 Computing Best Profile Covers Using Hypergraphs

Let us first recall some useful definitions regarding hypergraphs. For more details about hypergraphs theory, we refer the reader to [18,19].

Definition 4. ***hypergraph and transversals*** *[19]*
An hypergraph $\mathcal{H}$ is a pair (Σ, Γ) of a finite set $\Sigma = \{V_1, \ldots, V_n\}$ and a set Γ of subsets of Σ. The elements of Σ are called vertices, and the elements of Γ are called edges.
A set $T \subseteq \Sigma$ is a transversal of $\mathcal{H}$ if for each $\varepsilon \in \Gamma$, $T \cap \varepsilon \neq \emptyset$. A transversal T is minimal if no proper subset T' of T is a transversal. The set of the minimal transversals of an hypergraph $\mathcal{H}$ is noted $Tr(\mathcal{H})$.

In the rest of this section, we briefly sketch how we can compute best profile covers using hypergraphs theory.

4.1 Reduction of the Best Profile Covering Problem to Hypergraphs

In the context of languages with structural subsumption, [17] shows that:

- each concept description C can be expressed in a given normal form, called Reduced Clause Form (RCF), as a conjunction of atomic clauses (e.g., $c_1 \sqcap \ldots \sqcap c_m$), and
- the difference $C - D$ between two concepts descriptions C and D can be computed using the simple *set difference* operation between the sets of atomic clauses of C and D.

Based on this result, we can show that the best profile covering problem can be interpreted in the framework of hypergraphs as the problem of finding the minimal transversals with a minimal cost. Given a query Q and an ontology of Web services $\mathcal{T}$, the first step is to build an associated hypergraph $\mathcal{H}_{\mathcal{T}Q}$ as follows:

- each Web service S_i in $\mathcal{T}$ becomes a vertex V_{S_i} in the hypergraph $\mathcal{H}_{\mathcal{T}Q}$.
- each clause A in the normal form description of the output $O(Q)$ of the query Q becomes an edge in the hypergraph $\mathcal{H}_{\mathcal{T}Q}$. The edge is populated by those services that have in their outputs a clause A' that is equivalent to A.
- Let $X = \{V_{S_i}, \ldots, V_{S_j}\}$ be a set of vertices of the hypergraph $\mathcal{H}_{\mathcal{T}Q}$. We define the notion of a cost of a set of vertices as: $cost(X) = |Pmiss_{(S_i \sqcap \ldots \sqcap S_j)}(Q)|$.

Then, one can prove that computing the best profile covers of Q using $\mathcal{T}$ can be reduced to the computation of the minimal transversals with the minimal cost of the associated hypergraph $\mathcal{H}_{\mathcal{T}Q}$. More details about the reduction of the best covering problem to hypergraphs can be found in [13].

4.2 The Service Discovery Algorithm

Based on hypergraph theory, we propose an algorithm called *computeBProfile-Cov* that solves the best profile covering problem. *computeBProfileCov* is an adaptation of the *computeBCov* algorithm proposed in [13] to solve the general best covering problem.

A naive approach to compute the minimal transversals with the minimal cost of a hypergraph would be: *(i)* to compute all the minimal transversals using existing algorithms for computing the minimal transversals of an hypergraph (e.g., see [18,19]), and then *(ii)* to choose those transversals which have the minimal cost. A simple algorithm to compute the minimal transversals of an hypergraph $\mathcal{H}$ is proposed in [20]. The algorithm is incremental and works in n steps where n is the number of edges of the hypergraph $\mathcal{H}$. Starting from an empty set of transversals, the basic idea is to explore each edge of the hypergraph, one edge at each step, and generate a set of candidate transversals by computing all the possible unions between the candidates generated in the previous step and each vertex in the considered edge. At each step, the non-minimal candidate transversals (i.e., the candidates in which at least one other candidate is strictly included) are removed.

The algorithm *computeBProfileCov* makes an improvement over the naive approach in two ways:

1. it reduces the number of candidates in the intermediary steps of the algorithm by generating only the minimal transversals, and
2. it uses a combinatorial optimization technique (Branch-and-Bound) in order to prune, at the intermediary steps of the algorithm, those candidate transversals which will not generate transversals with a minimal cost.

Algorithm 1 ***computeBProfileCov*** (sketch)

Require: An ontology $\mathcal{T}$ and a query Q.
Ensure: The set of the best profile covers of Q using $\mathcal{T}$.
1: Build the associated hypergraph $\mathcal{H}_{\mathcal{T}Q} = (\Sigma, \Gamma)$.
2: $Tr(\mathcal{H}_{\mathcal{T}Q}) \leftarrow \emptyset$ – Initialization of the set of the minimal transversals.
3:
$$CostEval \leftarrow \sum_{e\in\Gamma'} \min_{V_{S_i}\in e}(|Pmiss_{S_i}(Q)|). \quad \text{– Initialization of CostEval}$$
4: **for all** edge $E \in \Gamma$ **do**
5: $Tr(\mathcal{H}_{\mathcal{T}Q}) \leftarrow$ the new generated set of the minimal transversals.
6: Remove from $Tr(\mathcal{H}_{\mathcal{T}Q})$ the transversals whose costs are greater than $CostEval$.
7: Compute a more precise evaluation of $CostEval$.
8: **end for**
9: **for all** $X = \{V_{S_i}, \ldots, V_{S_n}\} \in Tr(\mathcal{H}_{\mathcal{T}Q})$ such that $|Pmiss_{S_i\sqcap\ldots\sqcap S_n}(Q)| = CostEval$ **do**
10: return the concept $S_i \sqcap \ldots \sqcap S_n$ as a best profile cover of Q using $\mathcal{T}$.
11: **end for**

The first improvement, that allows to generate only good candidates (only minimal transversals) at each iteration (line 5 of the algorithm), uses a necessary and sufficient condition provided by Theorem 1 below. This condition characterizes a pair (X_i, s_j) that will generate a non minimal transversal at iteration i, where X_i is a minimal transversal generated at iteration $i-1$ and s_j is a vertex of the ith edge.

Theorem 1. *Let* $Tr(\mathcal{H}) = \{X_i, i = 1..m\}$ *the set of minimal transversals for the hypergraph* $\mathcal{H}$*, and* $E = \{s_j, j = 1..n\}$ *an extra edge of* $\mathcal{H}$*. Assume* $\mathcal{H}' = \mathcal{H} \cup E$*. Then, we have :* $X_i \cup \{s_j\}$ *is a non-minimal transversal of* $\mathcal{H}'$ $\Leftrightarrow$ *it exists a minimal transversal* X_k *of* $\mathcal{H}$ *such that* $X_k \cap E = \{s_j\}$ *and* $X_k \setminus \{s_j\} \subset X_i$*.*

Details and proof of Theorem 1 are given in [21].

The second improvement consists in a Branch-and-Bound like enumeration of transversals. First, a simple heuristic is used to efficiently compute a cost of a *good* transversal (i.e., a transversal expected to have a small cost). This can be carried out by adding, for each edge of the hypergraph, the cost of the vertex that has the minimal cost. The resulting cost is stored in the variable $CostEval$ (line 3 of the algorithm). As we have, for any set of vertices $X = \{V_{S_i}, \ldots, V_{S_n}\}$:

$$cost(X) = |Pmiss_{S_i\sqcap\ldots\sqcap S_n}(Q)| \leq \sum_{j\in[i,n]} |Pmiss_{S_j}(Q)| = \sum_{V_{S_j}\in X} cost(V_{S_j})$$

Hence, the evaluation $CostEval$ is an upper bound of the cost of an existing transversal. Then as we consider candidates in intermediate steps of the algorithm, we can eliminate from $Tr(\mathcal{H}_{\mathcal{T}Q})$ any candidate transversal that has a greater cost than $CostEval$, since that candidate cannot possibly lead to a transversal that is better than what we already know (line 6). Then, from each candidate transversal that remains in $Tr(\mathcal{H}_{TQ})$, we compute a new evaluation for *CostEval* by considering only remaining edges (line 7).

These two optimizations[6] have been implemented as separate options of the algorithm, namely option Pers for the first optimization and option BnB for the second one.

Hence, the algorithm *computeBProfileCov* can be used to allow dynamic discovery of DAML-S services based on their capabilities. According to the definitions 1 and 2 of Section 3, the algorithm selects the combinations of services that best match a given query and effectively computes the outputs of the query that cannot be satisfied by the available services (i.e., Prest) as well as the inputs that are required by the selected services and are not provided in the query (i.e., Pmiss).

5 Implementation and Experiments

To conduct experiments, we have developed a testbed prototype that allows to evaluate the performance of the *computeBProfileCov* algorithm. This prototype is implemented using the Java programing language. The prototype implements up to 6 versions of the *computeBProfileCov* algorithm corresponding to different combinations of optimization options. Moreover, it includes a tool that enables to generate random XML-based services ontologies and associated service requests that can be used to evaluate the *computeBProfileCov* algorithm. All experiments have been performed on a PC with a Pentium III 500 MHz and 384 Mo of RAM.

To test *computeBProfileCov*, we first have run *computeBProfileCov* on worst cases and then on a set of ontologies and queries randomly generated by our prototype. *computeBProfileCov* worst cases were built according to a theoretical study of the complexity of all versions of *computeBProfileCov*: two ontologies (and their associated query) have been built in order to maximize the number of minimal transversals of the corresponding hypergraph as well as the number of elementary operations of the algorithm (i.e., inclusion tests and intersection operations). In each case, there exists at least one version of *computeBProfileCov* that complete the execution in less than 20 seconds. We point out the fact that if these cases are very bad for *computeBProfileCov*, they are also totally unrealistic with respect to practical situations. Due to space limitation, we will not detail here the many parameters used in the generation of random ontologies. We just point out that we tried to generate larger but still realistic random ontologies. The modeling and random generating question is an hard issue that is far out from the scope of this paper. We focus here on three study cases which special feature is the varying size of the application domain ontology, of the Web service ontology and of the query. Their characteristics are given below:

[6] Other less significant optimization options have also been implemented.

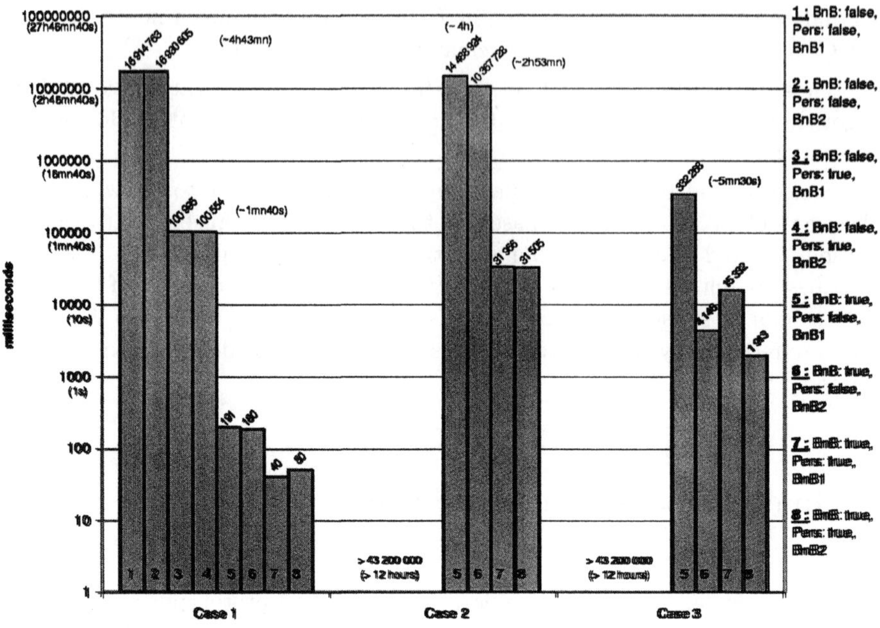

Fig. 1. Execution time

Configurations	Case 1	Case 2	Case 3
Number of concept descriptions in the application domain ontology	365	1334	3405
Number of Web services	366	660	570
Number of (atomic) clauses in the query	6	33	12

It is worth noting that the internal structures of these ontologies correspond to bad cases for the *computeBProfileCov* algorithm. We have run the 6 versions of the *computeBProfileCov* algorithm on each of these cases. The overall execution time results are given in Figure 1[7]. The Figure 1 shows that for the cases 1 and 3, there is at least a version of the algorithm that runs in less than two seconds, and in less than 30 seconds for the case 2. So, although the Figure 1 shows that there is a great difference in performance of the different versions of the algorithm, there is in each case one version of *computeBProfileCov* that allows us to be optimistic concerning the real-time execution of services discovery with quite large domain ontologies. All details concerning the implementation of *computeBProfileCov*, the theoretical study of worst cases, the parameterized ontology generation process and experimental results can be found in [21].

[7] Note that versions 1 and 2 of the algorithm (respectively, 3 and 4) are similar as both run *computeBProfileCov* without BnB, and what distinguishes 1 from 2 (respectively, 3 from 4) is the way the option BnB is implemented (BnB1 or BnB2).

6 Related Work and Concluding Remarks

There are some proposals of Web service discovery mechanisms that employ semantic Web technology for service description. For example, Bernstein et al. [10] proposes to use process ontologies to describe the behaviour of services and then to query such ontologies using a Process Query Language (PQL). Chakraborty et al. [8] defines an ontology based on DAML [22] to describe mobile devices and proposes a matching process, based on an advanced Prolog reasoning engine, to locate devices on the basis of their features. González-Castillo et al. [23] reports on an experience in building matchmaking prototype based on a description logic reasoning engine and operating on service descriptions in DAML+OIL. The proposed matching algorithm is based on simple subsumption and consistency tests. Paolucci et al. [11] proposes a matching algorithm between services and requests described in DAML-S. In this approach, a match between a service request and an advertised service is determined by comparing all the outputs of the query with the outputs of the advertisement and all the inputs of the advertisement with the inputs of the query. The proposed algorithm recognizes various degrees of matching that are determined by the minimal distance between concepts in the concept taxonomy. Based on a similar approach, the ATLAS matchmaker [24] operates on DAML-S ontologies and utilizes two separate sets of filters: *1)* Matching functional attributes to determine the applicability of advertisements (i.e., do they deliver sufficient quality of service, etc). *2)* Matching service functionalities to determine if the advertised service matches the requested service. A DAML-based subsumption inferential engine is used to compare input and output sets of requests and advertisements.

Finally, it should be noted that the problem of capabilities based matching has also been addressed by several other research communities, e.g., information retrieval, software reuse systems or multi-agent communities. More details about these approaches and their applicability in the context of the semantic Web service area can be found in [10,11].

Our work focuses on automatic discovery of Web services based on a semantic matching between declarative descriptions of services and requests. We adopt an approach similar to [11] for comparing requests with advertised services based on their inputs and outputs. However, we propose a rather different matching algorithm. Indeed, since we view the Web service discovery as a rewriting process, our algorithm is able to discover *combinations* of services that best match (cover) a given request. Furthermore, the difference between the query and its rewriting (i.e., Prest and Pmiss) is effectively computed and can be used to improve the Web service interoperability.

From the technical point of view, the best profile covering problem belongs to the general framework for *rewriting using terminologies* provided in [25]. This framework is defined as follows: given a terminology $\mathcal{T}$ (i.e., a set of concept descriptions), a concept description Q that does not contain concept names defined in $\mathcal{T}$ and a binary relation ρ between concept descriptions, can Q be rewritten into a description E, built using (some) of the names defined in $\mathcal{T}$, such that $Q \rho E$?

Additionally, some optimality criterion is defined in order to select the relevant rewritings. Already investigated instances of this problem are the minimal rewriting problem [25] and rewriting queries using views (e.g., [26,27]). In the former, ρ is instantiated by equivalence modulo $\mathcal{T}$ and the size of the rewriting is used as the optimality criterion. In the latter, the relation ρ is instanciated by subsumption and the optimality criterion is the inverse subsumption [25].

The *best profile covering problem* can be viewed as a new instance of the problem of rewriting concepts using terminologies where the goal is to rewrite a description Q into the closest description expressed as a conjunction of (some) concept names in $\mathcal{T}$ (hence, ρ is neither equivalence nor subsumption).

Our future work will be devoted to the extension of the proposed framework to hold the definition of the best profile covering problem for description logics where the difference operation is not semantically unique. After the very first results we got in this context, we argue that a restricted difference operator can be defined, and then the proposed framework can be extended to more expressive languages.

References

1. McIlraith, S., Son, T., Zeng, H.: Semantic Web Services. IEEE Intelligent Systems. Special Issue on the Semantic Web **16** (2001) 46–53
2. Fensel, D., Bussler, C., Maedche, A.: Semantic Web Enabled Web Services. In: International Semantic Web Conference, Sardinia, Italy. (2002) 1–2
3. Fensel, D., Bussler, C., Ding, Y., Omelayenko, B.: The Web Service Modeling Framework WSMF. Electronic Commerce Research and Applications **1** (2002)
4. Casati, F., Shan, M.C., Georgakopoulos, D.G., (editors): The VLDB Journal: Special Issue on E-Services. 10(1), Springer-Verlag Berlin Heidelberg (2001)
5. Weikum, G., (editor): Data Engineering Bulletin: Special Issue on Infrastructure for Advanced E-Services. 24(1), IEEE Computer Society (2001)
6. Casati, F., Shan, M.C.: Dynamic and adaptive composition of e-services. Information Systems **26** (2001) 143–163
7. Ding, Y., Fensel, D., M.C.A. Klein, B.O.: The semantic web: yet another hip? DKE **6** (2002) 205–227
8. Chakraborty, D., Perich, F., Avancha, S., Joshi, A.: DReggie: Semantic Service Discovery for M-Commerce Applications. In: Workshop on Reliable and Secure Applications in Mobile Environment, 20th Symposium on Reliable Distributed Systems. (2001) 28–31
9. The DAML Services Coalition: DAML-S: Web Service Description for the Semantic Web. In: The 1st International Semantic Web Conference (ISWC). (2002) 348–363
10. Bernstein, A., Klein, M.: Discovering Services: Towards High Precision Service Retrieval. In: CaiSE workshop on Web Services, e-Business, and the Semantic Web: Foundations, Models, Architecture, Engineering and Applications. Toronto, Canada. (2002)
11. Paolucci, M., Kawamura, T., Payne, T., Sycara, K.: Semantic Matching of Web Services Capabilities. In: Semantic Web Conference, Sardinia, Italy. (2002) 333–347
12. Hacid, M., Leger, A., Rey, C., Toumani, F.: Computing concept covers: A preliminary report. In: International Workshop on Description Logics (DL 2002). Toulouse, France. (2002)

13. Hacid, M.S., Leger, A., Rey, C., Toumani, F.: Dynamic Discovery of E-services (A Description Logics Based Approach). Report, LIMOS, Clemont-Ferrand, France (2002) see http://www.710.univ-lyon1.fr/~dbkrr/mshacid/publications.html.
14. Benatallah, B., Hacid, M.S., Rey, C., Toumani, F.: Semantic Reasoning for Web Services Discovery. In: WWW Workshop on E-Services and the Semantic Web, Budapest, Hungary. (2003)
15. Donini, F., M. Lenzerini, D. Nardi, A.S.: Reasoning in description logics. In: Gerhard Brewka, editor, Foundation of Knowledge Representation, CSLI-Publications (1996) 191–236
16. Horrocks, I., P.F.Patel-Schneider, van Harmelen, F.: Reviewing the Design of DAML+OIL: An Ontology Language for the Semantic Web. In: Proc. of the 18th Nat. Conf. on Artificial Intelligence (AAAI 2002). (2002)
17. Teege, G.: Making the difference: A subtraction operation for description logics. In Doyle, J., Sandewall, E., Torasso, P., eds.: KR'94, San Francisco, CA, Morgan Kaufmann (1994)
18. Berge, C.: Hypergraphs. Volume 45 of North Holland Mathematical Library. Elsevier Science Publishers B.V. (North-Holland) (1989)
19. Eiter, T., Gottlob, G.: Identifying the minimal transversals of a hypergraph and related problems. SIAM Journal on Computing **24** (1995) 1278–1304
20. Mannila, H., Räihä, K.J.: The Design of Relational Databases. Addison-Wesley, Wokingham, England (1994)
21. Rey, C., Toumani, F., Hacid, M.S., Leger, A.: An algorithm and a prototype for the dynamic discovery of e-services. Technical Report RR05-03, LIMOS, Clemont-Ferrand, France, http://www.isima.fr/limos/publications.htm (2003)
22. Hendler, J., McGuinness, D.L.: The DARPA Agent Markup Language. IEEE Intelligent Systems **15** (2000) 67–73
23. González-Castillo, J., Trastour, D., Bartolini, C.: Description Logics for Matchmaking of Services. In: KI-2001 Workshop on Applications of Description Logics Vienna, Austria. (2001) http://sunsite.informatik.rwth-aachen.de/Publications/CEUR-WS/Vol-44/.
24. Payne, T., Paolucci, M., Sycara, K.: Advertising and Matching DAML-S Service Descriptions (position paper). In: International Semantic Web Working Symposium, Stanford University, California, USA. (2001)
25. Baader, F., Küsters, R., Molitor, R.: Rewriting Concepts Using Terminologies. In: Proc. of KR'00, Colorado, USA. (2000) 297–308
26. Beeri, C., Levy, A., Rousset, M.C.: Rewriting Queries Using Views in Description Logics. In Yuan, L., ed.: Proc. of the ACM PODS , New York, USA. (1997) 99–108
27. Goasdoué, F., V. Lattès, M.C.R.: The Use of CARIN Language and Algorithms for Information Integration: The PICSEL System. IJICIS **9** (2000) 383–401

Learning to Attach Semantic Metadata to Web Services

Andreas Heß and Nicholas Kushmerick

Computer Science Department, University College Dublin, Ireland
{andreas.hess,nick}@ucd.ie

Abstract. Emerging Web standards promise a network of heterogeneous yet interoperable Web Services. Web Services would greatly simplify the development of many kinds of data integration and knowledge management applications. Unfortunately, this vision requires that services describe themselves with large amounts of semantic metadata "glue". We explore a variety of machine learning techniques to semi-automatically create such metadata.

We make three contributions. First, we describe a Bayesian learning and inference algorithm for classifying HTML forms into semantic categories, as well as assigning semantic labels to the form's fields. These techniques are important as legacy HTML interfaces are migrated to Web Services. Second, we describe the application of the Naive Bayes and SVM algorithms to the task of Web Service classification. We show that an ensemble approach that treats Web Services as structured objects is more accurate than an unstructured approach. Finally, we describe a clustering algorithm that automatically discovers the semantic categories of Web Services. All of our algorithms are evaluated using large collections of real HTML forms and Web Services.

1 Introduction

Emerging Web standards such as WSDL [w3.org/TR/wsdl], SOAP [w3.org/TR/soap], UDDI [uddi.org] and DAML-S [www.daml.org/services] promise an ocean of Web Services, networked components that can be invoked remotely using standard XML-based protocols. For example, significant e-commerce players such as Amazon and Google export Web Services giving public access to their content databases.

The key to automatically invoking and composing Web Services is to associate machine-understandable semantic metadata with each service. A central challenge to the Web Services initiative is therefore a lack of tools to (semi-)automatically generate the necessary metadata. We explore the use of machine learning techniques to automatically create such metadata from training data. Such an approach complements existing uses of machine learning to facilitate the Semantic Web, such as for information extraction [7,9,3] and for mapping between heterogeneous data schemata [5].

The various Web Services standards involve metadata at various levels of abstraction, from high-level advertisements that facilitate indexing and matching

D. Fensel et al. (Eds.): ISWC 2003, LNCS 2870, pp. 258–273, 2003.

relevant services, to low-level input/output specifications of particular operations. The various metadata standards are evolving rapidly, and the details of current standards are beyond the scope of this paper. Rather than committing to any particular standard, we investigate the following three sub-problems, which are essential components to any tool for helping developers create Web Services metadata.

1. To automatically invoke a particular Web Service operation, metadata is needed to indicate the overall "domain" of the operation, as well as the semantic meaning of each of the operation's input parameters. For example, to enable automatic invocation of a Web Service operation that queries an airline's timetable, the operation must be annotated with metadata indicating that the operation does indeed relate to airline timetable querying, and each parameter must be annotated with the kind of data that should be supplied (departure date, time and airport, destination airport, return date, number of passengers, etc). In Sec. 2, we propose to *automatically assign a Web Form to a concept in a domain taxonomy, and to assign each input parameter to a concept in a data-type taxonomy.*
2. A Web Service is a collection of operations, and Web Services must be grouped into coherent "categories" of services supporting similar operations. For example, many airlines may each export a Web Service that supports similar operations such as querying for flights, checking whether a flight is delayed, checking a frequent-traveller account balance, etc. To enable the retrieval of appropriate Web Services, in Sec. 3 we describe techniques to *automatically assign a Web Service to a concept in a category taxonomy.*
3. Finally, when Web Services are widely deployed, it may well be infeasible to agree a category taxonomy in advance. We therefore propose in Sec. 4 to *cluster Web Services in order to automatically create a category taxonomy.*

Fig. 1 describes the relationship between the category, domain and datatype taxonomies that motivate our research. In more detail, our work can be characterized in terms of the following three levels of metadata. First, we assume a *category* taxonomy $\mathcal{C}$. The category of a Web Service describes the general kind of service that is offered, such as "services related to travel", "information provider" or "business services". Second, we assume a *domain* taxonomy $\mathcal{D}$. Domains capture the purpose of a specific service operation, such as "searching for a book", "finding a job", "querying a airline timetable", etc. Third, we assume a *datatype* taxonomy $\mathcal{T}$. Datatypes relate not to low-level encoding issues such as "string" or "integer", but to the expected semantic category of a field's data, such as "book title", "salary", "destination airport", etc.

A fundamental assumption behind our work is that there are interdependencies between a Web Service's category, and the domains and datatypes of its operations. For example, a Web Service in the "services related to travel" category is likely to support an operation for "booking an airline ticket", and an operation for "finding a job" is likely to require a "salary requirement" as input. The structure of Fig. 1 indicates the main ways in which these constraints inter-

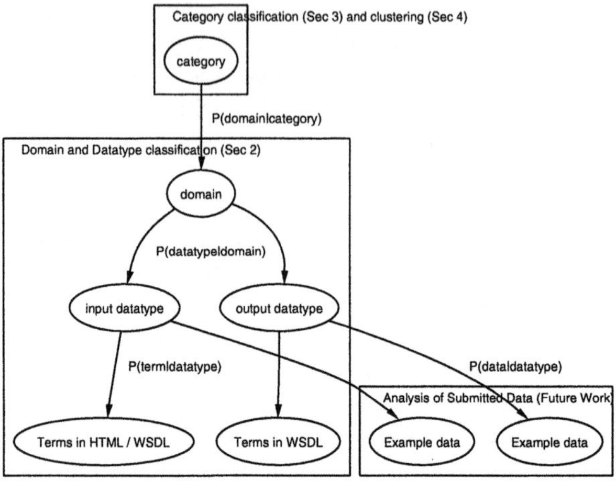

Fig. 1. A Web Service's category is dependent on the domains and datatypes of its operations.

act. The edges of the graph indicate conditional probabilities between entities, or the flow of evidence.

Finally, the boxes in Fig. 1 indicate the actual algorithms that we describe in this paper. As indicated above, in Sec. 2 focuses on the domain and datatype taxonomies, while Secs. 3–4 focus on the category taxonomy. Note that we do not exploit the additional evidence that the category gives us for the classification at the domain and datatype level. As part of our future work, we intend to exploit this connection, as well as additional evidence (e.g., the data actually sent to/from the Web Service).

2 Supervised Domain and Datatype Classification

We begin by describing an algorithm for classifying HTML forms into semantic categories, as well as assigning semantic labels to each form field. These techniques are important as legacy HTML interfaces are migrated to Web Services.

2.1 Problem Formulation

Web form instances are structured objects: a form comprises one or more fields, and each field in turn comprises one or more terms. More precisely, a *form* F_i is a sequence of *fields*, written $F_i = [f_i^1, f_i^2, \ldots]$, and each field f_i^j is a bag of *terms*, written $f_i^j = [t_i^j(1), t_i^j(2), \ldots]$.

The Web form learning problem is as follows. The input is set of labeled forms and fields; that is, a set $\{F_1, F_2, \ldots\}$ of forms together with a domain $D_i \in \mathcal{D}$ for each form F_i, and a datatype $T_i^j \in \mathcal{T}$ for each field $f_i^j \in F_i$. The output is a form classifier; that is, a function that maps an unlabeled form F_i, to a predicted domain $D_i \in \mathcal{D}$, and a predicted datatype $T_i^j \in \mathcal{T}$ for each field $f_i^j \in F_i$.

We assume a domain taxonomy $\mathcal{D}$ and a datatype taxonomy $\mathcal{T}$. We use SMALLCAPS to indicate domains, so we might have $\mathcal{D} = \{$SEARCHBOOK, FINDJOB, QUERYFLIGHT, ...$\}$. SansSerif style indicates datatypes, so we might have $\mathcal{T} = \{\mathsf{BookTitle}, \mathsf{Salary}, \mathsf{DestAirport}, \ldots\}$.

2.2 Generative Model

Our solution to the Web form classification is based on a stochastic generative model of a hypothetical "Web service designer" creating a Web page to host a particular service. First, the designer first selects a domain $D_i \in \mathcal{D}$ according to some probability distribution $\Pr[D_i]$. For example, in our experiments, forms for finding books were quite frequent relative to forms for finding colleges, so $\Pr[\text{SEARCHBOOK}] \gg \Pr[\text{FINDCOLLEGE}]$.

Second, the designer selects datatypes $T_i^j \in \mathcal{T}$ appropriate to D_i, by drawing from some distribution $\Pr[T_i^j|D_i]$. For example, presumably $\Pr[\mathsf{BookTitle}|\text{SEARCHBOOK}] \gg \Pr[\mathsf{DestAirport}|\text{SEARCHBOOK}]$, because services for finding books usually involve a book's title, but rarely involve airports. On the other hand, $\Pr[\mathsf{BookTitle}|\text{QUERYFLIGHT}] \ll \Pr[\mathsf{DestAirport}|\text{QUERYFLIGHT}]$.

Finally, the designer writes the Web page that implements the form by coding each field in turn. More precisely, for each selected datatype T_i^j, the designer uses terms $t_i^j(k)$ drawn according to some distribution $\Pr[t_i^j(k)|T_i^j]$. For example, presumably $\Pr[\mathtt{title}|\mathsf{BookTitle}] \gg \Pr[\mathtt{city}|\mathsf{BookTitle}]$, because the term `title` is much more likely than `city` to occur in a field requesting a book title. On the other hand, presumably $\Pr[\mathtt{title}|\mathsf{DestAirport}] \ll \Pr[\mathtt{city}|\mathsf{DestAirport}]$.

2.3 Parameter Estimation

The learning task is to estimate the parameters of the stochastic generative model from a set of training data. The training data comprises a set of N Web forms $\mathcal{F} = \{F_1, \ldots, F_N\}$, where for each form F_i the learning algorithm is given the domain $D_i \in \mathcal{D}$ and the datatypes T_i^j of the fields $f_i^j \in F_i$.

The parameters to be estimated are the domain probabilities $\hat{\Pr}[D]$ for $D \in \mathcal{D}$, the conditional datatype probabilities $\hat{\Pr}[T|D]$ for $D \in \mathcal{D}$ and $T \in \mathcal{T}$, and the conditional term probabilities $\hat{\Pr}[t|T]$ for term t and $T \in \mathcal{T}$. We estimate these parameters based on their frequency in the training data: $\hat{\Pr}[D] = N_{\mathcal{F}}(D)/N$, $\hat{\Pr}[T|D] = M_{\mathcal{F}}(T,D)/M_{\mathcal{F}}(D)$, and $\hat{\Pr}[t|T] = W_{\mathcal{F}}(t,T)/W_{\mathcal{F}}(T)$, where $N_{\mathcal{F}}(D)$ is the number of forms in the training set $\mathcal{F}$ with domain D; $M_{\mathcal{F}}(D)$ is the total number of fields in all forms of domain D; $M_{\mathcal{F}}(T,D)$ is the number of fields of datatype T in all forms of domain D; $W_{\mathcal{F}}(T)$ is the total number of terms of all fields of datatype T; and $W_{\mathcal{F}}(t,T)$ is the number of occurrences of term t in all fields of datatype t.

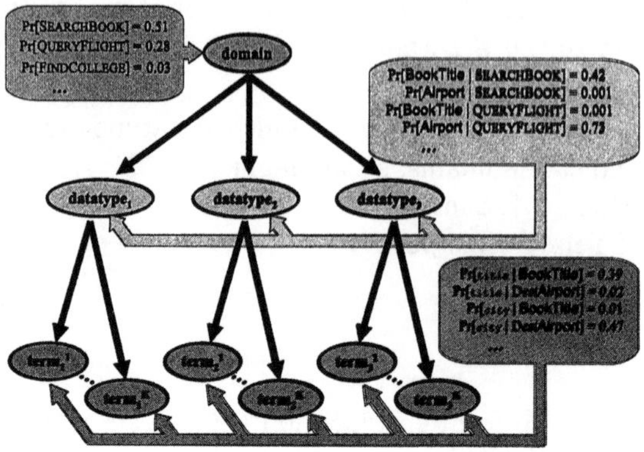

Fig. 2. The Bayesian network used to classify a Web form containing three fields.

2.4 Classification

Our approach to Web form classification involves converting a form into a Bayesian network. The network is a tree that reflects the generative model: a root node represents the form's domain, children represent the datatype of each field, and grandchildren encode the terms used to code each field.

In more detail, a Web form to be classified is converted into a three-layer tree-structured Bayesian network as follows. The first (root) layer contains just a single node **domain** that takes on values from the set of domains $\mathcal{D}$. The second layer consists of one child $\mathbf{datatype}_i$ of **domain** for each field in the form being classified, where each $\mathbf{datatype}_i$ take on values from the set $\mathcal{T}$.

The third (leaf) layer comprises a set of children $\{\mathbf{term}_i^1, \ldots, \mathbf{term}_i^K\}$ for each $\mathbf{datatype}_i$ node, where K is the number of terms in the field. The term nodes take on values from the vocabulary set $\mathcal{V}$, defined as the set of all terms that have occurred in the training data.

Fig. 2 illustrates the network that would be constructed for a form with three fields and K terms for each field. (Each field contains the same number K of terms/field for simplicity; in fact, the number of term nodes reflects the actual number of terms in the parent field.)

The conditional probability tables associated with each node correspond directly to the learned parameters mentioned earlier. That is, $\Pr[\mathbf{domain} = D] \equiv \hat{\Pr}(D)$, $\Pr[\mathbf{datatype}_i = T | \mathbf{domain} = D] \equiv \hat{\Pr}(T|D)$, and $\Pr[\mathbf{term}_i^k = t | \mathbf{datatype}_i = T] \equiv \hat{\Pr}(t|T)$. Note that the conditional probabilities tables are identical for all datatype nodes, and for all term nodes.

Given such a Bayesian network, classifying a form $F_i = [f_i^1, f_i^2, \ldots]$ involves "observing" the terms in each field (i.e., setting the probability $\Pr[\mathbf{term}_i^k = t_i^j(k)] \equiv 1$ for each term $t_i^j(k) \in f_i^j$), and then computing the maximum-likelihood form domain and field datatypes consistent with that evidence.

Domain taxonomy $\mathcal{D}$ and number of forms for each domain

SearchBook (44)	FindCollege (2)	SearchCollegeBook (17)
QueryFlight (34)	FindJob (23)	FindStockQuote (9)

Datatype taxonomy $\mathcal{T}$ (illustrative sample)

Address	NAdults	Airline	Author	BookCode	BookCondition	BookDetails
BookEdition	BookFormat	BookSearchType	BookSubject	BookTitle	NChildren	City
Class	College	CollegeSubject	CompanyName	Country	Currency	DateDepart
DateReturn	DestAirport	DestCity	Duration	Email	EmployeeLevel	...

Fig. 3. Subsets of the domain and datatype taxonomies used in the experiments.

2.5 Evaluation

We have evaluated our approach using a collection of 129 Web forms comprising 656 fields in total, for an average of 5.1 fields/form. As shown in Fig. 3, the domain taxonomy $\mathcal{D}$ used in our experiments contains 6 domains, and the datatype taxonomy $\mathcal{T}$ comprises 71 datatypes.

The forms were manually gathered by manually browsing Web forms indices such as InvisibleWeb.com for relevant forms. Each form was then inspected by hand to assign a domain to the form as a whole, and a datatype to each field.

After the forms were gathered, they were segmented into fields. We discuss the details below. For now, it suffices to say that we use HTML tags such as `<input>` and `<textarea>` to identify the fields that will appear to the user when the page is rendered. After a form has been segmented into fields, certain irrelevant fields (e.g., submit/reset buttons) are discarded. The remaining fields are then assigned a datatype.

A final subtlety is that some fields are not easily interpreted as "data", but rather indicate minor modifications to either the way the query is interpreted, or the output presentation. For example, there is a "help" option on one search services that augments the requested data with suggestions for query refinement. We discarded such fields on a case-by-case basis; a total of 12.1% of the fields were discarded in this way.

The final data-preparation step is to convert the HTML fragments into the "form = sequence of fields; field = bag of terms" representation. The HTML is first parsed into a sequence of tokens. Some of these tokens are HTML field tags (e.g., `<input>`, `<select>`, `<textarea>`). The form is segmented into fields by associating the remaining tokens with the nearest field. For example, "`<form> a <input name=f1> b c <textarea name=f2> d </form>`" would be segmented as "`a <input name=f1> b`" and "`c <textarea name=f2> d`".

The intent is that this segmentation process will associate with each field a bag of terms that provides evidence of the field's datatype. For example, our classification algorithm will learn to distinguish labels like "Book title" that are associated with BookTitle fields, from labels like "Title (Dr, Ms, ...)" that indicate PersonTitle.

Finally, we convert HTML fragments like "`Enter name: <input name=name1 type=text size=20> <br>`" that correspond to a particular field, into the field's bag of terms representation. We process each fragment as follows.

First, we discard HTML tags, retaining the values of a set of "interesting" attributes, such as an `<input>` tag's `name` attribute. The result is "`Enter name: name1`". Next, we tokenize the string at punctuation and space characters, convert all characters to lower case, apply Porter's stemming algorithm [11], discard stop words, and insert a special symbol encoding the field's HTML type (text, select, radio-button, etc). This yields the token sequence [`enter`, `name`, `name1`, **TypeText**]. Finally, we apply a set of term normalizations, such as replacing terms comprising just a single digit (letter) with a special symbol **SingleDigit** (**SingleLetter**), and deleting leading/trailing numbers. In this example the final result is the sequence [`enter`, `name`, `name`, **TypeText**].

2.6 Results

We begin by comparing our approach to two simple bag of terms baselines using a leave-one-out methodology. For domain classification, the baseline uses a single bag of all terms in the entire form. For datatype classification, the baseline approach is the naive Bayes algorithm over its bag of terms.

For domain prediction, our algorithm has an F1 score of 0.87 while the baseline scores 0.82. For datatype prediction, our algorithm has an F1 score of 0.43 while the baseline scores 0.38. We conclude that our "holistic" approach to form and field prediction is more accurate than a greedy baseline approach of making each prediction independently.

While our approach is far from perfect, we observe that form classification is extremely challenging, due both to noise in the underlying HTML, and the fact that our domain and datatype taxonomies contain many classes compared to traditional (usually binary!) text classification tasks.

While fully-automated form classification is our ultimate goal, an imperfect form classifier can still be useful in interactive, partially-automated scenarios in which a human gives the domain or (some of) the datatypes of a form to be labelled, and the classifier labels the remaining elements.

Our first experiment measures the improvement in datatype prediction if the Bayesian network is also provided as evidence the form's domain. In this case our algorithm has an F1 score of 0.51, compared to 0.43 mentioned earlier.

Our second experiment measures the improvement in domain prediction if evidence is provided for a randomly chosen fraction α of the fields' datatypes, for $0 \leq \alpha \leq 1$. $\alpha = 0$ corresponds to the fully automated situation in which no datatype evidence is provided; $\alpha = 1$ requires that a person provide the datatype of every field. As shown in Fig. 4, the domain classification F1 score increases rapidly as α approaches 1.

Our third investigation of semi-automated prediction involves the idea of ranking the predictions rather than requiring that the algorithm make just one prediction. In many semi-automated scenarios, the fact that the second- or third-ranked prediction is correct can still be useful even if the first is wrong. To formalize this notion, we calculate F1 based on treating the algorithm as correct if the true class is in the top R predictions as ranked by posterior probability. Fig. 4 shows the F1 score for predicting both domains and datatypes, as a

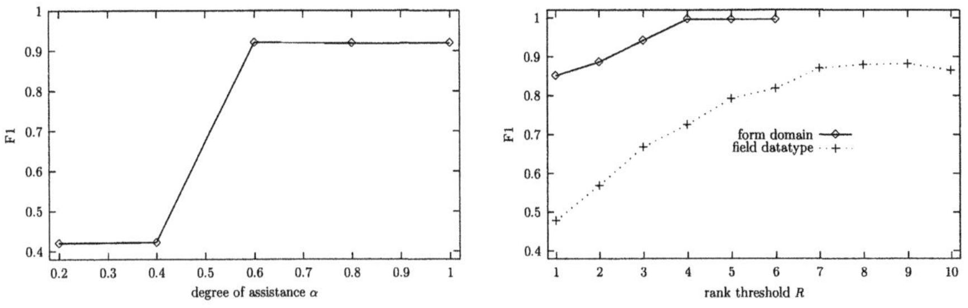

Fig. 4. F1 as a function of (left) the fraction α of field datatypes supplied by the user, and (right) the rank threshold R.

function of R. $R = 1$ corresponds to the cases described so far. We can see that relaxing R even slightly results in a dramatic increase in F1 score.

So far we have assumed unstructured datatype and domain taxonomies. However, domains and datatypes exhibit a natural hierarchical structure (e.g., "forms for finding something" vs. "forms for buying something"; or "fields related to book information" vs. "fields related to personal details"). It seems reasonable that in partially-automated settings, predicting a similar but wrong class is more useful than a dissimilar class.

To explore this issue, our research assistants converted their domain and datatype taxonomies into trees, creating additional abstract nodes to obtain reasonable and compact hierarchies. We used distance in these trees to measure the "quality" of a prediction, instead of a binary "right/wrong". For domain predictions, our algorithm's prediction is on average 0.40 edges away from the correct class, while the baseline algorithm's predictions are 0.55 edges away. For datatype prediction, our algorithm's average distance is 2.08 edges while the baseline algorithm averages 2.51. As above, we conclude that our algorithm outperforms the baseline.

3 Supervised Category Classification

The previous section addressed the classification of Web forms and their fields. We now address how to categorize Web Services. Since Web Services can export more than one operation, a Web Service corresponds loosely to a set of Web forms. As described in Sec. 1, we are therefore interested in classifying Web Services at the higher *category* level ("Business", "Games", etc.), rather than the lower *domain* level ("search for a book", "purchase a book", etc.) used for classifying Web forms.

3.1 Problem Formulation

We assume a set $\mathcal{C} = \{C_1, C_2, \ldots\}$ of Web Service categories. Each C_i corresponds formally to a subset of some domain ontology $\mathcal{D}$: $C_i \in 2^{\mathcal{D}}$ for each i.

Category taxonomy C and number of Web Services for each category			
BUSINESS (22)	COMMUNICATION (44)	CONVERTER (43)	COUNTRY INFO (62)
DEVELOPERS (34)	FINDER (44)	GAMES (9)	MATHEMATICS (10)
MONEY (54)	NEWS (30)	WEB (39)	*discarded* (33)

Fig. 5. Web Service categories C.

For example, the "Business" category would include any Web Service whose operations are related in some way to business.

We treat the determination of a Web Service's category as a text classification problem, where the text comes from the Web Service's WSDL description. Unlike standard texts, WSDL descriptions are highly structured. Our experiments demonstrate that selecting the right set of features from this structured text improves the performance of a learning classifier. By combining different classifiers it is possible to improve the performance even further, although for both the feature selection and the combination no general rule exists.

In the following sections, we describe our Web Service corpus, describe the methods we used for classification, and evaluate our approach.

3.2 Web Services Corpus

We gathered a corpus of 424 Web Services from SALCentral.org, a Web Service index. These Web Services were then manually classified into a hierarchical taxonomy C. To avoid bias, the person was a research student with no previous experience with Web Services. The person has the same information as given on SALCentral.org, and was allowed to inspect the WSDL description if necessary. The person was advised to adaptively create new categories while classifying the Web Services and was allowed to arrange the categories as a hierarchy.

The 424 Web Services were classified by our assistant into 25 top level categories. As shown in Fig. 5, we then discarded categories with less than seven instances, leaving 391 Web Services in eleven categories that were used in our experiments. The discarded Web Services tended to be quite obscure, such as a search tool for a music teacher in an area specified by ZIP code. Even for a human classifier, these services would be extremely hard to classify. Note that the distribution after discarding these classes is still highly skewed, ranging from nine Web Services in the "Games" category, to 62 services in the "Country Information" category.

3.3 Ensemble Learning

As shown in Fig. 6, the information available to our categorization algorithms comes from two sources. First, the algorithms use the Web Service description in the WSDL format, which is always available to determine a service's category. Second, in some cases, additional descriptive text is available, such as from a UDDI entry. In our experiments, we use the descriptive text provided by

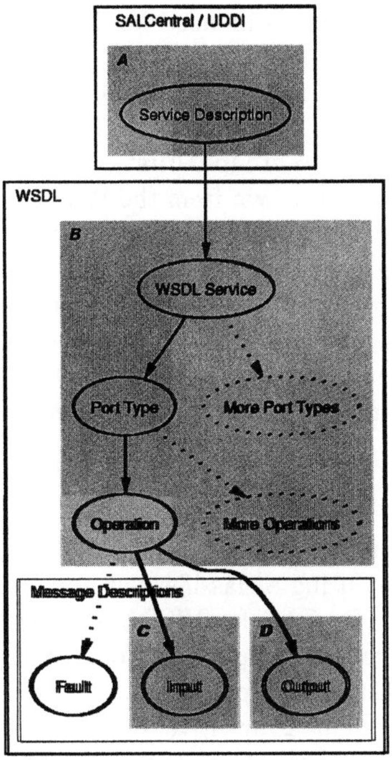

Fig. 6. Text structure for our Web Service corpus

SALCentral.org, since UDDI entries were not available. We parse the port types, operations and messages from the WSDL and extract names as well as comments from various "documentation" tags. We do not extract standard XML Schema data types like string or integer, or informations about the service provider. The extracted terms are stemmed with Porter's algorithm, and a stop-word list is used to discard low-information terms.

We experimented with four bags of words, denoted by *A*–*D*. The composition of these bags of words is marked in Fig. 6. We also used combinations of these bags of words, where e.g. *C+D* denotes a bag of words that consists of the descriptions of the input and output messages. We converted the resulting bag of words into a feature vector for supervised learning algorithms, with terms weighted based on simple frequency. We experimented with more sophisticated TFIDF-based weighting schemes, but they did not improve the results.

As learning algorithms, we used the Naive Bayes, SVM and HyperPipes algorithms as implemented in Weka [15]. We combined several classifiers in an ensemble learning approach. Ensemble learners make a prediction by voting together the predictions of several "base" classifiers. Ensemble learning has been shown in a variety of tasks to be more reliable than the base classifiers: the whole is often greater than the sum of its parts. To combine two or more classifiers, we multiplied the confidence values obtained from the multi-class classifier implementation. For some settings, we tried weighting of these values as well, but this did not improve the overall performance. We denote a combination of different algorithms or different feature sets by slashes, e.g. Naive Bayes($A/B+C+D$) denoting two Naive Bayes classifiers, one trained on the plain text description only and one trained one all terms extracted from the WSDL.

We split our tests into two groups. First, we tried to find the best split of bags of words using the terms drawn from the WSDL only (bags of words B–D). These experiments are of particular interest, because the WSDL is usually automatically generated (except for the occasional comment tags), and the terms that can be extracted from that are basically operation and parameter names. Note that we did not use any transmitted data, but only the parameter descriptions and the XML schema. Second, we look how the performance improves, if we include the plain text description (bag of words A).

3.4 Evaluation

We evaluated the different approaches using a leave-one-out methodology.

Our results show that using a classifier with one big bag of words that contains everything (i.e. $A+B+C+D$ for WSDL and descriptions, or $B+C+D$ for the WSDL-only tests) generally performs worst. We included these classifiers in Fig. 7 as baselines. Ensemble approaches where the bags of words are split generally perform better. This is intuitive, because we can assume a certain degree of independence between for example the terms that occur in the plain text descriptions and the terms that occur in the WSDL description. What is a bit more surprising is that for some settings we achieve very good results if we use only a subset of the available features, i.e. only one of the bags of words. So, in these cases, sometimes one part is greater than the whole. However, we could not find a generic rule for how to best split the available bags of words, as this seems to be strongly dependent on the algorithm and the actual data set.

Space restrictions prevent us from showing all our results, so in Fig. 7 we give the accuracy for the classifiers that performed best. Note that SVM generally performs better than Naive Bayes, except for the classifier where we used the plain text descriptions only. An ensemble consisting of three SVM classifiers performs good for both the WSDL-only setting and also when including the descriptions. However, the best results are achieved by other combinations.

In a machine learning setting with a split feature set it is also possible to use Co-Training [1] to improve classification accuracy, if unlabeled data is present. In preliminary experiments we added 370 unlabeled Web Services. In this particular setting we could gain no advantage using Co-Training, but due to time restrictions we were not able to fully explore this area.

For a semi-automatic assignment of the category to a Web Service, it is not always necessary that the algorithm predicts the category exactly, although this is of course desirable. A human developer would also save a considerable amount of work if he or she only had to choose between a small number of categories. For this reason, we also report the accuracy when we allow near misses. Fig. 7 shows how the classifiers improve when we increase this tolerance threshold. For our best classifier, the correct class is in the top 3 predictions 82% of the time.

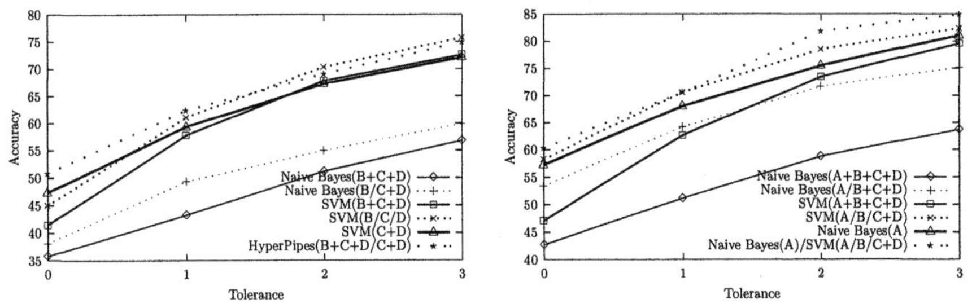

Fig. 7. Classification accuracy for WSDL only (left), and both WSDL and descriptions (right).

4 Unsupervised Category Clustering

As a third approach towards our goal of automatically creating Web Services metadata, we explored the use of unsupervised clustering algorithms to automatically discover the semantic categories of a group of Web Services.

4.1 Clustering Algorithms

We tested five clustering algorithms on our collection of Web Services. First, we tried a simple k-nearest-neighbour algorithm. Hierarchical group average and complete link algorithms (e.g. [14,12]) serve as representatives of traditional approaches. We also tried a variant of the group average clusterer that we call Common-Term, and the Word-IC algorithm [16]. The Word-IC algorithm, unlike the other clustering algorithms, does not rely on a traditional cosine based similarity measure between the documents (i.e. in the web services in our case), but hierarchically merges clusters based on the number of intersecting words and a global quality function. The global quality function also serves as a halting criterion. The Common Term algorithm halts, when the top level clusters do not share any terms. For the group average and complete link algorithms, we used a minimum similarity between documents as a halting criterion. As a baseline, we partition the Web Services into eleven random clusters.

Our Common-Term algorithm differs from the standard group average clustering in the way the centroid document vector is computed. Instead of using all terms from all the sub-clusters, only the terms that occur in all sub-clusters form the centroid are used. Like the Word-IC algorithm, our hope is that this leads to short and concise cluster labels.

We use the standard cosine approach with TFIDF weighting to measure the similarity $\sigma(a, b)$ between two "documents" a and b.

4.2 Quality Metrics for Clustering

Evaluating clustering algorithms is a task that is considerably harder than evaluating classifications, because we cannot always assign a cluster to a certain reference class. Several quality measures have been proposed; see [13] for a recent survey.

We have evaluated our clustering algorithms using Zamir's quality function [16], and the normalized mutual information quality metric described in [13]. We also introduce a novel measure inspired by the well-known precision and recall metrics that correlates well with other quality measures and has a simple probabilistic interpretation.

In the literature on evaluating clustering algorithms, precision and recall have only been used on a per-class basis. This assumes that a mapping between clusters and reference classes exists. The fraction of documents in a cluster that belong to the "dominant" class, i.e. the precision assuming the cluster corresponds to the dominant class, is known as purity. Usage of the purity measure is problematic, if the cluster contains an (approximately) equal number of objects from two or more classes. This clustering might not even be unintuitive, if it is merely the case that the granularity of the clustering is coarser than that of the reference classes.

We modify the definitions of precision and recall to consider *pairs* of objects, rather than individual objects. Let n be the number of objects. Then there are $\frac{n(n-1)}{2}$ pairs of objects. Each such pair must fall into one of four categories: the objects are put in the same class by both the reference clusters and the clustering algorithm, they are clustered together but in difference reference clusters, etc.

clustered together?		yes	no
in same reference class?	yes	a	b
	no	c	d

If a, b, c and d are the number of object pairs in each case, then $a+b+c+d = \frac{n(n-1)}{2}$. Precision and recall can now be computed the same way as in standard information retrieval: precision $= a/(a+c)$ and recall $= a/(a+b)$. Other metrics such as F1 or accuracy are defined in the usual way.

Note that there is a simple probabilistic interpretation of these metrics. Precision is equivalent to the conditional probability that two documents are in the same reference class given they are in the same cluster. Recall is equivalent to the conditional probability that two documents are in the same cluster given they are in the same reference class. Let $\mathcal{R}$ denote the event that a document pair is in the same reference class and $\mathcal{C}$ denote that a document pair is in the same cluster. Then we have that precision $= P(\mathcal{R} \wedge \mathcal{C} \mid \mathcal{C}) = P(\mathcal{R} \mid \mathcal{C})$, and recall $= P(\mathcal{R} \wedge \mathcal{C} \mid \mathcal{R}) = P(\mathcal{C} \mid \mathcal{R})$.

Note that precision is biased towards small clusters, but because we are considering document pairs it is not trivially maximized by placing every document in its own cluster. Recall is biased against large clusters, as it reaches the maximum when all documents are placed in one cluster. Finally, we observe that precision and recall are symmetric, in the sense that precision$(A, B) =$ recall(B, A) for any two clusterings A and B.

4.3 Evaluation

Fig. 8 shows the precision and F1 scores of the clusters generated by the various algorithms we tried. We do not report Zamir's quality measure $Q(\mathrm{C})$ or the normalized mutual information measure $Q(\mathrm{NMI})$, because they are highly correlated with our precision metric. Precision is biased towards a large number of small clusters, because it is easier for a clusterer to find a small number of similar services multiple times than to find a large number of similar clusters. Therefore we believe that also $Q(\mathrm{C})$ and $Q(\mathrm{NMI})$ are in fact biased towards small clusters, although it is claimed that $Q(\mathrm{NMI})$ is not biased, and although they do not reach their optimal value for singleton clusters.

Not surprisingly, none of the algorithms does particularly well, because the Web Services clustering problem is quite challenging. In many cases even humans disagree on the correct classification. For example, SALCentral.org manually organized its Web Services into their own taxonomy, and their classification bears little resemblance to ours. Furthermore, we have 11 categories in our reference classification, which is a rather high number. However, in terms of precision, all our algorithms outperform the random baseline.

All clustering algorithms tend to "over-refine", meaning that they produce far more clusters than classes exist in the reference data. For the group average and complete-link algorithms, the number of clusters could be decreased if we set a lower minimum similarity, but especially the group average algorithm then tends to produce very large clusters with more than 100 Web Services.

Note that recall is strongly affected by such an over-refinement. In our experiments, it turns out that the F1 (see Fig. 8), is largely dominated by recall. However, precision is more important than recall in the application scenarios that motivate our research. Specifically, consider generic automatic data integration scenarios in which Web Services that have been clustered together are then automatically invoked simultaneously. For example, a comparison shopping agent would invoke operations from all Web Services that were clustered into a "E-Commerce" category. Precision is more important than recall for the same reason why precision is more important in today's document search engines: in a Web populated by millions of Web Services, the danger is not that a relevant service will be missed, but that irrelevant services will be inadvertently retrieved.

We conclude from these data that Web Service category clustering is feasible based just on WSDL descriptions, through clearly hand-crafted text descriptions (e.g., SALCentral.org's description or text drawn from UDDI entries) produce even better results.

5 Discussion

Future Work. We are currently extending our classification and clustering algorithms in several directions. Our approaches ignore a valuable sources of evidence—such as the actual data passed to/from a Web Service—and it would

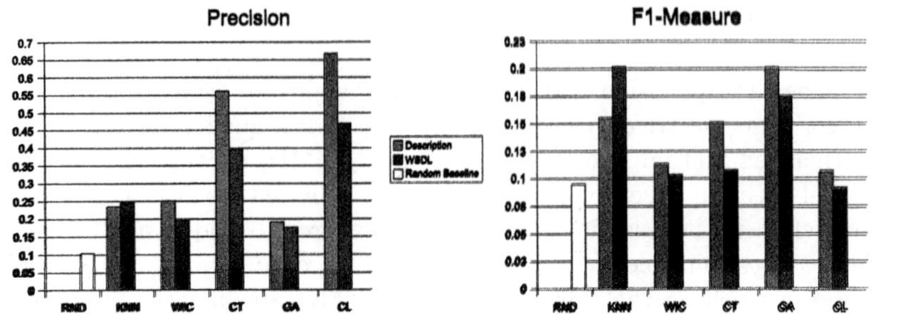

RND: Random baseline, KNN: k-Nearest-Neighbour, WIC: Word-IC, CT: Common Term, GA: Group Average, CL: Complete Link

Fig. 8. Precision and F1 for the various clustering algorithms.

be interesting to incorporate such evidence into our algorithms. Our clustering algorithm could be extended in a number of ways, such as using statistical methods such as latent semantic analysis as well as thesauri like WordNet.

We envision a single algorithm that incorporates the category, domain, datatype and term evidence shown in Fig. 1. To classify all the operations and inputs of a Web Service at the same time, a Bayesian network like the one in Fig. 2 could be constructed for each operation, and then a higher-level category node could be introduced whose children are the domain nodes for each of the operations.

Ultimately, our goal is to develop enabling technologies that could allow for the semi-automatic generation of Web Services metadata. We would like to use our techniques to develop a toolkit that emits metadata conforming to Semantic Web standards such as DAML/DAML-S.

Related Work. There has been some work on matching of Web Services (e.g. [10,2]), but they require manually-generated explicit semantic metadata.

Clustering is a well-known technique, although it has not yet been applied to Web Services. Besides the traditional group-average or single-link approaches, newer algorithms like Word-IC or the Scatter/Gather-algorithms [4] exist.

The search capabilities of UDDI are very restricted, though various extensions are available or under development (e.g. UDDIe [www.cs.cf.ac.uk/user/A.-Shaikhali/uddie]). Kerschberg et al are planning to apply the techniques they introduced in WebSifter [6] to UDDI.

When we actually want to simultaneously invoke multiple similar Web Services and aggregate the results, we encounter the problem of XML schema mapping (e.g., [5,8]).

Conclusions. The emerging Web Services protocols represent exciting new directions for the Web, but interoperability requires that each service be described by a large amount of semantic metadata "glue". We have presented three approaches to automatically generating such metadata, and evaluated our approach on a collection of Web Services and forms.

Although we a far from being able to automatically create semantic metadata, we believe that the methods we have presented here are a reasonable first step. Our preliminary results indicate that some of the requisite semantic metadata can be semi-automatically generated using machine learning, information retrieval and clustering techniques.

Acknowledgments. This research was supported by grants SFI/01/F.1/C015 from Science Foundation Ireland, and N00014-03-1-0274 from the US Office of Naval Research.

References

1. Avrim Blum and Tom Mitchell. Combining labeled and unlabeled data with co-training. In *COLT: Proceedings of the Workshop on Computational Learning Theory, Morgan Kaufmann Publishers*, 1998.
2. J. Cardoso. *Quality of Service and Semantic Composition of Workflows.* PhD thesis, Department of Computer Science, University of Georgia, Athens, GA, 2002.
3. F. Ciravegna. Adaptive information extraction from text by rule induction and generalization. In *17th Int. Joint Conference on Artifical Intelligence*, 2001.
4. D. Cutting, J. Pedersen, D. Karger, and J. Tukey. Scatter/gather: A cluster-based approach to browsing large document collections. In *Proceedings of the Fifteenth Annual International ACM SIGIR Conference on Research and Development in Information Retrieval*, pages 318–329, 1992.
5. A. Doan, P. Domingos, and A. Halevy. Reconciling schemas of disparate data sources: A machine-learning approach. In *Proc. SIGMOD Conference*, 2001.
6. L. Kerschberg, W. Kim, and A. Scime. Intelligent web search via personalizable meta-search agents. pages 1345–1358, 2002.
7. N. Kushmerick. Wrapper induction: Efficiency and expressiveness. *Artificial Intelligence*, 118(1–2):15–68, 2000.
8. S. Melnik, H. Molina-Garcia, and E. Rahm. Similariy flooding: A versatile graph matching algorithm. In *Proc. of the International Conference on Data Engineering (ICDE), 2002.*
9. I. Muslea, S. Minton, and C. Knoblock. A Hierachical Approach to Wrapper Induction. In *Proc. 3rd Int. Conf. Autonomous Agents*, pages 190–197, 1999.
10. M. Paolucci, T. Kawamura, T. Payne, and K. Sycara. Semantic matchmaking of web services capabilities. In *Int. Semantic Web Conference*, 2002.
11. M.F. Porter. An algorithm for suffix stripping. *Program*, 14(3):130–137, 1980.
12. G. Salton and M. McGill. *Introduction to Modern Information Retrieval.* McGraw-Hill, 1983.
13. Alexander Strehl. *Relationship-based Clustering and Cluster Ensembles for High-dimensional Data Mining.* PhD thesis, University of Texas, Austin, 2002.
14. C.J. van Rijsbergen. *Information Retrieval.* Butterworths, London, 2nd edition, 1979.
15. Ian H. Witten and Eibe Frank. *Data Mining: Practical machine learning tools with Java implementations.* Morgan Kaufmann, San Francisco.
16. Oren Zamir, Oren Etzioni, Omid Madani, and Richard M. Karp. Fast and intuitive clustering of web documents. In *Knowledge Discovery and Data Mining*, pages 287–290, 1997.

Semantic Markup for Semantic Web Tools: A DAML-S Description of an RDF-Store

Debbie Richards[1] and Marta Sabou[2]

[1] Div. of I.C.S., Macquarie University, Sydney, Australia
richards@ics.mq.edu.au
[2] Dept. of AI, Vrije Universiteit, Amsterdam, The Netherlands
marta@cs.vu.nl

Abstract. Easy integration of available tools will be a key success factor for the future of the Semantic Web. We envision that semantic descriptions of the tools themselves will play an important part in addressing this issue. Motivated by this vision we used DAML-S (a key initiative to support automated management of Web services) to describe Sesame (an RDF(S) storage and query engine). This paper discusses the major problems that we encountered as well as suggested solutions. This work is relevant to other Semantic Web research groups who wish to annotate their tools or to use annotated tools. Also, we hope to offer helpful input to the DAML-S coalition in the further development of their standard.

1 Introduction

Interest in the Semantic Web (SW) and Web services is increasing. SW technology promises to support a second generation of the World Wide Web by turning it from a repository for human consumption to a source of information and services that can be utilized by software agents. The need for easy discovery and integration of web-accessible services has fuelled the rapid development of the Web Services field. While many standards have been offered to support inter-operability of Web services, SW technology promises to increase automation in service discovery and integration on the basis of semantic markup. A major initiative in this direction is DAML-S [7], a DAML+OIL ontology which allows describing Web services in a machine interpretable way. It is claimed that DAML-S descriptions will automate the discovery, invocation, composition, interoperation and monitoring of web services [7].

As a result, an increasing number of efforts have been reported which involve the usage of DAML-S, however many of them do not use the whole language. Several projects use only certain parts of the DAML-S ontology, eg. matchmaking research tends to focus on the Profile ontology ([6], [14], [11]) while composition only requires the Process ontology [17]. Often, these parts are heavily extended rather then reused: [4] enriches the Process ontology, [18] extends the Profile ontology with bio-informatics related properties, [13] extends the specification of conditions. Finally, some papers mention use of complete DAML-S as is but give no details about their experiences.

The variety of application domains where DAML-S is used is also increasing. The first described services were fictitious (ex. the examples offered on the DAML-S site), just

D. Fensel et al. (Eds.): ISWC 2003, LNCS 2870, pp. 274–289, 2003.

like the services used for demonstrating solutions for complex tasks such as composition or matchmaking ([17], [11], [12]). However, recently different communities have started to experiment with describing their own real-life services, such as the merging of agent technology with DAML-S ([9], [15]). Important developments are reported in the field of bioinformatics as well [18]. Also, wishing to describe mathematical services, [3] concludes that DAML-S offers a good base, however they define their own description language - Mathematical Service Description Language (MSDL). Last but not least, e-commerce services are described: a currency converter and a description of Amazon[1]. Another class of services consists of Semantic Web services, such as ontology storage facilities (Sesame [5]), validators[2], annotation tools[3]. Surprisingly however, even if many Semantic Web related tools are made available as web-services, to our knowledge there is no work for describing such services.

We address this lack by using the entire DAML-S[4] ontology and WSDL to describe a typical SW Tool, Sesame [5][5]. We found that Sesame exhibits a set of characteristics which were not previously discussed for any particular group of services and therefore made its modelling non-trivial. First, it has a modular architecture composed of independent components which can be used in arbitrary combinations to fulfill certain tasks. In contrast, Web services described to-date, even if modular, have a well-defined workflow model and their components are not usable stand-alone. Second, it uses complex data types requiring a shift from the current practice of perceiving inputs and outputs as atomic values. Third, there are several constraints between its Input/Output parameters.

Naturally, the question arises: *Is DAML-S expressive enough to model these characteristics?* This paper attempts to answer this question since it is likely that such characteristics exist for other (SW) tools as well. Therefore the problems that we encountered are likely to be typical of the problems other people will encounter with publishing their tools as a web-service. Thus we provide our solutions and recommendations in terms of usage guidelines and language extensions to DAML-S.

We start with two introductory sections about the languages used (2) and about Sesame (3). Our findings relate to three main topics and are grouped in the next three sections (4, 5, 6). We conclude and suggest topics for future work in 7.

2 Languages for (Semantic) Service Description

2.1 DAML-S

The DAML-S ontology is conceptually divided into three sub-ontologies for specifying *what a service does*, *how the service works* and *how the service is implemented.* Accordingly, each DAML-S description has three major parts.

The *Profile*[6] describes what the service does so that it can be discovered at matchmaking time. It contains the contact information of providers, an extensible set of features

[1] http://www.daml.org/services/.

[2] DAML Validator at http://www.daml.org/validator/.

[3] Annotea – http://annotest.w3.org/annotations.

[4] This paper was written for DAML-S v.0.7. and updated for v0.9.

[5] Latest version available at http://www.cs.vu.nl/~marta/services/sesame/owl/.

[6] http://www.daml.org/services/daml-s/0.7/Profile.daml

that specify characteristics of the service and a functionality description by specifying the inputs, outputs, preconditions and effects (IOPE's) of the service.

The *Process*[7] presents the internal working of the service in terms of the internal processes, their process model and the internal data-flow. This information can be used during matchmaking but is aimed to assist execution monitoring. The Process describes the IOPE's of the service from a different perspective, but naturally links between the Profile and the Process of the model exist. Taken together they represent the conceptual level description of the service.

The *Grounding*[8] specifies the operational level details of the service by linking the conceptual level descriptions to the WSDL (Web Services Description Language) description of the service. The WSDL file contains the implementation details of the service such as message exchange formats and network protocols so that automatic invocation of the service is possible.

This layered description is used in the following way. First the Profile is inspected to see if the service has the desired capability. Further, the Process Model can give more detailed information about how the service works internally. This description can also be inspected during matchmaking. Finally, if the service conforms to the requirements, the Grounding specifies the implementation details needed for executing the service.

2.2 WSDL

WSDL is an industry standard for describing web-accessible services. WSDL has considerable support from industry and increasing tool-support (WSDL generators, editors). As an XML-based language, WSDL is machine processable: it is a structured (and standardized) way to describe web-interfaces. However the intended meaning (semantics) of the interface elements is interpretable only by human readers.

In WSDL a service is seen as a collection of network endpoints which operate on messages. Each WSDL document specifies an abstract description of the main components of the service and then binds this interface to concrete implementation details.

At the abstract description level types, messages, operations and portTypes are defined. First, one can define complex data types using XML Schema. Then a set of messages are specified by describing the name and the type of their parts. These messages represent either an input parameter set or the output of some abstract operations. Operations are conceptually grouped together in a PortType.

Through the binding part of the description the elements of the abstract interface are bound to concrete network protocols and message formats (SOAP, HTTP) and the actual network address of the service is specified.

3 Sesame

This section briefly introduces Sesame (3.1) and states some issues that we want our modelling to reflect (3.2).

[7] http://www.daml.org/services/daml-s/0.7/Process.daml

[8] http://www.daml.org/services/daml-s/0.7/Grounding.daml

3.1 Description

Sesame is an RDF(S) repository and query engine [5]. As such it can provide valuable support for ontology-based applications. It can be used either as a part of an application or it can be accessed via a web-interface. Currently both HTTP and SOAP communication protocols are available. Sesame's HTTP interface[9] makes available six different functionalities at six different URLs. We shortly present these functionalities including in brackets the URL extension where they are published.[10]

A Sesame server contains a set of password-protected repositories. So called public repositories are accessible without any login information. Through the server's HTTP interface one can request a list of all repositories which are available for a specified login, including the public ones (*listRepositories*). As a storage facility Sesame offers functionality to upload data and to interact with it. The data upload functionality adds data with a specified URL or sent as a string (*addData*). The content of a repository can be deleted completely (*clearRepository*). Further, deletion at the statement level is also supported (*removeStatements*). The user can retrieve the whole content of the repository (*extractRDF*) or alternatively only the schema information, only the instance information or both. A more refined data extraction method, the query method (*performRQLQuery* and *performRDQLQuery*), transforms Sesame into a query engine. There is no predefined way in which these functionalities should be used. In fact, they are highly self-contained and can be used stand-alone rather than in combination with other functionalities.

3.2 Modelling Requirements

We expect that our service markup will be used by intelligent agents which will reason with the provided semantic data. Also, for operational level integration all needed technical information must be properly captured. This requirement is fulfilled by DAML-S which allows both conceptual and syntactic level specifications (through WSDL).

At the conceptual level the ***semantics of the offered functionality*** has to be specified. There are multiple ways to do this. First, one can specify a service by *describing its parameters*. This issue is treated throughout the paper but mostly in section 6. Second, the meaning of a service depends on its relation to other services. It is desirable to describe how these components relate to each other so that an intelligent service could determine usage patterns for fulfilling certain tasks. One dependency between services is that of *composition*, when a certain service is composed out of multiple other services. Since this is the case of Sesame we investigate this issue in section 4. Another way to describe interdependencies is to specify *algebraic properties*. Examples are:

- DeleteStatement is idempotent: doing it twice is the same as doing it once. (Same for addStatement).
- Querying for a statement after having added it gives the statement back as a result.
- Querying for a statement after having deleted it gives a null result.
- Removing a statement after having added it is a null operation.

[9] See detailed description at http://sesame.aidministrator.nl/publications/users/ch06s02.html.

[10] A base URL of the form "http://HOSTNAME/SESAMEDIR/servlets" proceeds each extension – capitalized words depend on the server installation.

These are the real semantics of the operations, i.e. these properties really specify what it means to delete a statement, or to add one. We do not treat them in this paper.

Another issue is ***linking between the semantic and syntactic descriptions*** of a service. It is desirable that a single conceptual description can be mapped to descriptions of different technical implementations of the same service. In Sesame's case, it should be possible to ground its semantic description to the syntactic descriptions of all its different interfaces (HTTP, SOAP, RMI). We only experimented with linking to a WSDL description of an HTTP interface, however we encountered some problems (5.2).

Still related to grounding, technical descriptions used in combination with semantic ones should undergo minor changes so that they are still usable by tools which do not require semantic data. More on this in section 6.2.

4 Specifying Service Semantics

4.1 Splitting up Sesame

In order to satisfy the various needs of service providers, DAML-S does not impose a particular modelling style leaving a gap between conceptual considerations and the actual modelling. This happens with the very notion of service. Conceptually, they define web services as "Web sites that [...] allow one to effect some action or change in the world" [7]. Further they differentiate between simple and complex services. A simple service invokes a single web-accessible program and there is no interaction with the user during its execution. Request-response services are regarded as simple services. A complex service is composed of multiple simple services.

In the light of these definitions Sesame and each of its functionalities are web-services, where the functionalities are simple services and Sesame is a complex service. Deciding on the actual modelling was not so trivial. We present two of a number of alternatives we tried, underlining their benefits and disadvantages.

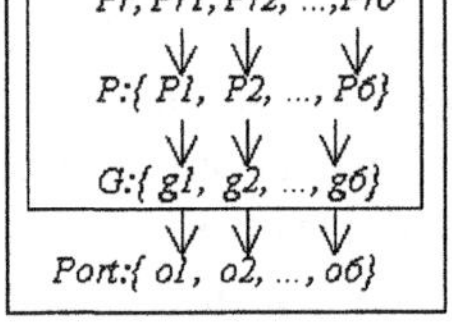

Fig. 1. Traditional Service Modelling

We first adopted the modelling style used in the existing DAML-S examples (see schematic representation in fig. 1). Accordingly, we have created a single *Service* instance, *Sesame*. The component functionalities were modelled as *AtomicProcesses (P1, ...P6)* within the *ProcessModel (P)*. Because, there is no fixed workflow between the components of Sesame, i.e. the six functionalities can be used in arbitrary ways to solve tasks, the workflow model that was closest to our needs was *process:choice*. This expresses very little about the relationships between the components and thus its semantic value is very weak. We tried to compensate this at the *Profile* (*Pr*) level where we have associated multiple *Profile* instances with the service, one for each functionality *(Pr1, ...Pr6)* and one for the global functionality of Sesame (*P* as an *OntologyStore*). Finally, the *Grounding (G)* of Sesame contains six *AtomicProcessGrounding* entities *(g1, ..g6)*, one for each internal process and its corresponding WSDL operation *(o1, ...o6)*.

This approach has the following limitations. First, several of the simple services offered alternative interfaces and implementations. Because only the *Service* concept can have different groundings (and not atomic processes), a different implementation of an atomic service results in a different grounding for the whole service. Therefore we face a combinatorial explosion of groundings for the general service whenever a component offers a new implementation. Second, at the *Profile* level, there is no indication of the relationship between the seven services. Third, even if all services are visible at matchmaking time (since their *Profile* is explicitly mentioned), one needs to interpret the full description of the complex service when using just a simple service.

Note that this style of description works fine for web services composed of simple services which (1) do not have meaning outside the service and (2) are used according to a fixed workflow. In such cases a single Profile suffices to describe the task their execution can achieve. There is no need to advertise all of them since they cannot be used stand-alone anyway. However, none of these assumptions apply to Sesame: its functionalities can be used in any combination and also just alone.

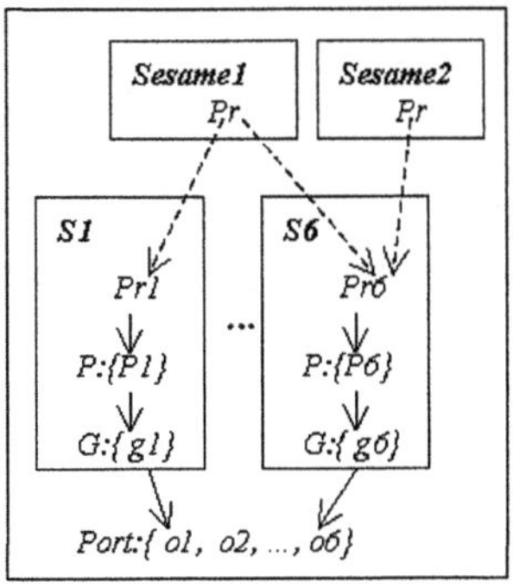

Fig. 2. Our Modelling

Due to these considerations we decided to model each functionality as a *Service (S1,...S6)*, as represented in fig. 2. Two of the limitations of the previous model are solved: (1) the overhead of declaring a new implementation of a simple service is reduced to declaring a single atomic grounding and (2) when using a service only its own description needs to be interpreted. However, the issue of expressing how these services inter-relate is still open. Optimally we would like to express that sets of these services can be used upon a certain Sesame server. Depending on the exposed services, different Sesame servers can have different type: some can offer only storage functionality (*OntologyStore - Sesame2*), some offer querying facilities (*QueryEngine*), some offer both (*OntologyStore and QueryEngine - Sesame1*). We want to express composition at the *Profile* rather than the *Process* level. We implemented this by building a domain ontology in which we enrich some of the DAML-S concepts as discussed in the next section.

4.2 The Role and Use of Domain Knowledge

Externally defined knowledge plays a major role in each DAML-S description. DAML-S offers a generic framework to describe a service, but to make it truly useful, domain knowledge is required. As DAML-S supports the inclusion of external knowledge in the service descriptions we are not addressing a problem in this section. Instead, since ontology acquisition is itself a difficult and time-consuming task we are offering the ontology we developed to support the description of Sesame and our reasoning leading to its development. Also, we show how this domain knowledge allowed us to model Sesame in the desired way.

The Domain Ontology. Matchmaking and integration of a set of web-services becomes easy if they are defined using the same rich domain ontology. A widely used domain ontology (1) should reflect terms accepted by a large community while (2) being easy to extend with new knowledge and (3) straightforward to integrate in the service descriptions. We tried to achieve all this in our domain ontology[11].

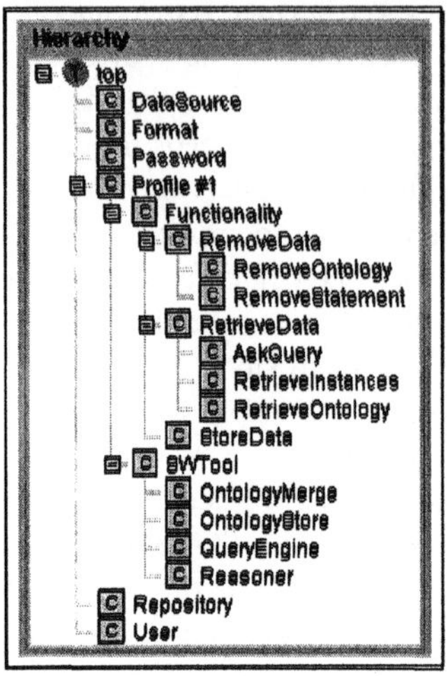

Fig. 3. The Domain Ontology[12]

Previously (section 4.1) we have motivated the need to express composition of services not at the *Process* but rather at the *Profile* level. To achieve this, in our domain ontology we make a conceptual difference between tools and their functionalities and define tool-profiles in terms of the functionality-profiles they provide. In terms of modelling this involved two inter-related constructions.

First, we specialized the DAML-S *profile:Profile* into *SWTool* and *Functionality*. The subclasses of the first concept reflect the main tool categories described by a thorough survey of existing Semantic Web Tools[10]. The second concept is the superclass for all functionalities. For now we have declared the functionality types relevant for Sesame and grouped them under more generic concepts. For example, we consider *RetrieveOntology* and *AskQuery* as methods for data retrieval. Their superclass, *RetrieveData*, can be extended with other methods specific to other tools which fulfill the same function.

Second, we have declared the new property, (*hasFunctionality*), which allows us to specify the kind of functionalities that a certain tool offers (depicted as part of the DomainOntology in fig.4). This construction allows us to define SWTool-s by imposing constraints on the type of functionalities they have. For example, an *OntologyStore* might allow a functionality of type *StoreData* and *must* offer a *RetrieveOntology* functionality. Also, a *QueryEngine* must provide an *AskQuery* functionality. Further, the ontology contains a set of terms needed to describe Sesame, such as *Repository, User, Password* etc. See the hierarchy of the main concepts in fig. 3.

We fulfilled the requirements for a widely used domain ontology. First, we used concepts from the largest survey about Semantic Web tools within the SW community and extended the concepts of DAML-S, which is growing into a standard. Second, our model is easy to extend: new functionality types can be added and new tool types can be defined using existing or newly added functionality. The third issue, that of easy use for service description is demonstrated in the next section.

Using Domain Knowledge in DAML-S Descriptions. Domain concepts are used for several reasons in a DAML-S description. First, they express the meaning of the offered functionality at the *Profile* level. This section is devoted to this first issue. Second, domain knowledge can be used to describe the IOPE's both at the *Process* and the *Profile* level, as will shortly be demonstrated in section 5.1. Finally, during the grounding process, WSDL descriptions are enriched with domain knowledge (as shown in section 6.2).

[11] http://www.cs.vu.nl/~marta/services/swTools.owl

[12] Image created with OilEd3.5, http://oiled.man.ac.uk/

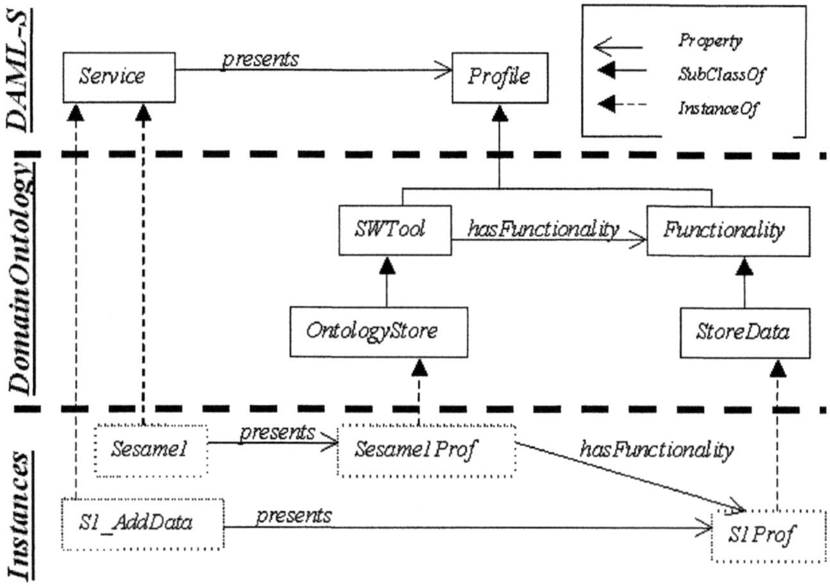

Fig. 4. Use of Domain Knowledge in Profiles

One indicates the overall functionality of a service by declaring its *Profile* as being of a type documented in the Domain Ontology. Figure 4 demonstrates this process. *Sesame1* is a *Service* instance and its *Profile*, *Sesame1Prof* is of the type *OntologyStore* which was declared in the domain ontology. Similarly, each individual functionality is declared as a service. For example, for the AddData functionality, we declared a *Service* instance, *S1AddData*, and associated with it a *Profile* instance of type *StoreData*.

By declaring Sesame's *Profile* of type *OntologyStore* we inherit the *hasFunctionality* property defined for any *SWTool*. At the instance level, we used this property to associate *Sesame1Prof* with *S1Prof*. This indicates that the functionality offered by the *Sesame1* service relies on the functionality of the *S1AddData* service.

It is very easy to define different Sesame instances with different combinations of these functionalities. This is useful in practical scenarios when different user groups can access different functionality. For example, a company which stores its data in Sesame may wish to make it available both for its customers and employees. Customers will only be allowed to read the stored data. Therefore, that particular service instance of Sesame will only advertise a data reading capability. On the contrary, employees can both add and read data, therefore their service instance will point to both functionalities.

We managed to express composition (interdependency) at the *Profile* rather than just at the *Process* level, as originally possible with DAML-S. At matchmaking time, if someone wants to use Sesame he gets a list of all needed service profiles and can discover the individual services associated to those profiles.

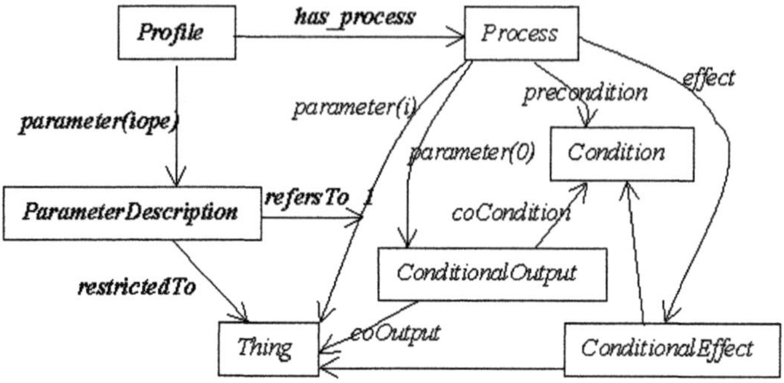

Fig. 5. Profile to Process bridge

5 Linking between Parts of the Description

The *ServiceProfile, ServiceModel* and *ServiceGrounding* are three different but linked descriptions of the same service. Identifying these links and specifying them correctly ensures the consistency of the description.

5.1 Profile to Process Bridge

A *Profile* contains several links to the *Process*. Figure 5 shows these links, where terms in bold-face belong to the *Profile* ontology and the rest to the *Process* ontology. Firstly, a *Profile* states the *Process* it describes through the unique property `has_process`. Secondly, the IOPE's of the *Profile* correspond to the IOPE's of the *Process*. Understanding this correspondence is not so trivial given the fact that the IOPE's play different roles for the *Profile* and for the *Process*. In the *Profile* ontology they are treated equally as parameters of the *Profile* (they are subproperties of the *profile:parameter* property - suggested with IOPE's between brackets in the figure). In the *Process* ontology only IO's are regarded as subproperties of the *process:parameter* property. The PE's are just simple properties of the *Process*. While technically the IOPE's are properties both for *Profile* and *Process*, the fact that they are treated differently at a conceptual level is misleading. In the DAML-S *Profile* ontology each *ParameterDescription refersTo* exactly one element of type *process:paramater*.

Several aspects of this mapping can be critiqued. First, one would expect that *Profile* parameters of a certain type can only refer to *Process* parameters of the same type. However, this is not enforced. With the current specification one can easily make a link between parameters of different types (eg. *profile:input* and *process:output*). Second, because the *Process* ontology does not model PE's as subproperties of *process:paramater*, it is inconsistent to use entities of this type as values for *profile:refersTo*. Therefore PE's defined for the *Profile* cannot refer to the corresponding PE's of the *Process*.

The DAML-S coalition acknowledges the possibility of inconsistencies between *Profile* and *Process* and that they will be discovered at some point [7]. Since matchmaking is based on the *Profile* description, the break may occur during (attempted) usage of the

Table 1. Sesame addData Service - the HTTP Interface

Parameter	Required	Description
repository (rep)	yes	Specifies the id of the repository to which data is added
data	for method1	The data that should be added to the repository
dataURL (URL)	for method2	The URL of the data that should be added to the repository
baseURL (base)	for method 1	Specifies the base URL for the data. Needed for method1 as Sesame does not know where the data came from. For method2 the baseURL defaults to dataURL
user	no	The user's login name. Needed to gain access to non-public repositories.
password (pass)	no	The user's password is only required in the case the user parameter is supplied
format	no	Determines the response format. Legal values are xml (the default) and html

service. The rationale for this design decision is not clear. We conclude that this link between the IOPE's at two distinct levels of specification should be corrected and made more explicit.

As an addition to the previous section on the use of domain knowledge, each parameter of the *Profile* has a *ParameterDescription* which mandates describing the parameter through the *profile:restrictedTo* property. This property has an unspecified range, therefore it can refer both to a DAML+OIL concept or to a data type. We recommend specifying a domain level concept: this gives the "semantics" of the parameter. For the *Process*, we have used domain concepts to specify the range of inputs and outputs in order to indicate their semantics.

5.2 DAML-S/WSDL Mapping

In this section we present our modelling experiences when writing the *Grounding* for the *addData* service and motivate the issues discussed in section 6.

The *ServiceGrounding* builds a bridge between the *ProcessModel* and the WSDL description of the service according to three rules[7]. First, each DAML-S *AtomicProcess* corresponds to a WSDL operation. Second, following from the previous rule, each input of the DAML-S *AtomicProcess* is mapped to a corresponding message-part in the input message of the WSDL operation. Similarly for DAML-S outputs, each output of the DAML-S *AtomicProcess* is mapped to a corresponding message-part in the output message of the WSDL operation. Third, the type of each WSDL message part can be specified in terms of a DAML-S parameter (an XML Schema data type or a DAML+OIL concept).

The Sesame *addData* service allows RDF(S) data to be uploaded to Sesame through an HTTP interface described in Table 1. This service can acquire the RDF(S) source either (1) by uploading the data itself (*method1*) or (2) by uploading a URL referring to the data (*method2*). The parameters specified will determine which method to use. Intuitively, this situation is similar to a specific kind of ad-hoc polymorphism, that of *overloading*: a certain method allows different signatures, but essentially it executes the same function.

The available documentation about DAML-S provided little guidance on how to model this situation. Some coalition members have considered the problem of supporting multiple interfaces and offered a solution for the situation where the number of arguments are the same and in the same order but where the data types may differ [2]. The solution offered is to define a higher level concept that covers all possible alternative data types. This solution guided us in our own modelling.

The effect of the service is not altered by the input parameters, that is, in all but error situations (such as an invalid password or a URL site that cannot be found). Therefore we consider that, conceptually, we have a single service which provides a means of adding some RDF(S) data to a Sesame repository, even if two slightly different implementations exist for the same service. In modelling terms we define a single service with two groundings, one for each implementation.

In modelling the conceptual part we took into consideration the solution presented in [2] by defining a *DataSource* concept to generally define the source of the RDF(S) data. This concept covers the two different data sources: (1) the data supplied as an URL (dataURL) and (2) the combination of a data stream (data) and its associated URL (baseURL). Below we show the inputs, expressed in terms of domain ontology concepts, expected by the *AtomicProcess P1* of the ProcessModel:

```
*ProcessModel:
   AtomicProcess:P1(I(Repository), I(DataSource),I(User),
                    I(Password), I(Format))
```

Our WSDL representation of the service consists of a *PortType (addData)* with two *operations (method1, method2)* which differ through their input messages: the first operation expects the actual data *(data)* and a base URL *(base)*, while the second receives the URL of the actual data *(URL)*.

```
*Service(
   PortType:addData(
       method1 (IMsg(rep, data, base, user, pass, format), OMsg(stream))
       method2 (IMsg(rep, URL, user, pass, format), OMsg(stream)))
```

Specifying the grounding to *method2* was easy. For grounding *method1* we need to express a one-to-many mapping between the *DataSourse* input of the *AtomicProcess P1* and two input message parts of this method: *data* and *base*. However, this is not possible since the DAML-S/WSDL mapping imposes that "each atomic process input and output corresponds to a (single) WSDL message part" [7]. While, the DAML-S coalition acknowledge that this could be a possible limitation, they do not give a concrete example of a problematic scenario. Our example shows that the assumption prohibits modelling of ad-hoc polymorphism (overloading). Therefore we encourage its revision.

The new version of DAML-S (v.0.9)[13] is less restrictive, but nevertheless does not solve this issue. There is a possibility of defining XSLT transformations between the *Process* parameters and the WSDL message parts. In case of inputs multiple input parameters can be mapped to a single WSDL message part. Still, we cannot solve our particular problem where we need to map one input parameter *(DataSource)* to multiple message parts (*data* and *baseURL*).

As can be seen in table 1, the *addData* service has several optional input parameters, three of which become mandatory depending on certain conditions. We will take up the issue of defining constraints on inputs in section 6.1.

[13] Version 0.9 was released after we submitted our paper thus our findings refer to v.0.7.

6 IO Specification

We have previously been concerned about the service as a whole and the links between the layers of its specification. We continue with details about how the parameters of the service can be specified. The first part of this section proposes a more flexible modelling of input parameters so that inputs depending on a condition can be specified as well. In the second we propose an alternative to complex data type specification.

6.1 Conditional Inputs

DAML-S does not cover cases when inputs depend on a certain condition. Currently one can only indicate whether an input is mandatory or optional by relying on the DAML+OIL cardinality restriction mechanism . For each mandatory input a cardinality restriction must enforce its existence. However, we have encountered situations when an input is only required in combination with another input. For example, when specifying the log-in information, a *password* is only mandatory when the *user* parameter is supplied. Further, in case of the *addData* service if the actual data is supplied, rather than a *URL*, then a *baseURL* must be specified.

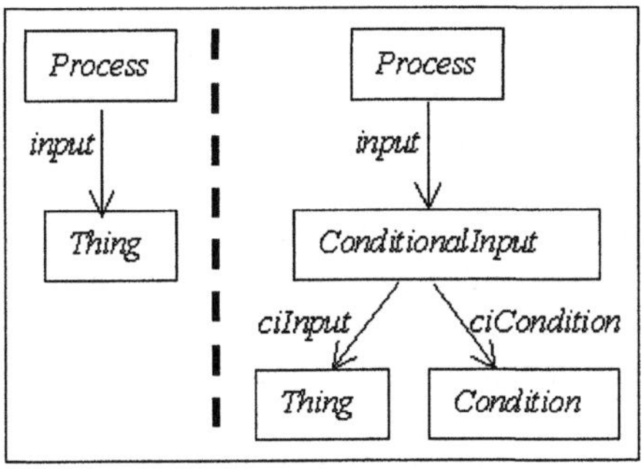

Fig. 6. Current and proposed modelling of inputs

A solution that appears to be the most consistent with the current version of DAML-S is to extend the *Process* ontology to support conditional inputs in the same way that outputs and effects may be conditional (see fig 6). Following the general template of defining conditional elements, we propose defining the *ConditionalInput* class which simply bundles a *Condition* and an input, using two properties: the condition of the conditional input (*ciCondition*) and the input of the conditional input (*ciInput*). A conditional input is an input that only occurs when a condition is true.

This modelling allows specifying a wider range of inputs than currently possible. First, inputs depending on factors external to the process can be described. For example, customers from outside the USA do not need to provide the zipcode input. In this case the customers geographic location conditions whether the zipcode input is needed or not. Second, we can capture situations exemplified before where an input is conditioned by the existence of another input, or generally a condition that involves other inputs. Third, we propose an alternative way to specify mandatory inputs by conditional inputs with a condition that is always "True". Finally, optional inputs can be modelled as UnconditionalInputs, i.e. inputs that do not depend on any condition. This list is not complete, however we think these cases are likely to appear in other tools (and services) as well. Note however that we did not deal with how conditions should be specified. In fact this is a thorny issue for the whole community.

6.2 Complex Data Types: XML Schema or DAML+OIL?

To support automatic discovery and operational integration of web services, their markup should provide information about (1) the semantics of their methods and parameters as well as (2) their syntactic signature (ex. method names, data format of parameters). The issue of how one can best specify complex data types (both at a syntactic and semantic level) has a major importance for Sesame where four methods provide complex output data types. As a concrete example, consider the simplest functionality of Sesame: *requestRepository*. It's output conforms to the DTD specified below.

```
<!ELEMENT repositorylist (repository)*>
<!ELEMENT repository(title)>
<!ELEMENT title          (#PCDATA)>
<!ATTLIST repository
         id       ID           #REQUIRED
         readable (true|false) #REQUIRED
         writable (true|false) #REQUIRED>
```

Such complex data formats are defined in the "types" section of a WSDL document. For maximum platform independence XML Schema(XSD) is used to specify the format of complex data types. The syntactic information provided by XSD allows other tools to easily parse any output that conforms to this DTD, therefore allowing an easy integration between web services. However this information has no semantics.

The DAML-S solution to this is to replace the syntactic XSD definitions with semantic definitions written in DAML+OIL, since WSDL allows using any XML-based type definition language in its "types" section. The claim is that this would use DAML+OIL's rich data typing feature [1].

We felt that this recommendation had limitations when applied to the complex types in Sesame. First, we found it difficult to express the complex syntax of the data type solely with DAML+OIL elements. We even considered using an OWL-based type definition as it provides more advanced ways for data typing than its ancestor. Even so we did not achieve our goal. This is understandable since DAML+OIL (and OWL) is an ontology language and as such it delegates the data type representation to XSD. Users are encouraged to refer to XSD complex types in their models rather then defining them using DAML+OIL.

Second, a WSDL document using purely DAML+OIL based data types would be useless for those users of the service which do not understand DAML+OIL. Ideally, an existing WSDL description should undergo minor changes when enabled for use with semantic technology to ensure its backward compatibility with traditional applications. We expect that many tools would use the XSD definitions of Sesame's WSDL description and only very few would understand DAML+OIL. Therefore we want to extend XSD types rather than to replace them.

Third, for some applications, not all parts of a complex data type were interesting semantically. For example, the syntax of the previous output is very complex, but semantically we are not interested in all its parts. We want to specify that objects of type *Repository* are returned but we do not want to specify further details.

With these considerations in mind, we used an alternative for complex type definition. We used XML Schema to specify the syntax of the output, just like for a traditional

WSDL description. To add semantics to this type we have augmented its components with references to corresponding DAML+OIL concepts. The *xsd:annotation* tag has exactly this function. We wrote the following XSD definition and augmented it with concepts defined in the domain ontology.

```
<xsd:element name="repositorylist">
 <xsd:complexType>
  <xsd:element name="repository">
   <xsd:annotation>
     <xsd:documentation>do:Repository</xsd:documentation>
   </xsd:annotation>
   <xsd:complexType>
     <xsd:element name="title" type="xsd:string"/>
     <xsd:attribute name="id" type="xsd:string" use="required"/>
     <xsd:attribute name="readable" type="xsd:boolean" use="required"/>
     <xsd:attribute name="writeable" type="xsd:boolean" use="required"/>
   </xsd:complexType>
  </xsd:element>
 </xsd:complexType>
</xsd:element>
```

This method satisfies all of our requirements. Using XML Schema to define complex types is straightforward since the language was designed for this purpose. We can easily add semantics to any parts of the description in such a way that it remains usable for non-semantic based applications.

7 Conclusions and Future Work

The goal of this paper is to assess the expressivity of DAML-S for certain service characteristics which were not discussed previously in the literature and are likely to be exhibited by Semantic Web Tools. Our global conclusion is that DAML-S offers a useful set of terms for describing semantic web tools however, we needed to make some extensions in order to achieve more expressivity. Indeed, the given properties of Sesame triggered many of these extensions. We think that research on how certain facets of web-services require certain type of modelling can be a valuable future work.

One observation is that Sesame combines a set of self-contained services which can be used in any combination in contrast to other services with a well-defined workflow of processes which cannot be used outside the composite service. While traditional DAML-S modelling favors the latter case, we were able to provide a work-around by allowing a composition mechanism between profiles of tools and functionalities within our domain ontology in section 4. The proposed construct may be appropriate beyond Sesame and a useful extension for DAML-S.

Major issues in this area still require some future work. First, the mentioned revision to DAML-S can be considered. Second, the whole conceptual view on this problem could be made clearer by aligning DAML-S with an upper level ontology such as DOLCE [8]. Third, we envision that in the future more standard domain ontologies will emerge and be adopted by large communities. This will make the task of defining ones own domain ontology much easier. Also, it would ensure inter-operability between the different descriptions and ensure effective matchmaking. Work on such ontologies (and in particular on an ontology of semantic web tools) is highly relevant future work. Fourth, we consider that the specification of algebraic properties between services would add much more semantics to the descriptions. However, work in this area is linked to developments in rule specification.

Specifying inputs and outputs is at least as important as specifying the semantics offered by the service. Sesame introduces the issue of expressing conditional inputs and complex data types which we treated in section 6. We proposed a novel modelling to allow more flexible specifications of different types of inputs and suggested an alternative specification of complex data types that would ensure minimal changes to existing WSDL documents. Specifying the content of such conditions is left to the user. While we can express some constraints with the built-in restriction mechanisms of DAML+OIL, defining generic rules remains as future work.

Finally, we discussed in section 5 some limitations/inconsistencies of DAML-S which are generally valid but hindered us in carrying out our particular descriptions. For a more detailed argumentation of these observations, see [16], where we report on the modelling of two simple web-services.

The automatic discovery, composition and execution of web-services by software agents potentially involves the use of web accessible SW tools which themselves must be semantically described. By offering our experiences with marking up Sesame we hope to assist others to markup their SW tools and to assist the DAML-S coalition in the development of their standard.

Acknowledgements. The authors would like to thank Annette ten Teije and Frank van Harmelen for their helpful comments on an earlier draft of this paper.

References

1. A. Ankolekar. DAML-S: Web Service Description for the Semantic Web. In I. Horrocks and J. A. Hendler, editors, *The Semantic Web – ISWC 2002, First International Semantic Web Conference*, volume 2342 of *Lecture Notes in Computer Science*, Sardinia, Italy, 2002.
2. A. Ankolenkar, F. Hutch, and K. Sycara. Concurrent Execution Semantics for DAML-S with Subtypes. In I. Horrocks and J. A. Hendler, editors, *The Semantic Web – ISWC 2002, First International Semantic Web Conference*, volume 2342 of *Lecture Notes in Computer Science*, pages 348–363, Sardinia, Italy, 2002.
3. W. Barbera-Medina, J. Padget, and M. Aird. Brokerage for Mathematical Services in MONET. In *AAMAS Workshop on Web Services and Agent-Based Engineering*, Melbourne, Australia, July 2003.
4. J. Brison, D. Martin, S.I. McIlraith, and L. A. Stein. *Agent-Based Composite Services in DAML-S: The Behavior-Oriented Design of an Intelligent Semantic Web.* Springer-Verlag, Berlin, 2002.
5. J. Broekstra, A. Kampman, and F. van Harmelen. Sesame: A generic architecture for storing and querying rdf and rdf schema. In I. Horrocks and J. A. Hendler, editors, *The Semantic Web – ISWC 2002, First International Semantic Web Conference*, volume 2342 of *Lecture Notes in Computer Science*, pages 348–363, Sardinia, Italy, 2002.

6. J. Cardoso and A. Sheth. Semantic e-Workflow Composition. Technical report, LSDIS Lab, Computer Science, University of Georgia, July 2002.
7. DAML Services Coalition. DAML-S: Semantic Markup for Web Services. DAML-S v. 0.7 White Paper, October 2002.
8. A. Gangemi, N. Guarino, C. Masolo, A. Oltramari, and L. Schneider. Sweetening Ontologies with DOLCE. In *Proceedings of EKAW*, Siguenza, Spain, 2002.
9. N. Gibbins, S. Harris, and N. Shadbolt. Agent-based Semantic Web Services. In *The Twelfth International World Wide Web Conference*, Budapest, Hungary, 2003.
10. A. Gomez Perez. A survey on ontology tools. OntoWeb Delieverable 1.3, May 2002.
11. M. Laukkanen and H. Helin. Composing Workflows of Semantic Web Services. In *AAMAS Workshop on Web Services and Agent-Based Engineering*, Melbourne, Australia, July 2003.
12. L. Lei and I. Horrocks. A Software Framework For Matchmaking Based on Semantic Web Technology. In *The Twelfth International World Wide Web Conference*, Budapest, Hungary, 2003.
13. A. Lopes, S. Gaio, and L.M. Botelho. From DAML-S to Executable Code. In *Proc. of the Workshop Challenges in Open Agent Systems AAMAS 2002*, 2002.
14. M. Paolucci, T. Kawamura, T. Payne, and K. Sycara. Semantic Matching of Web Services Capabilities. In I. Horrocks and J. A. Hendler, editors, *The Semantic Web – ISWC 2002, First International Semantic Web Conference*, volume 2342 of *Lecture Notes in Computer Science*, Sardinia, Italy, 2002.
15. D. Richards, S. van Splunter, F. Brazier, and M. Sabou. Composing Web Services using an Agent Factory. In *AAMAS Workshop on Web Services and Agent-Based Engineering*, Melbourne, Australia, July 2003.
16. M. Sabou, D. Richards, and S. van Splunter. An Experience Report on Using DAML-S. In *Workshop on E-Services and the Semantic Web*, Budapest, Hungary, May 2003.
17. M. Sheshagiri, M. desJardins, and T. Finin. A Planner for Composing Services Described in DAML-S. In *AAMAS Workshop on Web Services and Agent-Based Engineering*, Melbourne, Australia, July 2003.
18. C. Wroe, R. Stevens, C. Goble, A. Roberts, and M. Greenwood. A Suite of DAML+OIL Ontologies to Describe Bioinformatics Web Services and Data . *Journal of Cooperative Information Science*, 2003.

The DAML-S Virtual Machine*

Massimo Paolucci, Anupriya Ankolekar, Naveen Srinivasan, and Katia Sycara

Carnegie Mellon University
Pittsburgh, Pennsylvania, USA
{paolucci,anupriya,naveen,katia}@cs.cmu.edu

Abstract. This paper introduces the DAML-S Virtual Machine (DS-VM): an embedded component that uses the DAML-S Process Model to control the interaction between Web services. We provide a proof of the validity of the implementation of the DAML-S Virtual Machine by proving a mapping from the rules used by the DS-VM to the DAML-S Operational Semantics. Finally, we provide an example of use of the DS-VM with a DAML-Sized version of Amazon.com's Web service, and we conclude with an empirical evaluation that shows that the overhead required by the DS-VM during the interaction with Amazon is only a small fraction of the time required by a query to Amazon. The DS-VM provides crucial evidence that DAML-S can be effectively used to manage the interaction between Web Services.

1 Introduction

Web services are emerging as the core technology for e-business transactions. The wide spread use of XML, WSDL and SOAP supports interoperation between Web services, by abstracting implementation details such as programming language and transport protocol that plagued the earlier attempts to achieve distributed computation such as CORBA and Jini. On the other hand, Web services interoperation requires more than abstraction from implementation details, rather Web services should also share the same interpretation of the information that they exchange. This shared interpretation can be achieved only through a semantic description of the information that Web services exchange. Unfortunately, the Web services infrastructure does not provide a semantic layer where the content of the information exchanged by Web services can be expressed. As a consequence, the Web services infrastructure requires that programmers hardcode the interaction between Web services, furthermore the resulting Web services are inherently brittle since they will break whenever the content or the format of their messages change.

DAML-S attempts to overcome the limitations of the Web Services infrastructure by leveraging on DAML+OIL ontologies to provide a semantic specification of what Web services do and the information that they exchange. DAML-S

* The research was funded by the Defense Advanced Research Projects Agency as part of the DARPA Agent Markup Language (DAML) program under Air Force Research Laboratory contract F30601-00-2-0592 to Carnegie Mellon University.

D. Fensel et al. (Eds.): ISWC 2003, LNCS 2870, pp. 290–305, 2003.

adopts the prospective that any interaction between Web services involves at least two parties: a provider and a requester, where the requester needs some information or a service that can be provided by the providers. Furthermore, it is the responsibility of the requester to locate the provider and initiate the interaction; while it is the responsibility of the provider to publish a description of its capabilities, or in other words the service that it provides. A typical capability description involves description of how the service is performed, and what information the provider expects from the requester, and finally, how such information is delivered.

The management of the information exchange is specified in the Process Model and Grounding of DAML-S. Operationally, a Process Model is defined as an ordered collection of processes organized on the basis of a workflow, which specifies the sequence of processes performed by the provider during the transaction. Each process is defined as a transformation between an initial state and a final state, where the initial state is specified by the inputs required by the process and the preconditions for the process to run successfully. The final state is described as a set of outputs, or information that results from the execution of the process, and a set of effects that represent physical changes that result from the execution of the process.

During the interaction with the provider, the requester executes the Process Model published by the provider. Each (atomic) process corresponds to an (atomic) information exchange, where the inputs of the process describe the information that the provider expects from the requester, while the outputs correspond to information that the requester will receive in answer from the provider. Ultimately, by following the Process Model, the requester can infer the interaction protocol with the provider.

The contribution of this paper is the description of the DAML-S Virtual Machine (DS-VM) that uses DAML-S descriptions of Web services and DAML ontologies to control the interaction between Web services. The DS-VM described in this paper is one of a kind, because its a complete framework starting from parsing a DAML-S description, executing the process model consistently with the DAML-S operational semantics [2]. Furthermore, the DS-VM uses the DAML-S Grounding to transform the abstract description of the information exchanges between the provider and the requester into WSDL operations and ultimately bits of information that can be exchanged over the net.

To test the DS-VM we generated a DAML- S description of the web service provided by Amazon.com. The result was the automatic generation of a client for the web service that can manage the interaction and automatically interpret the results it obtained from the Web service to select the cheapest book, among all the responses it receives. Ultimately, this corresponds to a net improvement over the Web services infrastructure based on WSDL, because the web service did not require any hand coding of the interaction protocol, as it was automatically derived from the DAML-S description of the web service. Furthermore, by using the Semantic Web to interpret the results, the client was able to draw some inferences and make its selections.

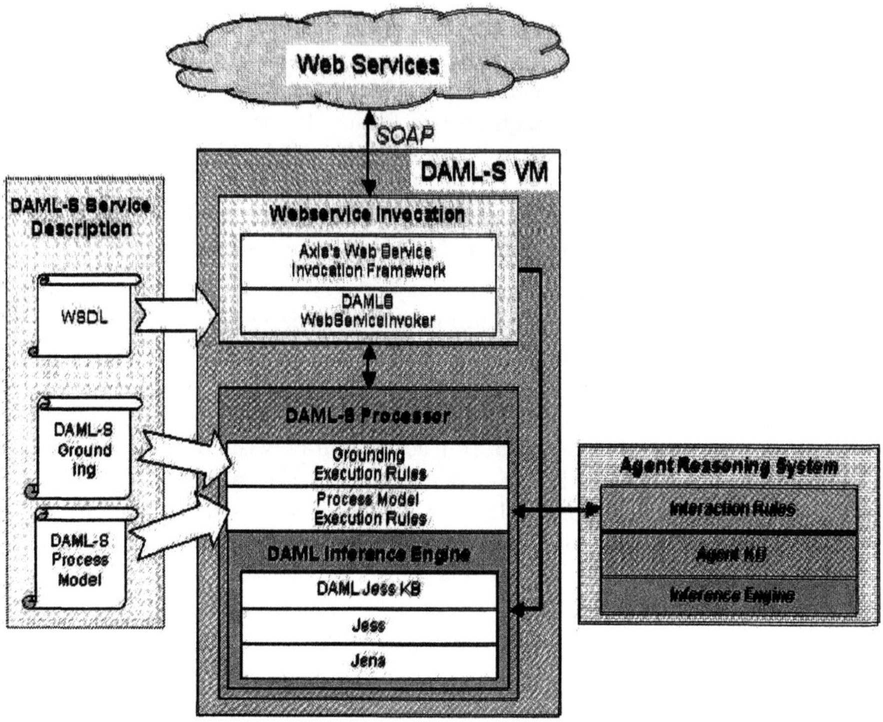

Fig. 1. Architecture of the DS-VM

In the rest of the paper we will discuss in details the theory and the implementation of the DS-VM. In section 2 we describe the architecture of the implementation of the DS-VM. In section 2.2 we show how the implementation maps on the Operational Semantics defined in [2]. In section 3 we describe the generation of the DAML-S description of Amazon.com's Web service; and in section 4 we provide performance measures of the DS-VM and we show that the use of DAML-S is not a computational burden, rather the performance of the DS-VM is equivalent to the performance of the hard coded Web service client provided by Amazon.com and anyway greatly overshadowed by the performance of a HTTP call to the Web service. Finally in section 5 we conclude.

2 Architecture of DS-VM

The architecture of the DS-VM and its relation with the rest of the Web service is described in figure 1. The figure is logically divided in three parts: on the left side the *DAML-S Service Description* specifies the knowledge used by the DS-VM to control the interaction with other Web services. This knowledge is composed by the DAML-S Process Model and Grounding as well as a WSDL description of the bindings. The DS-VM is displayed in the center of the picture. It is logically divided in two modules: the first one is the *DAML-S Processor* which uses the

DAML Inference Engine and a set of rules implementing the operational semantics of the DAML-S Process Model and Grounding to manage the interaction with the provider. The second component is the *Web service Invocation* module that is responsible for the information transfer with the provider. The last component of the DS-VM is shown on the right side of the figure. It is the *Web service Reasoning System* that is responsible for a number of decisions during the interaction. In the rest of this section we will concentrate on the DS-VM module, and specifically on the DAML-S Processor; we will describe in some details the role of the inference engine and the rules that it adopts to execute the Process Model and Grounding. We will conclude the section by analyzing its relation between the DAML-S Processor and the agent reasoning system, this relation highlights the assumptions that DAML-S makes on the whole Web service.

2.1 DAML-S Processor

The DAML-S Processor is the core of the DS-VM. It is responsible to "drive" the interaction with the provider on the basis of the specification of its Process Model and Grounding. More precisely, the DAML-S Processor derives the sequence of processes to be executed dealing with the intrinsic non-determinism of the DAML-S Process Model. Furthermore, it compiles the inputs to send to the provider and extracts its responses from the outputs.

The DAML-S Processor relies on a DAML inference engine to draw inferences from the DAML-S description of Web services, as well as deriving inferences from the ontologies that it loads. The current implementation is based on the DAML-Jess-KB [9], an implementation of the DAML axiomatic semantics that relies on the Jess theorem prover [6] and the Jena parser [10] to parse ontologies and assert them as new facts in the Jess KB.

In addition to making inferences on the definitions loaded from the Semantic Web, the DAML-S Processor is also responsible to derive the execution of the Process Models and the mappings defined by the Grounding. To perform these inferences, the Process Model uses the rules shown in table 1[1] that implement the execution semantics of of the Process Model, as defined in [3] and [2], which formalize the DAML-S specifications [1].

2.2 Implementation of the Process Model Operational Semantics

The main requirement on the DAML-S Processor is to be faithful to the intended semantics of the Process Model. In this section we review the semantics of each type of process by providing first an informal description, followed by a formal semantics as specified by tables 5 and 6, and finally we will show the mapping into the implementation shown in table 1. The mapping will provide an informal reason of why the rules in table 1 preserve the semantics of the process. Due to lack of space, we omit the full details of the proof. In the rest of this section,

[1] For ease of explanation the rules are expressed in a Prolog style. In our implementation they are expressed as OPS5 forward chaining rules.

we will assume familiarity with the syntax and semantics of *DAML-S Core* [3,2] and defer a brief review of DAML-S Core to the appendix.

Atomic. Atomic processes are executed by invoking the Grounding and information transfer with the provider. The implementation of atomic processes is shown by rule (1) in table 1. The semantics of atomic processes is shown by the rule (FUNC) in table 5 which specifies that p is a symbol that is mapped onto an actual operation $p_{\mathcal{A}}$ over a specified domain of values. The function $p_{\mathcal{A}}$ essentially corresponds to an operation invocation on the Web service. In practice such an invocation results in a call to the grounding as specified by rule (1).

sequence. A sequence of processes is executed by executing the processes in the order established by the sequence. Sequences are implemented by rule (2) in table 1. The semantics of sequences is shown by the rule (SEQ) in table 6 is formalized as follows:[2]

$$\texttt{sequence(Process,}\{p_1,\ldots p_n\}\texttt{)} = \texttt{do}\ \{p_1\texttt{;}\ldots\texttt{;}p_n\}$$

Notice that this is equivalent to the unraveling of

$$\texttt{do}\ \{p_1\texttt{;}\ldots\texttt{;}p_n\}\ \text{into}\ p_1\ \texttt{>>}\ \texttt{do}\ \{p_2\texttt{;}\ldots\texttt{;}p_n\}$$

where the first process of the list p_1 is evaluated first and then the rest of the list do $\{p_2\texttt{;}\ldots\texttt{;}p_n\}$ which is exactly what is expressed by rule (2) in table 1.

split. A split describes the spawn of multiple concurrent computation of processes skipping the wait for their completion. Splits are implemented by rule (3) in table 1. The semantics of sequences is shown by the rule (SPAWN) in table 6. Formally, a `split(Process,List)`, where `List` consists of the processes $p_1,\ldots p_n$ is expressed as:

$$\texttt{split(Process,}\{p_1,\ldots p_n\}\texttt{)} = \texttt{do}\ \{\texttt{spawn}\ p_1\texttt{;}\ldots\texttt{;spawn}\ p_n\}$$

As with `sequence`, this is equivalent to launching the first process in the `List` p_1 while concurrently the spawning off the remaining processes of the `List` $\{p_2,\ldots,p_n\}$ as concurrent processes as it is expressed by rule (3) in table 1.

[2] For simplicity, we use the imperative-style do-notation here. as defined in [7]:

$$\texttt{do}\ \{x\ \texttt{<-}\ e\texttt{;}s\} = e\ \texttt{>>=}\ \backslash x\ \texttt{->}\ \texttt{do}\ \{s\}$$
$$\texttt{do}\ \{e\texttt{;}s\} = e\ \texttt{>>=}\ \backslash\_\ \texttt{->}\ \texttt{do}\ \{s\}$$
$$\texttt{do}\ \{e\} = e$$

Table 1. Rules of the Process Model Processor

```
(1) executed (atomic(Process)) ⇐
            callGrounding(Process), assert(complete(Process))

(2) executed (sequence(Process,List)) ⇐
            executed(first(List)),
            executed(sequence(Process,rest(List)))
            assert(complete(sequence(Process,List)))

(3) executed (split(Process,List)) ⇐
            exec(first(List)), exec(split(Process,rest(List))),
            assert(complete(split(Process,List)))

(4) executed (splitJoint(Process,List)) ⇐
            exec(first(List)), exec(splitJoint(Process,rest(List))),
            complete(first(List)), complete(splitJoint(Process,rest(List)))
            assert(complete(splitJoint(Process,List)))

(5) executed (if(Cond,ThenProcess,ElseProcess)) ⇐
            ( Cond, executed(ThenProcess) ) XOR executed(ElseProcess)
            assert(complete(if(Cond,ThenProcess,ElseProcess)))

(6) executed (choice(Process,List)) ⇐ executed(oneOf(List))
            assert(complete(choice(Process,List)))
```

splitJoint. A splitJoint extends split by describing the spawn of multiple concurrent computation of processes with a coordination point at the end of the execution. SplitJoints are implemented by rule (4) in table 1. In our semantics the processes are spawned off sequentially, and the completion of the splitJoint depends on the completion of every process.

$$\texttt{splitJoint(Process,}\{p_1, \ldots, p_n\}\texttt{)}$$

is modeled as the following, where each p'_i =`do` $\{$ p_i`;`t`!done`$\}$:

```
do { t <- newport;
     split(Process,{p'1,... ,p'n};
     t?; ... t? }
```

This rule is equivalent to the split rule, with the only exception that the spawning process listens on port t for n messages, where n is the number of sub-processes that were initially spawned. Similarly, rule (4) in table 1 used by the DAML-S Processor to control the execution of a splitJoint differs from those for split only in that the splitJoint is complete only when each one of the sub-processes signals its own completion. Such a signal is produced by asserting the completion of the process as the last step of its execution as shown by all the rules in table 1.

if-then-else. An if-then-else conditional triggers the execution of the `then` process when the condition is true, or the `else` process when the condition is false. if-then-else are implemented by rule (5) in table 1. The semantics of sequences is shown by the rule (COND-TRUE) in table 6 and by a symmetrical rule for (COND-FALSE) which is not shown. The if-then-else conditional can be formalized as:

`if(Cond,ThenProcess,ElseProcess)` = `(cond Cond ThenProcess ElseProcess)`

The two XOR conditions in rule (5) of table 1 correspond to the two rules (COND-TRUE) and (COND-FALSE) of table 6, which essentially proves the equivalence between the two sets of rules.

choice. A choice represents a non-deterministic choice among a set of processes which may be forced by the execution context. The execution of a choice consists of executing one of the processes in its list. Choices are implemented by rule (6) in table 1, while the semantics of the construct is shown by the rule (CHOICE-LEFT) and (CHOICE-RIGHT) of table 6. A choice `choice(Process,List)` where `List` consists of processes $p_1, \ldots, p_n$, is formalized as:

$$\texttt{choice(Process,}\{p_1,\ldots p_n\}\texttt{)} = \texttt{(choice (choice } p_1\ p_2\texttt{) \ldots}\ p_n\texttt{)}$$

The DAML-S Processor rule (6) in table 1 for the processing of the choice construct executes one of the set of processes in the choice on the basis of some non-deterministic choice outside its control and is clearly equivalent to the semantics of the `choice` construct of DAML-S Core.

2.3 The Grounding and the Invocation of the Provider

The semantics of atomic processes, as described above, forces the execution of the DAML-S Grounding. The rules for the Grounding are stored in the *Grounding Execution Rules* module of the DAML-S Processor. These rules allow the compilation of atomic processes into WSDL operations that can be directly invoked by the *Web service Invocation* module.

In addition, the Grounding rules are used to extract the XSLT [5] transformations that are required when the provider does not use DAML as a transmission language. Essentially, these transformations provide a translation from the serialization of the data sent over the network, to the representation of the content of that data. The rationale of the translation is that the information contained by the data types and the information contained by the DAML ontologies should be equivalent. They are just presented in very different ways. The use of XSLT transformations adds a new level of abstraction to DAML-S allowing the description to be specified in terms of ontological classes and instances, whereas the actual data transmission can adopt any arbitrary format. Furthermore, it allows any Web service to be represented by DAML-S independently of its own internal use of DAML.

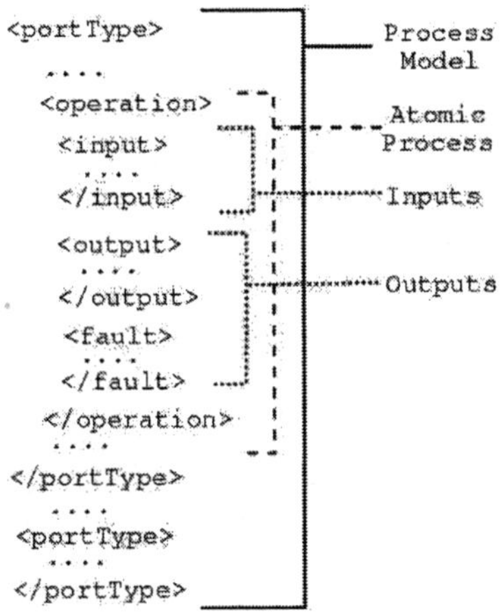

Fig. 2. Rationale of the translation from WSDL to DAML-S

From the implementation point of view, the XSLT transformations required by the Grounding are performed by XALAN [4] and then transformed into WSDL messages using JROM [8]. Finally, after the messages are constructed the WSDL operation is invoked using the AXIS framework. Outputs follow the opposite path, the data streams corresponding to the WSDL output messages are returned by the AXIS tools, and fed into JROM and finally transformed into DAML using XALAN. The DAML data is then parsed with the Jena DAML/RDF parser and finally asserted in the Jess KB where they are available for inference and interact with the rest of the knowledge of the Web service.

2.4 Interaction with the Reasoning System

The semantics discussed in the previous sections is mute on the Web service Reasoning System and concentrates on the specifications of the interaction between Web services. Nevertheless, the Reasoning System is responsible for many of the decisions that have to be made while using DAML-S. For instance, the application level is responsible for the use of the information extracted from the messages received from other Web Services or to decide what information to send to other Web Services. In order to take advantage of the flexibility supported by DAML-S, the Reasoning System should support non-deterministic choices while maintaining efficiency and control on the behavior of the Web Service. In ultimate analysis, DAML-S requires applications that look more like intelligent software agents than traditional e-commerce applications.

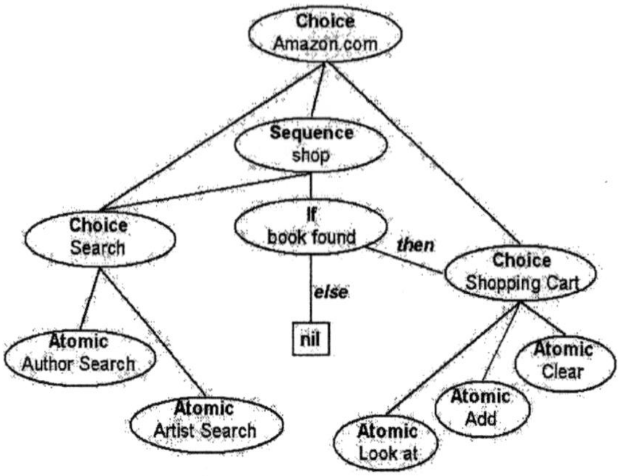

Fig. 3. The Process Model of Amazon.com's Web service

3 Using DAML-S to Interact with Amazon.com

Amazon.com provides a widely available Web service[3] which allows users to browse Amazon's databases, locate books and other products and put them in a shopping cart that can be accessed from the Amazon Web site. Through the Web service, users or programs can perform a wide range of keyword searches on the Amazon data bases, for example they are able to search for books with a given author, or look for products of a manufacturer, or search for DVD of movies of a given director. Keyword searches available, span over the whole set of data provided by Amazon, from customer's reviews to Seller profiles.

Amazon provides a SDK to build clients for its Web service, and many tutorials are available to implement the clients using different development kits from Microsoft .Net to IBM's Web Sphere. Amazon also provides a WSDL specification of its Web service that describes operations that can be performed with Amazon, using remote procedure call type of interaction.

We generated a DAML-S specification of the Amazon Web Service generalizing the WSDL description using WSDL2DAMLS [11]. WSDL2DAMLS is a tool that parses the WSDL specification and automatically generates a process model with an atomic process for each WSDL operation, and a complete specification of the grounding and a partial Profile. The translation scheme used by WSDL2DAMLS is shown in figure 2. Furthermore, WSDL2DAMLS generates DAML ontologies by mapping each abstract complex type in the WSDL specification to a DAML class.

Since DAML-S requires more information than the information available in WSDL, for example WSDL does not specify any control relation between the operations that could be invoked in any arbitrary order, the mapping produced

[3] For more information visit http://www.amazon.com/webservices

by WSDL2DAML-S is only a partial, and it still requires the intervention of a programmer to complete the generation of the Process Model and the Profile.

The use of WSDL2DAMLS saved us a great deal of effort in translating every single message type and operation, furthermore it provided us an automatic generation of the Grounding. The only problem with the translation was the generation of the DAML ontology from the complex types, the types used in the WSDL specification are totally arbitrary. While they may have facilitated the work of Amazon's programmers, in general they do not provide an ontological description of books or book selling. For example, the centerpiece of Amazon's Web service type structure is a complex type called *Details* which provides details about every type of product sold by Amazon. Details can be used to describe books, DVDs and other products, with the exception that only some fields apply to books, while others apply only to DVDs and so on. Hence we have to write an XSL stylesheet to transform Amazon's Details complex type to instances of our Ontologies.

As the last step, we completed the process model for the Amazon Web service by adding the control flow among the different operations. The result of this work is shown in figure 3. The main operation of the Process Model is a choice between three types of operations [4]. The first one is *browsing* the Amazon data bases which can be done either by Author search, or by Artist search. The second operation is *shopping* that can be done by first browsing, if anything is found, then adding the item to the shopping cart. The last set of operations allows analysis and modification of the shopping cart by clearing it or adding new items or looking at its content. Finally, we fed the generated Process Model, Grounding and Amazon's WSDL to the DS-VM to invoke the Amazon web service and we were able to perform arbitrary searches for books and CDs using DAML-S as the only specification of the server.

The last problem of interacting with the Amazon Web service has been the implementation of a principled set of rules to make a selection between the different choices in the Process Model. For instance, the Amazon's Process Model allows browsing, shopping or looking at the shopping cart. This type of decisions show that a Web service client has two type of problems: the first one is to decide how to use a Process Model, the second one is to implement those decisions. In our case, the first problem corresponds to deciding whether to browse or shop, the second one is to actually interact with Amazon to browse or shop. We assume that the DS-VM solves only the second problem, while the first one is relegated to the *Agent Reasoning System* shown figure 1, which contains a set of *Interaction Rules* that control the decisions of the agent. Specifically, the rules we implemented take into account the information available to the agent,

[4] Amazon's Web service allows many more types of searches than the set that we implemented. The problem we faced is that all of these searches are keyword based and they do not guarantee the type of the result and it is virtually impossible to know what type of object is returned. We therefore decided in our first attempt to limit to searches that are guaranteed to return books and CDs. Further analysis of the details type may allow us to perform additional types of searches.

Table 2. Execution time of Amazon Client and DS-VM (time in milliseconds)

	Amazon Client	DS-VM
Average Execution Time	2007 ms	2021 ms
Standard Deviation	1134 ms	776 ms

and goals it wants to achieve, and then it selects a path in the Process Model that can be executed with only the information available, and that provide the expected results.

4 Performance Measure

In the paper so far we demonstrated the correctness of the execution rules used in the DS-VM and we provided an example of usage of the DS-VM to connect to the Amazon Web service. In this section we provide a performance evaluation of the DS-VM and we show that, at least in the case of interacting with Amazon, the use of the DS-VM does not produce a performance penalty.

To estimate the performance of the DS-VM we performed two experiments. In the first one, which was restricted to the browsing operation, we compared the execution time of the DS-VM with the time required by the client provided by Amazon[5]. In the second experiment we provide the average time of the execution of the DS-VM when both browsing and reserving a book. In this experiment we could not compare with the Amazon client reserving books is beyond what the capabilities of the client that Amazon provides. In the second experiment we then compared the total time the DS-VM spent in processing DAML-S information with the total time of the interaction with the Amazon Web service. We repeated the experiments during different time of the day to account for the different load conditions both on our side and on Amazon's side. Also, in all experiments we requested books from the same author.

4.1 Experimental Results

In the first experiment was run 98 times over 4 days in varying load conditions. The results of the experiment are shown in table 2.

The first experiment shows that the DS-VM has virtually the same performance of the client distributed by Amazon, with only 14 milliseconds of difference on average.

In the second experiment we analyze how time is distributed in an interaction with Amazon when browsing and reserving a book. We computed three times: first the time required by the DS-VM to make a decision on the path to take in the process model, create the instances of the processes, and executing the processes; the second time is the time required by the data transformation from DAML to the format required by Amazon, and finally the invocation time. As

[5] The Amazon's client requires an input from the user, we hardcoded that input to avoid penalties due to the human interaction

Table 3. Distribution of time during the execution

	DS-VM	Data Transformation	Invocation
Average Time	83 ms	156 ms	2797ms
Percentage	3%	5%	92 %
Standard Deviation	107 ms	146 ms	1314 ms

in the first experiment we report the average times, and the standard deviation. We also report the percentage of the three averages compared to the total time required by the interaction. The data is shown in table 3[6].

Consistently with the first experiment the time required by the DS-VM is minimal with respect to a call to the Amazon web site requiring only 3% of the whole interaction time.

The experiments show that the use of the DS-VM **does not** produce a performance penalty. Indeed the average time of the required by the DS-VM for browsing is virtually equivalent to the time required by the Amazon client. This equivalence is explained by the second experiment that shows that the time required by the DAML-S is about 8% of the interaction time, and the majority of that time was required by the XSLT transformations between the XML format required by Amazon and DAML required by the DS-VM.

5 Conclusions

In this paper we introduced the DAML-S Virtual Machine, which, as far as we know, is the first complete implementation of DAML-S consistent with the operational semantics of the DAML-S Process Model. In the paper we discussed the architecture of the DS-VM and the rules that it uses to regulate the interactions with the providers. Furthermore, we showed that those rules are consistent with the semantics of the Process Model. Finally, we discussed the use of the DS-VM to interact with Amazon's Web service.

This paper provides an opportunity to analyze the contribution of DAML-S and the Semantic Web to the Web services infrastructure. Specifically, three questions emerge: the first one is whether there is any use of ontological information in the Web services representation; the second one is whether DAML-S representation of Web services is adequate or even useful. The last question is whether DAML-S can be effectively used in the interaction with Web services. The paper provides an answer to the last question showing that DS-VM is as efficient as the Amazon's own clients, but it also provides an initial answer the previous two questions.

Our experience with Amazon shows that ontological information facilitates the representation and use of Web services. For example, Amazon represents its products using only one data structure that does not distinguish between books, Cd's or electronic devices. That data structure depends on Amazon's internal

[6] The data does not account for the loading of the Process Model and the related ontologies since no similar operation was performed by the Amazon's client

way to represent products and it does not have any ontological status. As a consequence any client is forced to implement translation rules between Amazon's representation and their own. In practice, the result is an explosion of mappings, one for each provider. The Semantic Web provides a natural *interlingua* that is understood by all clients. As a consequence, using DAML-S, Amazon publishes its own internal mapping from its own data structure to DAML leaving to the clients the task of mapping from DAML to their own data structure. The result is that each client needs only one mapping to the ontology and then it can interact with any book selling web service.

The last question is whether there is a need for DAML-S representation. DAML-S requires the specification of the consequences that result from the execution of a process. This is probably the main contribution of DAML-S representation to the description of Web services. We made an essential use of this feature when our Amazon client had to make a selection between the different activities: look for books vs look for Cd's vs other types of products. To make the selection, the client needs to know what are the consequences of each choice, then match them against its own goals. Ultimately, this is possible only because DAML-S supports the representation of such consequences. Other Web service representation languages such as WSCI and BPEL4WS that do not support the representation input, outputs preconditions and effects of processes executed by Web services force programmers hardcode these choices in the clients leading to overspecialization which leads to brittleness and maintenance problems.

References

1. A. Ankolekar, M. Burstein, J. R. Hobbs, O. Lassila, D. L. Martin, S. A. McIlraith, S. Narayanan, M. Paolucci, T. Payne, K. Sycara, and H. Zeng. Daml-s: Web service description for the semantic web. In *ISWC 2002*, Sardegna, Italy, 2002.
2. A. Ankolekar, F. Huch, and K. Sycara. Concurrent execution semantics for daml-s with subtypes. In *ISWC, 2002*, Sardegna, Italy, 2002.
3. A. Ankolekar, F. Huch, and K. Sycara. Semantics for the web services specification language daml-s. In *Proceedings of the Fifth International Conference on Coordination Models and Languages,, 2002*, 2002.
4. Apache Foundation. XALAN, (http://xml.apache.org/xalan-j/).
5. J. Clark. XSL transformations (XSLT) version 1.0. Technical report, W3C, 1999.
6. E. Friedman-Hill. Jess.
7. S. Haskell and J. Peyton. Tackling the awkward squad: monadic input/output, concurrency, execptions and foreign-language calls. Lecture Notes for a tutorial given at Marktoberdorf Summer School, 2002.
8. IBM Corporation. JROM – java record object model.
9. J. Kopena and W. Regli. DAMLJessKB: A tool for reasoning with the semantic web. In *ISWC 2003*, 2003.
10. B. McBride. Jena: Implementing the rdf model and syntax specification. In *Semantic Web Workshop, WWW2001*, 2001.
11. M. Paolucci, N. Srinivasan, K. Sycara, and T. Nishimura. Towards a semantic choreography of web services: from WSDL to DAML-S. In *ICWS 2003*, Las Vegas, USA, 2003.

A DAML-S Core

In this section, we present a brief review of the syntax and formal semantics of DAML-S Core, as presented in [2].

A.1 Syntax

The set of *DAML-S Core expressions*, $Exp(\Sigma)$, over Σ, which represents a set of symbols for basic operations, is defined in Table 4. Given a type expression τ, the set of expressions of type τ is denoted by $Exp(\Sigma)^\tau$.

A.2 Operational Semantics of DAML-S Core

In a Σ-Interpretation $\mathcal{A} = (A, \alpha)$, A is a T-sorted set of concrete values and α an interpretation function that maps each symbol in Ω, the set of all constructors defined through DAML+OIL, to a function over A.

Definition 1 (State). *A* state *of execution within DAML-S Core is defined as a finite set of agents: State* $:= \mathcal{P}_{fin}(Agent)$ *An* agent *is a pair* (e, φ)*, where* $e \in Exp(\Sigma)$ *is the DAML-S Core expression being evaluated and* φ *is a partial function, mapping port references onto actual ports:*

$$Agent := Exp(\Sigma) \times \{\varphi \mid \varphi : \texttt{PortRef} \longrightarrow \texttt{Port}^{\mathfrak{A}}_\tau\}$$

for all τ*, where* $\texttt{Port}^{\mathfrak{A}}_\tau := (A^\tau)^*$ *and* $\texttt{PortRef}$ *is an infinite set of globally known unique port references, disjoint with* A*. Since no two agents can have a common port, the domains of their port functions* φ *are also disjoint.*

Definition 2 (Evaluation Context). *The set of* evaluation contexts $\mathcal{EC}$ *for DAML-S Core is defined by the context-free grammar*

$$E := [\,] \mid \phi(v_1, \ldots, v_i, E, e_{i+2}, e_n) \mid (E\ e) \mid (v\ E) \mid E \texttt{ >>= } e$$

for $v \in A$, $e, e_1, e_2 \in Exp(\Sigma)$, $\phi \in \Omega \cup S \backslash \{\texttt{spawn}, \texttt{choice}\}$.

Definition 3 (Operational Semantics). *The* operational semantics *of DAML-S is* $\longrightarrow \subset$ State $\times$ State *is defined in Tables 5 and 6. For* $(s, s') \in \longrightarrow$*, we write* $s \longrightarrow s'$*, denoting that state* s *can transition into state* s'.

The application of a defined service is essentially the same as the application rule, except that the arguments to s must be evaluated before they can be substituted into e. In a [SEQ], if the left-hand side of `>>=` returns a value v, then v is fed as argument to the expression e on the right-hand side.

Evaluating `spawn` e results in a new parallel agent being created, which evaluates e and has no ports, thus φ is empty. Creating a new port with port descriptor p involves extending the domain of φ with p and setting its initial value to be the empty word ϵ. The port descriptor p is returned to the creating agent. The

Table 4. DAML-S Core Expressions

Σ	$\Sigma \subseteq Exp(\Sigma)$
var	$Var^{\mathcal{T}} \subseteq Exp(\Sigma)^{\mathcal{T}}$
abs	$\backslash x$ `->` $e \in Exp(\Sigma)^{\tau_1 \to \tau_2}$ for $x \in Var^{\tau_1}$, $e \in Exp(\Sigma)^{\tau_2}$
appl	$(e_1\ e_2) \in Exp(\Sigma)^{\tau_2}$ for $e_1 \in Exp(\Sigma)^{\tau_1 \to \tau_2}$, $e_2 \in Exp(\Sigma)^{\tau_1}$
cond	`cond` $e\ e_1\ e_2 \in Exp(\Sigma)^{\mathtt{IO}\ \tau}$ for $e \in Exp(\Sigma)^{\mathtt{boolean}}$, $e_1, e_2 \in Exp(\Sigma)^{\mathtt{IO}\ \tau}$
return	`return` $e \in Exp(\Sigma)^{\mathtt{IO}\ \tau}$ for $e \in Exp(\Sigma)^{\tau}$
seq	e_1 `>>=` $e_2 \in Exp(\Sigma)^{\mathtt{IO}\ \tau_2}$ for $e_1 \in Exp(\Sigma)^{\mathtt{IO}\ \tau_1}$, $e_2 \in Exp(\Sigma)^{\tau_1 \to \mathtt{IO}\ \tau_2}$
send	$e_1 ! e_2 \in Exp(\Sigma)^{\mathtt{IO}\ ()}$ for $e_1 \in Exp(\Sigma)^{\mathtt{Port}\ \tau}$, $e_2 \in Exp(\Sigma)^{\tau}$
rec	$e? \in Exp(\Sigma)^{\mathtt{IO}\ \tau}$ for $e \in Exp(\Sigma)^{\mathtt{Port}\ \tau}$
port	$\mathtt{newPort}\tau \in Exp(\Sigma)^{\mathtt{IO\ Port}\ \tau}$ for $\tau \in \mathcal{T}$
spawn	`spawn` $e \in Exp(\Sigma)^{\mathtt{IO}\ ()}$ for $e \in Exp(\Sigma)^{\mathtt{IO}\ \tau}$
choice	`choice` $e_1\ e_2 \in Exp(\Sigma)^{\mathtt{IO}\ \tau}$ for $e_1, e_2 \in Exp(\Sigma)^{\mathtt{IO}\ \tau}$
serv	$s\ e_1 \cdots e_n \in Exp(\Sigma)^{\tau}$ for $e_i \in Exp(\Sigma)^{\tau_i}$, $s \in \mathcal{S}^{\tau_1 \to \cdots \to \tau_n \to \tau}$

Table 5. Semantics of DAML-S Core - I

$$\text{(FUNC)}\ \frac{\phi \in \Omega}{\Pi, (E[\phi v_1 \cdots v_n], \varphi) \longrightarrow \Pi, (E[\phi_{\mathfrak{A}} v_1 \cdots v_n], \varphi)}$$

$$\text{(APPL)}\ \frac{\text{free}(u) \cap \text{bound}(e) = \emptyset}{\Pi, (E[(\backslash x \texttt{ -> } e)\ u)], \varphi) \longrightarrow \Pi, (E[e[x/u]], \varphi)}$$

$$\text{(CONV)}\ \frac{y \text{ is a fresh free variable}}{\Pi, (E[\backslash x \texttt{ -> } e], \varphi) \longrightarrow \Pi, (E[\backslash y \texttt{ -> } e[x/y]], \varphi)}$$

$$\text{(SERV)}\ \frac{s x_1 \cdots x_n := e \in \mathcal{S}}{\Pi, (E[s v_1 \cdots v_n], \varphi) \longrightarrow \Pi, (E[e'[x_1/v_1, \ldots, x_n/v_n]], \varphi)}$$

evaluation of a receive expression $p?$ retrieves and returns the first value of p. The port descriptor mapping φ is modified to reflect the fact that the first message of p has been extracted. Similarly, the evaluation of a send expression, $p!v$, results in v being appended to the word at p. Since port descriptors are globally unique, there will only be one such p in the system.

Table 6. Semantics of DAML-S Core - II

$$(\text{SEQ})\frac{-}{\Pi, (E[\texttt{return}\ v\ \texttt{>>=}\ e], \varphi) \longrightarrow \Pi, (E[(e\ v)], \varphi)}$$

$$(\text{SPAWN})\frac{-}{\Pi, (E[\texttt{spawn}\ e], \varphi) \longrightarrow \Pi, (E[\texttt{return}\ ()], \varphi), (e, \emptyset)}$$

$$(\text{PORT})\frac{p \text{ new } \texttt{PortRef} \qquad \varphi'(x) = \begin{cases} \epsilon & \text{if } x = p; \\ \varphi(x) & \text{otherwise.} \end{cases}}{\Pi, (E[\texttt{newPort}\ \tau], \varphi) \longrightarrow \Pi, (E[\texttt{return}\ p], \varphi')}$$

$$(\text{REC})\frac{p \in Dom(\varphi) \qquad \varphi(p) = v \cdot w \qquad \varphi'(x) = \begin{cases} w & \text{if } x = p; \\ \varphi(x) & \text{otherwise.} \end{cases}}{\Pi, (E[p?], \varphi) \longrightarrow \Pi, (E[\texttt{return}\ v], \varphi')}$$

$$(\text{SEND})\frac{p \in Dom(\varphi_2) \qquad \varphi_2(p) = w \qquad \varphi_2'(x) = \begin{cases} w \cdot v & \text{if } x = p; \\ \varphi_2(x) & \text{otherwise.} \end{cases}}{\Pi, (E[p\texttt{!v}], \varphi_1), (e, \varphi_2) \longrightarrow \Pi, (E[\texttt{return}\ ()], \varphi_1), (e, \varphi_2')}$$

$$(\text{COND-TRUE})\frac{-}{\Pi, (E[\texttt{cond True}\ e_1\ e_2], \varphi) \longrightarrow \Pi, (E[e_1], \varphi)}$$

$$(\text{CHOICE-LEFT})\frac{\Pi, (E[e_1], \varphi) \longrightarrow \Pi', (E[e_1'], \varphi')}{\Pi, (E[\texttt{choice}\ e_1\ e_2], \varphi) \longrightarrow \Pi', (E[e_1'], \varphi')}$$

The rules for (COND-FALSE) and (CHOICE-RIGHT) are similar to the rules for (COND-TRUE) and (CHOICE-LEFT) given in Table 6. If the condition b evaluates to `False`, then the second argument e_2 is evaluated next, instead of e_1 For a choice expression e_1+e_2, if the expression on the left e_2 can be evaluated, then it is evaluated.However, the choice of which one is evaluated is made non-deterministically.

IRS–II: A Framework and Infrastructure for Semantic Web Services

Enrico Motta[1], John Domingue[1], Liliana Cabral[1], and Mauro Gaspari[2]

[1] Knowledge Media Institute, The Open University, Milton Keynes, UK
{E.Motta,J.B.Domingue,L.S.Cabral}@open.ac.uk
[2] Dipartimento di Scienze dell'Informazione, University of Bologna, Italy
gaspari@cs.unibo.it

Abstract. In this paper we describe IRS–II (Internet Reasoning Service) a framework and implemented infrastructure, whose main goal is to support the publication, location, composition and execution of heterogeneous web services, augmented with semantic descriptions of their functionalities. IRS–II has three main classes of features which distinguish it from other work on semantic web services. Firstly, it supports one-click publishing of standalone software: IRS–II automatically creates the appropriate wrappers, given pointers to the standalone code. Secondly, it explicitly distinguishes between tasks (what to do) and methods (how to achieve tasks) and as a result supports *capability-driven* service invocation; flexible mappings between services and problem specifications; and dynamic, knowledge-based service selection. Finally, IRS–II services are web service compatible – standard web services can be trivially published through the IRS–II and any IRS–II service automatically appears as a standard web service to other web service infrastructures. In the paper we illustrate the main functionalities of IRS–II through a scenario involving a distributed application in the healthcare domain.

1 Introduction

Web services promise to turn the web of static documents into a vast library of interoperable running computer programs and as such have attracted considerable interest, both from industry and academia. For example, IDC [8] predicts that the Web Services market, valued at $416 million in 2002, will be worth $2.9 billion by 2006.

Existing web service technologies are based on a manual approach to their creation, maintenance and management. At the centre of the conceptual architecture is a registry which stores descriptions of published web services. Clients query the registry to obtain relevant details and then interact directly with the deployed service. The descriptions, represented in XML based description languages, such as WSDL [17] and UDDI [16], mostly focus on the specification of the input and output data types and the access details. These specifications are obviously not powerful enough to support automatic discovery, mediation and composition of web services. A software agent cannot find out what a web service actually does, by reasoning about a WSDL specification. Analogously the same agent cannot locate the appropriate

D. Fensel et al. (Eds.): ISWC 2003, LNCS 2870, pp. 306–318, 2003.

service in a UDDI registry, given the specification of a target functionality. As a result, existing web service infrastructures by and large support a manual approach to web service management: only manual discovery is supported and only 'static', manually configured web applications are possible.

The above issues are being addressed by ongoing work in the area of *semantic web services* [3, 5, 14]. The basic idea here is that by augmenting web services with rich formal descriptions of their competence many aspects of their management will become automatic. Specifically, web service location, composition and mediation can become dynamic, with software agents able to reason about the functionalities provided by different web services, able to locate the best ones for solving a particular problem and able to automatically compose the relevant web services to build applications dynamically. Research in the area is relatively new and although a number of approaches have been proposed, such as DAML-S [3] and WSMF [5], no comprehensive tool infrastructures exist, which support the specification and use of semantic web services.

In this paper we describe IRS–II (Internet Reasoning Service) a framework and implemented infrastructure which supports the publication, location, composition and execution of heterogeneous web services, augmented with semantic descriptions of their functionalities. IRS–II has three main classes of features which distinguish it from other work on semantic web services.

Firstly, it supports *one-click publishing* of 'standard' programming code. In other words, it automatically transforms programming code (currently we support Java and Lisp environments) into a web service, by automatically creating the appropriate wrappers. Hence, it is very easy to make existing standalone software available on the net, as web services.

Secondly, the IRS–II builds on knowledge modeling research on reusable components for knowledge-based systems [2, 6, 9, 10], and as a result, its architecture explicitly separates task specifications (the problems which need to be solved), from the method specifications (ways to solve problems), from the domain models (where these problems, which can be generic in nature, need to be solved). As a consequence, IRS–II is able to support *capability-driven* service invocation (find me a service that can solve problem X). Moreover, the clean distinction between tasks and methods enables the specification of flexible mappings between services and problem specifications, thus allowing a n:m mapping between problems and methods and a dynamic, knowledge-based service selection.

Finally, IRS–II services are web service compatible – standard web services can be trivially published through the IRS–II and any IRS–II service automatically appears as a standard web service to other web service infrastructures.

The paper is organized as follows: in the following section we outline our overall approach. We then describe the IRS–II framework in detail and illustrate its main components through a scenario involving a distributed healthcare application. The final section of the paper contains our conclusions.

2 The IRS–II Approach

Work on the IRS–II began in the context of the IBROW project [1], whose overall goal was to support on-the-fly application development through the automatic configuration of reusable knowledge components, available from distributed libraries on the Internet. These libraries are structured according to the UPML framework [6], which is shown in figure 1. The UPML framework distinguishes between the following classes of components:

- *Domain models.* These describe the domain of an application (e.g. vehicles, a medical disease).
- *Task models.* These provide a generic description of the task to be solved, specifying the input and output types, the goal to be achieved and applicable preconditions. Tasks can be high-level generic descriptions of complex classes of applications, such as Classification or Scheduling, as well as more 'mundane' problem specifications, such as Exchange Rate Conversion.
- *Problem Solving Methods (PSMs).* These provide abstract, implementation-independent descriptions of reasoning processes which can be applied to solve tasks in specific domains. As in the case of task models, these can be high-level, generic PSMs such as Heuristic Classification [2] and Propose&Revise [9], or they can be specialized methods applicable to fine-grained tasks, such as Exchange Rate Conversion.
- *Bridges.* These specify mappings between the different model components within an application. For example, the refinement process in heuristic classification may be mapped onto a taxonomic hierarchy of attributes within some domain, in order to construct a specific application.

Each class of component is specified by means of an appropriate *ontology* [7].

The main advantage of this framework from an epistemological point of view is that it clearly separates the various components of knowledge-based applications, thus providing a theoretical basis for analyzing knowledge-based reasoners and an engineering basis for structuring libraries of reusable components, performing knowledge acquisition, and carrying out application development by reuse [10].

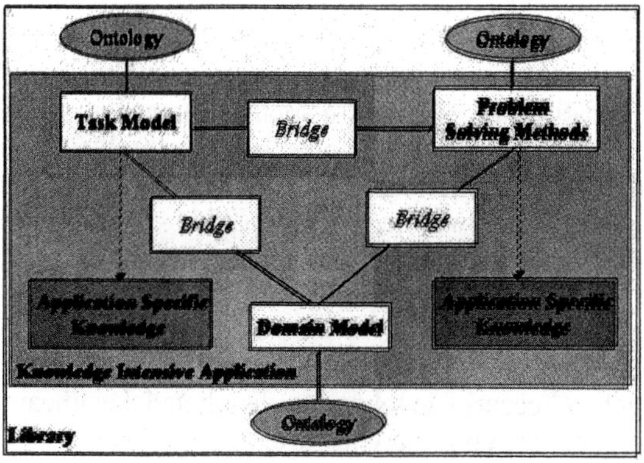

Fig. 1. The UPML framework

The application of the UPML framework to semantic web services also provides a number of advantages and in our view our framework compares favorably with approaches such as DAML-S, where services are arranged in hierarchies and no explicit notion of task is provided – tasks are defined as service-seeking agents. In

DAML-S tasks are always application specific, no provision for task registries is envisaged. In contrast in our approach, tasks provide the basic mechanism for aggregating services and it is possible to specify service types (i.e., tasks), independently of specific service providers. In principle this is also possible in DAML-S. Here a task would be defined as a service class, say S, and its profile will give the task definition. However, this solution implies that all instances of S will inherit the task profile. This approach is not very flexible, given that it makes it impossible to distinguish (and to reason about) the differences between the profile of a task (service class) and the profile of a method (specific service provider) – attributes are inherited down is-a hierarchies. In particular, in some cases, a method may only solve a weaker form of a task, and it is therefore important for a brokering agent to be able to reason about the task-method competence matching, to decide whether it is OK to use the weaker method in the given scenario. For instance, in a currency conversion scenario, a task specification may define currency conversion rates in terms of the official FT quotes, but different service providers may adopt other conversion rates. By explicitly distinguishing between tasks and methods we provide a basic framework for representing these differences and for enabling *matchmaking agents* [15] to reason about them.

The separation between tasks and methods also provides a basic model for dealing with ontology mismatches. While in DAML-S subscribing to a Service Class implies a strong ontological commitment (i.e., it means to define the new service as an instance of the class), the UPML framework assumes that the mapping between methods and tasks may be mediated by *bridges*. In practice this means that if task T is specified in ontology A and a method M is specified in ontology B, which can be used to solve T, it is still possible to use M to solve T, provided the appropriate bridge is defined.

Finally, another advantage of our approach is that the task-method distinction also enables capability-driven service invocation. While this is also possible in principle in approaches such as DAML-S, as discussed above, our approach provides both an explicit separation between service types and service providers and more flexibility in the association between methods and tasks.

3 IRS–II Architecture

The overall architecture of the IRS–II is shown in figure 2. The main components are the IRS Server, the IRS Publisher and the IRS Client, which communicate through a SOAP-based protocol [13].

3.1 IRS Server

The IRS server holds descriptions of semantic web services at two different levels. A knowledge level description is stored using the UPML framework of tasks, PSMs and domain models. These are currently represented internally in OCML [10], an Ontolingua-derived language which provides both the expressive power to express task specifications and service competencies, as well as the operational support to reason about these. Once rule and constraint languages are developed for OWL [12], we will provide the appropriate import/export mechanisms. In addition we have also special-purpose *mapping mechanisms* to connect competence specifications to specific web services. These correspond to the notion of *grounding* in DAML-S.

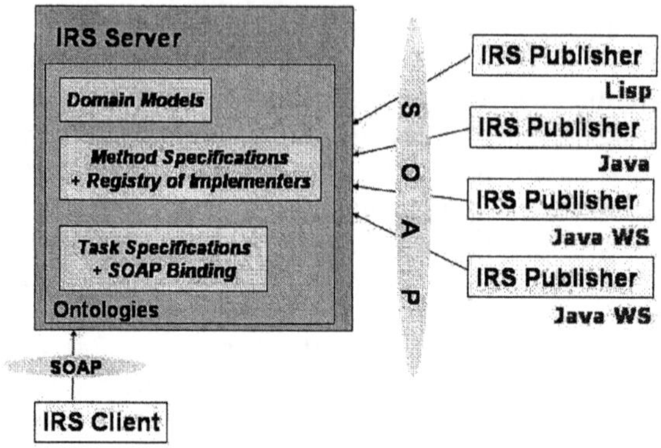

Fig. 2. The IRS–II architecture

3.2 Task Descriptions

An example task description, `exchange_rate_provision`, is shown in figure 3. As can be seen in the figure the task has two input roles, a `source_currency` and a `target_currency`, and one output role, the `exchange_rate`. The supporting definitions, such as `currency` and `positive_number`, are defined in the task ontology associated with this task, or in ontologies included by it.

```
(def-class exchange_rate_provision (goal-specification-task)
  ?task
  ((has-input-role  :value has_source_currency
                    :value has_target_currency)
   (has-output-role :value has_exchange_rate)
   (has_source_currency :type currency :cardinality 1)
   (has_target_currency :type currency :cardinality 1)
   (has_exchange_rate :type positive_number)
 (has-goal-expression
    :value (kappa (?psm ?sol)
                 (= ?sol (the_official_exchange_rate
                       (role-value ?psm has_source_currency)
                       (role-value
                       ?psm has_target_currency)))))))
```

Fig. 3. Definition of the `exchange_rate_provision` task

Web service mediation and composition are supported by task preconditions and goal expressions. No precondition is specified for this task, although the specifications of the input roles implicitly state that one (and no more than one) source and target currency have to be specified. The goal expression states that the output for the task must be compliant with the "official exchange rate", as specified in the relevant ontology.

```
(def-irs-soap-bindings
 exchange_rate_provision_ontology              ;;ontology name
 exchange_rate_provision                       ;;task name
 ((has-source-currency "xsd:symbol")           ;;source currency
  (has-target-currency "xsd:symbol"))          ;;target currency
 "xsd:float")                                  ;;output
```

Fig. 4. The soap-bindings for the `exchange_rate_provision` task

The integration of semantic specifications and web service descriptions is achieved at the task level by means of *SOAP bindings*. A SOAP binding maps the input and output roles onto SOAP types - the soap binding for the `exchange_rate_provision` task is shown in figure 4. The binding specifies that the input roles, `source_currency` and `target_currency`, are mapped to the SOAP type `xsd:symbol` and the output role is mapped to the SOAP type `xsd:float`. The relation between SOAP types and ontological input and output types is analogous to the distinction between knowledge and symbol level in knowledge-based systems [11]. The ontology specifies what knowledge is required and produced; the SOAP types specify the way this knowledge is effectively encoded in the symbol-level communication mechanism. Hence, any web service which solves a particular task must comply with both knowledge and symbol level requirements, or alternatively, bridges need to be defined to ensure interoperability.

3.3 Problem Solving Methods

The IRS server holds both the method descriptions (PSMs) and a registry of web services, which implement them. An example PSM, which tackles the `exchange_rate_provision` task, is shown in figure 5. We can see that the type of the input roles has been constrained from currency to `european_currency`. Also pre and post conditions have been introduced.

The precondition states that the bank must have available stock of the target currency, whilst the post-condition states that the rate provided is the one supplied by the European Central Bank (ECB). Hence, this particular service may or may not 'solve' the exchange provision task, depending on whether the exchange rate provided by ECB is the same as the one required by the task, or whether the matchmaking agent is happy to consider them as 'close enough'. The explicit distinction between tasks and PSMs makes it possible to precisely specify, by means of ontologies, both the problems to be addressed and the different ways to address them and provides a basis to matchmaking agents to reason about the method-to-to-task mapping and to mediation services to try and 'bridge the gap' between service requirements and service providers.

In a similar fashion to tasks, web service discovery is supported by the pre and post conditions. For instance, the conditions formulated in the `MM_Bank_exchange_rate_provider` PSM can be used to answer agent queries such as "which exchange rate services focus on European currencies" and "which exchange rate services are able to change 250K pounds into euros?".

```
(def-class MM_Bank_exchange_rate_provider (primitive-method)
 ?psm
 ((has-input-role
    :value has-source-currency
    :value has-target-currency)
 (has-output-role
  :value has-exchange-rate)
 (has-source-currency :type european_currency :cardinality 1)
 (has-target-currency :type european_currency :cardinality 1)
 (has-exchange-rate :type positive_number)
 (has-precondition
    :value (kappa (?psm) (stock-available
                          (role-value ?psm has-target-currency))
 (has-postcondition
    :value (kappa (?psm ?sol)
             (= ?sol (the-European-Central-Bank-exchange-rate
                   (role-value ?psm has-source-currency)
                   (role-value ?psm has-target-currency)))))))
```

Fig. 5. A PSM which addresses the `exchange_rate_provision` task

3.4 IRS Publisher

The IRS Publisher plays two roles in the IRS–II framework. Firstly, it links web services to their semantic descriptions within the IRS server. Note that it is possible to have multiple services described by the same semantic specifications (i.e., multiple implementation of the same functionality), as well as multiple semantic specifications of the same service. For instance, the same exchange rate converter can be described using two different ontologies for the financial sector.
Secondly, it automatically generates a set of wrappers which turn standalone Lisp or Java code into a web service described by a PSM. Standalone code which is published on the IRS appears as a standard java web service. That is, a web service endpoint is automatically generated.

Web services can be published using either the IRS Java API or the Publisher form based interface. Figure 6 shows an IRS–II user publishing a web service which implements the `MM_Bank_exchange_rate_provider`. As it can be seen from the figure, publishing a standard web service through the IRS is very easy. All the web service developer has to do to is:

1. Specify the location of the IRS server via a host and port number.
2. Indicate the PSM implemented by the service by providing its name and ontology. The menu of available PSMs is generated automatically once the location of the IRS server has been specified.
3. Specify the endpoint for the web service. If the 'service' in question is a piece of java code, specified as <java class, java method>, then the appropriate wrapper and an end-point are automatically generated by the IRS publisher.

Once the 'Publish Web Service' button has been pressed, a SOAP message encoding the information in the form is sent to the IRS server where an association between the PSM and the web service endpoint is stored in the registry of implementers. A Java API, which replicates the functionality of the form, also exists.

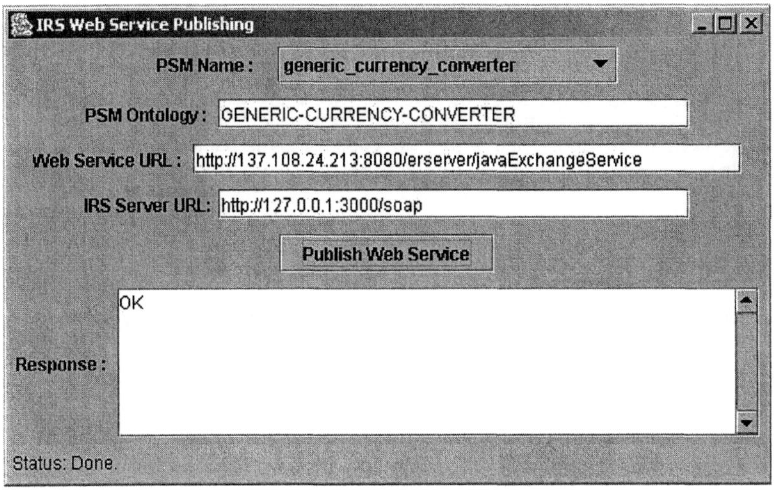

Fig. 6. The IRS–II form based interface for publishing a web service

As we mentioned earlier the IRS Publisher also allows standalone Java and Lisp code to be turned into a web service and associated with a PSM through a simple API. For Lisp a macro `irs-method-registration` is used - an example for the `MM_Bank_exchange_rate_provider` PSM is given in figure 7. When the form in figure 7 is executed, a set of wrappers are generated which make the function `mm-exchange-rate` available as a web service. Executing a second IRS form (`publish-all-services`) sends the description and location of all the newly created web services to the IRS server. The IRS Server automatically generates an endpoint, which enables the Lisp function to be accessed as a standard web service.

```
(irs-method-registration
 MM_Bank_exchange_rate_provider_ontology ;; the ontology
 MM_Bank_exchange_rate_provider          ;; the PSM
 mm-exchange-rate)                       ;; the Lisp function
```

Fig. 7. Registering the lisp function `mm-exchange-rate` as an implementation of the `MM_Bank_exchange_rate_provider` PSM.

A similar API is provided for Java. Figure 8 below shows how a Java method implementing the `MM_Bank_exchange_rate_provider` PSM could be published through the IRS publisher.

```
IRSPublisher irsPublisher =
   new IRSPublisher
        ("http://137.108.24.248:3000/soap");        //IRS server URL

irsPublisher.PublishPSM(
    "MM_Bank_exchange_rate_provider",               //PSM Name
    "MM_Bank_exchange_rate_provider_ontology",      //PSM Ontology
    "MM_Bank",                                      //Class name
    "exchangeRate");                                //method name
```

Fig. 8. The `exchangeRate` method of the Java class `MM_bank` published as an implementation of the `MM_Bank_exchange_rate_provider` PSM through the IRS Publisher.

3.5 IRS Client

A key feature of IRS–II is that web service invocation is *capability driven*. The IRS Client supports this by providing an interface and a set of APIs which are task centric. An IRS–II user simply asks for a task to be achieved and the IRS–II broker locates an appropriate PSM and then invokes the corresponding web service - see section 4 for an example. The same functionality can also be invoked programmatically, through appropriate APIs associated with the current client platforms, currently Lisp and Java.

4 The Patient Shipping Healthcare Scenario

To illustrate how the IRS can be used to develop applications in terms of a number of co-operating, distributed semantic web services, we will describe a scenario taken from the health-care domain. This scenario covers a UK health care policy which was introduced in 2002. The policy was to reduce waiting lists for the treatment of some non-urgent medical problems by giving patients who were expected to wait more than 6 months for an operation the option to be treated in mainland Europe. Figure 9 graphically illustrates how we have implemented the scenario, which we dub "patient shipping", within the IRS–II. To limit the scope of the application we focused on the medical condition of arthritis which can sometimes require surgery.

As can be seen in figure 9 five main types of web services are supported. Starting from the top left of the figure and proceeding clockwise these are:

- A diagnostic and recommender service able to diagnose a condition, for example a type of arthritis, from a set of symptoms, and to recommend a therapy such as a particular kind of surgery.
- A yellow pages service able to indicate which hospitals around Europe perform specific medical services.
- Services associated with individual hospitals able to answer queries about the availability and cost of the specific medical treatments they offer.
- Ambulance services able to provide prices for shipping patients from one hospital to another across international boundaries.
- An exchange rate service for converting prices into local currencies.

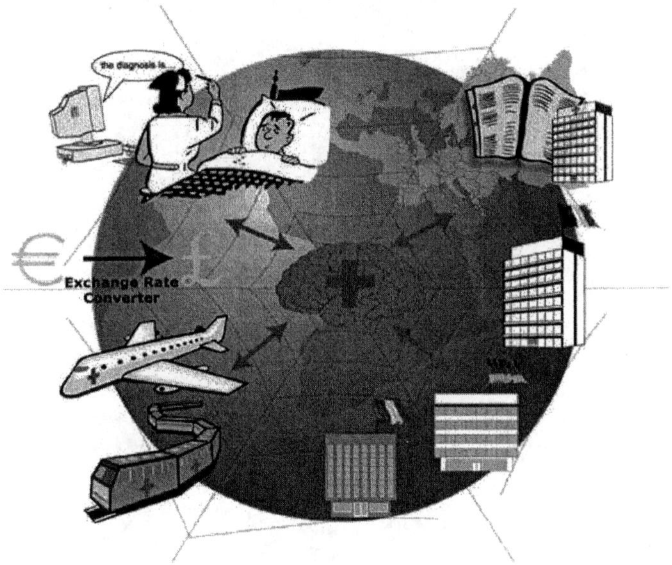

Fig. 9. A graphical overview of the patient shipping scenario

Task and PSM descriptions were created for the above services within the IRS server, using our knowledge modelling tool, WebOnto [4]. The services were then implemented in a mixture of Java Web Services (exchange rate, ambulance services and a number of the hospitals) and Lisp (all the remaining), and published using the IRS Publisher. Finally, a patient shipping web service which integrates the above services was implemented and published.

The patient shipping task has five input roles. The first four are the symptoms which the patient displays and the fifth is the location of the patient.

Figure 10 shows a visualization of the distributed application during the execution. The visualization is composed of two columns showing the IRS server and eleven published services. Each published web service is displayed in a panel containing a) the name of the PSM, b) an iconic representation of the status of the web service, and c) a log of the messages the web service sends and receives. The meanings of the icons are:

 - the web service is currently idle.

 - the web service is currently processing.

 - the web service is sending a message.

We can see in figure 10 that a number of services have been called with the following results:

- The patient has been diagnosed with *severe osteoarthritis* by the `Arthritis-Diagnosis-Service`.
- The `Arthritis-Therapy-Service` recommends that the patient is treated by means of Arthroplasty, a synonym for hip-replacement.

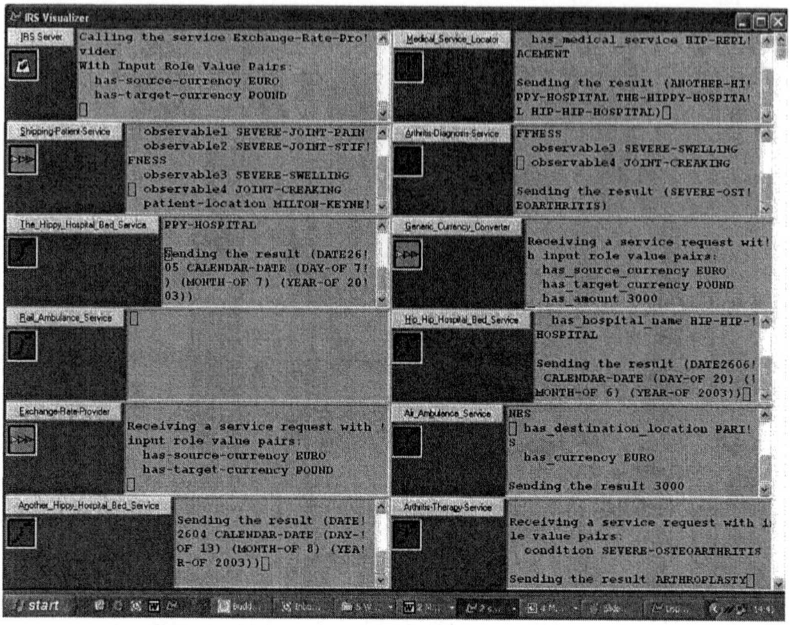

Fig. 10. A visualization of the patient shipping web service in mid execution

- The `Medical_Service_Locator` service has found three hospitals which offer hip-replacement as a medical service, specifically `Another-Hippy-Hospital`, `The-Hippy-Hospital`, and the `Hip-Hip-Hospital`.
- The `Hip-Hip-Hospital` can treat the patient first (on the 20th of June, 2003).
- The `Air_Ambulance_Service` can move the patient from Milton Keynes to Paris, the location of the `Hip-Hip-Hospital`, for 3000 Euros.

We can also see from figure 10 that three web services are currently running: the `Shipping-Patient-Service`; the `Generic_Currency_Converter` and the `Exchange-Rate-Provider`. The IRS server has just sent a message to the `Exchange-Rate-Provider` requesting an exchange rate between the Euro source currency and the Pound target currency. Three more steps will occur before the application terminates. First, the `Exchange-Rate-Provider` will send an exchange rate to the `Generic_Currency_Converter`. Second, the `Generic_Currency_Converter` will convert the 3000 Euros to 1920 pounds. Finally, the `Shipping-Patient-Service` will send the result back to the client interface (shown in figure 10).

This application illustrates some of the advantages of semantic web services in general and our approach in particular. Service discovery is carried out using semantic descriptions. For instance, once a need for hip replacement has been ascertained, the appropriate hospitals are identified, which can provide hip replacement, using a directory of hospitals and interrogating each hospital agent in turn. Thanks to the availability of semantic descriptions, it is not necessary to invoke hospital web services directly. Instead, a semantic query for hospitals providing hip replacement services is sent to the IRS and the IRS broker is then able to match this query against the semantic descriptions of the various hospital service providers. The other important aspect is the use of capability-driven service invocation. For instance, once a hospital has been identified, which can treat the patient in Paris, the application client simply sends an "achieve-task" message to the IRS server, asking the latter to find the cheapest provider of ambulance services between Milton Keynes and Paris.

5 Related Work

The framework used by the IRS–II has much in common with the *Web Service Modelling Framework (WSMF)* [5], as both the IRS–II and WSMF build on research in knowledge modelling and in particular on the UPML framework. As a result both approaches emphasize the importance of separating goal and service descriptions to ensure flexibility and scalability. The main difference between IRS–II and WSMF is that while the latter is exclusively a framework, the IRS–II is also an implemented infrastructure, providing publishing support, client APIs, brokering and registry mechanisms.

The IRS–II also differs from the DAML-S work in a number of ways, as already discussed in section 2. In particular, DAML-S does not include flexible tasks-to-methods mappings and relies instead on hierarchies of services, thus limiting the possibilities for flexible, n:m mediation between problems and services. Indeed no service-independent notion of problem type is present in DAML-S. Another difference is that IRS–II represents descriptions in OCML, while DAML-S uses DAML+OIL. This is likely to be a temporary difference, given that both approaches plan to move to OWL-based representations in the near future.

Regarding W3C Web Services standards, there are differences in the approach we take towards application development and in the roles of architecture components. For example, unlike UDDI registries, when a service description is published to IRS, the code for service invocation is automatically generated and later used during task achievement.

6 Conclusions

In this paper we have described IRS–II, a framework and an infrastructure which supports the publication, discovery, composition and use of semantic web services. IRS–II provides one-click publishing support for different software platforms, to facilitate publishing and semantic annotation of web services. Like WSMF, IRS–II capitalizes on knowledge modelling research and is based on a flexible framework separating service from problem specifications.

Future work on IRS–II will improve error handling, which at the moment is very basic. We also want to facilitate automatic mediation, in order to exploit the separation of tasks and methods more fully. Another important goal is to move away from a built-in matchmaking facility and generalize this to a matchmaking infrastructure, essentially providing hooks for different matchmaking approaches to be integrated. Finally, we plan to OWL-ify the infrastructure, to ensure its compliance with emerging semantic web standards.

Acknowledgements. This work has been partially supported by the Advanced Knowledge Technologies (AKT) Interdisciplinary Research Collaboration (IRC), which is sponsored by the UK Engineering and Physical Sciences Research Council under grant number GR/N15764/01. The AKT IRC comprises the Universities of Aberdeen, Edinburgh, Sheffield, Southampton and the Open University.

References

1. Benjamins, V. R., Plaza, E., Motta, E., Fensel, D., Studer, R., Wielinga, B., Schreiber, G., Zdrahal, Z., and Decker, S. An intelligent brokering service for knowledge-component reuse on the World-Wide Web. In Gaines, B. and Musen, M. (Editors), 11th Workshop on Knowledge Acquisition, Modeling and Management, Banff, Canada, 1998. http://ksi.cpsc.ucalgary.ca/KAW/KAW98/benjamins3/
2. Clancey W. J. (1985). Heuristic Classification. Artificial Intell*igence, 27*, pp. 289 –350.
3. DAML-S 0.7 Draft Release (2002). DAML Services Coalition.. Available online at http://www.daml.org/services/daml-s/0.7/.
4. Domingue, J. (1998) Tadzebao and WebOnto: Discussing, Browsing, and Editing Ontologies on the Web. 11th Knowledge Acquisition for Knowledge-Based Systems Workshop, April 18th–23rd. Banff, Canada.
5. Fensel, D., Bussler, C. (2002). The Web Service Modeling Framework WSMF. Available at http://informatik.uibk.ac.at/users/c70385/wese/wsmf.bis2002.pdf
6. Fensel, D. and Motta, E. (2001). Structured Development of Problem Solving Methods. IEEE Transactions on Knowledge and Data Engineering, 13(6), pp. 913–932.
7. Gruber, T. R. (1993). A Translation Approach to Portable Ontology Specifications. *Knowledge Acquisition, 5(2).*
8. IDC (2003) IDC direction 2003 Conference, Boston, March 2003
9. Marcus, S. and McDermott, J. (1989). SALT: A Knowledge Acquisition Language for Propose and Revise Systems. *Journal of Artificial Intelligence, 39(1)*, pp. 1–37.
10. Motta E. (1999). Reusable Components for Knowledge Modelling. IOS Press, Amsterdam, The Netherlands.
11. Newell A. (1982). The knowledge level. *Artificial Intelligence, 18(1)*, pp. 87–127.
12. Semantic Web. W3C Activity. Available online at http://www.w3.org/2001/sw/
13. Simple Object Access Protocol (SOAP) (2000). W3C Note 08. Available online at http://www.w3.org/TR/SOAP/.
14. McIlraith, S., Son, T. C., and Zeng, H. Semantic Web Services. IEEE Intelligent Systems, Mar/Apr. 2001, pp.46–53.
15. Sycara, K., Lu, J., Klusch, M. and Widoff, S. Matchmaking among Heterogeneous Agents on the Internet. Proceedings of the 1999 AAAI Spring Symposium on Intelligent Agents in Cyberspace, Stanford University, USA, 22–24 March 1999.
16. UDDI Specification. Available online at http://www.uddi.org/specification.html
17. Web Services Description Language (WSDL) (2001). W3C Note 15. Available online at http://www.w3.org/TR/wsdl

Towards a Knowledge-Based Approach to Semantic Service Composition

Liming Chen[1], Nigel R. Shadbolt[1], Carole Goble[2], Feng Tao[1], Simon J. Cox[3], Colin Puleston[2], and P.R. Smart[4]

[1] Department of Electronics and Computer Science, University of Southampton
Highfield, Southampton, SO17 1BJ, U.K.
{lc,nrs,ft}@ecs.soton.ac.uk

[2] Department of Computer Science, University of Manchester
Oxford Road, Manchester, M13 9PL, U.K.
{carole,colin.puleston}@cs.man.ac.uk

[3] School of Engineering Sciences, University of Southampton
Highfield, Southampton, SO17 1BJ, U.K.
sc@ecs.soton.ac.uk

[4] Epistemics Ltd., Strelley Hall, Nottingham NG8 6PE, U.K.
paul.smart@epistemics.co.uk

Abstract. The successful application of Grid and Web Service technologies to real-world problems, such as e-Science [1], requires not only the development of a common vocabulary and meta-data framework as the basis for inter-agent communication and service integration but also the access and use of a rich repository of domain-specific knowledge for problem solving. Both requirements are met by the respective outcomes of ontological and knowledge engineering initiatives. In this paper we discuss a novel, knowledge-based approach to resource synthesis (service composition), which draws on the functionality of semantic web services to represent and expose available resources. The approach we use exploits domain knowledge to guide the service composition process and provide advice on service selection and instantiation. The approach has been implemented in a prototype workflow construction environment that supports the runtime recommendation of a service solution, service discovery via semantic service descriptions, and knowledge-based configuration of selected services. The use of knowledge provides a basis for full automation of service composition via conventional planning algorithms. Workflows produced by this system can be executed through a domain-specific direct mapping mechanism or via a more fluid approach such as WSDL-based service grounding. The approach and prototype have been used to demonstrate practical benefits in the context of the Geodise initiative [2].

1 Introduction

The Grid [3] has been developed to support a vision of e-Science [1] where the sharing and coordinated use of diverse resources in dynamic, distributed virtual organizations is commonplace. Web services [4] have been designed to wrap and expose resources and provide interoperability between diverse applications. The combination of these technologies has seen Grid technologies evolving towards an

D. Fensel et al. (Eds.): ISWC 2003, LNCS 2870, pp. 319–334, 2003.

Open Grid Services Architecture (OGSA) [5] (a service-oriented distributed computing paradigm), which sees the Grid as providing an extensible set of services that virtual organizations can aggregate in various ways to solve domain specific problems.

Scientific computing in e-Science usually involves very complicated processes. A process is normally composed of many steps of computation. Each scientific computation is a resource that may come from different organizations and most probably is represented in different models and terminologies. Apart from this, other features of scientific computing include: (1) different disciplines have different problems, each dependent on different aspects of domain-specific knowledge; (2) the nature of the problem being dealt with often changes as the computation process proceeds, a fixed workflow is therefore nearly impossible for all but the most simple cases; and (3) both the underlying computing resources and the information input for the process are dynamic. Obviously an effective realization of the Grid computing paradigm, namely to promote the seamless integration of highly flexible and distributed coalitions of service-oriented components, requires not only an explicit description of resources so that they can be discovered, shared, understood and processed by both humans and machines, but also domain specific knowledge about how these resources should be composed, configured and executed to achieve some problem-solving goals.

Service discovery, description and messaging have been tackled in the web services community with introduction of a set of 'industry-standard' protocols (e.g. UDDI [6], WSDL [4] and SOAP [7]). However, none of these standards defines the meaning of services and their parameters in a way that transcends the tendency of agents to use their own terms and frame of reference. Furthermore, these protocols do not address the need to coordinate the sequencing and execution of services as part of some larger information processing tasks. Some industry initiatives have been developed to address this issue, such as WSFL [8], XLANG [9] and BPEL4WS [10]; however, such initiatives generally focus on representing service compositions where the flow of the process and the bindings between the services are known *a priori*. For scientific computations the knowledge required to select and coordinate the activity of available services is usually specific to the application domain. It is often the case that resource selection cannot be specified in advance of the execution of individual components of the more global workflow specification. As such it is apparent that pre-defined service sequencing and binding is not sufficient in scientific computing contexts.

Research on resource reuse on the Web has also been done in the knowledge engineering community in a different guise such as the IBROW project [11]. In IBROW resources are organized as component libraries and their competences are described using the language UPML [12]. This language uses logical formalisms and ontologies to describe the problem solving capabilities of the components. The central idea of the IBROW project is that of brokering [13] between libraries of software components and a user. Whilst IBROW has come up with a number of approaches to library organization, component specification, broker architectures and brokering mechanisms, it is not clear where domain knowledge can fit in the generic brokering service paradigm and how that knowledge is exploited in component selection and configuration. At this point IBROW concentrates on component discovery and configuration rather than component composition for problem solving.

Recently the Semantic Web technologies [14] have been used to provide more explicit and expressive descriptions for web services [18]. The purpose of semantic service descriptions is to facilitate service discovery based on underlying semantics that is enriched by means of ontologies using ontology description languages such as DAML+OIL [15], DAML-S [16] and OWL [17]. Obviously semantic service descriptions are not intended to provide the knowledge about when and how such services should be used to solve a problem, for example in the case of service composition. Some research [19] has exploited semantic matching via ontology-driven reasoning to conduct service composition. However, for some domains there is not always a well-structured high-level ontology that can be used to characterize the domain activities. Furthermore, for complex computations there may be multiple choices for the next step of a workflow sequence. The selection and configuration of a service for a specific problem are usually dependent on rich nexuses of domain knowledge.

We argue that both semantic service descriptions and domain-specific knowledge-based decision support services are essential ingredients for resource synthesis in e-Science. Semantic service descriptions support effective service discovery, seamless resource integration and reuse on the Grid. Knowledge-based decision-making support systems can suggest what should be done next during a service composition process and which service should be chosen once a number of services are discovered. All decisions can be made dynamically by taking into consideration the problem characteristics, service performances and previous computation results. Furthermore, once a service is selected, knowledge support can be further provided for the configuration of that service. As such we contend that web-based service–oriented applications, both e-Science and e-Business, ought to exploit semantic service descriptions and domain knowledge in order to solve complex problems through automatic, seamless resource synthesis on the Web/Grid.

This paper introduces a knowledge-based approach and framework for semantic service composition. In section 2 we briefly discuss semantic resource description using the DAML-S service ontology. Section 3 describes the knowledge-based advice system, in particular, its recommendation strategy and implementation architecture. Section 4 presents the semantic service composition framework for the knowledge-based approach. An implementation prototype is given in section 5 to demonstrate the approach with respect to an example problem taken from the GEODISE initiative. We conclude in section 6 with some initial findings and possible future work.

2 Modeling Resources with Semantics

Web/Grid services are used to model resources for scientific activities, which include not only information but also assets (data storage and specialized experimental facilities), capabilities (computational systems) and knowledge (recommendation and advice). They are represented and described using the WSDL, which uses XML [20] to describe services as a set of endpoints operating on messages. The implementation of WSDL during service design is usually more concerned with the signature of a service, i.e. the identifiers of the service and its parameters. Based on this description, it is usually impossible for software agents to figure out the precise meaning of the service identifiers and functionality provided by the service. The lack of semantics in the abstract functionality description of the service, i.e. the capabilities of the service, makes it difficult for machines to discover and use the service at the right time.

Ontological engineering plays a central role in incorporating semantics into service descriptions. An ontology is an explicit, shared specification of the various conceptualization in a problem domain. It not only provides a common language for interoperability but also adds meaning and relations to service descriptions. Ontology representation languages, such as RDF Schema [21], DAML+OIL or the ontology web language OWL, can be used to characterise the service-portfolio offered by a web service in a more expressive manner than the existing WSDL, thereby opening up the possibilty of automatic service discovery and use.

Semantically-enriched service descriptions can also be provided by the DAML Service ontology language DAML-S – a service description language that is itself written in RDF. DAML-S partitions a semantic description of a web service into three components: the service profile, process model and grounding. The Service Profile describes what a service does by specifying its inputs, outputs, preconditions, effects and other properties. The Process Model describes how a service works; each service is either an Atomic Process that is executed directly or a Composite Process that is a combination of other sub-processes. The Grounding contains the details of how an agent can access a service by specifying the details of the communication protocol, i.e. the parameters to be used in the protocol and the serialization techniques to be employed for the communication.

DAML-S allows the definition of classes of related services and can establish links to other concepts that describe specific service types and their properties. This makes service discovery much easier in terms of the built-in links, thus facilitating resource reuse. For example, in the engineering design domain a mesh generation service has a geometry file as its input, which is linked to a geometry generation service, and a mesh file as its output, which leads to the code analysis service. The mesh generation service itself uses the Gambit meshing tool as its process model.

3 A Knowledge-Based Advice System for Service Composition

Scientific activities often involve constructing a workflow either manually or automatically to realize a particular experiment or series of computations. In the service-oriented Grid computing paradigm this process amounts to discovering services on the Grid and composing those services into a workflow. Some domains such as a supermarket demand-supply chain have a fixed flow of process and stationery bindings between services. However, for most scientific disciplines a workflow is both domain-specific and problem-dependent. The appropriate selection of services at each point in the workflow often depends on the results of executing the preceding step. Moreover, the selection of a service from a set of competing services with similar capabilities is usually determined by the exact nature of the problem as well as the performances of the services available. As a result, it is not practical to specify, a priori, the precise sequence of steps for a problem goal. The successful orchestration of component services into a valid workflow specification is heavily dependent on bodies of domain knowledge as well as semantically enriched service descriptions.

A knowledge-based advice system aims to support automatic or semi-automatic service composition by providing advice constrained by bodies of domain-specific knowledge. It is described in detail below.

3.1 Strategies for Knowledge-Based Advice

There are two approaches to providing service composition advice. One is based on the semantic service descriptions, i.e. the conceptual links between services and their properties [18] [22]. It makes use of available information about service profiles such as the preconditions, constraints and outputs of the service in order to assess the potential fit of each service to a particular role in the workflow specification. The expressive description logic of DAML+OIL enables a suitable reasoning engine, such as FaCT [29], to automatically retrieve a service that matches the semantic description. External agents can use the outcome of such reasoning engines to select a service commensurate with their information processing goals. Often, however, such systems are limited with respect to the appropriate selection of services suited for a specific task or with the appropriate configuration of service parameters.

The knowledge-based approach to the provision of service composition advice can often succeed in situations where ontology-driven reasoning proves inadequate. For example, in the domain of engineering design search and optimization there are over a hundred different optimization methods, each of which is geared to solving a specific type of engineering problem. Even with a single method, different configurations of control parameters may produce very different results. Knowledge about the correct method to choose in a particular situation as well as the appropriate configuration of method parameters is an important feature of expert-level performance and a vital ingredient of problem-solving success. Any system concerned with the appropriate selection of optimization methods, therefore requires access to an exquisitely detailed representation of the knowledge contingencies relating problem characteristics and design goals with the appropriate selection and configuration of available methods.

The knowledge-based approach builds on the classical model of knowledge-based decision support systems that make extensive use of domain knowledge. Therefore, it relies heavily on the techniques of knowledge engineering [23]. The development of knowledge-based systems usually involves (1) the identification of knowledge-intensive task areas, and the gaining of a detailed insight into the ways in which knowledge is used to yield favorable decision outcomes, (2) the elicitation of, or indirect acquisition of, domain knowledge using knowledge acquisition (KA) techniques, (3) The modeling of human-level knowledge in formal, symbolic structures and the representation of that knowledge using a range of representational formalisms, (4) The use and reuse of knowledge in the knowledge-based system to meet the user requirements, and finally (5) The update and maintenance of both the formalized knowledge and knowledge-based systems. One feature of the latest knowledge engineering methodologies, such as CommonKADS [23], and knowledge engineering tools, is that they place special emphasis on the way in which knowledge is modeled so as to promote knowledge re-use across diverse problem-solving contexts.

Knowledge-based advice systems for service composition have the advantage of providing specific advice at multiple levels of granularity during the service composition process. At the highest level, the system can help determine what kind of service is required against a contextual backdrop that includes problem-solving goals and procedural knowledge. Once all the services that can fulfill the required function are discovered, the advice system can recommend an appropriate service, taking into account both problem characteristics and performance considerations. More specialized, in-depth advice can also be given, for example, how to initialize and configure the control parameters of a service. Such knowledge is usually only available from experienced users or domain experts.

In order to deploy, share and re-use knowledge-based advice systems in the Grid computing paradigm, the system has been developed with three important innovations. Firstly, ontologies are used as knowledge models for representing knowledge. Second, ontologies are exploited to conceptualize knowledge systems with commonly accepted vocabulary, thus facilitating knowledge sharing and re-use. Third, knowledge systems themselves are exposed as services within the service-oriented framework of the Grid.

3.2 A Service-Oriented Architecture for Knowledge-Based Advice Systems

Traditionally, knowledge intensive systems are constructed anew for each knowledge project. There is often little reuse of existing knowledge structures and problem-solving elements. The reasons for this are legion, including the diversity of domain knowledge, the close coupling of domain knowledge with reasoning processes and the different terminologies and modeling views adopted by different users for a single domain. It is obvious that the exploitation of knowledge technologies on the Web/Grid requires that these obstacles be successfully surmounted, an insight that has led to a variety of new tools, techniques and research agendas [14] [24] [25] [26].

Based on the above consideration we have developed a generic architecture for knowledge-based advice systems that is intended to operate on the Grid (see Figure 1) [27]. The architecture has three distinguishing features. The first is that it separates domain knowledge and reasoning functions into the Application Side and Knowledge Service Side respectively. The Application Side cares about the acquisition, modeling (knowledge engineer's work) and usage (end users' requirements) of domain knowledge. Knowledge services on the Service Side provide reasoning mechanisms, advice representation and communication. This feature enables the effective re-use of domain-specific knowledge across different problem-solving contexts and the application of common reasoning processes to diverse domain-specific problems. Such an approach has many advantages in terms of ease of maintenance and re-use of knowledge components.

A second feature of the architecture is its use of multiple layers. These layers enable the effective separation of reasoning, communication and representation components into the Inference, Communication and the Application Layers. The Application Layer uses domain ontologies from the Application Side to define an application-dependent state model that is then converted to a frame-like XML schema used as a placeholder for state variables. A state model contains the description of all possible factors that can potentially affect the advice delivered by the knowledge service. It holds the state space of an application on the Application Side and uses the state information as the input to the reasoning engine in the Inference Layer. The Communication Layer deals with the transmission protocols and serialization of messages between the Application Side and the Knowledge Service Side, i.e.

transmission of the XML schema of the state model and the state information requests. The Inference Layer provides a domain-independent inference capability via a reasoning engine. The availability of a domain-specific knowledge base enables the reasoning engine to drive inferential processes that operate on the state information.

A third feature of the architecture regards its use of ontologies – the web-oriented knowledge models. Not only are the state variables of an application denoted using ontology vocabularies, as discussed above, but also the axioms, facts and rules of the knowledge base are formalized with respect to the shared repository of common terms. The use of ontology enables different users and machines to share and reuse domain-specific knowledge. These features make the proposed advice system different from traditional standalone knowledge-based systems, and contribute to its acceptability in a Grid computing environment.

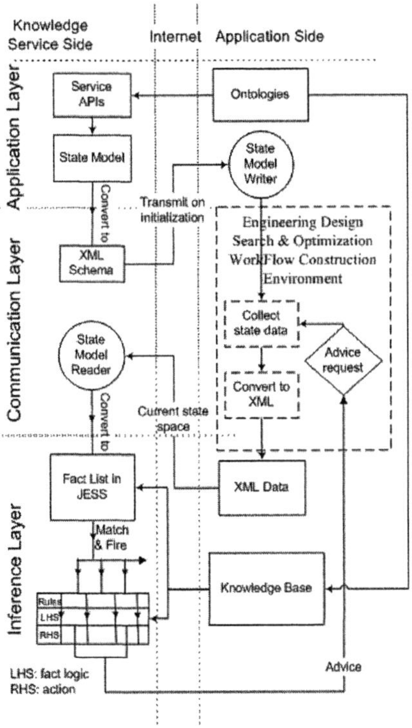

Fig. 1. The Architecture of Knowledge-based Advice System

The generic knowledge-based advice system is actually a web service, which operates as follows. The service user in the Application Side supplies domain knowledge, i.e. ontologies and knowledge bases. The knowledge service in the Knowledge Service Side creates the state model and corresponding XML schema. The state XML schema is passed onto the Application Side during knowledge service initialization. The State Model Writer in the Application Side monitors the progress of the application and collects relevant states to fill in the state XML schema. Whenever the application requests advice, the state information in the state model, i.e. an instantiated XML schema, will be sent to the knowledge service. Once the state information of the application reaches the Knowledge Service Side, it will be parsed and converted to facts. The reasoning engine in the Inference Layer will reason against these facts to provide domain-specific, context-sensitive decision support.

Figure 1 illustrates the implementation of the proposed architecture in the context of engineering design search and optimization. In this implementation, the Application Side (the user) is concerned with advice on EDSO workflow construction. Domain knowledge in this example application assumes the form of EDSO ontologies and knowledge-rich contingencies represented in a production rule-like format. The reasoning of the Inference Layer is based on JESS [28], a Java-based implementation of the CLIPS expert system shell. Outside of this domain, the aforementioned system architecture is applicable to any area of domain expertise, providing that a suitable characterization of the domain-specific knowledge is available.

4 Knowledge-Based Service Composition Framework

We have developed and partially implemented a knowledge-based service composition framework (see Figure 2) to provide a practical demonstration of our approach. This framework uses domain knowledge and advice services to provide advice and guidance with respect to the selection, sequencing and correct configuration of services as part of constructing a workflow specification. It additionally uses semantically-enriched service descriptions to assist in the process of discovering available services for workflow specification. This ability to exploit service descriptions facilitates the workflow specification process with respect to existing descriptions of Web/Grid resources.

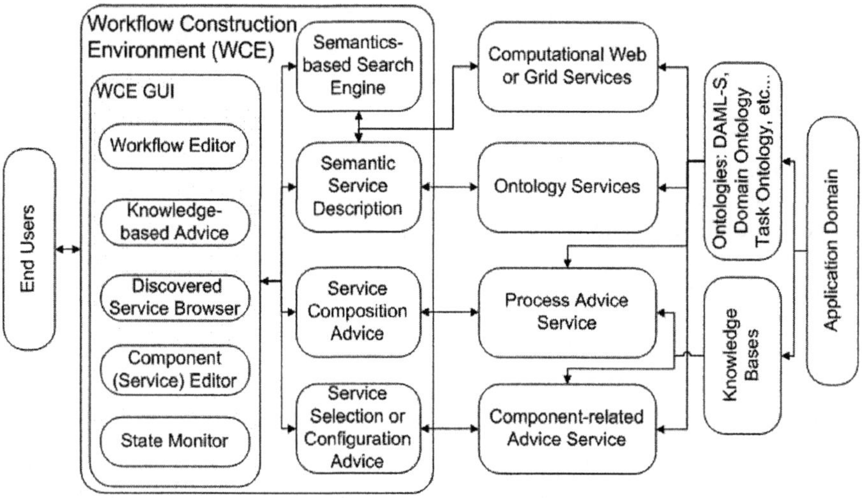

Fig. 2. The Knowledge-based Semantic Service Composition Framework

The framework consists of a set of components, mainly a Workflow Construction Environment, a set of diverse web services, Knowledge Bases and Ontologies. The Ontology component contains domain-related ontologies that provide an explicit shared conceptualization of the target domain, i.e. concepts, terms and relations. They serve as a conceptual backbone to underpin the service composition framework by supplying a common vocabulary and establishing semantic links among service properties. The ontologies were developed through ontological engineering and are exposed through the Ontology Services component. The Ontology Services provide complete access to any DAML+OIL ontology available over the Internet. Users can perform common ontological operations, such as subsumption checking, class and/or property retrieval and navigation of concept hierarchies through a set of ontology service APIs in conjunction with the FaCT reasoner [29]. Ontology Services are implemented as standard SOAP-based web services and can be accessed, shared and re-used through the WSDL standard.

The cornerstone of the service composition framework lies in the exploitation of domain-specific knowledge contained in the knowledge bases. These knowledge bases consist of concepts, axioms and rules acquired through KAs, which conceptualize the target domain. The availability of knowledge bases is a prerequisite for advice provision during the workflow construction process.

Advice services are actually knowledge-based systems that are implemented as web services [27] such as the Process and Component-related Advice Services. They provide advice based on service requests. Users can obtain advice in two ways. First, a user may request advice according to his/her epistemic needs and requirements during the workflow construction process. Secondly, a software agent can be used to monitor the service composition process as it unfolds, and provide advice and/or recommendations along the way. Both approaches need to monitor the progress of the composition process and collect snapshots of states when advice is requested. These states are then fed into the reasoning engine to retrieve context-sensitive advice as with traditional knowledge-based systems. Advice can be provided at multiple levels of granularity, for example the process level and/or the component level, dependent on the availability of knowledge in the underlying knowledge bases.

At the core of the framework is Workflow Construction Environment (WCE) It consists of a set of WCE GUIs and tools to facilitate workflow construction. Semantic service description is undertaken using ontologies accessed via the ontology services. As the DAML-S service ontology only provides the basic schema for describing a web service, it does not provide the vocabulary with which to describe specific services in different scientific domains. Therefore, domain specific ontologies are used to incorporate domain specific functions and terminology in creating semantic service descriptions. The process of specifying semantic service descriptions is carried out in two steps. Firstly, domain ontologies, such as the task ontology and the function ontology, are created. Then, the domain specific service ontology is built using concepts from the domain ontologies. The semantic descriptions of domain-specific services are actually instances of concepts from the service ontology. Semantic service descriptions are stored in the Semantic Service Description component.

Service discovery is accomplished by the use of a Semantic-based Search Engine. It is realized through reasoners such as FaCT or MatchMaker [19] acting on the semantic descriptions of services. The services that fulfill users' requirements will be returned to users as the basis for selection in the context of workflow specification.

The WCE GUI consists of five graphical tools to assist workflow construction. Each of them presents relevant structures and information via a control panel. The Component (Service) Editor is a frame-like data-storage structure. It can be used to specify a service description for service discovery or to define a service directly by filling in the required data fields. The structure of the Component Editor is dynamically generated in accordance with the service ontology. The Discovered Service Browser displays services returned by the search engine. Users can choose a service from the panel based on the advice given for a particular workflow composition. The State Monitor monitors the workflow construction process, and collects and maintains a workflow state space. During the workflow construction process, whenever a request for advice is made, the state space can be fed into the underlying knowledge-based advice services. Advice as to what to do next and which service should be used is then provided as output by these services. The results are shown in the Knowledge-based Advice panel. Workflows are built in the Workflow Editor where different services are connected together. Details of the workflow construction process will be described in the next section in the context of a real application.

5 Example Application: Workflow Construction in Geodise

Engineering design search and optimization (EDSO) is the process whereby engineering modeling and analysis are exploited to yield improved designs. An EDSO process usually comprises many different tasks. Consider the design optimization of a typical aero-engine or wing. It is necessary (1) to specify the wing geometry in a parametric form which specifies the permitted operations and constraints for the optimisation process, (2) to generate a mesh for the problem, (3) decide which analysis code to use and carry out the analysis, (4) decide the optimisation schedule, and finally (5) execute the optimisation run coupled to the analysis code. Apparently a problem solving process in EDSO is a process of constructing and executing a workflow.

Grid enabled engineering design search and optimization (Geodise) aims to aid engineers in the EDSO process by providing a range of internet-accessible web services comprising a suite of design optimization and search tools, computation packages, data, analysis and knowledge resources. A desirable feature of Geodise is that it should allow for users to compose a suite of EDSO algorithms (web services) into a workflow, i.e. to create a design solution to a specific EDSO problem. To provide such a capability we have applied our approach and the corresponding framework in Geodise. The detailed work is described below.

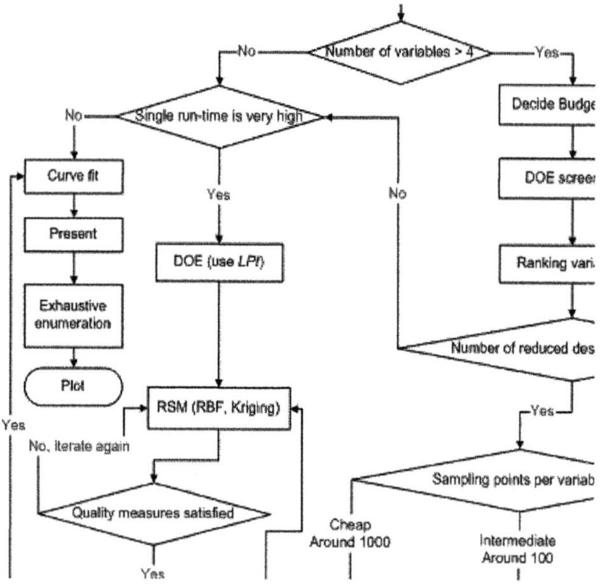

Fig. 3. Fragment of EDSO Design Process Flowchart

We have undertaken extensive knowledge and ontological engineering using CommonKADS methodology in the domain of EDSO. A substantial amount of domain knowledge has been acquired and modelled [30], for example the EDSO process knowledge in Figure 3. A number of ontologies have also been developed using OilEd [31] including the EDSO basic domain ontology, the optimization function ontology and the DAML-S-based task service ontology.

We have developed ontology services that use the emerging web ontology standard, DAML+OIL, as the underlying representation language. The services provide a set of Java APIs for common ontological operations. Ontology services are realized as a standard SOAP-based web service in Java and deployed using Apache Tomcat & Axis technologies.

We have developed a process knowledge base for EDSO design processes based on the knowledge model in Figure 3. Table 1 and Table 2 show a small subset of facts and rules in the knowledge base. We have implemented a knowledge-based advice system (discussed in 3.2) which is driven by the EDSO process knowledge [27]. The advice system monitors the design process and provides context-sensitive help at each stage of the process. This process is described in more detail below.

Table 1. Fragment of the facts in the process knowledge base

```
  … …
  f-6  (MAIN::resource (name "step_file") (location "d:/geodise/res/airFoilStepFile"))
  f-7  (MAIN::resource (name "gambit_jou_file") (location "d:/geodise/res/gambit.jou"))
  f-8  (MAIN::workflow_task (name "geometry") (input nil) (output "step_file") (relevant_commands nil) (finished? nil) (constrains nil) (dependance ))
  f-9  (MAIN::workflow_task (name "mesh") (input "step_file" "gambit_jou_file") (output "mesh_file") (relevant_commands nil) (finished? nil)
(constrains nil) (dependance ))
 … …
```

Table 2. Fragment of the rules in the process knowledge base

```
    … …
   (defrule rule1
          (not (state_panel (available_resources $?x "step_file" $?y)))      ?taskID<-(workflow_task(input $?a "step_file" $?b))
=>        (retract ?taskID)
          (printout t ?taskID " Retract this workflow task because it needs step_file as input, which is not available according to the state model. "  crlf))
   (defrule rule2
          (not (state_panel (available_resources $?x "gambit_jou_file" $?y)))   ?taskID<-(workflow_task(input $?a "gambit_jou_file" $?b))
=>        (retract ?taskID)
          (printout t ?taskID " Retract this workflow task because it needs gambit_jou_file as input,  which is not available according to the state model. "  crlf))
   … …

   (defrule workflow-answer-1
          (declare (salience -10))  (workflow_task (name ?n))
=>        (printout t "In term of the work flow, next step you can do: " ?n crlf))
```

As there are currently no semantically described EDSO task services available on the Grid, it makes no sense to search the Internet for any required task services. Therefore, we have not implemented the Semantics-based Search Engine of the service composition framework. In Geodise, the process of service discovery amounts to loading the EDSO task service ontology into the workflow construction environment. Users can then browse the service hierarchy and define appropriate services.

We have developed a workflow construction environment prototype for the framework as shown in Figure 4. The left panel is used to specify ontology services and the task service ontology. It presents the task service hierarchy through the Ontology Concept Browser. The right panel is the Component Editor. Its lower part is used to specify the properties of a task service and its upper part is used to search for task services that match the semantic description defined in the lower part. As we have not implemented the search mechanisms, the Component Editor is actually used to define a service directly. The middle panel is the Workflow Editor where services are composed and edited. The bottom panel is the State Monitor while the right top panel is used to display knowledge-based advice on service composition. The knowledge-based advice system has not yet been wrapped up as a set of web services. It currently runs as a standalone knowledge-based system, which is directly integrated with the workflow construction environment. Despite this difference from the architectural specification detailed above, the decision support provided for service composition is the same.

A workflow specification represents a design solution to a specific EDSO problem. The general procedure for composing services as a workflow using the workflow construction environment is described step by step below. This process is also illustrated in Figure 4.

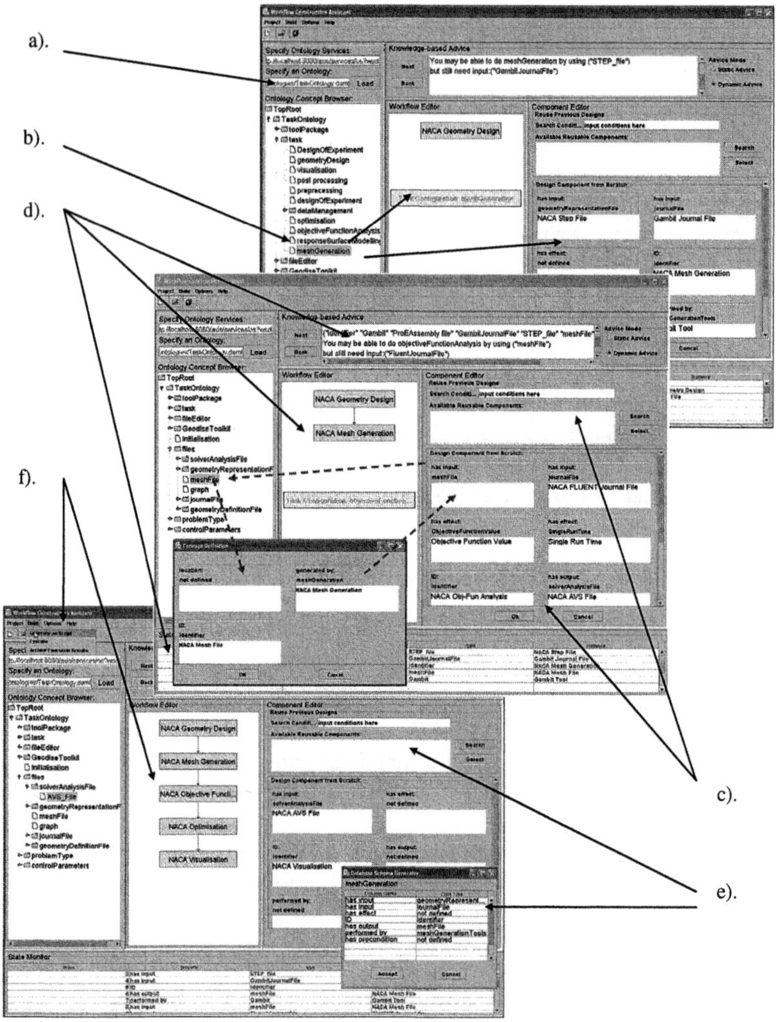

Fig. 4. Screenshots of Workflow Construction Environment

a). Specify and load the Geodise task service ontology via ontology services in the left panel. The Geodise task services will be presented in a hierarchy in the Ontology Concept Browser.

To start a workflow construction process, users need to provide an initial description of the problem at hand, e.g. the problem type and its characteristics. The knowledge-based advice system can then give advice on what to do first to solve the problem via the advice panel. Alternatively a static knowledge support system will suggest to users what should be done first.

b). Select a suitable primitive task service by navigating the service hierarchy utilizing the initial advice, and drag and drop it into the Workflow Editor. A task service description form will appear in the Component Editor for defining the service.

c). Define a task service by filling in the property values of the task service description form. Users can follow the ontological concept links from the semantic task service description to define each property. For example, to define a mesh file for the objective function analysis task, the semantic link of the property "meshFile" will bring you to the "MeshFile" concept in the Geodise task service ontology. Dragging and dropping the concept into the property's input area will in turn open a concept definition dialog box for users to input relevant values. This process is demonstrated by the red dashed arrows in Figure 4.

Alternatively users can partially describe the properties of a service using the service description form. The semantic-based search engine (at the top of the Component Editor) will enable users to discover similar task services on the Grid. This feature has not been implemented at present.

d). Once a task service is defined or discovered and selected in the Component Editor, two key operations will follow. First, an instantiated task service with embedded semantics will be added to the Workflow Editor. It will form a step of the workflow specified for the current problem. This is shown as a yellow box in Figure 4. Second some property information of the task service, in particular, the input, effect and output parameters, will be added to the state memory of the Workflow Construction Environment. These states are, in turn, passed on to the underlying advice system and displayed in the State Monitor. The recommendation on what one should/can do next is subsequently displayed in the knowledge advice panel. This advice guides users to select a suitable service from the service hierarchy.

e). A database schema for any task service can be generated automatically by dragging and dropping the service from the task service ontology. The instantiated service can then be archived in the database. By collecting all the services created for different problems a semantically-enriched knowledge base can be built over a period of time. This provides semantic content for the search engine to work on for future service discovery.

f). After an arbitrary number of loops, i.e. advice on required services, service discovery/configuration, and service composition, the user can construct a workflow that solves the specific problem. The generated workflow can be submitted to the underlying enactment engine where various resources will be bound together to form an executable. The executable will run in a domain specific execution environment. In Geodise, the executable is a Matlab .m script and the execution environment is the Matlab environment [32]. A full discussion of workflow enactment and execution issues is beyond the scope of this paper.

Each time a workflow is constructed for a particular design problem, it can be archived to form a semantically enriched problem/solution within a knowledge repository. This facilitates the re-use of previous designs, while avoiding the overhead of manually annotating the solution with respect to semantic content.

6 Conclusions

This paper has described an approach, a framework and its implementation towards the delivery of knowledge-based service composition, or more generally, resource synthesis, in a web-enabled or Grid computing environment. A central feature of the approach discussed herein is the exploitation of domain-specific knowledge to compose web/Grid services into a workflow specification specifically geared to a core set of problem-solving objectives based on best practice knowledge and expertise. In developing this approach we have emphasized the importance of DAML-S, and related technologies, in providing semantically-enriched characterizations of available services as the basis for dynamic service discovery and appropriate resource utilization. We have further outlined a service-oriented architecture for knowledge-based systems operating in the context of the technological infrastructure provided by Grid-computing platforms and the semantic web. Our approach co-opts traditional knowledge-based systems engineering with the current state-of-the-art in ontology specification and XML web services. The prototype system, developed to provide a concrete demonstration of our approach, exemplifies this close merger of previously disparate technologies, availing itself of both a knowledge-based decision support facility and exploitation of semantically-enriched service descriptions in a single unitary environment. Such systems empower problem-solving agents by enabling maximal exploitation of available resources to meet a diverse set of complex problem-solving goals.

The approach and the example prototype have both been developed in a specific application context, namely that of design search and optimization. While the full evaluation of this system awaits further investigation and user feedback, our initial results have been promising. We have not seen any reasons to prevent this approach from being applied to other types of Grid applications.

The importance of domain knowledge and expertise to problem-solving success is nowhere more apparent than in the field of scientific computation and scientific discovery. We have demonstrated the importance of domain knowledge with respect to one aspect of expertise, namely the selection and configuration of services as part of a workflow specification. While this system is as yet only partially automated – users still need to manually construct workflows based on knowledge-system output – we firmly believe the current results are an important milestone on the way to providing a fully automatic means of intelligent service discovery and resource utilization in the context of Grid computing and the Semantic Web.

Acknowledgements. This work is supported by the UK EPSRC Geodise e-Science pilot (GR/R67705/01). The authors gratefully acknowledge the contributions from and discussion with EPSRC projects MyGrid (GR/R67743/01) [33] and AKT (GR/N15764/01(P)).

References

1. Hey, T. and Trefethen, A. E.: The Data Deluge: An e-Science Perspective. To appear in "Grid Computing – Making the Global Infrastructure a Reality", Wiley, January 2003
2. Geodise project: http://www.geodise.org/
3. Foster, I. and Kesselman, C.: The Grid: Blueprint for a New Computing Infrastructure. Morgan Kaufmann (1999)
4. Chinnici, R., Gudgin, M., Moreau, J. and Weerawarana, S.: Web Services Description Language (WSDL) 1.2, *W3C Working Draft*. http://www.w3.org/TR/wsdl12/ (2002)
5. Foster, I., Kesselman, C., Nick, J. and Tucke S.: The Physiology of the Grid: An Open Grid Service Architecture for Distributed Systems Integration. http://www.globus.org/ogsa/ (2002)
6. UDDI. The UDDI technical white paper. 2000. http://www.uddi.org/
7. SOAP 1.2 Working draft, http://www.w3c.org/TR/2001/WD-soap12-part0-20011217/
8. WSFL 1.0 http://www-3.ibm.com/software/solutions/webservices/pdf/WSFL.pdf
9. XLANG http://www.gotdotnet.com/team/xml_wsspecs/xlang-c/default.htm
10. Curbera, F., Goland, Y., Klein, J., Leymann, F., Roller, D., Thatte, S. and Weerawarana, S. Business Process Execution Language for Web Services, Version 1.0. http://www-106.ibm.com/developerworks/webservices/library/ws-bpel/
11. IBROW project: http://www.swi.psy.uva.nl/projects/ibrow/home.html
12. Fensel, D., Benjamins, V.R., Motta, E. and Wielinga, B.: UPML: A Framework for knowledge system reuse. In Proceedings of the International Joint Conference on AI (IJCAI-99)
13. Benjamins, V.R., Plaza, E., Motta, E., Fensel, D., Studer, R., Wielinga, B., Schreiber, G. and Zdrahal, Z: IBROW3 – An Intelligent Brokering Service for Knowledge-Component Reuse on the World Wide Web. In proceedings of KAW'98 (1998)
14. Berners-Lee, T., Hendler, J. and Lassila, O.: The Semantic Web, Scientific American, May 2001
15. DAML+OIL http://www.daml.org.
16. DAML Services Ontology. DAML-:Web Service Description for the Semantic Web. In 1st International Semantic Web Conference (ISWC2001). http://www.daml.org/services/
17. OWL Web Ontology Language 1.0 Reference, http://www.w3.org/TR/owl-ref/
18. Sirin, E., Hendler, J. and Parsia, B.: Semi-automatic Composition of Web Services Using Semantic Descriptions. "Web Services: Modeling, Architecture and Infrastructure" workshop in conjunction with ICEIS2003 (2002)
19. Paolucci, M. Kawmura, T., Payne, T. and Sycara, K.: Semantic Matching of Web Services Capabilities. In The First International Semantic Web Conference (2002)
20. Extensible Markup Language, http://www.w3.org/XML/
21. Resource Description Framework (RDF) Model and Syntax Specification. W3C Recommendation Standard, http://www.w3.org/TR/1999/REC-rdf-syntax-19990222/
22. Wroe, C., Stevens, R., Goble, C., Roberts, A. and Greenwood, M.: A Suite of DAML+OIL Ontologies to Describe Bioinformatics Web Services and Data. International Journal of Cooperative Information Systems, Editor(s): Prof. Bukhres, O. ISSN: 0218-8430 (2003)
23. Schreiber S., Akkermans H., Anjewierden A., Hoog R., and Shadbolt N.: Knowledge Engineering and Management. The MIT Press, London (1999)
24. Advanced Knowledge Technologies (AKT) project: http://www.aktors.org/
25. Cannataro, M. and Talia, D.: The Knowledge Grid. Communication of the ACM, Vol.46 No.1, pp89–93 (2003)
26. Chen, L., Cox, S.J., Goble, C., Keane, A.J, Roberts, A., Shadbolt, N.R., Smart, P. and Tao, F.: Knowledge Services for Distributed Service Integration. In Proceedings of UK e-Science all hands meeting (2002)

27. Tao, F., Chen, L., Shadbolt, N.R., Pound, G. and Cox, S.J.: Towards the Semantic Grid: Putting Knowledge to Work in Design Optimization. In Proceedings of the 3rd International Conference on Knowledge Management, Industry meets Science, pp555–566. (2003)
28. Jess, the rule engine for the Java platform, http://herzberg.ca.sandia.gov/jess/
29. Horrocks, I., Sattler, U. and Tobies, S.: Practical reasoning for expressive description logics. Lecture Notes in Artificial Intelligence, No.1705 pp.161–180. Springer-Verlag (1999)
30. Chen, L., Cox, S.J., Goble, C., Keane, A.J., Roberts, A., Shadbolt, N.R., Smart, P., Tao, F.: Engineering Knowledge for Engineering Grid Applications [http://www.geodise.org/VPO/Files/Papers/euroweb02Final-submission-version.doc]. In Proceedings of Euroweb 2002 Conference, The Web and the GRID: from e-science to e-business, pp12–25 (2002)
31. Bechhofer, S., Horrocks, I., Goble, C. and Stevens, R.: OilEd: a Reason-able Ontology Editor for the Semantic Web DL2001, 14th International Workshop on Description Logics (2001)
32. Pound, G., Eres, H., Wason, J., Jiao, Z., Keane, A.J., and Cox, S.J.: A Grid-enabled Problem Solving Environment (PSE) for Design Optimization within Matlab. International Parallel and distributed Processing Symposium IPDPS-2003 (2003)
33. MyGrid project: http://mygrid.man.ac.uk/index.shtml

Security for DAML Web Services: Annotation and Matchmaking*

Grit Denker[1], Lalana Kagal[2], Tim Finin[2], Massimo Paolucci[3], and Katia Sycara[3]

[1] SRI International, Menlo Park, California, USA
denker@csl.sri.com
[2] University of Maryland Baltimore County, Baltimore, Maryland, USA
{lkagal1,finin}@cs.umbc.edu
[3] Carnegie Mellon University, Pittsburgh, Pennsylvania, USA
{paolucci, katia}@cs.cmu.edu

Abstract. In the next generation of the Internet semantic annotations will enable software agents to extract and interpret web content more quickly than it is possible with current techniques. The focus of this paper is to develop security annotations for web services that are represented in DAML-S and used by agents. We propose several security-related ontologies that are designed to represent well-known security concepts. These ontologies are used to describe the security requirements and capabilities of web services providers and requesting agents. A reasoning engine decides whether agents and web service have comparable security characteristics. Our prototypical implementation uses the Java Theorem Prover from Stanford for deciding the degree to which the requirements and capabilities match based on our matching algorithm. The security reasoner is integrated with the Semantic Matchmaker from CMU giving it the ability to provide security brokering between agents and services.

1 Introduction

Today's Internet is a vast information resource. However, its lack of structure and computer understandable metadata make it difficult to extract the desired information in a reasonable time. The Semantic Web is a vision of a future Internet in which web resources are enriched with machine-processable metadata, which describes their meaning. This metadata will enable software agents or search engines to find and interpret web content much more quickly and precisely than is possible with current techniques, such as keyword search or data mining. The DARPA Agent Markup Language DAML+OIL [1] is a language that allows the annotation of web pages to indicate their meaning. One of the advantages of DAML+OIL over other markup languages like XML or RDF is its expressiveness through built-in semantic concepts. For instance, DAML+OIL allows

* Supported by the Defense Advanced Research Projects Agency through the Air Force Research Laboratory under Contract F30602-00-C-0168 to SRI and contract F30602-00-2-0592 to CMU and DARPA contract F30602-97-1-0215 to UMBC.

D. Fensel et al. (Eds.): ISWC 2003, LNCS 2870, pp. 335–350, 2003.

the definition of relationships between classes such as inheritance (subclassing), equivalence, or construction of classes as boolean combinations of other classes (e.g., intersection or union of classes). These features allow to capture relevant semantic information in an ontology that proves useful when reasoning about ontologies and web resources that are marked-up with such ontologies.

In this paper, we are bridging the gap between the Semantic Web and security through DAMLized security annotations and by providing brokering over these annotations. Information security plays an increasingly critical role in society. Given the increased importance of the World Wide Web for business, industry, finance, education, government and other sectors, security will play a vital role in the success of the Semantic Web. It is essential to have tools and techniques in place that will allow the storage, maintenance, and processing of information of the Semantic Web in ways that meet security requirements such as authentication, authorization, and data integrity.

Our work focuses on security aspects for DAML web services. DAML-S [2] is a set of ontologies that support the description of Web services at three levels of abstraction: capability, process and invocation. The *capabilities* of a Web service are expressed by the *Service Profile* which describes high level features of the Web service and, most importantly, input/output transformations produced by the invocation of the Web service. The *process*, expressed by the *Service Model* describes what the service does. Finally, the invocation is described by the *Service Grounding* that describes how to contact the service, for example through asynchronous messaging or remote procedure call, and the format of the information to exchange.

In this paper, we aim to provide a framework that will allow the annotation of web services and agents with security information on a very high abstraction level. Motivating examples are given in Section 2. In Section 3 we propose several security-related ontologies that are designed to represent well-known security techniques in terms of their characteristics like credentials, mechanisms supported, notations used, etc. These ontologies are used to describe the security requirements and capabilities of web services and requesting agents. The requirements and capabilities can be specific by stating the particular standards/protocols supported or more generally in terms of the security mechanisms used, the credentials required or notations specified. Security markup adds value to the semantic web when used in connection with inference systems that support the process of deciding which web services matches a request. In Section 4 we propose an algorithm that decides whether agents and web service have comparable security characteristics by verifying that the agent's requirements are satisfied by the web service's capabilities and the service's requirements are met by the agent's capabilities. Our prototypical implementation uses JTP, the Java Theorem Prover from Stanford [3], for deciding the degree to which the requirements and capabilities match based on our matching algorithm. The security reasoner is integrated with the Semantic Matchmaker from CMU [4,5] giving it the ability to provide security brokering between agents and services.

An extended example explains the working of the system. Section 5 concludes with a brief summary and future work.

1.1 Related Work

Over the last couple of years many security-related frameworks for web applications have been proposed. A fair number of them are based on XML, like XML Signature [6,7], SAML [8], and WS-Security [9]. Our work aims to provide an layer of abstraction on top of the various existing security-related standards, addressing general security mechanisms (such as confidentiality etc.) without re-defining all the details for specific implementation choices (such as XMLSignature Syntax).

To our best knowledge, no integrating formal framework for this wide array of security-related approaches exists. An overview about security formats by G. Klyne [10] mentions many of the security notions that we formally specified in our ontologies. The openness of the semantic web dictates that there will be no such thing like one standard for security that will be adopted. Rather we expect that new protocols or mechanisms for security will emerge as research progresses. Nevertheless, we think that languages like DAML+OIL could be used to provide bridges between different formalism and enable interoperability. This is our motivation in providing a security ontology that is able to describe security mechanism of various different kinds on a very high abstraction level. Another advantage of using an ontological approach and a language like DAML+OIL is, that our approach is extensible. As new mechanisms become available, we can extend the existing classes and instances in order to incorporate the latest developments.

Most web based application servers like Apache, Tomcat, and Websphere include basic security functionality including authenticating users (via username/password, certificate, etc.), securing the communication (via https, ssl, etc.), support for sessions, etc. We are modeling these commonly present security features and services so that our ontologies can be used to describe and reason about a wide range of security related concepts.

2 Context and Motivating Example

Our work is targeted toward situations in which agents and web services have security markup as well as other more functionally-oriented markup. An agent has the task to find a web service with a specific functionality. Additionally, the agent is interested only in those web services that fulfill certain security properties, such as communicating via encrypted messages without needing authentication, to name an example. The agent itself has capabilities such as the credentials it holds or protocols it is able to use, that will determine which web services are a possible match for the agent's request. Similarly, a web service has capabilities including which security mechanism it utilizes, which credentials it is able to accept etc. Along with capabilities, a web service may also have its own requirements on agents that it is willing to communicate with. For example, a web service might have the capability to sign all outgoing messages and it might require subscribing agents to authenticate using a login. Therefore, though the web service may provide the functional capabilities that the agent is looking for (for instance, an online reservation service), the web service and agent may not match in terms of their security requirements and capabilities.

Our work defines necessary notations to express security-related capabilities and requirements of web services, so that they can be exploited by a special-purpose reasoner and matched against agent requests. Web services register with a matchmaker service describing both their functional capabilities (such as name, parameters, etc.) as well as security-related information. The ontologies we suggest in Section 3 can be used for this purpose. Examples for security requirements are "authentication by X.509 certificates" or "use of SSH protocol". Examples for security capabilities are "possession of a login" or "possibility to authenticate oneself." An agent making a request essentially fills out a web service template, describing the desired characteristics of the requested-service. Along with describing its own security capabilities, it includes requirements for the requested service. The request is sent to a matchmaker who, after finding services that meet the functional requirements of the agent, will utilize the security reasoner to decide the subset of all discovered services that also meet the security requirements of the requester agent.

Here are some examples how one can make use of security capability and requirement markups. For our work we are assuming that the matchmaker is trusted.

Example: Match. An agent, A, is looking for a travel web service. Agent A, using a matchmaker interface, fills out a template for a requested web service, describing the desired functionality of the web service as well as the agent's security requirements and capabilities. Let's assume that the agent is only capable of performing Open-PGP encryption and requires that the travel service be capable of authenticating itself and communicating in XML. A travel web service, T, registers with the same matchmaker. It provides its name, description, functional capabilities, security requirements and security capabilities. We assume that the travel service requires an agent to be able to perform encryption and the service itself is capable of the XKMS protocol for message exchanges.

When the agent submits its request, the matchmaker goes through the description of all services registered with it to find a set of services that provide travel functionality. So, the matchmaker finds service T as a functional match and checks the security requirements and capabilities of agent A against those of the web service T. In this case there is a match, because the agent's requirements are fulfilled by the service's capabilities and the service's requirements are met by the agent's capabilities. But what happens if the security capabilities and the security requirements are not subsumptions of each other? This brings us to the next scenario.

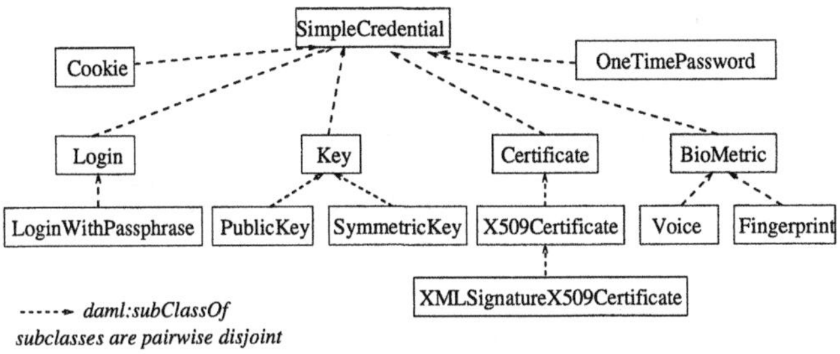

Fig. 1. A credential ontology (class hierarchy I)

Example: Negotiation. We do not assume that agents and services always register with their full capabilities. For example, an agent registers with the capability of having some certificate but the web service requires specifically X.509 certificates. The requirement of the web service is a stronger condition than what can be asserted by the capabilities of the agent and, thus, there is no match. Cases like this might be useful when agent or service first want to go through another protocol in which they establish some level of trust before they release specifics about the credentials or other capabilities they hold. Protocols for negotiation in the context of our work will be subject of future work.

3 DAML Ontologies

Our goal is to define security ontologies in DAML+OIL that allow the annotation of agents and web services with respect to various security related notions such as access control, data integrity and others. These ontologies are the basis for doing automatic subsumption reasoning over security annotations. All ontologies can be found at `www.csl.sri.com/users/denker/daml-sec/`. We start with an ontology that summarizes various ways in which authentication using credentials can take place.

3.1 Credentials

The process of establishing and verifying the identity of a requesting party in a web application, so-called authentication, is often the basis of the decision whether access is granted or not. Authentication is based on some token, also called credential, that the requesting party would know or have. Credentials are one of the various well-known authentication techniques such as name-passphrase login, public and private keys or certificates. Our goal is to be able to specify access control restrictions of web pages or web services that use authentication as a requirement for authorized access.

Different types of credentials are at the core of access restrictions. Thus, our first ontology in DAML+OIL defines the kind of credentials that are most commonly used in today's Internet security.

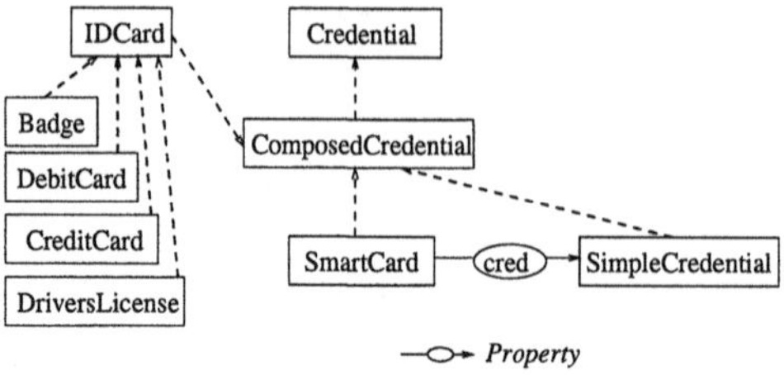

Fig. 2. A credential ontology (class hierarchy II)

We distinguish between "SimpleCredential" and "ComposedCredential". The top-level class "SimpleCredential" (see Figure 1) is subclassed to "Cookie, Login, Key, Certificate, BioMetric", and "OneTimePassword" (subclass relationships are depicted using dotted arrows). All subclasses are pairwise disjoint. "Public Key" and "Symmetric Key" are disjoint subclasses of the key class. The certificate class is specialized to "X509Certificate", and further to the specific class of X509 certificates in the XML Signature [7].

We have defined some of the most commonly existing classes of composed credentials (see Figure 2), such as "IDCard" and "SmartCard". For example, a smart card can contain data such as keys, biometric templates or PINs for authentication. Thus, composed credentials often contain simple credentials, as modeled in our ontology with a property "cred". Various specializations of identity cards are given. A simple credential is also a subclass of the composed credential class. Our ontology is extensible to allow for more credential classes or further properties.

Figures 1 and 2 only depict classes and their inheritance relationships. Properties and other restrictions are defined in the ontologies as well. For example the LoginWithPassphrase class has two datatype properties defined, "loginName" and "passphrase", both of type string (see Figure 3). We are using the DAML "restriction" concept to express that the cardinality on these properties for the login class is constrained to one. That means each LoginWithPassphrase-credential comes along with exactly one name and one passphrase. For the certificate class we defined an object property, that is a property with a DAML class as its range type. The property "assoc" associates with each certificate some data (such as issuer name, serial number, etc). In the special case of an XML Signature certificate, the object property is restricted to be of type "X509Data". This class is defined to be equivalent to the X509 element of the XML Signature definition in [7]. This way we tie our ontology into an ontology that is being standardized. For instance, a certificate that complies with the syntax of the XML Signature X509 key data element can be defined as follows:

```
<daml:ObjectProperty rdf:ID="assoc">
  <daml:range rdf:resource="CertificateData"/>
</daml:ObjectProperty>

<daml:Class rdf:ID="XMLSignatureX509v3Certificate">
  <daml:subClassOf rdf:resource="#Certificate">
```

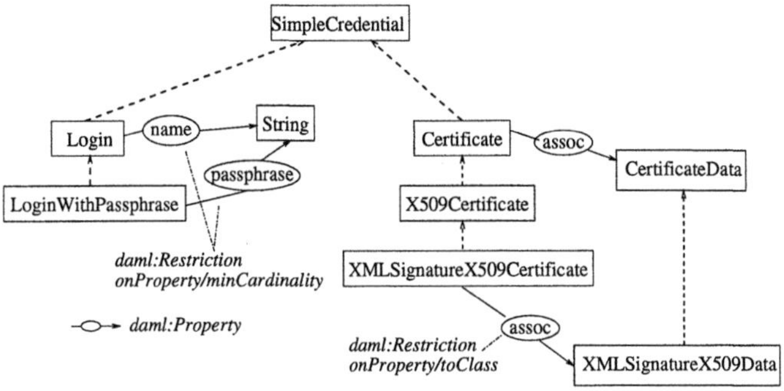

Fig. 3. A credential ontology (some properties)

```
  <daml:Restriction daml:cardinality="1">
    <daml:onProperty rdf:resource="#assoc"/>
    <daml:hasClass rdf:resource=
                     "http://www.w3.org/2000/09/xmldsig#X509Data"/>
  </daml:Restriction>
</daml:Class>
```

The tie into the standardized specifications is useful to (1) exploit other concepts of widely-distributed specifications or (2) to express more detailed security policies. As an example for (1) one could use the `KeyInfo` element in an XML `Signature` element. `KeyInfo` indicates the keys that need to be used in order to validate the signature. XML Signature has syntax elements to define key data related to X509 certificates [7], to PGP public key pairs [11], and SPKI public key pairs [12]. We can exploit those structures by defining specific instance of the class `Credential` in our security ontology. As an example for (2) one can imagine situations in which a web page only accepts X509 certificates that have been issued by a particular certification authority such as VeriSign or Thawte. Such information will be extremely helpful in directing software agents to web resources that are available to them. A software agent that searches for a particular web service could be equipped with a collection of certificates. Whenever the agent encounters a service that satisfies other functional aspects of its request, it may do some simple computation to conclude whether the service will be available.

3.2 Security Mechanisms

With our ontologies for security mechanism we aim to capture high-level security notations that are commonly used in describing user, agent or service security policies.

We propose an ontology that allows to interface on a high level of abstraction among various security standards and notations. Several properties are defined for the top class "SecurityMechanism" (not shown in Figure). For example, the ontology defines an object property "syntax" that has the class "Syntax"

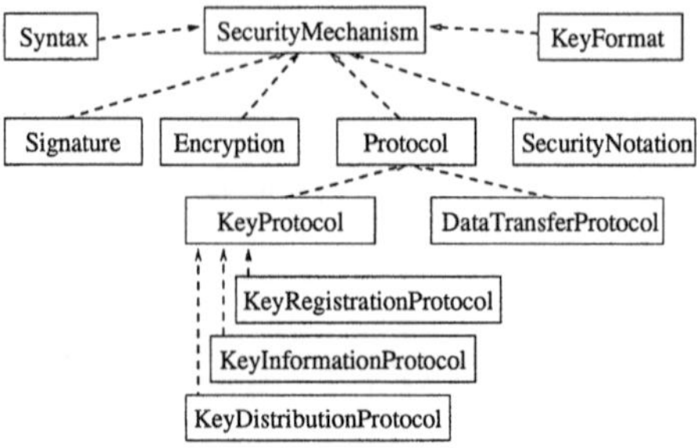

Fig. 4. A security ontology I

as range, another property "relSecNotation" has the class "SecurityNotation" as its range, and "reqCredential" has the credential class as range. There are various instances for the defined classes. For example, instances of syntax are "ASCII, DAML+OIL, OWL, XML, MIME"; security notations are "Authentication, Authorization, AccessControl, DataIntegrity, Confidentiality, Privacy, ExposureControl, Anonymity, Negotiation, Policy, KeyDistribution," and "X.509" is an instance of the KeyFormat class. "XML-DSIG" is an instance of the signature class and "OpenPGP-Enc" is of type "Encryption." Specific protocols such as "X-KRSS, X-KISS, Kerberos," or "SOAP" are defined as instances of the appropriate protocol subclasses that satisfy certain restrictions.

Restriction classes are classes in which we constrain the range of one of the object properties "reqCredential, syntax, relSecNotation" etc. Restriction classes are used as "patterns" for certain security notations. For example, an "AuthenticationSubClass" is a class that has as one of its related security notations "Authentication".

```
<daml:restriction rdf:ID="AuthenticationSubClass">
     <daml:onProperty rdf:resource="#relSecNotation"/>
     <daml:hasValue rdf:resource="#Authentication"/>
</daml:restriction>
```

Thus, if a web service has the authentication class as one of its requirement then it means that the service requires the user to authenticate.

One can define other restriction classes. For example, one can define a class where one of the required credentials is X.509 or where one of the syntax used is XML. We defined protocols in terms of their characteristics. For example, XKMS is specified as follows in our ontology.

```
<security:KeyProtocol rdf:ID="XKMS">
  <daml:intersectionOf rdf:parseType="daml:collection">
    <daml:Class rdf:ID="#AuthenticationSubClass"/>
    <daml:Class rdf:ID="#KeyDistributionSubClass"/>
    <daml:Class rdf:ID="#XMLSubClass"/>
  </daml:intersectionOf>
  <security:documentation rdf:resource="#XKMS-Ref"/>
</security:KeyProtocol>
```

XKMS is a protocol that provides authentication and key distribution and it uses XML as syntax. For more examples of restriction classes and protocols see `www.csl.sri.com/users/denker/daml-sec/security.daml`. How web services can make use of the restriction classes is illustrated in the next section.

We choose to define restriction classes to represent security requirements because we want to make use of the inherent features of description logic (DL), on which DAML+OIL is based, and the tools that are available for DL approaches. Subsumption reasoning is one of the well-defined techniques for description logics we which employ for our purposes. It allows to decide whether security capabilities and requirements are identical or whether they are in an appropriate inheritance relationship. Thus, we spare ourselves to define special-purpose algorithms that could achieve the same for lists of specific capabilities. Our approach takes advantage of the current technology to the best of its ability.

3.3 Merging Security Ontologies and DAML-S

The missing link between our security ontologies and web services is introduced next. We define a SecurityMechanism to be a subclass of ServiceParameter. Then we can declare two new properties for web services, namely "securityRequirement" and "securityCapability" of type SecurityMechanism.

An agent requesting a web service that is able to do authentication would result in the following "requested web service markup."

```
<security:KeyProtocol rdf:ID="Sec2">
      <security:relSecNotation rdf:resource="&security;#Authentication"/>
</security:KeyProtocol>

<profile:Profile rdf:ID="RequestServiceProfile1">
  <profile:serviceName> ... </profile:serviceName>
  <profile:textDescription> ... </profile:textDescription>
  <sec-requirement rdf:resource="#Sec2"/>
</profile:Profile>
```

A registered web service claims to be able to communicate using the XKMS protocol.

```
<security:XKMS rdf:ID="Sec1"/>

<profile:Profile rdf:ID="RegisteredServiceProfile1">
  ...
  <sec-capability rdf:resource="#Sec1"/>
</profile:Profile>
```

The question is, whether the registered service is a match for the request. Here is where our security reasoner comes into play. For the given example, a subsumption reasoner like JTP can resolve that the requirements of the request are fulfilled by the capabilities of the registered web service. The security reasoning algorithm that handles security matching requests is discussed below.

4 Security Reasoner

Consider the example from Section 2. Agent A that is capable of performing Open-PGP encryption and requires a communicating service to be capable of authenticating itself and communicating in XML, makes a request to the matchmaker for a travel web service. A travel web service T, registered with the same matchmaker, meets the requirements of the agent A. It requires an agent to be capable of encryption and itself to be capable of the XKMS protocol for message exchanges. Our security reasoner accepts as input the requirements and capabilities of the agent and of the service and decides to what degree they match. In this case, the reasoner finds that there is a close match as the capabilities of the service meet the requirements of the agent and the capabilities of the agent meet the requirements of the service.

Requirements and capabilities of agents and services are described using our security ontologies. They can be either instances of defined security protocols like XKMS and Open PGP or collections of instantiated characteristics of these protocols like encryption and authentication. Every agent and service can have more than one requirement and capability. For ease of development, we assume that they are disjunctively related. Adding conjunction does not involve redesign only additional coding. Our security reasoner is implemented in Java and uses Java Theorem Prover (JTP) and our matching algorithm to decide the relationship between the requirements and capabilities. This relationship can be either *perfect match, close match, general match, negotiation possible* or *no match.* Perfect match is the best match possible and no match is the worst.

4.1 Security Matching Algorithm

In this section we describe the algorithm used to decide whether two security descriptions are related. The matching algorithm exploits the subsumption capability of JTP to extract the most specific type of a requirement and a capability and then proceeds to match them. The most specific type is the lowest class in the security ontology that the requirement/capability is an instance of. However, the requirement and/or capability need not be of a certain protocol type, but instead can be a collection of characteristics associated with protocols. The matching algorithm considers three general cases : when both the requirement and the capability are instances of a protocol, when one of them is an instance of a protocol, and when neither is an instance of a protocol. The algorithm is as follows:

- Case I: Both the requirement and the capability are instances of a security protocol
  - Perfect Match: A capability and a requirement are perfectly matched if they are both instances of the same specific type. For example, if a capability and a requirement are of type XKMS, then there is a perfect match. However, if a capability is of type XKMS and a requirement is of a type which is a subclass of XKMS, then it is not a perfect match.

  - Close Match: If the most specific type of capability is lower in the hierarchy than the most specific type of the requirement, it is said to be a close match. The requirement in this case is more general than the capability. For example, if the requirement is of type XKMS and the capability is of a type which is a subclass of XKMS.
  - Possibility of Negotiation: If the requirement is more specific than the capability, there is a possibility of negotiation as the capability may not adequately represent the entities actual abilities. The most specific type of capability is lower in the hierarchy than the most specific type of the requirement.
  - No Match: If the most specific types of the requirement and capability are not related, then there is no match.

- Case II: Either capability or requirement are instances of a security protocol
  - General match: The capability is an instance of a protocol but the requirement is not. There is a general match if the characteristics of the requirement are a subset of the characteristics of the specific type of the capability. Let us assume that SSH is the most specific type of the capability and the requirement only has authorization as its related security notation, then, as the protocol SSH has authorization as related notation, there is a general match.
  - Possibility of Negotiation: If the requirement has a protocol as its most specific type and the capability does not, then there is a possibility of negotiation if every characteristic of the protocol type of requirement is also a characteristic of the capability. For example, the requirement is Kerberos, which includes authentication and key distribution, and the capability has the key distribution feature.
  - No Match: If there is no general match or a possibility of negotiation in this case, then there is no match.
- Case III: Neither capability or requirement are instances of a security protocol
  - General Match: This is the case if the features of the requirement are a subset of the features of the capability. Consider as an example, the requirement includes only authentication and the capability has authentication as one of its features.
  - No Match: If in case III there is no general match, then it is considered a no match. If for example, the requirement is for authorization and the capability is authentication and key distribution.

4.2 Integration into the Service Matchmaker

The main objective of Agents and Web services is to perform tasks such as providing information about a stock quotes, or Weather patterns, or purchasing and exchanging goods. To this extent, agents have two types of capabilities: a functional capability that describes the tasks performed by the agent and what the agent achieves; and security capabilities that specify constraints on agent and Web services communications. Any Internet wide registry of agents and Web services should provide a matching mechanism that applies to both dimensions: matching functional capabilities allows requesters to locate providers on the bases of what they do, security matching guarantees that the requester and the provider can interact.

The DAML-S/UDDI Matchmaker greatly improves on current web services registries, specifically UDDI. First, it expands UDDI by supporting the representation of capabilities of Web services; in addition, via the ontologies and security reasoning algorithm presented in this paper, it allows the representation of security capabilities and requirements that restrict the ability of two agents or Web services to interact.

The security reasoner has been integrated with the DAML-S/UDDI Matchmaker [4,5] which uses DAML-S to empower the UDDI web services registry [13] with functional capability matching. The DAML-S Matchmaker performs two tasks, the first one is to store advertisements of capabilities expressed as DAML-S profiles, the second one is to locate which advertisement matches the requests of capabilities the matchmaker received from requesting agents. Currently, the matchmaker uses only input and output information of DAML-S profile specifications. Thus, currently the matchmaker would not be able to handle our security specifications if we would specify them as preconditions of the web service. Moreover, the matchmaker does only consider subsumption on classes, whereas in our example (see Section 4.3) it is necessary to also include subsumption reasoning on instances of classes. For these reasons, we decided to use JTP's subsumption reasoning in connection with our restriction classes. Moreover, we proposed the security matching algorithm in Section 4.1 because we wanted to support a broader range of subsumption decisions, from perfect match, over close or general match and possibility of negotiation to no match, that are not supported in the current Matchmaker implemenation.

When matching advertisements and requests, the DAML-S/UDDI Matchmaker first locates those web services that satisfy the capabilities that the requester expects, second it removes all the web services that do not match the security requirements imposed by the requester. The latter test requires two matches, the first one is that the requester's requirements are satisfied by the provider's capabilities, then that the requirements that the provider are satisfied by the requester. For this purpose, the DAML-S/UDDI Matchmaker calls twice the security reasoning algorithm with the corresponding parameters. Depending on the result of the security reasoning algorithm, the matchmaker accepts a web service as a possible match or not.

4.3 Walk-Through Example

This section is a walk through of two examples of how security annotations of web services and agents are used by our system to provide security specific brokering. The examples demonstrate several features of our security ontology and illustrate the operation of the security reasoner.

Example 1 : We revisit Example 1 from Section 2. Agent A is looking for a travel web service and registers its functional requirements (what it wants the functional description of the matched service to be) and its security requirements (what it expects the security capabilities of a matched service to be) and capabilities (what security functionality it is capable of) with the DAML-S Matchmaker. Agent A is capable of performing OpenPGP encryption and requires a communicating service be capable of authenticating itself and communicating in XML. The following is the a part of the request made by agent A.

```
<security:OpenPGP-Enc rdf:ID="Capability1" />
<security:KeyProtocol rdf:ID="Requirement1">
    <security:relSecNotation rdf:resource="#Authentication" />
    <security:syntax rdf:resource="#XML" />
</security:KeyProtocol>
<Agent rdf:about="#A">
    <securityCapability rdf:resource="#Capability1" />
    <securityRequirement rdf:resource="#Requirement1" />
</Agent>
```

A web service T registers its functional description as travel and its security capabilities (what the service is capable of) as XKMS and its requirements (what it expects communicating agents to use) as encryption. The following is a portion of the service's description

```
<security:XKMS rdf:ID="Capability2" />
<security:KeyProtocol rdf:ID="Requirement2">
    <security:relSecNotation rdf:resource="Encryption" />
</security:KeyProtocol>
<profile:Profile rdf:about="#T">
    ...
    <securityCapability rdf:resource="#Capability2" />
    <securityRequirement rdf:resource="#Requirement2"/>
</profile:Profile>
```

The DAML-S Matchmaker uses the functional requirements of the agent to extract a list of registered agents that match in functionality. Then the Matchmaker uses the security reasoner to decide whether the agent matches any of the services in terms of security characteristics. Both the agent's request and the description of the service are input to the security reasoner. The following steps are taken by the security reasoner to decide whether the agent and service match in terms of their security annotations and to what degree.

- Based on the input the security reasoner makes the following inferences.
  - A's capability has OpenPGP-Enc as the most specific type
  - A's requirement does not have a most specific type and instead has a list of features of a security protocol (authentication and xml)
  - T's capability has XKMS as the most specific type
  - T's requirement does not have a most specific type and is a list of features of a security protocol (encryption)

- The reasoner tries to find the degree of matching between A's requirement and T's capability.
  - As T's capability has a most specific type (XKMS) and A's requirement (authentication and xml) does not, the reasoner selects Case II.
  - The reasoner tries General Matching, which is the first case of Case II.
  - It locates all the features associated with XKMS, which are authentication, xml and key distribution.
  - The features of the requirement are a subset of the features of XKMS, so General Matching holds.
- The reasoner tries to find the degree of matching between T's requirement and A's capability.
  - As A's capability has a most specific type (OpenPGP-Enc) and T's requirement. (encryption) does not, the reasoner selects Case II.
  - The reasoner tries the General Matching case of Case II.
  - It locates all the features associated with OpenPGP-Enc, among which encryption is.
  - The features of the requirement are a subset of the features of A's capability, so General Matching holds.
- The security reasoner decides that the agent and service match in terms of their security annotations and the degree is *general match.*

The DAML-S Matchmaker uses the above result of the security reasoner to decide that the agent and the service match in both functionality and security and informs the agent A that the service T *generally matches* its request.

Example 2 : As another example, consider a web service W1 looking for a banking service. It registers its functional description, security capability (SSH) and security requirement (authorization) with the Matchmaker. The security portion of its description is as follows

```
<security:SSH rdf:ID="Capability3" />
<security:KeyProtocol rdf:ID="Requirement3">
    <security:relSecNotation rdf:resource="#Authorization" />
    <security:syntax rdf:resource="#XML" />
</security:KeyProtocol>
<profile:Profile rdf:about="#W1">
    <profile:serviceName>... </profile:serviceName>
    <profile:textDescription>...</profile:textDescription>
    <securityCapability rdf:resource="#Capability3" />
   <securityRequirement rdf:resource="#Requirement3" />
</profile:Profile>
```

The Matchmaker finds a matching service, W2, with the functional description of personal banking and SSH as both its security requirement and capability.

```
<security:SSH rdf:ID="Capability4" />
<security:SSH rdf:ID="Requirement4" />
<profile:Profile rdf:about="#W2">
   ...
```

```
  <securityCapability rdf:resource="#Capability4" />
  <securityRequirement rdf:resource="#Requirement4" />
</profile:Profile>
```

5 Concluding Remarks

As shown in this paper, the formal definition of ontologies that will enable interoperability of various security frameworks has several advantages. The uniform representation becomes amenable to formal reasoning and it supports agents in selecting appropriate web services. We have presented a security ontology for DAML+OIL that is extensible in that it allows the definition of further security aspects as well as new links to existing standards and frameworks. With the given security framework for DAML+OIL many of the common access control, authentication, and data integrity measures of existing web services can be described. We described our prototype implementation that uses JTP and the DAML-S Matchmaker to enable security matching between DAML+OIL-aware software agents and services.

The current work is restricted to annotation and matchmaking of services with respect to security requirements. In the future we will address the connection between a service's profile and its implementation as defined in the grounding.

In the current framework, we focus on some common security notations. These are often embedded into the broader context of trust policies. We plan to extend our work and prototype to allow for security policy specifications. Logics for trust management is another topic of future investigations. There exists already a large body of work on trust management, e.g., [14,15,16] to name a few. Recent work on frameworks for distributed trust management and policy in multi-agent systems [17,18] and existing authentication and delegation logics have to be taken into consideration for future logical extensions of DAML+OIL. The first step will be the development of further basic ontologies for deontic concepts (permissions, obligations, and rights), as well as a basic agent and action ontology (requesting a resource, delegating rights, etc) [19]. A theory for reasoning about trust relations will be at the core of decision procedures for web agents that search for reliable information.

Another direction for future work is to extend our framework to composed services. Composition of security features from atomic services is non-trivial and the derivation of security features of a composite service on the basis of the security descriptions of its components will be addressed in future work.

Acknowledgements. We thank the anonymous reviewers for their comments that helped to improve the paper.

References

1. DAML+OIL Committee: DAML+OIL.
   `http://www.daml.org/2001/03/daml+oil.daml` (2001). See `http://www.daml.org/committee/` for committee members
2. DAML Services. (`http://www.daml.org/services`)
3. Fikes, R., Jenkins, J., Frank, G.: JTP: A System Architecture and Component Library for Hybrid Reasoning. http://www.ksl.stanford.edu/KSL-Abstracts/KSL-03-01.html (2003)
4. Paolucci, M., Kawamura, T., Payne, T.R., Sycara, K.: Semantic Matching of Web Services Capabilities. In: ISWC2002. (2002)
5. Paolucci, M., Kawamura, T., Payne, T.R., Sycara, K.: Importing the Semantic Web in UDDI. In: Proceedings of E-Services and the Semantic Web Workshop. 2002
6. IETF W3C XMLSignature Working Group: XML Signature. (`http://www.w3.org/Signature/`)
7. Bartel, M., Boyer, J., Fox, B., LaMacchia, B., Simon, E.: XML-Signature Syntax and Processing Rules.
   `http://www.w3.org/TR/2001/PR-xmldsig-core-20010820/`, 2001
8. OASIS Security Service Technical Committee: Security Assertion Markup Language (SAML). (`http://www.oasis-open.org/committees/security/`)
9. Atkinson, B., Della-Libera, G., Hada, S., Hondo, M., Hallam-Baker, P., Klein, J., LaMacchia, B., Leach, P., Manferdelli, J., Maruyama, H., Nadalin, A., Nagaratnam, N., Prfullchandra, H., Shewchuk, J., Simon, D.: WS-Security (2002).
   `http://www-106.ibm.com/developerworks/webservices/library/ws-secure/`
10. Klyne, G.: Framework for Security and Trust Standards.
    (`http://www.ninebynine.org/SWAD-E/Security-formats-20021202.html`)
11. Zimmermann, P.: The Official PGP User's Guide. MIT Press (1995)
12. SPKI: Simple Public Key Infrastructure.
    `http://www.ietf.org/html.charters/spki-charter.html`
13. UDDI: `http://www.uddi.org/pubs/whitepapers`.
14. Abadi, M., Burrows, M., Lampson, B., Plotkin, G.: A calculus for access control in distributed systems. ACM Transactions on Programming Languages and Systems, 15:706–734, 1993
15. Blaze, M., Feigenbaum, J., Lacy, J.: Decentralized Trust Management. In: Proc. 1996 IEEE Symposium on Security and Privacy, IEEE Computer Society (1996), 164–173
16. Li, N., Grosof, B., Feigenbaum, J.: A Practically Implementable and Tractable Delegation Logic. In: Proc. 2000 IEEE Symposium on Security and Privacy (S&P'00), IEEE Computer Society (2000), 27–42
17. Kagal, L., Finin, T., Joshi, A.: Developing Secure Agent Systems Using Delegation Based Trust Management. In: Security of Mobile MultiAgent Systems (SEMAS 02) held at Autonomous Agents and MultiAgent Systems (AAMAS 02), 2002
18. Bradshaw, J., Uszok, A., Jeffers, R., Suri, N., Hayes, P., Burstein, M., Acquisiti, A., Benyo, B., Breedy, M., Carvalho, M., Diller, D., Johnson, M., Kulkarni, S., Lott, J., Sierhuis, M., Hoof, R.V.: Representation and Reasoning for DAML-Based Policy and Domain Services in KAoS and Nomads. In: *Submitted to* AAMAS'03, July 14–18, 2003, Melbourne, Australia, 2003
19. Kagal, L., Finin, T., Joshi, A.: A Policy Language for A Pervasive Computing Environment. In: IEEE 4th International Workshop on Policies for Distributed Systems and Networks, 2002

Trust Management for the Semantic Web

Matthew Richardson[1*], Rakesh Agrawal[2], and Pedro Domingos[1]

[1] University of Washington, Box 352350, Seattle, WA 98195-2350
{mattr, pedrod}@cs.washington.edu,
[2] IBM Almaden Research Center, 650 Harry Road, San Jose, CA 95120-6099
ragrawal@acm.org

Abstract. Though research on the Semantic Web has progressed at a steady pace, its promise has yet to be realized. One major difficulty is that, by its very nature, the Semantic Web is a large, uncensored system to which anyone may contribute. This raises the question of how much credence to give each source. We cannot expect each user to know the trustworthiness of each source, nor would we want to assign top-down or global credibility values due to the subjective nature of trust. We tackle this problem by employing a web of trust, in which each user maintains trusts in a small number of other users. We then compose these trusts into trust values for all other users. The result of our computation is not an agglomerate "trustworthiness" of each user. Instead, each user receives a personalized set of trusts, which may vary widely from person to person. We define properties for combination functions which merge such trusts, and define a class of functions for which merging may be done locally while maintaining these properties. We give examples of specific functions and apply them to data from Epinions and our BibServ bibliography server. Experiments confirm that the methods are robust to noise, and do not put unreasonable expectations on users. We hope that these methods will help move the Semantic Web closer to fulfilling its promise.

1 Introduction

Since the articulation of the Semantic Web vision [9], it has become the focus of research on building the next web. The philosophy behind the Semantic Web is the same as that behind the World-Wide Web – anyone can be an information producer or consume anyone else's information. Thus far, most Semantic Web research (e.g., [6][27]) has focused on defining standards for communicating facts, rules, ontologies, etc. XML, RDF, RDF-schema, OWL and others form a necessary basis for the construction of the Semantic Web. However, even after these standards are in wide use, we still need to address the major issue of how to decide how trustworthy each information source is. One solution would be to require all information on the Semantic Web to be consistent and of high quality. But due to its sheer magnitude and diversity of sources, this will be nearly impossible. Much as in the development of the WWW, in which there was no attempt made to centrally control the quality of information, we believe that it is infeasible to do so on the Semantic Web.

---

* Researched while at IBM Almaden Research Center.

D. Fensel et al. (Eds.): ISWC 2003, LNCS 2870, pp. 351–368, 2003.

Instead, we should develop methods that work under the assumption that the information will be of widely varying quality. On the WWW, researchers have found that one way to handle this is to make use of "statements" of quality implicit in the link structure between pages [23][26]. This collaborative, distributed approach is far more cost-effective than a centralized approach. We propose that a similar technique will work on the Semantic Web, by having each user explicitly specify a (possibly small) set of users she trusts. The resulting web of trust may be used recursively to compute a user's trust in any other user (or, more precisely, in any other user in the same connected component of the trust graph). Note that, unlike PageRank, the result of our computation is not an agglomerate "trustworthiness" of each user. Instead, each receives her own personalized set of trusts, which may be vastly different from person to person. In this paper, we propose and examine some methods for such a computation.

In Section 2 we formulate a model that explicitly has the dual notions of *trust* and *belief*. Then, in Sections 3, 4, and 5, we define the meaning of belief combination under two different interpretations, and show an equivalence between the two. We also show a correspondence between combining beliefs and trusts that allows the use of whichever is more computationally efficient for the given system. We then give experimental results that show that our methods work across a wide variation of user quality and noise. We conclude with a discussion of related and future work.

2 Model

We assume content on the Semantic Web is (explicitly or implicitly) in the form of logical assertions. If all these assertions are consistent and believed with certainty, a logical calculus can be used to combine them. If not, a probabilistic calculus may be used (e.g., knowledge-based model construction [25]). However, our focus here is not on deriving beliefs for new statements given an initial set of statements. Rather, we propose a solution to the problem of establishing the degree of belief in a statement that is explicitly asserted by one or more sources on the Semantic Web. These beliefs can then be used by an appropriate calculus to compute beliefs in derived statements. Our basic model is that a user's belief in a statement should be a function of her trust in the sources providing it. Given each source's belief in the statement and the user's trust in each source, the user's belief in the statement can be computed in many different ways, corresponding to different models of how people form their beliefs. The framework presented in this paper supports a wide variety of combination functions, such as linear pool [17][18], noisy OR [28], and logistic regression [4]. We view the coefficients in these functions (one per source) as measuring the user's trust in each source,[1] and answer the question: how can a user decide how much to trust a source she does not know directly? Our answer is based on recursively propagating trust: if A has trust u in B and B has trust v in C, then A should have some trust t in C that is a function of u and v. We place restrictions on allowable methods for combining trusts that enable the efficient and local computation of derived trusts.

[1] Trust is, of course, a complex and multidimensional phenomenon, but we make a start in this paper by embodying it in a single numeric coefficient per user-source pair.

Similar restrictions on belief combination allow it to also be done using only local information.[2]

Consider a system of N users who, as a whole, have made M statements. Since we consider statements independently, we introduce the system as if there is only one.

Beliefs. Any user may assert her *personal belief* in the statement, which is taken from [0,1]. A high value means that the statement is accurate, credible, and/or relevant. Let b_i represent user i's personal belief in the statement. If user i has not provided one, we set b_i to 0. We refer to the collection of personal beliefs in the statement as the column vector $\mathbf{b}$ (see Section 8 for a discussion on more complex beliefs and trusts).

Trusts. User i may specify a *personal trust*, t_{ij}, for any user j. Trust is also a value taken from [0,1], where a high value means that the user is credible, trustworthy, and/or shares similar interests. If unspecified, we set t_{ij} to be 0. Note that t_{ij} need not equal t_{ji}. The collection of personal trusts can be represented as a N×N matrix $\mathbf{T}$. We write $\mathbf{t}_i$ to represent the row vector of user i's personal trusts in other users.

Merging. The web of trust provides a structure on which we may compute, for any user, their belief in the statement. We will refer these as *merged beliefs* ($\mathcal{B}$), to distinguish them from the user-specified *personal beliefs* ($\mathbf{b}$). The trust between any two users is given by the *merged trusts matrix* ($\mathcal{T}$), as opposed to the user-specified *personal trusts matrix* ($\mathbf{T}$).

3 Path Algebra Interpretation

In order to compute merged beliefs efficiently, we first make the simplifying assumption that a merged belief depends only on the paths of trust between the user and any other user with a personal belief in the statement. In Section 4 we consider an alternative probabilistic interpretation. For the moment, we consider only acyclic graphs (we generalize later to cyclic graphs).

Borrowing from generalized transitive closure literature [3], we define merged beliefs under the path algebra interpretation with the following conceptual computation:

1. Enumerate all (possibly exponential number of) paths between the user and every user with a personal belief in the statement.
2. Calculate the belief associated with each path by applying a *concatenation function* to the trusts along the path and also the personal belief held by the final node.
3. Combine those beliefs with an *aggregation function.*

---

[2] While this may not guarantee the probabilistic soundness of the resulting beliefs, we believe it is necessary for scalability on the size of the Web, and our experiments indicate it still produces useful results. Scalable probabilistic approximations are a direction for future research.

(See Figure 1). Some possible concatenation functions are multiplication and minimum value. Some possible aggregations functions are addition and maximum value. Various combinations lead to plausible belief-merging calculations such as measuring the most-reliable path or the maximum flow between the user and the statement.

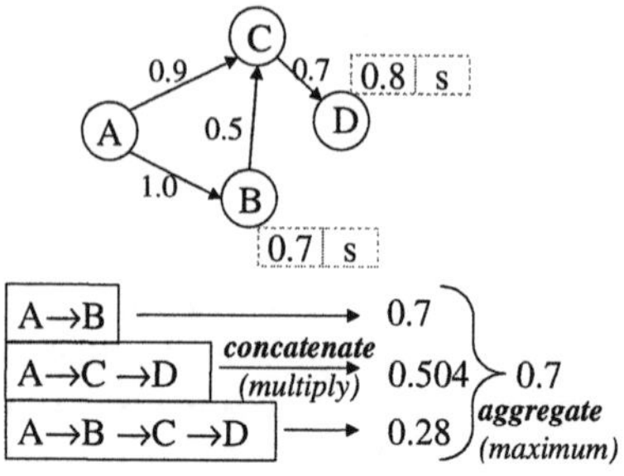

Fig. 1. Path Algebra belief merging on an example web of trust

Let ∘ and ◊ represent the concatenation and aggregation functions respectively. For example, $t_{ik} \circ t_{kj}$ is the amount that user *i* trusts user *j via k*, and the amount that *i* trusts *j* via any single other node is $\Diamond(\forall k: t_{ik} \circ t_{kj})$. If ◊ is addition and ∘ is multiplication, then $\Diamond(\forall k: t_{ik} \circ t_{kj}) \equiv \sum_k t_{ik} t_{kj}$. We define the matrix operation **C=A•B** such that $\mathbf{C}_{ij} = \Diamond(\forall k: A_{ik} \circ B_{kj})$. Note that for the previous example, **A•B** is simply matrix multiplication.

3.1 Local Belief Merging

The global meaning of beliefs given above assumes a user has full knowledge of the network including the personal trusts between all users, which is practically unreasonable. Can we instead merge beliefs locally while keeping the same global interpretation? Following [3], let *well-formed decomposable path problems* be defined as those for which ◊ is commutative and associative, and ∘ is associative and distributes over ◊ (The above examples for ◊ and ∘ all result in well-formed path problems). These may be computed using *generalized transitive closure* algorithms, which use only local information. One such algorithm is as follows:

1. $\mathcal{b}^{(0)} = \mathbf{b}$
2. $\mathcal{b}^{(n)} = \mathbf{T} \bullet \mathcal{b}^{(n\text{-}1)}$, or alternatively, $\mathcal{b}_i^{(n)} = \Diamond(\forall k: t_{ik} \circ \mathcal{b}_k^{(n\text{-}1)})$
3. Repeat step 2 until $\mathcal{b}^{(n)} = \mathcal{b}^{(n\text{-}1)}$

(where $\mathcal{b}^{(i)}$ represents the value of $\mathcal{b}$ in iteration *i*. Recall $\mathcal{b}$ are the merged beliefs)

Notice that in step 2, the user needs only the merged beliefs of her immediate neighbors, which allows her to merge beliefs *locally* while keeping the same *global* interpretation. We will use the term *belief combination function* to refer to the above algorithm and some selection of ∘ and ◊.

3.2 Strong and Weak Invariance

Refer to Figure 2 (*Case I*). Suppose a node is removed from the web of trust, and the edges to it are redirected to its trusted nodes (combining the trusts). If the merged beliefs of the remaining users remain unchanged, we say the belief combination function has *weak global invariance*. The path interpretation has this important property.

We can imagine another property that may be desirable. Again refer to Figure 2 (*Case II*). If we add an arc of trust directly from A to C, and the trust between A and C is unchanged, we say that the belief combination function has *strong global invariance.* Any belief combination function with weak invariance for which the aggregation function is also *idempotent* (meaning, $\Diamond(x, x) = \Diamond(x)$), will have strong invariance. This follows from the fact that the aggregation function is associative. Interestingly, whether or not the aggregation function must be idempotent is the primary difference between Agrawal's well-formed decomposable path problems [3] and Carre's path algebra [11] (also related is the definition of a closed semiring in [5]). One example of a belief combination function with strong global invariance is the one defined with $\Diamond$ as maximum and $\circ$ as multiplication.

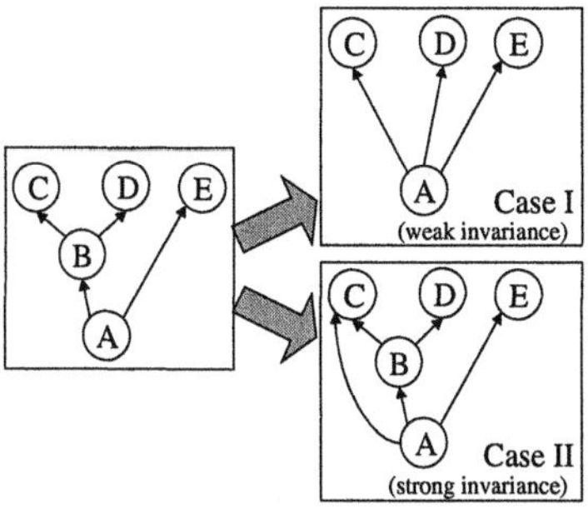

Fig. 2. Strong and weak invariance

3.3 Merging Trusts

The majority of the belief merging calculation involves the concatenation of chains of trust. Beliefs only enter the computation at the endpoint of each path. Instead of merging beliefs, can we merge trusts and then reuse these to calculate merged beliefs?

We define the interpretation of globally merged trusts in the same way as was done for beliefs: the trust between user i and user j is an aggregation function applied to the concatenation of trust along every path between them. It falls directly from path algebra that, if $\Diamond$ is commutative and associative, and $\circ$ is associative and distributes over $\Diamond$, then we can combine trusts locally while still maintaining global meaning:

$$\mathcal{T}^{(0)} = \mathbf{T}, \qquad \mathcal{T}^{(n)} = \mathbf{T} \bullet \mathcal{T}^{(n-1)} \quad , \qquad \text{Repeat until } \mathcal{T}^{(n)} = \mathcal{T}^{(n-1)}$$

($\mathcal{T}^{(i)}$ is the value of $\mathcal{T}$ in iteration i. Recall $\mathcal{T}$ is the matrix of merged trusts). To perform the computation, a user needs only to know her neighbors' merged trusts. This leads us to the following theorem, which states that, for a wide class of functions, merging trusts accomplishes the same as merging beliefs (the proof is in the Appendix)

Theorem 1: If $\Diamond$ is commutative and associative, and $\circ$ is associative and distributes over $\Diamond$, and $\mathbf{T}$, $\mathcal{T}$, $\mathbf{b}$, and $\mathcal{b}$ are as above, then $\mathbf{T} \bullet \mathcal{b} = \mathcal{T} \bullet \mathbf{b}$.

3.4 Cycles

Thus far, we have assumed the graph is acyclic. However, it is improbable that a web of trust will be acyclic. Indeed, the Epinions web of trust (see Section 6.1) is highly connected and cyclic. Borrowing terminology from path algebra, we define a combination function as *cycle-indifferent* if it is not affected by introducing a cycle in the path between two users. With cycle indifference, the aggregation over infinite paths will converge, since only the (finite number of) paths without cycles affect its calculation.

Proposition 1: All of the results and theorems introduced thus far are applicable to cyclic graphs if $\lozenge$ and $\circ$ define a cycle-indifferent path problem.

On cyclic graphs, a combination function that is not cycle-indifferent has the questionable property that a user may be able to affect others' trusts in him by modifying her own personal trusts. However, requiring a cycle-indifferent combination function may be overly restrictive. In Section 4 we explore an alternative interpretation that allows the use of combination functions that are not cycle-indifferent.

3.5 Selection of Belief Combination Function

The selection of belief combination function may depend on the application domain, desired belief and cycle semantics, and the expected typical social behavior in that domain. The ideal combination function may be user-dependent. For the remainder of the paper, we will always use multiplication for concatenation, though in the future we would like to explore other functions (such as the minimum value). The following is a brief summary of three different aggregation functions we have considered.

Maximum Value. Using maximum to combine beliefs is consistent with fuzzy logic, in which it has been shown to be the most reasonable function for performing a generalized *or* operation over [0,1] valued beliefs [8]. Maximum also has the advantages that it is cycle-indifferent, strongly consistent, and naturally handles missing values (by letting them be 0). With maximum, the user will believe anything believed by at least one of the users she trusts – a reasonable, if not overly optimistic, behavior.

Minimum Value. Minimum is not cycle-indifferent. In fuzzy logic, minimum value is used to perform the *and* operation. With minimum, the user will only believe a statement if it is believed by all of the users she trusts.

Average. Average does not satisfy the requirements for a well-formed path algebra outlined above (average is not associative). However, average can still be computed by using two aggregation functions: sum and count (count simply returns the number of paths by summing 1's). By passing along these two values, each node can locally compute averages. Average is not cycle-indifferent.

3.6 Computation

Since cycle-indifferent, weakly consistent combination functions are well-formed path problems, $\mathcal{B}$ and $\mathcal{T}$ may be computed using standard transitive closure algorithms. The simplest of these is the semi-naïve algorithm [7], which runs in $O(N^4)$ time, and essentially prescribes repeated application of the belief update equation. If running as a peer-to-peer system, the semi-naïve algorithm may be easily parallelized, requiring $O(N^3)$ computations per node [2]. Another algorithm is the Warshall algorithm [33], which computes the transitive closure in $O(N^3)$. Some work on parallel versions of the Warshall algorithm has been done in [2]. There has also been much research on optimizing transitive closure algorithms, such as for when the graph does not fit into memory [3]. In practice most users will specify only a few of the users as neighbors, and the number of iterations required to fully propagate information is much less than N, making the computation quite efficient. Theorem 1 allows us to choose whether we wish to merge trusts or merge beliefs. The most efficient method depends on, among other things, whether the system is implemented as a peer-to-peer network or as a server, the number of neighbors for a given user, the number of users, the number of statements in the system, and the number of queries made by each user.

4 Probabilistic Interpretation

In this formulation, we consider a probabilistic interpretation of global belief combination. The treatment is motivated by random walks on a Markov chain, which have been found to be of practical use in discovering high-quality web pages [26]. In what follows, we assume the set of personal trusts for a given user has been normalized.

Imagine a random knowledge-surfer hopping from user to user in search of beliefs. At each step, the surfer probabilistically selects a neighbor to jump to according to the current user's distribution of trusts. Then, with probability equal to the current user's belief, it says "yes, I believe in the statement". Otherwise, it says "no". Further, when choosing which user to jump to, the random surfer will, with probability $\lambda_i \in [0,1]$, ignore the trusts and instead jump directly back to the original user, *i*. We define a combination method to have a *global probabilistic interpretation* if it satisfies the following:

1) $\mathcal{T}_{ij}$ is the probability that, at any given step, user *i*'s random surfer is at user *j*.
2) $\mathcal{b}_i$ is the probability that, at any given step, user *i*'s random surfer says "yes".

The convergence properties of such random walks are well studied; $\mathcal{b}$ and $\mathcal{T}$ will converge as long as the network is irreducible and aperiodic [24]. λ_i can be viewed as a *self-trust*, and specifies the weight a user gives to her own beliefs and trusts. The behavior of the random knowledge-surfer is very similar to that of the intelligent surfer presented in [32], which is a generalization of PageRank that allows non-uniform transitions between web pages. What personalizes the calculation to user *i* is the random restart, which "grounds" the surfer to *i*'s trusts. The resulting trusts may be drastically different than using PageRank, since the number of neighbors will typically be small.

4.1 Computation

User i's trust in user j is the probability that her random surfer is on a user k, times the probability that the surfer would transition to user j, summed over all k. Taking λ_i into account as well, we have $\mathcal{T}_{ij} = \lambda_i \delta(i-j) + (1-\lambda_i)\sum_k \mathcal{T}_{ik} t_{kj}$, where $\delta(0)=1$ and $\delta(x \neq 0)=0$ and each row of $\mathbf{t}$ is normalized. In matrix form:

$$\mathcal{T}_i = \lambda_i \mathbf{I}_i + (1-\lambda_i)\mathcal{T}_i \mathbf{T}, \tag{1}$$

where $\mathbf{I}_i$ is the ith row of the identify matrix. In order to satisfy the global probabilistic interpretation, $\mathcal{b}_i$ must be the probability that user i's random surfer says "yes". This is the probability that it is on a given user times that user's belief in the statement:

$$\mathcal{b}_i = \sum_k \mathcal{T}_{ik} b_k, \quad \text{or,} \quad \mathcal{b}_i = \mathcal{T}_i \mathbf{b} \tag{2}$$

4.2 Local Belief and Trust Merging

As in section 3.1, we wish to perform this computation using only local information. We show that this is possible in the special case where $\lambda_i = \lambda$ is constant.
Unrolling Equation 1:

$$\mathcal{T} = \lambda\left[\sum_{m=0}^{\infty}(1-\lambda)^m \mathbf{T}^m\right]. \tag{3}$$

Note that $\mathbf{T}^0=\mathbf{I}$. Substituting into Equation 2,

$$\mathcal{b} = \lambda\left[\sum_{m=0}^{\infty}(1-\lambda)^m \mathbf{T}^m\right]\mathbf{b}, \tag{4}$$

which is satisfied by the recursive definition:

$$\mathcal{b} = \lambda\mathbf{b} + (1-\lambda)\mathbf{T}\mathcal{b} \tag{5}$$

Thus we find that in order to compute her merged belief, each user needs only to know her personal belief, and the merged beliefs of her neighbors. Besides having intuitive appeal, it has a probabilistic interpretation as well: user i selects a neighbor probabilistically according to her distribution of trust, $\mathbf{T}_i$, and then, with probability $(1-\lambda)$, accepts that neighbor's (merged) belief, and with probability λ accepts her own belief. Further, Equation 3 is also equivalent to the following, which says that a user may compute her merged trusts knowing only the merged trusts of her neighbors:

$$\mathcal{T} = \lambda\mathbf{I} + (1-\lambda)\mathbf{T}\mathcal{T} \tag{6}$$

The probabilistic interpretation for belief combination is essentially taking the weighted average of the neighbors' beliefs. We will thus refer to this belief combination as *weighted average* for the remainder of the paper. Note that for weighted average to make sense, if the user has not specified a belief we need to impute the value. Techniques such as those used in collaborative filtering [30] and Bayesian networks [13] for dealing with missing values may be applicable. If only relative rankings of beliefs are necessary, then it may be sufficient to use 0 for all unspecified beliefs.

5 Similarity of Probabilistic and Path Interpretations

There are clearly many similarities between the probabilistic and path interpretations. In both, beliefs may be merged by querying neighbors for their beliefs, multiplying (or concatenating) those by the trust in each neighbor, and adding (or aggregating) them together. Both interpretations also allow the computation of merged beliefs by first merging trusts. If we let the aggregation function be addition, and the concatenation function be multiplication, then the only difference between the two interpretations is due to the factor, λ. If $\lambda=0$, then Equation 5 for computing b is functionally the same as the algorithm for computing b in the path algebra interpretation. However, consider this: If λ is 0 then Equation 1 for computing T_i simply finds the primary eigenvector of the matrix **T**. Since there is only one primary eigenvector, this means that T_i would be the same for all users (assuming the graph is aperiodic and irreducible). How do we reconcile this with the path algebra interpretation, in which we expect different trust vectors per user? The answer is that the corresponding path algebra combination function is not cycle indifferent, and as a result the user's personal beliefs will get "washed out" by the infinite aggregation of other users' beliefs. Hence, as in the probabilistic interpretation, all users would end up with the same merged beliefs.

Both methods share similar tradeoffs with regards to architectural design. They may easily be employed in either a peer-to-peer or client-server architecture. We expect the system to be robust because a malicious user will be trusted less over time. Further, since the default trust in a user is 0, it is not useful for a user to create multiple pseudonyms, and users are motivated to maintain quality of information.

The web of trust calculation is not susceptible to "link-spamming," a phenomenon in PageRank whereby a person may increase others' trust in him by generating hundreds of virtual personas which all trust him. In PageRank, the uniform random jump of the surfer means that each virtual persona is bestowed some small amount of PageRank, which they 'give' to the spammer, thus increasing her rank. With a web of trust, this technique gains nothing unless the user is able to convince others to trust her virtual personas, which we expect will only occur if the personas actually provide useful information.

6 Experiments

In this section, we measure some properties of belief combination using the methods from this paper. We present two sets of experiments. The first uses a real web of trust, obtained from Epinions (www.epinions.com), but uses synthetic values for personal beliefs and trusts. We wanted to see how *maximum* (path interpretation) compared with *weighted average* (probabilistic interpretation) for belief combination. We also wanted to see what quality of user population is necessary for the system to work well, and what happens if there are mixes of both low and high quality users. Finally, these methods would have little practical use if we required that users be perfect at estimating trusts of their neighbors, so we examine the effect that varying the quality of trust estimation has on the overall accuracy of the system. For the second experiment, we implemented a real-world application, now available over the web (BibServ, www.bibserv.org). BibServ provides us with both anecdotal and experimental results.

6.1 Experiments with the Epinions Web of Trust

For these experiments, we used the web of trust obtained from Epinions, a user-oriented product review website. In order to maintain quality, Epinions encourages users to specify which other users they trust, and uses the resulting web of trust to order the product reviews seen by each person[3]. In order to perform experiments, we needed to augment the web of trust with statements and real-valued trusts.

We expected the information on the Semantic Web to be of varying quality, so we assigned to each user i a *quality* $\gamma_i \in [0,1]$. A user's quality determined the probability that a statement by the user was true. Unless otherwise specified, the quality of a user was chosen from a Gaussian distribution with $\mu = 0.5$ and $\sigma = 0.25$. These parameters are varied in the experiments below.

The Epinions web of trust is Boolean, but our methods require real-valued trusts. We expected that over time, the higher a user's quality, the more they were likely to be trusted. So, for any pair of users i and j where i trusts j in Epinions:

$$t_{ij} = \text{uniformly chosen from } [\max(\gamma_j - \delta_{ij}, 0), \min(\gamma_j + \delta_{ij}, 1)] \qquad (7)$$

where γ_i is the quality of user i and δ_{ij} is a noise parameter that determines how accurate users were at estimating the quality of the user they were trusting. We supposed that a user with low quality was bad at estimating trust, so for these experiments we let $\delta_{ij}=(1-\gamma_i)$.

We generated a random world that consisted of 5000 true or false "facts" (half of the facts were false). Users' statements asserted the truth or falsity of each fact (there were thus 10,000 possible statements, 5000 of which were correct). A user's personal belief (b_i) in any statement she asserted was 1.0.

The number of statements made by a user was equal to the number of Epinions reviews that user wrote. The few users with highest connectivity tended to have written the most reviews, while the majority of users wrote few (or none).

For each fact, each user computed her belief that the fact was true and her belief that the fact was false. For each user i, Let S_i be the set of statements for which $b_i > \tau$. If a user had non-zero belief that a fact was true and a non-zero belief that a fact was false, we used the one with highest belief. Let G_i be the set of correct statements "reachable" by user i (A statement is reachable if there is a path in the web of trust from user i to at least one user who has made the statement). Then $S_i \cap G_i$ is the set of statements that user i correctly believed were true, so $precision_i = | S_i \cap G_i | / | S_i |$ and $recall_i = | S_i \cap G_i | / | G_i |$. Precision and recall could be traded off by varying the belief threshold, τ. We present precision and recall results averaged over all users, and at the highest recall by using τ=0.

---

[3] The trust relationships can be obtained by crawling the site, as described in [31]. Though the full graph contains 75,000 users, we restricted our experiments to the first 5000 users (by crawl-order), which formed a network of 180,000 edges.

Table 1. Average precision and recall for various belief combination functions, and their standard deviations.

Comb. Function	Precision	Recall
Maximum	0.87 ± 0.13	0.98 ± 0.13
Weighted Average	0.69 ± 0.06	0.98 ± 0.15
Local	0.57 ± 0.13	0.44 ± 0.32
Random	0.51 ± 0.05	0.99 ± 0.11

Comparing Combining Functions. In Table 1, we give results for a variety of belief combination functions. The combination functions *maximum* and *weighted average* are the same as introduced earlier (unless otherwise specified, λ is 0.5 for weighted average). With *random*, T_{ij} was chosen uniformly from [0,1]. Since the average quality is 0.5, half of the facts in the system are true, so *random* led to a precision of (roughly) 0.5. *Local* means that a user incorporated only the personal beliefs of her immediate neighbors, and resulted in a precision of 0.57. *Weighted average* and *maximum* significantly outperformed the baseline functions, and *maximum* outperformed *weighted average*. We found that (data not presented) the precision differed only slightly between users with high quality and users with low quality. We believe this is because a low quality user would still have good combined beliefs if all of her neighbors had good combined beliefs.

Varying the Population Quality. It is important to understand how the average precision is affected by the quality of the users. We explored this by varying μ, the average population quality (see Figure 3). Overall, m*aximum* significantly outperformed *weighted average* ($p<0.01$), with the greatest difference at low quality.

We also explored the effect of varying λ for *weighted average*. In Figure 4, we see that λ had only a small effect on the results. We found that the better the population, the lower λ should be, which makes sense because in this case, the user should put high trust in the population. Because *maximum* seemed to consistently outperform *weighted average*, and has the additional advantage of being cycle-indifferent and producing absolute beliefs, we restricted the remaining experiments to it.

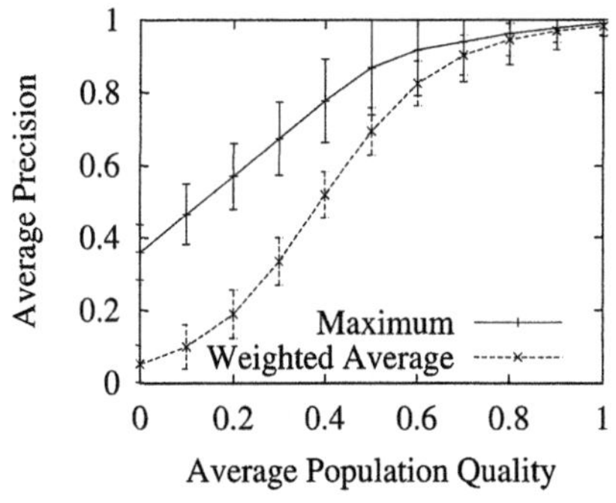

Fig. 3. Average precision ($\pm\sigma$) for *maximum* and *weighted average*

Good and Bad Users. To measure the robustness of the network to bad (or simply clueless) users, we selected user qualities from two Gaussian distributions, with means of 0.25 (*bad*) and 0.75 (*good*) (both had the same standard deviation as earlier, 0.25). We varied the fraction of users drawn from each distribution.

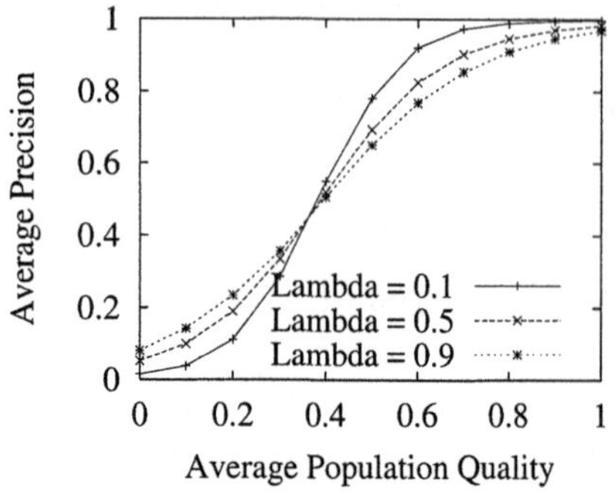

Fig. 4. Effect of λ on the precision when combining with *weighted average*

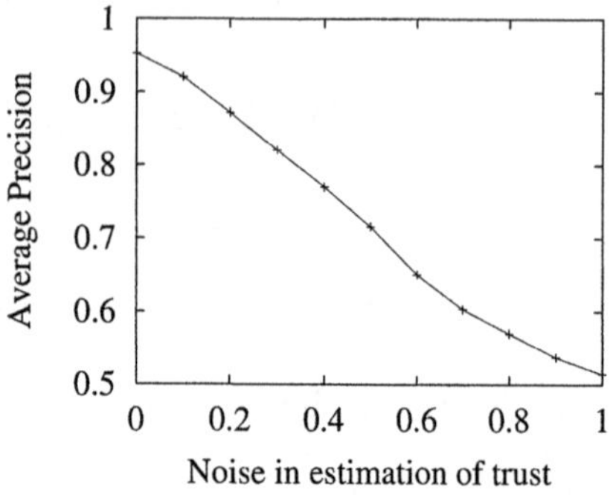

Fig. 5. Precision for various fractions of good people in the network, using *maximum* belief combination

We found the network to be surprisingly robust to bad users (see Figure 5). The average precision was very high (80-90%) when only 10-20% of the users were good. Consider also the network for which the fraction of good people is 0.5. This network has the same average population quality as the network used for Table 1, except in this case the population is drawn from a bimodal distribution of users instead of a unimodal distribution. The result is a higher precision, which shows that it is better to have a few good users than many mediocre ones.

Varying Trust Estimation Accuracy. We also investigated how accurate the trusts must be in order to maintain good quality beliefs. We let the trust noise parameter be the same for all users (δ_{ij}=δ) and varied δ (see Equation 7). Note that when δ=0, t_{ij} was γ_j, and when δ=1, t_{ij} was chosen uniformly from [0,1]. Figure 6 shows the average precision for various values of δ. Even with a noise level of 0.3, acceptable precision (>80%) was maintained.

The results show that the network is robust to noise and low quality users. Also, *maximum* outperformed *weighted average* in these experiments.

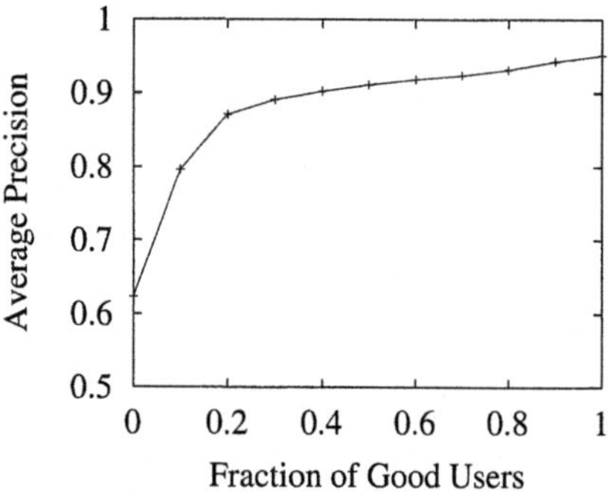

Fig. 6. Effect of varying the quality of trust estimation

6.2 Experiments with the BibServ Bibliography Server

We have implemented our belief and trust combination methods in our BibServ system, which is publicly accessible at www.bibserv.org. BibServ is a bibliography service that allows users to search for bibliography entries for inclusion in technical publications. Users may upload and maintain their bibliographies, create new entries, use entries created by others, and rate and edit any entry.

Why Bibliographies? We felt that bibliographies have many characteristics that make them a good starting point for our research into the Semantic Web. The bibliography domain is simple, yet gives rise to all of the issues of information quality, relevance, inconsistency, and redundancy that we desire to research. The BibServ beta site currently has 70 users, drawn mainly from the UW computer science department and IBM Almaden, and over half a million entries, of which 18000 entered by the users.

Implementation. BibServ is implemented as a centralized server, so we chose to store the merged trusts $\mathcal{T}$ and compute the merged beliefs as needed. This requires O(NM) space. Since there are many more bibliography entries than users, this is much less than the $O(M^2)$ space that would be required if we instead stored the merged beliefs.

By our definition, a user's merged belief in a bibliography entry represents the quality and relevance of that entry to them. Hence, search results are ordered by belief.[4] The computation of merged trusts and beliefs is implemented in SQL and, in the case of beliefs, is incorporated directly into the search query itself. The overhead of computing beliefs is typically less than 10% of the time required to perform the query itself. Experiments were performed using weighted average (λ=0.5) as well as maximum as belief combination functions.

Belief as Quality and Relevance. The relation of belief combination to BibServ is as follows. When performing a search on BibServ, a user presumably is looking for a good bibliographic entry (e.g. has all of the important fields filled in correctly) that is related to her own field of study. Our concept of "belief" corresponds to this – a good and relevant entry should have high belief. We treat each entry as a statement. Users may set their beliefs explicitly, and we implicitly assume a belief of 1.0 for any entry in their personal bibliography (unless otherwise explicitly rated). This forms the vector **b** for each entry. BibServ users are also presented with a list of other users whom they may rate. A high rating is intended to mean they expect the user to provide entries which are high quality and relevant. This forms the trust matrix **T**.

Experimental Results. We asked BibServ users to think of a specific paper they were interested in, and use BibServ to search for it using keywords. We returned the search results in random order, and asked the user to rate each result for quality (0-5) and relevance (either "yes, this is the paper I was looking for" or "no, this is not"). We required the user to make the search general enough to return at least 5 entries, and to rate them all. We used two metrics to evaluate the results. The first is whether there was a correlation between beliefs and either the rated quality or relevance of the

[4] Incorporating traditional measures of query relevance (for instance, TFIDF) may lead to a better ordering of entries. One probabilistic-based technique for this is that of query-dependent PageRank [32].

entries. In many cases, such as ordering search results, we only care whether the best k results may be determined by belief. We thus calculated the ratio of the average rating of the top k results (ordered by belief) vs. the average rating of all results. Unfortunately, we could do this experiment with only a small number of users. The data set consists of 405 ratings of quality and relevance on 26 searches by 13 users. The average user involved in the study specified 9 trusted users. Because the results are based on a small quantity of data, they should at best be considered preliminary.

The highest correlation was obtained with weighted average, which produced beliefs that had a correlation of 0.29 with the quality ratings (λ=0.03). The other correlations were 0.10 (weighted average vs. relevance), 0.16 (maximum vs. quality), and -0.01 (maximum vs. relevance). These results are not as positive as we had hoped for. Many factors can contribute to a low correlation, such as having little variance in the actual quality and relevance of the entries. Currently, almost all of the entries in BibServ are related to computer science, and all of the users are computer scientists, so the web of trust gives little predictive power for relevance. We expect that as BibServ accumulates users and publications on more varying topics, the correlation results will improve.

The average ratio of the top k results to the rating of all results (across different searches) for relevance ranged from 1.2 to 1.6 for a variety of k (1-5) and for either belief combination function. The average ratio ranged from 0.96 to 1.05 for quality. The ratio rapidly tended toward 1.0 as k increased, indicating that, while belief was a good indicator for relevance, the data contained a lot of noise (making it possible only to identify the very best few entries, not order them all). This is consistent with the low relevance correlation found above.

The most interesting result of these experiments was with regard to λ. We found that the best results when measuring beliefs vs. quality ratings were when λ was very small, though still non-zero. On the other hand, the best results for relevance were when λ was very large, though not equal to one. This indicated that 1) Most users shared a similar metric for evaluating the quality of a bibliography entry, and 2) Users had a widely varying metric for evaluating an entry's relevance. The best λ was not 0 or 1, indicating that both information from others and personalized beliefs were useful.

7 Related Work

The idea of a *web of trust* is not new. As mentioned, it is used by Epinions for ordering product reviews. Cryptography also makes use of a web of trust to verify identity [10]. In Abdul-Rahman's system, John's trust in Jane, and John's trust in Jane's ability to determine who is trustworthy, are separate, though discrete and only qualitatively valued [1]. Such a separation would be interesting to consider in our framework as well.

The analog of belief combination for the WWW is estimating the quality and relevance of web pages. Information retrieval methods based solely on the content of the page (such as TFIDF [20]) are useful, but are outperformed by methods that also involve the connectivity between pages [12][23][26].

Gil and Ratnaker [19] present an algorithm that involves a more complex, though qualitative, form of trust based on user annotations of information sources, which are then combined. One shortcoming of such an approach is that it derives values of "trustworthiness" that are not personalized for the individual using them, requiring all users – regardless of personal values – to agree on the credibility of sources. Secondly, by averaging the statements of many users, the approach is open to a malicious attacker who may submit many high (or low) ratings for a source in order to hide its true credibility. By employing a web of trust, our approach surmounts both of these difficulties (assuming users reduce their trust in a user that provides poor information).

Kamvar et. al's EigenTrust algorithm [21], which computes global trusts as a function of local trust values in a peer-to-peer network, is very similar to our probabilistic interpretation of trusts presented in section 4. One key difference is that we allow trusts and beliefs to vary; they are personalized for each user based on her personal trusts. In contrast, EigenTrust computes a global trust value (similar to PageRank) and emphasizes security against malicious peers who aim to disturb this calculation.

Pennock et. al. looked at how web-based artificial markets may combine the beliefs of their users [29]. Social network algorithms have been applied to webs of trust in order to identify users with high network influence [16][31]. Applying the same methods to the Semantic Web's web of trust may prove fruitful in identifying useful contributors, highly respected entities, etc. Also in a similar vein is the ReferralWeb project, which mines multiple sources to discover networks of trust among users [22]. Also interesting is collaborative filtering [30], in which a user's belief is computed from the beliefs of users she is similar to. This can be seen as forming the web of trust implicitly, based solely on similarity of interests.

8 Future Work

In this work, we assumed that statements are independent. We would like to investigate how dependencies between statements may be handled. For example, if we consider a taxonomy to be a set of class-subclass relationships, and consider each relationship to be an independent statement, then merging such taxonomy beliefs is not likely to lead to a useful taxonomy. We would like to be able to merge structural elements like taxonomies; [14] and [15] may provide useful insights into possible solutions.

The path algebra and probabilistic interpretations were shown to be nearly identical, and the probabilistic interpretation is a generalization of PageRank. Considering PageRank works so well on web pages, it would be interesting to apply the ideas developed here back to the WWW for the purposes of ranking pages. For instance, might we find it useful to replace the sum with a maximum in PageRank? In general, we would like to consider networks in which not all users employ the same belief combination function, perhaps by modifying the global interpretation in order to relax the requirements put on the concatenation and aggregation functions.

There are many tradeoffs between computation, communication, and storage requirements for the different architectures (peer to peer, central server, hierarchical, etc.), algorithms (semi-naïve, Warshall, etc.), and strategies (merge beliefs on demand, store all beliefs, etc.). We would like to formalize these tradeoffs for better understanding of the efficiency of the various architectures.

We considered only single valued beliefs and trusts. In general, a belief could actually be multi-valued, representing a magnitude in multiple dimensions, such as 'truth', and 'importance', and 'novelty'. We would also like to consider multi-valued trusts, such as those used by Gil and Ratnakar [19], which may represent similar dimensions as beliefs (but applied to users). It may be possible to combine beliefs and trusts into one concept, 'opinion', which may be similarly applied to both statements and users. Similarly, we would also like to allow users to specify *topic-specific* trusts. With topic-specific trusts, the normalized sum combination function would probably be similar to query-dependent PageRank [32].

9 Conclusions

If it is to succeed, the Semantic Web must address the issues of information quality, relevance, inconsistency and redundancy. This is done on today's Web using algorithms like PageRank, which take advantage of the link structure of the Web. We propose to generalize this to the Semantic Web by having each user specify which others she trusts, and leveraging this "web of trust" to estimate a user's belief in statements supplied by any other user. This paper formalizes some of the requirements for such a calculus, and describes a number of possible models for carrying it out. The potential of the approach, and the tradeoffs involved, are illustrated by experiments using data from the Epinions knowledge-sharing site, and from the BibServ site we have set up for collecting and serving bibliographic references.

Acknowledgements. An off-hand discussion with Jim Hendler at the Semantic Web Workshop at WWW 2002 provided the initial impetus for this work. We also thank Ramanathan Guha for discussions on the web of trust and James Lin for his help with BibServ's site design. This research was partially supported by an IBM Ph.D. Fellowship to the first author, and by ONR grant N00014-02-1-0408.

References

[1] Abdul-Rahman, A., & Hailes, S. (1997). A distributed trust model. *Proceedings of New Security Paradigms Workshop* (pp. 48–60).

[2] Agrawal, R., & Jagadish, H. V. (1988). Multiprocessor transitive closure algorithms. *Proceedings of the International Symposium on Databases in Parallel and Distributed Systems* (pp. 56–66). Austin, TX.

[3] Agrawal, R., Dar, S., & Jagadish, H. V. (1990). Direct transitive closure algorithms: Design and performance evaluation. *ACM Transactions on Database Systems, 15*, 427–458.

[4] Agresti, A. (1990). *Categorical data analysis*. New York, NY: Wiley.

[5] Aho, A. V., Hopcroft, J. E., & Ullman, J. D. (1974). *The design and analysis of computer algorithms*. Reading, MA: Addison-Wesley.

[6] Ankolekar, A., Burstein, M. H., Hobbs, J. R., Lassila, O., Martin, D., McDermott, . V., McIlraith, S. A., Narayanan, S., Paolucci, M., Payne, T. R., & Sycara, K. P. (2002). Daml-s: Web service description for the Semantic Web. *International Semantic Web Conference* (pp. 348–363).
[7] Bancilhon, F. (1985). Naive evaluation of recursively defined relations. *On Knowledge Base Management Systems (Islamorada)* (pp. 165–178).
[8] Bellman, R., & Giertz, M. (1973). On the analytic formalism of the theory of fuzzy sets. *Information Sciences, 5*, 149–156.
[9] Berners-Lee, T., Hendler, J., & Lassila, O. (May 2001). The Semantic Web. *Scientific American.*
[10] Blaze, M., Feigenbaum, J., & Lacy, J. (1996). Decentralized trust management. *Proceedings of the 1996 IEEE Symposium on Security and Privacy* (pp. 164–173). Oakland, CA.
[11] Carre, B. (1978). *Graphs and networks.* Oxford: Claredon Press.
[12] Chakrabarti, S., Dom, B., Gibson, D., Kleinberg, J., Raghavan, P., & Rajagopalan, S. (1998). Automatic resource compilation by analyzing hyperlink structure and associated text. *Proceedings of the Seventh International World Wide Web Conference* (pp. 65–74). Brisbane, Australia: Elsevier.
[13] Chickering, D. M., & Heckerman, D. (1997). Efficient approximations for the marginal likelihood of Bayesian networks with hidden variables. *Machine Learning, 29*, 181–212.
[14] Doan, A., Madhavan, J., Domingos, P., & Halevy, A. Y. (2002). Learning to Map between Ontologies on the Semantic Web. *Proceedings of the Eleventh International World Wide Web Conference* (pp. 662–673).
[15] Doan, A., Domingos, P., & Halevy, A. (2001). Reconciling schemas of disparate data sources: A machine-learning approach. *Proceedings of the 2001 ACM SIGMOD International Conference on Management of Data* (pp. 509–520). Santa Barbara, CA: ACM Press.
[16] Domingos, P., & Richardson, M. (2001). Mining the network value of customers. *Proceedings of the Seventh ACM SIGKDD International Conference on Knowledge Discovery and Data Mining* (pp. 57–66). San Francisco, CA: ACM Press.
[17] French, S. (1985). Group consensus probability distributions: A critical survey. In J. M. Bernardo, M. H. DeGroot, D. V. Lindley and A. F. M. Smith (Eds.), *Bayesian statistics 2*, 183–202. Amsterdam, Netherlands: Elsevier.
[18] Genest, C., & Zidek, J. V. (1986). Combining probability distributions: A critique and an annotated bibliography. *Statistical Science, 1*, 114–148.
[19] Gil, Y., & Ratnakar, V. (2002). Trusting information sources one citizen at a time. *International Semantic Web Conference* (pp. 162–176). Sardinia,Italy.
[20] Joachims, T. (1997). A probabilistic analysis of the Rocchio algorithm with TFIDF for text categorization. *Proceedings of the Fourteenth International Conference on Machine Learning (ICML–97)* (pp. 143–151). San Francisco, CA: Morgan Kaufmann.
[21] Kamvar, S., Schlosser, M., & Garcia-Molina, H. (2003). The EigenTrust algorithm for reputation management in P2P networks. *Proceedings of the Twelfth International World Wide Web Conference.*
[22] Kautz, H., Selman, B., & Shah, M. (1997). ReferralWeb: Combining social networks and collaborative filtering. *Communications of the ACM, 40*, 63–66.
[23] Kleinberg, J. M. (1998). Authoritative sources in a hyperlinked environment. *Proceedings of the Ninth Annual ACM-SIAM Symposium on Discrete Algorithms* (pp. 668–677). Baltimore, MD: ACM Press.
[24] Motwani95 Motwani, R., & Raghavan, P. (1995). *Randomized algorithms.* Cambridge University Press.
[25] Ngo, L., & Haddawy, P. (1997). Answering queries from context-sensitive probabilistic knowledge bases. *Theoretical Computer Science, 171*, 147–177.

[26] Page, L., Brin, S., Motwani, R., & Winograd, T. (1998). *The PageRank citation ranking: Bringing order to the web* (Technical Report). Stanford University, Stanford, CA.

[27] Patel-Schneider, P., & Simeon, J. (2002). Building the Semantic Web on XML. *International Semantic Web Conference* (pp. 147–161).

[28] Pearl, J. (1988). *Probabilistic reasoning in intelligent systems: Networks of plausible inference.* San Francisco, CA: Morgan Kaufmann.

[29] Pennock, D. M., Nielsen, F. A., & Giles, C. L. (2001). Extracting collective probabilistic forecasts from Web games. *Proceedings of the Seventh ACM SIGKDD International Conference on Knowledge Discovery and Data Mining* (pp. 174–183). San Francisco, CA: ACM Press.

[30] Resnick, P., Iacovou, N., Suchak, M., Bergstrom, P., & Riedl, J. (1994). GroupLens: An open architecture for collaborative filtering of netnews. *Proceedings of the ACM 1994 Conference on Computer Supported Cooperative Work* (pp. 175–186). New York, NY: ACM Press.

[31] Richardson, M., & Domingos, P. (2002). Mining knowledge-sharing sites for viral marketing. *Proceedings of the Eighth ACM SIGKDD International Conference on Knowledge Discovery and Data Mining* (pp. 61–70). Edmonton, Canada: ACM Press.

[32] Richardson, M., & Domingos, P. (2002). The intelligent surfer: Probabilistic combination of link and content information in PageRank. In T. G. Dietterich, S. Becker and Z. Ghahramani (Eds.), *Advances in Neural Information Processing Systems 14*, 1441–1448. Cambridge, MA: MIT Press.

[33] Warshall, S. (1962). A theorem on boolean matrices. *Journal of the ACM*, *9*, 11–12.

Appendix

Here we give a proof of Theorem 1. We are assuming $\Diamond$ is commutative and associative, $\circ$ is associative and distributes over $\Diamond$, and $\mathbf{T}$, $\mathcal{T}$, $\mathbf{b}$, and $\mathscr{b}$ are defined as in Section 3. Also from Section 3, $(\mathbf{A}\bullet\mathbf{B})_{ij}=\Diamond(\forall k\text{: } \mathbf{A}_{ik}\circ\mathbf{B}_{kj})$.

We first prove that $\bullet$ is associative. Let $\mathbf{X}=(\mathbf{A}\bullet\mathbf{B})\bullet\mathbf{C}$. Then:

$$\begin{aligned}
\mathbf{X}_{ij} &= \Diamond(\forall k\text{: } \Diamond(\forall l\text{: } \mathbf{A}_{il}\circ\mathbf{B}_{lk}) \circ \mathbf{C}_{kj}) && \text{from the definition of } \bullet \\
&= \Diamond(\forall k\text{: } \Diamond(\forall l\text{: } \mathbf{A}_{il}\circ\mathbf{B}_{lk}\circ\mathbf{C}_{kj})) && \text{since } \circ \text{ distributes over } \Diamond \text{ and } \circ \text{ is associative} \\
&= \Diamond(\forall l\text{: } \Diamond(\forall k\text{: } \mathbf{A}_{il}\circ\mathbf{B}_{lk}\circ\mathbf{C}_{kj})) && \text{since } \Diamond \text{ is associative} \\
&= \Diamond(\forall l\text{: } \mathbf{A}_{il}\circ \Diamond(\forall k\text{: } \mathbf{B}_{lk}\circ\mathbf{C}_{kj})) && \text{since } \circ \text{ distributes over } \Diamond \\
&= \Diamond(\forall l\text{: } \mathbf{A}_{il}\circ (\mathbf{B}\bullet\mathbf{C})_{lj}) && \text{by definition of } \bullet
\end{aligned}$$

This implies that

$$\mathbf{X} = \mathbf{A}\bullet(\mathbf{B}\bullet\mathbf{C}) \qquad \text{by definition of } \bullet.$$

We have $\mathscr{b}^{(0)} = \mathbf{b}$ and $\mathscr{b}^{(n)} = \mathbf{T}\bullet \mathscr{b}^{(n-1)}$, so $\mathscr{b}^{(n)} = \mathbf{T}\bullet(\mathbf{T}\bullet(\ldots \bullet(\mathbf{T}\bullet\mathbf{b})))$. Since $\bullet$ is associative,

$$\mathscr{b}^{(n)}= \mathbf{T}^{n}\bullet\mathbf{b} \tag{8}$$

(where $\mathbf{T}^{n}$ means $\mathbf{T}\bullet\mathbf{T}\bullet\mathbf{T}\ldots$ n times, and $\mathbf{T}^{0}$ is the identity matrix). We have $\mathcal{T}^{(0)} = \mathbf{T}$ and $\mathcal{T}^{(n)} = \mathbf{T}\bullet\mathcal{T}^{(n-1)}$, so $\mathcal{T}^{(n)} = \mathbf{T}\bullet(\mathbf{T}\bullet(\ldots \bullet(\mathbf{T}\bullet\mathbf{T})))$. Hence,

$$\mathcal{T}^{(n)}= \mathcal{T}\bullet\mathbf{T}^{n} \tag{9}$$

Combining Equations 8 and 9, $\mathbf{T}\bullet \mathscr{b}^{(n)} = \mathcal{T}^{(n)}\bullet\mathbf{b}$

Since we run until convergence, this is sufficient to show that $\mathbf{T}\bullet \mathscr{b} = \mathcal{T}\bullet\mathbf{b}$.

Signing RDF Graphs

Jeremy J. Carroll

Hewlett-Packard Labs, Bristol, UK, BS34 12QZ
jjc@hpl.hp.com

Abstract. Assuming **P<GI<NP**, the creation and verification of a digital signature of an arbitrary RDF graph cannot be done in polynomial time. However, it is possible to define a large class of canonicalizable RDF graphs, such that digital signatures for graphs in this class can be created and verified in O(*n*log(*n*)). Without changing its meaning, an arbitrary RDF graph can be nondeterministically pre-canonicalized into a graph of this class, before signing. The techniques in this paper are key enablers for the use of digital signature technology in the Semantic Web.

1 Introduction

Digital signatures permit a user of a document to verify that some named party has vouched for it. This is a key technology for reducing the trust barriers to e-business and e-commerce.

For use within the Semantic Web, it is necessary for the user of an RDF graph [1] to be able to verify a signature, either for that graph or for a subgraph.

All obvious methods for doing this have exponential worst-case behaviour.

We present a method that involves:

- a class of canonical RDF documents,
- a canonicalization algorithm that runs in O(*n*log(*n*)) but fails on worst-case inputs, for which there is no corresponding canonical RDF document,
- a precanonicalization algorithm, applicable to any RDF graph, that makes nondeterministic modifications to the input graph, if there is a danger that it is one of the worst-case inputs.

Signing a graph then involves running the precanonicalization algorithm, which may modify the graph, canonicalization the modified graph and signing the resulting canonical RDF.

Verifying a signature involves extracting the signed subgraph, canonicalizing this subgraph, and verifying the signature for the canonical RDF. If the canonicalization algorithms fails, then the graph was not signed.

It is crucial that we can make significant syntactic modifications to the graph that are explicitly meaningless

Section 2 demonstrates that RDF canonicalization is graph isomorphism (GI) complete. Section 3 introduces some preliminary notions needed in sections 4 and 6 which contains the principle algorithm of this paper. Section 5 defines canonical RDF, on the basis of the naïve algorithm of section 4. Section 6 shows how to patch up the problems caused by the naivety. Section 7 details some more sophisticated

D. Fensel et al. (Eds.): ISWC 2003, LNCS 2870, pp. 369–384, 2003.

techniques which are not necessary but may be desirable. Section 8 shows that all the techniques used are O($n$log$n$). Section 9 focuses on practical use of the techniques and reports on some test results.

2 Verifying Signatures of Arbitrary RDF

In a Semantic Web application, there is likely to be an RDF graph. If we wish to verify that either it, or a subgraph of it, has been digitally signed in some way, then we have to solve at least one well-known hard problem. Note this way of stating the problem rules out one scenario which is that *B* has read the graph from a file signed by *A*. If *B* has done this, then *B* can simply verify the signature on the file, and has no need to verify the signature for the graph, as a graph.

We follow [2] and assume the graph isomorphism problem is strictly harder than polynomial time, and strictly easier than nondeterministic polynomial time. (i.e. $P < GI < NP$). We also note that the subgraph isomorphism problem is well known to be NP complete. These results are applicable to RDF, see section 2.3.

Thus, if *A* wishes to sign an RDF graph and *B* wishes to verify the signature, then *A* needs to serialize the graph in some form, sign the serialization, and *B* needs to verify that signature. This overall process of signature verification permits a comparison (either for isomorphism or for subgraph) between the graph that *A* signs, and the graph that *B* verifies. This overall process solves the graph isomorphism problem or the subgraph isomorphism problem. Thus either the algorithm for signing the graph, or the algorithm for verifying the signature of the graph must be of complexity class GI or NP. It would possibly be best to make the signer do the hard work. Messmer and Bunke [3] show that graph and subgraph isomorphism with respect to a fixed graph, of size m, comparing with a varying graph of size n, can be performed in $O(n^3)$ time, but needs $O(3^m)$ space for the verification algorithm, computed in $O(m^m)$ time. Note that *A* would calculate this large algorithm, and *B* would have to execute it (without downloading all of it). This method could be used to give signature verification algorithms of cubic complexity; but creating the signature is of exponential complexity.

These worst-case scenarios are bad, and the solution for signing RDF needs to avoid them. The solution we present is based on not attempting to sign or verify signatures of *arbitrary* RDF.

2.1 Meaningless Changes

The key insight of this paper is that while in general signing RDF Graphs is GI complete, all interesting RDF graphs can be slightly modified (typically by adding a few, explicitly meaningless, triples) to be in a class of RDF graphs which can be canonicalized, and hence both signed and verified, in O($n$log$n$). Moreover, the class of easily canonicalizable RDF graphs can be large enough so that 90% of 'interesting' RDF graphs lie within it, and most of the other interesting graphs require only slight modification.

For the purpose of signing an RDF graph, since such modifications are meaningless, the social act of signing the unmodified graph is the same as the social act of signing the modified graph. Thus we always sign modified graphs, that can be canonicalized in O($n$log(n)). For signature verification, if the graph requires modification, then the signature to be checked was incorrect, since the only graphs that get signed have been modified and do not require further modification.

The reader should judge whether these modifications are merely a dirty hack or an elegant engineering compromise.

An alternative engineering approach of simply deleting problematic parts of the graph is also explored.

2.2 A Simple Example

Consider an RDF Graph with two triples, represented in N-Triples 4 as either:

```
# Here is a graph
_:aBlankNode <eg:prop>   "3" .
_:aBlankNode <eg:prop>   "5" .
```

or

```
_:ax       <eg:prop> "5"    .
_:ax  <eg:prop> "3" .
```

The two files are different, but the graph they describe is the same. The differences between the files are *insignificant*. These include: the comment; the whitespace; the order of the lines; the choice of blank node identifiers (e.g. *aBlankNode* or *ax*)

Other aspects of the N-Triples are *significant* in that they represent the intended abstract RDF Graph [1]. Significant aspects include: the presence or absence of a triple; the string in each literal; the URIs for each property or resource.

Our approach to signing a graph is to: specify a class of canonical RDF documents; and to sign an RDF graph by signing a canonical RDF document which is a serialization of either that graph, or a different graph which both entails and is entailed by the graph to be signed.

Canonical RDF is chosen so that there is at most one representation of that graph in Canonical RDF. Thus, we can check that these two are the same by converting both into canonical RDF and doing a character-by-character comparison. This might fail, if the graph proves difficult (which the above example does not).

Of the insignificant differences highlighted, only two present any interesting difficulties: the order of the lines, and the blank node identifiers.

2.3 RDF C14N Is GI Complete

The techniques in this paper cannot canonicalize arbitrary RDF graphs without making some modifications to them. This reflects the underlying difficulty of RDF canonicalization.

As discussed by Carroll [5], RDF graph equality and the graph isomorphism problem have equivalent complexity.

Any unlabelled undirected graph can be encoded in RDF by replacing each node with a blank node, and replacing each arc by two arcs (in each direction) always using a single property (e.g. `<eg:x>`). So a simple triangle (three nodes, three arcs) can be encoded in N-Triples as:

```
_:a <eg:x> _:b .          _:a <eg:x> _:c .
_:b <eg:x> _:a .          _:b <eg:x> _:c .
_:c <eg:x> _:b .          _:c <eg:x> _:a .
```

If we could fully solve RDF canonicalization in polynomial time, then we could compare two RDF graphs for equality in polynomial time (by comparing their canonical representations). This would provide an (unlikely) polynomial time solution to the Graph Isomorphism problem [2], [6], [7].

2.4 What's the Difficulty?

The graph isomorphism problem is deceptive. It really doesn't look hard! We will informally explore the problem of a canonical representation of a simple graph, with two disconnected components shown in Fig. 1.

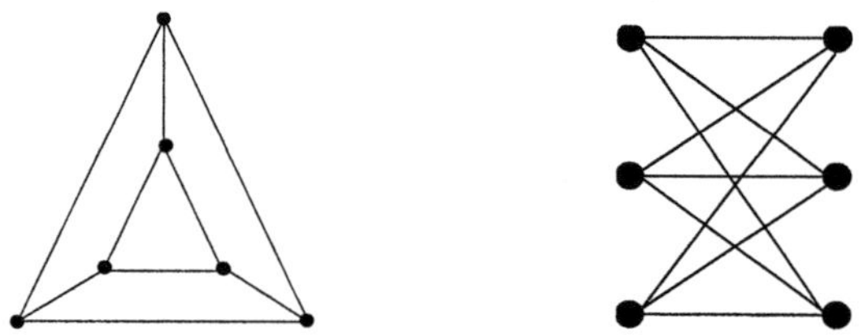

Fig. 1. A 12 vertex graphs

The graph consists of 12 nodes and 18 edges. Each node has three neighbours, and two nodes at a distance of two away. Each node is in a connected component of six nodes.

If we try and canonicalize this, we will start by writing some node before all the other nodes. That node will either come from the component on the left or that on the right. The canonicalization algorithm needs to make a deterministic choice. There is no intuitively obvious rationale for choosing one or the other, and which ever choice we make seems to require considerations not just about the node, but also its neighbours, and their neighbours, and …

A good solution to this problem is provided by McKay [8], [9]. He uses an analysis of the automorphism group of a graph to construct canonical representatives. His solution is of non-polynomial complexity and complicated to program. It is not a plausible candidate for an infrastructural component within the semantic web.

3 Preliminaries

3.1 Syntactic

For clarity of exposition the algorithms described in this paper are based around the lexicographic sorting of N-Triples [4] files. N-Triples is an ASCII format.

We use numbered gensym identifiers during the algorithm. These are created with just sufficient leading zeros so that lexicographic ordering and integer ordering are the same. (The number of leading zeros required is computed from the number of blank nodes in the RDF graph being considered).

3.2 Semantic

The techniques in this paper rely on being able to make meaningless changes to an RDF graph. This is done in accordance with the RDF formal semantics [10], by using a special property, which we conventionally refer to as **c14n:true** defined here:

```
<rdf:RDF xml:base="&c14n;" xmlns:c14n="&c14n;#">
  <rdfs:Property rdf:ID="true">
     <rdfs:description>This property is true whatever
resource is its subject, and whatever literal is its object.
    Thus triples with literal objects, and c14n:true as
predicate, can arbitrarily be added to and deleted from an RDF
graph without changing its meaning. </rdfs:description>
  </rdfs:Property>
<rdf:RDF>
```

(Omitting namespace declarations and the definition of the entity **&c14n;** as the URL `http://www-uk.hpl.hp.com/people/jjc/rdf/c14n)`.

By specifying this predicate as being always true, adding or deleting triples with this predicate does not alter the entailments under the RDF model theory. Formally the semantics of the document are unchanged.

If desired, an alternative would be to use OWL (Full) to define a trivially true predicate which holds between all resources and all long integers. The following cardinality constraint, in the OWL abstract syntax 11, expresses this condition:

```
class(rdfs:Resource complete restriction(c14n:true cardinality=2^64))
dataValuedProperty( c14n:true range( xsd:long ) )
```

3.3 N-Triples to Canonical XML

In this paper, we concentrate on creating canonical representations of RDF graphs in N-Triples [4].

However, for full integration with tools built on Canonical XML [12] it is necessary to transform these files into XML, and, moreover, we wish the XML produced to canonically depend on the original RDF graph.

This needs to be done by specifying a canonical method for turning an N-Triple document into RDF/XML. This must: preserve the order of the triples; prohibit the many variants in the grammar; specify the whitespace precisely.

3.4 RDF C14N without Blank Nodes

To create a canonical N-Triples file for an RDF graph without any blank nodes we can simply reorder the lines in the N-Triples document to be in lexicographic order.

(This could be implemented simply with Unix™ **sort**[1]). We may wish to canonicalise the lexical forms of typed literals first.

4 Labelling Blank Nodes

If we have blank nodes in the graph then life is somewhat trickier.

In N-Triples blank nodes are represented using blank node identifiers, which can appear in subject or object position.

Unfortunately, these identifiers are gensyms created during the writing of the N-Triples, and are not an intrinsic part of the graph. Hence, it is an error if the canonicalization depends on these gensyms. In contrast, the canonicalization algorithm must deterministically choose new blank node identifiers.

In this part of our approach, we first write out the file using arbitrarily chosen blank node identifiers; then we sort the document (mostly) ignoring those identifiers. On the basis of this sorted document, we then rename all the blank nodes, in a (hopefully) deterministic fashion.

Since the level of determinism is crucial to the workings of the canonicalization algorithm, we start by defining a deterministic blank node labelling algorithm. This suffers from the defect of not necessarily labeling all the blank nodes.

Deterministic, in this context, means dependent only upon significant parts of the initial representation of the graph, and *nondeterministic* means dependent, in part, upon insignificant parts of the initial representation of the graph.

4.1 One-Step Deterministic Labelling

In RDF [1], a single triple can contain zero, one or two blank nodes (the property must be specified by a URI reference).

We present an algorithm that labels some blank nodes on the basis of the immediate neighbors of that blank node (the one-step in the name of the algorithm).

1. Canonicalize the typed literals in the graph according to XML Schema [13].
2. Write the graph as an N-Triples document. Each line of the document is a complete distinct triple of the graph.
3. For each line with a blank node identifier in subject position (e.g. `_:subj`), replace the blank node identifier with `"~"` and add a comment `"# _:subj"` to the end of the line, indicating the original identifier.
4. For each line with a blank node identifier in object position (e.g. `_:obj`), replace the blank node identifier with `"~"` and add a comment `"# _:obj"` to the end of the line, indicating the original identifier.
5. Reorder the lines in the N-Triples document to be in lexicographic order. (This could be implemented with Unix™ **sort**).
6. Use a gensym counter, initialized to 1, and a lookup table, initially empty. Go through the file from top to bottom:

---

[1] **sort** in Unix uses a locale dependent ordering. To use US-ASCII order, it is necessary to set the environment variable `LC_ALL=C`.

   a. If this line is the same as the next or previous line excluding any trailing comment, continue to the next line in the file.
   b. If there is a "~" in object position:
      i. Extract the blank node identifier from the final comment in the line. Remove the comment.
      ii. Look the identifier up in the table.
      iii. If there is no entry, insert a new entry formed from **"_:g"** concatenated with the value of the gensym counter. Increment the counter.
      iv. Replace the "~" with the value from the table.
   c. If there is a "~" in subject position, use the same subprocedure to replace it with a consistently chosen gensym.
7. Using the same lookup table. Go through the file from top to bottom:
   a. If there is a "~" in object position:
      i. Extract the blank node identifier from the final comment in the line. Remove the comment.
      ii. Look the identifier up in the table.
      iii. If there is an entry, replace the "~" with the value from the table.
   b. If there is a "~" in subject position, use the same subprocedure to possibly replace it with a consistently chosen gensym.
8. Lexicographically sort the N-Triples again.

The only nondeterminism here is that the sort may depend on the blank node labels in pairs of triples for which the rest of the triple is identical. Such pairs are studiously avoided (step 6.a) in the assignment of labels, and so the order in which such pairs appear does not effect the labels chosen. Notice that step 7, which does deal with the incomparable lines, does not choose any labels and is hence deterministic.

The algorithm will deterministically label some of the blank nodes, for others it leaves them unlabelled. These nodes are referred to as *hard to label* nodes.

The operation of the deterministic labeling algorithm depends on triples that can distinguish one blank node from another. These *distinctive triples* are characterized by being unique in the graph even when all blank nodes are treated as identical.

The hard to label nodes do not participate in any distinctive triples.

Example 1, is fully labeled by this algorithm:

<eg:a> <eg:foo> _:a . _:a <eg:prop> "val" . <eg:b> <eg:prop> _:b .	→	<eg:a> <eg:foo> _:g1 . <eg:b> <eg:prop> _:g2 . _:g1 <eg:prop> "val" .

On the other hand, **example 2** is not fully labelled:

_:a <eg:zee> "why" . _:a <eg:prop> "val" . <eg:b> <eg:prop> _:b . _:b3 <eg:prop> "val" .	→	<eg:b> <eg:prop> _:g1 . _:g2 <eg:prop> "val" . _:g2 <eg:zee> "why" . ~ <eg:prop> "val" . # _:b3

5 Canonical RDF

The algorithm above has the desired property of being of a low complexity class O($n$log(n)), and hence optimizable to be sufficiently quick.

Thus we will define canonical RDF on the basis of this algorithm.

A canonical N-Triples document is one (without any comments) which is unchanged under the application of the one-step deterministic labeling algorithm.

That is canonical RDF in N-Triples has the following features:

- There are no hard to label nodes.
- Every blank node identifier has the form gNNN where NNN is some number of digits. The number of the digits is the same for every blank node identifier. At least one identifier has a non-zero first digit.
- After deleting all triples which are not distinctive, the first occurrences of each blank node identifier appear in numeric order, starting at 1, without gaps.
- The file is in lexicographic sort order.

Such files are unchanged under the one-step deterministic labeling.

If one-step deterministic labeling successfully labels all the nodes, then the resulting output will be canonical RDF. In such cases, one-step deterministic labeling is idempotent. So the resulting file in example 1 above is in canonical RDF.

6 Pre-canonicalization

We seek to make such a definition useable in all cases. Instead of defining the set of canonical RDF documents, such that *every* RDF document has a canonical representative, we set out to modify RDF graphs which do not have a canonical representative into ones that do, by ensuring that there are no hard to label nodes. This process of making nondeterministic modifications to the input in order to make it easier to canonicalize is not acceptable in a true canonicalization algorithm. Thus we refer to this step as precanonicalization. We try to minimize the changes made; and to be informed by the application needs as to what sort of changes are acceptable (this paper concentrates on the digital signature application).

Since many of the steps involved in precanonicalization are identical to those in the one step deterministic labeling algorithm already presented, we continue to consider complete algorithms involving both precanonicalization and the labeling.

6.1 Nondeterministic Pre-canonicalization

Applications of digital signatures usually require that the meaning of the document is fully captured in the object that is signed. A (somewhat tired) example would be signing a purchase order. In terms of the RDF semantics [10], the signed object should both entail and be entailed by the document presented for signature. The **`c14n:true`** predicate presented in section 3.2 has been designed so that arbitrary triples with this predicate can be added or deleted, without modifying the meaning. Using such triples we can make sure that none of the nodes are hard to label.

The version described here uses many passes of the file – the three important passes:

- identify the hard to label nodes;
- create additional distinctive triples for those nodes
- deterministically label the resulting graph.

Thus, we can perform the following steps:

A. Perform a one-step deterministic labeling
B. If there are no hard to label nodes, then stop. [Ensures idempotence]
C. Delete all triples with predicate **c14n:true** . [B ensures idempotence]
D. Perform a one-step deterministic labeling.
E. Using a new lookup table from step D, and a new counter, scan the file from top to bottom, performing these steps on each line:
   a. If there is a **"~"** in object position:
      i. Extract the blank node identifier from the final comment in the line. Remove the comment.
      ii. Look the identifier up in the table.
      iii. If there is no entry: add an entry **"x"** to the table; and add a new triple to the graph with subject being the blank node identified by the identifier from the comment, predicate being **c14n:true** and object being the string form of the counter; increment the counter.
   b. If there is a **"~"** in subject position, use the same subprocedure to possibly create a distinctive triple for the subject as well.
F. Perform a one-step deterministic labeling (of the new modified graph, with a new lookup table and counter). Since all nodes participate in a distinctive triple, every table lookup will find an entry.

This algorithm is nondeterministic in step E, which is hence the precanonicalization step, but that nondeterminism is fairly limited, because even with the rather naïve one-step deterministic labeling algorithm almost all nodes in almost all (practically occurring) RDF graphs will have been classified.

So again continuing with example 2, we find:

```
<eg:b> <eg:prop> _:g1 .
_:g2 <eg:prop> "val" .
_:g2 <eg:zee> "why" .
_:g3 <eg:prop> "val" .
_:g3 <http://www-uk.hpl.hp.com/people/jjc/rdf/c14n#true> "1" .
```

An application scenario in which this is useable is that of signing an OWL ontology 14. The ontologist creates the ontology in a tool, and then asks the tool to generate a signature using a private key. The tool:

- applies this algorithm, possibly adding additional triples to the ontology.
- creates a canonical RDF graph with the same meaning as the original ontology.
- computes the signature for the canonical RDF graph.
- adds additional triple(s) to the graph with the ontology URI as subject, and the signature as object.

The resulting graph (with additional triples both as a result of canonicalization and reflecting the signature) then replaces the original ontology. It is this graph (which can be canonicalized without any changes) that the ontologist publishes. Users of this ontology can then:

- find the signature in the graph.
- find the public key using some public key infrastructure
- delete the triple(s) carrying the signature from the graph.
- apply the deterministic labeling to form a canonical representation of the graph
- verify the signature of this canonical RDF using the public key.

6.2 Further Discussion

The one-step deterministic labeling algorithm used had the following characteristics:

- Reasonably fast (subquadratic)
- Deterministic
- Labels 'enough' blank nodes in realistic RDF
- Easy to explain and implement

The last point is helpful in a paper, but not a hard requirement. Thus in a deployed system we can imagine using a variant of the algorithm here.

It is a practical engineering problem to choose a near-optimal deterministic classification algorithm that gets the best trade off between speed of classification and practical utility. The deterministic labeling algorithm used in this paper is probably a touch naïve, but only a touch. We can be sure that those used by Mackay [8] are too expensive, given their non-polynomial complexity.

7 Advanced Methods

The methods in the previous sections are sufficient to solve the problem of signing RDF graphs. However, some additional techniques may improve the solution. These are discussed in this section.

7.1 Multistep Deterministic Labelling

The one-step deterministic labeling only considers the immediate neighbours of any node. In some graphs, particularly those arising in OWL ontology definitions [14], this may leave too many nodes unlabelled.

A solution is to choose a fixed depth e.g. two or three, and to consider the neighbours of a node up to that distance away. Thus we can consider the two-step and three-step deterministic labeling algorithms. Since for a fixed k a k-step method will, in essence, be k applications of the one step method, we will expect a linear slow down as we increase k. The underlying complexity class remains $O(n\log n)$. (It is straightforward to optimize k-step methods to make the slow down much less than linear).

To consider neighbours at distance N+1 we resort the partial labeled output of a deterministic labeling based on neighbours at distance N.

Having resorted the output, which will take into account those labels already deterministically chosen, we can then apply the one pass deterministic labeling algorithm, which effectively considers neighbours at an additional step removed.

For example, the full two-step deterministic labeling is as follows:

A. Perform a one step deterministic labeling.
B. Repeat steps 6, 7, 8 from the one step deterministic labeling algorithm, without reinitializing the table or counter.

For a k-step labeling, we need to repeat B k-1 times.

7.2 Optimizations

This paper has avoided issues to do with optimizing the algorithm presented, but concentrates on the complexity class of the algorithms.

Systems would benefit from merging steps presented here as sequential to reduce the total number of passes of the graph required. Also, given that most canonicalization is for objects that are small enough to fit in memory, the exposition in terms of sorting files is probably misleading. In-memory structures such as b-trees [15] should be used, and maintaining them in sort order, may be more efficient than permitting them to become unsorted and resorting them as a separate algorithmic step.

The multistep methods in particular are susceptible to optimization. Often the first stage will completely label the blank nodes of the graph. The subsequent stages are then redundant. Moreover, during the first stage we can identify those triples in the graph that require more work. The ones that do not need further work, play no further role in the algorithm, except being included, in a final merge, into the output.

7.3 Deterministic Precanonicalization

Other applications of digital signatures have a greater need for determinism than the exact preservation of meaning. Lynch [16] argues that canonicalization is a "Fundamental Tool to Facilitate Preservation and Management of Digital Information." The scenario he discusses is the need to reformat a digital object which is being preserved in an electronic library. The need for reformatting occurs as the software and hardware required to view the original object become obsolete.

Lynch uses (lossy) canonicalization as a way of defining the essence of a document. This essence, if sufficient unimportant details are discarded, will be invariant with reformatting. Thus we can compute this essence of the original document, and the original author can sign this essence to vouch for its authenticity.

Later, after the death of the author, and a sequence of many transformations of the original byte sequence, the essence of the document is unchanged, and we can still verify that the author signed it.

With this application canonicalization is intended to be lossy, but must be deterministic. A variant precanonicalization is simply to delete all hard-to-label nodes. This is deterministic, but loses meaning.

7.4 Multiple Arcs in a Single Comparison

The methods presented, have been constrained for simplicity, to those that can easily be implemented using Unix **`sort`** and **`awk`** over N-Triples.

On larger graphs it may be the case that there are nodes that do not participate in distinctive triples, but for which the set of triples in which they participate is distinctive. A simple example is:

```
_:a <eg:eat> "apple" .        _:a <eg:eat> "pear" .
_:b <eg:eat> "apple" .        _:b <eg:eat> "banana" .
_:c <eg:eat> "pear" .         _:c <eg:eat> "banana" .
```

None of the triples is distinctive, but `_:a` is the only blank node eating both apples and pears.

For some real RDF data (see section 9.1) it is advantageous to collect all the triples in which a node participates and use the set of labels on those triples as a key to attempt to distinguish the node.

8 Complexity

All the steps in this paper either involve lexicographically sorting a file, for which the best known algorithms are O($n$log$n$) [17] or involve stepping through a file line by line and doing either the same simple modification, or a modification involving a table lookup (e.g. step 6.b.ii in section 4). The former steps are O(n), the latter O($n$log$n$) (table lookup is O(log$n$), see [15]). Since any particular variant of the techniques involves a constant number of such sort or modification steps the overall complexity is O($n$log$n$) where n is the number of triples in the RDF graph.

9 Practical Issues

The nondeterministic algorithm potentially triples the size of the graph (worst case). This paper is predicated on that potential occurrence not actually happening. The deterministic part of the algorithm will label almost all the nodes in a typical RDF graph

Both of the preconicalization methods, (addition or deletion) change the RDF graph. In this sense the algorithms presented are not canonicalization algorithms. However, we have argued that for practical applications these changes are acceptable, as long as: they happen relatively rarely; they are expected; and that the choice between the deleting method or the adding method has been made appropriately for the application.

A further difficulty is found when canonicalizing multiple subsets of an RDF graph, using the nondeterministic method. The required changes for one such canonicalization will most likely be incompatible with the required changes for another. This can be addressed by using super-properties of `c14n:true` to create the distinctive triples.

9.1 Test Results

To assess how often these changes are made, we applied some of the algorithms in this paper to various test data sources. Specifically, we use the one step, two step and three step deterministic labeling algorithms[2] on the test data; and then further analyzed some of the problem cases.

Source	1	2	3	*
RDF test data [4]	130	0	0	0
OWL test data [19]	45	2	0	0
OWL guide [20]	0	0	0	1
DAML ontology library [21] (part)	93	10	5	40

The last line shows that of the files tested from the DAML ontology library 93 were deterministically labeled by the one-step algorithm. A further 10 were deterministically labeled using the two-step algorithm, but that 40 were not fully labeled even with the three step algorithm. The first two lines show that the N-Triples files include with test cases for RDF and OWL are not sufficiently challenging to be good tests for canonicalization.

The Baseball ontology [22] was one of the more difficult ontologies. The specific problem concerned the definition of `#LineUpEvent` and `#Start.` The four restrictions shown each have a blank node, and none of the triples used in the four are distinctive. This is a more complicated variant of the example in section 7.4.

```
<rdfs:Class

rdf:about="#LineupEvent">
 <rdfs:subClassOf>
  <daml:Restriction>
   <daml:onProperty
      rdf:resource="#position"/>
     <daml:toClass
       rdf:resource
="#Position"/>
  </daml:Restriction>
 </rdfs:subClassOf>
 <rdfs:subClassOf>
  <daml:Restriction>
   <daml:onProperty
      rdf:resource="#player"/>
   <daml:toClass
      rdf:resource="#Player"/>
  </daml:Restriction>
 </rdfs:subClassOf>
</rdfs:Class>
```

```
<rdfs:Class
         rdf:about="#Start">
 <rdfs:subClassOf>
  <daml:Restriction>
   <daml:onProperty
      rdf:resource="#position"/>
     <daml:toClass
       rdf:resource
="#Position"/>
  </daml:Restriction>
 </rdfs:subClassOf>
 <rdfs:subClassOf>
  <daml:Restriction>
   <daml:onProperty
      rdf:resource="#player"/>
   <daml:toClass
      rdf:resource="#Player"/>
  </daml:Restriction>
 </rdfs:subClassOf>
</rdfs:Class>
```

This observation prompted the use of a multiple arc comparison algorithm.

The algorithm: first did an N-step deterministic labeling (using single arcs); then performed a single multiple arc labeling, only on the as yet unlabelled nodes; then to finish off did a further M-step deterministic labeling. This algorithm was tested on the 56 files (from the DAML ontology library and the OWL Guide) that had proved difficult. The results were as in this table:

[2] We used a small prototype implementation [18] written in AWK on a Unix system.

	Post (M) 0	1	2	3
Pre (N) 0	12	9	7	6
1	9	7	6	6
2	8	6	6	6
3	7	6	6	6

The N and M values show the number of deterministic labellings before and after the multiple arc labeling. The entries show how many of the 56 files were not completely labeled by such an approach.

These show that the multiple arc method, even without the one step method, was effective in all but twelve of the difficult cases. Since these were about a third of the sample from the ontology library, the multiple arc method, used by itself, may be effective in 90% of the cases.

9.2 Redundancy

The test results pointed to a core of six difficult examples. These were analyzed further. One was the OWL Wine ontology from the OWL Guide [20]. The specific construct that caused the problem was the innocent looking:

```
<owl:Class rdf:ID="Wine">
 <rdfs:subClassOf>
  <owl:Restriction>
   <owl:onProperty rdf:resource="#hasMaker" />
   <owl:cardinality
          rdf:datatype=
 "http://www.w3.org/2000/10/XMLSchema#nonNegativeInteger"
   >1</owl:cardinality>
  </owl:Restriction>
 </rdfs:subClassOf>
```

The problem with this construct is that, presumably by error, it is repeated and occurs two times in the wine ontology. This gives rise to two blank nodes, one for each restriction. Each participates in four triples (with properties `rdfs:subClassOf`, `owl:onProperty`, `rdf:type`, `owl:cardinality`). These two blank nodes are indistinguishable.

The other five difficult cases all had examples of such repeated structures.

These repeated constructs add no meaning. The repeat, if detected, could simply be deleted. Unfortunately, detecting a repeated substructure within an RDF graph can be shown to be at least as hard as the graph isomorphism problem. Mugnier and Chein [23] show that the somewhat harder problem of removing all redundant arcs from a conceptual graph is NP complete. (In the RDF context this would include deletion of partial repeated substructures).

9.3 Problems Concerning rdf:Collection

It is conjectured that lists formed with the `rdf:parseType="Collection"` construct may present greater problems than has been revealed in this study.

The `rdf:parseType="Collection"` syntax [24] when used for lists with two or more elements, creates a number of blank nodes which:

- Are the subject of a triple with predicate **`rdf:type`**, and object **`rdf:List`**.
- Are the subject of an **`rdf:first`** triple with object being a blank node.

- Are the subject of an **rdf:rest** triple with object being a blank node.
- Are the object of an **rdf:rest** triple with subject being a blank node.

Since none of these triples is distinctive, and the node does not participate in any others, the one pass deterministic labeling will not label such nodes. Moreover the multiple arc label (section 7.4) does not help.

Given the importance of OWL in the semantic web, and the desire to canonicalize and digitally sign ontologies, this is a disadvantage with one-step methods. Moreover, additional distinctive arcs on such nodes, added as a result of the nondeterministic precanonicalization algorithm, would cause the resulting graph to be one that cannot use the compact `rdf:parseType="Collection"` syntax.

The multistep methods will often distinguish the blank nodes in a typical OWL ontology (possibly requiring the multiple arc label method). This is because while the elements of the list may all be blank, for example a list of restrictions, enough of these elements will participate in distinctive triples, for example, distinctive **owl:hasValue** triples. When adding further distinctive triples it is best to try and exploit the multistep canonicalization and to avoid adding them to the blank nodes carrying the list structure, but instead to add them to the members of the list (e.g. to a blank node of type **owl:Restriction**).

9.4 Summary of Test Results

The test results show that:

- The one step deterministic algorithm is usable but may require nondeterministic modification of many graphs arising from OWL.
- Methods involving comparisons between multiple arcs are applicable to almost all of the RDF data studied.
- Duplicate subgraphs could not be labeled deterministically, and cannot even be detected in polynomial time. The approach of nondeterministic graph modification to deal with these seems appropriate.

10 Conclusions

While we might expect that signing RDF graphs involves exponential worse case behaviour, this paper has shown that there are $O(n \log n)$ solutions.

The key is a preparedness to modify the graph prior to signing. Such modifications can be justified by the observation that the signature endorses the meaning of the graph, rather than the graph itself. The modifications can be chosen so as not to change the meaning of the RDF graph.

Judging from the test results, these modifications are, in practice, only needed for handling the problem of duplication within the graph to be signed. These results suggest that the naïve definition of canonical RDF in section 5 should be augmented with considerations of labels from multiple arcs (section 7.4).

References

1. Klyne, G., Carroll, J. J. (eds.): RDF Concepts and Abstract Syntax. W3C (2003)
2. Köbler, J., Schöning, U., Torán, J.: The Graph Isomorphism Problem: Its Structural Complexity. Birkhauser (1993)
3. Messmer, B.T., Bunke, H.: Subgraph Isomorphism Detection in Polynomial Time on Preprocessed Model Graphs. ACCV (1995) 373–382
4. Grant, J., Beckett, D. (eds.): RDF Test Cases. W3C Working Draft (2002) http://www.w3.org/TR/2002/WD-rdf-testcases-20021112/
5. Carroll, J.J.: Matching RDF Graphs. In: Horrocks, I. and Hendler, J. (eds.): ISWC 2002, LNCS 2342 (2002) 5–15.
6. Read, R.C., Corneil, D.G.: Graph Isomorphism Disease. Journal of Graph Theory (1977) 339–363
7. Fortin, S.:The Graph Isomorphism Problem, Technical Report TR 96–20, Department of Computer Science, University of Alberta (1996) ftp://ftp.cs.ualberta.ca/pub/TechReports/1996/TR96-20/TR96-20.ps.gz
8. McKay, B.D.: Practical Graph Isomorphism. Congressus Numerantium 30 (1981) 45–87 http://cs.anu.edu.au/~bdm/papers/pgi.pdf
9. McKay, B.D.: Nauty (1994) http://cs.anu.edu.au/~bdm/nauty/
10. Hayes, P. (ed.): RDF Semantics. W3C Working Draft (2003)
11. Patel-Schneider, P.F., Hayes, P., Horrocks, I. (eds.): OWL Semantics and Abstract Syntax. W3C Working Draft (2003)
12. Boyer, J. (ed.): Canonical XML. W3C Recommendation (2001)
13. Biron, P.V., Malhotra, A. (eds.): XML Schema Part 2: Datatypes. W3C Rec. (2001)
14. Dean, M., Schrieber, G.: OWL Reference. W3C Working Draft (2003)
15. Adel'son-Vel'skii, G.M., Landis, E.M.: An algorithm for the Organization of Information. Doklady Akademia Nauk SSSR, vol. 146 (1962) 263–266. English translation in Soviet Mathematics Doklady, vol. 3, pp. 1259–1263.
16. Lynch, C.: Canonicalization: A Fundamental Tool to Facilitate Preservation and Management of Digital Information. D-Lib 5(9) (1999) http://www.dlib.org/dlib/september99/09lynch.html
17. Knuth, D.E.: The Art of Computer Programming, V.3: Sorting and Searching (1973)
18. Carroll, J.J.: Awk scripts for canonicalizing N-Triples (2002) http://www-uk.hpl.hp.com/people/jjc/rdf/c14n-impl/
19. Carroll, J.J., de Roo, J. (eds.): Web Ontology Language (OWL) Test Cases, W3C Working Draft (2002) http://www.w3.org/TR/2002/WD-owl-test-20021024/
20. Smith, M.K., Welty, C., McGuinness, D. (eds): OWL Web Ontology Language, Guide. W3C Working Draft (2003) http://www.w3.org/TR/2003/WD-owl-guide-20030331/
21. Dean, M.(librarian): DAML Ontology Library http://www.daml.org/ontologies/
22. Dean, M.: Baseball Ontology, http://www.daml.org/2001/08/baseball/baseball-ont
23. Chien M., Mugnier, M.-L.: Conceptual Graphs: Fundamental Notions. Revue d'Intelligence Atificielle, Vol 5, n° 4 (1992) 365–406
24. Beckett, D. (ed.): RDF/XML Syntax Specification (Revised). W3C Working Draft (2003)

A Semantic E-Wallet to Reconcile Privacy and Context Awareness

Fabien L. Gandon and Norman M. Sadeh

School of Computer Science - Carnegie Mellon University
5000 Forbes Avenue, Pittsburgh, PA 15213-3891, USA
{Fabien.Gandon,Norman.Sadeh}@cs.cmu.edu
http://www-2.cs.cmu.edu/~sadeh/

Abstract. Increasingly, application developers are looking for ways to provide users with higher levels of personalization that capture different elements of a user's operating context, such as her location, the task that she is currently engaged in, who her colleagues are, *etc.* While there are many sources of contextual information, they tend to vary from one user to another and also over time. Different users may rely on different location tracking functionality provided by different cell phone operators; they may use different calendar systems, *etc.* In this paper, we describe work on a Semantic e-Wallet aimed at supporting automated discovery and access of personal resources, each represented as a Semantic Web Service. A key objective is to provide a Semantic Web environment for open access to a user's contextual resources, thereby reducing the costs associated with the development and maintenance of context-aware applications. A second objective is, through Semantic Web technologies, to empower users to selectively control who has access to their contextual information and under which conditions. This work has been carried out in the context of *my*Campus, a context-aware environment aimed at enhancing everyday campus life. Empirical results obtained on Carnegie Mellon's campus are encouraging.

1 Introduction

Increasingly, application developers are looking for ways to provide users with added levels of convenience and ease of use through functionality that is capable of capturing the context within which they operate. This may involve knowing where the user is located, the task she is currently engaged in, her eating preferences, who her colleagues are as well as a variety of other contextual attributes. While there are many sources of contextual information, they tend to vary from one user to another and also over time. Different users may rely on different location tracking functionality provided by different cell phone operators; they may use different calendar systems, *etc.* Traditionally, context aware applications and services have been hardwired to predefined sources of contextual information (e.g. relying on a particular set of sensors and protocols to track a user's locations). As a result, they remain prohibitively expensive to build and maintain and are few and between. We argue that what is needed is a more open environment, where context-aware applications can automatically discover and access a user's personal resources such as her calendar or location tracking functionality. This can be done by viewing each source of contextual

D. Fensel et al. (Eds.): ISWC 2003, LNCS 2870, pp. 385–401, 2003.

information (or personal resource) as a Web service. Unfortunately, current Web Services standards such as UDDI [15] or WSDL [25] are not sufficient when it comes to describing a user's personal resources and to enabling automated access to them by context aware applications. Another challenge, as we move towards more open platforms for access to a user's personal information, revolves around privacy issues. Users should be able to retain control over who has access to their personal information under different conditions. For instance, I may be willing to let my colleagues see where I am or access my calendar activities between 8am and 5pm on weekdays but not over the weekend. In addition, I may want to fine tune the granularity of the answer provided to a given query, depending on the context of that query. For instance, I may be willing to disclose the room that I am in to some people but only the city where I am to others. In fact, I may even want to give different answers to different people, telling my secretary I am off to see my dentist, while telling my customers I am in a meeting.

In this paper, we introduce a Semantic Web architecture aimed at supporting the automated discovery and access of personal resources in support of a variety of context-aware applications. Within this architecture, each source of contextual information (e.g. a calendar, location tracking functionality, collections of relevant user preferences, organizational databases) is represented as a Semantic Web service. A central element of our architecture is its *semantic e-Wallet*, which acts as a directory of contextual resources for a given user, while enforcing his/her *privacy preferences*. Privacy preferences enable users to specify what information can be provided to whom in different contexts. This also includes *obfuscation rules* that allow users to fine-tune the accuracy or inaccuracy of the information provided in response to different queries under different conditions.

We have validated our architecture in the context of *my*Campus, a context-aware environment aimed at enhancing everyday campus life at Carnegie Mellon University (CMU). The environment revolves around a growing collection of task-specific agents capable of automatically accessing a variety of contextual information about their users (e.g. context-aware restaurant concierge, context-aware message filtering agent, *etc.*). This includes accessing their locations, calendar activities as well as a variety of other attributes and preferences Students access the environment from PDAs over the campus's 802.11 wireless LAN. Empirical results obtained with a group of students over a period of several days are briefly summarized at the end of this article. While, in this paper, we focus on scenarios involving individual users, it should be noted that our architecture extends to scenarios where users are entire organizations. In this context, both organizations and individual users could each have one or more Semantic e-Wallets capable of leveraging a variety of individual or organizational knowledge subject to a rich set of privacy constraints.

The remainder of this article is organized as follows. Section 2 provides a brief overview of the state of the art in context awareness, privacy, Web Services and the Semantic Web, emphasizing limitations of the work reported so far in the literature. In Section 3, we provide an overview of our Semantic Web environment for context awareness and privacy. Section 4 focuses more specifically on the Semantic e-Wallet and includes a high-level scenario outlining its operation in response to a query about the current location of a user. Section 5 introduces the three layers of knowledge required to support the e-Wallet functionality. Section 6 discusses the e-Wallet's current implementation, which is based on OWL Lite [24], XSLT transformations [27], and JESS [10]. Sections 7 and 8 provide further details on the e-Wallet's three layers. Section 9 summarizes what we view as the main contributions of our work. It includes a brief discussion of experiments carried out in our *my*Campus environment along with some concluding remarks.

2 Prior Work

Prior efforts to develop context aware applications are many. Early work in context awareness includes the Active Badge System developed at Olivetti Research Lab to redirect phone calls based on people's locations [23]. The ParcTab system developed at the Xerox Palo Alto Research Center in the early nineties relied on PDAs to support a variety of context-aware office applications (e.g. locating nearby resources such as printers, posting electronic notes in a room, *etc.*) [20, 21]. Other relevant applications that have emerged over the years range from location-aware tour guides to context-aware memory aids. More recent research efforts in context awareness include MIT's Oxygen [6], CMU's Aura [11] and several projects at Berkeley's GUIR (e.g. [14]) to name just a few.

While early context-aware applications relied on *ad hoc* architectures and representations, it was quickly recognized that separating the process of acquiring contextual information from actual context-aware applications was key to facilitating application development and maintenance. Georgia Tech's Context Toolkit represents the most significant effort in this direction [7, 8]. In the Context Toolkit, widgets act as wrappers that provide access to different sets of contextual information (e.g. user location, identity, time and activity), while insulating applications from context acquisition concerns. Each user (as well as other relevant entities such as physical objects or locations) has a context server that contains all the widgets relevant to it. This is similar to our notion of e-Wallet, which serves as a directory of all personal resources relevant to a given user (e.g. relevant location tracking functionality, relevant collections of preferences, access to one or more calendar systems, *etc.*). Our Semantic e-Wallet however goes one step beyond Dey's Context Toolkit. It makes it possible to leverage much richer models of personal resources - what personal information they give access to, when to access one rather than the other, how to go about accessing these resources. In addition, it includes access control and obfuscation functionality to enforce user privacy preferences. This richer model is key to supporting automated discovery and access of a user's personal resources by agents. In other words, while the Context Toolkit focuses mainly on facilitating the development of context-aware applications through off-line, re-use and integration of context-aware components (i.e. widgets), our architecture emphasizes real-time, on-the-fly queries of personal resources by context-aware agents. These queries are processed through several layers of functionality that support automated discovery and access of relevant personal resources subject to user-specified privacy preferences.

The notion of e-Wallet as introduced in systems such as Microsoft's .NET Passport is not new. However current implementations have been limited to storing a very small amount of information and offer very restricted control to the user when it comes to specifying what information can be made available to different services. For instance, in Passport, users can specify whether or not they are willing to share parts of their profiles with all participating sites but cannot distinguish between different participating sites. Our notion of Semantic e-Wallet lifts these restrictions and allows users to control access to any of their personal resources. It also allows for multiple sources of similar information (e.g. multiple calendars or multiple location tracking functionality) and for functionality that can dynamically select which of these resources to tap based on the context and the nature of the query at hand (e.g. using your car's GPS system when you are driving and your cell phone operator's location tracking functionality when you are not).

Our notion of semantic e-Wallet extends recent efforts to develop rich languages for capturing user privacy preferences such as P3P's APPEL language [26]. It does so by making it possible to leverage any number of domain ontologies and by allowing for preferences that relate to any number of contextual attributes. In addition, it allows users to specify obfuscation rules through which they control the level of accuracy (or inaccuracy) at which their contextual information is disclosed to different parties under different conditions. This includes telling some people which room you are in, while simply telling others whether you are at work or not, or whether you are in town or not. It also includes scenarios where you might want to pretend you are in one place, while you are really elsewhere.

Last but not least, while the security community has developed powerful languages to capture access control privileges such as the Security Assertion Markup Language (SAML) [16], the XML Access Control Markup Language (XACML) [17] and the Enterprise Privacy Authorization Language (EPAL) [22], these languages do not take advantage of Semantic Web concepts. Our work builds directly on recent efforts aimed at moving the Web from an environment where information is primarily made available for human consumption to one where it is annotated with semantic markup that makes it understandable to computers (and intelligent agents). These efforts are part of a long-term vision generally referred to as the *Semantic Web* [1, 13]. They have already resulted in a succession of semantic markup languages [4, 24] as well as early efforts to define Web Service ontologies and markup in the context of languages such as DAML-S [5]. In our work, we have relied on the use of DAML+OIL [4] and more recently OWL [24] to represent contextual information (e.g. location, calendar activities, social and organizational relationships, *etc.*) and privacy preferences and on Semantic Web service concepts to support the automated discovery and access of personal and public resources.

3 Overall System Architecture

We consider an environment where, over time, users purchase (or subscribe to) different sets of task-specific agents. These agents are each intended to assist them in the context of different activities (e.g. scheduling meetings with colleagues, reminding them of purchases they need to make, arranging trips or filtering incoming messages). To function, each agent needs to access some information about its user as well as possibly other users. Access to a user's personal (or contextual) information is controlled by that user's e-Wallet subject to privacy enforcement rules. The e-Wallet Manager (or simply e-Wallet) serves as a repository of static knowledge about the user – just like .NET Passport, except that here knowledge is represented using OWL. In addition, the e-Wallet contains knowledge about how to access more information about the user by invoking a variety of resources, each represented as a Web Service.

This knowledge is stored in the form of rules that map different contextual attributes onto one or more possible service invocations, enabling the e-Wallet to automatically identify and activate the most relevant resources in response to queries about the user's context (e.g. accessing the user's calendar to find out about her availability, or consulting one or more location tracking applications in an attempt to find out about her current location). Privacy enforcing rules, also stored in the e-Wallet, ensure that information about the user is only disclosed to authorized parties, taking into account the context of the query. They further adjust the accuracy or inaccuracy of the information provided subject to obfuscation rules set by the user.

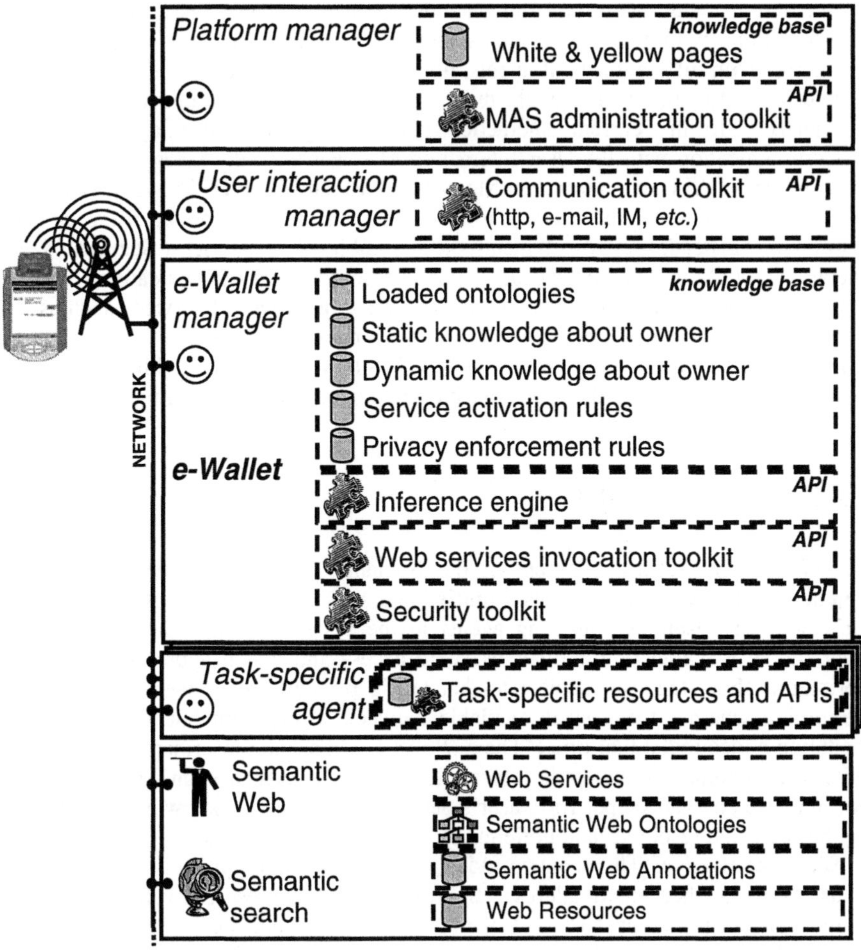

Fig. 1. *my*Campus architecture: a user's perspective - the smiley faces represent agents.

Figure 1 provides an overview of our Semantic Web environment. It illustrates a situation where access is from a PDA over a wireless network, as is the case in *my*Campus, the environment in which we have instantiated our architecture. However, our architecture extends to fixed Internet scenarios and more generally to environments where users can connect to the infrastructure through a number of access channels and devices – information about the particular access device and channel can actually be treated as part of the user's context and be made available through her e-Wallet. As can be seen in Figure 1, other key elements of our architecture include:

- One or more *Platform Managers* that build on top of Directory Facilitators and Agent Management Systems, as defined in FIPA [9]. They manage the agents running at their sites, and maintain white and yellow page directories of these agents and the services they provide.
- *User Interaction Managers* - typically one per user - that are responsible for interactions with the user. This includes managing login sessions as well as interactions with the user's agents and her e-Wallet. Because different users interact with different sets of agents, this also includes the dynamic generation of interfaces for interacting with these agents and the customization of these interfaces to the current interaction context (e.g. particular access device). Communication with the User Interaction Manager typically takes place through a number of APIs, e.g. an Instant Messaging API, an HTTP/HTML API, *etc.*

Clearly, agents are not limited to accessing information about users in the environment. Instead, they also typically access public Web Services, Semantic Web annotations, public ontologies and other public resources. On CMU's campus, where we have deployed *my*Campus, this includes access to a variety of services such as 23 restaurant web services or a pubic weather forecasting web service.

In the following sections, we focus on the e-Wallet functionality. Additional details on *my*Campus and some of the agents we have deployed can be found in [19].

4 A Semantic E-Wallet

The e-Wallet is a central element of our Semantic Web architecture for context awareness and privacy. It provides a unified and secure semantic interface to all the user's personal resources, enabling agents in the system, whether working for the owner of the e-Wallet or for other users, to access and, when appropriate, modify information about the user subject to that user's privacy preferences (e.g. not just determining whether the user is available between 3 and 4pm but also, possibly, scheduling a meeting at that time). The e-Wallet is *not* a static information repository. While it does contain some static information about the user, it is an agent acting as clearinghouse and gatekeeper for a user's personal resources. Its knowledge about the user, her personal resources and preferences falls into four categories:

- *Static knowledge*. This context-independent knowledge typically includes the user's name, her email address, employer, home address as well as context-independent preferences (e.g. "I like spicy vegetarian cuisine"). This knowledge, like all other in the e-Wallet, can be edited by the user via the User Interaction Manager.
- *Dynamic knowledge*. This is context-sensitive knowledge about the user, often involving a variety of preferences such as "When driving, I don't want to receive instant messages".
- *Service invocation rules*. These rules help leverage information resources external to the e-Wallet – both personal and public. They effectively turn the e-Wallet into

a semantic directory of personal resources that can be automatically discovered and accessed to process incoming queries. Specifically, service invocation rules provide a mapping between contextual attributes and personal resources available to access these attributes, viewing each personal resource as a Semantic Web service. An example of one such mapping is a rule indicating that a query about the user's current activity can be answered by accessing her Microsoft Outlook calendar. We have developed Web Service wrappers for a variety of personal resources such as Microsoft Outlook Calendar or location tracking functionality. Service invocation rules are not limited to providing a one-to-one mapping between contextual attributes and personal resources. Instead, they can leverage rich ontologies of personal resources, enabling the e-Wallet to select among a number of possible personal resources based on availability, accuracy and other relevant considerations. For instance, in response to a query about the user's location, the rules can specify that, when the user is driving, the best method available is the GPS in her car. If she is at work and her wireless-enabled PDA is on, her location can be obtained using location tracking functionality running over the enterprise's wireless LAN. If everything else fails, her calendar might have some information about her location. Finally, it should be noted that to answer queries about the user, additional mapping rules that support automated discovery and access of public services may also be needed. For instance, a query like "Tell me whether Fabien is in a sunny place right now" will typically require accessing Fabien's location as well as a public weather service.

- *Privacy preferences*. These preferences encapsulate knowledge about what information about herself the user is willing to disclose to others under different conditions. These preferences themselves fall into two categories:
  - *Access control rules*. These rules simply express who has the right to see what information under different conditions e.g. "My location should only be visible to members of my team during week days between 8am and 5pm".
  - *Obfuscation rules*. Often user privacy preferences are not black-and-white but rather involve different levels of accuracy or inaccuracy: *Obfuscation by abstraction* is about abstracting away some details about the user's current context such as telling people whether or not you are in town without giving your exact location. *Obfuscation by falsification* is about scenarios where the user may not want to appear as if she is withholding information but would rather provide false information. For instance, a user may not want to reveal her true email address to a web service for fear of getting spammed.

All the above knowledge (including rules) is represented in OWL. It can leverage a number of relevant ontologies (e.g. ontologies about contextual attributes, personal resources, as well as more specific knowledge such as cuisine types and food preferences or message types and message filtering preferences).

Before delving deeper into the details of the e-Wallet, a scenario will help illustrate the key steps it goes through in processing incoming queries (Figure 2). For the sake of argument, we will assume a query submitted by a user (Norman) to the e-Wallet of a second user (Fabien) inquiring about that second user's current location. The main steps are as follows:

1. *Asserting the query's context*: As a first step, facts about the context of the query are asserted – namely they are loaded into the e-Wallet's inference engine for possible use as part of inferences to be made in processing the query. In our example, one such assertion is that "the sender of the query is Norman".

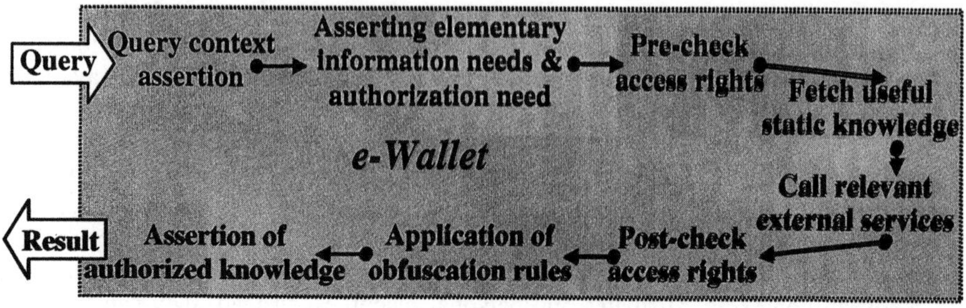

Fig. 2. Main steps involved in processing a query submitted to an e-Wallet.

2. *Asserting elementary information needs and the need to go through an authorization process*: Here the query is translated into an aggregate goal that includes (a) a combination of elementary information needs – in our example the need to find "Fabien's location", along with (b) a requirement to go through an authorization process. The authorization process, which is distributed across some of the following steps, results in the request being either denied or cleared, the latter possibly following the application of obfuscation rules. In our example, the authorization goal requires checking that Norman is entitled to having access to Fabien's location and that the level of resolution at which the query is answered is compatible with Fabien's privacy preferences.
3. *Pre-checking whether the query is allowable*: A first check is performed to see whether the query is allowable based on access rights considerations. In our example, the e-Wallet checks whether Norman is allowed to inquire about Fabien's location. Fabien's e-Wallet might include a privacy preference specifying that his colleagues at work can see the building that he is in, when he is on campus, but that no one else should be given access to his location. In this first check, the e-Wallet might be able to determine that Norman is indeed a colleague of Fabien's – e.g. based on organizational knowledge stored in the static knowledge base of Fabien's e-Wallet. At this stage, because it has not yet determined whether Fabien is on campus or not, the e-Wallet has no ground for denying the request. Therefore, it continues processing it, as detailed below.
4. *Checking the e-Wallet's local knowledge base*: Some queries can be answered in whole or in part, using facts in the e-Wallet's local knowledge base, which, as we have seen in Section 3, contains both static (namely, context-independent) and dynamic (namely, context-sensitive) knowledge about the user. In our particular example, such knowledge is not particularly helpful and the e-Wallet needs to turn to outside sources of personal information to answer the query (see next step).
5. *Invoking personal resources as Web services*: When local knowledge is not sufficient to answer a query, the e-Wallet turns to its service invocation rules to identify external resources that might help answer it. This may involve accessing one or more of the user's personal resources such as his calendar and/or one or more trusted public services. In our example, the campus where Fabien works has a wireless LAN that supports location tracking. This functionality can be invoked by the e-Wallet to obtain Fabien's location. The actual invocation takes place through the web service invocation toolkit already introduced in Figure 1.

6. *Post-checking whether the query is allowable*: armed with additional knowledge obtained by invoking one or more external resources, the e-Wallet is now in a better position to check whether the query is allowable. In our example, colleagues of Fabien's are only allowed to see his location when he is on campus. Assuming that Fabien is on campus, the request is now deemed allowable. This does not mean however that the authorization process required as part of the goals set in step 2 has been fully completed. Obfuscation rules may still need to be applied.
7. *Application of Obfuscation Rules*: suppose that the location tracking functionality used to answer our query about Fabien's location returned the specific room he is in, while Fabien is only willing to disclose the buildings that he is in. This latter requirement is captured by the e-Wallet in the form of an obfuscation rule that returns the building in which Fabien is rather than the exact room. Application of this rule will typically involve accessing ontologies about rooms and buildings as well as annotations about the campus where Fabien works.
8. The query has now been fully processed and an acceptable answer generated. This answer (e.g. "Fabien is in Smith Hall") can be returned to Norman.

5 A Three-Layer E-Wallet Implementation

As shown in Figure 3, we developed a three-layer implementation of our e-Wallet:

- *Core Layer*: At the most basic level, the e-Wallet's knowledge includes an OWL meta-model – required to interpret OWL statements. In addition, it maintains both static (context-independent) and dynamic (context-dependent) knowledge about the user. This knowledge is obtained by loading available annotations about the user along with relevant ontologies and is currently completed using forward chaining reasoning – to avoid having to infer the same facts over and over again. Knowledge in this layer is represented using a (core) triple template:

  `(predicate, subject, object)`$_{\text{TRIPLE}}$
- The *Service Layer* completes the e-Wallet's core knowledge with invocation rules that map information retrieval goals about contextual attributes onto external service invocations. These are modeled as backward chaining rules. Given an information retrieval goal such as "Give me Fabien's location", they help identify and invoke one or more relevant information resources, each modeled as a Web service, as already discussed in Section 4. Knowledge in this layer is represented using a special type of triple called "service triple" denoted:

  `(predicate, subject, object)`$_{\text{SERVICE TRIPLE}}$

  Service triples reside in the service layer and are created in either of two ways. They can result from the migration of a triple from the core layer or from the activation of an invocation rule (e.g. an assertion about Fabien's location as returned by a call to a location tracking service). Migration between the core layer and the service layer is implemented by rules specifying that any (core) triple can be used to generate an equivalent service triple.
- The outer layer is referred to as the *Privacy Layer*, as this is where privacy enforcing rules are applied. Assertions in this layer are represented as another special type of triple called "authorized triple":

  `(predicate, subject, object)`$_{\text{AUTHORIZED TRIPLE}}$

Only authorized triples can be sent in response to queries. Authorized triples are generated by applying privacy enforcing rules to service triples, thereby ensuring that information about the user is only disclosed to authorized parties and in accordance with relevant obfuscation rules.

Privacy enforcing rules are encoded as backward chaining rules. These rules map needs for authorized triples onto needs for service triples to be post-processed subject to the privacy enforcing rules. Upon receiving an incoming query, the e-Wallet generates a need for one or more authorized triples. This need in turn typically triggers needs for service triples and core triples, eventually resulting either (a) in the generation of authorized triples that can be returned in response to the query or (b) in an exception, if the query is found unallowable (e.g. an unauthorized party requesting your location or trying to schedule a meeting in your calendar). In summary, security in our architecture is directly enforced through the typing mechanisms.

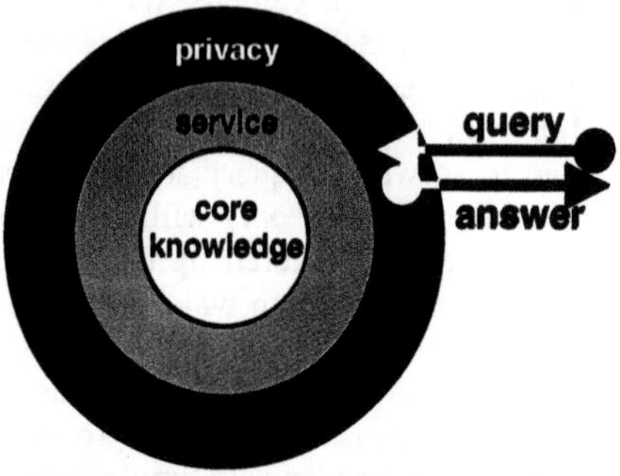

Fig. 3. e-Wallet 3-layer implementation

6 Additional Implementation Considerations

The current implementation of our e-Wallet is based on JESS, a high-performance Java-based rule engine that supports both forward and backward chaining – the latter by reifying "needs for facts" as facts themselves, which in turn trigger forward chaining rules. The e-Wallet's knowledge base is initialized with: (a) a model of RDF [28] triples, (b) a model of specialized triples used in our three layers (core triples, service triples and authorized triples) along with associated migration rules between the layers, and (c) an OWL meta-model.

Additional knowledge is loaded into the e-Wallet by translating OWL input files into JESS assertions and rules, using a set of XSLT stylesheets. The OWL input files include ontologies and annotations that are transformed into (core) triple assertions, forward chaining rules (used to complete knowledge at the core layer) as well as service invocation rules and privacy enforcing rules – both represented as backward chaining rules. The XSLT templates act as meta-rules that generate the body, head and type of the triples used by the JESS rules.

Once all this knowledge has been loaded and the forward chaining rules have been applied to complete the core knowledge base, the e-Wallet is ready to process incoming queries. A query is transformed into the need for an authorized triple. This in turn triggers privacy enforcing rules and generates needs for service triples. The service triples are generated by either migrating core triples or activating service invocation rules or a combination of both. This further detailed below.

1. Queries have two components (see Figure 4): (a) an annotation about the query providing its context (e.g., who the sender of the query is), and (b) the query itself in the form of a pattern using a special namespace to identify variables. The

context of a query is asserted for the time it takes to process it – later, clean up rules take care of removing all assertions created while processing it. We assume that security protocols (e.g., using digital signatures) are used to verify assertions about the query's context (e.g. verifying the identity of the sender). The query itself is transformed into a set of authorized triples in the privacy layer. These authorized triples form the body of a backward-chaining rule, whose head is a function that stores the results each time the rule is triggered and that generates RDF results in XML syntax.

2. The need of the query for authorized triples triggers privacy enforcing rules. As illustrated in Figure 5, these rules have two roles. First, they check that the sender of the query has the required access rights. In addition, they also apply obfuscation rules to triples to ensure that the level of accuracy or inaccuracy provided in answers to queries is compatible with the user's privacy preferences. The need for authorized triples in combination with privacy enforcing rules generates a need for service triples.
3. The need for service triples in turn triggers service rules. First a generic service rule is applied that checks whether the needed service triple is not already available as a core triple. If this is the case an equivalent service triple is simply created. If there is no equivalent core triple, the e-Wallet looks for matching rules that trigger internal function calls (e.g. getting the current time and date). If that fails too, it looks for matching (external) Web Services. To support this, we have extended the Jess library with internal functions (e.g. time) and functions to call external services. An example of a service invocation rule is given in Figure 6.

The system has been designed with efficiency in mind. For instance, query processing stops as soon as a security check violation is identified. Also, at the service layer, rules ensure that the system first checks for available core triples before attempting to invoke external resources.

We currently use RDF-S/OWL to represent rules. We do not reify the role of the relation and its arguments. We simply use triples to represent rules and take advantage of the typing mechanism of the XML syntax. We use a special namespace to identify variables. While we are following ongoing developments in RuleML [2] and DAML Rules, our current focus in on the use of rules that apply to OWL assertions. Later we could easily extend our system, for instance using XSLT stylesheets [27] to translate between our representation of rules in OWL and RuleML representations.

As shown in Figure 5, *privacy enforcing rules* are defined using three tags: the content of the *target tag* describes the piece of knowledge to which this rule applies; the content of the *check tag* describes the conditions under which the read access is granted; the content of the *revision tag* describes the obfuscation to be applied before migrating triples to the authorized layer.

As shown in Figure 6 the *service rules* can have up to three children tags: the content of the *output tag* describes the piece of knowledge that this rule can produce; the content of the *precondition tag* describes the knowledge needed for calling the service; the content of the *call tag* describes the function to trigger and its parameters.

```
<qowl:Query rdf:ID="">
  <qowl:sender rdf:resource="http://cs.cmu.edu/~nsadeh"/>
</qowl:Query>
<mc:Person rdf:about="http://cs.cmu.edu/~fgandon">
  <mc:location rdf:resource="http://sadehlab.cs.cmu.edu/Variable#location" />
</mc:Person>
```

Fig. 4. Query issued by the user 'nsadeh' requesting the location of user 'fgandon'

```
<sowl:ReadAccessRule>
  <rdf:label>people can only know whether or not I am on campus</rdf:label>
  <sowl:target>
    <mc:Person rdf:about="&variable;#owner">
      <mc:location rdf:resource="&variable;#location"/>
    </mc:Person>
  </sowl:target>
  <sowl:check>
   <rowl:And>
     <rowl:condition>
       <mc:E-Wallet rdf:about="&variable;#e-Wallet">
         <mc:owner>
          <mc:Person rdf:about="&variable;#owner"/>
         </mc:owner>
       </mc:E-Wallet>
     </rowl:condition>
     <rowl:condition>
       <mc:Place rdf:about="http://www.cmu.edu">
          <mc:include rdf:resource="&variable;#location" />
       </mc:Place>
     </rowl:condition>
     <rowl:not-condition>
       <qowl:Query rdf:about="&variable;#query">
         <qowl:sender rdf:resource="&variable;#owner" />
       </qowl:Query>
     </rowl:not-condition>
   </rowl:And>
  </sowl:check>
  <sowl:revision>
    <mc:Person rdf:about="&variable;#owner">
      <mc:location rdf:resource="http://www.cmu.edu"/>
    </mc:Person>
  </sowl:revision>
</sowl:ReadAccessRule>
```

Fig. 5. Privacy rule obfuscating the location of the owner

```
<wowl:ServiceRule wowl:salience="50">
  <rdf:label>provide location for IP Address</rdf:label>
  <wowl:output>
    <mc:Entity rdf:about="&variable;#entity">
      <mc:location rdf:resource="&variable;#location" />
    </mc:Entity>
  </wowl:output>
  <wowl:precondition>
    <mc:Entity rdf:about="&variable;#entity"><mc:ip>&variable;#ip</mc:ip>
    </mc:Entity>
  </wowl:precondition>
  <wowl:call>
   <wowl:Service wowl:name="call-web-service">
     <wowl:parameter>http://cmu.edu/location_tracking#</wowl:parameter>
     <wowl:parameter>&variable;#ip</wowl:parameter>
   </wowl:Service>
  </wowl:call>
</wowl:ServiceRule>
```

Fig. 6. Service rule for location-tracking invocation

7 Static Knowledge and Domain-Specific Rules

As indicated earlier, the RDF triple meta-model is defined as a template used in forward chaining rules. The OWL meta-model is asserted as a list of unordered facts such as the one shown in Figure 7. The semantics attached to properties is translated into rules such as the one shown in Figure 8.

```
(triple
   (predicate "http://www.w3.org/1999/02/22-rdf-syntax-ns#type")
   (subject   "http://www.w3.org/2002/07/owl#equivalentProperty")
   (object    "http://www.w3.org/2002/07/owl#SymmetricProperty")
)
```

Fig. 7. Declare property equivalence as a symmetric property

```
(defrule equivalent-property (declare (salience 100))
   (triple
     (predicate "http://www.w3.org/2002/07/owl#equivalentProperty")
     (subject   ?p1)
     (object    ?p2))
   (triple (predicate p1?) (subject ?s) (object ?o))
   (not (triple (predicate p2?) (subject ?s) (object ?o)))
   =>
   (assert (triple (predicate p2?) (subject ?s) (object ?o)))
)
```

Fig. 8. Rule for forward-chaining completion of property equivalence

As far as the OWL meta-model is concerned, we are focusing on those aspects of OWL-Lite relevant to our application scenarios. More precisely the current system handles: `Resource`, `Class`, `Property`, `type`, `subClassOf`, `subPropertyOf`, `ObjectProperty`, `TransitiveProperty`, `SymmetricProperty`, `inverseProperty`, `equivalentProperty`, `equivalentClass`, `sameIndividualAs`, `DatatypeProperty`, `FunctionalProperty`, `InverseFunctionalProperty`. – results obtained by running our OWL engine on top of the official OWL test cases are available at http://mycampus.sadehlab.cs.cmu.edu/tests/.

Likewise, triples in the ontologies and annotations loaded into the e-Wallet are asserted as unordered facts. Often, additional domain-dependent rules are needed such as the one in Figure 9 which defines colleagues as members of the same team. Such rules can help enforce context-sensitive preferences such as 'My colleagues can see my location when I am at work'.

```
<rowl:Rule direction="forward">
  <rdf:label>Members of the same group means colleagues</rdf:label>
  <rowl:head>
    <mc:Person rdf:about="&variable;#person1">
      <mc:colleague rdf:resource="&variable;#person2"/>
    </mc:Person>
  </rowl:head>
  <rowl:body>
    <mc:Team rdf:ID="&variable;#group">
      <mc:include><mc:Person rdf:about="&variable;#person1"/></mc:include>
      <mc:include><mc:Person rdf:about="&variable;#person2"/></mc:include>
    </mc:Team>
  </rowl:body>
</rowl:Rule>
```

Fig. 9. Rule defining colleagues as members of the same team

The inference engine is used to complete the base applying all the rules, thus saving time during the query solving process and providing a rollback point if needed.

8 Service Layer Processing

As indicated earlier, needs for service triples can be satisfied by either migrating a matching core triple or by activating a matching service invocation rule. For obvious efficiency reasons, it makes sense to always look for core triples first. This can be enforced by assigning a high priority (salience in JESS terminology) to rules that look for matching core triples and lower priority to service invocation rules. Service invocation rules are themselves given different priorities, based on the nature of the resource they invoke. This is further detailed below.

- If the needed service triple can be obtained by invoking an internal function (e.g. getting the current time), that function will be activated;
- If no internal service can provide the triple (or if internal calls have failed) but there is a personal service that can possibly provide the needed triple (e.g., obtaining the user's current activity from her personal calendar), the corresponding backward invocation rule is fired, calling that personal resource's Web Service wrapper;
- If no personal resource can provide the needed triple or if the calls failed, the engine looks for invocation rules involving public web services. This can include invoking public Semantic Web search engines (e.g. CORESE [3] or distributed search architecture such as TAP [12]) or public matchmaking services such as the one in [18] – this step is not currently implemented.
- If everything fails, the query is considered to have failed.

In summary, the body of each rule requires a need for a particular piece of information or triple (e.g. Fabien's location) along with the availability of a specific set of arguments (e.g. knowledge of the IP address of Fabien's PDA). The salience of the rules is used to decide the order to follow when trying to obtain the information (e.g. if multiple sources of location information are available). In general, we envision having a set of rules, where, should everything else fail, the e-Wallet reverts to a low salience rule that invokes one or more semantic search engines and/or one or more public matchmaking services (e.g. [18]). Clearly, as users acquire new personal resources (e.g. a new calendar), they will have to register them with their e-Wallets (e.g. using predefined service profiles that are provided with the resource itself).

9 Summary and Concluding Remarks

In this paper, we have presented a Semantic Web architecture for context awareness and privacy. A key element of our architecture is its e-wallet, which supports the automated discovery and access of a user's personal resources subject to user-specified privacy preferences. Personal and public resources are represented as web services. Service invocation rules along with service ontologies and service profiles enable the e-Wallet to dynamically identify the most promising resources available to answer a query. When one resource is unavailable, service invocation rules can help identify the next most relevant resource (e.g. using a calendar resource instead of a location tracking resource to estimate the user's current location). Public matchmaking services and semantic search engine functionality can also be leveraged through low salience rules that amount to reverting to these services when everything else has failed. Another innovation introduced in our e-Wallet is its support for a rich set of privacy preferences, including obfuscation rules that enable users to selectively adjust the accuracy or inaccuracy of responses they provide depending on the context of each query. We have described a three-layer implementation of our e-Wallet using JESS, OWL-Lite and XSLT stylesheets. A query to the e-Wallet successively results in the creation of needs for authorization triples and service triples. The latter can be satisfied through the identification of matching core triples and/or the activation of service invocation rules.

An early version of our architecture has been validated in *my*Campus, a context-aware environment aimed at enhancing campus life at CMU. The environment is accessible to members of the campus community from their PDAs over the university's wireless LAN. An example of a *my*Campus agent we have developed is a "restaurant concierge" that gives users suggestions on where to have lunch, depending on their food preferences, their location on campus and the weather. For instance, when it rains, the concierge might look for places that do not require walking outside – depending on how the user sets her preferences. Another task-specific agent that has proved particularly popular among students during the course of a 3-day study is a context-aware message filtering agent. The agent filters incoming alerts, taking into account a profile of topics a user is interested in as well as contextual attributes such as the user's current activities (e.g. "when in class, only show me emergency alerts"). Experiments with *my*Campus indicate that different students are interested in different task-specific agents and that, to be effective, many agents require access to a great variety of contextual resources. Our experiments also confirmed that users are concerned about protecting access to their personal information. The need for leveraging a variety of contextual attributes and the students' demand for privacy strongly argue for Semantic e-Wallets such as the one presented here. A key challenge however remains to reconcile the power of these Semantic environments with all important usability requirements that demand systems that are flexible, yet easy to configure. We are experimenting with different approaches to editing and learning user profiles, which we hope will help alleviate this problem.

Acknowledgments. This material is based on research conducted as part of the DAML initiative and has been sponsored by the Air Force Research Laboratory under contract F30602-02-2-0035 and, earlier, by the Defense Advanced Research Project Agency under contract F30602-98-2-0135. The US Government is authorized to reproduce and distribute reprints for Governmental purposes notwithstanding any copyright notation thereon. This work was also in part supported by grants from IBM, HP, Symbol, Boeing, Amazon and Fujitsu and the IST Program (SWAP project).

References

1. Berners-Lee, T., Hendler, J., Lassila, O.: The Semantic Web, Scientific American, May (2001)
2. Boley, H., Grosof, B., Tabet, S., Wagner, G.: RuleML DTDs, The Rule Markup Initiative RuleML, http://www.dfki.uni-kl.de/ruleml/indtd0.8.html
3. Corby, O., Faron-Zucker, C., Corese: A Corporate Semantic Web Engine, Workshop on Real World RDF and Semantic Web Applications, WWW Conference, Hawaii, (2002)
4. DAML Joint Committee: DAML+OIL language, 27 March 2001, http://www.daml.org/2001/03/daml+oil-index.html
5. DAML Services Coalition: DAML-S: Web Service Description for the Semantic Web, First International Semantic Web Conference, ISWC'02, Sardinia, Italy, LNCS 2342, (2002) 348–363
6. Dertouzos, M.: The Future of Computing, Scientific American, August (1999)
7. Dey, A.K., Abowd, G.D.: Toward a Better Understanding of Context and Context-Awareness, GVU Technical Report GIT-GVU-99-22. College of Computing, Georgia Institute of Technology, (1999)
8. Dey, A., Salber, D., Futakawa, M., Abowd, G.: An Architecture to Support Context Aware Computing, Technical Report GIT-GVU-99-23. College Computing, Georgia Institute of Technology, Nov. (2000)
9. FIPA, Specifications (2002) http://www.fipa.org/repository/fipa2000.html
10. Friedman-Hill, E.: Jess in Action: Java Rule-based Systems, Manning Publications Company, June 2003, ISBN 1930110898, http://herzberg.ca.sandia.gov/jess/
11. Garlan, D., Siewiorek, D., Smailagic, A., Steenkiste P.: Project Aura: Towards Distraction-Free Pervasive Computing, IEEE Pervasive Computing, Special Issue on Integrated Pervasive Computing Environments, Vol. 1, Number 2, April–June (2002) 22–31
12. Guha, R., McCool, R., Miller E.: Semantic Search, to be published in proceedings of WWW Conference, Budapest (2003)
13. Hendler, J.: Agents on the Web, IEEE Intelligent Systems, Special Issue on the Semantic Web, Vol. 16, No. 2, pp. 30–37, March/April, (2001)
14. Hong, J., Llanday, J.: A Context/Communication Information Agent, in Personal and Ubiquitous Computing Special Issue Situated Interaction and Context-Aware Computing, Vol. 5(1) (2001) 78–81
15. OASIS: Universal Description, Discovery and Integration standard, http://www.uddi.org/
16. OASIS: Security Assertion Markup Language (SAML), Technology Reports, April 14 (2003) http://xml.coverpages.org/saml.html
17. OASIS: Extensible Access Control Markup Language (XACML), Technology Reports, March 28 (2003) http://xml.coverpages.org/xacml.html
18. Paolucci, M., Kawamura, T., Payne, T., and Sycara, K.: Semantic Matching of Web Service Capabilities, Proceedings of the 1st International Semantic Web Conference, Eds. I. Horrocks and J. Hendler, LCNS 2342, Springer Verlag, 2002.
19. Sadeh, N., Gandon, F., Chan, T., Van, L., Kwon O., Takizawa, K.: Context-Aware m-Commerce: A Semantic Web Approach, Proceedings of the 5th International Conference on Electronic Commerce, Pittsburgh, PA, (2003)
20. Schilit, W.: A System Architecture for Context-Aware Mobile Computing, Ph.D. Thesis, Columbia University, 1995.
21. Schilit, B., Adams, N., Want, R.: Context-Aware Computing Applications. Proc. of the Workshop on Mobile Computing Systems and Applications, IEEE Computer Society, Santa Cruz, CA, (1994) 85–90
22. Schunter, M., Powers, C., The Enterprise Privacy Authorization Language (EPAL 1.1), IBM Research Laboratory, http://www.zurich.ibm.com/security/enterprise-privacy/epal/
23. Want, R., Hopper, A., Falcao, V., Gibbons, J.: The Active Badge Location System, ACM Transactions on Information Systems 10(1) (1992) 91–102.

24. W3C: OWL Web Ontology Language Reference, Working Draft 31 March 2003, http://www.w3.org/TR/owl-ref/
25. W3C: Web Services Description Language (WSDL) 1.1, Note 15 March 2001 http://www.w3.org/TR/wsdl
26. W3C: The Platform for Privacy Preferences 1.0 (P3P1.0) Specification, Recommendation 16 April 2002, http://www.w3.org/TR/P3P/
26. W3C: XSL Transformations (XSLT) Version 1.0, Recommendation 16 November 1999, http://www.w3.org/TR/xslt
28. W3C: RDF Vocabulary Description Language 1.0: RDF Schema, Working Draft 23 January (2003) http://www.w3.org/TR/rdf-schema/

A Policy Based Approach to Security for the Semantic Web*

Lalana Kagal, Tim Finin, and Anupam Joshi

Computer Science and Electrical Engineering Department
University of Maryland Baltimore County
Baltimore, Maryland, USA
{lkagal1,finin,joshi}@cs.umbc.edu

Abstract. Along with developing specifications for the description of meta-data and the extraction of information for the Semantic Web, it is important to maximize security in this environment, which is fundamentally dynamic, open and devoid of many of the clues human societies have relied on for security assessment. Our research investigates the marking up of web entities with a semantic policy language and the use of distributed policy management as an alternative to traditional authentication and access control schemes. The policy language allows policies to be described in terms of deontic concepts and models speech acts, which allows the dynamic modification of existing policies, decentralized security control and less exhaustive policies. We present a security framework, based on this policy language, which addresses security issues for web resources, agents and services in the Semantic Web.

1 Introduction

The Semantic Web is a future generation of the current Web, where resources are annotated with machine understandable meta-data, allowing the automation of the retrieval and usage of these resources in their correct contexts. The focus of much of the existing semantic web work [1,2] has been on the creation of languages for knowledge representation such as DAML+OIL (`http://www.daml.org/`) and OWL (`http://www.w3.org/TR/webont-req/`), of systems that reason over these semantic descriptions for information retrieval [3,4], and tools to help annotate web pages with semantic markup [5,6]. However, with the increase in interest in web based e-commerce, banking and travel services, the amount of business that is transacted online, and the explosion in the amount of services available, a key need for the vision of the Semantic Web to succeed is the ability to handle security and privacy and the ability to automate these protocols for the use of all web entities alike. The obvious solution is to extend security mechanisms applicable to distributed systems (e.g. Kerberos, PGP, SPKI etc.) for the semantic web. However, we believe that this

* This research was supported in part by Hewlett-Packard Labs, Palo Alto, DARPA contract F30602-97-1-0215, NSF career award 9875433 and NSF award 0242403.

D. Fensel et al. (Eds.): ISWC 2003, LNCS 2870, pp. 402–418, 2003.

is difficult given the completely decentralized nature of the web, the extremely large number of resources, services, agents and users, and their heterogeneity. In addition, the set of entities that access an information source or interact with a given web entity (a web entity includes web pages, agents and services) cannot be enumerated a priori. Along with this is the problem of the semantic meaning of the security information; it is not feasible to expect all entities to use the same terminology to represent security protocols and information. This forces the use of a semantic language like RDF-S, DAML+OIL or OWL whose constructs help entities better understand the meaning of the security information. Based on this, we conclude that a security framework for the Semantic Web needs to be flexible, semantically rich and simple enough to automate.

We propose the use of two main components in order to secure the Semantic Web; a semantic policy language for defining security requirements and a distributed policy management approach. As the Semantic Web is composed of web entities like web services, agents, and human users, security should be uniformly applied to and be applicable to all. It is important for web entities to be able to express their security information in a clear and concise manner so that its meaning is unambiguous. Towards this end we suggest the use of a policy language, based on RDF-S, to markup security information. Though, DAML+OIL and OWL include better semantics, they are still evolving and as part of our future work, we are working towards developing a mapping from our policy language into one of them. In distributed policy management, every entity in the system can specify and enforce its own policy as there is no central policy. Policies can be specified in terms of properties of users, agents, services and resources and not just their identities as it may not always be possible to authenticate all entities on the web. The framework attempts to overcome several deficiencies of current security mechanisms by providing access control to resources from a large number of requesting entities that may be unknown to the former, providing security without necessarily authenticating requesters completely, providing flexibility in specifying security requirements and giving every entity a certain amount of autonomy in making their own security decisions. Given the inherently distributed nature of the semantic web, our framework supports several speech acts that allow entities to automatically update existing policies : the delegations of permissions, by which web entities can delegate to other entities certain rights that they possess bound by constraints, the revocation of permissions to remove existing rights, the requesting of actions to be performed and rights to be delegated and the cancellation of previous requests.

In Section 2 we describe some related security work and in Section 3 we discuss the overview of our approach. The details of the policy language, including the constructs, conflict resolution and speech acts supported, follow in Section 4. As delegation is an important aspect of our framework, in Section 5 delegation management is discussed. We discuss the details of our framework with respect to different web entities in Section 6 and we conclude with a summary.

2 Existing Security Mechanisms

There have been some efforts in adapting data exchange formats and protocols related to security in distributed systems to the Semantic Web like XML digital signatures [7], XML encryption [8], and X.509 Public Key Certificates [9]. These systems, based on XML [10], tend to be for authentication and accountability rather than authorization that our framework addresses. Though XML is probably the best exchange format for the Web, it only provides limited interoperability and scalability. Semantic languages like RDF-S, DAML+OIL or OWL that describe ontologies and provide interoperability across applications are more suitable for the Semantic Web. However, as these XML-based frameworks address issues different from our system, it is possible to use them in parallel with ours.

Extensible Access Control Markup Language (XACML) [11] is a language in XML for expressing access policies. This work is similar to ours; in that it allows control over actions and supports resolution of conflicts. However, (i) it does not provide support for speech acts, (ii) adding domain specific information is time consuming (In our framework, adding application/domain specific information involves importing those ontologies or extending our policy ontology.), (iii) it does not allow *types* of actions to be defined (Our policy language allows policies to be written for types of actions that satisfy a certain set of conditions.), (iv) its conflict resolution is not across policies, (v) it can only be used for authorization policies (Our policy language can be used for policies about authorization, privacy, conversation etc.), and (vi) as it is based in XML, it does not benefit from the interoperability and extensibility provided by a semantic language.

The Platform for Privacy Preferences (P3P) is a standard developed by the World Wide Web Consortium (W3C) that enables websites to describe their privacy policies and allows browsers to reason over these policies to decide whether they match the user's preferences [12]. This work tries to reduce Internet users' concerns about the personal information they reveal when visiting various websites. A website specifies its privacy policy and a user is not allowed access to it or warned of conflict if his preferences do not match the policy. The specifications are not designed for information privacy but for the information gathered by websites, and they cannot be used to describe privacy policy for agents and services on the web.

Role Based Access Control (RBAC)[13,14,15,16] is one of the better known methods for access control, in which relations are established between users - roles, and permissions - roles. However it is difficult to apply the RBAC model for systems in which it is not possible to assign roles to all users in advance. In addition it is typically not possible to change access rights of a particular entity without modifying the roles. Simple Role Based Access Control is rather restrictive, as every time access rights of an agent change, its role has to change as well. Our policy language allows access rights (and the other deontic constructs) to be associated with different credentials and properties of entities, and not roles alone. More sophisticated RBAC models include work on delegation between roles [17] and assigning roles to users that are outside the system [18,19]. This research considers delegating the entire set of permissions associated with a set of roles of the delegator (the entity doing the delegation) to the delegatee (the entity receiving the delegation). Our work allows the the policy to dictate what subset of permissions a delegator is able to delegate, to whom and under what conditions. In fact, our policy language is able to represent most RBAC models. Herzberg [18] uses properties of certificates to map users outside the domain to domain specific roles. This is very similar to our work, however instead of mapping properties of certificates to roles, we map properties of the user to access rights directly. Though this may seem like a drawback, we have found that this provides greater control in specifying access rights to foreign users as certain *types* of rights can be given, like the read rights on a certain resource, the right to print to all the color printers on the fifth floor, and the right to delete all the files belonging to your colleague.

The Strongman project uses KeyNote [20] to build secure information systems by automating key and policy management [21]. KeyNote is a trust management system, which binds public keys to access rights. It does not verify certificates or signatures, but allows the functionality to be handled by an external program making integration with existing PKI infrastructures possible. The system is versatile but rather too closely bound to digital certificates as it cannot handle other domain information or link into non PKI systems. It includes a rather simple notion of delegation and uses a programming language instead of a semantic language making its integration with the semantic web difficult.

3 Our Approach

Drawing from our experience with security issues associated with widely distributed systems [22,23,24], we propose a security framework for the Semantic Web based on distributed policy management through the use of a semantic policy language. By distributed policy management, we mean every web entity can specify policies for its access, for privacy, for entities it wants to communicate with etc., which are enforced either by an internal policy engine or the policy engine on the platform it is running on or registered with. A policy includes a set of rules that associate a required set of credentials with a certain ability or right; implying that only entities with the specified credentials can possess the ability. A credential is any property associated with a entity: affiliation, age, certificate, login/password, membership in a certain organization, etc. An entity that meets the requirements of a policy rule is trusted to use the associated action. The policy language, based on deontic concepts, consists of constructs that are flexible and that allow different kinds of policies (security, privacy, management, conversation etc.) to be specified. The language is not tied to any specific application and permits domain specific information to be reasoned over. As the framework is geared towards environments that consist of several domains the language includes meta-policies for specifying mechanisms for handling conflicts.

Though policies associate credentials with actions or services, the process of verifying credentials is handled outside the system. This allows existing mechanisms like PKI, Kerberos etc. to be integrated into the framework.

Our work is similar to role based access control - in that a user's access rights are computed from his/her properties. However, we propose to use additional ontologies that include not just a fixed property, role, but any properties and constraints expressed in an semantic language including elements of both description logics and declarative rules. Consider the earlier example of an employee delegating his *speaker* role to a visiting speaker. In our work, the employee is able to delegate just his rights on the projector and coffee maker to the speaker instead of all the rights associated with the speaker role. This provides greater control on delegation. It also allows rights to be assigned dynamically to a person, who has no role within that organization, without creating a new short term role specific to this person. Similarly, rights can be revoked from a user without changing his/her role, making this approach more flexible and maintainable than role based access control.

The main points of our research work include

- Semantic Policy Language : Our framework provides a policy language based on deontic logic concepts for specifying entities, properties of entities, actions, speech acts, policies. These policies are based on properties of agents, and other domain specific conditions and are described in terms of permissions (what an agent can do), prohibitions (what an agent cannot do), obligations (what an agent should do), and dispensations (what an agent need no longer do). Each web entity is able to describe its security policies in an intelligible manner, so that the meaning is distinct. This allows all entities interacting with it to unmistakably understand its security requirements. The language has an ontology that allows policies (including meta policies) to be described in RDF-S [25], though policies in Prolog [26] are also accepted. Using the axiomatic semantics of RDF-S and the policy language, interacting entities are able to interpret the security information correctly.
- Modeling Speech Acts : We provide a specification of speech acts that can be used to extend the policies namely; delegation (add a permission), revocation (remove a permission or add a prohibition), request (causes an action to be performed or causes a delegation which leads to a permission) and cancel (cancels previous request). Our framework includes detailed delegation management that allows access rights to be transferred further decentralizing control and allowing policies to be less comprehensive. The inclusion of speech acts also allows conversation policies to be described, which is important for controlling communication.
- Distributed Security Framework : In most systems, policies are centralized, specified by single set of individuals, about a predetermined set of users and resources and in a single location with a central point of control. However the widely distributed, open systems that we are addressing require decentralized policies and distributed control, where every entity is responsible

for describing and enforcing its own policy, which our framework supports. We provide a security framework that uses the policy engine in a distributed way allowing a web entity flexibility in security support.
– Mechanisms for Conflict Resolution : Since our framework allows every entity to specify its own policy, and as the Semantic Web spans several domains there is a potential for conflicts. Towards this end, we provide constructs for resolving conflicts; namely setting priorities for rules or entire policies and specifying precedence between positive and negative modalities for policies grouped by agents or actions/services.

The following sections discuss the above mentioned points in greater detail.

4 Policy Language

Our policy language is modeled on deontic concepts of rights, prohibitions, obligations and dispensations [27]. We believe that most policies can be expressed as what an entity can/cannot do and what it should/should not do in terms of actions, services, conversations etc., making our language capable of describing a large variety of policies ranging from security policies to conversation and behavior policies. The policy language has some domain independent ontologies but will also require specific domain ontologies. The former includes concepts for permissions, obligations, actions, speech acts, operators etc. The latter is a set of ontologies, used by the entities in the system, which defines domain classes (person, file, deleteAFile, readBook) etc. and properties associated with the classes (age, num-pages, email).

The language includes two constructs for specifying meta-policies that are invoked to resolve conflicts; setting the modality preference (negative over positive or vice versa) or stating the priority between policies [28]. For example, it is possible to say that in case of conflict the Federal policy always overrides the State policy.

Another important aspect of the framework is that it models speech acts like delegation, revocation, request and cancel that allow policies to be less exhaustive and allow for decentralized security control. Delegations are very important to the internet because web entities may not be able to project who will use them or pre-establish all the desirable requirements of the entities who should use them. Delegations allow access rights of an entity to be propagated to a set of trusted entities, without explicitly changing its policy or requirements. Consider a DAML-S web service that is only accessible by users of a certain role in a certain organization. These users also have the right to delegate the ability to use this service to other users in the organizations for a certain time period. A delegation from one of these users to another employee of the organization permits the latter to use the web service without any explicit modification of the policy or code of the service, while the constraints associated with the delegation are met. The ability to delegate makes it possible to change access rights of web entities dynamically. A revocation speech act nullifies an existing right (whether policy based or delegation based) of an entity. An entity can request another entity for a right or to perform an action on its behalf and an entity can also cancel any previously made request.

The policy language supports individual policies as well as group and role based policies in a uniform manner by allowing domain dependent representations for roles and/or groups to be included in the conditions of the policy rules.

The policy language includes a RDF-S ontology for specifying entities, objects, policies, credentials, and domain specific information.

4.1 Representation of Actions and Conditions

Though the actual execution of services/actions is outside the system, the policy language includes a representation of them that allows more contextual information to be captured and allows for greater understanding of the action and its parameters. This allows policies to be defined over different aspects of an action and not just its identity. For example, it is possible to say all faculty members of the CS department have the right to all services (e.g. print, fax, xerox) on any color printer in the UMBC CS department. Action specifications include the target resources they act on, pre-conditions and effects. Complex actions can be composed using action operators of *sequence, non-deterministic choice, once* and *iteration.*

Simple conditions are built from domain specific information and complex conditions can be built from simple conditions using *and, or* and *not.* A condition is of the form "entity from UMBC" or "in the role of student".

Using these actions and conditions, a policy maker is able to create policy rules. There are four kinds of policy rules representing each deontic concept : right, obligation, prohibition, and dispensation. Each policy rule is a tuple of action and associated requirements. In order to associate these policy objects with users, the policy maker uses the *has* predicate in logic or the *grants* property of the *Policy* class in RDF-S creating rights, obligations etc. for the users.

Example 1 : Simple condition. A web service specifies that all graduate students from University of Maryland Baltimore County can access its service, which is identified by *service1.*

The policy rule in logic is as follows :

```
has(X, right(service1, graduateStudent(X, 'UMBC')))
```

where, service1 is an allowable action, UMBC is a constant for University of Maryland Baltimore County and graduateStudent(X, 'UMBC') is a domain dependent condition specified by the deployer. It is assumed that either the matchmaker, which the service is registered with, or the service itself it able to verify the attributes of an entity using traditional schemes like PKI, SPKI etc.

We are experimenting with ways to encode our simple policy rules in RDF and Notation3 [29]. Eventually, we hope to use whatever standard or standards emerge from the semantic web community for representing rules in RDF. Here is our N3 example in one framework we are using. We describe the rest of our examples in Prolog for conciseness.

```
@prefix rdfs:  <http://www.w3.org/2000/01/rdf-schema#> .
@prefix rei: <http://www.csee.umbc.edu/~lkagal1/rei-simplified#>.
@prefix univ: <http://www.csee.umbc.edu/~lkagal1/univ#>.
@prefix : <#>.
:v1 a rei:Variable.
:R a rei:Right;
        rei:agent :v1;
        rei:action univ:service1.
:cseepolicy a rei:Policy;
rei:grants [a rei:granting;
        rei:to v1;
        rei:deontic R;
        rei:oncondition [a rdfs:statement;
                rdfs:subject v1;
                rdfs:predicate rdfs:type;
                rdfs:object univ:GraduateStudent]].
```

Example 2 : Complex Condition. Consider a right associated with 'John'. *'John'* has the right to either perform action *printBW* followed by repeated executions of *printColor* or perform action *fax* once. He only has the right while he satisfies the associated conditions.

```
has('John', right(nond(seq( printBW, iteration(printColor)),
once(fax)),lab-member('John','AI')))
```

4.2 Speech Acts

The language models four speech acts that allow policies to be less exhaustive, allow for decentralized security control and are able to modify policies dynamically: delegate, revoke, cancel and request.

- Delegation : A delegation from an entity gives a right to another entity or group of entities. A delegation, if valid, causes a *Right* to be created. Only an entity with the *Right* to delegate can make a valid delegation. A delegator always retains the right to revoke the delegated right. (Please refer to Section 5 for more details about delegations)
  - *delegateSpeechAct(Sender, Receiver, right(Action, Condition))* and Receiver satisfies Conditions $\longrightarrow$ *has(Receiver,right(Action, Condition))*
- Request : There are two kinds of requests; a request for an action and a request for a right. The former, if accepted, causes an obligation on the part of the receiver. A request for a right, if valid and accepted, causes the receiver to delegate the right to the sender. However, the delegation allows the sender the permission to perform the action only if the receiver has the right to delegate.

  - *requestSpeechAct(Sender, Receiver, Action)* ⟶ disagree
    requestSpeechAct(Sender, Receiver, Action) ⟶ *has(Receiver, obligation(Action, Condition))*
  - *requestSpeechAct(Sender, Receiver, right(Action, Condition))* ⟶ disagree
    request(Sender, Receiver, right(Action, Condition)) ⟶
    delegateSpeechAct(Receiver,Sender, right(Action, XCondition))
- Revoke : Revocation is the removal of a right and acts as a prohibition. A revocation is allowed in two cases; an entity can revoke those rights to which it has the right to revoke or those rights that it has itself delegated.
  revokeSpeechAct(Sender, Receiver, right(Action, Condition)) ⟶ *revocation(Receiver, right(Action, Condition)) and Sender no longer has the right to perform Action*
- Cancel : An entity can cancel any request it has sent, and this nullifies any obligation or delegation caused by the request.
  - *cancelSpeechAct(Sender, Receiver, Action) AND has(Receiver, obligation(Action, true))* ⟶ *has(Receiver, dispensation(Action, Condition))*
  - *cancelSpeechAct(Sender, Receiver, right(Action, X))* ⟶ *Sender no longer has the right to perform Action*

Example 3 : Request. Continuing with Example 2, 'Jane' is not a lab member of 'AI' and she requests John to give her the right to perform *printBW*.

```
requestSpeechAct('Jane', 'John', right(printBW,_))
```

If accepted and if 'John' has the right to delegate, 'John' sends a delegation to 'Jane' giving her the right to use printBW as long as she is an employee of 'UMBC'.

```
delegateSpeechAct('John', 'Jane', right(printBW,employee('Jane','UMBC'))
```

4.3 Meta Policies

As there is a potential for conflicts, the language also contains meta-policy specifications for conflict resolution. Meta-policies are policies about how policies are interpreted and how conflicts are resolved dynamically. Conflicts only occur if the policies are about the same action, on the same target but the modalities (right/prohibition, obligation/dispensation) are different. Meta policies in our system regulate conflicting policies in two ways by specifying priorities and precedence relations [30]. Using a special construct, *overrides*, the priorities between any two rules or two policies can be set. In case of conflicts, the rule/policy with the higher priority is chosen. It also possible to indicate the order in which the priorities are checked; policy level or rule level first. The other way of resolving conflicts is by specifying which modality holds precedence over the other in the meta-policies. The deployer of the platform/agent can associate a certain precedence for all policies associated with a set of actions or a set of agents satisfying a certain set of conditions.

4.4 Policy Engine

Associated with the policy language is a policy engine that interprets and reasons over the policies, related speech acts and domain information expressed either in Prolog or RDF-S to make decisions about applicable rights, prohibitions, obligations and dispensations. It is possible to extend the policy ontology with other ontologies, which will be accepted and reasoned over by the policy engine. All domain specific information can be specified as separate ontologies and domain specific actions can be subclasses of DomainAction of the policy ontology.

If, while processing a request, the policy engine comes across a conflict, it uses associated meta-policies to resolve it. For example, 'John' wants to print to 'HPPrinter021', he sends a request to 'HPPrinter021'. "HPPrinter021' finds that 'John' has both a right to use it and is prohibited from using it. However, the right has been given higher priority than the prohibition and 'HPPrinter021' permits 'John' to print. The policy engine is able to answer questions about whether a request is valid, what the pending obligations of an agent are, under what conditions a request for a certain action is authorized etc. In order to make correct policy decisions, we assume the presence of a monitoring service that sends all relevant speech acts to the policy engine. The policy engine is implemented in Prolog with a Java interface.

The engine is used as a reasoning engine and is consulted before every request for an action/service and before taking any action. Based on the answer of the engine, the controller of the web entity (could be the entity itself) decides whether to allow or deny the request or go ahead with the action. The engine is also capable of answering other queries related to policy making: who can perform a certain action, who can perform any action on a certain resource, what conditions must an entity possess in order to use a certain action/resource, what unfulfilled obligations does entity X currently have, etc. These queries can be used to decide whether the policy does what it is supposed to and to check whether there are any inconsistencies in it.

5 Delegation Management

Our framework allows entities to delegate rights, with restrictions attached, to other entities. A delegation is in fact a transference of a right from one entity (delegator) to another entity (delegatee). However after the delegation, the delegator retains the right. The right to delegate is defined implicitly and explicitly. Implicitly, an entity can delegate rights to any service it offers and explicitly, an entity that has been given the right to delegate by another entity, who has the right, can perform valid delegations, as long as the delegation fulfills the constraints of the previous delegation. A delegation usually has constraints attached, such as one that limits the access to a certain period, or to whom the right can be re-delegated. A delegation consists of various information; delegator, right, constraints on delegatee, constraints on execution, constraints on re-delegation and time period. By using constraints on delegatee, the delegator can specify whom to delegate to. For example, a delegation could be conferred on all agents with certificates from a certain CA and that are registered with a certain platform. By restricting which delegatee can actually use the right, the delegator can prevent wrongful execution of the right. Constraints on re-delegation allow the delegator to decide whether the right can be re-delegated and to whom it can be re-delegated to.

In a delegation chain, an entity has the right to a certain action (including speech acts) if it possesses the right or if it has been delegated the right. It should satisfy the conditions associated with the innermost right of execution of every delegation in the chain. Each delegator should satisfy the condition on the delegation of the delegation before it in the chain and the delegatee conditions of all previous delegations. If any one entity fails any required delegator condition (whether caused by a change in circumstances or a new revocation or the expiration of a delegation), the delegations from that point on in the chain are invalid. We have developed rules that capture this information and enforce security by checking these constraints for all entities in a certificate chain.

Example 4 : Delegation. 'Amy' has the right to delegate the right to execute printOnePageHP and she delegates this right to 'Tim'. 'Tim' can only execute printOnePageHP if he satisfies both the condition associated with the speech act (employee('Tim', 'UMBC') and the condition associated with 'Amy''s delegation right (group-member(X, Group)).

```
has('Amy', right('Amy',
    delegate(right(X, print, group-member(X,Group))), employee('Amy', 'UMBC')))

delegateSpeechAct('Amy', 'Tim', right('Tim', print, employee('Tim', 'UMBC')))
```

6 Design Overview

In this section, we present a security framework that realizes our previously described ideas about distributed policy management with the help of our policy language. We describe the security functionality of the three main categories of entities prevalent on the semantic web; web services, agents and web resources like pages, servers, etc. The framework is similar for all three cases. A web entity specifies its security policy and consults a policy engine before every request for action by other entities and before any action it performs. This policy engine could be internal i.e. part of the web entity itself or it could belong to a broker or platform that the entity is running off. If the policy engine is external, then the entity has to inform the external engine module of its policy (either explicitly or as part of its markup) and has to trust the broker/platform to filter requests to it based on its policy. An entity also specifies a privacy policy, which is consulted before the entity or the broker/platform communicates any information about the entity.

6.1 Web Resources

In the internet of today there are a lot of pages (static and dynamic) that require some form of authentication and access control before allowing requests to go through, e.g. accessing bank statements, submitting news items etc. This number will keep growing as the amount of sensitive information accessible over the net will keep increasing. To allow agents, services and humans alike to use these secure pages, they are marked up with our policy language. The markup specifies what credentials are required for access in terms of username/password, certificate, and other credentials [31]. The web server that is hosting the web resource contains a policy engine module. The web server is trusted to perform the security functionality on behalf of the resource, which holds even in the current web. When a secure web resource is requested, the server reads the page and checks the security markup. It feeds this information along with the parameters associated with the request to the policy engine module. The policy engine module reasons over the request, the credentials of the requester and the policy of the web resource to decide whether the request should be allowed to go through. If the credentials don't match, the module could return the list of credentials required for access, in a form understandable by the requester otherwise it returns the requested resource data.

This framework is based on an earlier policy based system we developed for eHealthcare in pervasive computing environments [32], where electronic patient information is redacted according to the requester's credentials (including his role in the hospital, certificates etc.), his relationship to the patient and any delegations he possesses, providing different views of the same information to different hospital personnel.

Example 5 : As an example, consider a hospital web site that provides patient information. The patient information web page requires that all requests be accompanied by valid certificates provided by the hospital. One of the doctors, who is away on leave, is discussing a difficult case with one of his friends, who is also a doctor. His friend makes a suggestion the doctor has not tried as yet. The doctor uses his cellphone to retrieve certain information from the hospital's website. His cellphone sends an HTTP request to the website. The web server rejects the request because there is no certificate. The doctor then asks his web agent (which is running on a server at his home) to retrieve the information. When the website denies the agent's request, the agent asks for the required list of credentials. The web server replies that it requires a hospital authorized certificate. The agent is able to understand this credential perfectly and resends the request with the necessary certificate attached. This time the web server permits the request and the agent returns the information to the requesting doctor.

6.2 Agents

Agents that search the web for information/services have to semi-autonomously decide what web services, resources and agents to trust about certain information and services. Along with this, each agent also has to decide what entities to trust to use its own services and information.

We currently follow the the FIPA specifications for agents [33]. Agents exist within agent platforms, which provide middleware functionality to all registered agents. These platforms provide registration, and communication services to the agents, along with enabling them to provide and access services. The two core facilitator agents are Agent Management System (AMS), and the Directory Facilitator (DF). The AMS maintains a directory of registered agents, containing their Agent Identifiers (AIDs) and transport address, and provides a *white page* service. Each agent must register with an AMS in order to get a valid AID. The DF provides *yellow pages* services to other agents. Agents register their services with the DF or query the DF to find out what services are offered by other agents.

Deployers of agent platforms specify policies for accessing the agent platform. Specifically, a deployer describes policies for restricting access to four main actions: registration with the AMS, querying the AMS, registration with the DF, and querying the DF.

An agent specifies policies that a requester must satisfy in order to use its service. An agent can either use an internal policy engine module or trust the platform with which it is registered to enforce its policy.

Security is enforced at two levels: platform or agent. In *platform security*, the AMS and DF have additional security features. The AMS decides whether or not to allow an agent to register, search or use its other functions. Similarly, the DF also decides whether to allow an agent to register, modify or search for agents based on certain access control information. An agent, while registering, sends some access control information to the AMS specifying its security category; *private*, *secure* or *open*. A *private* agent's Agent Identifier (AID) is not displayed to any other agent by the AMS, a *secure* agent has to send some access control information so that the AMS can filter requests to the agent and *open* agent is visible to all agents. Similarly, while registering its services with a DF, the agent chooses a category for each service. For example, an agent A can register as an *open* agent with the AMS and register two services with the DF, an open GPS service and a secure navigator service. Agent A also specifies that only agents with certain credentials can access the navigator service. Using these policies, the AMS and the DF decide whether or not to provide a requesting entity information about the matched agent or service, depending on whether the entity meets the matched agent's/service's requirements. In *agent security*, the agent uses its own policy to decide how to further authenticate agents and how to authorize their service requests. The handling of queries by platforms to secure agents is illustrated in Figure 1.

If an agent cannot use the AMS/DF for making authorization decisions on its behalf, then the agent should contain a security/trust module to interpret its own policies. This makes the presence of the reasoning engine in an agent *optional*, allowing agents to run on smaller, lightweight devices. The AMS/DF has a list of conditions that an agent must satisfy in order to contact a particular

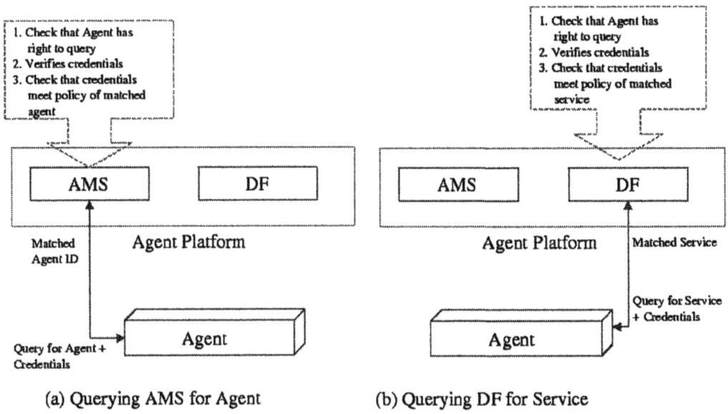

Fig. 1. An entity that queries a platform must satisfy the matched agent/service policy in order to get access to the agent/service.

agent or use a particular service. However, the AMS and DF do not have the agent's policy or have access to its knowledge base. It is upto the agent to make sure that these conditions are accurate and conform to its policy. If the AMS or DF is unable to understand the associated conditions, then based on the policy of the platform, the AMS and DF can decide to reject all requests for the agent or service or accept all requests and forward them to the agent for interpretation.

6.3 Web Services

Web services generally register themselves with a matchmaker [34] that interprets their functional description and provides brokering services for them. Similar to our agent security framework, web services either use an internal policy engine module to enforce their policy or register their policies along with their functional description with a matchmaker. If it is capable of providing security for itself, a web service filters all requests coming to it by verifying that they match its policy. If a web service does not have a policy engine, the matchmaker is responsible for filtering requests for the web service and only forwards those requests that meet the policy of the web service.

During registration, the web service sends the matchmaker its security policy along with its functional description. The matchmaker may have a policy on which credentials are required by a service to register with it. If the web service meets the matchmaker's requirements, the registration is permitted and the matchmaker stores the service's policy. On receiving a query that matches the functional requirements of the web service, the matchmaker checks if the requester's credentials/properties match the policy of the matched service. If the credentials do not match, the web service is not considered as an answer for the request. The web service can also use an internal policy engine to further filter requests received from the matchmaker. If the web service does not want to use the matchmaker for security, the web service does not register its security policy. In this case, the matchmaker allows all requests that match web service's

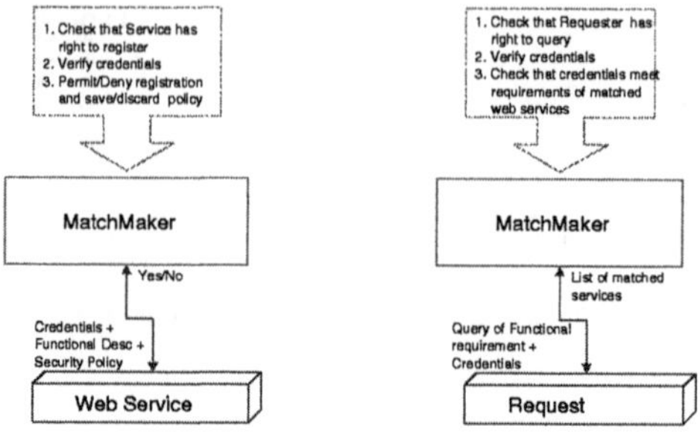

(a) Registering with MatchMaker (b) Querying MatchMaker

Fig. 2. The web service registers its functional description and security policy with a matchmaker. When the matchmaker receives a request that matches the web service, it verifies that the request meets the policy of the web service.

functionality to go through, and the service decides whether or not to accept it. Figure 2 illustrates the integration of security in a web service environment.

This framework is based on our earlier work, Vigil, a security framework, which provides access control to services in pervasive environments [22]. In Vigil, services register their functional description and security policy with the Service Manager of the environment. The Service Manager provides functional and security matchmaking between services and mobile users. Only users that meet a service's security requirements are allowed to view its interface or access it.

7 Current Work and Summary

This paper investigates security issues related to the Semantic Web. We believe that to secure the Semantic Web two main components are required: a semantic policy language for defining security requirements and a distributed policy management approach. In distributed policy management, every entity is able to specify its own policy for security and privacy. It is important for web entities to be able to express their security policies in a clear and concise manner so that its meaning is unambiguous. Towards this end we use a policy language based on a semantic language to markup security information for web entities. Given the inherently distributed nature of the semantic web, the framework includes speech acts like delegation, revocation, request and cancel that dynamically modify existing policies. The policy engine includes strong delegation management making it useful for dynamic systems, consisting of transient resources and users, and distributed systems, in which creating comprehensive policies may be time consuming.

We have developed the specifications of the policy language and a policy engine that reasons over policies in logic and RDF-S, accepts domain dependent information and speech acts, and answers security related queries. We have designed and developed two similar policy based security frameworks, (i) for pervasive environments [22] and (ii) for a supply chain management system [24], which was part of the IBM EECOMS project [35]. We have designed the security framework models for the different web entities including the interaction protocols, and are in the process of developing a security prototype for an agent framework [36].

In this paper, we described the specifications of a semantic policy language and the design of security models for web entities based on this language. We demonstrated through examples the usefulness of our policy language and of our framework based on distributed policy management. We believe that this methodology supports a stronger and more flexible base for securing web entities compared to conventional security mechanisms.

References

1. Cost, R., Finin, T., Joshi, A., Peng, Y., Nicholas, C., Soboroff, I., Chen, H., Kagal, L., Perich, F., Zou, Y., Tolia, S.: ITTALKS: A Case Study in DAML and the Semantic Web. IEEE Intelligent Systems Special Issue 2002 (2002)
2. Horrocks, I., van Harmelen, F., Patel-Schneider, P., Berners-Lee, T., Brickley, D., Connolly, D., Dean, M., Decker, S., Fensel, D., Fikes, R., Hayes, P., Heflin, J., Hendler, J., Lassila, O., McGuinness, D., Stein, L.A.: DAML+OIL Language Specifications. http://www.daml.org (2002)
3. Kopena, J.: DAMLJessKB. http://plan.mcs.drexel.edu/projects/legorobots/design/software/DAMLJessKB/
4. Dean, M., Barber, K.: DAML Crawler. (http://www.daml.org/crawler/)
5. Kalyanpur, A., Hendler, J.: RDF Web Scraper Version 1.1. http://www.ece.umd.edu/ adityak/running.html (2002)
6. Kogut, P., Holmes, W.: AeroDAML: Applying Information Extraction to Generate DAML Annotations from Web Pages. (In: First International Conference on Knowledge Capture (K-CAP 2001) Workshop on Knowledge Markup and Semantic Annotation, Victoria, 2001)
7. Eastlake, D., Reagle, J., Solo, D.: XML-Signature Syntax and Processing. (RFC 3275, March 2002)
8. Eastlake, D., Reagle, J.: XML Encryption Syntax and Processing. (W3C Candidate Recommendation, August 2002)
9. Housley, R., Polk, W., Ford, W., Solo, D.: Internet x.509 public key infrastructure certificate and certificate revocation list (crl) profile. (RFC 3280, April 2002)
10. W3C: Extensible Markup Language. (W3C Recommendation, http://www.w3c.org/XML/)
11. Godik, S., Moses, T.: Oasis extensible access control markup language (xacml). (OASIS Committee Secification cs-xacml-specification-1.0, November 2002)
12. Cranor, L., Langheinrich, M., Marchiori, M., Presler-Marshall, M., Reagle, J.: Platform for privacy preferences (p3p) (2002)
13. Ferraiolo, D., Kuhn, R.: Role-based access controls. In: 15th NIST-NCSC National Computer Security Conference. (1992) 554–563
14. Guiri, L.: A new model for role-based access control (1995)
15. Sandhu, R.S.: Role-based access control. In Zerkowitz, M., ed.: Advances in Computers. Volume 48. Academic Press (1998)
16. Yialelis, N., Lupu, E., Sloman, M.: Role-based security for distributed object systems (1996)

17. Barka, E., Sandhu, R.: Framework for role-based delegation models. In: Annual Computer Security Applications Conference. (2000)
18. Herzberg, A., Mass, Y., J.Mihaeli, D.Naor, Ravid, Y.: Access control meets public key infrastructure : Or assigning roles to strangers. In: 2000 IEEE Symposium on Security and Privacy, Oakland, May 2000. (2000)
19. Hildmann, T., Barholdt, J.: Managing trust between collaborating companies using outsourced role based access control. In: Fourth ACM workshop on Role-based access control, Fairfax, Virginia, United States. (1999)
20. Blaze, M., Feigenbaum, J., Ioannidis, J., Keromytis, A.: The keynote trust management system version (1999)
21. Keromytis, A., Ioannidis, S., Greenwald, M., Smith, J.: The strongman architecture. In: Third DARPA Information Survivability Conference and Exposition (DISCEX III), Washington, D.C. April 22–24. (2003)
22. Undercoffer, J., Perich, F., Cedilnik, A., Kagal, L., Joshi, A., Finin, T.: A Secure Infrastructure for Service Discovery and Management in Pervasive Computing. The Journal of Special Issues on Mobility of Systems, Users, Data and Computing (2003)
23. Kagal, L., Finin, T., Joshi, A.: Trust based security for pervasive computing enviroments. In: IEEE Communications, December 2001. (2001)
24. Kagal, L., Finin, T., Peng, Y.: A Framework for Distributed Trust Management. In: Proceedings of IJCAI-01 Workshop on Autonomy, Delegation and Control. (2001)
25. W3C: Resource Description Framework. W3C Recommendation, http://www.w3.org/TR/rdf-schema/ (2002)
26. Swedish Institute, S.I.o.C.S.: SICStus Prolog. http://www.sics.se/ sicstus/ (2001)
27. Kagal, L., Finin, T., Joshi, A.: A policy language for pervasive systems. In: Fourth IEEE International Workshop on Policies for Distributed Systems and Networks. (2003)
28. Moffett, J., Sloman, M.: Policy conflict analysis in distributed systems management. Journal of Organizational Computing (1993)
29. Berners-Lee, T.: Notation 3. http://www.w3.org/DesignIssues/Notation3 (2001)
30. Lupu, E.C., Sloman, M.: Conflicts in policy-based distributed systems management. IEEE Transactions on Software Engineering (1999)
31. Denker, G.: Access control and data integrity for daml+oil and daml-s. White paper (2002)
32. Chodhari, A., Kagal, L., Joshi, A., Finin, T., Yesha, Y.: Patientservice : A policy based information service for ehealthcare. In: Fifth International Workshop on Enterprise Networking and Computing in Healthcare Industry, Santa Monica, June. (2003)
33. FIPA: FIPA Agent Management Specification. In: FIPA website (http://www.fipa.org/specs/fipa00023/). (2001)
34. Paolucci, M., Kawamura, T., Payne, T.R., Sycara, K.: Semantic matching of web services capabilities. In: ISWC2002. (2002)
35. Ingersoll Rand (Woodcliff Lake, NJ) and QAD (Carpenteria, CA) and Berclain Group (Schaumburg, IL) and IBM Corporation (Somers, NY): CIIMPLEX Consortium, Consortium for Integrated Intelligent Manufacturing PLanning and EXecution. http://www.ciimplex.org (2000)
36. Kagal, L., Finin, T., Joshi, A.: Developing secure agent systems using delegation based trust management. In: Security of Mobile MultiAgent Systems held at Autonomous Agents and MultiAgent Systems. (2002)

Semantic Web Languages for Policy Representation and Reasoning: A Comparison of KAoS, Rei, and Ponder

Gianluca Tonti[1,2], Jeffrey M. Bradshaw[1], Renia Jeffers[1], Rebecca Montanari[2], Niranjan Suri[1], and Andrzej Uszok[1]

[1] Institute for Human and Machine Cognition (IHMC)
University of West Florida
40 S. Alcaniz Street, Pensacola, FL 32501 – USA
{jbradshaw,rjeffers,nsuri,gtonti,auszok}@ihmc.us
[2] Dipartimento di Elettronica, Informatica e Sistemistica
University of Bologna
Viale Risorgimento, 2 - 40136 Bologna - ITALY
{rmontanari,gtonti}@deis.unibo.it

Abstract. Policies are being increasingly used for automated system management and controlling the behavior of complex systems. The use of policies allows administrators to modify system behavior without changing source code or requiring the consent or cooperation of the components being governed. Early approaches to policy representation have been restrictive in many ways. However semantically-rich policy representations can reduce human error, simplify policy analysis, reduce policy conflicts, and facilitate interoperability. In this paper, we compare three approaches to policy representation, reasoning, and enforcement. We highlight similarities and differences between Ponder, KAoS, and Rei, and sketch out some general criteria and properties for more adequate approaches to policy semantics in the future.

1 Introduction

Until recently, the use of Semantic Web languages has been limited primarily to representing Web content and services. However the capabilities of these languages, coupled with the increasing availability of mature environments and tools to facilitate their use, make them well suited for many other kinds of applications. In this paper, we evaluate ongoing efforts to use Semantic Web languages to represent and reason about policies for multi-agent and distributed systems. In particular, we intend to show the strengths and limitations of such languages for policy representation and reasoning by comparing and contrasting three approaches: KAoS, Rei and Ponder.

Policies are a means to dynamically regulate the behavior of system components without changing code and without requiring the consent or cooperation of the components being governed [1, 2]. By changing policies, a system can be continuously adjusted to accommodate variations in externally imposed constraints and environmental conditions. The adoption of a policy based-approach for controlling a system requires an appropriate policy representation and the design and

D. Fensel et al. (Eds.): ISWC 2003, LNCS 2870, pp. 419–437, 2003.

development of a policy management framework. Policies will become increasingly more important to the real world implementation of Semantic Web Services [3, 4].

KAoS uses DAML[1] (and soon will use OWL[2]) as the basis for representing and reasoning about policies within Web Services, Grid Computing, and multi-agent system platforms [2, 3, 4, 5]. KAoS also exploits ontologies for representing and reasoning about *domains* describing organizations of human, agent, and other computational actors. Rei is a new deontic concept-based policy language that is currently implemented in Prolog with a semantic representation of policies in RDF-S. In the future, it is expected that Rei will support OWL and Notation3[3] ontologies [6, 7]. Ponder is an object-oriented policy language for the management of distributed systems and networks [1, 8]. The developers of Ponder pioneered many of the policy management concepts used in KAoS and Rei, though its implementation differs in important ways [9].

The paper is organized as follows. Section 2 describes the motivation and background of policy-based approaches for the management of software systems, beginning with the extensive research over the last decade about the management of network and quality of service and continuing to the present day in new application areas such as the control of multi-agent systems. Section 3 briefly presents the three different approaches for policy representation, reasoning, and enforcement. These are compared in Section 4 through the implementation of a common example of a communication policy. This is followed by a discussion of the approaches and of some of the open issues that must be resolved as a prerequisite to widespread adoption. Finally, in Section 5, we present some conclusions.

2 Motivation and Background for Policy-Based Management

Policies, which constrain the behavior of system components, are becoming an increasingly popular approach to dynamic adjustability of applications in academia and industry. Elsewhere [2], we have pointed out the many benefits of policy-based approaches, including reusability, efficiency, extensibility, context-sensitivity, verifiability, support for both simple and sophisticated components, protection from poorly-designed, buggy, or malicious components, and reasoning about component behavior. Policies have important analogues in animal societies and human cultures [10].

Policy-based network management has been the subject of extensive research over the last decade [11]. Policies are often applied to automate network administration tasks, such as configuration, security, recovery, or quality of service (QoS). In the network management field, policies are expressed as sets of rules governing choices in the behavior of the network. Multiple approaches for policy specification have been proposed that range from formal policy languages that can be processed and interpreted easily and directly by a computer, to rule-based policy notation using an if-then-else format, to the representation of policies as entries in a table consisting of multiple attributes [12, 13, 14]. There are also ongoing standardization efforts toward

---

[1] DARPA Agent Markup Language (http://www.daml.org)

[2] Web Ontology Language (http://www.w3.org/2001/sw/WebOnt/)

[3] http://www.w3.org/DesignIssues/Notation3.html

common policy information models and frameworks. The Internet Engineering Task Force, for instance, has been investigating policies as a means for managing IP-multiservice networks by focusing on the specification of protocols and object-oriented models for representing policies [15].

The scope of policy management is increasingly going beyond these traditional applications in significant ways. New challenges for policy management include:

- sources and methods protection, digital rights management, information filtering and transformation, capability-based access;
- active networks, agile computing, pervasive and mobile systems;
- organizational modeling, coalition formation, formalizing cross-organizational agreements;
- trust models, trust management, information pedigrees;
- effective human-machine interaction: interruption and notification management, presence management, adjustable autonomy, teamwork facilitation, safety; and
- intelligent retrieval of all policies relevant to some situation.

The management of multi-agent systems represents one of the most promising fields for the exploitation of policy-based approaches [2, 6, 16]. By their ability to operate independently without constant human supervision, agents can perform tasks that would be impractical or impossible using traditional software applications. On the other hand, this additional autonomy, if unchecked, also has the potential of effecting severe damage if agents are poorly designed, buggy, or malicious.

Controlling agent behavior is a complex task because agent behavior cannot be a-priori programmed to face any operative run-time situation, but requires dynamic and continuous adjustments to allow agents to act in any execution context in the most suitable way [2]. From a technical perspective, we want to be able to help ensure the protection of agent state, the viability of agent communities, and the reliability of the resources on which they depend. To accomplish this, we must guarantee, insofar as is possible, that the autonomy of agents can always be bounded by explicit enforceable policy that can be continually adjusted to maximize the agents' effectiveness and safety in both human and computational environments. From a social perspective, we want agents to be designed to fit well with how people actually work together. Explicit policies governing human-agent interaction, based on careful observation of work practice and an understanding of current social science research, can help assure that effective and natural coordination, appropriate levels and modalities of feedback, and adequate predictability and responsiveness to human control are maintained [17]. In short, interaction among humans and agents must be graceful and should enhance rather than hinder human work. All these factors are key to providing the reassurance and trust that are the prerequisites to the widespread acceptance of agent technology for non-trivial applications.

3 Policy Languages and Frameworks

Policies can be specified in many different ways and multiple approaches have been proposed in different application domains [11]. There are, however, some general requirements that any policy representation should satisfy regardless of its field of applicability: *expressiveness* to handle the wide range of policy requirements arising in the system being managed, *simplicity* to ease the policy definition tasks for administrators with different degrees of expertise, *enforceability* to ensure a mapping of policy specifications into implementable policies for various platforms, *scalabilty* to ensure adequate performance, and *analyzability* to allow reasoning about policies. The challenge is to achieve a suitable balance among the objectives of expressiveness, computational tractability, and ease of use.

The aim of this section is not to provide a general survey of the state-of-the-art in policy representation, but to describe selected technical aspects of a few policy approaches that have been specifically designed and extensively tested for management of multi-agent and distributed systems. We first present KAoS followed by Rei, both of which were originally designed for governing agent behavior, and finally Ponder which is one of the most well-known policy-based systems for network management and is being evaluated in several universities and industrial organizations.

3.1 KAoS

KAoS a collection of componentized policy and domain management services compatible with several popular agent frameworks, including Nomads [18], the DARPA CoABS Grid [19], the DARPA ALP/Ultra*Log Cougaar framework (http://www.cougaar.net), CORBA (http://www.omg.org), Voyager (http://www.recursionsw.com/osi.asp), and Brahms (www.agentisolutions.com). While initially oriented to the dynamic and complex requirements of software agent applications, KAoS services are also being adapted to general-purpose grid computing (http://www.gridforum.org) and Web Services (http://www.w3.org/2002/ws/) environments as well [3, 4]. KAoS has been deployed in a wide variety of applications, from coalition warfare [5, 16], to robustness and survivability for distributed systems [http://www.ultralog.net], to human-agent teamwork in space applications [17], to cognitive prostheses [2]. See [2] for a summary of these and other applications.

KAoS domain services provide the capability for groups of software components, people, resources, and other entities to be organized into domains and subdomains to facilitate agent-agent collaboration and external policy administration.

KAoS policy services allow for the specification, management, conflict resolution, and enforcement of policies within domains. Policies are currently represented in DAML+OIL as ontologies. The KAoS Policy Ontologies (KPO) distinguish between *authorizations* (i.e., constraints that permit or forbid some action) and *obligations* (i.e., constraints that require some action to be performed, or else waive such a requirement).

The following important features of KAoS are worth noting. First, the approach does not assume that the policy-governed system is comprised of a homogeneous set of components that have been designed in advance to work with KAoS services. Rather the goal is to be able to have KAoS services work with arbitrarily written components after the fact through support being added transparently at the platform level. Second, insofar as possible, the KAoS framework supports dynamic runtime policy changes and not merely static configurations determined in advance. Third, the framework is extensible to a variety of execution platforms that might be simultaneously running with different enforcement mechanisms—in principle any platform for which policy enforcement mechanisms may be written. Fourth, the KAoS framework is intended to be robust and adaptable in continuing to manage and enforce policy in the face of attack or failure of any combination of components.

Policy representation. Within the KAoS Policy Ontologies (KPO), a policy is an instance of the appropriate policy type (i.e., positive or negative authorization; positive or negative obligation) that defines the associated values for its properties, such as site of enforcement, priority, and update time stamp. Complex policy constructs such as delegation are built directly out of the four basic policy types rather than through special-purpose mechanisms (e.g., metapolicies). Through various property restrictions in the action type, the specific context for the action is defined (e.g., relations to target and other situation entities). A given policy can also be variously scoped, for example, either to individual components, to components of a given class, to components belonging to a particular group, or to components running in a given physical place or computational environment (e.g., host, VM). The current version of the core ontologies in KPO consists of more than 100 classes and related properties that together define basic ontologies for actions, actors, groups, places, various entities related to actions (e.g., computing resources), and policies. Application developers typically extend KPO with additional domain specific ontological elements. As the application runs, classes and individuals corresponding to new policies and application entities are also transparently added and deleted as needed. Figure 1 shows a fragment of a communication policy example stating that the members of a domain called A are permitted to communicate to members outside the domain using encrypted communication:

```
<daml:Class rdf:ID="ExampleAction">
  <rdfs:subClassOf rdf:resource="#EncryptedCommunicationAction" />
  <rdfs:subClassOf>
        <daml:Restriction>
                  <daml:onProperty rdf:resource="#performedBy" />
              <daml:toClass rdf:resource="#MembersOfDomainA" />
          </daml:Restriction>
   </rdfs:subClassOf>
   <rdfs:subClassOf>
         <daml:Restriction>
                  <daml:onProperty rdf:resource="#hasDestination" />
              <daml:toClass rdf:resource="#notMembersOfDomainA " />
           </daml:Restriction>
       </rdfs:subClassOf>
</daml:Class>
<policy:PosAuthorizationPolicy rdf:ID="Example">
 <policy:controls rdf:resource="#ExampleAction" />
 <policy:hasSiteOfEnforcement rdf:resource="#ActorSite" />
 <policy:hasPriority>10</policy:hasPriority>

<policy:hasUpdateTimeStamp>4237445645589</policy:hasUpdateTimeStamp>
```

Fig. 1. Example of DAML policy representation in KAoS. Note that the use of the KPAT GUI shields users from having to know and use DAML notations (see Figure 2).

Policy management features. KAoS provides the KAoS Policy Administration Tool (KPAT)[4] as a graphical interface (Figure 2). KPAT assists users in policy specification, revision, and application. In addition, KPAT can be used to browse and load ontologies and to analyze and deconflict newly defined policies. As policies, domains, and application entities are defined using the KPAT GUI, the appropriate DAML representations are generated automatically in the background and asserted into or retracted from the system, insulating the user from having to know DAML or from coding directly in a policy language as in Rei and Ponder. Policy templates allow various classes of policy definitions to be defined as high-level domain-specific abstractions. A rich set of queries is also available through KPAT or through programmatic interfaces.

KAoS detects potential conflicts between policies at specification time, whenever a user tries to add a new policy to the Directory Service. The KAoS algorithm for policy conflict detection is able to detect conflicts between policies by relying on algorithms implemented as extensions to Stanford's Java Theorem Prover (JTP) (http://www.ksl.stanford.edu/software/JTP/), which is integrated into KAoS. The engine identifies policy conflicts by using the subsumption mechanisms among relevant classes. KAoS tries to resolve conflicts by ordering policies according to their precedence and, where necessary and desired, generating new harmonized policies [4, 5].

In addition, KAoS provides a complete deployment model that consists of some basic services and components such as the Domain Manager, the Directory Service, and Guards. The KAoS framework is responsible for the management of domains of agents and assures policy consistency at all the levels of the domain hierarchy. The Directory Service is responsible for overall policy management, while Guards interpret policies and pass them on to Enforcers, which are platform-specific components that handle the actual policy enforcement. Before performing its function to allow or forbid a given action, Enforcers for authorization policies must obtain an answer to the question, "is a given action permitted or not?" or reasons of performance and robustness. KAoS typically provides the answer locally through intelligent lookup rather than inference. An action description is created by the Enforcer and passed to the Guard, which traverses policy storage and checks to see if the given action instance is in the range of actions controlled by any of its policies. If the authorization mechanism does not find any policy applicable to the action description passed to it, it answers the question consistent with whatever default authorization modality it has been given. Domain defaults either correspond to a *democracy,* where everything is permitted that is not explicitly forbidden, or a *tyranny,* where everything is forbidden that is not explicitly permitted. Enforcement mechanisms for obligation policies work in a similar fashion, however rather than preemptively prohibiting actions, either they monitor and respond as necessary to the performance or non-performance of obligation actions, or else they actively facilitate performance through types of enforcers called enablers.

---

[4] pronounced "KAY-pat"

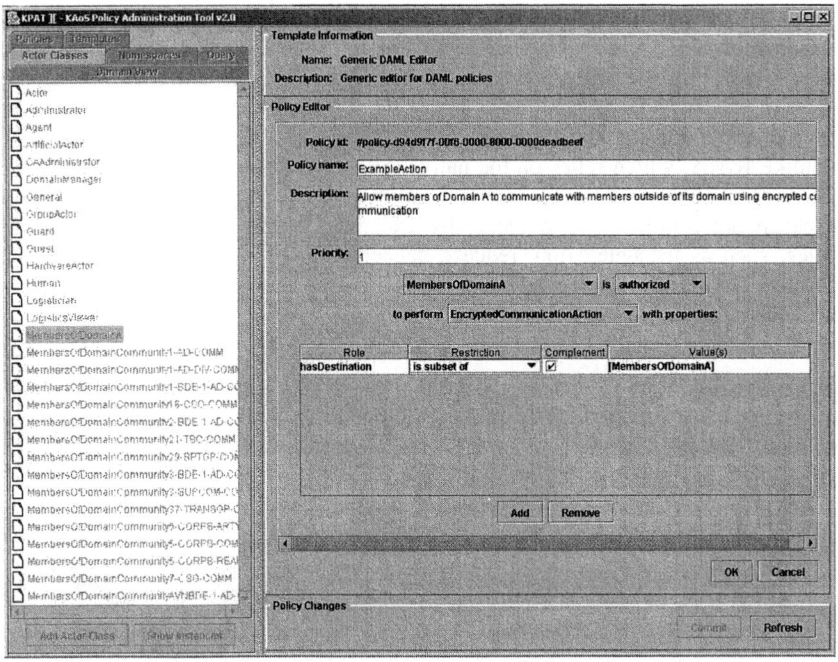

Fig. 2. KPAT hides the complexity of DAML through the use of a graphical user interface and a generic DAML template. Additional language-specific templates or domain-specific templates for common classes of policies can be easily defined.

3.2 Rei

Rei is a policy framework that integrates support for policy specification, analysis and reasoning in pervasive computing applications [6, 7]. Rei has been used in conjunction with the Vigil security framework [6], Fujitsu's Task Computing project, and with the Groove workspace [http://www.groove.net] within the DARPA Genoa II program [http://www.darpa.mil/iao/GenoaII.htm].

The Rei deontic concept-based policy language allows users to express and represent the concepts of *rights*, *prohibitions*, *obligations,* and *dispensations*. These concepts correspond, respectively, to the conditions of positive and negative authorization, and positive and negative obligation in KAoS and Ponder. In addition, Rei permits users to specify policies that are defined as rules associating an entity of a managed domain with its set of rights, prohibitions, obligations, and dispensations.

Rei relies on an application-independent ontology to represent the concepts of rights, prohibitions, obligations, dispensations, and policy rules. This allows different elements of a pervasive environment to understand and interpret Rei policies in the correct way. The basic ontology also includes the description of actions. A general action is described by its unique action identifier, the target objects on which the action can be performed, a set of pre-conditions that must be true before the action can be performed, and the effects that result from the action when it is performed.

Like KAoS, Rei allows users to extend the basic ontology with additional domain dependent ontologies to express concepts and resources that are peculiar to certain domains. For instance, if there is a need to model the specific action of printing a file on a local printer, the general action class of the Rei basic ontology can be customized to include more contextual information about specific printing options.

Unlike KAoS, which relies on the native APIs or message-passing facilities of the underlying platform in which its services reside, the Rei language relies on a rich set of speech act primitives to dynamically exchange rights and obligations between entities, such as the delegation, request, cancellation, or revocation of policies. Rei uses meta-policies to resolve policy conflicts that are automatically detected by the Rei policy engine.

Policy specification. Rei's concepts of rights, permissions, obligations, dispensations, and policy rules are represented as Prolog predicates. No GUI equivalent of KPAT is provided in the current version of Rei.[5] Table 1 reports some examples of Rei rights and policy specifications.

Table 1. Example of Rei policy specification.

	Rei Policy Constructs	Rei Policy Instance (example)
A	*PolicyObject (Action , Conditions)*	**right (examineStudent , professor (Var))**
B	*has (Subject , Policy Object)*	**has (Var , right (examineStudent, professor (Var))**
C	*action (ActionName, TargetObjects, Pre-Conditions, Effects)*	**action (examineStudent, Y, [student(Y)] , [])**

Row A describes a *Policy Object* that is used to model rights, permissions, obligations, and dispensations to perform a specific action under certain conditions. The right column of Row A shows a Policy Object instance that defines the right to perform the *examineStudent* action when the condition on the variable *Var* is true—that is, when Var is a professor. Row B illustrates the concept of a *Policy Rule*, which is used to define the association between the subject of a policy and a Policy Object via the *has* construct. In the example on Row B, the right defined in row A is now associated with a set of entities that are represented by the variable *Var*. These entities can examine students only if they satisfy the *professor(Var)* condition, i.e., the entities need to be professors. Finally, row C shows the definition of an action. In the right column, the action *examineStudent* is performed on all the entities (*Y* variable) that are students *(student(Y))* without producing any effect on the system *([])*. For additional detail, see [6].

Rei also permits users to specify role-based access control policies or policies relating not only to individuals but also to groups of entities. For instance, in row B the variable *Var* (all variables are denoted by a beginning capital letter) can be resolved by a role or group based set of entities that resolve the condition of the Policy Object, i.e. by all the members of the *professor* role or group. Roles and groups are not represented by specific constructs of the language and are not described in the basic Rei ontology. In making this design decision, the developers of Rei argue that roles do not receive a consistent interpretation in different applications, and may not

[5] A new GUI for Rei is under development in the form of a plug-in for Protégé.

always be required. Policy programmers deal with a smaller set of constructs and code domain-specific implementations of roles and groups when required.

Policy deployment model. The Rei framework provides a policy engine that reasons about the policy specifications. The engine accepts policy specification in both the Rei language and in RDF-S, consistent with the Rei ontology. Specifically, the engine automatically translates the RDF specification into triples of the form (subject, predicate, object). The engine also accepts additional domain-dependent information in any semantic language that can then be converted into this recognizable form of triple. The engine is consistent and complete [6] and allows queries according to the Prolog language about any policies, meta-policies, and domain dependent knowledge that have been loaded in its knowledge base.

The Rei policy engine can detect modality conflicts among policies. In particular, the engine marks two policies as conflicting if they are of conflicting modalities and if there is an overlap in subject, target, and action. In order to resolve the detected conflicts, Rei provides the possibility to specify meta-policies that define priorities on policies, and/or set precedence relations between policy modalities.

Rei decentralizes the policy control to system entities. Some constructs allow specification of speech acts to exchange policies between entities and comprehensive delegation management allows the rights of entities to be configured dynamically.

The Rei framework does not provide an enforcement model. In fact, the policy engine has not been designed to enforce the policies but only to reason about them and reply to queries. For example, the engine can say if an entity has the right or obligation to perform a certain action, but then it does not include mechanisms to ensure enforcement of the policy by, for example, forbidding the policy subject from performing unauthorized actions or by forcing the entity to execute required actions. Thus it provides limited or no protection from malicious or non-compliant components or agents.

3.3 Ponder

Ponder is a declarative, object-oriented language that supports the specification of several types of management policies for distributed object systems and provides structuring techniques for policies to cater for the complexity of policy administration in large enterprise information systems [1, 9, 14]. It has been widely deployed in many applications.

Ponder distinguishes between basic and composite policies. A basic policy is considered a rule governing the choices in system behaviour and is specified by a declaration between a set of *subjects* and a set of *targets*. These sets are used to define the managed objects that the policy operates over. Ponder uses the term subject to refer to users, principals, or automated manager components, which have management responsibility (i.e., have the authority to initiate a management decision). A subject can operate on target objects (resources or service providers) by invoking methods visible in the target interface. The fundamental policy types in Ponder are obligations and authorizations. For example, *obligation policies* define "the actions that policy subjects must perform on target entities when specific relevant events occur" while *authorization policies* define "what operations a subject is authorized to do on target objects" [14].

Composite policies allow the basic policies relating to organizational units to be grouped. Examples of composite policies are *role* and *relationships* policies. In Ponder, roles are groups of policies governing the behavior of the same subject by specifying its rights and duties while relationships group the policies defining the rights and duties of roles towards each other.

Ponder policies rely on the key concept of management domains. Domains provide a means of grouping objects on which policies apply and can be used to partition the objects in a large system as desired. Ponder policy subjects and targets are defined in terms of domain scope expressions that allow the combination of domains to form composite set of objects, but also to identify a single named object within a single domain.

Policy specification. Figure 3 illustrates an example of a Ponder authorization policy. The policy specifies that the professor principals have read access to all the exercise files of their students only during the opening hours of the school, i.e. from 7 am to 7 pm and from Monday to Friday.

```
type auth+ FileAccess (subject professor,
                       target  exerciseFiles )
  {
    action   read;
    when
          Time.between(0700, 1900) and
          Time.between('mon', 'fri');
  }
inst auth+ P1 = FileAccess ("professor/Green",
                       "NodeServer/StudentFiles");
```

Fig. 3. Ponder authorization policy specification

A *type* policy definition introduces a new user-defined policy type, from which one or more policy instances of that type can be created. Policy types can also be parameterized and the instances created with context-specific parameters, for example, the subject and target sets can be passed as actual parameters. A policy instance declaration creates an instance of a user-defined policy type. P1 is a policy instance that authorizes the professor principal called Green to access the student exercise files hosted on the NodeServer. The read action is a method of the target interface and can be neither refined nor specialized. The `when` clause is used to deny read access to the files during school closing hours.

Note that Ponder does not currently support the specification of default rules for policies. For example, if an authorization policy is not specified for an action, the default constraint on behavior (i.e., whether to permit or forbid the action) is implementation dependent.

Policy deployment model. Ponder provides various graphical tools for editing, updating, removing, and browsing Ponder policies [20]. There are also tools for syntactic and semantic analysis of policy specifications and for transforming Ponder language specifications directly into XML or Java code that can be interpreted at runtime.

In addition, the developers of Ponder have implemented a prototype conflict detection tool to detect overlaps and conflicts between policies. The tool distinguished between modality conflicts and application-specific conflicts [8]. Similar to KAoS and Rei, the former are inconsistencies in the policy specification that may arise among policies with modalities of opposite signs that refer to the same subjects, targets, and actions (e.g., conflicts between permissions and prohibitions or between obligations and prohibitions). However, the lack of an ontology limits its ability to deal with subjects, actions, and targets at varying levels of abstraction. The latter are inconsistencies between the policy content and external criteria (e.g. conflict between an obligation to access a resource and a limitation on the resource availability). More recent work on policy analysis in Ponder has focused on using abductive reasoning together with an event calculus representation of the policies to identify and detect the policy conflicts [21].

Ponder proposes a general-purpose deployment model [22]. At the end of the policy specification the policy is compiled by the Ponder compiler into a Java class and then represented at runtime by a Java object. The downside is that runtime changes to policy are not possible. The distribution and enforcement model distinguishes between authorization and obligation policies. Authorization policy objects are distributed closer to the target objects of the policy where an Access Controller Agent provides their runtime interpretation and enforcement by allowing or rejecting access requests to controlled target resources. Obligation policy objects are distributed closer to the subject objects of the policy where a Policy Management Agent provides their run-time interpretation and enforcement at policy-relevant event occurrence. Ponder provides the specification of the interfaces for the enforcement agents, i.e., for the Access Controller and Policy Management Agent, but no implementation is provided. There are some systems that implement the Ponder policy deployment model in different application domains [23].

4 Case-Study: Controlling Communication

This section compares the policy frameworks described in Section 3 with the main goal of highlighting their differences and of outlining some general key requirements for a comprehensive semantic approach to policies. The case of a communication policy among agents is considered for purposes of comparison. Communication in multi-agent systems has proven to be a very common application of policy. Let us consider the case of a multi-agent system modeling an academic institute where there is the need to rule the communication between professors and their students, both represented as agents. In the following sections we will use a policy that states that "*professors are permitted to communicate the final examination grade to their students using an encrypted communication only after the approval of the institute's director*" as a running policy example to show how the three approaches represent, analyze and deploy it.

4.1 Policy Representation

Table 2 shows the different representations of the policy example in KAoS, Rei and Ponder.

KAoS exploits a DAML-based representation of the policy example. In particular it is modeled as an instance of a positive authorization policy type with associated properties set to the desired values. For example, the *performedBy* property represents the sender and its value is restricted to the "AgentProfessors", while the *siteOfEnforcement* value is set to the "SubjectSite" meaning that the enforcement mechanisms will be associated with the professor agents that are the subject of the policy.

In Rei, the policy specification is based on a Prolog-like representation. The policy is modeled by means of three basic constructs. In particular, the *action* construct models the "gradeCommunication" action that involve "Professors" and "Students", the *right* construct models the right of executing this action when the set of policy conditions are verified, and finally the *has* construct assigns this right to the "Professors".

The exploitation of a Ponder authorization policy type for mapping the communication policy requires the identification of the resources that need protection and to know in advance their specific names and interfaces. For example, in the specification we assume that the resource to be protected is the communication channel (the "CommunicationChannel" target resource) and that the action that a policy subject can exploit to send data is the "communication" method of the "CommunicationChannel" object interface.

A major advantage of using KAoS for representing the policy is that any policy element (groups, actors, actions, action properties, conditions of applicability) is described by an appropriate ontology at the desired level of abstraction. KAoS policy specification is split into two parts. The first part defines the aspects of the controlled action. This part, represented within a single DAML class, is self-contained and includes information about the type of action, the class of subjects performing this action and additional context information. In comparison, other policy specification approaches separate information about the action type from the class of subjects, making analysis of the policy more complex. KAoS' approach allows users to analyze and compare action classes independently of policies and to apply the policy management information (e.g., policy modality, precedence), which is included in the second part of the policy specification, at the end of the decision process. Finally, KAoS provides a rich set of predefined ontologies that can be extended to accommodate specific application requirements and hides the potential complexity of policy representation and languages behind the KPAT graphical user interface.

In Rei the specification is more readable and compact than a semantic web language such as DAML. On the other hand, the Prolog-like syntax policy specification is not so easy for users with limited expertise in logic languages.

Finally, the Ponder policy specification is easy to understand thanks to its declarative specification. However, the low level of abstraction provided in Ponder by method calls may be a limitation to its use in multi-agent systems, where support for dynamic runtime changes and the need for simultaneously varying levels of description are usually important requirements.

Table 2. Policy Specification in KAoS, Rei, and Ponder

KAoS

```
<?xml version='1.0'?>
<rdf:RDF xmlns:rdf="http://www.w3.org/1999/02/22-rdf-syntax-ns#"
         xmlns:rdfs="http://www.w3.org/2000/01/rdf-schema#"
         xmlns:daml="http://www.daml.org/2001/03/daml+oil#"
         xmlns:xsd ="http://www.w3.org/2000/10/XMLSchema#"
         xmlns:policy="http://ontology.coginst.uwf.edu/Policy.daml#"
         xmlns="http://ontology.coginst.uwf.edu/ExamplePolicies/PolicyExample.daml#">
<daml:Ontology rdf:about="">
  .....
<daml:Class rdf:ID="ExaminationGradePolicyAction">
    <daml:intersectionOf rdf:parseType="daml:collection">
    <daml:Class rdf:about="http://ontology.coginst.uwf.edu/Action.daml#EncryptedCommunicationAction"/>
     <daml:Restriction>
        <daml:onProperty rdf:resource="http://ontology.coginst.uwf.edu/Action.daml#performedBy"/>
        <daml:toClass rdf:resource="http://ontology.coginst.uwf.edu/ActorClasses.daml#AgentProfessors"/>
     </daml:Restriction>
     <daml:Restriction>
        <daml:onProperty rdf:resource="http://ontology.coginst.uwf.edu/Action.daml#hasDestination"/>
        <daml:toClass rdf:resource="http://ontology.coginst.uwf.edu/ActorClasses.daml#AgentStudents"/>
     </daml:Restriction>
     <daml:Restriction>
        <daml:onProperty rdf:resource="http://ontology.coginst.uwf.edu/ Action.daml#hasApproval"/>
       <daml:toClass
            rdf:resource="http://ontology.coginst.uwf.edu/ActorClasses.daml#AgentInstituteDirector"/>
     </daml:Restriction>
    </daml:intersectionOf>
 </daml:Class>
 <policy:PosAuthorizationPolicy rdf:ID="ExaminationGradePolicy">
    <policy:controls rdf:resource="#ExaminationGradePolicyAction"/>
    <policy:hasSiteOfEnforcement rdf:resource="http://ontology.coginst.uwf.edu/Policy.daml#SubjectSite"/>
     <policy:hasPriority>10</policy:hasPriority>
     <policy:hasUpdateTimeStamp>446744445544</policy:hasUpdateTimeStamp>
 </policy:PosAuthorizationPolicy >
```

Rei

```
                          Action name (URI)   Target Objects
        action (gradesCommunication, [Stud, Prof], [ ],      Pre-conditions
                   communicated('grade', Stud, Prof))        Effects
        has(Prof,     Subject            Action
Policy       right( gradesCommunication,
rule  Policy Condition ( action(gradesCommunication, [Stud, Prof], X,Y),
      Object             professor(Prof), student(Stud, Prof),
                         commType('encrypted'),  dataType('Grade'),
                         approval(Prof,instituteDirector)   ))
```

Ponder

```
domain prof = /SysEntities/Agents/ProfessorAgents;
domain stud = /SysEntities/Agents/StudentsAgents;

inst auth+ ExamGradeComm {
   subject  s= prof;
   target  t = /SysEntities/SysServices/CommunicationChannel;
   action t.communication ("Encrypted", data, destination) ;
   when data.getType = "Grade"
     && destination == (stud -> select (st I st.professor == s))
     && s.receivedApproval(s.getInstituteDirector()) == 'true' ;
}
```

4.2 Policy Reasoning

In KAoS, various inferences can be performed for a variety of purposes, such as detecting and harmonizing conflicting policies (e.g., is any negative authorization policy denying the same action or a subclass of the same action?), disclosing related policies (e.g. which policies deal the approval of the institute director?), or reasoning about future actions based on knowledge of policies in force (e.g. which entity can read from or write to the database of examination grades?). The power and efficiency of description logics can be leveraged to their full extent, and the use of JTP allows going beyond description logic where necessary. Queries can also be written in Rei through its expressive query language. Rei relies on the Prolog reasoning engine to analyze the policies and can reason over domain-dependent ontologies by automatically translating the RDF policies into triples. In KAoS, this conversion is hidden from the users by Stanford's Java Theorem Prover that converts the knowledge base into triples before reasoning over them and providing only the end results. In Rei, the users have the ability to directly manage the intermediate form. For example, it is possible to create a policy by using the conversion to triple of any instance of a domain dependent class. Moreover, users have the capability to access the policy instances in this form by submitting some Prolog queries to the policy engine.

The increased representational power of DAML/OWL over RDF-S allows more powerful forms of policy inference to be used by developers and users. Moreover, because all aspects of KAoS representation are encoded purely in DAML/OWL, any third-party tool or environment supporting DAML/OWL can perform specialized analyses of the full knowledge base completely independent of KAoS itself, thus easing integration with an increasingly sophisticated range of new tools and language enhancements in the future.

Finally, Ponder can detect modality and application specific conflicts in policies, such as conflicts of duty. Ponder policy rules are translated into an event calculus representation that describes the semantics of the policy language. Abductive reasoning techniques are exploited to analyze the policy specifications to identify existing conflicts and provide explanations on how they might arise [21].

4.3 Policy Deployment

In KAoS, the abstract representation of actions (in contrast to the method calls in Ponder) is both a boon and a bane. On the one hand, this abstraction allows KAoS to be adapted for just about any platform that has the requisite enforcement hooks. On the other hand, deployment in any given platform requires the availability of a specific enforcer for the policy Action Class, i.e., in our example for the EncryptedCommunicationAction class. If such an enforcer does not already exist, it must be implemented. Its design is usually a non trivial task and requires programmers to have a deep understanding of the action class and its mapping to the platform. As libraries of enforcers for common actions across platforms are developed, this will become less and less of an issue.

Rei, as explained in Section 3.2, does not provide any enforcement support and this is one of the main drawbacks of exploiting this language for practical applications. In addition, even if the engine accepts ontology-based policy specification, the main policy management is over the Rei constructs. This is a constraint when compared to KAoS that manages the policy in its original form, leaving to the implementing platforms the possibility to choose the most appropriate run-time representation.

In Ponder, the main advantage of modeling policy actions at a low level of abstraction is that they can be directly implemented in Java with little additional effort. This is the reason for its wide adoption in many existing systems.[6] For example, the communication policy example can be simply implemented by a proxy object with the same interface of the CommunicationChannel object. When the 'communication' method is invoked by the policy subject, the proxy grants/denies the communication permission according to the caller identity and to the specified constraint.

For the sake of clarity, Table 3 reports and synthesizes some of the features of the three approaches discussed in the previous Sections.

Table 3. Features of KAoS, Rei, and Ponder

	KAoS	Rei	Ponder
Ontology-based	Yes	Yes	No
Specification language	DAML/OWL	Rei: (Prolog-like syntax + RDF-S)	Ponder (declarative specification)
Tools for policy specification	KPAT – Graphical editor for ontology and policy management	No** ** a GUI is being developed for the next Rei version	Graphical editor and compiler
Reasoning support	Java Theorem Prover	Prolog engine	Event calculus representation
Enforcement mechanisms	Need to write the code of appropriate enforcers and to insert them in entities to control ** ** Policy automation being explored for the next version	Action execution is outside the Rei engine	Java interfaces for enforcement agents are provided
Flexibility	Ontology can be extended with domain dependent descriptions of local entities	Ontology can be extended with domain dependent descriptions of local entities	Management domain as a structuring technique for partitioning complex object systems

4.4 Discussion

As the previous sections made clear, each form of policy representation exhibits pros and cons and thus the choice of an approach should be driven by the characteristics of the application domain and by the application requirements.

However, our experience to date seems to indicate quite clearly that, apart from the specific considerations of the representation employed, the adoption of Semantic Web representations provide more advantages than drawbacks. Table 4 compares generic Semantic Web approaches to policy specification (KAoS, Rei) to the Ponder approach that is used as a representative of the non-ontology-based languages. The comparison takes into consideration the basic language requirements pointed out in Section 3.

Ontologies simplify the task of governing the behavior of complex environments. The possibility of representing entities and behaviors at multiple levels of abstraction improves the global ***expressiveness,*** allowing flexibility in dealing with several kinds of contexts at different level of specifications. The use of ontologies permits the

[6] The automatic generation of native Java VM policies directly from KPAT is under development in KAoS.

policy framework to be easily extended simply adding new concepts to the ontology. In traditional languages this task is usually much trickier. For example in Ponder the specification of the communication policy example requires the non-trivial effort to extend the policy language or to convert the policy into a resource control policy. In addition, the possibility of modeling policies at a high level of abstraction allows users to focus their attention more on high-level management requirements than on implementation details, such as the method names in Ponder.

An ontology-based description of the policy enables the system to use concepts to describe the environments and the entities being controlled, thus simplifying their description and improving the ***analyzability*** of the system. Policy frameworks can take advantage of this powerful feature, such as policy conflict detection and harmonization. In addition, ontology-based approaches simplify access to policy information, with the possibility of dynamically calculating relations between policies and the environment, entities, or other policies based on ontology relations rather than fixing them in advance. Like databases, it is possible to access the information provided by querying the ontology according to the ontology schema. This is an advantage in comparison to traditional languages that provide only pre-defined queries to access information and static representations of policy. How to design the ontology is an application dependent problem. As in database design, ontologies should be designed and extended consistent with the application context and optimized for the most common queries. Finally, ontologies can also simplify the sharing of policy knowledge among different organizations and applications, thus increasing the possibility for entities to negotiate policies and to agree on a common set of policies.

However, the adoption of ontologies for policy specification requires addressing some technical difficulties.

Semantic web languages used for ontology representation still present a complex syntax, long declarative description, and hyperlinks and references to external resources that make the code very difficult to read (e.g., compare the readability of a Ponder policy with a DAML policy). To improve the ***ease of use*** of these languages, graphical interfaces or other tools for policy specification should be adopted. For example, KPAT provides a graphical interface for policy specification and management but such tool always exacts a price in continued development to keep up with significant changes in foundational ontologies; while Rei provides a simplified language for policy specification that hides the complexity of the semantic representation even if it burdens the user with the task of learning an additional language.

Finally, ***enforceability*** is a critical aspect for semantic web languages. Ontology-based policy specification can be difficult to implement in comparison to other policy specification such as Ponder, because of the high level specification of ontology-based policies can be far removed from the concrete implementation of the policy enforcement on the systems. Usually the gap between the specification and the implementation of policies cannot be completely overcome in an automated manner, but has to be resolved to a greater or lesser degree by human programmers consistent with the capabilities and features of each platform. For example, independent of the semantic representation adopted, the implementation of an enforcer for the policy example requires the enforcers to locate the Professor agents in the system to control, to intercept any attempt to send data to Student agents (this task might also require the addition of code in the agent), and to query the policy repository with an appropriate description of the action. Enforcement code generation facilities and libraries of enforcement mechanisms adapted to specific platforms are among the most important features for policy management frameworks to provide to enable their widespread implementation.

Table 4. Comparison between semantic web and traditional languages

	Semantic web languages for policy specification	Ponder ** ** used as example of non-semantic web language
Expressiveness	Capable of representing concepts and behavior of any complex environment	Capable of controlling specific sorts of behavior within object-oriented systems
	Multiple levels of abstraction	Low level of abstraction: object level
	Easy to extend policy ontology at runtime with new concepts	Extensibility supported by object-oriented inheritance at compile-time
Analyzability	Ontology representation simplifies and directly supports policy reasoning, conflict detection and harmonization	Conflict detection requires transforming policy specification into an event calculus representation
	Simplified access to policy information by querying the ontology	Access to single policy object by API – Access to policy repository to be designed
Ease-of-use	Need of specialized tools to assist unskilled users with policy specification and interpretation	Language specifically designed for simple policy specification and direct readability
Enforceability	High-level specification requires skilled programmers or sophisticated policy automation mechanisms for enforcement	Detailed specifications can be directly mapped into policy enforcement mechanisms
	Policy sharing among heterogeneous systems requires an agreement on a common ontology	Policy sharing among heterogeneous systems requires agreement on interfaces

5 Conclusion

Policy based approaches to systems management are of particular importance because they allow the separation of the rules that govern the behavior of a system from the functionality provided by that system [11]. Research into policy based systems management has focused on languages for specifying policies and architectures for managing and deploying policies in distributed environments and complex systems, such as multi-agent systems. This paper has described similarities and differences among three important policy management approaches: KAoS, Rei and Ponder.

Existing approaches have generated divergent solutions that tend to be best suited for particular ranges of applications and discourage a common approach for all situations. Ideally, a common approach to specifying and deploying policy for the management aspects of all application domains is desirable to simplify policy analysis and reduce policy inconsistencies and conflicts and to facilitate policy reuse across various systems. Notwithstanding this ideal, the concept of a universal programming language has never been successful and it is not clear why a common approach should succeed for policy specification and deployment. Although we hope to conduct more formal and thorough analyses in the future, our examination of the issues to date indicate promising advantages in the adoption of Semantic Web languages for policy representation and reasoning.

References

1. N. Damianou, N. Dulay, E. Lupu, M. Sloman: The Ponder Policy Specification Language. In proceedings of Workshop on Policies for Distributed Systems and Networks (POLICY 2001). Springer-Verlag, LNCS 1995, Bristol, UK, (2001)
2. J. M. Bradshaw, P. Beautement, L. Bunch, S. V. Drakunov, P. Feltovich, R.R. Hoffman, R. Jeffers, M. Johnson, S. Kulkarni, A.K. Raj, N. Suri, A. Uszok: Making Agents Acceptable to People. In N. Zhong and J. Liu (Eds.), Intelligent Technologies for Information Analysis: Advances in Agents, Data Mining, and Statistical Learning, Berlin: Springer Verlag, in press, (2003)
3. M. Johnson, P. Chang, R. Jeffers, J. Bradshaw, V-W. Soo, M. Breedy, L. Bunch, S. Kulkarni, J. Lott, N. Suri, A. Uszok: KAoS semantic policy and domain services: An application of DAML to Web-Services-based grid architectures. Proceedings of the AAMAS 03 Workshop on Web Services and Agent-Based Engineering, Melbourne, Australia, July, (2003)
4. A. Uszok, J. Bradshaw, R. Jeffers, N. Suri, P. Hayes, M. Breedy, L. Bunch, M. Johnson, S. Kulkarni, J. Lott: KAoS policy and domain services: Toward a description-logic approach to policy representation, deconfliction, and enforcement. In Proceedings of IEEE Fourth International Workshop on Policy (Policy 2003). Lake Como, Italy, 4–6 June, Los Alamitos, CA: IEEE Computer Society, pp. 93–98, (2003)
5. J. M. Bradshaw, A. Uszok, R. Jeffers, N. Suri, M. Burstein: Representation and reasoning for DAML-based policy and domain services in KAoS and Nomads. Proceedings of the Autonomous Agents and Multi-Agent Systems Conference (AAMAS 2003). Melbourne, Australia, New York, NY: ACM Press, pp. 835–842, (2003)
6. L. Kagal, T. Finin, A. Johshi: A Policy Language for Pervasive Computing Environment. In Proceedings of IEEE Fourth International Workshop on Policy (Policy 2003). Lake Como, Italy, 4–6 June, Los Alamitos, CA: IEEE Computer Society, pp. 63–76, (2003).
7. L. Kagal: Rei: A Policy Language for the Me-Centric Project. HP Labs Technical Report, HPL-2002-270, (2002)
8. E. C. Lupu, M. Sloman: Conflicts in policy-based distributed system management. IEEE Transaction on Software Engineering, Vol. 25, No. 6, (1999)
9. M. Sloman: Policy Driven Management for distributed Systems. Plenum Press Journal of Network and Systems Management, Vol. 2, No. 4, (1994), 333–360
10. P. Feltovich, J. M. Bradshaw, R. Jeffers, A. Uszok: Order and KAoS: Using policy to represent agent cultures. In Proceedings of the AAMAS 03 Workshop on Humans and Multi-Agent Systems. July, Melbourne, Australia
11. S. Wright, R. Chadha, G. Lapiotis (eds.): Special Issue on Policy Based Networking. IEEE Network, Vol. 16, No. 2, March, (2002), 8–56
12. J. Fritz Barnes, R. Pandey: CacheL: Language Support for Customizable Caching Policies. In Proceedings of 4th Interantional Web Caching Workshop, San Diego, CA, (1999)
13. J. Hoagland: Specifying and Implementing Security Policies Using LaSCO, the Language for Security Constraints on Objects. Ph.D. dissertation, UC Davis, (2000)
14. N. Damianou, N. Dulay, E. C. Lupu, M. Sloman: Ponder: A Language for Specifying Security and Management Policies for Distributed Systems. Imperial College, UK, Research Report Department of Computing 2001, (2000)
15. The IETF Policy Framework Working Group: Charter available at http://www.ietf.org/html.charters/policy-charter.html
16. D. N. Allsopp, P. Beautement, J. M. Bradshaw, E. H. Durfee, M. Kirton, C.A. Knoblock, N. Suri, A. Tate, C. W. Tompson: Coalition Agents Experiment: Multiagent Cooperation in International Coalitions. IEEE Intelligent Systems, Vol. 17, No. 3, (2002), 26–35

17. J. M. Bradshaw, M. Sierhuis, A. Acquisti, P. Feltovich, R. Hoffman, R. Jeffers, D. Prescott, N. Suri, A. Uszok, R. Van Hoof: Adjustable autonomy and human-agent teamwork in practice: An interim report on space applications. In H. Hexmoor, R. Falcone, & C. Castelfranchi (Ed.), Agent Autonomy. Dordrecht, The Netherlands: Kluwer, (2003), pp. 243–280
18. N. Suri, J.M. Bradshaw, M.R. Breedy, P.T. Groth, G.A. Hill, R. Jeffers: Strong Mobility and Fine-Grained Resource Control in NOMADS. In Proceedings of the 2nd International Symposium on Agents Systems and Applications and the 4th International Symposium on Mobile Agents (ASA/MA2000). Springer-Verlag, (2000)
19. M. Kahn, C. Cicalese: CoABS Grid Scalability Experiments. O.F. Rana (Ed.), 2nd International Workshop on Infrastructure for Scalable Multi-Agent Systems at the 5th International Conference on Autonomous Agents. Montreal, CA, New York: ACM Press, (2001)
20. N. Damianou, N. Dulay, E. Lupu, M. Sloman, T. Tonouchi: Tools for Domain-based Policy Management of Distributed Systems. In Proceedings of Network Operations and Management Symposium (NOMS'02). IEEE Press, Florence, Italy, (2002), 203–217
21. A. K. Bandara, E. Lupu, A. Russo: Using Event Calculus to Formalise Policy Specification and Analysis. In Proceedings of 4th IEEE workshop on Policies for Distributed Systems and Networks (POLICY 2003), Lake Como, Italy, (2003)
22. N. Dulay, E. Lupu, M Sloman, N. Damianou: A Policy Deployment Model for the Ponder Language. In Proceedings of IEEE/IFIP International Symposium on Integrated Network Management (IM'2001). IEEE Press, Seattle, May 2001
23. R. Montanari, G. Tonti, C. Stefanelli: A Policy-based Mobile Agent Infrastructure. In Proceedings of 2003 Symposium on Applications and the Internet (SAINT 2003). IEEE Press, Orlando, Florida, US, (2003), 370–379

An Agent Framework for Inter-personal Information Sharing with an RDF-Based Repository

Koji Kamei, Sen Yoshida*, Kazuhiro Kuwabara**, Jun-ichi Akahani, and Tetsuji Satoh

NTT Communication Science Laboratories, NTT Corporation
2-4 Hikaridai, Seika-cho, Soraku-gun, Kyoto 619-0237 Japan
kamei@cslab.kecl.ntt.co.jp

Abstract. In this paper, we propose a framework for personal agents that supports inter-personal information exchange and sharing. The framework offers a repository-centered architecture in which a user can store information resources and annotations. On this framework, applications work collaboratively with the help of the event notification mechanism.

The personal agent especially targets the collecting and utilizing of information that describes how the user handled information resources. The descriptions of interactions are obtained by applications on the agent framework and stored into the RDF repository as annotations to the original information resources. A personal agent consists of applications that utilize these "annotations about interaction" for infortion sharing.

We first discuss "annotation about interaction" in personal environments, then describe the current implementation of our framework that offers an RDF-based repository. The experimental implementation of both communication-oriented and information-sharing-oriented applications on this framework is introduced as a starting point for our approach.

1 Introduction

In collaborative activity between individuals, sharing and exchanging information play important roles in communication. We receive a great deal of information from other individuals, interpret it and reflect on it using our own knowledge, after which we produce new information and forward it to other individuals. We propose a framework for personal agents that aims to support this type of information sharing and exchange. We primarily target the phases of receiving information and its subsequent use; in other words, our framework aims to support the reflexive phase in an individual's activity. To realize this objective, the personal agent utilizes the user's personal annotations that each individual privately adds to information resources stored at hand.

Here, the annotations primarily include verbal annotations that users explicitly added to information resources, and in addition to them, descriptions of interaction between users and information. More specifically, the latter describes how one has handled a

* Presently with Research and Development Center, Nippon Telegraph and Telephone West Corporation.

** Presently with ATR Intelligent Robotics and Communication Laboratories.

D. Fensel et al. (Eds.): ISWC 2003, LNCS 2870, pp. 438–452, 2003.

resource, such as, "the timestamp when the user read a document," "the folder to which the user moved an e-mail," and "other users to whom the user introduced a Web page." In other words, the annotations that we are concerned with here, describe both the interaction between a user and items of information, and that between the user and other users. By adding such annotations of interaction, the agent system can organize and reuse information items for its user. Thus, by utilizing the organized knowledge, the agent can support its user's communication activities.

When annotations are added interactively and organization becomes complicated, it is appropriate to use a schema-less, semi-structured database [1,2]. We have employed the resource description framework (RDF) [3] to describe these types of annotations about interaction. In this case, individuals and documents are mapped as *resources* in an RDF statement, and interactions are mapped as *predicates*.

It is natural and easy to use RDF statements to describe annotations of interactions. However, ontologies on interaction and information handling have not been adequately discussed to date, due to the difficulty in defining the vocabulary of interaction dissociated from cases of actual use, as opposed to the clearly defined class hierarchies of vocabulary for knowledge representation. It is also addressed in [4] that ontologies must be able to evolve continuously. The current implementation status of our framework described in this paper supplies a means for developing RDF-based annotations of interaction, and contributes to refining the definition of vocabularies through actual implementation of application systems. Defining vocabularies about interaction is not only a challenge in ontology engineering, but also a challenge in information design [5]. In our approach, designing applications that help users to handle information resources is inseparable from defining vocabularies about information handling. In other words, defining ontologies about information handling and interaction will lead information designers to invent new applications.

In this paper, we describe an agent framework with an RDF-based personal repository. First, we discuss requirements for the personal repository and annotations in the personal environment, then describe the framework's current implementation status. We also describe the experimental implementation of two types of existing applications on our framework as a starting point for this approach: CommunityOrganizer [6] and Gleams of People [7] for communication-oriented applications, Nakif [8,9] and KVP2P [10] for information-sharing-oriented ones.

2 Personal Agent for Supporting Interaction

2.1 Personalized Information Repository

The aim of the personal agent is to support information exchange and sharing between individuals. This type of agent is classified as an information agent according to the agent technology roadmap [11]. To achieve this, it is necessary that an individual can easily utilize information resources that he or she has handled. We focus on information storage that is deployed beside the user, storing any type of information resources the user has handled.

A personal repository is essentially a storage system that privately accumulates the information resources a user has handled. The repository stores not only information resources such as documents, but also metadata as annotation to information resources. Here, metadata includes information about how the user handled information resources, since we are focusing on interaction between the user and information resources. The repository employs the resource description framework (RDF) to describe these semi-structured annotations.

The Haystack project is a well-known project that also employs semi-structured storage for accumulating and modeling personal information [12]. Haystack and our personal repository can share both the approach to back-end storage systems and the whole objective that the system supports personal information exchange. Both projects have recently focused on user interface matter; however, current interests seems to be different. Haystack is focusing on making use of RDF as a component architecture for re-configurable user interfaces; that is, how to develop user interfaces [13]. Their prototype interface, named Ozone, is dynamically constructed at runtime, and the programming language, named Adenine, supports the definition of the user interface in RDF. On the other hand, our personal repository focuses on what type of metadata should be stored and watched while a user interacts with the user interfaces; that is, how to design user interface and user interaction. The system architecture needs to support interaction between the repository and user interface modules, and ontologies that can describe the metadata about interaction should be defined. There exist differences between current interests, although these approaches do not conflict with each other.

Our proposed agent framework is designed to support communication activities on this RDF-based personal repository. The framework offers an event notification mechanism to help implement services and applications that constitute a personal agent. Since multiple application modules run collaboratively on a personal agent framework and share information items and RDF statements in the repository, they need to be notified when the data that they are referring to change.

2.2 Annotations in Personal Environments

In the context of the Semantic Web, annotations change Web pages from human-readable ones to machine-readable ones. The case introduced with the Semantic Web explains that the annotations to a Web page are added by the page's publisher and published world-wide. This model can be classified as a publisher-driven, open-style method of annotation.

On the other hand, information resources acquired by individuals are not limited to public items such as Web pages, but also include non-public items such as private e-mails. Moreover, private information is often more important than public information; therefore it would be natural to suppose that users would also add annotations to items of private information. Furthermore, it is important to pay attention to the receiver-side annotations in addition to publisher-side annotations.

Although both the RDF model and other existing implementations of the annotation server cover this type of receiver-side annotation, the use of personal annotations have not yet been mentioned. For example, the scenario described by the Annotea project [14] proposes a case for their use, in which an annotation server is deployed globally to collect and share the annotation statements, and clients then share the server. It also allows multiple servers to exist for different purposes and for different groups of users. It does not, however, address the concept of private annotation servers and collaboration.

Nejdl *et al.* [15] discussed collaborative annotation as a part of EDUTELLA, which is a framework that allows communication between different RDF repositories. They proposed a modification exchange language designed to keep decentralized repositories coherent. Although the language is useful for exchanging personal annotations, their interests seem to be directed toward coherency rather than individuality.

2.3 Design Problem in Personal Agents

Annotations are usually added by hand. To add annotations about information handling, however, it is desirable that annotations are added automatically by applications according to operations the user executed on those applications.

Two problems arise when dealing with such applications. One is to define vocabularies for describing interaction between individuals and information resources. This relates to the ontology definition problem in the Semantic Web. The other is to design applications that lead users to handle information resources along the defined vocabularies. The latter is covered by researches into both information design and interaction design.

Those two problems are mutually dependent and should be solved simultaneously; that is, information designers need to consider the defining ontology of interaction. To aid this design process, we propose a personal agent framework with an RDF-based personal repository that accumulates information resources and annotations, especially with vocabulary about interaction.

2.4 Information Sharing between Personal Environments

In the environment described above, information resources are assumed to be stored locally beside the user, and gradually shared through peer-to-peer information exchange.

Information items exchanged between people are not limited to messages they have written, but also include introductions to information items that another person has created. In other words, a message created by a user can be received by another person through peer-to-peer intentional message forwarding. In this sense, for example, *forwarded* and *introduced* can be included in information-sharing vocabularies.

Exchanging and sharing information is obviously an interaction between individuals, but at the same time, it is also an interaction between an individual and information resources. Keeping track of this kind of interaction is necessary to design applications for smooth information sharing and exchange.

3 Personal Repository

In this section, we describe the architecture and implementation of a personal repository that enables and utilizes the personal annotations.

A personal agent exists beside each user to support his or her activities, and a personal repository occupies the center of our personal agent framework; that is, a personal

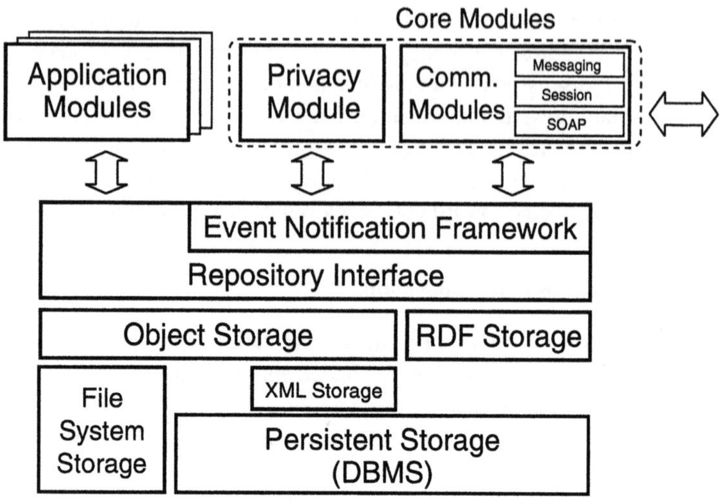

Fig. 1. Architecture of the personal repository

repository exists for each user and accumulates information and annotations that its owner has handled. A personal agent consists of groups of various programs that store and make use of information organized upon the personal repository.

The personal repository is currently implemented in a Java2 SDK 1.4 environment, and employs various open-source products relating to Web and XML technologies. The whole system architecture is shown in Figure 1. We first describe three core modules of the personal repository, then address its programming interface and a visual interface.

3.1 Back-End Storage

The personal repository needs to support the features of an RDF database, since relationships between resources can be described as RDF statements. Additionally, an auxiliary information storage is required to save these items and issue a URI to each one. Object-oriented database systems or XML database systems with Object-XML mapping features are suitable for this requirement.

Data in personal repositories are stored in both Object storage and RDF storage. The former assigns a URI to each object so that the items can be addressed using URIs from RDF statements, while the latter holds RDF statements that describe relationships between information items: items stored in Object storage and items defined outside the repository. Both types of storage possess specialized retrieval functions.

The RDF storage is implemented on a Jena Semantic Web toolkit [1]. For the back-end storage of Jena, PostgreSQL [2] is used for persistency. Objects are stored in several sub-storages. Messages that encoded into XML format are stored in an XML storage that

[1] http://www.hpl.hp.com/semweb/jena-top.html
[2] http://www.postgresql.org/

utilizes eXist[3], which implements XML:DB API [4] and shares the back-end PostgreSQL system with the RDF storage. Images and HTML files are stored into a file-system-based storage for ease of browsing from Web browsers. Other objects are currently stored in the PostgreSQL as text data.

3.2 Event Notification Framework

Since multiple applications run simultaneously on a personal agent framework and share RDF statements and information items in the repository, they need to be notified when the data that they are referring to have changed. An event notification framework enables application modules to collaborate with each other. That is, personal agent consist of multiple application modules that are activated by the event notification framework on the repository. The repository contains a group of core modules that are started when the repository is invoked. In addition, the repository can contain various modules that are registered by applications invoked by the user. Since multiple applications can listen to a repository simultaneously, a *write* operation (of an RDF statement or XML document) performed by a certain application module may trigger another application. As a result, coordination among applications can be realized.

The event notification framework is built upon both types of storage described in the previous section. This feature is based on the concept of the active database [16]. Referring to the ECA model, this framework monitors *write* operations to the storage as an *event*. It then notifies application modules of modifications such as registration of an RDF statement related to particular nodes and/or predicates, or registration of an XML document with a specific element and/or value. Each module registers a template pattern for each *condition* from which it desires to be notified of the change. The current implementation of the personal repository provides Java level API for event notification framework, therefore, the template pattern (condition) should be represented as a Java object. The syntax of the template pattern for the XML repository is defined as an XML element and represented as an instance of `org.w3c.dom.Element` class. For the RDF repository, the template is described as an RDF statement with wildcards. The `Template` class resembles to the `Statement` interface in Jena, but allows to set null value for each element (subject, predicate and object) to represent the wildcard value.

When the *condition* is satisfied, the *action* clause is processed. Currently the action clause should be written in Java as a callback function. Overall behavior of the agent and applications is realized as results of the interaction among those modules invoked by changes of data in the repository. The coordination between user interface modules and the repository is also implemented in this callback method.

The repository is considered as a type of a shared blackboard in the framework since a group of programs works collaboratively for the owner, although it does not offer any layered structure, unlike the (distributed) blackboard model [17]. The layers or structures will be defined as data by RDF statements when some program requires such kinds of structures.

[3] http://exist-db.org/

[4] http://www.xmldb.org/xapi/index.html

The event notification framework can also be compared with tuple-space-based systems such as Linda [18], especially while watching RDF statements. Our framework offers both a blocking and a non-blocking *read* operation. After a *read* operation has been processed, the matched element remains in the repository since it is not a discrete tuple but a part of organized structure of information. If it is necessary to remove some elements, users need to give instructions to remove them in the action clause of the rule.

3.3 Communication between Personal Agents

The communication layer between personal agents is based on the concept of peer-to-peer communication; that is, each agent can send messages directly to any other known agents, and in actual cases of group communication, messages may also be exchanged in a server-oriented manner.

The repository keeps acquintances' information, that is, mappings between the acquintance's name and his or her agent's address (a URL for inter-agent communication). The system does not actually define any hard limit to the number of entries, although the address list might usually contain handleds of users since this framework supports information exchange between acquintances. It does not mean that the system only supports communication in a closed community, because users can forward information from one acquintance to another, just like in our real-world experience. Information exchange between more than a thousand of repositories will be realized by multi-hop communication.

The address list is currently maintained in two ways. A user can maintain the list entries by hand through applications' user interfaces such as Gleams of People (described below). Another is the tentative use of peer discovery in a LAN, since acquintances with whom a user closely shares information exist in the same LAN. The current implementation of this function is implemented as a module upon the repository with Rendezvous technology[5]. It acquires mappings between an acquintance's name and its URL from Rendezvous, then updates information in the repository. Peer discovery from outside a LAN has not been implemented yet; however, it can be implemented as a similar module that refers global white/yellow pages and subsequently updates the repository.

The protocol for communication between personal repositories supports two features: one is connection management, which determines where the peer exists, and the other is a simple messaging feature that delivers an XML document to the peer. These protocols are implemented as messaging services on SOAP [6], which is a lightweight protocol intended for exchanging structured information in a decentralized, distributed environment. We defined the protocol using SOAP to keep the protocol itself independent of Java language in order to secure interoperability. Although SOAP provides a range of features, such as remote procedure calls, message forwarding, etc., we employ its message exchange feature on the HTTP protocol to exchange XML elements. Currently, the services are implemented with Apache Axis [7] SOAP library and deployed to Tomcat [8] servlet containers. Since inter-repository communication is performed in a

[5] http://developer.apple.com/darwin/projects/rendezvous/

[6] http://www.w3.org/TR/soap12-part0/

[7] http://xml.apache.org/axis/

[8] http://jakarta.apache.org/tomcat/

peer-to-peer manner, each repository needs to invoke its own servlet container to receive requests from other repositories.

At this communication level, each agent can request other agents to notify changes in their repositories by remotely registering notification conditions described in the previous section. When a listener registration request arrives from another agent on the communication layer, a listener proxy is created and registered to the repository. When the proxy listener is fired from the repository, the proxy listener composes a message that describes the event, and sends it to the remote listener. A privacy management module is deployed to protect privacy. This module monitors the registration of condition templates from other repositories and decides whether to acccept the registration of the listener.

3.4 Programming Interface

The programming interface to the repository is currently defined at the Java API level. Since it is a type of storage system, modification and query are primitive APIs. It is obviously necessary to define a query language independent from low-level APIs. We are currently in the process of designing a repository query language that supports not only the query/update function, but also our event notification framework. We also plan to implement a script engine for the language as a service on the event notification layer.

3.5 Repository Viewer

While developing modules for a personal repository, we also implemented a repository viewer as one of the development support tools. The repository viewer is a tool for browsing and/or authoring RDF statements and XML documents stored in a repository. When a user specifies the URI of a node in the repository, it retrieves RDF statements that describe the specified node as its subject or object. The result is represented in two forms: graphic representation in a two-dimensional plane, and list-like representation.

The graphical view in Figure 2a shows the resource node to which a user is paying attention located at the center of the view, while other nodes located around the view are resources that are arranged in two hops according to their relationship with the center node. By pointing to the edge with a mouse, the RDF triple of the edge is displayed at the bottom of the screen. By clicking a node on the view, the view is updated to place the clicked node at the screen's center. In the listing view (Figure 2b), the *predicate* of incoming edges is listed on the left of the screen, and outgoing edges on the right. A list of all subject nodes is also provided to support direct jumps to other nodes.

Although its current representation is limited, this tool is helpful in developing our application because it allows us to inspect and modify the items in the repository while in operation. Since the tool also monitors the repository's event notification framework, the the changes in the repository are immediately reflected in the view.

4 Existing Applications of Repository

In this section, we introduce several applications being implemented on the personal agent framework. Two types of applications are described: first, two communication-

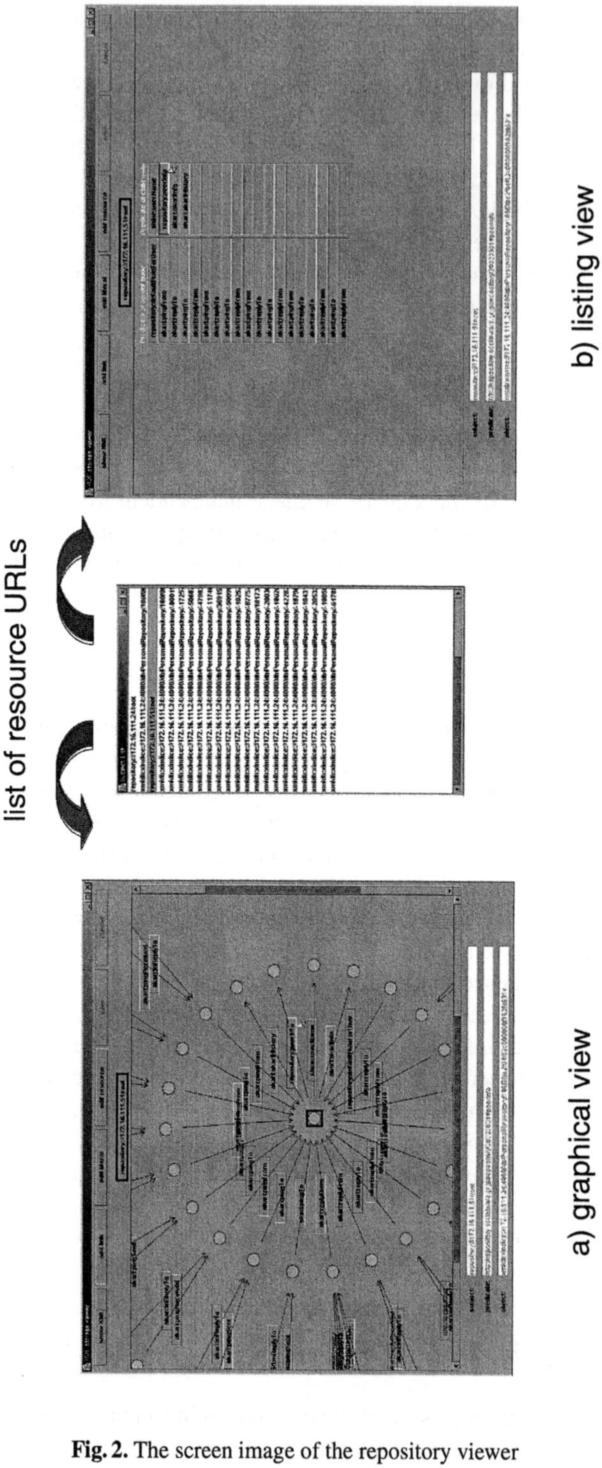

Fig. 2. The screen image of the repository viewer

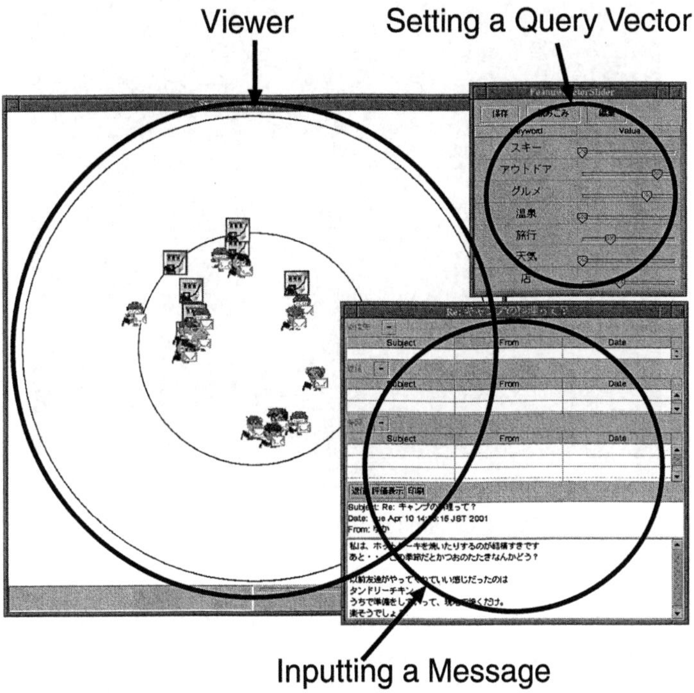

Fig. 3. CommunityOrganizer (screen image)

oriented applications, CommunityOrganizer and Gleams of People, then two information-sharing-oriented applications, Nakif and KVP2P.

4.1 CommunityOrganizer

CommunityOrganizer provides a shared space where public short messages and Web page introductions are exchanged, and in which people are made aware of possible communities of interests. Since the exchanged messages are similar to e-mail, they contain header information such as *sender*, *subject*, *timestamp of creation time*, etc. — fields that are represented as annotations to a message in RDF storage. Users can also introduce resources on the Web to their communities. In this case, the URI of the resource is described instead of verbal messages.

Figure 3 shows the primary component of CommunityOrganizer's user interface, on which information items relevant to the user's interests are shown as icons on the two-dimensional display. Icons are arranged so that relevant icons are located closer and form clusters, and the view is updated when new information items are added, enabling users to become aware of the dynamic formation of information clusters.

The event notification framework of the personal repository notifies the application module of messages' arrival to update the visualization. In other words, when several

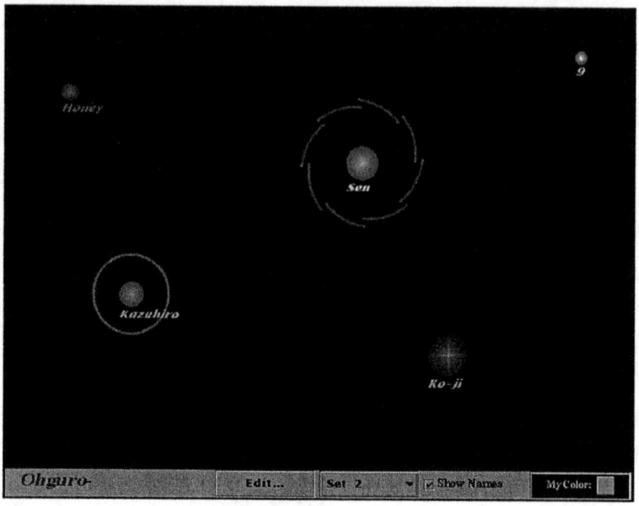

Fig. 4. Gleams of People (screen image)

messages concerning a topic are posted in a short period, the messages (and relevant resources) move to create an animated cluster.

To calculate the relevance between the view and resources, a feature vector is added for each resource to represent the content. The vector is described as an XML document consisting of a set of keyword-value pairs, and stored as an annotation (linked with the *content feature* predicate) to the original message.

4.2 Gleams of People

Gleams of People is a very lightweight communication medium that is designed to convey a simple greeting (such as "how are you?") or a message simply intended for keeping in touch [7]. Figure 4 shows a screen image of Gleams of People.

A message can be sent by touching the sphere corresponding to the intended receiver. The content of the message is just a "color," which represents the mood of the sender. When a message is received at the receiver's end, a sphere gleams with the color sent, then the receiver's agent automatically sends back its owner's mood. In this way, it conveys *things that are not so important to talk about, but that are still worth expressing*.

The spheres indicate presence and status information of corresponding users at a glance, and also unobtrusively indicate the history of communication activities; that is, the interval for which the sphere gleams reflects the number of messages received from the corresponding user, because it is important to present the communication history to the user in order to foster social relationships.

With a personal repository, the system can record the *akari status* that describes how the gleam is expressed, and the history of exchanged messages with respect to its user.

4.3 Nakif

Nakif is a hybrid filtering technique that incorporates a content-based method into a collaborative filtering system, thus it provides high-quality evaluations of communities of interests [8].

When a user evaluates a document in Nakif, that is, assigns a *positive* or *negative* score to the document, the evaluation is shared among members in the communities of interest. When a user receives an evaluation, Nakif appends the *evaluation* as an annotation to the evaluated resource, and updates the evaluator's *user profile* vector based on the *evaluation* and the *content feature* of the resource. The learning module in Nakif gathers those *user profile* vectors and treats the collection as a *user profile matrix*.

When an information resource or an evaluation of a resource arrives from another user, Nakif will be invoked by the repository. It then locally evaluates the resource (arrived or evaluated) and stores the calculated score as an annotation to the resource. The change will influence other applications, such as CommunityOrganizer.

One alternative application of Nakif is that a personal agent can automatically forward a newly received (or evaluated) information resource to other agents. With the user profile matrix described above, Nakif can estimate users who will evaluate the document positively. This inversed utilization of original Nakif enables information sharing with two-way information filtering.

4.4 KVP2P

KVP2P [10] appends two features to the personal agent. One is a personalized information retrieval method with a personalized concept-base, while the other is a method for collaborative information retrieval between personal repositories. A personal repository accumulates each user's information and its structure; therefore, it reflects its owner's interests and communication activities. Because such a system requires an IR mechanism as one of its basic functionalities, we employed a concept-based IR system as a search engine for personal repositories.

The "concept base" is an extended vector space model for information retrieval [19] that is grounded in co-occurrence to solve the above problem. This method first counts the word co-occurrences that occur in proximity in the documents, then constructs a word co-occurrence matrix. Second, it reduces the rank of the matrix using singular value decomposition (SVD) to yield the keywords' vector space. The vector for a document is represented as the sum of the keyword vectors generated from it, and in this method, documents having similar content have strong relevance even if the documents do not use the same expressions. Since the personal repository contains information resources that accurately describe its owner's interests, we have proposed a method for constructing a personalized co-occurrence-based concept-base on the personal repository [20].

The personalized concept-base facilitates information retrieval in a personal repository. However, a new problem arises when querying to other users' personal repositories: since the documents in personal repositories differ from each other, the derived concept-base for each repository also differs. That is, simply transferring query requests does not provide desirable results. To solve this problem, KVP2P offers an IR function that searches for documents in equalized vector spaces. A scheme for vector space equalization, the automated relevance feedback scheme, is proposed and implemented as a service on the repository-based personal agent framework. The idea is derived from the technique known as relevance feedback. Conventional relevance feedback is a human-to-computer feedback technique in which a human judges whether documents retrieved by a computer are desirable. On the other hand, in the proposed scheme, the caller's personal agent can judge the adequacy of the documents by using the concept-base to establish the feedback loop automatically.

4.5 Discussion

The applications described above have, except for KVP2P, developed once prior to the personal repository, and have been experimentally integrated. The experience influenced the design of personal repository architecture, which is a common framework based on a semi-structured and active database.

Shine, for example, is a peer-to-peer agent framework that provides basic vocabularies about agents, users, communication and communities [21]. Community Organizer and Gleams of People have been integrated on it. The vocabularies defined in Shine provide a start point for defining vocabularies in this personal agent frameworks. In Shine, the primary elements of the system are an agent and its user, so each agent has *agentID* and *username* attributes. From the perspective of the repository's owner, other users (in the repository) are represented as *acquaintances*.

Another example is the integration of Community Organizer and Nakif [8]. The implementation has changed the information sharing scheme from a server-centered model to a partially distributed model. Here, information sharing is achieved not merely by forwarding all the information obtained, but by filtering the information to be forwarded based on the metadata that describes both the evaluation and the feature of the content. Although the efficiency of collaboration filtering depends on the quality of the content feature vector, in the previous implementation of Nakif the content feature of the document was represented by word frequency. By integrating with personalized concept-base in KVP2P, the efficiency of collaborative filtering is expected to be improved.

5 Summary and Further Issues

In this paper, we described a framework for a communication support agent. In this framework, one personal agent exists for each user and supports his or her communication activities, especially information exchange and sharing. We considered collaboration between individuals as the results of shared annotations. It leads us to propose an RDF-based personal repository framework, the need for vocabularies about interaction, and information design with those vocabularies.

We described the current design and implementation of the personal repository onto which users can store information resources, personally create annotations to those resources, and with which they can exchange and share information resources and annotations. We also described four existing applications being re-implemented on the personal agent framework. They indicated example usages of our repository-based personal agent framework, and direction to define vocabularies for describing interaction.

The next step will require us to add ontology mapping and an approximation mechanism [22] on top of our framework, since application designers will themselves define or improve vocabularies. Vocabularies in this paper are extracted from existing weakly-tied applications, and as a result, the relationship between vocabularies is weakly defined. To support an ontology mapping mechanism, more investigation is required to precisely define the relationship between vocabularies. Future work will also include extracting base classes or properties for ontology structures, and defining causal relationships between vocabularies.

Acknowledgments. The concept of a personal repository arose through continuous discussions with Mr. Kaname Funakoshi and Mr. Takeshi Ohguro. They also gave us useful advice for incorporating their works Nakif and Gleams of People. KVP2P is a research result from collaboration with Dr. Takashi Yukawa at Nagaoka University of Technology. In addition, we wish to thank Mr. Takashi Kawachi and Mr. Koji Saito for the implementation of the personal repository framework and applications.

References

1. Abiteboul, S., Quass, D., McHugh, J., Widom, J., Wiener, J.L.: The Lorel query language for semistructured data. International Journal on Digital Libraries **1** (1997) 68–88
2. Buneman, P., Fernandez, M., Suciu, D.: UnQL: A query language and algebra for semistructured data based on structural recursion. VLDB Journal **9** (2000) 76–110
3. Lassila, O., Swich, R.R.: Resource description framework (RDF) model and syntax specification. Technical report, W3C Recommendation, http://www.w3.org/TR/1999/REC-rdf-syntax-19990222/ (1999)
4. Stojanovic, L., Motik, B.: Ontology evolution within ontology editors. In: EON2002 Evaluation of Ontology-based Tools. (2002) 53–62
5. Jacobson, R., ed.: Information Design. MIT Press (1999)
6. Kamei, K., Fujita, K., Jettmar, E., Yoshida, S., Kuwabara, K.: Effectiveness of spatial representation in the formation of network communities: Experimental study on community organizer. Interacting with Computer **14** (2002) 739–759
7. Ohguro, T.: Towards agents which are suggestive of "Awareness of Connectedness". Trans. IEICE **E84-D** (2001) 957–967
8. Funakoshi, K., Kamei, K., Yoshida, S., Kuwabara, K.: Incorporating content-based collaborative filtering in a community support system. In: Intelligent Agents: Specification, Modeling, and Applications (PRIMA2001 Proceedings). Number 2132 in LNAI (2001) 198–209
9. Funakoshi, K., Ohguro, T.: Evaluation of integrated content-based collaborative filtering. In: 2001 ACM SIGIR Workshop on Recommender Systems. (2001)
10. Yukawa, T., Yoshida, S., Kuwabara, K.: A vector space equalization scheme for a concept-based collaborative information retrieval system. In: Proc. of 16th International FLAIRS Conference. (2003)
11. Luck, M., McBurney, P., Preist, C.: Agent Technology: Enabling Next Generation Computing. AgentLink, http://www.agentlink.org/roadmap/index.html (2003)
12. Adar, E., Karger, D.R., Stein, L.A.: Haystack: Per-user information environments. In: Proc. of 8th International Conference on Information and Knowledge Management (CIKM1999). (1999) 413–422

13. Huynh, D., Karger, D., Quan, D.: Haystack: A platform for creating, organizing and visualizing information using RDF. In: Semantic Web Workshop. (2002)
14. Koivunen, M.R., Swick, R.: Metadata based annotation infrastructure offers flexibility and extensibility for collaborative applications and beyond. In: KCAP 2001 workshop on knowledge markup and semantic annotation. (2001)
15. Nejdl, W., Siberski, W., Simon, B., Tane, J.: Towards a modification exchange language for distributed RDF repositories. In: ISWC2002. Number 2342 in LNCS, Springer-Verlag (2002) 236–249
16. Widom, J., Ceri, S.: Active Database Systems. Morgan Kaufmann (1996)
17. Hayes-Roth, B.: A blackboard architecture for control. Artificial Intelligence **26** (1985) 251–321
18. Gelernter, D.: Generative communication in Linda. ACM Trans. on Programming Languages and Systems **7** (1985) 80–112
19. Schütze, H., Pedersen, J.O.: A cooccurrence-based thesaurus and two applications to information retrieval. Information Processing & Management **33** (1997) 307–318
20. Yoshida, S., Yukawa, T., Kuwabara, K.: Constructing and examining personalized cooccurrence-based thesauri on Web pages. In: Proc. WWW2003. (2003)
21. Yoshida, S., Kamei, K., Ohguro, T., Kuwabara, K.: Shine: A peer-to-peer based framework of network community support systems. Computer Communications (2003) 1199–1209
22. Akahani, J., Hiramatsu, K., Satoh, T.: Approximate query reformulation based on hierarchical ontology mapping. In: Proc. International Workshop on Semantic Web Foundations and Application Technologies. (2003) 43–46

An Environment for Distributed Ontology Development Based on Dependency Management

Eiichi Sunagawa, Kouji Kozaki, Yoshinobu Kitamura, and Riichiro Mizoguchi

The Institute of Scientific and Industrial Research, Osaka University
8-1 Mihogaoka, Ibaraki, Osaka, 567-0047 Japan
Tel: +81-6-6879-8416, Fax: +81-6-6879-2123
{sunagawa,kozaki,kita,miz}@ei.sanken.osaka-u.ac.jp
http://www.ei.sanken.osaka-u.ac.jp/

Abstract. This paper describes a system for supporting development of ontology in a distributed manner. By a distributed manner, we mean ontology is divided into several component ontologies, which are developed by different developers in a distributed environment. The target ontology is obtained by compiling the component ontologies. These component ontologies are identified according to their conceptual level or domain characteristics. The distributed development of ontologies applies to many situations such as cooperative development, reusing ontologies and so on. To support such a way of ontology development, we investigate the dependency between component ontologies and design some functions for management of these ontologies based on their dependencies. We next consider the influence of a change of one ontology to others through its dependencies and design a function to suggest a few candidate modifications of the influenced ontology for keeping the consistency. We also present some examples of how the system works.

1 Introduction

The more Semantic Web attracts attention, the more importance of ontology increases. In the Semantic Web, ontologies are developed by different developers in a distributed environment. So, Distribute Ontology Development is one of the most significant issues.

In general, ontology can be divided into several component ontologies. Building ontology means occasionally building portions and compiling them. These component ontologies are identified according to their conceptual level or domains.

For example, Fig.1 shows "Plant Ontology", which was built in the Human Media Project sponsored by the former Ministry of International Trade and Industry [1]. This ontology is separated into three parts: Top Level Ontology, Task Ontology and Domain Ontology. Furthermore, the domain ontology is divided into two ontologies: physical attribute and equipment. Equipment Ontology is further divided into ontologies of objects, plant parts and function. In Fig.1, arrows express the relation between an upper ontology and a lower ontology. This is named "*Super-sub* Relation" (discussed in section 2.1).

D. Fensel et al. (Eds.): ISWC 2003, LNCS 2870, pp. 453–468, 2003.

Development of ontology as a whole is achieved by editing and modification of its component ontologies individually. We call development of ontology in this manner "Distributed Ontology Development", and we aim to develop a system supporting it through our research. To support such a way of ontology development, we have been investigating the dependency management between component ontologies. We consider how a change of one ontology influences on others through its dependencies and what countermeasures are effective for the change in order to keep the consistency of them [2].

In this paper, we discuss more details of distributed ontology development. Section 2 discusses its basic philosophy and summarizes our work to date. Section 3 describes implementation of the proposed methods in Hozo [3, 4] followed by concluding remarks. In section 4, we discuss the future work.

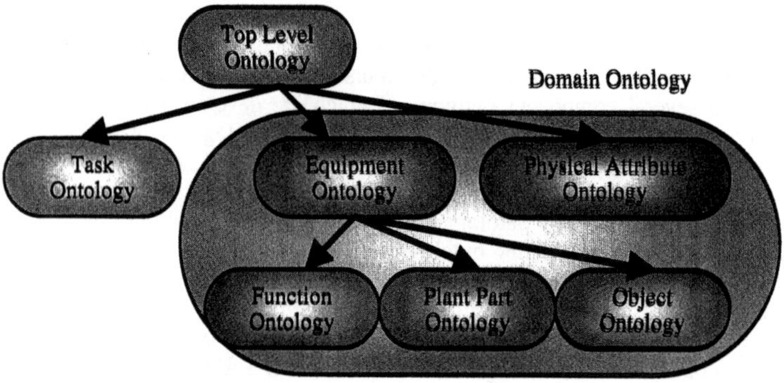

Fig. 1. Plant Ontology. It can be divided into several ontologies according to their conceptual levels or domains

2 Distributed Ontology Development

The purpose of our research is to realize a distributed ontology development. We assume a situation where target ontology is divided into several component ontologies and to construct each ontology individually (perhaps in parallel) by different developers in a distributed environment.

The distributed development of ontologies applies to many situations such as cooperative development, understanding the total picture of conceptual hierarchy, reusing ontologies and so on. For example, a developer would divide one ontology by categorizing concepts roughly, and then he/she builds each component ontologies in cooperation with other developers. He/she can divide in such a manner before and during the course of construction. In another case, he/she would carve out a constructed ontology for reusing it as a part of another one. In these cases, we can assume that such component ontologies are valuable on every phase of ontology development.

In this section, we argue requirements on developing ontology in such a distributed manner. We especially note how to keep the consistency of component ontologies which are constructed individually and we define the dependency between ontologies.

2.1 Dependencies between Ontologies and Their Management

In this paper, we treat basic concepts mainly syntactically or formally while we have argued a part of heavy weight ontology such as the role concept in [3]. The dependency this paper discusses is based on *is-a* relation and class constraint. As these relations can be treated in RDF(S) or OWL, our research will contribute to the development of ontologies for the Semantic Web.

Dependency between Ontologies. When constructing ontology, concepts are usually defined with reference to the definitions of other concepts. In collaborative construction, those referred concepts might exist in another ontology developed by another person. That means some concepts in ontology depend on other concepts in another ontology. This section discusses the dependency between ontologies which is defined as in terms of the dependency between concepts defined in respective ontologies. The kinds of them are:

1) *Super-sub* Relation (*is-a* relation): Two ontologies are said to be in "*super-sub* relation", if and only if there are at least two concepts in is-a relation and each of the two concepts belongs to a different ontology of the two. We named these ontologies "upper ontology" and "lower ontology" respectively. The lower ontology depends on the upper one at the point of inheriting definition. In the "Plant Ontology"(Fig.1), we can find this relation between "Top Level Ontology" and "Equipment Ontology", between "Equipment Ontology" and "Plant Parts Ontology", etc.
2) *Referring-to* Relation (class constraint): We define "referring-to relation" as the relation that a concept in one ontology refers to a concept in another as a class constraint. We named the ontology containing the slot being constrained "referring ontology" and the other "referred-to ontology". In the "Plant Ontology" (Fig.1), we can find this relation between "Plant Parts Ontology" and "Physical Attribute Ontology", etc.

These 4 types of component ontology based on dependencies, "lower", "upper", "referring" and "referred", are determined on the basis of conceptual dependency with each other. So, an ontology does not have its won type intrinsically. If there are several concept pairs making dependency between two ontologies, we can define several numbers (and kinds) of dependencies and each ontology takes multiple positions. In such a case, ontologies and their dependencies form a graph (rather than a tree) as a whole.

Management of Dependency between Ontologies. When editing ontology, we should pay attention to the change influencing on other ontologies. In some cases, that change may destroy the consistency between ontologies. We investigated two approaches to keep consistency of the dependency. One is to restrict the change which influences on others. The proactive restriction helps developers to avoid inconsistency. The other approach is to modify the influenced ontology according to the type of the change. This paper is mainly concerned with the latter approach, and the former is argued in section 4 as remaining work. 5 kinds of countermeasures taken in the influenced ontology are:

- **1-1)** ***To modify influenced ontology for accepting the change;*** The user makes agreement on the change of the ontology and tries to modify his/her ontology depending on it. The influenced ontology needs to be modified to adapt to the changed ontology. The way to reflect the change of the influencing ontology is mentioned later.
- **1-2)** ***To leave the depending ontology influenced by the change;*** In some cases, the influenced ontology is not need to be modified, as the changed ontology doesn't contradict it.
- **2-1)** ***To modify influenced ontology for rejecting the change;*** As far as keeping the consistency of the dependency, the user tries to modify his/her ontology against the change and reduce the influence. The way to negate the influence of the change is mentioned later.
- **2-2)** ***To stay compliant with the last version of the changed (depending) ontology;*** Under controlling the version of ontologies, the dependency is kept in this way. If influencing ontology would be changed again, influenced one could adapt to the change and the consistency would be recovered. However, this should be a temporal method to keep the dependency. Its problem is argued in section 4.
- **3)** ***To break the dependency;*** In order to make the influenced ontology independent of the others, concepts whose change influences on it are imported in it and cut the link of the dependency between the two.

1-1) and 1-2) are selected when the author agrees on the change and accept its influence on his/her ontology. 2-1), 2-2) and 3) are to reject the change. Then, he/she is able to deny the change influencing his/her ontology at least in itself. All but 3) of these countermeasures are selected in order to keep the dependency.

In either case of accepting or not accepting, modification of the influenced ontology should be supported because of its complexity. So, we began with conceiving the patterns of the change. And, for the influence of each pattern, we investigated the possible way of modification to keep the dependency. The influenced ontology is modified based on this framework.

We have two major kinds of patterns of the change: operation on the concept itself and changing its definition. The former includes the cases where a concept has been deleted or a sub concept has been added. The latter does the cases where the label has been changed, a slot such as a part of or an attribute of a concept has been deleted, added or a class constraint has been changed. In all, we have 17 types of the change of the concept according to the kind of dependency. And, as the countermeasures for the change, we have 67 ways of modification. Table.1 shows what type of the change are supported and how many countermeasures for each type are supported. We cannot always take all kinds of countermeasures. Some types of the change influence strongly and restrict the choices of authors.

Examples of Modifying ontology to Keep the Consistency of Its Dependency. In this section, we show two examples of the dependency management in "Plant Ontology" (described in section 1).

Ex.1: Fig.2 shows a portion of "Plant Ontology". "*Heat Exchanging Device*" is sub-concept of (*is-a*) "*Device*". are so, too. Then, we can define *super-sub* relation between "Equipment Ontology" and "Plant part ontology". Assume that the slot

"*Input Thing*" has been deleted from the concept "*Device*" in "Equipment Ontology". That change influences "Plant Part Ontology".

Table 1. The patterns of the change and countermeasure for them

patterns of the change	countermeasures for the change				
	accept the change		reject the change		
	keep the dependency				break the dependency
	modify	leave	modify	last version	
	1-1	1-2	2-1	2-1	3
super-sub relation					
operation of a concept					
deletion of a concept	1	-	1	1	1
addition of a sub concept	2	1	-	1	1
change of the definition					
change of the label	1	1	-	1	1
deletion of a slot	1	-	1	1	1
addition of a slot	2	1	-	1	1
change of the class constraint (inheriting)					
generalizing	1	1	-	1	1
specializing	-	1	-	1	1
different concept	-	1	-	1	1
change of the class constraint (overridden)					
generalizing	-	1	-	1	1
specializing	2	-	-	1	1
different concept	2	-	-	1	1
referring-to relation					
operation of a concept					
deletion of a concept	1	-	1	1	1
addition of a sub concept	1	1	-	1	1
change of the definition					
change of the label	1	1	-	1	1
deletion of a slot (referred by a role concept)	1	-	1	1	1
deletion of a slot (not referred by a role concept)	-	1	-	1	1
addition of a slot	2	1	-	1	1

According to Table.1, four ways are supported to cope with the change of "Deletion of a slot in *Super-sub* Relation". The developer of "Plant Part Ontology" can select a countermeasure out the followings:

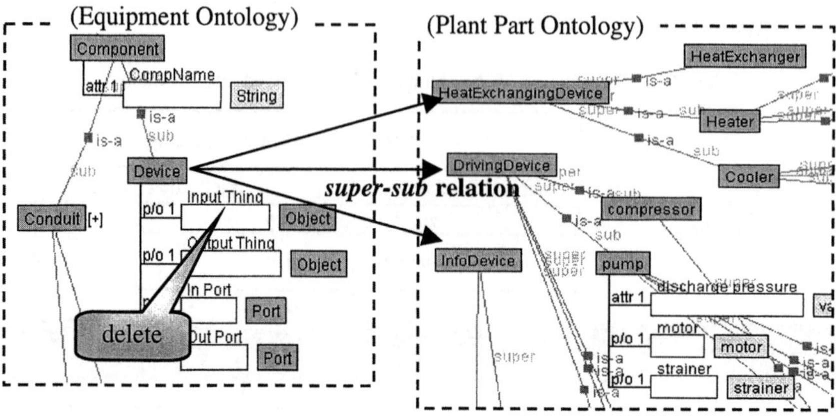

Fig. 2. An example of *super-sub* relation

- **1-2) To delete the slot in all influenced concepts (to accept the change):** Deletion of "*Input Thing*" is applied to all influenced concepts in "Plant Part Ontology". (In the case of this example, it is thought that manual change is needed because of importance of the deleted definition.)
- **2-1) To add the same as deleted slot to a depending concept in the lower ontology (to reject the change):** To reject the deletion of *"Input Thing"* in "Plant Part Ontology", the slot should be added to appropriate concepts which are inheriting it. (In this example, the slot *"Input thing"* is inherited by "*Heat Exchanging Device*", "*Driving Device*" and "*Info Device*". Then, we should add the slot to them.)
- **2-2) To stay compliant with the last version of the modified ontology (to reject the change):** The old version of "Equipment Ontology" has been saved in the ontology server (described in section 3.1). "Plant Part Ontology" can keep dependence on it under the version control.
- **3) To break the dependency (to reject the change):** Re-define *"Device"* with "*Input Thing*" in "Plant Part Ontology" and break the dependency between the ontologies. "Plant Part Ontology" is then changed to be independent of "Equipment Ontology".

Ex.2: Fig.4 shows part of "Plant Ontology" (in Fig.1). "*Liquid Thermometer*" in "Plant Part Ontology" is referring to "*Liquid*" in "Object Ontology" as a class constraint of "*M_Object*". Then, we can define *referring-to* relation between these ontologies. Assume that the concept "*Liquid*" has been deleted from "Object Ontology". It influences "Plant Part Ontology".

According to Table.1, four ways are supported to cope with the change such as "Deletion of a concept in *Referring-to* Relation". The developer of "Plant Part Ontology" can select a countermeasure out the followings:

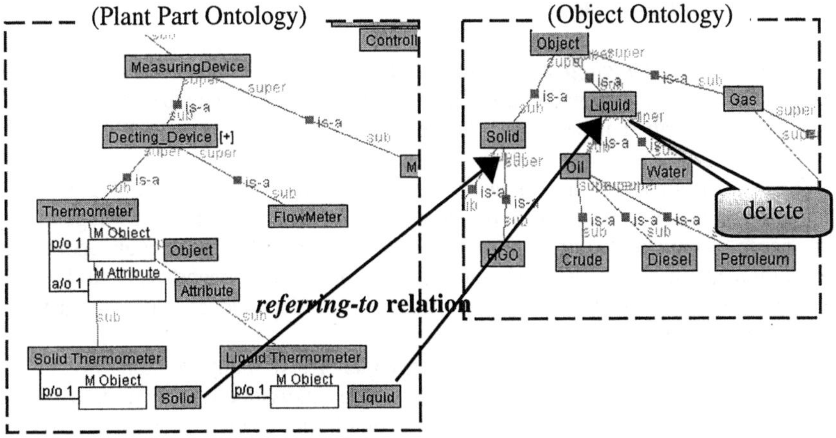

Fig. 3. An example of *referring-to* relation

- **1-1) To refer a super concept of the deleted concept (to accept the change):** As the class constraint of *"Liquid Thermometer"*, we can refer *"Object"* which is the super concept of *"Liquid"*. This means the class constraint to *"Measurement Attribute"* become looser a little.
- **2-1) To add the same as the deleted concept to the referring ontology (to reject the change):** This way means the deletion of *"Liquid"* is denied in "Plant Part Ontology". The author redefines *"Liquid"* in "Plant Part Ontology", and establishes newly *super-sub* relation between "Plant Part Ontology" and "Object Ontology" through *is-a* relation between *"Liquid"* and *"Object"*. (However, this method should be temporary adjustment. Because it is not desirable that only one concept, which is a *"Object"*, is defined in the different ontology from "Object Ontology", in which the other concepts of *"Object"* are defined.)
- **2-2) To stay compliant with the last version of the modified ontology (to reject the change):** It is the same as Ex.1.
- **3) To break the dependency (to reject the change):** It is the same as Ex.1.

2.2 Other Contentions

The management of dependencies between ontologies is not enough for realizing distributed ontology development smoothly because dependency is one of the aspects which appear particularly in the consistency management of conceptual hierarchy. So, we have to consider more general functions for supporting distributed development. In this section, we discuss the management of ontology from the point of *version control*, *updating* and *reusing*. Next, the management of developers is discussed together with cooperative development. Here, we need to note that component ontologies are managed together with their developers by each target ontology as a whole.

Management of Ontologies

Version Control of Ontologies. In distributed ontology development, each component ontology is updated independently. To manage the dependency between them with our method described in section 2.1, the system have to preserve old versions of ontologies.

When under construction, it is not hard to control the version of ontologies. An old version of ontology needs to be preserved in the system only if it has dependencies with some component ontologies. So, our system manages dependencies with information about the version of ontology which has the dependency. And, we can manage them more easily if ontology avoids having dependency with an old version of other ontology unnecessarily.

However, it is very hard to manage dependencies if many versions of the same ontology have dependencies with other ontologies individually. It causes a problem especially in a stage of compiling component ontologies to the target ontology. This is discussed in section 4.

Update of Ontologies. In our distributed ontology development system, its user constructs his/her own component ontologies on a local computer. And when he/she decides to publish them, the ontology is updated on a shared space of server computer. At the same time, the user can access to other published ontologies which other developers have developed, whenever he/she needs to check the dependency of his/her ontology. If it is needed to be refined, he/she modifies his/her ontology to cope with the change of ontologies it depends on. Then, he/she updates the modified ontology again.

Reuse of Ontologies. In our system published component ontologies are reused as some part of other ontologies. We support 3 types of reusing ontologies as follows

1) reusing ontology which is under construction
2) using a particular version of ontology
3) importing some version of ontology, and arranging it

In general, ontology reused should be of the final version because it is hard to develop ontology with keeping its consistency in several different target ontologies. For this reason 1) is not good way to reuse ontologies. On the other hands, if the developer uses a particular version of ontology, as 2), and ignores its evolution later on, the reuse of ontology becomes easier. 3) is an evolved case of 2) , and it is supposed the most practical way. In this case, arranged ontologies should be regarded not as the updated version of the imported ontology. To simplify the management of ontologies, it is regarded as a newly developed ontology rather than a new version of the original ontology. And its versions should be managed separately.

At any types, to reuse ontologies we should consider not only computer processing (e.g. management of consistency of the conceptual hierarchy) but also communication and agreement among the developers. To support reuse of ontology in the distributed ontology development, we will investigate more these topics.

Cooperative Development and User Management. It is very hard to manage the consistency of dependencies if several developers construct the same part of ontology at the same time. For this reason, our system does not allow multiple accesses to a concept by different developers at the same time.

When developers edit their ontology, the system manages and shows the information they need. For example, which ontologies are related it, how their relations are, the developer of related ontologies, and so on. Because the methodology of ontology development is still argued and outside of this paper, we do not describe detail of how this information support developers in cooperative development. But, at least, we can say that the information will be used in order to support communication between developers because it is difficult for them to make agreement about target ontology in a distributed manner.

However, we still have some issues to consider. Firstly, our approach might become unnecessarily complex when many developers divide a large ontology into many component ontologies and construct them in parallel. One solution to this problem is to control the access of developers at a conceptual level in ontologies. We will investigate it in the future work. Secondly, we can take some cases in which several developers would like to construct the same component ontology of target ontology. This issue is mentioned together with the construction of component ontologies in section 4.

3 Distributed Ontology Development with "Hozo"

On the basis of our consideration described in the above section, we designed two tools for supporting to practice distributed ontology development. First, we summarize our system "Hozo" developed as an environment for building ontologies. Next, we describe how distributed ontology development is realized in "Hozo" and how two tools works for supporting developers.

3.1 "Hozo", an Environment for Building Ontologies

We have developed an environment, named "Hozo" [3, 4], for building ontologies based on fundamental ontological theories. Hozo is composed of "Ontology Editor", "Onto-Studio" and "Ontology Server" (in Fig.4). Ontology Editor provides users with a graphical interface, through which they can browse and modify ontologies. This system manages properties between concepts in the *is-a* hierarchy. Onto-Studio is based on a method of building ontologies, named AFM (Activity-First Method) [5], and it helps users design ontology from technical documents. Ontology Server manages the built ontologies and models.

Because the architecture is implemented in Java and the Ontology Editor is an applet, it can work as a client through Internet. Hozo manages ontologies and models considering who its developer is. Models are built by choosing and instantiating concepts in the ontology and by connecting the instances. Hozo also checks the consistency of the model using the axioms defined in the ontology. The ontology and the resulting model are available in different formats (Lisp, Text, and XML/DTD) that make it portable and reusable.

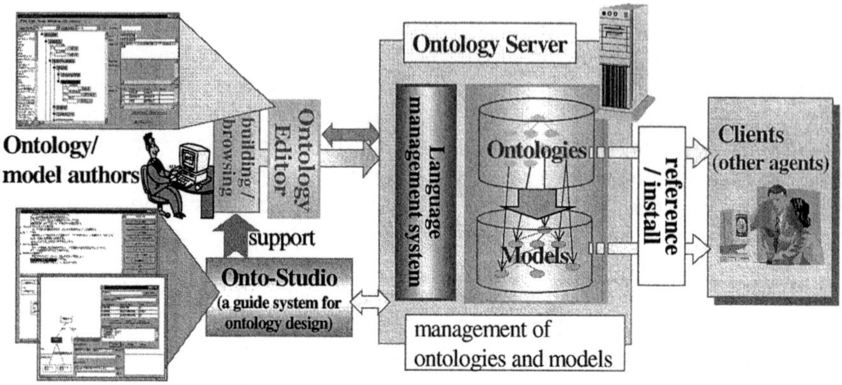

Fig. 4. Hozo, an Environment for Building Ontologies

3.2 Practice of Distributed Ontology Development

Flow of Distributed Ontology Development. Distributed ontology development is performed as described in section 2.2. The development has been done by the repetition of the following steps; **1)** a developer logins Hozo and runs Ontology Manager (described in section 3.3). Then, he/she can get a total picture of the target ontology and information of dependencies between component ontologies. One of the important information is which ontology has been changed. **2)** he/she selects ontology to edit and open it by Ontology Editor. At the same time, Ontology Editor accesses other component ontologies it depends on and compiles them temporarily. At this phase, a concept hierarchy is built up as one ontology (e.g. inheritance of the definition). Then, its dependencies are checked automatically and he/she knows their conditions. If their consistencies may be broken, he/she can select countermeasures listed on Tracking Panel (described in section 3.4) to cope with the change. **3)** he/she starts editing his/her ontology. In addition, dependency is checked whenever he/she needs it is under editing. **4)** After editing, he/she updates his/her ontology on Ontology Server and publishes it to others.

Data Structure and Its Use. To manage the dependencies, the system manages the information about each component ontology as follows:

- its name, its version, its developer and the last update time of itself
- the name and the version of ontologies it depends on
- a copy data of the definition of the concept it depends on in other ontology

A copy data of the definition is used to check the consistency of dependency and to identify the type of change of ontology (in Fig. 5). The copy data is mounted in ontology when its developer makes or rebuilds a dependency. Our system checks the change of influencing ontology by comparing the definition of depended concepts with its copy data the influenced ontology has. If the consistency of dependency may be broken, the system lists the kind of detected changes and countermeasures to keep consistency of the dependency based on the patterns in Table.1.

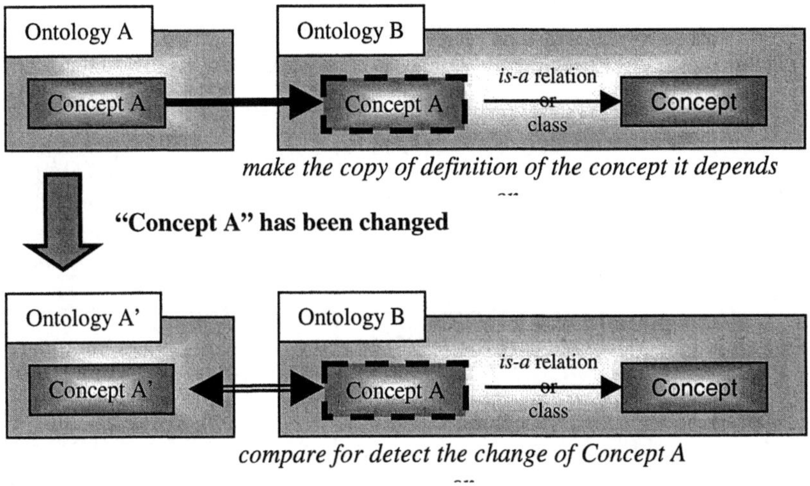

Fig. 5. Data Structure of dependency. When ontology B depends on concept A in ontology A, the system make the copy of definition of concept A in ontology B. This copy is used for detecting and identifying of the change of concept A

Operations for Distributed Ontology Development. Ontology Manager provides four operations for distributed ontology development; to create new component ontology, to divide a component ontology, to compile ontologies and to reuse ontology as a component. These are available mainly in the case where a developer specifies component ontologies and their dependencies before constructing every component ontology and then participants start development according to the specification. On the other hand, we can assume a case where a developer constructs each component ontology before its borderline and dependency is defined. In such a case, he/she has to make a dependency on occasions. Ontology Editor provides the functions to find a concept in other ontologies and make a dependency with it.

3.3 Ontology Manager

We have designed a tool, named "Ontology Manager". Fig.6 shows its interface. Ontology Manager consists of 4 panels:

- **Ontology List** shows a list of ontologies which is registered in Ontology Server. Users can select ontology, and then the information about it is shown in other panels.
- **Ontology Viewer** shows dependencies between ontologies graphically by using nodes and links each of which represents ontology and *super-sub* relation, respectively.
- **Ontology Information Panel** shows the name, file name, developer, version, last update of the selected ontology.
- **Dependency Panel** shows the list of ontologies which have a dependency with the selected ontology. They are classified in 4 types (described in section 2.1): *upper*,

lower, *referring-to* and *referred-to*. Users can select shown type by tabs. The table informs users the names of ontologies, concepts which constitute the dependency, version of ontologies and whether that concept is changed or not.

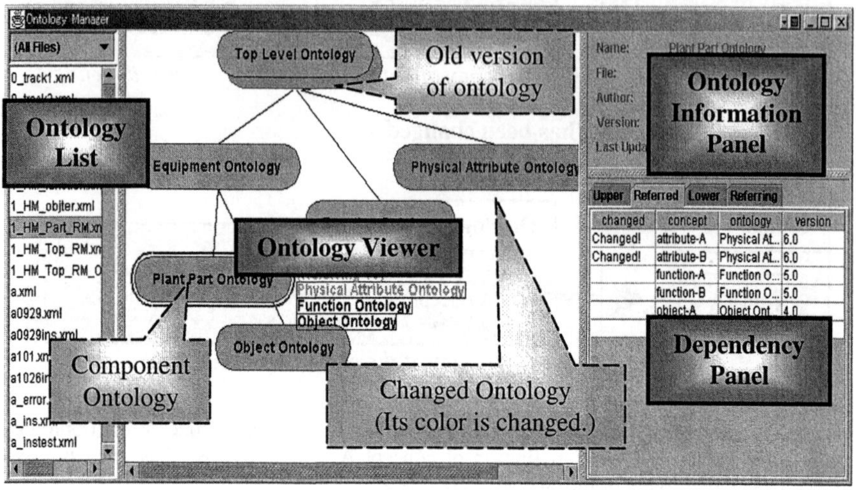

Fig. 6. Ontology Manager. It consists of 4 panels: Ontology List, Ontology Viewer, Ontology Information Panel and Dependency Panel

These panels are to show users a series of information about ontologies built by Hozo. Besides, Ontology Manager acts as a bridge between ontologies edited in local and ones open to the public (Fig.7). Furthermore, Ontology Manager carries out 3 functions as follows.

- **Management of Dependency.** In both local and public cases, only component ontologies exist and developers edit them individually. Ontology Manager compiles them virtually to form target ontology and shows its configuration on Ontology Viewer. It enables developers to grasp easily the outline of dependencies. And, if developers need to get details about dependencies, they can use Dependency Panel. In addition, this function is used as a first step for supporting modification to cope with changes as described in section 2.1. More details are described in section 3.4.
- **Version Control.** To manage dependency between ontologies, Ontology Manager treats their versions also. If some ontology depends on an old version of another, the caution is given graphically on Ontology Viewer. These old versions of ontologies are preserved in Ontology Server, if they have been open to the public. Ontology Manager searches Ontology Server and find necessary version of the ontology.
- **Management of Developers and Their Access.** Ontology Server has information about every target ontology together with its developer. The system manages the developer's access to ontologies by considering which target ontology he/she joins to construct and which component ontologies he/she may edit. A developer cannot edit every component ontology. As described in section 2.2, we assume that one component ontology is built by one developer. However, if a developer gives

permission, the system allows another to edit his/her ontology. In this case, unless he/she admit, the edited ontology cannot be updated.

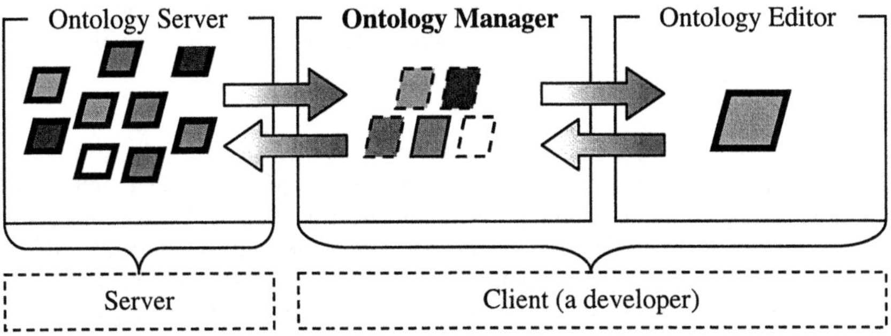

Fig. 7. Roles of Ontology Manager. It acts as a bridge between Ontology Editor and Ontology Server. Its roles are to: (1) download component ontologies of a target ontology from Ontology Server, (2) propagate the influences of the change to the ontology which is edited with Ontology Editor (3) upload the component ontology, which is edited in local, to Ontology Server

3.4 Tracking Panel: The Function to Keep the Consistency of the Dependency

Ontology Manager shows developers which ontology has been changed and might destroy the consistency of its dependency. To keep the consistency of dependency, the developer should get more information that how the influencing ontology has been changed and what countermeasures are supported. These are shown in Tracking Panel. The panel lists the change of the influencing ontology and the possible countermeasures for coping with each change. He/she selects the change of the ontology and the countermeasure form the list. Then his/her ontology is modified semi automatically and the dependency is kept its consistency. This function is available whenever he/she requests the change information of other ontologies.

4 Remaining Work

To advance distributed ontology development further, we have some issues to discuss. In this paper, we have already mentioned them a little. Here, we describe them in more details.

- *Keeping the Consistency from the Influencing Ontology*

In this paper we took an approach to keep the consistency from the depending ontologies. On the other hand, we can consider the approach to keep the consistency of the dependency from the influencing ontology. We plan two stages to realize this. In the first stage, a developer is informed of the influence of the operation on other ontologies by the system. It is exceedingly helpful for developers to know the effect of their operation to other ontologies and take a low-risk approach. This function is like to be realized easily by using the information our system has. In the next stage, the system constrains user's changing operation on their own ontology so that consistency between the current ontology and other ontology may not be broken. This will be hard to realize because it may disturb developers operations to evolve ontology unless the levels of prohibition is discussed full well. However, this topic is abstruse to discuss.

- *Consistency of the Target Ontology and Version Control*

In some situations, we cannot assume the consistency of the target ontology as a whole obtained by simply compiling these component ontologies. For example, it is a probable case that multiple component ontologies depend on several different versions of the same ontology. Then, we need to discuss the construction of component ontologies again from the view point of versions of ontology. We may have to construct the last version of ontology as different new ontology by dividing its several older versions.

- *Construction of Component Ontologies*

This topic is concerned with determination of borderlines among component ontologies. And it connected with so many aspects of distributed ontology development that we cannot fully comprehend it. Here, we mention just three topics.

One is related to cooperative development. We have already designed the framework to support several developers to construct the same part of target ontology (described in section 3.3). However, if they construct in parallel, we have still problems to argue. We would allow several ontologies to describe the same part of target ontology when we aim to compare them, switch them, choice the best one and so on. They may be built in parallel or may be imported from the other target ontology. They are not regarded as the same, but resemble to ontologies which are several versions of ontology. So, in constructing phase, we may be able to keep their consistency in the framework like a version control.

Next is connected with the kind of relations between ontologies. We have dealt with two types of dependency between ontologies such as "*super-sub*" relation and "*referring-to*" relation. And now, we can see other kinds of relations between ontologies based on concepts hierarchy they have. For example *inclusive* relation, *parallel* relation and so on. These relations may be available to discuss the construction of target ontology as a whole. Besides this, we can find more kinds of relations based on content of ontology; such as a *task-domain* relation, a *role concept-basic concept* relation and so on. It may be useful for supporting the development of ontology to accommodate developers with a framework to manage content relations.

Last topic is how to determine borderlines among ontologies. In the case of "Plant Ontology", we did not explain why it can be divided so. It is true that the component ontologies are identified according to their conceptual levels or domains, but we didn't discuss how to divide and integrate ontology in this paper. Especially in distributed development, it is related to the working domain each developer has.

5 Related Work

Our basic motivation and design philosophy share a lot with CVS [6]. CVS (Concurrent Version System) has been often used in system and software development. CVS manages objects (in general, they are source code files) and controls their update. To avoid confliction caused by concurrent work done by several developers, CVS needs them to merge their own object and shared object updated in a repository. Our system also provides developers with the space for sharing target ontology. Each developer finds the difference between his/her editing ontology and shared one and modifies his/her own ontology to avoid conflict. However, in general, a programmer edits a source code in many ways. So, it is hard to understand the difference of versions considering variety of coding ways of the same semantics. On the other hand, ontology description languages are systemized and well-structured. Then, system can manage developer's action and offer them possible modifications to keep the consistency of their own ontology.

Some other ontology building tools also have been developed with functions for supporting collaborative development. OntoEdit [7] allows multiple users control their access to the same ontology to develop it collaboratively. We don't allow such operation. Instead, we allow users to divide one ontology into several component ontologies. While developers in OntoEdit treat all parts of their target ontology, each developer in Hozo can construct his/her own part of the target ontology individually and in parallel.

The Karlsruhe Ontology and Semantic Web framework (KAON) has developed an application, which resembles our system [8]. They intend to support evolution of ontology with its consistency kept. Their approach is very similar to ours. Both of them investigate the types of the change of ontology and strategies to keep the consistency. The differences between the two are as follows:

1) While KAON uses those strategies in the case of evolution of an ontology, we use them in different ontologies from the view point of distributed ontology development. But, their strategies seem to be also available in distributed development.
2) We discriminate dependency of "*Super-sub* Relation" and that of "*Referring-to* Relation".
3) Hozo can treat role concept unlike them.

6 Conclusion

In this paper, we discussed distributed ontology development and described our system to realize it. In our system, ontologies are managed based on their dependency among them. This relation is available also to keep the consistency of the dependency even if the change of ontology influences on another. These two aspects are located centrally in our research. Beside them, we discussed the framework for practicing distributed ontology development. Ontologies are managed from three view points; *version control*, *updating* and *reusing*. And with considering cooperative development, we argued also the management of developers and their access to ontologies.

Our framework is realized in "Hozo" which is the system we have developed as an environment for building ontologies. The prototype of this system has been implemented although some details have not been done yet. And, we still have remaining works to evolve our framework.

Distributed ontology development can apply to many situations such as collaborative development, cooperative development, reusing ontologies and so on. In each of them, it will support developers to construct their target ontology.

References

1. R. Mizoguchi, K. Kozaki, T. Sano, and Y. Kitamura: Construction and Deployment of a Plant Ontology, Proc. of the 12th International Conference Knowledge Engineering and Knowledge Management (EKAW2000), pp.113–128, Juan-les-Pins, France, October 2–6, 2000
2. E. Sunagawa, K. Kozaki, T. Kitamura, and R. Mizoguchi: Management of dependency between two or more ontologies in an environment for distributed development, Proc. of the International Workshop on Semantic Web Foundations and Application Technologies (SWFAT2003), pp.35–41, Nara, Japan, March 12, 2003
3. K. Kozaki, Y. Kitamura, M. Ikeda, and R. Mizoguchi: Development of an Environment for Building Ontologies Which Is Based on a Fundamental Consideration of "Relationship" and "Role", Proc. of the Sixth Pacific Knowledge Acquisition Workshop (PKAW2000), pp.205–221, Sydney, Australia, December 11–13, 2000
4. K. Kozaki, Y. Kitamura, M. Ikeda, and R. Mizoguchi: Hozo: An Environment for Building/Using Ontologies Based on a Fundamental Consideration of Role" and "Relationship", Proc. of the 13th International Conference Knowledge Engineering and Knowledge Management (EKAW2002), pp.213–218, Sigüenza, Spain, October 1–4, 2002
5. R. Mizoguchi, M. Ikeda, K. Seta, and V. Johontology for Modeling the World from Problem Solving Perspectives, Proc. of IJCAI–95 Workshop on Basic Ontological Issues in Knowledge Sharing, pp. 1–12, 1995
6. http://www.cvshome.org/
7. Y. Sure, M. Erdmann, J. Angele, S. Staab, R. Studer, and D. Wenke: OntoEdit: Collaborative Ontology Development for the Semantic Web, Proc. of the First International Semantic Web Conference (ISWC2002), Sardinia, Italy, June 9–12, 2002
8. L. Stojanovic, M. Maedche, B. Motik, N. Stojanovic: User-driven Ontology Evolution Management, Proc. of the 13th International Conference Knowledge Engineering and Knowledge Management (EKAW2002), pp.213–218, Sigüenza, Spain, October 1–4, 2002

Beyond Ontology Construction; Ontology Services as Online Knowledge Sharing Communities

Yang Li, Simon Thompson, Zhu Tan, Nick Giles, and Hamid Gharib

Intelligent Systems Lab, BTexact
MLB1/PP12, Orion Building
Adastral Park, Ipswich, UK,IP5 3RE
{yang.li,simon.2.thompson,zhu.tan,nick.giles,hamid.gharib}
@bt.com

Abstract. There are a number of different ontology server implementations available, Their functionality focuses on editing, browsing and storing ontologies. In some cases the ontology server also provides an inference engine that allows statements about the relationships between entities in different ontologies to be tested or retrieved. These functions are certainly required for a practical deployment of an ontology service in an organization but when an ontology service is to be deployed in an open environment, such as the Semantic Web, a number of other considerations become apparent. This paper describes ACOS (Agent Cities Ontology Service), during the development of ACOS we have explored some aspects of creating a collaborative, community-oriented ontology server, in an open environment.

1 Introduction

Ontology servers create a collaborative environment for managing, developing and sharing ontologies. Without such an environment, it is much more difficult for agents to interconnect their ontologies. Ontology servers enable the exchange and re-use of ontologies with minimal effort, possibly facilitating their use within practical system development environment [1].

In this paper we have developed a technically novel ontology service that introduces some new reasoning facilities to verify the consistency of ontologies and to support their construction and the construction of relationships within the ontologies (intra ontology relationships) and between ontologies (inter-ontology relationships). Simultaneously we have developed a management system for ontologies that draws inspiration from the Slashdot web site's method of managing comments on stories [9].

Within this environment, users are willing to use and develop ontologies collaboratively. In turn, ontologies become well developed and attract more users. The ontology server allows users to control access to their ontologies, such as allowing only specified users to read their ontology, or allowing some users to alter their ontology. In addition, more flexible access controls can be used, allowing certain categories or qualities of users a set of permissions. For instance, one can allow highly rated users to modify ontologies, on the basis that they are acknowledged to be good at managing other ontologies, and can therefore assist in the development of

D. Fensel et al. (Eds.): ISWC 2003, LNCS 2870, pp. 469–483, 2003.

yours'. User ratings might be based upon the level of use of the ontologies that they own, allowing those users that produce ontologies the community needs to be recognized.

Ontology management is clearly important, but it is not clear who should do it, or how they will be paid. In the WWW where information repositories are used by millions, their management is paid for only by advertising, or in some cases by state compelled subscription (CCTV, BBC). Trusted knowledge sources are significant and useful, but no one is willing to pay for them.

This is not to say that there is no money to be made from providing an ontology service. It is our belief that a subscription to access the shared space would be acceptable to its users, provided that a premium is being obtained by the subscriber. We think this because the ontologies are business critical resources. While there is no study to confirm this, our intuition and experience of open system development for example during the construction of the demonstration applications during the Agentcities project, shows that an ontology is not only central to the local development effort, it is central to ensuring that the developed system is interoperable with other systems. This value means that there is a business case for paying for access to an ontology server.

The question is: how much? The cost of a resource is determined by the cost of the infrastructure required to provide it and the cost of the effort that will maintain it. Those that deploy an ontology service will rapidly discover (as we have) that there is a great deal of work to be done in deleting test deployments, checking updates are acceptable, retrieving lost data and so on. The work is comparable (unsurprisingly) to the work that a DBA undertakes. It is therefore significant to note that there are no public sql databases, accessible for query and update, that are in widespread use for development in internet systems. Our point is: in terms of private resources for in house development efforts a business case for an highly managed ontology server can be made. As a mode of service provision to a community that is paying via subscription it is much harder to see that this is the case.

It is this insight that motivated us to develop an automated consistency checking and community based management algorithms that are used to maintain the ACOS ontology server. These mechanisms mean that the users who need the ontologies: those that make most use of them and have the highest stake in them are able to maintain them.

The contributions that we report here are:

- An ontology service that uses a specific set of semantics for the construction of ontologies and inter-ontology connections.
- An ontology service with novel validation & consistency checking abilities.
- An ontology service with a novel management interface.

The rest of this paper is organized as follows.

- Section 2 introduces the design and infrastructure of our ontology server; it discusses the knowledge representation that we chose and the mechanism for connecting ontologies.
- Section 3 describes the mechanism which is used to construct individual ontologies.
- Section 4 describes the consistency checking capabilities of ACOS

- Section 5 describes the mechanisms for community based management of the ontology service
- Section 6 is a comparison between ACOS and other ontology servers
- In section 7 we draw conclusions from the work that we have done and suggest directions for future work.

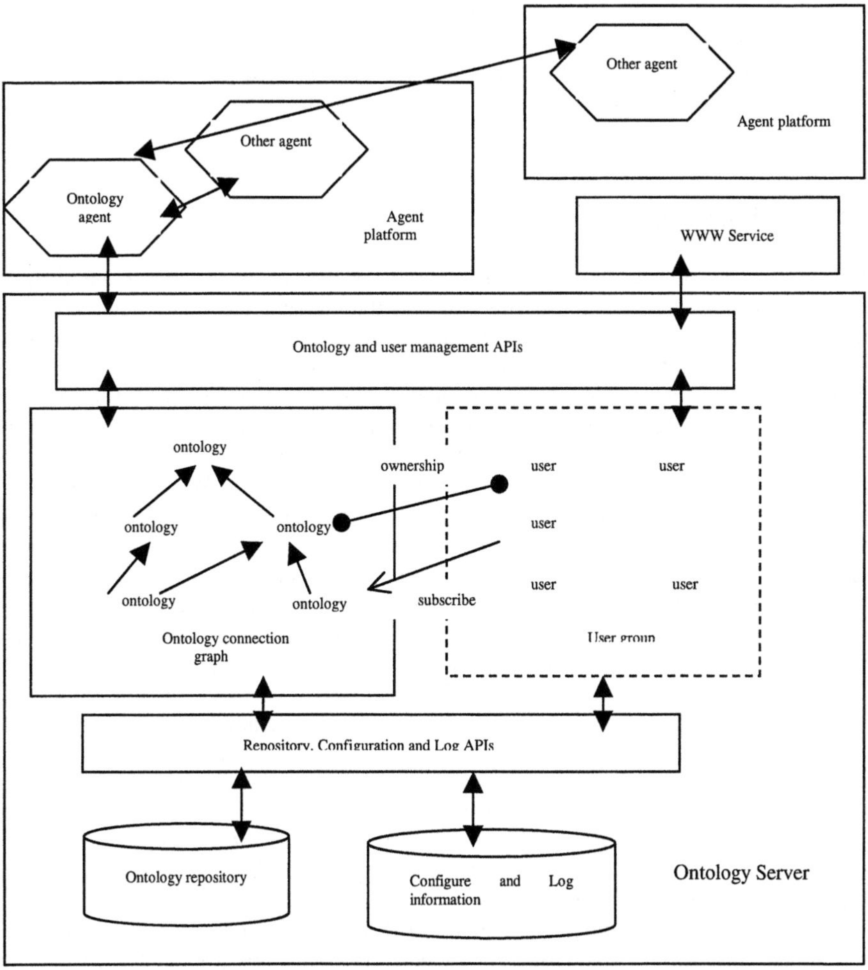

Fig. 1. ACOS Architecture

2 ACOS Architecture

The architecture of the ACOS sever is shown in Figure 1. Two central data structure held in the ontology server are ontology connection graph and user group. Ontology connection graph is the internal ontology representation managed by the ontology server; whilst the latter is the data structure used for user access control management.

These two components are linked with each other through a system of ownership and subscription relations. Ontology and user access management APIs are the implementation of interfaces that provide functions of ontology management and user access control management to external clients such as a web browser user or a software agent. In the latter case, an Ontology Agent will act as a middle-man, connecting between ontology server and other agents, using agreed Agent communication language. The other agents can reside on either the same or different agent platforms. Repository, configuration and log APIs provide functions to put the in-memory data into persistent storage, in our case, files in the format of DAML+OIL and XML in the hard disk. In the rest of this section, we will discuss the internal ontology representation.

2.1 Knowledge Representation

Designing a suitable knowledge representation is the first step towards building an ontology server. Various knowledge representation schemas have been proposed including logic, semantic nets, neural nets, production rules, cases, frames & object-oriented representations [2]. In 1970s and 1980s, the booming of expert systems highlighted production rules & frames, and made them popular in both knowledge engineering and software engineering communities [3]. This trend has bled into the semantic web community, as AI and Networking communities are collaborating to bring knowledge representation and reasoning capabilities to the WWW [4, 5, 6].

An expert system is designed for capturing special domain knowledge and using it, in combination with an inference engine, for simulating the automatic reasoning process of a human expert. The knowledge embedded in the expert system is not used for knowledge sharing across diverse communities. Some researchers have raised doubts that this change in the context of use of the knowledge system, from single interactions in a closed community of knowledge to interactions by many users in an open environment may render knowledge representation, such as Frames [7, 5], inappropriate for use in the semantic web [8, 10]. A typical example from the W3C for informally describing "person", using DAML+OIL, is: "*a person is a subclass of animal, whose parent is also a person, who has only one father, and whose shoe size is at least 1*" [11]. The question is: if another agent defines a person as "*subclass of animal, whose parent is also a person, who has only one mother, and whose hat size is at least 1*", are these concepts of *Person* compatible? Can an interaction between these two agents be conducted?

The Foundation for Physical Agents (FIPA) is a standards body which has developed interaction standards for agents in open environment. During the production of its standards set FIPA identified ontology integration problem as a major issue for communicating agents [6]. It believes that "even if two agents adopt the same vocabulary, there is no guarantee that they can agree on a certain information unless they commit to the same conceptualization" [6]. Assuming that each agent has its own conceptualization, "a necessary condition in order to make an agreement possible is that the intended models of both conceptualization overlap" [12].

Accordingly, FIPA introduced an important classification dimension for ontologies – their level of detail: a *fine-grained ontology* that has very rich axioms, written in a very expressive language like full first order logic, gets closer to specifying the intended meaning of a vocabulary, but usually very hard to develop and hard to reason on; a coarse ontology that consists of minimal set of axioms written in a language of minimal expressivity, to support only a limited set of specific services [6]. These two categories are also termed as *off-line/reference ontologies* and *on-line/shareable ontologies*, respectively: the former are only accessed from time to time for reference purposes, while the latter support core system's functionality that is the overlap of local ontologies [13].

ACOS is designed to be an on-line community in which a diverse of software agent groups can contribute and use ontologies at run time. A key enabler to this scenario is a high degree of "shareness" of the ontologies maintained by the server. To achieve shareness, it is required that local features of an ontology be removed. Example constructors that can bring in local features include *property* in DAML+OIL [5] or *slot* in Ontolingua [7] that can be used to describe product attributes [8]. It is normally easy to define and agree on a particular product that can be represented as a class in a Framework language; it is, however, hard to agree on the attributes of a product. For instance, a mobile phone model produced by Motorola may contain features that Nokia does not provide or vice verse; can we still recognize a model as a Mobile Phone, if some of the product features are missing in that model? In this case, we tend to treat products as shareable ontologies and attributes reference ontologies.

Other example constructors that bring in local effect are *part-of* in Framework [7] and *disjoint-with* in Description Logic [14]. Constructor part-of is normally used to specify the compositional feature of a product/process. Such a composition is often due to a local requirement, for instance, a network card needs to be installed on a computer or using a swipe card is needed to get access to a building. A computer without a network card or getting access to a building without using a swipe card does not deny the fact that it is still a computer or a process of getting access to a building. Constructor disjoint-with is normally used to specify the property that two classes are disjoint with each other. An example can be found in W3C: (disjoint-with Man Woman) [11], which indicates that Man should be disjoint with Woman. As more discoveries are made in science, and as society and culture gradually advance, the boundary between Man and Woman could become blur, i.e., the above property may not hold given changed definitions on Man and Woman.

To achieve a high degree of shareness, we need to capture ontologies that are in coarse-grain and are more stable in the process of evolution. We believe that constructors *Class*, *subClassOf* offer such good features. Constructor Class is used to specify a concept in a coarse-grain (compared to attributes that are in fine-grain); Constructor subClassOf is used to document the evolutionary history of concepts and history, having time as its horizon axis, is resistant to changing its past. In addition to Class and SubClassOf, we also introduced *SuperClassOf*, *sameClassAs* and *instanceOf* as the constructors in ACOS. The definitions of these constructors are in accordance with those described in FIPA ontology service specification [6]. We will not present them separately.

2.2 Constructing an Ontology Hierarchy

To facilitate collaborative, on-line ontology development, we implemented *import* mechanism that is equivalent to *extension* relationship described in the FIPA ontology service specification [6].

In a collaborative development, an ontology developer normally focuses on a particular sub-domain. For instance, a restaurant ontology developer may be only interested in building concept hierarchy related to restaurant industry rather than automobile industry. In the meantime, to build sound restaurant ontology, substantial supporting knowledge is needed from food industry, cookery industry, interior design engineering, management science, etc. A component architecture can best suit for this scenario, where individual domain expert develops ontology in a particular sub-domain and reuse the ontology developed by other domain experts.

Informally, the semantics of "Ontology O1 imports O2" is that (1) all the concepts and instances that are defined in O2 are also found in O1; (2) all the relationships between entities in O2 are also found in O1. It is noted that the constructor import is transitive, i.e., if "O1 imports O2" and "O2 imports O3", we also have "O1 imports O3" or "O1 imports both O2 and O3". It is also noted that circular dependencies are allowed in the import chain. For instance, while restaurant ontology needs support from management science ontology for describing its human resource, the management science ontology may also needs support from restaurant ontology for describing health and safety issues. Formally speaking, the import relationship constructs a *cyclic graph*. To identify all the supporting/imported ontologies of O1, we can simply compute the transitive closure of O1 by following the import chain.

Seemingly an easy mechanism, "import" has intrinsic implication in maintaining the consistency of ontology system, even in the ACOS where ontology constructors are simplified, to a maximum degree. By gluing disparate ontologies together, one faces the issue that properties in different ontologies may contradict with each other. The issue becomes even serious when changes are made in an existing ontology that may invalidate many properties of the ontology system that previously hold.

The issue of knowledge base maintenance was well documented in the field of knowledge engineering. Three strategies for consistency-checking are notable: (1) allowing the existence of "inconsistency" by relaxing the criteria of consistency-checking; (2) reducing the effort of consistency-checking by enforcing modified model that can control the ripple effect [15, 16]; (3) resolving inconsistency by allowing humans intervene, in workshops [7].

To facilitate collaborative, on-line ontology development, we employed a fourth strategy: automatically checking the consistency of ontology system in the process of ontology development. The algorithm for consistency checking will be discussed in Section 4.0. In addition to facilitating ontology construction, the import mechanism is also used to evaluate the relative importance of ontologies. In the next section we present the ontology construction services that are provided to ACOS users.

3 Ontology Development Services

In conformance to FIPA ontology service specification [6], ACOS also provides functions that allow software agents to assert, retract and query on predicates. The predicates are in the form of (subClassOf C1 C2), (superClassOf C1, C2), (sameClassAs C1, C2) and (instanceOf I1, C1) that were described in Section 2.

The semantics of action ASSERT, as specified by FIPA, is to "add, create, or define the said predicate in an ontology. The syntax of ASSERT action is as follows: (ASSERT (predicate)). The ontology agent is responsible to respect the consistency of the ontology and it can refuse to do the action if the result would produce an inconsistent ontology" [6]. In addition to preserving this semantics, we also make two extensions of ASSERT in the Agentcities ontology service, which are tailored for needs of facilitating collaborative, on-line agent community. First, allowing asserting predicate that is involved in two ontologies. Second, refining the result "failure" for action ASSERT into two reasons: "the predicate already explicitly exists", "the predicate is already implied". The former capability facilitates component-based ontology development; the latter is used to evaluate and manage agent's behaviour. For instance, a user who asserts a predicate that has already explicitly existed in an ontology may be less experienced than the user who asserts a predicate that can only be implied by the ontology. An analogy to this scenario is the difference between copyright and patent, where identifying infringement of a patent is undoubtedly more difficult than claiming the violation of a copyright.

The semantics of action RETRACT, as specified by FIPA, is to "remove, delete or detach the said predicate in the ontology definition. The ontology agent is responsible to respect consistency of the ontology and it can refuse to do the action if the result would produce an inconsistent ontology" [6]. Similarly, we also extend the semantics of RETRACT by allowing a predicate that is involved in two ontologies be retracted and refining the result "failure" for action RETRACT into two reasons: "the predicate does not exist", "implied predicate is not retractable".

Once an ontology system is developed, queries can then be made to the ontology server asking about the relationship between classes or between a class and an instance, the ontologies that contain a certain class/instance, the subclasses/superclasses of a given class, etc. The applications of these ontology services are significant in the real world. For instance, a shopper at a supermarket who intends to buy a pack of apples may end up with having a bag of oranges in his/her hand! The real world is full of fuzziness & uncertainty and well-organized ontology systems should help to accommodate it.

In addition to the functions of ontology construction and query, the ACOS also offers services of uploading and downloading ontologies. Currently we support DAML+OIL as an external format.

4 Consistency Checking Capability

As mentioned earlier, consistency-check is essential to ensuring the integrity of an ontology system. Informally, we say an ontology system is consistent iff there is no contradiction between classes/relationships in the ontology. The consistency-check mechanism of ACOS is built on top of its query capability. A key query function is to decide whether the predicate (subClassOf C1 C2) holds. Agrawal developed an efficient algorithm for deciding the "is-a" relationship between entities by computing a "compressed transitive closure of a graph". To compute the compressed transitive closure, a post-order traverse of the graph is needed, which incurs a computational complexity of O(n), where n is the size of the graph. Once the closure is in hand, only a simple integer range comparison is needed to decide whether the is-a relationship holds or not. This result generally applies to acyclic graph and the compressed transitive closure is incrementally maintainable, at a higher cost [17].

There is always a trade-off between the effort spent in using a structure and that in maintaining the structure. Another common method for deciding the is-a/subsumption/subClassOf relation is to trace through the relation chain. In this case, the effort of maintaining the graph is reduced significantly, in the best case, one operation, at the cost of increased effort in computing the query, in the worst case, O(n), where n is the size of the graph.

Since ACOS supports both on-line ontology construction and on-line ontology query, it needs to strike a balance between the effort for maintaining ontology and that for using ontology. We believe that a non-compressed graph representation can provide such a good trade-off.

To check whether a subClassOf, superClassOf, instanceOf or sameClassAs relationship holds between two classes in an acyclic graph that contains multiple kinds of relationships like $\underline{\text{subClassOf}}$, $\underline{\text{sameClassAs}}$ and $\underline{\text{instanceOf}}$, we use grammar-guided analysis method:

$$
\begin{aligned}
sameClassAs(C1, C2) ::= \;& \underline{sameClassAs}(C1, C2) \\
\mid\;& \underline{sameClassAs}(C1, C3) \wedge sameClassAs(C3, C2) \\
\mid\;& sameClassAs(C2, C1) \\
subClassOf(C1, C2) ::= \;& \underline{subClassOf}(C1, C2) \\
\mid\;& \underline{subClassOf}(C1, C3) \wedge subClassOf(C3, C2) \\
\mid\;& sameClassAs(C1, C3) \wedge subClassOf(C3, C2) \\
\mid\;& subClassOf(C1, C3) \wedge sameClassAs(C3, C2) \\
superClassOf(C1, C2) ::= \;& subClassOf(C2, C1) \\
instanceOf(I1, C1) ::= \;& \underline{instanceOf}(I1, C1) \\
\mid\;& instanceOf(I1, C2) \wedge subClassOf(C2, \mathrm{C1})
\end{aligned}
$$

It is noted that we use Relation and $\underline{\text{Relation}}$ to denote the relation that we want to query and the relation that is denoted in the ontology file respectively. From the grammar above we can also see that Relation sameClassAs satisfies transitive law, commutative law; Relation subClassOf satisfies transitive law.

The consistency of ontology system maintained by ACOS is enforced by checking a set of rules that are given below:

$$
\begin{aligned}
&SubClassOf(C1, C2) \wedge subClassOf(C2, C1) = false \\
&SameClassAs(C1, C2) \wedge subClassOf(C1, C2) = false \\
&Class(CI1) \wedge Instance(CI1) = false
\end{aligned}
$$

The consistency-check algorithm can be described as follows:

Input: ONTS (Ontologies involved in an assert or retract action)

Output: TRUE, if the action won't result in an inconsistency; FALSE, otherwise.

Step 1. Compute the transitive closures of import relation that has ONTS as starting points.

Step 2. Compute the combination of pairs of entities that occur in these closures.

Step 3. FOR each pair in Step 2, check the consistency-check rules given above. IF one of the rules fails, terminate the algorithm and return FALSE.

Step 4. Terminate the algorithm and return TRUE.

At Step 1, we decide the ontologies that may be affected by the change, this can be done at an effort of O(p), where p is the number of ontologies. The computation of pairs and the application of consistency-check rules at Step 2 and Step 3 involve a two-level loop, which needs an effort of $O(n \times n) \times M$, where n is the total number of entities in the ontology system and M is the effort of computing subClassOf(C1, C2) and sameClassAs(C1, C2). Since $O(p) \ll (O(n \times n)) \times M$, we have an overall computational complexity of the algorithm: $(O(n \times n)) \times M$.

5 Community Orientated Ontology Management

Once an ontology system has been created by one user using the methodology described above a key issue is how should it be maintained and managed. Previous work has taken the view that a particular user should continue to own and be responsible for all updates to the ontology. This view does not correspond to reality.

Ontology development is a communal activity, and it is an ongoing communal activity; we have come to this conclusion by observing the way in which standards (ontologies are standards) are developed and controlled by committees over a period of time. The membership of the committee is fluid, but controlled. A chairman may or may not have control of the committee. In short, the way in which an ontology should be managed is dependent on the use and community that the ontology has.

In ACOS, every ontology is associated with an owner, a user group, and a subscriber group. The owner is the user who created the ontology. They specify the access rules to their ontology and manage the user group. The user group of an ontology are the owner's trusted users, to whom the owner can give write permissions to create a team development environment. The subscriber group is those who subscribe the ontology as their interface ontology. A subscriber can talk to another subscriber using the terms in its interface ontology. Often, subscribers are the owner or a member of user group of the ontology.

After building the links between the ontology connection graph and user group, a collaborative development environment is established. To go a step further, we have built a flexible access control mechanism and rating system to create a community-oriented co-operation environment. The flexible access control system balances between on the one hand keeping an ontology internally consistent, which is done by maintaining a tight change control system, administered by a small group of people, and on the other hand maintaining the ontology's usefulness by allowing any user who has an interest to initiate changes. We have used the sort of concepts that power the management of the "Slashdot" web site to manage ontology services, however we have introduced some new concepts to cope with the fact that the resources that we are managing here are persistent and have different uses and significance & value.

5.1 Calculating Ontology Ratings

Ontology owners specify flexible criteria for accessing the ontology. Those "good users" who satisfy the criteria can access a ontology even though they are not a member of that ontology's user group. We believe this approach can maintain ontology's quality without restraining the ability of user to contribute to that resource. Additionally this has the benefit that the ontology may no longer the exclusive property of its contributor. In some cases the ontology contributor may wish to maintain exclusive control of the resource; for example a top-of-the-chain retailer may have the primary objective of forcing its suppliers to conform to its own standards and may simply want an ontology server as an open exchange control mechanism. Alternatively a large company may wish to create a standard to develop a market for exploitation through service products; in this situation its customers may be reassured by the fact that the ontology supplied now has a life of its own.

Consistency checking is applied prior to all the ontology modifying requests. Those requests that will cause inconsistency are not acted upon. Ontologies and users are rated, the ratings of them are connected to each other and are the foundation of flexible access control system. Ontologies will be mainly rated according to their popularity. Let S be an ontology system, O be an ontology, T be a transitive closure (following the relation "imported-by") of O in S, the popularity of O in S is computed as the sum of numbers of subscribed users in T. Figure 2 shows an example of an ontology connection system.

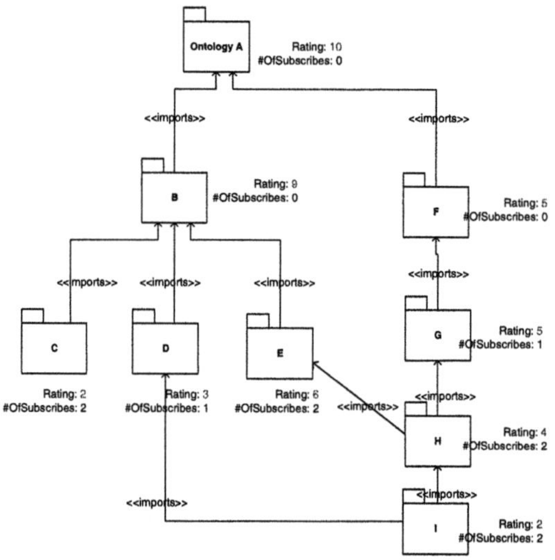

Fig. 2. Ontology Connection System

The calculation process is illustrated in Table 1.

We take the rating calculation of ontology E for example. The ontology E is directly imported by ontology H, and imported by implication into ontology I. Therefore the rating of ontology E (E_k) will be: ontology E's number of subscribers + ontology H's number of subscribers + ontology I's number's subscribers = 2 + 2 + 2 = 6.

From the example, we can see the rating of an ontology will represent the popularity of that ontology, i.e. some vocabularies in the ontology can be interpreted by six users.

Table 1. A rating calculation illustration

Ontology	Full imported set	# of subscriber	rating
A		0	10
B	A	0	9
C	A,B	2	2
D	A,B	1	3
E	A,B	2	6
F	A,	0	5
G	A,F	1	5
H	A,B,E,F,G	2	4
I	A,B,D,E,F,G,H	2	2

5.2 Calculating User Ratings

User ratings are based upon the level of use of the ontologies (ontology rating) that they own and their previous actions. These actions involve asserting and retracting predicates in an ontology. The more successful an action is, the higher rating the user will get; and vice verse. The degree of success for assertion is characterised by a real number that is in proportion to the rating of the ontology being modified. The rationale here is that the higher the rating of an ontology, the more popular it is among the users and it will require more expertise to add new knowledge to it. The degree of failure is in reverse proportion to the rating of the modified ontology and having the nature of the failure as a factor; the explanation is that an agent should receive higher penalty if it fails to add new knowledge in a less popular area. Also, failing to assert an already-implied predicate should receive less penalty than failing to assert an explicitly-exist predicate.

Since retracting a predicate does not affect the consistency of an ontology, the degree of success/failure is not in proportion to the rating of modified ontology. However, it does have the nature of failure as a factor: failing to retract a non-existent predicate will receive heavier penalty than failing to retract an implied predicate.

As updating ontology is considered as a critical activity, thresholds are set up as entry criteria that allow user to undertake the activity; only when the user's rating is higher than the threshold can it assert or retract a predicate.

6 Evaluation

6.1 Critique of Consistency Checking

We discussed, in Section 4, that the overall computational complexity of the algorithm is (O(n×n)) ×M, where n the total number of entities in the ontology system and M is the effort of checking subClassOf(C1, C2) and sameClassAs(C1, C2). The key factor here is M whose computation effort depends on the representation of the graph, i.e. linked format or compressed format. In the former case, which is also our choice, the computation effort is O(n) in the worst case and O(log(n)) on average.

6.2 Critique of Rating System

We have implemented & reported a straw man rating system with the intention of illustrating the principle of developing community administered resources. We have not considered the following factors :

- the computational cost of calculating ratings as part of the management system;
- the relevance and effectiveness of the heuristic for determining ratings

Further investigation is needed to validate the appropriateness of the algorithms adopted.

6.3 Comparison with Other Ontology Servers

Although there are many knowledge repositories since Knowledge Engineering established itself as field in 1970s, most of them were developed as knowledge Bases for expert system applications [3]. The knowledge embedded in these repositories are normally in fine-grained, understood only by few domain specialists and not for the purpose of sharing among general audience. Strictly speaking, according to FIPA definition, these kinds of knowledge are not called *shared ontology* [6].

Ontolingua server [18] is such kind a knowledge repository management system that has been running since 1995. It is a tool that supports distributed, collaborative editing, browsing and creation of Ontolingua ontologies. The ontolingua ontology uses the representation languages of both Ontolingua Frame Ontology [19] and KIF, which is a wide spectrum language capable of representing fine features of concepts. The ontolingua server supports ontology inclusion and circular dependencies [7]. Its consistency-check capability, however, is restricted to the functions similar to database schema checking. For instance, "all slots, slot values, facets and facet values are checked to make sure that they conform to the constraints that they apply (e.g., domain, range, slot value type, and cardinality constraints)" [7]. There is a reasonable choice, given the complicated knowledge structure that Ontolingua server supports; an automatic, on-line, complete consistency-check would be very difficult if not infeasible. The way Ontolingua server ensures knowledge base consistency is through human intervention, where "when someone has an ontology that they believe is ready for others to use, they can choose to publish their ontology in the ontology server. After the ontology has been *approved*, it becomes available to anyone with access to the ontology server through the library" [7]. In other words, the consistency checking is done in domain experts' heads. In comparison, ACOS supports ontologies that can be shared by a wide range of software agent communities and facilitate on-line ontology construction, consistency-check and use.

Driven by the needs and visions for Semantic Web, where ontology server is believed to be a key component [8], there is a surge of work related to ontology server development that is either under the way or in plan [20, 21, 22]. OntoRama [20] is an ontology editor for WebKB that is a web accessible Knowledge Base containing a type hierarchy and knowledge statements. The Knowledge Base supports a set of selected ontology constructors including subtypeOf, partOf, memberOf, urlOf, etc. The main functions of OntoRama include search, compare and modify WebKB ontologies [24]. At current stage, OntoRama does not support consistency-check and cross-ontology query; as a result, its capability of supporting on-line, collaborative ontology construction is restricted.

UKOLN [21] is an initiative to develop an ontology server for Agentcities.NET project. It proposed that a registry be established on UKOLN agent platform that provides a publication environment for the disclosure of metadata vocabularies and customised application-specific profiles of these vocabularies. As latest as in October 2002, it is still at research and investigation stage, such as investigation of JADE as agent platform, ontology constructors, functions of ontology services, etc. [21].

DOGMA [22], a new ontology server research project, is funded for 5 years by the Vrije Universiteit Brussel. The mission of its ontology server is to "assist the gathering and incremental growth of ontoloiges" [23]. The main novelty of the proposed ontology server, that is in line with the rationale of ACOS, is stated as "the use of the extremely simple structures should – we conjecture – achieve at least a degree of scalability not possible with more complex representations hitherto used in the literature and practice; this extensional approach will naturally lead to very large sets, thereby moving the issue to matters of ontology organisation, rather than of representational power or sophistication" [10]. The proposed ontology model consists of 5 basic elements: context, terms, concepts, roles and lexicons; constraints and derivation rules are intentionally left outside the ontology. At this stage, they are still experimenting with the ontology model and an early (and incomplete) version of ontology server is being implemented. In the first prototype they are building, consistency-check and user control is not included. DBMS, in particular, MSQL server 7.0, is used to store the ontology [23]. Table 2 summarises the features of these ontology services.

Table 2. Comparison of ontology services features

	ACOS	FIPA Ontology Service	Ontolingua	OntoRama	UKOLN	DOGMA
Knowl. Rep	Simple	Complex	Complex	Med	Under dev.	Medium
Import Mechanism	Yes	Yes	Yes	No	Not mentioned	No
Manner of Consistency Checking	Auto	Open	Human Approval, simple data type checking	Not mentioned	Not mentioned	Not mentioned
Ontology Repository Platform	Jena + DAML +OIL	Open	Ontolingua Server	Jena + RDF	Under dev.	DBMS
User Access Control	Yes	N/A	Yes	No	Not mentioned	No
Managemnt Provision	Comm unity	N/A	Central	Central	Central	Central
Status	Rolled out 2002	Spec.0/08/ 2001	Rolled out in 1995	Rolled out 2000	Under dev.	Being developed

7 Conclusion

The description of ACOS given above discloses a novel system for inferencing over ontologies and managing collections of them. We have discussed the usefulness and utility of ontology servers in engineering systems that operate in the Agentcities environment and that will operate in the Semantic Web in the future.

In the future we intend to investigate the issues of data & structure management and the impact and implications of the strategies that are adopted with respect to these issues. We will also examine how we can handle the uncertainty and ambiguity that arise within knowledge sources developed and used by groups of humans [25]. With respect to technical issues we intend to investigate transactional mechanisms that can be used to manage and resolve knowledge base conflicts in a real time environment and the implementation of a canonical web service interface to the server.

References

[1] *Willmott, S. and Burg, B. and O'Brien, P,.* "May your Information Service Live in Interesting Times: Engineering Dynamic Service Environments", In proceedings 3rd International Conference on Enterprise Information Systems (ICEIS2001), Setubal, Portugal, 7–10th July 2001. July, 2001.

[2] P.R. Cohen and E. Feigenbaum (eds.): "The Handbook of Artificial Intelligence", Morgan Kaufman, 1982.

[3] C.K. Chang, (ed.): "Handbook of Software Engineering and Knowledge Engineering", World Scientific Publishing Co., 2002.

[4] Tim Berners–Lee, James Hendler and Ora Lassila, "The Semantic Web, A new form of Web content that is meaningful to computers will unleash a revolution of new possibilities", Scientific American, May, 2001.

[5] http://www.daml.org/2001/03/daml+oil-index.html

[6] Foundation for Intelligent Physical Agents, FIPA Ontology Service Specification, http://www.fipa.org/specs/fipa00086/XC00086D.html

[7] A. Farquhar, R. Fikes and J. Rice, "The Ontolingua Server: a Tool for Collaborative Ontology Construction", in Proceedings of the 10th Knowledge Acquisition for Knowledge-based System Workshop, Baniff, Canada, Nov., 1996.

[8] R. Agrawal, "Making Semantic Web Real: Some Building Blocks", invited talk, in Proceedings of International Workshop on Semantic Web, Hawaii, 2002.

[9] The Slashdot community portal. www.slashdot.org

[10] Spyns P., Oberle D., Volz R., Zheng J., Jarrar M., Sure Y., Studer R. & Meersman R., "OntoWeb – a Semantic Web Community Portal", in Karagiannis D. & Reimer U., (eds.), in Proceedings of the Fourth International Conference on Practical Aspects of Knowledge Management (PAKM02), LNAI 2569, Springer Verlag, pp. 189–200.

[11] http://www.daml.org/2001/03/daml+oil-ex.daml

[12] Guarino, N., "Formal Ontology in Information Systems", in N. Guarino (ed.) Proceedings of FOIS'98, Trento, Italy, June, 1998.

[13] Gruber, T.R., "Toward Principle for the Design of Ontologies Used for Knowledge Sharing", International Journal of Human and Computer Studies, 43(5/6): 907–928.

[14] A. Borgida, R.J. Brachman, D.L. McGuinness, and L.A. Resnick, "CLASSIC: A Structural Data Model for Objects", in Proceedings of the ACM SIGMOD International Conference on Management of Data, pp. 58–67, Portland, OR, 1989.

[15] P. Compton and R. Jansen, "Knowledge in Context: A Strategy for Expert System Maintenance", C.J. Barter and M.J. Brooks, in Procs of the 2nd Australian Joint Artificial Intelligence Conf, pp.292–306, Adelaide, Aus, Nov., 1998.
[16] P. Compton and R. Jansen, "A Philosophical Basis for Knowledge Acquisition", Knowledge Acquisition 2(3), pp. 241–258.
[17] R. Agrawal, A. Borgida, H.V. Jagadish, "Efficient Management of Transitive Relationship in Large Data Bases", SIGMOD 1989.
[18] http://www-ksl-svc.stanford.edu:5915
[19] T.R. Gruber, "A Translation Approach to Portable Ontology Specifications", in Proceedings of the 2nd Japanese Knowledge Acquisition for Knowledge-based Systems Workshop, Kobe, 1992.
[20] http://www.ontorama.org/doc/intro.html
[21] An Ontology Server for Agentcities.NET, http://www.ukoln.ac.uk/metadata/agentcities/InterimReport.htm
[22] Ontology Server Research, http://www.starlab.vub.ac.be/research/dogma/OntologyServer.htm
[23] G. Zhao, J. Zheng and R. Meersman, "An Architecture Framework of Ontology Development and Deployment", in Proceedings of the E-Society IADIS International Conference, 2003.
[24] P. Martin and P. Eklund, "Knowledge Indexation and Retrieval and the World Wide Web", IEEE Intelligent Systems – Special Issue on "Knowledge Management and Knowledge Distribution over the Internet", July, pp. 18–25, 2000.
[25] Y. Li, H. Yang and W. Chu, "Clarity-Guided Belief Revision for Domain Knowledge Recovery in Legacy Systems", in Proceedings of the 12th International Conference on Software Engineering and Knowledge Engineering, Chicago, USA, Jul., 2000.

Semantic Annotation, Indexing, and Retrieval

Atanas Kiryakov, Borislav Popov, Damyan Ognyanoff, Dimitar Manov, Angel Kirilov, and Miroslav Goranov

Ontotext Lab, Sirma AI EOOD, 138 Tsarigradsko Shose, Sofia 1784, Bulgaria
{naso,borislav,damyan,mitac,angel,miro}@sirma.bg

Abstract. The Semantic Web realization depends on the availability of critical mass of metadata for the web content, linked to formal knowledge about the world. This paper presents our vision about a holistic system allowing annotation, indexing, and retrieval of documents with respect to real-world entities. A system (called KIM), partially implementing this concept is shortly presented and used for evaluation and demonstration.
Our understanding is that a system for semantic annotation should be based upon specific knowledge about the world, rather than indifferent to any ontological commitments and general knowledge. To assure efficiency and reusability of the metadata we introduce a simplistic upper-level ontology which starts with some basic philosophic distinctions and goes down to the most popular entity types (people, companies, cities, etc.), thus providing many of the inter-domain common sense concepts and allowing easy domain-specific extensions. Based on the ontology, an extensive knowledge base of entities descriptions is maintained.
Semantically enhanced information extraction system providing automatic annotation with references to classes in the ontology and instances in the knowledge base is presented. Based on these annotations, we perform IR-like indexing and retrieval, further extended using the ontology and knowledge about the specific entities.

1 Introduction

Semantic Web is about adding formal semantics (metadata, knowledge) to the web content for the purpose of more efficient access and management. Since its vitality depends on the presence of critical mass of metadata, the acquisition of this metadata is a major challenge for the Semantic Web community. Though, in some cases unavoidable, the manual accumulation of this explicit semantics is not considered a feasible approach. Our vision is that fully automatic methods for semantic annotation should be researched and developed. For this to happen, the necessary design and modeling questions should be faced and resolved, and the enabling complementary resources and infrastructure should be provided. To assure wide acceptance and usage of semantic annotation systems their tasks should be clearly defined, their performance – properly evaluated and communicated.

The semantic annotation offered here is a specific metadata generation and usage schema targeted to enable new information access methods and extend existing ones. The annotation scheme offered is based on the understanding that the named entities

D. Fensel et al. (Eds.): ISWC 2003, LNCS 2870, pp. 484–499, 2003.

(NE, see 1.1) mentioned in the documents constitute important part of their semantics. Further, using different sorts of redundancy, external or background knowledge, those entities can be coupled with formal descriptions and thus provide more semantics and connectivity to the web. We hope that the expectations towards the Semantic Web will be easier to realize if the following basic tasks can be defined and solved:

1. Annotate and hyperlink (references to) named entities in text documents;

2. Index and retrieve documents with respect to the referred entities.

The first task can be seen as an advanced combination of basic press-clipping exercise, typical IE[1] task, and automatic hyper-linking. The resulting annotations represent basically a document enrichment and presentation method, which can further be used to enable other access methods.

The second task is just a modification of the classical IR task – documents are retrieved based on relevance to NEs instead of words. However the basic assumption is quite similar – the documents are characterized by the bag of tokens[2] constituting their content, disregarding its structure. While the basic IR approach considers as tokens the word stems, for the last decade there was considerable effort towards using word-senses or lexical concepts (see [20] and [36]) for indexing and retrieval. The named entities can be seen as special sort of token to be taken care of. What we present here is one more (pretty much independent) development direction instead of alternative of the contemporary IR trends.

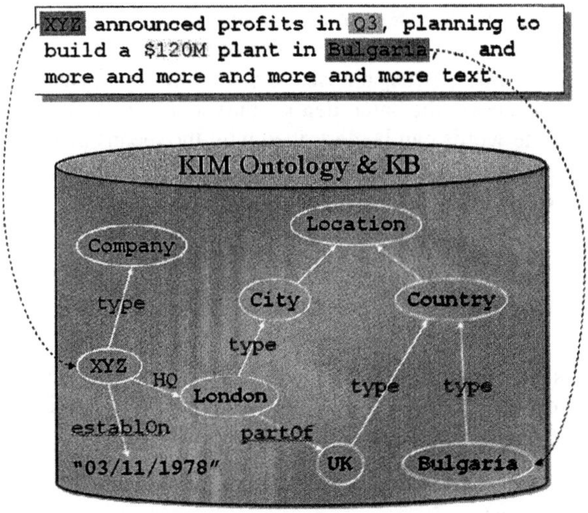

Fig. 1. Semantic Annotation

In a nutshell, Semantic Annotation is about assigning to the entities in the text links to their semantic descriptions (as presented on Fig. 1). This sort of metadata provides

---

[1] Information extraction, a relatively young discipline in the Natural Language Processing (NLP), which conducts partial analysis of text in order to extract specific information, [6].

[2] Or "atomic text entities" as those are referred in [17].

both class and instance information about the entities. It is a matter of terminology whether these annotations should be called "semantic", "entity" or some other way. To the best of our knowledge there is no well-established term for this task; neither there is a well-established meaning for "semantic annotation". What is more important, the automatic semantic annotations enable many new applications: highlighting, indexing and retrieval, categorization, generation of more advanced metadata, smooth traversal between unstructured text and available relevant knowledge. Semantic annotation is applicable for any sort of text – web pages, regular (non-web) documents, text fields in databases, etc. Further, knowledge acquisition can be performed based on extraction of more complex dependencies – analysis of relationships between entities, event and situation descriptions, etc.

This paper presents a schema for automatic semantic annotation, indexing and retrieval, together with a discussion on number of design and modeling questions (section 2) followed by discussion on the process (section 3). In section 4, we present a software platform, KIM, which demonstrates this model based on the latest Semantic Web and Information Extraction technology. The fifth section provides survey on related work. Conclusion and future work are discussed in section 6.

1.1 Named Entities

In the NLP and particularly IE tradition, **named entities** are considered: *people, organizations, locations*, and others referred by name. In a wider interpretation, those include also scalar values *(numbers,dates, amounts of money)*, *addresses*, etc.

The NEs require different handling because of their different nature and semantics[3] as opposed to the words (terms, phrases, etc.) While the former denote particulars (individuals or instances), the later denote universals (concepts, classes, relations, attributes). While the words can be described with the means of lexical semantics and common sense, the understanding and managing of named entities, requires more specific world knowledge.

2 Semantic Annotation Model and Representation

Here we discuss the structure and the representation of the semantic annotations, including the necessary knowledge and metadata. There are number of basic prerequisite for representation of semantic annotations:

- Ontology (or at least taxonomy) defining the entity classes. It should be possible to refer to those classes;
- Entity identifiers which allow those to be distinguished and linked to their semantic descriptions;
- Knowledge base with entity descriptions.

[3] Without trying to discuss what semantic means in general, we simplify it down to "a model or description of an object which allows further interpretation."

The next question considers an important choice for the representation of the annotations – "to embed or not to embed?" Although the embedded annotations seem easier to maintain, there are number of arguments providing evidence that the semantic annotations have to be decoupled from the content they refer to. One key reason is to allow dynamic, user-specific, semantic annotations – the embedded annotations become part of the content and may not change corresponding to the interest of the user or the context of usage. Further, embedded complex annotations would have negative impact on the volume of the content and can complicate its maintenance – imagine that page with three layers of overlapping semantic annotations need to be updated preserving them consistent. Those and number of other issues defending the externally encoded annotation can be found in [34] which also provides an interesting parallel to the open hypermedia systems.

Once decided that the semantic annotations has to be kept separate from the content, the next question is whether or not (or how much) to couple the annotations with the ontology and the knowledge base? It is the case that such integration seems profitable – it would be easier to keep in synch the annotations with the class and entity descriptions. However, there are at least two important problems:

- Both the cardinality and the complexity of the annotations differ from those of the entity descriptions – the annotations are simpler, but their count is usually much bigger than this of the entity descriptions. Even considering middle-sized document corpora the annotations can reach tens of millions. Suppose 10M annotations are stored in an RDF(S) store together with 1M entity descriptions. Suppose also that each annotation and each entity description are represented with 10 statements. There is a considerable difference regarding the inference approaches and hardware capable in efficient reasoning and access to 10M-statement repository and with 110M-statement repository.
- It would be nice if the world knowledge (ontology and instance data) and the document-related metadata are kept independent. This would mean that for one and the same document different extraction, processing, or authoring methods will be able to deliver alternative metadata referring to one and the same knowledge store.
- Most important, it should be possible the ownership and the responsibility for the metadata and the knowledge to be distributed. This way, different parties can develop and maintain separately the content, the metadata, and the knowledge.

Fig. 2. Distributed Heterogeneous Knowledge

Based on the above arguments we propose decoupled representation and management of the documents, the metadata (annotations) and the formal knowledge (ontologies and instance data) as depicted on Fig. 2.

2.1 Light-Weight Upper Level Ontology

We will shortly advocate the appropriateness of using ontology for defining the entity types – those are the only wide accepted paradigm for management of open, sharable, and reusable knowledge. According to our view, light-weight ontology (poor on axioms) is sufficient for simple definition of the entity classes, their appropriate attributes, and relations. In the same time it allows more efficient and scalable management of the knowledge (compared the heavy-weight semantic approaches.)

The ontology to support semantic annotation in a web context should address number of general classes which use to appear in texts in various domains. Describing these classes together with the most basic relations and attributes means that an upper-level ontology should be involved. The experience within number of projects[4] demonstrates that "logically extensive" upper-level ontologies are extremely hard to agree on, build, maintain, understand, and use. This seems to provide enough evidence that a light-weight upper level ontology is necessary for semantic annotations.

2.2 Knowledge Representation Language

According to the analysis of ontology and knowledge representation languages and formats in [11] and other authors it becomes evident that there is no much consensus beyond RDF(S), see [4]. The latter is well established in the Semantic Web community as a knowledge representation and interchange language. The rich diversity of RDF(S) repositories, APIs and tools, forms a mature environment for development of systems grounded in RDF(S) representation of their ontological and knowledge resources. Because of the common acceptance of RDF(S) in the Semantic Web community, it would be easy to reuse the ontology and KB, as well as enrich them with domain-specific extensions. The new OWL (see [9]) standard offers clear, relatively consensual and backward-compatible path beyond RDF(S), but still lacks sufficient tool support. Our experience shows (see the section on KIM) that for the basic purposes of light-weight ontology definition and entity description, RDF(S) provides sufficient basic expressiveness. The most critical nice-to-have primitives (equality, transitive and symmetric relations, etc.) are well covered in OWL Lite – the simplest first level of OWL. So, we suggest that RDF(S) is used in a way which allows easy extension towards OWL – this means avoiding primitives and patterns not included in OWL, http://www.w3.org/2002/07/owl.

2.3 Metadata Encoding and Management

The metadata has to be stored in a format allowing its efficient management; we are not going to prescribe a specific format here, but rather to outline number of principles and requirements towards the document and annotation management:

[4] For instance, Cyc (http://www.cyc.com) and the Standard Upper Ontology initiative (http://suo.ieee.org/)

- Documents (and other content) in different formats to be identifiable and their text content to be accessible;
- To allow non-embedded annotations over documents to be stored, managed and retrieved according to their positions, features, and references to a KB;
- To allow embedding of the annotations at least for some of the formats;
- To allow export and exchange of the annotations in different formats.

There are number of standards and initiatives related to encoding and representation of metadata related to text. Two of the most popular are TEI[5] and Tipster[6].

2.4 Knowledge Base

Once having the entity types, relations, and attributes encoded in an ontology, the next aspect of the semantic annotation representation are the entity descriptions. It should be possible to identify, describe and interconnect the entities in a general, flexible and standard fashion. We call a body of formal knowledge about entities a knowledge base (KB) – although a bit old-fashioned, this term reflects best the representation of non-ontological formal knowledge. A KB is expected to contain mostly instance knowledge/data, so, other names can also make a good fit for such dataset.

We consider that the ontology (defining all classes, relations and attributes, together with further constraints and dependencies) is a sort of schema for the KB and both should be kept into a semantic store – any sort of formal knowledge reasoning and management system which provides the basic operations: storage and retrieval according to the syntax and semantics of the selected formalism. The store may or may not provide inference[7], it can implement different reasoning strategies, etc. There are also more advanced management features which are not considered as a must: versioning, access control, transaction support, locking, client-caching. For an overview of those see [16], [15], [19] and [25]. Whether the ontology and knowledge base should be kept together – this is a matter of distributed knowledge representation and management which is outside the scope of this paper.

The KB can host two sorts of entity knowledge (descriptions and relationships):

- Pre-populated – such imported or otherwise acquired from trusted sources;
- Automatically extracted – such discovered in the process of semantic annotation (say via IE) or using other knowledge discovery and acquisition methods such as data-mining.

It is up to the specific implementation, whether or not and how much the KB to be pre-populated. For instance, information about entities of general importance (including their aliases) can significantly help the IE used for automatic semantic annotations – an extensive proposal about this can be found in the description of the KIM platform later on in this paper.

Further, domain and task specific knowledge could help the customization of a semantic annotation application – after extending the ontology to match the appliance

[5] The Text Encoding Initiative, http://www.tei-c.org/

[6] Tipster Architecture, http://www.cs.nyu.edu/cs/faculty/grishman/tipster.html

[7] For instance, there are experts who do not consider as inference the interpretation of RDF(S) according to its model-theoretic semantics, just because this one is simple compared to semantic and the inference methods in other languages.

domain, the KB could be pre-populated with specific entities. For instance, information about specific markets, customers, products, technologies and competitors could be of a great help for business intelligence and press-clipping; for company intelligence within UK it would be important to have more exhaustive coverage of UK-based companies and UK locations. It might also appear beneficial to reduce the general information that is not applicable in the concrete context and thus construct a more focused KB.

Since state of the art IE (and in particular named entity recognition, NER) allows recognition of new (previously unknown) entities and relations between them, it is reasonable to use this advantage for the enrichment of the KB. Because of the innate non-preciseness of these methods, the knowledge accumulated through them should be distinguishable from the one that was pre-populated. Thus the extraction of new metadata, can still be grounded in the trusted knowledge about the world, while the accumulated entities would be available for indexing, browsing and navigation. Recognized entities could be transformed to trusted ones at some point, through semi-automatic validation process. Important part of this enrichment would be the template extraction of entity relations, which could be referred to as some kind of content-based learning of the system. Depending on the texts that are being processed, the respective changes would occur in the recognized parts of the KB, and thus its projection of the world would change accordingly (e.g. processing only sport news articles, the metadata would be both rich for this domain and poor for the others.)

2.5 Unified Representation of Lexical Knowledge

The symbolic IE processing usually requires some lexica to be used for pattern recognition and other purposes. These are both general entries (such as various sorts of stop words) as well as such specific for the entity classes being handled. It is common that IE systems keep these in application-specific formats or directly hard-coded in the source code.

It's worth to represent and manage those in the same format used for the ontology and the entity knowledge base – this way the same tools (parsers, editors, etc.) can be used to manage both sorts of knowledge. For this purpose, part of the ontology (or just a separate one) could be dedicated to defining the types of lexical resources used by the natural language technologies involved.

The corresponding lexical resources part of the KB should be pre-populated to aid the IE process by providing clues for the entity and relation recognition, which goes beyond the already known instances. For instance, for efficient recognition of persons in the text one would need lists of first names (male and female), person titles, positions and professions. Some of these could be ontologically distinguishable by gender, as well. For the Organization lexica one should pre-populate possible suffixes (such as Ltd., GmbH, etc.), and terms appearing in the organization name (e.g. company, theatre, etc.). Additionally, time and date lexica ("a.m.", "Tue", etc.), currency units, address lexica and others should be included. The mature symbolic NER and IE systems already have coverage of such resources; the next step to integrate them in a system for automatic semantic annotation would be just to encode them in a formal ontology and present them in the KB.

3 Semantic Annotation Process

As already mentioned, we focus mainly on the automatic semantic annotation, leaving manual annotation to approaches more related to authoring web content. Even less accurate, the automatic approaches for metadata acquisition promise scalability and without them the Semantic Web will remain mostly a vision for long time. Our experience shows that the existing state-of-the-art IE systems have the potential to automate the annotation with reasonable accuracy and performance.

Although a lot of research and development contributed in the area of automatic IE so far, the lack of standards and integration with formal knowledge management systems was obscuring its usage. We claim that it is crucial to encode the extracted knowledge formally and according to well known and widely accepted knowledge representation and metadata encoding standards. Such system should be easily extensible for domain-specific applications, providing basic means for addressing the most common entities types, their attributes, and relations.

3.1 Extraction

It is a major problem with the traditional NER approaches that the annotations produced are not encoded in an open formal system and unbound entity types are used. The resources used are also traditionally presented in a proprietary form with no clear semantics. This hinders the reuse of both lexical resources and the resulting annotations by other systems, thus limiting the progress of the language technologies, since effortless sharing of resources and results is too expensive.

These problems can be partly resolved by an ontology-based infrastructure for IE. As proposed above, the entity types should be defined within an ontology, and the entities being recognized to be described (or at least kept) in accompanying KB. Thus the NLP systems with ontology support would more easily share both pre-populated knowledge and the results of their processing, as well, as all the different sorts of lexicons and other resources commonly used.

An important case demonstrating how ontologies can be used in IE are the so-called gazetteers used to look-up in the text predefined strings out of predefined lists. At present, the lists are being kept in proprietary formats. Typical result of the work of the gazetteers are annotations with some unbound strings used as types. A better approach presumes all the various annotation types and list values to be kept in a semantic store. Thus, the resulting annotation can be typed by reference to ontology classes and even further, point to specific lexeme or entity, if appropriate.

Since a huge amount of NLP research has been contributed in the recent years (and even decades), we suggest the reuse of existing systems with proven maturity, and effectiveness. Such system should be modified so to use resources kept in a KB and produce annotations referring to the latter. Our experience shows that such a change is not a trivial one. All the processing layers have to be re-engineered in order to get opened towards the semantic repository and depend on it for their inputs. However, there are number of benefits of such approach:

- All the various sorts of resources can be managed in a much more standard and uniform way;
- It becomes easier to manage the different sorts of linguistic knowledge at the proper level of generality. For instance, a properly structured entity type hierarchy

would allow that the entities and their references in the text are classified in the most precise way, but still easily matched in more general patterns. Thus, one can have a specific mountain annotated and still match it within a grammar rule which expects any sort of location;

- Wherever it is possible, any available further knowledge will be accessible directly with a reference from the annotation to the semantic store. Thus, available knowledge for an entity can be used for instance for disambiguation or co-reference resolution tasks.

A processing layer that is not inherent to the traditional IE systems can generate and store in the KB the descriptions of the newly discovered entities. When the same entity is encountered in the text next time, it can be directly linked to the already generated description. Further, extending the IE task to cover template relations extraction, another layer could enrich the KB with these relations.

3.2 Indexing and Retrieval

Historically, the issue of specific handling of the named entities was neglected by the information retrieval (IR) community, apart from some shallow handling for the purpose of Questions/Answering tasks. However, a recent large scale human interaction study on a personal content IR system of Microsoft (reported in [10]) demonstrates that, at least in some cases, the ignorance of the named entities does not match the user needs: "The most common query types in our logs were People/places/things, Computers/internet and Health/science. In the People/places thing category, names were especially prevalent. Their importance is highlighted by the fact that 25% of the queries involved people's names suggesting that people are a powerful memory cue for personal content. In contrast, general informational queries are less prevalent."

As the web content is rapidly growing, the demand of more advanced retrieval methods increases accordingly. Based on semantic annotations, efficient indexing and retrieval techniques could be developed involving explicit handling of the named entity references.

In a nutshell, the semantic annotations could be used to index both "NY" and "N.Y." as occurrence of the specific entity "New York" like if there was just its unique ID. Because of no entity recognition involved, the present systems will index on "NY", "N", and "Y" which demonstrates well some of the problems with the keyword-based search engines.

Given metadata indexing of the content, advanced semantic querying should be feasible. In a query towards a repository of semantically annotated documents, it should be possible to specify entity type restrictions, name and other attribute restrictions, as well as relations between the entities of interest. For instance, it should possible to make a query that targets all documents that refer to Persons that hold some Positions within an Organization, and also restricts the names of the entities or some of their attributes (e.g. a person's gender).

Further, semantic annotations could be used to match specific references in the text to more general queries. For instance, a query such as "company 'Redwood Shores'" could match documents mentioning the town and specific companies such as ORACLE and Symbian, but not the word "company".

Finally, although the above sketched enhancements look prominent, it still requires a lot of research and experiments to determine to what extent and how they could improve the existing IR systems. It is hard in a general context to predict how semantic indexing will combine with the symbolic and the statistical methods currently in use, such as the lexical approach presented in [20] and the latent semantic analysis presented in [18]. For this purpose, large scale experimental data and evaluation are required.

4 KIM Platform: Implementing the Vision

The Knowledge and Information Management (KIM) platform embodies our vision of semantic annotation, indexing and retrieval services and infrastructure. An essential idea in KIM, is the semantic (or entity) annotation, (as depicted on Fig. 1). It can be seen as a classical named-entity recognition and annotation process. However, in contrast to most of the existing IE systems, KIM provides for each entity reference in the text (i) a link (URI) to the most specific class in the ontology and (ii) a link to the specific instance in the knowledge base. The latest is (to the best of our knowledge) an unique KIM feature which allows further indexing and retrieval of documents with respect to entities.

For the end-user, the usage of a KIM-based application is straightforward and simple – requesting annotation from a browser plug-in, which highlights the entities in the current content and generates a hyperlink used for further exploring the available knowledge for the entity (as shown in Fig. 4). A semantic query web UI allows specification of a search query, that consists of entity type, name, attribute and relation restrictions (allowing queries such as **`Organization-locatedIn-Country`**, **`Person-hasPosition-Position-within-Organization`**, etc.)
This section provides a short overview of the main components of KIM, which is presented in bigger details in [27] and on its web site, http://www.ontotext.com/kim.

4.1 KIM Architecture

The KIM platform consists of KIM Ontology (KIMO) [8], knowledge base, KIM Server (with API for remote access, embedding, and integration), and front-ends (browser plug-in for Internet Explorer, Semantic Query web user interface, and Knowledge Explorer for KB navigation). KIM ontologies and knowledge bases are kept in the Sesame[9] RDF(S) repository and the Ontology Middleware Module[10] [16].

KIM provides a mature infrastructure for IE, annotation and document management, based on GATE[11] [7]. The Lucene[12] information retrieval engine has been adopted to index documents by entity types and measure relevance according

---

8 http://www.ontotext.com/kim/2003/03/kimo.rdfs

9 http://sesame.aidministrator.nl/, RDF(S) repository by Aidministrator b.v.

10 OMM (www.ontotext.com/omm) is an enterprise back-end for knowledge management.

11 General Architecture for Text Engineering (GATE), http://gate.ac.uk, leading NLP and IE platform developed in the University of Sheffield.

12 Lucene, http://jakarta.apache.org/lucene/, high performance full text search engine

entities, along with tokens and stems. It is important to mention that KIM, as a software platform, is domain and task independent as are Gate, Sesame and Lucene.

4.2 KIM Ontology (KIMO)

KIM uses a simplistic upper-level ontology starting with some basic philosophic distinctions between entity types (such as **`Object`**-s - existing entities such as locations and agents, **`Happening`**-s – defining events and situations, and **`Abstract`**-ions that are neither objects, neither happenings). Further on, the ontology goes in more details to such extent that real-world entity types of general importance are included (meetings, military conflicts, employment positions, commercial, government and other organizations, people, and various locations, etc.). The characteristic attributes and relations for the featured entity types, are defined (e.g. **`subRegionOf`** property for **`Location`**-s, **`hasPosition`** for **`Person`**s, **`locatedIn`** for organizations, etc.) Having this simplistic upper-level ontology as basis, one could add domain-specific extensions to it easily, for profiling the semantic annotation for concrete applications.

The distribution of the most commonly referred entity types varies greatly from domain to domain. As researched in [23], despite the difference of type distributions, there are several general entity types that appear in all corpuses – Person, Location, Organization, Money (amount), Dates, etc. The proper representation and positioning of those basic types was one of the objectives behind the design of KIMO. Further the ontology defines more specific entity types (e.g. **`Mountain`**, as a more specific type than **`Location`**.) The extent of specialization of the ontology is determined on the basis of research of the entity types in a corpus of general news (incl. political, sport, financial, etc.)

The KIM ontology (KIMO)[13] consists of about 250 classes and 100 properties. The top Entities could be seen in the type hierarchy of the KIM plug-in on Fig 4. The ontology is encoded in RDF(S). In addition number of "generative" (in the style of the RDFS MT semantics) axioms are defined, such as:

`<X, locatedIn, Y>` and **`<Y, subRegionOf, Z>`** => **`<X, locatedIn, Z>`**

This sort of axioms are supported by Sesame and provide easy to understand and manage consistent mechanism for "custom" extensions to the RDF(S) semantics with respect to specific ontology. Those axioms can be seen as an add-hoc but quite practical way to avoid the RDF(S) constraints without a need to implement some specific flavor of OWL or another language.

4.3 KIM Knowledge Base

The entity descriptions are being stored in the same RDF(S) repository as the KIM ontology. Each entity has information about its specific type, aliases (incl. a main alias, expressing the (most probable) official name), attributes (e.g. latitude of a **`Location`**), and relations (e.g. a **`Location subRegionOf`** another **`Location`**). A simplified schema of the entity representation is depicted on Fig. 3.

---

[13] http://www.ontotext.com/kim/2003/03/kimo.rdfs

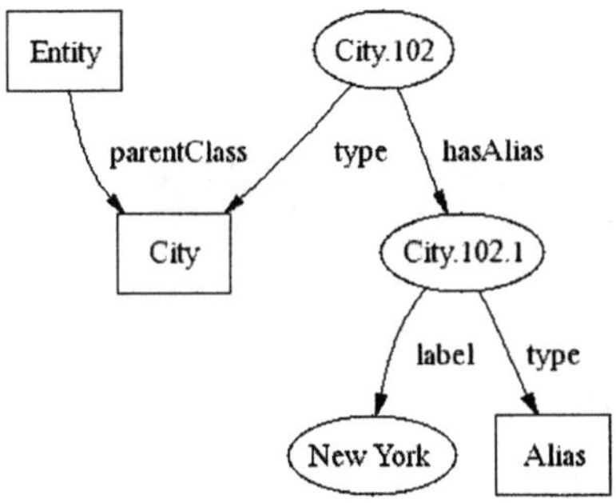

Fig. 3. Simplified entity description

KIM KB has been pre-populated with entities of general importance, that allow enough clues for the IE process to perform well on inter-domain web content. It consists of about 80,000 entities. Various relations between entities are also predefined (like position of a person in an organization or company's allocation.)

4.4 KIM Information Extraction

KIM IE is based on the GATE framework, which has proved its maturity, extensibility and task independency for IE and other NL applications. The essence of the KIM IE, is the recognition of named entities (NE) with respect to KIMO ontology. The entity instances all bear unique identifiers (URI) that allow annotations to be linked both to the entity type and to the exact individual in the KB. For new (previously unknown) entities, URIs are being generated and assigned, next minimal descriptions are stored in the semantic store. The annotations are kept separated from the annotated content, and an API for their management is provided.

The actual processing of the content goes through several steps, starting with tokenization, splitting to sentences, and part of speech tagging. These processing layers are provided by the GATE framework, along with grammars and other standard building bricks for construction of sophisticated IE applications. However, number of components and resources have been considerably re-engineered and new ones were developed.

4.5 Indexing and Retrieval

Once the NER process has finished, the content is indexed with respect to specific NE. This enables queries with restrictions over entities, entity types, names, attributes, and relations. Technically, Lucene is adapted to perform full-text indexing, which is uniquely addressing each entity disregarding the alias used in the text. The retrieval accuracy of KIM has not been evaluated against a traditional IR engine, and this is a topic that would be researched in the future.

4.6 KIM Front-Ends

Different KIM front-end user interfaces are possible given the KIM API, which provides the functionality and infrastructure for the semantic annotation, indexing and retrieval, as well as document management, and KB navigation. We have created a

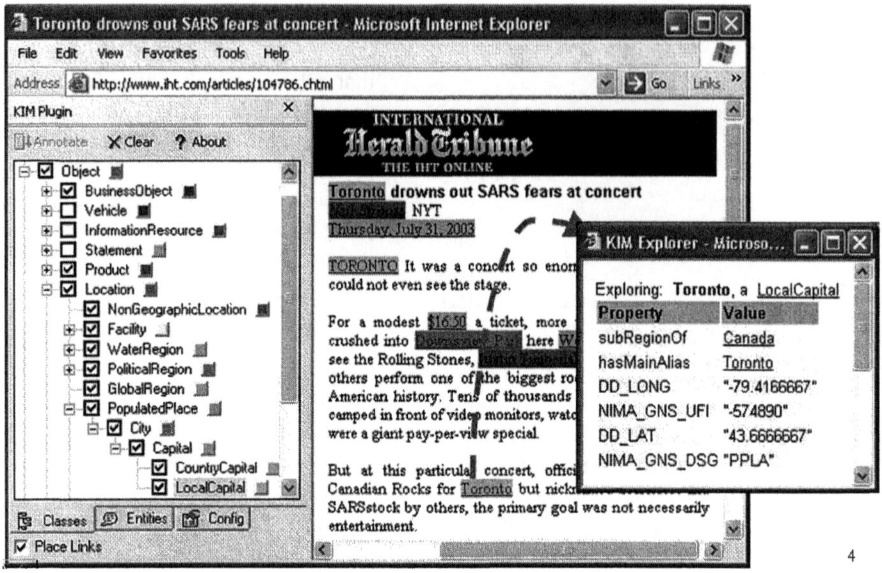

Fig. 4. The KIM plug-in with the top of the KIM Ontology, and KIM Explorer on top

plug-in (Fig. 4) for the Internet Explorer browser. The KIM plug-in provides lightweight semantic annotations delivery to the end user. On its first tab, the plug-in displays the entity type hierarchy (a branch of the KIM ontology). For each entity type there is an associated color used for highlighting the annotations of this type. Check boxes for each entity, allow the user to select the entity types of interest.

Upon invoking annotation of the current browser content, the plug-in extracts the text of the currently displayed document and sends it to an Annotation Server which is in its turn using the KIM Server NER API. The servers return the annotations with their offsets, type and instance information. The annotations are highlighted in the content (in the color of the respective entity type), and are hyperlinked to the KIM KB Explorer (Fig. 4). On the second tab of the plug-in there is a list of all the recognized entities for the current document, sorted by appearance frequency. Upon choosing from the list of entities, or following a hyperlink over an annotated entity in the text the user invokes the KIM KB Explorer, which provides a view of the part of the KB and the ontology that are related to the chosen entity (incl. type, aliases, relations and attributes). This way the user can directly navigate from the annotations to the instances that they are linked to in the KB. Via this explorer, the KB could be further explored by choosing one of the related entities, or the entity class.

5 Related Work

Semantic annotation of documents with respect to ontology and entity knowledge base is discussed in [5] and [14] – although presenting interesting and ambitious approaches, these do not discuss usage of information extraction for automatic annotation. The focus of [14] is manual semantic annotation for authoring web content, while [5] targets the creation of a web-based open hypermedia linking service, backed by a conceptual model of document terminology. Semantic annotation is used also in the S-CREAM project presented in [13] – the approach there is interesting with the heavy involvement of machine learning techniques for extraction of relations between the entities being annotated. Similar approach is taken also within the MnM project [35], where the semantic annotations can be placed inline in the document content and refer to an ontology and KB server (WebOnto), accessible via standard API. Another related approach is taken in OFF, [8], which puts an emphasize on the collaborative ontology development and annotation.

An interesting NE indexing and question/answering system is presented in [24]. Flat set of entity types is assigned to tokens and the annotations are incorporated in the content, in order to index by NE type later. Once indexed the content is queried via NL questions, with NE tagging over the question used to determine the expected answer type (e.g. When have the UN been established; UN here would be tagged with _ORG, specifying that the expected answer type is organization.) All the semantic annotation techniques above lack usage of upper-level ontologies and critical mass of world knowledge to serve as a trusted and reusable basis for the automatic recognition and annotation, as in the approach presented in [1] and discussed later on here.

Significant amount of research on information extraction (IE) has been performed in various projects within the GATE framework (see [6-7], [23]) with many existing tools and resources available. We build on those to provide language technology open to the Semantic Web standards and tools.

6 Conclusion and Future Work

This paper presented the notion of semantic annotation– an original meta-data model allowing ontology based named-entity annotation, indexing, and retrieval. Number of issues related to the representation and the usage of the semantic annotation were addressed. The KIM platform (addressed with more details in [27]) was shortly introduced to demonstrate an implementation of this vision.

The evaluation work done until now does not provide enough evidence regarding the approach, technology, and resources being used. The major obstacle is that there are neither test data nor well developed metrics for semantic annotation and retrieval.

Although naïve in some aspects, KIM platform provides a test bed and proves number of hypothesis and design decisions:

- It is worth using massive entity knowledge for. Even without comprehensive disambiguation, the precision drawbacks seem acceptable;
- It is possible to store and query tens of thousands of entities together with their descriptions in an RDF(S) repository (namely, Sesame);
- A simple but efficient technique for entity-aware IR is demonstrated;
- Few of light-weight front end tools can deliver in intuitive fashion the results of semantic annotation, indexing, and retrieval.

The challenges towards the general approach can be summarized as follows:

- Develop (or adapt) evaluation metric which properly measures the performance of a semantic annotation system;
- Experiment different approaches towards disambiguation of named-entity references: adaptation of a Hidden Markov Model learner successfully used for

non-semantic disambiguation is one of the first ideas; techniques similar to those used for word-sense disambiguation (namely, lexical-chaining); techniques for "symbolic" context management.

References

1. Bontcheva K., Kiryakov A., Cunningham H., Popov B., Dimitrov M. *Semantic Web Enabled, Open Source Language Technology.* In proc. of EACL Workshop "Language Technology and the Semantic Web", NLPXML-2003, 13 April, 2003
2. Brickley D, Guha R.V., eds. *Resource Description Framework (RDF) Schemas,* W3C http://www.w3.org/TR/2000/CR-rdf-schema-20000327/
3. Carr L., Bechhofer S., Goble C., Hall W. *Conceptual Linking: Ontology-based Open Hypermedia.* In The WWW10 Conference, Hong Kong, May, pp. 334–342.
4. Cunningham H., *Information Extraction: a User Guide* (revised version). Department of Computer Science, University of Sheffield, May, 1999
5. Cunningham H., Maynard D., Bontcheva K. and Tablan V., *GATE: A Framework and Graphical Development Environment for Robust NLP Tools and Applications.* In proc. of the 40th Anniversary Meeting of the Association for Computational Linguistics, 2002.
6. Collier N., Takeuchi K, Kawazoe A. *Open Ontology Forge: An Environment for Text Mining in a Semantic Web World.* In proc. of the International Workshop on Semantic Web Foundations and Application Technologies, Nara, Japan, 11th March.
7. Dean M., Connolly D., van Harmelen, F., Hendler J., Horrocks I., McGuinness D., Patel-Schneider P., Stein L.A., *Web Ontology Language (OWL) Reference Version 1.0.* W3C Working Draft 12 Nov. 2002, http://www.w3.org/TR/2002/WD-owl-ref-20021112/
8. Dumais S., Cutrell E., Cadiz J., Jancke G., Sarin R. and Robbins D. *Stuff I've Seen: A system for personal information retrieval and re-use.* In proc. of SIGIR'03, July 28 – August 1, 2003, Toronto, Canada, ACM Press, pp. 72–79.
9. Fensel D. *Ontology Language, v.2 (Welcome to OIL)* . Deliverable 2, On-To-Knowledge project, Dec 2001. http://www.ontoknowledge.org/downl/del2.pdf
10. Handschuh S., Staab St., Ciravegna F. *S-CREAM – Semi-automatic CREAtion of Metadata.* The 13th International Conference on Knowledge Engineering and Management (EKAW 2002), ed Gomez-Perez, A., Springer Verlag, 2002.
11. Kahan J., Koivunen M., Prud'Hommeaux E., Swick R. *Annotea: An Open RDF Infrastructure for Shared Web Annotations.* In The WWW10 Conference, Hong Kong, May, pp. 623–632.
12. Kampman A., Harmelen F., Broekstra J. *Sesame: A Generic Architecture for Storing and Querying RDF and RDF Schema.* In proc. of ISWC2002, June 9–12th, 2002, Italia.
13. Kiryakov A., Simov K. Iv., Ognyanov D. *Ontology Middleware: Analysis and Design* Del. 38, On-To-Knowledge, March 2002. http://www.ontoknowledge.org/downl/del38.pdf
14. Kiryakov A., Simov K. Iv. *Ontologically Supported Semantic Matching.* In proc. of "NODALIDA'99: Nordic Conference on Comp. Linguistics", Trondheim, Dec. 9–10, 1999.
15. Landauer T., and Dumais S. *A solution to Plato's problem: the Latent Semantic Analysis theory of acquisition, induction and representation of knowledge.* Psychological Review, 104(2), 1997, 211–240.
16. Maedche A., Motik B., Stojanovic L., Studer R. and Volz R. *Ontologies for Enterprise Knowledge Management* [http://kaon.semanticweb.org/docus/ieee-is-maedcheetal.pdf]. In IEEE Intelligent Systems, Vol. 18, Num. 2, pp. 26–33, 2003.
17. Mahesh K., Kud J., Dixon P. *Oracle at TREC8: A Lexical Approach,* In proc. of the Eighth Text Retrieval Conference (TREC-8), 1999.

18. Manov D, Kiryakov A, Popov B, Bontcheva K, Maynard D, Cunningham H. *Experiments with geographic knowledge for information extraction.* NAACL-HLT 2003, Canada. Workshop on the Analysis of Geographic References, May 31 2003, Edmonton, Alberta.
19. Maynard D., Tablan V., Bontcheva K., Cunningham H, and Wilks Y. *MUlti-Source Entity recognition – an Information Extraction System for Diverse Text Types.* Technical report CS–02–03, Univ. of Sheffield, Dep. of CS, 2003. http://gate.ac.uk/gate/doc/papers.html
20. Moldovan D., Mihalcea R. *Document Indexing Using Named Entities.* In "Studies in Informatics and Control", Vol. 10, No. 1, March 2001.
21. Noy N., Musen M. *Ontology Versioning as an Element of an Ontology-Management Framework.* IEEE Intelligent Systems, to appear, 2003.
22. Popov B., Kiryakov A., Kirilov A., Manov D., Ognyanoff D., Goranov M. *KIM – Semantic Annotation Platform.* In proc. of 2nd International Semantic Web Conference (ISWC2003), 20–23 October 2003, Florida, USA. To appear.
23. Pustejovsky J., Boguraev B., Verhagen, M., Buitelaar P., and Johnston M., *Semantic Indexing and Typed Hyperlinking.* In proc. of the AAAI Conference, Spring Symposium, NLP for WWW, Stanford University, CA, 1997, pp. 120–128.
24. van Ossenbruggen J., Hardman L., Rutledge L., *Hypermedia and the Semantic Web: A Research Agenda.* Journal of Digital information, volume 3 issue 1, May 2002.
25. Vargas-Vera M., Motta E., Domingue J., Lanzoni M., Stutt A. and Ciravegna F, *MnM: Ontology Driven Semi-Automatic and Automatic Support for Semantic Markup*, In Proc. Of EKAW 2002, ed. Gomez-Perez, A., Springer Verlag, 2002.
26. 36. Voorhees E. *Using WordNet for Text Retrieval.* In "WordNet: an electronic lexical database." Fellbaum, C. (editor), MIT Press, 1998.

An Approach for the Ranking of Query Results in the Semantic Web

Nenad Stojanovic[1], Rudi Studer[1,2,3], and Ljiljana Stojanovic[2]

[1] Institute AIFB, University of Karlsruhe, 76128 Karlsruhe, Germany
{nst,rst}@aifb.uni-karlsruhe.de
[2] FZI - Research Center for Information Technology at the University of Karlsruhe, 76131 Karlsruhe, Germany
Ljiljana.Stojanovic@fzi.de
[3] Ontoprise GmbH, Amalienbadstraße 36, 76227 Karlsruhe, Germany

Abstract. One of the vital problems in the searching for information is the ranking of the retrieved results, because users make typically very short queries (2-3 terms) and tend to consider only the first ten results. In traditional IR approaches the relevance of the results is determined only by analysing the underlying information repository (content and hyperlink structure), which leads to the weak relevance model. On the other hand, in the Semantic Web the querying process is supported by an ontology such that other important sources for determining the relevance of results can be considered: the structure of the underlying domain and the characteristics of the searching process.

In this paper we present a novel approach for determining relevance in ontology-based searching for information, which exploits the "full potential" of the semantics of such a semantically-based link structure. We present several analyses about how a Semantic Web querying mechanism can benefit of using our ranking approach.

1 Introduction

One of the main goals of the current Web is information sharing, i.e. the possibility to access information without considering a particular platform, language, protocol. It was the business need behind the current Web [1]. Consequently, the focus of the Web research in the last ten years was on the standards for ensuring that Web information resources can be accessed. The development of the Semantic Web and the layering in the Semantic Web architecture should enable more efficient inclusion of machine agents in the process of searching for information resources. Moreover, the higher layers in the architecture should enable the explanation of how a piece of information was found and the reason for trusting the information. Even the emerging industrial interest in the Web Services has to rely on the Semantic Web functionalities to find a service efficiently (semantically) [2].

In this paper, we elaborate on the benefits to be expected in searching for information, when exploiting Semantic Web technologies. More precisely, based on the experiences from Web information retrieval (IR), we analyse the challenges for Semantic Web IR and develop an approach that exploits the explicitly shared

D. Fensel et al. (Eds.): ISWC 2003, LNCS 2870, pp. 500–516, 2003.

semantics of the information for the more efficient searching in the Semantic Web. Besides the improvements in the precision and recall [3], we see two other very important and practical benefits of using an ontology in the searching for information: better possibilities for ranking and clustering the retrieved information. We present a novel approach for ranking the results of ontology-based searching and show its implications on Semantic Web IR. The approach combines the characteristics of the inferencing process and the content of the information repository used in searching. It relies on our previous work on ontology-based inferencing [4] and ontology-based information retrieval [5], as well as on our current efforts in developing a Semantic Web infrastructure [6] and research in the Semantic Web Mining [7]. The approach can be very easily extended with any additional information related to the search process, e.g. the frequency of usage of ontology-based information. We have implemented the approach in the Ontobroker inference engine (ontobroker.semanticweb.org) and incorporated it in the Semantic Portal of our Institute. We present an evaluation study about the performance of this approach.

The paper is structured as follows: In the second section we introduce the terminology we use in this paper. In section 3 we present our ontology-based ranking schema and discuss its advantages for searching in the Semantic Web, whereas in section 4 we give implementation details. Results of our evaluation study are presented in section 5. Related work is presented in section 7 and section 8 contains some concluding remarks.

2 Background

In this section we give the basic terminology we use in this paper. Due to lack of space some definition of lower importance for understanding this paper are omitted.

Definition 1: Ontology

A core ontology is a structure $O := (C, \leq_C, R, \sigma, \leq_r)$ consisting of

- two disjoint sets C and R whose elements are called concept identifiers and relation identifiers, resp.,
- a partial order $\leq_c$ on C, called concept hierarchy or taxonomy (without cycles)
- a function $\sigma : R \rightarrow C^+$, called signature
- a partial order $\leq_r$ on R called relation hierarchy, where $r_1 \leq_r r_2$ implies $|\sigma(r_1)| = |\sigma(r_2)|$ and $\pi_i(\sigma(r_1)) \leq_c \pi_i(\sigma(r_2))$ for each $1 \leq i \leq |\sigma(r_1)|$

Often we call concept identifiers and relation identifiers concepts and relations, respectively, for the sake of simplicity.

Definition 2: Domain and Range

For a relation $r \in R$ with $|\sigma(r)| = 2$, we define its domain and its range by $dom(r) := \pi_1(\sigma(r))$ and $range(r) := \pi_2(\sigma(r))$.

Definition 3: Axioms (Rules)
Let L be a logical language and $L(O)$ be the set of statements in L w.r.t. an ontology O. An L-axiom system for an ontology $O := (C, \leq_c, R, \sigma, \leq_r)$ is a pair $A := (AI, \alpha)$, where

- AI is a set whose elements are called axiom identifiers and
- $\alpha : AI \to L(O)$ is a mapping.

The elements of $\alpha(AI)$ are called axioms or rules.

An ontology with L-axioms is a pair (O, A), where O is an ontology and A is an L-axiom system for O.

Definition 4: Knowledge Base
A Knowledge Base is a structure $KB := (C_{KB}, R_{KB}, I, l_c, l_r)$ consisting of

- two disjoint sets C_{KB} and R_{KB}
- a set I whose elements are called instance identifiers (or instances or objects in brief)
- a function $l_C : C_{KB} \to I$ called concept instantiation
- a function $l_r : R_{KB} \to I^+$ called relation instantiation

A relation instance can be depicted as $r(I_1, I_2, ..., I_n)$, where $r \in R_{KB}, I_i \in I$. r is called a predicate and I_i is called a term.

Definition 5: Query
A (conjunctive) query is of the form or can be rewritten into the form:

$$forall\ \overline{X}\ \ \overline{P}(\overline{X}, \overline{k})\ \text{and}\ not(\overline{N}(\overline{X}, \overline{k}))$$

with $\overline{X}$ being a vector of variables $(X_1, ..., X_n)$, $\overline{k}$ being a vector of constants (concept instances), $\overline{P}$ being a vector of conjoined predicates (relations) and $\overline{N}$ a vector of disjoined predicates (relations). A query can be viewed as an axiom without a head.

For example, for the query "forall x worksIn(x, KM) and researchIn(x, KMsystems)" we have

$$\overline{X} := (x),\ k := (KM, KMsystems),\ \overline{P} := (P_1, P_2),\ P_1(u,v,w) := worksIn(u,v),$$
$$P_2(u,v,w) := researchIn(u,w).$$

Note: In this paper we consider only conjunctive queries. Since a disjunctive query can be represented as a disjunction of several conjunctive queries our approach can be easily extended to disjunctive queries.

Definition 6: Answers (results) of a query
Let Ω be the set of all relation instances which can be proven in the given ontology (this set can be obtained by the materialisation of all rules).

For a query Q " $forall\ \overline{X}\ \ \overline{P}(\overline{X}, \overline{k})$ and $not(\overline{N}(\overline{X}, \overline{k}))$ " an answer is an element (tuple) in the set $R(Q) = \{\overline{X}\} = \{(x_1, x_2, ... x_n)\}$, such that $\overline{P}(\overline{X}, \overline{k})$ and $not(\overline{N}(\overline{X}, \overline{k}))$ is provable, i.e. each of the relation instances $r(x_1, x_2, ..., x_n, k_1, ... k_l)$, $r \in \overline{P}$ exists in the set Ω and each of $l(x_1, x_2, ..., x_n, k_1, ... k_l), l \in \overline{N}$ does not exist in Ω.

3 The Ranking in the Semantic Web

3.1 Introduction

There are two crucial differences between Web IR and searching for information in the Semantic Web:

- Instead of searching for web documents, an agent in the Semantic Web searches for resources which satisfy some formally defined conditions, i.e. all resources which are retrieved are relevant for the given query. Consequently, the criteria precision and recall, which are very popular for the estimation of the quality of the Web IR, are not so much useful for the resource retrieval in the Semantic Web.
- Searching is treated as ontology-based inferencing, which enables retrieval of information that is not explicitly stored in the information repository. By using the background knowledge implied by the underlying domain ontology, some new, implicitly stated, statements can be inferred in the querying process. In that way, although all retrieved results are relevant for a given query, their inferencing processes can be different and used for ranking the results.

Both differences emphasize the role of ranking the results that are retrieved for a query in Semantic Web. Even when machine agents process the list of results automatically, it is not realistic to assume that they will inspect the whole list of thousands of retrieved results. Moreover, in real applications, e.g. skill management, the retrieved resources can be people, e.g. experts, and just several of them can be contacted.

The ranking of the results of a search process in the Semantic Web should benefit from all possible advantages implied by using the conceptual model of a domain, i.e. the domain ontology, in describing the information on the Web. The strength of an ontology lies in the formal and explicit specification of the constraints which exist between domain entities (an entity can be a concept or relation). One of the most powerful mechanisms for describing constraints between entities in a domain are rules (see Definition 3). The rules are part of the knowledge about a domain and are extensively used for deriving results of an ontology-based query, i.e. in the inferencing process. As we already mentioned in the previous section, the way in which a result of a query is derived can help in ranking the results of that query. Subsequently, we present such a ranking approach, which combines characteristics of the inferencing process and the content of the information repository used in searching. Due to the strong dependence on the usage of ontology background, we call it *ontology-based ranking*.

The importance of the rules for the ontologies on the web is already recognised in the Semantic Web community and several initiatives for representing rules in the RDF compatible format are already started, e.g. RuleML [8]. However, since the current W3C (proposal) standard for representing ontologies on the Web, OWL [9], does not cover the rules (yet), we have to use an ontology representation formalism which enables dealing with rules. Since our approach is partially implemented in the Ontobroker system [4], which relies on the F-Logic [10], in the rest of the paper we will use F-Logic notation for representing ontologies. However, the generality of our approach remains.

3.2 Motivating Example

In order to make the discussion more understandable, we will introduce and motivate the requirement for a ranking approach with an example, firstly. The example is taken from our evaluation study we present in section 5. In the rest of the text we will refer to it as the *institute example.*

Let us assume the following ontology:

```
1: Project::Object[hasTopic =>> Topic].
2: Lecture::Object[hasTopic =>> Topic].
3: Topic::Object[subtopicOf =>> Topic].
4: Researcher::Object.                                          (1)
5: Professor:: Researcher.
6: PhDStudent:: Researcher.
7: Researcher [worksIn =>> Project; researchIn =>> Topic; teaches =>> Lecture].
8: FORALL X,Y,Z   Z: Researcher [researchIn ->>Y] <- Z[worksIn ->>X] and
        X:Project[hasTopic ->>Y].
9: FORALL X,Y,Z   Z: Researcher [researchIn ->>Y] <- Z[teaches ->>X] and
        X:Lecture[hasTopic ->>Y].
10:FORALL X,Y,Z   Z:Project[hasTopic ->>Y] <- X:Topic[subtopicOf ->>Y] and
        Z[hasTopic ->>X].
```

To give an intuition of the semantic of the F-Logic statements, in line 1, one finds a concept definition for a `Project` being an `Object` with a relation `hasTopic`. The range of the relation is restricted to `Topic`. Ontology axioms as the one given in line 8 (1) use this syntax to describe regularities. Line 8 states that if a `Researcher` *Z* works in a `Project` *X* and *X* has topic *Y*, then *Z* does research in *Y*. Let us further assume the following knowledge base:

```
11: rst:Professor.
12: gst:Professor.
13: meh:PhdStudent.
14: nst:PhdStudent.                                             (2)
15: ysu:PhdStudent.
16: KM:Topic.
17: TextMining:Topic.
18: DataMining:Topic.
19: rst[worksIn->>OntoWeb; worksIn ->>DotCom; worksIn ->>OTK].
20: ysu[worksIn ->>OTK].
21: rst[teaches ->>KnowledgeManagement].
22: nst[teaches ->>KnowledgeManagement].
23: gst[teaches ->>KnowledgeManagement;worksIn->>DotCom].
24: gst[teaches ->>InfoA;teaches ->>InfoB].
25: gst[worksIn ->>OntoWeb; worksIn ->>DotCom; worksIn ->>SWAP].
26: meh[worksIn ->>SWAP;teaches->>InfoB].
27: OntoWeb:Project[hasTopic->>KM;hasTopic->>TextMining; hasTopic->>DataMining].
28: WonderWeb:Project.
29: OTK:Project[hasTopic->>KM].
30: DotCom:Project[hasTopic->>KM].
31: SWAP:Project[hasTopic->>TextMining].
32: TextMining[subtopicOf->>KM].
33: DataMining[subtopicOf->>KM].
34: KnowledgeManagement:Lecture[hasTopic->>KM].
35: InfoA:Lecture.
36: InfoB:Lecture.
```

Definitions of instances in the knowledge base are syntactically very similar to the concept definition in F-Logic. In line 11 the instance `rst` of the concept `Professor` is defined. Furthermore, in line 20, the relation `worksIn` is instantiated between `ysu` and `OTK`. Similarly, in line 29 it is stated that `OTK` is a `Project` related to the topic `KM`.

Now, an F-Logic query may ask for all people who research in KM by:

```
Qa: FORALL Y <- Y[researchIn ->> KM].
```
(3)

which may result in the set $R(Qa)$ = {(rst), (sst), (ysu), (meh), (gst), (nst)}.

By using the associations: $\overline{X} := (Y)$, $\overline{k} :=$ ("KM"), $\overline{P} := (P_1)$, $P_1(Y,"KM") :=$ Y[researchIn ->>"KM"], the query (3) can be represented in the formal manner (Definition 5) introduced in section 2.

Obviously, all answers are correct with regard to the given knowledge base and ontology, but the question is how these answers are related to each other. Let us consider the intuitive assumptions about the relevance of the different results in the following cases:

1) ysu vs. gst
- ysu works in just one project and that project is about KM
- gst works in three projects but just one of them is about KM

  => ysu is more relevant for KM than gst.

2) rst vs. ysu
- ysu works in just one project and that project is about KM
- rst works in three projects, all related to KM

  => rst is more relevant for KM than ysu.

3) gst vs. nst
- gst is a Professor and gives a lecture about KM
- nst is a PhDStudent and gives the same lecture as gst

  => gst is more relevant for KM than nst

4) nst vs. meh
- nst works in just one project and that project is about KM
- meh works in just one project and that project is about TextMining, which is a special part of KM research

  => nst is more relevant for KM than meh

5) ysu vs. nst
- ysu works in just one project and that project is about KM
- nst works in just one project and that project is about KM

  => the relevance of ysu and nst is the same,

Alternatively, we can use more semantic about these relations:
- ysu works in just one project and that project is about KM and he works alone
- nst works in just one project and that project is about KM and there are two other persons who support the research in that project

It could be concluded that ysu is more relevant than nst, but the following arguments might be applied:
- ysu works for the whole project => ysu puts a lot of efforts in the project
- nst works with two other persons in the project => nst benefits from the collaboration with two other persons

  Therefore, the relevance depends on additional factors, e.g. what is the proportional active participation of all three members in that project.

It is clear that a powerful, but flexible ranking schema is needed, in order to fulfil all requirements presented in this example. This is the goal of our ranking approach. In the discussion of the approach (cf. the end of the next section) we explain the solutions for the above mentioned requirements.

3.3 The Ontology-Based Ranking Schema

In this subsection we give the theoretical framework for calculating the relevance of the returned results for a query, which resolves the above mentioned cases.

Although a query returns the set of concept instances as an answer, the relevance of these answers is defined on the level of the relation instances. The reason is that the concept instance is treated as the identifier of an object (e.g. `rst`), whereas the relation instance (e.g. `rst[researchIn->>KM]`) represents the property of that object whose relevance for the query can be determined. It means that the relevance of an answer $a = \overline{X_1} = (x_1, x_2, ... x_n)$ for the query Q will be calculated on the substitution of this answer in the query Q, i.e. by considering the $\overline{P}(\overline{X_1}, \overline{k})$: $P_1(\overline{X_1}, \overline{k}), P_2(\overline{X_1}, \overline{k}), ..., P_k(\overline{X_1}, \overline{k})$ - the set of *returned relation instances*, depicted as $\Lambda(a)$, for an answer a. It is clear that $\forall a, \Lambda(a) \supset \Omega$ (for the used terminology see section 2).

For the given example and query (3) follows:

```
Λ(rst)={rst[researchIn->>KM]}, Λ(sst)={sst[researchIn->>KM]}
Λ(ysu)={ysu[researchIn->>KM]}, Λ(gst)={gst[researchIn->>KM]}
Λ(nst)={nst[researchIn->>KM]}, Λ(meh)={meh[researchIn->>KM]}
```

Since the returned relation instances for each answer can be proven in the ontology, the traditional definition of the relevance via a similarity function between returned relation instances [11] is useless (similarities between two arbitrary answers are equal).

There are two differences between *returned relation instances* for answers to a query:

(i) the specificity of the instantiation of the ontology (content of the knowledge base)
e.g. for the domain presented in the motivating example, for a query about researchers in KM, a useful information for ranking can be that a researcher works in three projects about KM and gives two lectures regarding KM

(ii) the inferencing process in which an answer is implied - the derivation tree of an answer (a returned relation instance)
e.g. the query for a researcher who researches in KM will return the researcher who researches in the `DataMining` as well, since `DataMining` is a subtopic of KM.

Therefore, we introduce the relevance function $\sigma: \Omega \rightarrow \Re$ that computes the relevance of a relation instance returned in the querying process, based on analysing (i) the knowledge base (criterion i) and the inferencing process (criterion ii). The relevance of an answer a, $\rho(a)$, $a \in R(Q)$, is the geometrical mean of the relevancies of the returned relation instances for that answer, i.e. $\rho(a) = \sqrt[|\Lambda(a)|]{\prod_{x \in \Lambda(a)} \sigma(x)}$, where $|S|$ denotes the cardinality of a given set S. Finally, the ranking of the answers for a query is achieved by ordering them according to their relevance. In the following two subsections we give in detail the calculation of the above mentioned relevancies.

3.3.1 The Content of the Knowledge Base

In this subsection we explain the calculation of the relevance of a relation instance for the user's query.

Definition 7: The ambiguity of a term in a relation instance
The ambiguity of a term (a concept instance) in a relation instance is defined as the number of interpretations of the given relation instance with respect to that term (i.e. when all other terms in the relation instance, except the considered term, are substituted with a variable).

$$Amb(I_j, r(I_1, I_2, \ldots, I_j, \ldots, I_n)) = \left| \{x, y, \ldots, w \mid \exists x, y, \ldots w \;\; r(x, \ldots, I_j, \ldots, w)\} \right| \qquad (4)$$

For example, $Amb(gst, worksIn(gst, OntoWeb)) = \left| \{x \mid \exists x \;\; worksIn(gst, x)\} \right| = 3$ (regarding motivating example, person `gst` works in three projects `OntoWeb, DotCom, SWAP`).

Definition 8: The specificity/relevance of a relation instance
The specificity of a relational instance is the reciprocal value of the ambiguity of each of its terms (concept instances). It is calculated as:

$$Spec(r(I_1, I_2, \ldots, I_n)) = \frac{1}{Amb(I_1, r(I_1, I_2, \ldots, I_n))} \cdot \ldots \cdot \frac{1}{Amb(I_n, r(I_1, I_2, \ldots, I_n))} \qquad (5)$$

For example, regarding the situation presented in (1), the specificity of the instance *workIn(gst, OntoWeb)* is as follows: $Spec(worksIn(gst, OntoWeb)) =$

$$\frac{1}{Amb(gst, worksIn(gst, OntoWeb))} \cdot \frac{1}{Amb(OntoWeb, worksIn(gst, OntoWeb))} = \frac{1}{3} \cdot \frac{1}{2} = \frac{1}{6} \qquad (6)$$

The specificity is maximal (i.e. = 1) when none of the terms from the relational instance can be found in any other relation instance of the same type[1]. For example, the relation instance `teaches(meh, InfoB)` (in F-Logic `meh[teaches->>InfoB].`) has the maximal specificity, because there is only one relation instance for the relation `teaches` which contains either `meh` or `InfoB`.

The specificity of a relation instance can be interpreted as the measure of its relevance for the user's query. When the specificity of a relation instance is higher, then the relevance is higher as well.

Hence, the relevance is calculated as: $Rel(r(I_1, I_2, \ldots, I_n)) = Spec(r(I_1, I_2, \ldots, I_n))$ (7)

When considering the case 5) from section 3.2, the treatment of factors which determine relevance is task-dependent. The formula (5) can be adapted to such task-dependent customisation by changing the reciprocity-effect of the ambiguity of a term on the relevance of the whole relation instance. For example, when the relevance of a participant of a project for the research related to that project increases with the number of participants of the project, then the statement (6) can be changed into (note that we have two participants in `OntoWeb`): $Spec(worksIn(gst, OntoWeb)) =$

$$\frac{1}{Amb(gst, worksIn(gst, OntoWeb))} \cdot Amb(OntoWeb, worksIn(gst, OntoWeb)) = \frac{1}{3} \cdot 2 = \frac{2}{3}$$

Our approach supports this kind of parameterised calculation of the relevance.

3.3.2 The Characteristics of the Inferencing Process

As showed in the motivating example, in querying an ontology the background knowledge about the domain is used for inferring new, implicitly stated facts in the knowledge base. Therefore, the query results might be extended by inference, which

---

[1] A relation type is defined by the relation that is instantiated in the relation instance.

uses rules from the domain ontology, i.e. the query process includes ontology-based inferencing. We omit here the detailed description of the different types of inferencing processes (evaluations) [12], but present instead the common inferencing structure which can be used for the proof of the returned results. Such a proof structure enables the reconstruction of the inferencing steps for a query's result and consequently the calculation of its relevance. This structure is described in the next three definitions.

Definition 9: AND-OR tree

An AND-OR tree is a tree structure, defined as the set T = $\{root, N, v\_and, v\_or\}$, where *root* is the root of the tree, *N* is the set of nodes in the tree, *v_and* and *v_or* are (irreflexive, anti-symmetric) relations between nodes (they define links in the tree and are called parent-child relations in the text), *v_and*: $N \rightarrow N$ (such a link is called an and_link and the node is called an and_connector), *v_or*: $N \rightarrow N^*$ (such a link is called an or_link and the node is called an or_connector).

Definition 10: Derivation tree of a query

Given an ontology O with axioms, the derivation tree of the query Q is an AND-OR tree whose root plays the role of an or_connector between the derivation trees of each result (resulting relation instance) *R*(Q) for the query Q, i.e.

$DTree(Q) = \{root, N, v\_and, v\_or\}$, $N = \bigcup_{r \in \Lambda(a) \wedge a \in R(Q)} DTree(r)$, *v_or*: root→N , *v_and* = { }.

Definition 11: Derivation tree of a relation instance (creating)

The derivation tree of a relation instance $r(I_1, I_2, \ldots, I_n)$ is defined as follows:

- Every relation instantiation *l* from KB is a derivation tree for itself; a single node with label *l*.
- Let *A* be the set of axioms from the given ontology O, whose heads contain the atomic formula which can be unified with the relation *r*.
- Let A = $p{:-}q_1, \ldots, q_n$, be an axiom from *A*, let d_i, $1 \le i \le n$, be relation instances with derivation trees T_i, let θ be the mgu[2] of $(q_1, \ldots, q_n)$ and $(d_1, \ldots, d_n)$. Then the following is a derivation tree for p[θ] (relation instance): the root is a node labelled with p[θ] and each T_i, $1 \le i \le n$, is a child of the root. The root plays an and_connector role.
- The derivation tree for *r* is the tree with the root which plays the role of an or_connector between the derivation trees for all axioms from *A*. It is labelled with p[θ]*

Fig. 1 depicts a derivation tree, created according to the definitions 9, 10 and 11.

[2] A substitution is a mapping from the set of variables of the language under consideration to the set of terms. Two terms t1 and t2 are said to be unifiable if there is a substitution σ such that t1[σ] = t2[σ]; σ is said to be a unifier of t1 and t2. Note that if two terms have a unifier, they have a most general unifier (mgu) that is unique up to renaming of variables.

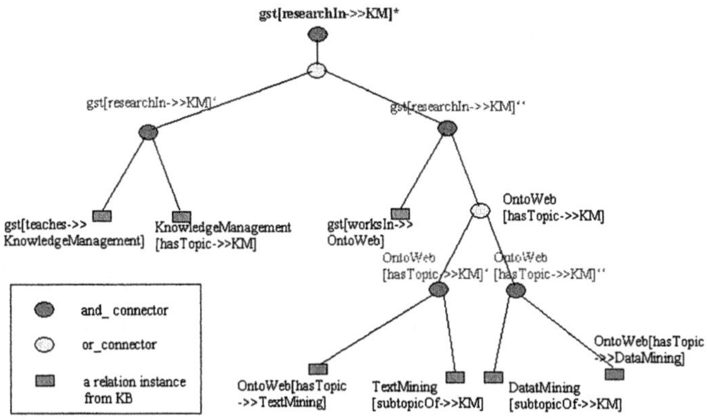

Fig. 1. The derivation tree for the relation instance `gst[researchIn->>KM]`, regarding the motivating example. The tree is generated according to the definitions 9, 10 and 11.

It is clear that a derivation tree represents the manner in which a result was inferred. The root is the disjunction of all results. Each node in a tree is a relation instance. Each or_connector node connects various ways in which a relation instance is derived, whereas an and_connector node defines a way in which the relation instance is derived. For a relation instance there are several and_connector nodes (the number is equal to the number of rules, whose head parts unify with that relation instance) and an or_connector, which connects those and _connector nodes.

For each and_connector node it is possible to define the query specificity as a measure of the relevance of that relation instance (using formula (5)). From the definition of the derivation tree it is clear that the relevance of a node depends on the relevance of its children's nodes. A relevance is propagated in two ways depending on the type of nodes:

- an and_connector multiplies the relevancies of its children (because each child is a part of a rule that infers the parent)
- an or_connector sums the relevances of its children (because children make an impact on the parent independently)

Such propagation corresponds to the propagation of the signals in a semantic network, so called node activation sequences [13].

The following formulas describe the processing done by a node:

(i) for an and_connector $node_i$: $Rel\_and(node_i) = Rel(node_i) \cdot \sum_{v\_or(node_i, node_j)} Rel\_or(node_j)$ (8)

for the root node *root*, we set $Rel(root) = 1$.

(ii) for an or_connector $node_i$: $Rel\_or(node_i) = \prod_{v\_and(node_i, node_l)} Rel\_and(node_l)$ (9)

(iii) for a leaf $node_i$: $Rel\_and(node_i) = Rel(node_i)$ (10)

Each node is in the form $r(I_i, I_2, ..., I_n)$, *Rel(node)* is the initial relevance, defined with formula (7), *Rel_and(node)* is the calculated relevance of the relation instance corresponding to *node*. Therefore, the relevance of a returned relation instance r for the answer a, i.e. $r \in \Lambda(a)$, is calculated as follows: $\sigma(r) = Rel\_and(r)$.

Finally, the relevance of the answer a is $\rho(a) = \sqrt[|\Lambda(a)|]{\prod_{r \in \Lambda(a)} Rel\_and(r)}$. (11)

Discussion:

(i) The ranking measure described with (11) deals with both factors for determining the relevance we mentioned in previous section (i.e. regarding content and inference)

(ii) In formula (5) we treat the inverse impact of the number of relations of the same type r as follows: when an instance is in several relations of the same type, then its relevance for that relation type is split into all of them. This enables resolving of the case 2) from section 3.2. However, when each of these relations are relevant for the given query, according to summing in formula (8) the instance has an impact "without losses" (= 1) on this relation. This is important for resolving case 1) from section 3.2.

(iii) Since for each transitive relation there is a rule which enables inferencing over the subconcepts, the derivation trees of two subconcepts, which are placed in the different depth in the hierarchy of a term, are different. Consequently, their relevancies (formula (11)) are different, i.e. the subconcepts placed deeper in the hierarchy are less relevant for the queries regarding the root concept. It enables resolving of the case 3) and 4) from section 3.2.

(iv) The case 5) form section 3.2 was treated in the discussion regarding Definition 8.

(v) The formula (5) for calculating the specificity of a relation instance is general enough to model other interpretations of the relevance (see the discussion in the case 5 in section 3.2) as well as to incorporate other factors which can determine the relevance, e.g. usage information. We see the calculation of the relevance as a task/problem-sensitive decision and we plan to develop task-oriented strategies for calculating relevance. For example, whether the number of the instances which are in the same relation should increase or decrease the relevance is a problem-sensitive decision and we assume that a user wants to have opportunity to set such an indicator for each relation, otherwise he/she will use default option.

4 Implementation

4.1 Ontobroker and Its Explanation Facility

We implemented the presented ranking approach in the Semantic Portal of our Institute. It is an ontology-based web application, which serves as the test-bed for our research related to ontologies and Semantic Web. The Semantic Portal (SEAL) [5] is an ontology-based application, which provides a "single-click" access to almost all information related to the organisation, people, research and projects of our Institute. It is widely used by our research and administrative staff as well as by our students.

One of the most usable features is the possibility to search for people, research areas and projects on the semantic basis, i.e. using the corresponding Institute Ontology. The hierarchy of research areas is especially comprehensive – more than 130 concepts. The example from section 3 is a part of it. The portal provides a very user-friendly interface, which enables formation of arbitrary queries using entities from the underlying ontology. The search is performed as an inference through metadata, which are crawled from the portal pages. As the inference mechanism we use the Ontobroker system [4], a deductive, object-oriented database system operating either in the main memory or on a relational database (via JDBC). Ontobroker uses the bottom-up fix-point evaluation procedure. It allows general recursion and negation is allowed in the clause body. The native logical language of the Ontobroker is F-Logic. More details about Ontobroker can be found in [4].

The latest version of Ontobroker (www.ontoprise.com) has a powerful explanation facility, which tracks the evaluation of the rules and the substitutions applied in them. The ranking approach is based on processing this explanation file. Out of it, the derivation tree for a query, according to the definitions 9-11, is generated. Since Ontobroker generates explanations in the form of F-Logic statements, the processing of the explanation file is logic-based. Indeed, we define a small ontology for processing explanation statements, including the set of rules which enables the generation of the desired AND-OR tree. Such an approach enables a very efficient customisation of the explanation process. The recursive rules and the negation do not impose any problems for the processing of the explanation file. The explanation file explains the original logic program, i.e. no optimisation technique (e.g. Magic set) affects the explanation process. Due to the lack of space we omit here more details.

The ranking approach is developed as an additional module for the Ontobroker system. The ranking module takes the list of results for the query and the explanation file as inputs. The output is the ranked list of results. Case studies show that the time delay introduced in the answering process is not significant.

4.2 Evaluation of Ranking Performances

In our previous work [5] we developed a module for ranking the results retrieved by Ontobroker, based on the calculation the similarity between terms in a hierarchy (i.e. for any transitive relation). The measure is based on the assumption, that the similarity between two objects (concepts or instances) may be computed by considering their relative place in a common hierarchy *H*. *H* may, but need not be a taxonomy. For instance, in our test domain we have a categorization of research topics – *H(subtopicOf)*, which is not a taxonomy. The similarity between two objects in a hierarchy is calculated using the so-called *Object Match* measure. In the following we describe very briefly this measure.

For each object we define *Upwards cotopy* (UC) as the number of objects on the paths between the given object and the root of the given hierarchy *H*. The *Object Match* (OM) between two objects, O_1, O_2, is defined as $OM(O_1,O_2,H) = \frac{UC(O_1,H) \cap UC(O_2,H)}{UC(O_1,H) \cup UC(O_2,H)}$. Basically, *OM* reaches 1 when two objects coincide; it degrades to the extent to which the discrepancy between intersections and unions increases (an *OM* between concepts that do not share common super-concepts yields value 0). More details can be found in [5].

The problem in such a calculation of the relevance is that a part of the domain model (i.e. the domain axioms) is not treated at all. It leads to a weak relevance model, which takes into account only the hierarchy of relations in the ontology. For example, the difference of the relevance for the research area `KM` between a `Researcher`, who is the leader of a `KM`-project and another `Researcher`, who is "only" a participant in a `KM`-project, cannot be expressed using our former ranking approach. For real-world applications we have developed using the Ontobroker, it was a very important issue, especially in the skill-management domain.

By involving more semantics about the domain (i.e. axioms) in calculating the relevance, we expected that the new approach for ranking will outperform the old one. Therefore, we set up an evaluation study in order to prove this claim.

Due to the subjective nature of relevance, it is very difficult to evaluate the performance of a ranking algorithm. Here we used a modification of the method for interactive comparing of two ranking algorithms, proposed in [14].

Our experiment is set up as follows: For a query, the set of predefined answers is determined. These answers are processed by both ranking algorithms. The returned rankings are mixed, so that at any point the top l results of the combined ranking contain the top ka and kb rankings from A and B, $\|ka - kb\| \leq 1$. The combined ranking for the given query is presented to the user, and the user is asked to select $l/2$ of the most relevant results. We calculate the number of these top $l/2$ results chosen from each of the two ranking algorithms, the so-called *top_results_ratio*, as:

$$top\_results\_ratio(X) = \frac{top(X)}{Num(X)},$$

where *top(X)* is the number of results from the ranking *X* in the selected top *l/2* results and *Num(X)* is the total number of results from the ranking *X* presented to the user, i.e. for X=A, *Num(X)= ka* and for X=B, *Num(X)= kb*. The ranking with higher *top_results_ratio* has the better ranking schema.

In the original method [14], the ranks are calculated in a different way: users just click on one or two results, these clicks are recorded and afterwards the clickstream data are analysed.

For this evaluation step we used the data from the Semantic Portal of our Institute.

For the experiment we selected the answers of 20 predefined queries and performed the ranking of these answers by both algorithms. The queries were about researchers who research in different research area, e.g. in the F-logic: `FORALL X, X[reserachIn->>"name_of_research_area"]`. The number of answers varies from 8 to 15. We set the values *l*, *ka* and *kb* to 16, 8 and 8, respectively. We used ten subject experts in the evaluation. They did not have previous knowledge about the system.

In order to evaluate the additional cost of our algorithm, we measured the processing time for all algorithms. The results of the evaluation study are given in table 1. In the table wins/total is the ratio of the number of trials in which the corresponding algorithm won and the total number of trials (=200).

Table 1. The results of the evaluation.

Algorithm	**Based only on hierarchy**	**Based on the full domain model**
Ranking (wins/total)	8/200	192/200
average process. time	703 ms	850 ms

Discussion: The experiment proved that using more semantics about the domain in a ranking algorithm improves the ranking drastically, without increasing the processing time significantly. The 8 losses, we accounted in the evaluation, were for the sets of answers which do not require a lot of semantics to be properly ranked. Moreover, the differences in results in these cases are very vague. For large data sets and more complex domain models (more rules) we expect even better results.

Comprehensiveness of the approach: It can be shown that calculating the similarity in a hierarchy (e.g. the hierarchy of topics) we used in [5], is equivalent to determining the relevance by applying our approach only on the transitive relation which models that hierarchy (e.g. on the relation `subtopicOf`). Since the transitivity of a relation is modelled in an ontology through the transitivity axiom, the derivation tree which corresponds to the query regarding that relation (e.g. "`CBR` is a `subtopicOf KM`") is equal to the path between these two nodes in the hierarchy. This path is used as the key factor for calculating similarity in our previous approach [5]. In other words, our previous approach for calculating similarity can be treated as a special case (when only the transitive axiom exists in the domain ontology) of our new approach (which uses more semantics - all axioms from the domain ontology).

Complexity of the approach: Our approach is general and can be applied to any type of evaluation which relies on an abstract model of the derivation tree (like Definitions 7–11). However, the prerequisite for the approach is the external readability of derivation trees of answers which are returned for a query. Here we discuss only the complexity of the processing the derivation trees, but not the complexity of producing (externalisation) of these structures. As the results presented in the table 1 show, in the case of the Ontobroker system, the externalisation of derivation trees is not a time-consuming activity.

For computing the time-complexity of our approach we make the following assumptions:

- Since the number of instances in an ontology can be very large, they should be stored in a database. It means that the access to the ontology has to be considered as a time-consuming activity.
- The size of the ontology can be approximated using: $\boldsymbol{l}$ (average number of the premises in a rule), $\boldsymbol{k}$ (the average arity of an ontological relation), $\boldsymbol{g}$ (average number of the instantiations of a relation), $\boldsymbol{m}$ (average depth of a derivation tree)
- We consider the case that $\boldsymbol{n}$ results are retrieved for the user's query

The time-complexity for the calculation of the *Ambiguity parameter*, (4), is $\Omega(\boldsymbol{g}*(\boldsymbol{k}-1))$ – it is the number of accesses to the ontology. The time-complexity for the calculation of the *Specificity parameter*, (5), is $\Omega(\boldsymbol{g}*(\boldsymbol{k}-1)*\boldsymbol{k})$. The complexity for processing the derivation tree of a result, (8)-(10), is $\Omega(l^m *\boldsymbol{g}*(\boldsymbol{k}-1)*\boldsymbol{k})$.

Finally, the time-complexity of ranking all $\boldsymbol{n}$ results is $\Omega(\boldsymbol{n}* l^m *\boldsymbol{g}*(\boldsymbol{k}-1)*\boldsymbol{k})$.

However, the exponential parameter, $\boldsymbol{m}$ - the average depth, is in practice very low (<10), as well the parameter $\boldsymbol{l}$. Further, for our application domain, Semantic Web, the value of the parameter $\boldsymbol{k}$ is 2. The only parameter which can be very large is the number of instances, $\boldsymbol{g}$, i.e. $\boldsymbol{m}$, $\boldsymbol{l}$, $\boldsymbol{k}$ $l^m << \boldsymbol{g}$. Therefore, the time-complexity of our ranking approach is $\Omega(n*g)$, i.e. it is linear regarding g. It means that our approach scales well with increasing the number of instances in the ontology.

5 Related Work

Semantic methods in Information Retrieval. Using more structured and machine readable information about a web document for improving searching for information is very promising research area in the Semantic Web community. In [15] is presented an approach for information retrieval over documents that consist of both free text and semantic annotations with statements in DAML+OIL. These statements provide both structured and semi-structured information about the documents and their content. The developed framework advocates the interdependency of search (text retrieval/extraction methods) and inference for the precise retrieval over the semantic content. However, the approach does not consider the ranking of retrieved documents.

Ontologies. Although the ideas for ontology-based ranking come from our research in ontology-based systems, it is difficult to compare it in that context, since, as far as we know, none of the inference engines performs ranking of inferred results. Regarding the ranking algorithm itself, we can compare our measure of similarity for the transitive relations (similarity in the hierarchy) with the work done in the NLP community [16] which refers to the similarity between two concepts in a `isA`-taxonomy such as the WordNet or CYC upper ontology. Our approach differs from this notion of similarity in two main aspects: Firstly, our similarity measure is applicable to a hierarchy which may, but need not be a taxonomy and secondly it takes into account not only similarities but also differences between the items being compared, expressing both in semantic-cotopy terms. The second property enables the measuring of self-similarity and subclass-relationship similarity, which are crucial for comparing results derived from the inferencing processes.

A very interesting approach for processing ontology-based information is given in [17]. It exploits the connectionistic structure of an ontology in order to define connectedness metrics between instances in the ontology. The approach is applied for defining communities of practice in the system called ONTOCOPI. The insight behind the approach ONTOCOPI is that if an ontology of the working domain of an organisation is created, then the links between the instances can be measured to indicate which are closely related. However, this approach does not exploit all the semantics of a domain expressed in an ontology (e.g. rules) or which can be induced from the usage of the link structure.

In [18] authors describe an interesting approach for querying Semantic Associations on the Semantic Web, which capture complex relationships between entities that capture a connectivity of entities or a pattern of entities and relationships between them based on a specific notion of an isomorphism called ρ-isomorphism. The approach builds upon a formal model for RDF, which uses a graph data model and also provides a type system for RDF data. Since this model do not encompass the notion of rules, all captured associations are derived from the explicit information existing in a RDF graph. On the other side, the strength of our approach lies in exploiting implicit knowledge, captured in the ontology axioms, for determining relevance. By materialising all implicit knowledge, lots of information important for determining relevance of facts is lost. Obviously, the differences arise due to different tasks of the approaches: their approach detects complex associations that may be buried deep in the data, whereas our approach is focused on assessing existing associations. Moreover, by allowing querying for relations (e.g. FORALL X <-rst[X->>KM]) our ranking approach could be adapted to this detection task as well.

6 Conclusion

Since the strength of an ontological structure lies in the formal and explicit semantics of the relationships between ontological entities, the Semantic Web has to exploit the full potential of the semantic-based hyperlink structure between web resources, in order to improve the efficiency of resource retrieval. The determination of the relevance of a web resource for a user's query is the issue which can be significantly improved in the Semantic Web, especially the relevance based on the analysis of the inferencing process. In this paper we presented a novel approach for determining relevance in the ontology-based searching for information. This approach is oriented towards the determination of the link relevance and reflects the semantic link-based nature of the Semantic Web. It easily enables the incorporation of any additional information related to a link, such as the usage of that link. Moreover, we see the calculation of the relevance as a task/problem-sensitive decision and we plan to develop task-oriented strategies for calculating relevance.

Acknowledgement. The research presented in this paper would not have been possible without our colleagues and students at the Institute AIFB, University of Karlsruhe. Special thanks to the Jürgen Angele from Ontoprise GmbH for developing the explanation features in the Ontobroker. Research for this paper was partially financed by BMBF in the project "SemIPort" (08C5939) and by EU in the IST-2000-28293 project "Ontologging".

References

[1] Berners-Lee, T.: Business Model for the Semantic Web. W3C, October 2001.

[2] Fensel, D., Bussler, C Y. Ding, and B. Omelayenko: The Web Service Modeling Framework WSMF, Electronic Commerce Research and Applications, 1(2), 2002.

[3] Guarino, N., Masolo, C. and Vetere, G. "OntoSeek: Content-Based Access to the Web", IEEE Intelligent Systems, 14(3), pp. 70–80, (May 1999).

[4] Decker, S., Erdmann, M., Fensel, D. and Studer, R. Ontobroker: Ontology Based Access to Distributed and Semi-Structured Information. In R. Meersman et al., editors, Database Semantics: Semantic Issues in Multimedia Systems, pages 351–369. Kluwer, 1999.

[5] Stojanovic, N., Maedche, A., Staab, S., Studer, R. and Sure, Y. "SEAL — A Framework for Developing SEmantic PortALs", ACM K-CAP 2001. October, Vancouver, 2001.

[6] Bozsak, E., Ehrig, M., Handschuh, S., Hotho, A., Mädche, A., Motik, B., Oberle, D., Schmitz, C., Staab, S., Stojanovic, L., Stojanovic, N., Studer, R., Stumme, G., Sure, Y., Tane, J., Volz, R. and Zachariasm V. KAON – Towards a large scale Semantic Web. In: Proceedings of EC-Web 2002. Aix-en-Provence, France, September 2–6, 2002. LNCS, Springer, 2002.
[7] Stojanovic, N., Stojanovic, L., Gonzalez, J. On Enhancing Searching for Information in an Information Portal by Tracking Users' Activities, First International Workshop on Mining for Enhanced Web Search (MEWS 2002), held in conjunction with 3rd International Conference on Web Information System Engineering WISE 2002, Singapore, 2002, IEEE Press.
[8] Boley, H., Tabet, S., Wagner, G. Design Rationale of RuleML: A Markup Language for Semantic Web Rules, SWWS'01, Stanford University, July/August 2001.
[9] OWL Web Ontology Language 1.0 Reference, W3C Working Draft 29 July 2002.
[10] Kifer, M., Lausen, G., Wu, J.: Logical Foundations of Object-Oriented and Frame-Based Languages, Journal ACM, 42:741–843, 1995.
[11] Kulyukin, V., Settle, A Ranked retrieval with semantic networks and vector spaces. JASIST 52(13): 1224–1233 (2001).
[12] Ullman J. D. Principles of Database and Knowledge-based Systems. Computer Science Press, Rockville.
[13] Martin, C. Direct memory access parsing (Tech. Rep. No. CS93-07). Chicago, IL: The University of Chicago, Department of Computer Science.
[14] Joachims, T. Evaluating Retrieval Performance Using Clickthrough Data, Proceedings of the SIGIR Workshop on Mathematical/Formal Methods in Information Retrieval, 2002.
[15] Shah, U., Finin, T., Joshi, A., Cost S. and Mayfield, J. Information Retrieval on the Semantic Web, ACM CIKM'02, 2002.
[16] Resnik, P. Using information content to evaluate semantic similarity in a taxonomy. In Proceedings of IJCAI-95, Montreal, Canada, 1995.
[17] O'Hara, K., and Alani, H. and Shadbolt, N. Identifying Communities of Practice: Analysing Ontologies as Networks to Support Community Recognition, IFIP-WCC 2002, Montreal, 2002, Kluwer.
[18] Anyanwu K. and Sheth A. r-Queries: Enabling Querying for Semantic Associations on the Semantic Web, The Twelfth International World Wide Web Conference, Budapest, Hungary, pp. 690–699, May 2003

Querying Semantic Web Resources Using TRIPLE Views

Zoltán Miklós[1], Gustaf Neumann[1], Uwe Zdun[1], and Michael Sintek[2]

[1] Vienna University of Economics,
Department for Information Systems
{zoltan.miklos,gustaf.neumann,uwe.zdun}@wu-wien.ac.at
[2] DFKI GmbH, Kaiserslautern,
sintek@dfki.de

Abstract. Resources on the Semantic Web are described by metadata based on some formal or informal ontology. It is a common situation that casual users are not familiar with a domain ontology in detail. This makes it difficult for such users (or their user tools) to formulate queries to find the relevant resources. Users consider the resources in their specific context, so the most straightforward solution is to formulate queries in an ontology that corresponds to a user-specific view. We present an approach based on multiple views expressed in ontologies simpler than the domain ontology. This allows users to query heterogeneous data repositories in terms of multiple, relatively simple, view ontologies. Ontology developers can define such view ontologies and the corresponding mapping rules. These ontologies are represented in Semantic Web ontology languages such as RDFS, DAML+OIL, or OWL. We present our approach with examples from the e-learning domain using the Semantic Web query and transformation language TRIPLE.

1 Introduction

On the Semantic Web, resources are annotated with ontology-based metadata. Ontologies are formal, explicit specifications of a shared conceptualization. Ontologies play a central role on the Semantic Web because they represent the relations between semantic information, hence all query or reasoning services have to be based on ontologies. Several ontology languages have been proposed and investigated recently, such as RDFS [18], DAML+OIL [4], or OWL [17].

There are several problems that make it hard to query Semantic Web resources:

– *User Perspective:* Users who are interested in finding resources formulate queries related to some ontology. The user's (or their agent's) view of a domain is often different from an ontology developer's view. On the other hand, users are expected be be familiar enough with the domain ontology to efficiently formulate queries. Users would not have to learn the domain ontology if they could formulate their queries in an ontology that corresponds to their domain-specific view.

D. Fensel et al. (Eds.): ISWC 2003, LNCS 2870, pp. 517–532, 2003.

- *Application Integration:* In the current state of the Semantic Web, ontologies are developed from scratch, which means that many ontologies exist that describe the same domain. It is widely believed, that in the future development of the Semantic Web, this heterogeneity of ontologies will remain and multiple ontologies for many particular domains will coexist. Applications face the problem of obtaining information from sources which are described by different, independently developed ontologies.
- *Performance Overhead:* In many Semantic Web domains there are large or very large data sets. Queries can produce a considerable performance overhead. Problem-specific views of the resources could potentially minimize this problem.
- *Lack of Formal Definitions:* Various standardized vocabularies for metadata exist, such as IEEE LOM [11] for learning resources, but these are often only informally defined and do not allow for deeper reasoning.

In this paper, we propose an approach to overcome the problem of heterogeneous ontologies. Rather than defining a single large ontology, we propose to distinguish one or more "source ontologies" and a number of "target ontologies". The source ontologies describe the resource instances and are usually rather complex. The target ontologies individually cover certain aspects of the application domain. A user who wants to query heterogeneous data sources can formulate queries in terms of (multiple) relatively simple target ontologies. In other words, a view of the resources described in the source ontologies is created. In this view the resources are expressed using the target ontologies. For expressing ontologies, resources, and views, we use the Semantic Web query and transformation language TRIPLE [19].

We present our approach in Section 2 using an introductory example from the e-learning domain. In Section 3 we outline our solution. In Section 4 we give a short overview of the language TRIPLE. Section 5 describes our approach using the previously introduced scenario in TRIPLE. In Section 6 we give a description logic specification for our mappings. Section 7 presents related work, and Section 8 concludes the paper with our plans for future research.

2 Example: E-learning Scenario

In this section we describe a typical e-learning scenario that we use for the examples in this paper. The Semantic Web is used in our examples to support a search for relevant resources. These resources include online courses, online books, different kinds of exercises, etc.

The Learn@WU system[1] is an e-learning system that supports these kinds of resources and presents them on the Web. A subsystem of Learn@WU allows students to interactively try out exercises in tests which are randomly chosen from the learning resources.

[1] see `http://learn.wu-wien.ac.at/`

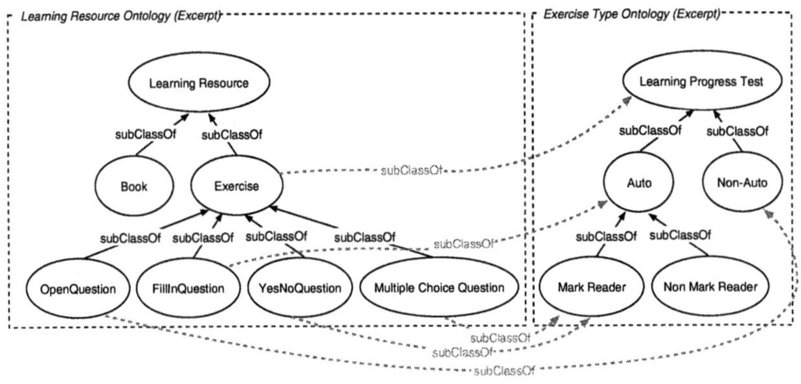

Fig. 1. The learning resource ontology, the exercise ontology and possible mappings

Students are not aware of the learning resource ontology and are not interested in how e-learning experts organize the learning resources; instead, they have their own view of exercises. The interactive test system only requires this limited view of exercises, not the whole learning resource ontology.

An excerpt of the learning resource ontology is depicted on the left hand side of Figure 1. The ontology of exercise types, as depicted on the right hand side of the figure, is a typical smaller ontology that only consists of a part of the learning resources in a particular context. There is a set of correspondences between these two ontologies that have to be considered during a mapping, as depicted by dotted lines in the figure.

3 Creating Views in a Target Ontology

Our approach relies on the distinction between two kinds of ontologies, *source ontologies* and *target ontologies*. Source ontologies are developed by domain experts for representing the Semantic Web resources in a particular domain. In contrast, target ontologies reflect a user's perspective or a domain-specific or problem-specific view of Semantic Web resources. Note that this distinction between source and taget ontologies is only conceptual; of course, any ontology can be a source ontology and target ontology as well.

Throughout this paper we use the following terms:

Source ontology: A (pre-existing) ontology that was developed specifically for a certain application.

Target ontology: This is an ontology that covers a small aspect of an application domain. Examples of a target ontology from the e-learning domain are various kinds of online exercises that can be automatically corrected or are suited for a mark reader. Another example is an ontology that contains the formats suitable for various delivery machines.

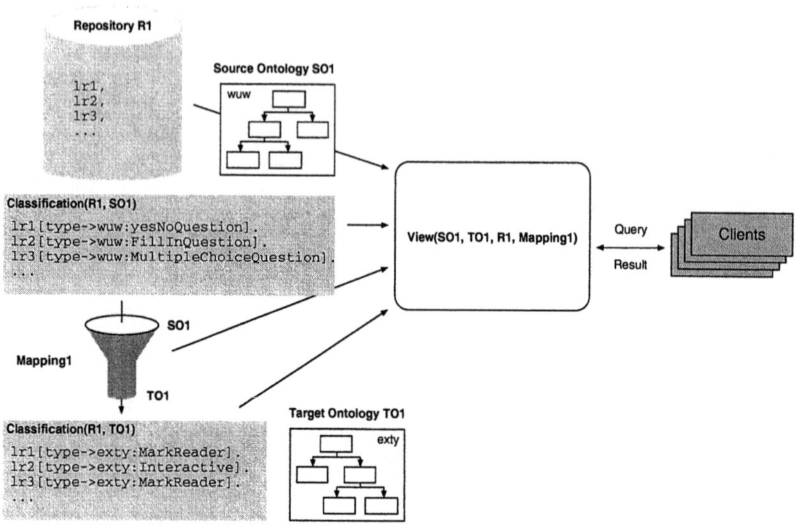

Fig. 2. Mapping Ontologies into Views

Metadata repository: Resource metadata, defined in terms of some (source) ontologies. There might be multiple repositories using the same source ontology.

Mapping model and view model: The specification to map the resources in the source ontologies to one or more target ontologies. The mapping model is specific to its source ontologies and target ontologies. Different view models can be defined on top of a mapping.

View: A set of resources, expressed in the target ontology. The view is created according to a mapping model and a view model.

The ontology editors provide a set of *mapping rules* between the resources and their properties in the source ontologies and target ontologies. The *view rules* are applied using the ontologies involved, mapping rules, and instance resources. The result is a context-specific view, expressed in the application ontologies. Clients can query the view using the application ontology only, without further knowledge of the more complex source ontologies (see Figure 2).

More than two ontologies can also be involved in a view. We depicted this situation in Figure 3. In the examples of Section 5 we use only two ontologies for reasons of simplicity and brevity. The examples use the language TRIPLE, which is briefly explained in the next section.

4 Overview of TRIPLE

TRIPLE [19] is a rule language for the Semantic Web which is based on Horn logic and borrows many basic features from F-Logic [13] but is especially designed for querying and transforming RDF models.

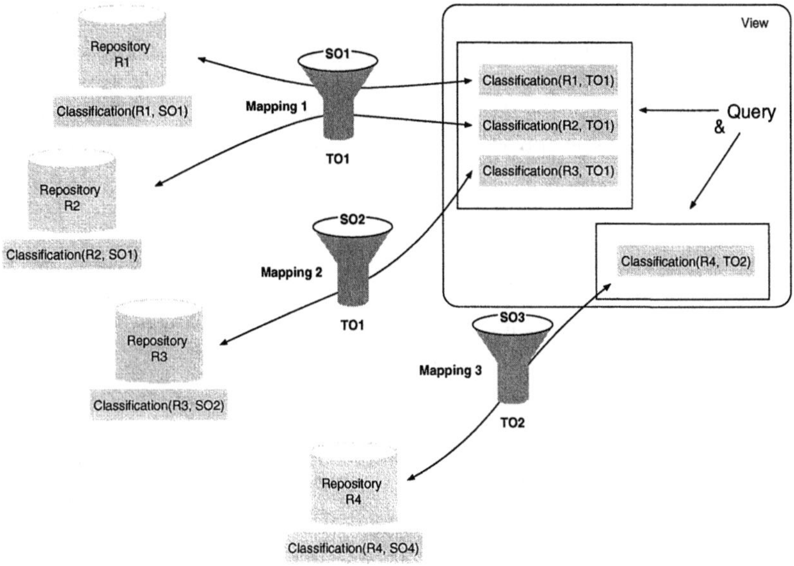

Fig. 3. View with Multiple Ontologies

TRIPLE can be viewed as a successor of SiLRI (Simple Logic-based RDF Interpreter [5]). One of the most important differences to F-Logic and SiLRI is that TRIPLE does not have fixed semantics for object-oriented features like classes and inheritance. Its modular architecture allows such features to be defined for object-oriented and other data models like UML, Topic Maps, or RDF Schema. Description logic extensions of RDF (Schema) like OIL, DAML+OIL, and OWL that cannot be fully handled by Horn logic are provided as modules that interact with a description logic classifier, e.g., FaCT [10], resulting in a hybrid rule language.

Namespaces and Resources: TRIPLE has special support for namespaces and resource identifiers. Namespaces are declared via clause-like constructs of the form *nsabbrev* := *namespace.*, e.g.:

```
rdf := "http://www.w3.org/1999/02/22-rdf-syntax-ns#".
```

Resources are written as *nsabbrev:name*, where *nsabbrev* is a namespace abbreviation and *name* is the local name of the resource.

Statements and Molecules: Inspired by F-Logic object syntax, an RDF statement (triple) is written as: *subject*[*predicate* → *object*]. Several statements with the same subject can be abbreviated as "molecules":

```
stefan[hasAge->33;isMarried->yes;...].
```

RDF statements (and molecules) can be nested, e.g.:

```
stefan[marriedTo->birgit[hasAge->32]].
```

Models: RDF models, i.e., sets of statements, are made explicit in TRIPLE ("first class citizens").[2] Statements, molecules, and also Horn atoms that are true in a specific model are written as *atom@model* (similar to Flora-2 module syntax), where *atom* is a statement, molecule, or Horn atom and *model* is a model specification (i.e., a resource denoting a model), e.g.:

```
michael[hasAge->35]@factsAboutDFKI.
```

TRIPLE also allows Skolem functions as model specifications. Skolem functions can be used to transform one model (or several models) into a new one when used in rules (e.g., for ontology mapping/integration):

```
O[P->Q]@sf(m1,X,Y) <- ...
```

If all (or many) statements/molecules or Horn atoms in a formula are from one model, the following abbreviation can be used: *formula@model.* All statements/molecules and Horn atoms in *formula* without an explicit model specification are implicitly suffixed with @*model.*

Logical Formulae: TRIPLE uses the usual set of connectives and quantifiers for building formulae from statements/molecules and Horn atoms, i.e., $\wedge$, $\vee$, $\neg$, $\forall$, $\exists$, etc.[3] All variables must be introduced via quantifiers, therefore marking them is not necessary (i.e., TRIPLE does not require variables to start with an uppercase letter as in Prolog).

Clauses and Blocks: A TRIPLE clause is either a fact or a rule. Rule heads may only contain conjunctions of molecules and Horn atoms and must not contain (explicitly or implicitly) any disjunctive or negated expressions. To assert that a set of clauses is true in a specific model, a model block is used: @*model* {*clauses*}, or, if the model specification is parameterized: $\forall$ *Mdl* @*model(Mdl)* {*clauses*}.

5 Examples of Querying Using TRIPLE Views

In this section we provide examples for resolving typical problem scenarios in TRIPLE using the view concepts presented in Section 3.

5.1 Simple Views

At first, we have to define the ontologies under consideration. The excerpt from the Learn@WU ontology for learning resources introduced in Section 2 can be defined by the following TRIPLE statements:

[2] Note that the notion of *model* in RDF does not coincide with its use in (mathematical) logics.

[3] For TRIPLE programs in plain ASCII syntax, the symbols AND, OR, NOT, FORALL, EXISTS, <-, ->, etc. are used.

```
@wuw:ont {
   wuw:LearningResource[rdfs:subClassOf -> rdfs:Resource].
   wuw:Book[rdfs:subClassOf -> wuw:LearningResource].
   wuw:Exercise[rdfs:subClassOf -> wuw:LearningResource].
   wuw:OpenQuestion[rdfs:subClassOf -> wuw:Exercise].
   wuw:FillInQuestion[rdfs:subClassOf -> wuw:Exercise].
   wuw:YesNoQuestion[rdfs:subClassOf -> wuw:Exercise].
   wuw:MultipleChoiceQuestion[rdfs:subClassOf -> wuw:Exercise].
   ...
}
```

Here we define a class hierarchy of learning resources which is expressed in a TRIPLE model `wuw:ont`. The RDF Schema [18] semantics (for `rdfs:subClassOf`, `rdf:type` etc.) are defined as shown in the appendix (model `rdfschema(Mdl)`).

Next, we define a sample metadata repository using this ontology:

```
question1_1[rdf:type -> wuw:OpenQuestion; wuw:difficulty -> low].
question1_2[rdf:type -> wuw:FillInQuestion;
            wuw:difficulty -> medium].
question1_3[rdf:type -> wuw:YesNoQuestion; wuw:difficulty -> high].
question2_1[rdf:type -> wuw:YesNoQuestion; wuw:difficulty -> low].
question2_2[rdf:type -> wuw:MultipleChoiceQuestion;
            wuw:difficulty -> medium].
question3_1[rdf:type -> wuw:MultipleChoiceQuestion;
            wuw:difficulty -> high].
book1[rdf:type -> wuw:Book].
...
```

Now consider a second ontology which defines exercise types and which is used by the web test subsystem of Lean@WU. This ontology is much simpler than the learning resource ontology and uses fewer resources and properties. For instance, all `difficulty` properties and all resources that are not exercises (like the book resource in the above example) can be omitted. The ontology is expressed as a second TRIPLE model:

```
@exty:ont {
    exty:LearningProgressTest[rdfs:subClassOf -> rdfs:Resource].
    exty:Auto[rdfs:subClassOf -> exty:LearningProgressTest].
    exty:NonAuto[rdfs:subClassOf -> exty:LearningProgressTest].
    exty:MarkReader[rdfs:subClassOf -> exty:Auto].
    exty:NonMarkReader[rdfs:subClassOf -> exty:Auto].
}
```

The method of integrating these two ontologies is to use the `wuw` ontology as source ontology and the `exty` ontology as target ontology. Clients only use views expressed in the target ontology for the queries. We first define a mapping between the two ontologies and then define view models based on the mapping. A very simple mapping uses only the `subClassOf` relationship to model the relationships between the two ontologies. The mapping is placed in a separate mapping model:

```
@exty:mappings {
   wuw:MultipleChoiceQuestion[rdfs:subClassOf -> exty:MarkReader].
   wuw:YesNoQuestion[rdfs:subClassOf -> exty:MarkReader].
   wuw:FillInQuestion[rdfs:subClassOf -> exty:Auto].
   wuw:Exercise[rdfs:subClassOf -> exty:LearningProgressTest].
   wuw:OpenQuestion[rdfs:subClassOf -> exty:NonAuto].
}
```

For any given set of models, we can now—in a next step—define the rules for creating a view model `view(Ont1, Ont2, Mappings)`:

```
FORALL Ont1, Ont2, Mappings  @view(Ont1, Ont2, Mappings) {
  FORALL R,P,O  R[P -> O] <- R[P -> O]@Ont2.
  FORALL R,P,O  R[P -> O] <-
      R[P -> O]@rdfschema(view(Ont1, Ont2, Mappings)).
  FORALL R,C1,C2  R[rdf:type -> C1]
      R[rdf:type -> C2]@rdfschema(Ont1) AND
       C2[rdfs:subClassOf -> C1]@Mappings.
}
```

The view model is parameterized by taking two ontologies and a mapping between the ontologies as parameters. In this example `Ont1` is the source and `Ont2` the target ontology. The first rules states that everything in `Ont2` holds. Then, in the second rule, the RDF schema semantics defined before are applied to the view model. Finally we use the mapping model with its `subClassOf` relationships to create a view of the two ontologies according to the mapping.

Note that the definitions above are typically implemented by different roles, such as providers of ontologies and providers of view models. The actual resources are usually produced by the users of the system. The users (or the user tools) are usually interested in creating queries as well, but here it is important to be able to generate queries by very simple means. For instance, a user might compose queries in GUI-based tools. The view concept helps us to limit the query syntax and yet produce usable and user-customizable results.

For instance, a typical query using the above ontology view definition might be that the web test system requires those resources that are of type `MarkReader` (i.e., exercises that it can automatically test in web forms). The system simply has to query the view for resources of the particular type and receives all resources in the view that are exercises of type `MarkReader`. Note that the simplicity of the query is due to the view definition described above.

```
FORALL R  <- (R[rdf:type -> exty:MarkReader])@view(wuw:ont,
  exty:ont, exty:mappings).
```

The output of the TRIPLE engine for the example above is:

```
R = question3_1
R = question2_2
R = question2_1
R = question1_3
```

5.2 Constraining the Views with Property Values

As already mentioned in Section 2, the simple mapping rules used in the previous section might not be enough. Sensible views often have to be created under consideration of the (property) values of the data. Consider a simple example as an extension of the scenario in the previous section: the web test system should create a shuffled mix from the set of exercises that are the basis for test questions. Further assume that the test questions are defined as being either of type `FillInQuestion`, `YesNoQuestion`, or `MultipleChoiceQuestion`, and are not of the difficulty `low`. Moreover, the web test system should only use those questions from the result set that it can automatically correct in web forms (i.e., those of type `MarkReader`).

We have to use a more complex mapping rule to implement the definition of test questions:

```
@exty:mappings {
  ...
  FORALL R  R[rdf:type -> exty:TestQuestion] <-
     ((R[rdf:type -> wuw:MultipleChoiceQuestion] OR
       R[rdf:type -> wuw:YesNoQuestion] OR
       R[rdf:type -> wuw:FillInQuestion])  AND
      (R[wuw:difficulty -> medium] OR
       R[wuw:difficulty -> high]))@rdfschema(wuw:ont).
}
```

Note that the `exty:TestQuestion` definition is simply composed of `AND` and `OR` expressions, which means it can easily be created, say, by a tool that allows users to compose ontologies graphically.

The query for the view created with this mapping again is quite simple. It simply adds the new test question type definition to the previous `MarkReader` query by composition with `AND`:

```
FORALL R  <- (R[rdf:type -> exty:TestQuestion]
              AND R[rdf:type -> exty:MarkReader])
             @view(wuw:ont, exty:ont, exty:mappings).
```

The output of the TRIPLE engine for this query is:

```
R = question2_2
R = question3_1
R = question1_3
```

6 Description Logic Specification of Mappings

An interesting class of mappings is those that can be specified with a standard description logic like $\mathcal{SHIQ}$ [9] or its Semantic Web variants (OIL, DAML+OIL, OWL). The advantage of this approach is that users can create relatively interesting mappings with a simple point-and-click interface, since description logic expressions do not use any variables and therefore only class and property (role) names plus a small set of connectives (conjunction, disjunction, negation, etc.) have to be dealt with.

The mappings are specified by connecting class expressions of the source (Ont_S) and target (Ont_T) ontology with the usual implication:

$$C^{Ont_S} \sqsubseteq C^{Ont_T}$$

The most simple case is where C^{Ont_S} and C^{Ont_T} are class names ("primitive concepts"), e.g.:

$$\text{wuw:MultipleChoiceQuestion} \sqsubseteq \text{exty:MarkReader}$$

The corresponding RDFS/OWL expression (in TRIPLE syntax) uses the `rdfs:subClassOf` to relate the two classes:

```
wuw:MultipleChoiceQuestion[rdfs:subClassOf -> exty:MarkReader].
```

The view definition `@view(Ont1, Ont2, Mappings)` contains the following rule to map instances from C^{Ont_S} to C^{Ont_T}:

```
FORALL R,C1,C2  R[rdf:type -> C2] <-
      R[rdf:type -> C1]@rdfschema(Ont1) AND
      C1[rdfs:subClassOf -> C2]@Mappings.
```

For the case of complex class expressions, it is much simpler to create TRIPLE rules (via an automatic mapping) instead of writing rules that handle these class expressions directly.[4] For expressions of the form $C^{Ont_S} \sqsubseteq C^{Ont_T}$, C^{Ont_S} becomes the body and C^{Ont_T} becomes the head of a TRIPLE rule:

$$\text{TRIPLE}(C^{Ont_T}) \leftarrow \text{TRIPLE}(C^{Ont_S}).$$

As a consequence, C^{Ont_T} can only be a very simple class expression (i.e., no disjunction or negation is allowed).

As the following example shows, the mapping from the description logic expression to the corresponding TRIPLE rule is straightforward:

$$\begin{array}{l}(\text{wuw:MultipleChoiceQuestion} \\ \ \sqcup \text{wuw:YesNoQuestion} \\ \ \sqcup \text{wuw:FillInQuestion}) \\ \sqcap \exists\text{wuw:difficulty}.\{\text{medium}, \text{high}\}\end{array} \sqsubseteq \text{exty:TestQuestion}$$

[4] An alternative would be to access a description logic classifier from within the TRIPLE engine.

```
FORALL R  R[rdf:type -> exty:TestQuestion] <-
     ((R[rdf:type -> wuw:MultipleChoiceQuestion] OR
       R[rdf:type -> wuw:YesNoQuestion] OR
       R[rdf:type -> wuw:FillInQuestion])  AND
      (R[wuw:difficulty -> medium] OR
       R[wuw:difficulty -> high]))@rdfschema(wuw:ont).
```

7 Related Work

Our work follows the mediator architecture suggested by Wiederhold [21]. He addresses the problem in the database context that for end users the lack of abstraction and the need to understand the representation of data hinders the access to the available data. Another motivation for mediator architectures is the problem of combining information from multiple databases or other information sources where the representation and structure is different. In mediator architecture, a mediator plays the role of a virtual database: Users might formulate queries as if the data were available in a mediator database and the mediator translates the queries to the data sources. The mediator then synthesizes the answers from the sources and returns the answer to the user. In our approach it is possible for users to formulate their queries only in terms of the target ontology.

Several approaches have been proposed and implemented to build mediators over relational databases, for example [3].

Calvanese et al. [1] analyze the problems of ontology integration. They describe the ontologies with Description Logics. They argue that for capturing the mappings between ontologies the use of Description Logic is not sufficient and suggest a notion based on queries which is similar to our approach using rule-based views.

The subset of possible mappings we can define in description logics, as described in section 6, is still relevant in many practical situations, especially since they are easier to specify via a graphical user interface.

Mitra et al. [15] investigate the integration of heterogeneous sources (UML, DAML+OIL). They define articulation rules that establish correspondence between concepts in different ontologies. These articulation rules are used to rewrite queries. They use a common ontology format called the ONION conceptual model.

The currently available ontology editors for the Semantic Web also support some form of ontology mapping. Noy et al. [16] surveys ontology mapping support of these tools.

Recently several researchers investigated different aspects of ontology mappings for the Semantic Web. The mappings in these investigations are used not to query for resources using views but for information integration, where essentially the same problems have to be solved.

Halevy et al. [8] developed a data management infrastructure for Semantic Web applications. The main focus of their work was to enable interoperability of XML sources. They developed a mapping language based on XQuery. The mappings are also used to support query answering, which is possible in both directions using their query-answering algorithm. We use a specific class of Horn rules for expressing the mapping rules.

On the Semantic Web the data from heterogeneous sources is described by different ontologies. Doan et al. [6] argue that, in the case of information processing, the mapping between ontologies should happen (semi-)automatically. They developed a system that employs machine learning techniques to find the mappings.

Catarci and Lenzerini [2] described interschema knowledge using description logic. Their work focuses on how to use this interschema information for reasoning tasks, for example, to check the consistency of integrated information systems.

Data integration problems and possible solutions are extensively analyzed in database literature. Wache [20] provides a classification of the problems. The schematic and data heterogeneity conflicts are described in [14]. Semantic conflicts are analyzed by Kashyap et al. [12] and Goh [7]. Structural or semantic heterogeneity or data inconsistency can cause integration conflicts:

- Structural conflicts occur if we compare the structure of the data models of different information sources. In the case of structural conflicts, the semantic structure of the data is the same, the difference is in the representation structure. Structural conflicts are, for example, label conflicts, where the data attributes are equivalent but different labels are used.
- In the case of a semantic conflict, the equivalent structural elements have to be interpreted with different semantics. A typical semantic conflict is the unit and scale conflict, when two numeric values have the same semantics, but the values have a different meaning. An example would be "price", if it is represented in one information system implicitly in Euros, while in other systems in Dollars. Another typical semantic conflict is when two information sources use different data representation types.

Because of the large number of possible conflicts, individual treatment of the problems is often necessary. We have only concentrated on a subset of these problems that can be resolved with mapping rules between resources and their properties in two (or more) ontologies.

8 Conclusion and Future Work

On the Semantic Web, resources are described with metadata related to some ontology. Using our approach, users or applications can express their queries for resources with respect to an ontology that reflects a user-specific or application-specific view of the domain (i.e., in the application ontologies). We demonstrated with some typical application cases from the e-learning domain how mapping rules and views can be defined using the language TRIPLE. These views allow clients to formulate queries only in the target ontologies. The mapping rules connect the instances described by the "source ontology" with the terminologies (classes and properties) of the "target ontology". The ontologies, the mappings, and the queries are specified in TRIPLE. Simple mappings can also be formulated in Description Logic; we demonstrated a specific class of mappings which is relevant in many practical situations.

Our approach has several advantages:

- Users can formulate their queries in the target ontology in a more natural way than in the source ontology. The mappings in our method are developed by ontology developers and usually not by the users who submit queries. Our objective was not to require the user to be familiar with the domain expert's ontology; mapping rules can be created in any case only by persons who are familiar with the source ontology.
- If the source ontology evolves, the application ontology often remains the same, and only the mappings have to be updated or rewritten. In this way the users are not affected by changes in the source ontology.
- As in other mediator approaches, our approach can be used to integrate data described in different, independently developed ontologies.
- Integration with other software systems is possible.
- Queries based on views can potentially be more efficient than queries based on the source ontologies.
- Because our implementation uses TRIPLE, the ontologies we connect with views can be represented in different ontology languages like RDFS or DAML +OIL.
- The method could also be used for integrating information sources. Our paper demonstrates the opposite direction: In the examples we have only one information source and several (possible) views. When integrating information sources the automatic creation of mappings is much more important, in our examples the mappings are created manually.

Of course, our approach has some limitations:

- Our approach assumes that some mapping between different ontologies can be found. If it is not (easily) possible, other data integration approaches (e.g., imperative approaches) may be more appropriate. Specifically if programmatic specification of data integration is constantly required (e.g., by the end user), rule-based approaches might be cumbersome.
- The possibly increased efficiency using a view has to be contrasted with the effort of creating the view. Specifically, when the resources in source ontology often change, creating views can cause problems. This problem can be resolved by introducing caching structures in the view computation.

In our future research we plan to address more mapping conflicts, e.g., semantic conflicts. We also want to investigate how to integrate our approach with other data integration approaches and how to optimize query execution.

Acknowledgement. This work was supported by the Elena project and is partly sponsored by the European Commission (IST-2001-37264).

References

1. Calvanese, D., De Giacomo, G., Lenzerini, M.: Ontology of Integration and Integration of Ontologies. In *Proceedings of the 2001 Description Logic Workshop (DL 2001)*.
2. Catarci, T., Lenzerini, M.: Representing and Using Interschema Knowledge in Cooperative Information Systems. *Journal of Intelligent and Cooperative Systems*, 2(4):375–398, 1993.
3. Chawathe, S., Garcia-Molina, H., Hammer, J., Ireland, K., Papakonstantinou, Y., Ullman, J., Widom, J.: The TSIMMIS Project: Integration of Heterogeneous Information Sources. In *Proceedings of IPSJ Conference*, pp. 7–18, Tokyo, Japan, October 1994.
4. DAML+OIL. http://www.w3.org/TR/daml+oil-reference.
5. Decker, S., Brickley, D., Saarela J., Angele, J.: A query and inference service for RDF. In *The Query Languages Workshop, QL'98*, WorldWideWeb Consortium (W3C), Boston, USA, 1998., http://www.w3.org/TandS/QL/QL98/.
6. Doan, A., Madhavan, J., Domingos P., Halevy, A.: Learning to Map between Ontologies on the Semantic Web. In *11th International World Wide Web Conference (WWW'2002)*, Hawaii, USA, 2002.
7. Goh, C.: Representing and Reasoning about Semantic Conflicts in Heterogeneous Information Systems. Ph.D. Thesis, MIT Sloan School of Management, 1996.
8. Halevy, A., Ives, Z., Tatarinov, I., Mork, P.: Piazza: Data Management Infrastructure for Semantic-Web Applications. In *Proceedings of the Twelfth International World Wide Web Conference*, Budapest, Hungary, May 2003.
9. Horrocks, I., Sattler, U., Tobies, S.: Practical Reasoning for Expressive Description Logics. In *Proceedings of the 6th International Conference on Logic for Programming and Automated Reasoning (LPAR'99)*, 1999.
10. Horrocks, I.: The FaCT System. 2001., http://www.cs.man.ac.uk/~horrocks/FaCT/
11. IEEE Learning Technology Standards Committee: *IEEE LOM Draft 6.1*, http://ltsc.ieee.org/doc/index.html, 2001.
12. Kashyap, V., Sheth, A. P.: Semantic and Schematic Similarities Between Database Objects: A Context-Based Approach. In *VLDB Journal* 5(4): 276–304(1996).
13. Kifer, M., Lausen, G., Wu, J.: Logical Foundations of Object-Oriented and Frame-Based Languages, In *Journal of the ACM*, Jul. 1995., vol 42, pp. 741–843.
14. Kim, W., Seo, J.: Classifying Schematic and Data Heterogeneity in Multidatabase Systems. *IEEE Computer*. Vol 24. No. 12. December, 1991.
15. Mitra P., Wiederhold G., Decker S.: A scalable framework for the interoperation of information sources. In *Semantic Web Working Symposium*, pp. 317–329, 2001.
16. Noy, N. F., Musen, M. A.: Evaluating Ontology-Mapping Tools: Requirements and Experience. In *Workshop on Evaluation of Ontology Tools at EKAW'02 (EON2002)*. 2002. http://www.smi.stanford.edu/pubs/SMI_Reports/SMI-2002-0936.pdf.
17. OWL. http://www.w3.org/TR/owl-ref/.
18. RDF Schema. http://www.wcatarci93representing3.org/TR/rdf-schema/.
19. Sintek, M., Decker, S.: TRIPLE–A Query, Inference, and Transformation Language for the Semantic Web. In *Proceedings of the First International Semantic Web Conference (ISWC)*, Sardinia, June 2002.
20. Wache, H.: Semantische Mediation fur heterogene Informationsquellen. Akademische Verlagsgesellschaft AKA GmbH, Berlin, Reihe "Dissertationen zur Künstlichen Intelligenz (DISKI)", Nr. 261, 2003. In German.

21. Wiederhold, G.: Mediators in the Architecture of Future Information Systems. In *IEEE Computer*, Vol. 25, No. 3. March, 1992.

Appendix: Complete Example

```
// 0. rdf schema semantics
FORALL Mdl @rdfschema(Mdl) {
  FORALL O,P,V   O[P->V] <- O[P->V]@Mdl.
  FORALL O,P,V   O[P->V] <- EXISTS S
      (S[rdfs:subPropertyOf->P] AND O[S->V]).
  FORALL O,P,V   O[rdfs:subClassOf->V] <-
      EXISTS W   (O[rdfs:subClassOf->W] AND W[rdfs:subClassOf->V]).
  FORALL O,P,V   O[rdfs:subPropertyOf->V] <-
      EXISTS W   (O[rdfs:subPropertyOf->W] AND W[rdfs:subPropertyOf->V]).
  FORALL O,T   O[rdf:type->T] <-
      EXISTS S   (S[rdfs:subClassOf->T] AND O[rdf:type->S]).
}

// 1. learning object ontology plus some resources at WUW

@wuw:ont {

   // ontology
   wuw:LearningResource[rdfs:subClassOf -> rdfs:Resource].
   wuw:Book[rdfs:subClassOf -> wuw:LearningResource].
   wuw:Exercise[rdfs:subClassOf -> wuw:LearningResource].
   wuw:OpenQuestion[rdfs:subClassOf -> wuw:Exercise].
   wuw:FillInQuestion[rdfs:subClassOf -> wuw:Exercise].
   wuw:YesNoQuestion[rdfs:subClassOf -> wuw:Exercise].
   wuw:MultipleChoiceQuestion[rdfs:subClassOf -> wuw:Exercise].

   // some instances
   question1_1[rdf:type -> wuw:OpenQuestion; wuw:difficulty -> low].
   question1_2[rdf:type -> wuw:FillInQuestion; wuw:difficulty -> medium].
   question1_3[rdf:type -> wuw:YesNoQuestion; wuw:difficulty -> high].
   question2_1[rdf:type -> wuw:YesNoQuestion; wuw:difficulty -> low].
   question2_2[rdf:type -> wuw:MultipleChoiceQuestion; wuw:difficulty -> medium].
   question3_1[rdf:type -> wuw:MultipleChoiceQuestion; wuw:difficulty -> high].
   book1[rdf:type -> wuw:Book].
}

// 2. exercise types ontology

@exty:ont {
    exty:LearningProgressTest[rdfs:subClassOf -> rdfs:Resource].
    exty:Auto[rdfs:subClassOf -> exty:LearningProgressTest].
    exty:NonAuto[rdfs:subClassOf -> exty:LearningProgressTest].
    exty:MarkReader[rdfs:subClassOf -> exty:Auto].
    exty:NonMarkReader[rdfs:subClassOf -> exty:Auto].
}

// 3. mapping definitions

@exty:mappings {

   wuw:MultipleChoiceQuestion[rdfs:subClassOf -> exty:MarkReader].
   wuw:YesNoQuestion[rdfs:subClassOf -> exty:MarkReader].
   wuw:FillInQuestion[rdfs:subClassOf -> exty:Auto].
   wuw:Exercise[rdfs:subClassOf -> exty:LearningProgressTest].
   wuw:OpenQuestion[rdfs:subClassOf -> exty:NonAuto].

   FORALL R  R[rdf:type -> exty:TestQuestion] <-
       ((R[rdf:type -> wuw:MultipleChoiceQuestion] OR
         R[rdf:type -> wuw:YesNoQuestion] OR
         R[rdf:type -> wuw:FillInQuestion])  AND
```

```
        (R[wuw:difficulty -> medium] OR
         R[wuw:difficulty -> high]))@rdfschema(wuw:ont).

}

// 4. view definition

FORALL Ont1, Ont2, Mappings  @view(Ont1, Ont2, Mappings) {

  FORALL R,P,O  R[P -> O] <- // everything in Ont2 holds
      R[P -> O]@Ont2.

  FORALL R,P,O  R[P -> O] <- // everything in mappings holds
      R[P -> O]@Mappings.

  FORALL R,P,O  R[P -> O] <- // apply rdf schema semantics on "self"
      R[P -> O]@rdfschema(view(Ont1, Ont2, Mappings)).

  FORALL R,C1,C2  R[rdf:type -> C1] <- // rdfs:subClassOf mapping
      R[rdf:type -> C2]@rdfschema(Ont1) AND
       C2[rdfs:subClassOf -> C1]@Mappings.
}

// 5. queries

// give me the types of all resources from the WUW ontology
// wrt. view ontology (i.e., in terms of exty ontology)
FORALL R,O  <- R[rdf:type -> O]@view(wuw:ont, exty:ont, exty:mappings).

// query Mark Readers for online system
FORALL R  <- (R[rdf:type -> exty:MarkReader])@view(wuw:ont, exty:ont, exty:mappings).
```

Automatic Annotation of Content-Rich HTML Documents: Structural and Semantic Analysis

Saikat Mukherjee[1], Guizhen Yang[2], and I.V. Ramakrishnan[1]

[1] Department of Computer Science
Stony Brook University, Stony Brook, NY 11794, U.S.A.
{saikat,ram}@CS.StonyBrook.EDU
[2] Department of Computer Science and Engineering
University at Buffalo, Buffalo, NY 14260, U.S.A.
gzyang@CSE.Buffalo.EDU

Abstract. Although RDF/XML has been widely recognized as the standard vehicle for representing semantic information on the Web, an enormous amount of semantic data is still being encoded in HTML documents that are designed primarily for human consumption and not directly amenable to machine processing. This paper seeks to bridge this semantic gap by addressing the fundamental problem of *automatically* annotating HTML documents with semantic labels. Exploiting a key observation that semantically related items exhibit consistency in presentation style as well as spatial locality in template-based content-rich HTML documents, we have developed a novel framework for automatically partitioning such documents into semantic structures. Our framework tightly couples structural analysis of documents with semantic analysis incorporating domain ontologies and lexical databases such as WordNet. We present experimental evidence of the effectiveness of our techniques on a large collection of HTML documents from various news portals.

1 Introduction

The Semantic Web espouses a vision [3] for next-generation information networks where content providers define and share machine processable data on the Web to empower a variety of automated tasks ranging from information integration to Web services. There have been significant activities in building the technological infrastructure for realizing the Semantic Web vision and applications based on it. Notable efforts include developing Semantic Web languages such as DAML+OIL [22,23] based on Description Logic, and DAML Rules [16], which seeks to extend the Semantic Web with rule-based and object-oriented capabilities. Prototype systems, such as FaCT [21], $\mathcal{F}$LORA-2 [31,30], and TRIPLE [28], are now available to drive the knowledge representation and reasoning component of the Semantic Web.

Semantic Web documents contain metadata to express the meaning of their content. Tools such as those pioneered by SHOE [20] and OntoBroker [13,29] facilitate manual annotation of HTML documents with semantic markups. However, an enormous amount of semantic data (such as product descriptions and

D. Fensel et al. (Eds.): ISWC 2003, LNCS 2870, pp. 533–549, 2003.

Fig. 1. New York Times Front Page

pricing information) is still being encoded in "plain" HTML documents. These documents are designed primarily for human consumption and hence, unlike annotated Semantic Web documents, are not machine understandable.

In this paper we address the relatively unexplored problem of *automatically* annotating HTML documents, especially those that are machine generated from templates and contain *rich* semantic data. These kinds of documents are increasingly common nowadays since most content-rich Web sites (*e.g.*, news portals, product portals, etc.) are typically maintained using content management software that creates HTML documents by populating templates from backend databases. Figure 1, depicting a screen shot of the New York Times front page, is an example of a template-based content-rich HTML document. Observe that it has a news taxonomy (on the left in the figure) which does not change and a template for major headline news items. Each of these items begins with a hyperlink labeled with the news headline (*e.g.*, "White House ...") followed by the news source (*e.g.*, "By REUTERS ..."), followed by a timestamp and a text summary of the article (*e.g.*, "The White House today ...") and (optionally) a couple of pointers to related news.

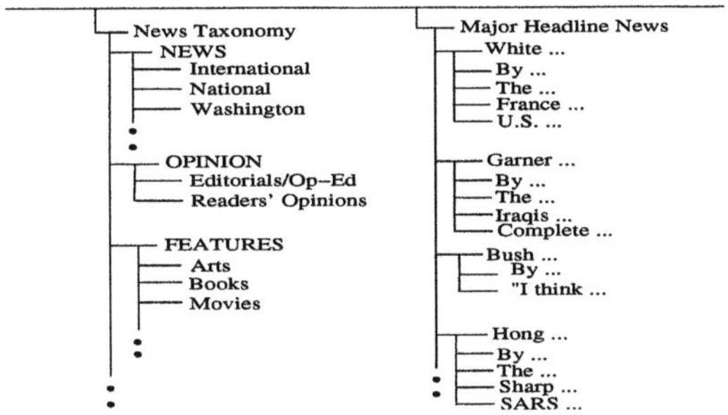

Fig. 2. A Fragment of the Semantic Partition Tree for New York Times Front Page

Usually a content-rich HTML document (such as the one shown in Figure 1) comprises many semantic concepts (*e.g.*, "News Taxonomy" and "Major Headline News") and concept instances. These concepts and concept instances can be organized into a *semantic partition tree* (such as the one shown in Figure 2) which represents the "semantics" of a HTML document. In a semantic partition tree each partition (subtree) consists of items related to a semantic concept. For example, in Figure 2 all the major headline news items are grouped under the subtree labeled "Major Headline News". The problem addressed in this paper is to automatically transform template-based content-rich HTML documents into their corresponding semantic partition trees. Note that once a semantic partition tree is created, it is relatively straightforward to generate a corresponding new document (in RDF/XML or some other suitable formats) with semantic annotations.[1]

There are two main tasks underlying the creation of a semantic partition tree from a HTML document: (i) identify segments of the document that correspond to semantic concepts; and (ii) assign labels to these segments. Informally, we say that several items are semantically related if they all belong to the same concept. Our solution to these problems is based on two important observations about semantically related items in template-based HTML documents, namely:

- *Semantically related items exhibit consistency in presentation style.* For example, observe the presentation styles of the items in the news taxonomy of the New York Times front page (on the left in Figure 1). The main taxonomic items, "NEWS", "OPINION", "FEATURES", ..., etc., are all presented in bold font. All the subtaxonomic items (*e.g.*, "International", "National", "Washington", ..., etc.) under a main taxonomic item (*e.g.*, "NEWS") are hyperlinks. A similar observation can also be made on all the major headline news items in the Figure 1.
- *Semantically related items exhibit spatial locality.* For example, when rendered in a browser (see Figure 1), all the taxonomic items are placed in close vicinity occupying the left portion of the page. Further observe that in the DOM tree (see Figure 3) corresponding to the HTML document, all these

[1] However, the final document generation step is not the main focus of this paper.

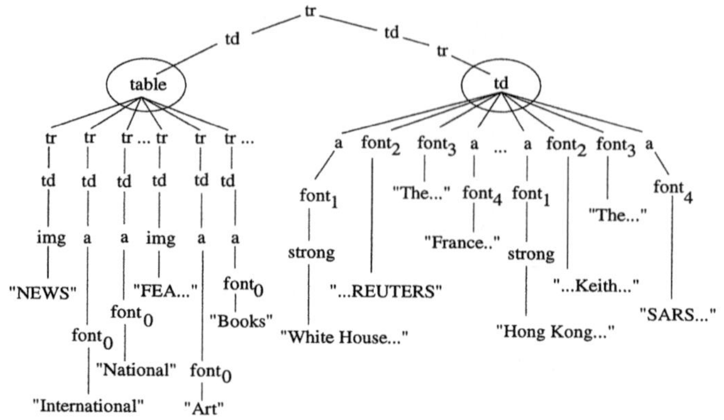

Fig. 3. DOM Tree Fragment of New York Times Front Page

taxonomic items are grouped together under one *single* subtree rooted at the *table* node (shown in circle). Similarly, all the major headline news items are clustered under a different subtree rooted at the *td* node (shown in circle in Figure 3).

Our solution to automatically creating semantic partition trees exploits the two key observations above. The first observation leads to the idea of associating a type with every leaf node in the DOM tree. The type of a leaf node consists of the root-to-leaf path of this node in the DOM tree and captures the notion of consistency in presentation style. The second observation gives rise to the idea of propagating types bottom-up in the DOM tree and discovering structural recurrence patterns for semantically related items at the root of a subtree. The reader is referred to Section 2.1 for more details.

Summary of Our Approaches and Contributions

- Based on the idea of types and type propagation, we develop structural analysis techniques for automatically partitioning HTML documents into semantic structures. Our algorithm can also discover semantic labels and associate them with partitions when they are present in the document (*e.g.*, "NATIONAL", "INTERNATIONAL", ..., etc. appearing in the third column in Figure 1). (See Sections 2.1 and 2.2.)
- We develop semantic analysis techniques to factor in structural variations in concept instances (*e.g.*, the absence of pointers to related news in the third major headline news item in Figure 1 in contrast to the others). Our semantic analysis makes lexical associations via WordNet to more accurately put the pieces of a concept instance together. To assign informative labels that are not present in a HTML document (*e.g.*, "Major Headline News" in Figure 2) to partitions our semantic analysis makes concept associations by classifying the content of a partition using an ontology encoding domain knowledge. (See Section 2.2.)

– To accurately separate and aggregate instances of a semantic concept as well as uncover higher level concept instances in a complex ontology we propagate lexical and concept associations by coupling structural and semantic analysis to work in tandem. (See Section 2.2.)

The rest of this paper is organized as follows. Our framework for automatic semantic partitioning is presented in Section 2. In Section 2.1 we introduce structural analysis techniques based on sequential pattern discovery. In Section 2.2 we show how structural analysis can be coupled with semantic analysis to improve accuracy of partitioning. Experimental results appear in Section 3. Related work is discussed in Section 4. Finally, Section 5 concludes this paper.

2 A Framework for Automatic Semantic Partitioning

As we point out in Section 1, the principal step in automatic semantic annotation is to transform HTML documents into semantic partition trees. This is achieved in our framework through a combination of structural and semantic analysis techniques. First we illustrate the ideas underlying structural analysis.

2.1 Structural Analysis

Structural analysis is based on the key observation that in template-based content-rich HTML documents semantically related items exhibit consistency in presentation style and spatial locality. Such a property can be captured by a simple typing system for the nodes in the DOM tree (and its corresponding semantic partition tree) of a HTML document. Formally, we have the following definition.

Definition 1 (Types) *Given a DOM tree: (i) Let* $t_1, t_2 \ldots, t_k$ *be the sequence of HTML tags, with their attribute values, on the path from the root of the DOM tree to a leaf node, then* $t_1 \cdot t_2 \ldots t_k$ *is a primitive type; (ii) If* $T_1, \ldots, T_k$ *are types, then* $seq(T_1 \ldots T_k)$ *is a compound type.*

Intuitively, a primitive type encodes the presentation style (including location and visual cues such as font type and size) of a piece of text that corresponds to a leaf node in a DOM tree. For example, in the DOM tree of Figure 3 (which corresponds to the HTML document shown in Figure 1, all the leaf nodes corresponding to the main taxonomic items, “NEWS”, “OPINION”, “FEATURES”, ..., etc., have the same primitive type, $tr \cdot td \cdot table \cdot tr \cdot td \cdot img$. Let us denote this type as T_1. Further observe that all the subtaxonomic items under each main taxonomic item, such as “International”, “National”, ..., etc., under the “NEWS” item, have the same primitive type, $tr \cdot td \cdot table \cdot tr \cdot td \cdot a \cdot font_0$.[2] Let us denote it using T_2.

[2] The *font* tags with different subscripts in Figure 3 (*e.g.*, $font_0$) denote *font* tags with different attributes such as type and size.

A compound type essentially summarizes the structural recurrence information at a subtree rooted at an internal node. Note that in Figure 3 the subtree rooted at the *table* node (shown in circle) groups together several main taxonomic items each of which is followed by a number of subtaxonomic items, *i.e.*, the entire taxonomy is clustered under this *single* DOM tree. This property of spatial locality combined with consistency in presentation style reveals evident structural recurrence information about semantically related items. If we cast all the primitive types of the leaf nodes in the subtree rooted at *table*, then we obtain the following string: $T_1T_2T_2 \ldots T_1T_2T_2 \ldots$. In this string the *sequential pattern*, $T_1T_2^*$ (here $*$ denotes Kleene closure), exactly captures the structural recurrence information of each semantically related item (*i.e.*, a main taxonomic item followed by a number of subtaxonomic items). In our type settings, the sequential pattern $T_1T_2^*$ is *generalized* as the compound type $seq(T_1T_2)$, which is assigned to the type of the *table* node (shown in circle) in Figure 3.

Therefore, as illustrated by the example above, the idea underlying structural analysis is to discover sequential patterns on the type sequence of nodes in a DOM tree. Given any two types as defined above, their equivalence is defined straightforwardly: two types are equivalent if and only if they are syntactically the same. Our structural analysis algorithm is built on the notion of *maximal repeating substrings*, which is defined below.

Definition 2 (Maximal Repeating Substrings) *Given a string S and a support threshold value θ, a substring α that repeats k times in S is a maximal repeating substring if and only if: (i) $k \geq 2$ and $|\alpha| \times k \geq \theta \cdot |S|$ ($|S|$ denotes the length of S); and (ii) $|\alpha| \times k$ is the maximum among all substrings that satisfy condition (i); and (iii) k is the maximum among all substrings that satisfy conditions (i) and (ii).*

Essentially the above definition says that a maximal repeating substring should be, first of all, a repeating substring that covers a majority of elements.[3] In addition, its coverage should be maximized and its length minimized (under the prerequisite that its coverage be maximized). In the sequel, we will use $MaximalRepeatingSubstring(S)$ to represent any algorithm that returns a maximal repeating substring of the input string S if there is one. Otherwise, we assume that it returns the empty string ε.

Since semantically related items exhibit spatial locality, structural analysis can be performed recursively bottom-up starting from the leaf nodes of the DOM tree of a HTML document. Specifically, to transform the DOM tree of a HTML document into a semantic partition tree, we simply invoke the top-level algorithm *PartitionTree* on the root of the given DOM tree. This algorithm first traverses the DOM tree top-down and then restructures it bottom-up.

[3] The support threshold value is used to filter out "noise" during structural analysis. Since our algorithm traverses a DOM tree bottom-up and multiple semantically related items can be dispersed in several subtrees, the "true" sequential pattern may not be discovered until our algorithm is invoked on an internal node closer to the root. Normally the support threshold value is set to 30% - 50% in our system.

```
Algorithm PartitionTree(n)
input
    n : a node in a DOM tree
begin
1.  if n is a leaf node then
2.      n.type = the sequence of HTML tags from the root to n
3.  else if n has only one child node c then
4.      PartitionTree(c)
5.      Replace n with c and remove n from the DOM tree.
6.  else
7.      for each child node x of n do PartitionTree(x) endfor
8.      Analyze(n)
9.  endif
end
```

We use the notation *n.type* to refer the type attribute of a node n. In the algorithm *PartitionTree*, Line 2 assigns primitive types to all leaf nodes. Internal nodes with only one child are handled in Lines 4–5. In such a case, the type of this only child node is computed and then simply propagated up the tree. However, for an internal node with multiple children, we first invoke *PartitionTree* on all of its children to collect their type information (Line 6). Then the algorithm *Analyze* is invoked upon this node to perform a pattern discovery on its children nodes (Line 7). (Here *Analyze* only does structural analysis. In Section 2.2 we will show how to extend it to do semantic analysis.)

```
Algorithm Analyze(n)
input
    n : an internal node in a DOM tree
begin
1.  S = the sequence of all the child nodes of n
2.  for each node c in S do
3.      if c.flatten = true then
4.          Replace c with the sequence of all the child nodes of c.
5.      endif
6.  endfor
7.  τ = ε
8.  do
9.      Collapse adjacent nodes in S which share the same type.
10.     α = MaximalRepeatingSubstring(TypeStr(S))
11.     if α ≠ ε then τ = α endif
12.     if |α| > 1 then
13.         for each substring ρ in S such that TypeStr(ρ) = α do
14.             Replace ρ with NewNode(ρ,seq(α)).
15.         endfor
16.     endif
17. while |α| > 1
18. if τ = ε then
19.     n.flatten = true
20. else
21.     Partition S into β_0γβ_1 ... γβ_m, where TypeStr(γ) = τ.
22.     for each γβ_i do Replace γβ_i with NewNode(γβ_i, NewType(τ)). endfor
23.     n.type = NewType(τ)
24. endif
25. Make the nodes in S the new children of n.
end
```

The algorithm *Analyze* takes an internal node, n, as input. Its main function is to discover structurally similar items among all the children of n and restructure the subtree rooted at n accordingly. Because our algorithm climbs up a DOM tree from leaf nodes to the root, structural similarity may not be discovered until it reaches a node close enough to the root. Therefore, we associate a boolean attribute, *flatten*, with each node to signal whether a structural similarity pattern has been discovered at this node. The value of this attribute is initialized to *false* for each node. However, if a pattern (or type) is not found at a node, then its *flatten* attribute is set to *true* (Line 19).

In Lines 1–6, all the child nodes of n are collected into a sequence, which will be partitioned into semantically related items later if they share structural similarity. But if we encounter a node, c, whose *flatten* attribute has the value *true* (which means a pattern is not found at this node), then we move all the child nodes of c into this sequence for further processing. Note that when the algorithm *Analyze* is invoked on a node, all of its descendant nodes are already typed. Intuitively, since the type of a node summarizes the structure of the subtree rooted at that node, analysis of the sequence of sibling types is essential for structural similarity pattern discovery, which is done in two stages by our algorithm.

In the first stage, consecutive nodes having equivalent types are collapsed into a single node (Line 9). The intuition behind this is that they all relate to the same item. Next, in Line 10, an attempt is made to find a maximal repeating substring of the string corresponding to the type sequence of S (returned by $TypeStr(S)$). If such a substring does not exist (hence no structural similarity), then the loop in Lines 8–17 is exited and the *flatten* attribute of the current node is set to *true* (Line 19). However, if a maximal repeating substring, α, is found and α contains at least two elements ($|\alpha| > 1$), then the sequence of consecutive nodes whose type sequence matches α is merged into a new node created by the procedure $NewNode$ (Lines 12–16). The first argument of $NewNode$ contains the sequence of nodes to be merged while the second argument indicates the type of this new node. The above collapsing-discovering-merging process is repeated until it cannot be performed any more.

In the second stage (Lines 21–23), the last pattern discovered during the first stage is used to partition the remaining sequence of nodes further. This is a simple heuristic that we apply to handle variations in document structures (*e.g.*, missing data items). Note that if τ contains only one type, then $NewType(\tau)$ returns τ directly; otherwise, it returns the compound type $seq(\tau)$.

Now we illustrate the working steps of the algorithm *Analyze* using an example. For simplicity, we will just show how it manipulates a sequence of types and omit other details. Suppose the type sequence of S is $T_1T_2T_3T_2T_3T_4T_1T_2T_3T_5$ immediately before the algorithm executes the loop starting at Line 8. T_2T_3 is a maximal repeating substring. Let us use a new type T_6 to denote $seq(T_2T_3)$. Then after the first iteration of the loop, the type sequence becomes $T_1T_6T_6T_4T_1T_6T_5$. The first two occurrences of T_6 can be collapsed into one, resulting in $T_1T_6T_4T_1T_6T_5$, in which T_1T_6 is a maximal repeating substring. Again, we use a new type T_7 to represent $seq(T_1T6)$. So after the second iteration the type sequence becomes $T_7T_4T_7T_5$ and the loop terminates. It is not hard to see that the first T_7 and the following T_4 will be put into one partition and the rest into another partition. T_7 is the type assigned to the current node.

2.2 Semantic Analysis

There are two main problems with structural analysis. Firstly, it may not, in general, *always* yield correct partitions corresponding to concept instances, especially when there are structural dissimilarities among them. In particular, the analysis based on maximal repeating substrings (immediately after Line 17 in the algorithm *Analyze*) does not guarantee complete partitions. For example, observe that in Figure 1 the third major headline news item starting with "Bush Backs ..." does not have any pointer to related news while all the others do. Invoking algorithm *Analyze* on the *td* node in Figure 3 (shown in circle which contains all major headline news items) renders a sequence S as follows: $\gamma \cdot T_4 \cdot \gamma \cdot T_4 \cdot \gamma \cdot \gamma \cdot T_4$, where $\gamma = seq(T_1T_2T_3)$; T_1, T_2, T_3, T_4 correspond to news title, source, text summary, and pointers to related news, respectively. (The correct partitions corresponding to the four major headline news items should be $P_1 = \gamma \cdot T_4$, $P_2 = \gamma \cdot T_4$, $P_3 = \gamma$, $P_4 = \gamma \cdot T_4$, such that $S = P_1 \cdot P_2 \cdot P_3 \cdot P_4$.)

The second problem with structural analysis is concerned with assigning semantic labels to partitions. Usually the labels of (small) partitions deep in a partition tree are provided by Web site designers in the document itself (*e.g.*, "NATIONAL," "INTERNATIONAL" ..., etc. appearing in the third column in Figure 1). When such a label is present in a document, it is usually the first text item in the partition. Applying this observation as a heuristic, we can extract labels for many partitions. On the other hand, we also have to deal with labeling concept instances using labels not present in the document (*e.g.*, "Major Headline News" in Figure 2). Such situations occur when smaller partitions are aggregated into bigger partitions (*e.g.*, "News Taxonomy" in Figure 2).

To address the problems above, we incorporate semantic analysis techniques into algorithm *Analyze* introduced in Section 2.1. Specifically, Lines 18–24 of algorithm *Analyze*, which serve as a rather straightforward heuristic to finally separate concept instances, will now be replaced with more general techniques for semantic analysis. Due to space limitation, here we will only outline the ideas.

Lexical Association. Lexical association is a light-weight linguistic processing technique for identifying small segments of related text. It semantically relates two *consecutive* pieces of free text by examining whether they share common words (after filtering out "stop" words such as "the" and "of") either directly or via synonym relationship. This process can be implemented using WordNet [1], a widely popular digital lexical reference database.

For instance, recall the example at the beginning of this section, where pure structural analysis produces the sequence $S = \gamma \cdot T_4 \cdot \gamma \cdot T_4 \cdot \gamma \cdot \gamma \cdot T_4$. At this point there is no justification to sort out the correct concept instances, $P_1 = \gamma \cdot T_4$, $P_2 = \gamma \cdot T_4$, $P_3 = \gamma$, $P_4 = \gamma \cdot T_4$, corresponding to the four major headline news items (in the second column of Figure 1) such that $S = P_1 \cdot P_2 \cdot P_3 \cdot P_4$. However, observe that in partition P_4, the texts associated with γ and the following T_4 share the common word "SARS". Therefore, by lexical association γ and T_4 can be semantically related and hence merged into one partition with high confidence.

Fig. 4. An Ontology for the News Domain

Concept Association. Concept association maps a partition to a semantic concept that succinctly summarizes the meaning of its content. The concept becomes the label of the partition. To make concept association we leverage domain knowledge encoded in an *ontology*. Informally an ontology describes concepts and their relationships, their features and attributes in a domain of interest. For instance, an ontology for the news domain is shown in Figure 4 and Table 1. Note that all the concepts and their subsumption hierarchy is depicted in Figure 4.

Recall the observation that the labels for (small) partitions may be present in the document itself. Moreover, they are usually the first text item of a partition. This observation leads to the following heuristic for discovering such labels. Suppose a type sequence $T\alpha$ corresponds to a partition. If T consists of short text (one to two words) and matches one of the keywords of a concept in the ontology, then it is extracted as the label for the corresponding partition (*e.g.*, "NATIONAL", "INTERNATIONAL" ..., etc. in the third column of Figure 1).

In cases where labels are not present in the document for the partitions, rules encoded in the ontology are used to classify the content of a partition. For instance, Table 1 shows the concept association rules for the news ontology. To determine if a partition can be classified as a major headline news item the ontology uses a rule which is a function of the key features associated with it, namely, (hyperlink) title, keywords for recognizing news sources (such as AP, Reuters, etc.), and features associated with news summaries such as constraints on the text length.[4]

Propagating Lexical and Concept Associations. In principle, the lightweight semantic analysis techniques introduced above are "incomplete" and hence not all concept instances can be identified. However, recall the key observation that semantically related items exhibit both consistency in presentation style and spatial locality. We can exploit this observation to *propagate* lexical as well as concept associations to other structurally similar items.

[4] More sophisticated classifiers such as Naive Bayes can also be used to make concept associations.

Table 1. Ontology Concepts and Their Mapping Functions

Ontology Concept	Mapping Function
Major Headline News	Rule: Function of Title, Source, Content
Minor Headline News	Rule: Function of Title, Content
National	Keyword: National, U.S.
International	Keyword: International, World
Science & Technology	Keyword: Science, Technology
Arts & Entertainment	Keyword: Arts, Movies, Music, Entertainment, Books, Travel
Business	Keyword: Business, Finance
Sports	Keyword: Sports, Baseball, Basketball
Health	Keyword: Health, Fitness
Detailed News	Rule: Function of Title, Content
News Taxonomy	Keyword: NEWS, OPINION

For instance, recall again the example illustrating lexical association above. In that example we determined via lexical association that γ and T_4 in P_4 are semantically related. Such an association between γ and T_4 can be propagated to other nearby (γ, T_4) pairs to form the partitions P_1 and P_2 (and so the remaining γ becomes P_3).

Structural Types vs. Semantic Types. Like lexical associations concept associations discovered can also be propagated to structurally similar items to assign semantic labels to partitions. In contrast to *structural* types (see Definition 1) that summarize the structural recurrence information about semantically related items, semantic labels can be viewed as *semantic* types that directly capture the semantics of partitions. Because semantic types factor out structural disparities, weaving structural and semantic types together enables our sequential pattern analysis process to uncover higher level concepts in a complex ontology.

Now each node in a DOM tree is associated with two types: a structural type and a semantic type. Once a semantic type (and the semantic label) is assigned to the root node of a partition, it will replace its structural type (if it exists) in the structural analysis process. However, its structural type is still retained in order to propagate concept associations. This will enable structural and semantic analysis to work in tandem. Specifically, immediately prior to invoking structural analysis on the root of a DOM subtree, the semantic type of a child node is propagated to all its siblings having the same structural type.

3 Experimental Results

We have implemented a prototype system and used it to create semantic partition trees from 50 sample HTML documents collected from 8 different news portals. The ontology used in our experiment is shown in Figure 4. These 50 sample HTML documents consist of 15 "front" pages (which contain multiple

Table 2. Complexity Measures of Sample HTML Documents

Portal	D	Major Headline News			Minor Headline News			Category News			Detailed News			News Taxonomy		
		N	MF	SD	N	MF	SD	N	MF	SD	N	MF	SD	N	MF	SD
New York Times	15	4	47	5.24	2	28	0.47	19	97	37.32	-	-	-	6	79	27.69
	16	-	-	-	1	16	2.26	-	-	-	1	26	14.88	-	-	-
CNN	14	1	23	5.00	-	-	-	12	13	29.55	-	-	-	1	23	8.04
	13	-	-	-	-	-	-	2	9	5.40	1	32	12.91	1	23	7.87
Yahoo News	18	-	-	-	-	-	-	11	49	49.66	-	-	-	1	24	9.68
	21	-	-	-	3	16	7.05	-	-	-	1	62	22.94	1	30	3.37
Google News	13	26	30	64.16	1	30	4.14	-	-	-	-	-	-	1	15	4.97
	16	-	-	-	2	25	56.30	-	-	-	1	25	20.70	1	34	0.90
ZdNet	13	15	35	12.47	3	6	4.76	-	-	-	-	-	-	-	-	-
	13	-	-	-	4	25	14.39	-	-	-	1	41	18.30	-	-	-
CNet	12	7	79	47.50	3	17	10.29	2	27	6.61	-	-	-	1	7	0
	11	-	-	-	1	22	10.80	-	-	-	1	43	27.26	1	7	0
Bloomberg News	21	7	31	31.10	-	-	-	-	-	-	-	-	-	1	37	5.31
	2	-	-	-	-	-	-	-	-	-	1	30	3.33	1	40	9.80
Recorder News	14	10	25	9.56	-	-	-	-	-	-	-	-	-	1	32	4.06
	5	-	-	-	-	-	-	-	-	-	1	46	1.12	-	-	-

concepts and concept instances such as news taxonomy and various headline news items) and 35 "detailed" news pages (which are usually characterized by a long text description).

To reflect the complexity of a HTML document in terms of its layout structure and content richness, we have collected statistics about all the 50 sample documents (see Table 2). Technically the complexity of a HTML document can be measured along four different dimensions: (1) Mean depth of the DOM tree (denoted by D). A large mean depth value usually implies complicated presentation style; (2) Number of concepts w.r.t. the ontology and their instances (denoted by N). Usually large values are observed on front pages reflecting their rich content; (3) Mean of the maximum fanout of subtrees in the DOM tree that are mapped to ontology concepts (denoted by MF). The maximum fanout of a tree is the max of all the fanout values of descendant nodes. A large value usually implies the presence of multiple concept instances that are clustered together in close vicinity; (4) Standard deviation of structural types of leaf nodes contained in the subtrees that are mapped to ontology concepts (denoted by SD). A larger values usually indicates a higher degree of structural variation among the concept instances.

We compute all the four metrics as defined above for each ontology concept in every HTML document in our sample data set. When each metric is finally tallied, we group together all documents collected from the same news portal and take the mean value of each group. Furthermore, each group is divided into front and detailed news pages and their corresponding mean values of each metric are shown in the top and bottoms rows, respectively, in Table 2 for every news portal. For instance, with respect to the documents from New York Times, the average mean depth of front (detailed) news pages is 15 (16); the average number of "Major Headline News" instances is 4 for front news pages. Note that in Table 2 the symbol "-" indicates that a metric is not applicable.

We measure two performance metrics: *recall* and *precision*. Recall value for a concept in a document is the fraction of the number of partitions correctly

Table 3. Recall and Precision Measures of Semantic Partitions

Portal	Major Headline News		Minor Headline News		Category News		Detailed News		News Taxonomy	
	Rec.%	Prec.%	Rec.%	Prec.%	Rec.%	Prec.%	Rec.%	Prec.%	Rec.%	Prec.%
New York Times	100	100	50	100	100	100	-	-	100	100
	-	-	25	100	-	-	100	100	-	-
CNN	100	100	-	-	100	100	-	-	100	100
	-	-	-	-	0	0	100	100	100	100
Yahoo News	-	-	-	-	81.8	100	-	-	100	50
	-	-	66.7	100	-	-	100	100	100	100
Google News	76.9	100	100	100	-	-	-	-	100	100
	-	-	-	-	-	-	100	100	100	100
ZdNet	93.3	100	66.7	100	-	-	-	-	-	-
	-	-	78.9	93.3	-	-	100	100	-	-
CNet	100	100	87.5	100	100	100	-	-	100	100
	-	-	0	0	-	-	100	100	100	100
Bloomberg News	100	100	-	-	-	-	-	-	100	100
	-	-	-	-	-	-	100	100	100	100
Recorder News	90	90	-	-	-	-	-	-	100	100
	-	-	-	-	-	-	100	100	-	-

labeled as instances of the concept over the actual number of concept instances present in the document. Precision value for a concept is the fraction of the number of partitions correctly labeled as instances of the concept over the total number of partitions (correctly and erroneously) labeled as instances of the concept. To collect recall and precision measures, first we manually identify all the ontology concepts and their correct instances for each document and thus obtain our reference model. When the semantic partition trees are rendered by our algorithm, we manually tally the number of partitions that are correct and erroneous w.r.t. the reference model and thereby compute the recall and precision values. As before, these recall and precision numbers are presented in Table 3 for every news portal and every concept w.r.t. the front and detailed news pages, respectively.

The recall and precision numbers presented in Table 3 show that our algorithm for automatically partitioning HTML documents works well in practice. On detailed news pages which typically contain few concepts and concept instances our algorithm shows high recall and precision. Even for front pages which normally include multiple concepts and instances our algorithm shows little degradation.

It is noteworthy pointing out that our algorithm almost always achieves 100% recall and precision on taxonomic news items, which typically show high structural homogeneity (see the low SD values in Table 2). For some complex pages (such as New York Times and Yahoo front page) the recall and precision for category news is high in spite of their complexity (see SD and MF values of these pages in Table 2 for category news). On the other hand the recall for major headline news in Google's front page is considerably lower than that of CNet's front page because of many more concept instances in Google. Also observe that in ZdNet's front page, in spite of the low complexity of minor headline news (see the low N, MF, and SD values) the recall value is low. This is due to the the "incompleteness" of our semantic analysis techniques.

The running time of our algorithm consists of two components: one is due to structural analysis while the other due to semantic analysis. The complexity of the structural analysis is dominated by $MaximalRepeatingSubstring$ whose worst case time complexity is quadratic in the length of the input sequence. During the bottom-up traversal of the DOM tree this procedure can be invoked at most n times where n is linear in the number of nodes in the DOM tree. The complexity of semantic analysis is dependent on the implementation technology used for doing lexical and concept associations. Currently in our prototype implementation the light-weight concept association rules have worst case time complexity linear in the number of concepts in the ontology.

Finally, we also measure the total running time that our algorithm takes for processing a document. On a Pentium III machine with a 800MHz processor and 256MB memory, the running times range from 60 milliseconds to 6289 milliseconds for documents with 96 nodes to 1709 nodes in their DOM trees.

4 Related Work

The problem studied in this paper is primarily concerned with automatically annotating HTML documents. The essence of this problem boils down to organizing the concepts and concept instances in a HTML document into a (labeled) semantic partition tree. There are a number of areas related to this problem, namely, XML schema discovery [15,26,14,27], schema inference from HTML documents [8,2], wrapper construction [17,7,25], record boundary detection in HTML documents [12,11,10,4], and semantic annotation of HTML documents [18,19,9]

However, our approach departs from all the related works above in several respects. Firstly, our main focus is on template-based content-rich HTML documents. Unlike the proposed approaches for XML schema discovery and schema inference from HTML documents, which require a collection of documents as input, we work on *individual* documents. Secondly, our techniques exploit the key observation that semantically related items exhibit consistency in presentation style as well as spatial locality.

Heuristics have been proposed to partition HTML documents into tree-like structures so as to facilitate Web browsing on small-screen devices [5], efficient Web search [33], and converting HTML documents into XML data [6,32]. However, the partitioning algorithms in these works do not perform complex sequential pattern analysis as proposed by us. The partitioning algorithm of [33] depends on *ad hoc* interpretation of HTML markups and hence does not scale well to arbitrary content-rich domains. In [5], a combination of keyword extraction and text summarization is used for semantic partitioning; but the implicit patterns in template-based Web documents are not exploited. The problem of assigning semantic labels to partitions was not addressed in [32]. Unlike our work, [6] did not propose general techniques for discovering semantic labels that are present in a document. Moreover, our work further complements these above works by introducing a novel semantic analysis framework based on discovering and propagating concept associations.

Relevant to our work is the problem of record boundary detection in HTML documents pioneered in [12]. Several heuristics were introduced in [12] for this problem and were later extended in [4]. More recently, a sophisticated framework for developing application ontologies and using them for delineating record boundaries was proposed in [10]. However, these techniques are not directly applicable to our problem due to the presence of rich content comprising multiple concepts and concept instances in one document. Furthermore, like most proposed wrapper construction techniques, [10] requires supervised training whereas our framework does not.

Recently, interesting works were reported in [20,18,19,9], which seek to enable the Semantic Web by enriching Web documents with semantic labels. In [20,18, 19] powerful ontology management systems form the backbone of systems that support *interactive* annotation of HTML documents. This is in contrast to our approach where annotation is *automatic* given a domain ontology. Even though annotation in [9] is automatic, it does not exploit the key observation that semantically related items exhibit spatial locality in DOM trees of HTML documents. Consequently, their partitioning algorithm may fail to properly identify concept instances in template-generated HTML documents containing multiple concept instances.

Finally, the fundamental difference between our approach and other works is that our framework tightly couples structural and semantic analysis techniques and propagates semantic associations discovered in order to identify concept instances.

5 Conclusion

There is scope for improving both structural and semantic analysis. In structural analysis we can incorporate more robust pattern discovery techniques based on minimum string edit distances. This can easily accommodate structural differences without requiring semantic analysis. We can enhance semantic analysis by incorporating more powerful classification techniques.

The idea of semantic partitioning has important implication to other data management problems. First, it eases the task of formulating (XPath and XQuery) queries to retrieve data from HTML documents. Semantic partitioning can be used to detect semantic changes in document content, an idea recently explored in [24]. Another application is audio-browsable Web content. By putting a dialog interface to the content of a HTML document which is reorganized based on the knowledge of its schema, a user can easily browse its content using voice commands. Audio browsable Web content can greatly expand the reach of the Web to visually challenged individuals. Finally, the idea of semantic partitioning can enable the creation of self-repairing wrappers.

Acknowledgement. This work was supported in part by the NSF grants CCR-0205376, CCR-0311512, and IIS-0072927. The authors would like to thank Wenfang Tan for implementing the algorithms and collecting experimental results.

References

1. WordNet. http://www.cogsci.princeton.edu/~wn/.
2. A. Arasu and H. Garcia-Molina. Extracting structured data from web pages. In *ACM SIGMOD*, 2003.
3. T. Berners-Lee and M. Fischetti. *Weaving the Web.* Harper San Francisco, 1999.
4. D. Buttler, L. Liu, and C. Pu. A fully automated object extraction system for the world wide web. In *International Confernece on Distributed Computing Systems (ICDCS)*, 2001.
5. O. Buyukkoten, H. Garcia-Molina, and A. Paepcke. Focussed web searching with PDAs. In *International World Wide Web Conference*, 2000.
6. C. Y. Chung, M. Gertz, and N. Sundaresan. Reverse engineering for web data: From visual to semantic structures. In *ICDE*, 2002.
7. W. Cohen, M. Hurst, and L. Jensen. A flexible learning system for wrapping tables and lists in html documents. In *International World Wide Web Conference*, 2002.
8. V. Crescenzi, G. Mecca, and P. Merialdo. Roadrunner: Towards automatic data extraction from large web sites. In *VLDB*, 2001.
9. S. Dill, N. Eiron, D. Gibson, D. Gruhl, R. Guha, A. Jhingran, T. Kanungo, S. Rajagopalan, A. Tomkins, J. Tomlin, and J. Yien. SemTag and Seeker: Bootstrapping the semantic web via automated semantic annotation. In *International World Wide Web Conference*, 2003.
10. D. Embley and L. Xu. Record location and reconfiguration in unstructured multiple-record web documents. In *ACM International Workshop on the Web and Databases (WebDB)*, 2000.
11. D. W. Embley, D. M. Campbell, R. D. Smith, and S. W. Liddle. Ontology-based extraction and structuring of information from data-rich unstructured documents. In *International Conference on Information and Knowledge Management (CIKM)*, 1998.
12. D. W. Embley, Y. Jiang, and Y.-K. Ng. Record-boundary discovery in web documents. In *ACM SIGMOD*, 1999.
13. D. Fensel, S. Decker, M. Erdmann, and R. Studer. Ontobroker: Or how to enable intelligent access to the WWW. In *11th Banff Knowledge Acquisition for Knowledge-Based Systems Workshop*, Banff, Canada, 1998.
14. M. Garofalakis, A. Gionis, R. Rastogi, S. Seshadri, and K. Shim. XTRACT: A system for extracting document type descriptors from xml documents. In *ACM SIGMOD*, 2000.
15. R. Goldman and J. Widom. DataGuides: Enabling query formulation and optimization in semistructured databases. In *VLDB*, 1997.
16. B. N. Grosof, I. Horrocks, R. Volz, and S. Decker. Description logic programms: Combining logic programs with description logic. In *International World Wide Web Conference*, 2003.
17. J. Hammer, H. Garcia-Molina, S. Nestorov, R. Yerneni, M. M. Breunig, and V. Vassalos. Template-based wrappers in the TSIMMIS system. In *ACM SIGMOD*, 1997.
18. S. Handschuh and S. Staab. Authoring and annotation of web pages in CREAM. In *International World Wide Web Conference*, 2002.

19. S. Handschuh, S. Staab, and R. Volz. On deep annotation. In *International World Wide Web Conference*, 2003.
20. J. Heflin, J. A. Hendler, and S. Luke. SHOE: A blueprint for the semantic web. In D. Fensel, J. A. Hendler, H. Lieberman, and W. Wahlster, editors, *Spinning the Semantic Web*, pages 29–63. MIT Press, 2003.
21. I. Horrocks. Benchmark analysis with FaCT. In *TABLEAUX*, 2000.
22. I. Horrocks. DAML+OIL: A description logic for the Semantic Web. *IEEE Bulletin of the Technical Committee on Data Engineering*, 25(1), March 2002.
23. I. Horrocks and S. Tessaris. Querying the semantic web: A formal approach. In *International Semantic Web Conference (ISWC)*, 2002.
24. S.-J. Lim and Y.-K. Ng. A automated change detection algorithm for HTML documents based on semantic hierarchies. In *ICDE*, 2001.
25. L. Liu, C. Pu, and W. Han. XWRAP: An XML-enabled wrapper construction system for web information sources. In *ICDE*, 2000.
26. S. Nestorov, S. Abiteboul, and R. Motwani. Extracting schema from semistructured data. In *ACM SIGMOD*, 1998.
27. Y. Papakonstantinou and V. Vianu. DTD inference for views of xml data. In *ACM PODS*, 2000.
28. M. Sintek and S. Decker. TRIPLE – a query, inference, and transformation language for the semantic web. In *International Semantic Web Conference (ISWC)*, 2002.
29. S. Staab, J. Angele, S. Decker, M. Erdmann, A. Hotho, A. Maedche, H.-P. Schnurr, R. Studerand, and Y. Sure. Semantic community web portals. In *International World Wide Web Conference*, 2000.
30. G. Yang and M. Kifer. $\mathcal{F}$LORA-2: User's Manual. http://flora.sourceforge.net/, June 2002.
31. G. Yang and M. Kifer. Well-founded optimism: Inheritance in frame-based knowledge bases. In *International Conference on Ontologies, Databases, and Applications of Semantics (ODBASE)*, 2002.
32. Y. Yang and H. Zhang. HTML page analysis based on visual cues. In *International Conference on Document Analysis and Recognition (ICDAR)*, 2001.
33. S. Yu, D. Cai, J.-R. Wen, and W.-Y. Ma. Improving pseudo-relevance feedback in web information retrieval using web page segnmentation. In *International World Wide Web Conference*, 2003.

Semi-automatic Semantic Annotation of Images Using Machine Learning Techniques

Oge Marques and Nitish Barman

Department of Computer Science and Engineering
Florida Atlantic University
777 Glades Road, Boca Raton, FL 33431–0991
{omarques,NBAR4294}@fau.edu

Abstract. The success of the Semantic Web hinges on being able to produce semantic markups on Web pages and their components, in a way that is cost-effective and consistent with adopted schemas and ontologies. Since images are an essential component of the Web, this work focuses on an intelligent approach to semantic annotation of images. We propose a three-layer architecture, in which the bottom layer organizes visual information extracted from the raw image contents, which are mapped to semantically meaningful keywords in the middle layer, which are then connected to schemas and ontologies on the top layer. Our key contribution is the use of machine learning algorithms for user-assisted, semi-automatic image annotation, in such a way that the knowledge of previously annotated images – both at metadata and visual levels – is used to speed up the annotation of subsequent images within the same domain (ontology) as well as to improve future query and retrieval of annotated images.

1 Introduction

The success of the Semantic Web hinges on being able to produce semantic markups on Web pages and their components, in a way that is cost-effective and consistent with adopted schemas and ontologies. A significant portion of the Web is comprised of images. And as yet, most of the images on the Web have not been marked-up with respect to their semantic content. Our work is an attempt to address this issue by providing an intelligent approach to expediting and facilitating the semantic annotation of images. We explore the issues of annotating, crawling, querying, and retrieving images in a way that extends our previous work in the related field of content-based image retrieval [16,17], and redirects our efforts toward a 'Semantic Web-ready' solution.

Recent developments in Web engineering, such as the popularization of XML and Web services, will allow easy packaging, discovery and communication of structured information such as metadata schemas and indexes for media data such as images. These new advances will not, however, enable the automatic generation of these metadata. In other words, it is still very costly and human intensive to generate powerful metadata and media descriptors to populate such

D. Fensel et al. (Eds.): ISWC 2003, LNCS 2870, pp. 550–565, 2003.

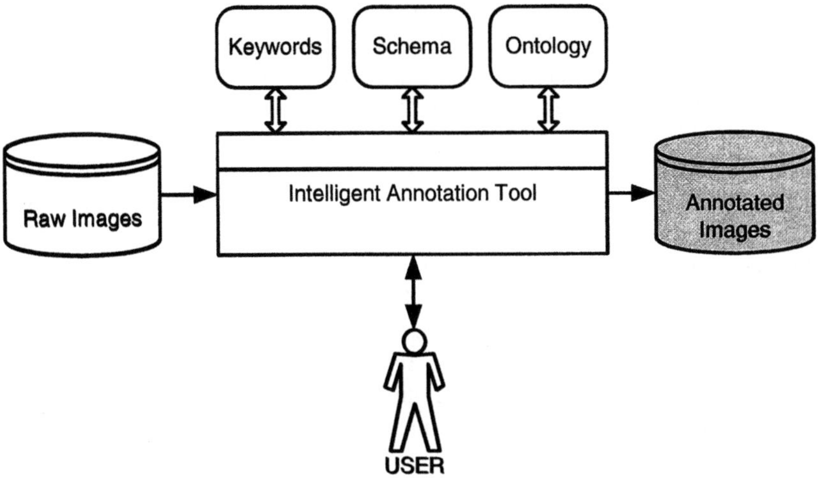

Fig. 1. Intelligent image annotation tool: conceptual diagram

metadata schemas and structures for very large media databases. Our research addresses this topic and suggests an intelligent, user-assisted, semi-automatic solution for annotating (potentially huge) repositories of raw images, and storing the result (e.g., in XML-formatted RDF-schema) in an 'annotated image' repository (Figure 1). The resulting annotated image archive would then be available for queries by visual content (giving an image as an example) and/or keywords as well as for data exchange with other Web-based applications.

In addition to its primary goals – consistent, cost-effective, fast, intelligent annotation of visual data – the method proposed in this paper also aims at improving the performance of subsequent image query and retrieval operations on the annotated image repository. The image retrieval problem has not been successfully solved yet, despite almost a decade of work [24] and dozens of research prototypes and commercial products developed as a result. The use of keywords only does not provide satisfactory results (as anyone who has used the 'Images' option in Google^{TM} [8] knows), mostly because the correlation between the keywords used in the query and the desired image file has to be established by unreliable, vague, not always available metadata, in the form of surrounding text and/or HTML tags, such as the contents of the **alt** attribute of the **img** element in the HTML document. Pure content-based image retrieval (CBIR) also falls short of providing an adequate solution to the problem, mostly due to the limitations of current computer vision techniques in bridging the gap between visual features and their semantic meaning. There is a clear need to cleverly combine the two in order to yield a better solution, and several researchers (e.g., [21]) have been working on techniques that combine textual and visual cues to improve retrieval results.

In previous work [17] we assumed a purely content-based scenario and dismissed the use of keywords because of the tedious, time-consuming, and subjective nature of human annotation and the ambiguous results it often produces. However, recent developments in RDF schemas, ontologies, and other Semantic Web-related efforts, have led us to look at the problem from a different perspective, one in which the use of metadata is a required part of the solution. We decided to concentrate our efforts in improving the efficiency of the annotation process, ensuring the meaningfulness of the chosen keywords, and preparing the framework for exchange and reuse of annotated visual data.

The content of this paper is structured as follows. Section 2 summarizes related work, particularly in the fields of image annotation and combination of textual and visual features for image retrieval. Section 3 explains the proposed architecture and its main components. Section 4 focuses on the techniques and algorithms for image annotation, and subsequent query and retrieval. Finally, Section 5 presents some concluding remarks.

2 Related Work

In this Section we discuss works related to semi-automatic annotation of textual data, image annotation, combination of keywords and visual features in image retrieval, and use of metadata for description of multimedia content, particularly images.

2.1 Semi-automatic Semantic Annotation of Text

There have been a number of papers on semi-automatic semantic annotation of natural language text. In [6], Erdmann et al. describe an ontology-based annotation tool developed under the KA^2-initiative. Since the raw data is in text format, their system uses a tokenizer, a lexical analysis component, and a chunk parser, in such a way as to associate single words or complex expressions with a concept from the ontology, connected through the domain lexicon linkage. Recognized concepts and dependency relations between concepts are highlighted as suggested annotations, so that all relevant information in the document with regard to the ontology is proposed to the annotator, whereas the actual process of annotation is delegated to the annotation tool. This work also addresses the need of treating document annotation and ontology maintenance in a cyclic fashion. Even though it focuses on textual information, it provided us some useful guidelines for the development of our work, such as the suggestion to keep the ontology simple and the need to support annotators with interactive GUIs. In subsequent papers [9,10], this work is extended to an annotation environment that allows construction of relational metadata, while maintaining the same strict guidelines of annotation for the sake of generating machine-understandable data, viz. to allow relational metadata, proper reference and consistency.

2.2 Image Annotation

Work on semantic image annotation is still in its infancy, and we found only two examples that relate more closely to the work proposed in this paper. One is Photo-RDF [15], a project for describing and retrieving JPEG pictures with (RDF) metadata. Photo-RDF describes the RDF schemas, offers a data-entry program (RDFPic) for quickly entering metadata for large numbers of photos, proposes a way to serve the photos and the metadata over HTTP, and suggests search methods to retrieve photos based on their descriptions. It uses the Dublin Core (DC) schema as well as additional optional schemas for technical data. Its data-entry tool (RDFPic) has a GUI that allows the user to reuse the annotation values that were entered for previous photos in a nice and friendly way, saving annotation time.

The other is CBSA [4], a content-based soft annotation tool that allows adding semantic labels to a small set of images. Machine learning algorithms extend the labels to larger image sets, based on the visual similarity between the new (unlabeled) images and previously labeled images. This work is one of the most recent relevant results in combination of visual and textual features in image retrieval, but it does not rely on ontologies and/or schemas.

2.3 Combining Visual and Textual Features in Image Retrieval

Researchers in the field of visual information retrieval have recognized the many difficulties in retrieving images from large repositories using only visual contents. It is also widely accepted that the retrieval of images annotated with keywords may provide potentially better results, which unfortunately depend on the amount, quality, and consistency of the metadata associated with each image. In very well-controlled annotation environments, the use of keywords, even when hidden from the end user (see [5] for an example), is likely to provide better results than the sole reliance on visual properties extracted using current computer vision techniques.

The main drawbacks of image query and retrieval by keywords can be classified in three levels, in increasing degree of complexity. First, on a practical level, most of the images available over the Web – or the HTML pages in which they are embedded – are not annotated in a consistent, meaningful way. Secondly, when keywords are used, they are often isolated from any framework – such as schema or ontology – that could put them in context and allow further inference of relevant knowledge. Third, on a deeper level, the contents, meaning, and emotions associated with or evoked by a picture can hardly be adequately expressed in words [24].

One of the best-known efforts in combining visual and textual features in image retrieval is the work by Sclaroff et al. [21], in which textual and visual statistics from HTML documents are combined into a single index vector. Their system, ImageRover [13], enables the user to provide relevance feedback which is used to set the weights of the distance metrics used to compare the images. It relies on whatever textual information is available next to the image within the

HTML page in which it is embedded, using the Latent Semantic Indexing (LSI) method, which assigns different weights to words, depending on their importance; for instance, words found inside the **alt** attribute of the **img** element are assigned a higher weight than those found within a pair of **h2** tags. But this work also does not refer to schemas or ontologies.

2.4 Use of Metadata for Description of Multimedia Content

The standardization and widespread adoption of metadata for describing multimedia content has been a goal of many researchers and standard bodies in the field. It is widely recognized that the use of standardized descriptors, description schemes, etc., such as proposed in the MPEG-7 standard [12], will promote an easier integration of tools and applications without limiting the creative efforts of researchers involved in open topics such as efficient multidimensional indexing structures or faster search algorithms for multimedia data.

For the specific case of images, two recent developments toward metadata adoption and standardization are worth mentioning: the "Data Dictionary for Images" [19], a comprehensive list of technical data elements required to manage digital image collections, and the Adobe eXtensible Metadata Platform XMP [1] , an RDF-based framework for adding machine-readable labels, or semantic content to application files, databases and content repositories.

The adoption of RDF, XML, and other Semantic Web-oriented technologies and concepts in visual information retrieval can also be found in the description of European projects ARTISTE (An integrated Art Analysis and Navigation Environment) [3] and SCULPTEUR (Semantic and Content-based mULtimedia exPloiTation for EURopean benefit) [22].

3 Proposed Architecture

In this Section, we outline our proposed architecture. First, we present our holistic vision, which should put in perspective where our work fits in the grand scheme. Next, we describe our proposed three-layer model for annotation, query, and retrieval in more detail.

3.1 The Big Picture

The work described in this paper is part of a bigger vision, in which our intelligent image indexing and annotation solution is exposed as an Intelligent Image Indexing Web Service (I3WS) to potential clients. This Web service will take a raw image repository (plus a few optional constraints and parameters – schemas, keywords, ontologies, etc.) as an input and return its annotated version as a result. Clients of the service would save annotation time and manpower and get a free semantic mark-up, which they could use in any way (e.g., to improve the visibility and rank of their pages to a search engine).

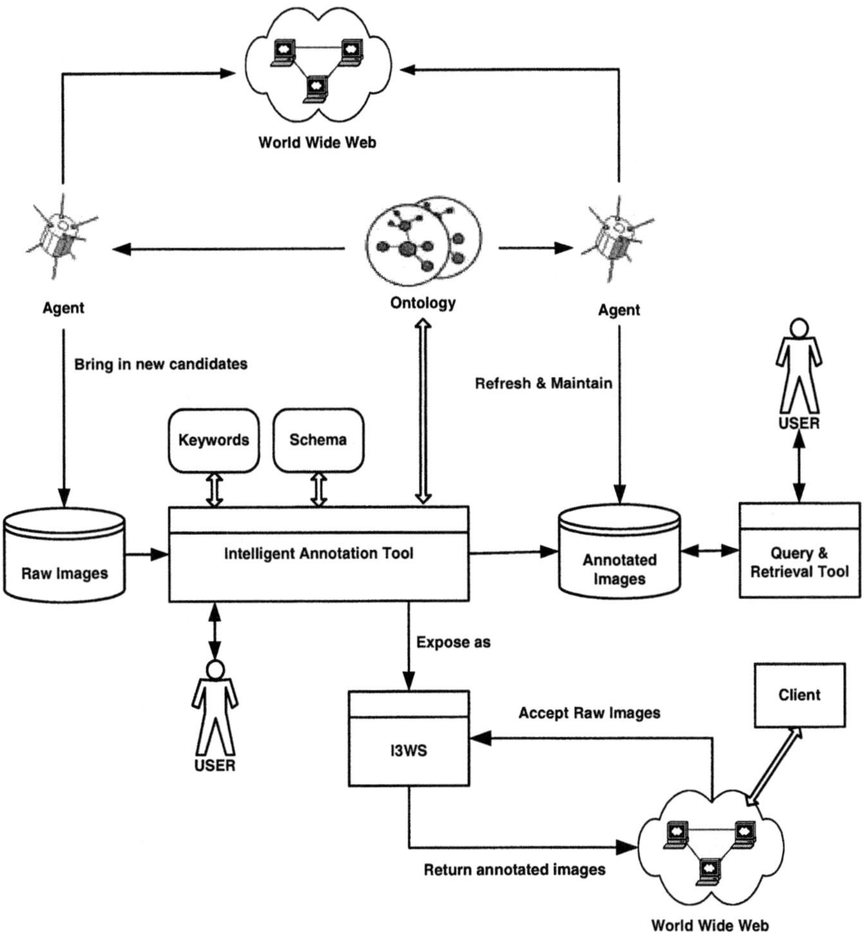

Fig. 2. The big picture.

In addition to annotating third-party repositories, our system keeps its own image repositories (with locally stored thumbnails and links to the actual images' locations on the Web) and a Web-based GUI for performing query and retrieval on them (see Section 4.3 for more details). In a future stage, we also plan to use ontology-focused agents [11] to crawl the Web and bring new candidate images that fit under a given ontology to the 'raw image repository' for subsequent annotation. The agents will also periodically update the annotated repository by checking the integrity of the links between our local thumbnails and the full-size images to which they correspond. Figure 2 depicts our overarching vision. The focus of our current work, however, is the development of the Intelligent Annotation Tool (IAT) and the Query and Retrieval Tool (QRT).

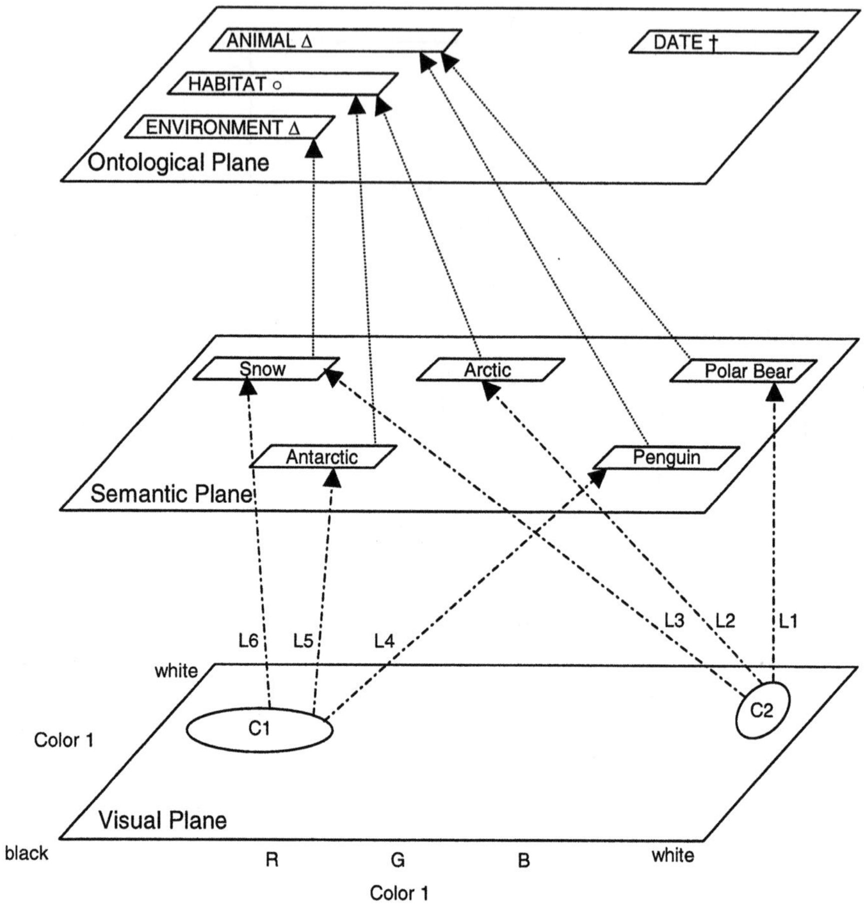

Fig. 3. The proposed three layer architecture, where: o = content-dependent metadata, △ = content-descriptive metadata, † = content-independent metadata.

3.2 The Three-Layer Model for Annotation, Query, and Retrieval

We propose a three-layer model, in which the inter-planar relationships are used as a basis for making inferences about the semantic content of not yet annotated images. The visual plane organizes visual information extracted from the raw image contents. The information in the visual plane is mapped to semantically meaningful keywords in the semantic plane. The keywords in the semantic plane, in turn, map to specific slots in the domain-specific schema(s) contained in the ontological plane.

The bottom layer (*visual plane*) is a *K-D* space containing the visual feature vectors corresponding to each image in the annotated database. The size and nature of these feature vectors is purely dependent on the visual feature extraction algorithms that one wishes to implement, from simple color-based measures such as color histograms, to complex and task-specific features, such as eigenfaces. Ideally, the extracted feature vectors should be compact (for the sake of both storage and processing) and discriminative, i.e., the distribution of the vectors in the *K-D* space should resemble the relative visual similarity among the images to which they map, in such a way that visually similar images should appear clustered together.

The middle layer (*semantic plane*) contains all the keywords that have been used to annotate the images.

The top layer (*ontological plane*) contains the schemas and ontologies to which the keywords belong. It contains information about the relationships (i.e. dependencies) between the various tags in the RDF schema. Storing this information in a separate plane allows us to easily extend the RDF schema and automatically re-annotate the images in the annotated images database with the new keyword-tag combinations used in the extended schema.

Figure 3 shows a simplified version of the model in which the visual plane is a *2-D* plane whose axes are the two predominant colors in the image, containing two clusters (C1 and C2). Each cluster maps to the keywords that have been used to annotate at least one image in that cluster. The weight of each link (L1, L2, ..., L6) is proportional to the number of images in that cluster which have been annotated with that keyword. The ontological plane depicts a very simple 4-slot schema, with different types of metadata: *content-dependent metadata* (e.g., *environment*, which may relate strongly to the predominant color in a picture), *content-descriptive metadata* (e.g., name of an *animal*), and *content-independent metadata* (e.g., the *date* when the photo was taken).

Note, also, that each keyword in the semantic plane maps to a slot in the schema contained in the ontological plane. The knowledge that visually similar images may map onto independent – maybe even mutually exclusive – keywords is modeled using a Bayesian network, whose details are explained in Section 4.1.

4 Detailed Description of Our Approach

Broadly, our application makes use of knowledge (semantic and visual) derived from previously annotated images to expedite and facilitate the annotation of subsequent images. The knowledge derived is also used to improve query and retrieval of annotated images.

In this Section, we describe our application in more detail. We begin by noting that the proposed approach assumes that meaningful visual features are extracted from the raw images, and that images that are sufficiently similar are grouped together in clusters. It is beyond the scope of this paper to discuss the implications behind the choice and design of feature extraction and clustering strategies, issues that have been addressed by [2,7,14,16,20,23], among many others. Next, we describe what we believe to be the most important and innovative aspect of our contribution – the Intelligent Inference Engine (IIE). Finally, we provide a more detailed procedural description of each phase of our application.

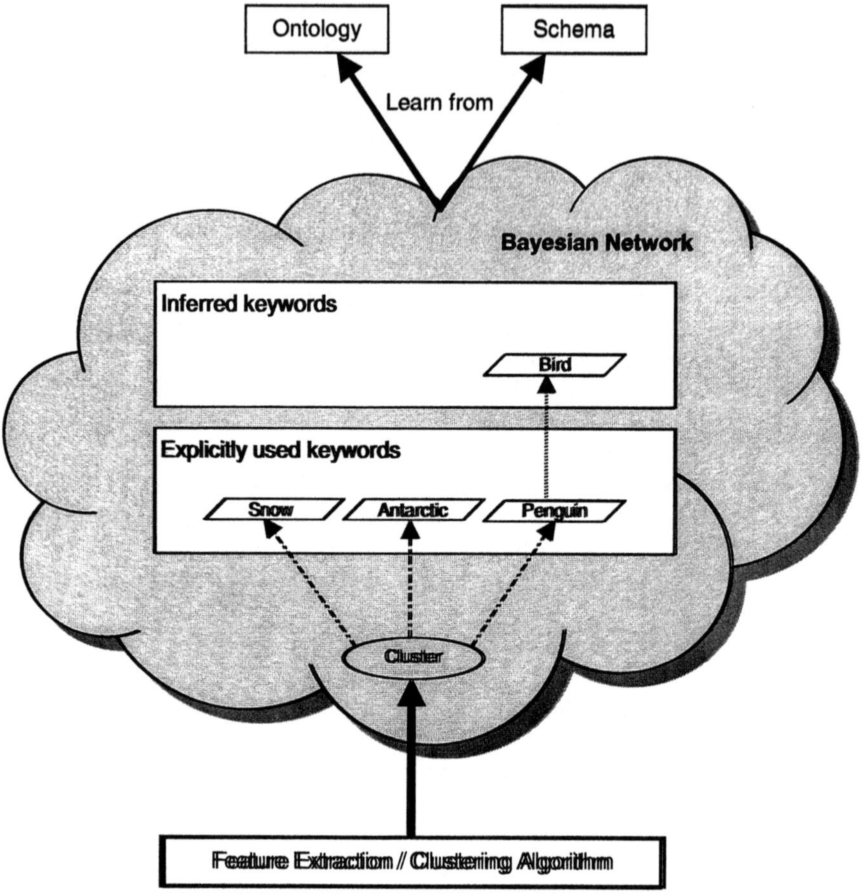

Fig. 4. The Bayesian network used to model relationships between low-level features and keywords – simplified view.

4.1 The Intelligent Inference Engine

We model the relationship between visual features and the keywords using a Bayesian network [18] (Figure 4), whose root node represents cluster membership and whose first level of nodes includes all the keywords explicitly used in the annotation process. The network can include additional levels which correspond to keywords that are not explicitly used in the annotation process.

The prior probabilities are derived from the clusters' sizes as the ratio of the size of cluster C_i and the total number of images in the repository (N). The mapping between clusters and explicitly used keywords is performed at the first level of the Bayesian network. The conditional probability of occurrence of any keyword given that the image belongs to a certain cluster in the visual plane can be easily computed and updated every time an individual image is annotated as can the conditional probabilities of keywords in other levels of the Bayesian network.

What distinguishes our approach from classical learning Bayesian networks is the fact that our system learns both from the ontologies and schemas from the top layer as well from the joint occurrence of visual features and keywords in annotated images. What makes our approach innovative is that we use not only the joint probabilities of various keywords in order to make inferences but we also use knowledge derived from the domain specific schema (e.g., which keywords are valid, how a keyword may be a subcategory of another, mutually exclusive keywords, etc.) to "validate" those inferences and derive additional inferences which could not be otherwise made.

We offer a few simple examples (see Figures 3 and 4) to help clarify what we mean.

Example 1: Using joint probabilities of keywords to make inferences. If several images have already been labeled with the keywords 'antarctic' and 'penguin', and the user labels the current image with the keyword 'penguin', the IAT can suggest that perhaps it should also be labeled with 'antarctic'.

Example 2: Using joint probabilities of keywords to prevent inconsistent or contradictory annotation. If the IAT has accumulated knowledge that keywords 'arctic' and 'penguin' never occur together, and the user tries to label the current image with both these keywords, the IAT can issue a warning against it.

Example 3: Validating an inference based on the knowledge of schemas. If the user attempts to label an image with both 'arctic' and 'antarctic', the IAT prevents him from doing so, based on the knowledge that both these keywords map onto the same slot in the schema (i.e., they are mutually exclusive).

Example 4: Extending keywords based on the knowledge of schemas. An image annotated with the keyword 'penguin' could also be associated with the keyword 'bird', without requiring explicit user intervention.

4.2 Annotation

The annotation phase is responsible for adding metadata to a collection of raw images. It takes a raw image and a set of keywords and returns the RDF-formatted description of the image. The annotation process is divided into two stages: initialization and cataloguing.

Initialization Stage. The initialization stage establishes and populates the Bayesian network. At the beginning of this stage the annotated image repository is empty. The purpose of this stage is to populate it with enough images to allow the IAT to make intelligent inferences. This is a human-intensive stage in that the user is required to annotate raw images without receiving any suggestions from the IAT. We do, however, attempt to reduce the burden on the user by offering him a pre-selected subset of allowed keywords that can be used during annotation, in such a way as to save annotation time, minimize ambiguities, and ensure compliance with the selected schema/ontology.

Once a raw image has been annotated, it is saved in the annotated image repository. At the end of this stage, we subject the annotated images to feature extraction and clustering algorithms. We then map these images and their attributes into the three-layer model described earlier. This process establishes our Bayesian network.

Cataloguing Stage. The cataloguing stage is similar to the initialization stage in that raw images are annotated with keywords and saved to the annotated image repository. However, this stage is not as human-intensive because the IAT offers suggestions about which keywords should be used to annotate the current (raw) image. The process of generating and offering suggestions is as follows. First, visual information (feature vectors) is extracted from the current image, using a combination of color-, texture, shape-based computer vision techniques. Next, the extracted feature vector is mapped onto the visual plane. We select the cluster (if any) that is closest to the feature vector of the current image and analyze the weights of the links from the cluster to the keyword vectors in the semantic plane. Based on that analysis (including calculation of relevant probabilities and knowledge inferred from the schema), we infer the most probable semantic content of the raw image and suggest the appropriate keywords to the user. As part of the ongoing learning process, at the end of the cataloguing stage (or after a certain percentage increase in the number of annotated images), the annotated images are re-clustered, the weights in the Bayesian network are updated, thus increasing the amount of empirical data available to us in order to make inferences.

4.3 Query and Retrieval

The other distinct phase in our application is the Query and Retrieval Phase. The application allows the user to search for an image or set of images that match the parameters specified in the user's query. The query could be either a textual description (i.e. a set of keywords) of the target image(s), an example image, or both. The query information (keywords, visual features extracted on-the-fly from the query image, or both) would then be compared with the data associated with the images in the annotated image repository. In all cases, a set of images that most closely match the parameters defined in the query would be returned (as thumbnails) to the user. If the desired image is among the set of

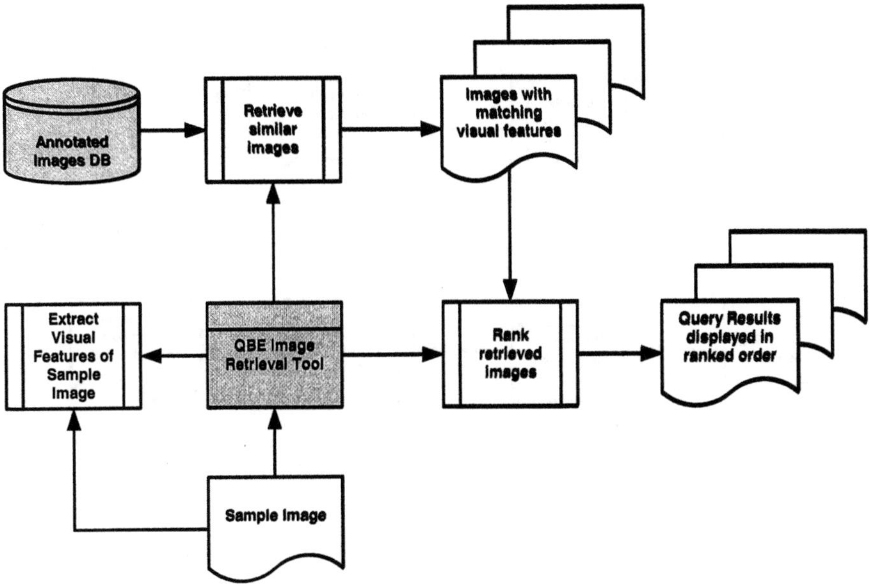

Fig. 5. Query by example

images returned, the search is completed. At any rate, the user can interactively browse and refine the results of the query.

Our proposed system supports four types of queries:

Query by example (QBE). In a QBE (Figure 5) the user provides the system with an example image and expects the system to retrieve similar images. The user may or may not have a target image in mind. The query is considered successful if the user selects one or more images returned as a result of the query. The QBE works as follows:

1. Extract visual information from the example image.
2. Map the extracted feature vector onto the visual plane.
3. Determine if there are any images (*not* clusters) within range (experimentally determined threshold) of the example image's feature vector.
4. Retrieve up to M images that are closest to the feature vector of the example image using an appropriate metric.
5. Rank the images based on their proximity to the example image's feature vector.
6. Display retrieved images in rank order.

Query by example – extended (QBEE). A QBEE is very similar to a QBE except that similarity of (inferred) semantic content, instead of visual similarity,

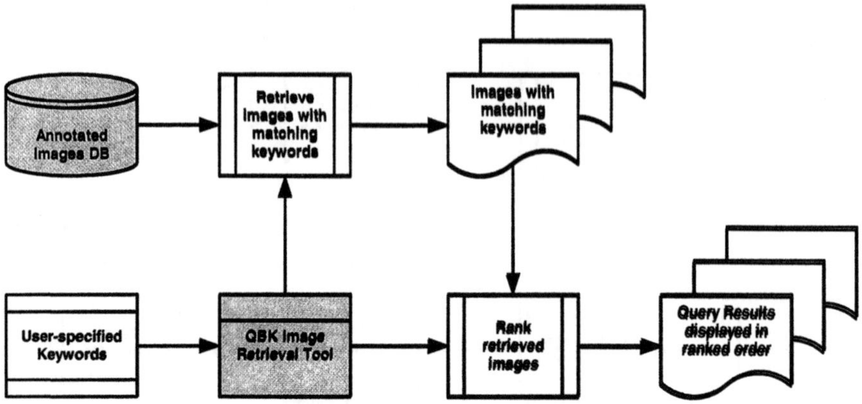

Fig. 6. Query by keyword

is the basis for measuring similarity to the example image. The process is outlined below:

1. Extract visual information from the example image.
2. Map the extracted feature vector onto the visual plane.
3. Determine if there are any image clusters within range (experimentally determined threshold) of the example image's feature vector.
4. Select the cluster (if any) that is closest to the feature vector of the example image.
5. Analyze the weights of the links from the images in the selected cluster to the keyword vectors in the semantic plane.
6. Based on the above analysis (including calculation of joint probabilities and probabilities of co-occurrence), infer the most probable semantic content of the example image.
7. Retrieve up to M images that are most similar to the inferred semantic content of the example image and rank accordingly.
8. Display retrieved images in rank order.

Query by keyword (QBK). In a QBK (Figure 6) the user types in one or more keywords, which are mapped to the schema(s) that characterize(s) the domain(s) to which the annotated images belong. The system is expected to retrieve those images that have at least one selected keyword associated with them. The process by which the system retrieves images based on a QBK is as follows:

1. Retrieve all images that have at least one of the specified keywords associated with them.
2. Rank the images based on the number of specified keywords associated with them as well as knowledge inferred from our Bayesian network.
3. Display retrieved images in rank order.

Query by both example and keyword (QBEK). Finally, in a QBEK the user provides a sample image as well as keywords in order to retrieve matching images. The procedure for retrieving images in this case is essentially analogous to a QBK followed by a QBE. The procedure is outlined below:

1. Extract visual information from the example image.
2. Map the extracted feature vector into the visual plane.
3. Select a subset of images that have at least one of the specified keywords associated with them.
4. From the subset of images selected in the step above, select all images that are within range of the example image's feature vector.
5. Rank the selected images based on both visual similarity to the example image and the semantic similarity to the set of query keywords.
6. Retrieve up to M images with the highest rank (score).
7. Display retrieved images in rank order.

5 Concluding Remarks

We have proposed a three-layer architecture for semi-automatic semantic annotation of images using machine learning techniques. This work extends and redirects our previous work in the related field of content-based image retrieval toward a Semantic Web-oriented solution.

The proposed architecture allows a good degree of independence among efforts in improving its supporting technologies and algorithms, such as:

- Development of better algorithms for extraction of visual features.
- Implementation of better clustering algorithms.
- Investigation of improved learning strategies.
- Deployment of ontology-focused intelligent agents.
- Enlargement and maintenance of ontologies and their mapping to keywords.

It is also acknowledged that the quality of the individual algorithms – particularly those used for visual feature extraction, clustering, similarity calculations, and mapping between the bottom and middle layer of our model – is a crucial factor to the success of the proposed methodology. A more systematic way of addressing these potential problems should be devised in future stages of this research.

In addition to its primary goals – consistent, cost-effective, fast, intelligent annotation of visual data – the method proposed in this paper also aims at improving the performance of subsequent image query and retrieval operations on the annotated image repository.

When fully implemented, the work described in this paper will provide an intelligent image indexing and annotation solution to Web-based clients, who will be able to save precious and costly annotation time and manpower and get a free semantic mark-up on their raw images.

Acknowledgments. The authors want to thank Dragutin Petkovic for his excellent comments and suggestions.

References

1. Adobe XMP. `http://www.adobe.com/products/xmp/main.html`.
2. S. Aksoy and R.M. Haralick. Graph-theoretic clustering for image grouping and retrieval. In *Proceedings of the IEEE Computer Society Conference on Computer Vision and Pattern Recognition*, pages 23–25, Fort Collins, CO, USA, 1999.
3. ARTISTE (An integrated Art Analysis and Navigation Environment). `http://www.ecs.soton.ac.uk/~km/projs/artiste/`.
4. E. Chang, K. Goh, G. Sychay, and G. Wu. CBSA: content-based soft annotation for multimodal image retrieval using bayes point machines. *IEEE Transactions on Circuits and Systems for Video Technology*, 13(1):26–38, January 2003.
5. I. J. Cox, M. L. Miller, T. Papathomas, J. Ghosn, and P.N. Yianilos. Hidden annotation in content based image retrieval. In *Proceedings of the IEEE Workshop on Content-Based Access of Image and Video Libraries*, pages 76–81, San Juan, Puerto Rico, 1997.
6. M. Erdmann, A. Maedche, H. Schnurr, and S. Staab. From manual to semi-automatic semantic annotation: About ontology-based text annotation tools. In *Proceedings of the COLING 2000 Workshop on Semantic Annotation and Intelligent Content*, Luxembourg, 2000.
7. Y. Gong, G. Proietti, and C. Faloutsos. Image indexing and retrieval based on human perceptual color clustering. In *Proceedings in IEEE Computer Society Conference on Computer Vision and Pattern Recognition*, pages 578–583, 1998.
8. Google^{TM} image search. `http://www.google.com/imghp`.
9. S. Handschuh, S. Staab, and F. Ciravegna. S-CREAM – Semi-automatic CREAtion of Metadata. In *Proceedings of the 13th International Conference on Knowledge Engineering and Knowledge Management (EKAW02)*, October 2002.
10. S. Handschuh, S. Staab, and A. Maedche. CREAM – creating relational metadata with a component-based, ontology-driven annotation framework. In *Proceedings of the International Semantic Web Working Symposium*, Stanford University, California, USA, 2001.
11. J. Hendler. Agents and the semantic web. *IEEE Intelligent Systems*, March/April 2001.
12. J. Hunter. Adding Multimedia to the Semantic Web – Building an MPEG-7 Ontology. In *Proceedings of the International Semantic Web Working Symposium*, Stanford University, California, USA, 2001.
13. ImageRover. `http://www.cs.bu.edu/faculty/sclaroff/ivc/ImageRover/Home.html`.
14. S. Krishnamachari and M. Abdel-Mottaleb. Image browsing using hierarchical clustering. In *Proceedings of the IEEE International Symposium on Computers and Communications*, pages 301–307, 1999.
15. Y. Lafon and B. Bos. Describing and retrieving photos using rdf and http. Technical report, W3C, April 2002. `http://www.w3.org/TR/photo-rdf`.
16. O. Marques and B. Furht. *Content-Based Image and Video Retrieval.* Kluwer Academic Publishers, Norwell, MA, 2002.
17. O. Marques and B. Furht. MUSE: A content-based image search and retrieval system using relevance feedback. *Multimedia Tools and Applications*, May 2002.

18. R.E. Neapolitan. *Learning Bayesian Networks.* Prentice-Hall, Upper Saddle River, NJ, 2004.
19. NISO Z39.87-2002 AIIM 20-2002 data dictionary – technical metadata for digital still images. `http://www.niso.org/committees/index.html`.
20. Y. Rui, T. S. Huang, and S.-F. Chang. Image retrieval: Current techniques, promising directions and open issues. *Journal of Visual Communication and Image Representation*, 10(1):1–23, March 1999.
21. S. Sclaroff, M. La Cascia, and S. Sethi. Unifying textual and visual cues for content-based image retrieval on the world wide web. *Computer Vision and Image Understanding*, 75(1/2):86–98, July/August 1999.
22. SCULPTEUR (Semantic and Content-based mULtimedia exPloiTation for EURopean benefit). `http://www.sculpteurweb.org/`.
23. G. Sheikholeslami, W. Chang, and A. Zhang. Semantic clustering and querying on heterogeneous features for visual data. In *Proceedings of the* 6th *ACM International Multimedia Conference*, pages 3–12, Bristol, England, 1998.
24. A.W.M. Smeulders, M. Worring, S. Santini, A. Gupta, and R. Jain. Content-based image retrieval at the end of the early years. *IEEE Transactions on Pattern Analysis and Machine Intelligence*, 22(12):1349–1380, December 2000.

Integrating Structure and Semantics into Audio-visual Documents

Raphaël Troncy[1,2]

[1] Institut National de l'Audiovisuel,
Direction de la Recherche, Équipe DCA
4, Av. de l'Europe - 94366 Bry-sur-Marne
rtroncy@ina.fr
http://www.ina.fr/
[2] INRIA Rhône-Alpes, Équipe EXMO
http://www.inrialpes.fr/exmo

Abstract. Describing audio-visual documents amounts to consider documentary aspects (the structure) as well as conceptual aspects (the content). In this paper, we propose an architecture which describes formally the content of the videos and which constrains the structure of their descriptions. This work is based on languages and technologies underlying the Semantic Web and in particular ontologies. Therefore, we propose to combine emerging Web standards, namely MPEG-7/XML Schema for the structural part and OWL/RDF for the knowledge part of the description. Finally, our work offers reasoning support on both aspects when querying a database of videos.

1 Introduction

The French institute INA[1] has to manage large multimedia and audio-visual (AV) databases. In order to allow an efficient access to the data stored, we describe and index most of the parts of these video documents by their content. This description process can be briefly summarized in three steps:

1. Identification of the content creator (author, title, producer, length, rights, etc.) and the content provider (broadcast channel, broadcast hour, title of the program group, etc.).
2. Structural decomposition in video segments (i.e. a spatial and/or temporal unit of multimedia) corresponding to the logical structure of the TV program.
3. Semantic description of these segments.

[1] INA (*Institut National de l'Audiovisuel*) has been archiving TV documents for 50 years and radio documents for 65 years. It stores more than 840 000 hours of broadcast programs (including 76 000 hours digitalized) and 940 000 hours of radio programs.

D. Fensel et al. (Eds.): ISWC 2003, LNCS 2870, pp. 566–581, 2003.

Putting this database on the Web raises typical Semantic Web [4] issues because the Web contains more and more multimedia data. For instance, allowing any individuals (i.e. non audio-visual professional) to retrieve and to access particular audio-visual sequences requires a precise and controlled description of the content of the documents. Moreover, browsing the database to retrieve the broadcast context of an AV sequence requires a controlled description of the logical structure of these documents. For that purpose, we propose in this article an architecture based on ontologies to describe formally the content of the videos, and documentary tools (XML languages family) to constrain their structure. This architecture combines Web emerging standards, namely MPEG-7/XML Schema for the structural part and OWL/RDF for the knowledge part of the description, and finally offers reasoning support on both aspects when querying the database.

This paper is organized as follows. In the next section, we give a complete example on how both structure and content have to be related. In section 3, we briefly introduce some basic components of MPEG-7 [8], that is, the Multimedia Description Schemes (MDS) and XML Schema which has been adopted as the schema language for the multimedia standard. Readers who are already familiar with these languages can skip this section. In section 4 we discuss which language is suitable for describing both the structure and the semantics of audio-visual materials, and for performing some reasoning on these descriptions. We introduce in section 5 our architecture proposal: the modeling of an AV ontology which aims to express the logical constrains for the structure of the videos, and the modeling of another domain-specific ontology to describe the content of each sequence (detailed in section 6). We show how the temporal decomposition of a video and the descriptions of each segment provide the statements that feed a knowledge base (section 7). Finally, we give our conclusions and outline future work in section 8.

2 Example and Requirements

For describing audio-visual materials, librarians currently watch the video, provide its metadata, decompose it into segments, and describe, in natural language, the meaning of each sequence. Moreover, a few keywords controlled by a thesaurus can be used as descriptors for the whole document. For instance, the example given in Table 1 contains a sample description of a French weekly sports magazine named "*Stade2*". To describe this magazine, the INA's documentalists identify its *report* and its *studio* sequences, and write short summaries including information such as events, participants, places, context, etc.

Now, let us imagine that someone wish to retrieve *all audio-visual sequences concerning the Paris-Nice cycling race in which Sandy Casar is interviewed.* A full text search on the description given in Table 1, with the keywords *Paris-Nice*, *Sandy Casar* and *interview* will effectively give the three sequences, but several limitations occur:

Table 1. A sample description of the French sports magazine "*Stade2*"

11 [**Outdoor set with guests** : Laurent Jalabert and Sandy Casar] at 18:37:56:00 - 00:02:43:00. - France 2 *Live from Nice, Jean Ren GODART interviews Laurent JALABERT and Sandy CASAR about the last stage of the Paris-Nice cycling race.*
12 [**Cycling** : Paris-Nice, the French who success] at 18:40:39:00 - 00:03:17:00 Rodolphe Gaudin. - France 2 *Report devoted to the Paris-Nice cycling race. For the French teams and for the riders, this competition is very important for preparing the Tour de France event. Commentaries on race pictures with some interviews with Jean Marie LEBLANC, Didier ROUS and Sandy CASAR.*
13 [**Indoor Set** : 6th part] at 18:43:56:00 - 00:09:06:00. - Eurosport *In studio, the second part of the interview, from Nice, of Sandy CASAR by Jean Ren GODART about the Paris-Nice cycling race and a few sports news with pictures commented by Alexandre BOYON and Laurent PUYAT.*

1. The sequence numbered 13 does not match precisely the query since it contains also some shots from the studio dealing with other sports and events. The problem raised here comes from the logical model that does not allow more than two levels (the whole document and its sequences).
2. The sequences numbered 11 and 13 are in fact the same interview, broadcasted in two parts, but this piece of knowledge is lost. The problem comes from the structural model since a sequence cannot be a non-connected temporal entity.
3. Finally, the query cannot be extended. For instance, if the query had been to retrieve *all the audio-visual sequences where a rider gives an interview about any cycling race with several stages* then the full text search engine would answer "no match".

One way to alleviate this problem is to make the AV descriptions more readily accessible to both human readers and automated processes. The Semantic Web aims at providing machine-processable data that improve the automatic manipulation of the information, in particular, offering some reasoning support when querying these data. Thus, we propose to use the languages and the technologies underlying the Semantic Web to improve the current way of describing. As seen with the example given above, our architecture has to fulfill the following requirements:

- To express models that constrain the logical structure of a description (e.g., identify an *interview* inside a particular *report* of a given *sports magazine*).
- To represent the meaning contained in this structure in a machine-accessible fashion to make inferences (e.g., deduce that a *Cartoon* is a *Fiction* with no real characters).
- To describe semantically the content of each sequence, again in a formal way, to perform some reasoning (e.g., deduce that in case of a cycling race with several stages the *Prologue* is always an *individual time trial* numbered *stage 0*).

The question arising is then: which languages are the most suitable to perform all these tasks? We will introduce briefly in the next section the natural candidate from an audio-visual standpoint, MPEG-7, which aims at describing the content of multimedia documents. But if this language is well suited for document manipulation, it falls short at embedding semantic constructs.

3 MPEG-7: The Standard for Describing Multimedia Documents

According to [3], the most important barrier for accessing efficiently multimedia data has been the lack of a standard, comprehensive and flexible representation that enables intelligent and interoperable multimedia applications. In 1996, the MPEG committee at the Tampere meeting has emphasized the need for a powerful solution for quick and efficient identification (searching, filtering, etc.) of these information. A new standard for "*Multimedia Content Description*", widely known as MPEG-7 [8], emerged from the result of their discussion.

MPEG-7 standardizes *tools* or ways to define multimedia *Descriptors* (Ds), *Description Schemes* (DSs) and the relationships between them. The descriptors correspond to the data features themselves, generally low-level features such as visual (e.g. texture, camera motion) or audio (e.g. melody), while the description schemes refer to more abstract description entities. These tools as well as their relationships are represented using the *Description Definition Language* (DDL), the core part of the language. According to the MPEG-7 Requirements Document, the DDL allows the modification of existing Description Schemes and the creation of new ones. Finally, the W3C XML Schema recommendation [16] has been adopted as the most appropriate schema for the MPEG-7 DDL[2] [15].

MPEG-7 provides the tools for describing any multimedia document, but the standard puts largely emphasis on audio-visual data. The Part 5 of the standard, named *Multimedia Description Schemes*, covers a broad range of descriptors including tools for content description (structure and semantics), but also for content management (media, creation and production, access rights), navigation and access (browsing, summarization), content organization (collection) or even user interaction with multimedia content (preferences, usage history).

3.1 Structure and Semantics in MPEG-7

Intuitively, the content of video data is adequately described if both their *structural* and *semantic* aspects are highlighted. For this reason, the integration of both structure and semantic features is generally considered as the most important contribution of the MPEG-7 standard. More precisely, the structural description of the content is based on the idea of *segment*. The abstract segment type specified in the *SegmentDS* is specialized into concrete types depending

[2] Several extensions (array and matrix datatypes) have been added in order to satisfy specific MPEG-7 requirements.

on the media (audio, image, video, multimedia). These types use either media locator or masks (for non-connected segments in space and time) to describe the formation and boundaries of the segments. Furthermore, the segments can be recursively decomposed temporally, spatially or by their constituents like the audio tracks and thus, form a tree hierarchy of segments, that is the hierarchical organization of the video.

The semantic description (*SemanticDS*) deals with the narrative world depicted or related to the audio-visual content. The MPEG-7 approach is focused on the events, understood as occasions upon which something happens. Objects, people and places can populate such occasions, as well as their date. Furthermore, all these entities can have properties. Finally, the background, the other events and entities provide the context for the description [3]. Therefore, the components of the semantic descriptions roughly fall into entities of the narrative world (*ObjectDS*, *EventDS*, *SemanticPlaceDS*, *SemanticDateDS*), their attributes (label, comments, abstraction level) and their relations. Normative semantic relations describe how semantic entities relate in a story (*agent*, *cause*, *goal*), how they relate to each other (*specializes*, *exemplifies*) and how they are linked to the media (*depicts*, *symbolizes*).

3.2 MPEG-7 Extension Mechanisms

We have seen that the MPEG-7 framework consists in a huge amount of descriptors and descriptions schemes. Moreover, the standard provides two ways to extend them. The first is to use the extension mechanism provided by XML Schema which has been chosen as the MPEG-7 DDL. The XML Schema language provides powerful and flexible means for specifying constrains on XML documents. Basically, XML Schema allows to define simple and complex types, to declare the elements and their attributes with some cardinality indicators that will be used in an XML instance document, and to import or reuse schema components previously defined in external documents. The derivation mechanism makes easy to construct type definitions by specifying only the method of derivation and the differences between the base and derived type definitions. With this simple inheritance mechanism, new user-defined data types can be created, extending or restricting the built-in data types. The standardized Description Schemes of the MPEG-7 language are mostly defined with this facility, and should be themselves, in theory, expandable. However, the conformity and the validity of the new "derived" Description Schemes is rather fuzzy in the standard and should be studied more precisely in future version.

The second extension facility of MPEG-7 deals with the definition of simple taxonomy named *Classification Schemes* (CS). According to the standard, "*a CS is a set of standard terms that describe some domain and may organize the terms it contains with a set of terms relations*". However, a CS is closer to a thesaurus than a formal ontology because the constructs provided are very limited[3] with respect to the current proposed ontology languages. Furthermore,

[3] Only five relationships can be used to form the classification hierarchy: *use*, *used for*, *broader term*, *narrower term* and *related term*.

if CS can be used inside a description, they cannot be used in models to constrain the semantics of collection of multimedia documents.

Despite these two extension mechanisms, it is still impossible to define precisely the semantics of the descriptors added. For instance, one may want to define with necessary and sufficient conditions a `StudioProgram` *as exactly* a `HomogeneousProgram` whose all sequences are `StudioSequence`. Let us consider the `Program#123`, described with the theme `Cycling` and whose sequences are all identified with the genre `StudioSequence`. If a user looks for all `StudioProgram` with the theme `Sports`, he expects to retrieve the `Program#123`. The problem is that this simple result is impossible to infer with MPEG-7 or XML Schema.

To conclude, we notice that the descriptors standardized by MPEG-7 or obtained by extension are not formally defined, but formal semantics is necessary in order to enable the access and the exchange of the multimedia content. XML Schema allows to add some structure, but it cannot express the meaning of this structure. Which language is then suitable for representing the video content both in a machine and a human-understandable format and for performing reasoning on these descriptions?

4 Which Language for Reasoning on Audio-visual Descriptions?

The MPEG-7 descriptors are closely related to the physical features of audio-visual data. For instance, it is not possible to constrain, at the schema level, the segments according to their genre (e.g. report, studio, interview) or their general themes (e.g. sports, sciences, politics, economy). Similarly, the standardized descriptors are too restrictive to cover all the possible descriptions of the content and specially to describe precisely a particular scene of the video. In this section, we will discuss how we can create new descriptors, with a formal meaning, in order to perform some reasoning: with the extension mechanism included in MPEG-7 (section 4.1) or with a knowledge representation language like OWL+RDF (section 4.2). This will lead us to conclude that the best solution is to combine these two approaches.

4.1 MPEG-7 + XML Schema

As we have seen in section 3.2, the MPEG-7 language can be extended in two ways: using the *DDL* (that is, XML Schema) or using the *Classification Schemes* (CS).

XML Schema allows to construct new type definitions extending or restricting already defined data types. For instance, TV Anytime[4] uses this language for

[4] The TV Anytime Forum (`http://www.tv-anytime.org/`) is an association of organizations which seeks to develop specifications to provide value-added interactive services, such as the electronic program guide, in the context of TV digital broad-

building higher-level descriptors, such as the intended audience of a program or its broadcast conditions [12]. We can also use this mechanism for building our own description schemes. For example, the code below defines a type for `TVNews`, a kind of `TVProgram`, `hosted` by somebody, and which contains an unbounded ordered sequence of `studio` and `report` segments.

```
<xsd:complexType name="TVNewsType">
 <xsd:complexContent>
  <xsd:extension base="TVProgramType">
   <xsd:sequence maxOccurs="unbounded">
    <xsd:element name="Studio" type="StudioType"/>
    <xsd:element name="Report" type="ReportType"/>
   </xsd:sequence>
   <xsd:attribute name="host" type="xsd:string" use="required"/>
  </xsd:extension>
 </xsd:complexContent>
</xsd:complexType>
```

However, the problem is not solved because it is still impossible to reason, here, on the structural part of the audio-visual description. Actually, XML Schema provides the means to have very rich structure but is rather limited when expressing the meaning of this structure as the language is (only) concerned with providing typing and structuring information for isolated chunk of data. As we have seen, it is not possible to define (with necessary and sufficient conditions) a `StudioProgram` *as exactly* a `HomogeneousProgram` whose all sequences are `StudioSequence`. It is also not possible to express basic axioms such as "a `TVProgram` cannot be both a `HomogeneousProgram` and a `HeterogeneousProgram`[5]."

The other way to extend the set of MPEG-7 descriptors is the Classification Schemes. TV Anytime has defined in this way a thesaurus describing the possible genres and themes of a TV program. The COALA (Content-Oriented Audio-visual Library Access) project uses also the CS to build a framework for the retrieval of audio-visual TV news documents [6]. But as we have seen in section 3.2, the CS can only be referred to inside a description and they cannot be used to constrain the structure of a collection of documents. More important, the constructs provided by the CS are thesauric relations and cannot express simple axioms allowing efficient inference calculus. Consequently, using only documentary languages like MPEG-7 and XML Schema to describe formally the structure and the content of audio-visual documents seems not enough. However, the knowledge representation languages under development by the Semantic Web Activity of the W3C, are good candidates for solving our problem.

casting. The forum identified the metadata as one of the key technologies enabling their vision and have adopted MPEG-7 as the description language.

[5] A definition of `HomogeneousProgram` and `HeterogeneousProgram` is given in section 6.1.

4.2 OWL + RDF

For alleviating the lack of semantics of MPEG-7, Jane Hunter has already proposed an ontology expressing the semantics of the MPEG-7 metadata terms [7]. This ontology, represented in DAML+OIL[6], is built by reverse-engineering of the existing XML Schema definitions together with the interpretation of the english-text semantic descriptions. It contains the class and property hierarchies corresponding to the segment entities classified by media, their possible decomposition, the non-multimedia entities (e.g. Agent, Role, Place, Instrument), etc.

In the same way, we can define the classes and properties still missing in MPEG-7. OWL (*Ontology Web Language*) [10], a language under the W3C recommendation process, can be used to explicitly represent the meaning of terms in vocabularies and their relationships. It is therefore a language for representing, encoding and sharing ontologies on the Web. The expressive power of OWL allows us to define (in the Description Logics sense) classes. For instance, the code below illustrates the definition of the `StudioProgram` class in OWL.

```
<owl:Class rdf:ID="StudioProgram">
 <owl:intersectionOf rdf:parseType="Collection">
  <owl:Class rdf:about="#HomogeneousProgram"/>
  <owl:Restriction>
   <owl:onProperty rdf:resource="#hasSequence"/>
   <owl:allValuesFrom rdf:resource="#StudioSequence"/>
  </owl:Restriction>
 </owl:intersectionOf>
</owl:Class>
```

Furthermore, it is possible to express basic axioms such as "a `TVProgram` cannot be both a `HomogeneousProgram` and a `HeterogeneousProgram`" (with the construct `owl:disjointWith`). OWL ontologies are encoded and written as RDF graphs, which are in turn sets of RDF triples [13]. These triples are the statements feeding a knowledge base on which it is now possible to perform some reasoning.

So, the use of a knowledge representation language seems to satisfy our needs from the knowledge standpoint. However, the structure of the audio-visual documents is completely lost. Now, it is impossible to retrieve the sequence preceding, following, embedding or embracing a given sequence, that is, the necessary context to interpret any video sequence. The problem, as shown in [11], comes here from the modeling foundations of the languages used: whereas XML (and XML Schema) are based on a tree model where nodes are totally ordered, OWL (and RDF) are based on a directed graph model where edges are unordered. In other words, the notion of regular expression, used to constrain the structure of XML documents, is missing in OWL. Patel-Schneider and Simon [11] proposed to represent the ordering information between the relationships that are related to a

[6] DAML+OIL results from the joint efforts of the DAML group (US) and the OIL proposal (EU), and provides a language for expressing far more sophisticated classifications and properties of resources than RDFS.

common resource. Thus, the formal definition of their SWOL proposal language allows to capture document order in XML documents, but this is only a partial solution for the documentary problem.

Consequently, we propose to use MPEG-7/XML Schema for expressing the structural meaning of audio-visual documents, while OWL/RDF is used for expressing the ontological meaning of the constructs. A transformation, from the ontological syntax (OWL) into the schema syntax (XML Schema), is performed. The following sections detail our proposed architecture and its resources.

5 Architecture Proposal

We have already expressed:

1. The need to make inferences on both structural and conceptual aspects of the audio-visual descriptions.
2. The need to have a good documentary model, that is, sufficiently expressive to constrain the structure of the documents.

To achieve the first goal, we propose to build two ontologies: an audio-visual ontology modeling the classes and properties useful to describe the audio-visual structure of the documents (e.g. genre, general theme), and a domain-specific ontology modeling the classes and properties useful to describe the content of each sequence. These classes are derived in XML Schema types, which are combined in order to form description schemes. This process provides the material for constraining collection of audio-visual descriptions. An overview of our proposed architecture is shown in Figure 1.

The audio-visual ontology aims at representing the meaning of the structural constructs of the descriptions. For instance, the ontology contains the definition of the `StudioProgram` class seen previously. Parts of this ontology are then translated into XML Schema types. At this stage, these types may include additional knowledge that is not modeled in the audio-visual ontology. For instance, the type `TVNewsType` points out that this kind of program is composed of an unbounded sequence (ordered) of `studio` and `report sequences`. As a result, the structural knowledge is divided between the ontology and the description schemes composed of XML Schema types. That does not really matter since it is still possible to make inferences with the ontology and since the description schemes obtained are in a final state. Finally, the XML Schema types derived from the ontology are linked (when it is possible) with the existing MPEG-7 types. For instance, the `TVNewsType` becomes a subtype of the `VideoSegmentType` defined in MPEG-7.

The temporal decomposition of a particular audio-visual program provides a skeleton of description. It is an XML document that has to be validated with the description scheme on which it relies. Sequences of interest are *time-coded* (i.e. spatio-temporally located), and are described in terms of concepts derived from the audio-visual ontology. So, they provide the instances that are encoded in RDF triples that feed our knowledge base. It is now possible to make inferences

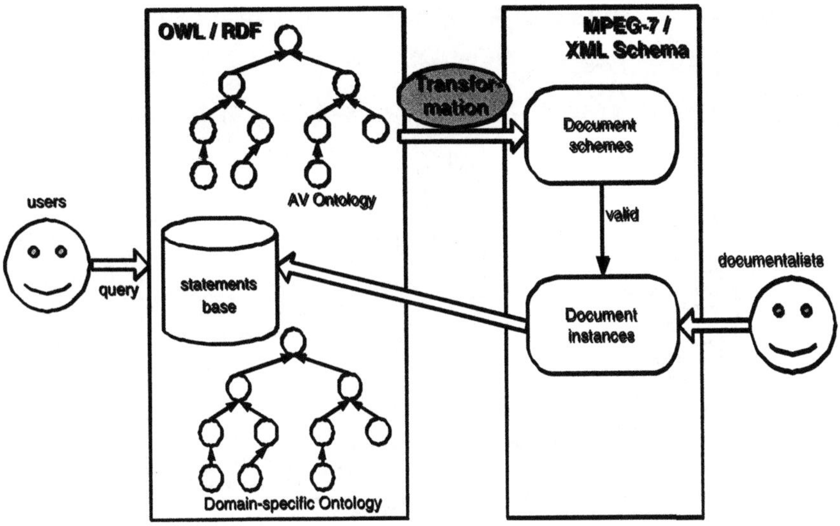

Fig. 1. Overall architecture offering reasoning support on audio-visual descriptions. The transformation between the AV ontology (OWL) and the document schemes (XML Schema) could be carried out with XSLT (see discussion in Section 6.2)

on the structural elements of the description. Moreover, it is still possible to retrieve the context of a given sequence through the documentary structure of the program. Finally, the domain-specific ontology aims at representing the content of each audio-visual sequences. Again, instances of concepts used in the description provide the statements that will be a part of the knowledge base.

6 Ontologies and Documents

The general architecture described above needs some resources. In section 6.1, we present how we have modeled and formalized the audio-visual ontology. We show in section 6.2 how parts of this ontology are translated into XML Schema types that are the building blocks of document schemes. Finally, we briefly present in section 6.3 another ontology dealing with the cycling sport. This domain-specific ontology provides the necessary concepts for describing the content of audio-visual sequences.

6.1 The Audio-visual Ontology

For constraining the structure of the descriptions while performing reasoning on this structure, we have proposed to model and formalize an audio-visual ontology. Many approaches (for a complete survey, the reader can refer to the OntoWeb Technical RoadMap[7]) have been reported to build ontologies, but few

[7] `http://babage.dia.fi.upm.es/ontoweb/wp1/OntoRoadMap/index.html`

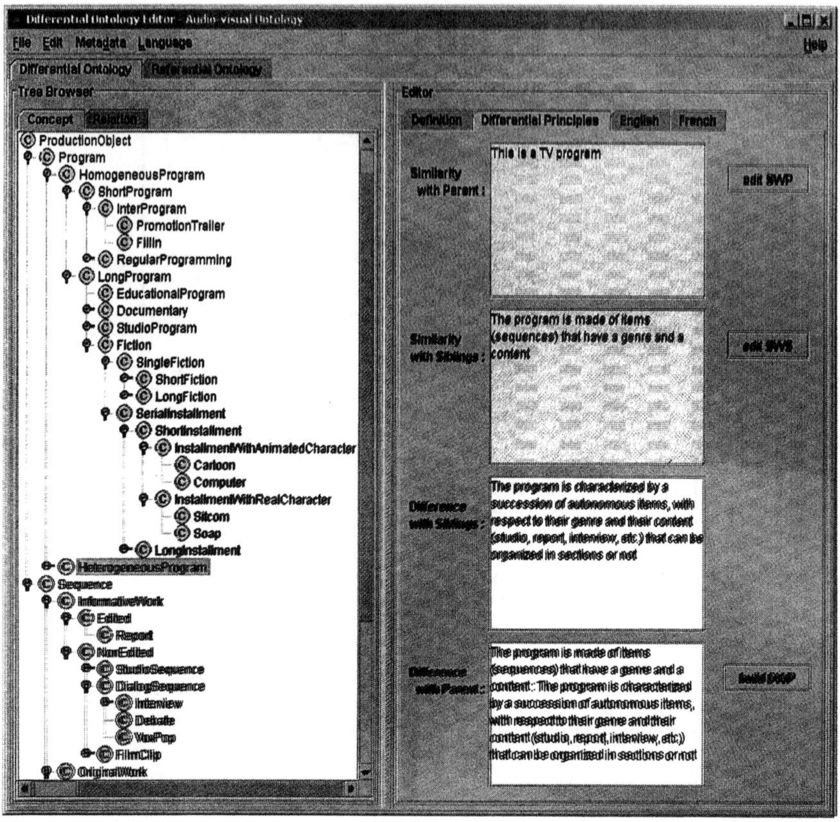

Fig. 2. The differential principles bound to the concept *HeterogenousProgram* in the *DOE* tool

fully detail the steps needed to obtain and structure the taxonomies. This observation has lead us to propose a methodology entailing a semantic commitment to normalize the meaning of the concepts. This methodology, detailed in [1], is implemented into the **DOE**[8] (*Differential Ontology Editor*) tool, an ontology editor complementary to other existing tools like **OilEd** or **Protégé2000** (Figure 2).

The audio-visual ontology[9] has been elaborated from real guidelines used to teach professional documentalists how to describe the TV and radio programs. The ontology can roughly be divided into three parts. One contains all the concepts that characterize a program or its sequences. The first criteria used in

[8] DOE, available for free at `http://opales.ina.fr/public/`, has been partially funded by the OPALES consortium under a PRIAMM grant from the French Ministry of Industry.

[9] This ontology is available in several formats (RDFS, OWL) at `http://opales.ina.fr/public/ontologies/`.

the ontology modeling process is the audio-visual genre. In the first move, we distinguish the "whole" program from its sequences. A program can be homogeneous or heterogeneous. Actually, a *heterogeneous program* is characterized by a sequence of autonomous elements in form and in content (e.g. *studio*, *report*, *interview*) unlike a *homogeneous program* (Figure 2). Then, the classes *magazine*, *TV news* or *best-of* will be subsumed by the *heterogeneous program* while the classes *documentary*, *fiction* or *studio program* will subsume the *homogeneous program*. The second criteria used to describe an audio-visual sequence is its general themes. We have then classify about 40 themes such as *sports*, *sciences*, *art* or *tourism* under the branch *qualia* of the ontology. Finally, classes dealing with the intended audience, the public participation or the broadcast conditions allow to complete the characterization of the video sequences. The second part of the ontology lists numerous roles of persons involved in the making of the programs while the third part deals with production activities. Here, these classes concern the shooting and recording (e.g. *sound pick-up*, *camera motion*), the editing (e.g. *fade*, *cut*) or the post-production (e.g. *special effects*, *subtitle*).

The audio-visual ontology, once well-conceptualized in DOE, is exported into the RDFS language. We use then the **OilEd** editor [2] to complete the formalization process, that is, to define some classes (see the `StudioProgram` previous example) or to add some basic axioms, and to produce the final OWL files.

6.2 Building Formalized Description Schemes

The audio-visual ontology contains formal definitions for all the concepts used in the structural descriptions of the documents. We have proposed then to translate parts of this ontology into XML Schema types. This translation can be made from the ontology editor or from the formal definition of each element expressed in the ontology web language. For instance, OWL *classes* become *complex types*, the *subClassOf* relationship becomes an *extension* of a base type, the *property restriction* becomes an *element* of a type content model, or the *union* of class expressions becomes a *choice* of this content model, etc. We wonder if this transformation can be made automatically through simple XSLT stylesheet but it seems that this process is not deterministic.

These XML Schema types are linked (when it is possible) with the existing MPEG-7 types. For instance, all the types related to audio-visual genres are considered as a specialization of the MPEG-7 `VideoSegmentType`. Thus, these new types inherit its content model and benefit from the available decomposition for the segments. Finally, types are combined in order to form description schemes[10]. The expressive power of XML Schema allows us to add knowledge which is not modeled in the ontology, such as a regular expression of sequences symbolizing the structural constrains of a collection of programs. The description

[10] These schemes could also contain some constructs from the VRA Core categories (`http://www.vraweb.org`) in order to describe all the necessary metadata for each sequence, thus enhancing the interoperability between processors aware of at least a part of the description.

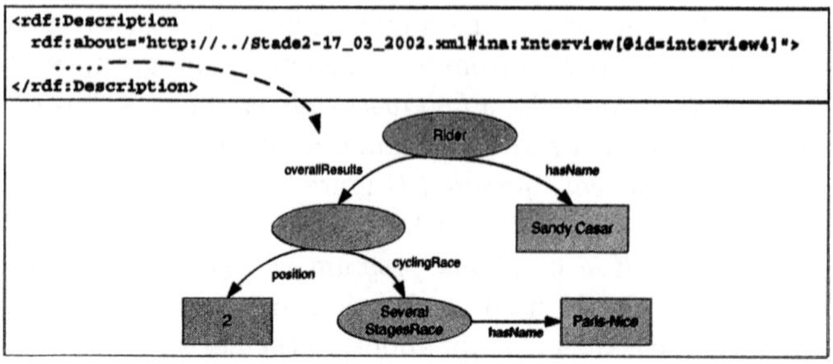

Fig. 3. Graph for RDF/XML example

schemes contain embedded MPEG-7 constructs, thus making easier the exchange of descriptions between MPEG-7 aware applications.

6.3 Domain Ontology and Statements

Besides the audio-visual ontology, we have proposed to model a domain-specific ontology in order to provide the necessary concepts for describing the content itself of audio-visual sequences. For example, we have modeled a cycling ontology [1] which describes the *Tour de France* event or the related sports news and magazines broadcasted on TV.

Furthermore, we use a base of conceptual facts bound to the cycling ontology. These statements were obtained automatically by natural language extraction on textual resources dealing with this event [9]. For instance, the statement: *the rider Sandy Casar has the position 2 in the overall results of the Paris-Nice cycling race* can be represented, in terms of the cycling ontology, as a RDF graph (Figure 3).

7 Implementation

The final goal of the architecture proposed in section 5 is the creation of a base of statements. Actually, it provides the instances of the concepts for the two ontologies (audio-visual and cycling) that will be used inside the descriptions of the video documents. Two sources allow us to enlarge the knowledge base. As seen in the previous section, the first source is obtained automatically by conceptual information extraction on texts dealing with cycling. Moreover, the temporal decomposition of a specific program provides the instance of a description scheme and consequently, the instances of the audio-visual ontology.

Actually, the description of an audio-visual document begins with the localization of entities of interest. Each segment is located in space and time in order to be characterized in terms of genre and theme and then, be described by the content. The description has also to be valid with respect to the description scheme on which the video document belongs. At INA, we use **SegmenTool**[11] to

[11] SegmenTool is developed by the DCA team of INA and has been funded by the CHAPERON project under a PRIAMM grant from the French Ministry of Industry.

Fig. 4. Video segmentation inside **SegmenTool**

segment temporally the audio-visual documents and to build MPEG-7 descriptions (Figure 4).

Each segment is time-coded and characterized according to a genre and a general theme. The resulting description reflects then the logical structure of the program. For instance, the code below shows the skeleton of a description where an *interview* of Sandy Casar is located temporally inside a *report* of the sports magazine *Stade2*.

```
<ina:Report id="aa23c647c-6517-4aee-8bce-870ae52a01af">
 ...
 <mp7:TemporalDecomposition>
  <ina:Interview id="adb23ab65-f8e7-4b2a-8c98-807197da600a">
   <mp7:MediaTime>
    <mp7:MediaTimePoint>T00:24:19:10160640F14112000</MediaTimePoint>
    <MediaDuration>PT00H00M07S9031680N14112000F</MediaDuration>
   </mp7:MediaTime>
   <ina:Themes value="Cycling"/>
  </ina:Interview>
 </mp7:TemporalDecomposition>
</ina:Report>
```

This fragment of description contains some descriptors that have their corresponding concept in the audio-visual ontology. Hence, we can generate automatically the instances of these classes from this fragment. For instance, from the code above, we can generate an instance of the class `Interview` and give a value for its attributes:

```
<Interview rdf:ID="interview4">
 <hasStartTime rdf:datatype="xsd:string">T00:24:19</hasStartTime>
 <hasDuration rdf:datatype="xsd:string">PT00H00M07S9</hasDuration>
 <hasThemes rdf:resource="#Cycling"/>
 ...
</Interview>
```

Finally, other statements describing the content of video sequences (such as the one shown in Figure 3) can be linked – via an XPATH expression – with a particular fragment of the structural description. Hence, Figure 3 asserts that it exists an *interview* in the program where Sandy Casar talks about his position in the overall results of the Paris-Nice cycling race. All these statements can be represented by RDF triples that feed the knowledge base on which we will make inferences.

We use the **Sesame** architecture [5] for storing and querying the ontologies and the statements. Currently, this architecture supports only RDF Schema as the ontology language, but support for OWL Lite semantics is planned for the next releases. Enhanced inference services are possible with the **BOR** reasoner [14] that has been integrated with Sesame within the On-To-Knowledge project. Actually, the BOR reasoner implements the semantics of DAML+OIL. Thus, it is closed to what could be achieved with OWL inference engines in terms of reasoning performance. With the Sesame-integrated-BOR system, answers for the query given at the end of section 3.2 can be retrieved. The system can infer that the `Program#123` is a `StudioProgram` (thanks to the ontology definition) and deals with `Sports` (as its theme is `Cycling`). In the same way, for the query given in section 2 – *find all the audio-visual sequences where a rider gives an interview about any cycling race with several stages* – the system can infer that the sequence *interview*, as described in the Figure 3, matches the query.

8 Conclusion and Future Work

In this paper we have proposed a general architecture for reasoning on descriptions of video documents. We have modeled an audio-visual ontology that contains the concepts of *genre*, of *theme* and of *technical process* for the production of TV programs. We have also translated parts of this ontology into XML Schema types which specialize MPEG-7 descriptors. Those XML Schema types can be combined inside description schemes that constrain the logical structure of collections of documents. Describing a particular TV program boils down to cut it out temporally in order to instantiate a description scheme, that provides the instances of the concepts of the audio-visual ontology which finally, feed the knowledge base.

We have now to test this architecture on a larger scale, that is, a few hours of video annotated and real users querying the database with the ontologies. We expect also tools that implement the semantics of OWL in order to exploit the full reasoning power of the ontologies modeled. Finally, we plan to compare and merge the MPEG-7 ontology proposed by Hunter with our audio-visual ontology.

References

1. B. Bachimont, A. Isaac, and R. Troncy. Semantic Commitment for Designing Ontologies: A Proposal. In *Proc. of the 13th International Conference on Knowledge Engineering and Knowledge Management (EKAW'02)*, LNAI 2473, p. 114–121, Siguenza, Spain, 2002.
2. S. Bechhofer, I. Horrocks, C. Goble, and R. Stevens. OilEd: a Reason-able Ontology Editor for the Semantic Web. In *Proc. of KI2001, Joint German/Austrian conference on Artificial Intelligence*, LNAI 2174, p. 396–408, Vienna, Austria, 2001.
3. Ana B. Benitez, H. Rising, and C. Jörgensen. Semantics of Multimedia in MPEG-7. In *IEEE Conference on Image Processing (ICIP'02)*, Rochester, New York, 2002.
4. T. Berners-Lee, J. Hendler, and O. Lassila. The Semantic Web. In *Scientific American*, 284(5):34–43, 2001.
5. J. Broekstra, A. Kampman, and F. van Harmelen. Sesame: a Generic Architecture for Storing and Querying RDF and RDF Schema. In Ian Horrocks and James Hendler, editors, *Proc. of the first International Semantic Web Conference (ISWC'02)*, LNCS 2342, p. 54–68, Sardinia, Italia, 2002.
6. N. Fatemi, and O. Abou Khaled. COALA: Content-Oriented Audiovisual Library Access. In *Proc. of the 8th International Conference on Multimedia Modeling (MMM'2001)*, p. 59–71, Amsterdam, The Netherlands, 2001.
7. J. Hunter. Adding Multimedia to the Semantic Web – Building an MPEG-7 Ontology. In *Proc. of the First International Semantic Web Working Symposium (SWWS'01)*, p. 261–283, Stanford, California, 2001.
8. ISO. Information Technology – Multimedia Content Description Interface (MPEG-7). Standard No. ISO/IEC 15938:2001, International Organization for Standardization(ISO), 2001.
9. E. Le Roux. Extraction d'information dans des textes libres guide par une ontologie. PhD Thesis, 2003.
10. OWL, Web Ontology Language Reference Version 1.0. W3C Working Draft, 31 March 2003. `http://www.w3.org/TR/owl-ref/`
11. P. F. Patel-Schneider, and J. Siméon. Building the Semantic Web on XML. In Ian Horrocks and James Hendler, editors, *Proc. of the first International Semantic Web Conference (ISWC'02)*, LNCS 2342, p. 147–161, Sardinia, Italia, 2002.
12. S. Pfeiffer, and U. Srinivasan. TV Anytime as an application scenario for MPEG-7. In *Proc. of Workshop on Standards, Interoperability and Practice of the 8th International Conference on Multimedia*, ACM Multimedia, Los Angeles, California, 2000.
13. RDF, Ressource Description Framework Primer. W3C Working Draft, 23 January 2003. `http://www.w3.org/TR/rdf-primer/`
14. K. Simov, and S. Jordanov. BOR: a Pragmatic DAML+OIL Reasoner. Deliverable 40, On-To-Knowledge Project, 2002.
15. E. Terzi, A. Vakali, J. Fan, and M.-S. Hacid. The MPEG-7 Multimedia Content Description Standard and the XML Schema Language. In *Proc. of the 7th International Conference on Distributed Multimedia Systems (DMS'01)*, Taipei, Taiwan, 2001.
16. XML Schema. W3C Recommendation, 2 May 2001. `http://www.w3.org/XML/Schema`

SCULPTEUR: Towards a New Paradigm for Multimedia Museum Information Handling

Matthew Addis[1], Mike Boniface[1], Simon Goodall[2], Paul Grimwood[1], Sanghee Kim[2], Paul Lewis[2], Kirk Martinez[2], and Alison Stevenson[1]

[1] IT Innovation, University of Southampton,
SO16 7NP, UK
{mja,mjb,pg,as}@it-innovation.soton.ac.uk
[2] Department of Electronics and Computer Science,
University of Southampton, SO17 1BJ, UK
{sg02r,sk,phl,km}@ecs.soton.ac.uk

Abstract. This paper describes the design and prototype implementation of a novel architecture for integrated concept, metadata and content based browsing and retrieval of museum information. The work is part of a European project involving several major galleries and the aim is to provide more versatile access to digital collections of museum artefacts, including 2-D images, 3-D models and other multimedia representations. An ontology for the museum domain, based on the CIDOC Conceptual Reference Model, is being developed as a semantic layer with references to the digital collection as instance information. A graphical concept browser is an integral component in the user interface, allowing navigation through the semantic layer, display of thumbnails, or full representations of artefacts and textual information in appropriate viewers and the invocation of conventional content based searching or combined querying. Semantic Web technologies are used in system integration to describe how tools for analysis and visualisation can be applied to different data types and sources. This supports flexible and managed formulation, execution and interpretation of the results of distributed multimedia queries. Combined searches using concepts, content and metadata can be initiated from a single user interface.

1 Introduction

Within Europe there are many hundreds of digital heritage archives of special scientific and cultural interest containing information that is diverse in both type and organisation. There is a clear need for scientists, researchers, curators and historians to contribute to, develop and exploit these archives. It is equally important to make the archives available electronically, both to increase public access for enjoyment and learning, and to enable scientific study for conservation and restoration. The SCULPTEUR project [1], supported by the European Union under the Fifth Framework Programme, aims to fulfil these needs by building on the achievements of the ARTISTE [2] project by developing a system for integrated navigation and searching of gallery and museum collections using textual metadata, content-based analysis and ontological classification.

D. Fensel et al. (Eds.): ISWC 2003, LNCS 2870, pp. 582–596, 2003.

Five major European galleries are involved in the project: the Uffizi in Florence, the National Gallery and the Victoria and Albert Museum in London, the Musee de Cherbourg, and the Centre de Recherche et de Restauration des Musées de France (C2RMF) which is the Louvre related restoration centre. By taking an ontological approach to the semantics of search and retrieval, and to system integration, SCULPTEUR will enable these institutions to develop, manage, visualize, navigate, search and exploit their valuable digital resources. This paper presents the design and the first of a series of prototype implementations of SCULPTEUR.

2 Motivation

Museums and galleries often own several different digital representations of some, or all, of the hundreds of thousands of works of art in their trust. These representations include public access images, specialized high-resolution scientific images used for conservation purposes, 3D models of individual artefacts and short movies showing artefacts in their gallery location. Data held in the collections owned by one gallery or museum is frequently relevant to the work performed at other galleries or museums. For example, when a museum conducts a programme of conservation and restoration it is beneficial to access information on the condition and treatments of similar works of art in other museums and galleries. However, discovery and access to this information is currently a manual and time-consuming process.

Different types of representation and digital textual metadata are often stored in separate collections and legacy systems. The heterogeneity of information and systems for museum collections creates several challenges for any system designed to support search and retrieval across that information, especially if the system needs to provide such services to other organisations or the general public.

The first, and most fundamental challenge is that the metadata terms used to describe and structure collections often differ from institution to institution. Previous approaches to this problem have focused on either imposing a common structure on the metadata to create a standard across a small number of institutions (Van Eyck project [3]), or imposing a standard interface technique (z39.50 [4], AQUARELLE [5]). However, these approaches fail to accommodate the diversity of specialized collections in the museum domain and fail to provide a schema that is sufficiently descriptive of the relationships therein.

The second challenge is to provide access in a way that enables the searcher (member of the public, or museum curator alike) to fully exploit the richness of the data available. Many existing digital library systems have a single entity, the digital text, at the centre of all user interactions with the system. The users search by specifying a word or phrase for the items of associated metadata, for example 'date of publication'. Similarly, previous multimedia digital libraries and image retrieval systems [28], such as ARTISTE, place the digital image at the centre of all user interactions with the system. The users search by specifying a value for one of the items of metadata associated with the image, for example "Find all images of art works where the artist's name is Raphael", or by specifying a content-based search in which case the user supplies a query image and asks to see, for example, "images of a similar colour".

A singular focus to the search specification and the objects returned does not allow the diversity of information often contained in a multimedia digital library to be fully exploited. For example, a typical museum library will contain metadata about art works (e.g. title, medium, state of restoration), the creators of those art works (e.g. name, date of birth), and digital representations of the art as well as metadata about those representations (e.g. angle of lighting, full or sub image), information about locations (e.g. as the place the art work is stored, or as the artist's country of origin) and dates (e.g. as the date of artist's death, or the date of creation digital image). If access is solely centred on the digital image, then the user is forced to follow a single path through the data that obscures the multi-directional relationships that exist therein. If access is given to the full complexity of the information in a user's collection, or in other collections, then the complexity needs to be presented and navigated in a manageable way. As a result, graphical tools are required for ontological browsing of the concepts, relationships and instances within collections.

A third challenge arises when using content-based search techniques [20,23,30] such as searching the colour, texture, shape etc of the digital representations. There is significant value to the user when content-based techniques are combined with textual metadata searching [19,21,24,25]. However, content-based analysis and comparison techniques are highly specialised, often computationally intensive, and have little or no support for describing their semantics in current tools and standards. Furthermore, it is unreasonable to expect all museums and libraries to support a common set of content-based search techniques. Therefore, if a user seeks to search a collection they need to first determine the search capabilities supported and then formulate an appropriate query. Whilst this is manageable for occasional searches of single collections, there are clearly problems when looking to automate distributed queries across multiple collections. Of course, the use of a common query language syntax and a common protocol for search and retrieval is not precluded, and indeed these can be used to provide the backbone of interoperability.

Finally, information about museum collections is sometimes incomplete or may even contain inaccuracies. Semantic Web [8] and Agent technologies offer a way to find additional information on the Web. This additional information may be missing items of metadata associated with an artefact or artist, or may be additional narrative and supplementary information of interest to end-users such as artist biographies or further sources of information available on remote Web Sites. Augmenting museum collections is not limited to adding information from external sources. Existing content can be analysed to further classify the items in the collection, for example classifier agents could monitor the collection and use known associations between content descriptors (colour, texture, shape, volume) to aid classification of existing objects or new acquisitions.

Overall, there is a clear need for galleries and museums to be able to better augment, navigate, exploit and share the rich information in their digital collections. Galleries and museums will wish to maintain autonomy over the way their content is structured and they will want control over what services are provide to their users, both internal and external. This requires SCULPTEUR to abstract the complexity and heterogeneity of their legacy systems to provide simple browsing and search facilities for the user using a combination of ontological, textual metadata and content-based analysis techniques. Furthermore, published semantics and interoperability protocols are needed to allow individual SCULPTEUR systems to interoperate to achieve seamless cross-collection searching.

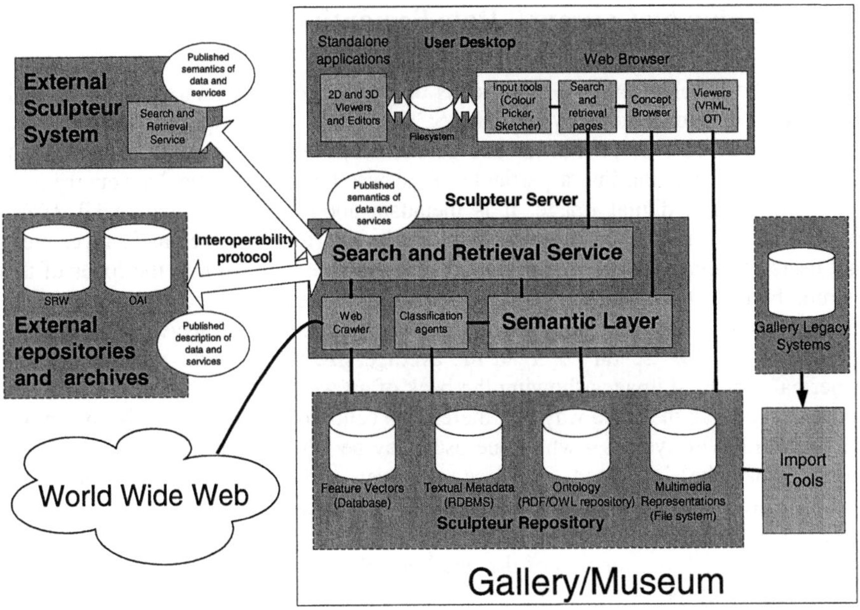

Fig. 1. Sculpteur Architecture

3 Architecture

The SCULPTEUR architecture is designed to provide integrated concept, metadata and content based browsing, retrieval and analysis of museum information. The architecture includes components for augmenting the knowledge about the museum's collections through semi-automated classification of its content and through information extraction from external sources such as the Web.

As Fig. 1 illustrates, SCULPTEUR will include tools for importing data (new images, 3-D models and other digital representations of museum artefacts, data from other gallery systems and information from the web) and for interoperating with external systems (remote SCULPTEUR installations, gallery legacy systems or remote digital libraries supporting standard interfaces such as OAI[6] or SRW[7]).

The question of how the ontologies used in the semantic layer map to the instance information introduces the possibility of various refinements to the architecture. The integration of the legacy museum information with the semantic layer can be achieved either by the storage of instance information within a knowledge base, or through mapping concepts in the ontology directly to attributes of the data source. An example of the latter is the mapping of the 'author' concept in the ontology to the 'createdBy' column of a particular database table. We take a centralised approach to mapping between ontologies and data sources. All data from museum and gallery legacy systems are mirrored in a central location, and a mapping between the ontology and this central data source is created. A user can query the system or other SCULPTEUR knowledge bases using a uniform interface. Further details of the components of the SCULPTEUR architecture can be found below.

4 Navigating by Concept – Data Semantics

To solve the problem of a singular focus obscuring potential interesting information to be derived from links between data, SCULPTEUR will employ a semantic layer that makes explicit those entities and relationships which are implicit in the data. Clearly the information that a particular artist was born in a particular country is not metadata about a digital image, it is metadata about that artist and SCULPTEUR makes that logical ordering of data visible in its interface. The semantic layer means that users can make any of the entities identified in the collection as the focus of their search, both in terms of the search specification and the objects returned by the search. Example searches might include "Find all countries that have produced artists working in the 19th Century", "Find the average size of art works made of stone in America", or "Find images showing the back of art works where those art works have been restored". In the same way that there is no centre of the Web there is no centre of the SCULPTEUR system – while one user may be interested in searching for artists, another may be interested in place and yet another in the art works. The SCULPTEUR system will enable users to approach the same data in multiple different ways using a single interface.

The semantic layer consists of the ontology [9] and instance information. Instance information may be held directly in the ontology or by references, e.g. a URL, to external physical locations. Legacy metadata tends to use domain-specific and often museum specific terms making it difficult to search multiple collections. Ontologies make use of vocabularies to define and organize related information. By using common vocabularies, it makes it easier to share and re-use the concepts across museums. An ontology also allows the user to search and retrieve information of interest through various layers of complexity (i.e. abstract or concrete). While it is evident to see many benefits of using ontology-driven information management, ontology creation and maintenance are labour-intensive and time-consuming tasks since it is necessary to make sure the hierarchies of the concepts are structured accurately and without duplications. This observation, combined with the desire to use existing common vocabularies where possible, led us to base the SCULPTEUR prototype data ontology on the CIDOC CRM.

The CIDOC Conceptual Reference Model (CRM) developed by CIDOC Documentation Standards Working Group is concerned with cultural heritage information describing concepts and relations relevant to all types of material collected and displayed by museums [10]. The CRM aims to support the exchange of relevant information across museums through coherent semantics and common vocabularies. SCULPTEUR has extended the CRM by adding concepts and relationships and by including multimedia representations as artefact instances. Protégé [11] was used for such modifications. The ontology is represented in RDF/RDFS. Fig. 2 shows part of the CRM and shows how we have made extensions. For example, the CRM 'Information Carrier' concept is used to denote physical things such as art objects in a museum. We added 'has_thumbnail_location' and 'has_image_location' properties (bottom left of Fig. 2) to identify the location (e.g. a URL) of digital images that represent these physical things.

The associations between object representations and concepts in the ontology allow enhanced retrieval possibilities by facilitating broadening or narrowing of the search scope through broader and narrower concepts. It will also permit enhanced content

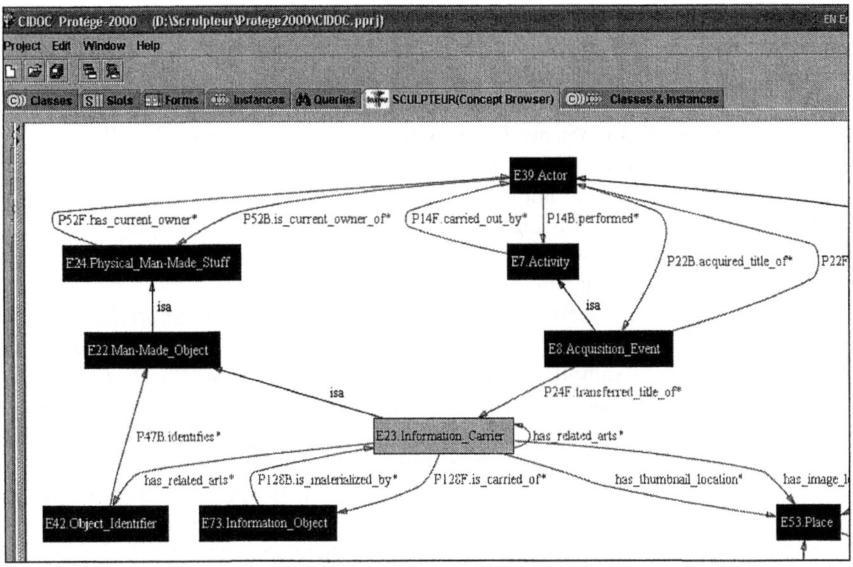

Fig. 2. Protégé screen shot showing an example of extensions to the CRM

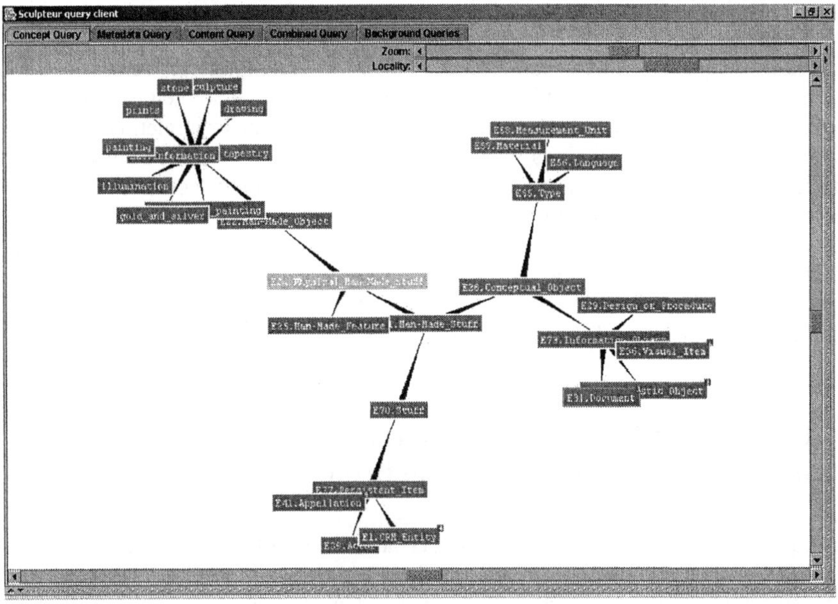

Fig. 3. SCULPTEUR Concept Browser showing extensions to CIDOC CRM

based searches since a content match with an object associated with a concept will allow other objects associated with the concept to be retrieved whether or not they are visually similar.

As shown in Fig. 3, we have also developed a graphical Concept Browser to allow navigation through the ontology as a semantic layer. The Concept Browser in particular aims to assist users whose domain expertise is relatively low for example, members of the public visiting a museum web site or gallery terminal, or perhaps a art historian or painting conservationist looking to understand the contents of a museum's collection. In Fig. 3, the CRM 'Information Carrier' concept has been sub-classed into the different types of art objects found within a particular museum collection, e.g. 'prints', 'drawings' and 'paintings' (top right corner of Fig. 3)

Within SCULPTEUR, the ontology is mostly based on existing museum databases of images and metadata and using semi- or automatic database mapping tools, users can populate an initial knowledgebase which structures the data gathered according to concepts and relations defined in the ontology.

Missing instances can occur when galleries hold large numbers of artefacts and the relevant information is scattered in different places, which makes it difficult to collect and locate all values. Examples might be missing dates when works were created or names of places where artists were born or worked. In addition, the knowledge required for identifying and validating such knowledge is generally held by a small number of people. Hence, the development of tools for automatically finding missing instances is useful in order to reduce human efforts and time in processing related information. The Web, in particular, is potentially useful for gathering such missing information, but sites conforming to semantic web standards are limited. Information processing is required for extracting the missing relations from the Web. Whereas search engines (e.g. 'Google' or 'Yahoo') can retrieve pages which are possibly relevant to the information required, the extraction of the specific relations within the pages can be better served by knowledge extraction techniques. We are developing searching "agents" which can identify and, where possible, retrieve missing information automatically. GATE [12] and WordNet [13] are applied to retrieved web pages in order to extract named-entities for identifying and completing the missing instances. Since these relations generally link two concepts conforming to ontology specifications, it is necessary to construct any semantic connections between identified entities. A syntactic and semantic analysis, based on a natural language processing, can structure the extracted annotations according to their roles in a given sentence (e.g. 'subject' or 'object'). Based on subject-verb or object-verb associations, a set of potential relations are created. Human experts are used to validate correctness of information before it is committed to the knowledgebase.

5 The Concept Browser – An Interface for Combined Semantic and Content-Based Queries and Browsing

A graphical concept browser provides user access to parts of the ontology allowing searchers to navigate easily to representations of interest. Combined with algorithms for multimedia object matching (based on feature vectors extracted from the representations) and menus for metadata selection, the system facilitates individual or combined concept, metadata and content-based searches.

Several HCI issues exist in SCULPTEUR when employing collection navigation via graphical ontology. Firstly, the complexity of the ontology and the method of navigation needs to be matched to the needs and ability of the user. For example, a school child navigating a museum Web site for material to use in a School project has

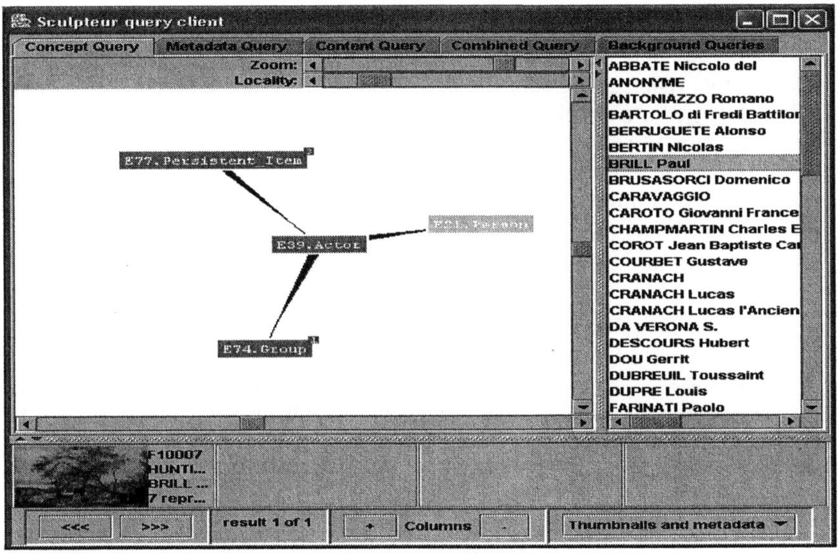

Fig. 4. User Interface to the Concept Browser

very different requirements to an art historian who wants very specific details about the works of art for just one artist or period. As a result, SCULPTEUR is investigating the use of different 'views' over the underlying CRM ontology as a way of exposing or hiding complexity as necessary. We are also looking at how graphical ontologies can be used alongside more traditional and familiar search and retrieval interfaces such as the use of text-based forms. Another HCI issue is how to allow people to form a query composed of a semantic term plus a content-based query in the form of a choice of image and algorithm. In our prototype interface (Fig. 4) three different information areas are displayed as tabbed panels: concept, metadata (i.e. things which are not extracted into the concept layer) and image content queries. By selecting items from each panel a combined query can be composed such as "made of wood" and "like this image in terms of colour histogram".

Each panel can be used individually and the concept panel is particularly interesting as it gives a visual representation of the ontology. Clicking on a concept puts it into the centre and shows concepts close to it. Changing the "locality" allows more distant terms to be seen together. Right-clicking on a concept allows the user access to request all the instances, as shown in Fig. 4 above. The Concept Browser proved to be a useful test interface and it was found that the approach was relatively intuitive. However, plenty of screen space is required and the location of concepts on the screen was not fixed which made "visual hunting" necessary. The visibility of the current query context was also not good as the user had to switch to the combined view.

6 Defining the Semantics of Search and Retrieval

It is important to model the semantics of the search and retrieval processes to support systems integration and to assist the user in the search and retrieval process.

Queries supported in SCULPTEUR are: **textual metadata** (existing descriptions of objects in a collection stored in relational database tables); **representation content** (feature vectors representing shape, colour, texture etc.); and **concepts** (things in the domain ontology, for example 'painting', 'sculpture', 'style'). For example, a user can retrieve museum objects according to associated textual metadata by filling in required values in a form. Content-based analysis can be used to return similar representations (2D images, 3D models, image movies) to one supplied by the user. Browsing or searching through concepts enables a user to locate and retrieve museum objects according to the concepts with which they are associated, or by relationships to other concepts.

These three apparently different areas can all be treated in the same way by considering them all to be ontological concepts, i.e. by building a unifying model of all aspects of the search and retrieval domain. In doing this all searches can be done in an integrated and uniform way. Single statements can be used to specify sophisticated queries such as 'find the 2-D thumbnails for all oil paintings that are authored by Van Gogh, where the painting contains colours similar to the oranges and yellows that I select'.

However the SCULPTEUR system needs to do more than simply integrate different types of query since SCULPTEUR incorporates a diverse range of tools for use in the formulation, execution and interpretation of the results of a query. This complexity is illustrated in Fig. 5.. For example, the inputs to a multimedia search and retrieval query can be supplied in a variety of ways such as query images or 3D models, textual metadata, concepts found by browsing an ontology, or free text. Similarly, the outputs could be images, models, concepts, or textual information. Furthermore, it needs to be possible to view these outputs in many ways such as 2D thumbnails ordered by similarity to a query image, art object titles chronologically ordered on a timeline, or paintings presented in a virtual gallery. Other ways of presenting results could include locations on a museum floor plan, or a street map showing gallery locations. A range of tools will be required to support this diversity of inputs and outputs.

SCULPTEUR has a system ontology which includes concepts such as the digital representation of art objects (JPEG, TIFF, VRML, 3D models), feature vectors of those digital representations (colour histograms etc), algorithms used to produce and compare feature vectors, tools to construct queries (colour picker, 3D editor) and to display digital representations (2 and 3 D viewers), and other components of the search and retrieval process such as QueryRepresentation (2D or 3D representation supplied as input to a query) and ResultSet (things returned as results of the query).

We have prototyped the system ontology using Protégé [11]. We then developed queries to determine if the ontology could be used successfully to support the search and retrieval process. Some of the classes and relationships in the system ontology are presented in Fig. 6. This diagram shows the high-level system concepts and their relationships. Not all of the ontology is shown, in particular the range of representation types and formats is limited, and the link to the museum domain is not shown. Specific relationships such as 'the Colour Coherence Vector algorithm can be applied to 2D colour images to produce a Colour Histogram'. These relationships are modelled through the idea of DigitalAttributes. A DigitalAttribute (e.g. has colour) captures the specific requirements of each Algorithm and also describes Representation types that are suitable for providing this input.

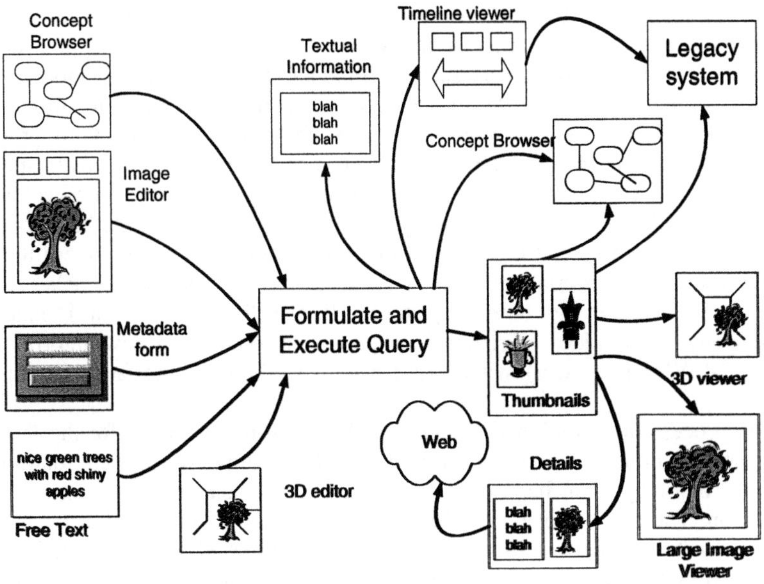

Fig. 5. Inputs and outputs of the SCULPTEUR search and retrieval process

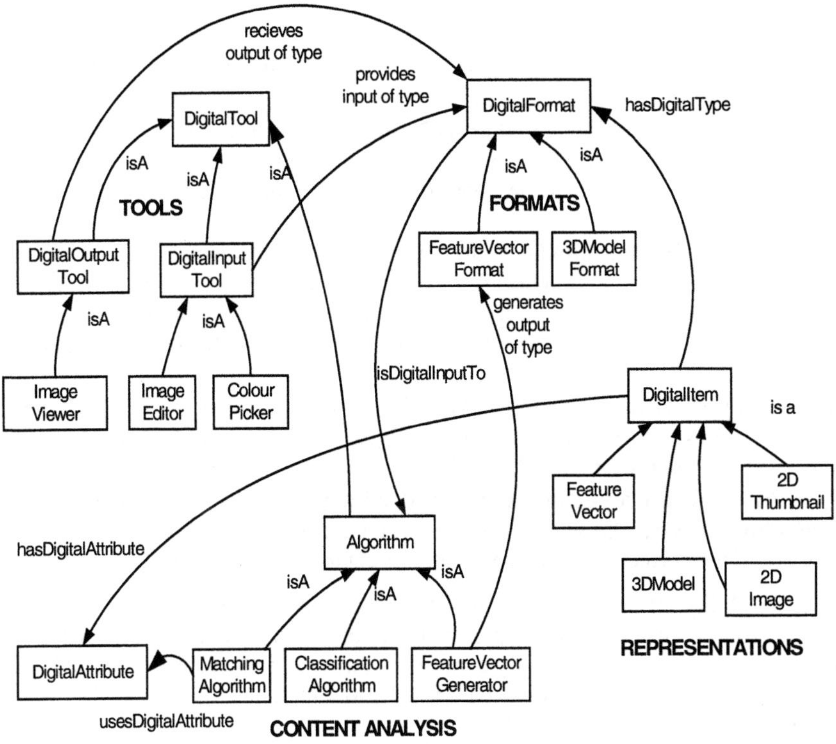

Fig. 6. Extract from Sculpteur system ontology

SCULPTEUR will use the system ontology to determine the right tools, data and algorithms to use for a particular query. The process of execution of a combined concept and content-based query such as "Find and then show me 3D models of vases that are similar to a 3D model of a vase in my collection" illustrates this idea. The system would interpret the users intentions and use the ontology to present the appropriate tools to the user: (i) a 3D viewer or editor and (ii) a means to specify the concept Vase. An appropriate algorithm for the comparison of feature vectors of 3D models would be selected by using relationships that link media formats and associated algorithms that can process them. On completion of the query the system would use the appropriate tool capable of displaying the 3D models. A further advantage of an ontology describing the SCULPTEUR system is that it enables new components to be added as required to the system (such as a new algorithm, or an additional VRML viewer) without extensive recoding of interfaces or application servers.

The process of a combined metadata and content-based search for the 'Van Gogh painting' example given earlier further illustrates how the system ontology and domain ontology can be combined to facilitate query composition and query execution. The query process can be broken down into a number of steps as outlined below. Each of these steps were developed and tested using Protégé against a combined system and domain ontology, and therefore some of the description below refers to concepts not shown in Fig. 6. In the full system, the users will not be subject to this query process since it will be transparently and automatically executed behind a much more intuitive user interface.

- **Q1: Find all 'MatchingAlgorithm' that 'usesDigitalAttribute' Colour.** This would return the appropriate matching algorithm.
- **Q2: Find all 'DigitalFormat' that 'isDigitalInputTo' Q1.** This would return the ColourHistogramFormat instance of 'FeatureVectorFormat' concept. This is necessary information to find appropriate tools and to limit the feature vector space during query execution
- **Q3: Find all 'DigitalInputTool' that 'generatesDigitalFormat' Q2.** This would return instances of the ColourPicker concept. The ontology has been now been used to specify the correct tools available for use with a particular query.
- **Q4: Find all 'Painting' that 'wasCreatedBy' Van Gogh.** This is a metadata search.
- **Q5: Find all '2DImage' 'represents' Q4.** The system concerns itself with digital representations rather than original art objects so we need to find those that represent the paintings returned by Q4.
- **Q6: Find 'FeatureVector' that 'hasDigitalType' Q2 & 'FeatureVector' 'isFeatureOf' Q5.** The search space has been constrained to those feature vectors that are of the correct type and that represent 2D images of painting by Van Gogh.

The feasibility of using ontologies for these system aspects of SCULPTEUR depends strongly on the availability of suitable tools and standards. We believe that RDF and RDFS [32] are sufficiently expressive, and that both suitable tools and query languages [31] exist to allow SCULPTEUR to automatically query the system ontology for the information it needs.

As well as support for the facilitation of systems integration, the approach taken of defining aspects of the SCULPTEUR system within the ontology also provides important support for the search and retrieval process. Query execution in SCULPTEUR will often be an iterative process: A user performing an initial search may wish to then either broaden or narrow the set of returned results, or use one of the returned images in a subsequent query. This search process would flow until the correct item/s are found. Containing the semantics and provenance of aspects of the search and retrieval process - such as a QueryRepresentation or ResultSet - within the ontology provides for a powerful iterative search and retrieval process. Moreover, defining semantics of search and retrieval provides specific support for interoperability and cross-collection searching.

7 Interoperability

The extensive use of semantic web technologies in SCULPTEUR provides a way to establish common semantics between heterogeneous digital libraries containing multimedia collections. These common semantics include how to perform, content-based analysis and searching by concept as well as conventional textual metadata searching. This goes a long way towards interoperability between multiple digital libraries. In fact, this would be sufficient to enable cross-collection search and retrieval between SCULPTEUR systems. However, common semantics are not enough to provide interoperability with third-party systems. To achieve this requires adoption of standard protocols for the process of search and retrieval.

In order for the digital heritage resources contained within a museum or gallery collection to be incorporated into the semantic web, it is essential that both the digital resources themselves and the features of the system be made available in a machine understandable way. By describing aspects of the system and the search and retrieval process – such as the algorithms supported and the nature of the results of a search – as concepts in the ontology, the necessary semantics for interoperability are provided. In essence, the system has to describe what is available and how to use it.

The Search and Retrieve Web Service (SRW) [7] is an initiative based on the z39.50 protocol [4] for searching databases that contain metadata and objects. It proposes a query language, Common Query Language (CQL) [15] and currently represents the emerging standard in the area of distributed data access for digital libraries. However being traditionally concerned with text based searching, CQL provides no formal method to specify searches for similar images or 3D models using particular content-based algorithms [14]. Although many multimedia oriented query languages exist [16][17][18] for content-based searching, there is no one language that has been accepted as the standard multimedia query language and that addresses the issues related to searching distributed collections. ARTISTE was one of the early implementers of SRW [27] and worked in close contact with the z39.50 community to develop the SRW specifications to extend the capabilities to combined image content and metadata based searches over multiple collections. CQL was expanded to provide support for image content queries by adding image operator (img-op), image analyser (img-analyser) and an image expression (img-exp) to the language.

```
primary ::=result-set-expression | [index-name rel-op]
adj-expr | index-name img-op img-analyser img-exp
```

The SRW CQL specification of result-set-expression and index-name remains unchanged in the SCULPTEUR CQL. The SCULPTEUR CQL further specifies elements necessary to an image content query

```
img-op ::= "SimilarTo" | "PartOf"
img-analyser ::= identifier
img-expr ::= url
```

It can be seen from the definition of img-expr above that query images are specified as URLs. The same approach is used for query result images. Some examples of SCULPTEUR CQL queries are given below.

```
dc.Creator contains Vinci and
sculpteurCore.VisibleLightImage SimilarTo CCV
http://scutlpeur.it-
innovation.soton.ac.uk/test_images/test.jpg
```

This query combines a Dublin Core [29] 'Creator' metadata search with an image content-based query that uses the 'CCV' (Colour Coherence Vector) algorithm to find images that are 'SimilarTo' the referenced query image 'test.jpg'.

```
dc.Subject = TEXTILE and
sculpteurCore.VisibleLightImage PartOf MCCV
http://sculpteur.it-
innovation.soton.ac.uk/test_images/test.jpg and
dc.Creator contains Morris and William
```

This query combines a textual metadata search involving the Dublin Core attributes 'Subject' and 'Creator' with an image content-based query that uses the 'MCCV' (Multiscalar Colour Coherence Vector [22]) algorithm to find images that have the referenced query image as 'part of' them, i.e. as a sub-image.

8 Conclusion

In this paper we have presented a new approach to the design and implementation of a system that provides searching, navigating and querying of the diverse multimedia information held by museums and galleries. A coherent architecture is achieved by using ontologies to describe both the domain of the stored information and the features and facilities of the system itself. Agents are being developed to extract missing information using semantic web and natural language processing.

We support content, metadata and concept based approaches to querying a collection and viewing the results. The ontology for the museum domains can be navigated using a graphical concept browser, which also gives direct access to the multimedia representations. This approach differentiates SCULPTEUR from other multimedia information retrieval systems where searches are typically specified using a text-based interface and results are typically only presented as an ordered list of matches.

We have begun to show that it is possible to use a combination of system and data ontologies to define and publish the semantics of search and retrieval. In this way we are moving towards the semantic web ideal of a self-describing digital heritage archive, accessible to anyone who can read these published semantics.

Acknowledgements. The authors wish to thank: the European Commission for support through the SCULPTEUR project under grant IST-2001-35372; the collaborators on the project for many useful discussions, use of data and valuable help and advice; P Dibdin, A Pillinger, R Sadotra, A Smithson and T Wirdyanto who, as Master of Engineering students, contributed substantially to the development of the SCULPTEUR prototype; TouchGraph (www.touchgraph.com) for software used in the concept browser; and Hewlett Packard's Art & Science programme for the donation of server equipment.

References

[1] SCULPTEUR IST-2001-35372 http://www.sculpteurweb.org
[2] ARTISTE IST-1999-11978 http://www.artisteweb.org/
[3] J. H. E. van der Starre, "Visual Arts Network for the exchange of cultural knowledge: Van Eyck Project", Information Services & Use, Vol.13, pp 347–355, 1993.
[4] z39.50 http://lcweb.loc.gov/z3950/agency/
[5] A. Michard, V. Christophides, M. Scholl, M. Stapleton, D. Sutcliffe, A.M. Vercoustre, "The Aquarelle resource discovery system", Computer Networks and ISDN Systems, Vol. 30, 1185–1200, 1998.
[6] Open Archives Initiative http://www.openarchives.org/
[7] ZING Search and Retrieve Web service http://www.loc.gov/z3950/agency/zing/srw/
[8] The Semantic Web http://www.semanticweb.org/
[9] T. R. Gruber. Toward principles for the design of ontologies used for knowledge sharing. Presented at the Padua workshop on Formal Ontology, March 1993
[10] N. Crofts, I. Dionissiadou, M. Doerr, M. Stiff, Definition of the CIDOC Object-Oriented Conceptual Reference Model, V.3.1, July 2001
[11] J. Gennari, M. A. Musen, R. W. Fergerson, W. E. Grosso, M. Crubézy, H. Eriksson, N. F. Noy, S. W. Tu, The Evolution of Protégé: An Environment for Knowledge-Based Systems Development. 2002. Technical Report, SMI-2002-0943
[12] H. Cunningham, D. Maynard, K. Bontcheva, V. Tablan, GATE: A Framework and Graphical Development Environment for Robust NLP Tools and Applications. Proceedings of the 40th Anniversary Meeting of the Association for Computational Linguistics (ACL'02), Philadelphia, US.,2002
[13] G. Miller, R. Beckwith, C. Fellbaum, D. Gross, K. Miller, Introduction to WordNet: An On-Line Lexical Database, In Technical Report, University of Princeton, U.S.A., 1993
[14] ARTISTE D6.2 Impact on World-Wide Metadata Standards http://www.it-innovation.soton.ac.uk/artiste/documentation/D6.2.final.pdf
[15] CQL http://www.loc.gov/z3950/agency/zing/cql/cql-syntax.html
[16] J.Z. Li, M. Tamer Ozsu, D Szafron, V. Oria. MOQL: A Multimedia Object Query language. The 3rd Intl. Workshop on Multimedia Information Systems, 19–28, 1997
[17] A.Henrich, G Robbert. POQL: A Query Language for structured multimedia documents. Proceedings 1st Intl Workshop on Multimedia Data and Document Engineering, 17–26, 2001
[18] G. Amato, G. Mainetto, P. Savino. A Query Language for Similarity-based Retrieval of Multimedia Data. Advances in Databases and Information Systems, 1–13, 1997.
[19] Addis, M., Lewis, P., Martinez, K. "ARTISTE image retrieval system puts European galleries in the picture", Cultivate Interactive http://www.cultivate-int.org/issue7/artiste/

[20] F. S. Abas and K. Martinez (2002) Craquelure Analysis for Content-Based Retrieval. IEEE DSP 2002 conference. July 2002.

[21] Dobie, Mark R. and Tansley, Robert H. and Joyce, Dan W. and Weal, Mark J. and Lewis, Paul H. and Hall, Wendy (1999) A Flexible Architecture for Content and Concept Based Multimedia Information Exploration. In Harper, David J. and Eakins, John P., Eds. Proceedings The Challenge of Image Retrieval, Newcastle, 1999, pages 1–12.On Fri, 2 May 2003,

[23] M. Addis, M. Boniface, S. Goodall, P. Grimwood, S. Kim,P. Lewis, K. Martinez, A. Stevenson, Integrated image content and metadata search and retrieval across multiple databases, To be presented at CIVR2003, July 24–25, 2003, University of Illinois at Urbana

[24] J Stevenson, A Review of the Artiste Project, International Conference on the Challenge of Image and Video Retrieval CIVR2002 July 19, 2002, London, UK http://www.civr2002.org

[25] P. Allen, M. Boniface, P. Lewis, K. Martinez "Interoperability between Multimedia Collections for Content & Metadata-Based Searching", 11th WWW Conference, Hawaii. 7–11 May 2002 http://www2002.org/CDROM/alternate/196/index.html

[27] ARTISTE SRW Service demonstration http://artiste.it-innovation.soton.ac.uk/srw

[28] R.C. Veltkamp and M. Tanase. Content-based image retrieval systems : A survey. Technical report UU-CS-2000-34, Department of Computing Science, Utrecht University, October 2000. 34

[29] Dublin Core http://www.dublincore.org/

[30] Arnold W. M. Smeulders, M Worring, S Santini, A Gupta, and R Jain. Content-Based Image Retrieval at the End of the Early Years. In Transactions On Pattern Analysis And Machine Intelligence, volume 22 of 12, pages 1349–1380. IEEE, December 2000.

[31] RQL: A Functional Query Language for RDF, G. Karvounarakis, A. Magkanaraki, S. Alexaki, V. Christophides, D. Plexousakis, M. Scholl, K. Tolle, to be published at Functional Approaches to Computing With Data, P.M.D.Gray, L.Kerschberg, P.J.H.King, A.Poulovassilis (eds.), LNCS Series

[32] RDF Resource Description Framework http://www.w3c.org/RDF/

Towards Ontology-Driven Discourse: From Semantic Graphs to Multimedia Presentations

Joost Geurts, Stefano Bocconi, Jacco van Ossenbruggen, and Lynda Hardman

CWI, P.O. Box 94079, 1090 GB Amsterdam, The Netherlands,
{Firstname.Lastname}@cwi.nl

Abstract. Traditionally, research in applying Semantic Web technology to multimedia information systems has focused on using annotations and ontologies to improve the retrieval process. This paper concentrates on improving the presentation of the retrieval results.

First, our approach uses ontological domain knowledge to select and organize the content relevant to the topic the user is interested in. Domain ontologies are valuable in the presentation generation process, because effective presentations are those that succeed in conveying the relevant domain semantics to the user. Explicit discourse and narrative knowledge allows selection of appropriate presentation genres and creation of narrative structures, which are used for conveying these domain relations.

In addition, knowledge of graphic design and media characteristics is essential to transform abstract presentation structures into real multimedia presentations. Design knowledge determines how the semantics and presentation structure are expressed in the multimedia presentation. In traditional Web environments, this type of design knowledge remains implicit, hidden in style sheets and other document transformation code. Our second use of Semantic Web technology is to model design knowledge explicitly, and to enable it to drive the transformations needed to turn annotated media items into structured presentations.

1 Introduction

When applying Semantic Web technology to data-driven Web sites, the typical focus is either on annotation of the data to improve information retrieval, or on structuring the data, using Semantic Web modeling techniques as an alternative to database-oriented (including ER) or software-oriented (including UML) modeling techniques [7,9,10,13]. The presentation of the retrieved and structured data is seen as a "detail" that is best left to CSS or XSLT style sheets. We claim that this approach grossly underestimates the importance and complexity of effective presentation design.

To do their work properly, we expect human professional designers to at least understand:

1. the underlying semantics of the client's information;
2. the most effective order, grouping and priorities for structuring this information;
3. the most effective means of using the chosen medium to convey the information.

D. Fensel et al. (Eds.): ISWC 2003, LNCS 2870, pp. 597–612, 2003.

Information presentation design is thus an inherently knowledge-driven process. It also requires sufficient knowledge about the domain to be able to convey the essential semantic relations in the presentation. It requires knowledge about how to order, group and prioritize this information effectively, for example by organizing the information into a coherent storyline with a clear introduction, main body and conclusion. Finally, it requires knowledge about media design. First, the designer needs to be able to select the most appropriate medium and, second, to understand the characteristics of that medium to find the most effective means of using its characteristics to achieve the communication goal.

Unfortunately, deploying professional designers to design data-driven Web sites is only feasible if the underlying data, its semantics and target audience are relatively homogeneous. The variety of data sources and semantic relations, combined with a variety of output devices and different user profiles, quickly leads to a combinatorial explosion that forces content providers into a one-size-fits-all approach that ignores the different types of knowledge sketched above. Clearly, some form of automation is needed, and this automated process will need to take this knowledge into account.

While we do not claim that we can even approach the quality of human designers, this paper explores to what extent Semantic Web technology can be used to model the knowledge sketched above, and to what extent this can be used to create an ontology-driven transformation process that generates a coherent multimedia presentation which conveys the relationships within the information to the end user. This paper is explicitly *not* about new models of genre, discourse or narrative. The discourse models presented are used as an example and are inspired by existing communication modeling techniques [11]. The same applies to the document and graphic design models used, which were inspired by general text books on design [19,27].

We assume that the multimedia items of our presentation are properly annotated, and that these annotations represent the domain relations between the items in some sort of semantic graph (e.g. in RDF). We then use this graph, and the associated ontology, to select, order, group and prioritize the information. In addition, we use a *Discourse* ontology to guide this process. This ontology contains information about different document genres and the building blocks for creating documents for each genre. The resulting data structure is, following Rutledge et al. [20], called a *structured progression*. This data structure is then used as the basis for generating a multimedia presentation. In addition to discourse knowledge, this process is also guided by media design knowledge from the *Design* ontology.

Figure 1 illustrates our approach, emphasizing the two focal points of this paper: (1) the process that uses domain and discourse knowledge to transform a semantic graph into a structured progression, and (2), the process that uses discourse and design knowledge to transform this into a multimedia presentation.

The remainder of this paper is structured as follows. Section 2 presents a working example, based on a semantic graph modeling the life and works of the painter Rembrandt van Rijn. This graph is used as a basis to generate a multimedia biography automatically. We use the example to illustrate the processing steps involved and which knowledge sources are used when. Section 3 describes the first process in more depth. We show how domain relations can be mapped to discourse structures, a technique which makes

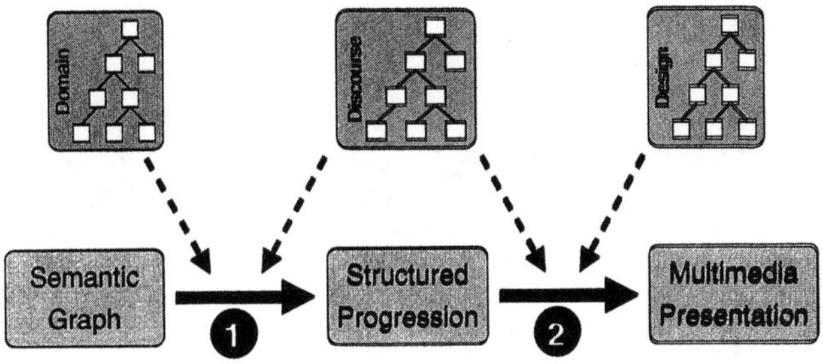

Fig. 1. The two-step, ontology-driven transformation process

our approach extensible to other domains. In addition, we report on our experience using existing Semantic Web technologies. In Section 4 we describe the second process, which transforms a structured progression to a real multimedia presentation. This step is based on transformation rules whose application is guided by the discourse and design ontologies, and also by the constraints on the final multimedia presentation. The rules use the grouping, ordering and priorities of the material defined in the structured progression to create a coherent multimedia presentation. In Section 5, we describe related work and examine the design choices of other systems with respect to the main points of our approach. Finally, conclusions and future work are given in Section 6.

2 Example Scenario

Our user queries for "life and work of Rembrandt" using a Web browser. The user has also selected the preferred types of the structured progression. This type will define the *genre* of the presentation. Examples of genre include disc:Biography and disc:CV[1]. Our user has chosen disc:Biography among the preferred genres. Finally, the user selects the output medium, e.g. printed paper, interactive hypermedia presentation, non-interactive multimedia, a slide show, etc. In our case the user has chosen a non-interactive multimedia presentation.

The results returned by the retrieval component (outside the scope of this article), combined with the associated semantic relations from the domain ontology, form the semantic graph that is the main input to our system (shown at the left of Figure 2). Based on this graph, the system selects a matching genre type from the ones specified by the user, in our case the disc:Biography. It then uses a set of rules to transform the graph into a structured progression representing the biography. At this stage, the information in the semantic graph has been ordered, grouped and prioritized (center of Figure 2).

The structured progression contains some typical facts about Rembrandt, such as his full name, place and date of birth, etc. This is followed by information about his career and finally some information about his personal life, that is, about his son Titus and wife Saskia. In the next step, media items which represent the concepts are retrieved. The

[1] Schema level information is typeset in sans-serif font, with a namespace-like qualifier to indicate the ontology used. So disc:Biography refers to the Biography class of the discourse ontology, and dom:Artist to the Artist class of the domain ontology.

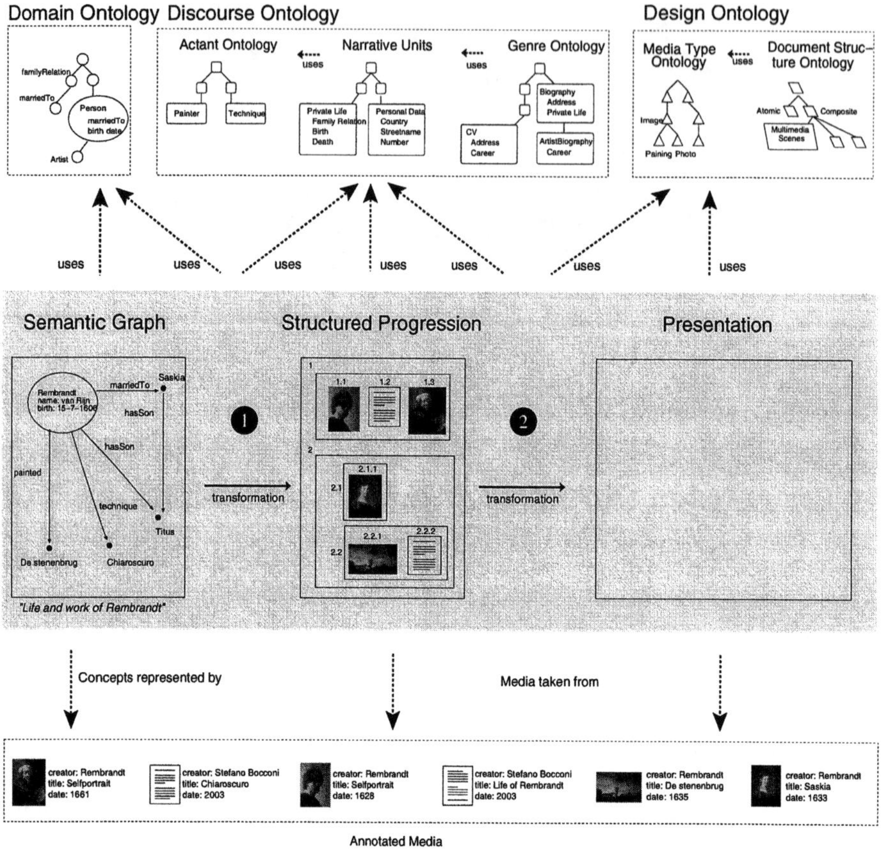

Fig. 2. Sketch of the processing of the example scenario. The middle layer shows an example semantic graph (left) that is first transformed to a biography structure (middle) and then to a multimedia presentation (right). The upper layer shows the ontologies involved, while the lower layer represents the annotated media items used.

chosen output medium defines how the biography is conveyed to the user. A multimedia presentation, for example, will use sequentially ordered scenes and possibly sub-scenes. Transitions between scenes can be realized by using links or by placing them one after the other using appropriate fade in/out effects. In our case the latter is used. Finally the user chooses a format for the presentation. For the timed multimedia presentation generated, the system supports SMIL and HTML+TIME. The presentation is serialized using the selected output format and sent to the user's Web client (on the right of Figure 2).

3 From Semantic Graph to Structured Progression

This section discusses the first transformation step. In terms of the example, this is the step that transforms the semantic (RDF) graph representing the relevant media items and their annotations into a target biography structured progression.

Note that traditional document processing chains usually *start* at this point. For example, one could apply an XSLT transformation or CSS style sheet to the biography structure to produce presentation formats such as HTML. These methods are, however, not well suited to generate RDF and XML structures from RDF graphs. When applied to RDF, languages such as CSS and XSLT operate purely on the XML level of RDF's serialization syntax, without any understanding or support for the semantics of the RDF data model. Since domain knowledge is essential for conveying the underlying message, the transformation process also needs access to knowledge on the RDF Schema level to be able to query the underlying domain ontology. In addition, since the discourse knowledge is also stored in an RDF Schema ontology, RDF Schema support is also required to gain access to the transformation's own "operating" knowledge.

We have prototyped several transformations in both Java and Prolog environments that have direct access to a Sesame RDF Schema-based repository [5,6]. We use a Sesame server to store all RDF and RDF Schema knowledge used. The key advantage of this approach is that our transformation no longer needs to access the RDF on the XML syntax level, but can gain direct access on the RDF instance level and RDF Schema level using any of the query languages supported by Sesame (currently RQL [14], RDQL [18] and SeRQL [1]).

This approach allows us to make all domain and discourse knowledge explicit that usually remains implicit in the XSLT (or, in our case, Java or Prolog) transformation code, by modeling it in the appropriate ontology. As a consequence, the transformation process itself uses (declarative) domain and discourse-specific knowledge, while the (procedural) transformation code remains generic.

For example, given the instance `Rembrandt`[2], from the semantic graph on the left of Figure 2 on page 600, the transformation code uses an RQL query to retrieve the classes this instance belongs to, and selects a structured progression type from the discourse ontology that can be applied to this class. In our example, `Rembrandt` turns out to be an instance of dom:Artist, and the discourse ontology defines an instance of disc:ArtistBiography that has a disc:Subject property with value dom:Artist.

Each structured progression, including disc:ArtistBiography, has a disc:narrativeUnits property that specifies the disc:NarrativeUnits that can be used to construct the structured progression. In our example, the applicable narrative units are instances of the classes disc:Personal Data, disc:Private Life and disc:Career.

Narrative units have associated rules which are inspired by the work of Greimas [11] (see Table 1 on page 602) and are used to select matching content. An instance of disc:Private Life, for example, contains rules to select information about family relations from the semantic graph. In our case, the semantic graph includes an dom:isMarried relation between `Rembrandt` and `Saskia_Uylenburgh`. Rule # 3 in the table, for example, can use this domain relation to select Saskia in the disc:Role of disc:Spouse.

[2] Instance level information is typeset in courier font.

Table 1. Narrative units and their associated rules (simplified for readability)

PersonalData

#	Current Role	Relation	Progression	New Role	Relevant Properties
1	MainCharacter	none	none	none	[descriptionText, portrait, ...]
...					

PrivateLife

#	Current Role	Relation	Progression	New Role	Relevant Properties
2	MainCharacter	none	none	none	[name, birthDate, ...]
3	MainCharacter	isMarried	privateLife	spouse	[marriedPlace, marriedDate]
4	MainCharacter	parentOf	none	child	[birthPlace, birthDate]
5	spouse	none	none	none	[name, daughterOf]
...					

Career

#	Current Role	Relation	Progression	New Role	Relevant Properties
6	MainCharacter	none	none	none	[workPlace, ...]
7	MainCharacter	taughtBy	career	master	[stylePeriod]
8	master	style	career	technique	[styleDescription]
...					

```
<rdf:RDF xmlns:rdf="http://www.w3.org/1999/02/22-rdf-syntax-ns#"
        xmlns    ="http://www.cwi.nl/~media/ns/discourse#"
        xmlns:d  ="http://www.cwi.nl/~media/ns/discourse#">

    <discourse d:type='biography'>
        <narrativeunit rdf:parseType='Resource'>
            <type>PersonalData</type>
            <actant>Rembrandt_van_Rijn</actant>
            <role>MainCharacter</role>
            <data rdf:parseType='Resource'>
                <descriptiveText>Rembrandt Harmensz. van Rijn is the most famous...</descriptiveText>
                <portrait rdf:resource='http://www.rijksmuseum.nl/SK-A-4691.Z.jpg'/>
            </data>
        </narrativeunit>
        <narrativeunit rdf:parseType='Resource'>
            <type>Career</type>
            <actant>Rembrandt_van_Rijn</actant>
            <role>Painter</role>
            <data>....</data>
            <narrativeunit rdf:parseType='Resource'>
                <type>Career</type>
                <actant>Chiaroscuro</actant>
                <role>Technique</role>
                <data rdf:parseType='Resource'>
                    <descriptiveText>Clair-obscur (French) and chiaroscuro (Italian)...</descriptiveText>
                    <painting rdf:resource='http://www.rijksmuseum.nl/SK-A-1935.ORG.jpg'/>
                    <painting rdf:resource='http://www.rijksmuseum.nl/SK-A-4691.Z.jpg'/>
                </data>
            </narrativeunit>
        </narrativeunit>
        <narrativeunit rdf:parseType='Resource'>
            <type>PrivateLife</type>
            <actant>Rembrandt_van_Rijn</actant>
            <role>PrivatePerson</role>
            <data>....</data>
            <narrativeunit rdf:parseType='Resource'>
                <type>PrivateLife</type>
                <actant>Saskia_Uylenburgh</actant>
                <role>Spouse</role>
                <data rdf:parseType='Resource'>
                    <descriptiveText>In 1634 Rembrandt married...</descriptiveText>
                    <portrait rdf:resource='http://www.rijksmuseum.nl/SK-A-4057.jpg'/>
                </data>
            </narrativeunit>
        </narrativeunit>
    </discourse>
</rdf:RDF>
```

Fig. 3. RDF/XML representation of the biography

Selecting roles is the main task of the rules each narrative unit contains. Each rule states that if a given instance with a given role (e.g. Rembrandt in the role of disc:MainCharacter) has a certain domain relation with another instance (e.g. relation dom:isMarried with Saskia_Uylenburgh), the latter instance could become a new character in the story with the role specified in the rule (in this case Saskia enters the story in the role of disc:Spouse).

Rules can be applied recursively to define how to further expand the story with the new character. In our example, rule # 3 not only assigns to Saskia_Uylenburgh the role of disc:Spouse, but it also specifies that PrivateLife is the narrative unit that can be used for a subsequent nested story line. The engine would then look whether PrivateLife contains rules that can be applied to disc:Spouse. If there is such an applicable rule, a nested narrative unit about e.g. the son of Saskia_Uylenburgh would be added to the presentation. This process continues until no more rules can be applied or no more elements satisfy the current rule. A rule can also specify that no further expansion should happen.

Note that since each narrative unit uses different rules and different roles, the same instance can play a different role in the story fragments generated. For example, Saskia_Uylenburgh with role disc:MainCharacter would generate a different story from Saskia_Uylenburgh in the role of disc:Spouse.

A rule also defines, for each specific role, the information from the domain ontology that needs to be incorporated in the narrative unit. For example, rule # 1 specifies that for the disc:MainCharacter in disc:PersonalData extra slots should be added: disc:descriptionText and disc:portrait. The rules also define (not shown in the table) which properties from the domain ontology contain the corresponding information. Rules, as well as all the other concepts used in the structured progression, are explicitly encoded in the discourse ontology.

After all rules have been applied to the initial arbitrary semantic graph structure, the result is the structured progression represented graphically at the center of Figure 2 on page 600 and in RDF in Figure 3. This is a biography with three narrative units: disc:PersonalData with Rembrandt in the role of disc:MainCharacter with two other units, disc:Career containing Chiaroscuro in the role of disc:Technique and disc:PrivateLife containing Saskia_Uylenburgh in the role of disc:Spouse. The information contained within the initial semantic graph has been grouped, ordered and prioritized in terms of the disc:Biography discourse. This hides the specific details of the domain ontology from the next phase of the transformation. The structured progression, therefore, has to pass on sufficient semantics for the next step which transforms the structure progression into a playable multimedia presentation.

4 From Structured Progression to Multimedia Presentation

This section discusses the second transformation step shown in Figure 1 and 2. In terms of the example, this transforms the biography in Figure 3 about Rembrandt into a final form presentation. Although the structure of the information is known at this point, by what means it is conveyed to the user is still open. In this section we show how both discourse and design knowledge are used to transform the structured progression into a final form multimedia presentation.

First, the structured progression is transformed into a so-called *document structure*. In this step, decisions are made about the output medium (e.g. traditional text, interactive hypermedia or "passive" multimedia[3]). For traditional text, this step would map the biography-specific elements to a more generic document structure, defined in terms of chapters, sections etc. similar to the structure in LaTeX or HTML documents. Similar structures can be defined for other output media, such as the multimedia presentation used in the example, that are defined in terms of scenes and sub-scenes.

Second, the document structure is transformed into a tree of formatting objects. In this step, the more detailed layout and formatting decisions are made. For traditional text, this would involve the decisions related to typesetting normally made by word processors or typesetters such as TeX. For the multimedia presentation, this also includes determining the exact timing of the presentation, the interaction style, transition effects etc.

Note that the advantages of this two-step process are similar in both the text and multimedia cases. By mapping the discourse-specific narrative units to more general document elements, the second step can be defined in more commonly applicable formatting rules. In the text case, this means that we do not have to define the precise formatting of the disc:PrivateLife unit. Instead, it can be mapped onto the document section element, relying on the common formatting rules for section-level elements. Similar advantages apply to the multimedia case. For example, instead of specifying explicitly what transition effects have to be applied between disc:PrivateLife, disc:Career and all the other units, we prefer to specify this once on the more generic scene and sub-scene level, after the narrative units have been mapped to these multimedia document structures.

Unfortunately, the disadvantages of this approach are also similar. The main drawback is that when one looks in more detail, there always comes a level that can no longer be effectively specified in terms of the document structure. In the case of text, this article for example, the section, subsection and paragraph level can be conveniently expressed in LaTeX. Even the content and structure of the tables can be effectively represented, because LaTeX defines a sufficiently rich document structure. Figure 2, however, has a level of detail that can no longer be conveniently expressed in LaTeX. Instead, it was created in an external drawing tool and included as a PostScript figure. As a result, from the perspective of the document structure, the figure is a black box. All semantics of the figure remain implicit, and all formatting within that black box has been done manually. For the multimedia case, the situation is even worse. As a relatively new output medium, multimedia documents have not yet evolved a common structure as rich as textual documents. When zooming into a multimedia document, one thus sooner reaches the moment where one can no longer conveniently represent the intended semantics in the document structure.

In practice, one reaches this point so often, that the option of leaving the formatting of material that is too detailed for the document structure to a human designer is not even feasible. Instead, in the first step the detailed structures are copied directly into the document structure, so we can then define specific rules in the second step to deal with their formatting directly.

[3] At the time of writing, our prototype supports only multimedia output.

Table 2. Example mapping from narrative units to document structure.

Narrative unit	Biography Type	Role	Document structure Paper	Multimedia
1	PersonalData	MainCharacter	Section	Scene
2	PrivateLife	MainCharacter	Section	Scene
3	Career	MainCharacter	Section	Scene
2.1	PrivateLife	Spouse	SubSection	Sub-scene
3.1	Career	Master	SubSection	Sub-scene
2.2	PrivateLife	Child	SubSection	Sub-scene
3.2	Career	Technique	SubSection	Sub-scene
...	...	...	...	...

4.1 From Structured Progression to Document Structure

As described previously, a structured progression defines grouping, ordering and priorities of disc:narrative unit instances. It describes the main message an author wants to convey, and relates and organizes narrative units contributing relevant information to this message. It structures the information by defining a hierarchical ordering, differentiating between detailed and more general information. Information without presentation, however, remains abstract. A human author uses different mechanisms, depending on the context, to transform this information into a perceivable document. This includes the selection of media items and the choice of a output medium such as "multimedia presentation" or "paper document". The structure of a narrative, which in our case is modeled as a structured progression, is partly conveyed through the document structure. In traditional text documents, the chapters, sections and paragraphs reflect the underlying narrative structure, where chapters are more general than sections. Multimedia presentations have a similar structure (although less explicit) which we call *scenes* and *sub-scenes*. These are used as generic grouping mechanisms, for which appropriate formatting rules can be defined. One of the main goals of these rules is to identify the (sub)scene boundaries by using, for example, transition-effects or hyperlinks. The screendump on the right of Figure 2 on page 600 represents the first scene; the thumbnail images in the corner are hyperlinks to the two other scenes.

Table 2 shows an example mapping of discourse structures to appropriate document structures. For example, the narrative unit 'PersonalData' is represented as a 'section' in a paper document and as a 'scene' in a multimedia presentation.

Because narrative units can generate sub-narrative units, which subsequently can result in an arbitrary number of levels in the structured progression, the mapping in general cannot be made explicit. In addition, the document structure for paper documents (e.g. chapter, section, subsection) tends to be more fine-grained than a document structure for multimedia presentations (e.g. scene, sub-scene). As a consequence, when generating multimedia presentations, one has to partly bypass the document structure more often than for paper documents. Instead, one needs to be able to convey semantic and discourse relations directly by means of spatial and temporal layout. In our examples, the relation between paintings and their titles is too application-specific to be expressed in our generic document structure. As an escape-mechanism we still allow this information to be copied literally into the multimedia document structure, so that specific formatting rules can determine the formatting of these domain semantics directly.

4.2 Conveying Document Structure

The final step discussed here is the transformation of the document structure into a set of presentation constructs that specify all formatting decisions needed to generate the multimedia presentation. This includes assigning layout clues to allow a reader to recognize the document structure (and thus the underlying semantic relations). For paper documents this is typically realized by typographic conventions, such as using large bold-face fonts for headings to mark the beginning of a new section and chapter. Multimedia presentations can sometimes use similar typographic conventions, but also use more multimedia specific means. Scene boundaries, for example, can be conveyed by using transition effects, or by using hyperlinks to traverse from one scene to the other.

The process of transforming a document structure into presentation constructs uses our Cuypers library (see [23,24] for details). This library uses constraint solving techniques to verify whether a presentation construct conforms to the delivery-context constraints, such as screen size. If these constraints are violated then the library allows us to specify alternative formatting strategies, or indeed discard the construct as a whole. To anticipate formatting failure, the transformation process needs to proceed bottom up, requiring the transformation of leaf nodes of the document structure first.

Because a user may want to be able to distinguish visually between disc:PrivateLife and disc:Career the transformation needs knowledge about the type of narrative corresponding to the scene. In addition, the role of the characters in a scene also need to be specified: the presentation of a disc:Son may need to be different from the presentation of a disc:Spouse. A rule which transforms a document structure, corresponding to a narrative unit, into a presentation construct has thus two discourse parameters: disc:NarrativeType and disc:Role. These discourse parameters allow our system to adapt the formatting of the presentation to convey the message more effectively. Because both parameters are defined in the discourse ontology, we can use subsumption reasoning to generalize the rules, making them applicable for presenting multiple discourse relations. For example, a rule which presents a disc:Painter can be generalized to disc:Artist, in which case the same rule is also applicable to disc:Sculptors.

4.3 Conveying Discourse Semantics Directly

As mentioned before, almost every non-trivial application has some more specific details in the domain or discourse semantics that cannot be effectively expressed in the generic document structure. We allow these semantics to be copied into the document structure. As a result, the formatting step needs to have specific rules that can deal with this type of information, in addition to the rules discussed above that only deal with the document structure proper. We experimented with such specific rules and used different types of knowledge to determine the formatting.

Discourse Knowledge. In our example, disc:Portrait, disc:Painting and disc:DescriptiveText represent concepts directly by means of a media item, and these concepts are mapped directly onto equivalent concepts in the multimedia design ontology (e.g. mm:Painting etc.). Depending on their function in the discourse, we need to define how different media types are to be formatted. For example, the same image of a self-portrait of Rembrandt might require different formatting, one type of formatting when it functions as a disc:Portrait in the disc:PersonalData section, and another when it functions as an example disc:Painting illustrating the `Chiaroscuro` technique. In addition, the system needs knowledge about how to deal with media items that are related in the discourse, and how to group them in terms of presentation constructs that are specific for the output medium. In our example, it will need to be able to group the range of paintings used to illustrate `Chiaroscuro` into a slide show, but it would choose a different solution for a paper version.

Media Characteristics. When building a balanced and coherent presentation, one needs to be aware of the differences between the various media modalities used. Text, images, audio and video all have a very different impact on the way the presentation is perceived by the user, and the system needs to be aware of the differences[4]. In addition, different media types have different formatting requirements. The images of the paintings in our example have a fixed aspect ratio, while the text boxes used for the descriptions can have a wide range of acceptable aspect ratios.

On the other hand, some media types also share important characteristics. For example, the rules mentioned above discriminate between disc:Portrait and disc:Painting. When these rules fail or are missing, there would still be a fall back rule that defines a generic formatting for images. This rule would be applied because the media type ontology defines both mm:Painting and mm:Portrait to be subclasses of mm:Image. In addition, similar subsumption-based fall back rules are required for the groupings. That is, in the absence of specific rules to group paintings into slide shows, fall back rules specifying the generic formatting of a group of images are required.

In practice, the variety of document and discourse structures, media items and intended layout effects, and all the possible combinations, quickly result in an overwhelming number of rules if each of them has to explicitly specified. By using ontological knowledge, however, we can generalize rules, matching on entire subtrees instead of individual cases. For cases where these rules are too generic, more specific rules can be added later. This approach also provides a redundancy that can be exploited for backtracking. In the case that a rule cannot be applied, because of, for example, hardware constraints (e.g. the resulting presentation would not fit on the screen), an alternative rule is invoked automatically. Only if no rule is applicable does the presentation generation fail (see [23, 24] for details).

Once all levels of document structure have been represented by presentation constructs, a final step is required to generate the final presentation format. This is a relatively simple XSLT transformation. We currently support SMIL 1.0 [25], SMIL 2.0 [26] and HTML+TIME [21].

---

4 Most of this knowledge is, however, still implicit in the current version of the system.

5 Related Work

The common thread among the related work is the use of semantics to generate meaningful presentations. The Standard Reference Model for Intelligent Multimedia Presentations [4] provides a theoretical framework which many of these systems follow. It is, however, the different approaches to realizing the overall goal and the context in which they do this that differs. In discussing related work we focus on the issues of domain independence, explicit knowledge representation and the type of generated narrative.

Bateman et al. [2] describe a system (DArt$_{bio}$) that generates artist biographies based on a domain model containing information about several thousand artists. The presentation is created following presentation plans, which are a type of template expressed in terms of Rhetorical Structure Theory [17]. These plans are genre-specific (e.g. for biographies) and tailored to the information contained in the domain model. A natural language generator and a graphic generator create the information items and a layout component determines the layout.

DArt$_{bio}$ is domain dependent and focuses neither on the reuse of information nor on making the knowledge it uses explicit; in this regard it is a pre Semantic Web application, because the knowledge sources are not separate from the core functionality of the system. Furthermore, the narrative it can generate is based on templates (presentation plans) and, once the genre has been determined, has a fixed structure.

Artequakt [15] also generates artist biographies. The system uses a biography ontology, which defines the data for an artist biography. Information is collected by parsing text found on the Web and is subsequently presented using templates. Artequakt does not use annotated media items and, because of the parsing, is strongly text oriented. This allows, at least in theory, the reuse of all the textual information published on the Web about artists. On the other hand, Artequakt uses a domain dependent ontology as its knowledge base and domain dependent templates, which would need to be recreated to apply the system to other domains.

Rutledge et al. [20] describe the Topia system, which generates hypermedia presentations in a domain-independent way, using clustering of annotated media items. The clustering is made by grouping media items that have the same attributes with the same values. Topia does not use knowledge about a particular domain or a particular attribute because it only needs to know whether two attributes or values are equal or different. The advantage of the Topia approach is that the grouping algorithm is relatively simple and, more importantly, that it is domain independent. This is at the same time the limiting factor, because domain knowledge can contribute to the understanding of a topic since the frequency of an occurring relation does not necessarily indicate its importance and might not answer the question a user has. Topia has no explicit discourse knowledge, so that it cannot generate an evolving narrative such as, e.g. a biography or a fairy tale. Topia allows some flexibility because the user can indicate the most important relations, thus guiding the clustering algorithm to cluster media items on these relations. In this sense, we might say that Topia makes the knowledge and the reasoning it uses accessible to the user.

Little at al. [16] generate presentations using media items annotated with Dublin Core [8] metadata. Their focus is on inferring knowledge from the metadata, thereby creating and extending the semantic graph. Dublin Core has the advantage that large amounts of content have been annotated with it; moreover, because Dublin Core is generally applicable, the generation process has a certain degree of domain independence. The disadvantage is that Dublin Core is not a powerful standard to express semantics. Therefore only simple narratives can be generated, by using grammars to define which semantic relations can be put in an introduction, in a middle or ending section.

Some analogies exist between our work and Scholonto [22], even if the latter is not meant for presentation generation. ScholOnto is designed to enable researchers to describe via a semantic network the contributions a document makes and its relationship to the literature. They also use a discourse ontology, in their case to model at a general level the claims a researcher would want to make about a document, while our focus is more on narrative and on the single media item level. ScholOnto is domain specific, its domain being scientific documents, and requires documents to be annotated with the discourse ontology (in ScholOnto there is no domain ontology, or the domain ontology and discourse ontology are the same).

6 Conclusions and Future Work

This paper explores the use of Semantic Web technology for explicit domain, discourse and media knowledge for conveying domain and discourse relations in multimedia presentations. Including these different types of knowledge into the process explicitly also allows for the adaptability and extensibility required.

To date, we have generated only short presentations, based on a restricted domain ontology. We also focused on a single discourse structure (the biography) and a single document structure (a multimedia presentation). More research is needed to scale these aspects of the system to more realistic scenarios. We are also investigating the possibilities of taking explicit user profiles into account, and how knowledge about the user interacts with the discourse and design knowledge used in the current prototype.

We have focused on two characteristics that are important for a presentation generation system: 1) to be effective in conveying the relevant domain semantics, and 2) to be generally applicable. These two requirements are often conflicting. In order to present relevant domain relations but keep the process as general as possible, we query the domain ontology only when transforming the semantic graph into a structured progression. All important domain relations are then mapped to discourse relations. This explicit mapping localizes all specific domain knowledge in the first step. This has the advantage that the application in the remaining transformation always deals with known discourse concepts and is therefore reusable for different domain ontologies.

Our approach to explicit discourse knowledge uses rules with explicit roles to dynamically expand a story. This has the advantage that information presented can be adapted to the context in which it is presented, and helps to improve the coherence of the overall presentation. Using role-based rules can lead to narrative complexities such as recursive expansion of narrative units which need to be dealt with by the designer of the rules.

Another design goal was to strive for making all reasoning explicit, with the assumption this facilitates information sharing and flexibility. All the intelligence of the engine creating the presentation is RDFS-encoded. The discourse ontology not only allows our application knowledge to be made explicit, but is also used as a logical configuration tool (and also graphical, if using a graphical ontology editor like Protege-2000 [12])[5]. This is because all elements determining the behavior of the application are contained in the ontology and are defined in terms of each other: a genre is defined by its narrative units, which are defined by their rules, which are expressed in terms of roles. The ontology defines thus the framework a narrative designer would use to define his or her particular form of narrative.

The fact that an ontology editor can be used to configure the application is a secondary but interesting application of Semantic Web technology. The drawback of this approach is that ontology languages such as RDF Schema are not designed for expressing rules. As a result, our rules are forced to be simple. One cannot combine rules using logical AND or OR or make one rule dependent on the outcome of another. A next step is to investigate the use of more powerful languages such as RuleML [3] for expressing the rules within the system.

The second part of the system uses discourse knowledge to convey appropriate semantics for presenting information. Conveying semantics in terms of presentation is partly realized by document structure which materializes the structure of the information. The way this structure is made explicit changes for different types of document structure and modalities. Especially for multimedia presentations, document structure by itself is not sufficient to convey relevant semantics. This is mainly due to the fact that multimedia presentations, in contrast to paper documents, have a shallow document structure. To compensate for this, our system may bypass the document structure and use lay-out rules that operate directly on the discourse semantics.

The transformation of the structured progression to a final form presentation is carried out using two types of rules — those that allow a generic approach ensuring that some sort of presentation can be generated; and discourse specific rules, which convey important semantical relations, that can be added easily to the system. This contrasts to the approach in Artequakt and DArt$_{bio}$ where the domain dependent rules are deeply embedded within the system.

Acknowledgments. Part of the research described here was funded by the Dutch national NWO/NASH, ToKeN2000 I^{2}RP projects and by grant IST-2000-28767 from the European Union's Information Society Programme to the Question How project. Examples are taken from a ToKeN2000 demonstrator, and all media content has been kindly provided by the Rijksmuseum in Amsterdam. We like to thank Lloyd Rutledge, Frank Nack, Geert-Jan Houben (TU/e) and Martin Alberink (Telematica Instituut) for their useful feedback.

References

1. Aidministrator Nederland B.V. *SeRQL user manual*, April 4, 2003. `http://sesame.aidministrator.nl/publications/SeRQL%20user%20manual.pdf`

[5] Protege screenshots, the RDFS ontologies used, the online Sesame repositories, together with a demo, can be found at: `http://www.cwi.nl/~media/conferences/ISWC2003/`.

2. J. Bateman, J. Kleinz, T. Kamps, and K. Reichenberger. Towards Constructive Text, Diagram, and Layout Generation for Information Presentation. *Computational Linguistics*, 27(3):409–449, September 2001. `http://acl.ldc.upenn.edu/J/J01/`.
3. H. Boley, S. Tabet, and G. Wagner. Design Rationale of RuleML: A Markup Language for Semantic Web Rules. In *Semantic Web Working Symposium (SWWS)*, Stanford University, California, USA, July 30–August 1, 2001. `http://www.semanticweb.org/SWWS/program/full/paper20.pdf`.
4. M. Bordegoni, G. Faconti, M. Maybury, T. Rist, S. Ruggieri, P. Trahanias, and M. Wilson. A Standard Reference Model for Intelligent Multimedia Presentation Systems. *Computer Standards & Interfaces*, 18(6–7):477–496, December 1997. `http://www.dfki.uni-sb.de/imedia/lidos/papers/csi97/`.
5. J. Broekstra, A. Kampman, and F. van Harmelen. Sesame: An Architecture for Storing and Querying RDF Data and Schema Information. In D. Fensel, J. Hendler, H. Lieberman, and W. Wahlster, editors, *Semantics for the WWW*. MIT Press, 2001.
6. J. Broekstra, A. Kampman, and F. van Harmelen. Sesame: A Generic Architecture for Storing and Querying RDF and RDF Schema. In I. Horrocks and J. Hendler, editors, *The Semantic Web – ISWC 2002*, number 2342 in Lecture Notes in Computer Science, pages 54–68, Berlin Heidelberg, 2002. Springer. `link.springer.de/link/service/series/0558/papers/2342/23420054.pdf`.
7. S. Comai and P. Fraternali. A semantic model for specifying data-intensive Web applications using WebML. In *Semantic Web Working Symposium (SWWS)*, Stanford University, California, USA, July 30–August 1, 2001. `http://www.semanticweb.org/SWWS/program/full/paper19.pdf`.
8. Dublin Core Community. Dublin Core Element Set, Version 1.1, 1999. `http://www.dublincore.org/documents/dces/`.
9. K. Falkovych, M. Sabou, and H. Stuckenschmidt. UML for the Semantic Web: Transformation-Based Approaches. In B. Omelayenko and M. Klein, editors, *Knowledge Transformation for the Semantic Web*, pages 92–106. IOS Press, 2003. `http://www.cwi.nl/~media/publications/UML_for_SW.pdf`.
10. M. F. Fernandez, D. Florescu, J. Kang, A. Y. Levy, and D. Suciu. Overview of Strudel – A Web-Site Management System. *Networking and Information Systems Journal*, 1:115–14, 1998. `http://www.cs.wisc.edu/~jaewoo/pubs/NISJ98.pdf`.
11. J. Greimas. *Structural Semantics: An Attempt at a Method.* Lincoln: University of Nebraska Press, 1983.
12. W. Grosso, H. Eriksson, R. Fergerson, J. Gennari, S. Tu, and M. Musen. Knowledge Modeling at the Millennium (The Design and Evolution of Protege-2000). Technical Report SMI Report Number: SMI-1999-0801, Stanford Medical Informatics (SMI), 1999.
13. T. Isakowitz, E. A. Stohr, and P. Balasubramanian. RMM: A Methodology for Structured Hypermedia Design. *Communications of the ACM*, 38(8):34–44, August 1995.
14. G. Karvounarakis, S. Alexaki, V. Christophides, D. Plexousakis, and M. Scholl. RQL: A Declarative Query Language for RDF. In *Proceedings of the Eleventh International World Wide Web Conference (WWW2002)*, pages 592–603, Honolulu, Hawaii, USA, May 2002. ACM Press. `http://139.91.183.30:9090/RDF/publications/www2002/www2002.html`.
15. S. Kim, H. Alani, W. Hall, P. Lewis, D. Millard, N. Shadbolt, and M. Weal. Artequakt: Generating Tailored Biographies with Automatically Annotated Fragments from the Web. Presented at the Semantic Authoring, Annotation and Knowledge Markup (SAAKM) 2002 Workshop at the 15th European Conference on Artificial Intelligence (ECAI 2002), Lyon, France.

16. S. Little, J. Geurts, and J. Hunter. Dynamic Generation of Intelligent Multimedia Presentations through Semantic Inferencing. In *6th European Conference on Research and Advanced Technology for Digital Libraries*, pages 158–189. Springer, September 2002. `http://www.cwi.nl/~media/publications/ecdl2002.pdf`.
17. W. C. Mann, C. M. I. M. Matthiesen, and S. A. Thompson. Rhetorical Structure Theory and Text Analysis. Technical Report ISI/RR-89-242, Information Sciences Institute, University of Southern California, November 1989.
18. B. McBride. Jena: Implementing the RDF Model and Syntax Specification. See `http://www.hpl.hp.com/semweb/`.
19. M. Oldach. *Creativity for Graphic Designers*. North Light Books, Cincinnati, Ohio, 1995.
20. L. Rutledge, M. Alberink, R. Brussee, S. Pokraev, W. van Dieten, and M. Veenstra. Finding the Story – Broader Applicability of Semantics and Discourse for Hypermedia Generation. In *Proceedings of the 14th ACM conference on Hypertext and Hypermedia*, Nottingham, UK, August 26–30, 2003. `http://www.ht03.org/`. To be published.
21. P. Schmitz, J. Yu, and P. Santangeli. Timed Interactive Multimedia Extensions for HTML (HTML+TIME): Extending SMIL into the Web Browser. W3C Note are available at `http://www.w3.org/TR/1998/NOTE-HTMLplusTIME-19980918`, September 1998.
22. S. B. Shum, E. Motta, and J. Domingue. ScholOnto: an Ontology-Based Digital Library Server for Research Documents and Discourse. *International Journal on Digital Libraries*, 3(3), August/September 2000. `http://kmi.open.ac.uk/projects/scholonto/docs/ScholOnto-IJoDL-2000.pdf`
23. J. van Ossenbruggen, J. Geurts, F. Cornelissen, L. Rutledge, and L. Hardman. Towards Second and Third Generation Web-Based Multimedia. In *The Tenth International World Wide Web Conference*, pages 479–488, Hong Kong, May 1–5, 2001. IW3C2, ACM Press. `http://www10.org/cdrom/papers/423/index.html`.
24. J. van Ossenbruggen, J. Geurts, L. Hardman, and L. Rutledge. Towards a Formatting Vocabulary for Time-based Hypermedia. In *The Twelfth International World Wide Web Conference*, pages 384–393, Budapest, Hungary, May 20–24, 2003. IW3C2, ACM Press. `http://www2003.org/cdrom/papers/refereed/p383/p383-ossenbruggen.html`.
25. W3C. Synchronized Multimedia Integration Language (SMIL) 1.0 Specification. W3C Recommendation, June 15, 1998. `http://www.w3.org/TR/1998/REC-smil`. Edited by Philipp Hoschka.
26. W3C. Synchronized Multimedia Integration Language (SMIL 2.0) Specification. W3C Recommendation, August 7, 2001. `http://www.w3.org/TR/smil20`. Edited by Aaron Cohen.
27. R. Williams. *The Non-Designer's Design Book*. Peachpit Press, 1994.

Benchmarking DAML+OIL Repositories

Yuanbo Guo, Jeff Heflin, and Zhengxiang Pan

Department of Computer Science and Engineering, Lehigh University
19 Memorial Drive West, Bethlehem, PA 18015
{yug2,heflin,zhp2}@cse.lehigh.edu

Abstract. We present a benchmark that facilitates the evaluation of DAML+OIL repositories in a standard and systematic way. This benchmark is intended to evaluate the performance of DAML+OIL repositories with respect to extensional queries over a large data set that commits to a single realistic ontology. It consists of the ontology, customizable synthetic data, a set of test queries, and several performance metrics. Main features of the benchmark include a plausible ontology for the university domain, a repeatable data set that can be scaled to an arbitrary size, and an approach for measuring the degree to which a repository returns complete query answers. We also show a benchmark experiment for the evaluation of DLDB, a DAML+OIL repository that extends a relational database management system with description logic inference capabilities.

1 Introduction

DAML+OIL [6], built on RDF and RDF Schema [23] as a markup language for Web resources, is the subject of much research. One important issue in using DAML+OIL is to explore efficient and scalable mechanisms for storing and querying its semantic data. A variety of systems may be used as the repository, for example, relational databases, simple knowledge representation systems, deductive databases, and description logic systems. Furthermore, given a particular style of system such as relational database, numerous schemata are possible [1, 2, 11, 19].

Another issue, which is closely related to the previous one, is to exploit the semantics of DAML+OIL. DAML+OIL extends RDF and RDF Schema with richer modelling primitives and has a clear and well defined semantics [6]. Hence techniques like ontology reasoning could be integrated into the repositories in order to enhance them.

Clearly every approach has its pros and cons. Given so many potential combinations of systems, schemata and techniques for constructing DAML+OIL repositories, there is obviously a need for a standard and systematic way to evaluate those repositories in order to help users to choose an implementation that meets their needs.

This paper presents a first step to meet such a need. We have developed the Lehigh University benchmark (LUBM) to facilitate the evaluation of DAML+OIL repositories. The benchmark consists of a realistic ontology, customizable synthetic test data, a set of test queries, and several performance metrics. In order to use the

D. Fensel et al. (Eds.): ISWC 2003, LNCS 2870, pp. 613–627, 2003.

benchmark, we have also implemented related facilities. We show in the paper how we designed the benchmark and tailored it to the Semantic Web and DAML+OIL. In addition, based on the benchmark, we have successfully conducted an experiment to evaluate DLDB [20], a DAML+OIL repository developed by us, which extends a relational DBMS with description logic inference capabilities.

The rest of the paper is organized as follows: Section 2 details the design of the benchmark and talks about some implementation issues as well. Section 3 presents the aforementioned experiment. Section 4 discusses some related work. Section 5 concludes.

2 The Benchmark

As noted, the goal of the Lehigh University benchmark is to standardize and facilitate the evaluation of repositories for DAML+OIL. It has four major components: a benchmark ontology, benchmark data, test queries, and performance metrics. It also consists of a tool for synthetic data generation. We describe them in the following sections.

2.1 Benchmark Ontology

Recognizing that on the Semantic Web, data will by far outnumber ontologies, we wanted to develop a benchmark for this. Therefore, we chose to generate large amounts of data for a single ontology of moderate size. We aimed for this data to be as realistic as possible.

We have created the Univ-Bench ontology [13] as the benchmark ontology, based on which the benchmark data are generated. The ontology describes universities and departments and the activities that occur at them. It currently contains 43 classes and 32 properties. Its predecessor is the Univ1.0 ontology [12], which has been used to describe DAML data about actual universities and departments. We chose this ontology expecting that its domain would be familiar to most of the benchmark users. In creating the benchmark ontology, we have made some changes to the Univ1.0 ontology mainly to use more DAML+OIL features that are required by the benchmark. For instance, the Univ1.0 ontology states that GraduateStudent is a subclass of Student. In the Univ-Bench ontology, we have replaced that definition with what is shown in Fig. 1, using restriction. As a result, the subclass relationship between the two classes must be inferred using DAML+OIL semantics.

2.2 Benchmark Data

The benchmark data are the DAML+OIL data to be stored to the target repository. We have adopted a method of synthetic data generation. This serves multiple purposes. As with the Wisconsin benchmark [3, 4], a standard and widely used database benchmark, this allows us to control the selectivity and output size of each test query. However, there are some other DAML+OIL specific considerations:

```
<daml:Class ID="GraduateStudent">
   <rdfs:label>graduate student</rdfs:label>
   <daml:subClassOf>
      <rdfs:Class>
         <daml:intersectionOf rdf:parseType="daml:collection">
            <daml:Class rdf:about="#Person" />
            <daml:Restriction>
               <daml:onProperty rdf:resource="#takesCourse" />
               <daml:hasClass>
                  <daml:Class rdf:about="#GraduateCourse" />
               </daml:hasClass>
            </daml:Restriction>
         </daml:intersectionOf>
      </rdfs:Class>
   </daml:subClassOf>
</daml:Class>
<daml:Class ID="Student">
   <rdfs:label>student</rdfs:label>
   <daml:sameClassAs>
      <rdfs:Class>
         <daml:intersectionOf rdf:parseType="daml:collection">
            <daml:Class rdf:about="#Person" />
            <daml:Restriction>
               <daml:onProperty rdf:resource="#takesCourse" />
               <daml:hasClass>
                  <daml:Class rdf:about="#Course" />
               </daml:hasClass>
            </daml:Restriction>
         </daml:intersectionOf>
      </rdfs:Class>
   </daml:sameClassAs>
</daml:Class>
<daml:Class ID="GraduateCourse">
   <rdfs:label>Graduate Level Courses</rdfs:label>
   <rdfs:subClassOf rdf:resource="#Course" />
</daml:Class>
```

Fig. 1. Definition of classes Student and GraduateStudent

1. We would like the benchmark data to be of a range of sizes including considerably large ones. It is hard to find such data sources that are based on the same ontology.
2. We may need the presence of certain kinds of instances in the benchmark data. This allows us to design repeatable tests for as many representative query types as possible. These tests not only evaluate the storage mechanisms for DAML+OIL data but also the techniques that exploit DAML+OIL semantics. We may rely on instances of certain classes and/or properties to test against those techniques.

Data generation is carried out by UBA (Univ-Bench Artificial data generator), a tool we have developed for the benchmark. UBA features random and repeatable generation of DAML+OIL instances. A university is the minimum unit of data generation and for each university, a set of files describing its departments are generated. Instances of both classes and properties are randomly decided. To make the data as realistic as possible, some restrictions are applied based on common sense and domain investigation. Examples are "a minimum of 15 and a maximum of 25 departments in each university", "an undergraduate student/faculty ratio between 8 and 14 inclusively", "each graduate student takes at least 1 but at most 3 courses", and so on and so forth.

UBA identifies universities by assigning them zero-based indexes, e.g., the first university is named University0. Data generated by the tool are exactly repeatable in respect of universities. This is possible because the tool allows the user to enter an initial seed for the random number generator that is used in the data generation process.

UBA makes it possible to systematically produce the benchmark data. We may specify how many and which universities to generate. And information such as the number of instances of each class and property is provided so that we can easily determine how many universities to load to the repository in order to conduct the experiment on data of a specific size. In the benchmark, we choose data sets via looking at the total number of class instances. To help identify the data set, we introduce the following notation:

LUBM(N, S): The data set that contains N's universities beginning at University0 and is generated by the UBA tool starting with seed S.

We use this notation in section 3 when describing the experiment.

2.3 Test Queries

We have constructed thirteen queries for the benchmark, as shown at the end of the section. For each query, we first describe it in natural language and then in a KIF [10] like language, in which a query is written as a conjunction of atoms.[1] Then we analyze the characteristics of the query to show why it has been chosen.

In choosing the queries, first of all, we wanted them to be realistic. Meanwhile, we have mainly taken into account following factors:

1. *Input size.* This is measured as the proportion of the class instances involved in the query to the total class instances in the benchmark data. Here we refer to not just class instances explicitly expressed but also those that are entailed by the knowledge base. We define the input size as large if the proportion is greater than 5%, and small otherwise.
2. *Selectivity.* This is measured as the estimated proportion of the class instances involved in the query that satisfy the query criteria. We regard the selectivity as high if the proportion is lower than 10%, and low otherwise. Generally, we did the estimation based on DAML+OIL semantics, the Univ-Bench ontology, the benchmark data model, and the actual data sets. Whether the selectivity is high or low for a query may depend on the data set used. For instance, the selectivity of Queries 8, 11 and 12 is low if the data set contains only University0 while high if the data set contains more than 10 universities.
3. *Complexity.* We use the number of classes and properties that are involved in the query as an indication of complexity. Since we do not assume any specific implementation of the repository, the real degree of complexity may vary by systems and schemata. For example, in a relational database the number may

[1] As we will show later, the benchmark user is not restricted to use this query language. We use it here for the sake of the subsequent explanation and also because we use it in the experiment.

directly indicate the times of join, which is a significant operation, or may not depending on the schema design.

4. *Hierarchy information assumed.* This considers whether information of class hierarchy or property hierarchy is required to achieve the complete answer. (We define completeness in next section).
5. DAML+OIL inference *assumed.* This considers whether DAML+OIL inference is required to achieve the completeness of the answer. DAML+OIL features used in the test queries include subsumption, i.e., inference of implicit subclass relationship, TransitiveProperty, inverseOf, and realization, i.e., inference of the most specific concepts that an individual is an instance of. One thing to note is that we are not benchmarking complex description logic reasoning. We are concerned with extensional queries. Some queries use simple description logic reasoning mainly to verify that this capability is present.

We have chosen test queries that cover a range of types in terms of the above criteria. At the same time, to the end of performance evaluation, we have emphasized queries with large input and high selectivity. If not otherwise noted, all the test queries are of this type. Some subtler factors have also been considered in designing the queries, such as the depth and width of class hierarchies[2], and the way the classes and properties chain together in the query.

Query1: All the graduate students who take GraduateCourse0 at Department0 of University0.

(type GraduateStudent ?X)
(takesCourse ?X http://www.Department0.University0.edu/GraduateCourse0)

This query bears large input and high selectivity. It is the simplest in the query set: it queries about just one class and one property and does not assume any hierarchy information or DAML+OIL inference.

Query2: All the graduate students who are now studying at the university from which they obtained their bachelor's degrees.

(type GraduateStudent ?X)
(type University ?Y)
(type Department ?Z)
(memberOf ?X ?Z)
(subOrganizationOf ?Z ?Y)
(undergraduateDegreeFrom ?X ?Y)

This query increases in complexity: 3 classes and 3 properties are involved. Additionally, there is a triangular pattern of relationships between the objects involved.

Query3: All the publications of AssistantProfessor0 at Department0 of University0.

(type Publication ?X)
(publicationAuthor ?X
http://www.Department0.University0.edu/AssistantProfessor0)

This query is similar to Query 1 but class Publication has a wide hierarchy.

---

2 We define a class hierarchy as deep if its depth is greater than 3, and as wide if its average branching factor is greater than 3.

Query4: All the professors at Department0 of University0 and their email addresses and telephone numbers

(type Professor ?X)
(worksFor ?X http://www.Department0.University0.edu)
(name ?X ?Y1)
(emailAddress ?X ?Y2)
(telephone ?X ?Y3)

This query has small input and high selectivity. It assumes subClassOf relationship between Professor and its subclasses. Class Professor has a wide hierarchy. Another feature is that it queries about multiple properties of a single class.

Query5: All the members of Department0 of University0.

(type Person ?X)
(memberOf ?X http://www.Department0.University0.edu)

This query assumes subClassOf relationship between Person and its subclasses and subPropertyOf relationship between memberOf and its subproperties. Moreover, class Person features a deep and wide hierarchy.

Query6: All the students

(type Student ?X)

This query concerns only one class, but it assumes both the explicit subClassOf relationship between UndergraduateStudent and Student and the implicit one between GraduateStudent and Student. In addition, this query represents those with large input and low selectivity.

Query7: All the students who take the courses of AssociateProfessor0 at Department0 of University0.

(type Student ?X)
(type Course ?Y)
(teacherOf http://www.Department0.University0.edu/AssociateProfessor0 ?Y)
(takesCourse ?X ?Y)

This query is similar to Query 6 in terms of class Student but it increases in the number of classes and properties and its selectivity is high.

Query8: All the students of University0 and their email addresses.

(type Student ?X)
(type Department ?Y)
(memberOf ?X ?Y)
(subOrganizationOf ?Y http://www.University0.edu)
(emailAddress ?X ?Z)

This query is further more complex than Query 7 by including one more property. And as mentioned, the selectivity of this query and also Queries 11 and 12 depends on the data set.

Query9: All the students who take the courses of their advisors.

(type Student ?X)
(type Faculty ?Y)
(type Course ?Z)
(advisor ?X ?Y)
(takesCourse ?X ?Z)
(teacherOf ?Y ?Z)

Besides the aforementioned features of class Student and the wide hierarchy of class Faculty, this query is characterized by the most classes and properties in the query set. Like Query 2, there is a triangular pattern of relationships.

Query10: All the students who take GraduateCourse0 at Department0 of University0.
(type Student ?X)
(takesCourse ?X http://www.Department0.University0.edu/GraduateCourse0)
This query differs from Queries 6, 7, 8 and 9 in that it only requires the (implicit) subClassOf relationship between GraduateStudent and Student, i.e., subClassOf relationship between UndergraduateStudent and Student does not add to the results.

Query11: All the research groups at University0.
(type ResearchGroup ?X)
(subOrganizationOf ?X http://www.University0.edu)
Queries 11, 12 and 13 are intended to verify the presence of certain DAML+OIL reasoning capabilities in the repository. In this query, property subOrganizationOf is defined as transitive. Since in the benchmark data, instances of ResearchGroup are stated as a sub-organization of a Department individual and the later sub-organization of a University individual, inference about the subOrgnizationOf relationship between instances of ResearchGroup and University is required to answer this query. Additionally, input of this query is small.

Query12: All the department chairs of University0.
(type Chair ?X)
(type Department ?Y)
(worksFor ?X ?Y)
(subOrganizationOf ?Y http://www.University0.edu)
The benchmark data do not produce any instances of class Chair. Instead, each Department individual is linked to the chair professor of that department by property head. Hence this query requires realization, i.e., inference that that professor is an instance of class Chair because he or she is the head of a department. Input of this query is small as well.

Query13: All the alumni of University0.
(type Person ?X)
(hasAlumnus http://www.University0.edu ?X)
Property hasAlumnus is defined in the benchmark ontology as the inverse of property degreeFrom, which has three subproperties:
undergraduateDegreeFrom, mastersDegreeFrom, and doctoralDegreeFrom.
The benchmark data state a person as an alumnus of a university using one of these three subproperties instead of hasAlumnus. Therefore, this query assumes subPropertyOf relationships between degreeFrom and its subproperties, and also requires inference about inverseOf.

2.4 Performance Metrics

We have introduced four performance metrics for the evaluation of DAML+OIL repositories, defined as follows:

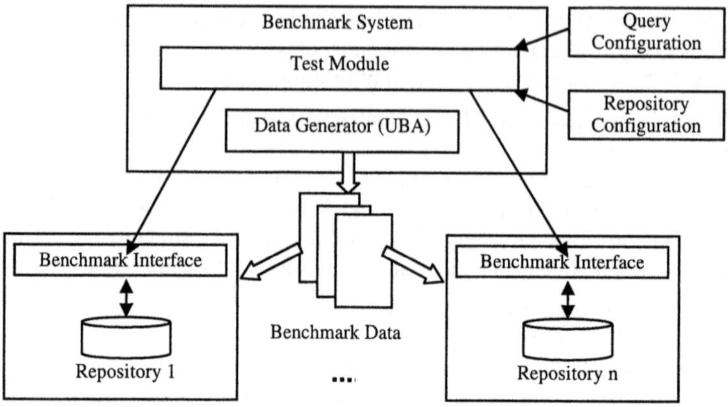

Fig. 2. Architecture of the Benchmark System

1. *Load time.* The stand alone elapsed time for storing the benchmark data to the repository. This also counts the time spent in any processing of the ontology and source files, such as parsing and reasoning.
2. *Repository size.* The consequent size of the repository after loading the specified benchmark data into it.
3. *Query response time.* The stand alone elapsed time of the query. The benchmark measures the time of each query on the target repositories as the following:

   For each target repository:

     For each test query:

       Open the repository.

       Execute the query on the repository consecutively for 10 times and compute the average response time. Each time:

         Issue the query, obtain the pointer to the result set, traverse that set sequentially, and collect the elapsed time.

       Close the repository.
4. *Completeness.* In logic, an inference procedure is complete if it can find a proof for any sentence that is entailed by the knowledge base. With respect to queries, we say a repository is complete if it generates all answers that are entailed by the knowledge base, where each answer is a binding of the query variables that results in an entailed sentence. However, on the Semantic Web, partial answers will often be acceptable. So it is important not to measure completeness with such a coarse distinction. Instead we measure degree of completeness of each query answer as the percentage of the complete results.

Among the above metrics, while the first three are standard (query response time was introduced in the Wisconsin benchmark [3, 4], and load time and repository size have been commonly used in other database benchmarks, e.g., the OO1 benchmark [5]), completeness is a new metric we developed for our benchmark.

2.5 Implementing the Benchmark on a Repository

Fig. 2 depicts the architecture of the benchmark system. The benchmark prescribes an interface to be implemented by each target repository. Through the interface, the benchmark system launches the loading process, requests operations on the repository (e.g. open and close), issues queries and obtains the results.

The benchmark user makes the benchmark system aware of the repositories by declaring them in a repository configuration file. The test queries are materialized via a specific language in a query configuration file. The language used depends on the functionality of the repository and the objective of the benchmarking task. The benchmark system just reads the lines of each query from the configuration file and passes them to each repository.

3 An Experiment Using the Benchmark

3.1 Introduction

DLDB [20] is a repository we have developed for the processing, storing and querying of DAML+OIL data. Its major feature is the extension of a relational database system with description logic inference capabilities. Specifically, DLDB uses Microsoft Access as the DBMS and FaCT [14, 15] as the DAML+OIL reasoner. It uses a database schema in which each class and property has its own table. Furthermore, views are employed to store hierarchy information of classes and properties. The view of each class is the union of its table and the views of all of its subclasses. Views of properties are implemented in a similar way by making use of the subproperty relationship.

The goal of the experiment is to evaluate DLDB and particularly the tradeoff between logical completeness and system performance. To this end, we have created two limited versions of DLDB and compared DLDB to them by using the benchmark. Therefore there are three repositories in the experiment, as follows:

1. *DLDB.* The aforementioned DLDB system.
2. *DLDB with No Reasoner (NR hereafter).* Same as DLDB except that the FaCT reasoning is not applied during loading the benchmark data. Thus the system does not have any implicit class hierarchy information.
3. *Plain.* A further simplified version of NR, wherein views are not used. Therefore the system does not explicitly use hierarchy information for classes or properties.

Test queries were shown in Section 2.3. The aforementioned benchmark interface was implemented in the three repositories respectively. Five different sizes of data sets containing 1, 5, 10, 20 and 50 universities were tested on those repositories. The experiment environment was the following:

Windows XP Professional Operating System;
1.80GHz Pentium 4 CPU;
256MB of RAM; 40GB of Hard Disk;
MS Access 2002 DBMS; JDBC/ODBC

We show the experiment results in next section.

Table 1. Load Time and Repository Sizes

Repository	Data Set	No. of Class Instances	Load Time (hh:mm:ss)	Repository Size (KB)
DLDB	LUBM(1, 0)	17,150	00:06:51	13,042
NR			00:06:46	13,042
Plain			00:06:46	12,943
DLDB	LUBM(5, 0)	107,421	00:42:39	73,925
NR			00:41:57	73,925
Plain			00:41:34	73,794
DLDB	LUBM(10, 0)	218,690	01:27:24	147,948
NR			01:25:32	147,948
Plain			01:26:02	147,816
DLDB	LUBM(20, 0)	462,316	03:06:32	311,099
NR			03:02:41	311,067
Plain			03:04:45	310,936
DLDB	LUBM(50, 0)	1,146,186	07:59:46	766,738
NR			07:49:40	766,738
Plain			07:52:19	766,607

3.2 Results and Analysis

Table 1 lists the time for loading the benchmark data to each repository and the consequent database sizes. To make them more comparable, we measured the database sizes after compacting the databases via using the MS Access database compacting utility, which rearranges how the database file is stored on the disk in order to improve the disk space efficiency.

Even though DLDB spends extra time in ontology reasoning, as displayed in the results there is no significant increase in its load time. This is unsurprising since DLDB only spends a fixed time doing reasoning at the start of loading so that the overhead is trivial and is quickly dominated by the time required to parse and load large amounts of data.

Overall, DLDB and NR have larger database sizes than Plain. This can be ascribed to the space overhead introduced by the use of views and the hierarchy information stored in the former two repositories. However the differences are minor: they are less than 1% for all the data sets. Moreover, it turns out that the overhead is stable as the data set size increases.

Table 2 shows the results of each test query on the three repositories, including the query response time, the number of answers and the answer completeness in percentage.

With respect to the completeness of answers, there are four patterns in the results, as described below. Meanwhile, we analyze the query response time inside each pattern and show some repesentative results via charts in Fig. 3.

1. The three repositories return the same number of answers. This happens when answering the query requires neither hierarchy information nor DAML+OIL inference. Queries 1, 2 and 3 belong to this pattern. As for the response time, the three repositories have close performance for Query 1. But as the chart of Query 2 shows, DLDB and NR takes significant longer time than Plain for the other two queries. This is not hard to understand if we refer to Section 2.3. Class Publication

Table 2. Results of Test Queries

Query	Repository & Data Set / Metrics	LUBM(1, 0) DLDB	LUBM(1, 0) NR	LUBM(1, 0) Plain	LUBM(5, 0) DLDB	LUBM(5, 0) NR	LUBM(5, 0) Plain	LUBM(10, 0) DLDB	LUBM(10, 0) NR	LUBM(10, 0) Plain	LUBM(20, 0) DLDB	LUBM(20, 0) NR	LUBM(20, 0) Plain	LUBM(50, 0) DLDB	LUBM(50, 0) NR	LUBM(50, 0) Plain
1	Time(ms)	32	48	43	200	201	209	396	396	420	881	885	885	2295	2106	2248
	Answers	2	2	2	2	2	2	2	2	2	2	2	2	2	2	2
	Completeness	100	100	100	100	100	100	100	100	100	100	100	100	100	100	100
2	Time(ms)	139	132	20	850	867	142	1823	1871	382	5020	5060	1132	17782	16635	3854
	Answers	0	0	0	9	9	9	28	28	28	59	59	59	130	130	130
	Completeness	100	100	100	100	100	100	100	100	100	100	100	100	100	100	100
3	Time(ms)	168	182	31	2545	2506	115	5535	5518	215	11948	11867	437	35334	35157	1129
	Answers	6	6	6	6	6	6	6	6	6	6	6	6	6	6	6
	Completeness	100	100	100	100	100	100	100	100	100	100	100	100	100	100	100
4	Time(ms)	281	268	7	1996	1981	9	5159	5243	15	12740	12562	21	23100	21440	76
	Answers	34	34	0	34	34	0	34	34	0	34	34	0	34	34	0
	Completeness	100	100	0	100	100	0	100	100	0	100	100	0	100	100	0
5	Time(ms)	270	306	3	2729	3734	3	6348	8639	3	14615	19306	3	44428	56970	3
	Answers	719	719	0	719	719	0	719	719	0	719	719	0	719	719	0
	Completeness	100	100	0	100	100	0	100	100	0	100	100	0	100	100	0
6	Time(ms)	85	50	3	1073	526	4	2332	1075	3	5151	2346	7	14590	6553	7
	Answers	7790	5916	0	48582	36682	0	99566	75547	0	210603	160120	0	519842	393730	0
	Completeness	100	76	0	100	76	0	100	76	0	100	76	0	100	76	0
7	Time(ms)	351	68	17	1398	817	57	3126	1806	120	7082	4087	254	20134	11334	340
	Answers	34	30	0	34	30	0	34	30	0	34	30	0	34	30	0
	Completeness	100	88	0	100	88	0	100	88	0	100	88	0	100	88	0
8	Time(ms)	418	360	25	2843	2139	26	5982	4756	20	14031	11829	34	39250	32120	98
	Answers	7790	5916	0	7790	5916	0	7790	5916	0	7790	5916	0	7790	5916	0
	Completeness	100	76	0	100	76	0	100	76	0	100	76	0	100	76	0
9	Time(ms)	298	239	6	4962	3906	10	11953	8857	18	32948	24845	23	115782	41604	54
	Answers	113	57	0	715	353	0	1345	671	0	2864	1421	0	7368	3587	0
	Completeness	100	50	0	100	49	0	100	50	0	100	50	0	100	49	0
10	Time(ms)	92	48	3	1031	512	3	2264	1073	3	5000	2501	3	14525	6776	11
	Answers	2	0	0	2	0	0	2	0	0	2	0	0	2	0	0
	Completeness	100	0	0	100	0	0	100	0	0	100	0	0	100	0	0
11	Time(ms)	7	7	6	12	12	10	18	21	15	32	23	18	73	59	36
	Answers	0	0	0	0	0	0	0	0	0	0	0	0	0	0	0
	Completeness	0	0	0	0	0	0	0	0	0	0	0	0	0	0	0
12	Time(ms)	14	15	4	37	36	4	67	68	4	262	264	4	600	600	7
	Answers	0	0	0	0	0	0	0	0	0	0	0	0	0	0	0
	Completeness	0	0	0	0	0	0	0	0	0	0	0	0	0	0	0
13	Time(ms)	156	201	3	1792	2882	1	3903	6298	3	9185	14056	4	26846	41360	4
	Answers	0	0	0	0	0	0	0	0	0	0	0	0	0	0	0
	Completeness	0	0	0	0	0	0	0	0	0	0	0	0	0	0	0

in Query 3 has a wide hierarchy, and DLDB and NR are implemented to search all the way along the hierarchy even though that will not add any answers since all publications in the benchmark data are of class Publication. In Query 2, though only memberOf has one subproperty, due to the complexity of the query, i.e., it has five more classes and properties, even extra consideration of just one subproperty in combination with those classes and properties can lead to significant time overhead. In this case, the extra work by DLDB and NR will not add any answers either since all relationships between GraduateStudent and Department in the benchmark data are of property memberOf.

2. DLDB and NR return the same number of answers while Plain returns no answers. Queries 4 and 5 exhibit this pattern, both of which require class hierarchy information. It is not surprising that the former two repositories have much longer response time than Plain. Chart of Query 4 is shown in Fig. 3.

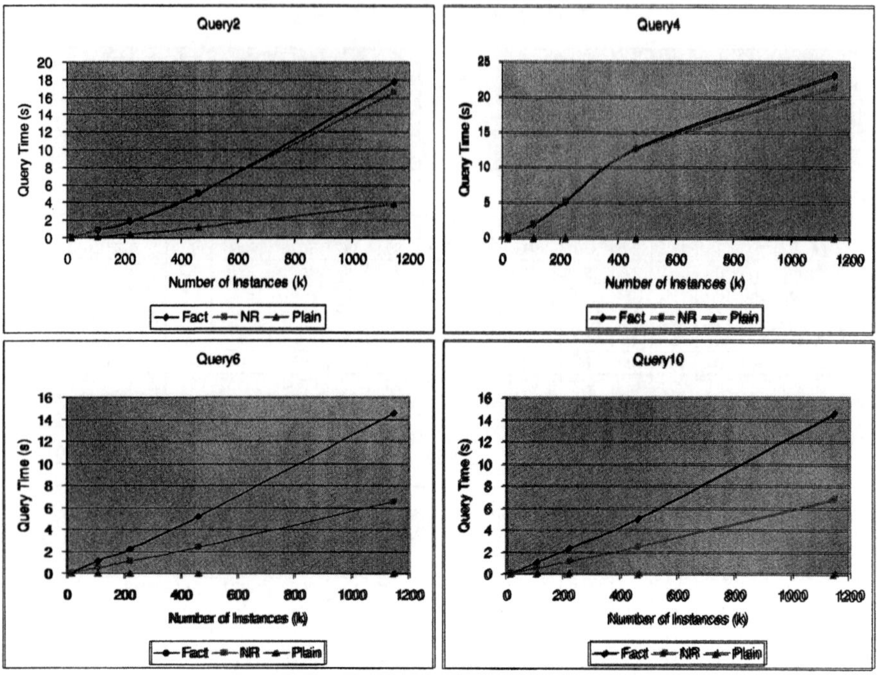

Fig. 3. Response Time for Queries 2, 4, 6 and 10

3. Both DLDB and NR return more than one answer while Plain returns no answers. In addition, DLDB returns more answers than NR. Queries of this kind include Queries 6, 7, 8 and 9. All of them require not only the hierarchy information but also DAML+OIL inference, which causes the difference among the three repositories. Response time for query 6 is shown in Fig. 3. We regard that the longer time DLDB takes than NR can mainly be ascribed to the larger answers it finds and handles.
4. DLDB returns multiple answers while both NR and Plain return no answers. Query 10 is the example, which requires inference capability to find any answer. Query 10's chart appears in Fig. 3. Again it is unsurprising that it costs DLDB longer time to handle more results than the others. In addition, it is notable that NR takes about half as long as DLDB to get no results.
5. None of the repositories is able to return any answers. Those queries include Queries 11, 12 and 13, which, as Section 2.3 shows, require certain DAML+OIL inferences that DLDB's reasoner is currently incapable of.

As far as the primary goal of this experiment is concerned, by the comparision of the three repositories, we see that the storage mechanism and the additional inference capabilities of DLDB have enabled it to achieve a considerably higher degree of the completeness of answers to many queries. Though this has to be traded off with performance mainly represented by the query response time, both for queries that can benifit from it and those that cannot, overall we consider the loss is small enough compared to what could potentially be gained.

More intensive analysis is possible when taking into account other charateristics of the queries that are described in section 2.3. In addition, the experiment results have hinted at some potential subjects. For one example, the curves for the queries as in Fig. 3 are all close to linear, suggesting the repositories are likely to scale. This motivates us to examine the issue with even larger data sets. For another, response time of NR for Queries 5 and 13 is outstandingly longer than that of DLDB, although we regard the two repositories are very similiar with respect to those two queries.[3] Also as shown above, even DLDB is unable to answer some queries with its current inference capability.

4 Related Work

To the best of our knowledge, the benchmark presented herein is the first one for DAML+OIL repositories in the Semantic Web area. There is a research work in benchmarking RDF schemata, which performs statistical analysis about the size and morphology of RDF schemata [18]. However this work does not provide a benchmark for evaluating a repository. [2] has developed some benchmark queries for RDF, however, these are mostly intensional queries, while we are concerned with extensional queries for DAML+OIL.

We have referred to several database benchmarks, including the Wisconsin benchmark [3, 4], the OO1 benchmark [5], and the SEQUOIA 2000 benchmark [22]. They are all DBMS-oriented benchmarks and storage benchmarks (vs. visualization benchmarks). The Lehigh University benchmark shares in spirit with them methodology and rationale in terms of the use of synthetic data, some criteria for choosing the test queries, and all but one of the metrics. However, our benchmark is tailored to the evaluation of DAML+OIL repositories and thus has many unique features. Particularly as shown in the previous sections, the benchmark contains an ontology, data sets, test queries and criteria that reflect special concepts, structures and concerns in the Semantic Web area such as classes and properties, logical completeness vs. system performance, etc. Moreover, our benchmark is intended to work with any DAML+OIL repositories, not just database systems.

Some attempts have been done to benchmark description logic systems [8, 16]. The emphasis of this work is to evaluate the reasoning algorithms in terms of the tradeoff between expressiveness and tractability in description logic. As noted before, our benchmark is not a description logic benchmark. We are more concerned about the issue of storing and querying large amount of data that are created for realistic Semantic Web systems. [8] and [16] test the systems with respect to knowledge bases composed of a Tbox and an Abox, which can essentially be viewed as the counterparts of the ontology and the data set in our benchmark respectively. [16] uses both synthetic and realistic Tboxes and uses a synthetic Abox. But its Abox is predetermined and not scalable. In contrast, our benchmark data are generated randomly and can scale to arbitrary size. [8] generates the Abox randomly. However, unlike our benchmark data, the Abox is not customizable and repeatable. It generates the Tbox randomly while our benchmark is based on a realistic ontology.

---

[3] Our initial investigation suggested that this was due to the difference in the structures of class Person's hierarchies in the two repositories.

Lastly, there exist some query languages for RDF or DAML+OIL such as DQL [9], RQL [17] and TRIPLE [21]. Since none of these has proven dominant, we decided to use a query language that could be easily translated into any of them.

5 Conclusions

In this paper we presented the Lehigh University benchmark. The benchmark is intended to evaluate the performance of DAML+OIL repositories with respect to extensional queries over a large data set that commits to a single realistic ontology. It supports the evaluation of arbitrary repositories. It facilitates the evaluation with synthetically generated data based on the Univ-Bench ontology and allows tests to be conducted on data of arbitrary size. The test queries and performance metrics are designed so that the benchmark could evaluate not only the underlying system and schema but functionalities integrated in the repository such as support for DAML+OIL entailment. Moreover, the benchmark includes a metric for the degree to which a repository returns complete query answers. Consequently, the benchmark could help the user to evaluate different repositories depending on the preference in the tradeoff between logical completeness and system performance. Those interested in obtaining the benchmark and supporting tools should visit http://www.cse.lehigh.edu/~heflin/research/.

Using the benchmark, we have conducted an experiment to evaluate DLDB, a DAML+OIL repository that extends a relational DBMS with description logic inference capabilities. We compared DLDB against two limited versions of it. The experiment showed that the storage mechanism adopted in DLDB plus the inference capabilities added to it could help increase the degree of completeness of query answers. It also showed that there was a tradeoff between the logical completeness and system performance. However the loss in the later appeared to be insignificant in light of the gain in the former. We also expect that the results in this experiment could be used as a baseline for other work on similar systems and schemata.

We intend to explore a number of ideas as future work. First, although designed for DAML+OIL, the benchmark can be easily adapted to OWL [7]. Second, we will use the Lehigh University benchmark to evaluate a variety of Semantic Web repositories with respect to performance and answer completeness. Third, as mentioned, we will examine the scalability of the repositories with even larger data sets. Fourth, we intend to develop another benchmark that includes multiple ontologies and supports ontology integration. Finally, we want to create benchmarks that are based on ontologies with different characteristics.

References

1. R. Agrawal, A. Somani, and Y. Xu. Storage and Querying of E-Commerce Data. In Proc. of VLDB 2001, the 27th International Conference on Very Large Data Bases. 2001.
2. S. Alexaki et al. On Storing Voluminous RDF Description: The case of Web Portal Catalogs. In Proc. of the 4th International Workshop on the Web and Databases (WebDB2001) in conjunction with ACM SIGMOD'01 Conference. 2001.

3. D. Bitton, D. DeWitt, and C. Turbyfill. Benchmarking Database Systems, a Systematic Approach. In Proc. of the 9th International Conference on Very Large Data Bases. 1983.
4. D. Bitton and C. Turbyfill. A Retrospective on the Wisconsin Benchmark. In Readings in Database Systems, Second Edition. 1994.
5. R.G.G.Cattell. An Engineering Database Benchmark. In Readings in Database Systems, Second Edition. 1994.
6. Dan Connolly et al. DAML+OIL (March 2001) Reference Description. http://www.w3.org/TR/daml+oil-reference
7. Mike Dean et al. Web Ontology Language (OWL) Reference Version 1.0. W3C Working Draft 12 November 2002. http://www.w3.org/TR/2002/WD-owl-ref-20021112
8. Quentin Elhaik, M-C Rousset, and Bernard Ycart. Generating Random Benchmarks for Description Logics. In Proceedings of DL'98. 1998.
9. Richard Fikes et al. DAML Query Language (April 2003). http://www.daml.org/2003/04/dql
10. Gensereth M., Fikes R. Knowledge Interchange Format. Stanford Logic Report Logic-92-1, Stanford Univ. http://logic.stanford.edu/kif/kif.html
11. M. Gertz and K. Sattler. A Model and Architecture for Conceptualized Data Annotations. Technical Report, Dept. of Computer Science, University of California, Davis. 2001.
12. Jeff Heflin. Univ1.0 Ontology. http://www.cs.umd.edu/projects/plus/DAML/onts/univ1.0.daml
13. Jeff Heflin and Zhengxiang Pan. Univ-Bench Ontology. http://www.lehigh.edu/~zhp2/univ-bench.daml
14. I. Horrocks. Benchmark Analysis with FaCT. In Proc. of TABLEAUX 2000. 2000.
15. I. Horrocks. The FaCT System. In Automated Reasoning with Analytic Tableaux and Related Methods: International Conference (Tableaux'98). 1998.
16. Horrocks, I. and Patel-Schneider, P. DL systems comparison. In Proceedings of DL'98. 1998.
17. G. Karvounarakis, V. Christophides, D. Plexousakis, and S. Alexaki. Querying Community Web Portals. Technical report, Institute of Computer Science, FORTH, Heraklion, Greece. 2000. http://www.ics.forth.gr/proj/isst/RDF/RQL/rql.pdf
18. A. Magkanaraki et al. Benchmarking RDF schemas for the Semantic Web. In Proc. of First International Semantic Web Conference. 2002.
19. S. Melnik. Storing RDF in a relational database. http://www-db.stanford.edu/~melnik/rdf/db.html
20. Zhengxiang Pan and Jeff Heflin. DLDB: Extending Relational Databases to Support Semantic Web Queries. Submitted to Workshop on Practical and Scaleable Semantic Systems, International Semantic Web Conference 2003.
21. Michael Sintek and Stefan Decker. TRIPLE – A Query, Inference, and Transformation Language for the Semantic Web. In Proc. of First International Semantic Web Conference. 2002.
22. M. Stonebraker et al. The SEQUIOA 2000 Storage Benchmark. In Readings in Database Systems, Second Edition. 1994.
23. World Wide Web Consortium. Resource Description Framework (RDF). http://www.w3.org/RDF/

DAMLJessKB: A Tool for Reasoning with the Semantic Web

Joseph B. Kopena and William C. Regli*

Geometric and Intelligent Computing Laboratory
Department of Computer Science
College of Engineering, Drexel University
3141 Chestnut Street
Philadelphia, PA, 19104
regli@drexel.edu
http://gicl.mcs.drexel.edu/

Abstract. We describe DAMLJessKB, a tool for reasoning with the DARPA Agent Markup Language (DAML) and performing inference on the Semantic Web. DAMLJessKB maps DAML's semantics into facts and rules for use in a production system, such as the Java Expert System Shell (Jess). This article presents our underlying methodology and provides a detailed example of how DAMLJessKB can be used to make decisions about DAML-encoded engineering design knowledge. We believe that tools like DAMLJessKB are needed to help realize the full potential of the Semantic Web and DAML.

1 Introduction

DAMLJessKB is a tool for reasoning with the Semantic Web. It is a description logic reasoner for performing inference with the DARPA Agent Markup Language (DAML). This is accomplished by using a production system to carry out the automated inferences entailed by the semantics of the DAML, Resource Description Framework Schema (RDF-S), and XML Schema: Datatypes (XSD) specifications. We show how DAMLJessKB can be used to implement the reasoning necessary to build Semantic Web applications and provide an example from the domain of engineering design.

The Semantic Web is a vision of the next generation World Wide Web, where all content is both machine and human interpretable. Currently, the Web is largely a presentation medium intended for human users [1,2]. While much of the existing work has focused on representation and semantics, DAMLJessKB addresses how to use these representations for making inferences. The representations and semantics for our current DAMLJessKB are based on the RDF W3C REC-rdf-syntax-19990222 proposed standard [3]. To define information structure, we use the proposed RDF-S standard CR-rdf-schema-20000327 [4] to create the basic relationships between classes of objects and properties. In addition, the proposed XSD standard REC-xmlschema-2-20010502 [5] is used to manipulate and reason on literal data (i.e., integer and floating point numbers, etc.) and define new classes of literal values. Lastly, DAML builds a description

* Also with the Department of Mechanical Engineering and Mechanics.

D. Fensel et al. (Eds.): ISWC 2003, LNCS 2870, pp. 628–643, 2003.

logic language on top of RDF-S and XSD where statements are expressed using RDF. DAMLJessKB currently uses the March 2001 DAML+OIL specification [6]. Using this language, the structure of complex information can be described through relationships between classes and properties of objects while maintaining tractable reasoning.

Creating Semantic Web applications requires applying the semantics of these languages to make decisions based on the entailments of their formal definitions. DAMLJessKB utilizes the Java Expert System Shell (Jess) [7] developed at Sandia National Laboratories to carry out this reasoning. Jess and DAMLJessKB are Java-based and well suited for incorporation into applications, applets, and servlets. Presently, DAMLJessKB is being employed in a number of research projects. Users and applications include: Penn State University's Industrial Engineering Department (product/process ontologies), UMBC's Agents group (information retrieval) [8], Coca Cola (enterprise integration), SRI, and Lockheed Martin's Advanced Technology Laboratories.

This article describes the development and use of DAMLJessKB in Semantic Web applications. The following section discusses and motivates some of the possible inferences and the role of such a reasoning capability in Semantic Web software. Then, we briefly describe related work and give an description of the DAMLJessKB tool. Finally, we present some prototype applications of this tool and some conclusions.

2 Motivation

DAML is a formal knowledge representation language, enabling the ability to perform automated inference with DAML-encoded knowledge. The formal semantics for DAML [9,10] can either be used directly, such as incorporating the axioms into a general theorem prover, or indirectly, such as in DAMLJessKB. With these formal semantics there is a precise correct interpretation of the standards, so we can characterize non-standard assumptions we make, prove the correctness of our reasoning, etc.

One class of automated inference this enables is the ability to perform basic consistency checking on input documents. This relates to many people making use of DAML as a schema-type language. This is useful, as XML DTDs, Schema, etc. are focused on the syntactic structure of the document. DAML allows you to impose a structure on information modeled in RDF. This frees you from having to worry about the particulars of how your document is transcribed, and lets you worry about the information present.

However, such automated inference can be used in more general, more powerful ways. For example, it can be used for knowledge translation as well as application-specific tasks. Translation comes from determining relationships between classes, properties, etc. Application tasks come from being able to perform reasoning on input information to do such things as determine relationships between classes and properties. This could also be used in translation, if there was an underlying base ontology.

Application Scenario: Engineering Design. Consider the problem of managing repositories of engineering designs, such as shown in Figure 1. Every design includes CAD data (i.e., the mechanical assembly model, joints, features, tolerances, etc), design intent and rationale, and documents describing the intended function and behavior of the artifact. Large engineering enterprises may have huge knowledge-bases of current and past

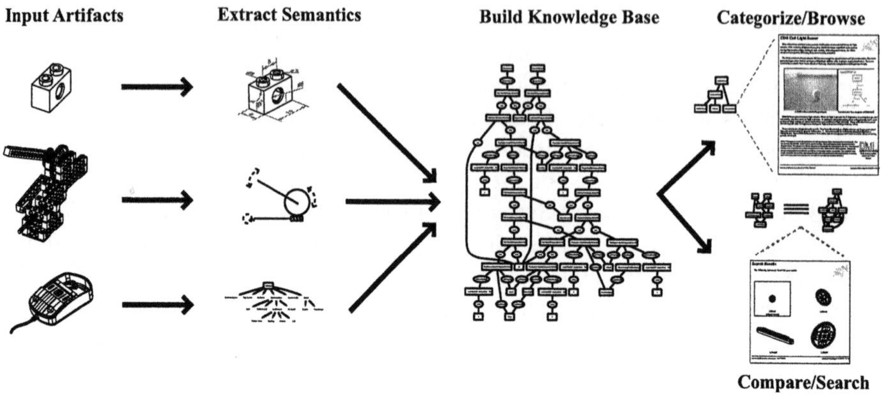

Fig. 1. Overview: Using DAMLJessKB to reason with engineering data

product information that engineers must interrogate throughout the product lifecycle. For example:

- Searching engineering repositories [11] to find models for use in variational design. Variational design is the task of adapting old designs to solve new requirements. This would require being able to make inferences about device behavior and function.
- Analyzing design and manufacturing data across different domains. This would require the specification of and inference with shared ontologies that capture the engineering or manufacturing semantics of a class of artifacts.
- Maintaining existing products, which requires being able to make inferences about stored design knowledge and design rationale.

It is our belief that DAML and similar languages could be the basis of new knowledge interchange standards that go beyond the current STEP standard for product data exchange (ISO 10303) [12]. Answering questions like those above requires more than the shared syntax of STEP. DAML-based representations that capture designs, parts and assemblies, tolerances, features, etc could form the basis of new representations that can be used in conjunction with automatic tools for inference and knowledge discovery. We show a detailed example of this sort of application in Section 6.

3 Related Work

In order to correctly input information modeled in DAML, applications need to implement the semantics of the language. This also enables the application to make use of the inferences entailed by those semantics in its own reasoning process. In this section we review work in providing reasoning for DAML and other Semantic Web languages.

Description Logic Reasoners. DAML has been designed as a description logic (DL) language with a syntax suitable for being embedded in Web documents. Other efforts at providing inference tools for the Semantic Web have built translators to existing DL reasoners, such as FaCT [13]. Compared to such efforts, DAMLJessKB attempts to support a broader set of relevant languages, including XSD, RDF-S, and DAML+OIL. DAMLJessKB's Java-based implementation also allows for easier incorporation into Java-based applications than many current DL systems. Notably, this provides a Semantic Web inference tool for use in applets, servlets, and Java-enabled embedded devices such as cell phones and PDAs. In addition, as opposed to most current DL implementations, DAMLJessKB does not draw a clear boundary between instances and terminologies in the knowledge base. More discussion on DAML and DAMLJessKB's support for reasoning on classes of classes is presented in Section 4.

A prominent distinction between DL reasoners and DAMLJessKB is that nearly all of the former make an open world assumption while the latter's use of an underlying production system entails a closed world assumption. We return to this issue in Section 4. DAMLJessKB's implementation approach does cost in terms of computational complexity as compared to results for basic description logics. However, reasoners supporting all of the DAML elements, such as `equivalentTo` and `TransitiveProperty`, will also suffer as compared to these results. In our experience, the expressiveness of the underlying production system has been sufficient for implementing the semantics of these languages in a closed world interpretation. We believe this to be demonstrable through the intersection of the subsets of first order logic corresponding to classes of description logics and production systems but present no analysis in this article.

Non-DL Reasoners. A variety of Semantic Web projects have taken an approach similar to DAMLJessKB of translating DAML semantics and content into forms suitable for use in non-description logic reasoners such as general first order theorem provers and production systems. A reasonably complete list of such efforts is presented at `http://www.daml.org/reasoning/`. Compared to DAMLJessKB, most of the efforts based on production systems have not attempted to implement as large a portion of the DAML semantics. Typically, they incorporate little terminological reasoning and support for the more expressive DAML elements. Few support XML Schema Datatypes. General first order theorem proving approaches often incorporate most of the more expressive DAML statements but not support for datatypes as many theorem provers are ill suited for reasoning on literal values. Such packages are subject to complexity results for the theorem prover, as well as the difficult problem often encountered in practice of tuning the system to control the search/search space and produce acceptable runtimes. Additonally, nearly all theorem provers operate under an open world assumption, an issue to which we will return in Section 4.

Programmatic Tools. Many initial and current Semantic Web-related applications and demonstrations simply operate on the XML structure of input data, or construct APIs based on an object-oriented view of RDF data. In these cases, any ontology developed for the application is misused as a schema for the XML data, or as a specification similar to class definitions in object-oriented programming languages, ignoring most of the semantics. Such approaches are, of course, limited in their ability to operate with other applications and data sources as they will only be able to process a small set of valid input documents. Constructing APIs for DAML will either suffer the same problem through ignoring most of the semantics or will effectively implement a description logic reasoner. In either case, when the semantics are ignored, the application suffers through limitations

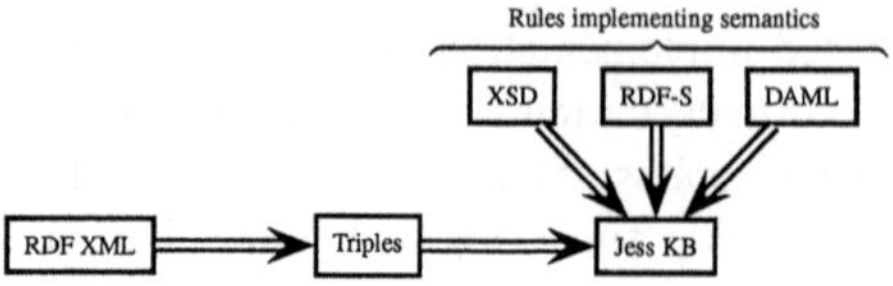

(a) Overview of DAMLJessKB process

```
<rdfs:Class rdf:about="#Artifact" />

<rdfs:Class rdf:about="#Part">
  <rdfs:subClassOf rdf:resource="#Artifact"/>
</rdfs:Class>

<eng:Part rdf:about="#Cog17" />
```

(b) RDF snippet in XML form

```
( (rdf:type eng:Artifact rdfs:Class)
(rdf:type eng:Part rdfs:Class)
(rdfs:subClassOf eng:Part eng:Artifact)
(rdf:type ex:Cog17 eng:Part) )
```

(c) Corresponding triple model

```
∀a, b, i (rdfs:subClassOf a b)
∧ (rdf:type i a)
⊃ (rdf:type i b)
```

(d) Rule implied by RDF-S semantics

```
( (rdf:type eng:Artifact rdfs:Class)
(rdf:type eng:Part rdfs:Class)
(rdfs:subClassOf eng:Part eng:Artifact)
(rdf:type ex:Cog17 eng:Part)
(rdf:type ex:Cog17 eng:Artifact) )
```

(e) Model derived from facts and rule

Fig. 2. The basic approach of DAMLJessKB.

on its ability to make interesting inferences, and consequently on its ability to accept valid inputs. DAMLJessKB avoids these problems by providing for such inferences. We see as one of its strengths the ability to add value to even simple Semantic Web applications by providing an easy to use DAML inference tool coupled with the excellent application building features of the underlying production system.

4 Approach

The DAMLJessKB mapping is illustrated in Figure 2. One of the basic properties of RDF is that no matter how complex its XML form, the underlying model can be seen simply as a list of triples. Each triple asserts a relation between a subject and an object through a predicate. DAMLJessKB maps these into facts in a production system.

Procedure. Given an XML source document (Figure 2(b)), an RDF parser generates a stream of triples (Figure 2(c)). These triples are asserted into the production system and rules derived from the semantics of the language are applied (Figure 2(d)) to populate the knowledge base with the additional facts which can be entailed from the input (Figure 2(e)). Additional methods are then invoked to carry out extra-logical aspects of the languages, such as loading ontologies from `daml:imports` statements, as well as tasks such as ontology debugging through looking for valid but probably unintended inputs.

The advantage of this approach is that information extracted and inferred from input documents is immediately available for use in the underlying production sytem. Such

```
<daml:Class rdf:about="#Piece" />

<daml:Class rdf:about="#Class">
 <daml:intersectionOf
   rdf:parseType="daml:collection">
  <rdfs:Class rdf:about="&daml;#Class" />
  <daml:Restriction>
   <daml:onProperty
     rdf:resource="&daml;#subClassOf" />
   <daml:hasValue rdf:resource="#Piece" />
  </daml:Restriction>
 </daml:intersectionOf>
</daml:Class>

<lego:Class rdf:about="#Brick" />

<daml:Class rdf:about="#Gear">
 <daml:subClassOf rdf:resource="#Piece" />
</daml:Class>

<lego:Brick rdf:about="#MyBrick" />
```

(a) A class of classes in DAML.

```
( (rdf:type lego:Brick daml:Class)
(rdfs:subClassOf lego:Brick lego:Piece)
(rdf:type lego:Gear lego:Class)
(rdf:type lego:MyBrick lego:Piece) )
```

(b) Relevant portion of corresponding inferred model.

Fig. 3. Example demonstrating a TBox/ABox intersection in DAML

systems are commonly used in knowledge-based applications and represent a powerful programming paradigm. DAMLJessKB allows developers to easily interwork the semantics of the input languages with their own application-specific reasoning.

Another advantage of this approach, as compared to many description logic implementations, is that it makes no distinction between the terminology of the ontologies being used and any instance data loaded. There is no "TBox/ABox" boundary in the description logic sense [14]. The syntax and semantics of RDF-S and DAML fully permit such reasoning—in fact, the language definitions make use of this sort of reasoning, for example in declaring `daml:Class` a subclass of `rdfs:Class`. A more complex example of reasoning on classes of classes is presented in Figure 3. In this example, DAMLJessKB correctly infers all entailments because terminological items are not treated specially, except that RDF-S and DAML symbols are present in the rulebase.

DAMLJessKB differs from most Semantic Web reasoners, which are built on description logic and general theorem provers, in that, by using a production system, it assumes a closed world (i.e., if a fact does not exist it is assumed to be false). This is in contrast to the RDF-S and DAML standards, which specify an open world assumption (i.e., all facts have to be proven either true or false). DAMLJessKB's closed world assumption has both positives and negatives. On the negative side, it makes some inferences suspect as they do not follow the exact semantics of the languages. On the positive side, closed world is often a reasonable assumption in practice: one can ask and answer many practical questions under the assumption that knowledge-bases used with DAMLJessKB will include all required data for making the needed inferences. If data is "unknown", the external application using DAMLJessKB can find out its value and assert if it is true or false. Indeed, we believe many real-world Semantic Web applications will need to make similar assumptions, albeit perhaps in different forms such as mechanically asserting closure axioms as a pre-reasoning step in reading input data—even if these are non-standard assumptions with respect to the language semantics. Indeed, closed world assumptions may prove necessary to enable wide acceptance and utility for Semantic Web applications.

5 Implementation

DAMLJessKB uses ARP ("Another RDF Parser") to load and parse XML documents containing RDF. ARP is part of the Jena toolkit [1] for parsing RDF documents, actively developed and supported by Hewlett Packard Labs. Amongst several available RDF parsers for Java, ARP was chosen because of its speed and support for DAML collection syntax. Unlike most parsers, ARP simply produces a stream of RDF triples from input triples. Other packages then make use of this stream, for example in the larger Jena package by constructing a graph model of the triples. This is ideal for use in DAMLJessKB as the only functionality required of the RDF parser is the generation of triples to be asserted into the production system. ARP supports `rdf:parseType="daml:collection"` syntactic constructs by creating the corresponding `daml:List` object and feeding it into the stream of triples.

As noted previously, DAMLJessKB uses Jess ("Java Expert System Shell") as its inference engine. Jess is actively developed and supported by Sandia National Laboratories. In many respects it can be seen as a Java version of CLIPS [15], the widely used C Language Interface Production System originally developed by NASA. The two share roughly the same architecture, expressiveness, and scripting capabilities. Jess was chosen over several other Java-based production systems because of its active development and support, tight interaction with Java programs, scripting language, and expressiveness. The Jess rule language includes elements not present in many other production systems, such as negation and arbitrary combinations of boolean conjunctions and disjunctions. We have found it necessary to use such capabilities in DAMLJessKB, for example using negation and conjunction in a rule to implement a form of universal quantification. Jess provides for excellent application development opportunities through utilizing features of the Java language and runtime environment to enable easy-to-use and powerful interaction with external programs. Its scripting language is also powerful enough to generate full applications entirely within the Jess system.

DAMLJessKB acts as a facade for the Jess object containing the knowledge base. The facade's primary purpose is to supply an interface for loading RDF documents into Jess and automatically applying RDF/RDF-S/XSD/DAML+OIL semantics. It also provides access to the knowledge base as if it were a normal Jess object while supplying additional general utility functionality, such as loading Jess files from Java archives (`jar` files) and alternate interfaces to the Jess query mechanism. The following subsections explain the process outlined in Section 4 in more detail.

5.1 Translation from Arp to Jess

Triples produced by ARP are collected and asserted into Jess. As the triples are collected, some simple manipulations on the stream are performed to handle syntactic translation, anonymous nodes, and datatypes. Most basic of these manipulations is translating URIs into valid Jess symbols by removing invalid characters. For example, tildes are replaced with an escape code. DAMLJessKB also inserts the dummy predicate `PropertyValue`

[1] Available at `http://www.hpl.hp.com/semweb/`

```
<daml:Datatype rdf:about="#AtLeast4">
  <xsd:minInclusive>
    <xsd:integer rdf:value="4" />
  </xsd:minInclusive>
</daml:Datatype>

<daml:Datatype rdf:about="#AtLeast6">
  <xsd:minInclusive>
    <xsd:integer rdf:value="6" />
  </xsd:minInclusive>
</daml:Datatype>
```

(a) Sample datatype definitions.

```
<lego:Brick rdf:about="#Brick1">
  <lego:length>12</lego:length>
</lego:Brick>

<lego:Brick rdf:about="#Brick2">
  <lego:length rdf:value="2" />
</lego:Brick>

<lego:Brick rdf:about="#Brick3">
  <lego:length><xsd:Integer rdf:value="8" />
  </lego:length>
</lego:Brick>
```

(b) Sample literal values.

Fig. 4. Example datatype definitions and literal values

in front of each triple, similar to the axiomatic DAML semantics [9]. This is necessary to enable variables and quantification on relations.

Anonymous objects present in the RDF XML are skolemized using a unique identifier generated by ARP. In addition, the unary predicate `anonymous` is asserted for each skolem symbol. In theory this could be used to incorporate some amount of reasoning about the existential nature of these nodes, as per the RDF specification. This marking has also proven useful in practice for doing such things as determining the relative importance of the object to the ontology designer or input source. For example, in generating class diagrams anonymous classes can be removed to reduce clutter as they are typically simply a means to the end of describing another class.

DAMLJessKB also looks for literal values as it collects triples and only allows them as objects of `rdf:value` statements. If they are encountered in other relations, a new `daml:Datatype` object is created and placed as the object of the statement. A new triple is then generated and incorporated into the stream stating that the `rdf:value` of the new datatype object is the literal which it replaced. This ensures a consistent `daml:Datatype` encapsulation for each literal without placing special demands on input ontologies or data. In addition, these literals remain compliant to the RDF and DAML standards such that triples containing literals can be reserialized from DAMLJessKB and used as input to another system. With literals treated in this consistent fashion it is possible to write rules implementing semantics for these datatype objects as well as other DAML elements containing literals, such as cardinality restrictions.

5.2 XML Schema Datatype Semantics

DAMLJessKB contains provisions for reasoning on literal values, implementing a form of `daml:Datatype` objects. These are based on Part Two of the XML Schema standard [5], Datatypes, using a non-standard RDF adaptation of XSD datatype definitions. Figure 4(a) shows some typical datatype definitions of this form while Figure 4(b) demonstrates some basic literal value syntax.

Figure 5(a) contains a rule for classifying literals as members of datatypes. From Figure 4(b), which shows CAD models for two Lego bricks, this rule will determine that `Brick3` and `Brick1` both have lengths of `AtLeast6` and `AtLeast4` in accordance with the two datatype definitions, as well as standard classes such as `xsd:positiveInteger`.

DAMLJessKB views datatypes as a class and therefore permits them to be used much as other classes might. For example, they can be combined through boolean oper-

```
(defrule mininclusive-classification
 (PropertyValue
  http://www.w3.org/1999/02/22-rdf-syntax-ns#type
  ?dt http://www.daml.org/2001/03/daml+oil#Datatype)
 (PropertyValue
  http://www.w3.org/2000/10/XMLSchema#minInclusive
  ?dt ?anon)
 (PropertyValue
  http://www.w3.org/1999/02/22-rdf-syntax-ns#value
  ?anon ?value)

 (PropertyValue
  http://www.w3.org/1999/02/22-rdf-syntax-ns#type
  ?inst
  http://www.w3.org/1999/02/22-rdf-syntax-ns#Literal)
 (PropertyValue
  http://www.w3.org/1999/02/22-rdf-syntax-ns#value
  ?inst ?ival)
 (test (and (integerp ?ival) (integerp ?value)
   (>= ?ival ?value)))

=> (assert
 (PropertyValue
  http://www.w3.org/1999/02/22-rdf-syntax-ns#type
  ?inst ?dt)))
```

(a) Sample rule for classifying literals

```
(defrule mininclusive-subclassing
  (PropertyValue
   http://www.w3.org/1999/02/22-rdf-syntax-ns#type
   ?dt1 http://www.daml.org/2001/03/daml+oil#Datatype)
  (PropertyValue
   http://www.w3.org/2000/10/XMLSchema#minInclusive
   ?dt1 ?anon1)
  (PropertyValue
   http://www.w3.org/1999/02/22-rdf-syntax-ns#value
   ?anon1 ?value1)

  (PropertyValue
   http://www.w3.org/1999/02/22-rdf-syntax-ns#type
   ?dt2&~?dt1
   http://www.daml.org/2001/03/daml+oil#Datatype)
  (PropertyValue
   http://www.w3.org/2000/10/XMLSchema#minInclusive
   ?dt2 ?anon2)
  (PropertyValue
   http://www.w3.org/1999/02/22-rdf-syntax-ns#value
   ?anon2 ?value2)

  (test (and (integerp ?value1) (integerp ?value2)
    (>= ?value1 ?value2)))
=>
  (assert (PropertyValue
    http://www.w3.org/2000/01/rdf-schema#subClassOf
    ?dt1 ?dt2)))
```

(b) Sample rule for terminological reasoning on datatypes

Fig. 5. Examples of DAMLJessKB's treatment of literals and datatypes

```
(defrule subclass-instances
  (PropertyValue
    http://www.w3.org/2000/01/rdf-schema#subClassOf
    ?child ?parent)
  (PropertyValue
    http://www.w3.org/1999/02/22-rdf-syntax-ns#type
    ?instance ?child)
=>
 (assert
  (PropertyValue
    http://www.w3.org/1999/02/22-rdf-syntax-ns#type
    ?instance ?parent)))
```

(a) Rule implementing basic notion of subclassing.

```
(defrule rdfs-domain
  (declare (salience -100))
  (PropertyValue
    http://www.w3.org/2000/01/rdf-schema#domain
    ?p ?c)
  (PropertyValue ?p ?i ?o)
  (not (PropertyValue
    http://www.w3.org/1999/02/22-rdf-syntax-ns#type
    ?i ?c))
=>
  (assert (PropertyValue
    http://www.w3.org/1999/02/22-rdf-syntax-ns#type
    ?i ?c))
  (gentle-warning "Set object '" ?i "' type to '" ?c
    "' due to a domain restriction on '" ?p "'"))
```

(b) One rule corresponding to semantics of `rdfs:domain`.

Fig. 6. Examples of DAMLJessKB's instance reasoning

ations to create new classes. In addition, special subsumption relationships are defined based on the particular semantics of the datatypes. This is very similar to the use of `daml:Restriction` classes, discussed later. Figure 5(b) demonstrates a rule implementing subsumption between `minInclusive` constraints. Given the two definitions in Figure 4(a), this rule will assert that `AtLeast6` is a subclass of `AtLeast4`.

5.3 Instance Data Reasoning

The set of rules implementing DAMLJessKB's reasoning can be roughly seen as falling into two categories. One concerns reasoning on instances of classes. The second concerns terminological reasoning, determining relationships between the classes themselves. This is roughly analogous to ABox and TBox reasoning in description logic systems.

Two examples have already been shown in regards to XSD semantics. The rule shown in Figure 5(a) can be seen as falling into the former, determining the relationships between instances and classes. Figure 5(b) contains a rule which corresponds to the latter category of rules, determining relationships between classes.

One of the most basic elements of the RDF-S and DAML languages are the `rdfs:subClassOf` and `daml:subClassOf` statements, which are defined to be equivalent. These properties are used to specify a subclass relationship between two classes. One of the intuitive notions of this relation is that any instance of a subclass is an instance of the parent class. Figure 6(a) implements this portion of the semantics of the relation, a very basic inference to perform on instances. Despite its simplicity, even this basic inference is extremely useful in practice and adds a great of capability to any application reading in data encoded according to a DAML or RDF-S ontology. For example, this rule provides for inferring that an object explicitly stated to be of a class in a taxonomy is also an instance of all the ancestors of that class.

One of the benefits of having formal semantics for DAML is that interpretations and assumptions of the language elements can be identified, characterized, and validated. Such assumptions can often be seen in practice, especially when the language is used by developers more accustomed to traditional programming than knowledge representation. A small but interesting example of this concerns `rdfs:domain` statements.

This property is used to assign a domain to another property, specifying the constraint that only instances of the domain class may have values for this property. Nearly all programmers are familiar with type-checking and this constraint is easily interpreted as a form of this. Many would make the assumption, based on their familiarity with traditional programming languages, that if an object has been asserted to have a value for such a constrained property but is not a member of the domain, then there is an error.

However, the actual inference in such a situation is that if an object, not otherwise of the domain, has been explicitly asserted to have a value for the constrained property, then it is indeed a member of the domain. Figure 6(b) contains a rule corresponding to this inference entailed by the semantics of the `rdfs:domain` property. The rule implements the actual semantics of the language element, however, recognizing that there is a common assumption about this property it also generates a warning. This warning indicates that such a situation exists and provides for some use of the domain constraint as a basic consistency checking device.

We note that such inconsistencies are formally characterizable using DAML. For example, if an instance of a class was found to have a value for a property constrained to a domain disjoint with the class, an actual inconsistency would be raised because the object would be a member of two mutually exclusive classes. However, at least currently, many DAML ontologies are not defined formally and exhaustively enough to contain such information. Many DAML ontologies contain an assumption on the part of the developers that classes are disjoint unless stated or reasoned to be otherwise. Therefore, some special actions such as the warning generated by the rule in Figure 6(b) are warranted in practice to help identify such assumptions.

```
<daml:Class rdf:about="#RobotLabMotor">
 <daml:intersectionOf
  rdf:parseType="daml:collection">
   <daml:Class rdf:about="&lego;#Piece" />
   <daml:Class rdf:about="&artifact;#Motor" />
   <daml:Class rdf:about="&robotlab;#KitItem" />
 </daml:intersectionOf>
</daml:Class>
```

(a) DAML snippet defining an intersection of classes

```
(defrule intersection-of-subsumption
 (declare (salience -50))

 (PropertyValue
  http://www.daml.org/2001/03/daml+oil#intersectionOf
  ?topClass ?topList)
 (PropertyValue
  http://www.daml.org/2001/03/daml+oil#intersectionOf
  ?botClass&~?topClass ?botList)

 (not (and (list-item ?topList ?y)
  (not (or (list-item ?botList ?y)
   (and (list-item ?botList ?x)
    (PropertyValue
     http://www.w3.org/2000/01/rdf-schema#subClassOf
     ?x ?y))))))

=>
  (assert (PropertyValue
    http://www.daml.org/2001/03/daml+oil#subClassOf
    ?botClass ?topClass)))
```

(b) Rule implementing subsumption of class intersections

```
<daml:Restriction>
  <daml:onProperty rdf:resource="#input" />
  <daml:cardinalityQ rdf:value="1" />
  <daml:hasClassQ
    rdf:resource="&flow;#ElectricalFlow" />
</daml:Restriction>
```

(c) DAML snippet defining a cardinality constraint

```
(defrule mincardinalityq-subsumption
  (PropertyValue
    http://www.w3.org/1999/02/22-rdf-syntax-ns#type
    ?restriction1
    http://www.daml.org/2001/03/daml+oil#Restriction)
  (PropertyValue
    http://www.daml.org/2001/03/daml+oil#onProperty
    ?restriction1 ?prop1)
  (PropertyValue
    http://www.daml.org/2001/03/daml+oil#minCardinalityQ
    ?restriction1 ?lit1)
  (PropertyValue
    http://www.daml.org/2001/03/daml+oil#hasClassQ
    ?restriction1 ?class1)
  (PropertyValue
    http://www.w3.org/1999/02/22-rdf-syntax-ns#value
    ?lit1 ?val1)

  (PropertyValue
    http://www.w3.org/1999/02/22-rdf-syntax-ns#type
    ?restriction2&~?restriction1
    http://www.daml.org/2001/03/daml+oil#Restriction)
  (PropertyValue
    http://www.daml.org/2001/03/daml+oil#onProperty
    ?restriction2 ?prop2)
  (or (PropertyValue
    http://www.daml.org/2001/03/daml+oil#minCardinalityQ
    ?restriction2 ?lit2)
    (PropertyValue
      http://www.daml.org/2001/03/daml+oil#cardinalityQ
      ?restriction2 ?lit2))
  (PropertyValue
    http://www.daml.org/2001/03/daml+oil#hasClassQ
    ?restriction2 ?class2)
  (PropertyValue
    http://www.w3.org/1999/02/22-rdf-syntax-ns#value
    ?lit2 ?val2)

  (test (and (integerp ?val1) (integerp ?val2)
    (>= ?val2 ?val1)))
  (or (test (eq ?class2 ?class1))
    (PropertyValue
      http://www.w3.org/2000/01/rdf-schema#subClassOf
      ?class2 ?class1))
=>
  (assert (PropertyValue
    http://www.daml.org/2001/03/daml+oil#subClassOf
    ?restriction2 ?restriction1)))
```

(d) Rule implementing subsumption between cardinality restrictions

Fig. 7. Examples of DAMLJessKB's terminological reasoning

5.4 Terminological Reasoning

Utilizing the full power of the Semantic Web requires inference on the relationships between classes—terminological reasoning. Through the semantics of description logic, objects and classes can be automatically compared, contrasted, and otherwise reasoned on. In order to do so the classes of objects present in the ontology have to be defined using a description logic language, in this case DAML.

One of the most commmon elements in such descriptions is the definition of a class as the intersection of a set of classes—conjunction. Figure 7(a) contains a snippet using the `daml:intersectionOf` class expression to define such an intersection. In the snippet, the class `RobotLabMotor` is declared as consisting of those objects which are members of the classes `lego:Piece`, `artifact:Motor`, and `robotlab:KitItem`, which are either primitive terms or defined elsewhere.

A very common terminological inference is subsumption between such intersections. Figure 7(b) shows an element of DAMLJessKB's implementation of such reasoning. The rule determines subclass relationships between intersections of classes by implementing structural subsumption on classes consisting solely of such intersections. Intuitively, the rule implements the idea that a class composed of the intersection of a set of classes is a subclass of a class composed of the intersection of a subset of those classes or subclasses of those classes. In the case where the two intersections are equivalent, each class will be asserted as a subclass of the other. Note that for convenience the set of classes in the intersection are held in a closed world list form which corresponds to the open world `daml:List` object actually created by the RDF parser.

Another common descriptive element is to declare the cardinality of properties for classes of objects. DAML contains several mechanisms for asserting such constraints. Figure 7(c) demonstrates an anoymous class declared to be subject to the constraint that it has one value for the `input` property of type `flow:ElectricalFlow`, although instances of this class may have other values of other types for that property. `daml:Restriction` objects are DAML classes associated with various types of constraints, including cardinality and type qualification. These are expressed through properties such as `daml:cardinalityQ` to indicate a qualified cardinality and `daml:onProperty` which declares the property on which the restriction is being placed.

Figure 7(d) shows a rule implementing subsumption reasoning between qualified cardinality restrictions. This corresponds to the intuitive notion that a class declared to have more fillers for a given property of a given class is a subclass of of a class declared to have less fillers for the given property of the same class or a super-class of the type qualification. The inferences provided by the semantics for these cardinality restrictions and class intersections will be used extensively in the examples presented in Section 6.

6 Using DAMLJessKB

This section gives two basic demonstrations of DAMLJessKB. The first is a simple example of a tool which would be crippled without being able to reason on DAML semantics. Closer to the actual application areas in which we are working, the second example shows a variational engineering design problem to which we hope to apply DAML and the Semantic Web.

Simple Example: Inferring Subclasses. Tools for creating Semantic Web content require reasoning capabilities just as applications do. Whether authoring ontologies or modeling information, reasoning is necessary to fully support the user with such tasks as consistency checking, graphical displays, and navigation. This is why ontology authoring environments such as Ontolingua and Protegé incorporate reasoning mechanisms. DAMLJessKB is well positioned to enable such reasoning for even small tools. Such tools include ontology markup cross referencers, class graphers, and basic information extracters. A number of these tools have been developed for DAML and a list is maintained at `http://www.daml.org/tools/`. However, many of these tools include no or very simplistic reasoning and therefore can not accept many valid inputs or produce inaccurate results. DAMLJessKB provides one option for easily incorporating Semantic Web reasoning into such tools.

```
(defquery direct-subclasses
  (PropertyValue
    http://www.daml.org/2001/03/daml+oil#subClassOf
    ?y&~:(guess-standard ?y)
    ?x&~?y&~:(guess-standard ?x))
  (not (anonymous ?y)) (not (anonymous ?x))

  (not (and
    (PropertyValue
      http://www.daml.org/2001/03/daml+oil#subClassOf
      ?y ?z&~?x&~?y)
    (PropertyValue
      http://www.daml.org/2001/03/daml+oil#subClassOf
      ?z ?x)
    (not (or (anonymous ?z)
      (PropertyValue
        http://www.daml.org/2001/03/daml+oil#subClassOf
        ?z ?y)))))
)

(printout t "digraph g {" crlf crlf
  "node [shape=box,fontname=Helvetica,fontsize=10];"
  crlf "edge [dir=back];" crlf crlf)

(bind ?res (run-query direct-subclasses))
(while (call ?res hasNext)
  (bind ?triple (call (call (call ?res next) fact 1)
    get 0))
  (bind ?obj (nth$ 3 ?triple))
  (bind ?subj (nth$ 2 ?triple))

  (printout t "    " (guess-name ?obj) " -> "
    (guess-name ?subj) ";" crlf))

(printout t crlf "}" crlf)
```

(a) Jess program generating graph for `dot`

```
<daml:Class rdf:about="&func;#Function">
  <daml:disjointWith rdf:resource="&flow;#Flow" />
  <daml:disjointWith rdf:resource="&artifact;#Artifact" />
</daml:Class>

<daml:Class rdf:about="&func;#Convert">
  <daml:subClassOf rdf:resource="&func;#Function" />
  <daml:disjointWith rdf:resource="&func;#Branch" />
  <daml:disjointWith rdf:resource="&func;#Channel" />
  <daml:disjointWith rdf:resource="&func;#Connect" />
  <daml:disjointWith
    rdf:resource="&func;#ControlMagnitude" />
  <daml:disjointWith rdf:resource="&func;#Provision" />
  <daml:disjointWith rdf:resource="&func;#Signal" />
  <daml:disjointWith rdf:resource="&func;#Support" />
</daml:Class>

<daml:Class rdf:about="&func;#MotorFunction">
  <daml:intersectionOf rdf:parseType="daml:collection">
    <daml:Class rdf:about="&func;#Convert" />
    <daml:Restriction>
      <daml:onProperty rdf:resource="#input" />
      <daml:toClass
        rdf:resource="&flow;#ElectricalFlow" />
    </daml:Restriction>
    <daml:Restriction>
      <daml:onProperty rdf:resource="#output" />
      <daml:toClass rdf:resource="&flow;#Rotation" />
    </daml:Restriction>
  </daml:intersectionOf>
</daml:Class>

<daml:Class rdf:about="&func;#RobotLabActuatorFunction">
  <daml:subClassOf rdf:resource="&func;#Function" />
  <daml:unionOf rdf:parseType="daml:collection">
    <daml:Class rdf:about="&func;#MotorFunction" />
    <daml:Class rdf:about="&func;#SolenoidFunction" />
  </daml:unionOf>
</daml:Class>
```

(b) Snippet from an input ontology

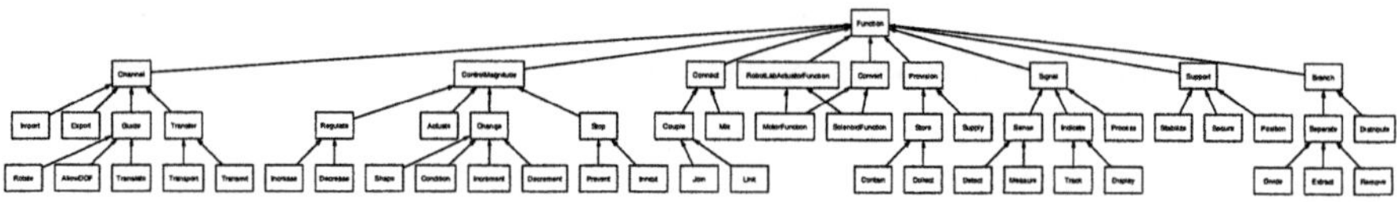

(c) Generated graph

Fig. 8. Simple application to generate subclass graph

For example, generating subclass graphs is a very simple capability which can greatly aid ontology authors and readers. Several programs and web services exist to generate such graphs, however most operate solely on explicit RDFS or DAML `subClassOf` statements. In order to accurately display all the subclass relationships and accept all valid ontology inputs (including such examples as that in Figure 3), the tool must be able to reason on the inputs. Figure 8 shows a simple version of such a tool which utilizes DAMLJessKB. Figure 8(a) contains a small program in Jess' scripting language for generating the subclass graph by generating output suitable for use with `dot`, an automatic graph layout tool[2]. The core of the program is a query for all the subclass relationships which have been inferred. Figure 8(b) contains a small portion of an input ontology and Figure 8(c) the generated graph.

[2] Available at `http://www.research.att.com/sw/tools/graphviz/`

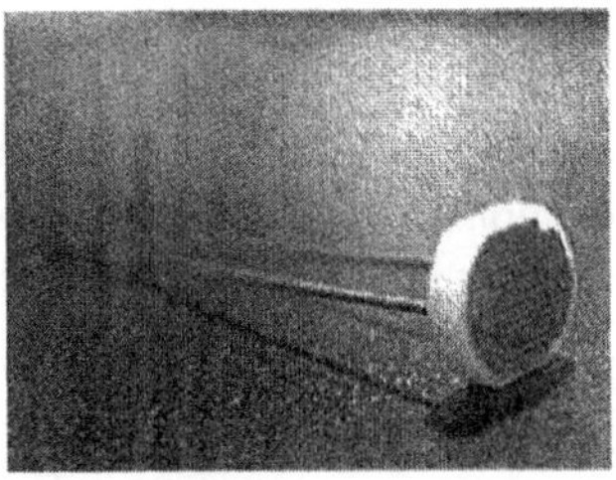

(a) A Cadmium Sulfide (CDS) cell

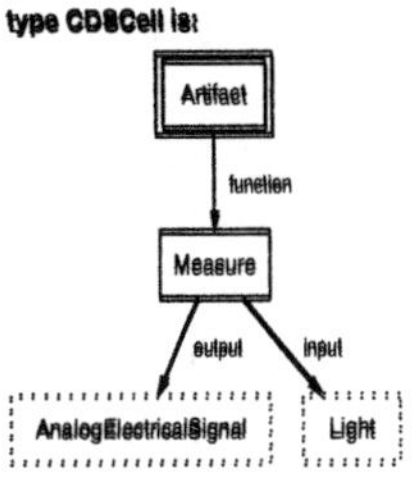

(b) CDS cell function and flow diagram

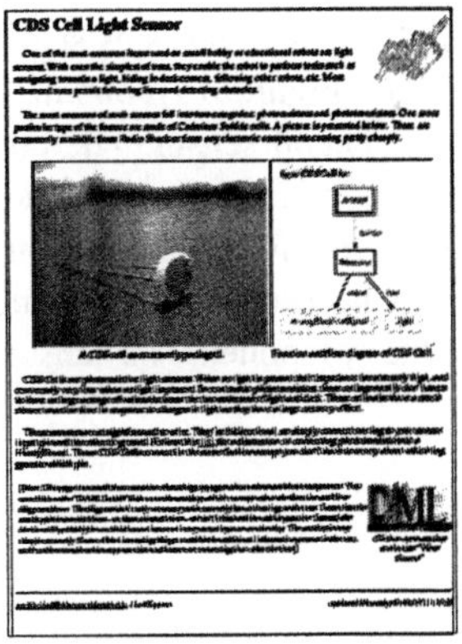

(c) Webpage for CDS cell

```
<daml:Class rdf:about="#Sensor">
 <daml:intersectionOf
   rdf:parseType="daml:collection">
  <daml:Class rdf:about="&eng;#Artifact" />

  <daml:Restriction>
   <daml:onProperty rdf:resource="&eng;#function"/>
   <daml:minCardinalityQ rdf:value="1" />

   <daml:hasClassQ>
    <daml:Class>
     <daml:intersectionOf
       rdf:parseType="daml:collection">
      <daml:Class rdf:about="&func;#Measure" />

      <daml:Restriction>
       <daml:onProperty
         rdf:resource="&eng;#output" />
       <daml:minCardinalityQ rdf:value="1" />
       <daml:hasClassQ
         rdf:resource="&flow;#MeasureSignal" />
      </daml:Restriction>

      <daml:Restriction>
       <daml:onProperty rdf:resource="&eng;#input"/>
       <daml:minCardinalityQ rdf:value="1" />
       <daml:hasClassQ rdf:resource="&flow;#Flow"/>
      </daml:Restriction>

     </daml:intersectionOf>
    </daml:Class>
   </daml:hasClassQ>
  </daml:Restriction>
 </daml:intersectionOf>
</daml:Class>
```

(d) DAML description of sensor class

Fig. 9. Artifact function and flow modeling and a comparison of two assembly models

Real-World Application: Variational Engineering Design. As outlined in Section 2, we are interested in reasoning about electromechanical assemblies and components. This includes tasks such as determining if an artifact performs a given function and searching for artifacts in design repositories to find similarities.

Consider the problem of designing LEGO robots, such as with the very popular Lego Mindstorms robot kits[3]. Figure 9(a) shows a typical light sensor component used in Lego robot kits; Figure 9(b) shows an engineering function and flow diagram [16,17] for this component. Function and flow diagrams provide an abstract representation of an assembly, its components and their intended behavior. This diagram notes that the sensor measures an input light source and outputs an electrical signal as the measure. However,

[3] http://mindstorms.lego.com/

function-flow models are typically lacking in formal semantics. Therefore we cannot automate such tasks as comparing these diagrams or searching large online repositories for functional patterns.

We have developed a formalization of these represenations by attributing description logic semantics to the diagrams. For example, the function and flow representation of the CDS sensor presented in Figure 9(b) can be mechanically interpreted as corresponding to the following description logic statement:

$$\text{CDSCell} \equiv (\text{Artifact} \wedge \exists \text{function}.(\text{Measure} \wedge \exists \text{output.AnalogElectricalSignal} \wedge \exists \text{input.Light})).$$

The use of DAML as the description logic language enables us to embed these formal representations into Web content or into an XML-based database schema. Figure 9(c) shows a web page used to provide information about these sensors to students in an introductory robotics class at Drexel University. By including DAML markup of such function and flow diagrams in Web pages we can perform such tasks as searching for components to perform specific functions. To illustrate this, Figure 9(d) contains a DAML version of a similar function and flow diagram for a general sensor. The component described by the webpage in Figure 9(c) can be compared to this class by loading both into the DAMLJessKB knowledge base and querying for relationships between the two. In this case the component is correctly incorporated into the terminology as a subclass of the general sensor; the software has determined that the component is a sensor without that information being explicitly stated.

7 Conclusions

Practical tools are needed for the vision of the Semantic Web to become fully realized. This paper introduced DAMLJessKB, which the authors believe is one such tool. With DAMLJessKB, users can perform inference based on semantics of the description logic which forms the basis of DAML. As more and more websites, network services, databases, and knowledge-bases look to DAML as a de facto representation syntax, DAMLJessKB will become one in a suite of tools that allow users to truly leverage the new-found shared semantics. In this way, we are hoping to contribute toward full reasoning with the Semantic Web.

DAMLJessKB is being actively used in a number of academic and government research projects. We have made DAMLJessKB publicly available under the GNU General Public License at
`http://edge.mcs.drexel.edu/assemblies/software/damljesskb/`.
We hope that this article broadens interest in DAMLJessKB and helps to create and grow a community of users who are working to improve it.

Acknowledgements. This work was supported in part by National Science Foundation (NSF) Knowledge and Distributed Intelligence in the Information Age (KDI) Initiative Grant CISE/IIS-9873005; Office of Naval Research Grant N00014-01-1-0618 and the National Institute of Standards and Technology (NIST) Grant 70-NAN-B2H0029. Any opinions, findings, and conclusions or recommendations expressed in this material are those of the author(s) and do not necessarily reflect the views of the National Science Foundation, Office of Naval Research, or other supporting organizations.

References

1. Berners-Lee, T., Hendler, J., Lassila, O.: The semantic web. Scientific American (2001)
2. Hendler, J.: Agents and the semantic web. IEEE Intelligent Systems (2001)
3. W3C: Resource Description Framework (RDF) model and syntax specification. http://www.w3.org/TR/1999/REC-rdf-syntax-19990222/ (1999)
4. W3C: Resource Description Framework Schema Specification (RDF-S). http://www.w3c.org/TR/2000/CR-rdf-schema-20000327/ (2000)
5. World Wide Web Consortium: XML Schema Part 2: Datatypes (XSD). http://www.w3.org/TR/xmlschema-2/ (2001)
6. DARPA: DAML march 2001 specifications (DAML+OIL). http://www.daml.org/2001/03/daml+oil-index (2001)
7. Friedman-Hill, E.: Jess: The rule engine for the Java platform. herzberg.ca.sandia.gov/jess/ (1995)
8. Shah, U., Finin, T., Joshi, A., Mayfield, J., Cost, R.: Information retrieval on the semantic web. In: ACM Conference on Information and Knowledge Management. (2002)
9. Fikes, R., McGuinness, D.L.: An axiomatic semantics for RDF, RDF Schema, and DAML+OIL. Technical Report KSL-01-01, Knowledge Systems Laboratory, Stanford University (2001)
10. van Harmelen, F., Patel-Schneider, P.F., Horrocks, I.: A model-theoretic semantics for DAML+OIL. http://www.daml.org/2001/03/model-theoretic-semantics (2001)
11. Szykman, S., Bochenek, C., Racz, J.W., Senfaute, J., Sriram, R.D.: Design repositories: Engineering design's new knowledge base. IEEE Intelligent Systems **15** (2000) 48–55
12. Szykman, S., Sriram, R.D., Regli, W.C.: The role of knowledge in next-generation product development systems. ASME Transactions, the Journal of Computer and Information Science in Engineering **1** (2001) 3–11
13. Horrocks, I.: The FaCT system. http://www.cs.man.ac.uk/~horrocks/FaCT/ (1999)
14. Baader, F., Calvanese, D., McGuinness, D., Nardi, D., Patel-Schneider, P., eds.: The Description Logic Handbook. Cambridge University Press (2002)
15. NASA: Clips: A tool for building expert systems. http://www.ghgcorp.com/clips/CLIPS.html (2002)
16. Szykman, S., Racz, J.W., Sriram, R.D.: The representation of function in computer-based design. In: ASME Design Engineering Technical Conferences, 11th International Conference on Design Theory and Methodology, New York, NY, USA, ASME, ASME Press (1999) DETC99/DTM-8742.
17. Pahl, G., Beitz, W.: Engineering Design – A Systematic Approach. 2nd edn. Springer, London, UK (1996)

Prolog-Based Infrastructure for RDF: Scalability and Performance

Jan Wielemaker[1], Guus Schreiber[2], and Bob Wielinga[1]

[1] University of Amsterdam
Social Science Informatics (SWI)
Roetersstraat 15, 1018 WB Amsterdam, The Netherlands
{jan,wielinga}@swi.psy.uva.nl
[2] Vrije Universiteit Amsterdam
Department of Computer Science
De Boelelaan 1081a, 1081 HV Amsterdam, The Netherlands
schreiber@cs.vu.nl

Abstract. The semantic web is a promising application-area for the Prolog programming language for its non-determinism and pattern-matching. In this paper we outline an infrastructure for loading and saving RDF/XML, storing triples, elementary reasoning with triples and visualization. A predecessor of the infrastructure described here has been used in various applications for ontology-based annotation of multimedia objects using semantic web languages. Our library aims at fast parsing, fast access and scalability for fairly large but not unbounded applications upto 40 million triples.
The RDF parser is distributed with SWI-Prolog under the LGPL Free Software licence. The other components will be added to the distribution as they become stable and documented.

1 Introduction

Semantic-web applications will require multiple large ontologies for indexing and querying. In this paper we describe an infrastructure for handling such large ontologies, This work was done on the context of a project on ontology-based annotation of multi-media objects to improve annotations and querying [13], for which we use the semantic-web languages RDF and RDFS. The annotations use a series of existing ontologies, including AAT [10], WordNet [8] and ULAN [14]. To facilitate this research we require an RDF toolkit capable of handling approximately 3 million triples efficiently on current desktop hardware. This paper describes the parser, storage and basic query interface for this Prolog-based RDF infrastructure. A practical overview using an older version of this infrastructure is in an XML.com article [9].

We have opted for a purely memory-based infrastructure for optimal speed. Our tool set can handle the 3 million triple target with approximately 300 Mb. of memory and scales to approximately 40 million triples on fully equipped 32-bit hardware. Although insufficient to represent "the whole web", we assume 40

D. Fensel et al. (Eds.): ISWC 2003, LNCS 2870, pp. 644–658, 2003.

million triples is sufficient for applications operating in a restricted domain such as annotations for a set of cultural-heritage collections.

This document is organised as follows. In Sect. 2 we describe and evaluate the Prolog-based RDF/XML parser. Section 3 discusses the requirements and candidate choices for a triple storage format. In Sect. 4 we describe the chosen storage method and the basic query engine. In Sect. 5 we describe the API and implementation for RDFS reasoning support. This section also illustrates the mechanism for expressing higher level queries. Section 7 describes visualisation tools to examine the contents of the database. Finally, Sect. 8 describes some related work.

Throughout the document we present metrics on time and memory resources required by our toolkit. Unless specified otherwise these are collected on a dual AMD 1600+ (approx. Pentium-IV 1600) machine with 2GB memory running SuSE Linux 8.1, gcc 3.2 and multi-threaded SWI-Prolog 5.1.11.[1] The software is widely portable to other platforms, including most Unix dialects, MS-Windows and MacOS X. Timing tests are executed on our reference data consisting of 1.5 million triples from WordNet, AAT and ULAN.

2 Parsing RDF/XML

The RDF/XML parser is the oldest component of the system. We started our own parser because the existing (1999) Java (SiRPAC[2]) and Pro Solutions Perl-based[3] parsers did not provide the performance required and we did not wish to enlarge the footprint and complicate the system by introducing Java or Perl components. The RDF/XML parser translates the output of the SWI-Prolog SGML/XML parser[4] into a Prolog list of triples using the steps summarised in Fig. 1. We illustrate these steps using an example from the RDF Syntax Specification document [5], which is translated by the SWI-Prolog XML parser into a Prolog term as described in Fig. 2.

We wanted our parser from the XML parse-tree to triples to reflect as closely as possible the RDF Syntax Specification to improve maintainability and simplify the implementation. The first parser-step uses a variation of DCG (Definite Clause Grammar), each ruleset translating a production from the Syntax Specification. Figure 3 shows part of the rules for *Production parseTypeCollectionPropertyElt*[5] into a Prolog term **collection**(*Elements*), where *Elements* holds an intermediate representation for the collection-elements. The body of the rules guiding this process consists of the term that must be matched, optionally followed by raw Prolog code between {...}, similar to DCG. The matched term can call rule-sets to translate a sub-term using a \ escape-sequence. In Fig. 3, the first rule (propertyElt) matches a term **element**(*Name, Attributes, Content*), iff

[1] `http://www.swi-prolog.org`

[2] `http://www-db.stanford.edu/~melnik/rdf/api.html`

[3] `http://www.pro-solutions.com/rdfdemo/`

[4] `http://www.swi-prolog.org/packages/sgml2pl.html`

[5] `http://www.w3.org/TR/rdf-syntax-grammar/#parseTypeCollectionPropertyElt`

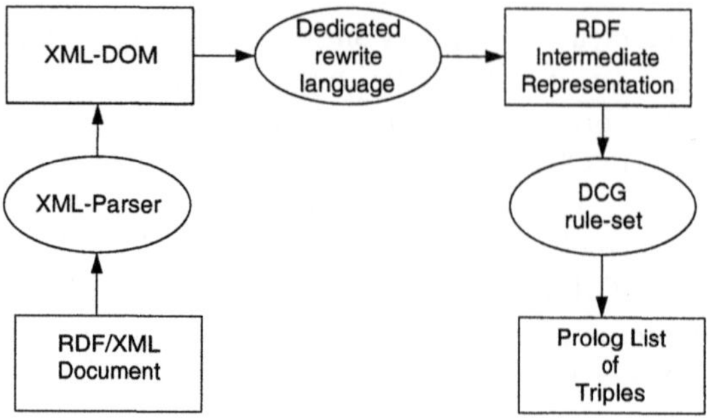

Fig. 1. Steps converting an RDF/XML document into a Prolog list of triples.

```
<rdf:RDF xmlns:rdf="http://www.w3.org/1999/02/22-rdf-syntax-ns#"
         xmlns:s="http://description.org/schema/">
  <rdf:Description about="http://www.w3.org/Home/Lassila">
     <s:Creator>Ora Lassila</s:Creator>
  </rdf:Description>
</rdf:RDF>
```

```
[ element('http://www.w3.org/1999/02/22-rdf-syntax-ns#':'RDF',
          [ xmlns:rdf = 'http://www.w3.org/1999/02/22-rdf-syntax-ns#',
            xmlns:s = 'http://description.org/schema/'
          ],
          [ element('http://www.w3.org/1999/02/22-rdf-syntax-ns#':'Description',
                    [ about = 'http://www.w3.org/Home/Lassila'
                    ],
                    [ element('http://description.org/schema/':'Creator',
                              [],
                              [ 'Ora Lassila'
                              ])
                    ])
          ])
]
```

Fig. 2. Input RDF/XML document and output of the Prolog XML Parser, illustrating the input for the RDF parser

Attributes matches the attribute specification and *Content* can be matched by the `nodeElementList` rule-set. The final step uses traditional DCG to translate the intermediate structure into a flat list of triples.

In the last phase the intermediate terms (e.g. **collection**(*Elements*) above) is translated into a list of triples using DCG rules.

Long documents cannot be handled this way as both the entire XML structure and the resulting list of RDF triples must fit on the Prolog stacks. To avoid this problem the XML parser can be operated in *streaming* mode and based on this mode the RDF parser handles RDF-Descriptions one-by-one, passing the resulting triples to a user-supplied Prolog goal.

```
propertyElt(Id, Name, collection(Elements), Base) ::=
        element(Name,
                \attrs([ \parseCollection,
                         \?idAttr(Id, Base)
                       ]),
                \nodeElementList(Elements, Base)).

parseCollection ::=
        \rdf_or_unqualified(parseType) = 'Collection'.

rdf_or_unqualified(Tag) ::=
        Tag.
rdf_or_unqualified(Tag) ::=
        NS:Tag,
        { rdf_name_space(NS), !
        }.
```

Fig. 3. Source code of the first phase, mapping the XML-DOM structure into a term derived from the RDF syntax specification. This fragment handles the `parseType=Collection` element

2.1 Metrics and Evaluation

The source-code of the parser is 1170 lines, 564 for the first pass creating the intermediate state, 341 for the generating the triples and 265 for the driver putting it all together. The time to parse the WordNet sources are given in Tab. 1.

The parser passes the W3C RDF Test Cases[6]. In the current implementation however it does not handle the `xml:lang` tag nor RDF typed literals using `rdf:datatype`.

Table 1. Statistics loading WordNet

File	Size (Kb)	Time (sec)	Triples	Triples/Sec.
wordnet-20000620.rdfs	3	0.00	37	–
wordnet_glossary-20010201.rdf	14,806	10.64	99,642	9,365
wordnet_hyponyms-20010201.rdf	8,064	10.22	78,445	7,676
wordnet_nouns-20010201.rdf	9,659	13.84	273,644	19,772
wordnet_similar-20010201.rdf	1,763	2.36	21,858	9,262
Total	34,295	37.06	473,626	12,780

[6] `http://www.w3.org/TR/2003/WD-rdf-testcases-20030123/`

3 Storing RDF Triples: Requirements and Alternatives

3.1 Requirement from Integrating Different Ontology Representations

Working with multiple ontologies created by different people and/or organizations poses some specific requirements for storing and retrieving RDF triples. We illustrate with an example from our own work on annotating images [12].

Given absence of official RDF versions of AAT and IconClass we created our own RDF representation, in which the concept hierarchy is modeled as an RDFS class hierarchy. We wanted to use these ontologies in combination with the RDF representation of WordNet created by Decker and Melnik[7]. However, their RDF Schema for WordNet defines classes and properties for the metamodel of WordNet. This means that WordNet *synsets* (the basic WordNet concepts) are represented as instances of the (meta)class `LexicalConcept` and that the WordNet hyponym relations (the subclass relations in WordNet) are represented as tuples of the metaproperty `hyponymOf` relation between instances of `wns:LexicalConcept`. This leads to a representational mismatch, as we are now unable to treat WordNet concepts as classes and WordNet hyponym relations as subclass relations.

Fortunately, RDFS provides metamodelling primitives for coping with this. Consider the following two RDF descriptions:

```
<rdf:Description rdf:about="&wns;LexicalConcept">
  <rdfs:subClassOf rdf:resource="&rdfs;Class"/>
</rdf:Description>

<rdf:Description rdf:about="&wns;hyponymOf">
  <rdfs:subPropertyOf rdf:resource="&rdfs;subClassOf"/>
</rdf:Description>
```

The first statement specifies that the class `LexicalConcept` is a subclass of the built-in RDFS metaclass `Class`, the instances of which are classes. This means that now all instances of `LexicalConcept` are also classes. In a similar vein, the second statement defines that the WordNet property `hyponymOf` is a subproperty of the RDFS subclass-of relation. This enables us to interpret the instances of `hyponymOf` as subclass links.

We expect representational mismatches to occur frequently in any realistic semantic-web setting. RDF mechanisms similar to the ones above can be employed to handle this. However, this poses the requirement on the toolkit that the infrastructure is able to interpret subtypes of `rdfs:Class` and `rdfs:subPropertyOf`. In particular the latter was important for our applications, e.g., to be able to reason with WordNet hyponym relations as subclass relations or to visualize WordNet as a class hierarchy (cf. Fig. 9).

---

[7] `http://www.semanticweb.org/library/`

3.2 Requirements

Based on experiences we stated the following requirements for the RDF storage formate.

Efficient subPropertyOf handling. As illustrated in Sect. 3.1, ontology-based annotation requires the re-use of multiple external ontologies. The `subPropertyOf` relation provides an ideal mechanism to re-interpret an existing RDF dataset.

Avoid frequent cache updates. In our first prototype we used secondary store based on the RDFS data model to speedup RDFS queries. The mapping from triples to this model is not suitable for incremental update, resulting in frequent slow re-computation of the derived model from the triples as the triple set changes.

Scalability. We anticipate the use of at least AAT, WordNet and ULAN in the next generation annotation tools. Together these require 1.5 million triples in their current form. We would like to be able to handle 3 million triples on a state-of-the-art notebook (512 MB).

Fast load/save. RDF/XML parsing and loading time for the above ontologies is 108 seconds. This should be reduced using an internal format.

3.3 Storage Options

The most natural way to store RDF triples is using facts of the format **rdf**(*Subject, Predicate, Object*) and this is, except for a thin wrapper improving namespace handling, the representation used in our first prototype. As standard Prolog systems only provide indexing on the first argument this implies that asking for properties of a subject is indexed, but asking about inverse relations is slow. Many queries involve reverse relations: "what are the sub-classes of X?". "what instances does Y have?", "what subjects have label L?" are queries commonly used on our annotation tool.

Our first tool solved these problems by building a secondary database following the RDFS datamodel. The cached relations included **rdfs_class**(*Class, Super, Meta*). **rdfs_property**(*Class, Property, Facet*), **rdf_instance**(*Resource, Class*) and **rdfs_label**(*Resource, Label*). These relations can be accessed quickly in any direction. This approach has a number of drawbacks. First of all, the implications of even adding or deleting a single triple are potentially enormous, leaving the choice between complicated incremental synchronisation of the cache with the triple set or frequent slow total recompute of the cache. Second, storing the cache requires considerable memory resources and third there are many more relations that could profit from caching.

Using an external DBMS for the triple store is an alternative. Assuming some SQL database, there are three possible designs. The simplest one is to use Prolog reasoning and simple `SELECT` statements to query the DB. This approach does not exploit query optimization and causes many requests involving large amounts of data. Alternatively, one could either write a mixture of Prolog and SQL or automate part of this process, as covered by the Prolog to SQL converter of Draxler [3]. Our own (unpublished) experiences indicate a simple database query is at best 100 and in practice often over 1,000 times slower than using the internal Prolog database. Query optimization is likely to be of limited effect due to poor handling of transitive relations in SQL. Many queries involve `rdfs:subClassOf`, `rdfs:subPropertyOf` and other transitive relations. Using an embedded database such as BerkeleyDB[8] provides much faster simple queries, but still imposes a serious efficiency penalty. This is due to both the overhead of the formal database API and to the mapping between the in-memory Prolog atom handles and the resource representation used in the database.

In another attempt we used ***Predicate***(*Subject, Object*) as database representation and stored the inverse relation as well in ***InversePred***(*Object, Subject*) with a wrapper to call the 'best' version depending on the runtime instantiation. This approach, using native Prolog syntax for fast load/safe satisfies the requirements with minor drawbacks. The 3 million triples, the software and OS together require about 600MB of memory. Save/load using Prolog native syntax is, despite the fast SWI-Prolog parser, only twice as fast as parsing the RDF/XML.

In the end we opted for a Prolog *foreign-language* extension: a module written in C to extend the functionality of Prolog.[9] A significant advantage using an extension to Prolog rather than a language independent storage module separated by a formal API is that the extension can use native Prolog atoms, significantly reducing memory requirements and access time.

4 Realising an RDF Store as C-Extension to Prolog

4.1 Storage Format

Triples are stored as a C-structure holding the three fields and 7 hash-table links for index access on all 7 possible instantiation patterns with at least one-field instantiated. The size of the hash-tables is automatically increased as the triple set grows. In addition, each triple is associated with a *source-reference* consisting of an atom (normally the filename) and an integer (normally the line-number) and a general-purpose set of flags, adding to 13 machine words (52 bytes on 32-bit hardware) per triple, or 149 Mbytes for the intended 3 million triples. Our reference-set of 1.5 million triples uses 890,000 atoms. In SWI-Prolog an atom requires 7 machine words overhead excluding the represented string. If we estimate the average length of an atom representing a fully qualified resource at 30 characters the atom-space required for the 1.8 million atoms in 3 million triples is about 88 Mbytes. The required total of 237 Mbytes for 3 million triples fits easily in 512 Mbytes.

[8] `http://www.sleepycat.com/`

[9] Extending Prolog using modules written in the C-language is provided in most todays Prolog systems although there is no established standard foreign interface and therefore the connection between the extension and Prolog needs to be rewritten when porting to other implementation of the Prolog language [1].

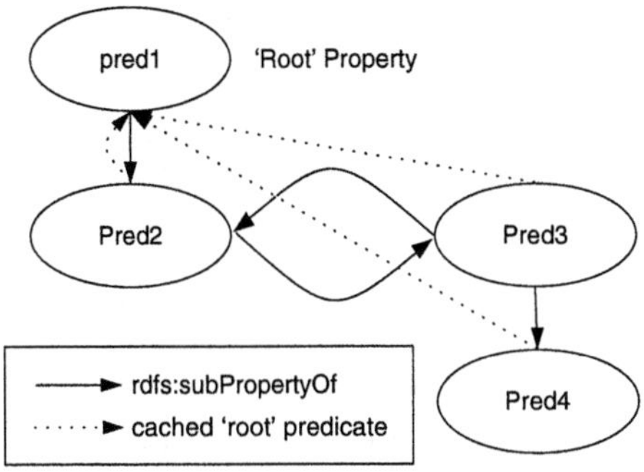

Fig. 4. All predicates are hashed on the root of the predicate hierarchy.

To accommodate active queries safely, deletion of triples is realised by flagging them as *erased*. Garbage collection can be invoked if no queries are active.

Indexing Subjects and resource *Objects* use the immutable atom-handle as hash-key. Literal *Objects* use a case-insensitive hash to speedup case-insensitive lookup of labels, a common operation in our annotation tool. The *Predicate* field needs special attention due to the requirement to handle `subPropertyOf` efficiently. The storage layer has an explicit representation for all known predicates which are linked directly in a hierarchy built using the `subPropertyOf` relation. Each predicate has a direct pointer to the *root* predicate: the topmost predicate in the hierarchy. If the top is formed by a cycle an arbitrary node of the cycle is flagged as the root, but all predicates in the hierarchy point to the same root as illustrated in Fig. 4. Each triple is now hashed using the root-predicate that belongs to the predicate of the triple.

The above representation provides fully indexed lookup of any instantiation pattern, case insensitive on literals and including sub-properties. As a compromise to our requirements, the storage layer must know the fully qualified resource for `subPropertyOf` and must rebuild the predicate hierarchy and hash-tables if `subPropertyOf` relations are added to or deleted from the triple store. The predicate hierarchy and index are invalidated if such a triple is added or deleted. The index is re-build on the first indexable query. We assume that changes to the constsubPropertyOf relations are infrequent.

4.2 Fast Save/Load Format

Although attractive, the Prolog-only prototype has indicated that storing triples using the native representation of Prolog terms does not provide the required speedup, while the files are, mainly due to the expanded namespaces, larger than the RDF/XML source. An efficient format can be realised by storing the atom-text only the first time. Later references to the same atom simply store this as the N-th atom. A hash-table is used to keep track of the atoms already seen. An atom on the file thus has two formats: `X` ⟨*integer*⟩ or `A` ⟨*length*⟩ ⟨*text*⟩. Loading

Table 2. Initial registered namespace abbreviations

rdf	http://www.w3.org/1999/02/22-rdf-syntax-ns#
rdfs	http://www.w3.org/2000/01/rdf-schema#
owl	http://www.w3.org/2002/7/owl#
xsd	http://www.w3.org/2000/10/XMLSchema#
dc	http://purl.org/dc/elements/1.1/
eor	http://dublincore.org/2000/03/13/eor#

requires an array of already-loaded atoms. The resulting representation has the same size as the RDF/XML within 10%, and our reference dataset of 1.5 million triples is loaded 22 times faster, or 5 seconds.

4.3 Namespace Handling

Fully qualified resources are long, hard to read and difficult to maintain in application source-code. On the other hand, representing resources as atoms holding the fully qualified resource is attractive because it is compact and compares very fast: the only test between two atoms as well as two resources is the equivalence test. Prolog optimises this test by ensuring there are no two atoms representing the same characters and therefore comparing atom-handles decides on equivalence.

To merge as much as possible of the advantages the API described in Tab. 3 is encapsulated in a macro-expansion mechanism based on Prolog **goal_expansion/2** rules. For each of the arguments that can receive a resource a term of the format ⟨*NS*⟩:⟨*Identifier*⟩, where ⟨*NS*⟩ is a registered abbreviation of a namespace and ⟨*Identifier*⟩ is a local name, is mapped to the fully qualified resource.[10] The predicate rdf_db:ns/2 maps registered short local namespace identifiers to the fully qualified namespaces. Declared as multifile, this predicate can be extended by the user. The initial definition contains the well-known abbreviations used in the context of the sematic web. See Tab. 2.

With these declarations, we can write the following to get all individuals of `http://www.w3.org/2000/01/rdf-schema#Class` on backtracking:

rdf(*X, rdf:type, rdfs:'Class'*)

4.4 Performance Evaluation

We studied two queries using our reference set. First we generated all solutions for **rdf**(*X, rdf:type, wns:'Noun'*). The 66025 nouns are generated in 0.0464 seconds (1.4 million alternatives/second). Second we asked for the type

[10] In our original prototype we provided a more powerful version of this mapping at runtime. In this version, output-arguments could be split into their namespace and local name as well. After examining actual use of this extra facility in the prototype and performance we concluded a limited compile-time alternative is more attractive.

Table 3. API summary for accessing the triple store

rdf(*?Subject, ?Predicate, ?Object*)
: Elementary query for triples. *Subject* and *Predicate* are atoms representing the fully qualified URL of the resource. *Object* is either an atom representing a resource or **literal**(*Text*) if the object is a literal value. For querying purposes, *Object* can be of the form **literal**(*+Query, -Value*), where *Query* is one of

 exact(*+Text*)
 : Perform exact, but case-insensitive match. This query is fully indexed.

 substring(*+Text*)
 : Match any literal that contains *Text* as a case-insensitive substring.

 word(*+Text*)
 : Match any literal that contains *Text* as a 'whole word'.

 prefix(*+Text*)
 : Match any literal that starts with *Text*.

rdf_has(*?Subject, ?Predicate, ?Object, -TriplePred*)
: This query exploits the `rdfs:subPropertyOf` relation. It returns any triple whose stored predicate equals *Predicate* or can reach this by following the transitive `rdfs:subPropertyOf` relation. The actual stored predicate is returned in *TriplePred*.

rdf_reachable(*?Subject, +Predicate, ?Object*)
: True if *Object* is, or can be reached following the transitive property *Predicate* from *Subject*. Either *Subject* or *Object* or both must be specified. If one of *Subject* or *Object* is unbound this predicate generates solutions in breath-first search order. It maintains a table of visited resources, never generates the same resource twice and is robust against cycles in the transitive relation.

rdf_subject(*?Subject*)
: Enumerate resources appearing as a subject in a triple. The reason for this predicate is to generate the known subjects *without duplicates* as one would get using **rdf**(*Subject, _, _*). The storage layer ensures the first triple with a specified *Subject* is flagged as such.

rdf_assert(*+Subject, +Predicate, +Object*)
: Assert a new triple into the database. *Subject* and *Predicate* are resources. *Object* is either a resource or a term **literal**(*Value*).

rdf_retractall(*?Subject, ?Predicate, ?Object*)
: Removes all matching triples from the database.

rdf_update(*+Subject, +Predicate, +Object, +Action*)
: Replaces one of the three fields on the matching triples depending on *Action*:

 subject(*Resource*)
 : Changes the first field of the triple.

 predicate(*Resource*)
 : Changes the second field of the triple.

 object(*Object*)
 : Changes the last field of the triple to the given resource or **literal**(*Value*).

of randomly generated nouns. This deterministic query is executed at 526,000 queries/second. Tests comparing **rdf/3** with **rdf_has/4**, which exploits the `rdfs:subPropertyOf` relation show no significant difference in performance.

```
rdfs_individual_of(Resource, Class) :-
        nonvar(Resource), !,
        rdf_has(Resource, rdf:type, MyClass),
        rdfs_subclass_of(MyClass, Class).
rdfs_individual_of(Resource, Class) :-
        nonvar(Class), !,
        rdfs_subclass_of(SubClass, Class),
        rdf_has(Resource, rdf:type, SubClass).
rdfs_individual_of(_Resource, _Class) :-
        throw(error(instantiation_error, _)).
```

Fig. 5. Implementation of **rdfs_individual_of/2**

5 Querying and RDFS

Queries at the RDFS level are implemented using trivial Prolog rules exploiting the primitives in Tab. 3. For example, Fig. 5 realises testing and generating individuals. The first rule tests whether an individual belongs to a given class or generates all classes the individual belongs to. The second rule generates all individuals that belong to a specified class. The last rule is called in the unbound condition. There is not much point generating all classes and all individuals that have a type that is equal to or a subclass of the generated class and therefore we generate a standard Prolog exception.

5.1 A Few User-Queries

Let us study the question 'Give me an individual of WordNet 'Noun' labeled *right*'. This non-deterministic query can be coded in two ways:

```
right_noun_1(R) :-
        rdfs_individual_of(R, wns:'Noun'),
        rdf_has(R, rdfs:label, literal(right)).

right_noun_2(R) :-
        rdf_has(R, rdfs:label, literal(right)),
        rdfs_individual_of(R, wns:'Noun').
```

The first query enumerates the subclasses of `wns:Noun`, generates their 66025 individuals and tests each for having the literal 'right' as label. The second generates the 8 resources in the 1.5 million triple set labeled 'right' and tests them to belong to `wns:Noun`. The first query requires 0.17 seconds and the second 0.37 milli-seconds to generate all alternatives.

A more interesting question is 'Give me a WordNet word that belongs to multiple lexical categories'. The program is shown in Fig. 6. The first **setof/3** generates the 123497 labels (a subproperty of `wns:wordForm`) defined in this WordNet version. Next we examine the labels one by one, generating the lexical categories and selecting the 6584 words that belongs to multiple categories. The query completes in 9.33 seconds after 2.27 million calls on **rdf_has/4** and **rdf_reachable/3**.

```
multi_cat(Label, CatList) :-
        setof(Label, wn_label(Label), Labels),
        member(Label, Labels),
        setof(Cat, lexical_category(Label, Cat), CatList),
        CatList = [_,_|_].

lexical_category(Label, Category) :-
        rdf_has(SynSet, rdfs:label, literal(Label)),
        rdfs_individual_of(SynSet, Category),
        rdf_has(Category, rdfs:subClassOf, wns:'LexicalConcept').

wn_label(Label) :-
        rdfs_individual_of(SynSet,  wns:'LexicalConcept'),
        rdf_has(SynSet, rdfs:label, literal(Label)).
```

Fig. 6. Finding all words that belong to multiple lexical categories

```
is_subclass_of(Class, Class).
is_subclass_of(Class, Super) :-
        rdf_has(Class, rdfs:subClassOf, Super0),
        is_subclass_of(Super0, Super).
```

Fig. 7. Coding a transitive relation

6 Declarativeness and Optimisation

As we have seen above, query optimisation by ordering goals in a conjunction is required for good performance. Future versions could perform reordering of conjunctions based on the instantiation pattern and cardinality statistics of the predicates.

Many types of reasoning involve transitive relations such as `rdfs:subClassOf` which are allowed to contain cycles. Using normal Prolog non-determinism to follow a transitive chain as illustrated in Fig. 7 will not terminate under these circumstances. This problem can be handled transparently in Prolog systems that provide tabling [11]. We have choosen for a dedicated solution with **rdf_reachable/3** described in Tab. 3 to stay within standard Prolog.

7 Visualisation

For our annotation application we developed interactive editors. We are reorganising these into a clean modular design for building RDF/RDFS and OWL tools. The current toolkit provides a hierarchical browser with instance and class-view on resources and a tool to generate classical RDF diagrams. Both tools provide menus that exploit the registered source-information to view the origin of a triple in a text-editor. Currently these tools help developers to examine the content of the database. Figure 8 and Fig. 9 visualise the WordNet resource labeled *right* in one of its many meanings.

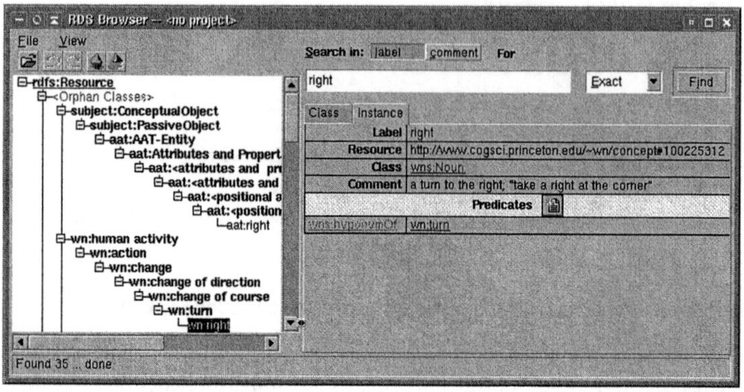

Fig. 8. The RDF browser after searching for *right* and selecting this term as a refinement of *turn*. The right tabbed-window can show a resource from various different viewpoints. This resource can be visualised as a generic resource or as a class.

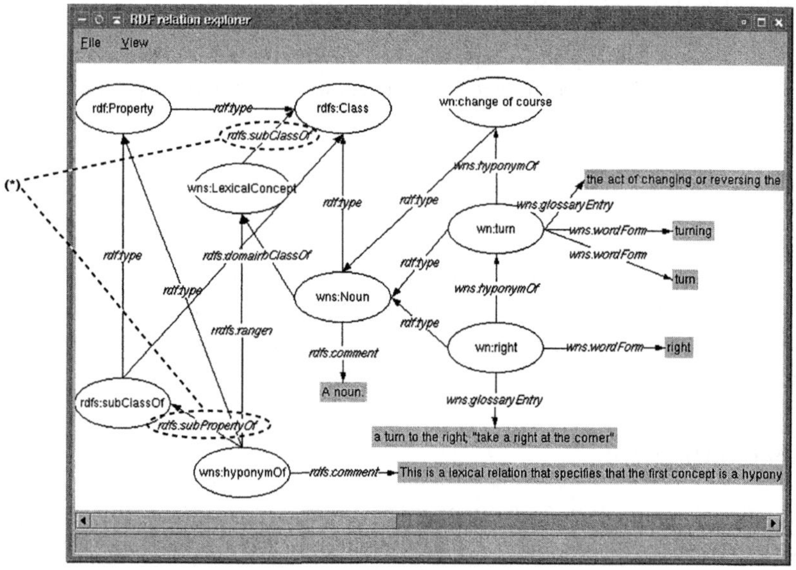

Fig. 9. From the browser we selected the *Diagram* option and expanded a few relations. The grey boxes represent literal values. The two marked relations turn WordNet into an RDFS class-hierarchy as explained in Sect. 3.1.

8 Related Work

Protege [4] is a modular Java-based ontology editor that can be extended using plugins. We regard Protege as complementary, providing interactive editing where we only provide simple interactive browsing. The Protege ontology language does not map one-to-one to RDFS, providing both extensions (e.g. cardinality) and limitations (notably in handling `subPropertyOf`). New versions of Protege and the introduction of OWL reduce this mismatch.

Jena [7] is a Java implementation for basic RDF handling. It aims at standard compliance and a friendly access from Java. Although its focus and coverage are slightly different the main difference is the choice of language.

Sesame [2] is an extensible Java-based architecture realising load/save of RDF/XML, modify the triple model and RQL [6] queries. It stresses a modular design where notably the storage module can be replaced. Although scalable, the modular approach with generic DBMS performs poorly (section 6.5 of [2]: Scalability Issues).

9 Discussion and Conclusions

We have outlined alternatives and an existing implementation of a library for handling semantic web languages in the Prolog language. We have demonstrated that this library can handle moderately large RDF triple sets (3 million) using 237 MB memory, ranging upto 40 million on 32-bit hardware providing a 3.5 GB address-space to applications. Further scaling either requires complicated segmentation of the store or hardware providing a larger (e.g. 64-bit) address-space. The library requires approx. 220 sec. to read 3 million triples from RDF/XML and 10 sec. from its proprietary file-format. Updating the `subPropertyOf` cache requires 3.3 sec. on this data-set. The library requires approx. 2 μs for the first answer and 0.7 μs for providing alternatives from the result-set through Prolog backtracking. All measurements on AMD Athlon 1600+ with 2 GB memory. The perfermance of indexed queries is constant with regard to the size of the triple set. The time required for not-indexed queries and cache-updates is proportional with the size of the triple set.

Declarativeness and optimisation by automatic reordering of conjunctions as discussed in Sect. 6 are omissions in the current design. Declarativeness can be achieved using tabling [11], a direction for which we should compare scalability and useability to dedicated solutions such as **rdf_reachable/3**. The use of an external database could provide query optimisation, but the lack of support for transitive relations is likely to harm optimisation and having two languages (Prolog and SQL) is a clear disadvantage. Automatic reordering of conjunctions of primitive RDF queries is a promising direction.

Experience with our first prototype has indicated that the queries required for our annotation and search process are expressed easily and concise in the Prolog language. We anticipate this infra structure is also suitable for the prototyping and implementation of end-user query langages.

References

1. Roberto Bagnara and Manuel Carro. Foreign language interfaces for Prolog: A terse survey. *ALP newsletter*, Mey 2002.
2. Jeen Broekstra and Arjohn Kampman. Sesame: A generic architecture for storing and querying RDF and RDF Schema. Technical Report OTK-del-10, Aidministrator Nederland bv, October 2001.
URL: http://sesame.aidministrator.nl/publications/del10.pdf.
3. C. Draxler. Accessing relational and NF^2 databases through database set predicates. In Geraint A. Wiggins, Chris Mellish, and Tim Duncan, editors, *ALPUK91: Proceedings of the 3rd UK Annual Conference on Logic Programming, Edinburgh 1991*, Workshops in Computing, pages 156–173. Springer-Verlag, 1991.
4. W. E. Grosso, H. Eriksson, R. W. Fergerson, J. H. Gennari, S. W. Tu, and M. A. Musen. Knowledge modeling at the millennium: The design and evolution of Protégé-2000. In *12th Banff Workshop on Knowledge Acquisition, Modeling, and Management. Banff, Alberta*, 1999.
URL: http://smi.stanford.edu/projects/protege (access date: 18 December 2000).
5. RDFCore Working Group. RDF/XML Syntax Specification (Revised)a. W3C Working Draft, World Wide Web Consortium, February 2003.
http://www.w3.org/TR/rdf-syntax-grammar/.
6. G. Karvounarakis, V. Christophides, D. Plexousakis, and S. Alexaki. Querying community web portals.
URL: http://www.ics.forth.gr/proj/isst/RDF/RQL/rql.html.
7. Brian McBride. Jena: Implementing the rdf model and syntax specification. 2001.
8. G. Miller. WordNet: A lexical database for english. *Comm. ACM*, 38(11), November 1995.
9. Bijan Parsia. RDF applications with Prolog. O'Reilly XML.com, 2001.
http://www.xml.com/pub/a/2001/07/25/prologrdf.html.
10. T. Peterson. *Introduction to the Art and Architecture Thesaurus*. Oxford University Press, 1994. See also: http://www.getty.edu/research/tools/vocabulary/aat/.
11. I. V. Ramakrishnan, Prasad Rao, Konstantinos Sagonas, Terrance Swift, and David S. Warren. Efficient tabling mechanisms for logic programs. In Leon Sterling, editor, *Proceedings of the 12th International Conference on Logic Programming*, pages 697–714, Cambridge, June 13–18 1995. MIT Press.
12. A. Th. Schreiber. The web is not well-formed. *IEEE Intelligent Systems*, March/April 2002.
13. A. Th. Schreiber, B. Dubbeldam, J. Wielemaker, and B. J. Wielinga. Ontology-based photo annotation. *IEEE Intelligent Systems*, 16(3):66–74, May/June 2001.
14. ULAN: Union List of Artist Names. The Getty Foundation.
URL: http://www.getty.edu/research/tools/vocabulary/ulan/, 2000.

Cooking the Semantic Web with the OWL API

Sean Bechhofer[1], Raphael Volz[2], and Phillip Lord[1]

[1] University of Manchester, UK
seanb@cs.man.ac.uk,p.lord@russet.org.uk
http://www.cs.man.ac.uk
[2] Institute AIFB, University of Karlsruhe, Germany
rvo@aifb.uni-karlsruhe.de
http://www.aifb.uni-karlsruhe.de

Abstract. This paper discusses issues that surround the provision of application support using OWL ontologies. It presents the OWL API, a high-level programmatic interface for accessing and manipulating OWL ontologies. We discuss the underlying design issues and illustrate possible solutions to technical issues occurring in systems that intend to support the OWL standard. Although the context of our solutions is that of a particular implementation, the issues discussed are largely independent of this and should be of interest to a wider community.

1 Introduction

To realize the vision of the Semantic Web, the Web Ontology Working Group [21] has been chartered to develop a standard language for expressing semantics on the web. The Web Ontology Language (OWL) comprises a standardized syntax for exchanging ontologies and specifies the semantics of the language, i.e. how the syntactic structures are to be interpreted.

However, it is unclear precisely how to slice the pie between the disciplines of syntax and semantics in applications. Support for OWL in applications involves understanding how syntax and semantics interact (i.e., their interface). A number of issues relating to this split continually re-occur in the design of Semantic applications, e.g. in the development of OntoEdit [19], OilEd [3] and KAON [6].

This paper discusses a number of the technical issues encountered when "implementing OWL" and introduces the OWL API, with which we can provide a high-level programmatic interface for both accessing and manipulating OWL ontologies. Besides presenting the underlying design issues we illustrate solutions to these issues in systems that intend to support the OWL standard.

The provision of APIs allows developers to work at a higher level of abstraction, and isolate themselves from some of the problematic issues related to serialization and parsing of data structures. Our experience has shown that application developers can interpret language specifications such as DAML+OIL in subtly different ways, and confusion reigns as to the particular namespaces and schema versions used[1]. The direct use of higher level constructs can also help

[1] **Quiz Question:** Without checking the schemas, can you be sure whether `type`, `comment` and `Property` belong to the RDF or RDF(S) vocabularies?

D. Fensel et al. (Eds.): ISWC 2003, LNCS 2870, pp. 659–675, 2003.

to alleviate problems with "round tripping"[2] that occur when using concrete transport syntaxes based on RDF [2].

The OWL API attempts to present a highly reusable component for the construction of different applications such as editors, annotation tools and query agents. Besides allowing them to "talk the same language", it ensures that they share underlying assumptions about the way that information is presented and represented. Thus a cornerstone to the successful implementation and delivery of the Semantic Web, namely the *interoperability* of applications is achieved.

We draw inspiration from the impact that has been made by the provision of the XML Document Object Model (DOM) [20]. The DOM, along with freely available implementations (such as the Java implementations in Sun's JDK [18]) has allowed a large number of developers to use and manipulate XML in applications, which has in turn facilitated the widespread adoption of XML. Our hope is that a similar effect can be achieved with an API for OWL.

There is a long tradition for providing programmatic access to knowledge based systems, however most of the previous work has been centered around protocols, such as Open Knowledge Base Connectivity (OKBC) and Generic Frame Protocol (GFP), which are application programming interfaces for accessing knowledge bases stored in knowledge representation systems. Such protocol-centric approaches, automatically assume a client-server architecture for application development. However, our approach is rather component-based since our intention is to develop a reusable component for developing OWL-based applications, in style of DOM for XML-based applications. To our knowledge, there are no current existing implementations of APIs for the OWL language, however there have been previous related approaches.

DAML+OIL interfaces. There have been a number of similar initiatives to provide application interfaces aimed at precursors of OWL such as DAML+OIL[1]. Jena [9] supplies a DAML+OIL interface that provides convenience wrappers around their RDF interface in order to increase the efficiency of manipulating the DAML+OIL fragments embedded in a particular RDF file. Naturally, this approach gives a rather syntax-centric view of DAML+OIL. Additionally the implementation is bound to a particular RDF implementation. The DAML API by AT&T government solutions is an additional interface to DAML ontologies. It defines a structural interface for the manipulation and accessing of DAML ontologies that is not bound to a particular syntactic representation such as RDF.

Semantic applications. KAON [6] is an open-source ontology management infrastructure targeted for business applications. It includes a comprehensive tool suite allowing easy ontology creation and management, as well as the building of ontology-based applications. To the latter extent it defines a standard interface

[2] *Round tripping* refers to the process where a data structure (e.g. an ontology) is serialized and deserialized to/from some concrete syntax without loss of information.

to access semantic structures – the KAON API[3] – and multiple implementations there of, e.g. on top of relational databases. However, the ontology model supported in KAON is much less expressive than that described by OWL since an important focus of KAON is performance on large knowledge bases [13]. However, many of our underlying design considerations conceptually follow the KAON design.

Ontology Editors. OilEd [3] provided a collection of data structures representing DAML+OIL ontologies[4]. The OilEd data structures suffer in a number of ways however – some of the relevant issues are covered in other sections of this paper. One drawback is that the functionality is supplied as implementation *classes* rather than *interfaces*, which binds the client to a particular implementation of the model. In addition, support for tracking and recording change is minimal. Other ontology editors such as OntoEdit and Protege also expose their internal APIs to offer access to the underlying data structures but experience similar problems since their design is heavily influenced by the application purpose.

Ontology Versioning and Evolution. Since an API for manipulating ontologies has to address change in ontologies, previous work focused on this subject has been considered. [14] addresses change in DAML+OIL documents by providing diff-style comparison of individual documents and identification of changes by analysis of the differences, e.g. identifying the renaming of classes. [17] takes a different stance and identifies a change ontology, which captures the different types of changes that can occur in ontology modelling. The implementation within KAON encapsulates these different change types and allows the modification of changes via appropriate strategy objects (See Section 3.2), ensuring that change is carried out according to user specifications.

The remaining sections of the paper are structured as follows. Section 2 motivates some of the fundamental decisions taken in our design. Sections 3 and 4 discuss the design itself. Section 5 briefly describes examples of the use of the API, and we conclude with a summary of our contribution.

2 Separating Functionality

The OWL specification provides a description of the underlying language along with a formal semantics, giving a precise interpretation of the meaning of OWL documents or ontologies. What it means to be "an OWL Implementation" is, however, less clear. Indeed, an examination of the WebOnt Working Group [21] mail archives suggests that opinions differ widely as to what one can claim to be an implementation.

Different classes of application require, and provide, different aspects of functionality (See Figure 1). For example, a format/syntax translator acts as a client

[3] Available at `http://kaon.semanticweb.org`

[4] Available at `http://oiled.man.ac.uk`

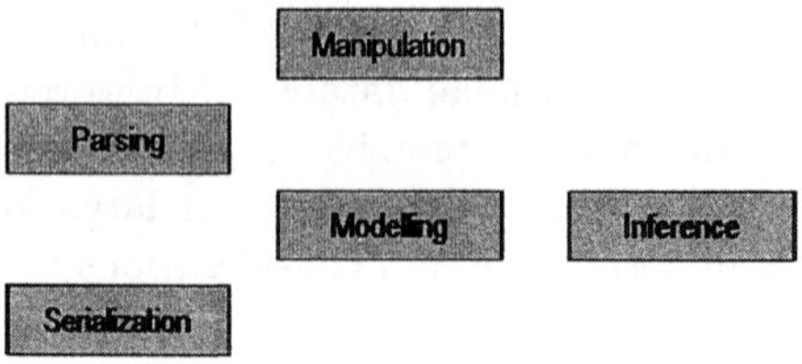

Fig. 1. Aspects of Implementation Support

```
A rdf:type rdfs:Class.
B rdf:type rdfs:Class.
B rdfs:subClassOf A.
b rdf:type B.
```

Fig. 2. Simple RDF Inference

of the API and requires the ability to parse, represent the results of the parsing in some way, and then serialize. An editing application would also require manipulation capabilities to allow construction and editing of ontologies (i.e. definitions of classes, properties and so on). A simple editor, however, need not actually require any functionality relating to semantics or inference, e.g. the facility for checking the consistency of class definitions, or whether subsumption relationships can be inferred. Alternatively, an application that simply deploys an ontology to client applications may not require any functionality that supports serialization, manipulation or extension of the ontology, but does support query of the ontology and its entailments. Turning to components that provide functionality, a reasoner will support inference, but need not be concerned with issues relating to serialization and parsing.

The following sections describe a number of examples that illustrate some of the issues we consider to be important. These include the need for explicit characterizations of functionality, the requirement for change support, identification of asserted and inferred information and preservation of ontological structure. These examples, along with the considerations above have motivated design decisions in our API as discussed in Section 3.

2.1 Entailment

Consider the RDF triples given in Figure 2. What might we expect when this collection of triples is given to an RDF-API and we then ask whether `b rdf:type A`? If the implementation simply represents the asserted facts as in the collection of triples, the answer is no. If, however, the implementation implements RDF entailment, then the answer is yes. It is not always clear in existing RDF implementations whether or not such entailments can be expected.

```
I)   Class(CarDriver partial
             Person
             restriction(drives someValuesFrom Vehicle))

II)  SubClassOf(CarDriver Person)
     SubClassOf(CarDriver restriction(drives someValuesFrom Vehicle))
```

Fig. 3. Explicit Class Definition and Class Definition through Axioms

2.2 Explicit Change Operations

The ability to track change is important for a number of ontology-based applications. Editors must be able to record the actions that the user is performing if they are to be able to provide effective change management and versioning functionality. Similarly, clients of a central ontology service will need to be informed of updates and changes to the ontologies served by the server. Explicitly representing changes as first-class objects can support this (and more).

2.3 Information Grouping

Different application uses of OWL ontologies require different characteristics of the ontologies. For example, an application using an ontology in order to perform, say, search or indexing of information may only be interested in the underlying inferences that can be drawn from the axioms in the model. An editing application, or one that provides a graphical view on the ontology in order to support query, may have different requirements in that the application may need to know the way in which the information has been structured or grouped. A particular short-coming identified in DAML+OIL [2] was the inability to distinguish the way that information had been presented by the original modeller or ontologist. The OWL abstract syntax, however, allows the definition of classes using both a definitional style, i.e. the use of class definitions, and through general axioms, i.e. the use of axioms.

As an example, consider Figure 3: I) shows the use of a class definition. In this case, the class of `CarDrivers` is defined as a subclass of the intersection of `Person` and those things that `drive` a `Vehicle`. This definition could also be made through a pair of subclass axioms as in Figure 3 II). Both definitions have the same *semantic* effect (in terms of the underlying model), but we can argue that these are, in fact, different. The way in which the information is presented is part of the OWL ontology, and an API for the language should try and preserve this wherever possible.

As a more complicated example, consider the three alternative definitions shown in Figure 4. Again, all three of these provide exactly the same semantics in terms of the inferences that can be drawn. However, they convey slightly different ways of modelling the world in terms of how the ontologist thinks things fit together. As discussed in [3], the issue here is that we would like to ensure that not only do we capture the correct semantics of the ontology, but also the *semiotics* [7].

```
I)   Class(CarDriver complete
             Person
             restriction(drives someValuesFrom Car))
     SubClassOf(CarDriver PersonOver17)


II)  Class(CarDriver partial
             PersonOver17)
     EquivalentClasses(CarDriver
             intersectionOf(Person
                            restriction(drives someValuesFrom Car)))


III) SubClassOf(CarDriver Person)
     SubClassOf(CarDriver restriction(drives someValuesFrom Car))
     SubClassOf(CarDriver PersonOver17)
     SubClassOf(intersectionOf(Person
                              restriction(drives someValuesFrom Car))
               CarDriver)
```

Fig. 4. Alternative Class Definitions

The ability to preserve these distinctions within the API is an important one, particularly if the API is to support not only the deployment of ontologies to applications but also applications that bring the user closer to the actual ontology, such as editors.

2.4 Assertions and Inferences

We consider that a separation of assertion and inference is important for applications such as editors. To illustrate this, we draw on our experiences with the implementation of OilEd [3].

OilEd used a DL reasoner to compute the inferred subsumption hierarchy of a DAML+OIL model[3]. There are a number of scenarios where this can prove useful. For example, one use case is the enhancement of RDF Schemas. The Schema is read into the tool, and the increased expressivity of DAML+OIL can be used to provide more detailed descriptions of the classes (for example the definition of `CarDriver` as a person who drives a vehicle in Figure 3). Once the descriptions have been applied, we can then export the schema in RDF(S) again. The original language (RDF(S)) is not rich enough to represent many of the constructs available in DAML+OIL, so these class definitions will be lost in the resulting output. Before exporting, however, we can use the reasoner to compute the inferred hierarchy (which may well include new subclass relationships due to the assertions), and then serialize the schema with the additional relationships. In this way the inferred sub/superclasses can be made accessible to simple RDF applications.

During the development of the tool, users expressed a desire to have the ability to add this inferred information back into the ontology. Thus a "commit

```
Class(Vehicle)
Class(Car partial Vehicle)
Class(Person)
ObjectProperty(drives)
Class(Driver complete
 intersectionOf(
  Person
  restriction(drives
    someValuesFrom Vehicle)))
Class(CarDriver complete
 intersectionOf(
  Person
  restriction(drives
    someValuesFrom Car)))
```

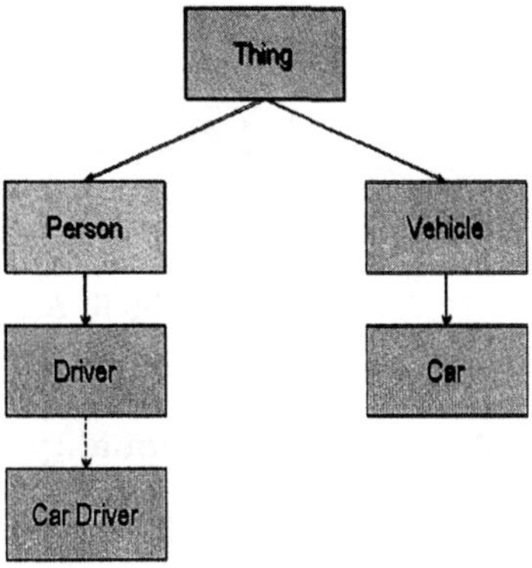

Fig. 5. A Simple Ontology and Inferred Hierarchy

changes" button was added, which did precisely this. In OilEd's implementation, this was achieved by adding the information to the assertions which make up the model.

Although the addition of the inferred relationships does not change the underlying semantics of the ontology (as they are already inferred, we are simply adding redundant information), over time our experience was that this was a confusing process, in particular when users then wanted to further edit the amended ontology. For example, take the simple ontology[5] shown on the left of Figure 5. This produces a hierarchy as shown on the right of Figure 5

In this example we find an inferred subclass relationship between `CarDriver` and `Driver` (shown as a dotted line). A simple approach would be to add this relationship back into the ontology. Consider the situation now, however, where the user is presented with the concept hierarchy in a Graphical User Interface (GUI), and tries to use the hierarchy to directly manipulate the underlying ontology, for example removing the relationship between `CarDriver` and `Driver`. How should we interpret this within the application? In order to *truly* remove the relationship between the two classes, we would need to alter their definitions, rather than simply removing some sub/superclass link between them. In this example, the user could remove the sub/superclass relationship and then find that it "comes back" after a reclassification.

The key issue here is that the information regarding the class hierarchy can be considered as *inferred* information which can be calculated from the *asserted* information which is present in the axioms of the ontology. We consider it to be of benefit to explicitly represent this split in the API.

In this way, in our example, the user interface can inform the user that more action than simply removing the super/subclass link is required.

---

[5] Our examples use the OWL Abstract Syntax[15] for presentation of ontology fragments

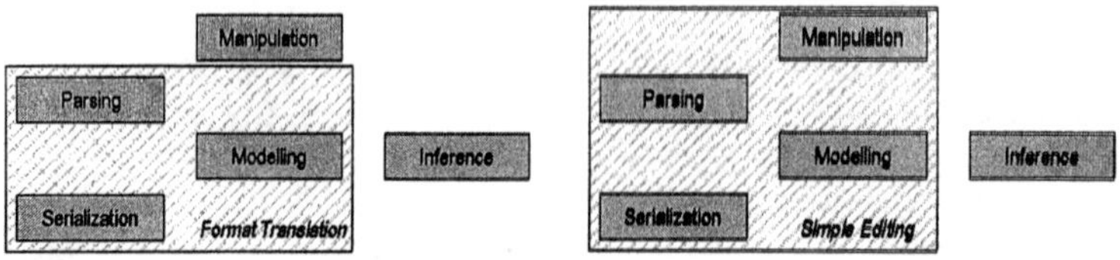

Fig. 6. Aspects and Applications

2.5 Aspects of Functionality

In the light of the preceding discussion, we can consider a number of different tasks that applications may perform which could be thought of as providing "OWL implementation". These include:

Serializing. Producing OWL concrete syntax (for example as RDF triples or using the OWL presentation syntax) from some internal data structure or representation;

Modelling. Providing data structures that can represent/encode OWL documents. This representation should be at an appropriate level. An XML string would provide a representation of the information in an ontology, but is unlikely to facilitate access to that information;

Parsing. Taking a concrete representation of an OWL document (e.g. an RDF-XML serialization of an OWL document) and building some internal representation that corresponds to that document;

Manipulation. Providing representation along with mechanisms for manipulation of those documents;

Inference. Providing a representation that in addition implements the formal semantics of the language.

We can think of these different tasks as providing different aspects of support for OWL (See Figure 1). Some aspects will (in general) require support from others, although this is not entirely the case. For example, serialization can be seen as a minimal level of support that does not necessarily require the implementation to "understand" or represent the entire language.

As introduced above, different classes of application will need differing combinations of these classes of functionality, as illustrated in Figure 6. We see this separation of the classes of functionality an application provides as crucial if we are to be confident that the implementation supplies appropriate functionality. Our API design explicitly reflects this through the separation of functionality into distinct packages.

3 API Design

The API contains a number of different packages, each of which reflects an aspect of functionality as introduced above.

3.1 Model

The `model` package provides basic, read-only access to an OWL ontology. Thus there are methods for accessing the Classes defined or used in the ontology (and their definitions), the Properties defined or used, Axioms asserted and so on.

The data structures and accessor methods defined within this package reflect the requirements expressed in Section 2.3 for the explicit preservation of information grouping. Although this introduces a certain amount of redundancy into the data structures (as there are multiple ways of representing information) it allows us to ensure that no information loss occurs when representing ontologies using the API.

For the situations where applications are not concerned with the grouping or structuring of information, we can provide alternative "views" of the information in the ontology, e.g. an axiom-centric view that simply presents all the assertions relating to class definitions as subclass axioms. This can be achieved through the use of `helper` classes.

3.2 Change

The `model` package described above provides read-only access to ontologies. The `change` package extends this to allow manipulation of those structures, e.g. the addition and removal of entities, changes to definitions, axioms and so on.

The `change` package achieves this through the use of the **Command** design pattern [8] which encapsulates a change request as an object. Changes are then enacted by a ChangeVisitor. See Section 4.2 for further discussion.

3.3 Inference

The OWL specification includes a detailed description of the semantics of the language. In particular, this defines precisely what entailment means with respect to OWL ontologies, and provides formal descriptions of properties such as consistency. The implementation of these semantics is a non-trivial matter, however, and providing a *complete* OWL reasoner, effectively requires the implementation of a Description Logic (DL) theorem prover. By separating this functionality, we can relieve implementors of the burden of this, while allowing those who do provide such implementations to be explicit about this in their advertised functionality. The `inference` package is intended to encapsulate this and provide access to functionality relating to the process of *reasoning* with OWL ontologies.

In addition, the `inference` and `model` packages partition functionality along the lines described in Section 2.4 above. This does not completely solve all the associated problems of supporting user editing of the ontology via graphical means, but by exposing the particular kinds of information that are present in the ontology, we are making it clear to applications what they can, and can not, do.

Of course, providing method signatures does not go all the way to advertising the functionality of an implementation – there is no guarantee that a component implementing the `inference` interface necessarily implements the semantics correctly. However, signatures go some way towards providing an expectation of the operations that are being supported. Collections of test data (such as the OWL Test Cases [4]) can allow systematic testing and a level of confidence as to whether the implementation is, in fact, performing correctly.

4 Detailed Design Decisions

The following sections discuss our design decisions in more detail.

4.1 Modelling the Language

Syntax vs. data model. The API represents the OWL language by modelling the language constructs in a data model. Often, such a data model might closely reflect the syntax of the language. Since OWL has several so-called presentation syntaxes, however (XML and RDF for the time being), the syntactic constructs available in the language cannot be used as the basis for establishing the data model. Adopting a bias towards a particular presentation syntax, e.g. the RDF representation, imposes major difficulties for access since it involves many syntactic overspecifications that are due to the particularities of the data model. For example, n-ary language constructs such as intersection and union, are broken down into several triples in the RDF graph. It is easier to access and manipulate these constructs, if they are presented as n-ary ones. Since any presentation syntax relates to the abstract syntax of the language [15], our decision is that the data model should follow this abstract syntax. In consequence, the mapping between serializations and data model is carried out by the parser and serialization implementations.

Interface vs. Implementation. The data model itself is represented as an interface, allowing user applications to provide alternative implementations of the interfaces with different properties. The use of interfaces is, of course, standard practice in Object Oriented design. It is however worth mentioning here, though, as it ensures that client applications can use the API without being concerned about the particular implementation strategy. Thus an implementation could provide simple in-memory storage of the ontologies (as is the case with our draft implementation), or could provide some persistent storage mechanism, with the interface sitting on top of a relational database, or an RDF store.

The data model is represented as an extensive interface hierarchy (see Figure 7 for an overview). This allows the simplification of a possible implementation by reusing abstract implementations for similar behaviour. For example, an implementation of functionality for traversing the property hierarchy can be used for both datatype properties and object properties.

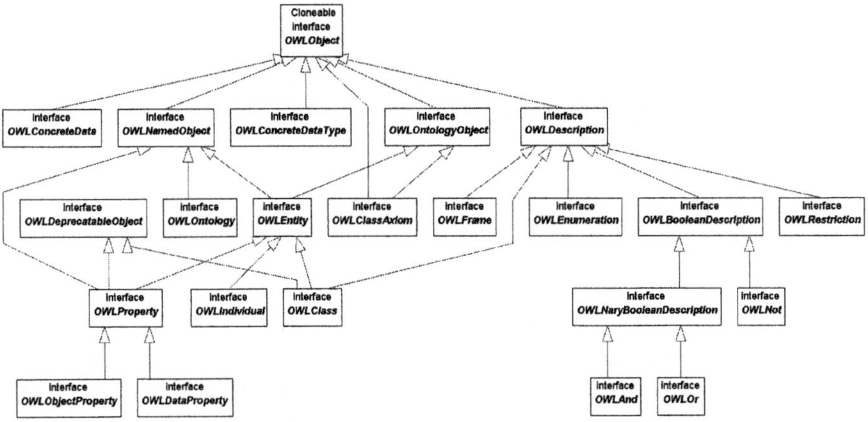

Fig. 7. OWL Data Model Excerpt

Locality of Information. All assertions are associated with a particular ontology, and OWL allows different ontologies to make different assertions about the same classes and properties. In order to support this, we require the ability to distinguish the source of information. The methods specified in interfaces maintain such information. For example, iterators for the declared superclasses of a given class can take an ontology as an argument, which restricts the iteration to those declarations made within the context of the given ontology.

4.2 Change

A critical point in applying ontologies to real-world problems is that domains are dynamic, and change over time – new concepts evolve, concepts change their meaning etc. Thus, the support for change is a crucial feature in an OWL API. Change support has to meet several aspects.

Granularity of change. Change in ontologies occurs at differing granularities. Besides basic changes, such as adding and removing entities, (classes, class restrictions or properties) change also happens at a higher granularity. For example, a user may decide to create a new class `Vehicle` that subsumes existing classes such as `Bike` and `Car`. A user may achieve this through successive application of fine grained changes. In the above example, 3 operations might be required: adding `Vehicle`, adding two superclass axioms and additional changes to keep the class hierarchy consistent, e.g. moving common existing superclasses of `Bike` and `Car` to `Vehicle`.

However, it can be beneficial to capture the high level intention of the above changes in a composite change operation tailored for this purpose. The impedance mismatch between the intention of change and its achievement is then removed, and the possibility of conceptual errors is decreased. Table 1 presents some composite changes supported by the API.

Table 1. Some composite changes (following [17])

Composite change	Description
Merge classes	Replace several classes with one aggregating their instances
Extract subclasses	Split a class into several classes and distribute properties among them
Extract superclass	Create a common superclass for a set of unrelated classes and transfer common properties to it
Pull up properties	Move property domains from a class to its super class

Dependency of Change. As we can see from the above example changes are not isolated – on the contrary most basic changes are performed in response to other basic changes. This creates a natural chain of changes. The API supports this by allowing the representation of chains of changes. This information often proves useful if a given change should be undone at a later stage, since it indicates the context within which the change was carried out. Composite changes are automatically decomposed into basic changes in the implementation and chained appropriately.

User intention. The above information is not always sufficient to capture the intention of a change completely, due to its incomplete specification. Hence, users are able to specify different change strategies. The choice made for a given strategy allows customization of the way that changes are processed depending on the particular situation and strategy.

For example, a user may choose to compute additional changes to keep a consistent structure of the ontology. For example, when deleting a class all instances may be chosen to be deleted as well, or to be moved to other classes. The particular choice here will be application, task, or context specific.

Change strategies. Change strategies can be used to support various aspects of customizable implementation behaviour. For example, a problem during the evolution of a Description Logic ontology is implicit meaning change in classes. Changes in axioms or definitions may effect the inferences that can be drawn from an ontology, implicitly impacting the "meaning" of classes. Reasoning may come into play during the enactment of evolution strategies in order to control this. For example, an implementation may choose to prevent any changes that cause inconsistencies to occur within the ontology.

Design decisions. The API acknowledges the above issues by separating the representation of change from the processing of changes. Change representation, e.g. the addition and removal of entities, changes to definitions, axioms and so on, is achieved through the use of the **Command** design pattern [8] which encapsulates a change type as a class. While the API "ships" with a complete set of basic change commands for all elements of the language, it also provides an elementary set of composite change commands such as represented in Table 1.

Users can provide their own change commands by subtyping an existing change class, and extending the processing of changes accordingly.

The processing of changes are then enacted by a ChangeVisitor. This approach has also been used with success in the KAON architecture and API. Along with the use of the command pattern, we can use the **Strategy** pattern [8] and employ customizable change strategies in a ChangeVisitor, which can edit or manipulate streams of change events to ensure that the internal models are kept in consistent states. For example, a particular implementation of the OWL Ontology interface may expect that before any axioms involving a class can be added to the ontology, the ontology must contain a (possibly empty) definition of the class. This is not necessarily something that we wish to be true of **all** implementations. However, we want to preserve the possibility to do so in a particular implementation, which can employ an appropriate strategy that takes any such axiom additions and first ensure that the classes used in the axiom are added to the ontology, thus preserving the internal consistency of the data structures.

Advanced Features. The use of the command pattern facilitates support for operations such as undo or redo, and the encapsulation of changes as operations provides a mechanism with which to track changes and support version management. The change objects also provide a convenient place for storing metadata about the changes, for example the user who requested the change – information which is again crucial in supporting the ontology management and editing process. In future versions of the API, changes may be encapsulated in transactions, which are processed as such, meeting the basic properties of transactions in databases, i.e. Atomicity, Consistency, Isolation and Durability.

4.3 Parsing

Since OWL possesses several presentation syntaxes, parsing is decoupled from particular implementations of the data model. A given file or stream is consumed by parser components, which issue a sequence of change events to the API in order to build an in-memory representation of an ontology.

Parsing RDF. Parsing RDF is a non-trivial effort. If possible, parsing should be done in a streaming manner to avoid large memory consumption while parsing large ontologies. However, with RDF this is, in the general case, impossible, since the graph is not serialized in any particular order. We *cannot* guarantee that all information required to process a particular syntactic construct is available until the entire model has been parsed.

Additionally, RDF ontologies are, in our experience, prone to errors due to their dependency on URIs. In many DAML+OIL ontologies inconsistent use of URIs was made. For example, namespaces are often misspelled. Hence, a series of heuristics are required in practice that try to ameliorate user errors by implicitly correcting such misspellings.

Another source of difficulty for parsing are missing definitions of classes or properties used within the ontology. For example, in the case of OWL Lite and OWL DL, properties must be explicitly typed as object properties or datatype properties. We can not tell from the URI what the correct type of the property, i.e. datatype or object property, is. Instead, a series of heuristics must be applied, e.g. inspecting all property instantiations and deducing from usage what the correct type could be.

However, the applied parsing heuristics must be optional and their usage must be specified by user applications. For example, a species validator (see Section 5) does not want to receive a cleaned ontology, since it could not detect the correct species of the initial source if definitions have been tampered with.

Inclusion The OWL language provides a simple mechanism for inclusion and import. Inclusion in the API is dealt with by registering all open ontologies within a housekeeping facility in the API. This facility manages all available parsers, thereby allowing the inclusion of XML-based ontologies into RDF-based ontologies, and manages the formal dependencies between open ontologies. This avoids the re-parsing of multiply used ontologies.

The parsing of included ontologies is handled in a depth-first manner. However, in case of RDF, the complete parsing of a certain RDF model is required, since the triple stating an inclusion could be the very last triple parsed in the model. The necessity to keep all RDF models in an inclusion hierarchy in-memory requires large amounts of main memory. This raises question about the suitability of RDF for large ontologies, which can be processed with low memory footprint in the XML-based syntax.

Inclusion is another fragile component of OWL due to the dependency on URIs. For example, a draft version of the OWL Guide `wine` ontology [16] contained an incorrect `imports` reference to the OWL Guide `food` ontology. To lessen this problem we adopt a solution in the OWL API of distinguishing between logical and physical URIs. The logical URIs are the base names for most URIs in the ontology, while the physical URIs refer to the actual locations that ontologies can be retrieved from.

The base name can be set in an explicit serialization via the `xml:base` attribute. This helps to enforce good practise with respect to relative URIs, since they do not then change if the ontology physically moves. If `xml:base` is not used, relative URIs are resolved relatively against the physical file URI.

The implementation keeps track of both logical URIS and physical URIS and can locate ontologies by either URI. In an extension of the OWL API, we could provide a further means for locating ontologies, by means of a registry as described in [10]. In the example above, if the implementation is unable to find the ontology by physical URI, it can try to locate instead by logical URI.

4.4 Implementation Language

The use of Java introduces a number of limitations on the API. For example, without generic collections, it is difficult to guarantee type safety without introducing a large number of extra helper classes to represent, for example, collections of Classes or collections of Properties. In our design, we have chosen simplicity over type safety, and a large number of methods simply return `Sets` when collections of objects are expected. It is then up to client applications to cast to the appropriate objects. However, this situation is remedied with the upcoming version of Java which supports generic collections.

5 Example: Species Validation

Finally, we present an example application that has been built using our draft implementation[6]. Species Validation[4] is the process whereby we identify the particular OWL sub-species (Lite, DL or Full) that an ontology belongs to. Species identification requires two stages:

1. parsing the OWL document;
2. a post-process to ensure that the various conditions for membership of the species hold. Examples of the validation conditions are: OWL Lite ontologies should not contain `unionOf`, `complementOf` or `oneOf` expressions; OWL DL/Lite ontologies cannot include properties specified as transitive with a super property specified as functional; OWL DL/Lite ontologies must separate Classes, Properties and Individuals, and cannot make use of metamodelling devices such as "Classes as instances".

Parsing requires access to the `model` and `change` interfaces, while the post processing stage is simply read-only and thus only uses the `model` interface. We have implemented a simple OWL Validator that performs validation and which is accessible as a Java Servlet.

The validator has been tested using the OWL Test Suite [4] and a draft version of the wines ontology from the OWL Guide [16]. In the wines ontology, a number of minor errors were detected. These included misuse of vocabulary (e.g. `hasClass` rather than `someValuesFrom`) and inconsistency in capitalization. In the latter case, the miscapitalization leads to the ontologies being flagged as outside the DL subspecies as the resulting IndividualIDs are not then explicitly typed (one of the conditions for OWL DL). The tool was also able to identify a number of minor errors in proposed tests. The validator was also able to read, check and detect errors in a draft version of a large ontology[7] containing some 500,000 RDF triples.

6 Conclusion

As a result of our work the OWL API is a readily available Standard Application Programming Interface (API)[8] that allows developers to access data structures

[6] See `http://wonderweb.semanticweb.org/owl/` for updates on the API development, current documentation, and links to applications using the API.

[7] The National Cancer Institute Thesaurus `http://www.mindswap.org/2003/CancerOntology/nciOncology.owl`

[8] It is available at `http://wonderweb.man.ac.uk/owl/`

and functionality that implement the concepts and components needed to build the Semantic Web. The higher-level abstractions of the API help to insulate application developers from underlying issues of syntax[9] and presentation.

The OWL Test Cases [4] provide general notions of OWL syntax and consistency checkers, but this is a somewhat coarse-grained idea – an OWL consistency checker takes a document as input, and outputs one word being `Consistent`, `Inconsistent`, or `Unknown`. Real applications need a finer notion of what is being implemented along with richer descriptions of functionality. Our design facilitates this through the explicit characterization of different aspects of functionality.

An exemplar of this approach is the XML Document Object Model (DOM) [20]. The DOM provides "a platform- and language-neutral interface that will allow programs and scripts to dynamically access and update the content, structure and style of documents." In practice, implementations of the DOM, such as the Java implementations encapsulated in the `org.w3c.dom` packages included in the latest releases of Sun's Java Software Development Kit (SDK) [18] (along with associated parsing libraries) have allowed a large number of developers to use and manipulate XML in applications. Similarly, APIs for the Resource Description Framework (RDF) [5] such as Jena [9] and the Stanford RDF API [12] have helped to push deployment of RDF technology into applications.

Our hope is that the OWL API will become a predominant component in the Semantic Web application world and gain a similar status as the standard SAX and DOM [20] interfaces for XML (or at least serve as a starting point for discussion about the design of such infrastructure).

Acknowledgments. The authors would like to thank Angus Roberts, who contributed to the early design of a prototype API. This work was supported by the European FET project WonderWeb (EU IST-2001-33052) and the myGrid E-science pilot (EPSRC GR/R67743). Raphael Volz was supported by DAAD.

References

1. Joint US/EU ad hoc Agent Markup Language Committee. Web Ontology Language, Reference Version 1.0. `http://www.daml.org/2001/03/daml+oil-index.html`.
2. S. Bechhofer, C. Goble, and I. Horrocks. DAML+OIL is not enough. In *SWWS-1, Semantic Web working symposium*, Jul/Aug 2001.
3. S. Bechhofer, I. Horrocks, C. Goble, and R. Stevens. OilEd: a Reason-able Ontology Editor for the Semantic Web. In *Proc. of KI2001, Joint German/Austrian conference on Artificial Intelligence*, volume 2174 of *LNAI*, pages 396–408, Vienna, Sep 2001. Springer-Verlag.
4. J. Carroll and J. De Roo. Web Ontology Language (OWL) Test Cases. `http://www.w3.org/TR/owl-test/`, 2003.

[9] **Quiz Answer:** `type` and `Property` are in the RDF vocabulary, `comment` is in RDF(S). Bonus point if you got all three.

5. World Wide Web Consortium. Resource Description Framework (RDF). http://www.w3.org/RDF/.
6. E. Bozsak et.al. KAON – Towards a Large Scale Semantic Web. In K. Bauknecht, A. Min Tjoa, and G. Quirchmayr, editors, *EC-Web 2002*, volume 2455 of *Lecture Notes in Computer Science*, pages 304–313. Springer, September 2002.
7. J. Euzenat. Towards formal knowledge intelligibility at the semiotic level. In *Proc. of ECAI 2000 Workshop Applied Semiotics: Control Problems*, pages 59–61, 2000.
8. E. Gamma, R. Helm, R. Johnson, and J. Vlissides. *Design Patterns: Elements of Reusable Object-Oriented Software.* Professional Computing Series. Addison-Wesley, 1995.
9. Hewlett Packard. Jena Semantic Web Toolkit. http://www.hpl.hp.com/semweb/jena.htm.
10. A. Maedche, B. Motik, L. Stojanovic, R. Studer, and R. Volz. An infrastructure for searching, reusing and evolving distributed ontologies. In *To Appear In Proc. of WWW 2003*, 2003.
11. R. Meersman and Z. Tari et. al, editors. *Proc. of the International Conference on Ontologies, Databases and Applications of SEmantics ODBASE 2002*, volume 2519 of *LNCS*, University of California, Irvine, USA, 2002. Springer.
12. S. Melnik. Stanford RDF API. http://www-db.stanford.edu/~melnik/rdf/api.html.
13. B. Motik, A. Maedche, and R. Volz. A conceptual modeling approach for building semantics-driven enterprise applications. In Meersman and et. al [11].
14. N. Noy and M. Klein. Ontology evolution: Not the same as schema evolution. *Knowledge and Information Systems*, 5, 2003.
15. P. Patel-Schneider, P. Hayes, and I. Horrocks. OWL Web Ontology Language (OWL) Abstract Syntax and Semantics. http://www.w3.org/TR/owl-semantics/, 2003.
16. M. Smith, C. Welty, and D. McGuinness. OWL Web Ontology Language Guide. http://www.w3.org/TR/owl-guide/, 2003.
17. L. Stojanovic, A. Maedche, B. Motik, and N. Stojanovic. User-driven ontology evolution management. In *Proc. of EKAW 2002*, page 285 ff., 2002.
18. Sun Microsystems, Inc. Java^{TM}Platform. http://java.sun.com/j2se/.
19. Y. Sure, S. Staab, and J. Angele. OntoEdit: Guiding ontology development by methodology and inferencing. In Meersman and et. al [11].
20. W3C DOM Working Group. Document Object Model. http://www.w3.org/DOM/.
21. W3C WebOnt Working Group. http://www.w3.org/2001/sw/WebOnt.

WebScripter: Grass-Roots Ontology Alignment via End-User Report Creation

Baoshi Yan, Martin Frank, Pedro Szekely, Robert Neches, and Juan Lopez

Information Sciences Institute, University of Southern California
4676 Admiralty Way, Marina del Rey, California 90292
{baoshi,frank,szekely,rneches,juan}@isi.edu

Abstract. Ontologies define hierarchies of classes and attributes; they are meta-data: data about data. In the "traditional approach" to ontology engineering, experts add new data by carefully analyzing others' ontologies and fitting their new concepts into the existing hierarchy. In the emerging "Semantic Web approach", ordinary users may not look at anyone's ontology before creating theirs - instead, they may simply define a new local schema from scratch that addresses their immediate needs, without worrying if and how their data may some day integrate with others' data. This paper describes WebScripter, a tool for translating between the countless mini-ontologies that the "Semantic Web approach" yields. In our approach, ordinary users graphically align data from multiple sources in a simple spreadsheet-like view without having to know anything about ontologies. The resulting web of equivalency statements is then mined by WebScripter to help users find related ontologies and data, and to automatically align the related data with their own.

1 WebScripter Overview

WebScripter is a tool that enables ordinary users to easily and quickly assemble reports extracting and fusing information from multiple, heterogeneous Semantic Web sources in RDF Schema (RDFS) format[1]. Different Semantic Web sources may use different ontologies. WebScripter addresses this problem by (a) making it easy for individual users to graphically align the attributes of two separate externally defined concepts, and (b) making it easy to reuse others' alignment work. At a high level, the WebScripter concept is that users extract content from heterogeneous sources and paste that content into what looks like an ordinary spreadsheet. What users implicitly do in WebScripter (without expending extra effort) is to build up an articulation ontology containing equivalency statements. We believe that in the long run, this articulation ontology will be more valuable than the data the users obtained when they constructed the original report. The equivalency information reduces the amount of work future WebScripter users have to perform. Thus, in some sense, you do not just use the Semantic Web when you use WebScripter, you help build it as you go along.

[1] We will use RDFS for brevity in the remainder of the paperal though our tool and discussions equally apply to DAML(+OIL) and OWL.

D. Fensel et al. (Eds.): ISWC 2003, LNCS 2870, pp. 676–689, 2003.

2 System Description

This section describes the current implementation of WebScripter by walking through a step-by-step example. In order to use WebScripter, users do not need to have knowledge of ontological languages. In this section we will describe how WebScripter help ordinary users locate RDFS sources, build a report and customize the representation of a report. We then show how the resulting ontology alignment data benefits other users in constructing similar reports by identifying related sources and aligning data.

2.1 Constructing a First Report from Scratch

Step 1: Load RDFS Data. In this example our job is to maintain a list of researchers working on the Semantic Web. The first task is to find the URLs where the researchers put their data (which we presume to be in some RDF-based format for this example). Although locating RDFS sources is not WebScripter's focus, WebScripter provides some support for it by wrapping Teknowledge's Semantic Search Engine [1]. This search engine accepts queries in the format of triple patterns, and returns matches from the BBN's crawled ontology library [2]. Our wrapper helps users by transforming their keyword-based queries into triple patterns, submitting them to Teknowledge's Semantic Search Engine and extracting source URL's from the results. Later on we will discuss how WebScripter can help identify related RDFS sources in a collaborative filtering fashion. In this example, we will use two RDFS data sources, ISWC'2002 annotated author data [3] and ISI's Distributed Scalable Systems Division personnel data [4].

Step 2: Create a Report. Figure 1 shows WebScripter just after loading the ISWC'2002 data. On the left side is a class hierarchy pane. Users can select a class to view its content in the lower right pane. The upper right pane is the report-authoring area. WebScripter offers three options for users to add a column to a report. (1) In the simplest case, users can select a column from a class and add it to the report, as shown in Figure 1. (2) Users can also type example data in the report-authoring area; WebScripter will then try to guess which column in which class the user is referring to. This is useful when users are lost in the class hierarchy. (3) In the most complicated case, users want to include information from different classes into a single report. We do not want to require users to understand the domain ontology in order to do that. For example, suppose users have already specified "name" and "email" for the instances of class "Person" in a report, and now they want to add information about the project a person works on, which is in the "Project" class. Instead of requiring users to specify how to go from the "Person" class to the "Project" class step by step, WebScripter will try to infer the ontological paths between these two classes, rank the paths first based on path length (shortest first) then by number of instance matches (more first), and lets users select (Figure 2). In our experience, the first entry listed

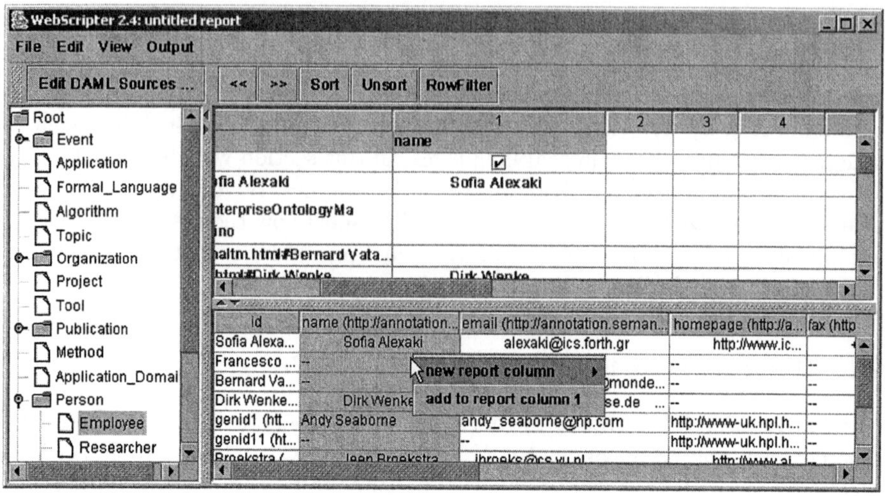

Fig. 1. WebScripter GUI: The left pane shows the class hierarchy of ISWC'2002 data; the lower right pane shows all the instance data for the selected class. Users can add columns from this pane to their report in the upper right pane.

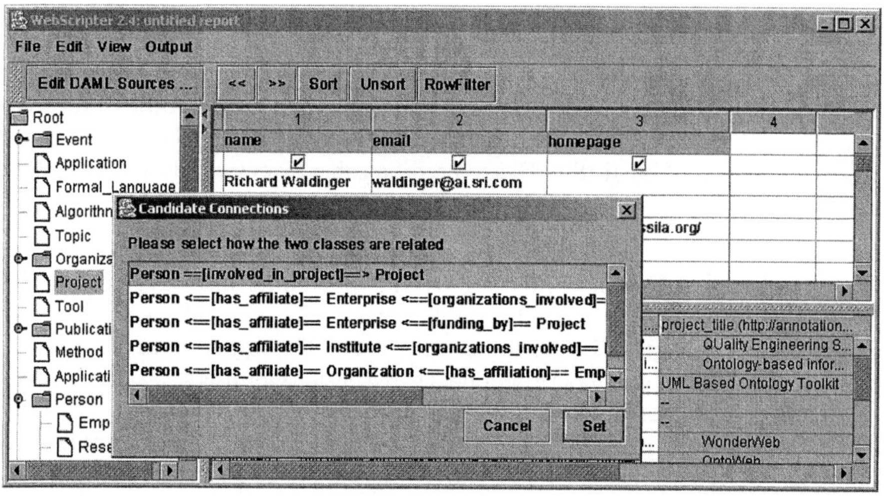

Fig. 2. Ontological Path Inference: When users add a column to the report that represents a new class, WebScripter detects the possible paths between these two classes and lets the user choose.

(the one with the shortest ontological path and which fills the most blanks in the report) is virtually always the desired choice.

Step 3: Align data from multiple sources. In our running example, the user is now done with adding ISWC'2002 author information to the report. Assume

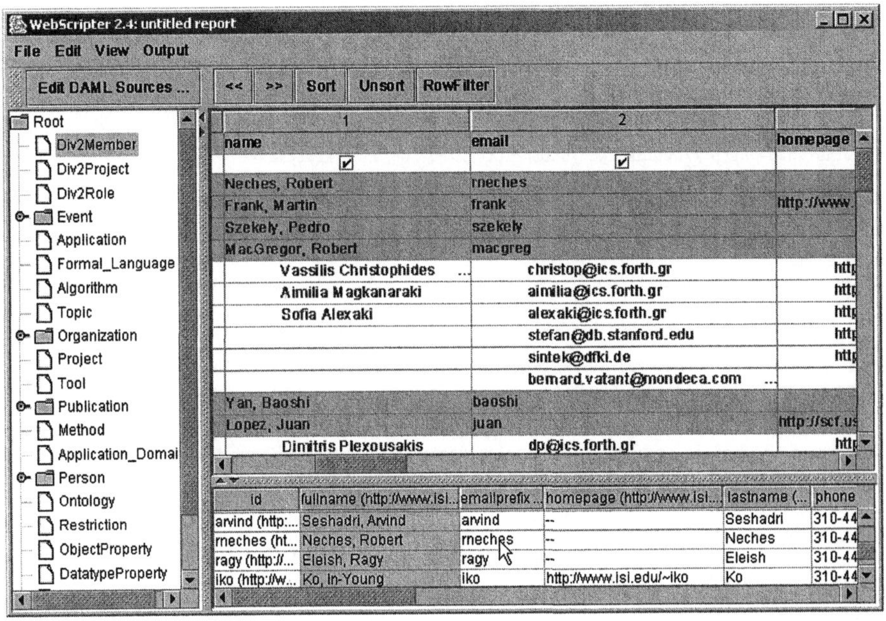

Fig. 3. Aligning Data: In the upper right pane, the shaded data is from ISI, the light data from ISWC.

they happen to find ISI's researcher information via Teknowledge's Semantic Search Engine and want to include that in the report also. They basically repeat the previous steps of adding columns but this time they add the columns from ISI "Div2Member" class to the corresponding columns of the ISWC data (rather than adding it as new columns). Figure 3 shows the combined data from the two groups.

When users compose a report by putting together information from heterogeneous sources, there is some implicit and valuable information that can be inferred. First, by composing a report, users imply a (weak) association between sources, i.e., "one user who use this source also used that one", somewhat analogous to Amazon's book recommendations ("customers who bought this book also bought that one"). This association can help future users locate relevant RDFS sources. Second and more interestingly, by putting heterogeneous information together, users also imply a (similarly weak) equivalency between concepts from different ontologies. For example, from the report in Figure 3 WebScripter could infer that ISI's "Div2Member" class is equivalent to ISWC's "Person" class, ISI's "fullname" property is equivalent to ISWC's "name" property, and so on. Table 1 shows the equivalency information inferred from the report in DAML format.

The alignment axioms shown above are the simplest ones, a direct alignment between two named classes or properties. Since WebScripter also supports joins (between two classes) and filtering (of instances), the alignment axioms can

Table 1. Resulting alignment axioms.

```
<?xml version="1.0" encoding="UTF-8"?>
<rdf:RDF  xmlns:rdf ="http://www.w3.org/1999/02/22-rdf-syntax-ns#"
  xmlns:rdfs="http://www.w3.org/2000/01/rdf-schema#"
  xmlns:daml="http://www.daml.org/2001/03/daml+oil#"
  xmlns:wseq="http://www.isi.edu/WebScripter/2002/06/equivalencies#"
>
<rdfs:Class rdf:about="http://annotation.semanticweb.org/iswc/iswc.daml#Person">
  <daml:sameClassAs rdf:resource=
        "http://www.isi.edu/webscripter/div2-org.o.daml#Div2Member"/>
</rdfs:Class>
<rdfs:Property rdf:about="http://annotation.semanticweb.org/iswc/iswc.daml#name">
  <daml:samePropertyAs rdf:resource=
        "http://www.isi.edu/webscripter/div2-org.o.daml#fullname"/>
</rdfs:Property>
<rdfs:Property rdf:about="http://annotation.semanticweb.org/iswc/iswc.daml#email">
  <daml:samePropertyAs rdf:resource=
        "http://www.isi.edu/webscripter/div2-org.o.daml#emailprefix"/>
</rdfs:Property>
<rdfs:Property rdf:about="http://annotation.semanticweb.org/iswc/iswc.daml#homepage">
  <daml:samePropertyAs rdf:resource=
        "http://www.isi.edu/webscripter/div2-org.o.daml#homepage"/>
</rdfs:Property>
<rdfs:Property rdf:about=
        "http://annotation.semanticweb.org/iswc/iswc.daml#involved_in_project">
  <daml:samePropertyAs rdf:resource=
        "http://www.isi.edu/webscripter/div2-org.o.daml#workson"/>
</rdfs:Property>
<rdfs:Property rdf:about="http://annotation.semanticweb.org/iswc/iswc.daml#project_title">
  <daml:samePropertyAs rdf:resource=
        "http://www.w3.org/2000/01/rdf-schema#label"/>
</rdfs:Property>
</rdf:RDF>
```

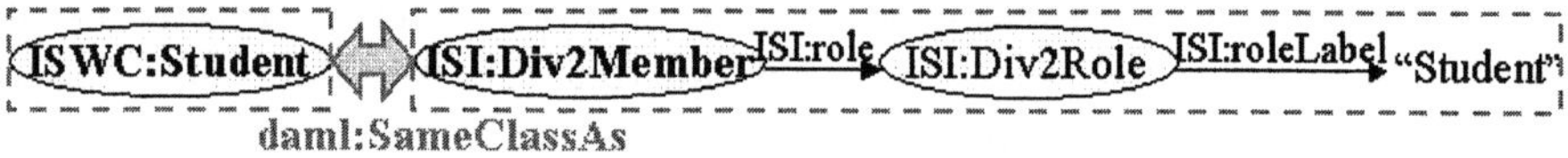

Fig. 4. Constructed-Class Alignment: An equivalency between a named class and a class defined by a join and subsequent fiter operation.

also be more complex. For example, if users want to build a report of just the ISI students, users need to add "Div2Member" instances to the report, do a join to their roles ("Div2Role") and filter the roles by "Student". The resulting equivalency is visualized as in Figure 4.

Figure 5 shows an axiom that defines the equivalency between two property sequences. This type of axiom can be captured with WebScripter (but we do not yet make use of it for our own alignment suggestions). To obtain the project name for a person, in the first case users simply follow the link "foo:projectName"; in the second case users need to follow the link "ISWC:involved_in_project", then the link "ISWC:project_title". Such "role chaining" is not expressible in current DAML or OWL. We are looking at RuleML [5] as an alternative.

Current semi-automatic ontology mapping tools (see [26] for a good survey) are good at one-to-one element mapping and tend to deal less with alignment axioms as complex as shown in Figures 4 and 5, which WebScripter in some

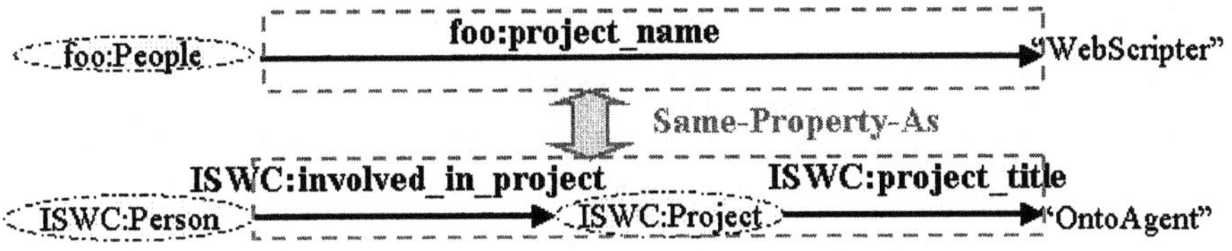

Fig. 5. Constructed-Property Alignment: An equivalency between two property sequences.

sense captures "for free" by providing an easy way for users to perform join and filtering during report authoring.

2.2 Constructing a Report with Automatic Alignment Support

The alignment axioms can be automatically published on a Web site and registered as a new DAML content root in BBN's DAML content library. Consequently, it can be used by Teknowledge's DAML search engine to extend user queries, and we expect it would benefit other applications as well. We also use the WebScripter-generated alignment axioms in WebScripter itself. WebScripter reads its default alignment axioms from a fixed location on our Web site to which anyone can contribute via WebScripter's "Easy Publish" menu. In this section we will quickly walk through an example of how the alignment axioms help users in report authoring.

In a nutshell, if users add any class or attribute to their report for which there are known equivalencies, WebScripter will mark them with a red "light bulb". If users click on the light bulb they can choose to import equivalencies. Accepting equivalencies can also automatically load known sources of the data, and then automatically aligns the attributes of the discovered classes. In this example, a user has constructed a new report which contains Stanford personnel data (the light area of the upper-right pane in Figure 6). She has just now manually aligned the Stanford and ISI names in the same column, and WebScripter responded by putting a lightbulb next to the the column name. This is an indication that WebScripter has equivalency information about the data she just added.

When the user clicks on the light bulb, WebScripter lists the equivalence or equivalencies and asks the user to accept or reject them (upper window of Figure 7). In this example, WebScripter knows where ISWC people data is located, and also knows how the ISWC aligns with the ISI data; it knows that because they were aligned by someone else before (in Figure 3) and because that user chose to share the alignment information.

If the user accepts an equivalency, WebScripter displays a further dialog box that lets users decide which of the known source files of the equivalent classes/properties they could add to their report (lower window Figure 7). None, some, or all of the rows can be selected with the mouse, clicking the Load File button then adds the selected URLs to the data sources that are imported by the WebScripter report. In this example, if the user accepts the ISI/ISWC equiva-

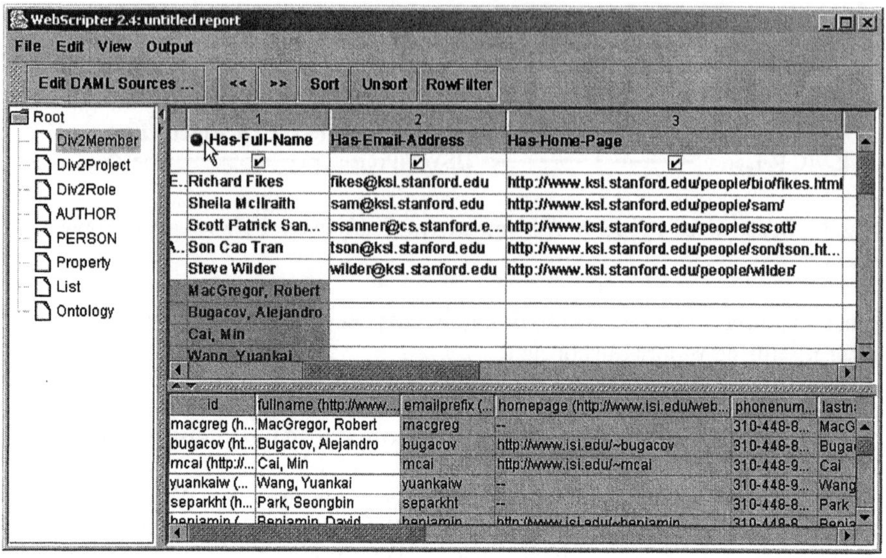

Fig. 6. Light bulbs tell the user that WebScripter can auto-align data for them.

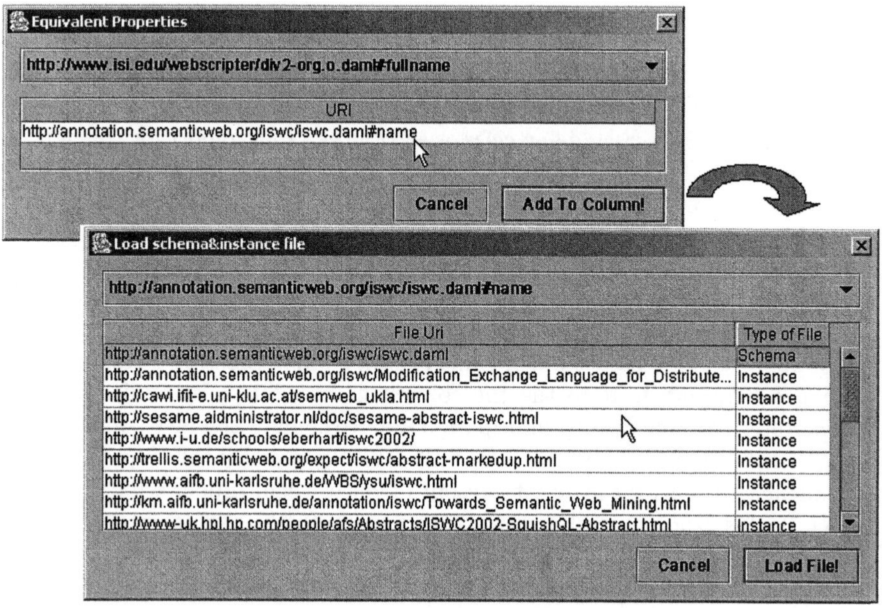

Fig. 7. The upper window lets users accept or reject an equivalency per se. The lower window lets users decide if they also want to add data sources to their reports that contain aligned data.

lencies and completes the Standord/ISI equivalencies and published those, WebScripter can now translate between all three ontologies.

2.3 Customizing WebScripter Reports

WebScripter reports can be published in various formats including HTML and plain text. WebScripter first generates an XML representation of the report. Various XSL stylesheets are part of the WebScripter distribution, and you can define your own variation to customize the presentation. We are also currently working on a new version that will allow accessing WebScripter reports on mobile devices such as PDAs by intelligently reformatting the HTML to smaller screen sizes [20].

3 Applications

WebScripter has turned out to be a valuable practical tool for the simple single-ontology case where there is only one schema but the instance data is distributed over many Web pages. For example, the Distributed Scalable Systems Division at ISI automatically pulls together its people page from many different DAMLized Web pages: some information is maintained by individuals themselves (such as their research interests), other information is maintained by the division director (such as project assignments), and some information is maintained at the institute level (such as office assignments); this relieved the division's administrative assistant from manually maintaining everyone's interests [4]. WebScripter has also been used externally, for example to maintain a Semantic Web tools list [6], and a DAML publications list [7]. WebScripter can be downloaded from [8].

As of the time of writing, one issue we encountered is that there is not really that much interesting, continuously updated RDF Schema, much less DAML or OWL, available on the Web today.[2] What made the original Web take off was that there was an immediate incentive for producers to use the technology because it was an easy way to publish information. We currently see little motivation for Web page authors to put work into producing RDF in addition to their regular HTML pages (as others have noted also, maybe most eloquently in [17]). In this section, we will describe a novel WebScripter application, which not only makes use of WebScripter but also incentivizes web authors to produce RDF contents.

3.1 Using WebScripter for Collaborative Semantic Weblogs

We're now in the process of applying WebScripter technology to weblogs. Such a "blog" is a "frequent, chronological publication of personal thoughts and Web links" [10]. It is an easy way to publish a piece of information with a single click.

[2] One notable exception are RSS 1.0 [9] headline exchange files such as *slashdot.org/slashdot.rdf.*

It is estimated that there were already from 500,000 to 1 million web bloggers since 1999 and that the number of bloggers is still expanding rapidly [12].

Weblogs, though very popular nowadays, have no semantic structure, which brings about several shortcomings. A weblog is a collection of posts. Each post is a segment of natural language text in HTML format. There is no metadata describing individual posts. The lack of semantic structure makes it difficult to organize weblogs. For example, suppose you have two weblogs, one is about the Semantic Web, the other about Java programming. Hence, you would want to add a discussion of Jena [22] to both weblogs. However, currently you have to either only add it to one weblog, or copy the same content over to the other blog, neither of which is satisfactory. The lack of semantics also rules out queries like "what are posts about Java programming for the Semantic Web". Weblogs quickly become clumsy for information retrieval as the volume of data increases because their only native indexing is by reverse chronological order.

WebScripter, coupled with an easy-to-use metadata publishing tool, could greatly enhance the functionality of weblogs. A weblog with no data other than the text and the entry date of a post can be viewed as a two-column WebScripter report. Additional columns can then be used for additional semantic mark-up about the posts. WebScripter by itself supports RDFS report authoring not original RDFS data entry. Thus, we also developed ISI Annotator, which provides an easy-to-use way to produce metadata. Annotator lets users define their own classes and properties for describing their posts.[3] The posts users publish are in RDFS format and can thus be post-processed by WebScripter (or any other RDFS tool, of course).

Figure 8 shows the chain of producing RDFS content in Annotator, post-processing it as a WebScripter report, and finally presenting it as a Web page with (invisible) RDFS mark-up via a stylesheet. Note that it is perfectly possible to define multiple WebScripter reports of that data, say one that only picks up posts marked as Java-related or as personal.

One common phenomenon in weblogs is cross-referencing between web bloggers with similar interests, which form a community where they read each other's blog, comment and share blogs. When a user builds a new report by aligning someone else's semantic weblog with her own, the immediate result is that she now will have other's semantic weblog content in her semantic weblog, but there are other important implications. First, the implicit alignment axioms inferred from her alignment would benefit other bloggers in doing the same work. Second, by adding aother's semantic weblog to hers, the user implies that there are shared interests. Such information could in turn facilitate the discovery of bloggers with similar interests, thus expediting the forming of a blogger community.

[3] Annotator also allows users to annotate existing Web pages with RDFS, hence its name, but that is not further discussed in this paper.

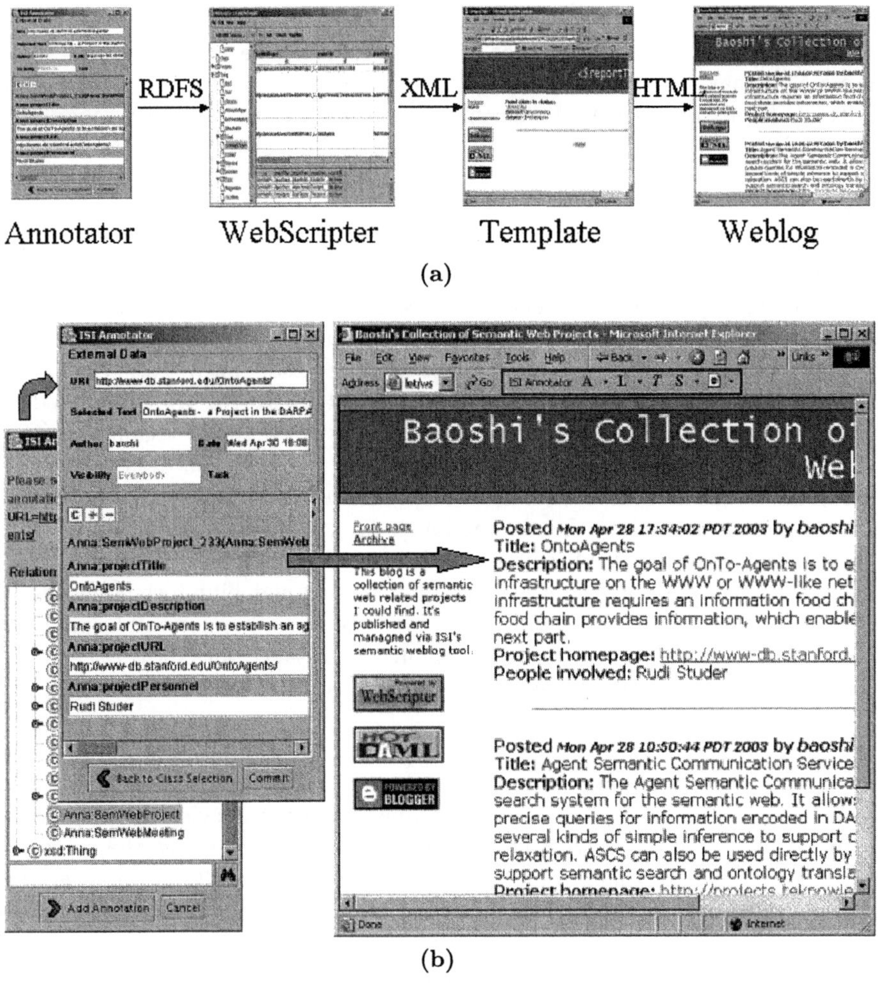

Fig. 8. Semantic Weblogs: (a) ISI's Annotator Tool can produce RDFS that is then run through a WebScripter report and produces the final Web page that contains both human and machine-readable mark-up. (b) ISI's Annotator(on the left) and the web page of a semantic weblog

4 Related Work

WebScripter's approach to ontology alignment is extreme: terms from different ontologies are always assumed to mean different things by default, and all ontology mapping is done by humans (implicitly, by putting them into the same column of a report) – in that sense, there is no automated inference.

This is similar in spirit to Gio Wiederhold's mediation approach to ontology interoperation [27], which also assumes that terms from different ontologies never mean the same thing unless committees of integration experts say they are. WebScripter pushes that concept to the brink by replacing the experts with ordinary users that may not even be aware of their implicit ontology alignment contributions. (Note, however, that we cannot yet proof that this collective alignment data is indeed a useful source for automatic ontology alignment on an Internet scale – we lack sufficient data from distributed WebScripter use to make that claim.)

Most schema matching techniques (see [26] for a survey) take a semi-automated approach to ontology interoperation: the system guesses likely matches between terms of two separately conceived ontologies, a human expert knowledgeable about the semantics of both ontologies then verifies the inferences, possibly using a graphical user interface. Such guesses can be based on name and structure similarity in schemas (ONION [24] , PROMPT [25]), plus data instances (LSD [14] GLUE [15]), or integrated use of different techniques (CUPID [21], COMA [13]). In WebScripter human users rely purely on the *data instances* to decide what collates and what does not (because they are just not expert enough to analyze the abstractions). That being said, incorporating the above techniques into WebScripter would clearly be beneficial if the rate of correct guesses is sufficiently high. Unlike other schema matching techniques, WebScripter is not suitable for alignment tasks where the only information available are the two schemas to be matched (without any instance data for the schemas). Rather, it relies on shared reuse and reasoning with other users' implicit and often imprecise ontology alignments.

OBSERVER [23], SIMS [11], TSIMMIS [16] and the Information Manifold [19] are all systems for querying multiple data sources of different schemata in a uniform way; however, they all rely on human experts to devise the ontological mappings between the sources to our knowledge. This is because they mediate between structured dynamic data sources (such as SQL/ODBC sources) without run-time human involvement where a higher level of precision is required to make the interoperation work. In contrast, WebScripter is targeted towards mediating between different ontologies in RDF-based Web pages with run-time human involvement, where the need for precision in the translation is naturally lower.

Another difference between WebScripter and the above systems is its philosophy of creating the Semantic Web while using it. Our vision and hope is that semantics can emerge from large-scale collaborative use of numerous, previously isolated ontologies.

5 Discussion

More appropriate Semantics for Alignment Axioms. Strictly speaking, the alignment axioms inferred from WebScripter should not be DAML or OWL equivalence statements, which are very strong claims: "x equivalent to y" means everything that applies to x also applies to y and vice versa. The WebScripter alignment axioms should really just imply equivalence within some context – two concepts are equivalent for the purposes of the report that some individual

Table 2. Sketch of a graphical user interface for better end-user control over alignment.

Class	Hops	Origin	Author	Rows	Date	Users
Person	1	stanford.e...	Smith	235	10/6/02	12
Employee	1	stanford.e...	Smith	57	10/6/02	6
Staff	1	stanford.e...	Smith	697	10/6/02	0
Member	2	www.isi.e...	Chen	15	3/4/01	17
Person	2	cmu.edu/...	Miller	973	12/7/01	4
Member	2	cmu.edu/...	Miller	107	12/7/01	9

created. Thus on the one hand, we need more work on judging the likelihood of two contexts being compatible, possibly according to report contents, user profile, or user report-authoring history. On the other hand, we need to evaluate how generic an alignment axiom is. We would propose a more grass-roots, somewhat Darwinian theory. The theory is that relatively small groups will use these axioms to align their semantics and eventually you will get alignment among groups of groups, and for a few things this will lead to alignment among really big groups. Nevertheless, we believe approximate alignment axioms in the spirit of Hovy's "generally accoiated with" links [18] will be a common phenomenon in the Semantic Web as it is unlikely that concepts casually developed by end users would meet as strong requirements as implied by the DAML or OWL equivalency statements.

Will WebScripter scale? The current implementation of WebScripter does not scale well because (a) all alignment axioms are stored in and retrieved from a single central server, and because (b) all processing occurs in the main memory of the user's machine. (Essentially, we chose not to worry about scalability until we got to a compelling application and a substantial number of users.) We believe that scalability for the former could be achieved with a server-farm approach as demonstrated by e.g. Google and Yahoo, or with a peer-2-peer approach to distribute equivalency data across the users' machines. The latter is already being addressed by RDF toolkits that can connect to back-end databases, such as Jena [22].

End-User Control over Auto-Alignment. Our current end-user interface for alignment (see Section 2.2) is unlikely to scale well for large numbers of alignment axioms. We see the following solutions to this problem (which are not mutually exclusive). *Social Filtering.* One approach would be to keep track of the authors of alignment axioms as well as the users of alignment axioms; this would enable users to say "I want to use the same equivalency data that Jim and Chris are using", a nicely implicit way to limit equivalencies to e.g. the accounting context if they are co-workers in accounting, without having to more formally define the context, which is a more abstract and difficult task. This would also allow cautious users to express "I am willing to use equivalency data that at least ten others are using" (which addresses the erroneous-alignment problem but not the context-mismatch problem). *Finer-Grained Control in the User Interface.* It would be nice to have a display (see Table 2) of the available equivalency information that presents more than just the equivalent URIs as we currently do (lower window of Figure 7). A related question is how users can lock out ill-intentioned sources of alignment axioms, addressing the general question of trust management on the Semantic Web. In a future stage of WebScripter, a Google-like social filtering mechanism and a Spam-blocking-like collaborative blacklist could help.

6 Conclusion

As an easy-to-use report authoring tool, WebScripter has proven its usefulness in several applications. As far as we know, WebScripter is currently the only interactive report generator for RDFS content. The most exciting application of WebScripter, as a collaborative ontology translation tool, has yet to prove its effectiveness due to the small number of casual Semantic Web users. Nevertheless, we are excited about this new approach to ontology alignment sharing. The key difference we see between "traditional" ontology translation and our approach is that non-experts perform all of the translation – but potentially on a global scale, leveraging each other's work.

Acknowledgments. We gratefully acknowledge DARPA DAML program funding for WebScripter under contract number F30602-00-2-0576. We thank Bob MacGregor and Stefan Decker for helpful discussions.

References

1. http://reliant.teknowledge.com/DAML.
2. http://www.daml.org/crawler.
3. http://annotation.semanticweb.org/iswc/ documents.html.
4. http://www.isi.edu/divisions/div2/. Click on People.
5. http://www.dfki.uni-kl.de/ruleml.
6. http://tools.semanticweb.org.
7. http://www.daml.org/publications/cite.html.
8. http://www.isi.edu/webscripter.
9. http://web.resource.org/rss/1.0.
10. http://www.marketingterms.com/dictionary/blog/.
11. Y. Arens, C. Knoblock, and W.-M. Shen. Query reformulation for dynamic information integration. *Intelligent Information Systems*, 6(2–3):99–130, 1996.
12. W. W. Conhaim. Blogging – what is it?, May 2002. http://www.infotoday.com/LU/may02/conhaim.htm.
13. H. Do and E. Rahm. Coma – a system for flexible combination of schema matching approaches. In *VLDB*, 2002.
14. A. Doan, P. Domingos, and A. Y. Halevy. Reconciling schemas of disparate data sources: A machine-learning approach. In *SIGMOD Conference*, 2001.
15. A. Doan, J. Madhavan, P. Domingos, and A. Halevy. Learning to map ontologies on the semantic web. In *The Eleventh International World Wide Web Conference*, 2002.

16. H. Garcia-Molina, Y. Papakonstantinou, D. Quass, A. Rajaraman, Y. Sagiv, J. Ullman, V. Vassalos, and J. Widom. The TSIMMIS approach to mediation: data models and languages. *Intelligent Information Systems*, 8(2):117–32, 1997.
17. S. Haustein and J. Pleumann. Easing participation in the semantic web. In *WWW-2002 Semantic Web Workshop*, Honolulu, Hawaii, May 7 2002.
18. E. Hovy. Using an ontology to simplify data access. *Communications of the ACM*, 46(1):47–49, 2003.
19. A. Levy, D. Srivastava, and T. Kirk. Data model and query evaluation in global information systems. *Intelligent Information Systems*, 5(2):121–43, 1995.
20. J. Lopez and P. Szekely. Web page adaptation for universal access. In *UAHCI-2001 Conference on Universal Access in Human Computer Interaction*, pages 690–694, New Orleans, 2001. Lawrence Erlbaum Associates, Mahwah, NJ.
21. J. Madhavan, P. A. Bernstein, and E. Rahm. Generic schema matching with cupid. In *The VLDB Journal*, pages 49–58, 2001.
22. B. McBride. Jena: Implementing the rdf model and syntax specification. Technical report, Hewlett-Packard, 2000.
http://www-uk.hpl.hp.com/people/bwm/papers/20001221-paper/.
23. E. Mena, A. Illarramendi, V. Kashyap, and A. Sheth. OBSERVER: an approach for query processing in global information systems based on interoperation across pre-existing ontologies. *Distributed and Parallel Databases*, 8(2):223–71, 2000.
24. P. Mitra and G. Wiederhold. An algebra for semantic interoperability of information sources. In *2nd Annual IEEE International Symposium on Bioinformatics and Bioengineering*, pages 174–82, Bethesda, MD, USA, November 4–6 2001.
25. N. F. Noy and M. A. Musen. PROMPT: Algorithm and tool for automated ontology merging and alignment. In *17th National Conference on AI*, 2000.
26. E. Rahm and P. Bernstein. On matching schemas automatically. Technical report, Microsoft Research, Redmon, WA, 2001. MSR-TR-2001-17.
27. G. Wiederhold. Interoperation, mediation, and ontologies. In *International Symposium on Fifth Generation Computer Systems, Workshop on Heterogeneous Cooperative Knowledge-Bases*, volume W3, pages 33–48. ICOT, Tokyo, Japan, December 1994.

Magpie – Towards a Semantic Web Browser

Martin Dzbor, John Domingue, and Enrico Motta

Knowledge Media Institute, The Open University, Milton Keynes, UK
{M.Dzbor,J.B.Domingue,E.Motta}@open.ac.uk

Abstract. Web browsing involves two tasks: finding the right web page and then *making sense* of its content. So far, research has focused on supporting the task of finding web resources through 'standard' information retrieval mechanisms, or semantics-enhanced search. Much less attention has been paid to the second problem. In this paper we describe Magpie, a tool which supports the interpretation of web pages. Magpie offers complementary knowledge sources, which a reader can call upon to quickly gain access to any background knowledge relevant to a web resource. Magpie automatically associates an ontology-based semantic layer to web resources, allowing relevant services to be invoked within a standard web browser. Hence, Magpie may be seen as a step towards a *semantic web browser*. The functionality of Magpie is illustrated using examples of how it has been integrated with our lab's web resources.

1 Introduction

Web browsing involves two basic tasks: (i) finding the right web page and (ii) *making sense* of its content. A lot of research has gone into supporting the task of finding web resources, either by means of 'standard' information retrieval mechanisms, or by means of semantically enhanced search [8, 14]. Less attention has been paid to the second task – supporting the *interpretation* of web pages. Annotation technologies [12, 17, 22] allow users to associate meta-information with web resources, which can then be used to facilitate their interpretation. While such technologies provide a useful way to support group-based and shared interpretation, they are nonetheless very limited; mainly because the annotation is carried out manually. In other words, the quality of the sensemaking support depends on the willingness of stakeholders to provide annotation, and their ability to provide valuable information. This is of course even more of a problem, if a formal approach to annotation is assumed, based on semantic web technology [1].

In this paper we describe Magpie, a tool supporting the interpretation of web pages. Magpie acts as a complementary knowledge source, which a user can call upon to gain instantaneous access to the background knowledge relevant to a web resource. Magpie follows a different approach from that used by the aforementioned annotation techniques: it automatically associates a semantic layer to a web resource, rather than relying on a manual annotation. This process relies on the availability of an *ontology* [7] – an explicit, declaratively specified representation of a discourse or problem matter. Ontologies are the cornerstone of the emerging semantic web: they provide conceptual interoperability, allow semantic agents to make sense of information on the web and to collaborate with other semantically aware agents. Magpie uses

D. Fensel et al. (Eds.): ISWC 2003, LNCS 2870, pp. 690–705, 2003.

ontologies in a similar way: to make it possible to associate meaning with the pieces of information found on a web page and then, on the basis of the identified meaning, to invoke the relevant services, or offer the user the appropriate functionalities.

The Magpie-mediated association between an ontology and a web resource provides an *interpretative viewpoint* or *context* over the resource in question. Indeed the overwhelming majority of web pages are created within a specific context. For example, the personal home page of a member of the Knowledge Media Institute would have normally been created within the context of that person's affiliation and organizational role. Some readers might be very familiar with such context, while others might not. In the latter case, the use of Magpie is especially beneficial, given that the context would be made explicit to the reader and context-specific functionalities will be provided. Because different readers show differing familiarity with the information shown in a web page and with the relevant background domain, they require different level of sensemaking support. Hence, the semantic layers in Magpie are designed with a specific type of user in mind.

In a seminal study of how users browse the web, Tauscher and Greenberg [21] presented the following statistics on the types of actions users may carry out:

- 58% of pages visited are revisits,
- 90% of all user actions are related to navigation,
- 30% of navigation actions are through the 'Back' button,
- less than 1% of navigation actions use a history mechanism

A fairly obvious conclusion from such statistics is that web users need support in capturing what they have seen previously. Current history mechanisms, 'Back' button aside, are of little help. Magpie is able to automatically track the items found during a browsing session using a *semantic log*. The semantic log allows *trigger services* to be subscribed to; they would be activated when a specific pattern of items has been found. One type of trigger service offered in Magpie is a *collector*, which collects items from a browsing session using an ontology-based filter. Examples of collectors are shown in the following section.

The rest of this paper is structured as follows. In the next section we give an overview of the functionality of Magpie through a scenario. Sections 3 and 4 discuss the Magpie design principles and architectural details. We then describe the different types of semantic services available in section 5. Finally, in sections 6 and 7, we review related research, and draw the conclusions from this research effort.

2 Scenario – Browsing the Web with Magpie

Imagine a journalist is writing an article on the Knowledge Media Institute (KMi) for a magazine. One of her tasks is to gather information about the important projects led by senior KMi staff. Using a web browser with a Magpie extension, she visits the home page of the lab's director Enrico Motta. After loading the page, she wants to highlight interesting concepts denoting researchers, collaborating organizations, projects, and research areas in the page. These concepts draw upon an existing ontology of academic and research organizations, which was populated by mining databases and web resources.

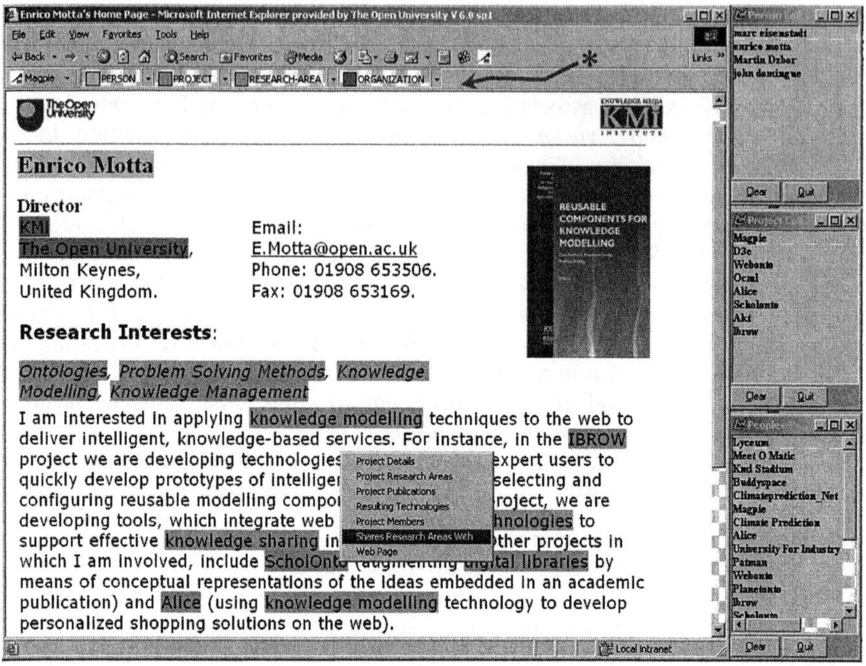

Fig. 1. Enrico Motta's home page viewed through Magpie. Known *people*, *organizations*, *projects* and *research areas* are highlighted using the Magpie toolbar (marked by '*'). On the right-hand side are three Magpie collectors – the top two log the people and projects found in the browsing session. The bottom one shows the (not explicitly mentioned) projects associated with the people found.

Fig. 1 shows the journalist's browser with the concepts of interest highlighted using the Magpie toolbar, which extends the functionality provided by Internet Explorer. As can be seen, Magpie preserves structure of the page, and only highlights the concepts upon user's request. This approach reduces the confusion, which may occur when the content and/or appearance of a web page are altered. Magpie toolbar (see close-up in Fig. 2) allows users to toggle highlighting for the specified types of entities, which were annotated in the page using an ontology-based lexicon. These types are ontology dependent – changing the ontology will modify the top-level headings displayed in the toolbar. As ontology represents an *interpretative viewpoint* we chose to leave the choice of ontology to the user. The button marked '♠' in Fig. 2 discretely hides the entire Magpie toolbar if not needed.

On the right-hand side of Fig. 1 are three Magpie *collectors*. These are automatically filled by Magpie *trigger services* as the user browses. During a browsing session, the entities found on accessed web pages are asserted into a *semantic log* knowledge base (KB). Collectors are set up to show a semantically filtered view of the semantic log. For instance, the top two collectors in Fig. 1 show the people and projects that have been recognized on the pages visited during the current browsing session. The bottom collector shows the projects associated with any people recognized during the browsing session, which were not mentioned explicitly in any page but originate from the populated domain ontology. Fig. 1 shows a number of projects the four researchers from the top-right collector are associated with.

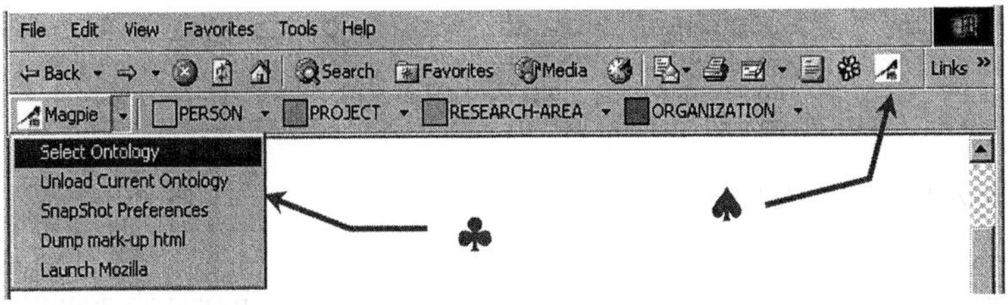

Fig. 2. Details of the Magpie toolbar showing four top-level classes that can be highlighted (*'Person'* through *'Project'*) in a page. The button marked '♠' toggles the toolbar on and off; Magpie menu (marked by '♣') enables the user to choose the ontology/viewpoint.

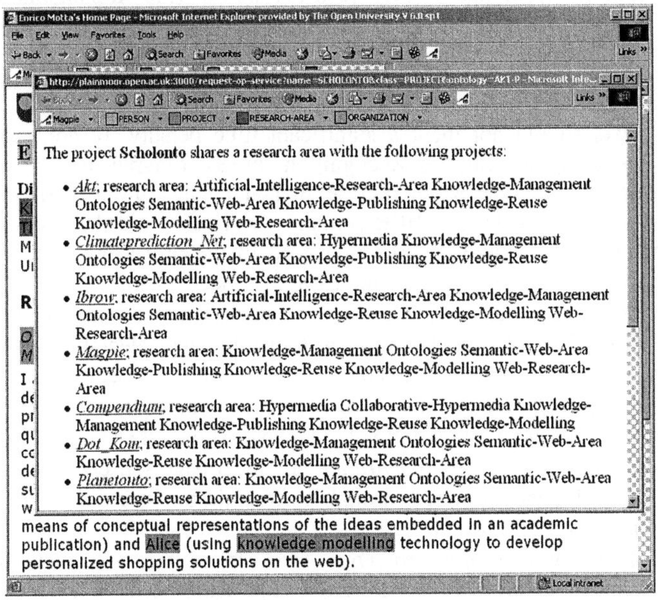

Fig. 3. Results of the *'Shares Research Areas With'* semantic query invoked for the *'ScholOnto'* project by the semantic menu action depicted in Fig. 1. Each bullet shows the name of a project followed by a list of overlapping research areas. Displayed answers are ordered according to the number of areas they have in common with *'ScholOnto'*.

Looking at the annotated page our journalist can see that the ScholOnto project might be suitable for her report, and she wonders if any related projects could be included in the same section. She right-clicks the 'ScholOnto' term, and the *semantic services menu* visible in Fig. 1 appears. The choices in the menu depend on the class (type) of the selected entity within the selected ontology. In our case, 'ScholOnto' is classified as a Project, so project-related options are displayed. Selecting an option labeled 'Shares Research Areas With' one can explore semantic neighbourhood that comprises projects sharing one or more research areas with ScholOnto. The results in Fig. 3 (foreground window) show which research areas has each 'neighbouring' project in common with ScholOnto. In our case, related projects include ClimatePrediction and Ibrow. To view details of the Ibrow project, our journalist may either select the 'Ibrow' record in the collector, or in the window shown in Fig. 3, and then the 'Web Page' option in the semantic menu. Selecting items in collectors brings up the same semantic services menu as if items were selected on a web page.

3 Basic Design Principles

The overall goal of this project is to support the interpretation of web documents with no a-priori mark-up through the addition of an ontology-derived semantic layer. This goal may be unfolded into a set of design principles and high-level functional requirements for providing ontology-based support for navigating and sensemaking. Each principle is listed and briefly justified below (the implementation is then detailed in sections 4 and 5):

- Magpie should extend a *standard web browser* to minimize the users' effort when learning to use the tool.
- Magpie users should not incur a significant time penalty. In contrast with most approaches to Named Entities Recognition (NER), Magpie must always provide *fast, real-time mark-up*. More precise mark-up can still be carried out in the background by a specialised NER semantic service, while the user browses. An additional mark-up would then be delivered to the user's browser *incrementally* (progressively), thus refining the simple but fast mechanisms.
- Magpie should allow users to select a particular *viewpoint* – i.e. the ontology used for mark-up and annotation should be customizable and selectable by the user[1] (the ontology may be downloaded from the web or read from a local disk).
- Magpie should *separate* the mark-up from the documents to facilitate different viewpoints (of different communities) to be layered over the same web resource.
- Magpie should *preserve the appearance* of a web page – users would quickly get confused if web pages browsed through a semantic browser did not look the same as when browsed traditionally.
- Magpie should process *any web page* – we assume the web documents are not 'pre-marked-up' by an author or librarian (e.g. using XML or RDF). However, if such a mark-up exists, Magpie should be able to make use of it.
- Magpie should provide an interface for a *simple publication of the semantic services* that can be deployed by the service authors, as well as an *easy subscription mechanism* for the service recipients/users.

4 Magpie Architecture

The architecture of Magpie is shown in Fig. 4. Magpie is essentially a bridge – a *mediator* between formal descriptions used by the ontology-based service providers and semantically unstructured HTML documents. In order to facilitate the aspect of servicing, the Magpie technology consists of a *Service Provider* component and a *Service Recipient* component. In a more traditional language of web development

---

[1] In our scenario, we worked with a single ontology but there is a mechanism for ontology selection built-in in the Magpie plug-in (see left-hand corner of Fig. 2).

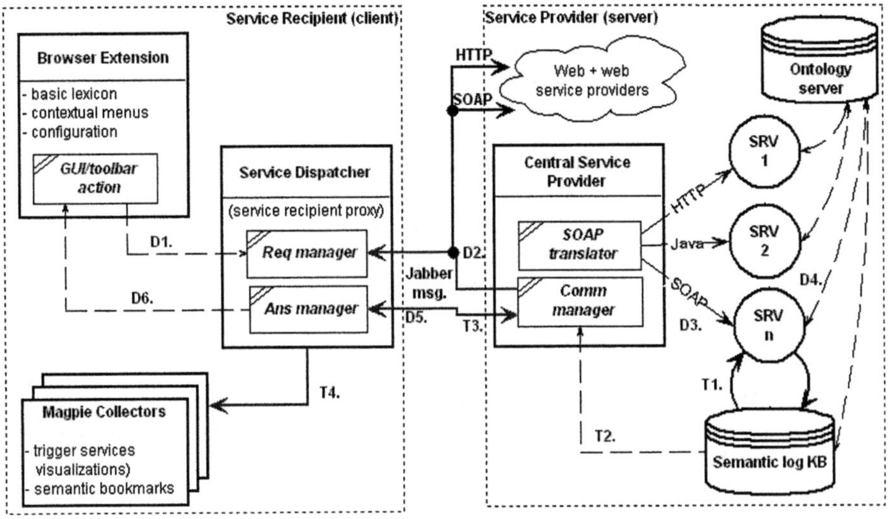

Fig. 4. Overall architecture of the Magpie framework for semantic browsing

these two components could be approximated as a server and a client, respectively. However, our notation emphasizes the fact that the document source (i.e. web server) and the source of a semantic service may not be one and the same computer. Similarly, a concept of 'client' suggests that an active role is always on the side of a browser with a server only passively serving requested data. In the context of semantic services, this is not appropriate. Mainly because (as we show below) there are circumstances where the server may become the element driving the conversation or providing the information that is semantically relevant but not explicitly requested.

In line with the web services paradigm there may be numerous providers of the same service and many different services [20]. Currently, the service provider component of Magpie is built around a suite of tools providing access to a library of knowledge models containing domain ontologies, populated KBs, semantic services and a semantic log KB. Some of the tools – e.g. a customized web server [19], which offers a library of methods to dynamically generate the appropriate content and reason about it – communicates via standard HTTP. In addition, there are tools communicating via SOAP – a popular protocol for web services [20]. In both cases, the underlying representation of the ontologies is shared.

Magpie accepts ontologies represented in RDF(S) [2], DAML+OIL [5], and OCML [16] (the latter being the internal representation for reasoning). In the future, we intend to include ontologies represented in OWL [18]. The services (cf. Fig. 1 and Fig. 3), are defined in one of the *Services* modules (SRV*) of the central Magpie service provider, and detailed in section 5.1. The purpose of the ontology of services is to abstract from the actual implementations, and enable the association of the semantic services with the object/entities on a web page. The *Semantic log KB* – one of the unique services in the Magpie suite, is used by the Magpie trigger services, which are described in section 5.2.

In order to use the services meaningfully, as well as to associate them with the appropriate terms, ontologies need to be regularly populated and updated. In our case, a set of techniques ('populators') was used to populate the domain ontology from heterogeneous data stored in web-accessible RDF documents, mined from organizational databases, or extracted from the standard web pages. The ontology population process is beyond the scope of this paper; for more information see [6].

4.1 Magpie Service Recipient Components

As shown in Fig. 4, the Magpie 'client'-side suite consists of a Magpie Browser Extension (of Internet Explorer), Magpie Collectors, and a Magpie Service Dispatcher. The primary purpose of the *Magpie Browser Extension* is to sit in the browser, and control the entire interaction with Magpie facilities. Specifically, it contains the user interface components, which visualize entities found in a web page, and enables users to interact with the semantic services through a simple contextual menu. The *Magpie Service Dispatcher* acts as a dedicated semantic proxy for the user's web browser. Its main task is to manage the communication between the menu in the Browser Extension and the appropriate dispatcher of the service providers. The Magpie Dispatcher delivers all the user's requests and the provider's responses in a uniform way in a form of customized XML messages.

4.1.1 Magpie Browser Extension (Plug-In)

As mentioned earlier, the Browser Extension is embedded in the user's web browser, and it is responsible for managing the interaction between the user and the semantically enriched browser. The plug-in is implemented in an unobtrusive way as a dynamically loaded library (DLL) that is registered to Internet Explorer. When the user wishes to turn the semantic capabilities and services on, s/he only activates the Magpie toolbar that forms an external GUI to the plug-in by pushing a single button.

The browser extension contains a small HTML parser that is able to highlight the entities from a particular ontology. A pre-condition of a successful parsing *within* the Magpie browser extension is the definition or download of an ontology-derived lexicon from an appropriate service provider. Although not as accurate as many existing NER techniques, simple lexicon-based parsing is extremely fast, and thus satisfies our low time overhead design constraint (see section 3).

In our case, the lexicon entries are generated overnight from the instances within the ontological knowledge base, which is populated from various sources (e.g. databases). We use several simple linguistic rules, such as the recognition of abbreviations or people's initials. Also, ontology specific transformation rules can be applied. For example, the classes in our ontology have `pretty-name` and `variant-names` slots, which can be included in the lexicon, and consequently, used to recognize the concepts of interest on a web page. Simple rules can then derive for example, variants "J. Bloggs" or "Bloggs, J." from a `pretty-name` "Joe Bloggs". The specific rules applicable to our scenario from section 2 use the AKT reference ontology[2].

We are investigating how other NER mechanisms can be incorporated into the parser to enhance its precision. To this extent, the web services paradigm seems to be a plausible way forward. Instead of adding more complex NER techniques to the browser extension, we suggest leaving the browser plug-in thin, and implementing the

---

[2] More information available at http://www.aktors.org.

advanced NER algorithms as (semantic web) services available upon a user's request. More on this topic follows in the next section.

The HTML annotation process in Magpie comprises a number of simple steps. When an entity of interest is recognized in the web page, the HTML annotator (a part of the visual interface), annotates it using <SPAN...> tags, and links it with a relevant ontological instance/class within the chosen ontology. This procedure creates essentially *a semantic layer* over the original document. The original content remains untouched; only the interesting concepts and the corresponding text on the page are highlighted.

This approach to visualizing the semantic layers means that users remain in control of what types of entities are visible at any time. We argue that this improves navigation through the content, and avoids the greatest danger of various link-recommending systems (see discussion e.g. in [15]) – overwhelming the users with too much information. When the recognized entities are highlighted, the Dispatcher also passes them to a *Semantic Log Updater*, which is one of our central semantic services. This service asserts the entities as facts into the *Semantic Log KB*. The purpose of semantic logging is addressed later in section 5.2, and more information about the delivery implementation is described in the next section.

The Magpie Browser Extension incorporates three user interface components, which enable users to interact with the semantic services. We mentioned the *Visual Component* for highlighting the matched entities found in the page. The second component features the *Semantic Services Menu* (shown in Fig. 1), which is created on the fly in a close interaction with the *Dispatcher* and the *Services* module of the Magpie service provider. The last component of the Service Recipient suite takes care of the Magpie *trigger services* – for instance, various *Collectors*, *Summarizers* and *Visualizers*. Trigger services and the individual components are described in section 5.2. We should note at this point that unlike the contextual menu-based services, the user does not explicitly request the trigger services. They are typically pushed from the service provider to reflect some recognized pattern in the recognized entities. The Magpie Browser Extension GUI in a form of a Magpie toolbar is shown in Fig. 2.

4.1.2 Magpie Service Dispatcher

The role of the Service Dispatcher is to handle all interactions between the user with the Magpie-enabled browser and the respective Magpie service providers. This approach is an alternative to the GET/POST requests available in the standard HTTP. Magpie still supports HTTP requests, but a growing number of services are available in formats that do not lend themselves for a seamless integration into a semantic web browser. Separating interface and communication gives us several advantages.

The clean separation enables us to implement interface so that it can abstract the user's actions and automatically generate appropriate XML form-based communication request. The XML forms needed for the communication are delivered together with the lexicon for a particular ontology upon the user's request. The form 'filling' occurs automatically – the user's right click generates a Semantic Services Menu consisting of the available services. Selection of one option in this menu basically 'fills in' the associated XML form with the data the user clicked on. Once filled in, the form is passed to the *Service Dispatcher* that delivers it on the user's behalf to the appropriate service provider (or its Dispatcher) for processing.

The second advantage becomes obvious when we take into account that it may take a while to process any particular request. Thus, instead of keeping a stream open to the specific service provider, the Magpie Dispatcher will wait until the provider is ready. In other words, the division enables us to implement the service request/response communication in an *asynchronous* way. This facilitates scalability, flexibility and enables more customized interaction.

Third, the Magpie Dispatcher has a direct access to the information pushed by the *trigger* services that the user subscribed to, because everything pushed towards the user passes through the dispatcher. Here, it is more practical to re-direct pushed information into a suitable window managed by the dispatcher rather than directly to the browser or browser plug-in. The main benefit is in lifting burden with managing the windows, connections and requests/responses from the browser, and enabling a service provider to address the user (this *bi-directional communication* is not possible with standard HTTP).

Finally, the Magpie approach is centered on the specific viewpoints onto the web facilitated by different ontologies. We envisage that users would select a particular ontology depending on their current task from a set of 'subscribed' ontologies. In this way, the interface will reflect the user's current needs and context. However, this is not everything. Because the Dispatcher is loosely connected to the web browser it can be easily used by other information accessing applications (e.g. word processors, eMail clients or instant messengers). Hence, the services could be made available in other environments in addition to the web browsers. For example, we have successfully implemented Magpie for Microsoft Word XP based on this architecture.

The flexibility of Magpie semantic services in respect to both, the selected ontology and the target user environment, is a strong and unique feature of our Magpie technology. It means that the content of a particular resource may be *re-interpreted* in the context of a new ontology (i.e. re-parsed and re-annotated). Consequently, different semantic services may become available to shed light on the particular aspects of the document. Presently, our main constraint in respect to the ontology flexibility is that at any time, one ontology is actively used for the annotation. This should avoid most of the consistency issues between multiple knowledge sources.

5 Semantic Services

In section 4, we presented the conceptual architecture of Magpie, and showed how a semantic layer is created, displayed and activated. The main benefits of using Magpie however are generated from the ability to deploy semantic services on top of the semantic layer. These services are provided to the user as a physically independent layer over a particular HTML document. Magpie distinguishes between two types of semantic services, each having a specific user interaction model. In Fig. 4, the two types of user interaction are shown using process paths labeled '**D***' and '**T***'.

According to the communication model in Fig. 4, the parser inside the browser identifies entities from a chosen ontological lexicon in the raw web page. Discovered entities are annotated, and using a sequence of arrows '**D1**' → '**D3**' recorded in semantic log. Meanwhile, the annotated page is displayed in the web browser (see also section 4.1.1). The path labeled with '**D***' represents services activated on a user's request; i.e. a user explicitly selects an entity s/he is interested in, and by a right mouse click invokes a contextual *Services menu.* This layer of *on-demand* semantic services is described in section 5.1. The initial point of the *on-demand* interaction ('**D1**') is always in the browser. Alternatively, semantic services may be based on patterns or *footprints* of the entities that co-occur in a particular document or browsing session (path with labels '**T***'). In section 5.2, we refer to this log-based functionality as *trigger services*, and these services originate always at the service provider's side.

5.1 On-Demand Semantic Services

Semantic services are enabled by clicking on the 'Magpie' button in the browser's main toolbar (see marker '♠' in Fig. 2). This action displays a dedicated toolbar, where a particular ontology can be selected, as shown in Fig. 2. Once the semantic services are activated, the contextual (right-click) menu of a web browser is overridden by an *on-demand services menu* whenever the mouse hovers over a recognized entity. The 'on-demand services' menu is also context-dependent as could be expected; however, in this case, we are dealing with a semantic context defined by the membership of a particular entity to a particular ontological class. The class membership of the entities is contained in the ontology or a lexicon generated from ontology.

In addition to domain ontologies that can be selected by the user (see marker '♣' in Fig. 2) to facilitate a viewpoint of a particular community, Magpie uses a special *Services* ontology. This ontology is part of the 'Ontology server' module (see top-right hand corner in Fig. 4), and it formally defines what operations/services can be performed for particular class(es) of entities, and the semantics of each operation. The semantic services are defined and published in line with standards of the emerging web services technology [20]. Thus, different groups of users may see different services to suit their knowledge or expertise. Generally speaking, the services may be published or revoked by their authors, and/or brokered to achieve richer interaction. In the scenario of using Magpie as a semantic portal for organizational research, the services were defined for the individual ontological classes directly in the 'Ontology server' without any specific publication or brokering mechanism. The services for the class *Project* are shown in the Semantic Menu displayed in the center of Fig. 1.

Similarly to parsing and annotation, the 'on-demand services' menu is generated on the fly. When a right click occurs, it is handled by the Magpie Browser Extension, and through the Magpie dispatcher the Magpie server proxy may be asked for the updated list of services that are available for a particular entity. This list may be cached in the browser to avoid delays. The request uses the information about class membership of a particular entity that was created while annotating the content (see section 4.1.1). If there are any applicable semantic services available, Magpie displays them in a menu, and lets the user choose what s/he is interested in. A selection of an option leads to a request to the Magpie dispatcher to contact the appropriate service provider and perform the requested reasoning. The knowledge-level reasoning facilitated by a particular service provider gives the requested context for a particular entity. This is delivered back to the web browser to be annotated and displayed. An example of a response is visible as a new browser window in the foreground of Fig. 3.

Hence, Magpie facilitates two complementary methods for web browsing. First, it implements syntactic browsing through the `<A HREF=...>` anchors inserted into a document by its author. A document accessed via anchors is parsed, annotated, and displayed with a Magpie toolbar to support semantically enriched user interaction (as described in section 4). The second browsing method follows the customized semantic anchors created during the automatic annotation, and the applicable, dynamically generated semantic services. While the first method gives access to physically linked content, the second method makes available the semantic context of a particular entity. The two methods are visually differentiated to minimize confusion, and provide complementary functionality. Fig. 1 shows a sample semantic services menu for term 'ScholOnto' (which according to the ontology, belongs to the 'Project' class). The semantic context corresponding to the user's request for similar projects is displayed in Fig. 3 *as if* the user followed a navigational link, and in this case contains a list of ontologically related and ordered projects.

5.2 Trigger Semantic Services

User-requested (on-demand) semantic services are one technique for interacting with the relevant background knowledge. A number of researchers stress the importance of active or push services, which we describe next in the context of Magpie. A background to this kind of services is discussed e.g. in [6]. The main feature distinguishing active services from the user-requested ones is that they tend to "look over the user's shoulder", gather facts, and present conclusions.

Such services are depicted in Fig. 4 by the interaction path containing labels '**T***' starting on the right hand side. As can be seen, a pre-condition for having active services is to keep *history logs* of browsing, particularly a log of the recognized entities. The label 'browsing history' is more than appropriate because a log accumulates findings not only from the current web page, but also from previously visited pages in the same browsing session.

The process of semantic logging runs in parallel with the web page annotation. While an annotated web page is displayed in a browser, the recognized entities are sent to the Magpie server component responsible for semantic log maintenance. The logged data are asserted as *facts* into a 'working' KB. Several *watchers* monitor and respond to patterns in the asserted facts. When the relevant assertions have been made for a particular watcher, a semantic service response is *triggered*, and applicable information delivered to the Magpie dispatcher on the client's side that in turn displays it in a dedicated window next to the user's web browser. This interaction is *asynchronous* – the service provider starts the communication, contacts the user's dispatcher, and pushes potentially relevant information.

A few examples of the results of a trigger service firing are shown on the right-hand side of Fig. 1 ('People', 'Projects' and 'People's Projects' collector windows). Definition of watchers underlying some trigger services has been published in [6], and we shall not repeat it here. However, generally speaking, when a web page is viewed in Magpie, one of the service providers responsible for the maintenance of the Semantic Log asserts `found-item` facts, for each of the lexical entities found, into the Semantic Log KB (see Fig. 4). The watcher, which may be implemented as an independent service provider, say "*SRV n*" in Fig. 4, triggers if a *Person* is found in the log, and s/he is a member of a *Project*, which is not yet present in the log. Once trigger fires, the *Project* and the URL of the page it relates to, are collected. Future work will enable Magpie users to create watchers using a direct publication interface, as well as subscribe to the watchers/triggers of interest.

The information deliverable in this way may range from simple collections of relevant items to sophisticated guidance on browsing or browsing history visualization. Since the service provider taps into a knowledge base constructed potentially from the logs of community members, the guidance or history visualization may draw on community knowledge and behaviors. This type of setup may seem surprising in our scenario presented earlier because a journalist is clearly *not a member* of KMi community. Does it make sense to send her community-relevant information?

Our view is yes – this setup may be seen as a journalist (an external agent) adopting the viewpoint of a specific community to *interpret* and *make sense* of a given web resource *from the perspective* of that community. Thus, a formal membership of a particular community and the utilization of their ontological viewpoints are two different roles, each of us can be involved in. Since a trigger service can be (in principle) selected and subscribed to, there is nothing wrong in tapping to the knowledge of a community of which the user is *not a formal member*. On the contrary, this enables him or her to see the document in its 'native' context.

This is clearly beneficial, especially if we follow Tauscher and Greenberg's argument [21] that 58% of all visits to web documents are to sites visited previously, but that history mechanisms are used infrequently. The large number of re-occurring visits calls for a sophisticated approach to the management of browsing histories. Indeed, one of design recommendations from their study was that bookmarks should have a *meaningful* representation. History management based on the semantics of the visited pages, and implemented by a *triggered* semantic layer may help to alleviate issues with the syntactic and linear (access time ordered) methods.

Although the design goal for our two types of services is the same – to provide users with additional knowledge to support the interpretation of web pages and to assist in information gathering – the underlying paradigms are different. The 'on-demand' services are invoked by a specific user request. Goal-driven reasoning from the user's query leads to a response, which is typically presented as a new web page. The trigger service is invoked when a watcher matches a pattern within the semantic log. The pattern is equivalent to data-driven reasoning, results of which are displayed by a change in the interface. In Fig. 1, trigger services amend one of the three collectors.

6 Related Work

One of the inspirations for Magpie was the COHSE system [3]. COHSE combines an Open Hypermedia System with an ontology server into a framework for ontological linking – an ontology-derived lexicon is used to add links to arbitrary web pages. The links are added either by proxy server or by an augmented Mozilla™ browser. The distinctions between Magpie and COHSE are due to their differing design goals. The design goals for COHSE were (i) to separate web links from the web pages and (ii) to make these links conceptual (i.e. potentially generated from ontology). The goal for

Magpie is to support interpretation and information gathering. Magpie's interface enables ontological differences to be highlighted, and the services provided are dependent on the class of entity found. Magpie also offers *trigger* services via semantic logs. Neither type of Magpie service is meant to replace traditional links; they act as an auxiliary knowledge source available at the user's fingertips.

In the last few years, a number of tools have emerged that support the annotation of web pages. A classic example is the Amaya HTML editor, which implements the Annotea infrastructure [12]. Annotea facilitates the RDF-based mark-up of documents as they are created. The authors or viewers may add various meta-statements to a document, which are separate from the document itself and are accessible to collaborating teams via a centralized annotation server. The annotation in this sense centers on attaching additional information to a chunk of content on an arbitrary web page. This feature of Annotea makes it a powerful tool for the joint authoring of documents where a small group of collaborating agents share a common goal. However, the same feature may make it more difficult to facilitate a similar form of annotation sharing in 'open' user communities. In these cases, there is no guarantee that a freely articulated annotation would convey the same meaning to the different users.

Another difference of the Annotea framework as compared to Magpie is the source of annotations. Annotea assumes that at least one author (human) is willing to invest additional effort into making a page semantically richer. Magpie is more liberal and assumes a reader subscribes to a particular domain ontology, which is then used to provide relevant background knowledge. It may be argued that ontology creation takes even more effort than manual document mark-up. This is true; however, an ontology is a domain model, a shared viewpoint that can be re-used for different purposes, not solely for the annotation of a single document. Thus, the effort spent on designing a shared ontology is greater in the short term but in the longer term, it is a more cost-effective way of recording a shared point of view. Moreover, ontologies are increasingly available for several domains, so in many cases, no development effort is actually required.

A similar approach to annotating documents can be found in other research projects. The CREAM-based Ont-O-Mat/Annotizer [9] is a tool similar to MnM [22], which integrates ontologies and information extraction tools. As with MnM, Amilcare [4] provides information extraction support, and ontologies are represented in DAML+OIL. Annotations in this framework are very close to those advocated in this paper. Any ontological instance, attribute or relation known in a particular ontology may be an annotation hook. A key feature of this tool is its use of *discourse representations* to structure the relatively flat output of Amilcare according to the chosen ontology, thus facilitating ontology population.

The CREAM research team show an important feature of ontology-based annotation and document enrichment. Namely, any annotating tool must be aware of already existing (i.e. recognized) entities and their relationships; otherwise harm can be done with redundancies and multiple definitions. CREAM's annotation inferences resemble our trigger services produced by a data-driven reasoning. On the other hand, our 'on-demand' services smoothly and seamlessly address the issue identified above – the awareness of the existing relationships and the actual context of ontological instances.

The SHOE project [11] proposed an extension to HTML to allow the specification of ontological information within common HTML-based documents. In addition to the inclusion of a semantically rich, ontological knowledge, SHOE tried to make these inclusions re-usable and understandable 'throughout the web'. An editor was developed to support the annotation. As with the tools mentioned above, and unlike our Magpie framework, SHOE relies on the offline mark-up of web documents. Once that is accomplished, the enriched documents are published, and dedicated tools may use the contextual knowledge (e.g. Exposé web crawler [10]).

7 Concluding Remarks

Reducing the information overload caused by the growing web is often cited as the premise for work on supporting the retrieval of relevant documents. But finding relevant documents is only half of the story. Their interpretation involves a reader in understanding the surrounding context, in which the document was created. In order to gain the full understanding, a reader will require knowledge of the specific terms mentioned and the implicit relationships contained both within the document and between the document and other external knowledge sources. Magpie addresses this issue by capturing context within an ontology, which then is used to enrich web documents with a semantic layer. Semantic services expose relevant segments of the ontology according to the user's needs. The choice of ontological viewpoint for interpreting a particular web page drives the interpretation bottom-up – by the user rather than domain expert or knowledge engineer.

Magpie users browse the web in a standard way with negligible differences in the user experience. Magpie achieves this by extending standard web browsers with standard mark-up languages, without altering the layout of the web page and imposing any significant time overhead. The key principle is that the user controls to what extent semantic browsing comes to the fore. The Magpie toolbar enables concepts to be made visible according to their ontological category, and the Magpie infrastructure enables arbitrary semantic actions to be triggered by patterns of items found within a semantic log. Trigger services also allow certain tasks to be delegated. In the scenario we showed how discovered entities could be used for a later inspection. However, Magpie allows more complex trigger services to be implemented. For example, the Magpie proxy may automatically parse web pages linked to the current page, thus allowing reconnaissance services similar to those found in Letizia [13] to be set up.

Attention as opposed to information is now widely acknowledged to be the scarce resource in the Internet age. Consequently, tools that can leverage semantic resources to take some of the burden of the interpretation task from the human reader are going to be of enormous use. We believe that Magpie is a step towards achieving this goal.

Our current effort is focused on deploying the Magpie suite of tools within the climate*prediction*.net project. Using the scheme that was successfully deployed in the SETI@home project, the idea of climate*prediction*.net is to exploit the idle time on PCs to run multiple versions of the UK Met Office climate model. Running large numbers of perturbed climate models (the project aims to collect 2M users) will overcome uncertainties present in the modeling (and hence prediction) process. During their participation in the project, the users would run climate models on their computers for several months. Magpie will be used for the purposes of interacting with and making sense of highly complex analyses of climate data that will be produced from running a statistical ensemble of perturbed climate models. Magpie will also enable lay members of the public to explore the rich scientific resources that exist in the domain of climatology and climate prediction. Thus, it is hoped that the semantic browsing capabilities of Magpie will serve as an *enabling technology* for the increased public understanding of science.

Acknowledgments. The Magpie effort is supported by the climate*prediction*.net and the Advanced Knowledge Technologies (AKT) projects. Climate*prediction*.net is sponsored by the UK Natural Environment Research Council and UK Department of Trade e-Science Initiative, and involves Oxford University, CLRC Rutherford Appleton Labs and The Open University. AKT is an Interdisciplinary Research Collaboration (IRC) sponsored by the UK Engineering and Physical Sciences Research Council by grant no. GR/N15764/01. The AKT IRC comprises the Universities of Aberdeen, Edinburgh, Sheffield, Southampton and The Open University.

References

1. Berners-Lee, T., Hendler, J., and Lassila, O., *The Semantic Web.* Scientific American, 2001. **279**(5): p. 34–43.
2. Brickley, D. and Guha, R., *Resource Description Framework (RDF) Schema Specification.* 2000, World Wide Web Consortium. (URL: http://www.w3.org/TR/2000/CR-rdf-schema-20000327).
3. Carr, L., Bechhofer, S., Goble, C., *et al. Conceptual Linking: Ontology-based Open Hypermedia.* In *Proc of the 10th Intl. WWW Conference.* 2001. Hong-Kong
4. Ciravegna, F. *Adaptive Information Extraction from Text by Rule Induction and Generalisation.* In *Proc. of the 17th Intl. Joint Conference on AI.* 2001. Washington, USA.
5. DAML.org, *Reference description of the DAML+OIL ontology mark-up language.* 2001, (URL: http://www.DAML.org/2001/03/reference.html).
6. Domingue, J., Dzbor, M., and Motta, E., *Semantic Layering with Magpie*, In *Handbook on Ontologies in Information Systems*, (Staab, S. and Studer, R., Editors). 2003, Springer Verlag.
7. Gruber, T.R., *A Translation approach to Portable Ontology Specifications.* Knowledge Acquisition, 1993. **5**(2): p. 199–221.
8. Guarino, N., Masolo, C., and Vetere, G., *OntoSeek: Content-Based Access to the Web.* IEEE Intelligent Systems, 1999. **14**(3): p. 70–80.
9. Handschuh, S., Staab, S., and Maedche, A. *CREAM – Creating relational metadata with a component-based, ontology driven annotation framework.* In *Proc. of the International Semantic Web Working Symposium.* 2001. California, USA.
10. Heflin, J. and Hendler, J., *A Portrait of the Semantic Web in Action.* IEEE Intelligent Systems, 2001. **16**(2): p. 54–59.
11. Heflin, J., Hendler, J., and Luke, S. *Reading Between the Lines: Using SHOE to Discover Implicit Knowledge from the Web.* In *Proc. of the AAAI Workshop on AI and Information Integration.* 1998.
12. Kahan, J., Koivunen, M.-R., Prud'Hommeaux, E., *et al. Annotea: An Open RDF Infrastructure for Shared Web Annotations.* In *Proc of the 10th Intl. WWW Conference.* 2001. Hong-Kong.
13. Lieberman, H., Fry, C., and Weitzman, L., *Exploring the web with reconnaissance Agents.* Communications of the ACM, 2001. **44**(8): p. 69–75.

14. McGuinness, D.L. *Ontological Issues for Knowledge-Enhanced Search.* In *Proc. of the Formal Ontology in Information Systems.* 1998.
15. Middleton, S., DeRoure, D., and Shadbolt, N. *Capturing knowledge of user preferences: Ontologies in recommender systems.* In *Proc. of the ACM K-CAP'01 Conference.* 2001. Victoria, Canada: ACM Press.
16. Motta, E., *Reusable Components for Knowledge Modelling.* Frontiers in AI and Applications. 1997, The Netherlands: IOS Press.
17. Ovsiannikov, I.A., Arbib, M.A., and Mcneill, T.H., *Annotation Technology.* International Journal of Human-Computer Studies, 1999. **50**(4): p. 329–362.
18. Patel-Schneider, P.F., Horrocks, I., and van Harmelen, F., *OWL Web Ontology Language 1.0 Abstract Syntax.* 2002, (URL http://www.w3.org/TR/owl-absyn/).
19. Riva, A. and Ramoni, M., *LispWeb: A Specialised HTTP Server for Distributed AI Applications.* Computer Networks and ISDN Systems, 1996. **28**(7–11): p. 953–961.
20. Sadiq, W. and Kumar, S., *Web Service Description (Usage Scenarios).* 2002, World Wide Web Consortium, (URL: http://www.w3.org/TR/2002/WD-ws-desc-usecases-20020604).
21. Tauscher, L. and Greenberg, S., *How People Revisit Web Pages: Empirical Findings and Implications for the Design of History Systems.* International Journal of Human Computer Studies, 2001. **47**(1): p. 97–138.
22. Vargas-Vera, M., Motta, E., Domingue, J., *et al. MnM: Ontology Driven Semi-automatic and Automatic Support for Semantic Markup.* In *Proc. of the 13th European Knowledge Acquisition Workshop (EKAW).* 2002. Spain.

Ontology-Based Resource Matching in the Grid – The Grid Meets the Semantic Web*

Hongsuda Tangmunarunkit, Stefan Decker, and Carl Kesselman

Information Sciences Institute
University of Southern California
{Hongsuda,Stefan,Carl}@isi.edu

Abstract. The Grid is an emerging technology for enabling resource sharing and coordinated problem solving in dynamic multi-institutional virtual organizations. In the Grid environment, shared resources and users typically span different organizations. The resource matching problem in the Grid involves assigning resources to tasks in order to satisfy task requirements and resource policies. These requirements and policies are often expressed in disjoint application and resource models, forcing a resource selector to perform semantic matching between the two. In this paper, we propose a flexible and extensible approach for solving resource matching in the Grid using semantic web technologies. We have designed and prototyped an ontology-based resource selector that exploits ontologies, background knowledge, and rules for solving resource matching in the Grid.

1 Introduction

The Grid is an emerging technology for enabling resource sharing and coordinated problem solving in dynamic multi-institutional virtual organizations [12,11]. Grids are used to join various geographically distributed computational and data resources, and deliver these resources to heterogeneous user communities [30,9,13]. These resources may belong to different institutions, have different usage policies and pose different requirements on acceptable requests. Grid applications, at the same time, may have different constraints that can only be satisfied by certain types of resources with specific capabilities. Before a resource (or a set of resources) can be allocated to run an application, the user or an agent must select resources appropriate to the requirements of the application [7]. We call this process of selecting resources based on application requirements *resource matching*. In a Grid environment, where resources may come and go, it is desirable and sometimes necessary to automate the resource matching to robustly meet specific application requirements.

Existing resource description and resource selection in the Grid is highly constrained. Traditional resource matching, as exemplified by the Condor Matchmaker [26] or Portable Batch System [23], is done based on symmetric, attribute-based matching. In these systems, the values of attributes advertised by resources are compared with

* This work was supported by National Science Foundation under grant EAR-0122464. Any opinions, findings, and conclusions or recommendations expressed in this material are those of the authors and do not necessarily reflect the views of the National Science Foundation.

D. Fensel et al. (Eds.): ISWC 2003, LNCS 2870, pp. 706–721, 2003.

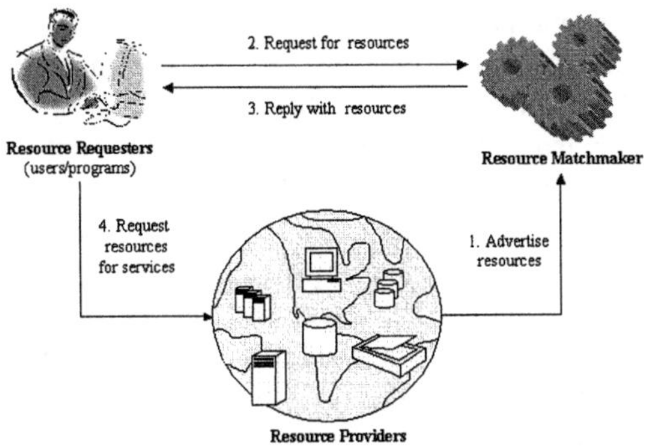

Fig. 1. Resource Matching: the matcher gathers resource information from resource providers. When a requestor submits a request to the matcher for a resource match, the matcher searches for the appropriate resource and returns the best result to the requestor. The requestor can then request the resource for its services or execution.

those required by jobs. For the comparison to be meaningful and effective, the resource providers and consumers have to agree upon attribute names and values. The exact matching and coordination between providers and consumers make such systems inflexible and difficult to extend to new characteristics or concepts. Moreover, in a heterogeneous multi-institutional environment such as the Grid, it is difficult to enforce the syntax and semantics of resource descriptions.

To illustrate, consider if a machine's operating system is described as "SunOS" or "Linux." To query for a machine that is "Unix" compatible, a user either has to:

1. explicitly incorporate the Unix compatibility concept into the request requirements by requesting a disjunction of all Unix-variant operating systems, *e.g.*, (OpSys="SunOS" || OpSys="Linux"), or
2. wait for all interesting resources to advertise their operating system as Unix as well as either Linux or SunOS, *e.g.*, (OpSys={"SunOS," "Unix"}), and then express a match as set-membership of the desired Unix value in the OpSys value set, *e.g.*, hasMember(OpSys, "Unix").

In the former case, the disjunctive requirements become unwieldy as more abstract concepts are developed. In the latter, the advertisements become more complex and all resources must be updated before a match can occur.

In this paper, we propose a flexible and extensible approach for performing Grid resource selection using an ontology-based matchmaker. Unlike the traditional Grid resource selectors that describe resource/request properties based on symmetric flat attributes (which might become unmanageable as the number of attributes grows), separate ontologies (*i.e.*, semantic descriptions of domain models) are created to declaratively describe resources and job requests using an expressive ontology language. Instead of exact syntax matching, our ontology-based matchmaker performs semantic matching using terms defined in those ontologies. The loose coupling between resource and request descriptions remove the tight coordination requirement between resource providers and consumers. In addition, our matchmaker can be easily extended, by adding vocabularies and inference rules, to include new concepts (*e.g.,* Unix compatibility) about resources and applications and adapted the resource selection to changing policies. These ontologies can also be distributed and shared with other tools and applications.

We have designed and prototyped our matchmaker using existing semantic web technologies to exploit ontologies and rules (based on Horn logic and F-Logic) for resource matching. In our approach, resource and request descriptions are asymmetric. Resource descriptions, request descriptions, and usage policies are all independently modeled and syntactically and semantically described using a semantic markup language; RDF schema. Domain background knowledge (*e.g.,* "SunOS and Linux are types of Unix operating system") captured in terms of rules are added for conducting further deduction (*e.g.,* a machine with "Linux" operating system is a candidate for a request of a "Unix" machine). Finally, matchmaking procedures written in terms of inference rules are used to reason about the characteristics of a request, available resources and usage policies to appropriately find a resource that satisfies the request requirements. Additional rules can also be added to automatically infer resource requirements from the characteristics of domain-specific applications (*e.g.,* 3D finite difference wave propagation simulation) without explicit statements from the user.

The rest of the paper is organized as follows. In Section 2, we summarize the semantic web technologies that we use in our work. Section 3 reviews related work to the resource selection problem. Section 4 describes the features and architecture of our ontology-based matchmaker and provides a matching example. Finally, we conclude our paper in Section 5.

2 Semantic Web Technologies

The Semantic Web [2] is the next generation of the web which evolves toward semantic knowledge representations and intelligent services (*e.g.,* information brokers, search agents) where information can be processed by machines. To fully realize this goal, standards for exchanging machine-understandable information have to be established. These standards define not only the syntactic representation of information, but also their semantic content. A technology stack, suggested by the W3C, that we use in our work consists of Resource Description Framework (RDF), which provides data model specification and an XML-based serialization syntax; ontologies, which enable the definition and sharing of domain vocabularies; and rules, which allow declarative processing of data.

2.1 The Resource Description Framework

At present, services on the Web are single islands. Common data models and data exchange standards are required in order to enable the fast integration of different datasources and to bridge semantic differences. The Web community has proposed the Resource Description Framework (RDF) [17] as a data model suitable for information integration tasks. The data model serves as a foundation for *ontology* languages.

2.2 Ontologies

An ontology is a specification of a conceptualization [14]. In this context, specification refers to an explicit representation by some syntactic means. In contrast to schema languages (like XML Schema or DTDs) ontologies try to capture the semantics of a domain by deploying knowledge representation primitives, enabling a machine to (partially) understand the relationships between concepts in a domain. Additional knowledge can be captured by axioms or rules. In the Web context, RDF-Schema [3] and OWL[1] are recommendations from the W3C for ontology modeling languages.

2.3 Rules

Rules, in combination with RDF and ontologies, are an active field of research. Rules can be used to capture domain knowledge. We have chosen TRIPLE [28] as the rule language for our approach. TRIPLE is based on Horn logic [21] and borrows many basic features from F-Logic [16]. It is especially designed for querying, transforming, and reasoning with RDF data. TRIPLE has no built-in support for knowledge representation languages, but can be configured by axioms to support arbitrary modeling languages (*i.e.,* RDF-Schema).

3 Related Work

3.1 Information Systems

Related to the resource selection problem are information systems for discovering, aggregating, publishing and querying against information about resources and services. Globus MDS [6] and UDDI [31] are two such examples; MDS has been widely used in the Grid community for resource discovery while UDDI has been used in the web community for business service discovery.

Both MDS and UDDI support simple query languages. However, they do not offer expressive description facilities, nor provide sophisticated matchmaking capabilities. In this environment, the usage scenario involves resource providers publishing descriptions of their properties to an information service/registry. A resource consumer then queries the registry to identify candidate resources prior to generating actual requests. Based on the returned queries, resource selection can be done either by a user or procedural algorithm. In this scenario, policy enforcement happens when a request is submitted to the resource/service providers. It is possible that a user request will fail, and hence prior resource selection effort is wasted.

3.2 Resource Matching in the Grid

We do not know of existing applications of ontological reasoning to matchmaking in the Grid. In the following, we review several variations on symmetric, attribute-based matchmaking technologies. These variations provide increasing levels of expressiveness but still require symmetric attribute models in their descriptive and constraint languages.

[1] See http://www.w3.org/2001/sw/WebOnt/ for more information.

Request ClassAd:
```
[ Type = "Job"; Owner = "user1";
  Constraint = other.Type == "Machine" && Arch == "INTEL"
    && OpSys == "SOLARIS251" && Disk >= 10000;
  Rank = other.Memory; ]
```

Resource ClassAd:
```
[ Type = "Machine"; Name = "m1"; Disk = 30000; Arch = "INTEL";
  OpSys = "SOLARIS251"; ResearchGrp = "user1", "user2";
  Constraint = member(other.Owner,ResearchGrp) && DayTime > 18*60*60;
  Rank = member(other.Owner,ResearchGrp) ]
```

Fig. 2. Two examples of Condor ClassAds. For each resource-request pair, constraint clauses are checked for compatibility against the other's properties. Rank is used to select among multiple matches.

Symmetric attribute-based matching. As part of Condor [5], Rajesh Raman *et. al* developed the classified advertisement (ClassAd) matchmaking framework for solving resource allocation problem in a distributed environment with decentralized ownership of resources [26]. This framework provides a bi-lateral match, allowing both resource consumers and providers to specify their matching constraints, *e.g.,* requirements and policy.

In this framework, properties of requests and resources are characterized in a form of arbitrary but common syntax (*e.g.,* attribute-value pairs) capable of representing both characteristics and policies (as shown in Figure2). A symmetric requirement (expressed as a *constraint* statement) is then evaluated to determine, for each request-resource pair, whether there is a match. For the matching to work, it is crucial that both requests and resources use the same attribute names and agree upon attribute values. When multiple resources match a job requirement, a function (expressed by a *Rank* expression) can be used to assign an order to resources and the highest ranked resource is returned as a match.

Gang-Matching. To overcome the binary matching limitation of Condor Matchmaker, Raman *et. al* later proposed the gang-matching extension [24,25], allowing a request ClassAd to specify a list of required bilateral matches. For example, a request may require one or more resources each of which must satisfy its described requirements, as well as, the inter-resource constraints. However, this extension does not support *set-matching* where resources are defined by their aggregate characteristics, *e.g.,* a set of computers with aggregate memory greater than 10 GB. Chuang Liu *et. al* proposed the set-extended ClassAd language and a technique for specifying and solving set-matching problem [20]. Although their set-matching system can be extended to solve the gang-matching problem, their system does not currently support this capability.

Constraint-satisfaction-based matching. Chuang Liu *et. al* recently proposed the Redline matching system: an alternative approach for doing resource selection in the Grid [19]. In this framework, the matching problem is first transformed into a constraint satisfaction problem [2], the set of constraints are then checked to make sure that no

[2] A constraint satisfaction problem (CSP) consists of a constraint C over variables $x_1, ..., x_n$ and a domain D that maps each variable x_i to a finite set of values, $D(x_i)$, that it is

conflicts occur, and finally existing constraint solving technologies [22] (such as integer programming) are used to solve the transformed problem. Similar to Condor matchmaker, the Redline matching system is based on symmetric description of resource and request (*i.e.*, the same description syntax is used to describe both resources and requests). However, comparing to ClassAd, the Redline language is more expressive. It supports both gang-matching and set-matching capabilities.

A common requirement among these systems is the symmetric syntactic description of resources and requests properties. As illustrated in the previous example in Section 1, it is difficult to introduce new concepts or characteristics into the system. Moreover, in the Grid environment, where resources and users span multiple organizations, it may be difficult to guarantee that resources and requests will use the same attribute names, and that the semantics of the same attributes are interpreted the same way by both resource providers and consumers.

Our ontology-based matchmaker, on the other hand, is based on an asymmetric description. The system uses ontologies to semantically describe requests and resources. Matching between request specification to resource capabilities is done in terms of rules. Different request description models, along with the mapping rules, can be easily added to our matchmaker. Similar to these matching systems, our matchmaker provides the ability to describe properties and matching preference. Our matchmaker also supports a binary matching and gang-matching. We plan to support set-matching in the future.

3.3 Matchmaking in Other Domains

We summarize existing work in other domains that, similar to our work, have developed matchmakers based on ontologies.

DAML+OIL based Matchmaking. DAML+OIL based Matchmaking [18] describes a matchmaking system based on Semantic Web Technology, using a Description Logic reasoner to compare ontology-based service descriptions. Service advertisements are expressed as class expressions. The elements of the class expressions are taken from a domain ontology and a specific service ontology. During the matchmaking process the advertisements are classified into a hierarchy. The next step is to classify the request's service profile and the complement of the service profiles. Classifying the service profile and its complement allows the matchmaker to determine which service advertisements are compatible with the requests service profile. Our approach is different from their approach in that instead of using classification, we write rules to both capture background knowledge and explicitly determine when a request (*i.e.*, advertisement) matches resources (*i.e.*, services).

InfoSleuth. InfoSleuth [1] is an agent-based information discovery and retrieval system. The system adopts broker agents for syntactic and semantic matchmaking. The broker matches agents that require services with other agents that can provide those services. Agent capabilities and services are described using a common shared ontology of attributes and constraints which all agents can use to specify advertisements and requests

allowed to take. The CSP represents the constraint $C.x_1D(x_1).....x_nD(x_1)$. For example $C = x_1 > 1, x_1 + x_2 < 4, D(x_1) = [1,2,3], D(x_2) = [1,2,3]$.

to the broker. The matchmaking is then performed by a deductive database system, allowing rules to evaluate whether an expression of requirements matches a set of advertised capabilities. This approach is similar to ours. We extend the InfoSleuth approach in several directions: first we use RDF based Semantic Web technology, and second we provide more detail for how ontology-based reasoning interacts with the matchmaking rules. Furthermore we introduce background knowledge to the matchmaking process, allowing for a more flexible matchmaking procedure.

LARKS/RETSINA. LARKS/RETSINA [29] is a multiagent infrastructure. LARKS is an Agent Capability Description Language (ACDL). LARKS offers the possibility to use domain knowledge by using an ontology written in the concept language ITL. Unlike our approach, LARKS does not use a declarative rules for matchmaking.

4 Ontology-Based Resource Matching

Our ontology-based matchmaker is developed based on semantic web technologies (described in section 2). In this section, we first summarize the desired features of our matchmaker, describe its architecture and finally the methodology.

Desired features of the ontology-based matchmaker are:

- *Asymmetric description of resource and request.* In our framework, the description of resources and requests are modeled and described separately. A semantic match between the two models will be provided. Due to the asymmetric description, no coordination between resource providers and consumers is required before new description vocabulary is added. This is not true for the symmetric attribute-based matching described in Section 3.
- *Sharing and Maintainability.* The ontologies are sharable and easier to maintain and to understand than flat attribute lists.
- *Bilateral Constraints.* A request description allows the request to specify its resource constraints in terms of requirements. At the same time, each resource can also independently express its usage policies (*e.g.*, identifying who is allowed the access) restricting matches to applications/requests. The matchmaker takes the policies of each resource and request constraints into accounts when searching for a match.
- *Ability to describe matching preference.* Both request and resource can specify its preference when multiple matches are found.
- *Multi-lateral matching.* A user can submit a request that requires multiple simultaneous resources, each matching its requirement clause. Set-matching [20] capability will also be added in the future.
- *Integrity Checking.* The matchmaker can use the domain knowledge to help identify inconsistencies in the resource descriptions before accepting it as an available resource. The integrity check can also be done for the request to make sure that there are no conflicts in the resource requirements. For example, a resource or request advertisement with `OperatingSystem="Windows2000"` and `CPUFamily="Sparc"` should be rejected.

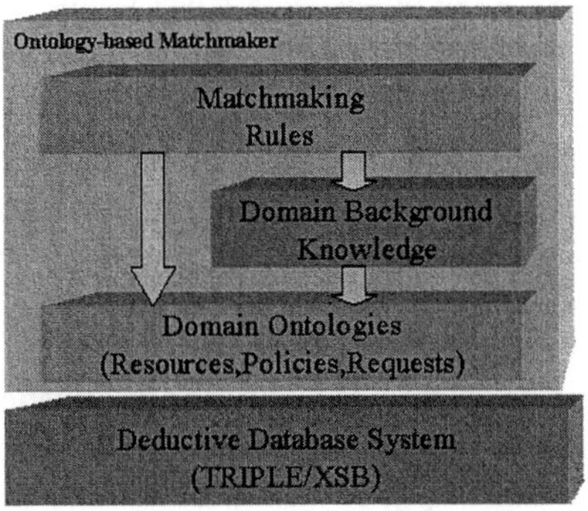

Fig. 3. Ontology-based Matchmaker

- *Expressiveness.* Due to the asymmetric description, the request can be modeled specifically for domain specific applications. The high-level application characteristics can be provided by the user. Furthermore, high-level characteristics can be automatically mapped to specific resource requirement configurations by the matchmaker.
- *Flexibility and Extensibility.* New concepts can be easily added into the ontology, *e.g.,* tightly-coupled machines or an MPI application. In addition, new constraints, *e.g.,* an MPI application requires tightly coupled machines, can be easily added in terms of rules.

4.1 Matchmaker Architecture

The ontology-based matchmaker consists of three components:

1. the *ontologies*, capturing the domain model and vocabulary for expressing resource advertisements and job requests,
2. *domain background knowledge*, capturing additional knowledge about the domain, and
3. *matchmaking rules*, defining when a resource matches a job description.

Figure 3 shows the relationship between these components. An arrow indicates the dependency between different components. For example, the background knowledge uses the vocabulary from the ontologies to capture background information. Matchmaking rules use both ontologies and background knowledge to match a request to resources. Our ontology-based matchmaker is built on top of TRIPLE/XSB deductive database system.

The matchmaking problem can be formally defined as follows. Let α be the set of all resource advertisements in a repository; $\mathcal{O}$, a domain ontology; $\mathcal{B}$ be a set of domain background knowledge; $\mathcal{R}$ be a set of matchmaking rules defining a binary predicate $match$; and $\models_{match}$ be a consequence operator (such as the usual consequence operator from classical logic). Then for a given query or advertisement q, matchmaking is computing the set $\{\alpha \mid \mathcal{O} \cup \mathcal{B} \cup \mathcal{R} \models_{match} match(\alpha, q)\}$. In the following we describe the components in more details.

Ontologies. We developed three initial ontologies. Using RDF-Schema, each ontology defines objects, properties of objects, and relationships among objects. These three ontologies are:

- *Resource ontology*. The resource ontology provides an abstract model for describing resources (*e.g.*, `ComputerSystem`, `OperatingSystem`), their capabilities (*e.g.*, `OperatingSystem.TotalPhysicalMemory=5000MB`) and their relationships (*e.g.*, `RunningOS(ComputerSystem` X`,OperatingSystem` Y`)`). Our initial model focuses on describing the capabilities of computational resources. The majority of our resource vocabularies are taken from the Common Information Model (CIM)—a conceptual information model for describing resource management that is neutral to vendors and implementation [4]. However, CIM focuses more on describing the physical elements of a system, not on abstract capability description. We started our resource model with a subset of CIM schema, modified and extended it to fit our requirements.
- *Resource Request ontology*. This ontology captures a request, properties of the request (*e.g.*, Request.Owner), characteristics of the request (*e.g.*, `JobType="MPI"`) and the resource requirements (*e.g.*, `MinPhysicalMemory=1G`, `NumberOfCPUs=16`). The ontology supports a request of multiple independent resources.
- *Policy ontology*. A model that capture the resource authorization and usage policies. For example, `AuthorizedAccounts=(ComputerSystem` X, `{user1,user2})` indicates a set of accounts that are authorized to access ComputerSystem X. Our model currently supports a simple authorization policy. We will expand the model to include usage policies in the future.

Ontology Creation. We use Protégé, an ontology editor which supports the RDF Schema, to develop our ontologies. Protégé [8] provides an integrated environment for editing ontology and instances. It hides the ontology language from the ontology developers allowing developers to work with high level concepts which as a result leads to rapid ontology development.

The Grid resources and users normally span across different organizations. The ability to share and exchange resource information is necessary for the creation of resource advertisements and job requests. Since our ontologies are represented by a semantic web standard, they can be easily exchanged and shared by other tools such as other rule-based engines or knowledge-based systems.

Domain Background Knowledge. The background knowledge captures additional knowledge about the domain (usually at the instance level) which is not captured by the ontology. This knowledge is used during the matchmaking process. We use TRIPLE, a rule system based on deductive database techniques, as an effective and expressive representation mechanism for implementing the background knowledge. The knowledge is captured in terms of rules. These rules use the vocabulary defined by the ontology to add additional axioms which cannot be expressed by the Ontology language and which typically influence the reasoning with instances. Figure 4 shows an example of typical background rules. These rules define which operating systems are compatible with each other and define `compatible` as transitive, reflexive, and symmetric. They also define

```
@gridBackground { // specifies grid background knowledge
  Linux[rdfs:subClassOf->GR:OperatingSystem].
  Unix[rdfs:subClassOf->GR:OperatingSystem].
  Debian[rdf:type->Linux].  Redhat[rdf:type->Linux].
  SunOS[rdf:type->Unix].    Linux[rdf:type->Unix].

  // transitivity axiom
  FORALL X,Y,Z X[compatibleWith->Z]<- X[compatibleWith->Y] AND Y[compatibleWith->Z].

  // identity axiom
  FORALL X X[compatibleWith->X].

  //symmetry axiom
  FORALL X,Y X[compatibleWith->Y]<- Y[compatibleWith->X].

  FORALL X,Y,Z X[substitutes->Z] <- (Y[rdf:type->Z] and
     X[substitutes->Y]) or X[compatibleWith->Z].
}
```

Fig. 4. Part of Grid Background Knowledge

`substitutes` in terms of `compatible`, to determine which operating systems can be substituted by each other.

Matchmaking Rules. The matchmaking rules define the matching constraints between requests and resources. These rules are implemented using TRIPLE rule language (Section 2.3). In additon to syntactic string/numeric equality and group membership rules which are primitive constraint expressions in existing attributed-based matchmakers, TRIPLE can reason about constraints in terms of object properties and their relationships specified in RDF data and background knowledge.

Figure 5 depicts part of the matchmaking effort. The rules require inputs—the set of advertisements `Data`, background knowledge `Background`, and domain ontology `Ontology`. The first rule defines the `match` property, which states when a `JobRequest` matches an advertisement of a ComputerSystem. This rule is defined in terms of other rules, *e.g.*, `matchesOS` (*match OperatingSystem*) and `matchesFS` (*match FileSystem*). The rule defining `matchOS` uses the Grid background knowledge by asking if the operating systems requested by the job can be substituted by the operating system provided by the `ComputerSystem` resource. The `matchesFS` rule checks whether the filesystem associated with the resource can satisfy the requested filesystem requirement. In the resource ontology, there are two classes of file systems (*i.e.*, LocalFileSystem and NetworkFileSystem) which are subclasses of the class `FileSystem`. The `matchesFS` rule invokes the reasoning with the ontology to check if its argument `Y` (associated with the resource) is an instance of the class `FileSystem`, and then performs simple arithmetic comparison to ensure that there is enough diskspace available for the request.

4.2 Deductive Database Engine for Ontology-Based Matchmaker

We use TRIPLE/XSB as a deductive database system [27]. TRIPLE/XSB supports RDF-Schema and TRIPLE rule language. It is implemented on top of the XSB deductive database system [32]. TRIPLE rules are first compiled into XSB rules, which are then further compiled into instructions for the XSB virtual machine. TRIPLE/XSB evaluates

```
FORALL Data, Background @match(Data,Background,Ontology){
 FORALL X,Y  X[matches->Y] <-
        X[rdf:type->GR:JobRequest]@Data
    and Y[rdf:type->GR:ComputerSystem]@rdfschema(Data,Ontology)
    and ((X.GR:RequestResource.GR:RequiredMemory)@Data)[matchesMEM->(Y.GR:RunningOS)@Data]
    and ((X.GR:RequestResource.GR:RequiredOS)@Data)[matchesOS->(Y.GR:RunningOS)@Data]
    and ((X.GR:RequestResource.GR:RequiredFS)@Data)[matchesFS->(Y.GR:HostedFileSystem)@Data]
    and ((X.GR:RequestResource.GR:RequiredCPU)@Data)[matchesCPU->Y].

// checking OperatingSystem requirement
 FORALL X,Y  X[matchesOS->Y] <-
        X[rdf:type->GR:OSRequirement]@Data
    and Y[rdf:type->GR:OperatingSystem]@Data
    and ((X.GR:OSType)@Data)[substitutes->(Y.GR:OSType)@Data]@Background.

// checking FileSystem Requirement
 FORALL X,Y  X[matchesFS->Y] <-
        X[rdf:type->GR:FSRequirement]@Data
    and Y[rdf:type->GR:FileSystem]@rdfschema(Data,Ontology)
    and (X.GR:MinDiskSpace)@Data =< (Y.GR:AvailableSpace)@Data.
}
```

Fig. 5. Part of Matchmaking Rules

matchmaking rules, in combination with background knowledge and ontologies, to find the best match for the request.

Performance. The number and complexity of the rules determine the performance of the matchmaker. In the case of non-recursive rules, the matchmaking process is equivalent to computing database queries and views, which is known to be efficient using conventional indexing and join techniques. In the case of recursive rules (as shown in our example), the evaluation may be time consuming. However, there are evaluation techniques developed for deductive databases (which are deployed by XSB) that can be used to avoid unnecessary rule evaluations. In addition, careful rule development can further optimize the system performance.

4.3 Methodology

The first step in developing an ontology-based matchmaker is to create domain ontologies. We have modeled and prototyped three ontologies mentioned in Section 4.1. Once the ontologies are defined, the vocabularies can then be used to generate background knowledge and matching rules. Ontology modeling is an iterative process. When new types of resources become available or when existing resources offer new capabilities, the resource ontology has to be updated to reflect the new status. Similarly, when the vocabularies change, the background knowledge and rules have to be adjusted accordingly. The ontologies, background knowledge and matching rules can be incrementally extended and maintained as the Grid evolves.

4.4 Matchmaking Framework

Resource Discovery. The matchmaking framework consists of ontology-based matchmakers, resource providers and resource consumers or requesters. Resource providers periodically advertise their resources and capabilities to one or more matchmakers (Step 1

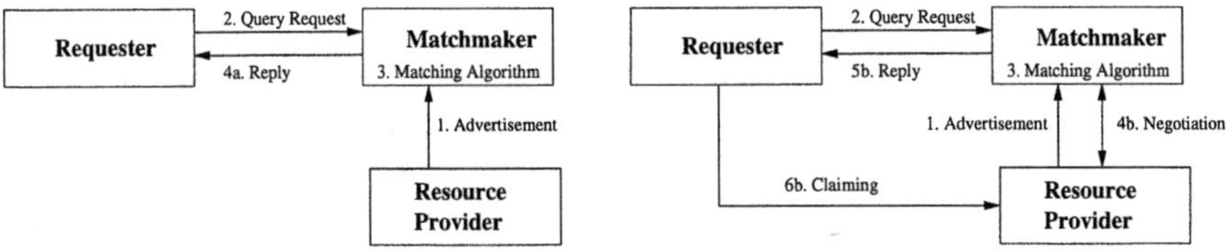

(a) Matchmaking Service (b) Brokering Service

Fig. 6. Actions involved in the two services provided by the matchmaker

in Figure 6). The advertisement is generated either due to system configuration, or in response to a query from the matchmaker. It is possible that resource providers may express their capabilities using a schema that is different from our ontology. In this case, we simply assume that a mapper between this schema to our ontology can be implemented. Upon receiving an advertisement, the matchmaker applies the appropriate mapper and then updates its list of available resources.

Each matchmaker maintains an aggregated list of available resources from the received advertisements. The list is based on soft-state updates from the providers. Each item on the list has an effective period associated with it. Whenever an advertisement is received, the effective period is appropriately set. When the effective period expires, the item is removed from the list. In the recently proposed Open Grid Services Architecture (OGSA) [10], the matchmaker could directly subscribe to service providers to get periodic XML-based status updates. The descriptive terms for services in that environment are extensible; this scenario is the central motivation for using extensible ontologies to map between evolving service descriptions and request models.

Matchmaker Services. There are two services provided by the matchmaker; the matchmaking and brokering services. The brokering service is built on top of the matchmaking service. One of the two services is invoked when a requester submits a job request to the matchmaker (Step2). A request is composed using vocabulary in the request ontology. Upon receiving a request, the matchmaker activates the matching rules to find a list of potential matches sorted according to the requester's preference criteria (Step3). If the request is for a matchmaking service, the matchmaker simply returns the matched list (or *NoMatchFound*) to the requester (Step4a).

In the case that the request is for a brokering service, there are two steps involved—negotiating and claiming. The matchmaker sends *negotiation* messages using the *negotiation protocol* to the highest-rank item in the list informing resources about a potential job request (Step4b). A resource provider can accept or deny the request. If it accepts the request, appropriate resources will be allocated for the future job. If the request is denied, the matchmaker then attempts to negotiate with the next highest-ranked item in the list until the matched list is exhausted. If no match is found, the matchmaker returns to the requester a *NoMatchFound* message, else it returns a list of matched resources and associated handles, and appropriately updates its list of available resources and their status (Step 5b). The requester can then contact the resource providers directly for their services using the *claiming protocol* (Step 6b).

4.5 Prototype Implementation

We have prototyped three initial ontologies (mentioned in Section 4.1) and an ontology-based matchmaker. Currently, the matchmaker reads instances of requests, available resources and authorization policies (described by vocabularies in the request, resource and policy ontologies, respectively) from an RDF file. Ontology instances are manually created using Protégé (which saves instances in the RDF format).

Our matchmaker currently offers only the matchmaking service. We plan to include the brokering service in the future. The user can activate the matchmaking service by submitting an instance file (in RDF) and a query asking for resources that satisfy the request specification. The query is then processed by the TRIPLE/XSB deductive database system using matchmaking rules, in combination with background knowledge and ontologies, to find the best match for the request.

Ongoing and future work is to implement the matchmaker as a Grid service. Once completed, a user will be able to submit a request specification (using our request ontology) from any client machine through a web service mechanism. The matchmaker service will notify the results to the user through similar mechanism.

4.6 Matching Example

We show a matching example by our matchmaker is this section. This matching example cannot be done easily by syntax-based matchmakers. Figure 7 shows examples of two instances of resources: a 64-CPU SunOS shared memory machine and a Linux cluster with 640 CPUs available. Due to space limitation, we are only showing a subset of resource properties that are relevant to the example. In this example, both resources belong to USC and only allow users who belong to "`rcf@usc.edu`" group to access the resources.

Figure 8 shows an example of a job request. The job request specifies that it wants one `ComputerSystem` resource for an MPI application. The resource requirements are specified with the prefix JobRequest.RequestResource. Since our background knowledge indicates that an MPI application can run on a tightly-coupled machine and both Linux cluster and shared memory are considered tightly-coupled machines, they both are candidate resources for an MPI application. Assuming that User1 has an account that belong to the "`rcf@usc.edu`" group, User1 is authorized to access both machines. The matchmaker then checks the capabilities of both resources against the resource requirements. Again, since our background knowledge specifies that both "`Linux`" and "`SunOS`" are types of "`Unix`", both resources pass the `OSType` requirement criteria. Because both resources are compatible with the resource requirements, the "`RankBy`" is used to select the best match. Finally, since the `MinClockSpeed` of "`Almaak.usc.edu`" is higher than that of "`Hpc.usc.edu`", the matchmaker returns "`Almaak.usc.edu`" as a match.

`RequestResource` is a relationship between `JobRequest` and `ResourceDescription` classes. We use this relationship to describe as many `ResourceDescription` instances as we want. For example, using the above request example, we can extend the above `JobRequest` to accommodate two resources by updating `NumberOfResources` to 2 and specifying another set of `JobRequest.RequestResource.*`.

Property Names	Property Values
UnitaryComputer.Name	"Almaak.usc.edu"
UnitaryComputer.AuthorizedGroup	"rcf@usc.edu"
UnitaryComputer.NumberOfAvailableCPUs	64
UnitaryComputer.ComputerSystemProcessor.MinClockSpeed	900
UnitaryComputer.HostedFileSystem.AvailableSpace	500
UnitaryComputer.RunningOS.OSType	"SunOS"
UnitaryComputer.RunningOS.Version	"5.8"
UnitaryComputer.RunningOS.FreeVirtualMemory	4000
UnitaryComputer.RunningOS.FreePhysicalMemory	4000
UnitaryComputer.RunningOS.MaxProcessCPUs	64
UnitaryComputer.RunningOS.MaxProcessMemorySize	2000

(a) A SunOS shared memory machine with 64 CPUs

Property Names	Property Values
LinuxCluster.Name	"Hpc.usc.edu"
LinuxCluster.AuthorizedGroup	"rcf@usc.edu"
LinuxCluster.NumberOfAvailableCPUs	640
LinuxCluster.MinClockSpeed	733
LinuxCluster.HostedFileSystem.AvailableSpace	5000
LinuxCluster.RunningOS.OSType	"Linux"
LinuxCluster.RunningOS.Version	"7.2"
LinuxCluster.RunningOS.FreeVirtualMemory	2000
LinuxCluster.RunningOS.FreePhysicalMemory	1000
LinuxCluster.RunningOS.MaxProcessCPUs	320
LinuxCluster.RunningOS.MaxProcessMemorySize	1500

(b) A linux cluster with 640 CPUs

Fig. 7. Available Resources

Property Names	Property Values
JobRequest.Name	"Request1"
JobRequest.Owner	"User1"
JobRequest.JobType	"MPI"
JobRequest.NumberOfResources	1
JobRequest.RequestResource.ResourceType	"ComputerSystem"
JobRequest.RequestResource.RankBy	"CPUClockSpeed"
JobRequest.RequestResource.RequiredOS.OSType	"Unix"
JobRequest.RequestResource.RequiredCPU.MinNumberCPUs	32
JobRequest.RequestResource.RequiredMemory.MinPhysicalMemory	1000
JobRequest.RequestResource.RequiredMemory.MinVirtualMemory	1000
JobRequest.RequestResource.RequiredFS.MinDiskSpace	200

Fig. 8. Job Request

5 Conclusion and Future Work

We have presented a prototype of an ontology-based resource matchmaker that exploits existing semantic web technologies. We have shown that Semantic Web technologies like RDF and RDF Schema can be used to build such a rule-based matchmaker. Since our matchmaker is built based on existing components, the effort to create and maintain the matchmaker is drastically reduced. So far, our experience with the ontology-based matchmaker is promising. We plan to expand the three ontologies and enhance the matchmaking capability.

For example, the resource model will be extended to cover other kinds of physical resources (*e.g.*, database and storage systems, network connections) and abstract services (*e.g.*, a specialized finite difference solver). We envision a consensus process possibly organized as a GGF working group which standardizes the vocabulary for expressing resource description in the Grid. We also plan to extend the resource request model and our matchmaker capability to support set-matching.

As mentioned in Section 4, one of the desired features of the matchmaker is to allow users to submit a request in terms of high-level application characteristics, which will in turn be mapped to specific resource requirement configurations by the matchmaker. We will start our investigation with earthquake applications (*e.g.*, finite different inelastic wave propagation simulations) in the SCEC/ITR project [15].

To show that our resource matchmaker can be efficiently used in the Grid environment, a practical performance evaluation of our matchmaker needs to be conducted. We plan to investigate the scalability and performance of our ontology matchmaker in terms of number of rules and number of resources in the ontologies. An evaluation comparison with the existing resource matchmaker in the Grid such as Condor will also be included.

References

1. R. J. Bayardo, Jr., W. Bohrer, R. Brice, A. Cichocki, J. Fowler, A. Helal, V. Kashyap, T. Ksiezyk, G. Martin, M. Nodine, M. Rashid, M. Rusinkiewicz, R. Shea, C. Unnikrishnan, A. Unruh, and D. Woelk. InfoSleuth: Agent-based semantic integration of information in open and dynamic environments. In *Proceedings of the ACM SIGMOD International Conference on Management of Data*, volume 26,2, pages 195–206, New York, 13–15 1997. ACM Press.
2. Tim Berners-Lee. *Weaving the Web*. Texere Publishing, NA, 2000.
3. Dan Brickley and R. V. Guha. Resource description framework (rdf) schema specification 1.0.
4. Common information model (cim) standards. http://www.dmtf.org/standards/standard_cim.php.
5. The condor project. http://www.cs.wisc.edu/condor.
6. K. Czajkowski, S. Fitzgerald, I. Foster, and C. Kesselman. Grid information services for distributed resource sharing. In *Proceedings of the Tenth IEEE International Symposium on High-Performance Distributed Computing (HPDC-10)*. IEEE Press, August 2001.
7. K. Czajkowski, I. Foster, C. Kesselman, V. Sander, and S. Tuecke. Snap: A protocol for negotiating service level agreements and coordinating resource management in distributed systems. In *Proceedings of 8th Workshop on Job Scheduling Strategies for Parallel Processing*, Edinburgh, Scotland, July 2002. Lecture Notes in Computer Science, 2537:153–183, 2002.
8. H. Eriksson, R. W. Fergerson, Y. Shahar, and M. A. Musen. Automatic generation of ontology editors. In *Twelfth Banff Knowledge Acquisition for Knowledge-based systems Workshop*, Banff, Alberta, Canada, 1999.
9. Eurogrid: Application testbed for european grid computing. http://www.eurogrid.org.
10. I. Foster, C. Kesselman, J. Nick, and S. Tuecke. The physiology of the grid: An open grid services architecture for distributed systems integration. In *Open Grid Service Infrastructure WG, Global Grid Forum*, June 2002. Extended version of Grid Services for Distributed System Integration.

11. I. Foster, C. Kesselman, and S. Tuecke. The anatomy of the grid: Enabling sdalable virtual organizations. *International J. Supercomputer Applications*, 15(3), 2001.
12. Ian Foster and Carl Kesselman, editors. *The Grid: Blueprint for A New Computing Infrastructure*. Morgan Kaufmann Publishers, San Francisco, 1999.
13. Griphyn – grid physics network. http://www.griphyn.org/index.php.
14. T. R. Gruber. A translation approach to portable ontology specifications. *Knowledge Acquisition*, 5(2):199–220, 1993.
15. T. H. Jordan and C. Kesselman *et al.* The scec community modeling environment – an information infrastructure for system-level earthquake research. http://www.scec.org/cme.
16. Michael Kifer, Georg Lausen, and James Wu. Logical foundations of object-oriented and frame-based languages. *Journal of the ACM*, 42(4):741–843, July 1995.
17. O. Lassila and R. R. Swick. Resource description framework (rdf) model and syntax specification. In *W3C Recommendation, World Wide Web Consortium*. February 1999. http://www.w3.org/TR/1999/REC-rdf-syntax-19990222.
18. Lei Li and Ian Horrocks. A software framework for matchmaking based on semantic web technology. In *Proceedings of the Twelfth International World Wide Web Conference (WWW 2003)*, 2003.
19. C. Liu and I. Foster. A constraint language approach to grid resource selection. Unpublished menuscripts.
20. C. Liu, L. Yang, I Foster, and D. Angulo. Design and evaluation of a resource selection framework. In *Proceedings of the Eleventh IEEE International Symposium on High-Performance Distributed Computing (HPDC-11)*, Edinburgh, Scottland, 2002.
21. J. W. Lloyd. *Foundations of Logic Programming*. Springer, Berlin, 2 edition, 1987.
22. Kim Marriott and J. S. Peter. *Programming with Constraints: An Introduction*. The MIT Press, Cambridge, Massachusetts, 1998.
23. The portable batch system. http://pbs.mrj.com.
24. R. Raman, M. Linvy, and M. solomon. Resource management through multilateral matchmaking. In *Proceedings of the Ninth IEEE Symposium on High Performance Distributed Computing (HPDC9)*, pages 290–291, Pittsburgh, Pennsylvania, August 2000.
25. R. Raman, M. Linvy, and M. solomon. Policy driven heterogeneous resource co-allocation with gangmatching. In *Proceedings of the twelfth IEEE Symposium on High Performance Distributed Computing (HPDC12)*, pages 80–89, Seattle, Washington, June 2003.
26. R. Raman, M. Livny, and M. Solomon. Matchmaking distributed resource management for high throughput computing. In *Proceedings of the Seventh IEEE International Symposium on High Performance Distributed Computing*, Chicago, IL, July 1998.
27. Michael Sintek and Stefan Decker. Triple – a query, inference, and transformation language for the semantic web. In Ian Horrocks and James Hendler, editors, *Proc. of the 13th Int. Semantic Web Conf. (ISWC 2002)*, number 2342 in Lecture Notes in Computer Science, pages 364–378. Springer-Verlag, 2002.
28. Michael Sintek and Stefan Decker. Triple – an rdf query, inference, and transformation language. In Ian Horrocks and James Hendler, editors, *Proc. of the 2002 International Semantic Web Conference (ISWC 2002)*, number 2342 in Lecture Notes in Computer Science. Springer-Verlag, 2002.
29. K. Sycara, S. Wido, M. Klusch, and J. Lu. Larks: Dynamic matchmaking among heterogeneous software agents in cyberspace, 2002.
30. The teragrid project. http://www.teragrid.org.
31. Universal description, discovery and integration of web services. http://www.uddi.org.
32. The xsb research group. http://xsb.sourceforge.net/.

A Q-Based Architecture for Semantic Information Interoperability on Semantic Web

Zhen-jie Wang, Huan-ye Sheng, and Peng Ding

Department of Computer Science and Engineering,
Shanghai Jiao Tong University, 200030 Shanghai, China
{wang-zj,sheng-hy,dingpeng}@cs.sjtu.edu.cn

Abstract. Semantic Web supports a fire-new infrastructure for solving the problem of semantic information interoperability, and it promises to support an intelligent and automatic information-processing platform for multi-agent system whose ultimate objective is to provide better services for end-users, for example, interoperable information query. Therefore, except agent-to-agent interaction in multi-agent system, there is human-to-agent interaction. To unify the two kinds of interaction, this paper introduces Q language - a scenario description language for designing interaction among agents and users. A Q-based architecture, which integrates ontology servers, ontology-mapping servers, semantic information sources, and multi-agent query system, is presented as a system solution to semantic information interoperability on Semantic Web. Furthermore, we investigate key technologies of interoperability: domain ontology, ontology-mapping service, and related multi-agent system, and give an implementation to demonstrate how our architecture works.

1 Introduction

On Semantic Web, a kind of new profiles including semantic information will be used to weave a fire-new infrastructure with machine-readable and machine-interpretable information [1], which supports many new functions, such as interoperability, fusion and integration of information. The idea for achieving information interoperability lies in that the meanings of the interchangeable information should be understood across the entire information infrastructure. A key basis of information interoperability is ontology, which makes it possible to abstract knowledge model of real world using concepts and annotate semantic information into web information sources. Obviously, domain ontology and annotated semantic information sources intend to improve information query and address semantic information interoperability. Semantic Web endowed with many ontology languages such as XML, RDF/S, and DAML+OIL [2,3,4], etc. These languages are foundation for ontology-based information query that will provide more effective information query service.

Because same information is widely applied in many domains, and users have different views for conceptualizing them, there must be different definitions of concepts and relationships for same information. To implement information

D. Fensel et al. (Eds.): ISWC 2003, LNCS 2870, pp. 722–737, 2003.

interoperability, concept-switching or concept-transformation function between different domain ontology is necessary.

Additionally, Semantic Web promises to support a semantic information-processing platform for multi-agent systems, on which agents will be first-class citizens. Therefore, besides domain ontology component and ontology-mapping component, another necessary component is multi-agent system that can automatically retrieve and manipulate semantic information for end-users. Thus, one of the most necessary requirements placed on agents is the capability to interact with end-users. To unify agent-to-agent and human-to-agent interaction, we introduce Q language - a scenario description language for describing interaction among agents and end-users [5].

The paper is organized as follows. Section 2 introuduces syntax facilities of Q language. In section 3, we present a Q-based architecture for implementing semantic information interoperability on Semantic Web, and then discuss its crucial components. Section 4 gives a prototype implementation of proposed Q-based architecture. Lastly, we conclude the paper and discuss related works.

2 *Q* Language Overview

Some inter-agent protocol description languages, such as KQML and AgenTalk [6], often regulate an agent's various actions on the basis of computational model of agent internal mechanisms. Obviously,these agents based on strict computational models have to be designed and developed by computer experts. It is necessary to design a new agent interaction description language, which makes it possible that those non-computer-professional application designers, such as sale managers and consumers, might write scenarios that describe and model the behaviors of agents, so that a practical multi-agent system can be easily established. Under the background, we start working on Q language - a scenario description language for designing interaction among agents and humans. This kind of scenario-based language is to design interaction from the viewpoint of scenario description, but not for describing agent internal mechanisms.

2.1 Syntax Facilities

Q extends Scheme by introducing sensing/acting functions and guard command to realize scenario description. Why Scheme [7] becomes Q's mother language is in that its Lisp-like characteristic: programs (here scenarios) can be handled as data. The basic facilities of Q language for scenario description include Cue, Action, Guard Command, Scenario, and Agent. Execution architecture of Q scenario consists of Execution Layer and Meta Layer [5].

Cue. A sensing function is defined as a cue, which represents agent's perception to its outside environment. A cue doesn't produce any side effect on the environment. The syntax of cue definition and its example are as follows.

```
(defcue cue-name {(parameter in|out|inout)}*)
(defcue ?receive (:sentence in) (:from out))
(?receive request :from user)
```

Action. An acting function is defined as an action, which may change and impose effects on the environment of agent system. The syntax and example of an action definition are showed below.

```
(defaction action-name {(parameter in|out|inout)}*)
(defaction querydaml (:damlquery in) (:queryresult out))
(!querydaml $queryrule $result)
```

Guard Command. A guard command is used for describing an agent's behavior control mechanism to await multiple cues. If one of cues is perceived, corresponding "form" will be performed. If no cue is perceived, the guard command will perform the "therwise" clause. The syntax and example of Guard Command are showed as follows.

```
(guard {(cue {form}*)* [(otherwise{form}*)]})
(guard ((?hear "Hello" Peedy) (!play "Greet")
                              (!speak "Hi, Nice to meet you"))
       ((?see-select 0) (!speak "Please input a query!")
                              (!askqueryinput $queryrule))
       (otherwise (!move 100 200) (!play "Wave")
                              (!speak "Bye-Bye")))
```

Scenario. A scenario is used for defining several different states represented by state1, state2, etc.

```
(defscenario scenario-name ({variable}*)
   (state1 {(cue {form}*)}*
           [(otherwise {form}*)])
   (state2 {(cue {form}*)}*
           [(otherwise {form}*)]))
```

An example of scenario is represented as follows, in which state transition is implemented by "form" (go state) between different states (state1, state2, etc.).

```
(defscenario query-agent-scenario (message)
   (let(($x #f))
      (state1((?equal $x Peedy)(!say message)(go state2))
             (otherwise (!say "Hello")(go state3)))
      (state2((guard
             ((?hear "Hello" Peedy)(!play "Greet")
                                   (!speak "Hi") (go state4))
             ((?see-select 0)(!askqueryinput $queryrule)
```

```
                                        (go state5))
         (otherwise (!move 100 200)(!play "Wave")
                    (!speak "Bye-Bye")))))))
```

Agent. Agent is defined together with a specified scenario that will be executed by the specified agent. An agent is defined as follows.

```
(defagent agent :scenario scenario-name {key value}*)
(defagent query-agent  query-agent-scenario
   :ip_address "192.168.100.188"
   :port_number 8080)
```

Conclusively, the most prominent property of Q Language is its simplicity on both design and application of agent systems with following characteristics: End-user-oriented, focusing on the interaction behavior of agent from the viewpoint of users, not agent; Error-allowed (no requirement for correctness); The complex behavior of agent can be realized by the combination of scenarios.

3 Semantic Information Interoperability

The basic architecture of semantic information interoperability on Semantic Web is described in Fig. 1. It is composed of end-users, agent system, ontology sources, and semantic information sources four parts. Agent system consists of user agent, query agent, wrapper agent, and facilitator agent. The interaction among these agents and interaction between end-user and agent system are described by a library of Q scenarios, each of which control an agent's behaviors and a group of which specify a multi-agent cooperation strategy to cope with a specific request. Ontology sources are ontology-mapping servers and domain ontology servers. Semantic information sources include web pages and web services and web databases, in which information providers have annotated semantic information using related domain ontology.

3.1 Domain Ontology

Ontology is generally defined as "a formal explicit specification of a shared conceptualization" [8], which is often used to abstract knowledge models of real world. Many advanced ontology languages, such as RDF/S, OIL and DAML+OIL, make it possible to describe domain ontology and annotate semantic information into web sources. Obviously, domain ontology that conceptualizes domain knowledge and corresponding semantic information sources intend to improve information query and address semantic information interoperability.

The decentralized characteristic of Semantic Web determines that users themselves are able to construct a large number of small domain ontology in much the same way that today's Web content is created [1]. These constructed domain ontology may be distributed in ontology servers of any physical web

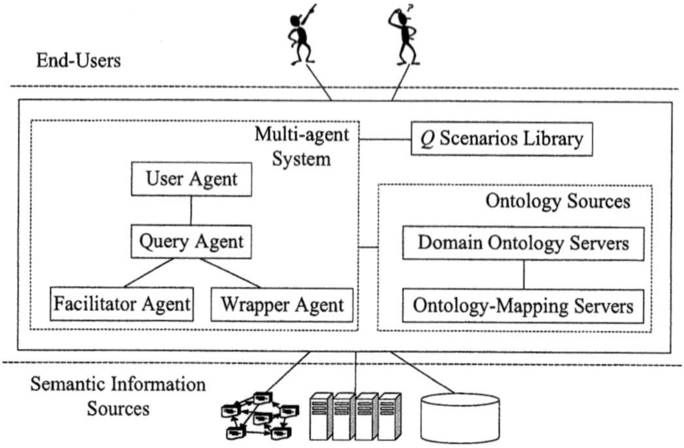

Fig. 1. Architecture for semantic information interoperability

sites. To same information applied in different domains, users have different views for conceptualizing them, so even if all domains' ontology is described in a common ontology language, there still exist different definitions of concepts and relationships for same objects. To implement information interoperability, concept-switching or concept-transformation function between different domain ontology is necessary. By different ontology definitions about the same objects Park and Service Advertisement respectively, we will clearly observe this necessary about concept transformation. These examples are represented by ontology language DAML+OIL.

The first example is about park information. One is about the definition of Park Ontology of Travel Domain in http://www.ichi.sjtu.edu.cn/Travel/Park-Ont. The other is about the definition of Garden Ontology of Administration Domain in http://www.Travel-Adm.com/Landscape/Garden-Ont.

```
Park Ontology:
<daml:Class ID="Park">
   <rdfs:subClassOf>
       <daml:Restriction daml:cardinality="1">
          <daml:onProperty rdf:resource="#Name"/>
       </daml:Restriction>
   </rdfs:subClassOf>
</daml:Class>
<daml:DatatypeProperty rdf:ID="Name">
   <rdfs:domain rdf:resource="#Park"/>
   <rdfs:range rdf:resource="#string"/>
</daml:DatatypeProperty>
<daml:DatatypeProperty rdf:ID="City">
   <rdfs:domain rdf:resource="#Park"/>
```

```
   <rdfs:range rdf:resource="#string"/>
</daml:DatatypeProperty>
<daml:DatatypeProperty rdf:ID="Country">
   <rdfs:domain rdf:resource="#Park"/>
   <rdfs:range rdf:resource="#string"/>
</daml:DatatypeProperty>
```

```
Garden Ontology:
<daml:Class ID="Garden">
   <rdfs:subClassOf>
      <daml:Restriction daml:cardinality="1">
         <daml:onProperty rdf:resource="#Name"/>
      </daml:Restriction>
   </rdfs:subClassOf>
</daml:Class>
<daml:DatatypeProperty rdf:ID="Name">
   <rdfs:domain rdf:resource="#Garden"/>
   <rdfs:range rdf:resource="#string"/>
</daml:DatatypeProperty>
<daml:DatatypeProperty rdf:ID="Place">
   <rdfs:domain rdf:resource="#Garden"/>
   <rdfs:range rdf:resource="#string"/>
</daml:DatatypeProperty>
```

The second example is about service advertisement of web service. One is about ServiceProfile Ontology of Service Domain in http://www.daml.com/Service/Profile-Ont. The other is about ServiceAdvertisement Ontology of Agent Domain in http://www.ichi.sjtu.edu.cn/Agent/Advertisement-Ont.

```
ServiceProfile Ontology:
<daml:Class ID="ServiceProfile">
   <daml:subClassOf rdf:resource="#Profile"/>
</daml:Class>
<daml:DatatypeProperty rdf:ID="ServiceName">
   <rdfs:domain rdf:resource="#ServiceProfile"/>
   <rdfs:range rdf:resource="#string"/>
</daml:DatatypeProperty>
<daml:DatatypeProperty rdf:ID="ServiceType">
   <rdfs:domain rdf:resource="#ServiceProfile"/>
   <rdfs:range rdf:resource="#Classification"/>
</daml:DatatypeProperty>
<daml:Class rdf:ID="Classification">
   <daml:oneOf rdf:parseType="daml:collection">
      <Type rdf:ID="Database-Query"/>
      <Type rdf:ID="E-Commence"/>
      <Type rdf:ID="Language-Translation"/>
   </daml:oneOf>
```

```
</daml:Class>
<daml:DatatypeProperty rdf:ID="Input">
   <rdfs:domain rdf:resource="#ServiceProfile"/>
   <rdfs:range rdf:resource="#string"/>
</daml:DatatypeProperty>
<daml:DatatypeProperty rdf:ID="Output">
   <rdfs:domain rdf:resource="#ServiceProfile"/>
   <rdfs:range rdf:resource="#string"/>
</daml:DatatypeProperty>

ServiceAdvertisement Ontology:
<daml:Class ID="ServiceAdvertisement">
   <daml:subClassOf rdf:resource="#Profile"/>
</daml:Class>
<daml:DatatypeProperty rdf:ID="ServiceName">
   <rdfs:domain rdf:resource="#ServiceAdvertisement"/>
   <rdfs:range rdf:resource="#string"/>
</daml:DatatypeProperty>
<daml:DatatypeProperty rdf:ID="ServiceType">
   <rdfs:domain rdf:resource="#ServiceAdvertisement"/>
   <rdfs:range rdf:resource="#Category"/>
</daml:DatatypeProperty>
<daml:Class rdf:ID="Category">
   <daml:subClassOf rdf:resource="#Classification"/>
</daml:Class>
<daml:DatatypeProperty rdf:ID="Precondition">
   <rdfs:domain rdf:resource="#ServiceAdvertisement"/>
   <rdfs:range rdf:resource="#string"/>
</daml:DatatypeProperty>
<daml:DatatypeProperty rdf:ID="Postcondition">
   <rdfs:domain rdf:resource="#ServiceAdvertisement"/>
   <rdfs:range rdf:resource="#string"/>
</daml:DatatypeProperty>
```

3.2 Ontology-Mapping Service

Furthermore, we discuss how to implement concept transformation through two concrete query examples. Supposed a user in Administration Domain wants to search for information about Yu Yuan Garden, and he sends Query A via a user agent to a query agent that will assist user in searching for information. A specific notation is used to identify concepts and specify ontology in users' query, for example, Query A is formalized by Garden Ontology with properties Name and Place. SEARCH <Administration:Garden> means that this user expects to search for objects of class Garden including all properties that are defined for this class, and searching results must be restricted to those objects with properties Name "Yu Yuan Garden" and Place "Shanghai, China".

```
Query A:
xmlns:Administration="http:// www.Travel-Adm.com /
                                              Landscape/Garden-Ont#">
SEARCH <Administration:Garden>
WHERE <Administration:Name>Yu Yuan Garden</Administration:Name>
      <Administration:Place>Shanghai,China</Administration:Place>
END
```

When the query agent browses a web page annotated with Park Ontology (see Annotation A), intuitively, if it is aware of equivalent mapping relation between property Place in Park Ontology of Travel Domain and properties City as well as Country in Garden Ontology of Administration Domain, it can find a object which includes information of Yu Yuan Garden in Shanghai of China.

```
Annotation A:
xmlns:Travel="http://www.ichi.sjtu.edu.cn/Travel/Park-Ont#">
<Travel:Park rdf:ID="YuYuan">
   <Travel:Name> Yu Yuan Garden</Travel:Name>
   <Travel:City> Shanghai</Travel:City>
   <Travel:Country> China </Travel:Country>
   <Travel:Area> 30 Acres </Travel:Area>
</Travel:Park>
```

In another example, a user in Agent Domain searches for information about a search engine, he sends Query B via a user agent to a query agent. Query B is formalized by ServiceAdvertisement Ontology. SEARCH <Agent:ServiceName> IN <Agent:ServiceAdvertisement> means that this user expect to search for property ServiceName in class ServiceAdvertisement, and searching results must be restricted to those objects with properties ServiceType "Language-Translation" and Postcondition "Web pages".

```
Query B:
xmlns:Agent="http://www.ichi.sjtu.edu.cn/
                                  Agent/Advertisement-Ont#">
SEARCH <Agent:ServiceName>
IN <Agent:ServiceAdvertisement>
WHERE <Agent:ServiceType rdf:resource="#Language-Translation"/>
      <Agent:Postcondition> Web Pages </Agent:Postcondition>
END
```

When the query agent contacts with facilitator agent, it acquires a service profile annotated with ServiceProfile Ontology (see Annotation B). If it is aware of mapping relations between ServiceAdvertisement Ontology of Agent Domain and ServiceProfile Ontology of Service Domain, for example, an equivalent mapping between properties Postcondition and Output, plus to a subsuming mapping between properties ServiceType and ServiceType, it can find a service with ServiceName "Google" in object GoogleProfile satisfies searching conditions.

```
Annotation B:
xmlns:Service="http://www.daml.com/Service/Profile-Ont#">
<Service:ServiceProfile rdf:ID="GoogleProfile">
   <Service:ServiceName> Google </Service:ServiceName>
   <Service:ServiceType rdf:resource="#Language-Translation"/>
   <Service:Input> Text of sentences </Service:Input>
   <Service:Output> Web pages </Service:Output>
</Service:ServiceProfile>
```

From above query examples, we conclude that ontology-mapping service, which accepts or collects mapping advertisement information from semantic information sources, and then updates and adds it in the form of mapping rules on ontology-mapping server, is a necessary component to implement information interoperability. The forms of mappings contain three types:

- Ontology-to-ontology: it specifies an equivalent or subsuming mapping between source ontology and target ontology.
- Class-to-class: it specifies an equivalent or subsuming mapping between classes of source ontology and target ontology.
- Property-to-property: it specifies an equivalent mapping between properties of class in source ontology and properties of class in target ontology.

A mapping rule has the form *r: Operator(o.c.p)* ***Rlation*** *Operator(o.c.p)*, where r is the rule's label, *Operator* is logical operator (AND, OR, or NOT), o represents ontology name, $o.c$ is a class of a ontology, and $o.c.p$ is a property of a class in a ontology. In symbol *()*, a set of ontology, classes, or properties is contained. ***Relation*** represents equivalent or subsuming relationships that are symbolized as: $=$, $\subseteq$. For example, the following rules represent the mappings between properties of Garden Ontology and Park Ontology.

```
R1:http://www.Travel-Adm.com/Landscape/Garden-Ont.Garden.Place =
   AND (http://www.ichi.sjtu.edu.cn/Travel/Park-Ont.Park.City,
        http://www.ichi.sjtu.edu.cn/Travel/Park-Ont.Park.Country)
R2:http://www.Travel-Adm.com/Landscape/Garden-Ont.Garden.Name =
   http://www.ichi.sjtu.edu.cn/Travel/Park-Ont.Park.Name
```

3.3 Multi-agent System

Multi-agent system including user agent, query agent, facilitator agent, and wrapper agent is to assist users in query inference and transformation, and it is used to connect users, ontology servers, ontology-mapping servers, and various semantic information sources (see Fig. 2).

In interoperable information query, query agent is used to assist users in query processing, for example concept extracting, ontology-mapping rules acquiring, query rewriting, knowledge finding, etc. Its primary function modules are depicted in Fig. 2. When end-users issue a query that is described by specified ontology to his user agent, user agent will submit it to query agent. Firstly,

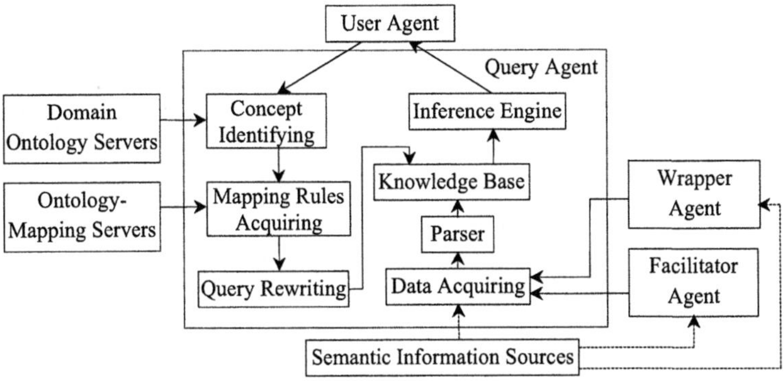

Fig. 2. Multi-agent query system

the query agent abstracts and identifies concepts in user's query; then it checks whether there are mappings between user ontology and ontology used by inspected semantic information. If query agent acquires ontology-mapping rules from ontology-mapping server, it will rewrite the user query. Parser is used to parse semantic data acquired from annotated semantic information sources. According to stored knowledge from Parser and rewritten query from Query Rewriting in Knowledge Base, Inference Engine will search and return corresponding query results to user agent.

If information source is a traditional Database, a wrapper agent is used to transform data in DB into semantic data according to its Database Schema. Here, wrapper agent acts as proxies for external information sources. Facilitator agent accepts semantic advertisements from services on Semantic Web, and matches service requests derived from a query agent.

In this multi-agent system, there is the interaction between users and user agent, for example, issuing query to user agent, returning results to user, reporting states of query; there are the interaction between query agent and user agent for transmission of query and results, the interaction between query agent and facilitator agent for searching service information, the interaction between query agent and wrapper agent for acquiring data from legacy system, and the interaction between query agent and domain ontology servers as well as ontology-mapping servers. All of interaction can be described by Q scenarios, which are used to control agents' behaviors and specify their cooperation strategy.

4 Implementation

The experimental environment consists of Q language, Microsoft Agent[1], Visual C++, and Prolog-based XSB[2]. The implementation architecture of query system is showed in Fig. 3. Q scenarios describe agents' behaviors (Cues and Actions)

[1] http://www.microsoft.com/msagent/.

[2] http://xsb.sourceforge.net/.

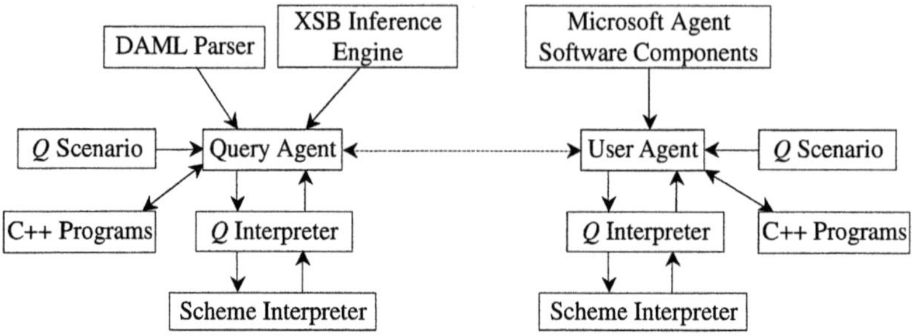

Fig. 3. Implementation architecture of query agent and user agent

Table 1. Main Cues and Actions of user agent

Cues and Actions	**Interpretation** (behaviors of user agent)
(?feel [:from user])	Checks whether to receive user's instruction, for example, quit, stop, etc.
(?receiveResult $Result [:from query-agent])	Checks whether to receive searching result from query agent.
(!speak Sentence [:to user])	Speaks to users, for example, query results.
(!play Animation)	Play some animations such as "GestureDown".
(!move X Y)	Moves to a point (x, y) in the screen with an appropriate manner, such as fly.
(!askqueryinput $Query[:from user])	Asks user to input query items, and variable $Query represents user's query.
(!submit $Requests [to: query-agent])	Submits user's requests to a query agent.

that are implemented by Visual C++. Designed on Microsoft Agent Software Components, our user agent is incorporated interactive abilities such as "speak", "play", "move", etc.

DAML+OIL is used to construct our domain ontology. Therefore, DAML Parser of query agent is designed to parse semantic annotation (DAML markup), and it is constructed on Repat[3]. According to RDF data model, this Parser should parse DAML annotation into triples, each of which includes three parts (Subject, Predicate, Object plus to their corresponding Namespace). These parsed triples are stored in Knowledge Base in a knowledge representation form that is consistent with XSB Inference Engine. As an efficient rule inference engine, XSB specifies ways of processing a pattern query and finding new knowledge from parsed semantic data.

Here, we will give two query examples mentioned in Query A and Query B. We assume that query agent directly acquires semantic information of "Yu Yuan Garden" from an annotated web page; in addition, it directly acquires semantic information of service "Google" from facilitator agent. We design user agent and query agent's main Cues and Actions as Table 1 and Table 2.

[3] http://www.daml.org/tools/repat.

Table 2. Main Cues and Actions of query agent

Cues and Actions	**Interpretation** (behaviors of query agent)
(?feel [:from user-agent])	Checks whether to get user agent's instruction.
(?receiveRequest $Query [:from user-agent])	Checks whether to get user agent's query request.
(?receiveRule $Mapping-rules [:from mapping-server])	Checks whether to receive ontology-mapping rules.
(!query-mapping $Mapping-rules [to: mapping-server])	Identifies concepts used in user query, and then queries mapping rules from ontology-mapping server.
(!query-rewriting $Mapping-rules $Query)	Rewrites this query according to mapping-rules.
(!parsedaml DAMLFile)	Parses a DAML file into triples.
(!querydaml $Query $Result)	Finishes Knowledge searching according to $Query, and stores query results in variable $Result.
(!return $Result [to: user-agent])	Returns query results in variable $Result to user agent.

The main states of user agent in a scenario are shown as follows. At the initial state state_Ask-query, user agent shows a dialog box and guides a user to input his query into the dialog box. After the user inputs the query, user agent's state shifts to state_Submit, in which the agent executes a action of sending a query to a query agent, and then user agent goes on shifting to state_MsgWait. In state_MsgWait, user agent waits for the user's instructions or the messages sent by query agent, and tells the user what is happening, and then shifts to the corresponding state. When user agent receives query results from query agent, it will speak results to user.

```
(state_Ask-query (otherwise
   (!speak " Hello! This is Agent Peedy!")
   (!play  "Greet")
   (!move 200 300)
   (!speak "Please input query in the dialog box!")
   (!askqueryinput $Query)  (go state_Submit)))
(state_Submit (otherwise
   (!submit $Query)(go state_MsgWait)))
(state_MsgWait
   ((?feel)(!speak "Please give me instructions!")
                            (go state_Instruction))
   ((?receiveResult $Result)
      (!speak "I receive results from query agent.")
      (!play "Read")
      (!move 300 450)
      (!speak $result) (go state_Ask-query))
   (otherwise
      (!speak "I am waiting message!" )(go state_MsgWait)))
```

The main states of query agent in a scenario are shown as follows. At the initial state state_MsgWait, query agent waits for the messages from user agent or ontology-mapping server, and then shifts to corresponding state. When query agent receives the query request from user agent, it shifts to state_Ask-rules, and acquires mapping rules from ontology-mapping server. After getting mapping rules, query agent shifts to state_Query for knowledge query.

```
(state_MsgWait
   ((?feel)  (go state_Instruction))
   ((?receiveRequest $query)  (go state_Ask-rules))
   ((?receiveRule $Mapping-rules) (go state_Query)
   (otherwise  (go state_MsgWait)))
(state_Ask-rules (otherwise
   (!query-mapping $Mapping-rules ServerName)(go state_MsgWait)))
(state_Query (otherwise
   (!query-rewriting $Mapping-rules $Query)
   (!parsedaml DAMLFile)
   (!querydaml $Query $Result)(go state_Return-result)))
```

Fig. 4 exhibits user input interface and respective query results of examples of Query A and Query B. Query examples show that query agent with capability of information interoperability exactly returns results.

5 Conclusion and Related Works

Essentially, our interoperable information query is an ontology-based searching approach. Compared with some related works of ontology-based searching, the advantage of our work is in that it introduces ontology-mapping function. For example, SHOE (Simple HTML Ontology Extension) was proposed, which allowed HTML developers to annotate useful semantic knowledge into their web pages, and then a web-crawling agent could capture knowledge from these annotated pages [9]. There were authors who developed an annotation strategy and tool to help formulating annotations and searching for specific images based on domain knowledge contained in ontology [10]. Because these ontology-based searching works neglected concept-switching or concept-transformation function, they only solved information interoperability in a limited degree. Also, there were researchers who investigated information query on the DAML-enabled web [11]. This work suggested ontology mapping, but it mainly examined the problem of inference in searching and addressed the issue of describing dynamic procedures and services in DAML on the Web, and the mechanism and details of how to utilize ontology mapping were unclear.

The decentralized feature of Semantic Web makes it inevitable that different communities will use their own ontology to annotate semantic information in their own information sources. In the sense, the inter-ontology mapping plays a crucial role for information interoperability. In addition, Semantic Web promises to support a semantic information-processing platform for multi-agent systems,

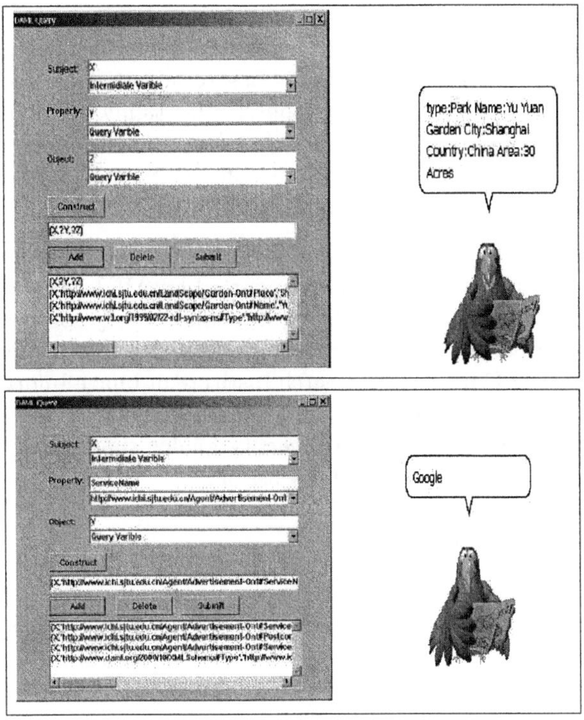

Fig. 4. Two query examples: find information about Yu Yuan Garden; find name of a web pages' search engine

on which agents will be first-class citizens. Considering the two points, many multi-agent systems have been proposed to cope with information interoperability issues, for example, in the areas of ontology heterogeneity, query reformulation, and data integration, etc. Even similar aims have been pursued by some multi-agent systems, such as BUSTER [12], KRAFT [13], Infosleuth [14], and Jeap [15]. Comparing them with our presented Q-based architecture for semantic information interoperability on Semantic Web, our architecture not only considers domain ontology servers and multi-agent system, but also introduces ontology-mapping services that provide concept switching or concept transformation function. Uniquely, we unify the two kinds of interaction: agent-to-agent and human-to-agent interaction in multi-agent query system by Q scenarios, through which end-users may control query agent's behaviors flexibly and interactively. Moreover, the property of Q language is in that it is more oriented to the non-computer professionals than KQML and FIPA ACL, which determines that application designers not only can use to Q scenarios model and describe the agents' behaviors, but also can use them to specify the multi-agent cooperation strategy by combining different Q scenarios in a library.

Next, further works need to be done for improving the practicability of our architecture. Firstly, a standard ontology-mapping representation and inference language have to be set up for make it easy to advertise and collect mapping information of semantic information sources. Certainly, mapping information may be fully manually specified in semantic information sources, or may be semi-automatically determined through some automatic mapping discover techniques, such as case-based reasoning technique.

Acknowledgement. This work was supported by AIEJ (Association of International Education, Japan). Q is being developed by Q consortium including Dept. of Social Informatics at Kyoto University, Dept. of Computer S&E at Shanghai Jiao Tong University, Research Institute of Image Information Science in Japan, and Japanese Science Technology Digital City Research Center. We thank Prof. Toru Ishida of Kyoto University for his supervising, and associate Prof. Zhi-qiang Gao for his detailed discussion.

References

1. J. Hendler. Agents and the semantic web. *IEEE Intelligent Systems*, 16(2): 30–37, 2001.
2. A. Gomez-Perez and O. Corcho. Ontology languages for the semantic web. *IEEE Intelligent Systems*, 16(2): 54–60, 2002.
3. T. Berners-Lee, J. Hendler, and O. Lassila. The semantic web. *Scientific American*, 284(5): 34–43, 2001.
4. J. Hendler and D. McGuinness. The darpa agent markup language. *IEEE Intelligent Systems*, 15(6): 72–73, 2000.
5. T. Ishida and M. Fukumoto. Interaction design language Q: the initial proposal. *Transactions of JSAI*, 17(2): 166–169, 2002.
6. K. Kuwabara, T. Ishida, and N. Osato. AgentTalk: coordination protocol description for multi-agent systems. In *Proceedings of the First International Conference on Multi-Agent Systems*, pages 455, 1995.
7. R. Kent Dybvig. The scheme programming language, second edition. Prentice Hall Inc., 1996.
8. M. Gruninger and J. Lee. Ontology applications and design. *Communications of the ACM*, 45(2): 39–41, 2002.
9. S. Luke, L. Spector, D. Rager, and J. Hendler. Ontology-based web agent. In *Proceedings of the First International Conference on Autonomous Agents*, Pages 59–66, 1997.
10. Th. Schreiber, B. Dubbeldam, J. Wielemaker, and B. Wielinga. Ontology-based photo annotation. *IEEE Intelligent Systems*, 16(3): 66–74, 2001.
11. G. Denker, J. R. Hobbs, D. Martin, S. Narayanan, and R. Waldinger. Accessing information and services on the DAML-enabled Web. In *Proceedings of the Second International Workshop on the Semantic Web*, 2001.
12. H. Stuckenschmidt, H. Wache, T. Vögele, and U. Visser. Enabling technologies for interoperability. In Ubbo Visser and Hardy Pundt, editors, *Workshop on the 14th International Symposium of Computer Science for Environmental Protection*, pages 35–46, 2000.

13. A. D. Preece, K. Hui, W. A. Gray, P. Marti, T. J. M. Bench-Capon, D. M. Jones, and Z. Cui. The KRAFT architecture for knowledge fusion and transformation. *Knowledge Based Systems*, 13(2–3): 113–120, 2000.
14. M. Nodine, J. Fowler, T. Ksiezyk, B.Perry, M. Taylor, and A. Unruh. Active information gathering in InfoSleuth. *International Journal of Cooperative Information Systems*, 9(1–2): 3–28, 2000.
15. M. Panti, L. Penserini, and L. Spalazzi. A multi-agent system based on the P2P model to information integration. Computer Science Institute, University of Ancona, 2002.

Haystack: A Platform for Authoring End User Semantic Web Applications

Dennis Quan, David Huynh, and David R. Karger

MIT Computer Science and Artificial Intelligence Laboratory
200 Technology Square, Cambridge, MA 02139 USA
{dquan,dfhuynh,karger}@ai.mit.edu

Abstract. The Semantic Web promises to open innumerable opportunities for automation and information retrieval by standardizing the protocols for metadata exchange. However, just as the success of the World Wide Web can be attributed to the ease of use and ubiquity of Web browsers, we believe that the unfolding of the Semantic Web vision depends on users getting powerful but easy-to-use tools for managing their information. But unlike HTML, which can be easily edited in any text editor, RDF is more complicated to author and does not have an obvious presentation mechanism. Previous work has concentrated on the ideas of generic RDF graph visualization and RDF Schema-based form generation. In this paper, we present a comprehensive platform for constructing end user applications that create, manipulate, and visualize arbitrary RDF-encoded information, adding another layer to the abstraction cake. We discuss a programming environment specifically designed for manipulating RDF and introduce user interface concepts on top that allow the developer to quickly assemble applications that are based on RDF data models. Also, because user interface specifications and program logic are themselves describable in RDF, applications built upon our framework enjoy properties such as network updatability, extensibility, and end user customizability – all desirable characteristics in the spirit of the Semantic Web.

1 Introduction

One reason underlying the initial success of the World Wide Web is the facility with which people can author Web pages and post them online. Web browsers proved to be an easy client-side platform on which to develop, due to the simplicity and forgiving nature of HTML syntax and the quick turnaround time of the edit-debug process of authoring HTML content. HTML was also sufficiently expressive as a layout language that creative page designs could be realized. Early adopters found a whole new medium in which to express and share their thoughts, designs, and artwork. As HTML matured, programming languages such as JavaScript were called upon to provide support for implementing client-side dynamic content, making HTML even more expressive.

Perhaps an even more important reason for the Web's success is the fact that HTML-based content is extremely easy to navigate. Using the almost ubiquitous Web browser, content located virtually anywhere in the world, regardless of the server on which it is hosted, can be browsed with point-and-click simplicity.

D. Fensel et al. (Eds.): ISWC 2003, LNCS 2870, pp. 738–753, 2003.

In contrast, the Resource Description Framework (RDF) [2], the corresponding standard language for the Semantic Web [3], enjoys none of these properties. Composition of RDF is difficult in its XML form, as is evidenced by the creation of several alternate syntaxes for RDF [5]. Separate from the syntax is the conceptual difficulty of crystallizing knowledge in terms of ontologies, a more complicated process than copying and pasting pieces of hypertext. Furthermore, there are no standard approaches to visualizing RDF, and the generalized approaches of graph visualization and key/value pair editing employed by many projects do not provide the intuitive interface presented by the Web [17].

For the Semantic Web to develop organically, various kinds of users must be able to participate in its growth. User interfaces must be constructed to facilitate the creation and distribution of RDF-encoded information and to visualize extant RDF metadata on the Semantic Web in an intuitive fashion. Developers will need tools for producing such user interfaces that give them easy access to RDF data and user interface components that are specially designed to handle the generality of RDF's data model.

An example of a user interface that gives normal humans the ability to interact with RDF is Haystack [1]. Haystack brings the Semantic Web to end users by leveraging key Semantic Web technologies that allow users to easily manage their documents, e-mail messages, appointments, tasks, etc. The Haystack user interface is capable of visualizing a variety of different types of information; meanwhile, the interface gives few clues to the notion that the underlying data model is represented in RDF. Presenting information in a manner familiar and intuitive to users is key, as few users are familiar with ontological vocabulary and descriptive logic. Additionally, users are unlikely to accept a system that requires them to explicitly shuttle information between their current systems and an RDF representation. In other words, end user Semantic Web applications need to be developed in such a way that users need not even be aware that the Semantic Web is involved!

In addition to serving as an exemplar, Haystack has been built as an extensible platform that allows various kinds of functionality to be developed easily and independently and incorporated seamlessly. In this paper we describe our observations on the kinds of tools that are needed by developers of RDF-based client software and demonstrate these key concepts of the Haystack system that can be reused by others.

2 Approach

The layers of Haystack's infrastructure are designed to tackle specific aspects of the problem of creating end user Semantic Web applications. Enabling the data layer of the system is Adenine, a new domain-specific programming language we have developed for manipulating RDF data. Like RDF/XML and Notation3 [5], it can be used to record RDF, but unlike them, it can express programming constructs that manipulate such data. Adenine adopts a combination of Python, Notation3, and Scheme [9] syntax in order to conveniently express frequently-used RDF operations. Furthermore, because Adenine can be compiled into an RDF representation, Adenine code and RDF data can be freely intermixed and distributed together.

The basis for the Haystack system is a layer that supports back-end components called services that are responsible for incorporating data from other systems and processing existing data in the background. Haystack's RDF information store holds all RDF data known to the system and serves as a blackboard that coordinates the workings of different services, allowing one service to build on the results produced by other services. Services can be written in a variety of languages, including Java, Python, and Adenine.

We turn our attention to the problems of presenting the RDF information that is managed by services to the user. As mentioned, one important part of the appeal of HTML is its expressiveness and ease in coding layout and presentation. Haystack supports an analogous, extensible user interface ontology called Ozone that exploits the power of RDF to describe on screen presentation. Using Ozone we can construct user interface elements called views that represent resources described in RDF on screen.

Not only do we need to present RDF data to the user, but we also need to give users intuitive tools with which to interact with such data. We allow users to manipulate resources with direct manipulation techniques such as context menus and drag and drop. The actual commands that are exposed by such techniques are specified according to an ontology for declaring operations on RDF data. Operations – akin to menu items and toolbar buttons in existing environments – can be defined to work on specific classes of RDF resources and are written in Adenine.

A special type of operation is object and document creation, which is the explicit means through which the user adds data to the system. We define the notion of a constructor, an adaptation of templates, factories, and other construction paradigms used in object-oriented systems [4], to the Semantic Web. Constructors, like operations, are Adenine functions that set up the basic properties of an object, potentially also displaying a user interface to prompt the user for necessary information in the process. We will show how this abstraction can address the issue of how users create new resources and describe existing resources to the system.

Our contributions can be reused in systems other than Haystack. Adenine, for instance, can code information processing algorithms on Web servers that handle RDF data. Haystack's UI framework can be adapted to serve Dynamic HTML pages built up by nesting HTML representations of pieces of RDF data. However, it is through the Haystack system that we wish to illustrate how the combined use of all of these techniques can ease the development of an environment that brings the benefits of the Semantic Web directly to end users.

3 Related Work

We believe that the availability of tools for prototyping and building programs that both produce content for and render content from the Semantic Web can help to improve the reception of Semantic Web technologies. The current generation of tools represents the first step in this direction in that they expose programming interfaces for manipulating information. Toolkits for generating, processing, and visualizing graphs of RDF data are widely available on most platforms [14] [15]. Tools for editing data according to specific ontologies, such as Ont-O-Mat and Protégé, give knowledge engineers powerful tools for creating and manipulating data that corresponds to specific schemata [10] [11]. Furthermore, server-side software packages have been developed to aggregate RDF information for presentation to users [13].

Building on these toolkits, Haystack exposes functionality to users for interacting with information at higher levels of abstraction. Rather than exposing information as a series of RDF statements, Haystack concentrates on the concepts that are important to users of that information: documents, messages, properties, annotations, etc. The Placeless Documents project at Xerox PARC [3] similarly developed an architecture for storing documents based on properties specified by the user and by the system. Both Haystack and Placeless Documents support arbitrary properties on objects and a collection mechanism for aggregating documents. It also specified in its schema access control attributes and shared properties useful for collaboration. We have taken advantage of many ideas that arose from this research in developing the user interface paradigms exposed to users in Haystack for working with RDF-encoded information.

4 Adenine Programming Language

In any system built upon an RDF data model, a sizeable amount of code – both in services and in user interface components – is devoted to the creation and manipulation of RDF-encoded metadata. We observed early on that the development of a language that facilitated the types of operations we frequently perform with RDF would greatly increase our productivity. This lead to the creation of Adenine. An example snippet of Adenine code is given below.

```
# Prefixes for simplifying input of URIs
@prefix : <urn:test-namespace:>

:ImportantMethod rdf:type rdfs:Class

method :expandDerivedClasses ;
rdf:type :ImportantMethod ;
rdfs:comment "x rdf:type y, y rdfs:subClassOf z => x rdf:type z"
        # Perform query
        # First parameter is the query specification
        # Second is a list of the variables to return,
        # in order
        = data (query {
                ?x rdf:type ?y
                ?y rdfs:subClassOf ?z
        } @(?x ?z))

        # Assert base class types
        for x in data
                # Here, x[0] refers to ?x
                # and x[1] refers to ?z
                add { x[0] rdf:type x[1] }
```

The impetus for creating this language is twofold. The first key motivation is having the language's syntax support the data model. Introducing the RDF data model into a standard object-oriented language is fairly straightforward; after all, object-oriented languages were designed specifically to be extensible in this fashion. Normally, one creates a class library to support the required objects. However, more advanced manipulation paradigms specific to an object model begin to tax the syntax of the language. In languages such as C++, C#, and Python, operator overloading allows programmers to reuse built-in operators for manipulating objects, but one is restricted to the existing syntax of the language; one cannot easily construct new syntactic structures. In Java, operator overloading is not supported, and this results in verbose APIs being created for any object-oriented system.

Arguably, this verbosity can be said to improve the readability of code. On the other hand, lack of syntactic support for a specific object model can be a hindrance to rapid development. Programs can end up being much longer than necessary because of the verbose syntactic structures used. This is the reason behind the popularity of domain-specific programming languages, such as those used in Matlab, Macromedia Director, etc. Adenine is such a language. It includes native support for RDF data types and makes it easy to interact with RDF stores and RDF-based services.

4.1 RDF Representation

The other motivation for creating Adenine was to be able to combine executable code with data in the same representation. To achieve this, Adenine is compilable directly into RDF according to the Adenine ontology. The benefits of this capability can be classified as portability and extensibility. Since 1996, bytecode-based virtual machine execution models have resurged as a result of Java's popularity. Their key benefit has been portability, enabling interpretation of software written for these platforms on vastly different computing environments. In essence, bytecode is a set of instructions written to a portable, predetermined, and byte-encoded ontology.

Adenine takes the bytecode concept one step further by making the ontology explicit and extensible and by replacing byte codes with RDF. In other words, instructions are represented as RDF resources, connected by "next instruction" predicates. Execution occurs by following a chain of such instruction resources. Instead of dealing with the syntactic issue of introducing byte codes for new instructions and semantics, Adenine takes advantage of RDF's ability to extend the directed "object code" graph with new instruction node types.

One recent example of a system that uses metadata-extensible languages is Microsoft's Common Language Runtime (CLR). In a language such as C#, *developer-defined* attributes can be placed on methods, classes, and fields to declare metadata ranging from thread safety to serializability. Compare this to Java, where serializability was introduced only through the creation of a new *language keyword* called "transient". The keyword approach requires knowledge of these extensions by the compiler; the attributes approach delegates this knowledge to the runtime and makes the language truly extensible.

In Adenine, RDF assertions can be applied to any statement, such as comments, classifications, authorship attributions, and information about concurrency safety. This fact enables a number of different features, from self-modifying code to automated object code analysis. Most importantly, it means that Adenine can be packaged together with schemas and other ontological metadata and manipulated in the same fashion as other RDF data. In particular, one feature that has proven to be highly useful is the ability to annotate functions with specialized types such as "asynchronous constructor" or "query operator". This feature is used heavily in the implementation of operations, which is discussed later in this paper.

Adenine's RDF representation and its treatment of the RDF triple as a native data type make Adenine very similar to Lisp, in that both support open-ended data models and both blur the distinction between data and code. However, there are some significant differences. The most superficial difference is that Adenine's syntax and semantics are especially well-suited to manipulating RDF data. Adenine is mostly statically scoped, but exposes dynamic variables that address the current RDF containers from which existing statements are queried and to which new statements are written. (An RDF container is simply a data structure that holds RDF statements.) Adenine's runtime model is also better adapted to being run off of an RDF container. Unlike most modern languages, Adenine supports two types of program state: in-memory, as is with most programming languages, and RDF container-based. Adenine in effect supports two kinds of closures, one being an in-memory closure as is in Lisp, and the other being persistent in an RDF container. This affords the developer more explicit control over the persistence model for Adenine programs and makes it possible for services written in Adenine to be distributed.

4.2 Defining Data in Adenine

RDF data is written in much the same way in Adenine as it is in Notation3. Double quotes enclose RDF literals and create instances of the `Literal` class. Angle brackets (<>) enclose URIs and create instances of the `Resource` class.

Prefixes can be declared as a convenient way of referring to frequently-used URIs. For example:

```
@prefix test: <http://test.org/>

if (== test:hi-there <http://test.org/hi-there>)
    print 'Success!'
```

The `rdf`, `rdfs`, `daml`, `xsd`, and `adenine` prefixes are predefined with their standard values.[1]

Collections of RDF statements are enclosed within curly braces (`{}`). The tokens within the `{}` operator are of the form:

```
{ [subject] [predicate] [object]
  [subject2] [predicate2] [object2] … }
```

No separator is required between consecutive statements, unlike Notation3. The semicolon (`;`) can be used in the subject field to refer to the last used subject. Expressions within the `{}` operator are handled as follows: Expressions that evaluate to `Resource` or `Literal` objects are used directly. Lists are expressed with the `@()` operator and are expressed as DAML+OIL lists. Other objects are converted into `Literal`'s. The `{}` expression itself evaluates to an object exposing the `IRDFContainer` interface.

---

[1] rdf: http://www.w3.org/1999/02/22-rdf-syntax-ns#
rdfs: http://www.w3.org/2000/01/rdf-schema#
daml: http://www.daml.org/2001/03/daml+oil#
xsd: http://www.w3.org/2001/XMLSchema#
adenine: http://haystack.lcs.mit.edu/schemata/adenine#

Anonymous nodes can be created from Adenine using the `${}` operator (the equivalent of the `[]` operator in Notation3). Syntactically, an anonymous node expression has type `Resource` and can be used anywhere a resource is needed. This feature is useful when you need a unique, "anonymous" URI for a set of statements. The following set of statements states that Mary's son is 15 years old and is named "Bob" (`add` is the command used to insert RDF statements into the store):

```
add {
    <urn:person:mary> <urn:person:hasSon> ${
        <urn:person:age> "15" ;
        <urn:person:name> "Bob"
    }
}
```

4.3 Writing Executable Code

The syntax of Adenine code resembles a combination of Python and Lisp. As in Python, indentation levels denote lexical block structure (indentation is ignored within `{}` expressions). Adenine is an imperative language, and as such contains standard constructs such as functions, for loops, arrays, and objects. Function calls resemble Lisp syntax in that they are enclosed in parentheses and do not use commas to separate parameters. Arrays are indexed with square brackets as they are in Python or Java. Also, because the Adenine interpreter is written in Java, Adenine code can call methods and access fields of Java objects using the dot operator, as is done in Java or Python. The execution model is quite similar to that of Java and Python in that an in-memory environment is used to store variables; in particular, execution state is *not* represented in RDF. Values in Adenine are represented as Java objects.

Adenine methods are functions that are named by URI and are compiled into RDF. To execute these functions, the Adenine interpreter is instantiated and passed the URI of the method to be run and the parameters to pass to it. The interpreter then constructs an initial in-memory environment binding standard names to built-in functions and executes the code one instruction at a time. Because methods are simply resources of type `adenine:Method`, one can also specify other metadata for methods, as was mentioned earlier. In the example given, an `rdfs:comment` is declared and the method is given an additional type, and these assertions will be entered directly into the RDF container that receives the compiled Adenine code.

Adenine methods are usually executed by interpretation of a method's instructions from an RDF store. A prototype interpreter has been implemented in Java and is used to run much of Haystack. However, to improve performance, a tool is available for compiling Adenine methods into Java Virtual Machine bytecode. While eliminating some of the dynamic nature of Adenine, translation into Java does provide a significant performance increase.

The top level of an Adenine file is used for data (i.e., `add` instructions) and method declarations and cannot contain executable code. This is because Adenine is in essence an alternate syntax for RDF. Within method declarations, however, is code that is compiled into RDF; hence, method declarations are like syntactic sugar for the equivalent Adenine RDF "bytecode".

Development on Adenine is ongoing, and Adenine is being used as a platform for testing new ideas in writing RDF-manipulating services and user interface components. More information about Adenine can be found at the following URL off of our website: http://haystack.lcs.mit.edu/documentation/adenine.pdf.

5 Services

In the past, programs that aggregated data from multiple sources, such as mail merge or customer relationship management, had to be capable of speaking numerous protocols with different back ends to generate their results. With a rich corpus of information described in a single format, namely RDF, the possibility for automation becomes significant because services can now be written against a single unified abstraction. In Haystack, *services* encapsulate key pieces of functionality that manipulate RDF data and execute independently of the user interface. Furthermore, services can be written to help users deal with problem such as information overload by extracting key information from e-mail messages and other documents and presenting the user with summaries. In short, services massage data of importance to the user for consumption by the user interface.

Services in Haystack are callable entities that expose a Java interface. (A Java-implemented stub class that calls Adenine methods is also available and frequently used.) The core services are mostly written in Java, but some are written in Adenine and some in Python (these services are hosted by the Jython interpreter). We utilize an RDF ontology derived from WSDL [6] for describing the interfaces to services as well as for noting which server processes hosts which services. As a consequence, we are able to support different protocols for communicating between services, from simply passing in-process Java objects around to using HTTP-based RPC mechanisms such as HTTP POST and SOAP [8]. In other words, Haystack services are in effect Web Services whose implementation implements the `edu.mit.lcs.haystack.server.service.IService` Java interface and where the appropriate WSDL metadata has been entered into the store; the system takes care of exposing services via whatever protocols are supported.

One specific class of service is of great importance in Haystack: the RDF store. RDF stores, as their name implies, hold RDF statements and allow clients to query their contents. As all persistent system state is described in RDF, Haystack uses RDF stores much as modern software uses the file system.

5.1 Core Infrastructure

Sitting at the core of the Haystack system is a service manager, a Java process that is responsible for starting up the services it hosts. At system startup the service manager reads an RDF configuration file to determine where the root RDF store is. The service manager then connects to this root store, much as a UNIX system mounts its root file system at startup, and determines what services should be started based on the values of the `config:hostsService` property of the service manager's resource (all service managers are named by URIs).

All services are run within the context of a root store and a service manager. The root store provides a container for services to persist their state. Furthermore, the service manager is responsible for allowing services to connect to one another. If a service requests to connect to a service running on the same service manager, the service manager can return a reference to the other service directly; otherwise, the service manager uses the information about the service encoded in the WSDL ontology to construct a proxy.

Because services in Haystack share an underlying store, services can interoperate with each other by treating the store as a "blackboard". Blackboard architectures permit multiple services to attack a problem by allowing services to use information on the blackboard to perform some specific analysis and to pose new information that is derived from that analysis. RDF stores have built-in support for registering events, which allows services to learn when new information (i.e., RDF statements) has been posted to the store. New functionality can be introduced by adding services that perform certain tasks when specific forms of information enter the system.

5.2 Automation

One useful application for services that is core to the Semantic Web is automation. Services are used in Haystack to automatically retrieve and process information from various sources, such as e-mail, calendars, the World Wide Web, etc. Haystack includes services that retrieve e-mail from POP3 servers, extract plaintext from HTML pages, generate text summaries, perform text-based classification, download RSS subscriptions on a regular basis, fulfill queries, and interface with the file system and LDAP servers.

Services are particularly useful for analyzing collections of documents and finding patterns, which can then aid the system when trying to present such a collection to the user. Modern information retrieval algorithms are capable of grouping documents by similarity or other metrics, and previous work has found these automatic classifications to be useful in many situations [19]. Additionally, users can build collections prescriptively by making a query. A service, armed with a specification of what a user is looking for, can create a collection from the results of a query, and it can watch for new data entering the system that matches the query. For example, one service that exists in Haystack automatically filters a user's e-mail for documents that appear to fit in one or more collections defined by the user, such as "Website Project" or "Letters from Mom" [19].

6 Ozone Presentation Ontology

We have defined an ontology called Ozone that can be used to encode page layout and content much like that expressible in HTML. The following code snippet illustrates how a simple page (Fig. 1) can be authored in Ozone:

```
@prefix slide:
<http://haystack.lcs.mit.edu/schemata/ozoneslide#>

= mySlide ${
   rdf:type            slide:Slide ;
   slide:margin               "10" ;
   slide:bgcolor              "lightGray" ;
   slide:color         "#444444" ;
```

Fig. 1. Sample slide

```
  slide:fontFamily           "Arial" ;
  slide:fontSize             "10" ;
  slide:child ${
    rdf:type          slide:Paragraph ;
    slide:children @(
     ${  rdf:type             slide:Text ;
         slide:text  "Welcome to Haystack" ;
         slide:fontSize       "120%" ;
         slide:fontBold       "true"
     }
     ${  rdf:type             slide:Break }
     ${  rdf:type             slide:Text ;
         slide:text  "The current user is:"
     }
     ${  rdf:type             slide:Block ;
         slide:marginLeft     "20" ;
         slide:borderWidth    "1" ;
         slide:child ${
           rdf:type  slide:Paragraph ;
           slide:children @(
             ${  rdf:type           ozone:ViewContainer ;
                 ozone:initialResource (__identity__.getResource) ;
                 ozone:viewPartClass   ozone:InlineViewPart
             }
           )
         }
     }
    )
  }
}
```

The code specifies a new *slide* (analogous to an HTML page) with all margins set to 10 pixels, the background color set to light gray, and the foreground (text) color set to a dark shade of gray as defined by an RGB triple. The text on the page will be in Arial, 10 point. These color and font settings are inherited by all descendant resources of the slide; they can also be overridden by the descendant resources when necessary, as is the case with Cascading Style Sheets.

The sample slide has one child, a slide:Paragraph resource (similar to the <P> tag in HTML). The slide:Paragraph resource has four child resources: two slide:Text resources, one slide:Break resource, and one slide:Block resource. The first slide:Text resource redefines its font size and boldens its text. The Block resource is like the <DIV> tag in HTML: it allows specification of block-specific attributes such as margins, borders, clearances, drop shadow, etc. Inside the Block resource is a placeholder for a view (discussed later), which renders the name of the current user. The current user is expressed by the Adenine expression (__identity__.getResource), which is embedded within the slide definition.

Note the hierarchical form of the code snippet: in this way, Ozone is very similar to HTML and should be somewhat familiar to HTML programmers who know RDF. Adenine makes it easy to write pieces of code that can both manipulate RDF data and generate Ozone data. This is important when, as in many cases, the Ozone data to be generated depends on data in the RDF store.

More information about Ozone can be found on our website at the following URL: http://haystack.lcs.mit.edu/documentation/ui.pdf.

7 Views as Representations of Resources

Using Ozone we can construct user interface elements called *views* that present information about resources in the RDF store. Specifically, a view is a component that displays certain types of resources in a particular way. A given RDF class may have any number of different views associated with it. Furthermore, views are described in RDF, allowing a view to be characterized according to the RDF classes it supports and how it displays resources (e.g., full screen, in a one line summary, as an applet-sized view, etc.). When a resource needs to be displayed in Haystack in a certain way, such as full screen, a view is chosen that possesses the necessary characteristics.

As components, views enable pieces of user interface functionality to be reused. The developer of a one line summary view for people (perhaps displaying a person's name and telephone number) provides an RDF description to the system that enables developers that need to display summaries of contacts to reuse the component. The best example of reuse can be seen in the case of views that embed views of other resources. For example, a view of an address book containing contacts and mailing lists needs not implement views for displaying contacts and mailing lists; Ozone provides a way for views to specify that a resource needs to be displayed at a certain location on the screen in a certain fashion (e.g., as a one line summary). In this way composite views can be constructed that leverage the specialized user interface functionality of the child views that are embedded.

When a view is instantiated, the system passes the view a *context object* that informs it of the resource to be displayed. The context object also contains a pointer to the parent view's context object, if one exists as a result of a view being embedded within another view. In this way views are made aware of the context in which they are displaying information. For example, if an address book view is displaying a list of people by embedding individual person views, the person view can know not to display the "Add to Address Book" button, since it knows that it is embedded within the address book's view and hence is displaying a resource that is already in the address book.

Also, because the system is responsible for instantiating views and keeping track of where child views are to be embedded within parent views, the system can provide default implementations of certain direct manipulation features for free. A good example is drag and drop: When the user starts to drag on a view, the system knows what resource is being represented by that view, such that when the view is dropped elsewhere in the user interface, the drop target can be informed of what resource was involved instead of simply the textual or graphical content of the particular representation that was dragged.

Take the example of filling in a list of meeting attendees on a form. Instead of retyping or copying and pasting names of people from an address book, a user can drag and drop contacts from an address book into the list. Because the views representing contacts in the address book are associated with the resources they represent and not just the names of the contacts, the identities of the contacts' resources can be preserved. The alternative opens the possibility for ambiguity because information is lost. For example, what if there are two people named "John Doe" known to the system? Specifying the text string alone is not sufficient to disambiguate which John Doe is intended, even though it is clear that the John Doe desired is the one that the user selected in the address book.

8 Operations

Most systems provide some mechanism for exposing prepackaged functionality that can be applied under specific circumstances. For example, in Java one can expose methods in a class definition that perform specific tasks when invoked. In C one can define functions that accept arguments of particular types. Under Windows, one can define verbs, which are bound to specific file types and perform actions such as opening or printing a document when activated through a context menu in the Windows Explorer shell. In general, these mechanisms all permit parameterized operations to be defined and exposed to clients.

In Haystack, the analogous construct is called an *operation*, which can accept any number of parameters of certain types and perform some task. Operations are Adenine methods annotated with key metadata such as parameter types [18]. The operation ontology is best explained in the context of an example. The definition of the "Browse To" operation is given in the following code snippet.

```
@prefix op: <http://haystack.lcs.mit.edu/schemata/operation#>

add { :target
    rdf:type            op:Parameter ;
    rdf:type            daml:ObjectProperty ;
    rdfs:label          "Target" ;
    op:required                "true" ;
    rdfs:range          daml:Thing
}

method :browseTo :target = target ;
rdf:type            op:Operation ;
dc:title        "Browse to" ;
ozone:icon      <http://haystack.lcs.mit.edu/icons/verbs/browseto.gif> ;
adenine:preload "true"
  ozone:navigate target[0]
```

The definition of an operation (e.g. `:browseToOperation`) includes basic information such as its name, an icon, as well as a set of named parameters. Notice that operations are defined using the method syntax; this is possible because operation is a subclass of Adenine method. Parameters (e.g. `:target`) are also given names, but in addition parameters can also be typed, in a variety of different ways. The most basic mechanism for typing is simply specifying an `rdfs:Class` as a parameter's class using the `rdfs:range` predicate. A parameter's type can also be constrained by giving an Adenine validator method, which given a value verifies that it can be used for that parameter. Finally, parameters can be specified to be either mandatory or optional.

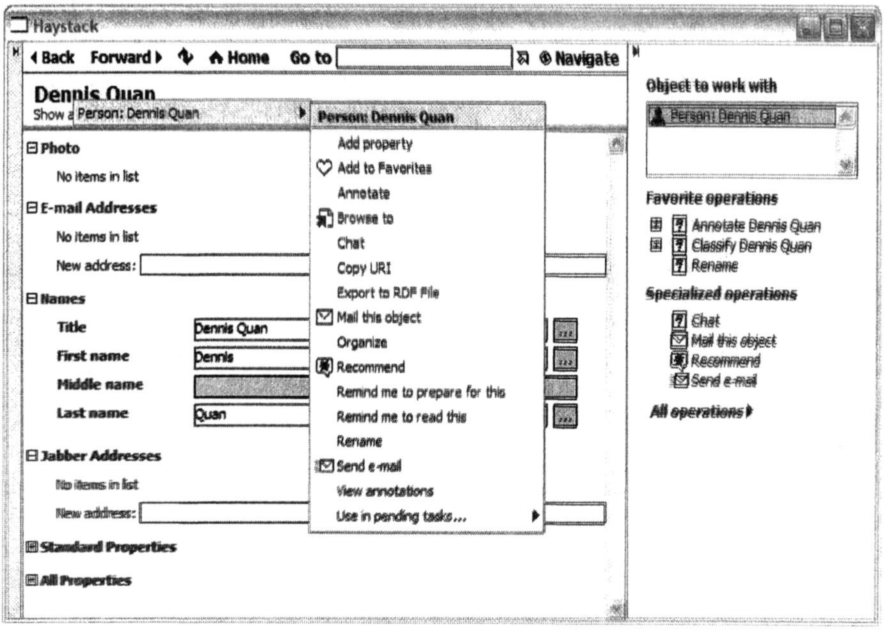

Fig. 2. Operations in Haystack

When an operation is invoked, the values assigned to the operation's parameters are passed to the operation. Parameters can have multiple values; for example, a send mail operation may allow multiple recipients to be specified. To allow for this, the Adenine method receives a list of all values for each named parameter.

The Haystack user interface exposes the operations installed in the system in various ways. Operations are displayed on the tool pane (the right hand pane) in Haystack as well as in context menus (Fig. 2). In fact, operations are also used for commands such as "Shutdown Haystack", where no parameters are needed. In this way, operations can play the roles normally played by menus and toolbars in applications today.

Furthermore, the Haystack framework eliminates the need for developers to create specialized user interfaces for user-performable operations in many cases. When an operation that requires parameters is activated, Haystack checks to see if the target object (in the case of the command being issued from a context menu or the tool pane) satisfies any of the operation's parameters. If there are unresolved parameters, Haystack presents a *UI continuation*, depicted in Fig. 3 [18].

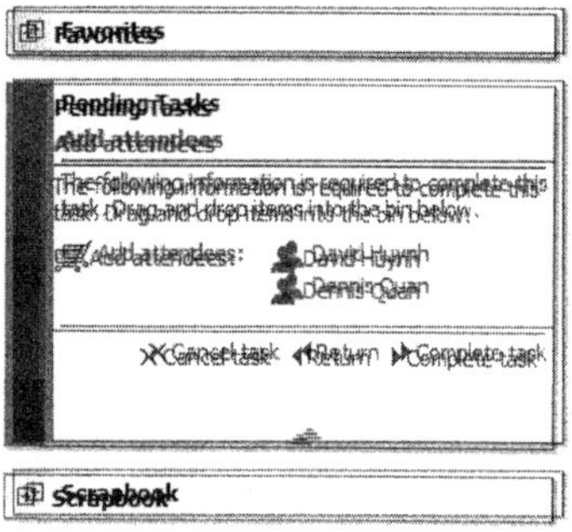

Fig. 3. Sample UI continuation (taken from left hand pane)

Like a dialog box, a UI continuation prompts the user for needed information – in this case, the unresolved parameters. However, unlike most dialog boxes, which are modal, UI continuations are modelessly placed on the left hand pane, allowing the user to use whatever tools in the system he or she is most familiar with to find the information needed to complete the operation. By default, the system takes the user to a convenient place to find the required information, such as in the case of a send e-mail operation, the user's address book. This interface is similar to a shopping cart on an e-business website: the user can drag and drop relevant items into the "bins" representing the operation's parameters. The user can even decide to perform other tasks and come back to the operation later. When the user has finished obtaining the necessary information and is ready to commence the operation, he or she can click the "Done" button on the UI continuation. The system then returns to the state that was present when the operation was initiated (hence the term continuation) and performs the operation. By providing UI continuation functionality, the system frees the developer from needing to design specialized, miniature user interfaces for retrieving information from within modal dialog boxes by reusing the existing browsing environment and at the same time providing the user with a seamless experience.

The operation abstraction allows the functionality of the system to be arbitrarily extended, without special plug-in interfaces or points of extensibility needing to be defined on a per-application basis. Furthermore, developers can declaratively specify new functionality to the system rather than modify monolithic dialog boxes, menus, or toolbars. However, since the UI continuation is displayed using Haystack's view technology, developers are free to customize the display of a UI continuation by defining new view parts.

9 Constructors

The operations ontology is able to describe a large portion of the functionality exposed by an application. However, one particular type of functionality provided by many applications deserves special focus: object creation. Object creation manifests itself in many different forms, ranging from the addition of a text box to a slide in a presentation graphics program to the composing of an e-mail. Applications that support object creation usually expose interfaces for allowing users to choose the appropriate type of object to create or to find a template or wizard that can help guide them through the process of creating the object.

In RDF, the process of creation can naïvely be thought of as the coining of a fresh URI followed by an `rdf:type` assertion. The corresponding choice list for creating objects in RDF could be implemented by displaying a list of all `rdfs:Class` resources known by the system. However, there are many issues not addressed by this solution. The user's mental model of object creation may map onto three distinct activities in the programmatic sense: (1) creation of the resource; (2) establishing some default view; (3) population of the resource with default data. For example, the creation of a picture album from the perspective of the data model is straightforward in that a picture album is simply a collection of resources that happen to be pictures. However, if the user begins viewing this blank picture album with an address book view, he or she may believe that the system has created the wrong object. With respect to the third point, Gamma et al. assert that object creation can come about in various ways, ranging from straightforward instantiation to creating objects according to some fixed pattern [4].

Furthermore, the classical framing of the object creation problem does not address the user interface implications entailed by certain kinds of instantiations. Some objects can be created without further input from the user, such as empty collections, while some objects require configuration data or other information to be properly initialized, such as a POP3 mail service.

To solve these problems, Haystack makes use of a constructor ontology, which describes resources called *constructors* that create objects. Constructors have type `construct:Constructor`, which derives from `adenine:Method`. (Constructors that are exposed to the user also have type `op:Operation`.) Like all other objects in Haystack, constructors can be browsed to in the user interface and have custom views associated with them. The default view for a constructor's UI continuation simply contains a button that invokes the constructor and browses to the created object. However, for constructors that require a custom user interface to be presented, a custom view part can be provided with specific controls for creating the object. Fig. 4 shows an example of the annotation pane in Haystack, which takes advantage of this functionality. Annotations in Haystack are not limited to text but can be constructed from any kind of object. The annotation pane exposes a drop down list of possible constructors; when the user completes the constructor, the newly created annotation is hooked to the object being annotated.

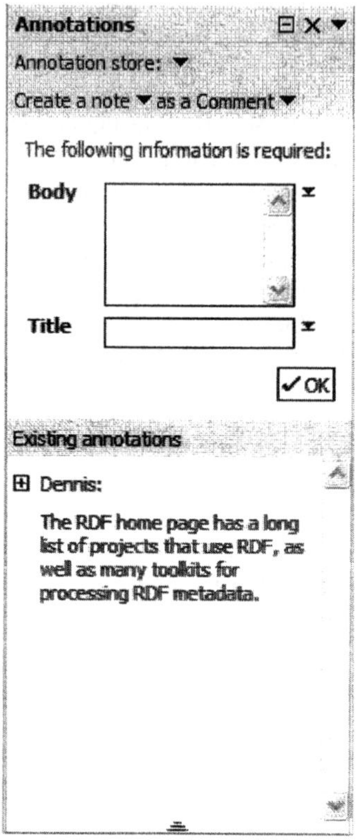

Fig. 4. Annotation UI

10 Conclusion

In this paper we have explored a number of the tools built into Haystack for developing Semantic Web applications for end users. These tools focus on applying RDF technology to improving the developer experience, by allowing developers to declaratively define concepts such as operations and user interface components. Many of these technologies have been built on top of Adenine, which facilitates the manipulation of RDF data and provides syntactic sugar for defining RDF ontologies and user interface designs. We believe these tools have lowered the barrier for creating truly usable and compelling applications that can deliver on the promises of automation and uninhibited data exchange on the Semantic Web.

Acknowledgements. This work was supported by the MIT-NTT collaboration, Project Oxygen, and IBM.

References

1. Huynh, D., Karger, D., and Quan, D.: Haystack: A Platform for Creating, Organizing and Visualizing Information Using RDF. Proceedings of Semantic Web Workshop, WWW2002. http://haystack.lcs.mit.edu/papers/sww02.pdf
2. Resource Description Framework (RDF) Model and Syntax Specification. http://www.w3.org/TR/1999/REC-rdf-syntax-19990222/
3. Berners-Lee, T., Hendler, J., and Lassila, O.: The Semantic Web. Scientific American, May 2001
4. Gamma, E., Helm, R., Johnson, R., and Vlissides, J.: Design Patterns. Boston: Addison Wesley, 1995
5. Berners-Lee, T.: Primer: Getting into RDF & Semantic Web using N3. http://www.w3.org/2000/10/swap/Primer.html
6. Christensen, E., Cubera, F., Meredith, G., and Weerawarana, S. (ed.): Web Services Description Language (WSDL) 1.1. http://www.w3.org/TR/wsdl
7. Dourish, P., Edwards, W.K., et al.: Extending Document Management Systems with User-Specific Active Properties. ACM Transactions on Information Systems, Vol. 18, No. 2, April 2000, 140–170
8. Box, D., Ehnebuske, D., Kavivaya, G., et al. (ed.): SOAP: Simple Object Access Protocol. http://msdn.microsoft.com/library/en-us/dnsoapsp/html/soapspec.asp
9. Abelson, H, Dybvig, R., Haynes, C., Rozas, G., et al.: Revised Report on the Algorithmic Language Scheme. Higher-Order and Symbolic Computation, Vol. 11, Issue 1, August 2000, 7–105
10. Eriksson, H., Fergerson, R., Shahar, Y., and Musen, M.: Automatic Generation of Ontology Editors. In Proceedings of the 12th Banff Knowledge Acquisition Workshop, 1999
11. Handschuh, S., Staab, S., and Maedche, A.: CREAM – Creating relational metadata with a component-based ontology-driven annotation framework. Proceedings of K-CAP '01
12. Horrocks, I. et al. (ed.): DAML+OIL. http://www.daml.org/2001/03/daml+oil-index.html
13. Stojanovic, N., Maedche, A., Staab, S., Studer, R., Sure, Y.: SEAL: a framework for developing SEmantic PortALs. Proceedings of the International Conference on Knowledge Capture, October 2001
14. Pietriga, E.: IsaViz. http://www.w3.org/2001/11/IsaViz/
15. Carroll, J.: Unparsing RDF/XML. Proceedings of WWW2002
16. Huynh, D., Quan, D., and Karger, D.: Haystack's User Experience for Interacting with Semistructured Information. Proceedings of WWW2003
17. Quan, D., Karger, D., and Huynh, D.: RDF Authoring Environments for End Users. Proceedings of Semantic Web Foundations and Application Technologies 2003
18. Quan, D., Huynh, D., Karger, D., and Miller, R.: User Interface Continuations. To appear in Proceedings of UIST 2003
19. Rosen, M.: E-mail Classification in the Haystack Framework, Master's Thesis, February 2003

Mangrove: Enticing Ordinary People onto the Semantic Web via Instant Gratification

Luke McDowell, Oren Etzioni, Steven D. Gribble, Alon Halevy, Henry Levy, William Pentney, Deepak Verma, and Stani Vlasseva

University of Washington, Department of Computer Science and Engineering, Seattle, WA 98195 USA,
{lucasm,etzioni,gribble,alon,levy,bill,deepak,stani}@cs.washington.edu
http://www.cs.washington.edu/research/semweb

Abstract. Despite numerous efforts, the *semantic web* has yet to achieve widespread adoption. Recently, some researchers have argued that participation in the semantic web is too difficult for "ordinary" people, limiting its growth and popularity.

In response, this paper introduces MANGROVE, a system whose goal is to entice non-technical people to semantically annotate their existing HTML data. MANGROVE seeks to alter the cost-benefit equation of authoring semantic content. To increase the benefit, MANGROVE is designed to make semantic content instantly available to services that consume the content and yield immediate, tangible benefit to authors. To reduce the cost, MANGROVE makes semantic authoring as painless as possible by transferring some of the burden of schema design, data cleaning, and data structuring from content authors to the programmers who create semantic services.

We have designed and implemented a MANGROVE prototype, built several semantic services for the system, and deployed those services in our department. This paper describes MANGROVE's goals, presents the system architecture, and reports on our implementation and deployment experience. Overall, MANGROVE demonstrates a concrete path for enabling and enticing non-technical people to enter the semantic web.

1 Introduction and Motivation

Numerous proposals for creating a *semantic web* have been made in recent years (e.g., [3,6,17]), yet adoption of the semantic web is far from widespread. Several researchers have recently questioned whether participation in the semantic web is too difficult for "ordinary" people [9,24,16]. Indeed, a key barrier to the growth of the semantic web is the need to *structure* data: technical sophistication and substantial effort are required whether one is creating a database schema or authoring an ontology. The database and knowledge representation communities have long ago recognized this challenge as a barrier to the widespread adoption of their powerful technologies. The semantic web exacerbates this problem, as the vision calls for large-scale and decentralized authoring of structured data. As

D. Fensel et al. (Eds.): ISWC 2003, LNCS 2870, pp. 754–770, 2003.

a result, the creation of the semantic web is sometimes viewed as a discontinuous divergence from today's web-authoring practices — technically sophisticated people will use complex tools to create new ontologies and services.

While utilizing such technical people will certainly yield many useful semantic web services, this paper is concerned with the non-technical people who drove the explosive growth of the HTML-based web. We consider the question *how do we entice non-technical people to structure their data?* This paper presents the architecture of MANGROVE, a system designed to enable and entice these "ordinary users" to contribute to the semantic web. In particular, MANGROVE seeks to emulate three key conditions that contributed to the rapid growth of the web:

- **Instant Gratification:** In the HTML world, a newly authored page is immediately accessible through a browser; we mimic this feature in MANGROVE by making annotated content instantly available to services. We posit that semantic annotation will be motivated by services that consume the annotations and result in immediate, tangible benefit to authors. MANGROVE provides several such services and the infrastructure to create additional ones over time.
- **Robustness:** When authoring an HTML page, authors are not forced to consider the contents of other, pre-existing pages. Similarly, MANGROVE does not require authors of semantic content to obey integrity constraints, such as data uniqueness or consistency. Data cleaning is deferred to the services that consume the data.
- **Ease of Authoring:** MANGROVE provides a graphical web-page annotation tool that enables users to easily and incrementally annotate existing HTML content.

As one example of the MANGROVE approach, consider the web site of our computer science department. The web pages at this site contain numerous facts including contact information, locations, schedules, publications, and relationships to other information. If users were enabled and motivated to semantically annotate these pages, then the pages and annotations could be used to support both standard HTML-based browsing as well as novel semantic services. For example, we have created a departmental calendar that draws on annotated information found on existing web pages, which describe courses, seminars, and other events. The calendar instantly consumes annotated facts as explained below. Because the calendar is authoritative and prominently placed in the department's web, events that appear in it are more likely to receive the attention of the department's community. As a result, people seeking to advertise events (e.g., seminars) are motivated to annotate their pages, which leads to their automatic inclusion in the department's calendar and in the semantic web.

The remainder of this paper is organized as follows. The next section introduces MANGROVE's architecture and explains how it supports its design goals. Section 3 describes our first semantic services and our initial experience from deploying MANGROVE. Section 4 discusses related work on this problem, and Section 5 concludes.

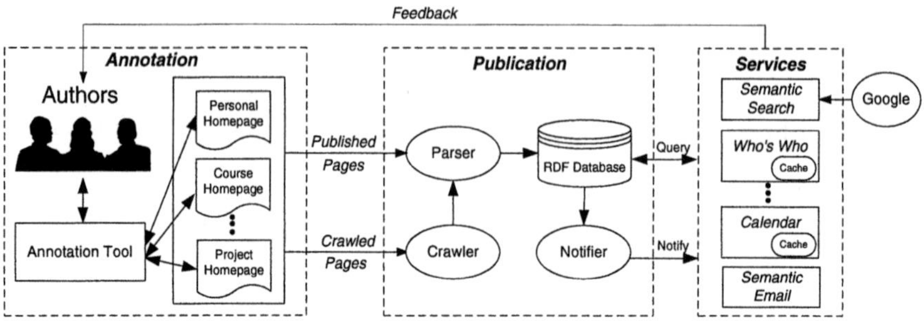

Fig. 1. The MANGROVE architecture and sample services.

2 The Architecture of MANGROVE

This section presents the high-level architecture of MANGROVE, details some of the key components, and relates them to MANGROVE's design goals.

2.1 Architecture Overview

Figure 1 shows the architecture of MANGROVE organized around the following three phases of operation:

- **Annotation:** Authors use our *graphical annotation tool* or an editor to insert annotations into existing HTML documents. The annotation tool provides users with a list of possible properties from a local schema based on the annotation context (e.g., describing a person or course), and stores the semantic data using a syntax that is simply syntactic sugar for basic RDF.
- **Publication:** Authors can explicitly *publish* annotated content, causing the *parser* to immediately parse and store the contents in a *RDF database*. The *notifier* then notifies registered services about relevant updates to this database. Services can then send *feedback* to the authors in the form of links to updated content (or diagnostic messages in case of errors). In addition, MANGROVE's *crawler* supplies data to the parser periodically, updating the database when authors forego explicit publishing.
- **Service Execution:** Newly published content is immediately available to a range of *services* that access the content via database queries. For example, we support semantic search, semantic email, and more complex services such as the automatically-generated department calendar.

These three phases are overlapping and iterative. For instance, after annotation, publication, and service execution, an author may refine her documents to add additional annotations or to improve data usage by the service. Supporting this complete life-cycle of content creation and consumption is important to fueling the semantic web development process.

Below, we describe MANGROVE in more detail. We focus first on architectural features that support instant gratification and robustness. Section 3 then describes the semantic services that make use of MANGROVE to provide instant gratification to content authors. We omit many aspects of components that use standard technology, such as our crawler, parser, and annotation tool. See [26] for more details.

2.2 Supporting Instant Gratification

In today's web, changes to a web page are immediately visible through a browser. We create the analogous experience in MANGROVE by enabling authors to *publish* semantically annotated content, which instantly transmits that content to MANGROVE's database and from there to services that consume the content.

MANGROVE authors have two simple interfaces for publishing their pages. They can publish by pressing a button in MANGROVE's graphical annotation tool, or they can enter the URL of an annotated page into a web form. Both interfaces send the URL to MANGROVE's parser, which fetches the document, parses it for semantic content, and stores that content in the RDF database. This mechanism ensures that users can immediately view the output of relevant services, updated with their newly published data, and then iterate either to achieve different results or to further annotate their data. In addition, before adding new content, the database purges any previously published information from the corresponding URL, allowing users to retract previously published information (e.g., if an event is canceled).

Crawling or polling all potentially relevant pages is an obvious alternative to explicit publication. While MANGROVE does utilize a crawler, it seems clear that crawling is insufficient given a reasonable crawling schedule. This is an important difference between MANGROVE and current systems (e.g., [6,17]) that do not attempt to support instant gratification and so can afford to rely exclusively on crawlers. MANGROVE's web crawler regularly revisits all pages that have been previously published, as well as all pages in a circumscribed domain (e.g., `cs.washington.edu`). The crawler enables MANGROVE to find semantic information that a user neglected to publish. Thus, publication supports instant gratification as desired, while web crawls provide a convenient backup in case of errors or when timeliness is less important.

Notification: Services specify data of interest by providing a query to the MANGROVE notifier.[1] When the database is updated by a new data publication or a web crawl, the notifier forwards data matching that query to the corresponding services for processing. For instance, the calendar service registers its interest in all pages that contain `<event>` properties (or that had such properties deleted). When it receives notification of relevant new data, the calendar processes that data and updates its internal data structures, ensuring that content authors see their new data on the calendar with minimal delay.[2]

[1] For simplicity, we assume in this paper that such a query consists of just a set of "relevant" RDF properties. More complex queries can be also supported efficiently [30].

[2] Note that while only registered services receive such notifications, any service that follows a simple API (of Mangrove or Jena[25]) may query the database for content.

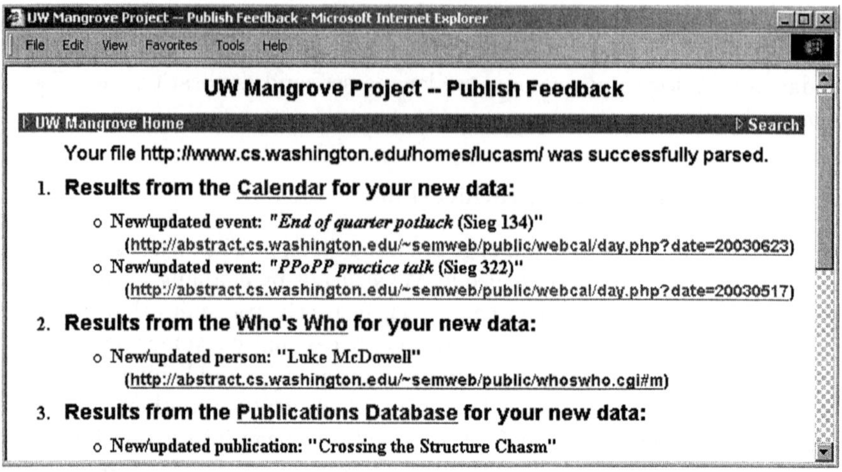

Fig. 2. Example output from the service feedback mechanism. Services that have registered interest in a property that is present at a published URL are sent relevant data from that URL. The services immediately return links to their resulting output.

Service feedback: MANGROVE provides a *service feedback* mechanism that is a key element of its architectural support for instant gratification. As noted earlier, services can register their interest in arbitrary RDF properties (e.g., `event`). Then, when a URL that contains such a property is published by an author, the services are automatically notified about the new information. Each notified service can return feedback to the author as shown in Figure 2. The feedback can identify problems encountered (e.g., a date was ambiguous or missing) or can confirm that the information was successfully "consumed" by the service.

The feedback mechanism supports instant gratification by making it easier for authors to immediately see the tangible output resulting from their new semantic data. Authors can click on any of the links shown in Figure 2 and they will be directed to a web page that shows how the information they *just* annotated is being used by a semantic service. For example, as soon as an event page is annotated and published, the organizer can click on a link and see her event appearing in the department's calendar. To be true to the 'instant' in 'instant gratification', publishing a page returns feedback to authors in about two seconds. We are working on further reducing that delay to a fraction of a second.

Because services and information are created independently in MANGROVE by different sets of people, there is the potential in the future for authors to be unaware of services that consume their information and that would provide further motivation for them to author more semantic information. The service feedback mechanism acts as a service discovery mechanism that addresses this problem. Once a service registers its interest in a particular property, an author that publishes relevant information will be notified about that service's interest in the property.[3] We expect that users will typically publish content with a particular service in mind, and then decide whether or not to investigate and possibly annotate additional content for the services that they learn of from this feedback. As the number of services grows, an author can avoid "feedback spam" by explicitly selecting the services that send her feedback, by limiting their number, or by filtering them according to the criteria of her choice (e.g., by domain or category). Additional techniques for supporting useful feedback across a very large numbers of services, content providers, and distinct ontologies is an interesting area for future work. Note that since the author is publishing information with the hope of making it broadly available, privacy does not seem to be a concern in this context.

The service feedback mechanism also supports robustness by helping authors to produce well-formed data. We discuss support for robustness further below.

2.3 Supporting Robustness

Database and knowledge base systems have a set of mechanisms that ensure that the contents of a database are clean and correct. For example, database systems enforce integrity constraints on data entry, thereby eliminating many opportunities for entering "dirty" data. In addition, database applications control carefully who is allowed to enter data, and therefore malicious data entry is rarely an issue. On the semantic web, such mechanisms are impractical. First, we do not have a central administration of the data on the semantic web, and hence integrity constraints are difficult if not impossible to define. Second, enforcing integrity constraints would create another hurdle preventing people from joining the semantic web, rather than enticing them. Third, on the semantic web authors who enter data may not be aware of which services consume their data and what is required in order for their data to be well formed. Hence, a design goal of MANGROVE is *robustness*: authors should be able to add content without considering constraints, and services should be able to consume data that is cleaned and consistent as appropriate for their needs. Furthermore, when users do intend their data to be consumed by certain services, there should be a feedback loop that ensures that their data was in a form that the service could consume. Below we describe how MANGROVE supports robustness in such a large-scale data sharing environment.

Deferring integrity constraints: On the HTML web, a user can put his phone number on a web page without considering whether it already appears anywhere else (e.g., in an employer's directory), or how others have formatted or structured that information. Despite that, users can effectively assess the correctness of the information they find (e.g., by inspecting the URL of the page) and interpret the data according to domain-specific conventions. In contrast, existing systems often restrict the way information may be expressed. For instance, in WebKB-2 [23], a user may not add information that contradicts another user unless the

[3] Very loosely speaking, this is analogous to checking which web pages link to your page – a service that is offered through search engines such as Google.

contradictions are explicitly identified first. Likewise, in SHOE [17], all data must conform to a specified type (for instance, dates must conform to RFC 1123).

MANGROVE purposefully does not enforce any integrity constraints on annotated data or restrict what claims a user can make. With the calendar, for instance, annotated events may be missing a name (or have more than one), dates may be ambiguous, and some data may even be intentionally misleading. Instead, MANGROVE *defers* all such integrity constraints to allow users to say anything they want, in any format. Furthermore, MANGROVE allows users to decide how extensively to annotate their data. For instance, the `instructor` property may refer to a resource with further properties such as `name` and `workPhone`, or simply to a string literal (e.g., "`John Fitz`"). Permitting such "light" annotations simplifies the annotation of existing HTML and allows authors to provide more detail over time.

To complement the deferral of integrity constraints, MANGROVE provides three mechanisms that facilitate the creation of appropriate data for services: service feedback (discussed earlier), data cleaning, and inspection of malicious information.

Data cleaning: The primary burden of *cleaning* the data is passed to the service consuming the data, based on the observation that different services will have varying requirements for data integrity. In some services, clean data may not be as important because users can tell easily whether the answers they are receiving are correct (possibly by following a hyperlink). For other services, it may be important that data be consistent (e.g., that an event have the correct location), and there may be some obvious heuristics on how to resolve conflicts. The source URL of the data is stored in the database and can serve as an important resource for cleaning up the data.

To assist with this process, MANGROVE provides a *service construction template* that enables services to apply a simple rule-based *cleaning policy* to the raw results obtained from the RDF database. For instance, for course events, our calendar specifies a simple policy that prefers data from pages specific to a particular course over data from general university-provided pages. Thus, factual conflicts (e.g., a location change not registered with the university) are resolved in the course-specific page's favor. The cleaning policy also helps the calendar to deal with different degrees of annotation. For instance, to identify the instructor for a course lecture, the calendar simply requests the value of the `<instructor>` property, and the template library automatically returns the `<name>` sub-property of the instructor if it exists, or the complete value of that property if sub-properties are not specified. Finally, the template also provides other rules to assist with data interpretation (e.g., to parse different formats of dates and times commonly found on the web, or those often found in a university setting, such as `''MWF 10-11 a.m.''`). To utilize these features, services may create their own cleaning policy or use a default from the service template.

Malicious information: Another reason that we store the source URL with every fact in the database is that it provides a mechanism for partially dealing with malicious information. The highly distributed nature of the web can lead

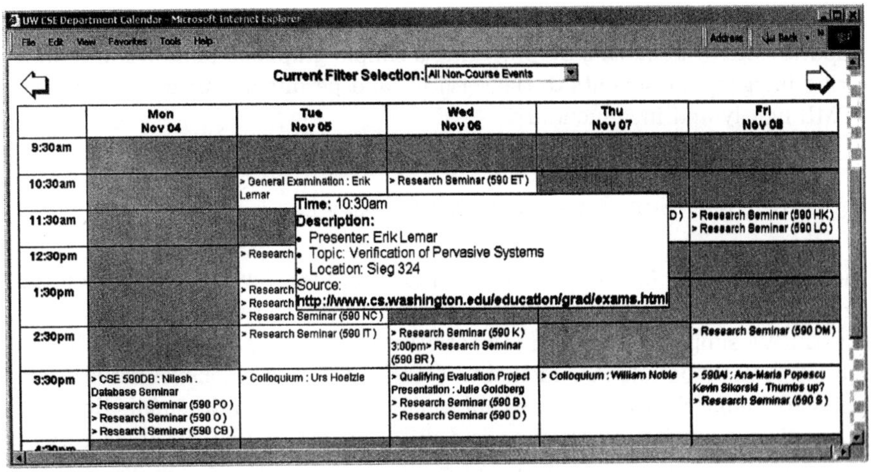

Fig. 3. The calendar service as deployed in our department. The popup box appears when the user mouses over a particular event, and displays additional information and its origin. For the live version, see `www.cs.washington.edu/research/semweb`.

to abuse, which popular services such as search engines have to grapple with on a regular basis. Potential abuse is an issue for semantic services as well. What is to prevent a user from maliciously publishing misleading information? Imagine, for example, that a nefarious AI professor purposefully publishes a misleading location for the highly popular database seminar in an attempt to "hijack" students and send them to the location of the AI seminar.

Thus, MANGROVE services associate an easily-accessible source (i.e., a URL) with each fact made visible to the user. For example, as shown in Figure 3, a user can "mouse over" any event in the calendar and see additional facts including one or more originating URLs. The user can click on these URLs to visit these pages and see the original context. Naturally, service writers are free to implement more sophisticated policies for identifying malicious information, based on freshness, URL, or further authentication. For instance, in case of conflict, our department calendar uses its previously mentioned cleaning policy to enable facts published from pages whose URL starts with `www.cs.washington.edu/education/` to override facts originating elsewhere.

2.4 Discussion

As noted in the introduction, MANGROVE is designed to enable and entice authors to structure their data by mimicking some of the conditions that led to the explosive growth of content creation on the web. First, MANGROVE supports *instant gratification* with a loop that takes freshly published semantic content to MANGROVE services, and then back to the user through the service feedback mechanism. Next, MANGROVE supports *robustness* by postponing the enforcement of integrity constraints, associating a source URL with every fact in the database, and with the service construction template, which assists services in cleaning and interpreting the data based on these URLs. Finally, MANGROVE supports *ease of authoring* by providing a simple graphical annotation tool, deferring integrity constraints to the services, and permitting authors to annotate HTML lightly and incrementally.

3 Semantic Services in MANGROVE

One of the goals of MANGROVE is to demonstrate that even modest amounts of annotation can significantly boost the utility of the web today. To illustrate this, MANGROVE supports a range of semantic services that represent several different web-interaction paradigms, including Google-style search, novel services that aggregate semantically annotated information, and semantic email. Below, we briefly discuss service construction and then consider each of the above services.

Services are written in Java and built on top of the MANGROVE service template that provides the basic infrastructure needed for service creation. Our implementation uses the Jena [25] RDF-based storage system, which enables our services to extract basic semantic information from the database by posing queries. In addition, the MANGROVE service template provides methods to assist with data cleaning and interpretation, as explained in Section 2.3. The template also aids service construction with support for incrementally computing and caching results. Overall, MANGROVE makes services substantially easier to write by encapsulating commonly-used functionality in this service template. At runtime, these services are then invoked by a Jakarta Tomcat servlet engine.

3.1 Semantic Search

We believe that annotation will be an incremental process starting with "light" annotation of pages and gradually increasing in scope and sophistication as more services are developed to consume an increasing number of annotations. It is important for this "chicken and egg" cycle that even light annotation yield tangible benefit to users. One important source of benefit is a Google-style search service that responds appropriately to search queries that freely mix properties and text. The service returns the set of web pages in our domain that contain the text and properties in the query.

The interface to the service is a web form that accepts standard textual search queries. The service also accepts queries such as "assistant professor" <facultyMember> <portrait>?, which combines the phrase "assistant professor" with properties. Like Google, the query has an implicit AND semantics and returns exactly the set of pages in our domain containing the phrase "associate professor" and the specified properties. The ? after the `<portrait>` property instructs the service to extract and return the HTML inside that property (as with the SELECT clause of a SQL query). Users select appropriate properties for the search from the simple schema available on the search page; future work will consider ways to make this selection even easier.

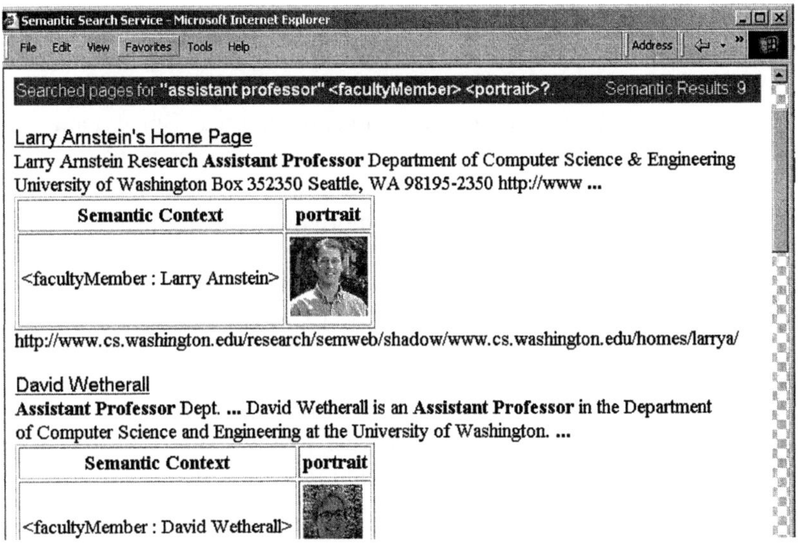

Fig. 4. The semantic search results page. The page reproduces the original query and reports the number of results returned at the top. Matching pages contain the phrase "assistant professor" and the properties <facultyMember> and <portrait>. The `?` in the query instructs the service to extract the <portrait> from each matching page.

The service is implemented by sending the textual portion of the query (if any) to Google along with instructions to restrict the results to the local domain (`cs.washington.edu`). The MANGROVE database is queried to return the set of pages containing all the properties in the query (if any). The two result sets are then intersected to identify the relevant set of pages. When multiple relevant pages are present, their order in the Google results is preserved to enable more prominent pages to appear first in the list. Finally, any extraction operations indicated by one or more question marks in the query are performed and included in the result (see Figure 4). Like Google, not every result provides what the user was seeking; the search service includes *semantic context* with each result — a snippet that assists the user in understanding the context of the extracted information. The snippet is the `name` property of the extracted property's subject. For instance, when extracting the `<portrait>` information as shown in Figure 4, the snippet is the name of the faculty member whose portrait is shown.

With its ability to mix text and properties, this kind of search is different from the standard querying capability supported by MANGROVE's underlying RDF database and other semantic web systems such as SHOE [17] and WebKB [23]. Our search service has value to users even when pages are only lightly annotated, supporting our goal of enticing users onto the semantic web.

3.2 Aggregation Services

Aggregation services provide useful views on data from the semantic web. We describe the aggregation services we implemented with MANGROVE below.

First, our Who's Who service compiles pictures, contact information, and personal data about people within an organization. In our department, a static Who's Who had existed for years, but was rarely updated (and was woefully out-of-date) because of the manual creation process required. Our dynamic Who's Who directly uses more up-to-date information from users' home pages, enabling users to update their own data at any time to reflect their changing interests.

Whereas Who's Who merely collects information from a set of web pages, our Research Publication Database compiles a searchable database of publications produced by members of our department based on the information in home pages and project pages. This service is able to infer missing information (e.g. the author of a paper) from context (e.g., the paper was found on the author's home page) and applies simple heuristics to avoid repeated entries by detecting duplicate publications. Only a single `<publication>` property enclosing a description of the publication is required in order to add an entry to the database, which facilitates light, incremental annotation. However, users may improve the quality of the output and the duplicate removal by specifying additional properties such as `<author>` and `<title>`.

Our most sophisticated service, the department calendar (shown in Figure 3), automatically constructs and updates a unified view of departmental events and displays them graphically. As with our other services, the calendar requires only a date and name to include an event in its output, but will make use of as much other information as is available (such as time, location, presenter, etc.).

Department members are motivated to annotate their events' home pages in order to publicize their events. (In fact, the current contents of the calendar are projected on the wall in the lobby of our department.) We initially seeded the calendar with date, time, and location information for courses and seminars by running a single wrapper on a university course summary page. Users then provide more detail by annotating a page about one of these events (e.g., users have annotated pre-existing HTML pages to identify the weekly topics for seminars). Alternatively, users may annotate pages to add new events to the calendar (e.g., an administrator has annotated a web page listing qualifying exams). Typically, users annotate and publish their modified pages, the calendar is immediately updated, and users then view the calendar to verify that their events are included. For changes (e.g., when an exam is re-scheduled), users may re-publish their pages or rely on the MANGROVE web crawler to capture such updates later.

3.3 Semantic Email

While the WWW is certainly a rich information space in which we spend significant amounts of time, many of us spend even more time on email. In the same spirit as the semantic web, adding some semantics to email also has the potential for increasing productivity. In fact, we often use email for tasks that are reminiscent of lightweight data collection, manipulation, and analysis. Because email is not set up to handle these tasks effectively, accomplishing them manually can be tedious, time-consuming, and error-prone. As another example of where instant gratification can entice people to add more semantic structure to their data, we developed *semantic email processes* (SEPs) [10] using MANGROVE.

As an example of semantic email, consider the process of organizing a potluck by sending an email to a list of people, asking who will attend and what dish they plan to bring, and then automatically collecting the responses and tallying them up. The benefits of such an automated process provide significant incentive for people to structure their original request.[4] We model a SEP as an RDF *data set* affected by *messages* from a set of *participants*, controlled by a set of *constraints* over the data set. For instance, when executing we may constrain the potluck so it results in a balanced number of appetizers, entrees, and desserts.[5]

Implementing SEPs within MANGROVE enables us to synergistically leverage data from the web and email worlds in one system. For instance, our calendar service accepts event information from annotated pages that are published via MANGROVE or via semantic email. Likewise, SEPs such as our "RSVP" process could accept event descriptions from an annotated web page, then monitor this web data for location or time changes to include in a reminder email. Finally, human responses to semantic email queries (e.g., requesting a phone number) can be used to gradually acquire semantic knowledge over time. See [10] for a more complete description of semantic email, including the formal model of SEPs and a description of important inference problems that arise in this context.

3.4 Discussion

MANGROVE and our services have been deployed in our department for only a few months, but already permit a few observations. First, simple services such as the calendar can offer substantial added value over other forms of accessing the same information. For instance, in the five months the online calendar has been operational, it has received more than 2700 distinct visits, with an average of about two page views per visit.[6] Second, users are willing to annotate their documents if the process is easy and interesting services exist to use the annotations. For instance, a small but growing number of users have annotated their personal home pages in order to be included in the WHO'S WHO and to promote their publications. In addition, administrators, students, and faculty have all utilized annotation to promote a wide range of events, ranging from official departmental events to visitor schedules to informal events at a local pub.

These observations are not meant to be conclusive: the system and its services are new and still evolving. Nonetheless, our initial experience strongly suggests that the MANGROVE system and services are both feasible and beneficial. See [26] for additional measurements demonstrating that simple annotation of existing documents is feasible and that it can potentially improve both the precision and recall of search compared to Google.

[4] While the *organizer* must perform some structuring, we do not require *participants* in this process to understand semantics or use any special tools; see [10] for details.

[5] This SEP and many others are available for public use, see http://www.cs.washington.edu/research/semweb/email.

[6] These statistics exclude traffic from webcrawlers and MANGROVE team members.

Scalability is an important design consideration for MANGROVE, and it has influenced several aspects of MANGROVE's architecture, such as our explicit publish/notification mechanisms. Nevertheless, the scalability of our current prototype is limited in two respects. First, at the logical level, the system does not currently provide mechanisms for composing or translating between multiple schemas or ontologies (all users annotate data with a common local schema). Second, at the physical level, the central database in which we store our data could become a bottleneck.

We address both scalability issues as part of a broader project described in [13]. Specifically, once a department has annotated its data according to a local schema, it can collaborate with other structured data sources using a *peer-data management system* (PDMS) [14]. In a PDMS, semantic relationships between data sources are provided using *schema mappings*, which enable the translation of queries posed on one source to the schema of the other. Our group has developed tools that assist in the construction of schema mappings [7,8], though these tools are not yet integrated into MANGROVE. Relying on a PDMS also distributes querying across a network of peers, eliminating the bottleneck associated with a central database.

4 Related Work

This paper is the first to articulate and focus on *instant gratification* as a central design goal for a semantic web system. Many of the key differences between MANGROVE's architecture and that of related semantic web systems follow from this distinct design goal. We discuss these differences in more detail below.

Haustein and Pleumann [16] note the importance of semantic data being "immediately visible" in a way that yields benefit to content authors. Their system, however, primarily provides this benefit by eliminating redundancy between HTML and semantic data, and then using this data and templates to dynamically generate attractive HTML or RDF content. While these features potentially make maintaining interrelated HTML and RDF data more convenient, their system is very different from MANGROVE. Specifically, they have a different architecture that doesn't support explicit publication, notification, or service feedback. In addition, we have identified and deployed a set of instant gratification services as an essential part of MANGROVE, which are absent from their system.

Two other projects most closely related to our work are OntoBroker [6] and SHOE [17], both of which make use of annotations inside HTML documents. SHOE's services, like those of many other systems, primarily consisted of tools to simply search or view semantic data, although their "Path Analyzer" [18] provided a convenient interface for exploring relationships among concepts. OntoBroker did implement a number of services, such as a Community Web Portal [31] and services intended to assist business processes [29]. SHOE and OntoBroker, however, primarily rely upon periodic web crawls to obtain new information from annotated HTML, thus preventing instant gratification and content creation feedback. In addition, MANGROVE has the advantage of enabling useful services even when content is only lightly annotated. For instance, while OntoBroker's "SoccerSearch" service [29] tries a semantic search and then a textual search if the former fails, MANGROVE's semantic+text search service can profitably combine both types of information.

As an alternative to crawling, some systems provide a web interface for users to directly enter semantic knowledge [23,6] or to instruct the system to immediately process the content of some URL [23]. However, we are aware of no existing systems that support this feature in a manner that provides instant gratification for typical web authors. For instance, the WebKB-2 system supports a command to load a URL, but this command must be embedded within a script, and existing data must be manually deleted from the repository before a (modified) document can be reprocessed.

Conceivably, we could leave the data in the HTML files and access them only at query time. In fact, several data integration systems (e.g., [11,1,19]) do exactly this type of polling. The difference between MANGROVE and such systems is that in the latter, the system is given *descriptions* of the contents of every data source. At query time, a data integration system can therefore prune the sources examined to only the relevant ones (typically a small number). In MANGROVE we cannot anticipate *a priori* which data will be on a particular web page, and hence we would have to access every page for any given query – clearly not a scalable solution. An additional reason why we chose publishing to a database over query-time access is that the number of queries is typically much higher than the number of publication actions. For example, people consult event information in the department calendar much more frequently than announcing new events or changing the events' time or location.

In MANGROVE we chose to store annotations within the original HTML pages, for simplicity and to enable easy updates of the annotations when the source data changes. However, the overall architecture is also consistent with external annotation, where a user may annotate any page and the annotations are transmitted directly to a semantic database, as possible with CREAM [15], Annotea [20], or COHSE [2]. A side effect of these tools is that they automatically aggregate data as with our explicit publish operation; MANGROVE completes the necessary features for instant gratification by providing service notification, feedback, and a host of useful services.

The TAP semantic search [12] executes independent textual and semantic searches based on traditional text queries. This service is easy to use but cannot currently exploit information from one search in the other, nor can the user specify the type of semantic information that is desired. Recently, QuizRDF [5] introduced a search service that does combine textual and semantic content. QuizRDF's searches are more restricted than those provided by MANGROVE's search service, making it more difficult to use as a building block for other services. However, QuizRDF has an elegant user interface that more readily assists users in identifying relevant properties.

Information Lens [22] used forms to enable a user to generate a single email message with semi-structured content that might assist recipients with filtering and prioritizing that message. Mangrove's SEPs generalize this earlier work by enabling users to create an email *process* consisting of a set of interrelated messages governed by useful constraints. In addition, Mangrove extends Information Lens's rule-based message processing to support more complex reasoning based on information from multiple messages and data imported from web sources. Consequently, Mangrove's SEPs support a much broader range of applications than those possible with Information Lens [10]. More recently, Kalyanpur et al. [21] proposed having users semantically annotate messages to improve mail search, sorting, and filtering. This approach can potentially result in rich semantic content, but requires users to invest significant annotation effort for some *potential* future benefit (e.g., in improved searching for an old email) or primarily for the benefit of the recipient. SEPs instead generate both the semantic content and the text of the email message directly from simple forms, and provide instant gratification by immediately utilizing this content for simple but time-saving email processes.

For storing and accessing RDF data, we utilize the Jena toolkit [25]. Other systems that also offer centralized RDF storage include Kaon [27] and Sesame [4]. Edutella [28] extends these approaches to provide RDF annotation, storage, and querying in a distributed peer-to-peer environment, and proposes some services, but primarily assumes the pre-existence of RDF data sources rather than considering the necessary architectures and services to motivate semantic web adoption. We view these systems as valuable modules for complete semantic web systems such as MANGROVE. In contrast, MANGROVE supports the complete cycle of content creation, real-time content aggregation, and execution of services that provide instant gratification to content authors.

5 Conclusion

This paper presented MANGROVE as a means of demonstrating how to entice non-technical people to contribute content to the semantic web. Specifically, the paper reports on the following contributions:

1. We highlighted three key conditions that are essential for the growth of the semantic web: *instant gratification* (*i.e.*, immediate, tangible value resulting from semantic annotation), *robustness* to malformed data and malicious misinformation, and *ease of authoring.*
2. We introduced the MANGROVE architecture that supports the complete semantic web "life-cycle" from content authoring to semantic web services. We demonstrated how elements of the architecture support each of our three design goals, particularly the explicit publish mechanism, service feedback, and deferral of integrity constraints.
3. We described several deployed semantic services that motivate the annotation of HTML content by consuming semantic information. We showed how these services can provide tangible benefit to authors even when pages are

only sparsely annotated. These are some of the first "semantic services" that are invoked by ordinary users as part of their daily routine. This deployment lends credence to the claim that our services are both feasible and beneficial.

Our goal in designing MANGROVE and in deploying it locally has been to test our design on today's HTML web against the requirements of ordinary users. Clearly, additional deployments in different universities, organizations, and countries are necessary to further refine and validate MANGROVE's design. New instant gratification services are necessary to drive further adoption, and a broad set of measurements is essential to test the usability and scalability of the system. Finally, we plan to incorporate MANGROVE as part of a peer-data management system to achieve web scale.

Acknowledgments. This research was partially supported by NSF ITR Grant IIS-0205635, DARPA contract NBCHD030010 for Oren Etzioni, NSF CAREER Grant IIS-9985114 for Alon Halevy, and by a NSF Graduate Research Fellowship for Luke McDowell. Thanks to Google and Corin Anderson for their assistance with our search service. We are also grateful to Abraham Bernstein, Natasha Noy, Valentin Razmov, Dan Weld, Oren Zamir, and the anonymous reviewers for their helpful comments on improving the paper. Mangrove's parser utilizes code from HTMLParser (http://htmlparser.sourceforge.net/) and Xerces-J (http://xml.apache.org/xerces-j/), and the calendar interface is based on WebCalendar (http://webcalendar.sourceforge.net/).

References

1. S. Adali, K. Candan, Y. Papakonstantinou, and V. Subrahmanian. Query caching and optimization in distributed mediator systems. In *Proc. of SIGMOD*, pages 137–148, Montreal, Canada, 1996.
2. S. Bechhofer and C. Goble. Towards annotation using DAML+OIL. In *K-CAP 2001 Workshop on Knowledge Markup and Semantic Annotation*, 2001.
3. T. Berners-Lee, J. Hendler, and O. Lassila. The semantic web. *Scientific American*, May 2001.
4. J. Broekstra, A. Kampman, and F. van Harmelen. Sesame: An architecture for storing and querying RDF data and schema information, 2001.
5. J. Davies, R. Weeks, and U. Krohn. QuizRDF: Search technology for the semantic web. In *Workshop on Real World RDF and Semantic Web Applications*, 2002.
6. S. Decker, M. Erdmann, D. Fensel, and R. Studer. Ontobroker: Ontology based access to distributed and semi-structured information. In *Eighth Working Conference on Database Semantics (DS-8)*, pages 351–369, 1999.
7. A. Doan, P. Domingos, and A. Halevy. Reconciling schemas of disparate data sources: a machine learning approach. In *Proc. of SIGMOD*, 2001.
8. A. Doan, J. Madhavan, P. Domingos, and A. Halevy. Learning to map between ontologies on the semantic web. In *Proc. of the Int. WWW Conf.*, 2002.
9. O. Etzioni, S. Gribble, A. Halevy, H. Levy, and L. McDowell. An evolutionary approach to the semantic web. In *Poster presentation at the First International Semantic Web Conference*, 2002.

10. O. Etzioni, A. Halevy, H. Levy, and L. McDowell. Semantic email: Adding lightweight data manipulation capabilities to the email habitat. In *Sixth International Workshop on the Web and Databases*, 2003.
11. H. Garcia-Molina, Y. Papakonstantinou, D. Quass, A. Rajaraman, Y. Sagiv, J. Ullman, and J. Widom. The TSIMMIS project: Integration of heterogeneous information sources. *Journal of Intelligent Information Systems*, March 1997.
12. R. Guha, R. McCool, and E. Miller. Semantic search. In *World Wide Web*, 2003.
13. A. Halevy, O. Etzioni, A. Doan, Z. Ives, J. Madhavan, L. McDowell, and I. Tatarinov. Crossing the structure chasm. In *First Biennial Conferenece on Innovative Data Systems Research, Asilomar, CA, January 5–8, 2003.*
14. A. Halevy, Z. Ives, I. Tatarinov, and P. Mork. Piazza: Data management infrastructure for semantic web applications. In *Proc. of the Int. WWW Conf.*, 2003.
15. S. Handschuh and S. Staab. Authoring and annotation of web pages in CREAM. In *World Wide Web*, pages 462–473, 2002.
16. S. Haustein and J. Pleumann. Is participation in the semantic web too difficult? In *First International Semantic Web Conference, Sardinia, Italy, June 2002.*
17. J. Heflin, J. Hendler, and S. Luke. SHOE: A knowledge representation language for internet applications. Technical Report CS-TR-4078, 1999.
18. J. Heflin, J. A. Hendler, and S. Luke. Applying ontology to the web: A case study. In *IWANN (2)*, pages 715–724, 1999.
19. Z. Ives, D. Florescu, M. Friedman, A. Levy, and D. Weld. An adaptive query execution engine for data integration. In *Proc. of SIGMOD*, pages 299–310, 1999.
20. J. Kahan and M.-R. Koivunen. Annotea: an open RDF infrastructure for shared web annotations. In *World Wide Web*, pages 623–632, 2001.
21. A. Kalyanpur, B. Parsia, J. Hendler, and J. Golbeck. SMORE – semantic markup, ontology, and RDF editor. http://www.mindswap.org/papers/.
22. T. Malone, K. Grant, F. Turbak, S. Brobst, and M. Cohen. Intelligent information-sharing systems. *Communications of the ACM*, 30(5):390–402, 1987.
23. P. Martin and P. W. Eklund. Large-scale cooperatively-built KBs. In *ICCS*, pages 231–244, 2001.
24. B. McBride. Four steps towards the widespread adoption of a semantic web. In *First International Semantic Web Conference, Sardinia, Italy, June 2002.*
25. B. McBride. Jena: Implementing the RDF model and syntax specification. http://www-uk.hpl.hp.com/people/bwm/papers/20001221-paper/, 2001. Hewlett Packard Laboratories.
26. L. McDowell, O. Etzioni, S. D. Gribble, A. Halevy, H. Levy, W. Pentney, D. Verma, and S. Vlasseva. Evolving the semantic web with Mangrove. Technical Report UW-CSE-03-02-01, February 2003.
27. B. Motik, A. Maedche, and R. Volz. A conceptual modeling approach for building semantics-driven enterprise applications. In *First International Conference on Ontologies, Dataases and Application of Semantics (ODBASE-2002)*, 2002.
28. W. Nejdl, B. Wolf, C. Qu, S. Decker, M. Sintek, A. Naeve, M. Nilsson, M. Palmér, and T. Risch. Edutella: a P2P networking infrastructure based on RDF. In *WWW*, pages 604–615, 2002.
29. Ontoprise. Demo applications. http://www.ontoprise.de/com/co_produ_appl2.htm
30. D. Reynolds. RDF-QBE: a Semantic Web building block. http://www.hpl.hp.com/semweb/publications.htm.
31. S. Staab, J. Angele, S. Decker, M. Erdmann, A. Hotho, A. Maedche, H.-P. Schnurr, R. Studer, and Y. Sure. Semantic community web portals. *WWW9 / Computer Networks*, 33(1–6):473–491, 2000.

FrameNet Meets the Semantic Web: Lexical Semantics for the Web

Srini Narayanan, Collin Baker, Charles Fillmore, and Miriam Petruck

International Computer Science Institute (ICSI),
1947 Center Street, Berkeley, CA 94704, USA,
snarayan@icsi.berkeley.edu
http://www.icsi.berkeley.edu/~framenet/

Abstract. This paper describes FrameNet [9,1,3], an online lexical resource for English based on the principles of frame semantics [5,7,2]. We provide a data category specification for frame semantics and FrameNet annotations in an RDF-based language. More specifically, we provide an RDF markup for **lexical units**, defined as a relation between a lemma and a semantic frame, and frame-to-frame relations, namely **Inheritance** and **Subframes**. The paper includes simple examples of FrameNet annotated sentences in an XML/RDF format that references the project-specific data category specification.

Frame Semantics and the FrameNet Project

FrameNet's goal is to provide, for a significant portion of the vocabulary of contemporary English, a body of semantically and syntactically annotated sentences from which reliable information can be reported on the valences or combinatorial possibilities of each item included. A semantic frame is a script-like structure of inferences, which are linked to the meanings of linguistic units (lexical items). Each frame identifies a set of frame elements (FEs), which are frame-specific semantic roles (participants, props, phases of a state of affairs). Our description of each lexical item identifies the frames which underlie a given meaning and the ways in which the FEs are realized in structures headed by the word. The FrameNet database documents the range of semantic and syntactic combinatory possibilities (valences) of each word in each of its senses, through manual annotation of example sentences and automatic summarization of the resulting annotations. FrameNet I focused on governors, meaning that for the most part, annotation was done in respect to verbs; in FrameNet II, we have been annotating in respect to governed words as well. The FrameNet database is available in XML, and can be displayed and queried via the web and other interfaces. FrameNet data has also been translated into the DAML+OIL extension to XML and the Resource Description Framework (RDF). This paper will explain the theory behind FrameNet, briefly discuss the annotation process, and then describe how the FrameNet data can be represented in RDF, using DAML+OIL, so that researchers on the semantic web can use the data.

D. Fensel et al. (Eds.): ISWC 2003, LNCS 2870, pp. 771–787, 2003.

Frame Semantic Background

In Frame Semantics [4,6,2,11], a linguistic unit, in our case, a word (in just one of its senses), **evokes** a particular frame and may **profile** some element or aspect of that frame.[1] An "evoked" frame is the structure of knowledge required for the understanding of a given lexical or phrasal item; a "profiled" entity is the component of a frame that integrates directly into the semantic structure of the surrounding text or sentence. The frames in question can be simple – small static scenes or states of affairs, simple patterns of contrast, relations between entities and the roles they serve, or possibly quite complex event types that provide the background for words that profile one or more of their phases or participants.

For example, the word *bartender* evokes a scene of service in a setting where alcoholic beverages are consumed, and profiles the person whose role is to prepare and serve these beverages. In a sentence like *The bartender asked for my ID*, it is the individual who occupies that role that we understand as making the request, and the request for identification is understood against the set of assumptions and practices of that frame.

Replacement: An Example Frame. A schematic description of the REPLACEMENT frame will include an AGENT effecting a change in the relationship between a PLACE (which can be a role, a function, a location, a job, a status, etc.) and a THEME. For example, in the sentence *Sal replaced his cap on his bald head*, *Sal* fills the role of AGENT, *his cap* instantiates the FE THEME, and *on his bald head* is the PLACE. The words defined in terms of this frame include, among others, *exchange.v, interchange.v, replace.v, replacement.n, substitute.v, substitution.n, succeed.v, supplant.v, swap.v, switch.v, trade.v.*

The REPLACEMENT frame involves states of affairs and transitions between them such that other situations are covered: an "old theme", which we refer to as OLD, starts out at the PLACE and ends up not at the PLACE, while a "new theme", which we call NEW, starts out not at the PLACE and ends up at the PLACE (as in *Factory owners replaced workers by machines*).

Syntactically, the role of AGENT can be expressed by a simple NP (as in *Margot switched her gaze to the floor*, a conjoined NP (as in *Margot and her admirer exchanged glances*), or two separate constituents, an NP and a PP (as in *Margot exchanged glances with her admirer*). Similarly, PLACE may be expressed as one PP or two. Compare *Ginny switched the phone between hands* and *Ginny switched the phone from one hand to the other.* And, if OLD and NEW are of the same type, they are expressed as a single FE (as in *The photographer switched lenses*).

The FrameNet Process

Using attested instances of contemporary English, FrameNet documents the manner in which frame elements (for given words in given meanings) are grammatically instantiated in English sentences and organizes and exhibits the results

[1] The term *profile* (used here as a verb) is borrowed from [8], esp. pp. 183ff.

of such findings in a systematic way. For example, in causative uses of the words, an expression about *replacing NP with NP* takes the direct object as the OLD and the oblique object as the NEW, whereas *substituting NP for NP* does it the other way around. A commitment to basing such generalizations on attestations from a large corpus, however, has revealed that in both UK and US English, the verb *substitute* also participates in the valence pattern found with *replace*, i.e. we find examples of *substituting* the OLD ***with*** the NEW.

In their daily work, FrameNet lexicographers record the variety of combinatorial patterns found in the corpus for each word in the FrameNet lexicon, present the results as the **valences** of the words, create software capable of deriving as much other information about the words as possible, from the annotations, and add manually only that information which cannot—or cannot easily—be derived automatically from the corpus or from the set of annotated examples.

FrameNet has been using the British National Corpus, more than 100,000,000 running words of contemporary British English.[2] In the current phase, we have begun to incorporate into our work the North American newswire corpora from the Linguistic Data Consortium (http://www.ldc.upenn.edu), and eventually we hope to be able to add the full resources of the American National Corpus (http://www.cs.vassar.edu/~ide/anc/).

Frame-to-Frame Relations

The FrameNet database records information about several different kinds of semantic relations, consisting mostly of frame-to-frame relations which indicate semantic relationships between collections of concepts. The two that we consider here are inheritance and subframes.

Inheritance. Frame **inheritance** is a relationship by which a single frame can be seen as an elaboration of one or more other parent frames, with bindings between the inherited semantic roles. In such cases, all of the frame elements, subframes, and semantic types of the parent have equally or more specific correspondents in the child frame. Consider for example, the CHANGE_OF_LEADERSHIP frame, which characterizes the appointment of a new leader or removal from office of an old one, and whose FEs include: SELECTOR, the being or entity that brings about the change in leadership (in the case of a democratic process, the electorate); OLD LEADER, the person removed from office; OLD ORDER, the political order that existed before the change; NEW LEADER, the person appointed to office; and ROLE, the position occupied by the new or old leader. Some of the words that belong to this frame describe the successful removal from office of a leader (e.g. *overthrow, oust, depose*), others only the attempt (e.g. *uprising, rebellion*). This frame inherits from the more abstract REPLACEMENT frame described

[2] Our use of the BNC is by courtesy of Oxford University Press, through Timothy Benbow. The version of the corpus we use was tokenized at Oxford, lemmatized and POS-tagged at the Institut für Maschinelle Sprachverarbeitung at the University of Stuttgart. Information about the BNC can be found at http://info.ox.ac.uk/bnc.

above, with the following FEs further specified in the child: OLD and NEW are narrowed to humans beings or political entities, i.e. OLD_LEADER and NEW_LEADER, respectively; and PLACE is an (abstract) position of political power, i.e. ROLE.

Subframes. The other type of relation between frames which is currently represented in the FN database is between a complex frame and several simpler frames which constitute it. We call this relationship (**subframes**). In such cases, frame elements of the complex frame may be identified (mapped) to the frame elements of the subparts, although not all frame elements of one need have any relation to the other. Also, the ordering and other temporal relationships of the subframes can be specified using binary precedence relations. To illustrate, consider the complex CRIMINAL_PROCESS frame, defined as follows: A Suspect is arrested by an AUTHORITY on certain CHARGES, then is arraigned as a DEFENDANT. If at any time the DEFENDANT pleads guilty, then the DEFENDANT is sentenced, otherwise the DEFENDANT first goes to trial. If the VERDICT after the trial is guilty, then the DEFENDANT is sentenced. In the end, the DEFENDANT is either released or is given a SENTENCE by a JUDGE at the sentencing. For each step in the process, there is a separate frame in the database, including ARREST, ARRAIGNMENT, TRIAL, SENTENCING, and so on. Each of these frames is related to the CRIMINAL_PROCESS frame via the SubFrame relation in the frame editor. Moreover, subframes (of the same complex frame) are related to each other through their ordering.

We have recognized the need to deal with other types of relations among frames, and, so far, have identified two, **SeeAlso**, and **Using**, but have not yet represented them in our database.

The FrameNet Product

The FrameNet database contains descriptions of more than 7,000 lexical units based on more than 130,000 annotated sentences. This information is available for a wide range of natural language processing applications, including question answering, machine translation, and information extraction.

The FrameNet database differs from existing lexical resources in the specificity of the frames and semantic roles it defines, the information it provides about relations between frames, and the degree of detail with which it describes, for each lexical item it covers, the possible syntactic realizations of semantic roles.

While Ide, et al., (2000) offers a representation scheme for dictionaries and other lexical data, the kind of information in the FrameNet database is not expressed in the same level of depth in any existing print dictionary or computational lexical resource. For instance, while WordNet describes semantic relations between words, it does not recognize conceptual schemas, i.e. frames, that mediate in these relations, and therefore does not have the means to link arguments of predicating words with the semantic roles they express. FrameNet also differs from WordNet in showing semantic relations across parts of speech, and in providing contextual information enriched with semantics (beyond the "Someone _s something" format of WordNet argument-structure representations).

The FN database can be seen both as a dictionary and a thesaurus. As a dictionary, each lexical unit (lemma in a given sense) is provided with (1) the name of the frame it belongs to and access to a description of the frame, (2) a definition (either original or from the Concise Oxford Dictionary, courtesy of Oxford University Press), (3) a valence description which summarizes the attested combinatorial possibilities in respect to both semantic roles and the syntactic form and function of the phrases that instantiate those roles (generated as a report from the database), and (4) access to annotated examples illustrating each syntactic pattern found in the corpus and the kinds of semantic information they contain.

The FN database can also be seen as a thesaurus by noting that lemmas are linked to the semantic frames in which they participate, and frames, in turn, are linked both to the full set of words which instantiate them and to related frames.

1 Criminal Process: A Full Example of Annotation and Representation

The FrameNet project is currently working on a very complex background frame called CRIMINAL_PROCESS, which contains many subframes, as a part of our analysis of texts in the crime domain.

The CRIMINAL_PROCESS frame is defined as follows: a SUSPECT is arrested by an AUTHORITY on certain CHARGES, then is arraigned as a DEFENDANT pleads guilty, then the DEFENDANT is sentenced, otherwise the DEFENDANT first goes to trial. If the VERDICT after the trial is guilty, then the DEFENDANT is sentenced. In the end, the DEFENDANT is either released or is given a SENTENCE by a JUDGE at the sentencing.

In addition to having a fairly large number of FEs, the CRIMINAL PROCESS frame, as its name suggests, represents a complex process with many parts. These are treated in FrameNet as subframes. Fig. 1 shows part of the subframe structure. The stages such as arrest, arraignment, and trial are subframe of CRIMINAL PROCESS and some of them (such as ARRAIGNMENT) have subframes of their own. The FE-to-FE links are not shown, but it should be clear that the person referred to as the SUSPECT in the Arrest frame is identified with the Defendant in the TRIAL frame, that (if justice is done) this will also be the OFFENDER in the OFFENSE frame, etc.

One step in the process depicted here is the arrest of a suspect. We have a frame called ARREST, which includes the verb *apprehend*. So part of the work of FrameNet on the ARREST frame will be collect corpus sentences containing *apprehend* and annotate them with FRs such as AUTHORITIES (those with the power to arrest), SUSPECT (the perso(s) who are arrested), CHARGES (the name

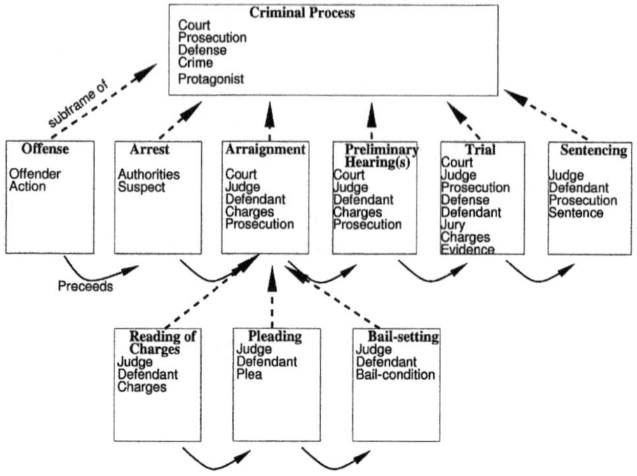

Fig. 1. The CRIMINAL PROCESS frame and some of its subframes

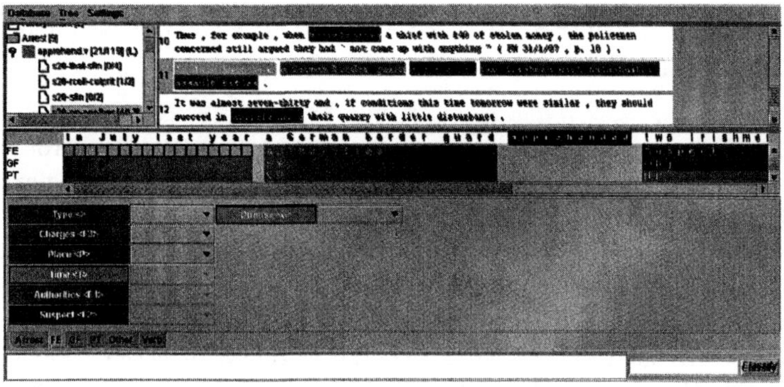

Fig. 2. Annotation of a sentence in the ARREST frame

of the offense which the Suspect is to be charged with), and more general FEs such as PLACE and TIME.

Fig. 2 shows the FrameNet annotation software in use. The user has selected the sentence *In July last year, a German border guard apprehended two Irishmen with Kalashnikov assault rifles*, and has marked the FEs TIME, AUTHORITIES, and SUSPECT. The resulting FE annotations can be displayed in a bracketed notation like this:

[$_{Time}$ In July last year] [$_{Authorities}$ a German border guard] apprehended^{Target} [$_{Suspect}$ two Irishmen with Kalashnikov assault rifle]

A Data Category Specification for Frame Semantics in RDF

The World Wide Web (WWW) contains a large amount of information which is expanding at a rapid rate. Most of that information is currently being represented using the Hypertext Markup Language (HTML), which is designed to allow web developers to display information in a way that is accessible to humans for viewing via web browsers. While HTML allows us to visualize the information on the web, it doesn't provide much capability to describe the information in ways that facilitate the use of software programs to find or interpret it. The World Wide Web Consortium (W3C) has developed the Extensible Markup Language (XML) which allows information to be more accurately described using tags. As an example, the word *crawl* on a web site might represent an *offline search* process (as in web crawling) or an exposition of a type of *animate motion.* The use of XML to provide metadata markup, such as for *crawl*, makes the meaning of the word unambiguous. However, XML has a limited capability to describe the relationships (schemas or ontologies) with respect to objects. The use of ontologies provides a very powerful way to describe objects and their relationships to other objects. The DAML language was developed as an extension to XML and the Resource Description Framework (RDF). The latest release of the language (DAML+OIL) (http://www.daml.org) provides a rich set of constructs with which to create ontologies and to markup information so that it is machine readable and understandable. Framenet-1 has been translated into DAML+OIL. We developed an automatic translator from FrameNet to DAML+OIL which is being updated to reflect FrameNet2 data. With periodic updates as the FrameNet data increases, we expect it to become useful for various applications on the Semantic Web. DAML+OIL is written in RDF (http://www.w3.org/TR/daml+oil-walkthru/#RDF1), i.e., DAML+OIL markup is a specific kind of RDF markup. RDF, in turn, is written in XML, using XML Namespaces (http://www.w3.org/TR/daml+oil-walkthru/#XMLNS), and URIs. Thus, our framenet declaration begins with an RDF start tag including several namespace declarations of the form:

```
<?Xml version='1.0' encoding='ISO-8859-1'?>
<!DOCTYPE uridef[
  <!ENTITY rdf
"http://www.w3.org/1999/02/22-rdf-syntax-ns">
  <!ENTITY rdfs
"http://www.w3.org/2000/01/rdf-schema">
  <!ENTITY xsd
"http://www.w3.org/2000/10/XMLSchema">
  <!ENTITY daml
"http://www.daml.org/2001/03/daml+oil">
  <!ENTITY daml
"http://www.daml.org/services/daml-s/0.9/process">
]>
```

```
<rdf:RDF
  xmlns:rdf =      "&rdf;#"
  xmlns:rdfs =     "&rdfs;#"
  xmlns:xsd =      "&xsd;#"
  xmlns:daml =     "&daml;#"
  xmlns:CYC =      "&cyc;#"
>
```

So in this document, the rdf: prefix should be understood as referring to things drawn from the namespace called http://www.w3.org/1999/02/22-rdf-syntax-ns#. This is a conventional RDF declaration appearing verbatim at the beginning of almost every rdf document. The second and third declarations make similar statements about the RDF Schema and XML Schema datatype namespaces. The fourth declaration says that in this document, elements prefixed with daml: should be understood as referring to things drawn from the namespace called http://www.w3.org/2001/03/daml+oil#. This again is a conventional DAML+OIL declaration. We use the XML entity model to use shortcuts with referring to the URIs.[3] The other DAML+OIL ontologies used in the FrameNet description include the DAML-S (http://www.daml.org/services) service ontologies, the OpenCYC DAML ontology (http:// www.cyc.com/2002/04/08/cyc.daml), and the SRI time ontology (http:// www.ai.sri.com/ daml/ontologies/ sri-basic/1-0/Time.daml) which is currently being revised with the new DAML+OIL time ontology effort. http://www.icsi.berkeley.edu/ snarayan/frame-2.daml has a complete namespace and imported ontology list.

The most general object of interest is a *frame*. We define the FRAME class as a *daml:class* We then define a bunch of bookkeeping properties on the FRAME class. An example of the name property is shown below.

```
<daml:Class rdf:ID="Frame">
  <rdfs:comment> The most general class </rdfs:comment>
</daml:Class>

<daml:ObjectProperty rdf:ID="Name">
  <rdfs:domain rdf:resource="#Frame"/>
  <rdfs:range rdf:resource="&rdf-schema;#Literal"/>
</daml:ObjectProperty>
```

In FrameNet, the basic relation between a word (Lemma) and a frame is the Lexical Unit (LU). The domain of the Lexical Unit is a Lemma or word and its range is a Frame. An LU is defined in DAML as a property.

```
<daml:ObjectProperty rdf:ID= "LU">
  <rdfs:domain rdf:resource="#Lexeme"/>
  <rdfs:range  rdf:resource="#Frame"/>
</daml:ObjectProperty>
```

[3] Note that all URIs are globally scoped, so without this the entire path has to be specified.

Roles are relations defined on frames ranging over the specific type of the *filler*. We use *daml:objectProperty* to define the roles of a frame. The domain of a role is its frame. We leave the type of the filler unrestricted at this level, allowing specific roles to specialize this further. Note that we use the *daml:samePropertyAs* relation to specify synonyms. The fragment below specifies that Frame Element, Role, and FE are synonyms.

```
<daml:ObjectProperty rdf:ID= "role">
  <rdfs:domain rdf:resource="#Frame"/>
  <rdfs:range  rdf:resource="&daml;#Thing"/>
</daml:ObjectProperty>

<daml:ObjectProperty rdf:ID="frameElement">
  <daml:samePropertyAs rdf:resource="#role"/>
</daml:ObjectProperty>

<daml:ObjectProperty rdf:ID="FE">
  <daml:samePropertyAs rdf:resource="#role"/>
</daml:ObjectProperty>
```

We use the various constructs *daml:maxCardinality*, *daml:minCardinality*, *daml:cardinalityQ*, etc. from DAML to specify cardinality restrictions on the fillers of a role property. The markup fragment below shows the specification of a single valued role.

```
<daml:ObjectProperty rdf:ID= "singleValuedRole">
  <rdfs:domain rdf:resource="#Frame"/>
  <rdfs:range>
   <rdfs:subClassOf>
    <daml:Restriction daml:maxCardinality="1">
      <daml:onProperty rdf:resource="#Role"/>
    </daml:Restriction>
   </rdfs:subClassOf>
</daml:Class>
```

The relation between frames (such as ARREST) and CRIMINAL PROCESS is often captured by a set of bindings between frame elements (such as the *arrested person* is the same individual as the *person charged* who is the same individual as the *defendant* in a criminal process).

By far the most important binding relation is the identification of roles (i.e. they refer to the same value (object)). This can be specified through the relation *identify* which is a *subProperty* of *bindingRelation*. Note that in order to do this, we have to extend the DAML+OIL language which does not allow properties to be defined over other properties. We use the DAML-S ontology (http://www.daml.org/services/daml-s/0.7/) primitive *daml-s:sameValues* to specify the *identify* relations.

```
<daml:ObjectProperty rdf:ID="identify">
  <rdf:subPropertyOf rdf:resource="&daml-s;#sameValues"/>
```

```
  <rdfs:domain rdf:resource="#Role"/>
  <rdfs:range rdf:resource="#Role"/>
</daml:ObjectProperty>
```

In FrameNet, a frame may inherit (A ISA B) from other frames or be *composed* of a set of subframes (which are frames themselves). For instance, the frame CRIMINAL PROCESS has subframes that correspond to various stages (ARREST, ARRAIGNMENT, CHARGE, etc.). Subframe relations are represented using the *daml:objectProperty.*[4]

```
<daml:ObjectProperty rdf:ID="subFrameOf">
  <rdfs:domain rdf:resource="#Frame"/>
  <rdfs:range rdf:resource="#Frame"/>
</daml:ObjectProperty>
```

A central relation between subframes is one of temporal ordering. We use *precedes* (in the sense of immediately precedes)) to encode this relation between subframes.

```
<daml:ObjectProperty rdf:ID="precedes">
  <rdfs:domain rdf:resource="#subFrame"/>
  <rdfs:range rdf:resource="#subFrame"/>
</daml:ObjectProperty>
```

We can define a property *temporalOrdering* that is the transitive version of *precedes.*

```
daml:TransitiveProperty rdf:ID="TemporalOrdering">
  <rdfs:label>TemporalOrdering</rdfs:label>
</daml:TransitiveProperty>
```

Note that the *temporalOrdering* property only says it is transitive, not that it is a transitive version of *precedes.* DAML+OIL does not currently allow us to express this relation. (see http://www.daml.org/2001/03/daml+oil-walkthru#properties).

Frame Elements may also inherit from each other. We use the rdfs:subPropertyOf to specify this dependences. For example, the following markup in DAML+OIL specifies that the role (Frame Element) MOTHER inherits from the role (Frame Element) PARENT. Note we can add further restrictions to the new role. For instance, we may want to restrict the filler of the MOTHER to be female (as opposed to animal for PARENT).

[4] The *subFrameOf* relation has a direct translation to a richer semantic representation that is able to model and reason about complex processes (such as buying, selling, reserving tickets) and services on the web. While the details of the representation are outside the scope of the this paper, the interested reader can look at [10] for an exposition of the markup language and its operational semantics.

```
<daml:ObjectProperty rdf:ID="mother">
  <rdfs:subPropertyOf rdf:resource="#parent"/>
  <rdfs:range rdf:resource="#Female"/>
</daml:ObjectProperty>
```

With these basic frame primitives defined, we are ready to look at an example using the Criminal Process frames.

An Example: The Criminal Process Frame

The basic frame is the CRIMINAL PROCESS Frame. It is a type of background frame. CP is used as a shorthand for this frame.

```
<daml:Class rdf:ID="CriminalProcess">
  <rdfs:subClassOf rdf:resource="#Frame"/>
</daml:Class>

<daml:Class rdf:ID="CP">
  <daml:sameClassAs rdf:resource="#CriminalProcess"/>
</daml:Class>
```

The CRIMINALPROCESS frame has a set of associated roles. These roles include that of COURT, DEFENDANT, PROSECUTION, DEFENSE, JURY, and CHARGES. Each of these roles may have a filler with a specific semantic type restriction. FrameNet does not specify the world knowledge and ontology required to reason about Frame Element filler types. We believe that one of the possible advantages in encoding FrameNet data in DAML+OIL is that as and when ontologies become available on the web (uch as OpenCYC), we can link to them for this purpose.

In the example fragment below we use the CYC *Court-Judicial* collection to specify the type of the COURT and the CYC *Lawyer* definition to specify the type restriction on the frame element DEFENSE. For illustrative purposes, the DAML+OIL markup below shows the use of a different ontology (from CYC) to restrict the defendant to be of type PERSON as defined in the example ontology. This restriction uses the DAML+OIL example from http://www.daml.org/2001/03/daml+oil-ex)

```
<daml:ObjectProperty rdf:ID="court">
  <rdfs:subPropertyOf rdf:resource="#FE"/>
  <rdfs:domain rdf:resource="#CriminalProcess"/>
  <rdfs:range rdf:resource="&CYC;#Court-Judicial"/>
</daml:ObjectProperty>

<daml:ObjectProperty rdf:ID="defense">
  <rdfs:subPropertyOf rdf:resource="#FE"/>
  <rdfs:domain rdf:resource="#CriminalProcess"/>
  <rdfs:range rdf:resource="&CYC;#Lawyer"/>
</daml:ObjectProperty>
```

```
<daml:ObjectProperty rdf:ID="defendant">
  <rdfs:subPropertyOf rdf:resource="#FE"/>
  <rdfs:domain rdf:resource="#CriminalProcess"/>
  <rdfs:range rdf:resource="&daml-ex;Person"/>
</daml:ObjectProperty>
```

The set of binding relations involves a set of role identification statements that specify that a role of a frame (subframe) has the same value (bound to the same object) as the role of a subframe (frame). We could specify these constraints either a) as anonymous subclass restrictions on the criminal process class (see http://www.daml.org/2001/03/daml+oil-ex for examples) or b) we could name each individual constraint (and thus obtain a handle onto that property). We chose the later method in our DAML+OIL encoding of FrameNet to allow users/programs to query any specific constraint (or modify it). Note also that the use of the dotting notation (A.b) to specify paths through simple and complex frames and is not fully supported in DAML+OIL (see http://www.daml.org/services/daml-s/2001/10/rationale.html and also [10] for more info).

```
<daml:ObjectProperty rdf:ID="prosecutionConstraint">
  <rdfs:subPropertyOf rdf:resource="#identify"/>
   <rdfs:domain rdf:resource="#CP.prosecution"/>
   <rdfs:range rdf:resource="#Trial.prosecution"/>
</daml:ObjectProperty>

<daml:ObjectProperty rdf:ID="defendantConstraint">
  <rdfs:subPropertyOf rdf:resource="#identify"/>
   <rdfs:domain rdf:resource="#CP.defendant"/>
   <rdfs:range rdf:resource="#Arrest.suspect"/>
</daml:ObjectProperty>
```

Subframes of the CRIMINALPROCESS frame are defined by their type (LexicalFrame or a BackgroundFrame). For example, ARREST and ARRAIGNMENT are Lexical Frames while TRIAL is a BackgroundFrame (all are subframes of CRIMINALPROCESS. We subtype the *subFrameOf* property to specify the individual subframe relations (shown below for the relation subframeOf(Criminal Process, Arraignment)).

```
<daml:Class rdf:ID="Arrest">
<rdfs:comment> A subframe </rdfs:comment>
  <rdfs:subClassOf rdf:resource="#LexicalFrame"/>
</daml:Class>

<daml:Class rdf:ID="Arraignment">
<rdfs:comment> A subframe </rdfs:comment>
  <rdfs:subClassOf rdf:resource="#LexicalFrame"/>
</daml:Class>
```

```
<daml:Class rdf:ID="Trial">
<rdfs:comment> A subframe </rdfs:comment>
  <rdfs:subClassOf rdf:resource="#BackgroundFrame"/>
</daml:Class>

<daml:ObjectProperty rdf:ID="arraignSubFrame">
  <rdfs:subPropertyOf rdf:resource="#subFrameOf"/>
   <rdfs:domain rdf:resource="#CP"/>
   <rdfs:range rdf:resource="#Arraignment"/>
</daml:ObjectProperty>
```

To specify the the relation *precedes(Arrest, Arraignment)* we restrict the property *precedes* within (the domain of) the ARREST frame to have as one of its range values the frame (class) ARRAIGNMENT. This is done using the property restriction feature with DAML+OIL as follows.

```
<daml:Class rdf:about="#Arrest">
  <rdfs:subClassOf>
    <daml:Restriction>
      <daml:onProperty rdf:resource="#precedes"/>
      <daml:hasClass rdf:resource="#Arraignment"/>
    </daml:Restriction>
  </rdfs:subClassOf>
</daml:Class>
```

With this markup of the ontology, we can create annotation instances for examples with targets that belong to the CRIMINALPROCESS (or its associated) frames.

Basic Annotation of Verb Arguments and Complements as Triplets

Consider the following sentence, which is annotated for the target *nab*, a verb in the ARREST frame; the frame elements represented are the arresting AUTHORITIES, the SUSPECT and the TIME when the event took place:

> [$_{Authorities}$Police] **nabbed** [$_{Suspect}$ the man], who was out on licence from prison, [$_{Time}$ when he returned home].

The phrase *who was out on licence from prison* provides additional information about the SUSPECT, but it is not syntactically an argument or complement of the target verb, nor semantically an element of the ARREST frame, so it is not annotated.

How do we propose to represent this in XML conforming to the proposed standards? The header of the file will refer to the FrameNet Data Category specification discussed in the last section:

```
1 <?xml version="1.0" encoding="UTF-8"?>
2 [DOCTYPE definitions like those shown in
  the preceeding section go here ]
3 <lexunit-annotation name="nab" frame="Arrest" pos="V">
4   <definition>COD: catch (someone) doing something
               wrong. </definition>
5  <subcorpus name="V-001-all">
```

The entity `<lexunit-annotation>`, which comprises the rest of the file includes attributes giving the name of the lexical unit (nab), the name of the frame (Arrest), and the part of speech of the lemma (verb). The first included element is a definition of the lemma within the frame, seen on line 4.

The entities contained within the lexunit-annotation are called subcorpora; we select sentences for annotation, according to their syntactic patterns, collocations, etc. Each such selectional pattern results in a subcorpus which is made available to the annotators; in our representation of the annotated sentences we want to preserve these groupings. In the case of *nab*, there are so few instances of the word that we have lumped them all into one subcorpus as shown on line 5.

It might seem logical that the entities within the subcorpus should be sentences, but in fact, we recognize the possibility that one sentence might be annotated several times, for several targets. There might even be several instances of the **same** target lemma in the same sentence in the same frame (e.g. *The FBI **nabbed** Jones in NYC, while the Mounties **nabbed** Smith in Toronto*), each with its own set of FEs. Therefore, the next smaller entity is the **annotation set** (line 6).

The annotation set, shown below, consists of the `<sentence>`, which thus far contains only the `<text>` of the sentence, and a set of layers, each consisting of a set of labels. Each label has attributes start and end, giving the stating and ending position in the text to which it is applied. This sentence is typical of the basic FrameNet annotation style, in that there are three main layers, one for frame elements ("FE", line 8), one for the phrase type (PT) of each FE (line 22), and one for the grammatical function (GF) of each FE (line 15). In each case, there are three coextensive labels; thus the word *Police*, in text positions 0-5 expresses the FE Authorities (line 10), has the phrase type "NP" (line 24) and is the subject of the verb *nab*, which we refer to as external argument "Ext" (line 17). The other two frame elements are shown by similar triplets, suspect-NP-Obj and Time-Swh-Comp, the latter meaning a complement of the verb consisting of a clause (S-node) introduced by a WH-relative.

```
 6 <annotationSet status="MANUAL">
 7  <layers>
 8    <layer name="FE">
 9      <labels>
10        <label name="Authorities" start="0"
                 end="5" />
11        <label name="Suspect" start="14" end="20" />
12        <label name="Time" start="61" end="81" />
```

```
      </labels>
    </layer>
    <layer name="GF">
      <labels>
        <label name="Ext" start="0" end="5" />
        <label name="Obj" start="14" end="20" />
        <label name="Comp" start="61" end="81" />
      </labels>
    </layer>
   <layer name="PT">
      <labels>
        <label name="NP" start="0" end="5" />
        <label name="NP" start="14" end="20" />
        <label name="Swh" start="61" end="81" />
      </labels>
    </layer>
    <layer name="Sent" />
    <layer name="Other" />
    <layer name="Target">
     <labels>
       <label name="Target" start="7" end="12" />
     </labels>
   </layer>
   <layer name="Verb" />
</layers>
<sentence aPos="34400709">
  <text>Police nabbed the man, who was out on
licence from prison,  when he returned home.
  </text>
</sentence>
</annotationSet>
```

There are three other layers shown in the example, none of which contain labels, called Sentence, Verb, and Other. The layer Target contains the single label Target; the fact that *nab* is the target word is indicated in the same way as the information about FEs.

As the basic unit of annotation is the label, which can be applied to anything ranging from a single character to an entire sentence, and there are no a priori constraints on labels overlapping, a great variety of information can be represented in this way. We will not be able to demonstrate all the possibilities here, but we will give a some representative examples.

In FrameNet, event nouns are annotated in the same frame (and hence with the same FEs) as the corresponding verbs; the main differences are that the syntactic patterns for the FEs of nouns are more varied, and (with rare exceptions), no FEs of nouns are **required** to be expressed. Consider the noun *arrest*, also in the ARREST frame, in the sentence:

> Two witnesses have come forward with information that could lead to [$_{Suspect}$the killer's] **arrest**.

In this case the SUSPECT is expressed as a possessive (*the killer's*; it could equally well have been in a PP headed by *of* (*the arrest of the killer*).

In addition to marking the FE SUSPECT from ARREST, we could also annotate the same sentence again in the CAUSATION frame with the target **lead**, which would create an annotation set listed under the the LU *lead_to*:

> Two witnesses have come forward with $[_{Cause}$information that$]$ could **lead** $[_{Effect}$to the killer's arrest$]$.

The same sentence would be annotated in two different frames, and the semantics of the two frames could (in theory) be combined compositionally to get the semantics of the phrase *information that could lead to the killer's arrest.* Similar processes of annotating in multiple frames with targets **come_forward** (and possibly **witness** as well) should yield a full semantics of the sentence.

At the current stage, we have converted all of FrameNet 1 data (annotations and frame descriptions) to DAML+OIL. The translator has also been updated to handle the more complex semantic relations (both frame and frame element based) in FrameNet 2. We plan to release both the XML and the RDF-based DAML+OIL versions of all FrameNet 2 releases.

Conclusion

The World Wide Web (WWW) contains a large amount of information which is expanding at a rapid rate. The information contained encompasses diverse ranges and types of data, from structured databases to text. While XML allows for the specification of metadata as a means to specify the structure and syntax of a URL, it does not provide much capability to describe the semantic relations between the different pieces of information in a manner that can be exploited by software programs for automation or interpretation. DAML+OIL is a widely used language related to the Semantic Web initiative that is poised to remedy this situation. The DAML+OIL language is being developed as an extension to XML and the Resource Description Framework (RDF). The latest release of the language (DAML+OIL) provides a rich set of constructs with which to create ontologies and to markup information so that it is machine readable and understandable. This rapid growth of the web also engenders a need for sophisticated techniques to represent lexical and sense distinctions in a machine readable and interpretable manner. The FrameNet database documents the range of semantic and syntactic combinatory possibilities (valences) of each word in each of its senses, through manual annotation of example sentences and automatic summarization of the resulting annotations. We believe that FrameNet offers promise as a potential resource to aid in the automatic identification and disambiguation of word meanings on the semantic web.

This paper described an encoding of FrameNet data in the DAML+OIL language. FrameNet 1 (both frame descriptions and annotations) has already been translated into DAML+OIL, and we reported on the updated translator which translates the richer set of frame and frame element relations in FrameNet 2 to DAML+OIL.

With periodic updates as the FrameNet data increases, we expect the DAML+OIL encoding of FrameNet to become useful for various applications on the semantic web. Conversely, as the set of DAML+OIL ontologies matures, FrameNet can directly link to the semantic web to incorporate domain-specific information including semantic typing of frame elements.

References

1. Collin F. Baker, Charles J. Fillmore, and John B. Lowe. 1998. The berkeley framenet project. In ACL, editor, *COLING-ACL '98: Proceedings of the Conference, held at the University of Montréal*, pages 86–90. Association for Computational Linguistics.
2. Charles J. Fillmore and B.T.S. Atkins. 1992. Towards a frame-based lexicon: The semantics of RISK and its neighbors. In Adrienne Lehrer and Eva Feder Kittay, editors, *Frames, Fields and Contrasts*. Lawrence Erlbaum Associates.
3. Charles J. Fillmore, Collin F. Baker, and Hiroaki Sato. 2002. The framenet database and software tools. In *Proceedings of the Third International Conference on Languag Resources and Evaluation*, volume IV, Las Palmas. LREC.
4. Charles J. Fillmore. 1976. Frame semantics and the nature of language. In *Annals of the New York Academy of Sciences: Conference on the Origin and Development of Language and Speech*, volume 280, pages 20–32.
5. Charles J. Fillmore. 1977a. The need for a frame semantics in linguistics. In Hans Karlgren, editor, *Statistical Methods in Linguistics*. Scriptor.
6. Charles J. Fillmore. 1977b. Scenes-and-frames semantics. In Antonio Zampolli, editor, *Linguistic Structures Processing*, number 59 in Fundamental Studies in Computer Science. North Holland Publishing.
7. Charles J. Fillmore. 1982. Frame semantics. In *Linguistics in the Morning Calm*, pages 111–137. Hanshin Publishing Co., Seoul, South Korea.
8. Ronald W. Langacker. 1987. *Foundations of Cognitive Grammar, Volume I: Theoretical Prerequisites*. Stanford University Press, Stanford, California.
9. John B. Lowe, Collin F. Baker, and Charles J. Fillmore. 1997. A frame-semantic approach to semantic annotation. In Marc Light, editor, *Tagging Text with Lexical Semantics: Why, What and How?* Special Interest Group on the Lexicon, Association for Computational Linguistics.
10. Srini Narayanan and Sheila McIlraith. 2002. Simulation, verification and automated composition of web services. In *Proc. Eleventh International World Wide Web Conference (WWW2002)*, May.
11. Miriam R. L. Petruck. 1996. Frame semantics. In Jef Verschueren, Jan-Ola Östman, Jan Blommaert, and Chris Bulcaen, editors, *Handbook of Pragmatics*. John Benjamins.

ScadaOnWeb – Web Based Supervisory Control and Data Acquisition

Thomas Dreyer[1], David Leal[2], Andrea Schröder[3], and Michael Schwan[3]

[1]RACOS Technische Informationssysteme
Max-Stromeyer-Str. 172, 78467 Konstanz, Germany
tdreyer@racos.com
[2]CAESAR Systems Limited
29 Somertrees Avenue, SE12 0BS, London, United Kingdom
david.leal@caesarsystems.co.uk
[3]Forschungsgemeinschaft für Elektrische Anlagen und Stromwirtschaft (FGH)
Postfach 81 01 69, 68201 Mannheim, Germany
{schroeder.andrea,schwan}@fgh-ma.de

Abstract. W3C envisages the future of the web as a "Semantic Web" – an extended web of machine-understandable information and automated services going far beyond current capabilities. The EC funded project ScadaOnWeb contributes to the Semantic Web by defining a new standard giving semantics to structured numeric data. An ontology for SCADA (supervisory control and data acquisition) applications is made available, enhancing semantics for the engineering domain. This ontology is defined in RDF, RDF schema and OWL. It comprises a basic ontology providing a general model for SCADA data, an ontology for physical quantities, units and data quality, and specific ontologies for different SCADA applications. Large amounts of structured numeric data inherent to most SCADA applications can either be stored within the XML file or within an external binary file referenced from within the XML file. The semantics wrapped around the structured numeric data enables the understanding of the numbers.

1 Introduction

Typically, SCADA Systems are used in industry to monitor and control plant status and provide data logging facilities. SCADA systems are highly configurable, and usually interface to the plant via PLCs (programmable logic controller). But process monitoring and control is a key technology in many areas of life. The process can be an environmental process, such as flows in a hydraulic basin or the dispersion of pollutants, an industrial production process, a transmission and distribution process carried out by a utility, or a commercial process such as the operation of the energy market. Today, in each of these areas, one-off systems are created using proprietary formats and systems with their inherent problems and disadvantages, e.g. lacking flexibility and high costs.

The ScadaOnWeb technology, developed within the EC funded project ScadaOnWeb [1] provides a standard platform that addresses this wider understanding of process monitoring and control applications that are distributed over

D. Fensel et al. (Eds.): ISWC 2003, LNCS 2870, pp. 788–801, 2003.

the web and make proprietary systems and formats superfluous. It extends current technologies by defining a standard for meta-data that gives semantics to engineering data and references standards for units of measure and ontologies for properties in different engineering domains. Standard transaction templates are developed to support process monitoring and control over the web and means for access control appropriate to process monitoring and control applications are provided [2].

In order to validate the ScadaOnWeb technology, the following prototype applications from different areas of process monitoring and control are developed:

- Flood warning system based upon remote sensors,
- Balance group energy management,
- Flexible metering of domestic and small industrial consumers,
- Condition based maintenance of remote equipment,
- Control of distributed wind and hydro electricity generation.

These are examples of a wide range of possible future applications in the area of engineering.

2 SCADA Web Data Type

Process monitoring and control can involve large amounts of numeric data with a regular structure. In order to process this type of data efficiently, it may be to the best advantage to maintain the structure as well as to hold the numbers in binary format, so that storage is minimized and computation is efficient. But information exchange also requires precision about the semantics of the data.

E.g. in a three-dimensional data-field data of many sensors can be stored for various time-steps. The binary file holds the measured value for time-step 10.000 and for sensor 1.000 in position (10.000, 1.000) of an array. It is necessary to know the identity of sensor 1.000 and where it is placed in the system, that time-step 10.000 was at 10:31:15 on 2001-12-14, and that the measured value is a flow expressed in $m^3 sec^{-1}$.

Using XML (Extensible Markup Language) [3] in conjunction with RDF (Resource Description Framework) [4] and RDFS provides the semantics, but a traditional XML approach may turn the data into millions of separate XML elements. Therefore, an approach was chosen which enables the information to be recorded and, where suitable, to be exchanged as a pair of files: An XML file which describes the semantics and a HDF5 (Hierarchical Data Format) [5] file with structured numeric data. HDF5 is a compact machine-independent binary file format developed by NCSA (National Center for Supercomputing Applications) and is used by NASA (North American Space Agency) and ESA (European Space Agency) in different applications.

This approach provides maximum flexibility: On server side, a ScadaOnWeb application with a high amount of recorded data may store it in a HDF5 file and keep the description of its semantic in a separate XML file or data-base referencing its respective HDF5 file (see Fig. 3). A similar application with a smaller amount of data recorded may choose to keep data and semantics in one and the same XML file. The same options hold if the server is queried by a client application: Depending on average amounts of data resulting from typical queries, the data may be exchanged in a single file or as a pair of files separating data and respective semantics. Fig. 1 symbolizes the case where large amounts of data are kept separate from its semantics in a structured HDF5 data block.

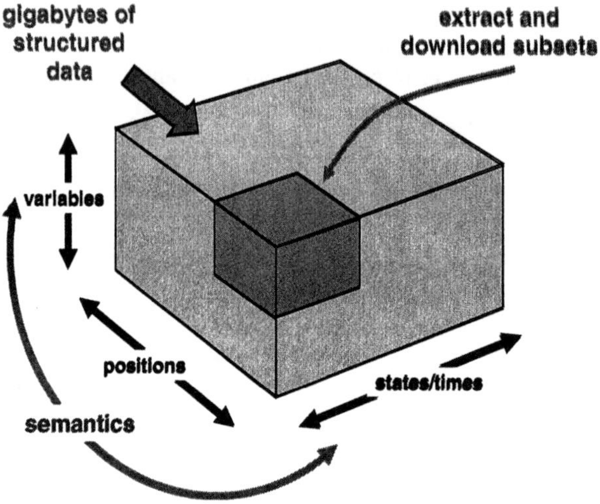

Fig. 1. SCADA web data type

The serialization in Fig. 2 is an example of a sensor 'sensor_xyz' making 96 measurements during a day. Each measurement is of the average electric power during the preceding 15 minutes. The distribution 'sensor_xyz_on_2002-05-02' is defined by the following equality:

$$\text{Distribution} = \text{Parameterization} \cdot \text{Table} \cdot (\text{Scale})^{-1} \qquad (1)$$

Each of "Distribution", "Parameterization", "Table" and "Scale" is a property. Hence the "Distribution" is described by a composition of the other three, as shown in the following serialization.

```
<?xml version="1.0"?>
<rdf:RDF
  <!-- Definition of namespaces and assignment of XML-Schema-->
    xmlns:rdf=http://www.w3.org/1999/02/22-rdf-syntax-ns#
    xmlns:rdfs="http://www.w3.org/2000/01/rdf-schema#"
    xmlns:owl="http://www.w3.org/2002/07/owl#"
    xmlns:po="http://www.scadaonweb.com/publications/ontologies/physicalObject.owl#"
    xmlns:ppqs="http://www.scadaonweb.com/publications/ontologies/physicalPropertyQuantityAndS
  cale.owl#"
    xmlns:pqs="http://www.scadaonweb.com/publications/ontologies/physicalQuantitySpaces.owl#"
    xmlns:snt="http://www.scadaonweb.com/publciations/ontologies/structureNumberAndText.owl#"
    xmlns:time="http://www.scadaonweb.com/publications/ontologies/time.owl#"
    xmlns:pods="http://www.scadaonweb.com/publications/ontologies/physicalObjectDecomposition
  AndSampling.owl#"
    xmlns:dist="http://www.scadaonweb.com/publications/ontologies/distributionAndDescription.owl
  #">
```

```
<po:Product rdf:ID="sensor_xyz"> </po:Product>

<po:ProductLifeSegment rdf:ID="sensor_xyz_on_2002-05-02">
 <po:lifeSegmentOfProduct rdf:resource="#sensor_xyz"/>
 <time:timeIntervalOfProductLifeSegment>
  <time:TimeInterval>
   <ppqs:closedLowerBoundOf1dPhysicalQuantitySpace>
    <time:Time>
     <time:utc>
      <time:UtcRepresentation>
       <snt:hasTerms rdf:parseType="Collection">
        <snt:Integer><snt:decimal>2002</snt:decimal></snt:Integer>
        <snt:Integer><snt:decimal>5</snt:decimal></snt:Integer>
        <snt:Integer><snt:decimal>2</snt:decimal></snt:Integer>
        <snt:Integer><snt:decimal>0</snt:decimal></snt:Integer>
        <snt:Integer><snt:decimal>0</snt:decimal></snt:Integer>
        <snt:Real><snt:decimal>0.0</snt:decimal></snt:Real>
        <snt:Boolean rdf:about="&snt;False"/>
       </snt:hasTerms>
      </time:UtcRepresentation>
     </time:utc>
    </time:Time>
   </ppqs:closedLowerBoundOf1dPhysicalQuantitySpace>
   <time:durationOfTimeInterval>
    <pqs:TimeDuration>
     <time:hour>
      <snt:Real>
       <snt:decimal>24.0</snt:decimal>
      </snt:Real>
     </time:hour>
    </pqs:TimeDuration>
   </time:durationOfTimeInterval>
  </time:TimeInterval>
 </time:timeIntervalOfProductLifeSegment>
</po:ProductLifeSegment>

<po:ProductLifeSegmentSet rdf:ID=" sensor_xyz_on_2002-05-02_at_15_minutes">
 <rdf:type rdf_resource="&pods;UniformlySizedProductLifeSegmentSet"/>
 <pods:lifeSegmentTemporalDecompositionOfProductLifeSegment
  rdf:resource="#sensor_xyz_on_2002-05-02"/>
 <pods:durationOfUniformlySizedSegments>
  <pqs:TimeDuration>
   <time:minute>
    <snt:Real><snt:decimal>15.0</snt:decimal></snt:Real>
   </time:minute>
  </pqs:TimeDuration>
 </pods:durationOfUniformlySizedSegments>
</po:ProductLifeSegmentSet>

<dist:PhysicalDistribution>
 <rdfs:domain rdf:resource="sensor_xyz_on_2002-05-02_at_15_minutes"/>
 <rdfs:range rdf:resource="&pqs;Power"/>
 <rdfs:subPropertyOf rdf:resource="&myPp;timeAveragePower"/>
 <dist:factorsInto>
  <dist:PhysicalDistributionDescriptionVector>
   <snt:hasTerms rdf:parseType="Collection">
    </dist:PhysicalParameterization>
     <rdf:type
       rdf:resource="&dist;DiscreteForwardTimeParameterisation"/>
```

```
    </dist:PhysicalParameterization>
    <snt:SymbolTable>
     <rdfs:domain>
      <snt:FiniteIntegerInterval>
       <snt:lowerBoundOfIntegerInterval>
        <snt:Integer><snt:decimal>1</snt:decimal></snt:Integer>
       </snt:lowerBoundOfIntegerInterval>
       <snt:upperBoundOfIntegerInterval>
        <snt:Integer><snt:decimal>96</snt:decimal></snt:Integer>
       </snt:upperBoundOfIntegerInterval>
      </snt:FiniteIntegerInterval>
     </rdfs:domain>
     </rdfs:range rdf:resource="&snt;Real"/>
     <snt:hasLinearizedSymbolTableTerms>
      <snt:SymbolVector>
       <snt:hasTerms rdf:parseType="Collection"/>
        <snt:Real><snt:decimal>2.4</snt:decimal></snt:Real>
        <snt:Real><snt:decimal>2.3</snt:decimal></snt:Real>
          ...
       </snt:hasTerms>
      </snt:SymbolVector>
     </snt:hasLinearizedSymbolTableTerms>
    </snt:SymbolTable>
    <dist:InverseCompoundScale>
     <owl:inverseOf>
      <ppqs:CompoundScale>
       <snt:compoundPropertyCompoundDomainComponents>
        <snt:PropertyVector>
         <snt:hasTerms rdf:parseType="Collection">
          <ppqs:Scale rdf:about="&myScales;kilowatt"/>
         </snt:hasTerms>
        </snt:PropertyVector>
       </snt:compoundPropertyCompoundDomainComponents>
      </ppqs:CompoundScale>
     </owl:InverseOf>
    </dist:InverseCompoundScale>
   </snt:hasTerms>
  </dist:PhysicalDistributionDescriptionVector>
 </dist:factorsInto>
</dist:PhysicalDistribution>

<rdf:RDF>
```

Fig. 2. XML-serialization for a temperature distribution

The prefixes of the tag names refer to namespaces in which the ontology is defined. For example the prefix “dist” refers to a file called http://www.scadaonweb.com/ publications/ontologies/distributionAndDescription.owl containing a part of the ontology that is relevant for distributions.

The table is defined explicitly in the XML document starting with the tag <snt:SymbolTable>. Alternatively if the table were much larger, a reference could be made to a table that is defined in a binary file, as shown in Fig. 3.

```
<snt:SymbolTable
  rdf:resource="http://www.company.eu/myFile.hdf5#myDataSet"/>
```

Fig. 3. Reference of data kept within an HDF5 file

In following chapters a basic understanding of the ontology referenced in the serialization of Fig. 2 is given. The main focus is the ontology of physical quantities, units and data quality.

3 Ontology

The ontology [6] underlying the example given in Fig. 2 serves as reference data dictionary for the SCADA web data type and is based on existing standards such as ISO 10303 (Industrial automation systems and integration - Product data representation and exchange) and ISO 15926 (Lifecycle data for process plant, including oil and gas production). It is defined in XML and is based on RDF, OWL (Web Ontology Language) [7] and MathML [8].

XML is unequalled as an exchange format on the Web but by itself, it doesn't provide what is needed for building the semantic web. Compared to RDF one of XML's drawbacks is that there are a lot of possible serializations for a statement. E.g. the statement "Otto Maier is the author of the web-site http://www.ottomaier.com" can be serialized as:

1. <Author>
    <uri> http://www.ottomaier.com</uri>
    <name>Otto Maier</name>
</Author>

2. <Document uri="http://www.ottomaier.com"
    <Author>Otto Maier</Author>
</Document>

3. <Document uri=http://www.ottomaier.com Author="Otto Maier"/>

For a human being all these serializations mean the same but an application interprets them differently because a parser generates different XML-trees. RDF in contrast has exactly one serialization matching a statement. Therefore RDF in combination with OWL that is layered on top of RDF is used to define an ontology for web-based SCADA applications.

The basic ontology can be referenced by specific ontologies, e.g. an ontology for an application in the field of condition based maintenance. This is shown in Fig. 4, Fig. 5, Fig. 6 and Fig. 7.

The basic ontology defines three principal types of physical objects: Product, Product life segment and Product at instant.

Product describes the complete lifetime of a physical object, e.g. the generator with the serial number 98/1234 is a product. Hence the class "Generator" is a specialization or subclass of "Product" (Fig. 4).

```
<rdfs:Class rdf:ID="Generator">
  <rdfs:subClassOf rdf:resource="&po;Product"/>
  <rdfs:comment>
    A product for producing electrical energy.
  </rdfs:comment>
</rdfs:Class>
```

Fig. 4. Definition of the class "Generator" as a subclass of "Product"

Product life segment describes a segment and an activity, respectively, in the life of a product. For example, the trip of the generator between 2002-02-28 T10:00:00 and 2002-02-28 T10:00:01 is a product life segment. Hence the class "GeneratorTrip" is a specialization or subclass of "ProductLifeSegment" (Fig. 5).

```
<rdfs:Class rdf:ID="GeneratorTrip">
  <rdfs:subClassOf rdf:resource="&po;ProductLifeSegment"/>
  <rdfs:comment>
    An activity that is a transition from a generating state to a non-generating state.
  </rdfs:comment>
</rdfs:Class>
```

Fig. 5. Definition of the class "GeneratorTrip" as a subclass of "ProductLifeSegment"

Product at instant describes an instant and state, respectively, in the lifetime of a product. The generation state of the generator at 2002-02-28 T10:00:00 is a product at instant. Therefore the class 'Generating' is a specialization or subclass of "ProductAtInstant" (Fig. 6).

```
<rdfs:Class rdf:ID="Generating">
  <rdfs:subClassOf rdf:resource="&po;ProductAtInstant"/>
  <rdfs:comment>A state that causes a flow of energy into an electrical network.</rdfs:comment>
</rdfs:Class>
```

Fig. 6. Definition of the class "Generating" as subclass of "Product at instant"

All classes are a specialization of these principal concepts and can be defined as their subclasses. According to these three principal physical objects, the following principal properties are defined: lifeSegmentOfProduct (assignment of a product life segment to a product), instantOfProduct (assignment of a state to a product), instanceOfLifeSegment (assignment of a state to a product life segment).

The example given in Fig. 4 is extended by defining that an activity of type 'GeneratorTrip' is only performed by a product of type "Generator". This is accomplished by formulating a restriction on the property "lifeSegmentOfProduct" (Fig. 7).

```
<rdfs:Class rdf:ID="GeneratorTrip">
  <rdfs:subClassOf rdf:resource="&po;ProductLifeSegment"/>
  <rdfs:subClassOf>
    <owl:Restriction>
      <owl:onProperty rdf:resource="&po;#lifeSegmentOfProduct"/>
      <owl:toClass rdf:resource="#Generator"/>
    </owl:Restriction>
  </rdfs:subClassOf>
  <rdfs:comment>
    An activity that is a transition from a generating state to a non-generating state.
  </rdfs:comment>
</rdfs:Class>
```

Fig. 7. Definition of a property restriction for the class "GeneratorTrip"

Except for the above described basic ontology for SCADA data and application specific SCADA ontologies, an ontology for physical quantity spaces and units is provided and can be referenced from XML files containing the data, e.g. "Power" and "kilowatt" as shown in Fig. 2. The definitions necessary for this ontology are described in the following paragraphs.

4 Physical Quantities and Properties

The value (e.g. 10 kg) of a physical quantity (e.g. mass) is a property of a physical object (e.g. transformer), that can be observed or measured. Additionally to the value (e.g. 10) the corresponding unit has to be given (e.g. kilogram). The RDF graph (Fig. 8) shows the definition of a physical quantity value and corresponds to the RDF serialization given in Fig. 9. An approach derived from MathML (rather than the approach used in XML Schema) has been used to specify the numeric value, because many physical properties are identified by complicated numeric values such as vectors or matrices.

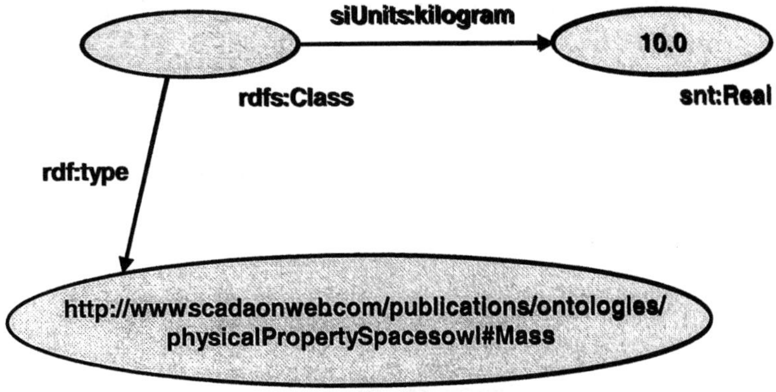

Fig. 8. Definition of a physical quantity value (graph)

```
<rdf:RDF
 ... (Definition of namespaces)>
  <rdfs:Class>
   <rdf:type rdf:resource="&pqs;Mass"/>
   <siUnits:kilogram>
     <snt:Real>
       <snt:decimal>10.0</snt:decimal>
     </snt:Real>
   </siUnits:kilogram>
  </rdfs:Class>
</rdf:RDF>
```

Fig. 9. Definition of a physical quantity value (serialization)

A scale for a physical quantity space is a property of the physical quantity space. The resulting RDF-graph shown in Fig. 10 corresponds to the RDF serialization given in Fig. 11.

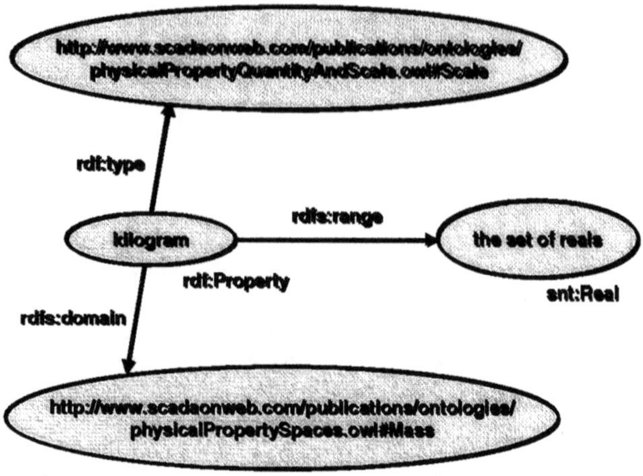

Fig. 10. Definition of a scale for a physical quantity space (graph)

```
<rdf:RDF
 ... (Definition of namespaces)>
  <rdf:Property rdf:ID="kilogram">
    <rdf:type rdf:resource="&ppqs;Scale"/>
    <rdfs:comment>kilogram scale defined by ISO 1000:1992</rdfs:comment>
    <rdfs:domain rdf:resource="&pqs;#Mass"/>
    <rdfs:range rdf:resource="&snt;Real"/>
  </rdf:Property>
</rdf:RDF>
```

Fig. 11. Definition of a scale for a physical quantity space (serialization)

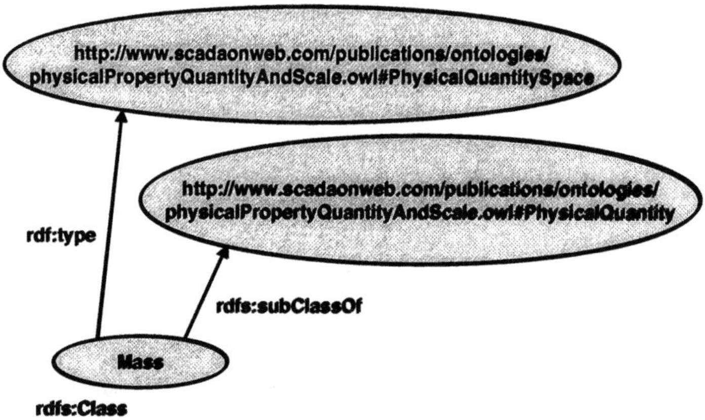

Fig. 12. Definition of a physical quantity space (graph)

A physical quantity space is a class containing all physical quantity values. E.g. "mass" is a physical quantity space and "10 kg" belongs to this class. The RDF graph in Fig. 12 defines a physical quantity space and corresponds to the RDF-serialization in Fig. 13.

```
<rdf:RDF
  ... (Definition of namespaces)>
  <rdfs:Class rdf:ID="Mass">
    <rdf:type rdf:resource="&ppqs;PhysicalQuantitySpace"/>
    <rdfs:subClassOf rdf:resource="&ppqs;PhysicalQuantity"/>
    <rdfs:comment>mass</rdfs:comment>
  </rdfs:Class>
</rdf:RDF>
```

Fig. 13. Definition of a physical quantity space (serialization)

Under the general term "possession of a physical property" the relationship between a physical object and a physical quantity is considered. A physical object is member of the class physical quantity space. E.g. the physical object "transformer at 10:30 h on 15.03.2002" is member of the class "10 kg". Fig. 14 shows an RDF-graph for a simple relationship for the physical property "massWhenEmpty". The corresponding RDF-serialization is given in Fig. 15.

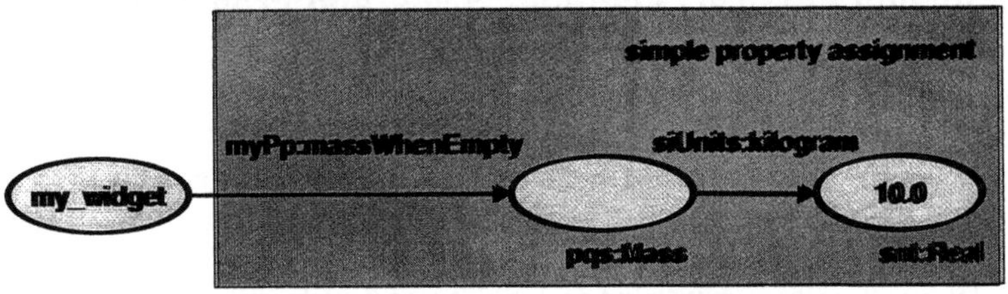

Fig. 14. Definition of a physical property (graph)

```
<rdf:RDF
  ... (Definition of namespaces)>
  <myPo:Widget rdf:ID="my_widget">
    <myPp:massWhenEmpty>
      <pqs:Mass>
        <siUnits:kilogram>
          <snt:Real>
            <snt:decimal>10.0</snt:decimal>
          <snt:Real>
        </siUnits:kilogram>
      </pqs:Mass>
    </myPp:massWhenEmpty>
  </myPo:Widget>
</rdf:RDF>
```

Fig. 15. Definition of a physical property (serialization)

5 Derived Physical Quantities, Scales, and Properties

Additionally to fundamental physical quantity spaces (e.g. mass, time, length), base units (e.g. kg, s, m) and simple physical properties (e.g. mass when empty), derived physical quantity spaces (e.g. velocity, acceleration, force) and their corresponding units (e.g. m/s, m/s^2, $kg{\cdot}m/s^2$) have been defined within the ScadaOnWeb ontology. Fig. 16 shows an example for a derived physical quantity.

```
<rdf:RDF
 ... (Definition of namespaces)>
  <ppqs:PhysicalQuantitySpace rdf:ID="Force">
   <rdf:type rdf:resource="#DerivedPhysicalQuantitySpace"/>
   <rdfs:label xml:lang="en">force</rdfs:label>
   <pqs:hasPhysicalDimension rdf:parseType="Literal">
    <mathml:apply>
     <mathml:times/>
     <ppqs:PhysicalQuantitySpace rdf:about="#Mass"/>>
     <ppqs:PhysicalQuantitySpace rdf:about="#Acceleration"/>
    </mathml:apply>
   </pqs:hasPhysicalDimension>
  </rdfs:Class>
</rdf:RDF>
```

Fig. 16. Definition of a derived physical quantity space (serialization)

6 Compound Physical Quantities, Scale, and Properties

A compound physical quantity value is a vector of two or more physical quantities (e.g. [2002-05-07 10:30 UTC, 20 degrees Kelvin]). Analogous to that, a compound physical quantity space and scale, respectively, can be defined by a vector of two or more physical quantity spaces (e.g. (instant in time, temperature)) and scales (e.g. [UTC, Kelvin]), respectively.

The identification of a compound physical quantity value is done with respect to a compound scale by a vector of numeric or text values (e.g. [(2002, 5, 7,10, 30), 20]). The serializations given in Fig. 17 and Fig. 18 show the definition of the compound physical quantity “InstantInTimeAndTemperature“ and the compound scale “utcAndKelvin“.

```
<rdf:RDF
 ... (Definition of namespaces)>
  <ppqs:PhysicalQuantityVectorSpace
     rdf:ID="InstantInTimeAndTemperature">
   <rdfs:label xml:lang="en">instant in time and temperature</rdfs:label>
   <snt:cartesianProductOf>
    <ppqs:PhysicalQuantitySpaceVector>
     <snt:hasTerms rdf:parseType="Collection">
     <ppqs:PhysicalQuantitySpace rdf:about="&time;#Time"/>
     <ppqs:PhysicalQuantitySpace rdf:about="&pqs;#Temperature"/>
     </snt:hasTerms>
    </ppqs:PhysicalQuantitySpaceVector>
   </snt:cartesianProductOf>
  </ppqs:PhysicalQuantityVectorSpace>
</rdf:RDF>
```

Fig. 17. Definition of a compound physical quantity

A compound physical property has a single physical object as its domain, and evaluates to give a compound physical quantity. As shown in Fig. 19 it can be defined by a vector of two or more physical properties (e.g. (time of instant, measured temperature)).

```
<rdf:RDF
 ... (Definition of namespaces)>
 <ppqs:CompoundScale rdf:ID="utcAndKelvin">
  <ppqs:unitSymbol>UTC, K</ppqs:unitSymbol>
  <rdfs:label xml:lang="en">UTC and Kelvin</rdfs:label>
  <rdfs:domain rdf:resource="#InstantInTimeAndTemperature"/>
  <rdfs:range>
   <snt:SymbolVectorSpace>
    <snt:cartesianProductOf>
     <snt:SymbolVector>
      <snt:hasTerms rdf:parseType="Collection">
       <snt:SymbolVector rdf:about="&time;#UtcRepresentation"/>
       <snt:MathsSpace rdf:about="&snt;Real"/>
      </snt:hasTerms>
     </snt:SymbolVector>
    </snt:cartesianProductOf>
   </snt:SymbolVectorSpace>
  </rdfs:range>
  <snt:compoundPropertyCompoundDomainComponents">
   <snt:PropertyVector>
    <snt:hasTerms rdf:parseType="Collection">
     <ppqs:Scale rdf:about="&time;utc"/>
     <ppqs:Scale rdf:about="&siUnits;kelvin"/>
    </snt:hasTerms>
   </snt:PropertyVector>
  </snt:compoundPropertyCompoundDomainComponents>
 </ppqs:CompoundScale>
</rdf:RDF>
```

Fig. 18. Definition of a compound scale

```
<rdf:RDF
 ... (Definition of namespaces)>
 <snt:CompoundPropertySingleDomain rdf:ID="timeOfInstantAndMeasuredTemp">
  <rdfs:label xml:lang="en">time of instant and measured temperature</rdfs:label>
  <rdfs:domain rdf:resource="&po;#ProductAtInstant"/>
  <rdfs:range rdf:resource="InstantInTimeAndTemperature"/>
   <snt:compoundPropertySingleDomainComponents>
    <snt:PropertyVector>
     <snt:hasTerms rdf:parseType="Collection"/>
      <rdf:Property rdf:about="&time;timeOfProductAtInstant"/>
      <rdf:Property rdf:about=&myProperties;measuredTemperature"/>
     </snt:hasTerms>
    </snt:PropertyVector>
   </snt:compoundPropertySingleDomainComponents>
 </snt:CompondPropertySingleDomain>
</rdf:RDF>
```

Fig. 19. Definition of a compound physical property

7 Data Quality

Except for the measured data value and the time of measurement the quality of the measured data is of relevance and must be considered in an ontology for the engineering domain. The ScadaOnWeb approach for defining quality is based on the common data attribute type "Quality" of IEC 61850-7-3 (Communication Networks and Systems in Substations, Part 7-3: Basic communication structure for substations and feeder equipment - Common data classes) which contains information on the validity, the detail quality (e.g. overflow, old data, etc.) and the source giving information related to the origin of a value. An XML/RDF file has been created for data quality and is part of the ScadaOnWeb ontology. It can therefore be referenced from within the definition of compound properties (e.g.: [time of instant, measured temperature, quality]).

8 Conclusion

Because of the lack of W3C standards for units, the Web has been little used for engineering data up to now. With the ontology for engineering data defined within the ScadaOnWeb project, containing the definitions for physical quantities and scales described above, an ontology for the engineering domain is finally available. These definitions, comprising a standardized XML Schema for physical quantities, units, data quality and co-ordinate systems, will be input to standardization bodies such as W3C and ISO. They form a basis for the handling of engineering data on the Web which applications in the engineering domain can reference. The ScadaOnWeb platform provides a generic solution to the efficient handling of SCADA data which can be used within applications, and which can replace proprietary systems. Five software applications of the ScadaOnWeb project use this generic platform in order to validate the technology. With the provision of a ScadaOnWeb plug-in it is expected to handle structured numeric data using web browsers in a simple way as it is possible for other standardized formats. Consequently, the use of the internet and intranet for SCADA applications is likely to become widespread.

9 Outlook

Basing itself on XML and Semantic Web technologies, ScadaOnWeb can be rightly said to be the first major project to apply Semantic Web technologies to the domain of engineering data opening thereby the way for a vast range of new non-proprietary applications. Already, the range of application domains covered by the ScadaOnWeb demonstrators is quite impressive:

- meteorology: disaster prediction
- supply of electrical power:
  - planning of power consumption
  - metering electrical power consumption
  - metering and control of small generators
  - maintenance of electrical supply networks
- electrical and process industries: maintenance of electrical machines and devices

But ScadaOnWeb technology is by no means limited to the range of application domains covered by the demonstrators: It has the potential to access and control in a many client, many server environment any device that supplies or receives data for which a standardized dictionary is available or can be made available. Therefore, future applications of ScadaOnWeb technology may be found in application domains as remote to each other as emission detection, disaster prediction, distributed power generation, supervision of off-shore installations and applications fed by non proprietary sources of stock market data.

Further in the future, a natural extension of the ScadaOnWeb technology will be to enrich it with rule-bases and build web services on top of it. Thus, ScadaOnWeb technology will be made available to and usable by agent software on the web. This work will be an important step towards realizing the vision of "Intelligent Web Services" build upon the "Semantic Web": In this context, rule-bases can play an important role as they can act as a means to draw inferences, to express constraints, to react to events/changes, etc. allowing applications to make deductions from the data supporting thereby the process of decision making.

Acknowledgement. This research project is sponsored by the European Community in the Information Society Technologies (IST) program and BBW (Bundesamt für Bildung und Wissenschaft, Bern, Switzerland).

References

[1] http://www.scadaonweb.com
[2] Bacher, R., Leal, D., Schröder, A.: "ScadaOnWeb – Modelling and Web-Exchange of Process and Engineering Information", International Semantic Web Conference, Cagliari, Italy, (2002)
[3] http://www.w3.org/XML/
[4] http://www.w3.org/RDF/
[5] http://hdf.ncsa.uiuc.edu/HDF5/
[6] Leal, D., Schröder, A.: "RDF reference data library format. Available online at: http://www.scadaonweb.com/publications/NOTE-RDL/NOTE-RDL.html
[7] http://www.w3.org/TR/owl-features/
[8] http://www.w3.org/Math/

ODESeW. Automatic Generation of Knowledge Portals for Intranets and Extranets

Oscar Corcho, Asunción Gómez-Pérez, Angel López-Cima, V. López-García, and María del Carmen Suárez-Figueroa

Laboratorio de Inteligencia Artificial
Facultad de Informática
Universidad Politécnica de Madrid
Campus de Montegancedo sn.
Boadilla del Monte, 28660. Madrid, Spain
{ocorcho,asun}@fi.upm.es
{alopez,vlopez,mcsuarez}@delicias.dia.fi.upm.es

Abstract. This paper presents ODESeW (Semantic Web Portal based on WebODE platform [1]) as an ontology-based application that automatically generates and manages a knowledge portal for Intranets and Extranets. ODESeW is designed on the top of WebODE ontology engineering platform. This paper shows the service architecture that allows configuring the visualization of ontology-based information for different kinds of users, establishing reading and updating access policies to its content, and performing consistency checking between the portal information and the ontologies underlying it.

1 Introduction

The terms *knowledge portal*, *semantic portal* and *community web portal* can be found in the literature ([6][10]) to indistinctly refer to knowledge-based web sites that allow corporate access to information and applications. A good definition of what they are can be found in [6], where they are defined as web applications that "*provide the means to select, classify and access, in a semantically meaningful and ubiquitous way, various information resources (e.g., sites, documents, data) for diverse target audiences (corporate, inter-enterprise, e-marketplace, etc.).*" From now on, we will use the term "knowledge portal" to refer to this kind of applications.

Knowledge portals present structured views of the web according to what it is usually called a knowledge catalogue [6]. A knowledge catalogue holds descriptions about the resources available to the community members, and is more flexible and complex than conventional (relational or object) databases. Ontologies are commonly used for this task of structuring knowledge, since they represent shared knowledge within a community.

The process of content provision in knowledge portals is usually performed collaboratively, normally with few resources (manpower, money) [10]. This supposes a great effort to maintain the Web portal and to integrate the information it contains (even if it is using ontologies to structure it). Besides, content presentation is always a

D. Fensel et al. (Eds.): ISWC 2003, LNCS 2870, pp. 802–817, 2003.

hard task, especially in knowledge-intensive web sites where content is continuously updated. To ameliorate the hard task of knowledge portal management, we need applications that automate these difficult knowledge workflow processes (content provision and integration, content presentation, and content access), as well as frameworks that support them.

Furthermore, in this knowledge intensive portals we distinguish between ontology developers and content (knowledge asset) providers versus Intranet and Extranet users. Ontology developers are in charged of developing the ontologies, which will be used by the content providers as a primary piece of knowledge for describing knowledge assets and by the end users as an index used to browse the knowledge portal. Regarding the end users, we distinguish between Intranet and Extranet users. Intranet users, which are also content providers, access content inserted by themselves or by others members. Different Intranet users have different permissions either for inserting content on the knowledge portal or for browsing the collected assets. Finally, extranet users, who scarcely include new content, but mainly access the allowed content by the knowledge portal administrator. Therefore, knowledge portals must be created having in mind that they have to act both as Intranets (private networks contained within an enterprise, whose main purpose is to share company information and computing resources among employees) and as Extranets (defined as collaborative extensions of an Intranet, which expands access to individuals outside the company) [1].

In this paper, we present ODESeW, an ontology-based application built inside the WebODE ontology engineering workbench, that allows managing knowledge-intensive ontology-based Intranets and Extranets, providing the following functions:

- *Knowledge modelling,* by means of an ontology development platform that integrates several ontology development services. As the knowledge portal will be used on the web, is highly recommend to use an ontology server (and not a stand-alone ontology editor) that allows to build cooperatively the ontologies as well as to access the ontologies through the web. The use of an ontology server as a basic infrastructure over which the knowledge portal is built will ease the management in a sync way of the assets with respect to the ontology changes. From a software perspective, the knowledge portal will benefit from the present and further services provided by the ontology server.
- *Content editing/provision* by means of ontology instances editing. ODESeW allows inserting, updating and removing class instances, their attributes and relation instances, in multiple interlinked ontologies and with different editing permissions for the portal users. As part of the instance editing functions, ODESeW can be also used as a document management tool, which allows handling electronic documents.
- *Content presentation/visualization* by means of highly-configurable user-defined visualizations of ontology classes, relations and instances, and with different browsing permissions for the portal users. The ontology is used for indexing the knowledge assets and for browsing them accordingly. The ontology provides structure on this content that helps the user find knowledge assets. The content stored in the portal can be accessed dynamically with menus automatically generated from ontologies according to the user's permission, visualizing

[1] Both definitions are obtained from http://www.scotsmist.co.uk/glossary_e.html

differently the different types of information stored in the knowledge assets; an example is the shallow natural language generation functions for Extranet users. The knowledge portal also provides annotated markup of its assets in RDF(S), DAML+OIL and OWL.

- *Content search and querying* functions, based on a hybrid approach based on ontologies and keywords. The content search and querying modules use the WebODE API for accessing and querying the contents of the ontologies.
- Easy web site *administration* services, which allow managing the knowledge portal users, editing and visualization permissions, and several other portal management needs. Such services are only accessed by the users belonging to the knowledge portal administration group.

As an important advantage of ODESeW over other similar Knowledge portals (we must cite the ontoweb portal) is the automatic synchronization between the contents of the portal and the ontologies in which it is based. So, if an ontology is modified with the WebODE ontology editor, the changes will be automatically seen in the knowledge portal either for ontology conceptualization itself or for its instances.

The paper is structured as follows: section 2 presents the software architecture of ODESeW, paying special attention to its integration with the WebODE ontology engineering workbench. Section 3 describes the most relevant functions of ODESeW, grouped in content editing, content presentation, content search and querying, and portal administration. Section 4 shows a case study of the use of ODESeW in a real application: the Intranet and Extranet of the European funded project Esperonto. In section 5, we describe some related work, and we conclude and present further work in sections 6.

2 ODESeW Architecture

ODESeW has been built in the framework of WebODE, a scalable ontology engineering workbench that gives support to the ontology building methodology METHONTOLOGY [5].

As shown in figure 1, the ODESeW portal is one of the two main front-end applications of the WebODE workbench. The other one is the WebODE ontology editor, which integrates all the ontology editing and management functions of the platform.

WebODE is platform-independent, since it is completely implemented in Java. To allow scalability and easy extensibility, it is supported by an application server, so that services can be easily created and integrated in the workbench by means of a management console. One important advantage of using this application server is that it allows deciding which users or user groups may access each of the services of the workbench.

The figure also shows the most relevant services currently available in the WebODE workbench. The core of the WebODE's ontology development services are: the cache, consistency and axiom services, and the ontology access service (ODE API), which defines an API for accessing WebODE ontologies. One of the main advantages of this architecture is that these services can be accessed remotely from any other application or any other instance of the WebODE workbench.

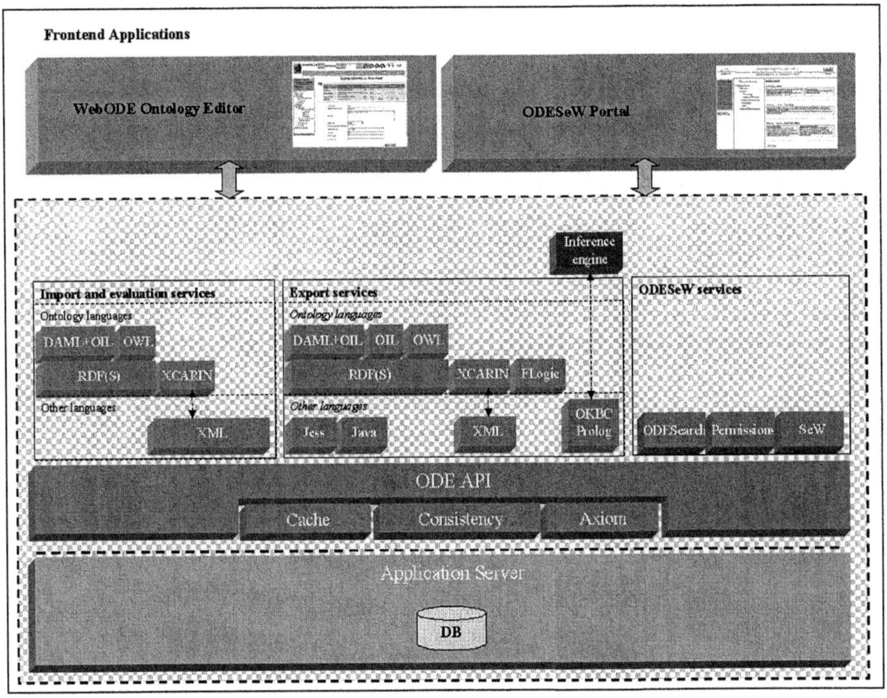

Fig. 1. WebODE ontology engineering workbench architecture.

Furthermore, ontologies are stored in a relational database, so they can manage huge ontologies quite efficiently. And it is also easily extensible, so that the database manager can be changed, or any backend system can be plugged in the bottom of the architecture. Finally, WebODE also provides backup management functions for the ontologies stored in the server.

The figure shows that the import, export and evaluation services are running on top of the ontology access service. These services import ontologies from XML, XCARIN, RDF(S)[3][7], DAML+OIL [11], and OWL [4]; and export ontologies to XML, FLogic, XCARIN, RDF(S), OIL, DAML+OIL, and OWL. Ontologies are also exported to languages that are not specifically created for defining ontologies, such as Prolog, Jess, and Java. For instance, the Prolog export service is used as a basis of the WebODE's inference engine. WebODE also evaluates ontologies written in RDF(S), DAML+OIL, and OWL.

Once described the main characteristics of the WebODE workbench, we will proceed to describe the services used by the ODESeW application. To implement ODESeW, we have built three more services on top of the ODE API, as shown in the right of the figure: *ODESearch*, *permission* and *SeW*.

- *ODESearch* allows querying the WebODE ontologies, by means of keywords or using the attributes of the ontology concepts as templates, as will be explained in section 3.3.
- The *permission* service is in charge of managing security in the access to the concepts, instances and attributes of the ontologies. It will manage both read and write access permissions to the content stored.

- *SeW* gives support to the administration functions of the ODESeW application. It allows selecting which ontologies will be published in the portal, which types of users can access it (administrators, guest users, etc.), how instances in the ontology will be visualized in the portal, etc. These functions are described in section 3.4.

There are many advantages of having built ODESeW on top of the WebODE workbench. First of all, ODESeW can use any of the WebODE workbench services. For example, with the ontology import services we can import other ontologies in the workbench, and these new ontologies can be easily selected for publication in the ODESeW portal. Consequently, we can create a complete new knowledge portal (including its Intranet and its Extranet) in a very short period of time.

Another advantage is that we can edit any of the ontologies published with ODESeW using the WebODE ontology editor, and observe at run-time the modifications in the knowledge portal, which means that there is auto-synching of the portal with respect to the ontology.

3 ODESeW Functions

ODESeW generates automatically knowledge portals for Intranets and Extranets, both of which use the same assets and knowledge. The knowledge portal provides different functions in each case:

- If the knowledge portal is being used as an Intranet, corporate users will be able to insert and update content in the portal as content providers, browse the content that they have inserted or that other corporate members have inserted there, and perform searches and queries on that content. The ontologies issues either for indexing knowledge asset or for searching them more efficiently.
- If the knowledge portal is being used as an Extranet, external users will usually be able to edit very restricted parts of the content stored in the portal, and browse, query and search only the content identified as public content by the content providers.

Apart from these content provision, visualization, and access functions, ODESeW provides management services that allow configuring them.

In this section, we will present the main functionalities of ODESeW, grouped in the four categories of: content editing/provision, content presentation/visualization, content querying and search, and administration services.

Another interesting function in a knowledge portal is the possibility to modify the published ontologies. ODESeW does not give support to this function, since for this task the WebODE ontology editor can be used. All the changes done to ontologies with the WebODE ontology editor are viewed in run-time execution in ODESeW, with no need to restart the web server.

3.1 Content Editing/Provision

In an ontology-based knowledge portal, the provision of content mainly consists of editing concept instances, that is, inserting, updating and removing instances of

ontology concepts. ODESeW gives support to this task by allowing users to edit concept instances and the values of their attributes, and to connect such instances by means of relations, even if they belong to different ontologies. The ontology conceptualization editing is delegating to the WebODE application.
This content provision task in ODESeW is mainly performed by Intranet users, although ODESeW does not restrict it to Extranet users (the administrator of the knowledge portal may decide whether to give Extranet users editing permissions to specific parts of the ontologies published in the portal).
ODESeW gives support to the following content provision functions:

- *Instance creation and removal.* Users can create instances of any concept in any of the ontologies published in ODESeW, provided that the users have enough permissions to create such instances. The same occurs with the removal of concept instances.
- *Instance editing.* To edit instances, users are presented with the attributes of the concept from which the instance is instance of, as well as the attributes inherited through the concept taxonomy (multiple inheritance is allowed in ODESeW). Figure 2 shows the instance editing form for the instance *Angel López-Cima* of the concept *PhD Student.* The user can insert one or several values of any of these attributes, provided that their maximum cardinality and value type constraints are respected. All these constraints are checked by the WebODE platform.

  Depending on the attribute types, ODESeW gives different fields to insert and update their values. For instance, if the value type of an attribute is *Date*, ODESeW will present a calendar from where the user can select a specific date. In figure 2, the attribute *Date Of Birth* has a link to a calendar next to the Add Value button.

  If the value type is URL, the user can either insert directly a URL or upload a file (an image, a PDF document, etc.) that is converted to a URL inside the knowledge portal. In the example of figure 2, we could insert the URL *http://delicias.dia.fi.upm.es/~alopez* as a value of the attribute *Homepage*, and we have inserted an image file as a value for the attribute *Photo*.
- *Relation instance editing.* The bottom of the instance editing form shows the relations that can be applied to the instance being edited. In figure 2, we can see that a *PhD Student* can *belong to* an *Organization* and could be the *contact Person* of an *Organization.* These relations appear in the form because their domain is the concept *Person*, which is a superclass of *PhD Student.*

  If a user decides to create any of these relation instances, (s)he will be shown a list of candidate instances from the same or from other ontologies that are instances of the concept that is the range of the relation. For instance, if we selected the relation *belong to* in figure 2, we would be shown a list of instances of the concept *Organization* or any of its subclasses. WebODE also checks the integrity constraints of these relations.

3.2 Content Presentation/Visualization

Content visualization in an ontology-based knowledge portal mainly consists of showing the ontology concepts and their related instances, presenting the details of

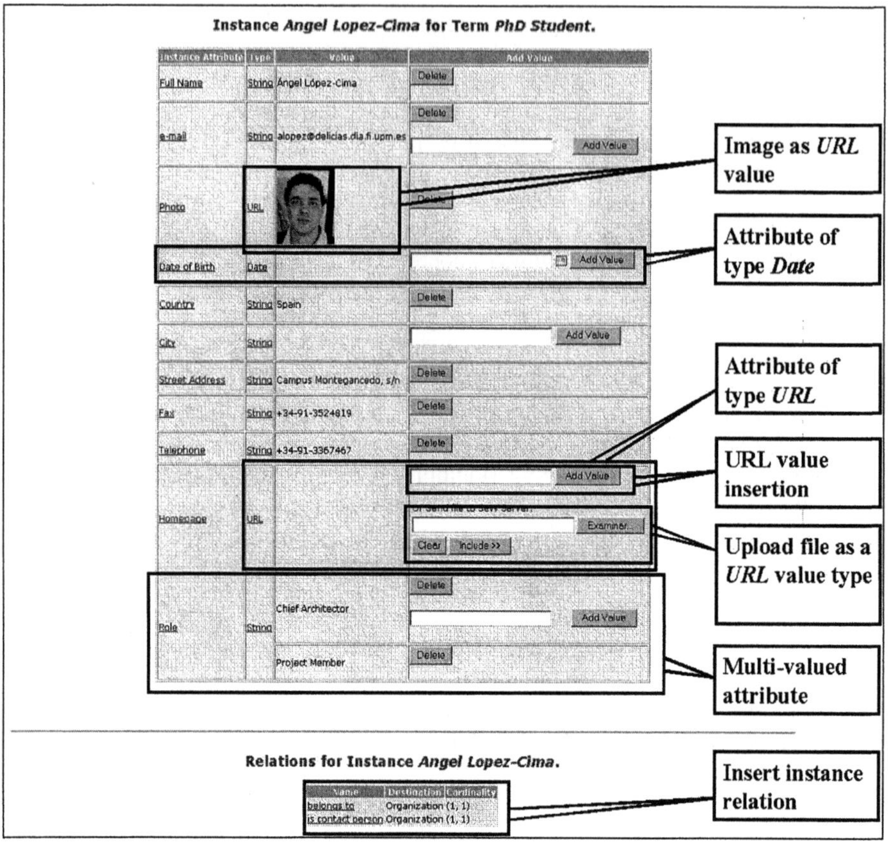

Fig. 2. Editing form for the instance *Angel López-Cima* of the concept *Phd Student* in an ontology about *persons*.

ontology instances and their relations with other instances, and allowing the navigation through these relations and between the different ontologies published in the portal. Although not related to the human-consumption, content visualization also consists of producing the annotated markup of all the knowledge stored in the portal.

It is important to mention again that the content is the same for Extranet and Intranet users, but ODESeW visualize differently depending on the two types of users.

On the one hand, if ODESeW is being used as an Extranet, that is, the user has not logged in the portal (from now on, we will refer to non-logged users as guest users), the portal "hides" all the knowledge representation terminology (words such as 'ontology', 'concept', 'instance', etc). So, external users do not need to know that the knowledge portal is internally based on ontologies. In fact, they do not need to know the terminology used in the knowledge representation field to use the portal. To present the content in a mode user-friendly way, ODESeW includes a shallow natural language generation functions.

On the other hand, if ODESeW is being used as an Intranet, that is, the user has logged in the portal, the portal shows all the information that the user has access to,

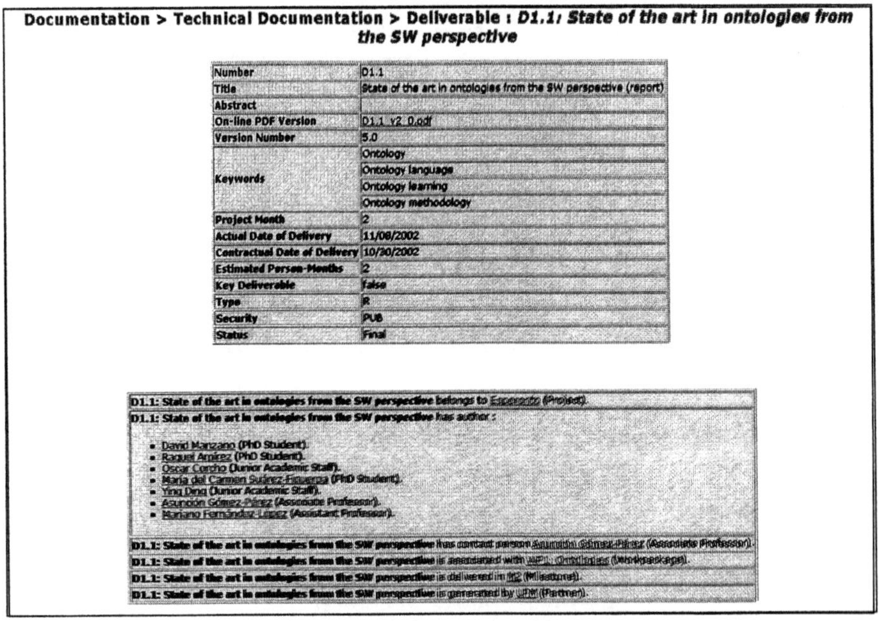

Fig. 3. Instance detail for the Extranet.

without hiding the knowledge representation terminology nor using natural language generation functions. Since different users may have different access and write permissions for the content in the portal, we can consider that there are as many different views of the information as type of users of the Intranet.

Figures 3 and 4 show different visualizations of the same instance (a deliverable in the European project Esperonto) at the Extranet and the Intranet, respectively. In figure 4, the Intranet user can see and access to the information of the attribute *On-line version*, but a guest user can not see the attribute as shows in figure 3 because this is a private attribute.

Apart from the previous functions, ODESeW has the following content provision features:

- *Automatically generated menus* to access the ontologies published in the portal.
- *Automatic generation of concept taxonomies from ontologies* to browse each of the published ontologies according to the permissions defined for each user. For Extranet users, apart from taking into account read permissions, the concept taxonomy will not show concepts that have not instances avoiding to the users access to a concept without any information (instances).
- *Instance lists visualization.* The instances of a concept (direct instances) and all its subconcepts (indirect instances) are shown by selecting the concept in the previous concept taxonomies. Each of the listed instances may have a description based on one or more of its attributes (as described in section 3.4). The portal only shows accessible instances according to the user read permissions. Figure 5 shows an example of an instance list where the instances of the concept Organization are described by their full name and their logo.

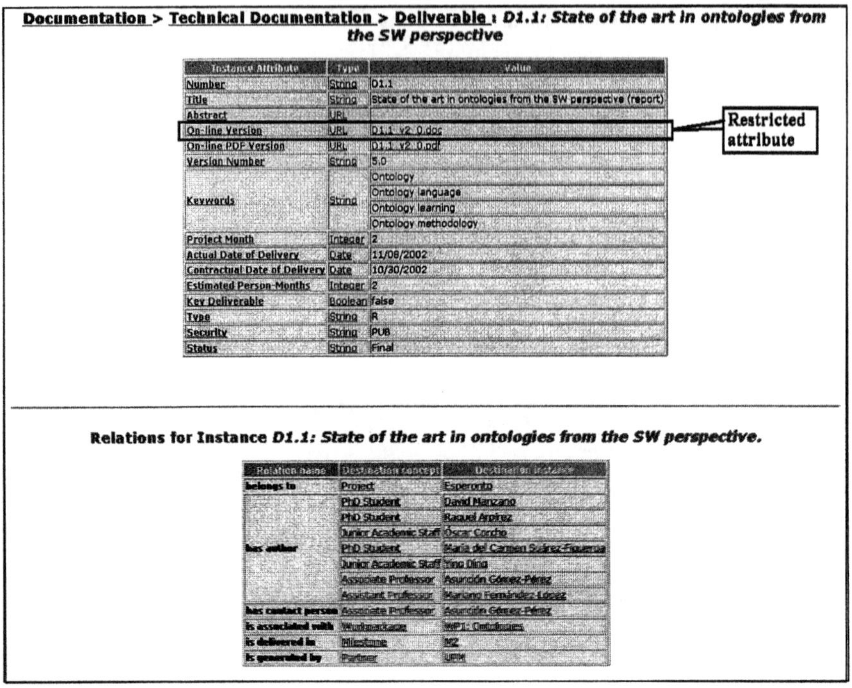

Fig. 4. Instance view for Intranets.

- *Instance details visualization.* When visualizing an instance, users can see the attributes and relation instances for which they have read permissions. The visualization of each attribute is different depending on its value type (String, Date, URL, etc.). For instance, in figure 3 and 4, the URLs appear as links and the rest of attribute values appear as text boxes. URL attributes that contain an image file are visualized as images, as was shown in the editing form of figure 2. Besides, the portal administrator can set the order in which the attributes of instances will be visualized, as we explain in section 3.4. By default, attributes are presented in alphabetical order.
- *Annotated ontology markup.* All the content visualized by the ODESeW is automatically generated as RDF code, and can refer to ontologies implemented in RDFS, DAML+OIL and OWL. To obtain this annotated markup, ODESeW uses the WebODE export services to these languages.

3.3 Content Search and Querying

In a data-intensive web-site, it is usually very difficult to find a specific piece of information, even in the case that content inside the portal is well structured. This problem is even more important in the case of the Extranet, since guest users do not need to have a clear idea of how the portal is structured.

For this reason, ODESeW includes a search engine that allows querying for information in one ontology or in all the ontologies of the portal. The search engine allows two kinds of search:

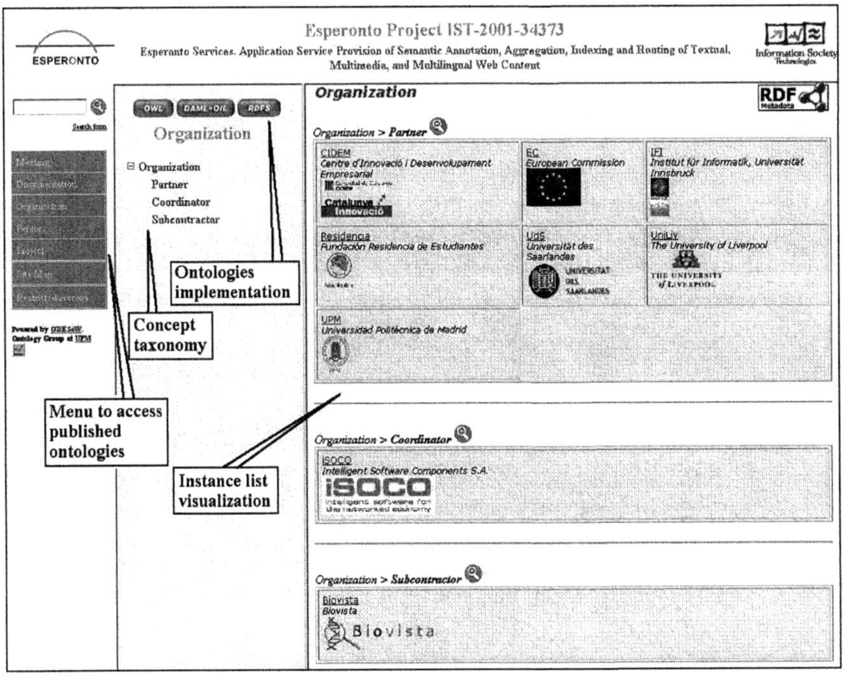

Fig. 5. Instance list visualization.

- *Keyword-based.* As in other conventional search tools, the search engine looks for instances or concept names that contain the keywords specified in the query.
- *Ontology-based.* ODESEW provides advanced search functions by means of a query form. The fields to be filled in at the query form are attributes and relations taken from the ontology. Once the user introduces the values (s)he is looking for, the search engines returns those instances that satisfy the conditions imposed in the attributes values specified in the form.

Though these are the most useful search and query facilities from the point of view of human-consumption, we must take into account that ODESeW also generates annotations in RDF for the content that it visualizes. This would allow other sites or agents to read the annotations and use that content in other environments.

3.4 Web Site Administration Functions

ODESeW provides a set of management tools that can only be accessed by the administrator user. This tool suite gives support to the basic management functions needed to maintain the knowledge portal, namely user management, permission management (security), ontology publication management, attribute ordering and instance list descriptions.

- *User management.* With this function, the knowledge portal administrator can insert, remove or modify the users of the Intranet.

- *Permission management.* With this function, the knowledge portal administrator can manage the read and write permissions for each user, including the guest users (that is, the Extranet users).
  Read permissions can be defined on an instance basis, which means that the administrator can decide whether a user can visualize an instance or some attributes of the instance. They can be also defined on a concept basis, which means that the administrator can decide whether a user can visualize a concept (and its instances) or some attributes of the concept. By default, any user can visualize all the concepts, instances, and attributes stored in the portal.
  Write permissions are defined on a concept basis, which means that the administrator can decide whether a user can insert, modify or remove an instance of a specific concept. By default, only the administrator can insert concept instances.
- *Ontology management.* With this function, the administrator decides which ontologies are published in the knowledge portal. Any WebODE ontology can be added or removed from the portal.
- *Attribute ordering.* With this function, the administrator can set, for each concept, the order in which the attributes of all its instances will be visualized. Once the administrator has set the order of the attributes of a concept, (s)he can impose this order to the subclasses of the concept.
- *Instance description.* With this function, the administrator can define the set of attributes to be used to describe instances of a concept in the instance list visualization, together with the order in which these attributes will appear. As in the previous case, the description and the order can be imposed to the subclasses of the concept. Figure 6 shows a screenshot of this function while setting the description of the instances of the concept *Documentation*, where we have selected the *Title* and the *instance description.*

4 Esperonto Web Site. A Case Study of the Application of ODESeW

Esperonto [2] (IST-2001-34373) is a European project funded by the European Commission. The aim of this project is to bridge the gap between the current World Wide Web and the Semantic Web by providing a service to "upgrade" existing Web content to Semantic Web content.

The project Web site[2] has been developed as a knowledge portal, powered by ODESeW, with a twofold function: first, to serve as an Intranet for the compilation of all the knowledge generated in the project, and second, to serve as an Extranet for the dissemination of the results of the project.

Five ontologies have been developed in WebODE for this portal: *project*, *documentation*, *person*, *organization*, and *meeting*. They describe respectively R&D projects and their structure, documents that are generated in a project, people and organizations participating in it, and meetings (administrative, technical, etc.) held during a project lifecycle. Figure 7 shows the relationships between all these

[2] http://www.esperonto.net

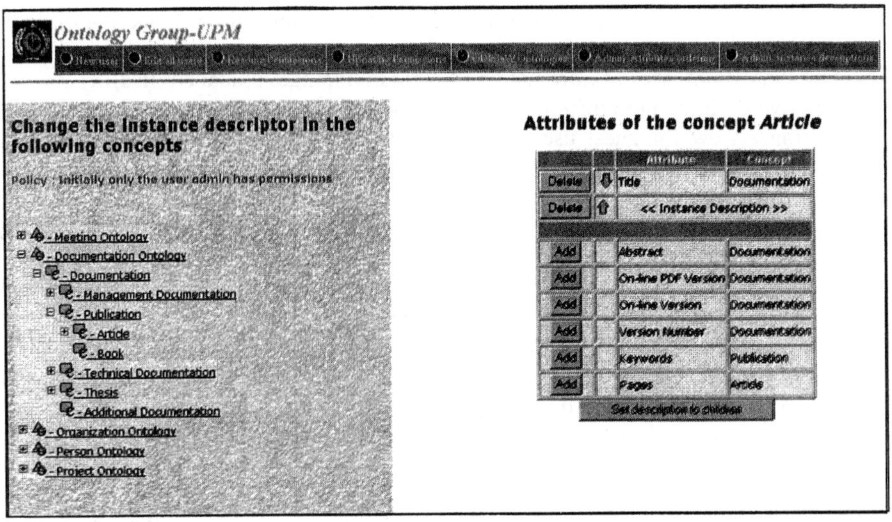

Fig. 6. **Selection of the attributes that will describe an instance in the instance list visualization.**

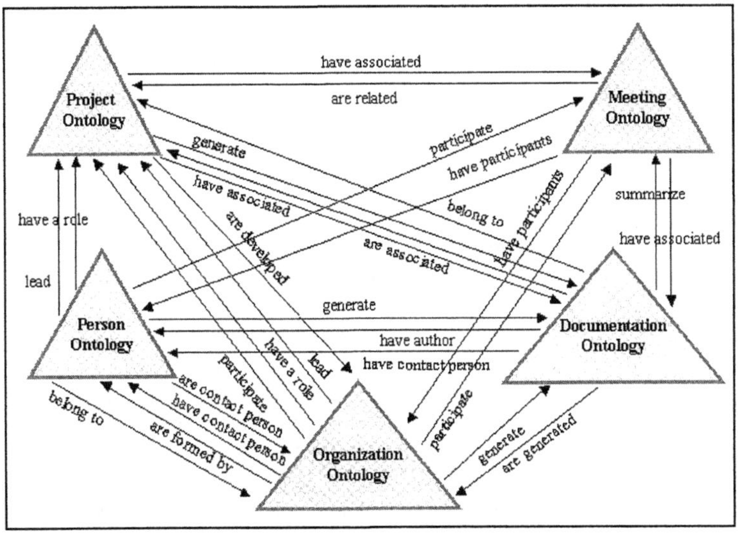

Fig. 7. Relations between the Esperonto knowledge portal ontologies.

ontologies (a project has associated meetings, a document belongs to a project, a document summarizes a meeting, people participate in a meeting and have a role in a project, etc.). These ontologies can be reused to describe any R&D project.

These ontologies were defined during the first months of the project life, and were used in the portal. Since then, they have experienced some modifications (adding and removing concepts, adding and removing attributes, etc.). Thanks to the strong interaction of ODESeW with WebODE, these modifications have not caused any consistency problems in the content stored in the portal.

As of July 2003, the Esperonto knowledge portal contains these 5 ontologies, with around 100 concepts, 200 attributes, 100 relations, 300 instances, which have resulted in more than 100Mbytes of information (this figure includes uploaded files).

We have defined three different visualizations of the Esperonto knowledge portal: the Extranet view for guest users, the Intranet view for the project partners, and a special view in the Intranet for the project officer. For each of these views, we have defined different levels of permissions in the portal. For instance, the guest user cannot insert instances in the portal, cannot access the restricted and private deliverables, can only access the PDF versions of public deliverables, etc.; the Intranet users have full read and write permissions for all the concepts, instances and attributes in the five ontologies; and the project officer view contains automatically generated reports of the project progress.

One of the advantages of using ODESeW on top of the WebODE ontology access service (ODE API) is that it is easy to access to the information in the portal programmatically, and that predefined queries can be easily constructed if needed. In the Esperonto portal home page, which is the only one that is usually modified manually by the portal administrator, we have defined several predefined queries, so as to generate automatically reports of public deliverables (which is the information most commonly looked for by the Extranet users, and even by the Intranet users), summarize the status of deliverables in the project, etc.

Finally, the Extranet of the Esperonto portal has undergone several usability tests by a third party company, which have allowed to improve most of its visualization functions.

5 Related Work

In this section we present related work in knowledge portals and languages that could be used to generate portals. We will focus on the similarities and differences with our approach.

A similar knowledge portal is the **OntoWeb portal**[3] [9], which is used as a dissemination tool of the European thematic network OntoWeb. Knowledge in this portal is structured according to one ontology, which contains information about organizations, persons, documentation, events, etc. There are two ways of inserting content in this portal: by means of forms and by syndicating content annotated in external web resources. In contrast with ODESeW, the OntoWeb portal provides a workflow for publishing information, it is supervised by a privileged user (a reviewer), and provides a syndicator system. However, it works only with one ontology, all the users have the same view on the content stored in the portal and there are not such advanced permission management functions.

The **OntoWebber** [12] is a tool to build portal based on ontology and it was used to build the Semantic Web Community Portal as part of the OntoAgents project [4]. This tool take the sources from ontologies in RDF or UML/XMI, or data based on HTML using corresponding data translator for these two last types of sources. In addition of the ontology domain of the portal, OntoWebber has other ontologies that's

[3] http;//www.ontoweb.org

[4] http://www-db.stanford.edu/Ontoagents/

defines the portal site: maintenance (rules for content maintenance), personalization (personalize content according the needs of users), presentation (look-and-feel of the Web pages), content (rendering Web pages with the ontology information) and navigation (links between Web pages) schemas. All these ontologies with a query engine generate a portal with statically or dynamically information. This tool can generate a portal fitting with the web developer necessity with all site-view ontologies and powered by a rule engine, but all information is centralized in the local server in contrast with ODESeW in which all functionality can be access remotely by web.

The **OntoRoadMap** portal[5] has been also developed in the context of OntoWeb. It includes six ontologies that describe ontology tools, languages, methodologies, applications, events and business scenarios. These ontologies were developed with WebODE and translated to a relational database schema, so that the portal was built on top of them. The main difference with respect to ODESeW is that the portal and the ontologies are not synchronized, in the sense that modifications in the ontologies cannot be seen at run-time in the portal.

KAON portal[6] is a tool that allows building ontology-based portals, based on the SEAL framework (SEmantic portAL) [8]. Once the ontologies and the visualization models for them have been built, KAON portal generates the ontology-based portal using HTML pages. In contrast with ODESeW, the KAON portal has a syndicator to acquire information from several sources. However, its main disadvantage is that whenever information is updated from the sources or the ontology is modified, the modifications are not seen in the generated portal at run-time, but it has to be regenerated again.

There are also two languages that deserve special attention, since they could be used for the generation and visualization of knowledge portals, apart from other kinds of portals: RSS and XTM.

RSS[7], also known as RDF Site Summary, Really Simple Syndication or Rich Site Summary, is a RDF-based language for describing news or other Web content that is available for distribution or syndication from a web site. Several tools based on RSS are available, which are mainly aimed at dynamically generating and syndicating news in a web site.

XML Topic Maps[8] (XTM) is an XML-based language that provides a model and grammar to represent the structure of information resources used to define topics and the associations between topics. The topic map paradigm was fully formalized as an ISO International Standard, ISO/IEC 13250:2000. Like with RSS, there are several tools for web visualization of topics and portals based on topics.

6 Conclusions

In this paper we have presented ODESeW, an ontology-based application built on top of the WebODE ontology engineering workbench that creates automatically knowledge portals that can be used as Intranets and Extranets.

---

[5] http://babage.dia.fi.upm.es/ontoweb/wp1/OntoRoadMap/index.html
[6] http://kaon.semanticweb.org/
[7] http://web.resource.org/rss/1.0/
[8] http://www.topicmaps.org/xtm/1.0/

ODESeW provides functions for content provision, content visualization, and content search and querying. It also provides an easy-to-use tool suite for the administration of the generated knowledge portals.

Due to its integration in WebODE, we have seen that any modification in the ontologies published in the knowledge portal can be seen at run-time in it, in contrast with other knowledge portal generation tools, and that any set of ontologies implemented in RDF(S), DAML+OIL, and OWL, among others, can be easily included in ODESeW to generate instantly a new knowledge portal. Besides, ODESeW allows establishing read and write permissions for all the content stored in it. Finally, it provides different visualizations for Intranet and Extranet users, so that Extranet users do not have the feeling that they are using a knowledge portal, but a conventional one.

We have also presented how we are using ODESeW as the Intranet and Extranet of the European project Esperonto.

Some of the aspects of our future work in ODESeW will be focused on (a) including better natural language generation for the instance detailed descriptions in the Extranet; (b) adding more editing functions for content provision, such as transferring instances from one concept to another; (c) providing configuration management and evolution support for the content stored in the portal; (d) and improving the current news system by integrating it with ontological information and with RSS technology.

Acknowledgements. This work has been supported by the Esperonto project (IST-2001-34373), by two research grants from UPM ("Becas asociadas a proyectos modalidad B") and by a research grant from MEC (AP-2002-3828).

References

1. Arpírez JC, Corcho O, Fernández-López M, Gómez-Pérez A (2001) WebODE: a scalable ontological engineering workbench. In: Gil Y, Musen M, Shavlik J (eds) First International Conference on Knowledge Capture (KCAP'01). Victoria, Canada. ACM Press (1–58113–380–4), New York, pp 6–13
2. Benjamins, VR., Contreras, J., Corcho, O., Gómez-Pérez. A. (2002). *Six Challenges for the Semantic Web.* In KR2002 Semantic Web Workshop. April 2002.
3. Brickley D, Guha RV (2003) *RDF Vocabulary Description Language 1.0: RDF Schema.* W3C Working Draft. http://www.w3.org/TR/PR-rdf-schema
4. Dean M, Schreiber G (2003). *OWL Web Ontology Language Reference.* W3C Working Draft. http://www.w3.org/TR/owl-ref/
5. Fernández-López M, Gómez-Pérez A, Juristo N (1997) *METHONTOLOGY: From Ontological Art Towards Ontological Engineering.* AAAI Symposium on Ontological Engineering (Stanford, 1997).
6. Karvounarakis G, Christophides V, Plexousakis D, Alexaki S (2000) Querying community web portals. Technical report, Institute of Computer Science, FORTH, Heraklion, Greece. See http://www.ics.forth.gr/proj/isst/RDF/RQL/rql.pdf
7. Lassila O, Swick R (1999) *Resource Description Framework (RDF) Model and Syntax Specification.* W3C Recommendation. http://www.w3.org/TR/REC-rdf-syntax/

8. Maedche, S. Staab, R. Studer, Y. Sure, and R. Volz. (2002) SEAL – Tying up information integration and web site management by ontologies. IEEE-CS Data Engineering Bulletin, Special Issue on Organizing and Discovering the Semantic Web, March 2002.
9. Spyns P, Oberle D, Volz R, Zheng J, Jarrar M, Sure Y, Studer R, Meersman R (2003). *Ontoweb – a Semantic Web Community Portal.* Fourth International Conference on Practical Aspects of Knowledge Management (PAKM), 2–3 December, 2002, Vienna, Austria, pp. 189–200, Publishing Year: 2002
10. Staab S, Angele J (2000) AI for the Web – Ontology-based Community Web Portals. 17th National Conference on Artificial Intelligence and 12th Innovative Applications of Artificial Intelligence Conference (AAAI 2000/IAAI 2000), Menlo Park/CA, Cambridge/MA, AAAI Press/MIT Press.
11. van Harmelen F, Patel-Schneider PF, Horrocks I (2001). *Annotated DAML+OIL* (March 2001) Markup Language. Technical Report. http://www.daml.org/2001/03/daml+oil-walkthru.html
12. Yuhui Jin, Stefan Decker, Gio Wiederhold. OntoWebber: *Model-Driven Ontology-Based Web Site Management.* The 1st International Semantic Web Working Symposium (SWWS'01), Stanford University, Stanford, CA, July 29–Aug 1, 2001.

Making Business Sense of the Semantic Web

Zavisa Bjelogrlic[1], Dirk-Willem van Gulik[2], and Alberto Reggiori[1]

[1] @Semantics. S.R.L., via Teulada 71, I00195 Rome, Italy
[2] Leiden office
{z,dirkx,albe}@asemantics.com
http://www.asemantics.com

Abstract. The Semantic Web and RDF offer a powerful platform for a wide range of applications. However, at this time, the semantic business is still in an embryonic stage. This paper analyses real-life applications: (i) A system in operation used to improve the presentation of corporate data, (ii) a prototype of a news clipping service and (iii) a feasibility analysis of a distributed, public administration database. Common to these applications is a "web database" model where resources are "URI-ed" - made available on the Web - and "RDF-ed" - described by one or multiple authorities. Descriptions are processed by RDFStore and made available to applications. The success factors of these three applications are analysed, and an application model is drawn up with requirements and desirable features for RDF Engines. In conclusion, we look at how and where the Semantic Web business can grow.

1 Introduction

The killer apps of the millenium web so far have been search engines, the deadliest of them all being Google, which tells you, as you search, what is most important to everybody. How it tells you that comes from a tiny bit of markup spread through the whole of the web, the link. The Semantic Web takes that idea a lot further: RDF provides a thread of meaning through the web, a golden thread of individualised meaning, making the web *your* web. Google is doing good business by telling us whats important to everybody. And in this paper, we show how good business can be done by telling you whats important to *you*.

The Semantic Web and its core technology RDF [1,2,3,4,5] offer a powerful platform for a wide range of applications. By "semantifying", the Web can be made searchable and browsable by computers and humans alike. This is the starting point for applications which are better and faster in presenting information to the user and which build new services by cross-correlating completely different data sources.

Talking about *the* Semantic Web can be misleading. The technology can be used for a wide variety of data resources in corporate intranets or even in standalone applications. Resources identified by a URI [22] ("URI-ed") and described in RDF ("RDF-ed"), can be searched and navigated through by following relations using so-called RDF engines. RDF engines have rapidly become an interesting alternative for a variety of database/data mining applications, knowledge

D. Fensel et al. (Eds.): ISWC 2003, LNCS 2870, pp. 818–833, 2003.

```
RDFBusiness = does_application_add_value &&
      willing_to_invest(date) &&
      better_than_classic_approach &&
      does_it_work( URIfy-ing, RDFy-ing, gathering_and_ingesting,
             indexing, searching_and_browsing, application_processing);
```

Fig. 1. Evaluation of success factors in the Semantic Web business.

management and documentation management systems, and other "classic" applications. The flexibility of RDF, its ability to gradually describe the resources and to keep different descriptions of the same resource is key to this. This makes the approach feasible for a range of different applications, some of which were up to now too fluid or simply lacking the regularity needed to fit into existing relational database models. To paraphrase Tim Berners-Lee[1], we had a situation where *anyone could say anything about anything without breaking the whole system.*

We characterise this idea as the Web Database approach. Of course, this is a marketing simplification and an attempt to define in as few words as possible the business use of the Semantic Web. Different attempts to integrate the Web and the database world are described in literature [6,7,8]. Our model can be described in five steps:

1. Resources are URIed and published on the Web.
2. Resources are annotated and described using RDF. Original resources are left untouched and can be protected or even partially hidden on their sites;
3. RDF descriptors are collected and processed by RDF engines;
4. Applications use a query language to search and navigate through RDF descriptors and perform additional processing over query results.
5. If needed and authorized, applications use the URI to access the "visible" part of the original resource.

At this time, the "semantic business" is still in an embryonic stage. Inhibitors for RDF to become the mainstream technology range from business to technical reasons. In this paper we will start with these inhibitors and analyse in chapter 2 those factors that are key to overcoming them. This is illustrated using three real-life RDF applications described in chapter 3. The analysis draws up a draft of an Application Model (chapter 4). More than a strictly technical model, it is a list of requirements and nice-to have features from a customer/business development point of view. Finally in chapter 5, we identify how and where the Semantic Web business can grow.

2 Success Factors

A simple evaluation of the success factors in the Semantic Web business is made in Figure 1 with a program statement (assuming left-to-right evaluation).

`does_application_add_value`: This is the first question. In the current situation, it is not so easy to make revenues out of data and services published on the Web. Why would somebody invest to semantify the Web? Does it really bring added value? Will an improved, semantic, Web be easier to sell? Semantifying can ease aggregation of data and, as an end result, reduce barriers between providers. Is this really wanted by the information providers? In the case of corporate use, does the semantic approach offer advantages which will pay off the investment made?

`willing_to_invest`: Supposing the first factor is True, and we have something valuable to offer, is somebody willing to invest in new technology? This may be a temporal factor: after years of the Internet boom, over-expectations and high figures in technology spending, we are not in the best situation today. Investment depends on the customer (or VC) policy on which we have little if any direct influence. There is one important point: is this investment in semantic technology something which will continue to yield results over the next years, or can it also produce just short term results? A technical characteristic of RDF is key here: RDF allows for almost complete separation of RDF descriptions from applications as URIs are used to reference the data. This implies that once RDFed the resources can be used years and years in one or in many, evolving applications, even if those applications do not have ready access to the data.

`better_than_classic_approach`: as for everything else in software, *"there are many ways to do it"* [9]. Why choose a new technology where only few adepts are experts and everybody else must learn new things? There are many academic answers, but it is not easy to find justifications for lack of programming skills and existing, mature tools, especially when you have on the other side XML technology and well-established RDBMS with JSP or ASP GUIs. We believe the right question here is not if Semantic is better but WHEN it is better.

`does_it_work`: at the end of the day, from a marketing point of view, the question is if all this stuff will work when put into real, day-to-day operation. What about the complexity of extracting metadata and defining them in RDF? Performance questions? What happens when data change daily or even faster? What happens in reality when data is distributed among networks of sites managed by different people? How appropriate is RDQL [13] for building more complex applications? How does it compare with SQL? Again, this is not a technical question but more a problem as to how fast an SQL programmer will be able to write applications in RDQL or in some other RDF query language.

3 Business Cases

Three cases are described in this paper. These are currently at different stages, ranging from a system in operation to a feasibility study.

3.1 Image Showcase

Image Showcase is a project developed for the European Space Agency ESA, ESRIN Frascati, `http://www.esa.int/`. The Agency publishes examples of satellite images acquired by different sensors of the ENVISAT satellite, the ERS-2 satellite and other satellites. These images are used as examples to explain and promote the use of earth observation techniques. The audience is the general public including youngsters and researchers not specialized in the use of remote sensing data. Images are annotated with text - which explains the background, the applications and provides some basic technical details about the images used. The image is normally published in several versions - a small thumbnail, a medium size quick-look suitable for slow downloading and a full size scientific quick-look of several megabytes in size. The main image is often augmented by as additional pictures that show annotated details of the larger images.

Cases are prepared by hand by different groups of experts following simple guidelines and using simple form templates. New case studies are added daily but, once published, they do not change. The total number of studies ranges between 500 and 1000 and grows each year. The studies are referenced or announced at different Agency portals and use different technical solutions. It is interesting to note that requests coming through Google from people searching for text contained in stories are among the *highest accesses to portals* .

The main objective of the project was to simplify and unify access to the Image Showcases for general public, in the “6-66 years range”. ESAs Image Showcase is a free service open to everybody. The objective was to avoid all complex interfaces, remote sensing jargon, various specialist map interfaces, java applets and browser plug-ins and simplify the interface to the extreme to make it compatible with all browsers. The example given to follow was Google: one field to fill out and immediate fast, relevant, results on the next click.

Approach. The approach adopted starts from parsing of the original, handwritten data, and creating RDF descriptions. One RDF “sister” file is created for every case. Part of the attributes are extracted automatically from available catalogue systems [10]. The vocabularies adopted for RDF are relatively simple.

1. each original showcase image is assigned the URL of the top level page. And each of the HTML pages and images which together make up the showcase are described with simple RDF properties;
2. each RDF description is made relative to the source HTML base i.e. ENVISAT or ERS-2 catalog;
3. simple Dublin Core (DC) [23] properties are used for the title, date, description (the story);
4. extended DC Terms (DCT) [23] properties are used to express the relationships between HTML pages, images and different versions of the images including thumbnails (appropriate for result lists) created on-the-fly during ingestion;
5. the space coverage, that is latitude and longitude, and the bounding rectangle of the image are described using DCT Box (from the extended Dublin Core Terms) and some ad-hoc OpenGIS Consortiums GML [11] vocabulary is used for the four-corner polygons;
6. RDF Schema [24] seeAlso property is used to link up different RDF descriptions about different HTML pages and images;

7. each image description is augmented with simple ad-hoc properties about its media content type, size and geometry, including presence of small thumbnails.

The conversion process is run regularly through a `make` command on every resource site to parse only recently changed files. Additional RDF descriptors are used to manually configure relations to other, non-semantic, Web resources. For example, so called "guide pages" for the satellites and sensors were defined in a separate RDF file parsed at query time. This was done as a first step to extending the Semantic Web to other data sources not included directly in the project. RDF descriptors are collected regularly from all sites where resources reside. This is done by a simple RDF gathering mechanism. After gathering, all descriptors are ingested in RDFStore [12].

Perl DBI is used to query all descriptors using RDQL language [13]. Queries are simple, corresponding to the extremely simple presentation required: (i) all showcases for a given collection sorted by date, (ii) free-text search over stories, (iii) limitation of the geographic region of search, (iv) path navigation for all images related to a case.

Different Web interfaces have been built over this query to provide a simple "Google" like interface with GEO specific details details.

Conclusion. Table 1 summarizes this case study. The system is well accepted but its full impact has not yet been evaluated. The semantic solution is seen as just another search engine, perhaps more flexible. This is also due to the fact that basically only*one type of data*, even if lost in different collections, is handled. An interesting extension will be to semantify other related data and to cross-correlate this with the semantic presentation of the showcases. We expect at this point to reach the critical mass and show how, with minimal effort, more complex applications can be built over the initial description of data. See `http://demo.asemantics.com/biz/isc/` for a demonstation.

3.2 LMN – Last Minute News

A variety of news clipping services are in operation today. These range from speciallist services such as Moreover to generic systems like Google News and others. A short overview of similar systems with references to more detailed information can be found in [15].

LMN is a prototype system of a real-time news clipping service. LMN was intended mainly as a technology demonstrator and as a mock-up for testing the dynamic aspects of RDF ingestion and indexing. The objective was to offer narrow search functions for fresh daily news, trying to reduce false-positives by considering additional information about sources and by offering to the user the ability to flavour the source express his/her rating of sources.

Approach. The news sources are harvested at regular intervals and parsed to create RSS1.0 compliant RDF descriptions of the contents available. Parsing is

Table 1. Factors Key Metrics for this Case Study

Type of Application	Web site management Unified access to sparse data. Portal service with free, unlimited access.
`does_application_add_value`:	Yes, it improves the access to data already published by different groups.
`willing_to_invest`:	Yes. In an evaluation phase to test if the new solution, already made public, improves the presentation of data, and the acceptance of data by the general public.
`better_than_classic_approach`:	Yes. No appropriate alternative solution found.
`does_it_work`:	
– URIfy-ing	Resources already published on the Web.
– RDFy-ing	Persing of manually-written text. Some 5 percent of erroneous parsing corrected by rewriting the originals.
– Gathering and ingesting	A hierarchical mother-index approach is used for guide gathering
– Indexing	RDFStore
– Searching and Browsing	RDQL free-text is combined with other parameters and spatial position. Navigation through all images.
– Application processing	Sorting. GUI and map handling (by a WMS compliant server [13])
Business Model	Software development and system integrations.

done on different sources, which, not surprisingly, show similar structure. Parsing extracts description, date, date of acquisition, author (when available), title and all images related to the article. In some cases, news articles offer a see-also section with related articles.

It is interesting to note that these see-also resources either belong to the same group or are very far and thus do not pose a competition threat to the provider in either case. This is an interesting indication of an inherent submission of Semantic Web to the data when used to aggregate data coming from different sources.

The whole parsing process is currently configured manually, typically by first defining a filter configuration and then cloning it for other sources. Parsing difficulties were encountered only for see-also links which use different patterns. Also, the headlines and front-page section of the origin Web site are more prone to manual editorial intervention - making it more error-prone to automatically harvesting.

Other attributes, such as section, type of source and flavour of the sources (e.g. serious newspaper vs gossip source, right/left or liberal/conservative or Republican/Democratic ratings) were defined at parser configuration time and assigned to a group/section of news.

The classification-flavouring of news-sources is subjective and depends on the orientation of the reader. To manage such diversity, the LMN user is allowed to define *his own flavouring of sources* which will override default settings. This is collected in a separate RDF description of sources that is parsed on-the-fly at search time and used to flavour the search results to rank the results according to the users preferences. Although this is just an experiment which does not show significant advantages to the user when only 10-15 sources are clipped, it might become of particular interest for analysis and intelligence work where not only information itself counts but also the *kind* of source and its *reliability* - trustworthiness is important.

Once parsed from the news sources, RDF data are ingested using RDFStore. That part of the data relating to user preferences is left undigested and used when flavoured search is invoked (i.e. parsed on-the fly). A simple RDF gathering protocol is used in this case as the RDF creation is done, after harvesting, in a single pass. The whole mechanism is managed by a series of make commands executed regularly.

Three interesting aspects were touched during ingestion and indexing:

1. A hot-swappable pool of RDFStore indexes was used to optimize updating of data without interrupting or slowing down the search and retrieval functions;
2. Depending on the provider site, news articles may disappear from the site after a short period, while others remain archived for a long time and can be retrieved later. This may lead to a *404 not-available* error badly perceived by the user of a aggregating service and to the erroneous ordering of hits. A simple solution was adopted here by defining the expiration time attribute for every section or group of resources. Following our baseline to try to keep things simple and efficient, we used a historic time-to-live acronym – TTL – for this attribute. This was an application level hack that uses RDF structure to define the TTL. Further work goes probably in favour of thinking about a more system-level solution: a TTL attribute on a triplet which might then be used for optimization of the RDF engine.
3. A special case is the RDF definition of user preferences and flavours of sources. This is implemented as RDF parsed on the fly at the query time and used for a single query. Being a preference only, these are small files not creating particular performance problems but again raising interesting questions about the usage of TTL on these flavoring triplets.

The query functions offered are (i) Free-text query on words contained in the description or title. (ii) Navigate (show) all pictures referenced by an article (or all pictures related to a group of hits, e.g. all images related to SARS). (iii) Navigate through see-also sources referenced by an article (iv) Flavour the search, i.e. consider the users classification of sources in ranking the hits.

Table 2. Factors / Key Metrics of Case Study II

Type of application	Unified access to external sources not participating in the initiative. News clipping service.
`does_application_add_value`:	Not clear yet. Demonstrator just open. As objective, added value should be in narrow search, and in user Flavoured search
`willing_to_invest`:	Not clear yet. Positive first comments.
`better_than_classic_approach`:	Not clear to the customer.
`does_it_work`:	
– URIfy-ing	Resources already Web published
– RDFy-ing	Parsing of HTML published data in a limited domain.
– Gathering and ingesting	A spider runs at regular intervals, parsing and keeping a local buffer of RDF data.
– Indexing	RDFStore
– Searching and Browsing	RDQL free-text combined with news/news-sources attributes. Navigation through graph for All images related to this/all news found and see-also articles.
– Application processing	Sorting/ranking, also taking user preferences into consideration (Flavored search). Presentation of results.
Business Model	Aggregator service or system development

The query is packed in one simple user interface and can operate both as a pull service and as a push service.

Conclusion. Table 2 summarizes this case study. Though we received positive first comments we also perceive reluctance to invest in new Internet services, even if such services seem to offer some added value as the difference is not immediate visible. Free-text search indexes + directory structure show similar results. Two aspects are positively considered: (i) application flexibility (another specialised service could easily be cloned) and (ii) user preferences and customization of the service. Also, and though easier then expected initially the latter requires more work for see-also data and headlines/front pages

It is difficult to draw conclusions for an application just open and still in finalisation and improvement phase. We believe the demonstrator can explain well the advantages of the Semantic Web and the ability to build different applications over RDF-described data. Such is also the case when operating on data belonging to different, non-participating, providers. `http://demo.asemantics.com/biz/lmn/`

3.3 Unemployment Records Database

Internet information systems aimed at supporting and streamlining employment procedures and ease the match of job requests with available offering were developed recently in Italy [16,17]. These systems cover the formal aspects related to the employment law in Italy and serve as exchange vehicles between employers and employment agencies/companies on one side and local administration on other side. The system also covers special rules fostering the employment of disabled people and are used to rank the candidates according to rules defined by local authorities for work offerings related to public services and administrations.

Todays systems started as stand-alone database applications, evolving through distributed database applications based on simple batch exchange of data and are evolving today to Internet services where a single, centralized service is used by various local authorities. Years of database development has led to a well-established data model and a good understanding of procedures. However the established model is commonly found lacking when:

1. Rules about employment and ranking algorithms change frequently and need to be tailored or modified by local authorities. This makes difficult to maintain a central service that offers up-to-date yet regional customized service to different local authorities.
2. Unemployment profile, skills, education and work experience descriptions vary from year to year according to the evolution of technology and society. The standard classification is a precise and rich thesaurus but always lags behind significantly, e.g. computer technology experience was only added recently.
3. Inadequacy or just slow evolution of the thesauri leads to use of free text to describe the employee his profile and, consequently, to the need for a free-text search. This is similar to a problem of semi-structured databases [7].
4. Operations are highly distributed among local offices. This requires either a central service or an efficient distributed database model.
5. Once ingested in the RDMBS, data is in practice lost and cannot be restructured. Technical solutions allow exchanging data saved in the RDBMS with other players and applications, tracking of changes and reconstruction of the change history but, in practice, this is costly and difficult to manage in case of multiple instances with changing data structure. Data are visible on the Web through forms and report pages but there we have the problem of opaqueness of the URI and data cannot easily be searched using this view.

These points were challenges for thinking about an upgrade of the solution based on Semantic Web technologies. Today, this is a feasibility analysis only.

Proposed Approach. Current data exist as SQL databases. The first step is to make this data Web-available. A nave approach [18] is proposed for this: SQL data are described as RDF equivalents of unemployment records. This can be done on-the-fly by any Web-SQL gateway. A natural primary key exists in the procedure the unique fiscal code assigned to every legal entity in Italy that can be used as URI. Published data need to be protected by authorization/authentication and proper encryption rules that guarantee full privacy of data. Publishing can also be *selective* and limited to part of the record for use by other systems (e.g. regional or central authority), keeping the rest for internal use (local authority).

Doing this only to allow cross-searches is not worth the effort and will probably be done better by a database solution or by ad-hoc applications. A point we think important is that records published are also available to other applications. Any other public administration system can access, if needed and authorised, the data published in RDF. For future use, existing SQL infrastructure can be upgraded with an intermediate

RDF (XML) step between the GUI and the SQL back-end. This will also allow to simplify the maintenance of the GUI for changes of procedures or customisation to local needs a costly process today.

In our view, RDF descriptors are published by a local office that is authoritative for a given geographic or domain area. These offices maintain the records and register all updates. The expandability of RDF allows defining of *basic data* by one authority, giving at the same time a *large flexibility to other authorities* to add additional attributes for the record involved. The schema proposed is:

1. Fiscal code used as URI to identify the unemployed person and his record;
2. A basic description is created with all formal data (full name, address/es, birth date and place, etc.). This is a short and fully standardized structure (no significant changes are expected here long term);
3. Basic data are extended by family structure records which contains all information about family status and similar information which can be used for ranking or subsidy calculation;
4. Education history and employment history is described by a sequence of related descriptors.

Descriptors are collected regularly by local instances of the RDFStore engines at the local office. Descriptors can also be collected by a regional centre to region-wide consultation services. The time-to-live attribute of the resource cannot be defined a priori the record changes when the unemployed person changes his status. There is however an expiration time - time for which the administration shall keep records or time for which subsidy is allowed. The gatherer must be able to detect updated or changed records to avoid full ingestion of data which might become, in this case, too heavy. The number of records foreseen for Rome and its suburbs, considering historic records saved, is on the order of 1m. Gathering is configured using a two-level mother-index for the domain (regional unemployment offices) and local mother-indexes. Time stamps need to be kept to select descriptions which will be ingested.

A more dynamic approach that uses on-the-fly conversion to RDF and maps RDQL queries into SQL queries could also be adopted. This will avoid gathering and is a good solution for integrating information coming from different data

Table 3. Factors / Key Metrics of Case Study III

Type of application	Improvement of a pure database application in case of a distributed/federated database.
`does_application_add_value`:	Yes, simplifies handling of records.
`willing_to_invest`:	Feasibility analysis only.
`better_than_classic_approach`:	Difficult to explain
`does_it_work`:	
– URIfy-ing	Needs a SQL2RDF or SQL to XML to RDF gateway and a mechanism for URI2URL mapping.
– RDFy-ing	Deterministic conversion, relatively simple to perform.
– Gathering and ingesting	Alternatively: a spider approach or on-the-fly conversion and RDQL2SQL gateway.
– Indexing	RDFStore. An efficient update mechanism is needed.
– Searching and Browsing	RDQL free-text combined search. Navigation through employment and education history is needed.
– Application processing	May become heavy due to complex combined queries and due to complex ranking algorithms.
Business Model	Software development.

models in SQL databases. It is too early to say now what will be the best choice. This will be a matter of query performances *versus* pre-processing load and defining what is an acceptable sync/delay with respect to real-time data.

Independently from the approach adopted, it is important to note that we need an *intermediate view* on the Web to exchange data among different administrations. The trend today seems to be XML. In our opinion, RDF or RDF described XML data will be a better solution allowing not only to *exchange* data but also to *query and navigate through information directly*, i.e. without moving data in XML from application to application and later integrating the applications. One can argue that RDF data also needs to be ingested or processed by an application. We believe that this is less costly, faster and more robust than ingesting in separate applications (1st step) and later integrating the applications (2nd step).

As a final step in the proposed approach, applications are developed over the local and regional centre mainly to provide search functions with criteria: (i) skill/education profile, both from controlled lists and free text description, (ii) work experience, both from controlled lists and free text description, (iii) age, (iv) belonging to special categories (e.g. disabled) and (v) preferences and willingness to move/relocate. A similar approach is used for creating ranked lists (e.g. for jobs in the public administration).

Conclusion. As summarized by Table 3 the approach shows intriguing advantages in data exchange, split of responsibilities between central and local authorities and offers flexible handling of semi-structured data.

The main benefit is not just simplifcation but also the improved exchange between actors, better customisation which directly causes a strong negative: management of data is more complex and technology change is too big. Part of the issue is that the same results could be obtained through improved RDBMS/Web approach.

It as a step ahead of XML data exchange: RDF will allow not only to exchange data but also to directly search and process data from third party applications. However, the approach requires a jump in a new technology and requires high training costs. And although the application brings valuable advantages, it is perceived as not yet mature. This makes it less realistic for operations in near future. It might be of interest for a more research-oriented pilot project.

4 Application Model

The cases presented show a common model which can be seen as the next, application, layer over the basic RDF Engine layer [12]. We can present the basic engine layer as a component dedicated to ingestion/update of RDF descriptors and fast, bullet search/navigation over the stored triplets. Looking at our real-life examples, the following basic components are needed to create a complete system:

1. *Compiler-gatherer system* which is able to collect RDF descriptors from controlled/cooperating sites, from external systems publishing RDF data or data from legacy applications (e.g. SQL database). Some of the gathering (or harvesting-Scutter) applications are described in [19,20,21]. The whole process of collecting and compiling data is more complex. Here we limit ourselves to feedback after building the first applications. For any real-life application, this must be optimized to reduce network traffic and engine ingestion load, e.g. by gathering only newly modified or expired resource descriptions only. The gathering system should be able to pull descriptors when expired, or to accept data pushed by an external unit (e.g. a robot collecting data and parsing them into RDF) and to immediately provide RDF data parsed on-the-fly and used for an on-going query. Gathering should be based on a protocol(s) which will simplify exchange of RDFs among different applications/providers.
2. An *Optimiser* component which is able to ignore/eliminate obsolete triplets in the engine and require new compiling when needed. This is more an internal component of the engine, but it needs information about the expiration of resources from the external world.
3. An optional application layer which uses the RDQL interface offered by the engine and provides intermediate level processing which may be used by applications. As an alternative, applications which need strong customisation

can directly use RDQL. A first example of this may be the sorting of data which is not covered today by RDQL.

4.1 Search Domain

In a more general model, complex applications may need to limit the search scope to a domain . More important, a domain must be kept up-to-date, i.e. checked for expiration by the optimiser and refreshed by compiler-gatherer. The RDFStore implementation today supports the concept of provenance as an orthogonal dimension to stored triplets [12]. To work efficiently, this context information will need to contain some time information (like TTL, date of acquisition, etc.) that is needed to check and optimise RDF compilation.

The protocol adopted for defining the domain cases described uses a simple mother-index solution. Mother-index is the starting point of the domain definition and it is defined by an URI. This top-level index contains information for the search engine and/or information for the gatherer where to start looking for RDF descriptors to collect. The mother-index contains a list of items which might be: (i) An URI of a sub-domain mother-index, (ii) An URI of a RDF description itself together with additional timing information, (iii) URI of a gateway where RDF(s) can be created on-the-fly from data in RDBMS and (iv)URI of an instance of the RDFStore engine which might accept the query and return results. Once defined, the domain can be used as part of the pattern to limit the scope of the search.

4.2 Optimiser

This component is introduced here as a missing part of the puzzle. The optimiser is still a vague definition for the next generation of RDFStore engines. A few functions are identified today, more will be added following requirements from on-going application development:

1. Check the context and mask/remove/garbage collect obsolete triplets.
2. Track the provenance of obsolete triplets and request from the compiler-gatherer to update information by checking original descriptors.
3. Perform optimization of indices and internal structures.

4.3 RDQL, SQL, and Application Layer

RDQL is defined to support a model where little if any a priori knowledge of original data is known at run time. This leads to a simple query language which offers basic functionality only and attempt to optimize as much as possible the performances.

Considering the type of applications searching and browsing the Web we believe this is a good approach. However, trying RDQL on a few real-life applications has shown a few limitations:

1. The current version of RDQL does not support empty matches. One can solve this by forcing, in RDF, empty property values, but this conflicts with the desire for basic separation from the original data structures. A modification of the syntax will help in building real-life applications without influencing the language basics.
2. Similar to this is the problem of OR-ing data in the search pattern. As defined today, the pattern allows only the conjunctive AND match criteria. As soon as we move to real applications, some kind of OR-ing is needed. Today, OR-ing is done on application level. This may be costly but, and it may lead to complex application code. Two solutions are possible here: allow OR in the search pattern of RDQL or build a higher-level layer to support these functions just below application level.
3. Free text supported search today is very primitive: only a simple word match is only. Considering the importance of free-text data (the easiest to parse and used in all cases when a controlled list is not available), a better model is needed. Alternatives could be to keep RDQL simple and do more sophisticated work in a higher, application level. Due to the strong tie with the way words are indexed and saved, it might become too costly in terms of time and memory use.
4. Sorting of hits according to some criteria is another interesting point. This is used in all applications we tried. In case of small number of matches, such is not a problem, sorting can easily be done by the application after getting the results back an RDQL query. Small means today even hundreds of thousands if not millions of hits. The problem occurs when a large number of nodes is hit. In this case, sorting outside the engine will become unacceptable. It is probably premature to discuss sorting here, but some way to instruct the RDF engine about the way results are ordered (especially if cursors or partial result returns are required) will be needed. This might be even an approximate ordering but it can help when huge amount of data is retrieved.
5. A point for future development is also related to special comparisons which might be needed (e.g. geographical position). As part of the next generation, we are thinking of ways to push low-level (i.e. inside the engine) special comparison functions.

These points also offer a first comparison with SQL. An important aspect is that RQDL, as well as the whole model, does not provide any form of the UPDATE statement. There is no way to change the RDF data, we can only search and browse through the graph. More than a *Web Database* model ours can be called a *Web Library*.

As a practical aspect, it was interesting to note that people with SQL experience and understanding of RDF were immediately able to write RDQL queries. This was straightforward. It was much more complex to understand and prepare good RDF descriptions.

5 Conclusions

After these first real application experiences, we believe that RDFBusiness is possible. It first needs to be defined well and then explained better to customers.

Unified Web management seems the most mature area of applications. This is easy to build, non-invasive and does not interfere with the providers organization. These solutions can significantly improve the usability of a portal with limited investment. Aggregation of external sources seems more complex as a business, mainly because of the business model and because of cost of RDFying external, non-cooperating sources. However, this is again a form of unified Web management and, using a proper model of business, we expect that it might become an interesting business area. The approach of *Flavouring the results* considering user ratings of sources at run-time, all done using RDF, is another characteristic which can be useful in more complex analyses or intelligence applications.

In both cases, critical mass was not reached. To explain the full potential of the Semantic Web we need different information RDFed. *The business will explode when we will be able to show how with few instructions we can link completely different data.*

Semantic Web as the next step in federated/distributed databases is probably an over-challenging area for business. However, there are some intriguing aspects to it. First, RDF is be a step ahead of XML as lingua franca for information interchange between database applications: XML+RDF annotated data will be immediately accessible by any application and can simplify and speed up the information life cycle. We are proposing in this area a pilot project aimed at governmental - public administration use in which the advantages of Semantic Web technologies can be evaluated.

For all applications, we believe RDFying is a long-term investment, however one which will generally have immediate payback which can make the initial application already of enough value to make the implementation process a win-win proposition. Once annotated in this way, data will be usable by different applications in forthcoming years thus safeguarding the investment for a long period of time. Also as RDF is gradual and allows multiple descriptions-views it is certainly not an all-or-nothing proposition commonly seen in most document-management solutions or knowledge/data mining applications. This is a promising path to take.

To make the applications really work, we need to consider context and provenance as well as dynamic aspects: many of the resources we are dealing with change frequently during the lifetime of the application. This and the application level processing are part of a more complex model which will crystallise better in the Next Generation of RDFStore [12] at it keeps up with the new application developed for our customers.

References

1. T Berners-Lee, J Hendler and O Lassila, The Semantic Web, Scientific American, May 2001, http://www.scientificamerican.com/2001/0501issue/0501berners-lee.html
2. T Berners-Lee: Semantic Web road Map, September 1998 http://www.w3.org/DesignIssues/Semantic.html
3. D Beckett: RDF/XML Syntax Specification (Revised) W3C Working Draft 23 January 2003 http://www.w3.org/TR/rdf-syntax-grammar/
4. O Lassila, RR Swick: Resource Description Framework (RDF) Model Syntax and Specification W3C Recommendation 22 February 1999 http://www.w3.org/TR/1999/REC-rdf-syntax-19990222/
5. J Grant, D Beckett: RDF Test Cases W3C Working Draft 23 January 2003 http://www.w3.org/TR/rdf-testcases/
6. SA Dobson: Lighweight Datatabases, WWW95 Conference, www.igd.fhg.de/archive/1995_www95/proceedings/papers/54/darm.html
7. A Levy: Putting Semi-structured Data to Practice, http://www.cs.washington.edu/homes/alon/cikm98.ppt
8. D Florescu, J Freira: "Querying the Web", http://www.pbnet.com.br/openline/cefet/tutoriais_sbbd_english.htm
9. L Wall: from the Interview with Tim O'Reilly around 1990, http://technetcast.ddj.com/tnc_program.html?program_id=52
10. ODISSEO: Open Distributed Information Services for Earth Observation, http://odisseo.esrin.esa.it/
11. OpenGIS: Geography Markup Language (GML) v1.0 and v2.0 http://opengis.net/gml/00-029/GML.html http://opengis.net/gml/01-029/GML2.html
12. A Reggiori, DW van Gulik, Z Bjelogrlic: Indexing and retrieving Semantic Web resources: the RDFStore model, Submitted to ISWC2003 Conference
13. L Miller, A Seaborne, A Reggiori: Three Implementations of SquishQL, a Simple RDF Query Language, www-uk.hpl.hp.com/people/afs/Papers/ISWC%202002%20-%20SquishQL.htm
14. Opengis Web map Server Specification, http://www.opengis.org/pressrm/summaries/20010219.TS.WMS.pdf
15. http://www.searchenginewatch.com/sereport/article.php/2175281
16. National-wide system developed by Italia Lavoro, Rome, Italy, http://www.italialavoro.it/
17. ETT: Regional systems, developed by ETT, Genova, Italy, http://www.ettdemo.com/domino/
18. W3C: Relational Databases on the Semantic Web, http://www.w3.org/DesignIssues/RDB-RDF.html
19. D Brickley: ScutterSpec http://rdfWeb.org/topic/ScutterSpec
20. All your FOAF pm module, http://frot.org/rdfweb/ayf.html
21. K Apsitis, RDF Crawler, http://ontobroker.semanticweb.org/rdfcrawl/
22. T. Berners-Lee, R. Fielding, L. Masinter August 1998 Uniform Resource Identifiers (URI): Generic Syntax http://www.ietf.org/rfc/rfc2396.txt
23. DC: Dublin Core Metadata Element Set, Version 1.1 http://dublincore.org/documents/dces/ and DCMI Metadata Terms http://dublincore.org/documents/2003/03/04/dcmi-terms/
24. Dan Brickley, R.V. Guha: RDF Vocabulary Description Language 1.0: RDF Schema W3C Working Draft

KIM – Semantic Annotation Platform

Borislav Popov, Atanas Kiryakov, Angel Kirilov, Dimitar Manov, Damyan Ognyanoff, and Miroslav Goranov

Ontotext Lab, Sirma AI EOOD, 138 Tsarigradsko Shose, Sofia 1784, Bulgaria
{borislav,naso,angel,mitac,damyan,miro}@sirma.bg

Abstract. The KIM platform provides a novel Knowledge and Information Management infrastructure and services for automatic semantic annotation, indexing, and retrieval of documents. It provides mature infrastructure for scaleable and customizable information extraction (IE[1]) as well as annotation and document management, based on GATE[2]. In order to provide basic level of performance and allow easy bootstrapping of applications, KIM is equipped with an upper-level ontology and a knowledge base providing extensive coverage of entities of general importance. The ontologies and knowledge bases involved are handled using cutting edge Semantic Web technology and standards, including RDF(S) repositories, ontology middleware and reasoning.
From technical point of view, the platform allows KIM-based applications to use it for automatic semantic annotation, content retrieval based on semantic restrictions, and querying and modifying the underlying ontologies and knowledge bases. This paper presents the KIM platform, with emphasize on its architecture, interfaces, tools, and other technical issues.

1 Introduction

The acquisition of masses of metadata for the web content would allow various Semantic Web applications to emerge and gain wide acceptance. Such applications would provide and use new access methods based on the associated metadata. At present there are various IE technologies available that allow recognition of named entities within the text, and even the relations, events, and scenarios in which they take part. Thus, metadata could be assigned to the document, presenting part of its information content, suitable for further processing. Such metadata can range from formal reference to the author of the document, to annotations of all the companies and amounts of money referred in the text. It is an important question how to make this metadata machine readable for the purposes of effective structuring, discovery, automation, integration, and reuse.

---

[1] Information extraction, a relatively young discipline in the Natural Language Processing (NLP), which conducts partial analysis of text in order to extract specific information.

[2] General Architecture for Text Engineering (GATE), http://gate.ac.uk, leading NLP and IE platform developed in the University of Sheffield.

D. Fensel et al. (Eds.): ISWC 2003, LNCS 2870, pp. 834–849, 2003.

The approach for automatic (versus manual) extraction of metadata is promising scalable, cheap, author-independent and (potentially) user-specific enrichment of the web content. However, at present there is no technology available to provide automatic semantic annotation in conceptually clear, intuitive, scalable, and accurate enough fashion. Even more, there is no clear vision regarding the approach and model for generation and representation of such annotations.

This paper presents first an innovative model for semantic content enrichment, named semantic annotation (section 2.) This model is implemented in the KIM platform which is presented in the third section with its architecture. KIM ontology and knowledge base are presented in sections 4 and 5. Section 6 offers a brief explanation of the semantic IE process. The indexing and retrieval by entities is outlined in section 7. In section 8 there is a brief overview of the KIM front-ends. The ninth section contains KIM performance and IE evaluation metrics. Short outline of the technologies used as basis for the KIM Platform is present in section 10. Discussion on related work is present in section 11. In the last section we present our conclusion and plans for future work.

2 Semantic Annotation

The semantic annotation offered here is a specific metadata generation and usage schema targeted to enable new information access methods and extend existing ones. It is based on the hypothesis that the named entities[3] mentioned in the documents constitute important part of their semantics (see [19], section 3.2 for discussion on this statement.) In a nutshell, we consider Semantic Annotation the idea of assigning to the entities in the text links to their semantic descriptions. The idea of this sort of metadata is to provide both class and instance information about the entities referred in the documents. It is a question of terminology whether these annotations should be called "semantic," "entity" or some other way. To the best of our knowledge there is no well established term for this task; neither there is a well established meaning for the term "semantic annotation"[4].

The automatic semantic annotations enable new applications: highlighting, indexing and retrieval, categorization, generation of more advanced metadata, smooth traversal between unstructured text and available relevant knowledge. Semantic annotation is applicable to any sort of text – web pages, regular (non-web) documents, text fields in databases, etc. Further, knowledge acquisition can be performed based on extraction of more complex dependencies – analysis of relationships between entities, event and situation descriptions, etc. We believe that, defined this way, semantic annotation is clearly specified, easy to understand, and can serve as a basis for number of useful applications (some of those demonstrated in KIM).

---

[3] Named entities are people, organizations, locations, and others referred by name. The wide interpretation of the term includes any tokens referring something specific in the world: numbers, addresses, amounts of money, etc.

[4] The term is previously used in [29] in a bit more general sense compared to what we propose, but it didn't got wide acceptance.

The automatic semantic annotation can be seen in this case as a classical named-entity recognition (NER) and annotation process. The semantic annotation is specific for providing more precise type information than the systems based on flat NE type sets (not bound to a taxonomy or other definitions.) The NE type is specified by reference to an ontology, and more important, the semantic annotation requires identification of the entity. While in a classical NER task, guessing the type is everything to be achieved, a semantic annotation needs to recognize the entity (either out of a set of known ones either as a new, unknown, one) and refer to it.

Considerations about the structure and the representation of the semantic annotations, including the necessary knowledge and metadata are not presented in detail. These issues (and many others, not directly related to KIM) are discussed in [19]; here we will only sketch the conclusions promoted there:

- Semantic annotation system requires a light-weight upper-level ontology focused on named entity classes (unlike Apple, Worm, Chair, Key, etc.);
- RDF(S) with compliance and possible extensions to OWL Lite is the best choice for knowledge representation language for the ontology and the KB – more power will unnecessarily degrade the scale and performance;
- the documents and the metadata (annotations) should be kept decoupled from each other and separate from the ontology and the knowledge base.

3 The KIM Platform

The KIM[5] platform provides services and infrastructure for semantic annotation, indexing, and retrieval. To do this in a consistent fashion, it performs information extraction based on an ontology and a massive knowledge base.

The traditional flat NE type sets consist of several general types (such as Organization, Person, Date, Location, Percent, Money). Although these represent the most important domain-independent NE types, still the entities with same type are dividable in more specific classes from the average educated human (e.g. public companies, sport teams, and syndicates are all organizations.) We identified an inter-domain NE type hierarchy from a corpus of general news and integrated it in the KIM Ontology (KIMO). The ontology contains definitions of entity classes, attributes, and relations, as well as a branch of lexical resource types (e.g. Title, PersonFirstName, etc.). The semantic descriptions of entities and relations between them are kept in a knowledge base (KB) encoded in the KIM ontology and residing in the same semantic repository. Thus KIM provides for each entity reference in the text (i) a link (URI) to the most specific class in the ontology and (ii) a link to the specific instance in the KB. Each extracted NE is linked to its specific type information (thus Arabian Sea would be identified as **`Sea`**, instead of the traditional – **`Location`**). The KB has been pre-populated with entities of general importance, and is iteratively enriched with entity individuals and relations as a result of the IE process. Thus the extracted named entities could be further used for semantic indexing and retrieval of content with respect to entity instance and type, as well as name and attribute restrictions, and

---

[5] http://www.ontotext.com/kim

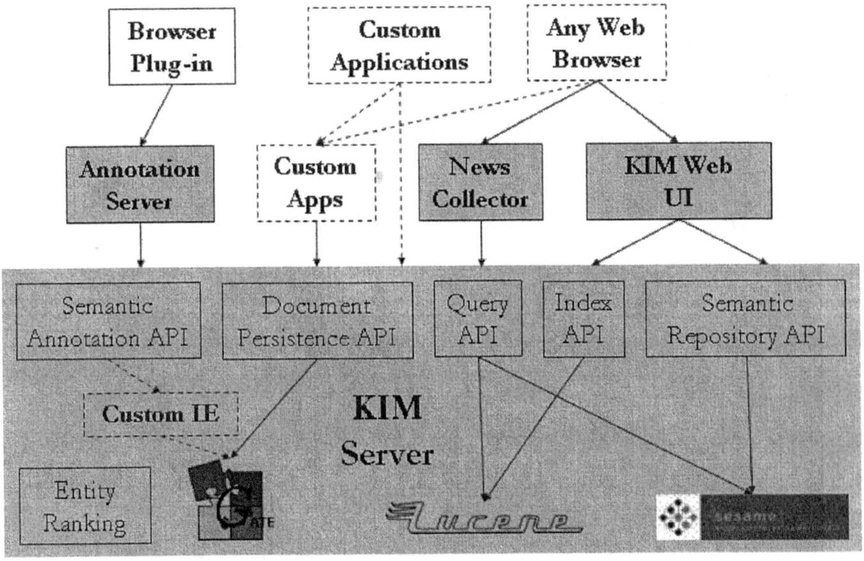

Fig. 1. KIM Architecture

expected relations between these entities (e.g. look for a `Sea` that is a sub region of the Indian Ocean).

For the end-user, the KIM IE functionality is straightforward and simple to use – requesting annotation from a browser plug-in, which highlights the entities in the current web page and generates a hyperlink used for further exploring the available knowledge for the entity (as shown on Fig. 1). Various access methods are also available – entity pattern search, entity lookup, keyword and document attribute search. There is also an opportunity to create a composite query consisting of atomic searches of the above types.

3.1 KIM Architecture

The KIM platform consists of KIM Ontology (KIMO), knowledge base, KIM Server (with API for remote access, embedding, and integration), and front-ends (browser plug-in for Internet Explorer, KIM web user interface with various access methods, and Knowledge Explorer for KB navigation). The KIM API provides semantic annotation, indexing and retrieval services and infrastructure. KIM ontologies and knowledge bases are kept in semantic repositories based on cutting edge Semantic Web technology and standards, including RDF(S) repositories (SESAME[6]), and ontology middleware[7] [16]. KIM provides a mature infrastructure for scalable and customizable information extraction, as well as annotation and document

[6] http://sesame.aidministrator.nl/, RDF(S) repository by Aidministrator b.v.

[7] OMM, http://www.ontotext.com/omm.

management, based on GATE [7]. The Lucene[8] information retrieval engine has been adopted to index documents by entity types and measure relevance according to entities, along with tokens and stems. It is important to mention that KIM, as a software platform, is domain and task independent as are Gate, Sesame, and Lucene. The KIM Architecture diagram is depicted on Fig. 1.

3.2 KIM API

The KIM Server API for remote access, embedding, and integration provides functionality and infrastructure for semantic annotation, indexing, and retrieval, as well as document management, and KB navigation. The modules of the KIM API can be seen at the middle layer on Fig. 1. The Semantic Annotation API allows annotation of documents with respect to KIM ontology and KB. It also provides infrastructure for content and annotations management. Documents and the associated annotations could be stored to/loaded from a data store via the Document Persistence API. The Index API is based on the Lucene IR engine, which has been modified to allow indexing with respect to named entities.

The Query API could be thought as a semantic IR API, which allows the specification of traditional key word searches, and also other ontology-aware access methods. It provides the infrastructure for constructing composite searches, combining entity search, keyword search, and entity pattern search. Due to the indexing with respect to entities, one could request all documents that are referring an entity described via restrictions over its name, class, and attributes. Even more, it is possible to specify a pattern of entities with the corresponding relations between them and ask for the documents that are referring the entities that satisfy the query.

For the means of managing and accessing the KB there is a Semantic Repository API, allowing access to the underlying KB through an RDF(S) compliant infrastructure and method set.

4 KIM Ontology

The rationale behind the KIM Ontology (KIMO) is to provide a minimal but sufficient ontology suitable for open-domain general purpose semantic annotations. It is designed from scratch for the purposes of KIM; inspirations are taken from number of upper-level resources: OpenCyc, WordNet 1.7, DOLCHE, EuroWordnet Top, and others. In order to keep it simple and easy to understand, it is kept small and naïve with respect to big number of philosophical, mathematical, and logical problems.

KIMO is a simplistic upper-level ontology starting with some basic distinctions between entity types (such as **`Object-`**s - existing entities such as locations and agents, **`Happening-`**s – defining events and situations, and **`Abstract-`**ions that are neither objects, neither happenings). Further on, the ontology goes in more details to such extent that real-world entity types of general importance are included (meetings,

---

[8] Lucene, http://jakarta.apache.org/lucene/, high performance full text search engine

military conflicts, employment positions, commercial, government and other organizations, people, and various locations, etc.). The characteristic attributes and relations for the featured entity types, are defined (e.g. **subRegionOf** property for **Location-**s, **hasPosition** for **Person**s, **locatedIn** for organizations, etc.) Having this ontology as basis, one could add domain-specific extensions to it easily, to profile the semantic annotation for concrete applications. The integration of multiple domain-specific ontologies for use within a single application is hardly possible without the intermediate role played by the upper-level ontology.

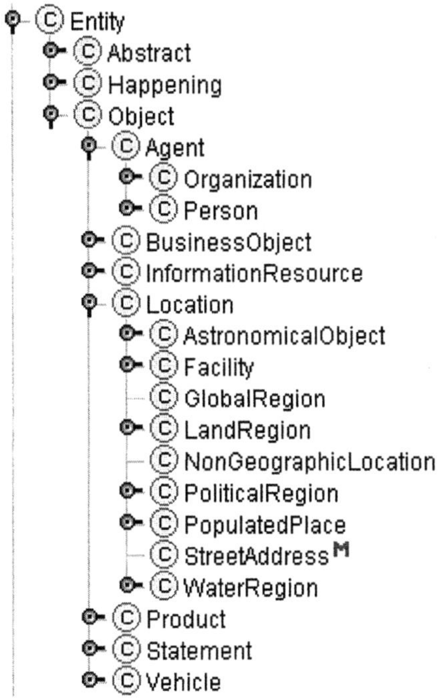

Fig. 2. The top of KIMO class hierarchy with expanded Entity branch. (on the left)

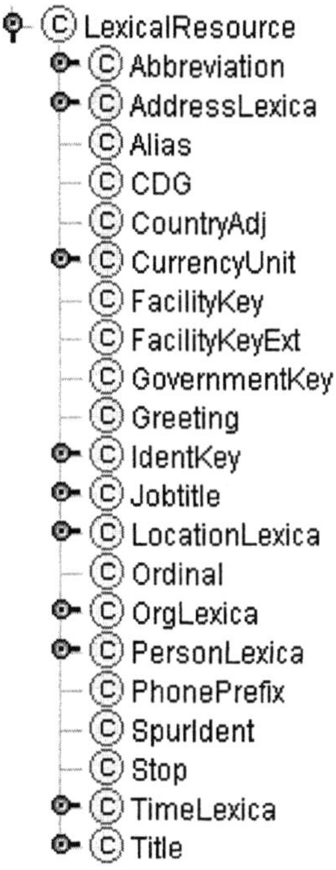

Fig. 3. The Lexical Resources top class hierarchy.

The distribution of the most commonly referred entity types varies greatly from domain to domain. As researched in [23], despite the difference of type distributions, there are several general entity types that appear in all corpuses – Person, Location, Organization, Money (amount), Dates, etc. The proper representation and positioning of those basic types was one of the objectives behind the design of KIMO. Further the ontology defines more specific classes, e.g. **Mountain**, as a sub-class of **Location** (the location-related classes are extensively covered, see [21] for more details.)

The extent of specialization of the ontology is determined on the basis of research of the entity types in a corpus of general news (incl. political, sport, financial, etc.) The KIM ontology (KIMO)[9] consists of about 250 entity classes and 100 attributes

---

[9] http://www.ontotext.com/kim/kimo.rdfs always refers to the most recent version

and relations. The top classes are **Entity**, **EntitySource** and **LexicalResource**. The top entities classes could be seen in the type hierarchy of the KIM plug-in on Fig. 6, and separately on Fig. 2.

The **LexicalResource** branch is dedicated to encoding various data aiding the IE process, such as company suffixes (AG, Ltd.), person first names, etc. (depicted on Fig. 3.) An important sub class of this branch is **Alias**, representing the alternative names for an **Entity** (see Fig. 4). The **hasAlias** relation is used to link an **Entity** to its alternative names. The official name of an entity is referred by the **hasMainAlias** property.

The instances of the **EntitySource** class are used to separate the trusted (pre-populated) information in the KB, from the automatically extracted one. This is indicated by the **generatedBy** property of the specific entity.

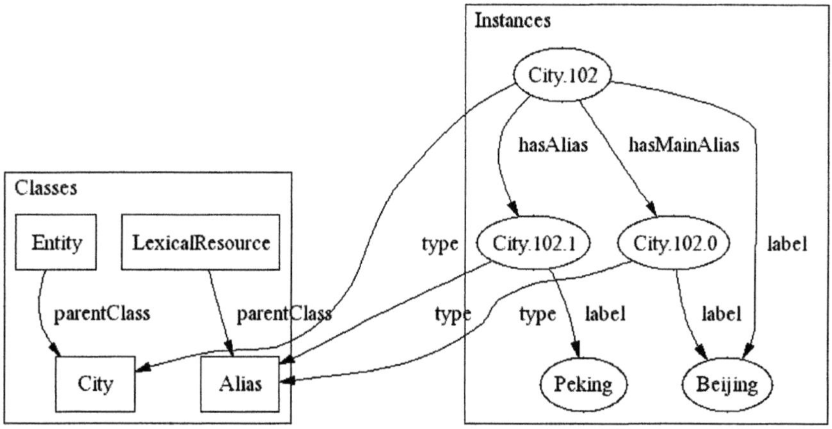

Fig. 4. RDF(S) Representation of an Entity description.

5 KIM Knowledge Base

No matter how sophisticated the automatic IE process is, one can still benefit from a starting KB to represent the entities that are important (popular, often cited, highly connected to others, etc) in the respective domain. Having a critical mass of trusted (in a sense handcrafted) knowledge can serve as a seed for further automatic population. Based on the determinism provided by this trusted knowledge, more advanced extraction methods could be applied to get it extended. In a sense, being able to grasp, learn, and infer is important, but knowing something in advance can be expected to improve the overall performance. Inferring or extracting with uncertain methods basic knowledge should be avoided in cases when it can be engineered in advance and maintained with reasonable efforts. This is the philosophy behind KIM, it reflects our intuition and can hardly be justified with something else than the overall performance of the KIM platform.

Combining the above philosophy with the aim of building a general-purpose, open-domain, semantic annotation platform leads us to genesis of the KIM KB. It is aiming to provide quasi exhaustive coverage of the most important entities in the world. In different words, the goal could be defined as: to cover what an undergraduate knows outside its country, specialization, and hobby. At the base line, this means the entities with their proper classes and aliases.

Obviously, building a domain-independent general knowledge base is too complex task and defined this way does not provide an obvious realization strategy. While still using various (including encyclopedic) sources and mental exercises, we substitute this task with an easier one which seems to serve as a good approximation: to provide good coverage of the entities mentioned in the international news. Here we mean those publications which use to cross the borders of the countries and feed the headlines of the global news wires. The specifics about this domain is that it covers (and also pre-determines) the most well known entities in the world.

KIM keeps the semantic descriptions of entities in the KIM KB, which is repeatedly enriched with newly recognized entities and relations. The entity descriptions are being stored in the same RDF(S) repository as the KIM ontology. Each entity has information about its specific type, aliases (incl. a main alias, expressing the most probable full or official name), attributes (e.g. latitude of a **Location**), and relations (e.g. a **Location subRegionOf** another **Location**). A schema of the entity representation in RDF(S) is depicted on Fig. 4.

5.1 Pre-population of KIM KB

KIM KB has been pre-populated with entities of general importance, that allow enough clues for the IE process to perform well on inter-domain web content. It consists of above 80,000 entities.

In its current state the KIM KB contains about 50,000 locations, including continents, global regions, 282 countries with their capitals, 4,700 cities (including all the cities with population over 100,000), mountains, big rivers, oceans, seas, and even oil fields. Each location has geographic coordinates and several aliases (usually including English, French, Spanish, and sometimes the local transcription of the location name) as well as co-positioning relations (e.g. **subRegionOf**.) Based on this spatial knowledge makes KIM a good basis for location-based services.

The organizations with highest general importance also have been pre-populated in the KB. Including the biggest world organizations (such as UN, NATO, OPEC), over 7,900 companies, and 140 stock exchanges for a total of 8,400 organization instances. For the public companies there are position relations of managing personnel. The organizations also have **locatedIn** relations to the corresponding **Country** instances. The additionally imported information about the companies consists of short description, URL, reference to an industry sector, reported sales, net income, and number of employees. A more extended report on the pre-population of the KIM KB can be found in [21].

Finally, in order to enable the IE process to recognize new entities and relations that are not a part of the KB, a collection of lexical resources is also presented in the KB. It covers organization suffixes, person names, time lexica, currency prefixes and others.

5.2 Controlling the Quality and Coverage of KIM KB

Ensuring the quality of the KB content, is not trivial and could not be performed manually (having more than 80,000 pre-populated entities, the manual approach simply not scale). The KIM KB is iteratively verified using an independently built KB of entities and relations collected manually from various web sources. An indirect verification is also performed during the evaluation of the performance of the KIM IE against a human annotated corpus.

The coverage of the KIM KB is being guaranteed through processing and analysis of the leading articles of the global news wires. The corpus of these articles is being constantly updated and bears on average 4000 documents per week – the top stories, as well as all other the economic and political news collected from about 15 sources. More details about the KIM KB are presented in [21]. On top of the corpus gathered this way, entity ranking is performed to detect the level of "popularity" of the specific entities. This allows proper manual handling at least of the most popular entities, as well, as early spotting of problems with the import strategy and sources.

6 Semantic Information Extraction

The essence of the KIM IE approach is the recognition of named entities with respect to a formal upper-level ontology (KIMO.) The NE annotations are typed with respect to the entity classes in the ontology. The entity instances all bear identifiers (URI,) that allow the annotations to be linked to the exact individual in the KB. The IE involved in KIM is currently concentrated mostly on the NER task, which is considered a step-stone for further attribute, relation, event, and scenario extraction. In order to identify the references of entity relations in the content, one should first have identified the related NE. Usually the entity references are associated with a NE type, such as Location, Person, etc. More and more hierarchical NE type sets appear, especially for domain-specific applications. This is due to the need for finer grained specification and identification of world concepts. For example, it would be natural for an IE application performing company intelligence to keep more specialized sub-classes of Organization (e.g. such as PublicCompany). A NE type taxonomy however brings in a new level of complexity and (as discussed in section 9) sets new challenges for the evaluation of the performance, since the traditional Precision/Recall metrics are not directly applicable.

The IE process presented here uses a light-weight ontology (KIMO) defining the entity classes. In addition to the hierarchical ordering, each class is coupled with its appropriate attributes. The relation types are also defined with their domain and range restrictions. Actually, the basic ontology language used (RDFS) considers both the relations and attributes as properties, which can also be organized in a hierarchy. Given the ontology, the entities in the text could be linked to their type, which is also feasible with just a type taxonomy. However we would like to go further, and identify not only the type of the NE but also keep its semantic description and extend it through the IE process. Thus, the NE references in the text are linked to an entity individual in the KB (section 5). The accessibility of the semantic descriptions of entities in the KB would allow the IE process to later base on attributes and relations as clues for recognition and disambiguation. For example, if a `Person` appears along with a **Company** in the content, and there are two companies that have the mentioned alias, we face an ambiguity. A possible approach would be to check whether the Person has some relations with one of the companies (e.g. working in it), and if so, the related **Company** to be chosen as a better candidate and associated with the NE reference in the content.

KIM IE is based on the GATE framework, which has proved its maturity, extensibility and task independency for IE and other NL applications. We have reused much of GATE's document management functionality, and generic NLP components as its Tokenizer, Part-of-Speech Tagger, and Sentence Splitter. These processing layers are provided by the GATE platform, along with pattern-matching grammars, NE coreference and others, as standardized building bricks for easy construction of sophisticated IE applications.

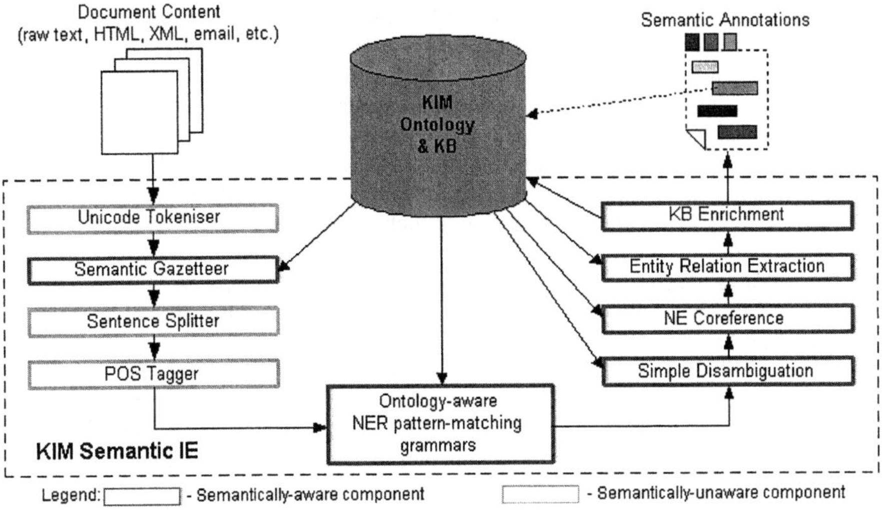

Fig. 5. KIM Semantic IE flow diagram.

For our purposes we changed the grammar components to handle entity class information and match rules according to it. The grammar rules are now based on the ontology classes, rather than on a flat set of NE types. This allows much more flexibility in the creation of NER rules at the most appropriate level of generality, giving both the opportunity to generalize and handle more specific NE types. A rule trying to extract relation between an organization and its point of presence can be specified at the level of the most general classes it applies to (Organization and Location) and still match a patterns with much more specific information (say, a radio station located in a county). On the other hand, instead of referring to all locations we could prefer to have rules that are especially applicable for Countries, Cities, or Seas.

The Semantic Gazetteer component is looking up in the text for entity aliases and lexemes loaded from the KB – its key role is to provide fast track for annotation of entities referred with known aliases. Along with it, all the reused components have been opened towards the semantic repository. For example, the NE co-reference module, in addition to the traditional ortho-matching techniques, handles the instance information of NE annotations and matches them according to it, as well as the traditional substring transformation matching. The Semantic Gazetteer, the simple disambiguation and annotation filtering components, as well as the final KB enrichment layer have been developed from scratch. These are not innate to a traditional NER and are inquired by the specifics of the Semantic IE, which takes care of the identification of NE references with respect to the ontology and KB.

The IE component flow diagram (Fig. 5) displays the sequential processing of content to the point where semantic annotations are produced over it. The semantic repository is also displayed and linked with the ontology and KB aware components.

7 Indexing and Retrieval

After semantic annotations of the documents, KIM allows those to be indexed with respect to the contained named entities. This allows later on document retrieval to be performed with respect to entities. One could specify the NEs that to be referred in the documents of interest, with name restrictions (e.g. a Person which name ends with 'Alabama'). Further, pattern of entities, relations between them and attribute restrictions can be specified. To answer the query, KIM applies semantic restrictions over the entities in the KB. Then the documents referring the resulting entities are being retrieved with relevance ranking according to NEs. Technically, Lucene is adapted to perform full-text indexing, which is uniquely addressing each entity disregarding the alias used in the text.

The retrieval accuracy of KIM has not been evaluated against a traditional IR engine, and this is a topic that should be researched in the future. However, KIM has the potential to perform better not only on reducing the unrelated documents in the result set while still retrieving the relevant ones (as a NE indexing system with flat entity types as in [24] and [29]), but also to increase the number of relevant documents, with such that do not contain the alias that was used for the entity name restriction, but have the same entity mentioned with another of its aliases.

8 KIM Front-Ends

The KIM API allows the implementation of various front-end tools providing access to the KIM Server functionality and infrastructure. We have created a web user interface (KIM Web UI) allowing traditional (key word search), as well as semantic access methods (entity search, pattern search.) Along with these the KIM Web UI generic content management and IR functionality allows indexing and storing of semantically annotated content. The entity and pattern searches return either a set of entities that satisfy the query, either a set of documents that refer to these entities. One could see the content with the associated metadata on the document level (title, author, etc.) The resulting entities are highlighted in the content and linked to their semantic descriptions in the KB.

KIM is also equipped with a plug-in (Fig. 6) for the Internet Explorer browser. It provides light-weight semantic annotations delivery to the end user. On its first tab, the plug-in displays the entity type hierarchy (a branch of the KIM ontology). For each entity type there is an associated color used for highlighting the annotations of this type. Check boxes for each entity, allow the user to select the entity types of interest. Upon invoking annotation of the current browser content, the plug-in extracts the text of the currently displayed document and sends it to an Annotation Server which is in its turn using the KIM Server Semantic Annotation API. The servers return the annotations with their offsets, type and instance information. The annotations are highlighted in the content (in the color of the respective entity type), and are hyperlinked to the KIM KB Explorer (Fig. 6.) On the second tab of the plug-in, there is a list of all the recognized entities for the current document, sorted by appearance frequency. Upon choosing from the list of entities, or following a hyperlink over an annotated entity in the text the user invokes the KIM KB Explorer, a web-form which provides a view of the part of the KB and the ontology that are directly related to the chosen entity (incl. type, aliases, relations, and attributes). This way, the user could easily navigate from the named entity annotations to the instances that they are linked to in the KB. Via this explorer, the KB could be further explored by choosing one of the related entities, or the entity type.

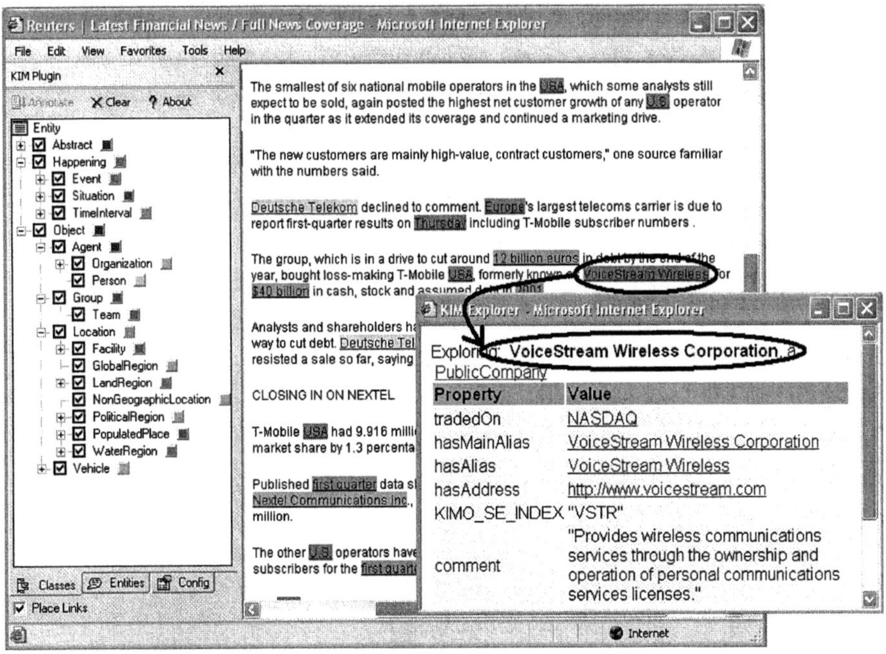

Fig. 6. The KIM plug-in with the top of the KIM Ontology, and KIM Explorer on top

The News Collector[10] is reusing some of the KIM Web UI and is an example of a KIM-based application which collects, annotates, and indexes news articles.

[10] A service which collects and semantically annotates the latest news from more than 10 of the most popular news sources. It is the one used to collect the corpus, further used for "entity ranking" and maintenance of the KIM KB. See http://news.ontotext.com

9 KIM Performance and IE Evaluation

Here we present brief performance metrics of the KIM Server and evaluation of KIM IE against a human annotated corpus. The evaluation corpus contains 100 documents of news articles from several UK media sources (Financial Times, Independent, Guardian) with total size close to 1 MB. We performed semantic annotation, indexing and storage of the metadata over the documents from the corpus on a dual-processor (1.13 GHz) PC server to acquire the following throughput metrics: annotation - 8kb/s; indexing 27 kb/s; storage 5kb/s; average 10 annotations/kb; 70 annotations/s. The speed of annotation depends on the document size, getting slower for bigger documents in a sort of logarithmic dependency.

The evaluation of the accuracy of the IE process has been performed over the same corpus human-annotated with the traditional flat NE types used by most of the NER systems. Despite the fact that KIM provides more specific type information, it is still possible to test it against the human annotated corpus (because something that is a `Mountain` is also a `Location`). In Table 1 we present the Precision, Recall and F-Measure of the automatically annotated corpus versus the human annotated one.

Table 1. KIM evaluation versus the human annotated corpus with respect to general NE types.

Annotation Type	Precision	Recall	F-Measure
Date	0.91	0.83	0.87
Person	0.90	0.85	0.87
Organization	0.77	0.56	0.64
Location	0.92	0.92	0.92
Percent	1	1	1
Money	1	1	1
Total	*0.86*	*0.82*	*0.84*

The above accuracy measures bear considerable distortion and only roughly approximate the accuracy of the semantic annotations. Sizeable semantically annotated corpus and new metrics are necessary for proper evaluation.

Given the complexity of the semantic IE process and the early development phase in which KIM is, these performance metrics encourage us to think that the automatic semantic annotation really could cope with the scale of the web content.

10 KIM Back-Ends

The technologies that KIM builds on have been carefully chosen, to be both mature enough, scalable and platform independent. The knowledge resources are kept in the Sesame RDF(S) repository, which provides storage and query functionality infrastructure. The Sesame repository is used with much over a million of RDF(S) statements. It is being queried by the semantic search methods to identify the entities according to the provided restrictions, and the result is further used for the retrieval of the referring documents. The IE process also relies on the semantic repository for its initialization and further processing.

The GATE platform has been used as a basis for the IE process and also for the management of content and annotations. It provided the basis text analysis technologies on top of which we have added the semantically aware extensions specific for KIM IE. The annotations and document management paradigms have been derived from the GATE infrastructure, but slightly simplified to avoid dependencies of the KIM clients on anything beyond the KIM API.

The Lucene IR engine has been adopted to perform indexing and retrieval with respect to named entities and evaluation of content relevance according to the entities which allows the semantic access methods described in section 7. The adoption of Lucene proves that it is easy to adjust a traditional IR engine to perform indexing with respect to metadata. Which means that there is no need of completely new technologies for the purposes of semantic indexing but rather the systems providing semantic IR could base on the existing quality IR engines.

11 Related Work

Semantic annotation of documents with respect to ontology and entity knowledge base is discussed in [5] and [14] – although presenting interesting and ambitious approaches, these do not discuss usage of information extraction for automatic annotation. The focus of [14] is manual semantic annotation for authoring web content, while [5] targets the creation of a web-based open hypermedia linking service, backed by a conceptual model of document terminology.

Semantic annotation is used also in the S-CREAM project presented in [13] – the approach there is interesting with the heavy involvement of machine learning techniques for extraction of relations between the entities being annotated. Similar approach is taken also within the MnM project [35], where the semantic annotations can be placed inline in the document content and refer to an ontology and KB server (WebOnto), accessible via standard API. Related to the previous is the project OFF, [9], which puts an emphasize on the collaborative ontology development.

Significant amount of research on IE has been performed in various projects related to GATE (see [22], [2], [6-8], [10], [23]). GATE provides tools such as tokenizers, part-of-speech taggers, gazetteer lookup components, pattern-matching grammars, coreference resolution tools and others that aid the construction of various NLP and especially IE applications. GATE is also a framework for content and annotation management. KIM's IE and content management is grounded in the GATE framework, and opens it towards Semantic Web knowledge representation and management technologies.

For some time now it has been obvious that the several general NE types used by the IE systems are not specific enough for many applications, that there are much more categories that matter. NE type hierarchies design has been discussed in [38].

All the semantic annotation techniques referred above lack the usage of upper-level ontologies and critical mass of world knowledge to serve as a trusted and reusable basis for the automatic recognition and annotation, as in the approach presented in [1] and discussed here. Also the IE processes involved in related work do not link the NE reference in the text with a NE individual in the KB. Because of this unique feature the semantic description of the entity instance reveals its attributes, aliases, type, origin source, and relations with other individuals.

12 Conclusion and Future Work

We had shortly introduced semantic annotations – an innovative notion for meta-data schema, generation and usage, discussed in more details in [19]. Next presented the KIM platform implementing it, based on GATE (which was substantially developed) and Sesame (which was substantially tuned to manage the size of the KB.)

Even linguistically simple, KIM platform provides a test bed and proofs number of hypothesis and design decisions: (i) its worth using almost-exhaustive entity knowledge (sort of super-gazetteers) for information extraction. The technology used (based on GATE) can manage the scale. Even without significant efforts on disambiguation, the precision drawbacks are acceptable for many applications; (ii) It is possible to adopt a traditional symbolic IE system to perform semantic annotations and thus provide its results in shape suitable for Semantic Web applications.

The implementation is currently under development, so, preliminary results are reported. In the future we would like to develop (or adapt) evaluation metric which properly measures the performance of a semantic annotation system; Experiment different approaches towards disambiguation of NE references; Make use of more advanced IE techniques for identification of relations, analysis of events and situations, etc. The KIM Ontology and KB as well as the methodology and procedure for their sustainable maintenance and improvement will be subject of future research.

References

1. Bontcheva K., Kiryakov A., Cunningham H., Popov B., Dimitrov M. *Semantic Web Enabled, Open Source Language Technology.* In proc. of EACL Workshop "Language Technology and the Semantic Web", NLPXML-2003, 13 April, 2003
2. Bontcheva K., Dimitrov M., Maynard D., Tablan V., Cunningham H., *Shallow Methods for Named Entity Coreference Resolution.* Chaînes de références et résolveurs d'anaphores, workshop TALN 2002, Nancy, France, 2002.
5. Carr L., Bechhofer S., Goble C., Hall W. *Conceptual Linking: Ontology-based Open Hypermedia.* In The WWW10 Conference, Hong Kong, May, pp. 334–342.
6. Cunningham H., *Information Extraction: a User Guide* (revised version). Department of Computer Science, University of Sheffield, May, 1999
7. Cunningham H., Maynard D., Bontcheva K. and Tablan V., *GATE: A Framework and Graphical Development Environment for Robust NLP Tools and Applications.* In Proc. of the 40th Anniversary Meeting of the Association for Computational Linguistics, 2002.
8. Cunningham, H. and Maynard D. and Tablan V., *JAPE: a Java Annotation Patterns Engine* (Second Edition). Technical report CS–00–10, Univ. of Sheffield, Department of Computer Science, 2000.
9. Collier N., Takeuchi K, Kawazoe A. *Open Ontology Forge: An Environment for Text Mining in a Semantic Web World.* In proc. of the International Workshop on Semantic Web Foundations and Application Technologies, Nara, Japan, 11th March.

10. Dimitrov M., Bontcheva K., Cunningham H., Maynard D., *A Light-weight Approach to Coreference Resolution for Named Entities in Text.* Proceedings of the Fourth Discourse Anaphora and Anaphor Resolution Colloquium (DAARC), Lisbon, September 2002.
13. Handschuh S., Staab St., Ciravegna F. *S-CREAM – Semi-automatic CREAtion of Metadata.*The 13th International Conference on Knowledge Engineering and Management (EKAW 2002), ed Gomez-Perez, A., Springer Verlag, 2002.
14. Kahan J., Koivunen M., Prud'Hommeaux E., Swick R.. *Annotea: An Open RDF Infrastructure for Shared Web Annotations.* In The WWW10 Conference, Hong Kong, May, pp. 623–632.
16. Kiryakov A., Simov K.Iv., Ognyanov D. *Ontology Middleware: Analysis and Design* Del. 38, On-To-Knowledge, March 2002. http://www.ontoknowledge.org/downl/del38.pdf
19. Kiryakov A., Popov B., Kirilov A., Manov D., Ognyanoff D., Goranov M. *Semantic Annotation, Indexing, and Retrieval.* In proc. of 2nd International Semantic Web Conference (ISWC2003), 20–23 October 2003, Florida, USA. To appear.
21. Manov D, Kiryakov A, Popov B, Bontcheva K, Maynard D, Cunningham H. *Experiments with geographic knowledge for information extraction.* NAACL-HLT 2003, Canada. Workshop on the Analysis of Geographic References, May 31 2003, Edmonton, Alberta.
22. Maynard D. ,Tablan D.,Ursu C., Cunningham H., Wilks Y., *Named Entity Recognition from Diverse Text Types.* RANLP 2001 Conference, Tzigov Chark, Bulgaria.
23. Maynard D., Tablan V., Bontcheva K., Cunningham H, and Wilks Y., *MUlti-Source Entity recognition – an Information Extraction System for Diverse Text Types.* Technical report CS–02–03, Univ. of Sheffield, Dep. of CS, 2003. http://gate.ac.uk/gate/doc/papers.html
24. Moldovan D., Mihalcea R.. *Document Indexing Using Named Entities.* In "Studies in Informatics and Control", Vol. 10, No. 1, March 2001.
29. Pustejovsky J., Boguraev B., Verhagen, M., Buitelaar P., and Johnston M., *Semantic Indexing and Typed hyperlinking.* In Proc. of the AAAI Conference, Spring Symposium, NLP for WWW, 120–128. Stanford University, CA, 1997.
35. Vargas-Vera M., Motta E., Domingue J., Lanzoni M., Stutt A. and Ciravegna F, *MnM: Ontology Driven Semi-Automatic and Automatic Support for Semantic Markup*, In Proc. Of EKAW 2002, ed Gomez-Perez, A., Springer Verlag, 2002.
38. Sekine S., Sudo K., Nobata Ch., *Extended Named Entity Hierarchy* (LREC 2002)

Ontology-Oriented Programming: Static Typing for the Inconsistent Programmer*

Neil M. Goldman

Teknowledge Corporation
4640 Admiralty Way, Suite 1001
Marina del Rey, CA 90292 USA
ngoldman@teknowledge.com

Abstract. Ontologies and object-oriented data models differ little in their *declarative characterization* of a domain. Differences in the *application* of these models, however, has led to quite different characteristics of the programming languages used to create and manipulate them – notably in the presence or lack of static typing.
Some ontology-reliant applications need to work with models that are *inconsistent* with the underlying ontology's declarative norms. Object-oriented languages preclude construction of such models. A secondary distinction is that ontologies, at least as used in the description logic community, provide a semantics that requires an *implicit* interpretation of extensional data, where possible, that retains consistency with the declarative norms, whereas object-oriented languages treat the norms as constraints that must be *explicitly* satisfied by a model.
An *ontology compiler*, currently targeting the Microsoft .Net language family, produces a traditional object-oriented class library that captures the declarative norms of an ontology. It enhances this library with additional methods that allow construction of models that are inconsistent with these norms. An application, rather than the library itself, determines when an operation should raise exceptions. *Annotations* to an ontology allow for tradeoffs between the flexibility of the generated library and its performance.

1 Introduction

Semantic annotations of web data will be both created and consumed by software acting on behalf of people or on behalf of other software agents. This paper is concerned with the nature of the programming languages and environments in which programmers compose such software. Some of these programs will be *generic* in nature – independent of any particular ontology. Validity checkers and query servers [1] fall into this category. Many more applications – e.g., a personal agent to manage bidding for an item at an online auction site – will require software that is written to deal with classes and properties of a specific ontology.

---

* This research was supported by DARPA contract F30602-00-C-0202.

D. Fensel et al. (Eds.): ISWC 2003, LNCS 2870, pp. 850–865, 2003.

The current generation of ontology based programming tools provides only weak support for programming the ontology-specific class of applications. Better support could be provided by *automatic generation* of software class libraries based on the content of the ontologies needed for such an application.

Section 2 describes the considerable overlap, as well as the few significant differences, between *object-oriented* (Ob-O) and *ontology-oriented* (On-O) data modeling. Section 3 looks at a specific, and I believe representative, example of applying a tool designed for implementing generic applications to the job of building an ontology-specific application, focusing on the absence of benefits afforded by static typing. Section 4 outlines a particular mapping from ontology-oriented models, as exemplified by the *OWL* family, to object-oriented class libraries, as exemplified by Microsoft's *.Net Framework.*

There may be more than one useful mapping from an ontology to a class library for manipulating the models allowed by that ontology. Section 5 illustrates several *annotations* that afford control over tradeoffs between flexibility and performance of the generated class library.

The objective of this technique is to support implementation of ontology-specific applications as depicted in Fig. 1, by automating the generation of ontology-specific class libraries for traditional object-oriented programming languages.

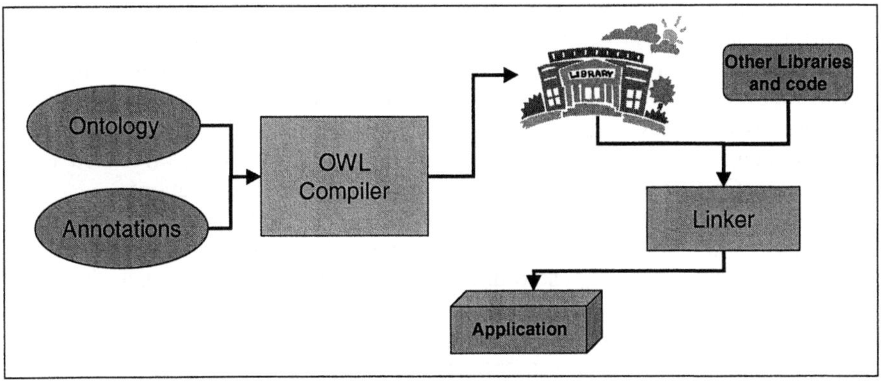

Fig. 1. Ontology-specific Application Development. An *ontology* and annotations are *compiled* to produce an ontology-specific *library*. This library is *linked* with other libraries and code to produce an *application*

2 On-O vs. Ob-O Data Modeling

Ontology languages, such as *OWL*[2], and object-oriented languages such as Microsoft's *.Net Framework* characterize a domain of discourse in quite similar fashion. In both we find a fundamental partitioning of the domain into *individuals* (**objects**) and *literals* (**values**). The universe of *individuals* (**objects**) is categorized into *classes* (**reference types**). The universe of *literals* (**values**) is categorized into *datatypes* (**value types**). OWL provides *ObjectProperties* to relate pairs of individuals, and *DatatypeProperties* to relate individuals to literals. .Net provides

fields[1] of **objects** for both purposes, but each field is used uniformly to relate an object to *either* another object *or* to a value, and so we could accurately partition them into **ObjectFields** and **DatatypeFields**.

Both *ObjectProperties* and *DatatypeProperties* can be given *domains* and *ranges*, restricting the individuals and literals that may be related by the properties. Every **field** also has a domain – some reference type – and a range.

Finally, both the On-O and Ob-O modeling languages provide intensional requirements of subsumption and disjointness[2] – that is, statements or implications of subsumption and disjointness that must hold for *all* model instances. The Ob-O reference types include both **class types** and **interface types**. It is the interface types that bear a considerable similarity to the *classes* of On-O models – in particular, if I_1 and I_2 are interface types, then I_1 may "inherit"[3] from I_2 (and thus be subsumed by it). Alternatively, if I_1 and I_2 have no common subtype, then they must be disjoint.

Another area of common concern is characterizing the number of *individuals* (**objects**) that may be related to a given *individual* (**object**) by a particular *ObjectProperty* (**field**). In particular, both On-O and Ob-O paradigms encourage a modeler to distinguish functional relationships (at most one range individual for a given domain individual) from others. The On-O paradigm cleanly isolates this issue, providing **restrictions** that allow cardinality restrictions other than "at most one" to be stated. The Ob-O paradigm confounds the characterization of cardinality with that of range. When a **field** is declared to have a reference type (e.g., Person) as its range, this means "at most one Person".[4] A programmer accommodates multiple range values by specifying a collection type (e.g., "array of Person") as the **field**'s range.[5]

The final commonality worth mentioning is that all the declarative information about classes (**reference types**), *datatypes* (**value types**), and *properties* (**fields**) in both paradigms is available in models of their own. This facility (referred to as **reflection** on Ob-O languages) is the basis for writing generic applications.

Although the commonalities are considerable, the Ob-O and On-O modeling paradigms are not isomorphs of one another. Each provides means of saying some things that the other cannot. These differences reflect the ways in which these two paradigms have been traditionally used. In particular, On-O models [3] evolved with the expectation that they would be consumed by software that supplies sophisticated (relative to traditional software, at least) *inference* capabilities. Ideally, such software makes no distinction, other than performance, between a model where a statement is

---

[1] Software engineering concerns – primarily encapsulation – lead Ob-O languages to provide **methods** (and, in .Net, **properties**) in addition to Fields. However, **fields** capture the fundamental modeling of relationships in the domain.

[2] *Owl Lite* does not provide a way to declare classes to be disjoint, but other *Owl* variants and description logic languages do provide this.

[3] "Inherit" in this context is the imposition of a requirement that any class that implements I_1 must also implement I_2.

[4] Ob-O languages traditionally support a Null object that can be stored in any reference-typed **field**. With very rare exceptions, use of the Null value is the means of saying "no range values for this domain object". There is no analog to the Null value for value types, so use of a value type as a **field** range means "exactly one."

[5] These collection types commit to more than just "multiple objects". They often commit to an ordering of the objects, or to allowing a bag rather than just a set.

explicit and one where the statement not explicit but is a logical consequence of other statements and the ontology. For example, if the *ObjectProperty* "hasNationality" is stated to have the *Class* "Country" as its range, and the statement "x hasNationality y" appears in a model, then the individual y has "Country" as one of its classes in the model, regardless of whether the fact "y hasClass Country" was ever explicitly added to the model. Designers of On-O modeling languages like *Owl* carefully limit the logical expressiveness of the language so that such expectations are plausible.

Ob-O modelers, on the other hand, do not expect much inference to be performed by the automatically generated software that implements their models. They do expect the software to enforce the logical implications of their data modeling, but to do by restricting what models can be built. In particular, models are built incrementally and an increment is not allowed if the result would be inconsistent. In the Ob-O world, the increment "x hasNationality y" would be rejected unless "y hasClass Country" were already present. One significant exception to this is supertype inference. The Ob-O modeler *does* expect "y hasClass PoliticalUnit" to be inferred whenever "y hasClass Country" is explicit (or inferable), assuming Country was declared to be a subtype of PoliticalUnit. Ob-O programming languages like Java[4] and the .Net[5] family actually exclude inconsistent models primarily through static typing, rejecting any program that could build an inconsistent model, rather than through runtime consistency checks. These languages provide *safe casts* to deal with circumstances where static type reasoning is too weak to ensure compliance. Programs that use reflection to build models are also subject to runtime exceptions from increments that would lead to inconsistent models.

The point of this discussion is that the On-O and Ob-O paradigms differ little in how they characterize a domain of discourse, but differ significantly in the anticipated use of that characterization by software. The one fundamental difference originates in the means by which *individuals* (**objects**) are categorized into *classes* (**reference types**). In the On-O paradigm, an individual may be explicitly (or implicitly) categorized into multiple classes. This *might* create an inconsistent model – e.g., if a pair of these classes had been declared disjoint in the ontology – but in general it is not a problem. In the Ob-O paradigm, however, each object belongs to a *single* most-specific, named, **class type**, and of course to any **class** or **interface** types that subsume it. As a consequence, the Ob-O data modeler must *anticipate* all possible intersections of types that may be needed by applications.

A second difference we shall have to confront in generating a class library suitable for manipulating models based on an ontology is the notion of identity. Owl has adopted from RDF the practice of using a URI as a globally shared "name" for an individual. While it is presumed that all uses of such a name refer to the same individual, it is *not* presumed that distinct names refer to distinct individuals. A given ontology and model will often justify neither the conclusion that the names refer to the same individual nor or that they refer to distinct individuals. In languages used to manipulate Ob-O models an individual is added to a model by applying a **New** operator, and each such individual is distinct, insofar as the language's innate reference equality semantics is concerned, from every other individual. As a result, an Ob-O model cannot contain both "a person named Will Shakespeare" and "a person named Francis Bacon" without making a commitment as to whether they are the same or distinct individuals. On-O models, on the other hand, have the option of stating that they are the same, stating that they are different, or reminaing noncommittal. [6]

3 Generic vs. Ontology-Specific Programming

If we accept that the primary value of the Semantic Web will come from software applications that can create and reason about ontology-based models, we need to ask whether existing programming languages are well-suited to building these applications.

The kinds of applications that are generally suggested for the Semantic Web seem to fall into two very different camps. Some applications – perhaps better thought of as tools – are generic in that their construction requires knowledge of the meaning of terms used in creating ontologies, such as 'subClassOf', but requires no knowledge of terms or semantics from any specific ontology. The kinds of tasks performed by such tools are things like consistency checking and query answering.

A second kind of application is one that deals with models based on one or more specific ontologies. [6] posits an agent that finds a suitable physician for a patient. This agent is concerned with some medical terms and some distance and time concepts. There are two reasons why non-generic applications are necessary:

- Some agents will need to supply semantics that cannot be expressed in the ontology language. Recall that ontology languages purposely limit their expressivity to retain decidability. The day may come when the additional semantics can be expressed in a standardized "declarative" language; it is possible today to supply them with procedural code.
- Even where the semantics expressed in an ontology is *logically* sufficient for an application, performance considerations will often dictate a non-generic implementation.

One approach to building Semantic Web tools and applications that has been popular is to rely on class libraries for mainstream object oriented languages (Java, .Net). The class library provides classes and fields that hold both ontologies and models built from them. Import/export methods provide a means to map between this representation and an XML-based "interchange" representation. The library provides two additional capabilities:

- a limited amount of inference, following the semantics expressed by the loaded ontology. Which of the authorized inferences are provided seems to be an ad-hoc implementation decision.
- a reflection-like set of methods that allow a programmer to index into a model using the types and properties of the ontologies on which it is based.

Fig. 2 exhibits the use of such a library to write a fragment of the sort of code that would be used in an ontology-specific application. The code uses the *Jena*[7,8] class library for Java, and is taken directly from a tutorial provided by the authors of that library. Jena is a library that can manipulate pure RDF models as well as models that use the DAML+OIL[9] extensions. The encoded algorithm is examining a model

[6] Typically Ob-O languages predefine a coarser-grained *Equals* equivalence operation that can be overridden on a class-by-class basis. But *Equals*, like reference equality, is boolean-valued; it does not provide "maybe" as a possible result.

based on the VCARD ontology[7], attempting to determine the name of a person whose email address is "amanda_cartwright@example.org".

```
DAMLModel model = … // code that loads the VCARD ontology
                    // and some data based on that ontology
DAMLClass vcardClass =
    (DAMLClass)model.getDAMLValue(vcardBaseURI+"#VCARD");
DAMLProperty fnProp =
   (DAMLProperty) model.getDAMLValue(vcardBaseURI+"#FN");
DAMLProperty emailProp = (DAMLProperty)
                 model.getDAMLValue(vcardBaseURI+"#EMAIL");
Iterator i = vcardClass.getInstances();
while (i.hasNext()) {
  DAMLInstance vcard = (DAMLInstance) i.next();
  Iterator i2 =
      vcard.accessProperty(emailProp).getAll(true);
  while (i2.hasNext()) {
     DAMLInstance email = (DAMLInstance) i2.next();
     if (email.getProperty(RDF.value).getString().equals(
                  "amanda_cartwright@example.org" ) ) {
       DAMLDataInstance fullname =
        (DAMLDataInstance) vcard.accessProperty(fnProp).
                            getDAMLValue();
       if ( fullname != null )
        System.out.println("Name: "+ fullname.getValue().
                                    getString());
     }
  }
}
```

Fig. 2. Jena code used for an ontology specific application

Several points stand out in an examination of this code.

- The Java types of the program's variables (**DAMLModel**, **DAMLClass**, **DAMLProperty**, **DAMLInstance**, **DAMLDataInstance**) are analogous to reflection types. They are *not* the classes introduced by the VCARD ontology. They *are* classes a programmer would want for writing generic applications.
- The names of classes and properties from the VCARD ontology appear as string literals (*VCARD*, *FN*, *EMAIL*).
- Datatype values stored in the model must be explicitly converted (getString) to an appropriate Java value type.

Fig. 3 displays the same algorithm, as it would appear in an object-oriented language using a VCARD class library. This example uses the syntax of VisualBasic.Net, but the code would isomorphic or nearly so in C# or even Java. In this case:

- The variable types (**VCARD, String**) and method names (*vcards*, *email*, *fn*) are those introduced or used by the VCARD ontology itself, not reflection types.
- Values of datatypes (in this example, strings) appear to the programmer as values from the value types of the embedding language.[8]

---

[7] http://www.hpl.hp.com/semweb/iswc2002/JenaTutorial.Alpha/DAML/solutions/vcard-daml.rdf

```
Dim model as VcardOntology.model
Dim vc as Vcard
for each vc in model.vcards
  dim eaddr as String
  for each eaddr in vc.emails
    if eaddr.equals("amanda_cartwright@example.org") then
      dim fullname as String = vc.fn
      if not fullname is Nothing then
         Console.Writeline("Name: " & fullname)
      end if
    end if
  next eaddr
next vc
```

Fig. 3. Statically typed code for an ontology specific application

The code in Fig. 3 is objectively more concise, and subjectively easier to comprehend, than that of Fig. 2. Programming in a statically typed environment conveys other important benefits. First, numerous programming errors that would only be detected by debugging in the Jena code will be caught by the compiler in the .Net code. These range from simple typographical errors, such as using "#*VCRD*" or "#vcard" instead of "#VCARD", to semantic errors that show up as type mismatches, such as using "#Orgname", a property whose domain is **Orgproperties**, rather than "VCard", in place of "#FN", a property whose domain is **Vcard**. In fact, such errors are often detected prior to compilation, or avoided entirely, in modern IDEs for statically typed languages, since programmers are offered menus and automatic name completion restricted to type-correct choices. Finally, the compilers of statically typed languages take advantage of the statically declared data model to produce smaller and more efficient code.

So far we have only observed that a *programmer* could take the same domain expertise required to write an ontology and could himself write an Ob-O class library that was more suitable for implementing many, if not all, ontology-specific applications for that domain. This is not surprising. The discussion in Section 0 goes beyond this, arguing that a well-written ontology already contains a declarative representation of the knowledge needed to construct that library – i.e., the library can be *generated* from the ontology automatically. The generated library can easily retain the correspondence between its types and fields and the corresponding concepts in the ontology as a mapping to the concept's URIs. Making this mapping available to an Ob-O language's reflection facilities enables a single *generic* program to import existing models encoded in their interchange syntax (RDF/XML) into the class library representation, and to export models created within the class library in interchange syntax. Thus no additional code needs to be written, or even generated, for the class libraries to share data with other web agents.

---

[8] Technically "string", unlike numeric types, is a reference type in the .Net languages as well as in Java. However, since strings have no mutable state, and provide a value-based equality operator, "string" acts for all practical purposes as an optimized value type.

Not so Fast...

Just what is the relationship between the Jena code in Fig. 1 and the .Net code in Fig. 3? Will they produce the same results across all possible model instances? Jena, after all, is capable of storing even inconsistent models. Furthermore, these code snippets contain no code that actually builds or increments models. Can the .Net statically typed library construct all possible models that could be constructed by the Jena code?

The answers to these questions depend on the issues of consistency and inference alluded to in section 851. A model, consisting of a finite set of assertions P(d,r) is *inconsistent* only if the negation of one of those assertions can be *inferred* from the model and the ontology. Since negations cannot be explicitly asserted, this must arise from an inferable negation. In the case of the Owl family this will involve at least one of the following:

- asserting that two individuals are distinct
- declaring that a property is functional (enabling inference of distinctness)
- declaring that two classes are disjoint
- declaring that one class is the complement of another (entailing their disjointness)

Many useful ontology specific applications do not rely on the ability to represent inconsistent models. Other suggested applications – particularly those that attempt to bring together data about the same domain of discourse from disparate sources – do seem likely to need to hold inconsistent models.[9]

At first blush the notion of static typing may seem incompatible with the ability to hold inconsistent models. In fact they are not incompatible. This will be addressed in greater detail in the following section of the paper. For now, simply observe that an Ob-O language can readily provide multiple methods that read and write the same data storage. By using run-time casts in their implementation, these methods can provide *different* views regarding the type of the storage. For example, what appears to be an "array of Thing" when viewed through some methods may appear as an "array of Person" when view through alternative methods. What allows this to work is that some of the casts used in the "array of Person" view will raise exceptions in the case that a non-Person has been added to the array through the "array of Thing" view. In summary, there is no reason why a class library cannot simultaneously provide a statically typed view of a model and simultaneously provide a statically typeless view of the same model. The typeless view would be capable, just like the Jena library, of holding an arbitrary set of explicit assertions.

Inference, on the other hand, is the ability to materialize assertions that are entailed by as well as those that are explicit in a model. Since any entailed assertion *could have been* explicitly asserted, inference does not introduce any added problems for the statically typed view of the model.

---

[9] In this regard, it is of concern that the interfaces through which people author ontologies and models to date seem to closely parallel the underlying language primitives, making it likely that desirable assertions of distinctness and declarations of disjointness will be inadvertently omitted.

4 Generating an Ob-O Class Library from an Ontology

The class library generator accepts as input an ontology (currently, DAML+OIL) and produces as output a .Net class library. It produces this library both in its binary form (an assembly) and in source code form (both VisualBasic and C#). Production of multiple source languages is handled by .Net's object model for code, which allows code generators to create abstract program models which can be both compiled and translated to the various concrete .Net languages.

The scheme by which this generator works was outlined above. The strategy is to provide pairs of typed and untyped fields for storage. Each typed field is associated with a .Net type T and holds a list of references each of which is a .Net instance of T – that is, `TypeOf r is T` would be true for every reference r in the list. T is a type in the generated library that serves as the "implementation" of a class in the ontology. The paired untyped field will hold references that need to be treated as instances of that type, but whose .Net type is not consistent with it. We will soon see where such instances arise. Corresponding to each such field pair, the library will provide one set of properties and methods that provide a statically typed view of the model and raise an exception if the untyped field is non-empty. A second set of properties and methods provides a typeless view that treats the concatenation of the pair of fields as a single collection of "Thing"s. The typeless view supports (portions of) applications that cannot abide the requirements of static typing.

In generating the types for a class library's fields, properties, and methods only *global* domain and range restrictions are taken into account. Implications about domain class that are conditional on range class and vice versa cannot be enforced statically and thus play no role in the assignment.

The descriptions below will refer to the accessibility of fields, methods, and properties as simply Public or Private. However, in many cases what is listed as Private actually uses the accessibility scope (called *Friend* in VisualBasic or *internal* in C#) that allows an element to be accessed from elsewhere in the library containing the element but not from outside that library.

Mapping Individual Classes

Suppose the ontology is named O. The class library will contain a public class **O.Model**. For each non-anonymous class C in O, the class library will contain a private class **O.C**. **O.C** will have a zero-argument constructor. The class **O.Model** will have a private field **my_Cs**, of type ArrayList[10]. This will hold only objects created by the constructor of **O.C**. The initial value is the empty list. A public method **O.Model.NewC()** implements allocation of new instances of **O.C**, calling its constructor and adding the result to **my_Cs**.

---

[10] This is an artifact of the absence of templates in the .Net languages. The only directly supported statically typed collection of Xs is "X()" (array of X), but these are not growable like ArrayLists. Thus we use a more flexible collection type and pay the price of a run-time cast (in the library code) each time an item is obtained from the list.

The library will also have a public interface **O.IC. O.C** will implement **O.IC.** We need the interface, as well as the class, because *multiple* inheritance only exists for interface types, not class types.

Mapping Subclassof

Suppose that the closest non-anonymous superclasses of C in O are $\{Sup_1 \ldots Sup_j\}$. Then for each $1 \leq i \leq j$, we will have **O.IC** inherits **O.ISup**$_i$. The net effect is that **O.C** now implements its direct interface, **O.IC**, which in turn inherits each interfaces paired with a superclass. Since this pattern is followed for *every* class, **O.C** is forced to implement the interface of every class in its superclass hierarchy. Fig. 4 depicts this mapping in a simple case.

Suppose also that the closest non-anonymous subclasses of C in O are $\{Sub_1 \ldots Sub_n\}$. There will be a public method **O.Model.EnumerateCs** that retuns a statically typed enumerator of **O.C**s. This enumeration will include objects in **my_Cs**, as well as objects produced by **EnumerateSub**$_1$**s**, etc. In other words, it will include objects created by the constructor of **O.C** or by the constructor of any of the classes corresponding to subclasses of C. In the case of DAGs, of course, this enumerator does *not* enumerate a class multiple times.

Mapping ObjectProperty and DatatypeProperty

Let $\mathcal{P}$(C) be the set of ObjectProperties in O whose global domain is declared to be C or a (not necessarily direct) superclass of C. If p is an ObjectProperty with no global domain declaration, then the domain is Thing, and we include p in $\mathcal{P}$(C).[11] In other words, $\mathcal{P}$(C) contains those properties applicable to *all* instances of C. For each $p \in \mathcal{P}$(C), we give **O.C** a private field **O.C.myps**. The field is assigned the type ArrayList, and initialized to the empty list. This provides a place to store the individuals whose .Net type is compatible with the declared range of p. A second field, **O.C.myps_nost**, is used to store other values for the range. Of course, if there is no declared range, or the range is Thing, the latter variable will always hold the empty list.

Let $\mathcal{P}$' (C) be the set of ObjectProperties in O whose global domain is declared to be C itself. For each p in $\mathcal{P}$' (C), **O.IC** is given two methods for adding a new range value for p. In one, **Addp**, the parameter type is the interface type corresponding to the range of p. In the other, **Addp_nost**, the parameter type is Thing. The implementations of the former simply add the parameter to **myps**. The implementations for the latter perform a run-time type test and add the parameter to **myps** if the reference has the right type, and to **myps_nost** if not.

---

[11] If p has multiple global domain declarations, then its domain is their intersection. We invent a name for this class and proceed as if the intersection class had been declared explicitly in the ontology and used as the domain of p.

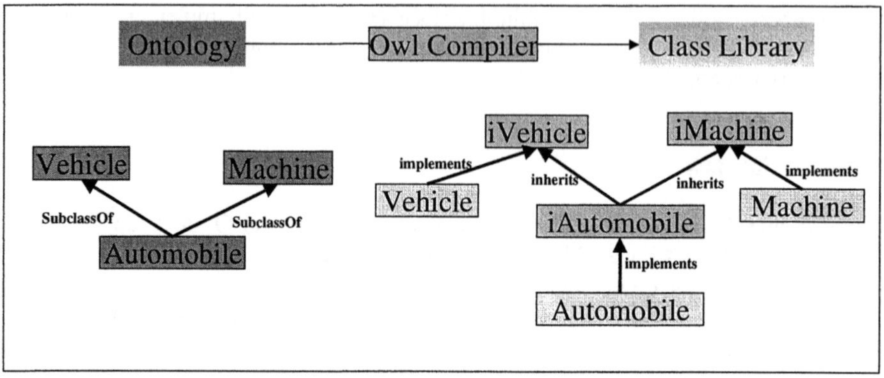

Fig. 4. For each ontology class, the generated library contains both a *class* and an *interface*. *SubclassOf* relationships between ontology classes are mirrored by *inherits* relationships among interfaces. Each library class *implements* the interface with which it is paired.

If p has a global maximum range cardinality of 1, then an additional pair of writing methods is included in **O.IC**. These (**Setp, Setp_nost**) provide a value that becomes the *sole* value in **myps** or **myps_nost.**

For reading, both statically typed and untyped iteration are provided. The statically typed method enumerates values from **myps**, but raises an exception if **myps_nost** is non-empty. The untyped iteration enumerates references from both lists.

If p has a global maxcardinality of 1, an additional statically typed reading method is provided. This method is prototyped as

```
GetP(byval ifnone as O.IR)as O.IR,
```

where R is global range restriction for p. The implementation consists of the following logic:

1. If **mypsnost** is nonempty, an exception is raised. Otherwise
2. If **myps** holds exactly one reference, that reference is returned. Otherwise
3. If **myps** holds no values, the "ifnone" parameter is returned. Otherwise
4. If **myps** holds multiple values, an exception is raised.

If p also has a global mincardinality of 1, an additional method is prototyped as

```
GetP()as O.IR
```

and functions identically to the other **GetP** method, except in case (3), where the second method raises an exception. An implementer's choice among these various methods reflects a decision on whether to treat inconsistency or incompleteness of a model as an *exceptional* situation or as a *normal* circumstance.

The mapping for Datatype properties is completely analogous. Because the fields that store range values always contain lists, regardless of any cardinality restrictions, the absence of a Null value for these types does not pose a problem.

What Is New and What New Is Not

We have just seen the how the class library increments a model with a single triple involving a property from O. But there are a few other kinds of triples that get added to Jena models, and we should look at their counterparts as well. Most interesting is the analog of the triple Jena uses to say "individual I belongs to class C." For Jena, there is nothing special about the ObjectProperty for "Type". But a statically typed language will somewhere have to treat this as other than just another property. To understand why there is a problem, we revisit the **New** operator mentioned earlier in conjunction with the Ob-O notion of identity. The New operator does more than give a new object an identity. It also gives the object a classification, which must be a single class (not interface) type C. The object returned by this operator is known to the Ob-O runtime to be an instance of that class, to be an instance of the class from which C inherits, etc, back to the built-in class **Object**, which is the root of all class inheritance. Furthermore, the runtime knows that if the object is an instance of any class type C, it is also an instance of the type I for every interface I implemented by C.

But while the **New** operator does a lot of classification, it will not do "additional" classification or "reclassification" or "specialization". If s is a variable bound to a Swimmer, we cannot write s.New.Bowler() to make s be a Bowler as well, or write s.New.NavySeal() to make s a particularly good swimmer. **New** just isn't used like a method; it is a syntactic primitive. So how do Ob-O languages perform these model increments, so straightforward in Jena and its ilk? As pointed out at the end of section 0, they *don't*. A tradeoff has been made in the runtime of these languages to favor performance over this flexibility. Our ontology compiler, in order to regain that flexibility, sacrifices performance.

For any object returned by **Model.NewC()**, we allow applications to create "proxies" of other types at any time. For example, having executed

```
ISwimmer s = m.NewSwimmer()
```

we can later execute

```
IBowler b = m.AsBowler(s)
```

The object created and stored in b is created when AsBowler uses m.NewBowler. The Bowler instance gets added to the **O.Model.my_Bowlers** list. We call the Bowler a *proxy* for the Swimmer instance, and we call the Swimmer a *principal* object of m and *the principal* object for the bowler instance. This information is recorded in private fields of the two instances. We also say that the Swimmer is its own principal object. Either the swimmer or the bowler may be used as the parameter of `m.AsSumoWrestler` to create another proxy. A principal object may end up with proxies of many other types, but at most one per type. If s had already had a proxy of the exact class bowler when we executed `m.AsBowler(s)`, the existing proxy would have been returned. Furthermore, a principal may not have a proxy of a class that is the same as or a superclass of the principal's own class. Having *created* s as a Swimmer, attempting to classify s as an athlete would have no affect on the model -- `m.AsAthlete(s)` would just return the Swimmer s.

The previous paragraph depicts a mechanism that in principal *stores* multiple classifications for a reference. We must also provide alternatives for the .Net runtime's operations that we wish were aware of this. In particular, applications that need proxies also need

- an equality test that treats all objects having the same principal as equivalent,
- a test of whether an object x is an instance of a type T that returns true if any object y having the same principal as x is an instance of T in the .Net sense, and
- a casting operator that will successfully cast x to T if any object having the same principal as x could be cast to T by a .Net cast.

The first method is a straightforward overloading of *Equals*. Since types are first-class objects in the .Net reflection API, the latter two are likewise easy to implement.

Note that this is *not* a matter of implementing inferences authorized by a model and ontology. The swimmer and bowler did not arise from descriptions with distinct ids. They fail the innate identity test solely because, to satisfy the requirements of static typing, two different invocations of the New operator were needed.

Retaining the URI Mapping

The .Net languages contain a weak but still useful means of extending the reflection API. By decorating the declarations of classes, interfaces, methods, etc. with some optional syntax, the .Net compiler arranges for the runtime to create objects called *custom attributes* whenever the library is loaded and associate these objects with the reflection instance corresponding to the decorated unit. There is very little restriction on what can go into classes used as custom attributes. So generating the code

```
<Resource("http://www.w3.org/2001/vcard-rdf/3.0#VCARD"> _
    Public Interface IVCARD  ...   End Interface
```

suffices to make the URI used for the class VCARD available via reflection to any application that loads the generated library.

5 Annotations

Ontologies do not address some issues that a programmer considers when designing an Ob-O class library. These are issues that rely on knowledge (or assumptions) about the applications that will actually be implemented using the library.

The four primary considerations that programmers bring to bear in these considerations are code size, data size, performance, and encapsulation. The latter is particularly important to Ob-O programmers, since it is central to their ability to provide structured explanations of algorithm correctness and security.

The scheme outlined in section 0 produces a library that is larger, slower, and less encapsulated than one that a programmer would likely produce manually. It will, on the other hand, be more flexible – that is, supply the functionality needed for a wider variety of possible applications – than the typical manually produced library. We now consider some *annotations* that can be asserted about the classes and properties of an ontology to control these tradeoffs. The list is meant only to be indicative of what is possible, not an exhaustive enumeration of what would be useful.

Class libraries do not always include a root object like *model* whose instances effectively partition the instances of all other objects. Even when they do, a root can generally enumerate the instances of few, if any, reference types in the library. A programmer can authorize the generator to omit the enumeration method for a type by marking the type as non-enumerable. A non-enumerable type may not have an enumerable supertype.

Ob-O programmers are comfortable with explicitly classifying an individual prior to using that individual in a context that requires (implies) its membership in the class -- they must circumvent the static typing system when this is not the case. Most programmers would argue that the value of trapping unintentional errors in the static type checker far outweighs the occasional inconvenience of having to provide explicit classifications. For most properties, a programmer would be happy to give up the flexibility of adding assertions about individuals not statically known to belong to the declared domain/range class. In other words, they are willing to allow the global domain and range declarations for a property be treated as static prerequisites for explicit assertions.

The .Net languages (and Java) allow a class not only to implement multiple interfaces, but to inherit the implementation of one other class. This means that it shares the implementation of any interfaces it has in common with that class, including fields. This has no impact on functionality or flexibility, but can result in drastically smaller code. Using annotations to indicate a single-inheritance thread through some of the classes in an ontology would significantly reduce the amount of code duplication needed to implement interfaces in the library's classes.

Many types in .Net programs exist *only* to be used as an interfaces – no class is needed that implements just that one interface. For example, an annotation could be used to indicate that "Vehicle" did not need to be supported as a class with its own implementation, but only as an interface implemented by its subclasses.

Classes in .Net programs can be marked as "MustInherit", meaning that any instance of the class must actually be created by instantiating some class that inherits from it. A class defined in an ontology as the union of other classes would be a likely candidate for this annotation.

Enumerated types in programming languages are generally implemented by assigning, at compile time, a distinct integer value to each enumeration member and using the integers as the run-time representation of the member. In .Net, programmers can choose these integers, and a common programming technique is to choose integers whose binary representation can be effectively used as a bit mask, thus enabling some logical set operations to be performed in constant time. This optimization could be expressed through annotations.

Table 1 summarizes the tradeoffs inherent in each of these annotations. The choice of the "default" flexibility to provide in a generated class library could be one that provided great flexibility and required annotations to give up some of that flexibility. Alternatively, the default could be for a relatively lean but inflexible library, requiring annotations to include the additional flexibility.

Table 1. Annotation Tradeoffs

Annotation	Code size	Data size	Perfor-mance	Encap-sulation
Enumerability	☺	☺	☺	
Domain/range as static requirements	☺	☺		☺
InheritsFrom	☺			
InterfaceOnly	☺			☺
MustInherit				☺
Bitmask		☺	☺	

6 Discussion

The idea of generating an Ob-O class library from an ontology is not new. A commercial product from Ontology Works[10] generates Java class libraries from a proprietary ontology language, apparently oriented toward use for accessing a database whose schema is also generated from the ontology. Mechanisms for dealing with multiple inheritance and inconsistency are not described, however.

A number of concerns for generating a viable class library implementation were omitted entirely from the design sketched in the previous sections. I will touch on several of them briefly here.

The generated code must supply *names* for classes, interfaces, properties, methods, and fields. The names must be legal, must avoid collisions with one another and with names in libraries on which the generated class library depends. The public names should be recognizable by a programmer who is familiar with the ontology being implemented. None of this is a serious problem. In both .Net and OWL ontologies, names consist of a namespace and a local part. Keeping a 1-1 correspondence between namespaces avoids most potential collisions, and relying on the local portion of the names from the ontology as the basis for the local portion of the class library names resolves the latter problem.

The discussion omitted operations that *remove* facts from a model. For the most part, those are just the obvious complements of the operations that add the same facts. The one exception is the classifications done by **New**, which inherently have the same lifetime as the object created. One could attempt to hide those classifications from the operations implemented by the library itself, but they would still be visible to the OO runtime system and so could not be effectively hidden from applications.

Scalability is a serious issue. The design presented here views the ontology to be implemented as a self-contained unit. Clearly we want to be able to reuse (share) the binary implementation of one ontology in the implementation of ontologies that import it. But there don't appear to be any restrictions in OWL on how an ontology that imports another one can use the terms of the imported one. The importing ontology may add new superclasses to the classes in the imported ontology, add new properties using classes of the imported ontology as their domain, or add global range requirements to imported properties. This is all very unlike the way class libraries use and extend one another.

The library generator description in this paper largely ignored *Datatypes and DatatypeProperties*. They are much simpler to deal with than Objects and ObjectProperties for three reasons. First, there no possibility of the equality of two datatype values being uncommitted. Second, there is no possibility of *asserting* the type of a datatype value. Third, there doesn't seem to be any practical need to store a datatype value in the range of a DatatypeProperty when the value is the wrong type – it seems that raising an exception in the case where there is no obvious conversion would be perfectly acceptable. It is also hard to imagine a use for a DatatypeProperty with no range type specified. The remaining problem is matching up the XSD types with the .Net value types, and the correspondence is straightforward for all the commonly used types, with the exception of fact that XSD integers have no size limit. Transparently mapping between an ontology's datatypes and built-in types opens up to the application programmer the large body of predefined methods on those types.

The use of proxies and principals in inadequate, as described, to fully deal with the problem of multiple explicit types for a single individual. Consider the example used earlier. Any property declared with Athlete as its domain would have ended up with explicit storage in both the principal, Swimmer, and in the proxy, Bowler, instances. If IsProfessional were such a property, we would have two values around. Of course we know it is possible to be both a professional basketball player and an amateur at baseball, so the same might be true for swimming and bowling. But this just shows the dangers of thinking you can understand the meaning of a property from its name – clearly the semantics of OWL requires that if IsProfessional is a property of athletes, there is no sense in which multiple values of the property can be assigned to an individual and differentiated based on a subclass when the individual happens to belong to more than one subclass.

References

1. DAML Query Language (DQL) : Abstract Specification, April 2003, Richard Fikes., Patrick Hayes, and Ian Horrocks, editors. URL: http://www.daml.org/2003/04/dql/dql
2. OWL Web Ontology Language Overview. Edited by Deborah L. McGuinness (Knowledge Systems Laboratory, Stanford University) and Frank van Harmelen (Vrije Universiteit, Amsterdam). URL: http://www.w3.org/TR/2003/WD-owl-features-20030331/.
3. The Description Logic Handbook: Theory, Implementation and Applications, Edited by Franz Baader, Diego Calvanese, Deborah McGuinness, Daniele Nardi, Peter Patel-Schneider, published by Cambridge University Press
4. James Gosling,Bill Joy,Guy Steele, and Gilad Bracha The Java Language Specification, Second Edition, Sun Microsystems, Inc, 2000
5. Don Box, Essential .NET Volume I: The Common Language Runtime,Addison-Wesley, November 2002
6. Tim Berners-Lee, James Hendler, Ora Lassila, The Semantic Web, Scientific American, May 2001
7. Brian McBride, Jena: A Semantic Web Toolkit, IEEE Internet Computing, Novermber, 2002, http://dsonline.computer.org/0211/f/wp6jena.htm
8. Mike Dean and Dave Rager, DAML dotnet API, URL: http://www.daml.org/2002/10/dotnetAPI/
9. Reference description of the DAML+OIL (March 2001) ontology markup language,2001, http://www.daml.org/2001/03/reference.html
10. OWL and the IODE, Ontology Works whitepaper, September 2001, http://www.ontologyworks.com/docs/whitepaper.pdf

Task Computing – The Semantic Web Meets Pervasive Computing

Ryusuke Masuoka[1], Bijan Parsia[2], and Yannis Labrou[1]

[1] Fujitsu Laboratories of America, Inc.,
8400 Baltimore Avenue, Suite 302, College Park, MD 20740, USA
{rmasuoka,yannis}@fla.fujitsu.com
http://www.flacp.fujitsulabs.com/
[2] MIND Lab, University of Maryland,
8400 Baltimore Avenue, Suite 200, College Park, MD 20740, USA
bparsia@isr.umd.edu
http://www.mindswap.org/

Abstract. Non-expert users have to accomplish non-trivial tasks in application and device-rich computing environments. The increasing complexity of such environments is detrimental to user productivity (and occasionally, sanity). We propose to reduce these difficulties by shifting focus to what users want to do (i.e., on the tasks at hand) rather than on the specific means for doing those tasks. We call this shift in focus "task computing"; we argue that "task computing" offers an incentive to device manufacturers to incorporate semantic web technologies into their devices in order to get the benefits of easier and more flexible use of their devices' features by end-users.

To support task computing, we developed an environment called a "Task Computing Environment" (TCE), which we have implemented using standard Semantic Web (RDF, OWL, DAML-S), Web Services (SOAP, WSDL) and pervasive computing (UPnP) technologies, we describe and evaluate our TCE implementation, and we discuss how it has been used to realize various device-usage scenarios.

1 Introduction

Fujitsu is an Information Technology company with a business that spans the entire range from chip design and manufacturing to integrated IT solutions. As a device manufacturer, Fujitsu is interested not only in designing and marketing devices (of various kinds) that deliver more functionality in each new product cycle but also in making this functionality user-accessible and incorporating it in higher value, integrated IT solutions. We discuss an application of Semantic Web and Web Services' technologies that supports these goals shared by many device manufacturers and IT solution providers.

Being knowledge workers ourselves we face the frustrations of trying to do simple things in the device and application-rich environments where we work. Let us consider the rituals of visiting a lab or a business unit in order to make a presentation and discuss collaboration with colleagues. We exchange printed business cards that end up in a desk drawer because we never have the time to enter them into our PIM,

D. Fensel et al. (Eds.): ISWC 2003, LNCS 2870, pp. 866–881, 2003.

we have to deal with capricious projectors that might or might not work as intended while we try to make a presentation, we promise to e-mail a soft copy of our presentation when we get back to our office or to follow-up with a new scheduled meeting, we search for addresses and directions to the restaurant for the business dinner or to the airport and print them on paper to take with us. Performing each of these simple tasks entails a complex choreography of interaction with a variety of devices and applications, cutting and pasting and a lot of time and frustration. The goal of the discussed work is to make it easy for the average user (who typically is neither the authors nor the readers of this paper) to perform each of these tasks with a few clicks; by focusing on the tasks that the user wants to accomplish, rather than the process of accomplishing them; we refer to our approach as Task Computing.

Several features of Window XP exhibit a very limited form of task orientation. For example, when the user inserts a music CD to the CD tray, a window pops up suggesting to the user tasks she can perform from that point on, such as "Play CD", or "Copy Music". In this case, the operating system uses a pre-specified list of actions, or tasks, that is associated with the occurrence of a specific event (i.e., inserting a music CD), so that when the event occurs, the relevant listing of actions is presented to the user to act upon. In Microsoft Office XP, the smart tags feature works similarly; it highlights text in the current document (while using Microsoft Word) and offers the user a drop down menu of actions that can be performed with the object that that text denotes. For example, if the text represents a name, then this feature may identify the object associated with that name to be a person, and may offer to send mail (to that person) or schedule a meeting (with that person). Microsoft XP and Microsoft Office are not the only examples of attempts to present to the user a more task-oriented view of the computing environment. When a user types an address in the search box of Google, the service will return (above the usual search results) a link to Yahoo maps or MapQuest that, if followed, will provide a map of the address.

These task-oriented systems exhibit three fundamental limitations:

- The functionality has been designed into the application; the application's programmers have programmed (hard-wired) the system's response.
- The system fragilely relies on correctly guessing the meaning of the input by its syntactic features.
- The system employs a cause-effect (or trigger-response) mechanism, in the sense that a certain type of input results to a single action (application invocation). There is no support for more complex user-composed and initiated workflows.

Task computing, as defined and elaborated in this paper, is an attempt to address these limitations. But we also believe that Task computing is an important step towards the realization of the pervasive computing vision [1] by enabling non-technical users to accomplish complex tasks in device-rich and service-rich pervasive computing environments. In the remainder of this paper we first elaborate on the notion of Task Computing and the set of technologies we have used in order to enable it. We discuss applications powered by Task Computing (specifically, the scenarios mentioned earlier in this section) and we present in detail our implementation of a Task Computing environment. We proceed to evaluate our accomplishment thus far and to discuss them in light of related work and we conclude with some of the future directions for this work.

2 Enabling Task Computing for Pervasive Environments Using Semantic Web Technologies

We define *Task Computing* as computation to fill the gap between tasks (what user wants to be done), and services (functionalities that are available to the user).

Task computing seeks to redefine how users interact with and use computing environments. We are particularly interested in pervasive computing environments, which typically involve multiple devices and services (functionalities) and non-technical users, with no a priori knowledge of the environment, operating mobile devices with limited interfaces. fundamental premise of Task Computing is to present to the user the tasks that are possible in the user's current context, to assist the user in creating more complex tasks by using simpler tasks as building blocks and to guide the user through the execution of the complex tasks. Once complex tasks are defined by the user (or perhaps by other users) such tasks can be re-used, very much like macros in popular applications today. Unlike macros (at least the ones that Microsoft Office users are familiar with), the building block tasks and the resulting complex tasks may span multiple applications and multiple computing platforms (not a single device). In fact, one of the goals of Task Computing is that the user does not need to know or care about how the actual constituent tasks are executed or where (on which machine) they might be executed on. The ultimate objective of Task Computing is to present to the user an abstract view of resources (devices and services) that can be used in an ad hoc manner by the user, in order to execute tasks of arbitrary complexity

2.1 Task Computing Framework (TCF) and Task Computing Environment (TCE) Definitions

A Task Computing Framework (TCF) is a framework that supports Task Computing, by providing support for:

- The workflows of Task Computing, i.e., at a minimum, Discovery, followed by Composition and Execution
- Semantic description of tasks and services
- Specification, Execution and Re-Usability of tasks by end-users
- Manipulation including creation and disposal of services by the end-users

Our definition of a Task Computing Framework does not make reference to computational components. We will refer to an embodiment of a Task Computing Framework as a Task Computing Environment (TCE). A TCE is a computational system that includes, at a minimum, the following components.

- One or more Task Computing Clients (TCCs),
- One or more Semantically Described Services (SDSs),
- One or more Semantic Service Discovery Mechanisms (SSDMs), and
- Optionally one or more Service Controls (SCs)

Later, we present in detail a Task Computing Client embodiment, called Semantic Task Execution EditoR (STEER), embodiments of multiple Semantically Described Services and Service Controls.

2.2 Technologies and Challenges of Designing a TCE

At the technical level, Task Computing relies on the on-the-fly discovery, selection, real-time (as opposed to design time) composition of services and execution of such compositions; the compositions represent end-users tasks. While any TCE ought to support these capabilities, and there are many ways to do so, in our TCE we chose to rely on Semantic Web Services technologies, in particular, DAML-S, OWL and Web Services technologies, specifically WSDL. While these choices addressed various issues facing our implementation (as described in Section 0), they introduced their own difficulties.

In assembling a TCE we faced multiple challenges:

- We had to assemble service discovery, composition and execution in a comprehensive framework where the selected technical choices needed to be mutually compatible. While the various Semantic Web/Web services standards went a long way toward interoperability, the standards and standard implementations thereof were in varying states of completeness. Over the course of developing our TCE, these standards changed and their implementations became more mature.
- We confronted the gap between the semantic layer of services and that of their execution.
- We had to design a user interface targeted to relatively unsophisticated end-users which would also work well and consistently across various devices and operating systems.
- We needed a plausible ontology translation mechanism to manage both interdevice-ontology mapping and the proliferation of services and tasks which use them. We had to develop techniques for managing highly dynamic sets of services, where many of the available services were created, advertised, hidden, or published by end users on an *ad hoc* basis.

Many difficulties were simply eliminated by our choice of Semantic Web and Web services technologies. For example, interlanguage function calls, even across the Internet, is trivial with WSDL described, SOAP based APIs. Web services provide a uniform interface for invoking program functionality across implementation and execution systems, whether these be language runtimes or actual computers. We currently use SOAP (in particular, the HTTP/RPC binding) as our wire protocol and direct invocation mechanism for all services. This approach provides language, operating system, and machine independence. We also use the Web Services Description Language (WSDL) for low level details of the service API. Both of these technologies provide excellent support for programmers and system integrators, but, by themselves, are not particularly suited for end users. Task computing, as we have presented it, relies extensively on service discovery and composition. The sorts of solutions for these needs offered by the Web services community (e.g., UDDI for discovery and BEPL4WS for composition) are similarly programmer oriented. These latter technologies are also less widely supported and are the focus of much less industry consensus.

3 Applications

Although we envision that Task Computing will gradually replace current personal computing experiences (those on desktop and laptop computers) as the main way to interact with computing devices, we currently focus on application environments where mobile users need to interact with transient devices and services. Examples of such environments include office spaces, home entertainment and healthcare.

Here we describe task computing application scenarios in office environment in favor of perspicuity and familiarity of the readers. The user is a salesperson (let us call her Alice) that meets Bob and his group for the first time in their conference room. Alice is allowed to wirelessly connect to the network provided for visitors. Alice's STEER (Semantic Task Execution EditoR, an implementation of TCC. See Section 0) on her PDA discovers many services in the room which can be used for interesting add-hoc compositions that can be executed in real time, via the Compose page of STEER.

Exchanging Business Cards
STEER infers a permissible composition of "Contact Provider" service for Bob running on his PDA and "Add into Contact List" on Alice's PDA. Alice hits the "Execute" button to execute [Contact Provider (on Bob's PDA) + Add into Contact List] to add Bob's contact into her PIM. Specifically, "Contact Provider" service for Bob is first executed and STEER acquires Bob's contact. Then STEER executes "Add into Contact List" running locally on Alice's PDA.

Showing and Sharing the Presentation
Alice is about to start the presentation of her product; the presentation file is stored on her PDA. Alice uses the composition of "Local File" service on her PDA and "View on Projector" service in the conference room [Local File + View on Projector]. As a result, Alice's presentation is projected on the screen and the control page shows up on her PDA. Using the control page, she can control her presentation wirelessly. Bob asks Alice for a copy of her presentation. Alice executes [Local File + Bank (File)] thus making the presentation file available through the "Bank (File)" service in the conference room. When someone later comes in the room, she can find the file to project it to the projector or copy it into her computing device even after Alice leaves the room.

Scheduling a Future Presentation
Bob and Alice schedule a future meeting in the same room. Bob creates the schedule item in his PIM on his PDA. He then composes and executes [Schedule from Scheduler + Bank (Schedule)] thus making the schedule item available as a service in the conference room environment. Alice can then execute [Schedule Provider (created by Bank (Schedule)) + Add into Schedule List] in order to add the newly scheduled future presentation into her PIM; other attendees can do the same, either now or later since the service will remain available in the room even after Bob leaves the room.

Checking and Printing Directions to the Airport
Alice asks Bob about how to get to the airport and Bob suggests that she use her STEER to see and print the directions. A map route service that displays on a public display the route between the office and other destinations is available in the conference room, along with services that provide the addresses of the nearby airports. Alice proceeds to perform a composition the [Map Router + Address of BWI airport], which when executed results to the route from the office to the BWI airport being displayed on the "Map Router" service's display. Alice can manipulate the display (zoom-in, zoom-out, pan, etc.) from her own PDA and she can even print the map route and directions.

It is important to note that each of these tasks can be performed in more than one ways. The services we have built can be deployed in any other environment and used by a user's TCE in that environment. Needless to mention that there are ways to achieve these tasks with today's technologies. What is unique though, is that none of the individual services was designed with these tasks in mind, that the existing services (40-50 in our demonstration environment) can be combined in a multitude of ways to perform interesting tasks (of which we only mention a handful) and finally, that the user need not discover, or familiarize themselves with the available services, in advance.

4 A TCE Embodiment

As mentioned in Section 0, a TCE consists of four components. In implementing each component, and assembling the components into a coherent whole, we have tried, as much as possible, to use Web standards with commodity like available implementations. In this, we were largely successful, modulo the relative immaturity of some of the standards we selected. This suggests that a reasonable TCE does not require special infrastructure support, but can be implemented almost entirely at the application level. This allowed us to make the various components self-contained, loosely coupled, and flexibly configurable and our TCE to be rapidly deployed in ad-hoc network environments. So, for example, our TCE still offers added value when dealing with plain UPnP services lacking rich semantic descriptions. Figure 1 shows the global architecture of our implemented TCE. Of course, this is just one of many possible TCEs.

4.1 STEER – Task Computing Client (TCC)

In this section, we describe how Semantic Task Execution EditoR (STEER), a Task Computing Client (TCC) works based on "Showing the Presentation" scenario described in Section 0. STEER offers a user interface for presenting to the user what she can do in the current context, and lets her define and execute the tasks.

We will attempt to describe the user experience of interacting with a TCE and simultaneously describe how the system accomplishes the user experience. Consider yourself to be a first time visitor to a company office. You are taken to the conference room and you get on the network provided for the visitors in the room. Then you want to give a presentation using the file on your computer. After you get the access to the network, you see a page in your Web browser on your computer like the one in the left side of Figure 2. This is the STEER Compose page, which shows the two-step service compositions as tasks you can do in this environment. This happens as follows.

First there is a discovery phase. STEER searches for the local and pervasive services[1] available and keep checking newly added or removed services.
STEER consults the local service manager (see Figure 1) for the available local semantic services such as "Local File" service which lets you choose a local file and expose it as a Web page. For each of those local services, STEER retrieves its Semantic Service Description (SSD) in DAML-S [3] from the local file system and feeds it into its inference engine (IE).

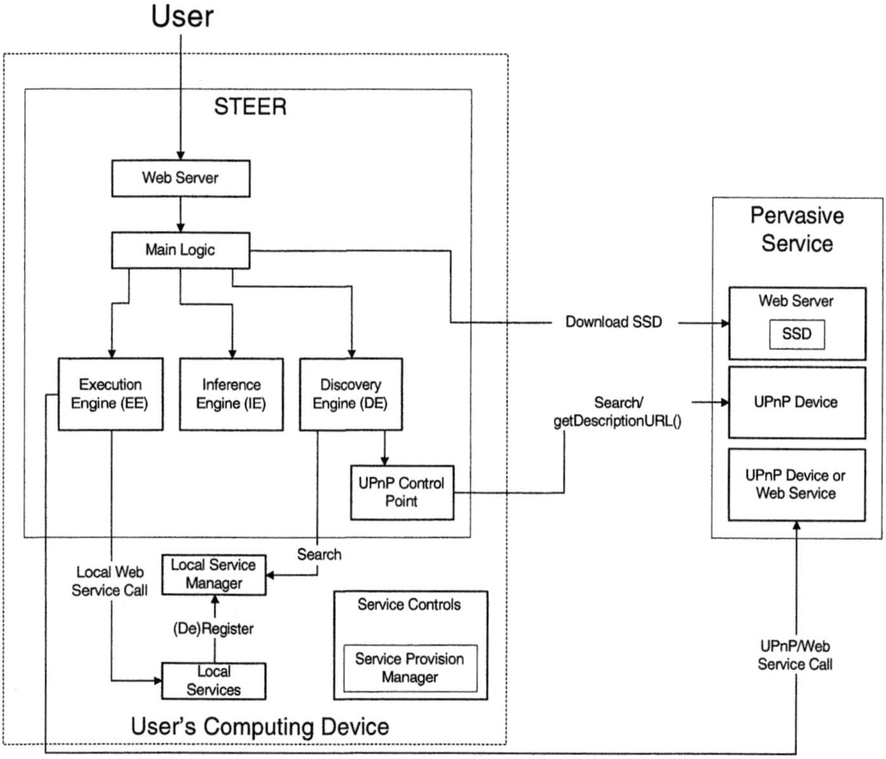

Fig. 1. Architecture of Task Computing Environment: User's computing device such as laptop and PDA runs STEER, a TCC, local service manager and optionally local services and service controls. Service controls may be running on other computers. A pervasive service consists of Web Server, UPnP device, and optionally Web Service. More details are given in the text.

---

[1] We define the local services as the services running on the user's computing device and private to the device. Pervasive services are defined as the services on the immediate network found through network service discovery mechanisms such as UPnP.

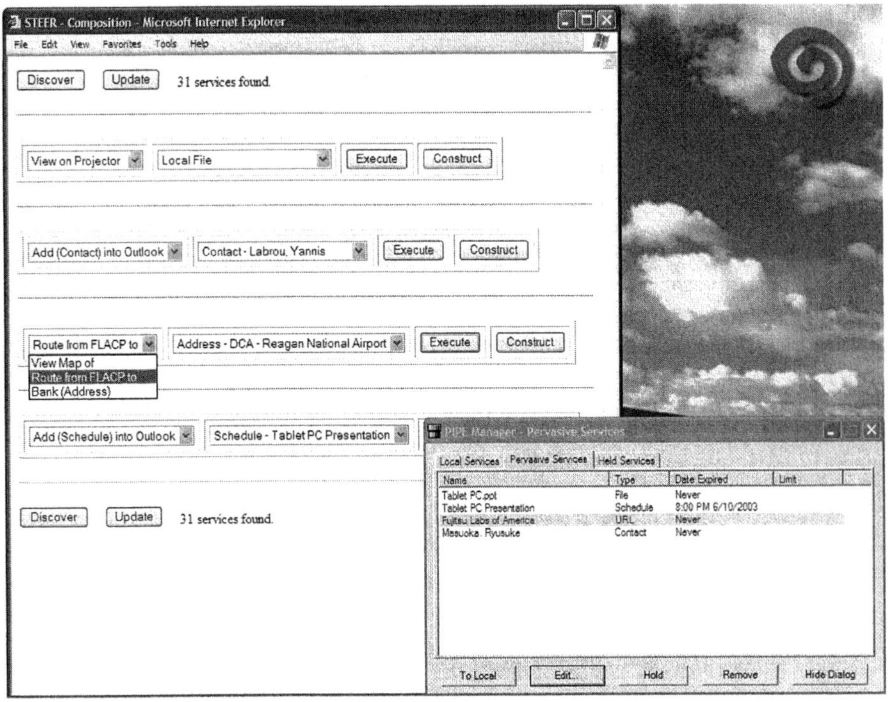

Fig. 2. Screenshot of Task Computing Environment (TCE) Client Desktop: STEER is a Web-server based TCC. STEER's Compose page is shown in the Web browser on the left. The compositions are categorized based on their semantic inputs and outputs. In each pair, any service on the right side drop-down menu can be combined with any service in the left side drop-down menu. The user uses the drop-down menu to choose the service and "Execute" button to execute the composition. The user can click "Construct" button to create a more complex composition starting from the two-service composition in this Compose page. The swirl on the upper right corner is the "White Hole." The user can drag and drop objects such as files, URLs, contacts and schedules from PIM to create services that provide semantic versions of the objects dropped into it. After the drag and drop, it swirls for a while to let the user know it is successfully dropped. Finally on the lower right corner a management GUI is shown; the user can use it to manage the services. Through this GUI, the user can make the services local or pervasive or hold temporarily those services for possible future use. The user can also control how those services are provided such as expiration time, etc.

STEER searches the services on the network using UPnP [2] device discovery protocol.[2] The UPnP architecture offers pervasive peer-to-peer network connectivity of devices and PCs. Pervasive services such as "View on Projector" respond to the search message as UPnP devices and are found by STEER. For each of those found UPnP devices, STEER makes a specific UPnP call (getDescriptionURL()) into it to get the URL of its SSD (expressed in DAML-S). STEER determines the service as a

---

[2] STEER acts as a control point and while pervasive services act as UPnP devices in UPnP terminology.

semantic service if it gets a result for this UPnP call. Then, STEER downloads its SSD in DAML-S from the URL returned. STEER feeds the SSD into its IE.

Then there is a composition phase. When STEER is asked for the Compose page, STEER asks its IE to compute prioritized two-step compositions starting with no-input services based on input and output matching. The order of compositions is prioritized based on various metrics including recentness of the service discovery and the exactness of matches. The IE returns possible compositions that are used by STEER to create the Web page which appears on the left in the Web browser in Figure 2. The Web page is dynamically created entirely from SSDs of found services. The menus are categorized based on the semantic objects handed between the services, such as "Web Page," contact, schedule, and address. The combination of "View on Projector" and "Local File" in the line for "Web Page" category is the composition you want to execute.[3]

Two-step composition starting with a no-input service has a couple of merits including: (1) The composition is always immediately executable with no input necessary to start, (2) Compositions allows interpretation as English sentences such as "View on Projector, Local File," and (3) Two-step composition, assuming that the constituent services are of the right granularity, are easy for the user to grasp.

Now you can immediately execute the composition by clicking the "Execute" button next to the particular composition. Or you can change the service to be executed, with any other compatible service by using drop-down menus. You can even construct longer compositions starting from any given two-step composition by clicking the "Construct" button in the same line as the composition. That leads you to the Construct page (figure not given in this paper) where you can modify the composition or add more services to the composition.

Let us assume that you decide to execute the service composition of "View on Projector" and "Local File" and click the "Execute" button. Figure 3 explains what happens when you click the "Execute" button. The Execution Engine of STEER (see Figure 1) handles the execution of the composition and makes the UPnP and Web Service call. Since the composition happens in the semantic layer, STEER needs to bridge the gap between the semantic objects in the semantic layer and parameters of and results from UPnP and Web Services. Using the grounding information in the SSDs of the services, STEER unmarshals the return values from UPnP and Web Service calls to the semantic object and marshals the semantic object to the parameters for those calls. This grounding mechanism, which happens in the Execution Engine, allows STEER to operate in the semantic layer and still to be able to execute all UPnP and Web services.

When the first service, "Local File" is executed, the service pops up a dialog box to let you to choose a file from your local file system. When you finish with the selection of the file, the service copies the file into a Web folder and returns the URL to the copied file as a string return value. The string is then unmarshaled into a "Web Page" semantic object by STEER internally.

---

[3] Note that "Local File" service, which has no-input, is the first service to be executed and the "View on Projector" is the second one to be executed.

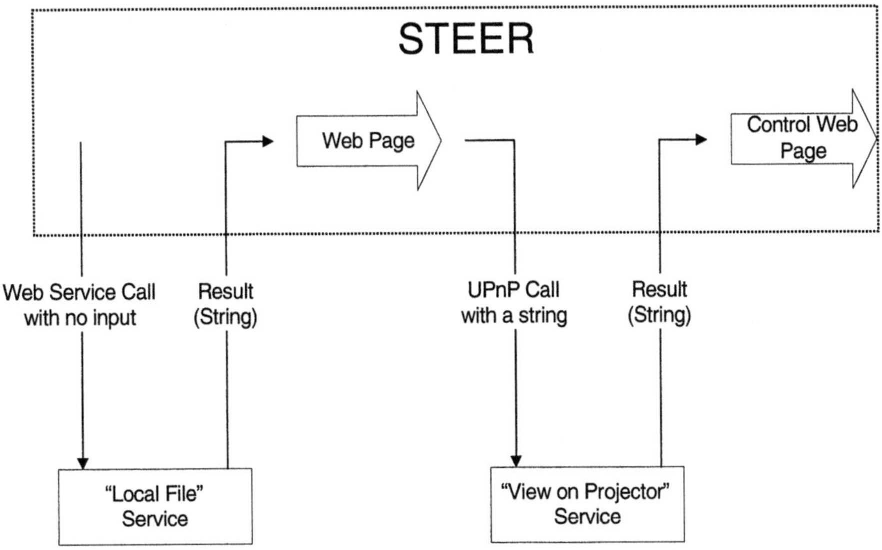

Fig. 3. Execution of the services by STEER: STEER uses the grounding information in their Semantic Service Descriptions (SSDs) to execute the services. In this case, the "Local File" service (which is a local service) is invoked through (local) Web Service call with no input based on WSDL/SOAP. The return value is just a string of URL, then STEER unmarshals it into a semantic object (which is "Web Page") using the grounding information in the SSD of "Local File" service. Then the "Web Page" semantic object is passed to the next service ("View on Projector") and marshaled into the string parameter for UPnP call. The same procedures apply if there are more services to follow in the composition to be executed.

The second service, "View on Projector" is executed with a string which is marshaled from the "Web Page" semantic object from the last service. "View on Projector" downloads the page from the given URL and displays it on the projector. Thus the execution of the composition enables you to show the file originally on your local disk on the projector in the room.[4]

An important point to note is that there has been no prior arrangement of those services and no knowledge of each other in advance. Both services happened to be found by STEER in a particular context, dynamically composed, and executed in a composition to accomplish a task.

Now let us turn to the issues of who and how to create those SSDs that makes it possible. The semantic object, "Web Page" in Figure 3 happens to be relatively simple with just one property of URL string. But STEER also needs to deal with other more complex semantic objects like address, schedule, and contact. While the

[4] You can actually control the "View on Projector" service so that you can give a decent presentation. This is possible since STEER automatically appends and executes "View Locally" service at the end of composition if the composition ends with a "Web Page" semantic object. The composition in this case ends with a "Control Web Page" to control "View on Projector" service. "View Locally" displays the "Control Web Page" (a subclass of "Web Page") in the Web browser locally on your computer.

grounding mechanism of marshalling and unmarshalling between semantic objects and parameters for the service invocations stays the same whether they are complex or simple, creating the grounding information for the complex semantic objects is substantially more difficult. Though we do not expect end-users of Task Computing create the grounding information, we foresee IT professionals at the device manufacturers and IT departments of large organizations will start to create the semantic service descriptions (SSDs) with grounding information for their devices and Web services.

We have created a tool called "OntoLink" to help such IT professionals to generate SSDs. "OntoLink" provides its user a GUI, which lets him visually create the SSD complete with the grounding of the semantic object in an ontology to the WSDL of the Web Service. Currently OntoLink supports grounding by XSLT scripts. The Execution Engine uses those XSLT scripts in the execution of services.

OntoLink also supports mapping (a kind of ontology translation) creation between the semantic objects in different ontologies. Grounding allows STEER to operate in the semantic layer, but it does not solve all the interoperability problems. Even though we expect that ontologies used in pervasive environment will be controlled mainly by device and software manufactures or consortia of such players and subsequent oligopoly of such ontologies, we will still need to have mapping between the semantic objects to freely compose the services which happened to be in different ontologies and many remote Web services. We see the efforts of creating the mappings fall on IT professionals as well. "OntoLink" lets its user open in its GUI two ontologies, which include the objects to be mapped. Through visual manipulation, the user produces the SSD of the mapping service.[5] Currently OntoLink supports semantic object mapping by XSLT scripts.

4.2 Services and Service Controls

In building up our TCE, we needed a reasonable set of "right-sized" services that would mesh appropriately with the sorts of objectives the particular set of end-users we had in mind (office workers) would have. Just as device manufacturers have to find the right grouping of functionalities to present to their users, so we had to provide services that were neither too packaged, nor too fine grained to fit in with our user's expectations and understanding. We had a further constraint of needing many services that made sense in no-input, two-step compositions.

In designing our services, we took inspiration from menu items commonly supplied across many sorts of office applications. Short term, adoption of TCEs will be by users already experienced with current applications, so it makes sense to provide them with familiar functionalities. Long term, it is clear that such ubiquitous presentation of functionality represents some degree of consensus understanding of the task in computer oriented offices.

We have implemented more than twenty kinds of services. They are categorized as follows:

[5] Though we do not go into the details in this paper, we treat semantic object mappings also as services and this decision made the whole architecture very consistent.

- Instance Selector: Lets the user select an item from a local system (file system, PIM, etc.) and outputs it as a semantic instance for other service to consume. This category includes such services as "Local File" and "Schedule from Scheduler."
- Instance Copier: Lets the user copy the semantic instance into a local system. This category includes such services as "Add into Contact List" and "Add into Scheduler."
- Instance Provider: Provides a semantic instance for other service to consume. This category includes such services as "Contact Provider" and "Schedule Provider."
- Instance Handler: Handles the semantic instance. This category includes "View on Projector" service as "Web Page" handler. "Map Router" service as "Address" handler, etc.

As in the right side of Figure 1, pervasive services have architecture with an UPnP device, a Web server, and optionally a Web service. UPnP device supports its discovery and returns the URL of its Semantic Service Description (SSD). The service provides the SSD by itself from its own Web server. The service which the SSD exposes is provided from its UPnP device or Web Service. One difficulty we needed to overcome is that its SSD may need to be created dynamically to accommodate the changes of environment the device happens to be in.

Other denizens of TCE are service controls. Service controls let you manage the services. You can create, hold temporarily, remove, or change how the services are provided.

In order to illustrate how the service controls are used, we describe how a business card exchange scenario works in TCE.[6] When you meet someone and want to give your business card to her, "White Hole" service control enables you to do so (see Figure 2). You first drag and drop your contact item from your PIM into the White Hole. Then the White Hole parses the contact item and creates a "Contact Provider" service for your contact. She finds this "Contact Provider" service and executes the composition of "Add into Contact List" and "Contact Provider" to insert your contact into his PIM. In the same way, you can share with her any other contact information as long as you have the contact in your PIM. By default, "White Hole" is configured to remove the service it created after a certain period of time, but you can remove it immediately or you can keep it forever by using the management GUI (see the lower right corner of Figure 2) if necessary.

With service controls, you can change the environment (which is defined here as the set of services available in your proximity) proactively for others as well as yourself. These service controls allows you to use the environment as communication medium. "Semantic Instance Bank" service controls let you to leave instances in the environment.[7] As in the "Scheduling a Future Presentation" scenario in Section 0, you can leave a schedule instance for the meeting in the conference room where the meeting will be held. The person who comes in the room later can find the schedule and insert it into her PIM if necessary.

The current list of implemented service controls includes:

---

[6] This is only one way to execute the "Exchanging Business Cards" scenario in Section 0 .

[7] "Instance Providing" services to be exact.

- White Hole: Lets the user drag and drop an item (file, contact, schedule, etc.) from local systems (file system, PIM, etc.) to create (and manage) a corresponding instance providing service
- Semantic Instance Bank: Semantic service for each type of semantic instances to create an instance providing service
- Image Service Control: Lets the user interact with image devices (scanner, DV/digital camera) and create an instance providing service for the image file captured.

We need to clearly state that this is all built already and that it works. We have installers for the complete TCE, so that a user can install the client environment on her machine in a couple of minutes and use it immediately once in a TCE environment.

5 Evaluation

In building this TCE, we wanted to build an end-to-end system, from discovery through composition to execution, all actually using the relevant technologies. This was often difficult as the maturity of the libraries (e.g., WSDL) or even the standards left a lot to be desired. We often traded "vertical" for "horizontal" completeness. For example, STEER only supports compositions of services with at most one input and/or output into sequences aligning those inputs and outputs. Thus, our DAML-S Process Model interpreter doesn't execute the more complex DAML-S control constructs, such as if-then-else, iteration, or split. However, given our target scenario – office workers without a lot of computer expertise – this limitation seemed not only acceptable, but desirable. It's unclear how to make more complex composing behavior feasible for our target audience.

Similarly, our reasoner isn't complete with regard to DAML+OIL semantics (much less supporting various useful, non-standard inferences), but given the relative simplicity of our matchmaking and selection needs, being lightweight and flexible trumped other features. Indeed, the success of such ad hoc reasoning services validates our framework. Often with component and assisted programming environments, there is difficulty in scaling down the implementation (and user) requirements. Just as regular programmers can build useful and interesting content management systems using Web standards and common components such as Apache, MySQL, and the like, we expect that regular programmers and system administrators will be able to build custom TCEs tuned to their particular situation and driven by their interests and needs.

Clearly, other scenarios would drive rather different design tradeoffs and thus rather different TCEs. However, it's pretty clear how to build those alternative TCEs out of ours. The easiest thing to change is the set of available services. As long as they can be cast into a single input/output model, our TCE will adapt automatically. But even if, say, in a Grid computing scenario, or a complex publishing one, the services supplied and the workflows desired were more elaborate, TCEs designed to handle such elaborations could easily reuse our discovery mechanisms, executor, inference engine (perhaps slightly extended), and even many of the services and meta-services (e.g., Service controls such as "White Hole" and "Semantic Instance Banks").

In general, TCEs are driven by the ordinary behavior of regular users focused on the job at hand. In this regard, one serious limitation in our current implementation is the lack, at least at the STEER UI level, of the ability to save and share compositions and generalized composition templates. We do have TCE clients that can do this, but we have not integrated that functionality into the overall system. The accretion of such embodied expertise in the system is critical to making the system truly dynamic. Merely having flexible, parameterized services is not enough, as they just generalize the predetermined set of actions somewhat. For a TCE to be user driven, it must allow for, support, indeed encourage the seamless expansion of the set of available, salient, task "conscious" services.

6 Related Work

Our work builds heavily on the convergence of the Semantic Web and Web services, particularly as supported by the DAML-S framework [3]. We use the DAML-S Profile upper ontology to represent and categorize our services for matchmaking and in-composition selection of services. All compositions are represented using the DAML-S process model, and executed directly by a process model interpreter. We extended the grounding ontology to directly handle UPnP, as well as providing support for marshalling and unmarshalling between XML schema and DAML+OIL. The latter extensions have been including in the lastest version of DAML-S.

Bussler, Maedche, and Fensel [4] suggest that, unlike the Semantic Web enabled Web Services (SWWS) conceptual architecture they propose, DAML-S doesn't present a "a mediated P2P environment" which requires every "trading partner to be able to mediate differences in document types, semantics or even business process behavior." To address this requirement, their architecture contains a "semantic transformation engine" as a critical component providing "ontology based mediation." Our TCE incorporates exactly such a mechanism without having to particularly extend the DAML-S framework. Our translators are just more services, albeit services of a specific type that a translation aware matching engine can make special use of. But this is no different than other classifications of services (in house vs. subcontracted, local vs. remote, UI vs. processing, information providing vs. world altering, etc.) that we might need to adopt for a variety of purposes. An advantage of our DAML-S based approached is that the system degrades smoothly when using more generic tools. Since ontology translators and mediators are just more services, a perfectly generic composer can use them.

Unlike much of the current work on "semantic matchmaking" (particularly in a DAML-S context), our approaches did not rely on either a broker or other repository mechanisms [7] or a sophisticated P2P scheme [4]. Given the limits imposed by the pervasive and local contexts, and the fact that we had only one fundamental scenario implemented, having every service announce itself to the client's knowledge base was quite feasible. The key discovery activities became selection of services in a particular composition context [5]. As we develop TCEs for more heterogeneous environments (e.g., where the user is moving from boardroom to coffee shop), we envision using more elaborate pervasive brokering schemes, such as described in [8]. Similarly, as remote services start to proliferate, we will need to find some way of finding and filtering them. We expect to have to support a number of mechanisms from enhanced

UDDI repositories [7], to user bookmarks, to RSS feeds, to a service aware Google, etc.

7 Conclusions and Future Work

We believe that Task Computing is a promising application of Semantic Web and Web Services technologies, especially in pervasive computing environment. What is unique about our Task Computing implementation is that we have implemented end-to-end system from discovery, to composition, and eventually execution of services, all of this driven by end-users, rather than by developers, via a user interface. In order to realize such a system and let the user define tasks at the semantic layer, we had to bridge the raw (in the sense of semantics) APIs that drive the execution layer and the semantic layer (the user-facing side) at all layers of the system (discovery, composition and eventually execution of composed services). But when completed we were able to provide the users with a task-oriented view of their environment that in turn minimizes the required knowledge and skills for accomplishing interesting tasks in that environment.

We see Task Computing as a business opportunity for both device manufacturers and IT solution providers. For device manufacturers, devices can be treated as Semantically Described Services (SSDs); someone will have to provide this semantic layer wrapper of the devices' functionality. In addition, the devices need to implement a service discovery mechanism (e.g., UPnP or Bluetooth) and make available a remote control API for accessing their functionality (e.g., UPnP). TCE clients such as STEER can be pre-configured with SSDs for well-known devices; or some web server in the network can provide SSDs for well-known devices; in other words, the provider of the semantic layer need to be the device manufacturer itself. Device manufactures will benefit from the newly found uses of their devices in flexible and ad-hoc Task Computing environment.

IT solution providers can combine the benefit of Task Computing-enabled devices with additional services, to provide interesting application is various verticals in an easier and faster manner than today. In a way, since the end-user becomes the application builder, the solution provider need only focus on the set of services to make available in the vertical environment and the user interface for that environment. The first task for the solution provider would be to select the web services, some of them, third party services that they want to make available to end users and create the semantic descriptions and grounding descriptions for them. Tools like OntoLink will help them with that task. The tangible advantage is not only the faster development cycle but the ease of maintenance and of adding functionality into the system, since they only need to add new services or to change the grounding of an existing service, in order to "upgrade" a service implementation.

Our system is the first version of a vision; as a result there are a lot of issues that we have barely considered thus far. Trust and security mechanisms, monitored execution of asynchronous, constantly-changing, or subscription services, deeper integration with location determination and other modalities for user interface such as voice, are just a few of the directions to further explore. Nevertheless, we believe that Task Computing has the potential to change how the end-users interact with their computing environments.

Acknowledgments. We want to thank Jim Hendler for his guidance and constructive criticism throughout this project and the writing of this paper. We also want to thank Mike Grove, Zhexuan Song, Wei-Lun Chen, Evren Sirin, and Aditya Kalyanpur for their hard work to make the Task Computing vision a reality.

References

1. Weiser, M.: The Computer of the 21st Century. Scientific American, vol. 265, no. 3, Sept. 1991, pp. 66–75
2. UPnP Forum: http://www.upnp.org/
3. The DAML Services Coalition (alphabetically Anupriya Ankolenkar, Mark Burstein, Jerry R. Hobbs, Ora Lassila, David L. Martin, Drew McDermott, Sheila A. McIlraith, Srini Narayanan, Massimo Paolucci, Terry R. Payne and Katia Sycara), "DAML-S: Web Service Description for the Semantic Web", The First International Semantic Web Conference (ISWC) , Sardinia (Italy), June, 2002.
4. Christoph Bussler, Alexander Maedche, Dieter Fensel, "A Conceptual Architecture for Semantic Web Enabled Web Services", ACM Special Interest Group on Management of Data: Volume 31, Number 4, Dec 2002
5. Evren Sirin, James Hendler, Bijan Parsia, "Semi-automatic Composition of Web Services using Semantic Descriptions", "Web Services: Modeling, Architecture and Infrastructure" workshop in conjunction with ICEIS2003, 2002
6. A. Flett. A comparison of daml-s and wsmf. In Internal Report, Vrije Universiteit Amsterdam, 2002.
7. Massimo Paolucci, Takahiro Kawamura, Terry R. Payne, and Katia Sycara, "Semantic Matching of Web Services Capabilities", The First International Semantic Web Conference (ISWC), Sardinia (Italy), June, 2002.
8. Harry Chen, Tim Finin, and Anupam Joshi, Using OWL in a Pervasive Computing Broker, Workshop on Ontologies in Open Agent Systems, AAMAS 2003.

A Semantic Infosphere

Michael Uschold[1], Peter Clark[1], Fred Dickey[1], Casey Fung[1], Sonia Smith[1], Stephen Uczekaj[1], Michael Wilke[1], Sean Bechhofer[2], and Ian Horrocks[2]

[1] Boeing, Phantom Works , P.O. Box 3707,m/s 7L-40
Seattle, WA USA 98124-2207,
michael.f.uschold@boeing.com

[2] Department of Computer Science, University of Manchester
Oxford Road, Manchester M13 9PL, UK,
seanb@cs.man.ac.uk

Abstract. We describe a prototype implementation of a semantic filtering capability added to an existing XML-based publish and subscribe infrastructure. An ontology is used to provide vocabulary for expressing both 1) the semantic annotations that characterize the published documents and 2) the subscriptions specifying the class of documents to be routed to a given client. A description logic (DL) classifier is used to determine which subscribers an incoming document is routed to. We outline the key elements of the ontology for the battlefield domain and give some sample annotations and subscriptions. This is the basis for describing a number of scenarios showing how this filtering capability could be used practice. We critically analyze the suitability of a DL language and reasoner in general, and the particular implementation choices (DAML+OIL, FaCT and OilEd) for performing this task. A key result of the work is to demonstrate the importance of testing semantics-based technologies on practical problems. We discovered a number of new and interesting areas for future work, which in turn can direct the focus of the research community.

1 Introduction

An infosphere is a platform of protocols, processes and common core services that permit stand-alone or web-based applications to submit, discover and share information over a network. An XML-based infosphere architecture called the Xinfosphere was developed at Boeing Phantom Works Seattle in 1999-2001. It was made available for download on the Boeing intranet.

The Xinfosphere supports two types of users and two types of core services. First, there are client users & applications that utilize data dissemination services such as publish, subscribe and query. Second, there are client administrators that utilize administration and security services such as configuration, monitoring and access control. Published items that can be subscribed to are called Information Data Objects (IDOs). They are in XML format. Each may have corresponding metadata, also in XML. Subscriber clients specify IDOs of interest by creating a filter. When an IDO is published, all the filters are checked to see which subscriber clients the IDO gets routed to. A given subscriber client only receives the IDOs that pass through their specified [subscription] filters.

D. Fensel et al. (Eds.): ISWC 2003, LNCS 2870, pp. 882–896, 2003.

The original mechanism for implementing the publish/subscribe component of the Xinfosphere is purely XML-based. All IDOs and metadata are in XML, filters are expressed in XPath, XSL or XQL [2,3,6]. As such, the approach is purely syntactic. The goal of this research is to explore the hypothesis that there are advantages to augmenting the Xinfosphere publish/subscribe component with a semantic filtering capability. Some potential advantages are as follows:

1. the subscriber will no longer be required to know the structure and syntax of the documents in order to create a filter, they focus instead on the semantics of the content;
2. [related to 1] a rich and powerful semantics-based mechanism can be used to express filters allowing greater selectivity and finer control;
3. the collection of filters from all the subscriber clients can be automatically classified, *a priori*, potentially resulting in faster routing;
4. a set of filters can be checked for internal consistency. This could be done for a single client, or for a group of clients;
5. the types of IDOs that can be subscribed to no longer need to be just a flat list; instead they may be arranged in a rich hierarchy that arises from an ontology in the domain of the IDOs.

We recognize that semantic approaches are not a panacea. In some circumstances, a syntactic approach may be adequate. The system has been architected to allow additional filtering mechanisms to be added. We have added one, leaving the original one in place. Other semantic filtering technologies can be added, for example, different description logic reasoners [1], or other ontology languages and inference engines. This gives clients the ability to choose the filtering technology most suitable to their needs.

Semantic Filtering: Subscriptions and Queries The Xinfosphere supports both publish/subscribe and answering queries from a static repository. Subscriptions and queries are closely related concepts, for example one can think of a subscription as a query to be applied in the future. In both cases, there is a description that an Information Data Object must match before it is passed along to the requester. The descriptions are the filters. We mainly focus on the publish/subscribe aspect of the Xinfosphere in this paper. We will usually not distinguish between queries and subscriptions, speaking only of semantic filters that could be used for either.

1.1 Approach

In this section we describe our approach for implementing a Semantic Infosphere. The existing Xinfosphere is architected to enable alternative filtering technologies. We added one that is semantics-based, rather than purely XML-based. We identify the main elements and comment briefly on our choice of which semantics technologies to use. Our approach includes the following key elements:

Ontology. Create an ontology that represents the key concepts and relationships in the domain of interest. Represent it in a formal language that has a corresponding inference engine.

Semantic Annotations. Augment documents with semantic annotations (i.e. metadata) using terms from the ontology, encoded in the ontology language. Documents are published along with their semantic annotations.

Semantic Filtering. This involves two steps. First, create semantic filters specifying which IDOs are of interest. Second, use an inference engine to determine which IDOs pass through the filters, thus ensuring that subscriptions route (or queries return) the correct documents to clients requesting them.

Our choice of technologies to use for these steps is summarized below.

- Use the description logic SHIQ [4] in DAML+OIL [11] syntax to represent the ontology, the semantic annotations and the filters;
- Use OilEd [8] to create the ontology;
- Use FaCT DL reasoner [10] both to 1) check the consistency of the ontology during its development, and 2) determine whether there is a match between the semantic annotations of a document and a semantic filter (subscription).

DAML+OIL was chosen because it was an emerging standard. OilEd was the only GUI ontology editor available that provided [nearly] full support for DAML+OIL, while FaCT was the natural choice for an inference engine as it was linked to OilEd. We discuss tools further in Section 5. For the remainder of this paper, we elaborate on the above steps, giving examples and scenarios illustrating the ideas. Finally, we consider some related and future work.

2 Ontology

The basis for a semantic infosphere is semantic publishing and filtering. In turn, the basis for semantic publishing and filtering is a formal ontology and associated inference engine. The ontology is represented in a formal language and captures the key concepts and relationships in the domain of interest. For example, in the battlefield ontology, we have concepts like 'units', 'movement' and 'place'.

2.1 Domain: Battlefield Reports

We used a scenario that was generated as a framework to support Natural Language Processing (NLP) techniques as part of the Boeing Real Time Information System (RTIMS) development [7]. The scenario is played on terrain which is Ft Lewis WA and vicinity. The US force was a standard J series Mechanized Battalion Task Force and the adversary was a defending Russian class motorized rifle battalion. A movement to contact framework was used to generate standard US Army spot report format (Date/Time,Location, Description, Reporting Unity, Info Evaluation) as the fictional situation developed. Outcomes, movements, incidents, casualties and losses were strictly arbitrary and scripted to generate a diversity of reports. Here is a simple spot report:

Spot Report 1
1. 220555Z Jun 92
2. 46 53' 25" N, 122 41' 40" W
3. Scout platoon completed recon of Rainier.
   No enemy contact.
   Sct platoon moving to battalion left flank.
4. 2-48 Inf

There are two main things being reported: 1) a reconnaissance event by a particular unit and 2) a movement by that same unit. In addition, there is information about time and location as well as the name of the unit. In general, a report can contain many different items of information. For example, a single report may have information about a unit engaging the enemy and destroying some of its equipment, the enemy abandoning a vehicle, the movement of a unit, and the fact that the unit is on watch.

This scenario data was ideal for our purposes. First, there were hundreds of messages available. Second, the ontology already existed. Finally, there was a set of semantic annotations for each message that had been *automatically generated* using natural language processing techniques, as noted above (see example below). We entered a portion of the ontology (initially represented in Prolog) into OilEd and exported it in DAML+OIL syntax.

There are four main kinds of information being reported on:
1. *Move*: for movement activities
2. *Event*: for other activities
3. *Situation Report*: to describe the status of a friendly force
4. *Enemy Order of Battle*: to describe enemy status and activities

Each has a corresponding template, for representing the semantic annotations. A single report can have one or more of each of the four kinds of template. For spot report 1, two templates were generated, an *Event* template and a *Move* template. For other spot reports, several could be generated.

2.2 The Domain Ontology

The ontology is based on the information that goes into each of the above four templates. As can been seen in the example above, each template consists of a fixed number of slot-filler pairs which represents the information contained in the message. Perhaps the most central concept is that of a unit. A unit has attributes such as Id, Size, Location, Force type (friendly/enemy), Function (e.g. recon, cavalry), Purpose (e.g. make contact, relieve), and Vehicles and Losses (e.g. equipment or personnel).

There are two roles for units: agent and object. The agent unit performs an activity. The object unit is the object of the agent activity. The agent does, and the object is done to. For example an agent unit may engage an enemy [object] unit. Note that an object role need not be filled by a unit, other things can be 'done to', e.g. a place might be the object of a recon activity. An agent unit has an additional attribute: instrument-of, indicating what is used to perform the action. For a unit in the object role, there is an attribute for response of object (e.g. abandon vehicle, hold position).

There is a wide variety of other things that are reported in these messages. When movement is being reported, the direction may be indicated. Reports on the status of friendly or enemy units will include the time of the report and various weapons and other equipment. For friendly units, a commander's assessment is included. Figure 2 depicts a number of these concepts in OilEd.

As part of the infrastructure for representing semantic annotations, we have a container for holding all the semantic annotations for a given spot report. This is a class called Message. As noted above, message has a number of templates associated with it. These are represented using a class called Template. It has four subclasses for the four template types (Event, Move, Situation Report, and Enemy order of Battle).

We use OilEd 'properties' (i.e. relations) to represent two main things:

1. The relation between Messages and Templates indicating which Templates are associated with a given Message.
2. The template slots. Every template slot has as its domain, a kind of Template. Some slots apply to all templates, others to two or more, and some to just one.

The relation for 1. is called 'hasTemplate'. Its domain is Message, and its range is Template. It has four sub-relations: hasMove, hasEvent, hasEoB and hasSitRep. All properties representing template slots have as their domain some kind of Template. If the slot applies to all templates, then the domain is exactly: Template. For those that apply to only some of the templates, the domain is a subclass of Template (e.g. Template-Event or Template-Move, or perhaps their union.). For example:

agentForce: Template → ForceType
objectUnitFunction: Template → UnitFunction
destination: Template-Move → Location

We use OilEd individuals to represent possible values for slots. For example, ForceType has two instances: friendly and enemy. UnitFunction has many instances such as: armor, cavalry and recon. This way of modeling the domain mirrored the way the metadata was represented and was chosen for expedience. There may be better modeling choices.

3 Semantic Annotations

Semantic annotations of the IDOs provide the foundation for semantic publishing. They are published along with the IDOs themselves. It is these annotations that are used to determine which IDOs pass through a given filter. The annotations may contain metadata about the document independent from its content, e.g. Dublin Core metadata such as date published and author. They may also describe the actual content of the document. In this paper, we focus mainly on the latter.

These annotations are like metadata in that they contain information augmenting the core IDO. However, they are different from metadata concerning the document as a whole (such as date published, author, number of words). Rather, the semantic annotations *formally represent portions of the content of the IDO in the syntax of the ontology language*. Each template is represented formally and linked to the IDO when it is published. As an example, templates generated for message 1 above are shown below. Slots with no data have been removed. This is the actual output of the metadata extraction program (RTIMS), generated from an internal Prolog representation.

```
sp-001

 1.  Template Type:                    EVENT
 2.  Message Nr:                       SP-001
 3.  Time of Event:                    220555Z JUN 92
 4.  Force Initiating:                 FRIENDLY
 5.  Agent Activity:                   RECON
 6.  Agent Location:                   046 53 25 N 122 41 40 W
 7.  Object Location:                  046 53 25 N 122 41 40 W
 8.  Agent:                            SCT PLT/2-48 INF
 9.  Agent Unit ID:                    SCT PLT/2-48 INF
10.  Agent Unit Function:              RECON
11.  Agent Unit Size:                  1:PLT
13.  Object:                           RAINIER
27.  General Result:                   NO ENEMY SIGHTED

 1.  Template Type:                    MOVE
 2.  Message Nr:                       SP-001
 3.  Time of Event:                    220555Z JUN 92
 4.  Maneuver Type:                    MOVE
 5.  Agent:                            SCT PLT/2-48 INF
 6.  Agent Force:                      FRIENDLY
 7.  Agent Unit ID:                    SCT PLT/2-48 INF
 8.  Agent Unit Function:              RECON
 9.  Agent Unit Size:                  1:PLT
11.  Agent Location:                   046 53 25 N 122 41 40 W
14.  Destination:                      2-48 INF LEFT FLANK
```

For the proof of concept demonstrator, we manually translated these informal annotations into DAML+OIL using OilEd. A better solution is to adapt the automatic metadata generator to output DAML+OIL instead of formatted templates in English.

As noted above, we use a class in the ontology called Message as a container for the semantic annotations. Logically, we wish to create instances of this concept for each spot report. In a publish/subscribe context, the semantic filtering inference will only be applied to one message at a time, as each message is published. After a message is routed to the right subscribers, it is either discarded, or placed in a data store for possible future query. For testing purposes, it is convenient to create a suite of messages and to determine all at once which messages get routed to which subscriptions. This is accomplished in OilEd by doing a complete classification (computing the class hierarchy) and realization (computing the most specific classes that individuals are instances of).

For our testing, we tried creating explicit instances in OilEd. This, however, resulted in unacceptable response times when we ran FaCT to do the classification and realization. As a workaround, we represented messages as concept descriptions instead of instances. Given the fact that we do not use the full expressive power of the logic w.r.t. individuals – in particular we never assert relationships between pairs of individuals – the realization computed using this workaround is indistinguishable from that which would be computed using "real" individuals: it can be viewed as an optimization rather than a workaround. To simplify this discussion, we will ignore such details for now – in Section 6 we discuss a proper solution using an *instance store* [9].

We created a new class called Message-Individual whose instances are particular messages. By convention, we prefix the name of all individuals with 'I' followed by a dash followed by an abbreviation of the class that it is an instance of. For example, 'I-

Aty-Recon' is an instance of the class 'Activity', and 'I-Ft-Friendly' is an instance of the class: 'ForceType'. An English rendition of the formal representation of some key portions of message 1 is given below. These annotations are created using OilEd and exported in DAML+OIL syntax. They are then added to the IDOs that are published in the Infosphere.

Message-001 is a subclass of Message-Individual with the following restrictions:

1. It has an Event template, with a filler restriction requiring that the Event template:
   a. has some agentForce that has value 'I-Ft-Friendly';
   b. has some eventActivity that has value 'I-Aty-Recon';
   c. has some agentUnitId that has value 'UID-`SCT PLT/2-48 INF`';
   d. has some agentUnitSize that is has value 'I-Sz-Platoon';
   e. has some generalResultOf that has value 'I-Rslt-NoEnembySighted';
   f. has some objectOf that has value 'I-Cty-Ranier'; *etc.*
2. It has a Move Template with a filler restriction requiring that the Move Template :
   a. has some agentForce that has value 'I-Ft-Friendly'
   b. has some eventActivity that has value 'I-Aty-Recon'.
   c. has some agentUnitId that has value 'UID-`SCT PLT/2-48 INF`'
   d. has some agentUnitSize that has value 'I-Sz-Platoon'
   e. has some agentLocation that has value
      'I-Grd-`046 53 25 N 122 41 40 W`'
   f. has some destination that has value '`2-48 INF LEFT FLANK`'

Next we discuss how subscribers create filters indicating which IDOs they are interested in. From here on in, we will use the term 'subscription' instead of 'filter', since that is our main emphasis.

4 Semantic Filtering

Recall that semantic filtering involves two steps: 1) creating the subscriptions and 2) performing the inference to determine which messages get routed to which subscribers. We express both the annotations and the subscriptions in DAML+OIL using the vocabulary from the ontology. The FaCT reasoner[1] is used to perform the semantic filtering inference. We have seen that each IDO is published along with a semantic annotation that logically represents an instance of the concept: Message-Individual. As a workaround, this is currently represented not as an instance, but as a [pseudo]-concept in DAML+OIL (see above). A subscription is a DAML+OIL concept representing a class of IDOs that a client is interested in. FaCT is used to answer the question: *"Is the DAML+OIL individual representing the message a member of the DAML+OIL class representing the subscription"?*

4.1 Creating Subscriptions

A subscription characterizes a particular subset of messages that a user is interested in seeing. For example, a client may subscribe to all messages where:

---

[1] http://www.cs.man.ac.uk/fact

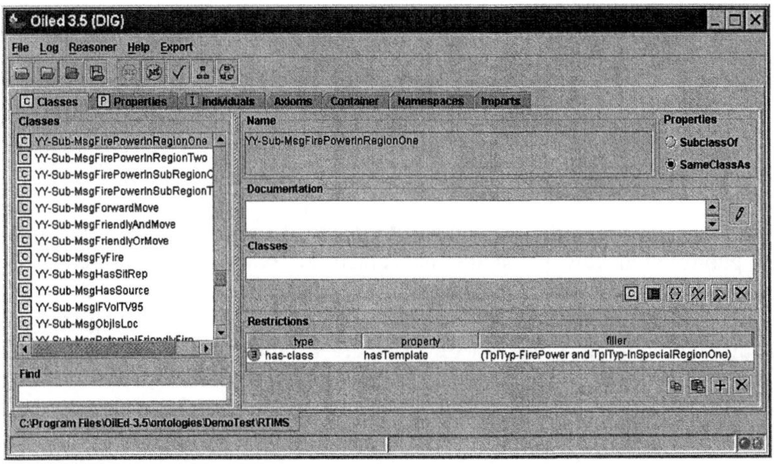

Fig. 1. Firepower in Region One

1. there is some firepower activity going on in a particular region;
2. a recon unit is engaging in a move activity;
3. an enemy unit is engaging in a move activity.

Here is an English rendition of the formal concept representing the first subscription:

- The class of all messages that have at least one template with a filler restriction requiring that the template type to be both TplTyp-FirePower Template and TplTyp-InSpecialRegionOne (see Figure 1).

In turn these template types are defined as:

- *TplType-FirePower*: the class of all templates that have at least one eventActivity with a filler restriction requiring that the activity be of type: FirePowerActivity. This concept has a number of member individuals including I-Aty-Attack, I-Aty-HitMine, and I-Aty-ReturnFire.
- *InSpecialRegionOne:* the class of all templates that have at least one agentLocation with a filler restriction requiring it to be of type: InRegionOne.

All of the subscriptions are defined in a similar manner using OilEd. To keep track of which concepts are subscriptions and which are part of the main ontology we create a special class called: YY-Subscription[2]. All subscriptions are defined to be subclasses of this.

Intermediate Vocabulary

Note the use of the concept: TplType-FirePower which was used to define the overall subscription. We anticipate that in practice, a client will create a variety of such concepts. They need not be part of the overall ontology, but are specific to a subscriber or group of subscribers' needs. They are used as an intermediate

[2] This name is used to force the subscriptions to be shown in OilEd after the main ontology concepts, all of which are in alphabetical order.

vocabulary for defining subscriptions. For concepts that are not going to be used again, it could be easier to just embed the concept definition in the subscription and not create it as an explicitly named concept.

4.2 Performing Semantic Filtering

The final step is to do the semantic filtering to determine which subscribers each newly published document should be routed to. Each document has a semantic annotation associated with it that is represented as a DAML+OIL individual. Formally, we need to find all the subscription concepts that a given semantic annotation individual is a member of. In Figure 2, all and only the nodes in italics are classes that the message for Spot Report 1 is a direct instance of.

In the testing phase, to make sure the messages would be routed properly, we represented all the messages and subscriptions in OilEd. By invoking the classifier, we automatically see which messages will get routed to which subscriber, as shown in Figure 2. Note that the message will be routed to all the subscription classes that are superclasses of the subscriptions of which the messages are direct instances. This is an advantage of semantic filtering.

4.3 A Set of Related Filters

Note that some of the subsuming subscriptions in Figure 1 are listed in the bottom window. These are the classes that directly subsume ZZ-Msg-001. In addition, there are all the subscriptions that subsume these. For example each of the following subsumes the prior subscription.

- ReconInSubRegionOne: any template with recon activity in SubRegionOne
- ReconInRegionOne: any template with recon activity in RegionOne
- ReconAty: any template related to Recon activity. which is in turn subsumed by Recon: any template having anything to do with Recon units or activities.

This illustrates one potential advantage of using classification to perform filtering. All the subscriptions themselves can be pre-classified. Figure 2 illustrates a set of related subscriptions that could be defined. These are pre-classified as indicated in the figure. This means that it can be faster to find all the matching subscriptions, than if each had to be tested one by one. We have not determined under what conditions this theoretical advantage would have practical import.

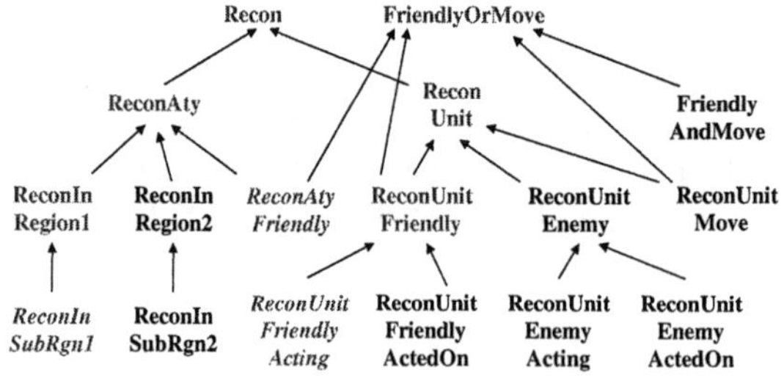

Fig. 2. Related Subscriptions

4.4 Usage Scenarios

For some brief scenarios whereby this semantic publish and subscribe system could be useful, consider a battle situation, where messages coming in from troops in the field. Different people have different jobs, and thus require different information. There would be a general in charge who needs to decide about moving troops to the best position. There will be other specialists, planners, recon experts etc. The recon specialist may need detailed information on a variety of recon units and activities, but possibly only in some regions. A pub/sub system running live would route the information to the right people at the right time. Different people could add or remove subscriptions dynamically.

5 Architecture and Tools

The XInfosphere is a platform of protocols, processes and common core services that permit applications and users to submit, discover and share information over a network. A core service of the XInfosphere is to allow for the exchange of XML information using a publish-subscribe-query model of data. Data producers publish XML data to an XInfosphere Information Data Object (IDO), which can be subscribed to by data consumers. Subscribers have the ability to filter information using the structural elements of the message.

The filtering mechanism used by the XInfosphere is extensible and allows additional message filtering techniques to be added. In order to adequately match information to user's needs based on content rather than structure, we extended the XInfosphere to support the semantic filtering of information. In this section, we discuss our selection of tools, and present the overall architecture.

5.1 System Architecture

The overall architecture is shown in Figure 3 and involves the following steps.

Ontology Creation. We loosely integrated OilEd, a graphical ontology editor developed at the University of Manchester, into XInfosphere. OilEd is bundled with the XInfosphere distribution software and can be launched from within XInfosphere. We used OilEd to develop a demonstration ontology in the domain of Army battlefield messages, exported in DAML+OIL syntax.

Semantic Publishing. We augmented the Army messages with semantic annotations using concepts and terms from the ontology. The messages, along with the semantic annotations are published to an IDO in an XInfosphere server.

Semantic Filtering. The Xfiltering mechanism was extended to allow for semantics based filtering, in addition to the existing XPath-based filtering. The messages containing semantic annotations contain a pre-defined metadata slot, which is recognized by the Xfiltering mechanism. We developed a FaCT client specifically for Xinfosphere. There are two steps: creating the filters, and performing the inference to determine which subscribers get which messages.

The filters (i.e. subscriptions) are created using OilEd. The subscriptions are included in the ontology that is loaded into FaCT. When a message is published, the FaCT client is asked to return all the subscription classes that the corresponding semantic annotation is a member individual of. Messages that successfully match the filter are forwarded to the subscriber.

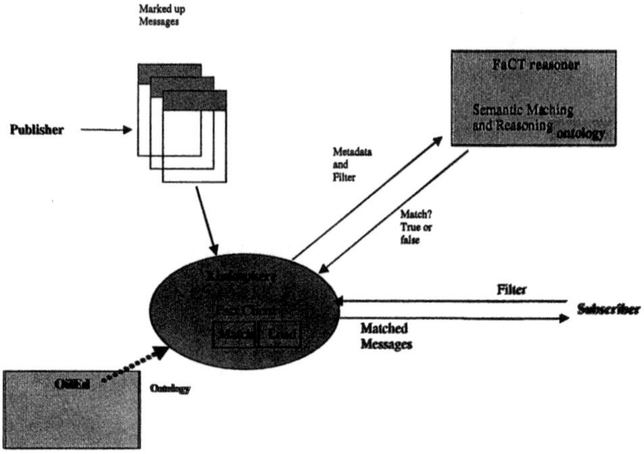

Fig. 3. System Architecture

5.2 Tools

We selected DAML+OIL as the language for representing the ontology because 1) it was highly expressive, 2) there was a fast inference engine for doing the semantic filtering (FaCT) and 3) it was an emerging W3C standard with the likely good tool support in the near future. OilEd was a natural choice for an ontology editor; the decision to use it followed from the decision to use a description logic reasoner to perform semantic filtering. OilEd was the only DAML+OIL tool ontology editor available at that time. Since then, a DAML+OIL plug-in for Protégé was developed [13]. However, it is very limited in the range of DL descriptions that you can create with it. To our knowledge, OilEd remains the only fully functional description logic ontology editor available.

We expressed both the annotations and the subscriptions in DAML+OIL using the vocabulary from the ontology. However, this was not strictly necessary, alternatives are possible. Nor did the decision to use DAML+OIL dictate what inference engine we would use. Prior to selecting OilEd to be the editor, we considered Rule-based matching in Jess as a way to do semantic filtering. This approach is used on a DAML-based publish/subscribe prototype called Ontology-Driven Knowledge Dissemination (ODKD)[3] developed as part of the Components for Ontology Driven Information

---

[3] http://www.daml.org/2002/02/iow/grci

Push (CODIP) program[4]. A set of rules is processed to find matches using the Rete algorithm. Logically, a matching rule is of the following general form:

If <Semantic Filter Pattern>
Then <Enable the Fetching and Routing of the appropriate document content>.

6 Discussion, Limitations, and Future Work

Using semantic rather than syntactic subscriptions provides a much more powerful mechanism for recognizing relevant messages. E.g., it might be possible to deduce from the ontology that if a unit is being engaged by a friendly unit, then it must be an enemy unit (even if this is not explicitly stated), and therefore that messages concerning such units should be routed to subscribers asking for information about enemy units.

A key message of this paper is that there is much to be learned by applying existing semantics-based technologies to solve challenging practical problems. The shortcomings of the current state of the art are highlighted. Some issues are readily resolved by good software engineering, others point to deeper issues and serve as useful feedback to the community in setting research goals. Here we discuss a variety of limitations with existing technologies and other ideas for future work.

Many limitations arose due to the fact that we were using research-ware, rather than commercial products. OilEd is a case in point; while being valuable for our proof of concept demo, we identified a variety of shortcomings that would need to be addressed in order to deploy a production system.

Individuals and Efficiency. As discussed above, performance problems arose when we tried to reason about messages represented as individuals in OilEd. This is because OilEd treats such individuals as *nominals* – singleton classes that can be used in forming ontology descriptions [14]. Reasoning with nominals is known to be hard. In this application, however, individuals are only used in a very restricted way, and it is possible to optimize reasoning (without any loss of inferential power) by treating individuals as classes.

It would obviously be convenient to have a reasoning tool that automatically provided optimized reasoning by exploiting our limited usage of individuals. This requirement has been recognized by the developers of FaCT, who have now developed a so called *instance store* for use in this and other similar applications [9]. As well as providing improved reasoning performance, the instance store uses a database to store individuals, and so is able to deal efficiently with very large numbers of individuals. This would also be of importance in a realistic application scenario where it might be necessary to deal with very large numbers of messages. Moreover, storing message individuals in a database will support not only subscriptions, but also ad hoc queries against all stored messages.

---

[4] http://grcinet.grci.com/maria/www/codipsite/codip.html

Scale. Whenever complex reasoning systems are used the question of scalability always arises. In this case, the number of different subscriptions is the crucial factor, as each subscription is represented as a class in the ontology. It seems reasonable, however, to assume that the number of different subscriptions would not grow without bound, and ontologies containing tens of thousands of subscription classes should not be a problem for the reasoner. In the current architecture, messages are not persistent, and so would not have a cumulative effect on performance. With the proposed new instance store solution, messages are persistent, but they are stored in a database which is able to cope with very large numbers of message instances.

Modularity. A limitation of OilEd is its lack of support for modularity. Formally, a subscription is just another class description which can be classified in the subsumption lattice. It is necessary to keep subscription [classes] separate from the lattice of classes in the ontology proper because the inference returns all classes in the lattice that a message individual belongs to. Only the subscription classes are of interest. There are many simple ways to address this, for example by creating a special class for subscriptions, and creating all subscriptions as subclasses of it. One could also use namespaces. More importantly, a user may need to save out to a separate file the subscriptions that they have created, with different users creating different sets of subscriptions using the same ontology. OilEd does not support this.

There is also a need to save out sets of messages (instances) associated with a given ontology. In OilEd, there is no way to create and export a single individual, or more generally, a specified portion of an ontology. Currently, we have to save out the whole ontology including all subscriptions and messages and extract the messages and subscriptions of interest in DAML+OIL format. This places a serious limitation on the ability to develop the ontology independently from a particular set of subscriptions. Other questions arise such as: "Do the subscriptions from different users get classified together"? and "can one user see the subscriptions created by another user"?

On-the-Fly Subscriptions. In a production setting a user will require the ability to create subscriptions and pass them along to the Xinfosphere on the fly. This requires 1) a special purpose GUI for creating subscriptions that exposes only those parts of an ontology editing tool that is of interest to an end user and 2) the ability to save out one or more individuals and/or subscriptions in a modeler manner. In general, there may be many different specialized GUIs required, one for each domain, or class of user. This will require customizable ontology editing functionality which is a layer above the GUI widget layer.

Semantic Bingo. There is a need for keeping track of multiple related messages that may come in over a period of time and which, when taken together, should result in their being routed to relevant subscribers. E.g., a risk of friendly fire might occur when: 1) friendly forces are engaging an enemy at a particular location; 2) reinforcements are moving to that location; 3) the enemy retreats. A set of messages indicating that all of these conditions have been met should be routed to battlefield commanders who can then take steps to avoid a friendly fire incident. This introduces some interesting technical challenges. One is reasoning over time – the above messages should indicate roughly contemporaneous actions; another is variable co-reference – a key element is that different messages refer to the same location. A possible solution might be to express information about time using a DAML+OIL datatype, and to use a more powerful query language such as the DAML Query Langue (see http://www.daml.org/dql/) to express complex subscriptions. Investigating this approach will be part of future work.

Limited Expressive Power. We also faced questions of expressivity requirements for the ontology language and inferencing. Two issues were particularly prominent:

Variables to enforce co-reference. As mentioned above, it is often useful for subscriptions to express interest in multiple occurrences of the same component (such as a location) in a message, without specifying any particular value. A possible solution would be the use of a more powerful query language.

Datatypes and values. Our domain requires the ability to incorporate computation with data values into the classification reasoning. A subscriber may be interested in certain regions as denoted by ranges of latitude and longitude. If a message is published with these coordinates, then numerical reasoning will be incorporated into the classification reasoning to conclude that this document should be passed along to that subscriber only if the actual coordinates fit into the specified region. Similar reasoning can be used to infer which dates fell into a certain range that a subscriber was interested in. Such information can be expressed in DAML+OIL using datatypes and values, but they cannot be reasoned with using FaCT. Full support for DAML+OIL datatypes will, however, be included in a future version of FaCT.

Plug and Play Semantic Filtering. We were successful in integrating a description logic based approach for publish and subscribe. The use of a DL in general, and of OilEd in particular provided the important advantage of using the classification engine to help ensure the consistency of the ontology. The ontology developer had no prior experience with building DL-based ontologies, nor therefore with this aspect of ontology checking. It was found to be extremely useful in spotting logical errors. The effect of this is to significantly increase confidence that the ontology correctly captures the developer's intuition about the structure of the domain.

In the long term, we do not want to force a particular ontology language, inference engine and tool suite onto a user community wishing to use a semantic filtering capability. Users may already be committed to a particular tool, or they may have special needs with respect to inference or expressive capabilities. Future work will include adding new semantic filtering technologies.

Semantic Heterogeneity. In a large or heterogeneous community, it cannot be assumed that all documents will be annotated using the same ontology. In general there will be more than one ontology that different publishers and/or subscribers use. If clients wished to subscribe to items from different publishers, or if their preferred ontologies were different from those of the publishers, then some form of ontology integration or mapping would be required [Kalfoglou and Schorlemmer 2003].

Acknowledgements. We are grateful to Deborah McGuinness, Volker Haarslev and Ralf Möller for discussions on how description logic might be used in a publish/subscribe environment. Liz Duncan, Heather Holmback, Steve Poteet and Herman Beuttel provided help with RTIMS and the battlefield scenario data.

References

[1] Franz Baader, Diego Calvanese, Deborah McGuinness, Daniele Nardi, and Peter F. Patel-Schneider, editors. *The Description Logic Handbook: Theory, Implementation and Applications*. Cambridge University Press, 2002.

[2] Anders Berglund, Scott Boag, Don Chamberlin, Mary F. Fernandez, Michael Kay, Jonathan Robie, and Jérôme Siméon. XML Path Language (XPath) 2.0. W3C Working Draft, May 2003. Available at http://www.w3.org/TR/xpath20/.

[3] James Clark. XSL Transformations (XSLT) Version 1.0. W3C Recommendation, Nov 1999. Available at http://www.w3.org/TR/xslt.

[4] Ian Horrocks, Ulrike Sattler, and Stephan Tobies. Practical reasoning for expressive description logics. In *Proc. of LPAR'99*, number 1705 in LNAI, pages 161–180. Springer, 1999.

[5] Peter F. Patel-Schneider, Patrick Hayes, and Ian Horrocks. Web ontology language (OWL) abstract syntax and semantics. W3C Working Draft, 3 February 2003. Available at http://www.w3.org/TR/2003/WD-owl-semantics-20030203/.

[6] Jonathan Robie. XQL (XML Query Language), Aug 1999. Available at http://www.ibiblio.org/xql/xql-proposal.html.

[7] Duncan, L., Holmback, H., Kau, A., Poteet, S., Miller, S., Harrison, P., Powell, J., & Jenkins, T. (1994). *Message processing and data extraction for the Real-Time Information Extraction System (RTIMS) project* (Boeing Technical Report BCSTECH-94–057).

[8] Sean Bechhofer, Ian Horrocks, Carole Goble, and Robert Stevens. OilEd: A Reasonable ontology editor for the semantic web. In Proc. of KI 2001, number 2174 in LNAI, pages 396–408. Springer, 2001.

[9] Sean Bechhofer, Ian Horrocks, and Daniele Turi. A simple DL instance store. In Submitted, May 2003. Available at http://www.cs.man.ac.uk/~horrocks/Publications/publications.html.

[10] Ian Horrocks. Using an expressive description logic: FaCT or fiction? In *Proc. KR'98*, pages 636–647, 1998.

[11] Ian Horrocks. DAML+OIL: a description logic for the semantic web. *Bull. of the IEEE Computer Society Technical Committee on Data Engineering*, 25(1):4–9, 2002.

[12] Peter F. Patel-Schneider, Patrick Hayes, and Ian Horrocks. Web ontology language (OWL) abstract syntax and semantics. W3C Working Draft, 3 February 2003. Available at http://www.w3.org/TR/2003/WD-owl-semantics-20030203/.

[13] W. E. Grosso, H. Eriksson, R. W. Fergerson, J. H. Gennari, S. W. Tu, and M. A. Musen. Knowledge modelling at the millenium (The design and evolution of Protégé-2000). In Proc. of KAW'99, 1999.

[14] Ian Horrocks and Ulrike Sattler. Ontology reasoning in the SHOQ(D) description logic. In *Proc. of IJCAI 2001*, pages 199–204, 2001.

Ontology-Based Information Integration in the Automotive Industry

Andreas Maier[1], Hans-Peter Schnurr[1], and York Sure[2]

[1] Ontoprise GmbH, Karlsruhe, Germany
{maier,schnurr}@ontoprise.de
http://www.ontoprise.de
[2] Institute AIFB, University of Karlsruhe, Germany
sure@aifb.uni-karlsruhe.de
http://www.aifb.uni-karlsruhe.de/WBS/

Abstract. Information integration is still one of today's hottest IT topics. Neither merging the information from different data sources nor preparing it for the end user's access has been completely solved. The goal of this paper is to present a holistic approach to integration by using ontologies and logic. There are several reasons for an ontology-based approach: Ontologies are able to cover all occurring data structures, for ontologies can be seen as nowadays most advanced knowledge representation model. They are able to cover complexity, for the combination with deductive logic extends the mapping and business logic capabilities. As the model is separated from the data storage, we get a higher degree of abstraction, whereby the semantics of the whole system is increased. Ontologies are extendible and highly reusable and deliver the user a better access to his relevant content.

In this paper we describe how current capabilities of knowledge representation, mapping of structures and description of the business logic are extended. In an elaborated case study of a specific R&D process in the automobile industry [Ste03] we demonstrate that the complex integration process can be realized much easier, faster, more understandable and less expensive than before, without changing the existing IT legacy environment.

1 Introduction

1.1 Motivation for Integrated IT Solutions

Today's users and IT professionals have high expectations towards software applications: They want to access the content they need and this content must be accurate and free of redundancy. The application must be intuitive and easy to use, reusable and extendable. It must be implemented in a short and inexpensive way and within the current IT legacy environment. To meet these expectations, the content has to be identified from the different sources (i.e. databases, applications, XML-Files, unstructured text files ...), and then to be integrated. But this means not building just connectors [Kre99] between applications, because

D. Fensel et al. (Eds.): ISWC 2003, LNCS 2870, pp. 897–912, 2003.

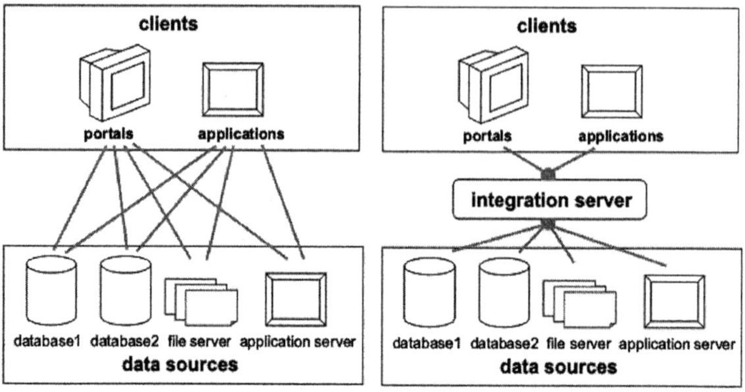

Fig. 1. Point-to-point-connections vs. a "real" integration solution

syntactical incompatibilities could be reduced by approaches like SQL [KK01] or XML; nor it's only tying up diverse data sources and displaying them on a common interface as shown in Figure 1 on the left side.

The goal of integration is to consolidate distributed information intelligently, free of redundancy, processed and operated by the right business logic to deliver the appropriate and condensed answer and offer the end user a simple access to it, without him needing knowledge about the underlying data structures (figure 1 right). We believe that with ontologies there's now a model at hand to fit for this goal. From the scientific direction it's the Semantic Web Initiative [FHLW03] which focuses the demand for a better information integration, i.e. by introducing common standards like RDF [LS99] and RDF schema [BG02]. From the market side software vendors and service provider target the customer's needs by promising solutions, which often lack of integrated data, i.e. solutions for Knowledge Management, Content Management, Data Warehousing or Business Intelligence.

1.2 Foundations I: What Is an Ontology?

An ontology is a knowledge representation model. Other models for example are extended entity relationship models, thesauri or topic maps. The most common definition of "ontology" is "An ontology is an explicit specification of a conceptualization." by Tom Gruber [Gru95].

Ontologies serve as a means for establishing a conceptually concise basis for communicating knowledge for many purposes. We restrict our attention to domain ontologies that describe a particular small model of the world as relevant to applications and have shown their usefulness in these application areas. Typically, an ontology is constructed and maintained in a collaborative effort of domain experts, end-users and IT specialists.

1.3 Foundations II: Deductive Logic

Logic models (i.e. Prolog [Spi96], Datalog [DL91], F-Logic [KLW95], Description Logic [Baa02]) help us to connect the different data sources by mapping or merging rules. As a second important point they help to easily build a deductive "business logic" upon our integrated information base and to check the consistence of the knowledge base. Deduction can also be very effective in a stand-alone application, but much more in an integration scenario. By consolidating applications and their underlying processes often new contexts are created and require a new business logic on top.

Especially F-Logic[1] acts as a bridge between models and logic, because it covers ontological (schema and instance) data as well as rules. Every object in the ontology (concepts, relations, attributes, instances) can be addressed by F-Logic atoms and, thus, be embedded into logical rules. Furthermore, F-Logic can also be used to query the system similarly to SQL. Besides efficient querying for instance data, F-Logic allows also for querying schema data itself and even for combinations of schema and instance data. In the following we will use F-Logic as logic format for the code examples.

1.4 Structure of This Paper

Initially we gave a motivation for our approach and describe the scientific foundations of ontologies and logic in Section 1. Next, we build up the requirement specification for the integration process in Section 2 which consists of the four main requirements, viz. (1) cover all existing data structures, (2) mapping, (3) modelling the business logic, and (4) providing a data storage. Based on these requirements we define structured procedure steps which will be illustrated in detail in Sections 3–6, viz. (I) schema import, (II) creating relations, (III) create mappings, (IV) rule modelling, (V) inferencing, (VI) schema export, and (VII) materialization. Our automotive case study will be subsequently worked out step-by-step, whereby it serves as a running example. Last, but not least, we conclude in Section 7.

2 Starting the Integration Process

2.1 Introducing the Case Study: PLM in the Automotive Industry

We now describe a setting from a case study performed at the German car manufacturer Audi AG, further details can be found at [Ste03]. A typical integration scenario found in the automobile industry is the management of product components data and its permitted configurations, which proves to be very difficult. These information lie widespread in different departments and there in different sources like CAD-, CAE- or CAT-systems or ERP/PPS -applications, databases, email programs, documents, organizers, etc., – often redundantly. All these IT

[1] see `http://www.ontoprise.de/documents/tutorial_flogic.pdf`

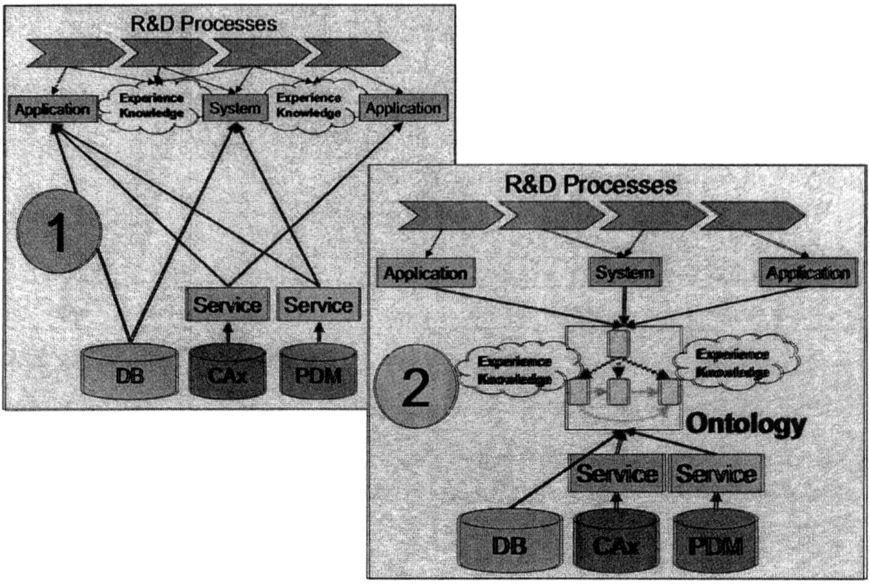

Fig. 2. A typical (1) and an integrated (2) R&D process

systems accompany the whole PLM[2]-process [Ber90], beginning with the product design and ending with the product release. To support this process, the contained information wants to be integrated for many reasons: The designer has to take constructional restrictions into account, the constructor must implement the designer's directives, the quality department wants to reduce the defect rate and the sales department has to meet the customer's request for individual pre-configured products.

An ontology could now catch up the different sources that we want to integrate. As Figure 2 shows, ontologies serve as a mediating meta model between the data sources and the user's access. Typically (see 1) different applications and systems support different process steps, the experience knowledge of engineers is crucial (i) to combine the different sources during the process, and (ii) to close the gap between different process steps and across application and system boarders. Ontologies (see 2) (i) formalize experience knowledge e.g. from engineers, and (ii) intermediate between different applications, systems and underlying services and data sources.

[2] PLM=product lifecycle management, CAD=Computer Aided Design, CAE=Computer Aided Engineering, CAT=Computer Aided Tests, ERP=Enterprise Resource Planning, PPS=Production Planning and Scheduling

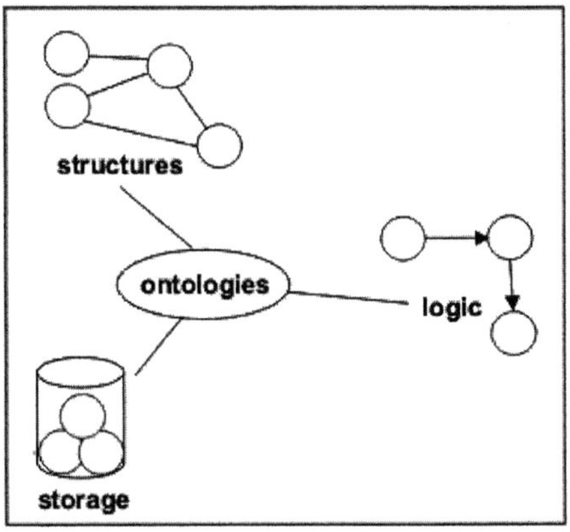

Fig. 3. Ontologies meet the requirements 1–4

2.2 Defining the Requirements

In our integration process we have to cover all existing data structures (*requirement 1*), which can be simple table structures up to complex hierarchical structured data with deep inheritance. After connecting to these structures we have to map them among each other (*requirement 2*). After this step we define the business logic for the whole new application (*requirement 3*) (hereby we will be supported by deductive inference mechanisms). If the data isn't kept in the origin sources, we have to provide an appropriate data storage for the information (*requirement 4*). As we will demonstrate in the coming sections, ontologies are a well-suited representation model to meet these requirements (see Figure 3).

2.3 Comparing Different Integration Approaches and Tools

A comparison of different approaches and tools for the information integration has one remarkable result: beside the ontology-based one, all approaches of information integration range on a pure syntactical level. They neither aim at building one common conceptual representation model (like an ontology), nor are they able to define a business logic based upon this model. Some tools (like e.g. the BizTalk Server of Microsoft) compensate this with rather focusing the transaction-oriented aspect of an integration process, than the information-oriented aspect outlined in the following Table 1.

2.4 Procedures

To the four requirements we allocate six procedure steps. Every step will be explained further below; together they form a process chain, which has to be worked out.

Table 1. Comparison of different approaches and tools

Approaches // Tools	**Covering existing data structures**	**Mapping**	**Business logic**	**Data storage**
relational databases				X
XSLT/XML	X	X		
RDF	X			
F-Logic	X	X	X	
BizTalk Server (Microsoft)		X		
Drag & Relate (SAP/Toptier)		X		
Clio (IBM)				
OntoEdit/Ontobroker (Ontoprise)	X	X	X	

1. Cover all existing data structures
   I Schema import
   II Creating relations
2. Mapping
   III Create mappings
3. Modelling the business logic
   IV Rule modelling
   V Inferencing
4. Providing a data storage
   VI Schema export
   VII Materialization

We use the case study in the automotive industry as a running example to illustrate our process model by a real-world scenario. Currently we provide tool support for the steps I–V, VI and VII are future work which remains to be done.

3 Requirement 1: Cover All Data Structures

We compared several knowledge representation models and discussed the advantages and weaknesses of them. As a conclusion we found that ontologies are the most advanced model of all of them, summing up most of the qualities of the others: Like Taxonomies [Pel89], ontologies are able to cover hierarchies. Like Thesauri [Med95], Semantic Nets [Hof86] and Topic Maps [PH02], ontologies contain relations. With them, complex contexts can be modelled and visualized in nets. Linguistic contexts (i.e. multi-lingualism or synonym relations), terminologies and classifications can be described, through which the semantic of the integration solution is increased. In comparison to ontologies and databases, these models have no data model. Thus they do not contain instances and attributes, which is necessary for the management of mass data. They also miss

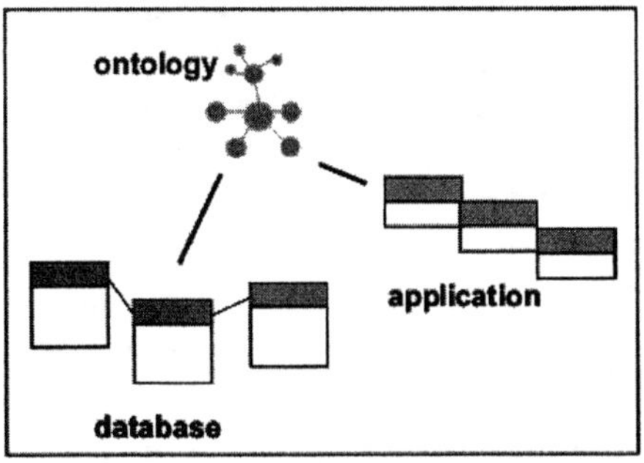

Fig. 4. Importing diverse schemas

a structured language like SQL to query the model. Taxonomies, Thesauri, Semantic Nets and the ER-model are comparatively old models. Topic Maps (an ISO standard) are the newest of them and potentially merge with the W3C efforts on ontologies. Like the Entity Relationship model (ER) [BCB91] and unlike the others mentioned above, ontologies have a data model distinguishing schema information from facts. This is essential for storing the facts (*requirement 4*: Provide a Data Storage). As relational databases do not provide an object model, they have some difficulties in picturing taxonomies and must define primary keys themselves. Every ER-model can be transformed in an ontology and, with some expense and limitations, vice versa. In comparison to databases, ontologies have a higher semantic, because they name the relations instead of linking primary keys and are multilingual. As an object based model, ontologies support inheritance and multiple inheritance of attributes and relationships.

3.1 Procedure Step I: Schema Import

By a schema import we connect a former independent data source to the ontology shown in Figure 4. Beneath other schema imports (i.e. for formats like RDF or OWL), the SQL import plays a very important role.

After an import of a database table into an ontology, this one is embedded as a concept into the concept taxonomy as shown in Figure 5. The former primary key from the attribute name has moved to the object id of the concept motor. Tables are interpreted as concepts, as they usually contain information about a distinct entity. Rows typically describe attributes of that entity and are coherently interpreted as attributes of concepts.

OntoEdit is an ontology engineering environment [SEA+02,SSA02]. An SQL import has already been realized in OntoEdit[3], e.g. for Microsoft SQL Server, IBM DB2, Oracle, and mySQL.

When importing a database table, OntoEdit creates an automatical connection to the database by the `dbaccessuser`-Built-in (Built-ins include e.g. connectors to various data structures etc.). For example there's a connection

[3] see `http://www.ontoprise.de/documents/tutorial_ontoedit.pdf`

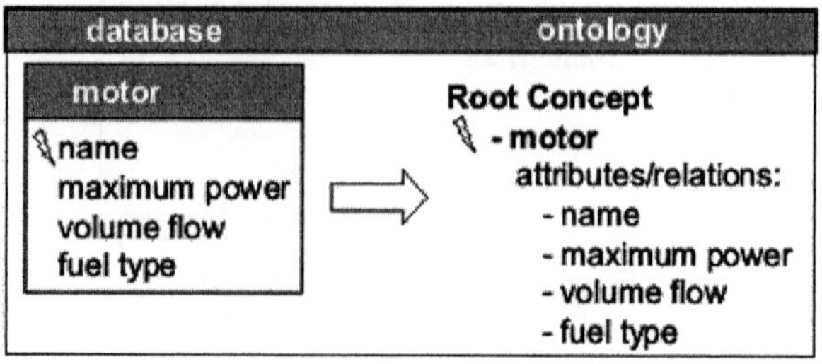

Fig. 5. Importing a database table

to the fields name, maximum_power, volume_flow and fuel_type from table table_motor at database database_motor of type MSSQLServer on computer server_motordata:

```
FORALL X, NAME, MAXIMUM_POWER, VOLUME_FLOW, FUEL_TYPE
    X:Motor[name->>NAME;
            maximum_power->>MAXIMUM_POWER;
            volume_flow->>VOLUME_FLOW;
            fuel_type->>FUEL_TYPE]
    <-
    dbaccessuser(
        "table_motor",
        F(  "name", NAME,
            "maximum_power", MAXIMUM_POWER,
            "volume_flow", VOLUME_FLOW,
            "fuel_type", FUEL_TYPE),
        "mssqlserver2000",
        "database_motor",
        "server_motordata:1433") AND
    concat("Motor", NAME, X).
```

The equivalent to the schema import is the schema export, that we will need for *requirement 3* (provide a data storage).

3.2 Procedure Step II: Creating Relations

If there have to be relations between so far unlinked concepts, i.e. because these were coming from different data sources, we can join them by logical rules. The new relations can be derived from very complex coherences. The concepts motor and catalyst for example are still unrelated, but catalyst has the attribute belongs_to_motor like shown in Figure 6 below. As the identifying numbers (121, 134, ...) are the same, a rule could be: If cnr_motor is the same number than the motor name without CNR_, then this catalyst belongs to that motor.

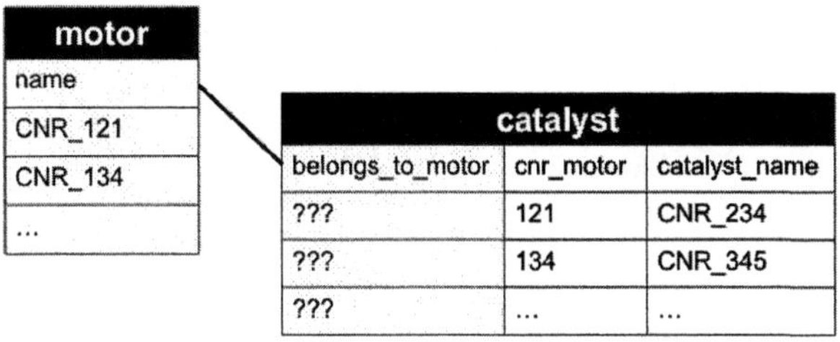

Fig. 6. Creating relations

In F-Logic, this would be expressed like:

```
FORALL X,Y,Z1,Z2
    X:catalyst[belongs_to_motor->Y:motor]
    <-
    X[cnr_motor->Z1] AND
    Y[name->Z2] AND
    concat("CNR_",Z1,Z2).
```

3.3 Continuing the Case Study: After the Schema Import

The import process should result in one or more ontologies that contain the complete model of all data sources. In our case study the created automobile ontology now contains the constituting concepts for the PLM system (see Figure 7).

4 Requirement 2: Create Mappings (Procedure Step III)

In practice there's often more than one core ontology. For this, mapping between them is needed. Also in a Semantic Web scenario, where the interaction between lots of ontologies is intended, mapping is very important. Ontology mapping connects not only primary keys and table rows, but is working on a more conceptual level, which leads to a higher degree of abstraction comparing to a simple database mapping. OntoMap, a mapping plug-in included in OntoEdit, supports the fundamental mapping types (i) concept-to-concept mapping, (ii) attribute-to-attribute mapping and (iii) attribute-to-concept mapping. Describing conditions and constraints (i.e. unit conversions) on the mapping rules is not explained further here. In the last section we will elaborate more on the difficulties found during the creation of the mappings in our case study.

4.1 Concept-to-Concept Mapping

An ontology mapping process is very similar to pure database respectively XML-mapping[4]. In each case the two schemas, which are going to be mapped, are

[4] cf. R. Bourret: Mapping DTDs to Databases, found at `http://www.xml.com/pub/a/2001/05/09/dtdtodbs.html`

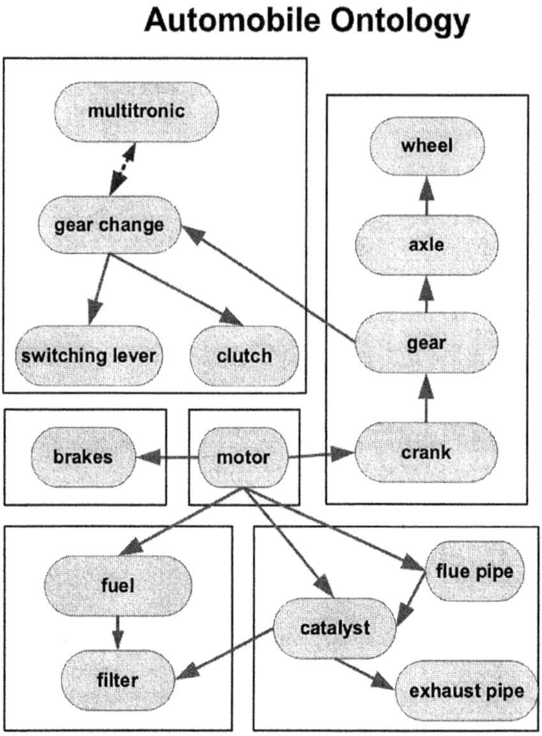

Fig. 7. Concepts of the automobile ontology

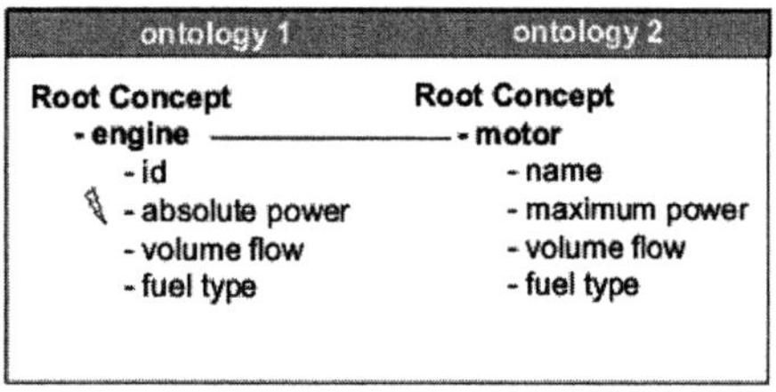

Fig. 8. Concept-to-concept-mapping

displayed in vertical rows parallel to each other (see Figure 8). If two concepts of two different sources contain the same type of information, a concept-to-concept mapping can be drawn (i.e. `engine` and `motor`).

The F-Logic syntax would be:

```
FORALL X
    X:ontology2#motor
    <-
    X:ontology1#engine.
```

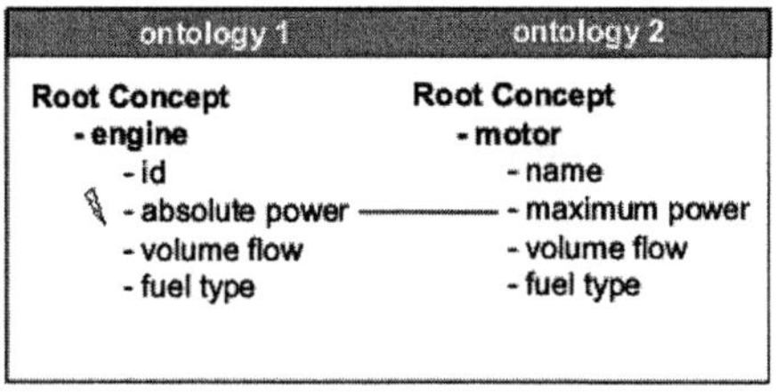

Fig. 9. Attribute-to-attribute-mapping

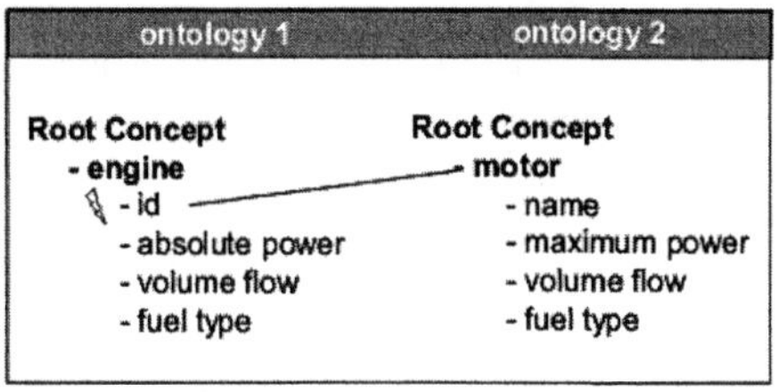

Fig. 10. Attribute-to-concept-mapping

4.2 Attribute-to-Attribute Mapping

An attribute-to-attribute mapping connects two attributes, stating that these contain the same information (i.e. `absolute power` and `maximum power`) (see Figure 9). A previous concept-to-concept mapping is prerequisite for that.

```
FORALL X,Y,Z
    Z:ontology2#motor[ontology2#maximum_power->>Y]
    <-
    X:ontology1#engine[ontology1#absolute_power->>Y].
```

4.3 Attribute-to-Concept Mapping

Another important aspect is the mapping of table rows (attributes) that are represented as concepts in other formats. The attribute-to-concept mapping shown below states that the primary key `id` of `engine` is connected to the object id of `motor` (see Figure 10).

```
FORALL X,Y,Z
    Y:ontology2#motor
    <-
    X:ontology1#engine[ontology1#id->>Y].
```

5 Requirement 3: Enhancing the Business Logic

Applications with lots of logical dependencies (i.e. configuration or variant management systems, solutions representing extensive knowledge domains, expert systems) can be realized much better with rule-based systems. Additionally, deductive logic reduces complexity. In really complex contexts with many relations between the concepts of the ontology the effort and complexity of implementation in pure SQL quickly gets too high. As another important reason for logic, the user doesn't need to know the underlying data structures. He only knows his question and not the whole conceptual structure that lies behind it.

5.1 Procedure Step IV: Rule Modelling

Having tied together the different data sources, we now illustrate the extendibility that logic rules offer to applications. Our basic ontology (see Figure 7) is now going to be enriched by five simple rules to expand the knowledge base:

- **Rule 1:** The tolerated transmission power of a car's crank N_crank must be higher than the power of the motor N_{motor}, but must not exceed the one of the gear N_{gear}. To sum up, the condition
  $$N_{motor} < N_{crank} < N_{gear} < N_{axle} < N_{wheel}$$
  has to be valid.
- **Rule 2:** The maximum power of the motor must not exceed the one of the brakes.
  $$P_{motor} < \mid P_{brakes} \mid$$
- **Rule 3:** For the volume flow VF_x there must be:
  $$VF_{motor} < VF_{fluepipe} < VF_{catalyst} < VF_{exhaustpipe}$$
- **Rule 4:** The filter installed in a catalyst must be able to filter the motor's fuel.
- **Rule 5:** If there's a gear change, then there has to be a switching lever and a clutch. If there is a multitronic instead, then there must be no gear change.

Rule 2 for example could be encoded in F-Logic as:

```
FORALL X,Y,Z1,Z2,Z3
    message("Warning: The motor's maximum power
            exceeds the one of the brakes!")
    <-
    X:motor[maximum_power->>Z1] AND
    Y:brake[maximum_power->>Z2] AND
    abs(Z1,Z3) AND
    lessorequal(Z2,Z3).
```

These five rules are now added to the ontology to provide them for the Inferencing process.

5.2 Procedure Step V: Inferencing

Inferences are information, that are derived by means of logical conclusions. Inferencing engines like Ontobroker[5] [DEFS99] use a formal logic calculus to

[5] see http://www.ontoprise.de/documents/tutorial_ontobroker.pdf

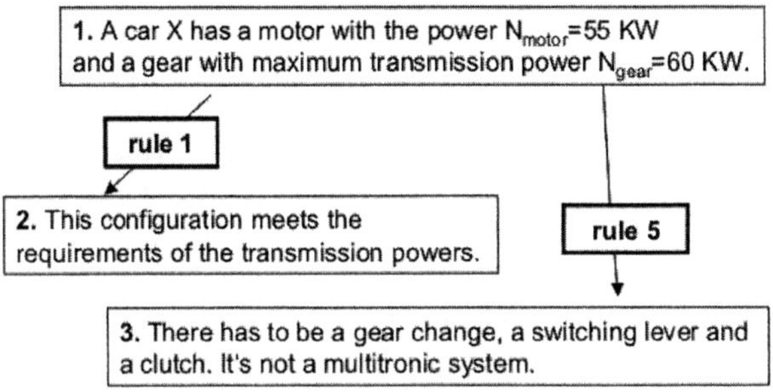

Fig. 11. An inferencing graph

generate new information out the input facts and rules. By an inferencing process the rules are applied to the given facts and extend the knowledge base by the newly created facts. Figure 11 visualizes this process.

The inference engine, running as a service on a computer, would now be able to deliver also the new facts to the user's access.

The remaining steps are at the moment of writing this paper not yet fully implemented. Therefore we will describe them in the next section as future work.

6 Future Work – Requirement 4: Provide a Data Storage

As a description for a mainly unchanging pool of information, the terms Knowledge Base or Repository are often used. We prefer to say data storage instead, emphasizing that in integration solutions the content is permanently changing. For maintenance reasons, the data itself should be kept only once, preferably in the origin application. If this is not possible for technical reasons (i.e. if the application isn't able being queried), we propose migrating it to a database. Although the ER-Model has its weaknesses (see previous section), we suggest using relational databases as storage because of their widely spread and mature solutions. The recently emerging repositories like the RDFS-repository Sesame [BKv02] offer an alternative to databases. But in comparison to repositories there's at the moment no alternative concerning performance and compatibility.

Procedure Step VI: Schema Export. To export an ontology schema or a part of it into a database, we need an SQL-Export, which creates the database schema out of the ontology and writes it into a new database. An SQL export has already been realized in OntoEdit and works in analogy to the SQL import (see Section 3).

Procedure Step VII: Materialisation. Before we start an inference server, we decide whether we want to materialize all attained new facts (i.e. to explicitly store all newly derived facts from rules). If not, all inferences are computed during runtime, when a query affords it. The decision whether to materialize or not depends on the data change rate. If it is high, materialisation doesn't make sense. The materialized facts can be written into a data storage, for example into a database. Ontobroker does this when using an internal database.

7 Conclusion

We have shown in a real-life industrial case study, viz. in the automotive industry at the car manufacturer Audi AG [Ste03], that the formalization of experience knowledge and the integration of heterogeneous data sources with the help of ontologies is feasible and beneficial. Key enabler in this case study are (i) OntoEdit [SEA+02,SSA02], an ontology engineering environment and its mapping extension OntoMap and (ii) Ontobroker [DEFS99], an F-Logic based inference engine.

Looking at today's available software for ontologies, [NM02] compare different tools. In particular, they distinguish ontology editors from ontology mappers. As we have shown above, this categorisation doesn't mean that it couldn't be combined in one product. In OntoEdit for example, there's a modelling component as well as a mapping plugin[6]. Another mapping mechanism between distributed ontologies (i.e. oriented towards the vision of the Semantic Web) is introduced in MAFRA [MMSV02], an interactive, incremental and dynamic framework for ontology mapping.

Of course, integration across different sources depends on the compatibility of their data structures. Just as you can't map Newton's 3-dimensional world by 100% to Einstein's 4-dimensional one, the result will always be an approximation. In the worst case, when ontologies are totally orthogonal to each other, a mapping can be impossible. But should a mapping be feasible, the manual approach described here might be supplemented by semi- or full automatic approaches. In our current point of view, these automatic approaches will bring in only a limited additional benefit. [DMDH02] delivers new findings on them.

In our practical setting, we were able to model all required mappings via F-Logic. All fundamental mappings were done (potentially by domain experts, here by ontology experts) with our graphical mapping plugin OntoMap, the more complex mappings required manual efforts in F-Logic by ontology experts.

Future development work includes the development of graphical tool support for more complex mappings. We have shown the feasibility of mappings for a practical setting in a (rather) closed domain, future work has to show the applicability for open domains such as envisioned by the Semantic Web.

References

[Baa02] F. Baader. *The description logic handbook: theory, implementation and applications.* Cambridge University Press, 2002.

[BCB91] C. Batini, S. Ceri, and C. Batini. *Conceptual Database Design: An Entity-Relationship Approach.* Addison Wesley Publishing Company, 1991.

[Ber90] T. Bernold. Product life: from design to disposal : life-cycle engineering: the key to risk management, safer products and industrial environmental strategies. In *International Conference on Industrial Risk Management*, Zürich, 1990. Elsevier.

[6] OntoEdit is based on a flexible plugin framework, further details can be found e.g. in [Han01].

[BG02] D. Brickley and R. V. Guha. RDF Vocabulary Description Language 1.0: RDF Schema. W3C Working Draft 12 November 2002, 2002. available at http://www.w3.org/TR/PR-rdf-schema/.

[BKv02] J. Broekstra, A. Kampman, and F. van Harmelen. Sesame: A generic architecture for storing and querying RDF and RDF Schema. In Horrocks and Hendler [HH02], pages 54–68.

[DEFS99] S. Decker, M. Erdmann, D. Fensel, and R. Studer. *Ontobroker: Ontology Based Access to Distributed and Semi-Structured Information*, pages 351–369. In Meersman et al. [MTS99], 1999.

[DL91] M. Dahr and K. Lautenbach. Towards a formal theory of datalog nets. Fachberichte informatik, Universitaet Koblenz-Landau, 1991.

[DMDH02] A. Doan, J. Madhavan, P. Domingos, and A. Halevy. Learning to map between ontologies on the semantic web. In *Proceedings of the World-Wide Web Conference (WWW-2002), Honolulu*, 2002.

[FHLW03] D. Fensel, J. Hendler, H. Lieberman, and W. Wahlster, editors. *Spinning the Semantic Web.* MIT Press, 2003.

[Gru95] T. R. Gruber. Towards principles for the design of ontologies used for knowledge sharing. *International Journal of Human-Computer Studies*, 43(5/6):907–928, 1995.

[Han01] S. Handschuh. OntoPlugins – a flexible component framework. Technical report, University of Karlsruhe, May 2001.

[HH02] I. Horrocks and J. A. Hendler, editors. *Proceedings of the First International Semantic Web Conference: The Semantic Web (ISWC 2002)*, volume 2342 of *Lecture Notes in Computer Science (LNCS)*, Sardinia, Italy, 2002. Springer.

[Hof86] H. Hoffmann. On the visualization of design notions, of notion instantiations, and of structural relationships in a design data base realized as a semantic net. In *Informatics and Psychology Workshop, Darmstadt*, 1986.

[KK01] K. Kline and D. Kline. *SQL in a Nutshell.* O'Reilly, 2001.

[KLW95] M. Kifer, G. Lausen, and J. Wu. Logical foundations of object-oriented and frame-based languages. *Journal of the ACM*, 42:741–843, 1995.

[Kre99] D. Kreuz. *Formale Semantik von Konnektoren.* PhD thesis, Technische Universitaet Hamburg, 1999.

[LS99] O. Lassila and R. Swick. Resource Description Framework (RDF). Model and Syntax Specification. W3C Recommendation 22 February 1999, 1999. available at http://www.w3.org/TR/REC-rdf-syntax.

[Med95] N. Meder. *Konstruktion und Retrieval von Wissen: Thesauri als Terminologische Lexika.* Indeks Verlag, Weilburg, 1995.

[MMSV02] A. Maedche, B. Motik, N. Silva, and R. Volz. MAFRA – a MApping FRAmework for distributed ontologies. In A. Gómez-Pérez and V. R. Benjamins, editors, *Proceedings of the 13th International Conference on Knowledge Engineering and Knowledge Management: Ontologies and the Semantic Web (EKAW 2002)*, volume 2473 of *Lecture Notes in Artificial Intelligence (LNAI)*, pages 235–250, Siguenza, Spain, 2002. Springer.

[MT+02] R. Meersman, Z. Tari, et al., editors. *Proceedings of the Confederated International Conferences: On the Move to Meaningful Internet Systems (CoopIS, DOA, and ODBASE 2002)*, volume 2519 of *Lecture Notes in Computer Science (LNCS)*, University of California, Irvine, USA, 2002. Springer.

[MTS99] R. Meersman, Z. Tari, and S. Stevens, editors. *Database Semantics: Semantic Issues in Multimedia Systems.* Kluwer Academic Publisher, 1999.

[NM02] N. Noy and M. Musen. Evaluating ontology mapping tools – requirements and experience. Technical report, Stanford University, 2002.

[Pel89] C. Peltason. *Wissensrepraesentation fuer Entwurfssysteme: d. Behandlung von Klassifikation und Taxonomie.* PhD thesis, Technische Universitaet Berlin, 1989.

[PH02] J. Park and S. Hunting. *XML Topic Maps.* Addison-Wesley Professional, 2002.

[SEA$^+$02] Y. Sure, M. Erdmann, J. Angele, S. Staab, R. Studer, and D. Wenke. OntoEdit: Collaborative ontology development for the semantic web. In Horrocks and Hendler [HH02], pages 221–235.

[Spi96] J. M. Spivey. *An introduction to logic programming through Prolog.* Prentice Hall London, 1996.

[SSA02] Y. Sure, S. Staab, and J. Angele. OntoEdit: Guiding ontology development by methodology and inferencing. In Meersman et al. [MT$^+$02], pages 1205–1222.

[Ste03] H. Stegmueller. Audi erprobt semantische Technologien – Zeit fuers Wesentliche. *Digital Engineering Magazin*, 2003(3):44–45, 2003.

Ontology-Based Query and Answering in Chemistry: OntoNova @ Project Halo

Jürgen Angele, Eddie Moench, Henrik Oppermann,
Steffen Staab, and D. Wenke

Ontoprise GmbH,
Amalienbadstraße 36,
76227 Karlsruhe, Germany
{angele,moench,oppermann,staab,wenke}@ontoprise.de

Abstract. The Project Halo has the long term objective of developing a *Digital Aristotle*, i.e. a knowledge system that is able to answer questions in a particular domain and give explanations for its answers. In this paper we report about the Ontoprise contribution to the Halo Pilot Project, in which various competing ontology engineering methodologies and knowledge system capabilities have been investigated. Concerning the first, we describe how we dealt with engineering a significant set of laws from chemistry that we had to let interact at different levels of generality and in varying orders. With regard to the latter, we report on the ability of our system to produce coherent and concise explanations of its reasoning. The importance of these two aspects can hardly be underestimated in the Semantic Web, as with future growth the interaction of large sets of laws will require dedicated management as well as the ability to let the user explore the trustworthiness of the ontology and the underlying data sources.

1 Introduction

The Halo Pilot Project[1] is the first phase of a projected multi-phase effort by Vulcan Inc.[2] whose ultimate goal is the creation of a "Digital Aristotle", an expert tutor in a wide variety of subjects. The Halo Pilot was a six-month effort intended to assess the state-of-the-art in question answering with an emphasis on deep reasoning. The effort was structured around the challenge of responding to variants of AP Chemistry questions that focused on a portion of the "Advanced Placement test: Chemistry".[3]

Our system, OntoNova, answers questions from this AP test. OntoNova justifies its answers in detail giving natural language explanations. The answers have been evaluated by expert graders according to the directives of the Educational Testing

[1] http://www.projecthalo.com

[2] http://www.vulcan.com

[3] The Advance Placement Program gives students the chance to try college-level work while still in high school. If one gets a "qualifying" grade on the AP Exam, many colleges give credit or advanced placement for these efforts (http://apcentral.collegeboard.com/program).

D. Fensel et al. (Eds.): ISWC 2003, LNCS 2870, pp. 913–928, 2003.

Services. Besides Ontoprise two other contenders, Cycorp Inc[4]. and SRI International[5], have built competing systems.

There are a number of issues that make the Halo Pilot Project as a whole and OntoNova as one of its parts extremely relevant for the Semantic Web:

1. The Halo Pilot constitutes a good match for some of the objectives that the Semantic Web community wants to achieve:
   a. Exploiting a rich ontology,
   b. Integrating various sources of knowledge,
   c. Giving justifications for deduced results.
2. The Halo Pilot Project was a controlled experiment with a cleanly defined setting, independent evaluators, freely available resources and re-produceable results from. Such settings are useful to
   a. Quantify costs, and
   b. Quantify adequacy of methods.
3. While the Halo Pilot still produced knowledge bases that appear to be too costly, it also showed that encoding knowledge by experts is "just" one order of magnitude more costly than writing the natural language text itself.

While the description of the overall Halo Pilot Project is currently put together by a joint committee consisting of representatives of Vulcan Inc. and the three teams, we here focus on number 1 shown in the list above and in particular on the description of OntoNova and the conclusions we could draw from our experiences building it. To do so, we first describe our technical approach to allow for the deduction of answers and justifications. In chapter 3, we present the architecture of our knowledge base that produced the answers and justifications. Chapter 4 briefly compares the overall results of the project as far as necessary to frame the OntoNova system. We conclude with some lessons learned.

2 Technical Approaches

Our technical approach builds on two main pillars. First (cf. Section 2.1), we build on the OntoBroker® technology that we have developed and that we have continuously improved for over a decade now [Ang93,DEFS99]. A complex ontology with rules, multiple representations of objects, and call-out functionality to particular problem-solving methods has been modeled in F-Logic [KLW95] to allow for infering answers posed to the system. Second (Secion 2.2), the deduction process has been extended and logged in F-Logic according to a particular trace ontology. This result could then be used by a second, but otherwise identical, inference engine in order to reason why a particular result had been achieved.

---

[4] http://www.cyc.com

[5] http://www.sri.com

2.1 Representing the Chemistry Domain in F-Logic

Conceptual (or Ontology) modeling deals with the question of how to describe in a declarative and abstract way the domain information of an application, its relevant vocabulary, and how to constrain the use of the data, by understanding what can be drawn from it. Corresponding abstract representation languages support the understanding of such descriptions, their rapid development, their maintenance and their reuse.

F-Logic ("F" stands for "Frames") combines the advantages of a conceptual high-level approach typical for frame-based languages and the expressiveness, the compact syntax, and the well defined semantics from logics. The original features of F-Logic [KLW95] include signatures, object identity, complex objects, methods, classes, inheritance, and rules. Our implementation of F-Logic by OntoBroker [DEFS99] introduced extensions and restrictions of the original features to make F-Logic a powerful and efficient language for many respective intended application domains.

Basic concepts of chemistry are represented as concepts in F-Logic and are arranged in an isa-hierarchy:

```
Molecule::Root.
Reaction::Root.
Ion::Molecule.
Anion::Ion.
Cation::Ion.
AlkaliMetalCation::Cation.
AlkalineEarthMetalCation::Cation.
PrecipitationReaction::Reaction.
GaseousReaction::Reaction.
```

Properties of these concepts and relations between these concepts are represented by methods. E.g.:

```
IonicMolecule[
      hasName=>>STRING;
      hasAnion=>>Anion;
      hasCation=>>Cation;
      hasAnionCoefficient=>>NUMBER;
      hasCationCoefficient=>>NUMBER;
      hasFormula=>>STRING].

HomogeniusMixture[hasComponent=>>PureSubstance].

Reaction[
      hasReactants=>>Molecule;
      hasReactantnames=>>STRING;
      hasProducts=>>Molecule;
      hasProductnames=>>STRING;
      hasEquation=>>STRING;
      fromMixture=>>Mixture;
      ...
      ].
```

Complex chemical relationships and axioms are represented by rules:

```
rule burnhydrocarbon: FORALL F,V1,V2,V3
burned(F):CombustionReaction[hasReactants->>{"O2",F};
           hasProducts->>{"H2O","CO2"}] <-
           burn(F) and hydrocarbon(F).
```

This rule states that if a formula *F* represents a hydrocarbon and is burned then the reaction is identified as a combustion reaction with the reactants O_2 and *F* and the products H_2O and CO_2 of the reaction equation .

Within these rules very often the arithmetic built-in functions of OntoBroker have been used:

```
FORALL R,C,C1,M,Re,Pr,L,L1,L2,Z
     R[coefficients->>C;
           hasReactantsList->>L1;hasProductsList->>L2]
           <-     reactants(R,Re) and products(R,Pr) and
                  and concatlists(Re,Pr,L) and
                  matrixbycols(L,M) and lessolve(M,C1)
                  wholenumbered(C1,C).
```

In this rule the reactants and products of a reaction are taken as lists, a matrix for a linear equation system is generated, solved and from the solutions vectors with integer coefficients are generated. Using this approach the problem to balance a chemical equation is solved.

The input for the answering process is either given as ground facts or as constants used in the query. For instance the input "methanol CH_3OH is burned" is given by the F-Logic fact:

```
burn("CH3OH").
```

Afterwards we can pose a question for the balanced reaction equation

```
FORALL Eq,R <- R:Reaction[hasEquation->Eq].
```

which results in the following answer:

```
R = burned("CH3OH")
Eq = "2O2 + 3CH3OH -> 4H2O + 2CO2"
```

As a conclusion it turned out, that F-Logic is very well suited for capturing the chemical domain. In contrast to the other teams OntoNova provided the most compact encoding of the knowledge base to cover the domain.

OntoBroker provides means for efficient reasoning in F-Logic. OntoBroker performs a mixture of forward and backward chaining based on the dynamic filtering algorithm [KL86] to compute (the smallest possible) subset of the model for answering the query. During forward chaining not only single tuples of variable instantiations but sets of such tuples are processed. It is well-known that set-oriented evaluation strategies are much more efficient than tuple oriented ones. The semantics for a set of F-Logic statements is then defined by a transformation process of F-Logic into normal logic (Horn logic with negation) and the well-founded semantics [GRS91] for the resulting set of facts and rules and axioms in normal logic.

2.2 Answer Justification

There are many reasons that users and applications in the Semantic Web need to understand the provenance of the information they get back from applications. One major motivating factor is trust. Trust and reuse of retrieval and deduction processes is facilitated when explanations are available. Ultimately, if users and/or applications are expected to trust, use and reuse application results, potentially in combination with other information or other application results, users and agents may need to understand where the derived and source information came from at varying degrees of detail. This information, sometimes called provenance, may be viewed as meta information about information told. Provenance information may include source name, date and author(s) of last update, authoritativeness of the source, degree of belief, degree of completeness, etc.

Even more, additional types of information may be required if users need to understand the meaning of terms or implications of query answers. If applications make deductions or otherwise manipulate information, users may need to understand how deductions were made and what manipulations were done. Information concerning derived or manipulated information may include term or phrase meaning, term inter-relationships (ontological relations including subclass, super-class, part-of, etc.), the source of derived information, reasoner description and others. In [McG03] an overview about requirements for answer explanation components may be found.

Recognition of the importance of explanation components for reasoning systems existed in a number of fields for many years. For example, expert systems researchers understood the need for systems that understood their reasoning processes and could generate explanations in a language understandable to its users [SHORT76]. A more detailed description about requirements and the necessity of answer explanation components can be found in [McG96], literature on explanations for expert systems [SWA91], theorem proving explanations [FeMi87] or [BOY95].

2.2.1 Approach

Our approach for answer justification is based on meta-inferencing. While processing a query the inference engine is producing a log-file of the proof tree for any given answer. This proof tree itself is represented in F-Logic. It contains the instantiated rules that were successfully applied to derive an answer. This file acts as input for a second inference run, where answers are produced, that are explaining the proof tree in natural language and by that how the answer to the original query was inferred.

We shortly will illustrate this approach with a sample question. The question asks for the K_a value if *mole* and *pH* of a substance is given

Encoded question:

```
<- exists Ka MPhKa(0.2,3.0,Ka).
```

An extract from the log-file of the proof tree:

```
a15106:Instantiation[ofRule->>kavalueMPhKa;
     dependsOnInstantiation->>{a15092};
     instantiatedVars->>{i(M,0.2),i(PH,3.0),
                    i(Ka,4.99E-6),i(H,0.0010),i(HH,1.0E-6)}].
a15092:Instantiation[ofRule->>phvaluephH;
     instantiatedVars->>{i(H,0.0010),i(Ph,3.0),i(R,-3.0)}].
```

The first statement means the rule *kavalueMPhKa* had been applied at the point in time logged here. Then, the variables *M* had been instantiated by 0.2, *PH* by 3.0, *Ka* by 4.99E-6, *H* by 0.0010 and *HH* by 1.0E-6 respectively.

Rules which are important for justifying results were named like "kavalueMPhKa" or "phvaluephH". For these rules certain explain rules are formulated which will be applied in the second, the meta-inference run. Frequently the named rules corresponded to important chemistry laws, which would also be found in the text book, while less important rules were typically required for technical reasons, e.g. in order to translate between two alternative representations of the same content, but were not important for the human to understand the solution proposed by the system.

For the first named rule of the proof tree, the corresponding explanation-rule is:

```
FORALL I,M1,PH1,Ka1,H1,HH1,EX1,Ka1R
explain(EX1,I) <-
    I:Instantiation[ofRule->>kavalueMPhKa;
    instantiatedVars->>{i(M,M1),i(PH,PH1),
    i(Ka,Ka1),i(H,H1),i(HH,HH1)}]and
    dround(Ka1,2,Ka1R) and EX1 is
    ("The equation for calculating the acid-dissociation
    constant Ka for monoprotic acids is <b>Ka=[H+][A-
    ]/[HA]</b>. For monoprotic acids the concentrations for
    hydrogen [H+] and for the anion [A-] are the same:
    <b>[H+]=[A-]</b>. Thus, we get <b>Ka= "+H1+" * "+H1+" /
    "+M1+" = "+Ka1R+" </b>for a solution concentration
    <b>[HA] = "+M1+" M</b>.").
```

An explanation-rule is specified by its reference to the rule (*kavalueMPhKa*), by accessing the instantiations of the variables of the answer producing rule, e.g. *M1* accesses the instantiation of variable *M*, and a text referring to these variables which is presented in the explanation.

These explanation rules are applied to the proof tree of our example and produce the following justification output:

- The equation for calculating the acid-dissociation constant Ka for monoprotic acids is **Ka=[H+][A-]/[HA]**. For monoprotic acids the concentrations for hydrogen [H+] and for the anion [A-] are the same: **[H+]=[A-]**. Thus, we get **Ka= 0.0010 * 0.0010 / 0.2 = 5.0E-6** for a solution concentration **[HA] = 0.2 M**.
    - The equation for calculating the pH-value is **ph=-log[H+]**. Thus we get pH-value **ph = 3, H+ concentration [H+] = 0.0010**.

2.2.2 Advantages of the Approach

This two-step process for creating explanations allows for applying the full power of inferencing to generate explanations. For OntoNova, we have developed an entire knowledge base for this purpose. Thus, one may (i) integrate additional knowledge, (ii) reduce redundancies of explanations, (iii) abstract from fine-grained explanations, and (iv) provide personalized explanations.

(i), when the proof tree does not contain enough information in itself, additional information will be needed to create comprehensible explanations. In our context, e.g., the proof tree contains the formulae of the different substances. However, in the explanations the names of the formulae are often necessary to produce understandable justifications. The generation of names from formulae then requires additional information not found within the proof tree.

(ii), in knowledge bases different paths often lead to the same result. For instance the acidity order of two substances may be determined by the pH-values that may be computed from the amount of substances in aqueous solutions – or they may be given by qualitative criteria like the number of oxygen elements in the formulae of the substances. Both criteria lead to the same ordering. As a consequence there are two different explanation paths for the same result. An explanation rule may rank these two explanation paths and ignore one of them when formulating the justification. Thus, redundancies in generated explanation may be reduced.

(iii), often it is necessary to come to different abstractions of explanations. E.g. for the purpose of debugging the knowledge base a very fine grained explanation level is necessary while for an expert a low grained explanation level is sufficient. The single inference steps and thus the proof tree which is a representation of these single inference steps provide the finest resolution of explanations. Additional rules may summarize these steps and may thus produce higher abstracted explanations. E.g. in our domain such rules may summarize the three different steps of a reaction like the (a) decomposition of the substances into their ionic compounds, (b) the composition of an insoluble substance out of these compounds and (c) the precipitation of the resulting substance from the solution as a precipitation reaction.

(iv), the three means (i)-(iii) just mentioned may all be used for generating specialized explanations for different contexts and for generating personalized explanations. Domain experts need other explanations than freshmen or novices and different types of explanations have to be given in different functional situations and contexts like science, research or in AP exam, respectively.

3 Encoding and Knowledge Base Architecture

3.1 Encoding of the KB

For testing purposes in the dry run Vulcan Inc. provided 50 Syllabus questions for each team. The encoding of the corpus (80 pages from [BLB2003]) has been done in three different phases. During the first phase the knowledge within the corpus has been encoded into the ontology and into rules, without considering the 50 Syllabus questions. This knowledge has been tested with some 40 exercises of [BLB2003]. For each of these exercises an encoded file and an output file by pair have been created. These pairs have been used for automatically testing the knowledge base.

In the next phase the Syllabus questions have been tested with a covering of around 30% of these questions. During this phase the knowledge base has been refined until coverage of around 70% of these questions has been reached. Additionally, in parallel during this phase, the explanation rules have been encoded. In the so-called dry run itself the encoded Syllabus questions have been sent to Vulcan, to test the installed systems. The remaining time to the challenge run then has been used to refine the encoding of the knowledge base and the explanation rules. During the entire process the library of test cases has been extended and used for automatic testing purposes. This ensured stability of the knowledge base against changes.

3.2 Question Encoding

The Syllabus contained two major types of questions: multiple choice questions and detailed answer questions.

Multiple Choice. An example for a multiple choice question is the following:

```
Which of the following compounds will produce a gas when HCl
is added to the solid compound? HCl is a strong acid
producing a yellow-green colored gas above the acid solution.
    a. Ba(OH)2 (s)
    b. CaCO3 (s)
    c. CuSO4 (s)
    d. Na3PO4(s)
    e. NaCl(s)
```

For multiple choices section two different encoding schemas have been used. The first schema encoded the multiple choice questions where our knowledge base could conclude the correct answer. E.g.:

```
//input facts
m1:Mixture[hasComponents->>{"HCl","Ba(OH)2"}].
m5:Mixture[hasComponents->>{"HCl","NaCl"}].
// encoding of the options
answer("A") <- exists P P:GaseousReaction[fromMixture->>m1].
answer("E") <- exists P P:GaseousReaction[fromMixture->>m5].
// query for the correct option
FORALL X <- answer(X).
```

The second schema encoded multiple choice questions where all but one of the options could be excluded by the knowledge base:

```
// all options
possibleanswer("A").
...
possibleanswer("E").
// encoding wrong options
FORALL X wronganswer("A") <- checkequation(ra,X).
...
FORALL X wronganswer("E") <- checkequation(re,X).
// exclude wrong options
FORALL Answer <-
    possibleanswer(Answer) and not wronganswer(Answer).
```

Detailed Answer Questions. The detailed answer questions, for which an exact answer like the pH-value had to be delivered, have been encoded as direct queries to the knowledge base. E.g.:

```
// give the pH-value of the buffer solution
FORALL Ph <- m1:BufferSolution[hasPHValue->>Ph].
```

3.3 Architecture of the Knowledge Base

The knowledge base has a three level architecture as shown in figure 1.

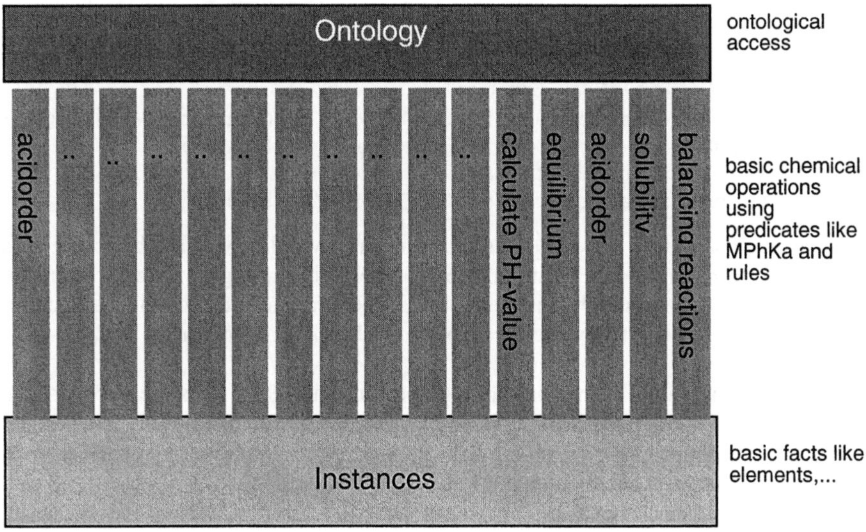

Fig. 1. Architecture of the knowledge base

The upper level contains the ontological information about concepts like elements, reactions, substances and mixtures together with their attributes and relationships. This layer provides the domain vocabulary and the domain structure and is target of the queries posed to the system. Let us illustrate this by an example.

The ontology for instance defines the concept *mixture* with attributes *hasPHValue, hasComponent, hasMole, and hasQuantitiy*. These attributes describe the formulae, the moles and the quantities of the components of the mixture. The attribute *hasPHValue* represents the pH-value of the mixture. Given such a mixture a query like

```
FORALL X <- m1:Mixture[hasPHValue->>X].
```

results in the pH-value of the mixture.

For the different types of mixtures different rules describe this pH-value. For instance, for strong acid-base titrations the pH-value is described by the following rule which represents one basic chemical operation (variable quantifications are skipped):

```
strongacidstrongbasetitration(Acid,AcidQuantity,AcidMole,
Base,BaseQuantity,BaseMole,PH)
<-   A:StrongAcid[hasFormula->>Acid]
     and B:WeakBase[hasFormula->>Base] and
```

```
multiply(BaseQuantity,BaseMole,OHMole) and
multiply(AcidQuantity,AcidMole,HMole) and
greater(HMole,OHMole) and
add(AcidQuantity,BaseQuantity,Volume) and
add(HAfterReaction,OHMole,HMole) and
multiply(HConc,Volume,HAfterReaction) and phH(HConc,PH).
```

Please remark that this rule uses in its body another basic chemical operation by the predicate *phH*.

This basic chemical operation is now attached to the ontology and thus defines the attribute *hasPHValue* of a mixture:

```
M:Mixture[hasPHvalue->>PH]
<-   M:Mixture[hasComponent->>{F1,F2}; hasQuantity->>c(F1,Q1);
     hasQuantity->>c(F2,Q2); hasMole->> c(F1,M1);
     hasMole->> c(F2,M2)] and
     strongacidbasetitration(F1,Q1,M1,F2,Q2,PH).
```

The advantages of this three level architecture are twofold. First the basic chemical operations are nearly independent from each other. This strongly reduces complexity of the knowledge base and the different chemical operations are decoupled and can be developed and tested independently. So each chemical operation is a stand-alone knowledge chunk.

Accessing the values using the ontology on the other hand frees the encoder from knowing all the specialized predicates and on the other hand enables an access to the different information pieces in a way that is much closer to natural language than the predicates of the basic chemical operations.

3.4 Encoding Sensitivity

Related to the methodology discussion above, it is worth to note that answer justification showed some sensitivity against our encoding. This is the logical consequence of our approach. As an example one may consider the following example of two different encodings for the same problem with, consequently, different justification outputs:

Original question:

```
The pH of a 1.0M solution of HCl is:
     a. 1.0
     b. 0.1
     c. 0.0
     d. less than zero
     e. between 0 and 1
```

Encoded question version a)

```
m1:Mixture[hasComponents->>"HCl"; hasMolarity->>c("HCl",1)].
answer("A") <- m1[hasPHValue->>1.0].
answer("B") <- m1[hasPHValue->>0.1].
answer("C") <- m1[hasPHValue->>0.0].
answer("D") <- exists Ph m1[hasPHValue->>Ph]
                 and less(Ph,0.0).
```

```
answer("E") <- exists Ph m1[hasPHValue->>Ph]
                    and less(Ph,1.0) and greater(Ph,0.0).
FORALL Answer <- answer(Answer).
```

Here we defined a mixture of *HCl* to be able to determine the pH value. Then we compared the calculated pH to the given values.

Answer version a): **C**

Justification version a)

- The equation for calculating the pH-value is **ph=-log[H+]**. Thus we get pH-value **ph = 0, H+ concentration [H+] = 1.**
- In the given mixture **the concentration of H3O-molecules(atoms) is 1 M**.
    - **HCl is a strong monoprotic acid** that completely splits into H+ and Cl-. A 1-molar mixture of HCl has therefore a 1-molar concentration of H+ and Cl- molecules.

Encoded question version b)

```
answer("A") <- phvalue(1,"HCl",1).
answer("B") <- phvalue(0.1,"HCl",1).
answer("C") <- phvalue(0,"HCl",1).
answer("D") <- exists Ph phvalue(Ph,"HCl",1)
                    and less(Ph,0.0).
answer("E") <- exists Ph phvalue(Ph,"HCl",1)
                    and less(Ph,1.0) and greater(Ph,0.0).
FORALL Answer <- answer(Answer).
```

In this encoding approach, we used the basic operation *phvalue* to compute the pH value of the given substance in an aqueous solution. Then we compared the calculated pH to the given values.

Answer version b): **C**

Justification version b)

- The pH-value of an acid is calculated by **ph=-log[H+]**. For **HCl** and the given data this leads to pH-value **ph=0,**H+ concentration **[H+]=1,**Molarity **M=1.**
    - As **HCl** is a strong acid (see page 122, table 4.2) and fully dissociates in water, the calculation of [H+] or molarity M is based on formula **[H+]=1*M**. With the given data this leads to H+ concentration **[H+]=1,** Molarity **M=1**
        - molecule **HCl** splits into **cation H** and into **anion Cl**

4 Challenge Results

After having encoded four chapters of [BLB2003] the competing systems have been sequestered by Vulcan Inc. and every team got 100 challenge questions which had to be encoded in each teams own representation formalism. After 14 days the encoding documents have been sent to Vulcan Inc. and each teams' system had to process these questions. In the following the results of this challenge run are presented.

4.1 Scores

In general, all teams showed up with similar good scores in the challenge run. There was no time limit for the answering process, so that the teams' systems did not take an AP exam under original conditions. The aim of the run was to test the general ability of the systems to answer questions of a complex domain.

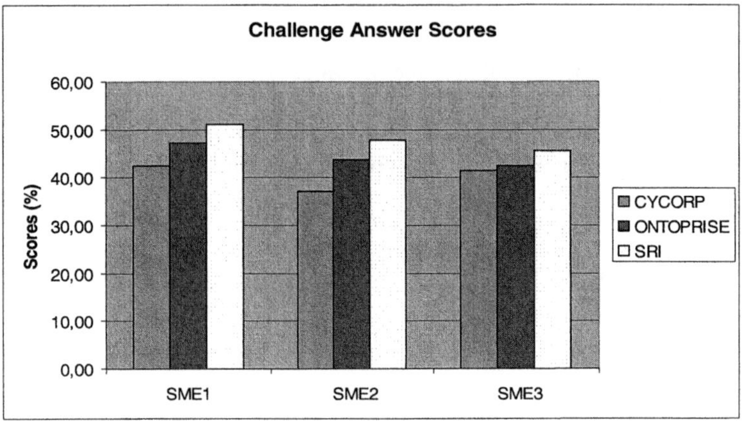

Fig. 2. Challenge answer scores

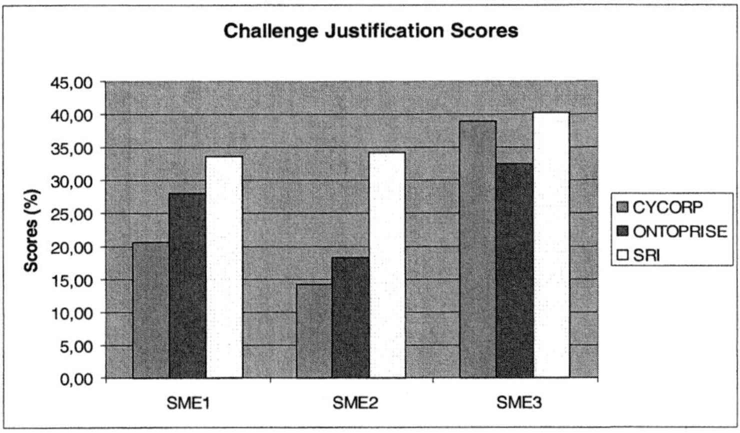

Fig. 3. Challenge justification scores

4.2 Fidelity

The project participants joined a fidelity committee which had the task to judge about the fidelity of the encodings. Most of the encodings were not matter of fidelity concerns. Nevertheless, some encodings not directly encoded the original information of/in the challenge question. Most violations simply ignored irrelevant information that was not encoded. Some cases encoded the formula of substances instead of their names and vice versa, as the substance name was not available but the formula could be still processed to derive an answer. As far as the question was encodable and the question's subject was covered by the KB, no major fidelity conflicts occurred. An example for a fidelity concern was stated for encoding the multiple choice question 12. In this case the knowledge engineer has interpreted that if a substance reacts with oxygen the corresponding reaction is a combustion reaction. Thus additional knowledge from the knowledge engineer is used here and a fidelity concern occurred:

```
When methane, CH4, gas reacts with oxygen, the following
     changes occur
burn("CH4"). // has been interpreted as combustion reaction
```

4.3 Coverage

Coverage means to what extend the questions could be encoded in the representation language. Coverage of challenge questions strongly correlates with the type of question. We had strong coverage in sections that we experienced in the sample questions for training purposes. We had 100% coverage in the MC-section and some 90% in the Detailed Answer Section (DAS). Sparse coverage was shown with unknown question types like in the Free Answer Section, where we only covered some 20% of the questions.

4.4 Brittleness

One outcome of the project is a brittleness taxonomy which classifies failures to different failure classes. As a summary one can state that the major part of failed answers belongs – in the case of OntoNova – to brittleness type "Modeling Error" (knowledge engineer fails to capture domain information properly in their modeling). This is true for answer generation and answer justification, respectively.

For example, we received the correct answer for the multiple choice question no. 19 (MC 19), but lost points for missing explanations. Though the explanation rule in general existed, but there was a typo in the rule that prevented the firing of the rule. There exist some other examples, where explanation rules were just missing, like in MC 2. MC 11 is an example, where parts of the knowledge base had slight bugs, but explanations fit pretty well. MC 23 is seen as an example where the corresponding part of the domain to answer the question was just not modeled at all. All these examples are modeling errors.

The second, major class of errors was the "Unexpected Question Type". This is especially true for the Free Form Section. The reason for the inability to answer those types of questions is based in the modeling of the knowledge base. In these cases the knowledge engineer did not forget to model a part of the domain, but lacked in modeling the different kinds of usage and application of the knowledge base. So in these cases one could often enough observe that certain operations could be done in a certain direction, but could not be operated in the other direction. For example, the calculation of the pH-value could be done by given ka-values but **not** vice versa:

```
Ascorbic acid, H2C6H6O6, is a diprotic acid
    with a Ka1 value of 8.9 x 10-5.
The pH of a 0.125 M solution of ascorbic acid is 2.48 and the
    concentration of C6H6O62- is 1.6 x 10-12 M.
Determine the value of Ka2.5
```

4.5 Performance

Processing performance of OntoNova has been much faster than its competitors, depending on the systems used to perform the challenge run. Our system for the official challenge run required about an hour to process the encodings. For a second, optional and not sequestrated run we slightly improved the knowledge base and brought down processing time to under 10 minutes.

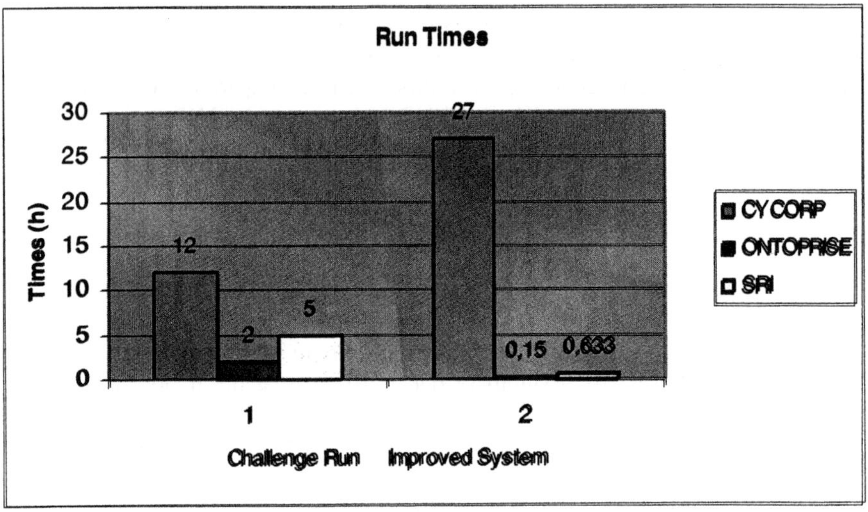

Fig. 4. Run times

5 Conclusion

From the development of OntoNova we gained a range of insights valuable for traditional knowledge systems – as well as for the Semantic Web.

1. F-Logic appeared as a representation language which is very well suited to be used in complex rule intensive domains. One obviously required addition to this language could be a package construct which divides the knowledge base into different parts. Our addition of namespace constructs is one step into F-Logic towards this objective (cf. [Onto03]).
2. Our inference engine OntoBroker has performed very well in answer and justification generation.

3. We also noticed that we have to improve our knowledge modeling environment by a better support for rule editing and rule debugging.
4. Another insight was that at the end of the knowledge base modeling domain experts should be able to extend and modify the knowledge base on their own. For that purpose a two-step process will be necessary. First the basic building blocks (like basic representation of formulas, basic chemical operations etc.) must be developed by a knowledge engineer in a general development environment like OntoEdit. In a second step such an environment must be specialized for a tool which comprises the special view of the domain expert and gives him the elementary building blocks as modeling primitives.

Concerning the evaluation results Ontoprise finished second according to the scores in answer generation and justification, respectively (see 4.1 Scores). This result seems very formidable, because we used just 2 person years instead of the 4 person years consumed by the other two teams and by that showed up with half the costs for encoding. Compared to other teams, our encodings are very compact and do not require specific hardware resources to be processed (experiments were performed on a standard current version of a Linux machine).

Processing performance of OntoNova has been faster than its competitors by factors between 5 and 30, depending on the systems used to perform the challenge run. The challenge run could have been done in some 3-4 minutes using a special twin-server that would have done answer generation and justification in parallel instead of sequentially. Additionally, we could have applied several optimization strategies to improve performance, so that there is much more potential for improvement – and will be needed for the Semantic Web to scale in size, scope and trust – matters advanced by the OntoNova in the Halo Pilot Project.

Acknowledgements. We gratefully acknowledge the fruitful interaction with all the other members of the Halo Pilot Project, in particular Noah Friedland (Vulcan) & Oliver Roup (previously at Vulcan), David Israel & Vinay Chaudhri (SRI), Bruce Porter (Univ. of Texas), Peter Clark (Boeing), G. Matthews, Michael Witbrock, Doug Lenat, (Cyc).

References

[Ang93] Jürgen Angele: Operationalisierung des Modells der Expertise mit KARL. DISKI, Infix Verlag, 1993.

[BLB2003] T.L. Brown, H.E. LeMay, B.E.Bursten, J.R.Burdge: Chemistry The Central Science, Ninth Edition, Prentice Hall, 2003.

[BOY95] Robert Boyer, Matt Kaufmann, and J. Moore. The Boyer-Moore Theorem Prover and Its Interactive Enhancement, Computers and Mathematics with Applications, 29(2), 1995, pp. 27–62.

[DEFS99] S. Decker, M. Erdmann, D. Fensel, and R. Studer. Ontobroker: Ontology based access to distributed and semi-structured information. In R. Meersman et al., editor, *Database Semantics: Semantic Issues in Multimedia Systems*. Kluwer Academic, 1999.

[FeMi87] Amy Felty and Dale Miller. Proof Explanation and Revision. University of Penn, Tech. Report MSCIS8817, 1987 http://cm.bell-labs.com/who/felty/abstracts/proof87.html.

[FHK97] J. Frohn, R. Himmer, P.-Th. Kandzia, C. Schlepphorst: How to Write F-Logic Programs in FLORID. Available from fpt://ftp.informatik.uni-freiburg.de/pub/florid/tutorial.ps.gz, 1997.

[GPQ97] Hector Garcia-Molina, Yannis Papakonstantinou, Dallan Quass, Anand Rajaraman, Yehoshua Sagiv, Jeffrey D. Ullman, Vasilis Vassalos, Jennifer Widom: The TSIMMIS Approach to Mediation: Data Models and Languages. JIIS 8(2): 117–132 (1997)

[GRS91] A. Van Gelder, K. A. Ross, and J. S. Schlipf. The well-founded semantics for general logic programs. *Journal of the ACM*, 38(3):620–650, July 1991.

[KL86] M. Kifer and E. Lozinskii. A framework for an efficient implementation of deductive databases. In *Proceedings of the 6th Advanced Database Symposium*, pages 109–116, Tokyo, August 1986.

[KLW95] M. Kifer, G. Lausen, and J.Wu. Logical foundations of object-oriented and framebased languages. *Journal of the ACM*, 42:741–843, 1995.

[McG03] Deborah L. McGuinness and Paulo Pinheiro da Silva. Inference Web: Portable and Shareable Explanations for Question Answering ". In the Proceedings of the American Association for Artificial Intelligence Spring Symposium Workshop on New Directions for Question Answering. Stanford University, Stanford, CA. March 2003.

[McG96] Deborah L. McGuinness. 1996. Explaining Reasoning in Description Logics. Ph.D. Thesis, Rutgers University, Technical Report LSCR-TR-277.

[Onto03] How to Write F-Logic Programs http://www.ontoprise.de/customercenter/support/tutorials

[SHORT76] Edward Hance Shortliffe. Computer-Based Medical Consultations: MYCIN. Elsevier/North Holland, New York, 1976.

[SWA91] W. Swartout, C. Paris, and J. Moore. "Explanations in Knowledge Systems: Design for Explainable Expert Systems". In IEEE Intelligent Systems, June 1991. http://www.computer.org/intelligent/ ex199/x3058abs.htm.

Author Index

Lecture Notes in Computer Science

For information about Vols. 1–2780
please contact your bookseller or Springer-Verlag

Vol. 2781: B. Michaelis, G. Krell (Eds.), Pattern Recognition. Proceedings, 2003. XVII, 621 pages. 2003.

Vol. 2782: M. Klusch, A. Omicini, S. Ossowski, H. Laamanen (Eds.), Cooperative Information Agents VII. Proceedings, 2003. XI, 345 pages. 2003. (Subseries LNAI).

Vol. 2783: W. Zhou, P. Nicholson, B. Corbitt, J. Fong (Eds.), Advances in Web-Based Learning – ICWL 2003. Proceedings, 2003. XV, 552 pages. 2003.

Vol. 2784: M. Genero, F. Grandi, W.-J. van den Heuvel, J. Krogstie, K. Lyytinen, H.C. Mayr, J. Nelson, A. Olivé, M. Piattini, G. Poels, J. Roddick, K. Siau, M. Yoshikawa, E.S.K. Yu (Eds.), Advanced Conceptual Modeling Techniques. Revised Papers, 2003. XVIII, 452 pages. 2003.

Vol. 2785: C. Peters, M. Braschler, J. Gonzalo, M. Kluck (Eds.), Advances in Cross-Language Information Retrieval. Revised Papers, 2003. XI, 828 pages. 2003.

Vol. 2786: F. Oquendo (Ed.), Software Process Technology. Proceedings, 2003. X, 173 pages. 2003.

Vol. 2787: J. Timmis, P. Bentley, E. Hart (Eds.), Artificial Immune Systems. Proceedings, 2003. XI, 299 pages. 2003.

Vol. 2788: S. Anderson, M. Felici, B. Littlewood (Eds.), Computer Safety, Reliability, and Security. Proceedings, 2003. XIX, 426 pages. 2003.

Vol. 2789: L. Böszörményi, P. Schojer (Eds.), Modular Programming Languages. Proceedings, 2003. XIII, 271 pages. 2003.

Vol. 2790: H. Kosch, L. Böszörményi, H. Hellwagner (Eds.), Euro-Par 2003 Parallel Processing. Proceedings, 2003. XXXV, 1320 pages. 2003.

Vol. 2792: T. Rist, R. Aylett, D. Ballin, J. Rickel (Eds.), Intelligent Virtual Agents. Proceedings, 2003. XV, 364 pages. 2003. (Subseries LNAI).

Vol. 2793: R. Backhouse, J. Gibbons (Eds.), Generic Programming. IX, 223 pages. 2003.

Vol. 2794: P. Kemper, W. H. Sanders (Eds.), Computer Performance Evaluation. Proceedings, 2003. X, 309 pages. 2003.

Vol. 2795: L. Chittaro (Ed.), Human-Computer Interaction with Mobile Devices and Services. Proceedings, 2003. XV, 494 pages. 2003.

Vol. 2796: M. Cialdea Mayer, F. Pirri (Eds.), Automated Reasoning with Analytic Tableaux and Related Methods. Proceedings, 2003. X, 271 pages. 2003. (Subseries LNAI).

Vol. 2798: L. Kalinichenko, R. Manthey, B. Thalheim, U. Wloka (Eds.), Advances in Databases and Information Systems. Proceedings, 2003. XIII, 431 pages. 2003.

Vol. 2799: J.J. Chico, E. Macii (Eds.), Integrated Circuit and System Design. Proceedings, 2003. XVII, 631 pages. 2003.

Vol. 2801: W. Banzhaf, T. Christaller, P. Dittrich, J.T. Kim, J. Ziegler (Eds.), Advances in Artificial Life. Proceedings, 2003. XVI, 905 pages. 2003. (Subseries LNAI).

Vol. 2803: M. Baaz, J.A. Makowsky (Eds.), Computer Science Logic. Proceedings, 2003. XII, 589 pages. 2003.

Vol. 2804: M. Bernardo, P. Inverardi (Eds.), Formal Methods for Software Architectures. Proceedings, 2003. VII, 287 pages. 2003.

Vol. 2805: K. Araki, S. Gnesi, D. Mandrioli (Eds.), FME 2003: Formal Methods. Proceedings, 2003. XVII, 942 pages. 2003.

Vol. 2806: J. Favela, D. Decouchant (Eds.), Groupware: Design, Implementation, and Use. Proceedings, 2003. XII, 382 pages. 2003.

Vol. 2807: V. Matoušek, P. Mautner (Eds.), Text, Speech and Dialogue. Proceedings, 2003. XIII, 426 pages. 2003. (Subseries LNAI).

Vol. 2808: E. Snekkenes, D. Gollmann (Eds.), Computer Security – ESORICS 2003. Proceedings, 2003. X, 345 pages. 2003.

Vol. 2810: M.R. Berthold, H.-J. Lenz, E. Bradley, R. Kruse, C. Borgelt (Eds.), Advances in Intelligent Data Analysis V. Proceedings, 2003. XV, 624 pages. 2003.

Vol. 2811: G. Karlsson, M.I. Smirnov (Eds.), Quality for All. Proceedings, 2003. XII, 295 pages. 2003.

Vol. 2812: G. Benson, R. Page (Eds.), Algorithms in Bioinformatics. Proceedings, 2003. X, 528 pages. 2003. (Subseries LNBI).

Vol. 2813: I.-Y. Song, S.W. Liddle, T.W. Ling, P. Scheuermann (Eds.), Conceptual Modeling – ER 2003. Proceedings, 2003. XIX, 584 pages. 2003.

Vol. 2814: M.A. Jeusfeld, Ó. Pastor (Eds.), Conceptual Modeling for Novel Application Domains. Proceedings, 2003. XVI, 410 pages. 2003.

Vol. 2815: Y. Lindell, Composition of Secure Multi-Party Protocols. XVI, 192 pages. 2003.

Vol. 2816: B. Stiller, G. Carle, M. Karsten, P. Reichl (Eds.), Group Communications and Charges. Proceedings, 2003. XIII, 354 pages. 2003.

Vol. 2817: D. Konstantas, M. Leonard, Y. Pigneur, S. Patel (Eds.), Object-Oriented Information Systems. Proceedings, 2003. XII, 426 pages. 2003.

Vol. 2818: H. Blanken, T. Grabs, H.-J. Schek, R. Schenkel, G. Weikum (Eds.), Intelligent Search on XML Data. XVII, 319 pages. 2003.

Vol. 2819: B. Benatallah, M.-C. Shan (Eds.), Technologies for E-Services. Proceedings, 2003. X, 203 pages. 2003.

Vol. 2820: G. Vigna, E. Jonsson, C. Kruegel (Eds.), Recent Advances in Intrusion Detection. Proceedings, 2003. X, 239 pages. 2003.

Vol. 2821: A. Günter, R. Kruse, B. Neumann (Eds.), KI 2003: Advances in Artificial Intelligence. Proceedings, 2003. XII, 662 pages. 2003. (Subseries LNAI).

Vol. 2822: N. Bianchi-Berthouze (Ed.), Databases in Networked Information Systems. Proceedings, 2003. X, 271 pages. 2003.

Vol. 2823: A. Omondi, S. Sedukhin (Eds.), Advances in Computer Systems Architecture. Proceedings, 2003. XIII, 409 pages. 2003.

Vol. 2824: Z. Bellahsène, A.B. Chaudhri, E. Rahm, M. Rys, R. Unland (Eds.), Database and XML Technologies. Proceedings, 2003. X, 283 pages. 2003.

Vol. 2825: W. Kuhn, M. Worboys, S. Timpf (Eds.), Spatial Information Theory. Proceedings, 2003. XI, 399 pages. 2003.

Vol. 2826: A. Krall (Ed.), Software and Compilers for Embedded Systems. Proceedings, 2003. XI, 403 pages. 2003.

Vol. 2827: A. Albrecht, K. Steinhöfel (Eds.), Stochastic Algorithms: Foundations and Applications. Proceedings, 2003. VIII, 167 pages. 2003.

Vol. 2828: A. Lioy, D. Mazzocchi (Eds.), Communications and Multimedia Security. Proceedings, 2003. VIII, 265 pages. 2003.

Vol. 2829: A. Cappelli, F. Turini (Eds.), AI*IA 2003: Advances in Artificial Intelligence. Proceedings, 2003. XIV, 552 pages. 2003. (Subseries LNAI).

Vol. 2830: F. Pfenning, Y. Smaragdakis (Eds.), Generative Programming and Component Engineering. Proceedings, 2003. IX, 397 pages. 2003.

Vol. 2831: M. Schillo, M. Klusch, J. Müller, H. Tianfield (Eds.), Multiagent System Technologies. Proceedings, 2003. X, 229 pages. 2003. (Subseries LNAI).

Vol. 2832: G. Di Battista, U. Zwick (Eds.), Algorithms – ESA 2003. Proceedings, 2003. XIV, 790 pages. 2003.

Vol. 2833: F. Rossi (Ed.), Principles and Practice of Constraint Programming – CP 2003. Proceedings, 2003. XIX, 1005 pages. 2003.

Vol. 2834: X. Zhou, S. Jähnichen, M. Xu, J. Cao (Eds.), Advanced Parallel Processing Technologies. Proceedings, 2003. XIV, 679 pages. 2003.

Vol. 2835: T. Horváth, A. Yamamoto (Eds.), Inductive Logic Programming. Proceedings, 2003. X, 401 pages. 2003. (Subseries LNAI).

Vol. 2836: S. Qing, D. Gollmann, J. Zhou (Eds.), Information and Communications Security. Proceedings, 2003. XI, 416 pages. 2003.

Vol. 2837: N. Lavrač, D. Gamberger, H. Blockeel, L. Todorovski (Eds.), Machine Learning: ECML 2003. Proceedings, 2003. XVI, 504 pages. 2003. (Subseries LNAI).

Vol. 2838: N. Lavrač, D. Gamberger, L. Todorovski, H. Blockeel (Eds.), Knowledge Discovery in Databases: PKDD 2003. Proceedings, 2003. XVI, 508 pages. 2003. (Subseries LNAI).

Vol. 2839: A. Marshall, N. Agoulmine (Eds.), Management of Multimedia Networks and Services. Proceedings, 2003. XIV, 532 pages. 2003.

Vol. 2840: J. Dongarra, D. Laforenza, S. Orlando (Eds.), Recent Advances in Parallel Virtual Machine and Message Passing Interface. Proceedings, 2003. XVIII, 693 pages. 2003.

Vol. 2841: C. Blundo, C. Laneve (Eds.), Theoretical Computer Science. Proceedings, 2003. XI, 397 pages. 2003.

Vol. 2842: R. Gavaldà, K.P. Jantke, E. Takimoto (Eds.), Algorithmic Learning Theory. Proceedings, 2003. XI, 313 pages. 2003. (Subseries LNAI).

Vol. 2843: G. Grieser, Y. Tanaka, A. Yamamoto (Eds.), Discovery Science. Proceedings, 2003. XII, 504 pages. 2003. (Subseries LNAI).

Vol. 2844: J.A. Jorge, N.J. Nunes, J.F. e Cunha (Eds.), Interactive Systems. Revised Papers, 2003. XIII, 429 pages. 2003.

Vol. 2846: J. Zhou, M. Yung, Y. Han (Eds.), Applied Cryptography and Network Security. Proceedings, 2003. XI, 436 pages. 2003.

Vol. 2847: R. de Lemos, T.S. Weber, J.B. Camargo Jr. (Eds.), Dependable Computing. Proceedings, 2003. XIV, 371 pages. 2003.

Vol. 2848: F.E. Fich (Ed.), Distributed Computing. Proceedings, 2003. X, 367 pages. 2003.

Vol. 2849: N. García, J.M. Martínez, L. Salgado (Eds.), Visual Content Processing and Representation. Proceedings, 2003. XII, 352 pages. 2003.

Vol. 2850: M.Y. Vardi, A. Voronkov (Eds.), Logic for Programming, Artificial Intelligence, and Reasoning. Proceedings, 2003. XIII, 437 pages. 2003. (Subseries LNAI)

Vol. 2851: C. Boyd, W. Mao (Eds.), Information Security. Proceedings, 2003. XI, 443 pages. 2003.

Vol. 2852: F.S. de Boer, M.M. Bonsangue, S. Graf, W.-P. de Roever (Eds.), Formal Methods for Components and Objects. Revised Lectures, 2003. VIII, 509 pages. 2003.

Vol. 2853: M. Jeckle, L.-J. Zhang (Eds.), Web Services – ICWS-Europe 2003. Proceedings, 2003. VIII, 227 pages. 2003.

Vol. 2855: R. Alur, I. Lee (Eds.), Embedded Software. Proceedings, 2003. X, 373 pages. 2003.

Vol. 2856: M. Smirnov, E. Biersack, C. Blondia, O. Bonaventure, O. Casals, G. Karlsson, George Pavlou, B. Quoitin, J. Roberts, I. Stavrakakis, B. Stiller, P. Trimintzios, P. Van Mieghem (Eds.), Quality of Future Internet Services. IX, 293 pages. 2003.

Vol. 2857: M.A. Nascimento, E.S. de Moura, A.L. Oliveira (Eds.), String Processing and Information Retrieval. Proceedings, 2003. XI, 379 pages. 2003.

Vol. 2858: A. Veidenbaum, K. Joe, H. Amano, H. Aiso (Eds.), High Performance Computing. Proceedings, 2003. XV, 566 pages. 2003.

Vol. 2859: B. Apolloni, M. Marinaro, R. Tagliaferri (Eds.), Neural Nets. Proceedings, 2003. X, 376 pages. 2003.

Vol. 2863: P. Stevens, J. Whittle, G. Booch (Eds.), «UML» 2003 – The Unified Modeling Language. Proceedings, 2003. XIV, 415 pages. 2003.

Vol. 2864: A.K. Dey, A. Schmidt, J.F. McCarthy (Eds.), UbiComp 2003: Ubiquitous Computing. Proceedings, 2003. XVII, 368 pages. 2003.

Vol. 2865: S. Pierre, M. Barbeau, E. Kranakis (Eds.), Ad-Hoc, Mobile, and Wireless Networks. Proceedings, 2003. X, 293 pages. 2003.

Vol. 2868: P. Perner, R. Brause, H.-G. Holzhütter (Eds.), Medical Data Analysis. Proceedings, 2003. VIII, 127 pages. 2003.

Vol. 2870: D. Fensel, K. Sycara, J. Mylopoulos (Eds.), The Semantic Web - ISWC 2003. Proceedings, 2003. XV, 931 pages. 2003.

Vol. 2871: N. Zhong, Z.W. Raś, S. Tsumoto, E. Suzuki (Eds.), Foundations of Intelligent Systems. Proceedings, 2003. XV, 697 pages. 2003. (Subseries LNAI)

Vol. 2881: E. Horlait, T. Magedanz, R.H. Glitho (Eds.), Mobile Agents for Telecommunication Applications. Proceedings, 2003. IX, 297 pages. 2003.

GPSR Compliance

The European Union's (EU) General Product Safety Regulation (GPSR) is a set of rules that requires consumer products to be safe and our obligations to ensure this.

If you have any concerns about our products, you can contact us on ProductSafety@springernature.com

In case Publisher is established outside the EU, the EU authorized representative is:

Springer Nature Customer Service Center GmbH
Europaplatz 3
69115 Heidelberg, Germany

Batch number: 10723231

Printed by Printforce, the Netherlands